African American
Literary Theory

African American Literary Theory

A Reader

Edited by
Winston Napier

NEW YORK UNIVERSITY PRESS ● **New York & London**

NEW YORK UNIVERSITY PRESS
New York and London

Library of Congress Cataloging-in-Publication Data
African American literary theory : a reader / edited by Winston Napier.
p. cm.
Includes bibliographical references (p.) and index.
ISBN 0-8147-5809-6 (acid-free paper)—ISBN 0-8147-5810-X (pbk. : acid-free paper)
1. American literature—Afro-American authors—History and criticism—Theory, etc. 2.
Afro-Americans in literature. I. Napier, Winston, 1953-
PS153.N5 A3425 2000
810.9'896073—dc21   00-25201

New York University Press books are printed on acid-free paper,
and their binding materials are chosen for strength and durability.

Manufactured in the United States of America

10 9 8 7 6 5 4 3 2

This book is dedicated to the memory of
Stephen E. Henderson, 1925–1997

Contents

Acknowledgments

I wish to thank several institutions for their availability and support in the production of this book. Howard University gave me the training and intellectual sensibilities that made possible my preparation for this project. Accordingly, I am especially grateful to its Department of English, as I am to its Department of Philosophy, where, as a graduate student, I delivered my first lectures on African American critical theory. Howard's Moorland-Spingarn Research Center and its African American Research Center were instrumental in providing much of the material included here. I extend my gratitude to the staff at the Moorland-Spingarn Center and express special thanks to E. Ethelbert Miller, Director of the African American Research Center, for his ready support and expeditious responses to my research requests. Special thanks are extended to the Higgins School for the Humanities at Clark University for its research grants and to its former director, Michael Spingler, for sharing my commitment to the celebration of African American intellectual culture. The Department of English at Clark University also provided unyielding support. The New York Public Library's Schomberg Research Center and the Elmer Bobst Library of New York University played important roles in providing information and material for this project, and it is to their staff that I now state my thanks. I am also indebted to John Johnson of Johnson's Publication for providing permission to reprint portions of its proprietary material.

Throughout my work on this project, a number of colleagues and friends have been helpful in a variety of ways. Karla Holloway spent much time discussing with me the selections included here. She always reaffirmed the need for this book and played no small role in stimulating my desire for its realization. Vincent Leitch was always available for stimulating discussion and sage advice. His vast knowledge of critical theory in general, as well as his willingness to share a seasoned familiarity with the publishing world, is forever appreciated. I wish to thank two of my colleagues at Clark University, SunHee Gertz and Virginia Vaughan, for their editorial readings of my introductory essay, as well as John Conron, Fern Johnson, and Stanley Sultan for their rewarding discussions on American literary culture. Other colleagues who warrant special mention are Angelyn Mitchell, who shared vital information that helped secure permission to reprint some of the pieces included here; Paula Rothenberg, who offered helpful advice during contractual negotiations; and Richard Feldstein, for his overall support of my work. I also thank Mitchell Lewis for his valuable discussions concerning the organization of the select bibliography, Emily Newton and Jarrett Brown for their diligence as my research assistants, and Denise Spriggs for always being there. Finally, this book would not have been published without the vision of Niko Pfund and the editorial guidance and patience of Eric Zinner, Despina Papazoglou Gimbel, and Daisy Hernandez; to them and their colleagues at New York University Press, I express deep appreciation.

Introduction

African Americans have, from their beginnings, been motivated to regard political empowerment and reform as central concerns. Starting life in the Americas with this sensibility, African Americans tempered their desire to reconfigure conventional American notions of race and inequality with a general concern for social acceptance and participation. The development of their artistic culture should be understood as deriving significantly from this reformative spirit and, accordingly, as regulated by a need to engage expressive culture as a form of protest.

The formal beginnings of African American literary speculation are located in the early part of the twentieth century. Writing mainly in magazines established to report on their society, African American literary thinkers from the start displayed concern with the use of literature as a means to counteract traditional European characterization of blacks as less than human. Publications such as the *Colored American Magazine*, founded in 1900, provided its editor, Pauline Hopkins, a forum with which to promote and sustain the literary principle stated in the preface to her 1900 novel *Contending Forces* that the value of black literature is to be located in its capacity to nurture positive self-images by accenting the forbearance and humanity of blacks in the face of adversity. At its best, fiction, she argued, should be regarded as "a record of growth and development from generation to generation." Hopkins's writing extended her position by expressing what we may term a functional principle of interdependence between authors and the reading community, for it was her belief that the black public at large has the responsibility of advancing the development and survival of black writers. She maintained that the strategic nurturing of writers was vital if black society was to redesign itself by undoing the psychocultural injury caused by racism. *"No one will do this for us,"* she declares with italicized emphasis in the preface to *Contending Forces; "we must ourselves develop the men and women who will faithfully portray the inmost thoughts and feelings of the Negro."* (Pp. 13–14).

Hopkins's functional aesthetics complemented W. E. B. Du Bois's concern with the self-promotional value of black literature. Like Hopkins, Du Bois used his position as editor of a magazine to disseminate his ideas on the purpose of black literature and the role of the black writer. *Crisis* magazine, established in 1910 as the literary vehicle for the National Association for the Advancement of Colored People, emerged under the control of Du Bois not only as a primary source of general and political information for the African American community but also as the most important means by which African American writers were able to reach a black readership. Himself a poet and novelist, Du Bois used *Crisis* to disseminate aesthetic proclamations on the value of literature as a source of political education and cultural celebration. His many essays on art and its use for the amelioration of black existence contributed significantly to the institutional onset of African American literary criticism and theory. Du Bois's efficient management of *Crisis*, with the support of his literary editor, Jesse Fauset, fueled the literary output of black writers in the 1920s and paved the road for other literary magazines such as *Opportunity*. Under the editorship of Charles S. Johnson, *Opportunity*, like *Crisis*, raised the level of cultural energy in black society and brought to the fore young writers who would be key to the realization of the Harlem Renaissance.

Considered by many the most dynamic cultural event in the history of black America, the Harlem Renaissance generated a literary and cultural explosion that would establish the black writer as a seminal social force. Accordingly, the role of writers and the value of their work to the improvement of African American identity became a popular concern. As a result, the continuing establishment of literary critical concerns and speculations became more central to the evolution and definition of black society. Writers such as Langston Hughes, Zora Neale Hurston, and George S. Schuyler produced essays that addressed issues of ideal literary themes, cultural identity, and psychological reconstruction. Their critical writings provided the black community lessons in identity and intellectual responsibility and created the canon upon which academic literary critics and theorists would later build.

Alain Locke, not unlike Du Bois, argued that literature should be used to reconstruct African Americans' social identities. He focused on black artistic culture as the means by which black self-image was to be reinterpreted and reshaped. Indeed, the first thing one notices in reading Locke's introduction to *The New Negro* is his confidence in young black artists' commitment to represent black America in new and progressive terms. The New Negro, he claims, has emerged full of vibrancy and with a "new psychology" that guarantees a future free from white America's definition of blacks as culturally barren and limited to imitative tendencies reflective of an inferior people. These young blacks, writes Locke,

> are the first fruits of the Negro Renaissance. Youth speaks, and the voice of the New Negro is heard. What stirs inarticulately in the masses is already vocal upon the lips of the talented few. . . . Here we have Negro youth with arresting visions and vibrant prophecies; forecasting in the mirror of art what we must see and recognize in the

streets of reality tomorrow, foretelling in new modes and accents the maturing speech
of full racial utterance. (P. 47)

The role of the black writer as he understood it was to use art to represent blacks in
a fresh light, a new "racial utterance" functioning not only as myth smasher but also,
and more important, as a means by which to fathom how positive self-identity could
be developed and regulated. According to Jeffery Stewart, writing in *The Critical
Temper of Alain Locke*, "Locke gave black art its 'critical temper' by correlating the
artistic and creative possibilities of the black experience with its social and political
realities. . . . [He] felt the purpose of culture and art was to educate and thus redefine
the meaning of Blackness in Western society" (p. xvii). Through this approach, blacks
could, for example, improve efforts to expel established images of themselves as
simple-minded "mammys," "Sambos," and happy accommodationists. In stressing
the importance of revised black identity and intellectual commitment, Locke, like
Hopkins, Johnson, and Du Bois, placed great emphasis on the role of black writers
in achieving such a reformation; he stated, in *The New Negro*, that they should
"prove the key to that revaluation of the Negro which must precede or accompany
any considerable further betterment of race relations" (p. 15). In fact, the section of
this text titled "Affirming a Black Aesthetic" affirms and documents the importance
of African American creative writers in establishing the speculative groundwork on
which contemporary African American literary theory depends. Black theorists may
trace their intellectual sensibilities to the political, cultural, and aesthetic concerns
articulated by the like of, to name but a few, Langston Hughes, Zora Neale Hurston,
Richard Wright, Ralph Ellison, Larry Neal, and LeRoi Jones (hereafter Amiri Baraka).

Thirty years after the Harlem Renaissance had passed, Baraka, in terms more
forceful than those of the literary prefects and cultural reconstructionists who had
come before him, championed nationalist ideals as key to the reclamation of an
African grandeur lost through European colonialism. Rhetorically affirming the
"Black Is Beautiful" principle and upholding literary art as the medium for its expression, Baraka in the 1960s inspired a cadre of writers who shared the assumption
that black literature must be reevaluated in terms of its social and political worth
to the black community. Reaching their audience through magazines such as *Liberator, The Journal of Black Poetry*, and, most especially, *Negro Digest* (edited by
Hoyt Fuller and renamed *Black World* in 1970), they spoke to the black community
as spiritual guides intent on displacing the European aesthetic values and assumptions that had negatively influenced African American cultural expression and identity. As Neal declares in "And Shine Swam On: An Afterword" (1968), "We will
have to alter our concepts of what art is, of what it is supposed to 'do.' The dead
form taught most writers in the white man's schools will have to be destroyed, or
at best, radically altered. We can learn more about what poetry is by listening to
the cadences in Malcolm's speeches, than from most of Western poetics." Operating
under the aegis of what Houston Baker terms the "index of repudiation," these
culturalist nationalist writers declared new aesthetic directives for the black artist.

"Our work at this stage," Carolyn Gerald wrote in "The Black Writer and His Role" (1969), "is clearly to destroy the zero and the negative image-myths of ourselves by turning them inside out. To do this, we reverse the symbolism, and we use that reverse symbolism as the tool for projecting our own image upon the universe."

For a growing number of black intellectuals, such as Houston Baker and Henry Louis Gates, the cultural nationalist movement eventually seemed too concerned with dictating an ideological platform, too concerned with establishing political agendas. Such an ideologically centered movement, Baker argued, lacked the methodological rigor necessary for serious analysis of black culture. In the introduction to his *The Journey Back: Issues in Black Literature and Criticism* (1980), he admits the following:

> Our stance was nationalistic; . . . and our results were sometimes dreary. The familiar terms were "Black Aesthetic," "Black Power," "Nation Time," and so on. If this working vocabulary was limited, so, too, was our perspective. We assumed we were fighting for survival, and we took Malcolm X's words quite literally: we proceeded "by any means necessary." (P. xi)

Even such a leading cultural nationalist artist as Larry Neal had by 1972 abandoned the nationalist school and had turned to structuralist theory in order to explore in painstaking detail what he understood to be the schematic elements of black America's expressive culture ("Some Reflections on the Black Aesthetic"). In 1976, in his essay "The Black Contribution to American Letters," Neal admitted that "the level of emotional rhetoric" present in nationalist critique was no longer viable. And Gates insisted, in 1979, that "The tendency of black criticism toward ideological absolutism, with its attendant Inquisition, must come to an end" ("Preface to Blackness: Text and Pretext").

By 1977 African American critics were self-consciously incorporating the ideas of structuralist theorists such as Lévi-Strauss, Roland Barthes, and Michel Foucault, to name a few. This resulted in speculative claims about the structural complexities grounding black American signification as individuals such as Neal, Baker, Gates, and Stephen Henderson embraced the dissecting opportunities structuralism offered. In the wake of the Black Arts Movement, they became more concerned in locating the foundational rules and paradigms specific to black cultural phenomena. Henderson, for example, while still maintaining traces of a nationalist sensibility, was nevertheless incorporating methodological principles of structuralism into his formalist study of black literature. His elaboration on this theory of saturation, in 1975, is contextualized by an underlying nationalist concern for black "Freedom and/or Liberation," "Black Transcendence," and "the communication of Blackness" and reminders that "the task of the present generation of critics [is] to make . . . 'our creative Brothers and Sisters . . . move on up a little higher.' " Nevertheless, showing his formalist training in New Criticism and structuralism, Henderson also has this to say:

If the critic is half worth his salt, then he would attempt to describe what occurs in the poem and to explain—to the extent that it is possible—how the "action" takes place. That is, how the elements of the work interact with one another to produce its effect. . . . Finally, he must place some value judgment on the work, on the totality of the work—not just its theme, its sociology, or its ideology, but also its structure. ("Saturation: Progress Report on a Theory of Black Poetry," in this volume)

Henry Louis Gates's explicit support of structuralist theory is apparent in "Preface to Blackness: Text and Pretext" when he writes that black critics "urgently need to direct [their] attention to the nature of black figurative language, to the nature of black narrative form of content, and to the arbitrary relations between the sign and its referent." Ironically, in the same essay Gates criticizes both Henderson and Baker for their connections with the cultural nationalist movement and for what he charges is their rhetorically inspired essentialist predisposition toward "Blackness." However, by then, both Henderson and Baker had more in common with Gates than Gates realized.

By the middle to late 1980s, African American literary theorists had begun incorporating the poststructuralist assumptions of French thinkers such as Jacques Derrida and Michel Foucault. Gates and Baker were among the first African American theorists to apply the radical poststructuralist principles of Derridean deconstruction to their scholarship. Baker's "Belief, Theory, and Blues: Notes for a Post-Structuralist Criticism of Afro-American Literature" (1986) established in print the beginnings of African American deconstructionist theory proper. And, while theorists such as Fredric Jameson and Hayden White figure into the thesis of Baker's 1988 book *Blues Ideology and Afro-American Literature*, it is Derrida's critique of universal truth, as well as his belief in the unstable nature of semantic signification, that rules the text. In Baker's words,

The guiding presupposition of my new book is that Afro-American culture is a complex reflexive enterprise which finds its proper figuration in blues conceived of as a matrix. A matrix is a womb, a network. . . . The matrix is a point of ceaseless input and output, a web of intersecting, crisscrossing impulses always in a productive transit [manifested *différance*]. Afro-American blues constitute such a network. They are what the French philosopher Jacques Derrida might describe as the "always ready" of Afro-American culture. ("Belief, Theory, and Blues," in this volume)

Deconstruction complemented Baker's belief that language—whether as the medium for literature, science, or philosophy—is a network of ideologically based and fleeting references, "ceaseless input and output," powerless to afford degree-zero signification or what Derrida calls "presence."

Ushering in a revolutionary epistemology, poststructuralism questioned with philosophic verve the belief in the linguistic sign as clear and distinct articulation. It derided the metaphysics of universal knowledge grounded in the Platonic defense of attainable Truth as inevitably confuted by the unbridgeable gap existing between any signifier (the word) and its signified (the meaning). Consequently the cultural values and political concerns of those who institutionalize knowledge became more readily perceived as determining factors in the very textualization, establishment, and dissemination of truth claims. The text came to be regarded as more than the published tome; whatever its form, it served as the cradle of histories, customs, and prejudices. The cultural nationalists had made this same claim in light of their Marxian sensibilities; however, they fell short in articulating an epistemology that questioned truth in general, for their main concern was to replace Eurocentric truths with Afrocentric truths.

Poststructuralism provided both Baker and Gates the philosophical support for the vernacular theories they developed to study black literary culture. Gates eventually emerged as the definitive black poststructuralist theorist. At that time, no other work published by a black critic engaged the ludic attitude and method of deconstruction to the extent Gates did in *The Signifying Monkey*. Writing in opposition to the domination of European cultural values, Gates developed an Afrocentric countermatrix that was, as he saw it, aesthetically more conducive to the analysis and valorization of Black culture. In the introduction to *The Signifying Monkey*, he states:

> I have tried to define a theory of Afro-American criticism not to mystify black literature, or to obscure its several delightful modes of creating meaning, but to begin to suggest how richly textured and layered that black literary artistry indeed is. By discussing explicitly that which is implicit in what we might think of as the logic of the tradition, I hope to enhance the reader's experience of black texts by identifying levels of meanings and expression that might otherwise remain mediated, or buried beneath the surface.

In other words, Gates conceived a resistant enterprise facilitating the political and existential empowerment of minority cultures, of gyno-cultures, of silenced voices. It gave way to semantic revolution and not to merely political reformation.

Implied in Gates's text is a denunciation of European oppression, as well as a celebration of African American cultural invention and survival. Throughout *The Signifying Monkey*, African American cultural invention is upheld as akin in spirit to the critique against European universalism that Derrida represents. For, as Gates maintains, at work in African American aesthetics, itself derived from West African ontological claims, was the appreciation of multiple meanings in a given signifier, the appreciation of the negative logics of *différance* articulated by Derrida. This helps explain the imaginative and traditionally deconstructive use of language in African American culture and its pervasive influence on the greater American linguistic discourse. The upshot is that Derrida's sense of language as a network of signifying play was a linguistic practicality in African American expressive culture, where semantic freeplay was a performative given. Gates's use of the Ibo god Esu Elegbara to symbolize this occurrence of semantic freeplay at work in African and African American linguistic phenomena may well be considered his introduction to the critical scene of a new form of cultural hermeneutics, what I term, *pace* Hermes, an "esuneutics." With metaphorical reference to the "the signifying monkey," Gates further locates the presence of esuneutic phenomena in African American linguistic discourse in such ludic forms of speech as "signifyin'," "playing the dozens," and other forms of verbal tricksterism and resistant signification.

Resistant signification—what Baker was identifying in the 1970s as indicative of an "index of repudiation"—has traditionally been a defensive maneuver in the formation and survival of African American culture. Such oppositional semantics represents arguably the first line of available systematic counteraction by Africans in the Americas and involves a traditional self-conscious play with language, a ready reception of signifying freeplay as a survivalistic tool of life. In the proto-deconstructive spirit of a trickster, African American slaves, for example, constantly had to deform signature, sign, and context in order to undermine and survive in a world where, leaving them at the mercy of tyrannical whimsy, laws negated the racial equality of black being. Perhaps one of the first published acts of cultural prototypical deconstruction in America is to be found in David Walker's *Appeal* of 1829. Employing the structural outline of the American Constitution, this book effectively deconstructs that document by highlighting its defense of slavery and racism even as it promotes the humanistic ideal of Enlightenment ethics. Walker's critique is a striking example of what Derrida would come to term the "double science," for here the central "text" of American political ideals is placed under moral indictment by being made to work ideologically and structurally against itself.

Deconstructive concepts, whether antecedent or coeval with European critical philosophy, have often been at work in the black community, intuitively as well as cognitively. And, while Derrida has given us a lexicon and has explicated poststructuralist epistemological principles, it is important to remember that his attack on the "Truth" of Western culture is an elaboration of insights and practices that were already functioning throughout African American history. African Americans have traditionally contributed to the development of poststructuralist theory by critiquing the status of "master narratives." Effectively, the spirit of deconstructionist critique has been at work throughout the history of blacks in the Americas, a point Gates develops in *The Signifying Monkey*. In fact, African American critical thought helped to highlight the mechanics of racial constructions and helped establish an interventonist legacy that has impelled even Derrida to address race, as he does on a rare occasion in his essay "Racism's Last Word," originally published in a special issue of *Critical Inquiry* edited by Gates in 1985.

Curiously, black intellectuals who employed poststructuralist theory often found themselves accused of compromising their political responsibilities to the black community in adopting abstruse terms and a complex analytical style that many still feel alienate the black community at large. These charges are especially apparent in Joyce Joyce's "The Black Canon: Reconstructing Black American Literary Criticism" (1987) and Barbara Christian's "The Race for Theory" (1988). Contrary to Joyce's charges, however, black poststructuralists see themselves as asserting the freedom to reject an imprisoning discourse of Euro-ideologies. Such freedom, they believe, is vital to an improved understanding of one's image of the world and self. Indeed, black poststructuralist theorists such as Michael Awkward, Mae Gwendolyn Henderson, and Hortense Spillers argue that the meanings and textualizations of language call for a recognition of the relevant ideology best suited to analyze and define the multiple meanings and values present in the literature of a culture. Black poststructuralist theorists therefore see themselves as gaining access to a meta-analysis of human knowledge. Consequently, Joyce's indictment has proved to be especially agitating to black poststructuralist theorists, especially Gates and Baker, who were explicitly targeted in her critique.

The two men produced firm responses to Joyce—Gates in his " 'What's Love Got to Do with It?': Critical Theory, Integrity, and the Black Idiom" and Baker in his "In Dubious Battle." Joyce then produced a meta-response with her " 'Who the Cap Fit': Unconsciousness and Unconscionableness in the Criticism of Houston A. Baker, Jr., and Henry Louis Gates, Jr.," thereby establishing the now notorious feud in *New Literary History*, where in 1987 the essays were all published seriatim in volume 18. This feud generated a flurry of comments from both white and black critics, including Sandra Adell, in "The Crisis in Black American Literary Criticism and the Postmodern Cures of Houston Baker, Jr., and Henry Louis Gates" (1994), and Deborah E. McDowell, in "Black Feminist Thinking: The 'Practice' of 'Theory' " (1995). In 1994 Joyce had yet another say with her "The Problems in Silence and Exclusiveness in the African American Literary Community," a little-known essay originally printed in *Black Books Bulletin* and reprinted here for the first time.

With the cultural revolution throughout the United States in the 1960s and 1970s came reformative opportunities that gave rise to feminist protest movements and to the eventual emergence of black feminist theory. Inaugurated in 1977 with Barbara Smith's essay "Toward a Black Feminist Criticism," black feminist theory evolved during the 1980s as an expression of antisexism qualified by racial protest. Smith's essay recognizes the revolutionary spirit associated with the Black Arts Movement; however, it stands out for its criticism of the male centeredness that qualified that movement and, as a rule, American society. Recognizing the special degree of alienation and oppression this causes black women, Smith called for analyses that take to task not only the racism of whites, including white feminists, but also, and most important, the sexism of both white and black males. Smith's inauguration of a black feminist critical discourse, specifically her added enunciation of black lesbian sensibilities, added a new dimension to black feminist concerns. Accordingly, homosexual themes and issues figure uninhibitedly in black feminist theory, as indicated here by Deborah McDowell's "New Directions for Black Feminist Criticism" (1980); Hazel Carby's "Woman's Era: Rethinking Black Feminist Theory" (1987); and Evelynn Hammonds's "Black (W)holes and the Geometry of Black Female Sexuality" (1994). In the case of black male critics, however, the professional establishment of queer theoretical concerns would not occur until the 1990s.

During the early 1980s, the scope of theoretical interests for black feminists widened further with Alice Walker's epigraphic introduction of the term "womanism" in her collection of essays *In Search of Our Mothers' Gardens* (1984). Defining this word, Walker sought to offer a strategy by which black men and black women might avoid divisions between themselves while pursuing political empowerment. In her essay "Some Implications of Womanist Theory" (1986), Sherley Anne Williams responds to Walker and defends reconciliatory concern for the quality of relationships between black men and black women. But Williams also maintains that feminist theory is by nature an egalitarian project, one that facilitates a variety of interests and themes specific to the greater American cultural scene. This womanist stance challenges the strictly gynocentric concerns in Smith's "Toward a Black Feminist Criticism" and in Deborah McDowell's "New Directions for Black Feminist Criticism," showing at once that black feminist thought is by no means homogeneous. Indeed, one may argue that the discourse of black womanist/feminist studies offers as inclusive an enterprise of theoretical adventure and participation as any experienced before in black or white American intellectual culture. As Mae Gwendolyn Henderson argues in "Speaking in Tongues" (1986), "it is the privileging (rather than repressing) of the other in ourselves" that commands the distinct thematic openings and behavioral expanse we have witnessed in many black womanists/feminists. Additionally, black American feminists' facile cross-cultural interaction with other feminist discourses, such as those in African, European, Hispanic, Asian, and Native American communities, promises opportunities for broader and more ethically progressive theoretical and practical possibilities worldwide. And, given black feminists' charges of racism, white feminists in general have taken stock, becoming more aware of and concerned with their own prejudices against women of color. For many women, this has resulted in an earnest pursuit of communitarian feminism on the American scene, one amplifying the multiethnic ethos found throughout its quarters.

Energized by critical mass and intercultural and interracial networks, as well as the spiritual legacies of, to name a few, Sojourner Truth, Pauline Hopkins, Anna Julia Cooper, Zora Neale Hurston, and Angelina Grimké, black women theorists throughout the 1980s and 1990s attended to issues of race, gender, politics, sexuality, and psychology as analytical perspectives from which to broaden their examination and interpretation of women's experiences. European theorists such as Hélène Cixous, Luce Irigaray, and Jacques Lacan have also offered black American feminists, as they have white American feminists, theoretical tools by which to gauge—at times problematically so—their own experiences. Such pursuit often involves theoretical daring and invention. Indeed, as Hortense J. Spillers puts it:

> [T]he move toward self-reflexivity demands a test of inherited portions of culture content in order to discover not only what tradition conceals but, as a result, also what one, under its auspices, is forced to blindside. Carrying out that line of thinking, we might be able to see in an apposite psychoanalytic protocol for the subjects of "race," broken away from the point of origin, which rupture has left a hole that speech can only point to and circle around, an entirely new repertoire of inquiry into human relations. (" 'All the Things You Could Be by Now,' " in this volume)

So influential is black feminist thought that black male critics such as Calvin Hernton, in *Sexual Mountain and Black Women Writers: Adventure in Sex, Literature and Real Life* (1987); Gates, in *Reading Black Reading Feminist: A Critical Anthology* (1990), and Baker, in *Workings of the Spirit: The Poetics of Afro-American Women's Writing* (1991) have attended to the canonical and aesthetic scope of black female literary culture, thereby contributing to and inspiring a growing body of self-identified black male feminists. Consider Michael Awkward's study of his feminist consciousness in "A Black Man's Place in Black Feminist Criticism" (1995).

One of the more recent developments in African American theory has been the steady emergence of black queer theorists who first began to make their presence known in growing numbers during the middle to late 1990s. Charles Nero's "Toward a Black Gay Aesthetic: Signifying in Contemporary Black Gay Literature" (1991) stands out as the first established call by a black academic for the development of black queer theory. It is no coincidence that Nero's essay reflects in its primary title a syntactic similarity to Barbara Smith's 1977 essay. Inspired by Smith, Nero was seeking to validate black gay studies in degrees similar to Smith's validation of black lesbian studies. The result in notable. In fact, the 1990s have witnessed a proliferation of scholarship by black theorists that addresses the black gay discourse, in particular. Examples of such studies included here are Robert F. Reid-Pharr's "Tearing the Goat's Flesh: Homosexuality, Abjection, and the Production of a Late Twentieth-Century Black Masculinity" (1996) and Marlon Ross's "Some Glances at the Black Fag: Race, Same-Sex Desire, and Cultural Belonging" (1997). Parallel to this growth of black queer theory is the proliferation of scholarship that addresses black masculinity in general.

The movement Nero helped inaugurate in African American literary and cultural theory complements the theoretical inroads made by black feminist theorists. Like the earlier work, it too is ethically corrective in its ethical assumptions and political goals. Displaying use of postmodern insights through conceptual revision, black queer thought demonstrates the role of theory in helping to widen our sensibilities to and our awareness of discourses that historically have been denounced by prejudiced voices within both the black and the white communities. Comparable to the black feminist movement, the black gay movement has forced scholars of black culture to address occurrences of bigotry beyond that inflicted by whites on blacks. In examining and theorizing on issues such as sexism and homophobia within the black community itself, African American critical theorists have effectively extended the investigative range of black cultural sensibilities and formations, keeping abreast of the moralistic dynamic at work in a discourse that calls for constant reappraisal of its evolution and its purpose.

Another striking development in the evolution of African American literary theory during the final years of the twentieth century concerns the expanded idea of the text. The text has come to represent any site of signification, and culture has come to represent a textual event that calls for the interpretive activities traditionally reserved for words on a page. This semiotic development has opened new avenues for theorists, leading them to read culture so as to identify its complex interplay of defining forces as yet another exercise in textual explication and decoding. More and more theorists find themselves breaking out of the conventional arena ascribed to the literary analyst, moving instead toward interpretation of the multiple forms of cultural presentations found in film, dance, music, and other modalities of cultural release. This move toward cultural studies in general has complicated the idea of the literary theorist in terms that force us to see such thinkers as responsible to a variety of disciplines and interests. As Wahneema Lubiano puts it, "Afro-American literary discourse is not now nor has it ever been monolithic; however, what has been consistent within the explicit and implicit terms of that discourse (as well as within Afro-American Studies in its institutional manifestations within the academy itself) is a concern with the relations of power and with social and economic history" ("Mapping the Interstices between Afro-American Cultural Discourse and Cultural Studies"). Lubiano makes clear what has always been connoted by the sociopolitical subtext located throughout the canon of African American literary criticism and theory. When, for example, we observe theorists such as Karla Holloway reading African American death rituals as text, or Hazel Carby and Phillip Brian Harper reading the black male as an indoctrinated site of discursive prejudices, we are compelled to see the ever available means by which African American theorists may contribute to the reading and analysis of American culture in order to, as Lubiano reminds us, "foreground the connection between 'culture' and Afro-American 'everyday life' " in a way that expands our understanding of the black experience as sociologically and historically prescribed. Such promotion of cultural criticism as a way to interpret the structural multiplicities of American society leads in turn to issues of methodology. This is Paul Taylor's concern, and it is appropriate that, in the final piece in this reader, Taylor urges us to consider new means by which to approach the study of African American culture. His call for a more decidedly philosophic method, one that self-consciously employs "aesthetics as a kind of cultural criticism," promises the theorist improved analytical means by which to excavate "the hidden ways in which history and culture condition our choices, beliefs, desires, and preferences" ("Malcolm's Conk and Danto's Colors; or, Four Logical Petitions Concerning Race, Beauty, and Aesthetics").

Finally, it remains to be said that the exponential increase in the quantity of published African American literary thought since the 1960s speaks to the occurrence of discursive events we have yet to comprehend satisfactorily. Admittedly, we still lack the retrospective distance to do so; accordingly, our work is laid out before us, challenging us further to approach African American critical theory as yet another dimension of the black experience replete with its own array of aesthetic affirmations and political expectations. It is my hope that this volume will contribute toward that end by highlighting the theoretical arguments that have regulated the development of twentieth-century African American intellectual discourse as expressed by those who have marked new analytical paths to improved understanding of America's ever expanding cultural forms.

Here before us, then, is a narrative of sweeping and, at times, dramatic proportions, one that continues to demand analytical decoding yet that guarantees a rich archive of details for those interested in exploring the emergence, formation, and development of twentieth-century African American literary thought. In effect, this collection not only illustrates the ways in which African American literary theorists express their cultural values and visions but also shows how these sentiments are constantly modified by the influx of theoretical "tools" and assumptions derived from a variety of sources. The reader can observe how generationally shifting intellectual proceedings affect the cultural spirit of the decades in which they dominate. For example, in comparing the dominant voices of the 1960s with those of the 1990s, one can discern the extent to which gender now contextualizes theoretical discussions of race, as well as the extent to which what was once a male-dominated enterprise has been dramatically qualified by female African American theorists, who have emerged in such numbers and with such influence that they are arguably the major force in *fin de siècle* African American literary culture.

Covering more than seventy years of African American literary culture, the essays included here are arranged chronologically and, except for the section titled "Affirming a Black Aesthetic," are grouped by the specific decade they represent. Where more than one essay by an author is included in a given decade, they are presented in order of publication dates so that the reader can more readily observe the scope of that author's ideas. This format works to reveal identifiable episodes throughout the domain of African American literary theory, while at the same time providing an important framework for those being introduced to the subject. For those already familiar with the canon, this arrangement highlights intertextual connections that may have previously been overlooked. In fact, the reader can simply scan the articles' titles to get a sense of the narrative details that their historically contextualized groupings provide. Another advantage of this arrangement is that the reader need not struggle with the task of deciding in what order to read the articles. By simply approaching them in the organized layout, the reader can follow the story of African American literary thought and the evolutionary momentum and intertextual debates (and, at times, feuds) that season this discourse. Given the intertextual scope and play blending these pieces together, with this collection we share moments of discursive agreements and conflicts, as well as a variety of strategies of methodological origination, appropriation, and qualification.

Such an array of harmony and tension discloses the interactive events and inevitable conflicts that add drama to this anthology's intended narration. Note, for example, the 1926 debate between Langston Hughes and George Schuyler. Observe the politically diverse voices of Ellison and Neal. Parallel Gates's "Preface to Blackness" (1979) with Baker's "Generational Shifts and the Recent Criticism of Afro-American Literature" (1981). Read Barbara Christian's "The Race to Theory" against Awkward's "Appropriative Gestures: Theory and Afro-American Literary Criticism" (1988), then compare it with Hortense Spillers's " 'All the Things You Could Be by Now, If Sigmund Freud's Wife Was Your Mother.' " Compare Deborah McDowell's "New Directions for Black Feminist Criticism" with Barbara Smith's "Toward a Black Feminist Criticism" before reading both against Sherley Anne Williams's "Some Implications of Womanist Theory." These suggestions offer only a hint of the intertextual feast awaiting the reader.

REFERENCES

Baker, Jr., Houston. *The Journey Back: Issues in Black Literature and Criticism.* Chicago: University of Chicago Press, 1980.

Hopkins, Paula. *Contending Forces: A Romance Illustrative of Negro Life North and South.* 1900; rpt. Miami, Mnemosyne, 1969

Locke, Alain, ed. *The New Negro.* 1925; rpt. New York: Atheneum, 1983.

Neal, Larry. "The Black Contribution to American Letters, Part II: The Writer as Activist— 1960 and After." In *The Black American Reference Book*, ed. Mabel M. Smythe. Englewood Cliffs, NJ: Prentice Hall, 1976.

Stewart, Jeffery C., ed. *The Critical Temper of Alain Locke: A Selection of His Essays on Art and Culture.* New York: Garland, 1983.

1

The 1920s to the 1960s

Affirming a Black Aesthetic

1 | Criteria of Negro Art

W. E. B. Du Bois

(1926)

I do not doubt but there are some in this audience who are a little disturbed at the subject of this meeting, and particularly at the subject I have chosen. Such people are thinking something like this: "How is it that an organization like this, a group of radicals trying to bring new things into the world, a fighting organization which has come up out of the blood and dust of battle, struggling for the right of black men to be ordinary human beings—how is it that an organization of this kind can turn aside to talk about Art? After all, what have we who are slaves and black to do with Art?"

Or perhaps there are others who feel a certain relief and are saying, "After all it is rather satisfactory after all this talk about rights and fighting to sit and dream of something which leaves a nice taste in the mouth."

Let me tell you that neither of these groups is right. The thing we are talking about tonight is part of the great fight we are carrying on and it represents a forward and an upward look—a pushing onward. You and I have been breasting hills; we have been climbing upward; there has been progress and we can see it day by day looking back along blood-filled paths. But as you go through the valleys and over the foothills, so long as you are climbing, the direction,—north, south, east or west,—is of less importance. But when gradually the vista widens and you begin to see the world at your feet and the far horizon, then it is time to know more precisely whither you are going and what you really want.

What do we want? What is the thing we are after? As it was phrased last night it had a certain truth: We want to be Americans, full-fledged Americans, with all the rights of other American citizens. But is that all? Do we want simply to be Americans? Once in a while through all of us there flashes some clairvoyance, some clear idea, of what America really is. We who are dark can see America in a way that white Americans can not. And seeing our country thus, are we satisfied with its present goals and ideals?

17

In the high school where I studied we learned most of Scott's "Lady of the Lake" by heart. In after life once it was my privilege to see the lake. It was Sunday. It was quiet. You could glimpse the deer wandering in unbroken forests; you could hear the soft ripple of romance on the waters. Around me fell the cadence of that poetry of my youth. I fell asleep full of the enchantment of the Scottish border. A new day broke and with it came a sudden rush of excursionists. They were mostly Americans and they were loud and strident. They poured upon the little pleasure boat,—men with their hats a little on one side and drooping cigars in the wet corners of their mouths; women who shared their conversation with the world. They all tried to get everywhere first. They pushed other people out of the way. They made all sorts of incoherent noises and gestures so that the quiet home folk and the visitors from other lands silently and half-wonderingly gave way before them. They struck a note not evil but wrong. They carried, perhaps, a sense of strength and accomplishment, but their hearts had no conception of the beauty which pervaded this holy place.

If you tonight suddenly should become full-fledged Americans; if your color faded, or the color line here in Chicago was miraculously forgotten; suppose, too, you became at the same time rich and powerful;—what is it that you would want? What would you immediately seek? Would you buy the most powerful of motor cars and outrace Cook County? Would you buy the most elaborate estate on the North Shore? Would you be a Rotarian or a Lion or a What-not of the very last degree? Would you wear the most striking clothes, give the richest dinners and buy the longest press notices?

Even as you visualize such ideals you know in your hearts that these are not the things you really want. You realize this sooner than the average white American because, pushed aside as we have been in America, there has come to us not only a certain distaste for the tawdry and flamboyant but a vision of what the world could be if it were really a beautiful world; if we had the true spirit; if we had the Seeing Eye, the Cunning Hand, the Feeling Heart; if we had, to be sure, not perfect happiness, but plenty of good hard work, the inevitable suffering that always comes with life; sacrifice and waiting, all that—but, nevertheless, lived in a world where men know, where men create, where they realize themselves and where they enjoy life. It is that sort of a world we want to create for ourselves and for all America.

After all, who shall describe Beauty? What is it? I remember tonight four beautiful things: The Cathedral at Cologne, a forest in stone, set in light and changing shadow, echoing with sunlight and solemn song; a village of the Veys in West Africa, a little thing of mauve and purple, quiet, lying content and shining in the sun; a black and velvet room where on a throne rests, in old and yellowing marble, the broken curves of the Venus of Milo; a single phrase of music in the Southern South—utter melody, haunting and appealing, suddenly arising out of night and eternity, beneath the moon.

Such is Beauty. Its variety is infinite, its possibility is endless. In normal life all may have it and have it yet again. The world is full of it; and yet today the mass of human beings are choked away from it, and their lives distorted and made ugly. This is not only wrong, it is silly. Who shall right this well-nigh universal failing? Who shall let this world be beautiful? Who shall restore to men the glory of sunsets and the peace of quiet sleep?

We black folk here may help for we have within us as a race new stirrings; stirrings of the beginning of a new appreciation of joy, of a new desire to create, of a new will to be; as though in this morning of group life we had awakened from some sleep that at once dimly mourns the past and dreams a splendid future; and there has come the conviction that the Youth that is here today, the Negro Youth, is a different kind of Youth, because in some new way it bears this mighty prophecy on its breast, with a new realization of itself, with new determination for all mankind.

What has this Beauty to do with the world? What has Beauty to do with Truth and Goodness—with the facts of the world and the right actions of men? "Nothing," the artists rush to answer. They may be right. I am but an humble disciple of art and cannot presume to say. I am one who tells the truth and exposes evil and seeks with Beauty and for Beauty to set the world right. That somehow, somewhere eternal and perfect Beauty sits above Truth and Right I can conceive, but here and now and in the world in which I work they are for me unseparated and inseparable.

This is brought to us peculiarly when as artists we face our own past as a people. There has come to us—and it has come especially through the man we are going to honor tonight*—a realization of that past, of which for long years we have been ashamed, for which we have apologized. We thought nothing could come out of that past which we wanted to remember; which we wanted to hand down to our children. Suddenly, this same past is taking on form, color and reality, and in a half shame-faced way we are beginning to be proud of it. We are remembering that the romance of the world did not die and lie forgotten in the Middle Age; that if you want romance to deal with you must have it here and now and in your own hands.

I once knew a man and woman. They had two children, a daughter who was white and a daughter who was brown; the daughter who was white married a white man; and when her wedding was preparing the daughter who was brown prepared to go and celebrate. But the mother said, "No!" and the brown daughter went into her room and turned on the gas and died. Do you want Greek tragedy swifter than that?

Or again, here is a little Southern town and you are in the public square. On one side of the square is the office of a colored lawyer and on all the other sides are men who do not like colored lawyers. A white woman goes into the black man's office and points to the white-filled square and says, "I want five hundred dollars now and if I do not get it I am going to scream."

Have you heard the story of the conquest of German East Africa? Listen to the untold tale: There were 40,000 black men and 4,000 white men who talked German. There were 20,000 black men and 12,000 white men who talked English. There were 10,000 black men and 400 white men who talked French. In Africa then where the Mountains of the Moon raised their white and snow-capped heads into the mouth of the tropic sun, where Nile and Congo rise and the Great Lakes swim, these men fought; they struggled on mountain, hill and valley, in river, lake and swamp, until in

*Carter Godwin Woodson, 12th Spingarn Medallist.

masses they sickened, crawled and died; until the 4,000 white Germans had become mostly bleached bones; until nearly all the 12,000 white Englishmen had returned to South Africa, and the 400 Frenchmen to Belgium and Heaven; all except a mere handful of the white men died; but thousands of black men from East, West and South Africa, from Nigeria and the Valley of the Nile, and from the West Indies still struggled, fought and died. For four years they fought and won and lost German East Africa; and all you hear about it is that England and Belgium conquered German Africa for the allies!

Such is the true and stirring stuff of which Romance is born and from this stuff come the stirrings of men who are beginning to remember that this kind of material is theirs; and this vital life of their own kind is beckoning them on.

The question comes next as to the interpretation of these new stirrings, of this new spirit: Of what is the colored artist capable? We have had on the part of both colored and white people singular unanimity of judgment in the past. Colored people have said: "This work must be inferior because it comes from colored people." White people have said: "It is inferior because it is done by colored people." But today there is coming to both the realization that the work of the black man is not always inferior. Interesting stories come to us. A professor in the University of Chicago read to a class that had studied literature a passage of poetry and asked them to guess the author. They guessed a goodly company from Shelley and Robert Browning down to Tennyson and Masefield. The author was Countée Cullen. Or again the English critic John Drinkwater went down to a Southern seminary, one of the sort which "finishes" young white women of the South. The students sat with their wooden faces while he tried to get some response out of them. Finally he said, "Name me some of your Southern poets." They hesitated. He said finally, "I'll start out with your best: Paul Laurence Dunbar"!

With the growing recognition of Negro artists in spite of the severe handicaps, one comforting thing is occurring to both white and black. They are whispering, "Here is a way out. Here is the real solution of the color problem. The recognition accorded Cullen, Hughes, Fauset, White and others shows there is no real color line. Keep quiet! Don't complain! Work! All will be well!"

I will not say that already this chorus amounts to a conspiracy. Perhaps I am naturally too suspicious. But I will say that there are today a surprising number of white people who are getting great satisfaction out of these younger Negro writers because they think it is going to stop agitation of the Negro question. They say, "What is the use of your fighting and complaining; do the great thing and the reward is there." And many colored people are all too eager to follow this advice; especially those who are weary of the eternal struggle along the color line, who are afraid to fight and to whom the money of philanthropists and the alluring publicity are subtle and deadly bribes. They say, "What is the use of fighting? Why not show simply what we deserve and let the reward come to us?"

And it is right here that the National Association for the Advancement of Colored People comes upon the field, comes with its great call to a new battle, a new fight and new things to fight before the old things are wholly won; and to say that the

Beauty of Truth and Freedom which shall some day be our heritage and the heritage of all civilized men is not in our hands yet and that we ourselves must not fail to realize.

There is in New York tonight a black woman molding clay by herself in a little bare room, because there is not a single school of sculpture in New York where she is welcome. Surely there are doors she might burst through, but when God makes a sculptor He does not always make the pushing sort of person who beats his way through doors thrust in his face. This girl is working her hands off to get out of this country so that she can get some sort of training.

There was Richard Brown. If he had been white he would have been alive today instead of dead of neglect. Many helped him when he asked but he was not the kind of boy that always asks. He was simply one who made colors sing.

There is a colored woman in Chicago who is a great musician. She thought she would like to study at Fontainebleau this summer where Walter Damrosch and a score of leaders of Art have an American school of music. But the application blank of this school says: "I am a white American and I apply for admission to the school."

We can go on the stage; we can be just as funny as white Americans wish us to be; we can play all the sordid parts that America likes to assign to Negroes; but for any thing else there is still small space for us.

And so I might go on. But let me sum up with this: Suppose the only Negro who survived some centuries hence was the Negro painted by white Americans in the novels and essays they have written. What would people in a hundred years say of black Americans? Now turn it around. Suppose you were to write a story and put in it the kind of people you know and like and imagine. You might get it published and you might not. And the "might not" is still far bigger than the "might." The white publishers catering to white folk would say, "It is not interesting"—to white folk, naturally not. They want Uncle Toms, Topsies, good "darkies" and clowns. I have in my office a story with all the earmarks of truth. A young man says that he started out to write and had his stories accepted. Then he began to write about the things he knew best about, that is, about his own people. He submitted a story to a magazine which said, "We are sorry, but we cannot take it." "I sat down and revised my story, changing the color of the characters and the locale and sent it under an assumed name with a change of address and it was accepted by the same magazine that had refused it, the editor promising to take anything else I might send in providing it was good enough."

We have, to be sure, a few recognized and successful Negro artists; but they are not all those fit to survive or even a good minority. They are but the remnants of that ability and genius among us whom the accidents of education and opportunity have raised on the tidal waves of chance. We black folk are not altogether peculiar in this. After all, in the world at large, it is only the accident, the remnant, that gets the chance to make the most of itself; but if this is true of the white world it is infinitely more true of the colored world. It is not simply the great clear tenor of Roland Hayes that opened the ears of America. We have had many voices of all kinds as fine as his and America was and is as deaf as she was for years to him. Then a foreign land heard Hayes and put its imprint on him and immediately America with all its imitative snobbery woke up. We approved Hayes because London, Paris and Berlin approved him and not simply because he was a great singer.

Thus it is the bounden duty of black America to begin this great work of the creation of Beauty, of the preservation of Beauty, of the realization of Beauty, and we must use in this work all the methods that men have used before. And what have been the tools of the artist in times gone by? First of all, he has used the Truth—not for the sake of truth, not as a scientist seeking truth, but as one upon whom Truth eternally thrust itself as the highest handmaid of imagination, as the one great vehicle of universal understanding. Again artists have used Goodness—goodness in all its aspects of justice, honor and right—not for sake of an ethical sanction but as the one true method of gaining sympathy and human interest.

The apostle of Beauty thus becomes the apostle of Truth and Right not by choice but by inner and outer compulsion. Free he is but his freedom is ever bounded by Truth and Justice; and slavery only dogs him when he is denied the right to tell the Truth or recognize an ideal of Justice.

Thus all Art is propaganda and ever must be, despite the wailing of the purists. I stand in utter shamelessness and say that whatever art I have for writing has been used always for propaganda for gaining the right of black folk to love and enjoy. I do not care a damn for any art that is not used for propaganda. But I do care when propaganda is confined to one side while the other is stripped and silent.

In New York we have two plays: "White Cargo" and "Congo." In "White Cargo" there is a fallen woman. She is black. In "Congo" the fallen woman is white. In "White Cargo" the black woman goes down further and further and in "Congo" the white woman begins with degradation but in the end is one of the angels of the Lord.

You know the current magazine story: A young white man goes down to Central America and the most beautiful colored woman there falls in love with him. She crawls across the whole isthmus to get to him. The white man says nobly, "No." He goes back to his white sweetheart in New York.

In such cases, it is not the positive propaganda of people who believe white blood divine, infallible and holy to which I object. It is the denial of a similar right of propaganda to those who believe black blood human, lovable and inspired with new ideals for the world. White artists themselves suffer from this narrowing of their field. They cry for freedom in dealing with Negroes because they have so little freedom in dealing with whites. DuBose Heyward writes "Porgy" and writes beautifully of the black Charleston underworld. But why does he do this? Because he cannot do a similar thing for the white people of Charleston, or they would drum him out of town. The only chance he had to tell the truth of pitiful human degradation was to tell it of colored people. I should not be surprised if Octavius Roy Cohen had approached the *Saturday Evening Post* and asked permission to write about a different kind of colored folk than the monstrosities he has created; but if he has, the *Post* has replied, "No. You are getting paid to write about the kind of colored people you are writing about."

In other words, the white public today demands from its artists, literary and pictorial, racial pre-judgment which deliberately distorts Truth and Justice, as far as colored races are concerned, and it will pay for no other.

On the other hand, the young and slowly growing black public still wants its prophets almost equally unfree. We are bound by all sorts of customs that have come down as second-hand soul clothes of white patrons. We are ashamed of sex and we lower our eyes when people will talk of it. Our religion holds us in superstition. Our worst side has been so shamelessly emphasized that we are denying we have or ever had a worst side. In all sorts of ways we are hemmed in and our new young artists have got to fight their way to freedom.

The ultimate judge has got to be you and you have got to build yourselves up into that wide judgment, that catholicity of temper which is going to enable the artist to have his widest chance for freedom. We can afford the Truth. White folk today cannot. As it is now we are handing everything over to a white jury. If a colored man wants to publish a book, he has got to get a white publisher and a white newspaper to say it is great; and then you and I say so. We must come to the place where the work of art when it appears is reviewed and acclaimed by our own free and unfettered judgment. And we are going to have a real and valuable and eternal judgment only as we make ourselves free of mind, proud of body and just of soul to all men.

And then do you know what will be said? It is already saying. Just as soon as true Art emerges; just as soon as the black artist appears, someone touches the race on the shoulder and says, "He did that because he was an American, not because he was a Negro; he was born here; he was trained here; he is not a Negro—what is a Negro anyhow? He is just human; it is the kind of thing you ought to expect."

I do not doubt that the ultimate art coming from black folk is going to be just as beautiful, and beautiful largely in the same ways, as the art that comes from white folk, or yellow, or red; but the point today is that until the art of the black folk compels recognition they will not be rated as human. And when through art they compel recognition then let the world discover if it will that their art is as new as it is old and as old as new.

I had a classmate once who did three beautiful things and died. One of them was a story of a folk who found fire and then went wandering in the gloom of night seeking again the stars they had once known and lost; suddenly out of blackness they looked up and there loomed the heavens; and what was it that they said? They raised a mighty cry: "It is the stars, it is the ancient stars, it is the young and everlasting stars!"

2 The Negro-Art Hokum

George S. Schuyler

(1926)

Negro art "made in America" is as nonexistent as the widely advertised profundity of Cal Coolidge, the "seven years of progress" of Mayor Hylan, or the reported sophistication of New Yorkers. Negro art there has been, is, and will be among the numerous black nations of Africa; but to suggest the possibility of any such development among the ten million colored people in this republic is self-evident foolishness. Eager apostles from Greenwich Village, Harlem, and environs proclaimed a great renaissance of Negro art just around the corner waiting to be ushered on the scene by those whose hobby is taking races, nations, peoples, and movements under their wing. New art forms expressing the "peculiar" psychology of the Negro were about to flood the market. In short, the art of Homo Africanus was about to electrify the waiting world. Skeptics patiently waited. They still wait.

True, from dark-skinned sources have come those slave songs based on Protestant hymns and Biblical texts known as the spirituals, work songs and secular songs of sorrow and tough luck known as the blues, that outgrowth of ragtime known as jazz (in the development of which whites have assisted), and the Charleston, an eccentric dance invented by the gamins around the public marketplace in Charleston, S.C. No one can or does deny this. But these are contributions of a caste in a certain section of the country. They are foreign to Northern Negroes, West Indian Negroes, and African Negroes. They are no more expressive or characteristic of the Negro race than the music and dancing of the Appalachian highlanders or the Dalmation peasantry are expressive or characteristic of the Caucasian race. If one wishes to speak of the musical contributions of the peasantry of the South, very well. Any group under similar circumstances would have produced something similar. It is merely a coincidence that this peasant class happens to be of a darker hue than the other inhabitants of the land. One recalls the remarkable likeness of the minor strains of the Russian mujiks to those of the Southern Negro.

As for the literature, painting, and sculpture of Aframericans—such as there is—it is identical in kind with the literature, painting, and sculpture of white Americans; that is, it shows more or less evidence of European influence. In the field of drama little of any merit has been written by and about Negroes that could not have been written by whites. The dean of the Aframerican literati is W. E. B. Du Bois, a product of Harvard and German universities; the foremost Aframerican sculptor is Meta Warwick Fuller, a graduate of leading American art schools and former student of Rodin; while the most noted Aframerican painter, Henry Ossawa Tanner, is dean of American painters in Paris and has been decorated by the French Government. Now the work of these artists is no more "expressive of the Negro soul"—as the gushers put it—than are the scribblings of Octavus Cohen or Hugh Wiley.

This, of course, is easily understood if one stops to realize that the Aframerican is merely a lampblacked Anglo-Saxon. If the European immigrant after two or three generations of exposure to our schools, politics, advertising, moral crusades, and restaurants becomes indistinguishable from the mass of Americans of the older stock (despite the influence of the foreign-language press), how much truer must it be of the sons of Ham who have been subjected to what the uplifters call Americanism for the last three hundred years. Aside from his color, which ranges from very dark brown to pink, your American Negro is just plain American. Negroes and whites from the same localities in this country talk, think, and act about the same. Because a few writers with a paucity of themes have seized upon imbecilities of the Negro rustics and clowns and palmed them off as authentic and characteristic Aframerican behavior, the common notion that the black American is so "different" from his white neighbor has gained wide currency. The mere mention of the word "Negro" conjures up in the average white American's mind a composite stereotype of Bert Williams, Aunt Jemima, Uncle Tom, Jack Johnson, Florian Slappey, and the various monstrosities scrawled by the cartoonists. Your average Aframerican no more resembles this stereotype than the average American resembles a composite of Andy Gump, Jim Jeffries, and a cartoon by Rube Goldberg.

Again, the Africamerican is subject to the same economic and social forces that mold the actions and thoughts of the white Americans. He is not living in a different world as some whites and a few Negroes would have us believe. When the jangling of his Connecticut alarm clock gets him out of his Grand Rapids bed to a breakfast similar to that eaten by his white brother across the street; when he toils at the same or similar work in mills, mines, factories, and commerce alongside the descendants of Spartacus, Robin Hood, and Eric the Red; when he wears similar clothing and speaks the same language with the same degree of perfection; when he reads the same Bible and belongs to the Baptist, Methodist, Episcopal, or Catholic church; when his fraternal affiliations also include the Elks, Masons, and Knights of Pythias; when he gets the same or similar schooling, lives in the same kind of houses, owns the same makes of cars (or rides in them), and nightly sees the same Hollywood version of life on the screen; when he smokes the same brands of tobacco, and avidly peruses the same puerile periodicals; in short, when he responds to the same political, social, moral, and economic stimuli in precisely the same manner as his white neighbor, it is sheer nonsense to talk about "racial differences" as between the American black man and the American white man. Glance over a Negro newspaper (it is printed in good Americanese) and you will find the usual quota of crime news, scandal, personals, and uplift to be found in the average white newspaper—which, by the way, is more widely read by the Negroes than is the Negro press. In order to satisfy the cravings of an inferiority complex engendered by the colorphobia of the mob, the readers of the Negro newspapers are given a slight dash of racialistic seasoning. In the homes of the black and white Americans of the same cultural and economic level one finds similar furniture, literature, and conversation. How, then, can the black American be expected to produce art and literature dissimilar to that of the white American?

Consider Coleridge-Taylor, Edward Wilmot Blyden, and Claude McKay, the Englishmen; Pushkin, the Russian; Bridgewater, the Pole; Antar, the Arabian; Latino, the Spaniard; Dumas, *père* and *fils*, the Frenchmen; and Paul Laurence Dunbar, Charles W. Chesnutt, and James Weldon Johnson, the Americans. All Negroes; yet their work shows the impress of nationality rather than race. They all reveal the psychology and culture of their environment—their color is incidental. Why should Negro artists of America vary from the national artistic norm when Negro artists in other countries have not done so? If we can foresee what kind of white citizens will inhabit this neck of the woods in the next generation by studying the sort of education and environment the children are exposed to now, it should not be difficult to reason that the adults of today are what they are because of the education and environment they were exposed to a generation ago. And that education and environment were about the same for blacks and whites. One contemplates the popularity of the Negro-art hokum and murmurs, "How come?"

This nonsense is probably the last stand of the old myth palmed off by Negrophobists for all these many years, and recently rehashed by the sainted Harding, that there are "fundamental, eternal, and inescapable differences" between white and black Americans. That there are Negroes who will lend this myth a helping hand need occasion no surprise. It has been broadcast all over the world by the vociferous scions of slaveholders, "scientists" like Madison Grant and Lothrop Stoddard, and the patriots who flood the treasury of the Ku Klux Klan; and is believed, even today, by the majority of free, white citizens. On this baseless premise, so flattering to the white mob, that the blackamoor is inferior and fundamentally different, is erected the postulate that he must needs be peculiar; and when he attempts to portray life through the medium of art, it must of necessity be a peculiar art. While such reasoning may seem conclusive to the majority of Americans, it must be rejected with a loud guffaw by intelligent people.

3 | The Negro Artist and the Racial Mountain

Langston Hughes

(1926)

One of the most promising of the young Negro poets said to me once, "I want to be a poet—not a Negro poet," meaning, I believe, "I want to write like a white poet"; meaning subconsciously, "I would like to be a white poet"; meaning behind that, "I would like to be white." And I was sorry the young man said that, for no great poet has ever been afraid of being himself. And I doubted then that, with his desire to run away spiritually from his race, this boy would ever be a great poet. But this is the mountain standing in the way of any true Negro art in America—this urge within the race toward whiteness, the desire to pour racial individuality into the mold of American standardization, and to be as little Negro and as much American as possible.

But let us look at the immediate background of this young poet. His family is of what I suppose one would call the Negro middle class: people who are by no means rich yet never uncomfortable nor hungry—smug, contented, respectable folk, members of the Baptist church. The father goes to work every morning. He is a chief steward at a large white club. The mother sometimes does fancy sewing or supervises parties for the rich families of the town. The children go to a mixed school. In the home they read white papers and magazines. And the mother often says "Don't be like niggers" when the children are bad. A frequent phrase from the father is, "Look how well a white man does things." And so the word white comes to be unconsciously a symbol of all the virtues. It holds for the children beauty, morality, and money. The whisper of "I want to be white" runs silently through their minds. This young poet's home is, I believe, a fairly typical home of the colored middle class. One sees immediately how difficult it would be for an artist born in such a home to interest himself in interpreting the beauty of his own people. He is never taught to see that beauty. He is taught rather not to see it, or if he does, to be ashamed of it when it is not according to Caucasian patterns.

For racial culture the home of a self-styled "high-class" Negro has nothing better to offer. Instead there will perhaps be more aping of things white than in a less cultured or less wealthy home. The father is perhaps a doctor, lawyer, landowner, or politician. The mother may be a social worker, or a teacher, or she may do nothing and have a maid. Father is often dark but he has usually married the lightest woman he could find. The family attend a fashionable church, where few really colored faces are to be found. And they themselves draw a color line. In the North they go to white theaters and white movies. And in the South they have at least two cars and a house "like white folks." Nordic manners, Nordic faces, Nordic hair, Nordic art (if any), and an Episcopal heaven. A very high mountain indeed for the would-be racial artist to climb in order to discover himself and his people.

But then there are the low-down folks, the so-called common element and they are the majority—may the Lord be praised! The people who have their nip of gin on Saturday nights and are not too important to themselves or the community, or too well fed, or too learned to watch the lazy world go round. They live on Seventh Street in Washington or State Street in Chicago and they do not particularly care whether they are like white folks or anybody else. Their joy runs, bang! into ecstasy. Their religion soars to a shout. Work maybe a little today, rest a little tomorrow. Play awhile. Sing awhile. O, let's dance! These common people are not afraid of spirituals, as for a long time their more intellectual brethren were, and jazz is their child. They furnish a wealth of colorful, distinctive material for any artist because they still hold their own individuality in the face of American standardizations. And perhaps these common people will give to the world its truly great Negro artist, the one who is not afraid to be himself. Whereas the better-class Negro would tell the artist what to do, the people at least let him alone when he does appear. And they are not ashamed of him—if they know he exists at all. And they accept what beauty is their own without question.

Certainly there is, for the American Negro artist who can escape the restrictions the more advanced among his own group would put upon him, a great field of unused material ready for his art. Without going outside his race, and even among the better classes with their "white" culture and conscious American manners, but still Negro enough to be different, there is sufficient matter to furnish a black artist with a lifetime of creative work. And when he chooses to touch on the relations between Negroes and whites in this country with their innumerable overtones and undertones, surely and especially for literature and the drama, there is an inexhaustible supply of themes at hand. To these the Negro artist can give his racial individuality, his heritage of rhythm and warmth, and his incongruous humor that so often, as in the Blues, becomes ironic laughter mixed with tears. But let us look again at the mountain.

A prominent Negro clubwoman in Philadelphia paid eleven dollars to hear Raquel Meller sing Andalusian popular songs. But she told me a few weeks before she would not think of going to hear "that woman," Clara Smith, a great black artist sing Negro folksongs. And many an upper-class Negro church, even now, would not dream of employing a spiritual in its services. The drab melodies in white folks' hymnbooks are much to be preferred. "We want to worship the Lord correctly and quietly. We don't believe in 'shouting.' Let's be dull like the Nordics," they say, in effect.

The road for the serious black artist, then, who would produce a racial art is most certainly rocky and the mountain is high. Until recently he received almost no encouragement for his work from either white or colored people. The fine novels of Chesnutt go out of print with neither race noticing their passing. The quaint charm and humor of Dunbar's dialect verse brought to him, in his day, largely the same kind of encouragement one would give a sideshow freak (A colored man writing poetry! How odd!) or a clown (How amusing!).

The present vogue in things Negro, although it may do as much harm as good for the budding colored artist, has at least done this: it has brought him forcibly to the attention of his own people among whom for so long, unless the other race had noticed him beforehand, he was a prophet with little honor. I understand that Charles Gilpin acted for years in Negro theaters without any special acclaim from his own, but when Broadway gave him eight curtain calls, Negroes, too, began to beat a tin pan in his honor. I know a young colored writer, a manual worker by day, who had been writing well for the colored magazines for some years, but it was not until he recently broke into the white publications and his first book was accepted by a prominent New York publisher that the "best" Negroes in his city took the trouble to discover that he lived there. Then almost immediately they decided to give a grand dinner for him. But the society ladies were careful to whisper to his mother that perhaps she'd better not come. They were not sure she would have an evening gown.

The Negro artist works against an undertow of sharp criticism and misunderstanding from his own group and unintentional bribes from the whites. "O, be respectable, write about nice people, show how good we are," say the Negroes. "Be stereotyped, don't go too far, don't shatter our illusions about you, don't amuse us too seriously. We will pay you," say the whites. Both would have told Jean Toomer not to write "Cane." The colored people did not praise it. The white people did not buy it. Most of the colored people who did read "Cane" hate it. They are afraid of it. Although the critics gave it good reviews the public remained indifferent. Yet (excepting the work of Du Bois) "Cane" contains the finest prose written by a Negro in America. And like the singing of Robeson, it is truly racial.

But in spite of the Nordicized Negro intelligentsia and the desires of some white editors we have an honest American Negro literature already with us. Now I await the rise of the Negro theater. Our folk music, having achieved world-wide fame, offers itself to the genius of the great individual American Negro composer who is to come. And within the next decade I expect to see the work of a growing school of colored artists who paint and model the beauty of dark faces and create with new technique the expressions of their own soul-world. And the Negro dancers who will dance like flame and the singers who will continue to carry our songs to all who listen—they will be with us in even greater numbers tomorrow.

Most of my own poems are racial in theme and treatment, derived from the life I know. In many of them I try to grasp and hold some of the meanings and rhythms of jazz. I am sincere as I know how to be in these poems and yet after every reading

I answer questions like these from my own people: Do you think Negroes should always write about Negroes? I wish you wouldn't read some of your poems to white folks. How do you find anything interesting in a place like a cabaret? Why do you write about black people? You aren't black. What makes you do so many jazz poems?

But jazz to me is one of the inherent expressions of Negro life in America: the eternal tom-tom beating in the Negro soul—the tom-tom of revolt against weariness in a white world, a world of subway trains, and work, work, work; the tom-tom of joy and laughter, and pain swallowed in a smile. Yet the Philadelphia clubwoman is ashamed to say that her race created it and she does not like me to write about it. The old subconscious "white is best" runs through her mind. Years of study under white teachers, a lifetime of white books, pictures, and papers, and white manners, morals, and Puritan standards made her dislike the spirituals. And now she turns up her nose at jazz and all its manifestations—likewise almost everything else distinctly racial. She doesn't care for the Winold Reiss portraits of Negroes because they are "too Negro." She does not want a true picture of herself from anybody. She wants the artist to flatter her, to make the white world believe that all Negroes are as smug and as near white in soul as she wants to be. But, to my mind, it is the duty of the younger Negro artist, if he accepts any duties at all from outsiders, to change through the force of his art that old whispering "I want to be white," hidden in the aspirations of his people, to "Why should I want to be white? I am a Negro—and beautiful!"

So I am ashamed for the black poet who says, "I want to be a poet, not a Negro poet," as though his own racial world were not as interesting as any other world. I am ashamed, too, for the colored artist who runs from the painting of Negro faces to the painting of sunsets after the manner of the academicians because he fears the strange un-whiteness of his own features. An artist must be free to choose what he does, certainly, but he must also never be afraid to do what he might choose.

Let the blare of Negro jazz bands and the bellowing voice of Bessie Smith singing Blues penetrate the closed ears of the colored near-intellectuals until they listen and perhaps understand. Let Paul Robeson singing Water Boy, and Rudolph Fisher writing about the streets of Harlem, and Jean Toomer holding the heart of Georgia in his hands, and Aaron Douglas drawing strange black fantasies cause the smug Negro middle class to turn from their white, respectable, ordinary books and papers to catch a glimmer of their own beauty. We younger Negro artists who create now intend to express our individual dark-skinned selves without fear or shame. If white people are pleased we are glad. If they are not, it doesn't matter. We know we are beautiful. And ugly too. The tom-tom cries and the tom-tom laughs. If colored people are pleased we are glad. If they are not, their displeasure doesn't matter either. We build our temples for tomorrow, strong as we know how, and we stand on top of the mountain, free within ourselves.

4 | Characteristics of Negro Expression

Zora Neale Hurston

(1934)

DRAMA

The Negro's universal mimicry is not so much a thing in itself as an evidence of something that permeates his entire self. And that thing is drama.

His very words are action words. His interpretation of the English language is in terms of pictures. One act described in terms of another. Hence the rich metaphor and simile.

The metaphor is of course very primitive. It is easier to illustrate than it is to explain because action came before speech. Let us make a parallel. Language is like money. In primitive communities actual goods, however bulky, are bartered for what one wants. This finally evolves into coin, the coin being not real wealth but a symbol of wealth. Still later even coin is abandoned for legal tender, and still later for checks in certain usages.

Every phase of Negro life is highly dramatized. No matter how joyful or how sad the case there is sufficient poise for drama. Everything is acted out. Unconsciously for the most part of course. There is an impromptu ceremony always ready for every hour of life. No little moment passes unadorned.

Now the people with highly developed languages have words for detached ideas. That is legal tender. "That-which-we-squat-on" has become "chair." "Groan-causer" has evolved into "spear," and so on. Some individuals even conceive of the equivalent of check words, like "ideation" and "pleonastic." Perhaps we might say that *Paradise Lost* and *Sartor Resartus* are written in check words.

The primitive man exchanges descriptive words. His terms are all close-fitting. Frequently the Negro, even with detached words in his vocabulary—not evolved in him but transplanted on his tongue by contact—must add action to it to make it do. So we have "chop-axe," "sitting-chair," "cook-pot," and the like because the speaker

31

has in his mind the picture of the object in use. Action. Everything illustrated. So we can say the white man thinks in a written language and the Negro thinks in hieroglyphics.

A bit of Negro drama familiar to all is the frequent meeting of two opponents who threaten to do atrocious murder one upon the other.

Who has not observed a robust young Negro chap posing upon a street corner, possessed of nothing but his clothing, his strength and his youth. Does he bear himself like a pauper? No, Louis XIV could be no more insolent in his assurance. His eyes say plainly "Female, halt!" His posture exults "Ah female, I am the eternal male, the giver of life. Behold in my hot flesh all the delights of this world. Salute me, I am strength." All this with a languid posture, there is no mistaking his meaning.

A Negro girl strolls past the corner lounger. Her whole body panging and posing. A slight shoulder movement that calls attention to her bust, that is all of a dare. A hippy undulation below the waist that is a sheaf of promises tied with conscious power. She is acting out "I'm a darned sweet woman and you know it."

These little plays by strolling players are acted out daily in a dozen streets in a thousand cities, and no one ever mistakes the meaning.

WILL TO ADORN

The will to adorn is the second most notable characteristic in Negro expression. Perhaps his idea of ornament does not attempt to meet conventional standards, but it satisfies the soul of its creator.

In this respect the American Negro has done wonders to the English language. It has often been stated by etymologists that the Negro has introduced no African words to the language. This is true, but it is equally true that he has made over a great part of the tongue to his liking and has had his revision accepted by the ruling class. No one listening to a Southern white man talk could deny this. Not only has he softened and toned down strongly consonanted words like "aren't" to "aint" and the like, he has made new force words out of old feeble elements. Examples of this are "ham-shanked," "battle-hammed," "double-teen," "bodaciously," "muffle-jawed."

But the Negro's greatest contribution to the language is: (1) the use of metaphor and simile; (2) the use of the double descriptive; (3) the use of verbal nouns.

1. METAPHOR AND SIMILE

One at a time, like lawyers going to heaven.
You sho is propaganda.
Sobbing hearted.
I'll beat you till: (*a*) rope like okra, (*b*) slack like lime, (*c*) smell like onions.
Fatal for naked.

Kyting along.
That's a lynch.
That's a rope.
Cloakers—deceivers.
Regular as pig-tracks.
Mule blood—black molasses.
Syndicating—gossiping.
Flambeaux—cheap café (lighted by flambeaux).
To put yo'self on de ladder.

2. THE DOUBLE DESCRIPTIVE

High-tall.
Little-tee-ninchy (tiny).
Low-down.
Top-superior.
Sham-polish.
Lady-people.
Kill-dead.
Hot-boiling.
Chop-axe.
Sitting-chairs.
De watch wall.
Speedy-hurry.
More great and more better.

3. VERBAL NOUNS

She features somebody I know.
Funeralize.
Sense me into it.
Puts the shamery on him.
'Taint everybody you kin confidence.
I wouldn't friend with her.
Jooking—playing piano or guitar as it is done in Jook-houses (houses of ill-fame).
Uglying away.
I wouldn't scorn my name all up on you.
Bookooing (beaucoup) around—showing off.

Nouns from Verbs

Won't stand a broke.
She won't take a listen.

He won't stand straightening.
That is such a complement.
That's a lynch.

The stark, trimmed phrases of the Occident seem too bare for the voluptuous child of the sun, hence the adornment. It arises out of the same impulse as the wearing of jewelry and the making of sculpture—the urge to adorn.

On the walls of the homes of the average Negro one always finds a glut of gaudy calenders, wall pockets and advertising lithographs. The sophisticated white man or Negro would tolerate none of these, even if they bore a likeness to the Mona Lisa. No commercial art for decoration. Nor the calender nor the advertisement spoils the picture for this lowly man. He sees the beauty in spite of the declaration of the Portland Cement Works or the butcher's announcement. I saw in Mobile a room in which there was an overstuffed mohair living-room suite, an imitation mahogany bed and chifforobe, a console victrola. The walls were gaily papered with Sunday supplements of the *Mobile Register*. There were seven calendars and three wall pockets. One of them was decorated with a lace doily. The mantel-shelf was covered with a scarf of deep homemade lace, looped up with a huge bow of pink crepe paper. Over the door was a huge lithograph showing the Treaty of Versailles being signed with a Waterman fountain pen.

It was grotesque, yes. But it indicated the desire for beauty. And decorating a decoration, as in the case of the doily on the gaudy wall pocket, did not seem out of place to the hostess. The feeling back of such an act is that there can never be enough of beauty, let alone too much. Perhaps she is right. We each have our standards of art, and thus are all interested parties and so unfit to pass judgment upon the art concepts of others.

Whatever the Negro does of his own volition he embellishes. His religious service is for the greater part excellent prose poetry. Both prayers and sermons are tooled and polished until they are true works of art. The supplication is forgotten in the frenzy of creation. The prayer of the white man is considered humorous in its bleakness. The beauty of the Old Testament does not exceed that of a Negro prayer.

ANGULARITY

After adornment the next most striking manifestation of the Negro is Angularity. Everything that he touches becomes angular. In all African sculpture and doctrine of any sort we find the same thing.

Anyone watching Negro dancers will be struck by the same phenomenon. Every posture is another angle. Pleasing, yes. But an effect achieved by the very means which an European strives to avoid.

The pictures on the walls are hung at deep angles. Furniture is always set at an angle. I have instances of a piece of furniture in the middle of a wall being set with one end nearer the wall than the other to avoid the simple straight line.

ASYMMETRY

Asymmetry is a definite feature of Negro art. I have no samples of true Negro painting unless we count the African shields, but the sculpture and carvings are full of this beauty and lack of symmetry.

It is present in the literature, both prose and verse. I offer an example of this quality in verse from Langston Hughes:

> I ain't gonna mistreat ma good gal any more,
> I'm just gonna kill her next time she makes me sore.
>
> I treats her kind but she don't do me right,
> She fights and quarrels most ever' night.
>
> I can't have no woman's got such low-down ways
> Cause de blue gum woman aint de style now'days.
>
> I brought her from the South and she's goin on back,
> Else I'll use her head for a carpet track.

It is the lack of symmetry which makes Negro dancing so difficult for white dancers to learn. The abrupt and unexpected changes. The frequent change of key and time are evidences of this quality in music. (Note the St. Louis Blues.)

The dancing of the justly famous Bo-Jangles and Snake Hips are excellent examples.

The presence of rhythm and lack of symmetry are paradoxical, but there they are. Both are present to a marked degree. There is always rhythm, but it is the rhythm of segments. Each unit has a rhythm of its own, but when the whole is assembled it is lacking in symmetry. But easily workable to a Negro who is accustomed to the break in going from one part to another, so that he adjusts himself to the new tempo.

DANCING

Negro dancing is dynamic suggestion. No matter how violent it may appear to the beholder, every posture gives the impression that the dancer will do much more. For example, the performer flexes one knee sharply, assumes a ferocious face mask, thrusts the upper part of the body forward with clenched fists, elbows taut as in hard running or grasping a thrusting blade. That is all. But the spectator himself adds the picture of ferocious assault, hears the drums and finds himself keeping time with the music and tensing himself for the struggle. It is compelling insinuation. That is the very reason the spectator is held so rapt. He is participating in the performance himself—carrying out the suggestions of the performer.

The difference in the two arts is: the white dancer attempts to express fully; the Negro is restrained, but succeeds in gripping the beholder by forcing him to finish the action the performer suggests. Since no art ever can express all the variations conceivable, the Negro must be considered the greater artist, his dancing is realistic suggestion, and that is about all a great artist can do.

NEGRO FOLKLORE

Negro folklore is not a thing of the past. It is still in the making. Its great variety shows the adaptability of the black man: nothing is too old or too new, domestic or foreign, high or low, for his use. God and the Devil are paired, and are treated no more reverently than Rockefeller and Ford. Both of these men are prominent in folklore, Ford being particularly strong, and they talk and act like good-natured stevedores or mill-hands. Ole Massa is sometimes a smart man and often a fool. The automobile is ranged alongside of the oxcart. The angels and the apostles walk and talk like section hands. And through it all walks Jack, the greatest culture hero of the South; Jack beats them all—even the Devil, who is often smarter than God.

CULTURE HEROES

The Devil is next after Jack as a culture hero. He can outsmart everyone but Jack. God is absolutely no match for him. He is good-natured and full of humor. The sort of person one may count on to help out in any difficulty.

Peter the Apostle is the third in importance. One need not look far for the explanation. The Negro is not a Christian really. The primitive gods are not deities of too subtle inner reflection; they are hardworking bodies who serve their devotees just as laboriously as the suppliant serves them. Gods of physical violence, stopping at nothing to serve their followers. Now of all the apostles Peter is the most active. When the other ten fell back trembling in the garden, Peter wielded the blade on the posse. Peter first and foremost in all action. The gods of no peoples have been philosophic until the people themselves have approached that state.

The rabbit, the bear, the lion, the buzzard, the fox are culture heroes from the animal world. The rabbit is far in the lead of all the others and is blood brother to Jack. In short, the trickster-hero of West Africa has been transplanted to America.

John Henry is a culture hero in song, but no more so than Stacker Lee, Smokey Joe or Bad Lazarus. There are many, many Negroes who have never heard of any of the song heroes, but none who do not know John (Jack) and the rabbit.

EXAMPLES OF FOLKLORE AND THE MODERN
CULTURE HERO

Why de Porpoise's Tail Is on Crosswise

Now, I want to tell you 'bout de porpoise. God had done made de world and everything. He set de moon and de stars in de sky. He got de fishes of de sea, and de fowls of de air completed.

He made de sun and hung it up. Then He made a nice gold track for it to run on. Then He said, "Now, Sun, I got everything made but Time. That's up to you. I want you to start out and go round de world on dis track just as fast as you kin make it. And de time it takes you to go and come, I'm going to call day and night." De Sun went zoonin' on cross de elements. Now, de porpoise was hanging round there and heard God what he tole de Sun, so he decided he'd take dat trip round de world hisself. He looked up and saw de Sun kytin' along, so he lit out too, him and dat Sun!

So de porpoise beat de Sun round de world by one hour and three minutes. So God said, "Aw naw, this aint gointer do! I didn't mean for nothin' to be faster than de Sun!" So God run dat porpoise for three days before he run him down and caught him, and took his tail off and put it on crossways to slow him up. Still he's de fastest thing in de water. And dat's why de porpoise got his tail on crossways.

Rockefeller and Ford

Once John D. Rockefeller and Henry Ford was woofing at each other. Rockefeller told Henry Ford he could build a solid gold road round the world. Henry Ford told him if he would he would look at it and see if he liked it, and if he did he would buy it and put one of his tin lizzies on it.

ORIGINALITY

It has been said so often that the Negro is lacking in originality that it has almost become a gospel. Outward signs seem to bear this out. But if one looks closely its falsity is immediately evident.

It is obvious that to get back to original sources is much too difficult for any group to claim very much as a certainty. What we really mean by originality is the modification of ideas. The most ardent admirer of the great Shakespeare cannot claim first source even for him. It is his treatment of the borrowed material.

So if we look at it squarely, the Negro is a very original being. While he lives and moves in the midst of a white civilization, everything that he touches is reinterpreted for his own use. He has modified the language, mode of food preparation, practice of medicine, and most certainly the religion of his new country, just as he adapted to suit himself the Sheik haircut made famous by Rudolph Valentino.

Everyone is familiar with the Negro's modification of the whites' musical instruments, so that his interpretation has been adopted by the white man himself and then reinterpreted. In so many words, Paul Whiteman is giving an imitation of a Negro orchestra making use of white-invented musical instruments in a Negro way. Thus has arisen a new art in the civilized world and thus has our so-called civilization come. The exchange and re-exchange of ideas between groups.

IMITATION

The Negro, the world over, is famous as a mimic. But this in no way damages his standing as an original. Mimicry is an art in itself. If it is not, then all art must fall by the same blow that strikes it down. When sculpture, painting, acting, dancing, literature neither reflect nor suggest anything in nature or human experience we turn away with a dull wonder in our hearts at why the thing was done. Moreover, the contention that the Negro imitates from a feeling of inferiority is incorrect. He mimics for the love of it. The group of Negroes who slavishly imitate is small. The average Negro glories in his ways. The highly educated Negro the same. The self-despisement lies in a middle class who scorns to do or be anything Negro. "That's just like a Nigger" is the most terrible rebuke one can lay upon this kind. He wears drab clothing, sits through a boresome church service, pretends to have no interest in the community, holds beauty contests, and otherwise apes all the mediocrities of the white brother. The truly cultured Negro scorns him, and the Negro "farthest down" is too busy "spreading his junk" in his own way to see or care. He likes his own things best. Even the group who are not Negroes but belong to the "sixth race," buy such records as "Shake dat thing" and "Tight lak dat." They really enjoy hearing a good bible-beater preach, but wild horses could drag no such admission from them. Their ready-made expression is: "We done got away from all that now." Some refuse to countenance Negro music on the grounds that it is niggerism, and for that reason should be done away with. Roland Hayes was thoroughly denounced for singing spirituals until he was accepted by white audiences. Langston Hughes is not considered a poet by this group because he writes of the man in the ditch, who is more numerous and real among us than any other.

But, this group aside, let us say that the art of mimicry is better developed in the Negro than in other racial groups. He does it as the mockingbird does it, for the love of it, and not because he wishes to be like the one imitated. I saw a group of small Negro boys imitating a cat defecating and the subsequent toilet of the cat. It was very realistic, and they enjoyed it as much as if they had been imitating a coronation ceremony. The dances are full of imitations of various animals. The buzzard lope, walking the dog, the pig's hind legs, holding the mule, elephant squat, pigeon's wing, falling off the log, seabord (imitation of an engine starting), and the like.

ABSENCE OF THE CONCEPT OF PRIVACY

It is said that Negroes keep nothing secret, that they have no reserve. This ought not to seem strange when one considers that we are an outdoor people accustomed to communal life. Add this to all-permeating drama and you have the explanation.

There is no privacy in an African village. Loves, fights, possessions are, to misquote Woodrow Wilson, "Open disagreements openly arrived at." The community is given the benefit of a good fight as well as a good wedding. An audience is a necessary part of any drama. We merely go with nature rather than against it.

Discord is more natural than accord. If we accept the doctrine of the survival of the fittest there are more fighting honors than there are honors for other achievements. Humanity places premiums on all things necessary to its well-being, and a valiant and good fighter is valuable in any community. So why hide the light under a bushel? Moreover, intimidation is a recognized part of warfare the world over, and threats certainly must be listed under that head. So that a great threatener must certainly be considered an aid to the fighting machine. So then if a man or woman is a facile hurler of threats why should he or she not show their wares to the community? Hence the holding of all quarrels and fights in the open. One relieves one's pent-up anger and at the same time earns laurels in intimidation. Besides, one does the community a service. There is nothing so exhilarating as watching well-matched opponents go into action. The entire world likes action, for that matter. Hence prize-fighters become millionaires.

Likewise lovemaking is a biological necessity the world over and an art among Negroes. So that a man or woman who is proficient sees no reason why the fact should not be moot. He swaggers. She struts hippily about. Songs are built on the power to charm beneath the bedclothes. Here again we have individuals striving to excel in what the community considers an art. Then if all of his world is seeking a great lover, why should he not speak right out loud?

It is all in a viewpoint. Lovemaking and fighting in all their branches are high arts, other things are arts among other groups where they brag about their proficiency just as brazenly as we do about these things that others consider matters for conversation behind closed doors. At any rate, the white man is despised by Negroes as a very poor fighter individually, and a very poor lover. One Negro, speaking of white men, said, "White folks is alright when dey gits in de bank and on de law bench, but dey sho' kin lie about wimmen folks."

I pressed him to explain. "Well you see, white mens makes out they marries wimmen to look at they eyes, and they know they gits em for just what us gits em for. 'Nother thing, white mens say they goes clear round de world and wins all de wimmen folks way from they men folks. Dat's a lie too. They don't win nothin, they buys em. Now de way I figgers it, if a woman don't want me enough to be wid me, 'thout I got to pay her, she kin rock right on, but these here white men don't know what to do wid a woman when they gits her—dat's how come they gives they wimmen so much. They got to. Us wimmen works jus as hard as us does an come home an sleep wid us every night. They own wouldn't do it and its de mens fault. Dese white men done fooled theyself bout dese wimmen.

"Now me, I keeps me some wimmens all de time. Dat's whut dey wuz put here for—us mens to use. Dat's right now, Miss. Y'all wuz put here so us mens could have some pleasure. Course I don't run round like heap uh men folks. But if my ole lady go way from me and stay more'n two weeks, I got to git me somebody, aint I?"

THE JOOK

Jook is the word for a Negro pleasure house. It may mean a bawdy house. It may mean the house set apart on public works where the men and women dance, drink and gamble. Often it is a combination of all these.

In past generations the music was furnished by "boxes," another word for guitars. One guitar was enough for a dance; to have two was considered excellent. Where two were playing one man played the lead and the other seconded him. The first player was "picking" and the second was "framming," that is, playing chords while the lead carried the melody by dexterous finger work. Sometimes a third player was added, and he played a tom-tom effect on the low strings. Believe it or not, this is excellent dance music.

Pianos soon came to take the place of the boxes, and now player-pianos and victrolas are in all of the Jooks.

Musically speaking, the Jook is the most important place in America. For in its smelly, shoddy confines has been born the secular music known as blues, and on blues has been founded jazz. The singing and playing in the true Negro style is called "jooking."

The songs grow by incremental repetition as they travel from mouth to mouth and from Jook to Jook for years before they reach outside ears. Hence the great variety of subject-matter in each song.

The Negro dances circulated over the world were also conceived inside the Jooks. They too make the round of Jooks and public works before going into the outside world.

In this respect it is interesting to mention the Black Bottom. I have read several false accounts of its origin and name. One writer claimed that it got its name from the black sticky mud on the bottom of the Mississippi river. Other equally absurd statements gummed the press. Now the dance really originated in the Jook section of Nashville, Tennessee, around Fourth Avenue. This is a tough neighborhood known as Black Bottom—hence the name.

The Charleston is perhaps forty years old, and was danced up and down the Atlantic seaboard from North Carolina to Key West, Florida.

The Negro social dance is slow and sensuous. The idea in the Jook is to gain sensation, and not so much exercise. So that just enough foot movement is added to keep the dancers on the floor. A tremendous sex stimulation is gained from this. But who is trying to avoid it? The man, the woman, the time and the place have met. Rather, little intimate names are indulged in to heap fire on fire.

These too have spread to all the world.

The Negro theatre, as built up by the Negro, is based on Jook situations, with women, gambling, fighting, drinking. Shows like "Dixie to Broadway" are only Negro in cast, and could just as well have come from pre-Soviet Russia.

Another interesting thing—Negro shows before being tampered with did not specialize in octoroon chorus girls. The girl who could hoist a Jook song from her belly and lam it against the front door of the theatre was the lead, even if she were as black as the hinges of hell. The question was "Can she jook?" She must also have a good belly wobble, and her hips must, to quote a popular work song, "Shake like jelly all over and be so broad, Lawd, Lawd, and be so broad." So that the bleached chorus is the result of a white demand and not the Negro's.

The woman in the Jook may be nappy headed and black, but if she is a good lover she gets there just the same. A favorite Jook song of the past has this to say:

SINGER: It aint good looks dat takes you through dis world.
AUDIENCE: What is it, good mama?
SINGER: Elgin[1] movements in your hips
      Twenty years guarantee.

And it always brought down the house too.

> Oh de white gal rides in a Cadillac,
> De yaller[2] gal rides de same,
> Black gal rides in a rusty Ford
> But she gits dere just de same.

The sort of woman her men idealize is the type that is put forth in the theatre. The art-creating Negro prefers a not too thin woman who can shake like jelly all over as she dances and sings, and that is the type he put forth on the stage. She has been banished by the white producer and the Negro who takes his cue from the white.

Of course a black woman is never the wife of the upper class Negro in the North. This state of affairs does not obtain in the South, however. I have noted numerous cases where the wife was considerably darker than the husband. People of some substance, too.

This scornful attitude towards black women receives mouth sanction by the mud-sills.

Even on the works and in the Jooks the black man sings disparagingly of black women. They say that she is evil. That she sleeps with her fists doubled up and ready for action. All over they are making a little drama of waking up a yaller wife and a black one.

A man is lying beside his yaller wife and wakes her up. She says to him, "Darling, do you know what I was dreaming when you woke me up?" He says, "No honey, what was you dreaming?" She says, "I dreamt I had done cooked you a big, fine dinner and we was setting down to eat out de same plate and I was setting on yo' lap jus huggin you and kissin you and you was so sweet."

Wake up a black woman, and before you kin git any sense into her she be done up and lammed you over the head four or five times. When you git her quiet she'll say, "Nigger, know whut I was dreamin when you woke me up?"

You say, "No honey, what was you dreamin?" She says, "I dreamt you shook yo' rusty fist under my nose and I split yo' head open wid a axe."

But in spite of disparaging fictitious drama, in real life the black girl is drawing on his account at the commissary. Down in the Cypress Swamp as he swings his axe he chants:

> Dat ole black gal, she keep on grumblin,
> New pair shoes, new pair shoes,
> I'm goint to buy her shoes and stockings
> Slippers too, slippers too.

Then adds aside: "Blacker de berry, sweeter de juice."

To be sure the black gal is still in power, men are still cutting and shooting their way to her pillow. To the queen of the Jook!

Speaking of the influence of the Jook, I noted that Mae West in "Sex" had much more flavor of the turpentine quarters than she did of the white bawd. I know that the piece she played on the piano is a very old Jook composition. "Honey let yo' drawers hang low" had been played and sung in every Jook in the South for at least thirty-five years. It has always puzzled me why she thought it likely to be played in a Canadian bawdy house.

Speaking of the use of Negro material by white performers, it is astonishing that so many are trying it, and I have never seen one yet entirely realistic. They often have all the elements of the song, dance, or expression, but they are misplaced or distorted by the accent falling on the wrong element. Every one seems to think that the Negro is easily imitated when nothing is further from the truth. Without exception I wonder why the blackface comedians *are* blackface; it is a puzzle—good comedians, but darn poor niggers. Gershwin and the other "Negro" rhapsodists come under this same axe. Just about as Negro as a caviar or Ann Pennington's athletic Black Bottom. When the Negroes who knew the Black Bottom in its cradle saw the Broadway version they asked each other, "Is you learnt dat *new* Black Bottom yet?" Proof that it was not *their* dance.

And God only knows what the world has suffered from the white damsels who try to sing Blues.

The Negroes themselves have sinned also in this respect. In spite of the goings up and down on the earth, from the original Fisk Jubilee Singers down to the present, there has been no genuine presentation of Negro songs to white audiences. The spirituals that have been sung around the world are Negroid to be sure, but so full of musicians' tricks that Negro congregations are highly entertained when they hear their old songs so changed. They never use the new style songs, and these are never heard unless perchance some daughter or son has been off to college and returns with one of the old songs with its face lifted, so to speak.

I am of the opinion that this trick style of delivery was originated by the Fisk Singers; Tuskeegee and Hampton followed suit and have helped spread this misconception of Negro spirituals. This Glee Club style has gone on so long and become so fixed among concert singers that it is considered quite authentic. But I say again, that not one concert singer in the world is singing the songs as the Negro song-makers sing them.

If anyone wishes to prove the truth of this let him step into some unfashionable Negro church and hear for himself.

To those who want to institute the Negro theatre, let me say it is already established. It is lacking in wealth, so it is not seen in the high places. A creature with a white head and Negro feet struts the Metropolitan boards. The real Negro theatre is in the Jooks and the cabarets. Self-conscious individuals may turn away the eye and say, "Let us search elsewhere for our dramatic art." Let 'em search. They certainly won't find it. Butter Beans and Susie, Bo-Jangles and Snake Hips are the only performers of the real Negro school it has ever been my pleasure to behold in New York.

DIALECT

If we are to believe the majority of writers of Negro dialect and the burnt-work artists, Negro speech is a weird thing, full of "arms" and "Ises." Fortunately we don't have to believe them. We may go directly to the Negro and let him speak for himself.

I know that I run the risk of being damned as an infidel for declaring that nowhere can be found the Negro who asks "am it?" nor yet his brother who announces "Ise uh gwinter." He exists only for a certain type of writers and performers.

Very few Negroes, educated or not, use a clear clipped "I." It verges more or less upon "Ah." I think the lip form is responsible for this to a great extent. By experiment the reader will find that a sharp "I" is very much easier with a thin taut lip than with a full soft lip. Like tightening violin strings.

If one listens closely one will note too that a word is slurred in one position in the sentence but clearly pronounced in another. This is particularly true of the pronouns. A pronoun as a subject is likely to be clearly enunciated, but slurred as an object. For example: "You better not let me ketch yuh."

There is a tendency in some localities to add the "h" to "it" and pronounce it "hit." Probably a vestige of old English. In some localities "if" is "ef."

In storytelling "so" is universally the connective. It is used even as an introductory word, at the very beginning of a story. In religious expression "and" is used. The trend in stories is to state conclusions; in religion, to enumerate.

I am mentioning only the most general rules in dialect because there are so many quirks that belong only to certain localities that nothing less than a volume would be adequate.

NOTES

1. Elegant(?).
2. Yaller (yellow), light mulatto.

5 | Blueprint for Negro Writing

Richard Wright

(1937)

1. THE ROLE OF NEGRO WRITING: TWO DEFINITIONS

Generally speaking, Negro writing in the past has been confined to humble novels, poems, and plays, prim and decorous ambassadors who went a-begging to white America. They entered the Court of American Public Opinion dressed in the knee-pants of servility, curtsying to show that the Negro was not inferior, that he was human, and that he had a life comparable to that of other people. For the most part these artistic ambassadors were received as though they were French poodles who do clever tricks.

White America never offered these Negro writers any serious criticism. The mere fact that a Negro could write was astonishing. Nor was there any deep concern on the part of white America with the role Negro writing should play in American culture; and the role it did play grew out of accident rather than intent or design. Either it crept in through the kitchen in the form of jokes; or it was the fruits of that foul soil which was the result of a liaison between inferiority-complexed Negro "geniuses" and burnt-out white Bohemians with money.

On the other hand, these often technically brilliant performances by Negro writers were looked upon by the majority of literate Negroes as something to be proud of. At best, Negro writing has been something external to the lives of educated Negroes themselves. That the productions of their writers should have been something of a guide in their daily living is a matter which seems never to have been raised seriously.

Under these conditions Negro writing assumed two general aspects: 1) It became a sort of conspicuous ornamentation, the hallmark of "achievement." 2) It became the voice of the educated Negro pleading with white America for justice.

Rarely was the best of this writing addressed to the Negro himself, his needs, his sufferings, his aspirations. Through misdirection, Negro writers have been far better

45

to others than they have been to themselves. And the mere recognition of this places the whole question of Negro writing in a new light and raises a doubt as to the validity of its present direction.

2. THE MINORITY OUTLOOK

Somewhere in his writings Lenin makes the observation that oppressed minorities often reflect the techniques of the bourgeoisie more brilliantly than some sections of the bourgeoisie themselves. The psychological importance of this becomes meaningful when it is recalled that oppressed minorities, and especially the petty bourgeois sections of oppressed minorities, strive to assimilate the virtues of the bourgeoisie in the assumption that by doing so they can lift themselves into a higher social sphere. But not only among the oppressed petty bourgeoisie does this occur. The workers of a minority people, chafing under exploitation, forge organizational forms of struggle to better their lot. Lacking the handicaps of false ambition and property, they have access to a wide social vision and a deep social consciousness. They display a greater freedom and initiative in pushing their claims upon civilization than even do the petty bourgeoisie. Their organizations show greater strength, adaptability, and efficiency than any other group or class in society.

That Negro workers, propelled by the harsh conditions of their lives, have demonstrated this consciousness and mobility for economic and political action there can be no doubt. But has this consciousness been reflected in the work of Negro writers to the same degree as it has in the Negro workers' struggle to free Herndon and the Scottsboro Boys, in the drive toward unionism, in the fight against lynching? Have they as creative writers taken advantage of their unique minority position?

The answer decidedly is *no*. Negro writers have lagged sadly, and as time passes the gap widens between them and their people.

How can this hiatus be bridged? How can the enervating effects of this long standing split be eliminated?

In presenting questions of this sort an attitude of self-consciousness and self-criticism is far more likely to be a fruitful point of departure than a mere recounting of past achievements. An emphasis upon tendency and experiment, a view of society as something becoming rather than as something fixed and admired is the one which points the way for Negro writers to stand shoulder to shoulder with Negro workers in mood and outlook.

3. A WHOLE CULTURE

There is, however, a culture of the Negro which is his and has been addressed to him; a culture which has, for good or ill, helped to clarify his consciousness and create emotional attitudes which are conducive to action. This culture has stemmed mainly from two sources: 1) the Negro church; 2) and the folklore of the Negro people.

It was through the portals of the church that the American Negro first entered the shrine of western culture. Living under slave conditions of life, bereft of his African heritage, the Negroes' struggle for religion on the plantations between 1820–60 assumed the form of a struggle for human rights. It remained a relatively revolutionary struggle until religion began to serve as an antidote for suffering and denial. But even today there are millions of American Negroes whose only sense of a whole universe, whose only relation to society and man, and whose only guide to personal dignity comes through the archaic morphology of Christian salvation.

It was, however, in a folklore moulded out of rigorous and inhuman conditions of life that the Negro achieved his most indigenous and complete expression. Blues, spirituals, and folk tales recounted from mouth to mouth; the whispered words of a black mother to her black daughter on the ways of men; the confidential wisdom of a black father to his black son; the swapping of sex experiences on street corners from boy to boy in the deepest vernacular; work songs sung under blazing suns—all these formed the channels through which the racial wisdom flowed.

One would have thought that Negro writers in the last century of striving at expression would have continued and deepened this folk tradition, would have tried to create a more intimate and yet a more profoundly social system of artistic communication between them and their people. But the illusion that they could escape through individual achievement the harsh lot of their race swung Negro writers away from any such path. Two separate cultures sprang up: one for the Negro masses, unwritten and unrecognized; and the other for the sons and daughters of a rising Negro bourgeoisie, parasitic and mannered.

Today the question is: Shall Negro writing be for the Negro masses, moulding the lives and consciousness of those masses toward new goals, or shall it continue begging the question of the Negroes' humanity?

4. THE PROBLEM OF NATIONALISM IN NEGRO WRITING

In stressing the difference between the role Negro writing failed to play in the lives of the Negro people, and the role it should play in the future if it is to serve its historic function; in pointing out the fact that Negro writing has been addressed in the main to a small white audience rather than to a Negro one, it should be stated that no attempt is being made here to propagate a specious and blatant nationalism. Yet the nationalist character of the Negro people is unmistakable. Psychologically this nationalism is reflected in the whole of Negro culture, and especially in folklore.

In the absence of fixed and nourishing forms of culture, the Negro has a folklore which embodies the memories and hopes of his struggle for freedom. Not yet caught in paint or stone, and as yet but feebly depicted in the poem and novel, the Negroes' most powerful images of hope and despair still remain in the fluid state of daily speech. How many John Henrys have lived and died on the lips of these black people? How many mythical heroes in embryo have been allowed to perish for lack of husbanding by alert intelligence?

Negro folklore contains, in a measure that puts to shame more deliberate forms of Negro expression, the collective sense of Negro life in America. Let those who shy at the nationalist implications of Negro life look at this body of folklore, living and powerful, which rose out of a unified sense of a common life and a common fate. Here are those vital beginnings of a recognition of value in life as it is *lived*, a recognition that marks the emergence of a new culture in the shell of the old. And at the moment this process starts, at the moment when a people begin to realize a *meaning* in their suffering, the civilization that engenders that suffering is doomed.

The nationalist aspects of Negro life are as sharply manifest in the social institutions of Negro people as in folklore. There is a Negro church, a Negro press, a Negro social world, a Negro sporting world, a Negro business world, a Negro school system, Negro professions; in short, a Negro way of life in America. The Negro people did not ask for this, and deep down, though they express themselves through their institutions and adhere to this special way of life, they do not want it now. This special existence was forced upon them from without by lynch rope, bayonet and mob rule. They accepted these negative conditions with the inevitability of a tree which must live or perish in whatever soil it finds itself.

The few crumbs of American civilization which the Negro has got from the tables of capitalism have been through these segregated channels. Many Negro institutions are cowardly and incompetent; but they are all that the Negro has. And, in the main, any move, whether for progress or reaction, must come through these institutions for the simple reason that all other channels are closed. Negro writers who seek to mould or influence the consciousness of the Negro people must address their messages to them through the ideologies and attitudes fostered in this warping way of life.

5. THE BASIS AND MEANING OF NATIONALISM IN NEGRO WRITING

The social institutions of the Negro are imprisoned in the Jim Crow political system of the South, and this Jim Crow political system is in turn built upon a plantation-feudal economy. Hence, it can be seen that the emotional expression of group-feeling which puzzles so many whites and leads them to deplore what they call "black chauvinism" is not a morbidly inherent trait of the Negro, but rather the reflex expression of a life whose roots are imbedded deeply in Southern soil.

Negro writers must accept the nationalist implications of their lives, not in order to encourage them, but in order to change and transcend them. They must accept the concept of nationalism because, in order to transcend it, they must possess and understand it. And a nationalist spirit in Negro writing means a nationalism carrying the highest possible pitch of social consciousness. It means a nationalism that knows its origins, its limitations; that is aware of the dangers of its position; that knows its ultimate aims are unrealizable within the framework of capitalist America; a nationalism whose reason for being lies in the simple fact of self-possession and in the consciousness of the interdependence of people in modern society.

For purposes of creative expression it means that the Negro writer must realize within the area of his own personal experience those impulses which, when prefigured in terms of broad social movements, constitute the stuff of nationalism.

For Negro writers even more so than for Negro politicians, nationalism is a bewildering and vexing question, the full ramifications of which cannot be dealt with here. But among Negro workers and the Negro middle class the spirit of nationalism is rife in a hundred devious forms; and a simple literary realism which seeks to depict the lives of these people devoid of wider social connotations, devoid of the revolutionary significance of these nationalist tendencies, must of necessity do a rank injustice to the Negro people and alienate their possible allies in the struggle for freedom.

6. SOCIAL CONSCIOUSNESS AND RESPONSIBILITY

The Negro writer who seeks to function within his race as a purposeful agent has a serious responsibility. In order to do justice to his subject matter, in order to depict Negro life in all of its manifold and intricate relationships, a deep, informed, and complex consciousness is necessary; a consciousness which draws for its strength upon the fluid lore of a great people, and moulds this lore with the concepts that move and direct the forces of history today.

With the gradual decline of the moral authority of the Negro church, and with the increasing irresolution which is paralyzing Negro middle class leadership, a new role is devolving upon the Negro writer. He is being called upon to do no less than create values by which his race is to struggle, live and die.

By his ability to fuse and make articulate the experiences of men, because his writing possesses the potential cunning to steal into the inmost recesses of the human heart, because he can create the myths and symbols that inspire a faith in life, he may expect either to be consigned to oblivion, or to be recognized for the valued agent he is.

This raises the question of the personality of the writer. It means that in the lives of Negro writers must be found those materials and experiences which will create a meaningful picture of the world today. Many young writers have grown to believe that a Marxist analysis of society presents such a picture. It creates a picture which, when placed before the eyes of the writer, should unify his personality, organize his emotions, buttress him with a tense and obdurate will to change the world.

And, in turn, this changed world will dialectically change the writer. Hence, it is through a Marxist conception of reality and society that the maximum degree of freedom in thought and feeling can be gained for the Negro writer. Further, this dramatic Marxist vision, when consciously grasped, endows the writer with a sense of dignity which no other vision can give. Ultimately, it restores to the writer his lost heritage, that is, his role as a creator of the world in which he lives, and as a creator of himself.

Yet, for the Negro writer, Marxism is but the starting point. No theory of life can take the place of life. After Marxism has laid bare the skeleton of society, there remains the task of the writer to plant flesh upon those bones out of his will to live. He may, with disgust and revulsion, say no and depict the horrors of capitalism encroaching upon the human being. Or he may, with hope and passion, say yes and depict the faint stirrings of a new and emerging life. But in whatever social voice he chooses to speak, whether positive or negative, there should always be heard or over-heard his faith, his necessity, his judgement.

His vision need not be simple or rendered in primer-like terms; for the life of the Negro people is not simple. The presentation of their lives should be simple, yes; but all the complexity, the strangeness, the magic wonder of life that plays like a bright sheen over the most sordid existence, should be there. To borrow a phrase from the Russians, it should have a *complex simplicity*. Eliot, Stein, Joyce, Proust, Hemingway, and Anderson; Gorky, Barbusse, Nexo, and Jack London no less than the folklore of the Negro himself should form the heritage of the Negro writer. Every iota of gain in human thought and sensibility should be ready grist for his mill, no matter how far-fetched they may seem in their immediate implications.

7. THE PROBLEM OF PERSPECTIVE

What vision must Negro writers have before their eyes in order to feel the impelling necessity for an about face? What angle of vision can show them all the forces of modern society in process, all the lines of economic development converging toward a distant point of hope? Must they believe in some "ism"?

They may feel that only dupes believe in "isms"; they feel with some measure of justification that another commitment means only another disillusionment. But any-one destitute of a theory about the meaning, structure and direction of modern society is a lost victim in a world he cannot understand or control.

But even if Negro writers found themselves through some "ism," how would that influence their writing? Are they being called upon to "preach"? To be "salesmen"? To "prostitute" their writing? Must they "sully" themselves? Must they write "prop-aganda"?

No; it is a question of awareness, of consciousness; it is, above all, a question of perspective.

Perspective is that part of a poem, novel, or play which a writer never puts directly upon paper. It is that fixed point in intellectual space where a writer stands to view the struggles, hopes, and sufferings of his people. There are times when he may stand too close and the result is a blurred vision. Or he may stand too far away and the result is a neglect of important things.

Of all the problems faced by writers who as a whole have never allied themselves with world movements, perspective is the most difficult of achievement. At its best, perspective is a pre-conscious assumption, something which a writer takes for granted, something which he wins through his living.

A Spanish writer recently spoke of living in the heights of one's time. Surely, perspective means just that.

It means that a Negro writer must learn to view the life of a Negro living in New York's Harlem or Chicago's South Side with the consciousness that one-sixth of the earth surface belongs to the working class. It means that a Negro writer must create in his readers' minds a relationship between a Negro woman hoeing cotton in the South and the men who loll in swivel chairs in Wall Street and take the fruits of her toil.

Perspective for Negro writers will come when they have looked and brooded so hard and long upon the harsh lot of their race and compared it with the hopes and struggles of minority peoples everywhere that the cold facts have begun to tell them something.

8. THE PROBLEM OF THEME

This does not mean that a Negro writer's sole concern must be with rendering the social scene; but if his conception of the life of his people is broad and deep enough, if the sense of the whole life he is seeking is vivid and strong in him, then his writing will embrace all those social, political, and economic forms under which the life of his people is manifest.

In speaking of theme one must necessarily be general and abstract; the temperament of each writer moulds and colors the world he sees. Negro life may be approached from a thousand angles, with no limit to technical and stylistic freedom.

Negro writers spring from a family, a clan, a class, and a nation; and the social units in which they are bound have a story, a record. Sense of theme will emerge in Negro writing when Negro writers try to fix this story about some pole of meaning, remembering as they do so that in the creative process meaning proceeds equally as much from the contemplation of the subject matter as from the hopes and apprehensions that rage in the heart of the writer.

Reduced to its simplest and most general terms, theme for Negro writers will rise from understanding the meaning of their being transplanted from a "savage" to a "civilized" culture in all of its social, political, economic, and emotional implications. It means that Negro writers must have in their consciousness the foreshortened picture of the whole, nourishing culture from which they were torn in Africa, and of the long, complex (and for the most part, unconscious) struggle to regain in some form and under alien conditions of life a whole culture again.

It is not only this picture they must have, but also a knowledge of the social and emotional milieu that gives it tone and solidity of detail. Theme for Negro writers will emerge when they have begun to feel the meaning of the history of their race as though they in one life time had lived it themselves throughout all the long centuries.

9. AUTONOMY OF CRAFT

For the Negro writer to depict this new reality requires a greater discipline and consciousness than was necessary for the so-called Harlem school of expression. Not only is the subject matter dealt with far more meaningful and complex, but the new role of the writer is qualitatively different. The Negro writer's new position demands a sharper definition of the status of his craft, and a sharper emphasis upon its functional autonomy.

Negro writers should seek through the medium of their craft to play as meaningful a role in the affairs of men as do other professionals. But if their writing is demanded to perform the social office of other professions, then the autonomy of craft is lost and writing detrimentally fused with other interests. The limitations of the craft constitute some of its greatest virtues. If the sensory vehicle of imaginative writing is required to carry too great a load of didactic material, the artistic sense is submerged.

The relationship between reality and the artistic image is not always direct and simple. The imaginative conception of a historical period will not be a carbon copy of reality. Image and emotion possess a logic of their own. A vulgarized simplicity constitutes the greatest danger in tracing the reciprocal interplay between the writer and his environment.

Writing has its professional autonomy; it should complement other professions, but it should not supplant them or be swamped by them.

10. THE NECESSITY FOR COLLECTIVE WORK

It goes without saying that these things cannot be gained by Negro writers if their present mode of isolated writing and living continues. This isolation exists *among* Negro writers as well as *between* Negro and white writers. The Negro writers' lack of thorough integration with the American scene, their lack of a clear realization among themselves of their possible role, have bred generation after generation of embittered and defeated literati.

Barred for decades from the theater and publishing houses, Negro writers have been made to feel a sense of difference. So deep has this white-hot iron of exclusion been burnt into their hearts that thousands have all but lost the desire to become identified with American civilization. The Negro writers' acceptance of this enforced isolation and their attempt to justify it is but a defense-reflex of the whole special way of life which has been rammed down their throats.

This problem, by its very nature, is one which must be approached contemporaneously from two points of view. The ideological unity of Negro writers and the alliance of that unity with all the progressive ideas of our day is the primary prerequisite for collective work. On the shoulders of white writers and Negro writers alike rest the responsibility of ending this mistrust and isolation.

By placing cultural health above narrow sectional prejudices, liberal writers of all races can help to break the stony soil of aggrandizement out of which the stunted plants of Negro nationalism grow. And, simultaneously, Negro writers can help to weed out these choking growths of reactionary nationalism and replace them with hardier and sturdier types.

These tasks are imperative in light of the fact that we live in a time when the majority of the most basic assumptions of life can no longer be taken for granted. Tradition is no longer a guide. The world has grown huge and cold. Surely this is the moment to ask questions, to theorize, to speculate, to wonder out of what materials can a human world be built.

Each step along this unknown path should be taken with thought, care, self-consciousness, and deliberation. When Negro writers think they have arrived at something which smacks of truth, humanity, they should want to test it with others, feel it with a degree of passion and strength that will enable them to communicate it to millions who are groping like themselves.

Writers faced with such tasks can have no possible time for malice or jealousy. The conditions for the growth of each writer depend too much upon the good work of other writers. Every first rate novel, poem, or play lifts the level of consciousness higher.

6 | What White Publishers Won't Print

Zora Neale Hurston

(1947)

I have been amazed by the Anglo-Saxon's lack of curiosity about the internal lives and emotions of the Negroes, and for that matter, any non-Anglo-Saxon peoples within our borders, above the class of unskilled labor.

This lack of interest is much more important than it seems at first glance. It is even more important at this time than it was in the past. The internal affairs of the nation have bearings on the international stress and strain, and this gap in the national literature now has tremendous weight in world affairs. National coherence and solidarity is implicit in a thorough understanding of the various groups within a nation, and this lack of knowledge about the internal emotions and behavior of the minorities cannot fail to bar out understanding. Man, like all the other animals fears and is repelled by that which he does not understand, and mere difference is apt to connote something malign.

The fact that there is no demand for incisive and full-dress stories around Negroes above the servant class is indicative of something of vast importance to this nation. This blank is NOT filled by the fiction built around upperclass Negroes exploiting the race problem. Rather, it tends to point it up. A college-bred Negro still is not a person like other folks, but an interesting problem, more or less. It calls to mind a story of slavery time. In this story, a master with more intellectual curiosity than usual, set out to see how much he could teach a particularly bright slave of his. When he had gotten him up to higher mathematics and to be a fluent reader of Latin, he called in a neighbor to show off his brilliant slave, and to argue that Negroes had brains just like the slave-owners had, and given the same opportunities, would turn out the same.

The visiting master of slaves looked and listened, tried to trap the literate slave in Algebra and Latin, and failing to do so in both, turned to his neighbor and said:

"Yes, he certainly knows his higher mathematics, and he can read Latin better than many white men I know, but I cannot bring myself to believe that he understands a thing that he is doing. It is all an aping of our culture. All on the outside. You are crazy if you think that it has changed him inside in the least. Turn him loose, and he will revert at once to the jungle. He is still a savage, and no amount of translating Virgil and Ovid is going to change him. In fact, all you have done is to turn a useful savage into a dangerous beast."

That was in slavery time, yes, and we have come a long, long way since then, but the troubling thing is that there are still too many who refuse to believe in the ingestion and digestion of western culture as yet. Hence the lack of literature about the higher emotions and love life of upperclass Negroes and the minorities in general.

Publishers and producers are cool to the idea. Now, do not leap to the conclusion that editors and producers constitute a special class of unbelievers. That is far from true. Publishing houses and theatrical promoters are in business to make money. They will sponsor anything that they believe will sell. They shy away from romantic stories about Negroes and Jews because they feel that they know the public indifference to such works, unless the story or play involves racial tension. It can then be offered as a study in Sociology, with the romantic side subdued. They know the skepticism in general about the complicated emotions in the minorities. The average American just cannot conceive of it, and would be apt to reject the notion, and publishers and producers take the stand that they are not in business to educate, but to make money. Sympathetic as they might be, they cannot afford to be crusaders.

In proof of this, you can note various publishers and producers edging forward a little, and ready to go even further when the trial balloons show that the public is ready for it. This public lack of interest is the nut of the matter.

The question naturally arises as to the why of this indifference, not to say skepticism, to the internal life of educated minorities.

The answer lies in what we may call THE AMERICAN MUSEUM OF UNNATURAL HISTORY. This is an intangible built on folk belief. It is assumed that all non-Anglo-Saxons are uncomplicated stereotypes. Everybody knows all about them. They are lay figures mounted in the museum where all may take them in at a glance. They are made of bent wires without insides at all. So how could anybody write a book about the nonexistent?

The American Indian is a contraption of copper wires in an eternal war-bonnet, with no equipment for laughter, expressionless face and that says "How" when spoken to. His only activity is treachery leading to massacres. Who is so dumb as not to know all about Indians, even if they have never seen one, nor talked with anyone who ever knew one?

The American Negro exhibit is a group of two. Both of these mechanical toys are built so that their feet eternally shuffle, and their eyes pop and roll. Shuffling feet and those popping, rolling eyes denote the Negro, and no characterization is genuine without this monotony. One is seated on a stump picking away on his banjo and singing and laughing. The other is a most amoral character before a sharecropper's shack mumbling about injustice. Doing this makes him out to be a Negro "intellectual." It is as simple as all that.

The whole museum is dedicated to the convenient "typical." In there is the "typical" Oriental, Jew, Yankee, Westerner, Southerner, Latin, and even out-of-favor Nordics like the German. The Englishman "I say old chappie," and the gesticulating Frenchman. The least observant American can know them all at a glance. However, the public willingly accepts the untypical in Nordics, but feels cheated if the untypical is portrayed in others. The author of *Scarlet Sister Mary* complained to me that her neighbors objected to her book on the grounds that she had the characters thinking, "and everybody know that Nigras don't think."

But for the national welfare, it is urgent to realize that the minorities do think, and think about something other than the race problem. That they are very human and internally, according to natural endowment, are just like everybody else. So long as this is not conceived, there must remain that feeling of unsurmountable difference, and difference to the average man means something bad. If people were made right, they would be just like him.

The trouble with the purely problem arguments is that they leave too much unknown. Argue all you will or may about injustice, but as long as the majority cannot conceive of a Negro or a Jew feeling and reacting inside just as they do, the majority will keep right on believing that people who do not look like them cannot possibly feel as they do, and conform to the established pattern. It is well known that there must be a body of waived matter, let us say, things accepted and taken for granted by all in a community before there can be that commonality of feeling. The usual phrase is having things in common. Until this is thoroughly established in respect to Negroes in America, as well as of [*sic*] other minorities, it will remain impossible for the majority to conceive of a Negro experiencing a deep and abiding love and not just the passion of sex. That a great mass of Negroes can be stirred by the pageants of Spring and Fall; the extravaganza of summer, and the majesty of winter. That they can and do experience discovery of the numerous subtle faces as a foundation for a great and selfless love, and the diverse nuances that go to destroy that love as with others. As it is now, this capacity, this evidence of high and complicated emotions, is ruled out. Hence the lack of interest in a romance uncomplicated by the race struggle has so little appeal.

This insistence on defeat in a story where upperclass Negroes are portrayed, perhaps says something from the subconscious of the majority. Involved in western culture, the hero or the heroine, or both, must appear frustrated and go down to defeat, somehow. Our literature reeks with it. Is it the same as saying, "You can translate Virgil, and fumble with the differential calculus, but can you really comprehend it? Can you cope with our subtleties?"

That brings us to the folklore of "reversion to type." This curious doctrine has such wide acceptance that it is tragic. One has only to examine the huge literature on it to be convinced. No matter how high we may *seem* to climb, put us under strain and we revert to type, that is, to the bush. Under a superficial layer of western culture, the jungle drums throb in our veins.

This ridiculous notion makes it possible for that majority who accept it to conceive of even a man like the suave and scholarly Dr. Charles S. Johnson to hide a black cat's bone on his person, and indulge in a midnight voodoo ceremony, complete with leopard skin and drums if threatened with the loss of the presidency of Fisk University, or the love of his wife. "Under the skin . . . better to deal with them in business, etc., but otherwise keep them at a safe distance and under control. I tell you, Carl Van Vechten, think as you like, but they are just not like us."

The extent and extravagance of this notion reaches the ultimate in nonsense in the widespread belief that the Chinese have bizarre genitals, because of that eye-fold that makes their eyes seem to slant. In spite of the fact that no biology has ever mentioned any such difference in reproductive organs makes no matter [*sic*]. Millions of people believe it. "Did you know that a Chinese has . . ." Consequently, their quiet contemplative manner is interpreted as a sign of slyness and a treacherous inclination.

But the opening wedge for better understanding has been thrust into the crack. Though many Negroes denounced Carl Van Vechten's *Nigger Heaven* because of the title, and without ever reading it, the book, written in the deepest sincerity, revealed Negroes of wealth and culture to the white public. It created curiosity even when it aroused skepticism. It made folks want to know. Worth Tuttle Hedden's *The Other Room* has definitely widened the opening. Neither of these well-written works take[s] a romance of upperclass Negro life as the central theme, but the atmosphere and the background [are] there. These works should be followed up by some incisive and intimate stories from the inside.

The realistic story around a Negro insurance official, dentist, general practitioner, undertaker and the like would be most revealing. Thinly disguised fiction around the well known Negro names is not the answer, either. The "exceptional" as well as the Ol' Man Rivers has been exploited all out of context already. Everybody is already resigned to the "exceptional" Negro, and willing to be entertained by the "quaint." To grasp the penetration of western civilization in a minority, it is necessary to know how the average behaves and lives. Books that deal with people like in Sinclair Lewis' *Main Street* [are] the necessary métier. For various reasons, the average, struggling, nonmorbid Negro is the best-kept secret in America. His revelation to the public is the thing needed to do away with that feeling of difference which inspires fear, and which ever expresses itself in dislike.

It is inevitable that this knowledge will destroy many illusions and romantic traditions which America probably likes to have around. But then, we have no record of anybody sinking into a lingering death on finding out that there was no Santa Claus. The old world will take it in its stride. The realization that Negroes are no better nor no worse, and at times just as boring as everybody else, will hardly kill off the population of the nation.

Outside of racial attitudes, there is still another reason why this literature should exist. Literature and other arts are supposed to hold up the mirror to nature. With only the fractional "exceptional" and the "quaint" portrayed, a true picture of Negro life in America cannot be. A great principle of national art has been violated.

These are the things that publishers and producers, as the accredited representatives of the American people, have not as yet taken into consideration sufficiently. Let there be light!

7 | Self-Criticism

The Third Dimension in Culture

Alain Locke

(1950)

The symposium section in this issue of *Phylon,* which I have had the opportunity of reading in manuscript, seems to signal the emergence of a long-awaited stage in Negro cultural development. For these eight essays analyzing our literary output and its implications mark a considerable step forward toward objective self-criticism. This is a necessary and welcome sign of cultural maturity. It was predicated twenty-five years ago as one of the objectives of the so-called Negro Renaissance, along with the companion aim of objective self-expression, but unfortunately such criticism was not forthcoming in any large volume. Its lack was unquestionably indicative of a certain lingering immaturity, the reasons for which it will be interesting to assess a little later on. For the moment it may be noted that the conditions which delayed it may also have been considerably responsible for the admitted shortcomings of our literary and artistic output in the Nineteen-twenties, thirties, and forties. Indeed this seems to be the present consensus of the new criticism which is so significantly emerging.

It is now obvious in retrospect, as many of these articles point out, that for many generations Negro creative expression was inevitably imitative and marked with a double provincialism of cultural immaturity and a racial sense of subordination. It ran a one-dimensional gamut from self-pity through sentimental appeal to hortatory moralizing and rhetorical threat—a child's gamut of tears, sobs, sulks and passionate protest. All of us probably expected too much of the Negro Renaissance, but its new vitality of independence, pride and self-respect, its scoff and defiance of prejudice and limitations were so welcome and heartening.

Like the adolescence it was, the New Negro era was gawky and pimply, indiscreet and over-confident, vainglorious and irresponsible; but its testy dynamic gave the Negro new spiritual stature and an added dimension of self-reliance. As several of the critics point out, adolescence was mistaken for manhood, so there was in the creative expression of the Twenties and Thirties pride without poise, vision without true perspective, self-esteem without the necessary tempering of full self-understanding.

Beginning with the broader social identifications of *Native Son,* and the social discoveries of common-denominator human universals between Negro situations and others, these critics rightly claim, artistic expression with Negroes has become increasingly sounder, more objective and less racialistic—in the limiting sense of chauvinism—but withal even more racial in the better sense of being more deeply felt and projected. This third dimension of objective universality, they feel, is the ultimate desideratum for a literature that seeks universal appeal and acceptance. I agree. In fact, have always agreed, though this is neither the time nor place for self-justifying quotations.

Suffice it to say that even in 1925, some original proponents of the "Negro Renaissance" forecast the position which seems to be the new consensus of the "new criticism." That is, that when the racial themes are imposed upon the Negro author either from within or without, they become an intolerable and limiting artistic ghetto, but that accepted by choice, either on the ground of best known material or preferred opportunity, they stake off a cultural bonanza. Mr. Gloster, for example, does well to inveigh against the triple snares of "race defense, protest and glorification," but it still remains that Negro life and experience contain one of the unworked mines of American dramatic and fictional material, overworked and shabby as their superficial exploitation has been. For both the white and the Negro author in this area, the era of pan-mining is about over or should be; the promising techniques are now deep-mining and better artistic smelting of the crude ore. In provincial and chauvinistic rendering, of which we have been offered far too much, especially from Negro authors, as Messrs. Redding and Reddick bravely point out, Negro materials pan out shallow, brittle and unrefined. But in objective, thoroughly humanized treatment they still promise artistic gold fit for universal currency. The necessary alchemy is, of course, universalized rendering, for in universalized particularity there has always resided the world's greatest and most enduring art.

Though rare, this quality has appeared sporadically in Negro writing. Mr. Chandler is right in giving us the proper historical perspective, however, by reminding us how long it took American literature itself to achieve this dimension of universalized power and insight. Perhaps it would be invidious to be too specific for the current generation, though I think all would agree that the first two chapters of *Native Son* had such quality, not to mention how and why the book as a whole lost these virtues as it became more and more involved in propagandist formulae. I am personally surprised that no one referred to the phenomenal early appearance of such "universal particularity" in Jean Toomer's *Cane* in 1923. Here was something admirably removed from what Mr. Chandler calls very aptly "promotional literature," but it is Negro through and through as well as deeply and movingly human. It was also exempt from any limitation of provincialism although it gave local color convincingly. To wish for more of this is to ask for the transmuting quality of expert craftsmanship combined with broad perspective or intuitive insight, one or the other.

For we must remember the two ways in which Russian literature achieved its great era; through the cosmopolitan way of Turgenev, Tolstoi and Chekov and the nativist way of Dostoievski, Gogol and Gorgki, each of which produced great writing and universal understanding for Russian experience.

Our problem now seems to be how to translate this new insight into creative action. So far as a body of sound criticism can point the way, we have in this group of critical essays the beginnings of a new objective criticism, and henceforth can have little excuse if a considerable part of our creative expression does not follow its lead and guidance. At least we have within our artistic grasp the final resolution of the old dilemma of the proper attitude of the Negro writer toward race materials. Agreeing that this should be, to quote Mr. Gloster, "to consider all life as his proper milieu, yet treat race (when he chooses) from the universal point of view, shunning the cultural isolation that results from racial preoccupation and Jim-Crow esthetics," we have as a net result, however, the mandate: Give us Negro life and experience in all the arts but with a third dimension of universalized common-denominator humanity.

A final word or so of constructive criticism may be in order. Let us start with the shameful fact that out of the whole range of Negro experience, the very areas on which the Negro author has almost monopolistic control, there has been little else than strange silence. On this matter, Mr. Reddick hints provocatively. I will venture to speak even more plainly on my own responsibility. Three tabus that seal doors that must be broken through to release greatly original and moving revelations about Negro life and experience remain unbroken, partly through convention-ridden cowardice, partly through misconceived protective strategy. If William March and Erskine Caldwell, Lillian Smith and William Faulkner can boldly break with the tribal tabus of the White South to release the full potentials of Southern drama and fiction, so in turn must the Negro author boldly break the seals of analogous Negro conventionality. Of course, easier said than done! The Negro intellectual is still largely in psychological bondage not only, as Reddick puts it, "to the laws and customs of the local (Southern) culture," but to the fear of breaking the tabus of Puritanism, Philistinism and falsely conceived conventions of "race respectability." Consciously and subconsciously, these repressions work great artistic harm, especially the fear of being accused of group disloyalty and "misrepresentation" in portraying the full gamut of Negro type, character and thinking. We are still in the throes of counter-stereotypes.

The releasing formula is to realize that in all human things we are basically and inevitably human, and that even the special racial complexities and overtones are only interesting variants. Why, then, this protective silence about the ambivalences of the Negro upper classes, about the dilemmas of intra-group prejudice and rivalry, about the dramatic inner paradoxes of mixed heritage, both biological and cultural, or the tragic breach between the Negro elite and the Negro masses, or the conflict between integration and vested-interest separatism in the present-day life of the Negro? These, among others, are the great themes, but they moulder in closed closets like family skeletons rather than shine brightly as the Aladdin's lamps that they really are.

To break such tabus is the crucial artistic question of the moment, the wrath of the Negro Rotarians, preachers, college presidents and journalists notwithstanding. It is this inner tyranny that must next be conquered, now that the outer tyrannies of prejudice and intellectual ostracism are being so suddenly relaxed. I am far from suggesting that even a considerable part of this revelation will be morally risqué or socially explosive; some of it will be, of course. But I do sense a strange and widely diffused feeling that many of these situations are Masonic secrets—things to be talked about, but not written or officially disclosed. Maybe, now that a few Negro authors have demonstrated the possibility of financial independence and success as writers, some of our younger talents can shake free of the white-collar servitudes of job dependency on the one hand and conventional "race loyalty" on the other. If so, we may confidently anticipate an era of fuller and more objective presentation by Negro authors of their versions of contemporary living in general and Negro life and experience in particular.

8 | Expressive Language

LeRoi Jones (Amiri Baraka)

(1963)

Speech is the effective form of a culture. Any shape or cluster of human history still apparent in the conscious and unconscious habit of groups of people is what I mean by culture. All culture is necessarily profound. The very fact of its longevity, of its being what it is, culture, the epic memory of practical tradition, means that it is profound. But the inherent profundity of culture does not necessarily mean that its uses (and they are as various as the human condition) will be profound. German culture is profound. Generically. Its uses, however, are specific, as are all uses . . . of ideas, inventions, products of nature. And specificity, as a right and passion of human life, breeds what it breeds as a result of its context.

Context, in this instance, is most dramatically social. And the social, though it must be rooted, as are all evidences of existence, in culture, depends for its impetus for the most part on a multiplicity of influences. Other cultures, for instance. Perhaps, and this is a common occurrence, the reaction or interreaction of one culture on another can produce a social context that will extend or influence any culture in many strange directions.

Social also means *economic*, as any reader of nineteenth-century European philosophy will understand. The economic is part of the social—and in our time much more so than what we have known as the spiritual or metaphysical, because the most valuable canons of power have either been reduced or traduced into stricter economic terms. That is, there has been a shift in the actual meaning of the world since Dante lived. As if Brooks Adams were right. Money does not mean the same thing to me it must mean to a rich man. I cannot, right now, think of one meaning to name. This is not so simple to understand. Even as a simple term of the English language, *money*, does not possess the same meanings for the rich man as it does for me, a lower-middle-class American, albeit of laughably "aristocratic" pretensions. What possibly can "money" mean to a poor man? And I am not talking now about those courageous products of our permissive society who walk knowledgeably into "poverty" as they would into a public toilet. I mean, The Poor.

I look in my pocket; I have seventy cents. Possibly I can buy a beer. A quart of ale, specifically. Then I will have twenty cents with which to annoy and seduce my fingers when they wearily search for gainful employment. I have no idea at this moment what that seventy cents will mean to my neighbor around the corner, a poor Puerto Rican man I have seen hopefully watching my plastic garbage can. But I am certain it cannot mean the same thing. Say to David Rockefeller, "I have money," and he will think you mean something entirely different. That is, if you also dress the part. He would not for a moment think, "Seventy cents." But then neither would many New York painters.

Speech, the way one describes the natural proposition of being alive, is much more crucial than even most artists realize. Semantic philosophers are certainly correct in their emphasis on the final dictation of words over their users. But they often neglect to point out that, after all, it is the actual importance, *power*, of the words that remains so finally crucial. Words have users, but as well, users have words. And it is the users that establish the world's realities. Realities being those fantasies that control your immediate span of life. Usually they are not your own fantasies, *i.e.*, they belong to governments, traditions, etc., which, it must be clear by now, can make for conflict with the singular human life all ways. The fantasy of America might hurt you, but it is what should be meant when one talks of "reality." Not only the things you can touch or see, but the things that make such touching or seeing "normal." Then words, like their users, have a hegemony. Socially—which is final, right now. If you are some kind of artist, you naturally might think this is not so. There is the future. But *immortality* is a kind of drug, I think—one that leads to happiness at the thought of death. Myself, I would rather live forever . . . just to make sure.

The social hegemony, one's position in society, enforces more specifically one's terms (even the vulgar have "pull"). Even to the mode of speech. But also it makes these terms an available explanation of any social hierarchy, so that the words them-selves become, even informally, laws. And of course they are usually very quickly stitched together to make formal statutes only fools or the faithfully intrepid would dare to question beyond immediate necessity.

The culture of the powerful is very infectious for the sophisticated, and strongly addictive. To be any kind of "success" one must be fluent in this culture. Know the words of the users, the semantic rituals of power. This is a way into wherever it is you are not now, but wish, very desperately, to get into.

Even speech then signals a fluency in this culture. A knowledge at least. "He's an educated man," is the barest acknowledgment of such fluency . . . in any time. "He's hip," my friends might say. They connote a similar entrance.

And it is certainly the meanings of words that are most important, even if they are no longer consciously acknowledged, but merely, by their use, trip a familiar lever of social accord. To recreate instantly the understood hierarchy of social, and by doing that, cultural, importance. And cultures are thought by most people in the world to do their business merely by being hierarchies. Certainly this is true in the West, in as simple a manifestation as Xenophobia, the naïve bridegroom of anti-human feeling, or in economic terms, Colonialism. For instance, when the first Africans were brought into the New World, it was thought that it was all right for them to be slaves because "they were heathens." It is a perfectly logical assumption.

And it follows, of course, that slavery would have been an even stranger phenomenon had the Africans spoken English when they first got here. It would have complicated things. Very soon after the first generations of Afro-Americans mastered this language, they invented white people called Abolitionists.

Words' meanings, but also the rhythm and syntax that frame and propel their concatenation, seek their culture as the final reference for what they are describing of the world. An A flat played twice on the same saxophone by two different men does not have to sound the same. If these men have different ideas of what they want this note to do, the note will not sound the same. Culture is the form, the overall structure of organized thought (as well as emotion and spiritual pretension). There are many cultures. Many ways of organizing thought, or having thought organized. That is, the form of thought's passage through the world will take on as many diverse shapes as there are diverse groups of travelers. Environment is one organizer of *groups*, at any level of its meaning. People who live in Newark, New Jersey, are organized, for whatever purpose, as Newarkers. It begins that simply. Another manifestation, at a slightly more complex level, can be the fact that blues singers from the Midwest sing through their noses. There is an explanation past the geographical, but that's the idea in tabloid. And singing through the nose does propose that the definition of singing be altered . . . even if ever so slightly. (At this point where someone's definitions must be changed, we are flitting around at the outskirts of the old city of Aesthetics. A solemn ghost town. Though some of the bones of reason can still be gathered there.)

But we still need definitions, even if there already are many. The dullest men are always satisfied that a dictionary lists everything in the world. They don't care that you may find out something *extra*, which one day might even be valuable to them. Of course, by that time it might even be in the dictionary, or at least they'd hope so, if you asked them directly.

But for every item in the world, there are a multiplicity of definitions that fit. And every word we use *could* mean something else. And at the same time. The culture fixes the use, and usage. And in "pluralistic" America, one should always listen very closely when he is being talked to. The speaker might mean something completely different from what we think we're hearing. "Where is your pot?"

I heard an old Negro street singer last week, Reverend Pearly Brown, singing, "God don't never change!" This is a precise thing he is singing. He does not mean "God does not ever change!" He means "God don't never change!" The difference, and I said it was crucial, is in the final human reference . . . the form of passage through the world. A man who is rich and famous who sings, "God don't never change," is confirming his hegemony and good fortune . . . or merely calling the bank. A blind hopeless black American is saying something very different. He is telling you about the extraordinary order of the world. But he is not telling you about his "fate." Fate is a luxury available only to those fortunate citizens with alternatives. The view from the top of the hill is not the same as that from the bottom of the hill. Nor are most viewers at either end of the hill, even certain that, in fact, there is any other place from which to look. Looking down usually eliminates the possibility of understanding what it must be like to look up. Or try to imagine yourself as not existing. It is difficult, but poets and politicians try every other day.

Being told to "speak proper," meaning that you become fluent with the jargon of power, is also a part of not "speaking proper." That is, the culture which desperately understands that it does not "speak proper," or is not fluent with the terms of social strength, also understands somewhere that its desire to gain such fluency is done at a terrifying risk. The bourgeois Negro accepts such risk as profit. But does *close-ter* (in the context of "jes a close-ter, walk withee") mean the same thing as *closer?* Close-ter, in the term of its user is, believe me, exact. It means a quality of existence, of actual physical disposition perhaps . . . in its manifestation as a tone and *rhythm* by which people live, most often in response to common modes of thought best enforced by some factor of environmental emotion that is exact and specific. Even the picture it summons is different, and certainly the "Thee" that is used to connect the implied "Me" with, is different. The God of the damned cannot know the God of the damner, that is, cannot know he is God. As no Blues person can really believe emotionally in Pascal's God, or Wittgenstein's question, "Can the concept of God exist in a perfectly logical language?" Answer: "God don't never change."

Communication is only important because it is the broadest root of education. And all cultures communicate exactly what they have, a powerful motley of experience.

9 | Brave Words for a Startling Occasion

Ralph Ellison

(1964)

First, as I express my gratitude for this honor which you have bestowed on me, let me say that I take it that you are rewarding my efforts rather than my not quite fully achieved attempt at a major novel. Indeed, if I were asked in all seriousness just what I considered to be the chief significance of *Invisible Man* as a fiction, I would reply: Its experimental attitude, and its attempt to return to the mood of personal moral responsibility for democracy which typified the best of our nineteenth-century fiction. That my first novel should win this most coveted prize must certainly indicate that there is a crisis in the American novel. You as critics have told us so, and current fiction sales would indicate that the reading public agrees. Certainly the younger novelists concur. The explosive nature of events mocks our brightest efforts. And the very "facts" which the naturalists assumed would make us free have lost the power to protect us from despair. Controversy now rages over just what aspects of American experience are suitable for novelistic treatment. The prestige of the theorists of the so-called novel of manners has been challenged. Thus after a long period of stability we find our assumptions concerning the novel being called into question. And though I was only vaguely aware, it was this growing crisis which shaped the writing of *Invisible Man*.

After the usual apprenticeship of imitation and seeking with delight to examine my experience through the discipline of the novel, I became gradually aware that the forms of so many of the works which impressed me were too restricted to contain the experience which I knew. The diversity of American life with its extreme fluidity and openness seemed too vital and alive to be caught for more than the briefest instant in the tight well-made Jamesian novel, which was, for all its artistic perfection, too concerned with "good taste" and stable areas. Nor could I safely use the forms of the "hard-boiled" novel, with its dedication to physical violence, social cynicism and understatement. Understatement depends, after all, upon commonly held assumptions and my minority status rendered all such assumptions questionable. There was also a problem of language, and even dialogue, which, with its hard-boiled stance and its monosyllabic utterance, is one of the shining achievements of twentieth-century American writing. For despite the notion that its rhythms were those of everyday speech, I found that when compared with the rich babel of idiomatic expression around me, a language full of imagery and gesture and rhetorical canniness, it was embarrassingly austere. Our speech I found resounding with an alive language swirling with over three hundred years of American living, a mixture of the folk, the Biblical, the scientific and the political. Slangy in one stance, academic in another, loaded poetically with imagery at one moment, mathematically bare of imagery in the next. As for the rather rigid concepts of reality which informed a number of the works which impressed me and to which I owe a great deal, I was forced to conclude that reality was far more mysterious and uncertain, and more exciting, and still, despite its raw violence and capriciousness, more promising. To attempt to express that American experience which has carried one back and forth and up and down the land and across, and across again the great river, from freight train to Pullman car, from contact with slavery to contact with a world of advanced scholarship, art and science, is simply to burst such neatly understated forms of the novel asunder.

A novel whose range was both broader and deeper was needed. And in my search I found myself turning to our classical nineteenth-century novelists. I felt that except for the work of William Faulkner something vital had gone out of American prose after Mark Twain. I came to believe that the writers of that period took a much greater responsibility for the condition of democracy and, indeed, their works were imaginative projections of the conflicts within the human heart which arose when the sacred principles of the Constitution and the Bill of Rights clashed with the practical exigencies of human greed and fear, hate and love. Naturally I was attracted to these writers as a Negro. Whatever they thought of my people per se, in their imaginative economy the Negro symbolized both the man lowest down and the mysterious, underground aspect of human personality. In a sense the Negro was the gauge of the human condition as it waxed and waned in our democracy. These writers were willing to confront the broad complexities of American life and we are the richer for their having done so.

Thus to see America with an awareness of its rich diversity and its almost magical fluidity and freedom, I was forced to conceive of a novel unburdened by the narrow naturalism which has led, after so many triumphs, to the final and unrelieved despair which marks so much of our current fiction. I was to dream of a prose which was flexible, and swift as American change is swift, confronting the inequalities and brutalities of our society forthrightly, but yet thrusting forth its images of hope, human fraternity and individual self-realization. It would use the richness of our speech, the idiomatic expression and the rhetorical flourishes from past periods which are still alive among us. And despite my personal failures, there must be possible a fiction which, leaving sociology to the scientists, can arrive at the truth about the human condition, here and now, with all the bright magic of a fairy tale.

What has been missing from so much experimental writing has been the passionate will to dominate reality as well as the laws of art. This will is the true source of the experimental attitude. We who struggle with form and with America should remember Eidothea's advice to Menelaus when in the *Odyssey* he and his friends are seeking their way home. She tells him to seize her father, Proteus, and to hold him fast "however he may struggle and fight. He will turn into all sorts of shapes to try you," she says, "into all the creatures that live and move upon the earth, into water, into blazing fire; but you must hold him fast and press him all the harder. When he is himself, and questions you in the same shape that he was when you saw him in his bed, let the old man go; and then, sir, ask which god it is who is angry, and how you shall make your way homewards over the fish-giving sea."

For the novelist, Proteus stands for both America and the inheritance of illusion through which all men must fight to achieve reality; the offended god stands for our sins against those principles we all hold sacred. The way home we seek is that condition of man's being at home in the world, which is called love, and which we term democracy. Our task then is always to challenge the apparent forms of reality—that is, the fixed manners and values of the few, and to struggle with it until it reveals its mad, vari-implicated chaos, its false faces, and on until it surrenders its insight, its truth. We are fortunate as American writers in that with our variety of racial and national traditions, idioms and manners, we are yet one. On its profoundest level American experience is of a whole. Its truth lies in its diversity and swiftness of change. Through forging forms of the novel worthy of it, we achieve not only the promise of our lives, but we anticipate the resolution of those world problems of humanity which for a moment seem to those who are in awe of statistics completely insoluble.

Whenever we as Americans have faced serious crises we have returned to fundamentals; this, in brief, is what I have tried to do.

—Address for Presentation Ceremony,
National Book Award, January 27, 1953.

10 And Shine Swam On

An Afterword

Larry Neal

(1968)

Just then the Captain said, "Shine, Shine, save poor me
I'll give you more money than a nigger ever see."
Shine said to the Captain: "Money is good on land and on sea,
but the money on land is the money for me."
And Shine swam on . . .
Then the Captain's lily white daughter come up on deck,
She had her hands on her pussy and her dress around her neck.
She say, "Shine, Shine, save poor me,
I'll give you more pussy than a nigger ever see."
Shine, he say, "There's pussy on land and pussy on sea,
but the pussy on land is the pussy for me."
And Shine swam on.

The quote is taken from an urban "toast" called the Titanic. It is part of the private mythology of Black America. Its symbolism is direct and profound. Shine is US. We have been below-deck stoking the ship's furnaces. Now the ship is sinking, but where will we swim? This is the question that the "New Breed" which James Brown sings about, asks.

We don't have all of the answers, but have attempted, through the artistic and political work presented here, to confront our problems from what must be called a radical perspective. Therefore, most of the book [*Black Fire: An Anthology of Afro-American Writing*] can be read as if it were a critical re-examination of Western political, social and artistic values. It can be read also as a rejection of anything that we feel is detrimental to our people. And it is almost axiomatic that most of what the West considers important endangers the more humane world we feel ours should be.

We have been, for the most part, talking about contemporary realities. We have not been talking about a return to some glorious African past. But we recognize the

69

past—the total past. Many of us refuse to accept a truncated Negro history which cuts us off completely from our African ancestry. To do so is to accept the very racist assumptions which we abhor. Rather, we want to comprehend history totally, and understand the manifold ways in which contemporary problems are affected by it.

There is a tension within Black America. And it has its roots in the general history of the race. The manner in which we see this history determines how we act. How should we see this history? What should we feel about it? This is important to know, because the sense of how that history should be felt is what either unites or separates us.

For, how the thing is felt helps to determine how it is played. For example, the 1966 uprising in Watts is a case of feeling one's history in a particular way, and then acting it out in the most immediate manner possible. The emotions of the crowd have always played an integral role in the making of history.

Again, what separates a Malcolm X from a Roy Wilkins is a profound difference in what each believes the history of America to be. Finally, the success of one leader over another depends upon which one best understands and expresses the emotional realities of a given historical epoch. Hence, we feel a Malcolm in a way that a Roy Wilkins, a King, and a Whitney Young can never be felt. Because a Malcolm, finally, interprets the emotional history of his people better than the others.

There is a tension throughout our communities. The ghosts of that tension are Nat Turner, Martin Delaney, Booker T. Washington, Frederick Douglass, Malcolm X, Garvey, Monroe Trotter, Du Bois, Fanon, and a whole panoply of mythical heroes from Br'er Rabbit to Shine. These ghosts have left us with some very heavy questions about the realities of life for black people in America.

The movement is now faced with a serious crisis. It has postulated a theory of Black Power; and that is good. But it has failed to evolve a workable ideology. That is, a workable concept—perhaps Black Power is it—which can encompass many of the diverse ideological tendencies existent in the black community. This concept would have to allow for separatists and revolutionaries; and it would have to take into consideration the realities of contemporary American power, both here and abroad. The militant wing of the movement has begun to deny the patriotic assumptions of the white and Negro establishment, but it has not supported that denial with a consistent theory of social change, one that must be rooted in the history of African-Americans.

Currently, there is a general lack of clarity about how to proceed. This lack of clarity is historical and is involved with what Du Bois called the "double-consciousness":

> this sense of always looking at one's self through the eyes of others, of measuring one's soul by the tape of a world that looks on in amused contempt and pity. One ever feels his two-ness—an American, a Negro—two souls, two thoughts, two thoughts, two unreconciled strivings; two warring ideals in one dark body, whose dogged strength alone keeps it from being torn asunder.

The history of the American Negro is the history of this strife—this longing to attain self-conscious manhood, to merge his double-self into a better and truer self.

This statement is from *The Souls of Black Folk*, which was published in 1897. The double-consciousness still exists, and was even in existence prior to 1897.

Nat Turner, Denmark Vesey, and Gabriel Prosser attempted to destroy this double-consciousness in bloody revolt.

In 1852, a black physician named Martin Delaney published a book entitled, *The Destiny of the Colored Peoples*. Delaney advocated repatriation—return to the Motherland (Africa). He believed that the United States would never fully grant black people freedom; and never would there be anything like "equal status with the white man."

Frederick Douglass, and many of the abolitionists, strongly believed in the "promise of America." But the double-consciousness and its resulting tension still exist. How else can we explain the existence of these same ideas in contemporary America? Why was Garvey so popular? Why is it that, in a community like Harlem, one finds a distinctly nationalistic element which is growing yearly, according to a recent article in *The New York Times*? And it is a contemporary nationalism, existing in varying degrees of sophistication; but all of its tendencies, from the Revolutionary Action Movement to the African Nationalist Pioneer Movement, are focused on questions not fully resolved by the established Negro leadership—questions which that leadership, at this stage of its development, is incapable of answering.

Therefore, the rebirth of the concept of Black Power opens old wounds. For the conflict between Booker T. Washington and W. E. B. Du Bois was essentially over the question of power, over the relationship of that power to the status of Black America. The focus of the conflict between Washington and Du Bois was education: What was the best means of educating black people? Should it be primarily university education, as advocated by Du Bois; or one rooted in what Washington called "craft skills"? Since education functions in a society to enforce certain values, both men found it impossible to confine discussion simply to the nature of black education. It became a political question. It *is* a political question. Therefore, what was essentially being debated was the political status of over ten million people of African descent who, against their wills, were being forced to eke out an existence in the United States.

Queen Mother Moore once pointed out to me that black people were never collectively given a chance to decide whether they wanted to be American citizens or not. After the Civil War, for example, there was no plebiscite putting the question of American citizenship to a vote. Therefore, implicit in the turn-of-the-century controversy between Washington and Du Bois is the idea that black people are a nation—a separate nation apart from white America. Around 1897, the idea was more a part of Washington's thinking than Du Bois'; but it was to haunt Du Bois until the day he died (in Ghana).

The educational ideas of both Washington and Du Bois were doomed to failure.

Both ideas, within the context of American values, were merely the extension of another kind of oppression. Only, now it was an oppression of the spirit. Within the context of a racist America, both were advocating a "colonialized" education; that is, an education equivalent to the kind the native receives, in Africa and Asia, under the imperialists. The fundamental role of education in a racist society would have to be to "keep the niggers in their place."

All of the Negro colleges in this country were, and, are even now, controlled by white money—white power. Du Bois recognized this after he was dismissed from Atlanta University. In 1934, he further proceeded to advocate the establishment of independent "segregated" institutions and the development of the black community as a separate entity. The advocacy of such ideas led to a break with the NAACP, which was committed to a policy of total integration into American society. Here then, is the tension, the ambiguity between integration and segregation, occurring in the highest ranks of a well-established middle-class organization. Hence, in 1934, Du Bois had not really advanced, at least not in terms of the ideas postulated above, but was merely picking up the threads of arguments put forth by Washington and Marcus Garvey. And the double-consciousness dominated his entire professional life.

He had been everything that was demanded of him: scholar, poet, politician, nationalist, integrationist, and finally in old age, a Communist. His had been a life full of controversy. He knew much about human nature, especially that of his people, but he did not understand Garvey—Garvey—who was merely his own double-consciousness theory personified in a very dynamic and forceful manner. Garvey was, in fact, attempting the destruction of that very tension which had plagued all of Du Bois' professional career.

It involved knowing and deciding who and what we are. Had Garvey an organizational apparatus equivalent to the NAACP's, the entire history of the world might have been different. For Garvey was more emotionally cohesive than Du Bois, and not as intellectually fragmented. Du Bois, for all of his commitment, was a somewhat stuffy intellectual with middle-class hangups, for which Garvey constantly attacked him. The people to whom Garvey appealed could never have understood Du Bois. But Garvey understood them, and the life-force within him was very fundamental to them. The NAACP has never had the kind of fervent appeal that the Garvey Movement had. It has rarely understood the tension within the black masses. To them, Garvey was a fanatic. But are these the words of a fanatic, or of a lover?

The N.A.A.C.P. wants us all to become white by amalgamation, but they are not honest enough to come out with the truth. To be a Negro is no disgrace, but an honor, and we of the U.N.I.A. do not want to become white. . . . We are proud and honorable. We love our race and respect and adore our mothers.

And, in a letter to his followers from prison:

My months of forcible removal from among you, being imprisoned as a punishment for advocating the cause of our *real emancipation* [emphasis mine], have not left me hopeless or despondent; but to the contrary, I see a great ray of light and the bursting of a mighty political cloud which will bring you complete freedom . . .

We have gradually won our way back into the confidence of the God of Africa, and He shall speak with a voice of thunder, that shall shake the pillars of a corrupt and unjust world, and once more restore Ethiopia to her ancient glory . . .

Hold fast to the Faith. Desert not the ranks, but as brave soldiers march on to victory. I am happy, and shall remain so, as long as you keep the flag flying.

So in 1940, Garvey died. He died in London, an exile. He was a proud man whose real fault was not lack of intense feeling and conviction, but an inability to tailor his nationalism to the realities of the American context. And also he was a threat to Europe's colonial designs in Africa, a much greater threat than the Pan-African conferences Du Bois used to organize. Garvey wanted a nation for his people. That would have meant the destruction of British, French and Portuguese imperialism in Africa. And since it was a movement directed by blacks here in this country, it would also have internally challenged American imperialism as it existed at that time.

But Garvey was no Theodor Herzl or Chaim Weizmann,[1] with their kind of skills and resources behind him. Had he been, he might have brought a nation into existence. But neither he nor his people had those kinds of resources, and, worse, the black bourgeoisie of the period did not understand him with the same intensity as the masses.

In 1940, the year Garvey died, Malcolm Little was fifteen years old. He caught a bus from Lansing, Michigan, and went to Boston to live with his sister Ella Collins, who is now head of the organization Malcolm started when he broke with the Nation of Islam. It is probably the most important bus ride in history.

Malcolm X, whose father had been a Garveyite, was destined to confront the double-consciousness of Black America. But his confrontation would be a modern one, rooted in the teachings of the Nation of Islam and in the realities of contemporary politics. That is to say, his ideas would be a synthesis of black nationalism's essential truths as derived from Martin Delaney, Du Bois, Garvey, the honorable Elijah Muhammed, Fanon, and Richard Wright. And his speech would be marked by a particular cadence, a kind of "hip" understanding of the world. It was the truth as only the oppressed, and those whose lives have somehow been "outside of history," could know it.

Civil rights and brotherhood were in vogue when Malcolm started "blowing"— started telling the truth in a manner only a deaf man would ignore. And many of us were deaf, or if not, in a deep sleep. He shot holes through the civil rights movement that was the new "in" for the white liberals. James Baldwin was also "in," pleading for a new morality to people who saw him as another form of entertainment. And there were sit-ins, pray-ins, sleep-ins, non-violence, and the March on Washington. And the voice of Malcolm cut through it all, stripping away the sham and the lies. He was the conscience of Black America, setting out, like a warrior, to destroy the double-consciousness. He did not eschew dialogue. He attempted, instead, to make it more meaningful by infusing some truth into it. For this reason, it was both painful and beautiful to listen to him.

Malcolm covered everything—nationhood, manhood, the family, brotherhood, history, and the Third World Revolution. Yet it always seemed to me that he was talking about a revolution of the psyche, about how we should see ourselves in the world.

But, just as suddenly as he was thrust among us—he was gone. Gone, just as Black America was starting to understand what he was talking about. And those who killed him, did so for just that reason. For Malcolm wanted to make real the internationalism of Garvey and Du Bois. Our problem had ceased to be one of civil rights, he argued, but is, instead, one of human rights. As such—he extended the argument— it belongs in an international context. Like Garvey and Du Bois before him, he linked the general oppression of Black America to that of the Third World. Further, he strongly advocated unity with that world, something few civil rights leaders have dared to do.

Hence, what has come to be known as Black Power must be seen in terms of the ideas and persons which preceded it. Black Power is, in fact, a synthesis of all of the nationalistic ideas embedded within the double-consciousness of Black America. But it has no one *specific* meaning. It is rather a kind of feeling—a kind of emotional response to one's history. The theoreticians among us can break down its components. However, that will not be enough, for like all good theories, it can ultimately be defined only in action—in movement. Essentially, this is what the "New Breed" is doing—defining itself through actions, be they artistic or political.

We have attempted through these historical judgments to examine the idea of nationhood, the idea, real or fanciful, that black people comprise a separate national entity within the dominant white culture. This sense of being separate, especially within a racist society with so-called democratic ideas, has created a particular tension within the psychology of Black America. We are saying, further, that this sense of the "separate" moves through much of today's black literature.

There is also a concomitant sense of being at "war." Max Stanford explains that this sense began the minute the first slaves were snatched from their lands. These two tensions, "separation" and "war," are pressing historical realities; both are leading to a literature of Armageddon.

We must face these ideas in all of their dimensions. In some cases, the literature speaks to the tension within, say, the family; or it deals with the nature of black manhood. At other times, especially in something like Jimmy Garrett's play *We Own the Night*, the "war" seems directed against an unseen white enemy; it is, in fact, an attack on the Uncle Tomism of the older generation.

The tension, or double-consciousness, is most often resolved in violence, simply because the nature of our existence in America has been one of violence. In some cases, the tension resolves in recognizing the beauty and love within Black America itself. No, not a new "Negritude," but a profound sense of a unique and beautiful culture; and a sense that there are many spiritual areas to explore *within* this culture. This is a kind of separation but there is no tension about it. There is a kind of peace in the separation. This peace may be threatened by the realities of the beast-world, but yet, it is lived as fully as life can be lived. This sense of a haven in blackness is found most often in the poetry selections.

But history weighs down on all of this literature. Every black writer in America has had to react to this history, either to make peace with it, or make war with it. It cannot be ignored. Every black writer has chosen a particular stance towards it. He or she may tell you that, for them, it was never a problem. But they will be liars.

Most contemporary black writing of the last few years, the literature of the young, has been aimed at the destruction of the double-consciousness. It has been aimed at consolidating the African-American personality. And it has not been essentially a literature of protest. It has, instead, turned its attention inward to the internal problems of the group. The problem of living in a racist society, therefore, is something that lurks on the immediate horizon, but which can not be dealt with until certain political, social and spiritual truths are understood by the oppressed themselves— inwardly understood.

It is a literature primarily directed at the consciences of black people. And, in that sense, it is a literature that is somewhat more mature than that which preceded it. The white world—the West—is seen now as a dying creature, totally bereft of spirituality. This being the case, the only hope is some kind of psychic withdrawal from its values and assumptions. Not just America, but most of the non-colored world has been in the process of destroying the spiritual roots of mankind, while not substituting anything meaningful for this destruction.

Therefore, many see the enslavement of the Third World as an enslavement of the Spirit. Marxists carefully analyze the material reasons for this kind of oppression, but it takes a Fanon to illustrate the spiritual malaise in back of this enslavement. I tend to feel that the answer lies outside of historical materialism. It is rooted in how man sees himself in the spiritual sense, in what he construes existence to mean. Most Western philosophical orientations have taken the force of meaning out of existence.

Why this has happened is not really known, at least not in any sense that is final. We do know that the Western mind construes reality differently from that of the rest of the world. Or should I say, feels reality differently? Western mythological configurations are even vastly different from other configurations. Such configurations lead to the postulation of certain ideas of what art is, of what life is. . . .

Let us take, for example, the disorientation one experiences when one sees a piece of African sculpture in a Madison Avenue art gallery. Ask yourself: What is it doing there? In Africa, the piece had ritual significance. It was a spiritual affirmation of the connection between man and his ancestors, and it implied a particular kind of ontology—a particular sense of being. However, when you see it in that gallery, you must recognize that no African artist desired that it be placed there. Rather, it was stolen by force and placed there. And the mind that stole it was of a different nature from the mind that made it.

In the gallery or the salon, it is merely an objet d'art, but for your ancestors, it was a bridge between them and the spirit, a bridge between you and your soul in the progression of a spiritual lineage. It was art, merely incidentally, for it was essentially functional in its natural setting. The same goes for music, song, dance, the folk tale and dress. All of these things were coalesced, with form and function unified. All of these were an evocation of the spirit which included an affirmation of daily life, and the necessity of living life with honor.

The degree to which the artists among us understand some of these things is the degree to which we shall fashion a total art form that speaks primarily to the needs of our people. The temptation offered by Western society is to turn from these essential truths and merge with the oppressor for solace. This temptation demands, not merely integration of the flesh, but also integration of the spirit. And there are few of us for whom this would not have dire consequences. Further, the tension, the double-consciousness of which we have already spoken, cannot be resolved in so easy a manner, especially when, within the context of the racist society, the merger has little chance of being a healthy one.

In an essay entitled, "Blue Print for Negro Writing," Richard Wright attempted to define all aspects of the writer's role—especially as it is related to his status as an oppressed individual. Wright saw the problem in the following manner: The black writer had turned to writing in an attempt to demonstrate to the white world that there were "Negroes who were civilized." I suppose, here, he meant people like Charles Chestnutt [*sic*] and William Braithwaite. The writing, Wright attempted to prove, had become the voice of the educated Negro pleading with white America for justice. But it was "external to the lives of educated Negroes themselves." Further, much of this writing was rarely addressed to black people, to their needs, sufferings and aspirations.

It is precisely here that almost all of our literature had failed. It had succumbed merely to providing exotic entertainment for white America. As Wright suggests, we had yet to create a dynamic body of literature addressed to the needs of our people. And there are a myriad of socio-economic reasons underlying this failure. The so-called Harlem Renaissance was, for the most part, a fantasy-era for most black writers and their white friends. For the people of the community, it never even existed. It was a thing apart. And when the money stopped, in 1929, to quote Langston Hughes: ". . . we were no longer in vogue, anyway, we Negroes. Sophisticated New Yorkers turned to Noel Coward. Colored actors began to go hungry, publishers politely rejected new manuscripts, and patrons found other uses for their money. The cycle that had charlestoned into being on the dancing heels of *Shuffle Along* now ended in *Green Pastures* with De Lawd. . . . The generous 1920's were over." For most of us, they had never begun. It was all an illusion, a kind of surrealistic euphoria.

Wright insisted on an approach to literature that would reconcile the black man's "nationalism" and his "revolutionary aspirations." The best way for the writer to do this, he wrote in "Blue Print," was the utilization of his own tradition and culture— a culture that had developed out of the black church, and the folklore of the people:

Blues, spirituals, and folk tales recounted from mouth to mouth; the whispered words of a black mother to her black daughter on the ways of men; the confidential wisdom of a black father to his black son; the swapping of sex experiences on the street corners from boy to boy in the deepest vernacular; work songs sung under blazing suns—all these formed the channels through which the racial wisdom flowed.

And what of the nationalism about which we spoke earlier? Here again, the tension arises. The question of nationalism occurs repeatedly in the works of Wright. Like Du Bois and other intellectuals, Wright found that he could not ignore it. Within Wright himself, there was being waged a great conflict over the validity of nationalism. In the essay under discussion, he forces the question out into the open, asserting the necessity of understanding the function of nationalism in the lives of the people:

> Let those who shy at the nationalistic implications of Negro life look at the body of folklore, living and powerful, which rose out of a common fate. Here are those vital beginnings of a recognition of a value in life as it is lived, a recognition that makes the emergence of a new culture in the shell of the old. And at the moment that this process starts, at the moment when people begin to realize a meaning in their suffering, the civilization that engenders that suffering is doomed.

A further reading of this essay reveals that Wright was not trying to construct a black ideology, but was, instead, attempting a kind of reconciliation between nationalism and Communism. The essay was written in 1937. By then, the Communists had discarded the "nation within a nation" concept and were working to discourage black nationalism among the Negro members of the Party. Wright was trying to re-link nationalism and Communism, but the two were incompatible. The Communists discouraged the construction of a black theoretical frame of reference, but did not substitute a theory that was more viable than the one some of its black Party members proposed. Hence, the double-consciousness was not resolved. Wright ended up splitting with the Party to preserve his own identity.

Even though he had failed, Richard Wright was headed in the right direction. But the conditions under which he labored did not allow success. The Party, for example, had never really understood the "Negro question" in any manner that was finally meaningful to black people. Further, the nationalistic models which Wright and a contemporary of his, Ralph Ellison, saw around them were too "brutal" and "coarse" for their sensibilities (Ras, in Ellison's novel). Ultimately, the tension within Wright forced him to leave America, to become a voluntary exile.

The last years of his life were spent explaining the psychology of the oppressed throughout the Third World. In *White Man Listen!*, he attempted to analyze, much like Fanon, the malaise accompanying the relationship between the oppressed and the oppressors. And the double-consciousness never left him. *White Man Listen!*, *Black Power*, and *The Color Line* are Wright's attempt to understand his own racial dilemma by placing it in an international context, thus linking it to the general affects of colonialism on the psychology of the oppressed. Therefore, these works, historically, link Wright with Garvey and Du Bois, as well as foreshadow the ideas of Fanon and Brother Malcolm. To be more germane to our subject, these latter works are certainly more pertinent to the ideas of the "New Breed" youth, than say, *Native Son*.

They are especially more pertinent than Ralph Ellison's novel, *Invisible Man*, which is a profound piece of writing but the kind of novel which, nonetheless, has little bearing on the world as the "New Breed" sees it. The things that concerned Ellison are interesting to read, but contemporary black youth feels another force in the world today. We know who we are, and we are not invisible, at least not to each other. We are not Kafkaesque creatures stumbling through a white light of confusion and absurdity. The light is black (now, get that!) as are most of the meaningful tendencies in the world.

> Let us waste no time in sterile litanies and nauseating mimicry. Leave this Europe where they are never done talking of Man, yet murder men everywhere they find them, at the corner of every one of their own streets, in all corners of the globe. For centuries they have stifled almost the whole of humanity in the name of a so-called spiritual experience. Look at them today swaying between atomic and spiritual disintegration. —FRANTZ FANON, *THE WRETCHED OF THE EARTH*

Our literature, our art and our music are moving closer to the forces motivating Black America. You can hear it everywhere, especially in the music, a surging new sound. Be it the Supremes, James Brown, the Temptations, John Coltrane, or Albert Ayler, there is a vital newness in this energy. There is love, tension and spiritual togetherness in it. We are beautiful—but there is more work to do, and just being beautiful is not enough.

We must take this sound, and make this energy meaningful to our people. Otherwise, it will have meant nothing, will have affected nothing. The force of what we have to say can only be realized in action. Black literature must become an integral part of the community's life style. And I believe that it must also be integral to the myths and experiences underlying the total history of black people.

New constructs will have to be developed. We will have to alter our concepts of what art is, of what it is supposed to "do." The dead forms taught most writers in the white man's schools will have to be destroyed, or at best, radically altered. We can learn more about what poetry is by listening to the cadences in Malcolm's speeches, than from most of Western poetics. Listen to James Brown scream. Ask yourself, then: Have you ever heard a Negro poet sing like that? Of course not, because we have been tied to the texts, like most white poets. The text could be destroyed and no one would be hurt in the least by it. The key is in the music. Our music has always been far ahead of our literature. Actually, until recently, it was our only literature, except for, perhaps, the folktale.

Therefore, what we are asking for is a new synthesis; a new sense of literature as a living reality. But first, we must liberate ourselves, destroy the double-consciousness. We must integrate with ourselves, understand that we have within us a great vision, revolutionary and spiritual in nature, understand that the West is dying, and offers little promise of rebirth.

All of her prophets have told her so: Sartre, Brecht, Camus, Albee, Burroughs and Fellini, have foretold her doom. Can we do anything less? It is merely what we have always secretly known—what Garvey, Du Bois, Fanon and Malcolm knew: The West is dying, as it must, as it should. However, the approach of this death merely makes the power-mad Magogs of the West more vicious, more dangerous—like McNamara with his computing machines, scientifically figuring out how to kill more people. We must address ourselves to this reality in the sharpest terms possible. Primarily, it is an address to black people. And that is not protest, as such. You don't have to protest to a hungry man about his hunger. You have either to feed him, or help him to eliminate the root causes of that hunger.

What of craft—the writer's craft? Well, under terms of a new definition concerning the function of literature, a new concept of what craft is will also evolve. For example, do I not find the craft of Stevie Wonder more suitable than that of Jascha Heifetz? Are not the sensibilities which produced the former closer to me than the latter? And does not the one indicate a way into things absent from the other?

To reiterate, the key to where the black people have to go is in the music. Our music has always been the most dominant manifestation of what we are and feel, literature was just an afterthought, the step taken by the Negro bourgeoisie who desired acceptance on the white man's terms. And that is precisely why the literature has failed. It was the case of one elite addressing another elite.

But our music is something else. The best of it has always operated at the core of our lives, forcing itself upon us as in a ritual. It has always, somehow, represented the collective psyche. Black literature must attempt to achieve that same sense of the collective ritual, but ritual directed at the destruction of useless, dead ideas. Further, it can be a ritual that affirms our highest possibilities, but is yet honest with us.

Some of these tendencies already exist in the literature. It is readily perceivable in LeRoi Jones's *Black Mass*, and in a recent recording of his with the Jihad Singers. Also, we have the work of Yusuf Rahman, who is the poetic equivalent of Charlie Parker. Similar tendencies are found in Sun-Ra's music and poetry; Ronald Fair's novel, *Many Thousand Gone*; the short stories of Henry Dumas; the poetry of K. Kgositsile, Welton Smith, Ed Spriggs, and Rolland Snellings; the dramatic choreography of Eleo Pomare; Calvin Hernton's very explosive poems; Ishmael Reed's poetry and prose works which are notable for a startling display of imagery; David Henderson's work, particularly "Keep On Pushin'," where he gets a chance to sing. There are many, many others.

What this has all been leading us to say is that the poet must become a performer, the way James Brown is a performer—loud, gaudy and racy. He must take his work where his people are: Harlem, Watts, Philadelphia, Chicago and the rural South. He must learn to embellish the context in which the work is executed; and, where possible, link the work to all usable aspects of the music. For the context of the work is as important as the work itself. Poets must learn to sing, dance and chant their works, tearing into the substance of their individual and collective experiences. We must make literature move people to a deeper understanding of what this thing is all about, be a kind of priest, a black magician, working juju with the word on the world.

Finally, the black artist must link his work to the struggle for his liberation and the liberation of his brothers and sisters. But, he will have executed an essential aspect of his role if he makes even a small gesture in the manner outlined. He will be furthering the psychological liberation of his people, without which, no change is even possible.

The artist and the political activist are one. They are both shapers of the future reality. Both understand and manipulate the collective myths of the race. Both are warriors, priests, lovers and destroyers. For the first violence will be internal—the destruction of a weak spiritual self for a more perfect self. But it will be a necessary violence. It is the only thing that will destroy the double-consciousness—the tension that is in the souls of the black folk.

NOTE

1. Herzl (1860–1904) and Weizmann (1874–1952) are two important thinkers in the history of Jewish Zionism. During the 19th century, Jewish intellectuals began to describe analytically the problem of the Jews since what is called the Diaspora—the dispersion of the Jews among the Gentiles after the Exile. The efforts of these two men and many others culminated in the erection of Israel. Because Garvey also advocated a "return," some writers have called his movement "Black Zionism."

11 The Black Writer and His Role

Carolyn F. Gerald

(1969)

> What is new (in black literature) is the deliberate desecration and smashing of idols, the turning inside-out of symbols . . . Bitterness is being replaced by wrath; a sense of frustration giving way before a sense of power.

Image is a term which we are using more and more in the black community because we are discovering that the image we have of ourselves controls what we are capable of doing. Image, in this sense, has the meaning of self-concept. We are giving cause and effect the same name. But the word image is properly speaking a concrete term meaning the projection or representation of an object; the image is the mirror of some aspect of reality.

At this point, we should draw a distinction between real and created images. Both are projections of reality, but the created image is projected by the imagination of man, and by the recall and associative power of his five senses. For instance, I can hold out a rose before you; the image of that rose is mirrored in your eye; it is a real image. Or I can describe a rose to you, and my words will create an image which you can visualize mentally. Perhaps you will even imagine the smell and the feel; the words I choose and the way I build them into the image will determine this. Usually a whole complex of associations builds up around an image, secondary images are evoked, until well-defined patterns of associations based upon sensory perceptions pervade in a very vague way the whole area of a man's experience.

Why is image so central to a man's self-definition? Because all images, and especially created images, represent a certain way of focusing on the world outside, and therefore they represent a certain point of view. Now, if we hold a certain point of view, we have automatically emphasized some aspects of reality, blocked out others, and glossed over the rest, and the image which we project or which we perceive is not objective reality but our own—or someone else's—reshaping of reality. If it is someone else's reshaping of reality which we perceive, then we are within that other person's sphere of influence and can be led to believe whatever he wishes us to believe: that a rosebush is pleasant because it has a fragrant smell, or that it is unpleasant because it has thorns. If these two images of the rosebush are combined into a metaphor, we have created images which lead us to make an association between the reality of the rosebush and another level of reality, and we can be influenced, for instance, on a moral level: "Pleasant-smelling roses have unpleasant thorns; therefore, beware the sweet fragrance of pleasure for underneath it lie hidden the thorns of destruction." In this way, the association made in the mind of the hearer or reader is controlled. By guiding, by controlling our associations, the image-maker can, and usually does, shape our view of reality, because the images the words conjure up when they are put together artistically provoke an immediate emotional response in us, and dim out of our consciousness all the untold other points of view at our disposal.

Image-making is part of all human experience. However, we are speaking here of the image created by the magic of words. We are considering image not so much as life but as literary art. Art reshapes the raw materials of nature and of human interaction and, in so doing, interprets reality in a non-analytical, non-intellectual way. Art thus makes a direct appeal to the senses and calls forth a spontaneous emotional identification with other men and with the universe. Therefore, the effects of the literary image are most often intuitive, deep beyond the threshold of reason and common sense. When we spoke of the sweet fragrance of pleasure and the thorns of destruction, we made an appeal not to reason but to the emotional attractiveness of the images. In this way, we develop, quite aside from our rational perception, an intuitive view of nature and of the cosmos, and our own relation to it. The rose is an old, familiar example of how our attitude toward the surrounding environment takes form and grows. The body of imagery surrounding the rose is rooted historically deep in Western cultural patterns of looking at the world. The rose symbolizes beauty on the physical level, and purity and freshness on the moral level. Because this imagery is traditional the associations are unquestioned, and because they are unquestioned, they take on the quality of myth. In the case of the rose, the imagery may seem harmless but we will see in a moment how such myth-building images can be the very death of self-concept.

Notice too, in the case of the rose, that man has projected himself into his imagery. The purity, beauty and freshness of the rose are usually compared to an idealized womankind. This is because the natural impetus of man is to impart to the whole cosmos the qualities which he possesses. Man's imagery is thus anthropomorphic; he sees himself or his behavior in every projection he makes. Thus, a flower *dances* in the breeze; the thunder rushes *angrily* through the skies; the sun *smiles* down on the *sleepy* noontime village; *Mother* earth *provides* for us. It follows that man's self-concept must inevitably be tied to his view of the universe, since he sees his own reflection in it at every moment. And a reflection of ourselves cannot be neutral; it cannot be objective; it is either positive or negative. How we regard the phenomena of nature is an indication of what we think of ourselves. The *howling* wind, for example, is not the same image as the *whining* wind. If our literary tradition stresses the howling wind, then we feel emotively that a mysterious prowling creature stalks through our universe. If the whining wind is stressed, we feel the presence of a weak but persistent creature following us constantly around.

We've said that man projects his image upon the universe. But man does not exist in isolation. It is far more accurate to say that man projects his cultural and racial images upon the universe and he derives a sense of personal worth from the reflection he sees gazing back at him. For he defines himself and the world in terms of others like him. He discovers his identity within a group.

And now we come to the heart of the matter, for we cannot judge ourselves unless we see a continuity of ourselves in other people and in things and concepts. We question our very right to exist without other existences like our own. This is why image is so important to African Americans. We are black people living in a white world. When we consider that the black man sees white cultural and racial images projected upon the whole extent of his universe, we cannot help but realize that a very great deal of the time the black man sees a zero image of himself. The black child growing into adulthood through a series of week-end movies, seeing white protagonists constantly before him projecting the whole gamut of human experience, is, in extreme cases, persuaded that he too must be white, or (what is more likely), he experiences manhood by proxy and in someone else's image. He sees, in other words, a zero image of himself. If there are black people on the screen, they are subservient to, uncomfortably different from, or busy emulating the larger, all-inclusive white culture. In that case, our young person sees a negative image of himself. Nor are the images which control personal worth always so direct or obvious. The very same image-myth process which we discovered through the example of the rose is present in the extensive body of color imagery in Western culture. Those associations with black and white have conditioned us to accept white as the symbol of goodness and purity; black as the symbol of evil and impurity.

This did not just happen. It is the result of white racial projection of its own best image upon the universe. Concomitant with that projection for several hundred years—ever since the black man has come within the sphere of influence of the white—the moral and aesthetic associations of black and white have been mixed up with race. Thus, the negative reflection of ourselves is, in the white man's system, the reverse side of his positive projection of himself. The white man has developed a myth of superiority based on images which compare him symbolically with the black man. The very fact of this interconnection is at once a holdover from previous bondage and the most effective means of perpetuating that bondage. We realize now that we are involved in a black-white war over the control of image. For to manipulate an image is to control a peoplehood. Zero image has for a long time meant the repression of our peoplehood.

Of course, the black American has not relied totally on the image projected by white culture. He has developed a literature, and that literature gives him a certain sense of self. We have, however, in spite of ourselves, not been successful in destroying zero image, for we have not been able to convince ourselves that our image is projected on any but a small and segregated strip of the universe. When a self-definition has proceeded spontaneously, the literature will reflect not only a group consciousness, shared points of view, common ancestry, common destiny and aspirations, but it reflects these in spiritual oneness with whatever natural and/or supernatural powers preside over and guide that destiny. For the black writer, the only possibility for spiritual oneness has been non-race or religious literature. But non-race or religious literature takes on insidiously the image projected by what is called the larger culture, and so takes on a white image. Black writers have also attempted to reflect spiritual oneness by writing within a totally black framework. But white images are implanted at the core of black life, the most obvious example being that of the Church, where God is white. Moreover, the black community is not self-sustaining, and a literature which would circumvent this essential feature of peoplehood cannot cope with the forces that shape us. For the most part though, black writers have avoided these two pitfalls, and our literature has been, as we have, slowly, painfully coming out of bondage and has been contributing to our growing sense of peoplehood. If black writers have historically concentrated on white-black animosity, it is because that animosity is an everyday fact of life and functional part of our universe.

The artist then, is the guardian of image; the writer is the myth-maker of his people. We still at times are not sure as to how much of our image is us; to what extent we are the sole authors of our myth, our peoplehood. There are those white people who would nullify any argument we advance on the basis that it is advanced in a white language. And it is true that languages project a specific cultural image. But I believe that we have arrived at a stage of self-awareness in our writing which sees this type of argument as irrelevant. Our very plain answer to this sophisticated argument is simply that we will not let white men define our peoplehood by telling us we're still using white tools to create it. Similarly, we must reject white attempts at portraying black reality. They are valid only in terms of the white man's projection of himself. They have no place in the definition of blackness, for they reveal the white writer's attempt to work through his own cultural guilt, fascination with blackness, or sense of spiritual emptiness. This includes all latterday Harriet Beecher Stowes. No one can hand us a peoplehood, complete with prefabricated images.

Even the word *black* is a translation from the Portuguese slave term *negro*, gone into the English language as Negro. But black is also the generalized term which we use to symbolize unity of origin, whether we are called Anglophone, Francophone, coloured, mulatto, West Indian or American Negro by the white image-makers. *Black* is the highly imagistic term we use to do away with all such divisionary euphemisms. It is the term we use to destroy the myth based on the complex of images which polarize black and white. These images must be mythically torn down, ritually destroyed. We cannot bury out heads before the existing body of myth, nor before our own Europeanization. Therefore, we cannot return nostalgically to a past heritage and pretend that historical continuity exists in anything but fragmentary form. We cannot block out the black-white struggle for control of image and create a utopianized world of all-black reflections. Our work at this stage is clearly to destroy the zero and the negative image-myths of ourselves by turning them inside out. To do this, we reverse the symbolism, and we use that reverse symbolism as the tool for projecting our own image upon the universe.

Zero image, and the need to work through it, is not a new concept. Many black writers have understood the importance of image, and Ralph Ellison in the early fifties stated the same intent metaphorically in the title and outer structure of his novel *Invisible Man*. What is new, I believe, is the deliberate desecration and smashing of idols, the turning inside-out of symbols, to which black writers are now proceeding with a vengeance. Bitterness, which runs through the whole of black literature, is being replaced by wrath; a sense of frustration is giving way before a sense of power. It is the sense of power which proceeds from a mythic consciousness based on a people's positive view of themselves and their destiny.

Perhaps we can best conclude with an illustration of the processes we've been discussing. The following poem attempts to desecrate the mythical and beautiful figure of the muse, entrenched in white culture since the time of its earliest flowering, Greco-Roman antiquity.

Dress the muse in black . . .
　No!
　　Kill her!

Make her jump
　Burning bright white bitch
　　From the pitched peaks of our houses
Let her shriek
　Pale old faded biddy . . .
Hear her?
　Stomping her feet round
　　On our rooftops all these years?

And we, inside. Yassuh meek
　Warming our hands by the fire (like sheep)

Phony 'fay!

Look at her!
　Running past
　　Blond flames waving in the wind

Blow on her!

Grab a torch up in your hand and come outside
　And watch her burn
　　And crackle
　　　And topple
　　　　And lie

Fallen
　Off our rooftops

Into the flame
Look up
   And gather round
      And shake your torch up at her!

Tease her like a yellow cat
   Crouching on the roof

Make her jump
   Make her howl
      Make her yowl
         Falling in the fire

Make it hot . . .
   Make it hate.
Clap and stomp round the fire
   And shout the spirit out of her.
      And draw your circle close
         For we'll kill us a devil tonight.

Come on away, now!
   Now!
      We'll find out own saint
         (or another name for her)
No need for hell's fire now

The fire's weak
   And burned out
      The universe is black again.

2 | The 1970s
The Onset of Theory and the Emergence of Black Feminist Critique

12 Some Reflections on the Black Aesthetic

Larry Neal

(1972)

Mythology	formal manifestation	1. RACE MEMORY (Africa, Middle Passage)
Spirit worship, Orishas, ancestors, African Gods. Syncretism/ catholic voodoo, macumba, Holy Ghost, Jesus as somebody you might know, like a personal deity. River spirits.	Samba, Calypso, Batucada, Cha-Cha, juba, gospel songs, jubilees, work song, spirituals.	Rhythm as an expression of race memory; rhythm as a basic creative principle; rhythm as an existence, creative force as vector of existence. Swinging
		2. MIDDLE PASSAGE (Diaspora) Race memory: terror, landlessness, claustrophobia: "America is a prison . . ." Malcolm X.
Neo-Mythology Shamans: Preachers, poets, blues singers, musicians, mackdaddies, and politicians.	formal manifestation All aspects of Black dance styles in the New World. Pelvic, Dress and walk.	3. TRANSMUTATION AND SYNTHESIS Funky Butt, Stomps, Jump Jim Crow, Buck n' Wing, Jigs, Snake, Grind, slow drag, jitterbug, twist, Watusi, fish, swim, boogaloo, etc. Dance to the *after* beat. Dance as race memory; transmitted through the collective folk consciousness.

Neo-Mythology
Legba, Oshun,
Yemaya, Urzulie,
Soul Momma, Evil
women, Good loving
women, woman as primarily
need/man as doer. Blues
singer as poet and moral
judge; bad man Earth
centered, but directed
cosmologically. Folk poet,
philosopher, priest, priestess,
conjurer, preacher,
teacher, hustler, seer,
soothsayer . . .

4. BLUES GOD/TONE AS MEANING
      AND MEMORY

Sound as racial memory, primeval. Life
breath. Word is perceived as energy or
force. Call and response Blues perceived
as an emanation outside of man, but yet
a manifestation of his being/reality.
Same energy source as Gospel, field
holler, but delineated in narrative
song. The African voice transplanted.
This God must be the meanest and the
strongest. He survives and persists
Once perceived as an evil force:
" . . . and I (Dude Botley) got to thinking about how many thousand of people
(Buddy) Bolden had made happy and all
of them women who used to idolize him
'Where are they now?' I say to myself.
Then I hear Bolden's cornet. I look
through the crack and there he is, relaxed back in the chair, blowing that
silver cornet softly, just above a
whisper, and I see he's got his hat
over the bell of the horn. I put my
ear close to the keyhole. I thought I
heard Bolden play the blues before,
and play hymns at funerals, but what
he is playing now is real strange and
I listen carefully, because he's playing
something that, for a while sounds like
the blues, then like a hymn. I cannot
make out the tune, but after awhile I
catch on. He is mixing up the blues
with the hymns. He plays the blues real
sad and the hymn sadder than the blues
and then the blues sadder than the hymn.
That is the first time that I had ever
heard hymns and blues cooked up together.
A strange cold feeling comes over me; I
get sort of scared because I know the
Lord don't like that mixing the Devil's
music with his music. . . . It sounded like
a battle between the Good Lord and the
Devil. Something tells me to listen and
see who wins. If Bolden stops on the
hymn, the Good Lord wins; if he stops
on the blues, the Devil wins."

HISTORY AS UNITARY MYTH

Shango, Nat Turner, Denmark,
Vesey, Brer' Rabbit, High John
the Conqueror, Jack Johnson, Ray
Robinson, Signifying Monkey,
Malcolm X, Adam Clayton Powell,
Garvey, Du Bois, Hon.
Elijah Muhammed, Martin L.
King, Rap Brown, Rev. Franklin,
Charlie Parker, Duke Ellington
James Brown, Bessie Smith
Moms Mabley, King Pleasure,
Raefilt Johnson. Son House.
Louis Armstrong. . . .
Voodoo again Ishmael Reed's
Hoodoo. Islamic suffis.
Third World's destiny.
The East as the Womb
and the Tomb. Fanon's
Third World, Bandung
Humanism. Revolution is the
operational mythology.
Symbol change. Expanded
metaphors as in the poetry
of Curtis Lyle and Stanley
Crouch; or L. Barrett's *Song
For MuMu* . . . Nigger styles and
masks such as Rinehart in the
Invisible Man. Style as in
James P. Johnson description
of stride pianists in the twenties.
Bobby Blue Bland wearing a dashiki
and a process. All of this links
up with the transmutation of
African styles and the revitalization
of these styles on the West.

5. BLACK ARTS MOVEMENT/BLACK
   ART AESTHETIC

Feeling/contemporary and historical.
Energy intensifies. Non-matrixed art
forms: Coltrane, Ornette, Sun Ra.
More concerned with the vibration of
the Word, than with the Word itself.
Like signifying.
The Black Nation as Poem. Ethical stance
as aesthetic. The synthesis of the above
presented outline. The integral unity of
culture, politics, and art. Spiritual.
Despises alienation in the European sense.
Art consciously committed; art addressed
primarily to Black and Third World people.
Black attempts to realize the world as
art by making Man more compatible to it
and it more compatible to Man. Styles
itself from nigger rhythms to cosmic
sensibility. Black love, conscious and
affirmed. Change.

13 | Cultural Strangulation
Black Literature and the White Aesthetic

Addison Gayle, Jr.

(1972)

> This assumption that of all the hues of God, whiteness is inherently and obviously better than brownness or tan leads to curious acts.
> —W. E. B. Du Bois

The expected opposition to the concept of a "Black Aesthetic" was not long in coming. In separate reviews of *Black Fire*, an anthology edited by LeRoi Jones and Larry Neal, critics from the *Saturday Review* and the *New York Review of Books* presented the expected rebuttal. Agreeing with Ralph Ellison that sociology and art are incompatible mates, these critics, nevertheless, invoked the clichés of the social ideology of the "we shall overcome" years in their attempt to steer Blacks from "the path of literary fantasy and folly."

Their major thesis is simple: There is no Black aesthetic because there is no white aesthetic. The Kerner Commission Report to the contrary, America is not two societies but one. Therefore, Americans of all races, colors and creeds share a common cultural heredity. This is to say that there is one predominant culture—the American culture—with tributary national and ethnic streams flowing into the larger river. Literature, the most important by-product of this cultural monolith, knows no parochial boundaries. To speak of a Black literature, a Black aesthetic, or a Black state, is to engage in racial chauvinism, separatist bias, and Black fantasy.

The question of a white aesthetic, however, is academic. One has neither to talk about it nor define it. Most Americans, black and white, accept the existence of a "White Aesthetic" as naturally as they accept April 15th as the deadline for paying their income tax—with far less animosity towards the former than the latter. The white aesthetic, despite the academic critics, has always been with us: for long before Diotima pointed out the way to heavenly beauty to Socrates, the poets of biblical times were discussing beauty in terms of light and dark—the essential characteristics of a white and black aesthetic—and establishing the dichotomy of superior *vs.* inferior which would assume body and form in the 18th century. Therefore, more serious than a definition, is the problem of tracing the white aesthetic from its early origins and afterwards, outlining the various changes in the basic formula from culture to culture and from nation to nation. Such an undertaking would be more germane to a book than an essay; nevertheless, one may take a certain starting point and, using selective nations and cultures, make the critical point, while calling attention to the necessity of a more comprehensive study encompassing all of the nations and cultures of the world.

Let us propose Greece as the logical starting point, bearing in mind Will Durant's observation that "all of Western Civilization is but a footnote to Plato," and take Plato as the first writer to attempt a systematic aesthetic. Two documents by Plato, *The Symposium* and *The Republic*, reveal the twin components of Plato's aesthetic system.

In *The Symposium*, Plato divides the universe into spheres. In one sphere, the lower, one finds the forms of beauty; in the other, the higher, beauty, as Diotima tells Socrates, is absolute and supreme. In *The Republic*, Plato defines the poet as an imitator (a third-rate imitator—a point which modern critics have long since forgotten) who reflects the heavenly beauty in the earthly mirror. In other words, the poet recreates beauty as it exists in heaven; thus the poet, as Neo-Platonists from Aquinas to Coleridge have told us, is the custodian of beauty on earth.

However, Plato defines beauty only in ambiguous, mystical terms; leaving the problem of a more circumscribed, secular definition to philosophers, poets, and critics. During most of the history of the Western world, these aestheticians have been white; therefore, it is not surprising that, symbolically and literally, they have defined beauty in terms of whiteness. (An early contradiction to this tendency is the Marquis DeSade who inverted the symbols, making black beautiful, but demonic, and white pure, but sterile—the Marquis is considered by modern criticism to have been mentally deranged.)

The distinction between whiteness as beautiful (good) and blackness as ugly (evil) appears early in the literature of the middle ages—in the Morality Plays of England. Heavily influenced by both Platonism and Christianity, these plays set forth the distinctions which exist today. To be white was to be pure, good, universal, and beautiful; to be black was to be impure, evil, parochial, and ugly.

The characters and the plots of these plays followed this basic format. The villain is always evil, in most cases the devil; the protagonist, or hero, is always good, in most cases, angels or disciples. The plot then is simple; good (light) triumphs over the forces of evil (dark). As English literature became more sophisticated, the symbols were made to cover wider areas of the human and literary experience. To love was divine; to hate, evil. The fancied mistress of Petrarch was the purest of the pure; Grendel's mother, a creature from the "lower regions and marshes," is, like her son, a monster; the "bad" characters in Chaucer's *Canterbury Tales* tell dark stories; and the Satan of *Paradise Lost* must be vanquished by Gabriel, the angel of purity.

These ancients, as Swift might have called them, established their dichotomies as a result of the influences of Neo-Platonism and Christianity. Later, the symbols became internationalized. Robert Burton, in *The Anatomy of Melancholy*, writes of "dark despair" in the seventeenth century, and James Boswell describes melancholia, that state of mind common to intellectuals of the 17th and 18th centuries, as a dark, dreaded affliction which robbed men of their creative energies. This condition—dark despair or melancholia—was later popularized in what is referred to in English literature as its "dark period"—the period of the Grave Yard School of poets and the Gothic novels.

The symbols thus far were largely applied to conditions, although characters who symbolized evil influences were also dark. In the early stages of English literature, these characters were mythological and fictitious and not representative of people of specific racial or ethnic groups. In the 18th century English novel, however, the symbolism becomes ethnic and racial.

There were forerunners. As early as 1621, Shakespeare has Iago refer to Othello as that "old Black ewe," attaching the mystical sexual characteristic to blackness which would become the motive for centuries of oppressive acts by white Americans. In *The Tempest*, Shakespeare's last play, Caliban, though not ostensibly black, is nevertheless a distant cousin of the colonial Friday in Daniel Defoe's *Robinson Crusoe*.

Robinson Crusoe was published at a historically significant time. In the year 1719, the English had all but completed their colonization of Africa. The slave trade in America was on its way to becoming a booming industry; in Africa, Black people were enslaved mentally as well as physically by such strange bedfellows as criminals, businessmen, and Christians. In the social and political spheres, a rationale was needed, and help came from the artist—in this case, the novelist—in the form of *Robinson Crusoe*. In the novel, Defoe brings together both Christian and Platonic symbolism, sharpening the dichotomy between light and dark on the one hand, while on the other establishing a criterion for the inferiority of Black people as opposed to the superiority of white.

One need only compare Crusoe with Friday to validate both of these statements. Crusoe is majestic, wise, white and a colonialist; Friday is savage, ignorant, black and a colonial. Therefore, Crusoe, the colonialist, has a double task. On the one hand he must transform the island (Africa—unproductive, barren, dead) into a little England (prosperous, life-giving, fertile), and he must recreate Friday in his own image, thus bringing him as close to being an Englishman as possible. At the end of the novel, Crusoe has accomplished both undertakings; the island is a replica of "mother England"; and Friday has been transformed into a white man, now capable of immigrating to the land of the gods.

From such mystical artifacts has the literature and criticism of the Western world sprung; and based upon such narrow prejudices as those of Defoe, the art of Black people throughout the world has been described as parochial and inferior. Friday was parochial and inferior until, having denounced his own culture, he assimilated another. Once this was done, symbolically, Friday underwent a change. To deal with him after the conversion was to deal with him in terms of a character who had been civilized and therefore had moved beyond racial parochialism.

However, Defoe was merely a hack novelist, not a thinker. It was left to shrewder minds than his to apply the rules of the white aesthetic to the practical areas of the Black literary and social worlds, and no shrewder minds were at work on this problem than those of writers and critics in America. In America, the rationale for both slavery and the inferiority of Black art and culture was supplied boldly, without the trappings of 18th-century symbolism.

In 1867, in a book entitled *Nojoque: A Question for a Continent*, Hinton Helper provided the vehicle for the cultural and social symbols of inferiority under which Blacks have labored in this country. Helper intended, as he states frankly in his preface, "to write the negro out of America." In the headings of the two major chapters of the book, the whole symbolic apparatus of the white aesthetic handed down from Plato to America is graphically revealed: the heading of one chapter reads: "Black: A Thing of Ugliness, Disease"; another heading reads: "White: A Thing of Life, Health, and Beauty."

Under the first heading, Helper argues that the color black "has always been associated with sinister things such as mourning, the devil, the darkness of night." Under the second, "White has always been associated with the light of day, divine transfiguration, the beneficent moon and stars . . . the fair complexion of romantic ladies, the costumes of Romans and angels, and the white of the American flag so beautifully combined with blue and red without ever a touch of the black that has been for the flag of pirates."

Such is the American critical ethic based upon centuries of distortion of the Platonic ideal. By not adequately defining beauty, and implying at least that this was the job of the poet, Plato laid the foundation for the white aesthetic as defined by Daniel Defoe and Hinton Helper. However, the uses of that aesthetic to stifle and strangle the cultures of other nations is not to be attributed to Plato but, instead, to his hereditary brothers far from the Aegean. For Plato knew his poets. They were not, he surmised, a very trusting lot and, therefore, by adopting an ambiguous position on symbols, he limited their power in the realm of aesthetics. For Plato, there were two kinds of symbols: natural and proscriptive. Natural symbols corresponded to absolute beauty as created by God; proscriptive symbols, on the other hand, were symbols of beauty as proscribed by man, which is to say that certain symbols are said to mean such and such by man himself.

The irony of the trap in which the Black artist has found himself throughout history is apparent. Those symbols which govern his life and art are proscriptive ones, set down by minds as diseased as Hinton Helper's. In other words, beauty has been in the eyes of an earthly beholder who has stipulated that beauty conforms to such and such a definition. To return to Friday, Defoe stipulated that civilized man was what Friday had to become, proscribed certain characteristics to the term "civilized," and presto, Friday, in order not to be regarded as a "savage under Western eyes," was forced to conform to this ideal. How well have the same stipulative definitions worked in the artistic sphere! Masterpieces are made at will by each new critic who argues that the subject of his doctoral dissertation is immortal. At one period of history, John Donne, according to the critic Samuel Johnson, is a second-rate poet;

at another period, according to the critic T. S. Eliot, he is one of the finest poets in the language. Dickens, argues Professor Ada Nisbet, is one of England's most representative novelists, while for F. R. Leavis, Dickens' work does not warrant him a place in *The Great Tradition.*

When Black literature is the subject, the verbiage reaches the height of the ridiculous. The good "Negro Novel," we are told by Robert Bone and Herbert Hill, is that novel in which the subject matter moves beyond the limitations of narrow parochialism. Form is the most important criterion of the work of art when Black literature is evaluated, whereas form, almost non-existent in Dostoyevsky's *Crime and Punishment,* and totally chaotic in Kafka's *The Trial,* must take second place to the supremacy of thought and message.

Richard Wright, says Theodore Gross, is not a major American novelist; while Ralph Ellison, on the strength of one novel, is. LeRoi Jones is not a major poet, Ed Bullins not a major playwright, Baldwin incapable of handling the novel form—all because white critics have said so.

Behind the symbol is the object or vehicle, and behind the vehicle is the definition. It is the definition with which we are concerned, for the extent of the cultural strangulation of Black literature by white critics has been the extent to which they have been allowed to define the terms in which the Black artist will deal with his own experience. The career of Paul Laurence Dunbar is the most striking example. Having internalized the definitions handed him by the American society, Dunbar would rather not have written about the Black experience at all, and three of his novels and most of his poetry support this argument. However, when forced to do so by his white liberal mentors, among them was the powerful critic, William Dean Howells, Dunbar deals with Blacks in terms of buffoonery, idiocy and comedy.

Like so many Black writers, past and present, Dunbar was trapped by the definitions of other men, never capable of realizing until near the end of his life, that those definitions were not god-given, but man-given; and so circumscribed by tradition and culture that they were irrelevant to an evaluation of either his life or his art.

In a literary conflict involving Christianity, Zarathustra, Friedrich Nietzsche's iconoclast, calls for "a new table of the laws." In similar iconoclastic fashion, the proponents of a Black Aesthetic, the idol smashers of America, call for a set of rules by which Black literature and art is to be judged and evaluated. For the historic practice of bowing to other men's gods and definitions has produced a crisis of the highest magnitude, and brought us, culturally, to the limits of racial armageddon. The trend must be reversed.

The acceptance of the phrase "Black is Beautiful" is the first step in the destruction of the old table of the laws and the construction of new ones, for the phrase flies in the face of the whole ethos of the white aesthetic. This step must be followed by serious scholarship and hard work; and Black critics must dig beneath the phrase and unearth the treasure of beauty lying deep in the untoured regions of the Black experience—regions where others, due to historical conditioning and cultural deprivation, cannot go.

14 | Inside the Funk Shop
A Word on Black Words

Stephen E. Henderson

(1973)

"Ain't it funky now!" James Brown screamed for days at the top on the Soul Brothers' Chart. "Ain't it funky!" The obnoxious word had been given a new Black meaning and public respectability. It wasn't a new word certainly, and it retained the original meanings which Black people had given it in the days of the Funky Hutt dance. But there were other meanings too, which jazz critics especially liked. In fact, they used the word so much that a decade ago Imamu Baraka (LeRoi Jones) declared it "almost useless." Now while the word "funky" is being revived, another Black word, "soul," that surfaced during the time Imamu wrote, is apparently on its way out—done in by overexposure and the Man.

Though both of these words have special Black meanings and are, in effect, Black words, they also have "standard" English meanings that both whites and Blacks know. The whites have, however, responded to the vital Black meanings in a way which epitomizes their historical response to Black culture: for although one may dismiss the emergence and popularity of words like these as linguistic fads, and the white imitations as merely innocuous, commercial, racist, or sick, that would be a grievous error, for this concern with Black language is part of a subtle system of co-optation and control which involves all major aspects of Black culture. If examined even with cursory attention, in fact, it epitomizes this system. It thus embodies (a) the virtual compulsion (personal and national) of whites to control Black distinctiveness, (b) the mythic and unconscious aspects of that control, (c) the commercial aspects of it, and especially, (d) the educational and political aspects of it.

First there is the level of fad—with the popularity and abuse of the words in question. The media plays an important role, chiefly in the dilution and distortion of Black meaning. The net effect is political control.

For example, a few years ago, *Time* magazine did a feature story on the word "soul," in which *Time* decided what that quality was and even determined the people and *literary characters* who possessed it. Among them were Jackie Kennedy, Caliban (but not Ariel), and other personages, white and Black. *Time* provided a kind of do-it-yourself kit and made the whole business a kind of game. *Newsweek*, not to be outdone, also sought for the mysterious essence of Black life encompassed in the word "soul." They were a bit less presumptuous and more pragmatic. They interviewed Black people themselves and published some, at least, of what they had to say, What the people said, in effect, was that "soul" was the Black lifestyle, the Black wisdom of the race, born in suffering, but proud, flexible, hip, shrewd, loving, tough, lyrical, patient, tender, and full of virtuoso elegance.

All of this, to be sure, wasn't obvious in the *Newsweek* story, and I flushed it out with a study which I conducted in Atlanta, Georgia in 1967–68. I pointedly asked people whether they thought that white folks had "soul." The responses were canny sometimes, at other times naive or hopeful, or just plain Christian democratic. That is to say, people regarded "soul" as a special something that Blacks possessed, but were often reluctant to press the point. Others defined "soul" in a quasi-religious sense, though again centering on the Black Experience. "Soul," for most, became deep-down feeling that Black people had which sometimes whites imitated. And if they wanted to call what they were doing and feeling "soul," why not let them. That's their business! Which, of course, was a most soulful way of dealing with the situation.

The response to "funk" can be seen in an article which appeared in the January 11 issue of the *Washington Post*, entitled "Funk Is in the Eye of the Beholder," by Henry Allen. Funk in the eye! Wow! But the author is certainly not uninformed. He knows something about the various meanings. He states: "Funk once meant a shameful condition shunned by millions, a quality (*sic*) linked to aging bedclothes, depression, various low-rent odors and incapacitating fear." "This," he declares, "is no longer true, and funk may become the hottest cultural property since organic food." He knows the usage of the jazz critics. He cites the music of Les McCann. Next, he examines current usage. "Funk is," he writes, "a way of life that only yesterday you no doubt considered tacky, old-fashioned, obnoxious or irrelevant. Funky is what things are before they become camp." Funk is not a "nostalgia for the mud, or a sentimental attraction for the lower classes," although these things are found in Thomas Wolfe, who uses the word "funk." Funk is doing the unexpected, but that which your "peer group" will also loathe. Getting high on a dollar-a-bottle wine, drinking beer out of the can, while sitting around in your undershirt listening to a ball game—all of this is very funky, especially if you also eat a peanut butter and jelly sandwich, which in fact, "comes about as close as anything to epitomizing the new funk." And, finally, "funk turns life into a costume party which you attend dressed just like everyone else."

The pattern is important. A word which has special significance for the Black community becomes useful or titillating to the white community. Then a process of justification and sanitizing begins. The media, the critics, and eventually the scholars take their roles. The chief thing, however, is to deny the original Blackness of the new usage out of ignorance or by design.

Here, as in the *Time* article on "soul," the point is to capitalize on the excitement aroused by Black usage and turn it into white ends. Just as *Time* reduced "soul" to a kind of do-your-own-thing game, the *Post* article reduces "funk" to a sentimental free-associational kitsch, and further links it to the stylized sensibility which produced the notion of camp. All of which has nothing to do basically with the Black Experience, and the proof is easy. Listen to James Brown. Or listen to the D.J. who says, "Oooooooo-Weeeeeeee! I'm fonky as I wanna be! Fonky as a can of Magic Shave! Can you dig it!" That kind of funk doesn't have anything to do with costume parties and campy old clothes. Sometimes Black folks wear old clothes because they want to be comfortable, but usually because they can't do any better. And Magic Shave is a thing unto itself.

The Black response to white imitation has been to ignore it, to tolerate it, to show whites what the real thing is by appearing to share it with them, to go back to the original basic meanings involved, to invent new meanings which defy white acceptance, or to discard the expression altogether and take up another. Thus, many Blacks didn't care whether white people said that they had "soul" or not, and black D.J.s even invented the tern "blue-eyed soul." And James Brown diplomatically allowed that Merv Griffin just might have "soul." And Dionne Warwick said that Dick Cavett had it. Aretha said Frank Sinatra had it too. And Jesse Jackson taught Mayor Daley the handshake. Finally, *Liberator* magazine got mad and said to hell with it, and declared that soul was useless—officially dead—and printed a picture of the gravesite to prove it. And so we became "funky"—like calling ourselves niggers in public. There are, of course, whites who try to call themselves "student niggers" and "new niggers" and "gay niggers" and "women's lib niggers" but Dick Cavett hasn't called Bill Russell "my main nigger" on TV yet. And Johnny Cash hasn't called Flip Wilson that either. And Johnny Carson hasn't called himself "funky" yet, and one doubts that any of the Presidential candidates would address Black voters as "my fellow funky Americans."

Thus, there is a temporary detente, so to speak, while the deodorizing machinery goes into action. The *Post* article shows how it works. Reduce the whole thing to a game played with "class" values—not racial ones—then retreat from the real world of the present to the nostalgic world of "O Mein Papa," in which everyone returns to the mythical melting pot of musical comedy and television commercials.

This would all be quite harmless and funny if we were merely talking about acculturation and if the pattern of white response merely indicated national emptiness, or neurosis, or greed. It would be hilarious if the only thing involved were the "Soulful Strut" and the "Funky Butt" finding their way to the White House, for a fascination with the Exotic African ranges through American—indeed, Western life and history, culminating in an all-pervasive Lust-Hate-Envy syndrome which is everywhere apparent. But it is part of a larger picture: the Imperialistic intrusion of Europe into the continent of Africa. The story is familiar by now: the initial peaceful contacts before the Industrial Revolution, the wondrous tales of wealth and exotic civilizations, the cancer of the slave trade, the coming of the missionaries and the settlers, and the wholesale dismembering of the continent and its people, and the bitter years of colonial subjugation. And on this side of the water, the need to justify the action—the system of exploitation and oppression, in a country supposedly democratic, founded on the assumption of universal human worth and the inalienable right to the pursuit of happiness.

What was needed was a mythology to justify slavery, and after that, segregation, and, as the truth becomes generally known the expansion and perpetuation of political and economic power through whatever means those in control have at their disposal. One of the chief means is education, both formal and informal—through the schools, through the churches, through the publishing industry, and through the communications media.

It is at this point that the question of language and of distinctive Black language and culture in the United States becomes crucial. It is here that we see in the apparently faddish concern with Black "slang" and lifestyle the powerful and subtle workings of a massive system of economic and political control. To view such questions as merely the concern of poets and academicians is dangerous, for as I noted earlier, the movement of unofficial and official response toward Black culture in this country has been toward the denial of Black distinctiveness. The point is to convince all people, white and Black, that everything of value which Black people possess they owe ultimately to the white man. In this manner it is possible to thwart any serious large scale organization of Blacks on a nationalistic basis.

This strategy has been employed whenever a distinctive feature of Black life seemed to resist the "melting pot." It has been used to discredit the originality of the blues, the spirituals, jazz, Black literature, and even large segments of Black folklore by pointing to European similarities or analogues. And the enormous energy spent in these attempts, sometimes by seemingly unwitting and "objective" scholars, has confused many of our people who not only fail to see our own strength but the devious weakness of our oppressors. Thus words like "funky" and "soul" are important indicators of our weakness as a unique people. They are important also because they signal that knowledge to the larger society which must control our identity images if it is ultimately to control us.

Historically, this has been done by raising certain kinds of "academic" and "scientific" questions with regard to our distinctiveness. The problem for the "scientists," then becomes one of measuring and defining and limiting and predicting that something which makes us distinctive. Quite understandably they have had problems with funk and soul. But they have also questioned the capacity of Blacks to master the "complex" European language which they were forced to adopt. They have questioned our capacity for "abstract" thought. In the process, they have conveniently forgotten Juan Latino, Phyllis Wheatley, Aesop, Terence, St. Augustine, Rameses II, Akhenaton, Paul Cuffey, Du Bois, and others. They have forgotten the pyramids and the Spirit World to the South.

The President of the United States himself—Thomas Jefferson—had his doubts about whether a Black man could master the Greek verb. And so we knocked ourselves out and learned Greek verbs and made Greek a requirement in our colleges for generations.

But underlying all that formal linguistic demonstration was the sheer poetic genius of the people which burst into the grandeur of the spirituals and the bitter precision of the blues. Funk and soul are part of this too. And the white response was predictable. They invented the minstrel tradition, both as a staged performance and as "literature," and they wrote in a language which, however entertaining they thought it to be, was certainly not Black. Imagine the popularity, for instance, of Hamlet's "to be or not to be" speech done up in "plantation English"! Yet such was the case.

On the other hand, the response toward the "Noble Savage" was one of appreciation for his simple broken, picturesque language which he mercifully dissolved in ineffable sweet, though "monotonous" song. Even "educated" Black people still accept that judgement of "an empty jingle in a broken tongue."

But the crucial response has been on the level of formal education with the myth of "Standard English" which all Americans had to learn if they were to get on in the world. In a somewhat disguised form it is still with us. It appears in conservative and liberal packages. The one believes in holding all noses to the same grindstone; the other saying, a fat nose is just as good as a long nose, as long as I'm selling the Kleenex, or doing the nose jobs. Accordingly there has grown up in this country over the past decade a dangerous collusion of forces in industry, government, private foundations, and professional language researchers and teachers. To date, their most seductive appeal has been the notion that the "culturally deprived" or "disadvantaged," i.e., Black child can be moved into the mainstream of American life—to use the cliché—if he is taught to be "bidialectical," that is, if he learns to use "standard" English in those situations which would guarantee success for him in the white world. He is to be taught that his own dialect, his social speech, is to be reserved only for private and intimate occasions. For his attempts at this kind of self-mutilation the child is rewarded with transistor radios and other products of the "Great Society." Industry has moved into the picture with the blandishments of contract teaching. Fortunately, its corruption has already been exposed and its premises and results brought under fire. But there is a more sophisticated operation afoot which involves professional linguists of national reputation. Although they are confronted with evidence that they are unprepared to produce real "double-speakers," they have a vested interest in the money and prestige and power involved. And if the Black child fails to become "bidialectical," the fault will be found in him, not in the system. And the final question is whether those who control the system and those who fund it are concerned with learning anyway, or with the circulation of money and the pacification of the Black Community.

So Black English worries these people. They know the political significance of language. They knew the power of "Ain' Gon' let Nobody Turn Me Round." They somehow co-opted it, but they have never been able to define "jazz" to say nothing of "soul." And it's not dead. We're just letting it rest a while, gathering up that ancestral energy, for as long as we have vital contact with that we can get it together. Well, it may be a costume party to Henry Allen, but it's real to us, and everything we do from now on gon' be FONKY!

15 Saturation

Progress Report on a Theory of Black Poetry

Stephen E. Henderson

(1975)

> (The) perception of Blackness, then, means that Blackness is, or can be, a value in the creation, in the description, and in the criticism of Black poetry. This is so . . . not because I say so, but because poets say so, musicians say so, either directly, or by implication.

In *Understanding the New Black Poetry* (Morrow, 1973), I attempted to sketch a critical framework which would help make the poetry accessible to a larger number of people. I tried to do this in a serious, nonpolemical fashion because, although some of the attacks on the poetry deserved to be simply blasted away by polemic, other attacks and misunderstandings were more challenging. And much of this misunderstanding was, frankly, in the minds of the Black people to whom the poetry was addressed. Not all of them were over 30, or reactionary, or brainwashed. Many of them were young, bright men and women who wanted to know more fully what was going on. Some of them were even poets themselves. I conceived the hook with them in mind, and, to be honest, in order to clarify some things for myself. The book has been generally well received, but like most attempts to explain or explicate or verbalize art, it also raised questions which need some systematic response.

These questions revolve mainly around one of the three categories that were basic to my discussion—saturation. The other two categories are theme and structure. Before I address those questions, however, I shall summarize briefly the entire argument. It says that there are two traditions or levels of Black poetry—the folk and the formal—which must be seen as a totality, since they often intersect and overlap one another, and since the people who create them are one people. It says further that the overriding theme of Black poetry is the idea of Freedom and/or Liberation, expressed in various ways and on various levels. This, of course, is not to deny the existence and importance of other themes—both public and personal; but the poetry reflects the concerns, the consciousness of the people—and Freedom/Liberation has been, and still is, obviously, the main objective of Black American life, and as a theme it virtually leaps from the pages of our poetry.

Structure is a crucial category because it is the one so loosely discussed and so open to damaging attack from enemies of the literature and enemies of the people, but sometimes even from well-meaning and "objective" friends of the literature and teachers of the people. Here are two examples: In a review of *Black Fire* (ed. LeRoi Jones and Larry Neal, Morrow, 1968), Peter Berek makes the following observation:

A few of the assembled works have a scatological energy that succeeds in impressing one with the violence and passion of the author's emotions, but the expression never achieves the precision and control which are the hallmarks of successful art (including the "black" arts of jazz and rhythm and blues). Characteristically (and sometimes ludicrously) the poet substitutes the announcement of an intention for its fulfillment. Thus Yusuf Rahman glorifies black womanhood by saying:

> naturally black & beautiful
> LOVE ME EBONY LADY
> Yes! I see blue-crystal teardrops
> burning scars on your soul's cheeks
> your tears splash acidly in my stomach of reality.

A burning heart is not the same as acid indigestion.
(*Saturday Review*, Nov. 30, 1968, p. 36.)

What makes the review damaging is the fact that the editors had compared the lines of this poem to a Charlie Parker solo. In another review, this one in *The New York Review of Books* (Dec. 19, 1968, p. 11), the same poem and the same statement are taken to task by Jack Richardson.

Neal can call a poet like Yusuf Rahman, who explodes in unconsidered bombast all over the page, the "poetic equivalent of Charlie Parker" without seeing that the former is haphazard and full of imagistic *non sequiturs*, while Parker was a lyric genius who, within an expanded chordal structure and method of substitution, produced music that was never randomly loose. He certainly never honked anything like these lines which end Rahman's poems, "Transcendental Blues":

> White maggots will not military your
>   babies down dead
>   again
> White maggots will not mercenary
>   your fertile Nile to ache with
>   pus
>   again
> My spears shall rain
> I-can't-give-them-anything-but-drops
> -of hate
> erasing them
> exterminating them
> so humanity can have a clear slate

>Just keep me constant
> ebony lady
>LOVE ME EBONY LADY
>LOVE ME EBONY LADY

However strongly one feels about racial unity, by no artistic legerdemain can one compare the author of the above with a man of abstract precision like Parker. Such a comparison goes beyond ebullience into a sort of critical madness.

Despite the implicit chauvinism in these reviews, polemic is certainly not sufficient to answer them. The question which they raise is structural and should be answered, if possible, in structural terms. If it cannot be, then the writer/critic/editor should be more careful with his similes. With these kinds of responses in mind, then, I tried to set down the structural patterns that I saw, and that I felt were identifiably Black. In the process, I assumed that anyone in the Western world who took the time to read a critical essay on poetry in the first place would already have some specific ideas about what European, specifically English, and Euro-American, specifically Anglo-American, poetic structures were.

This leaves, of course, the concept of saturation, which is the proper subject of this discussion. This category, while the most briefly discussed in my "Introduction: The Forms of Things Unknown," is actually the most important, in my thinking, of the categories, simply because it poses the most difficult questions on the one hand, and presents, on the other, a logical category in which they can be profitably discussed.

In the essay I observed that by saturation I mean "several things, but chiefly (a) the communication of Blackness in a given situation, and (b) a sense of fidelity to the observed and intuited truth of the Black Experience. I postulate this concept as a third category for describing and for evaluating Black poetry. As in the other two, theme and structure, this category exists only in relationship to the entire work and is employed merely to deal with an aspect of the poetry that warrants discussion and appreciation. In other words, just as it is misleading to speak of theme to the exclusion of structure, and vice versa, it is difficult, if not impossible, to speak honestly about saturation without considering these other two. In addition, one must not consider the poem in isolation but rather in relationship to the reader/audience, and the reader to the wider context of the phenomenon which we call, for the sake of convenience, the Black Experience" (*Understanding the New Black Poetry*, p. 62).

Saturation may thus be seen as (1) a perception, (2) a quality and (3) a condition of theme and structure. The perception occurs in the reader/audience in a situation of communication-involving the poem/poet/reader/performer. If the poem "works," then the reader perceives something in it which he identifies as Black and meaningful. He perceives this as being true to his knowledge of the experience recorded in the poem, according to his observation or according to his intuition. The important thing, at any rate, is that he considers the communication of this "Blackness" to be significant and his reception of it to be significant, whether he agrees with it or not. This communication of Blackness may be related to theme, or what is commonly called the subject or meaning of the poem; or it may be related to the structure of the poem—the way it is put together. With regard to theme, saturation may occur when the theme is simply, obviously, and naturally Black—as in a tiny poem by Sterling Plumpp, entitled "Heaven Here" (*Half Black Half Blacker*, Third World Press, 1970, p. 12).

> on asphalt
> dance floors
> in sure control
> o i see
> little alcindors
> be

On the other hand, as I point out in *Understanding the New Black Poetry* (p. 63), it may occur in poems which do not ostensibly deal with Black themes at all, which yet impress us somehow as Black, as having a Black "quality." The analogue in real life is the very fair-skinned person (who may or not be "black") whom we somehow take to be Black on the basis of some subliminal gesture, or tone, or "quality." I cite again two examples from Mari Evans' *I Am a Black Woman* (Morrow, 1970):

> I am not
> lazy . . . just
> . . . battered

And:

> where have you gone
> with your confident
> walk your
> crooked smile the
> rent money
> in one pocket and
> my heart
> in another

I noted that "In cases like these, the awareness is largely unverbalized and comes across as a 'typical' situation, which we identify as true-to-life or part of the Black Experience" (p. 63).

And there are poems which we simply draw into the dynamics of our Blackness because they do not contradict it but flow into it freely, stumped with our own personal and group impress. Many poems on love, for example, are of this variety, as are innumerable popular songs on the same theme.

But to return to my argument, poets can and have made Blackness—in a thematic and structural sense—the subject of their poems. And when they do so with the skill of Sterling Brown in "Ma Rainey," then the least the critic can do is to try to meet the work on its own terms. As far as I know, there are no traditional categories, or practices, or attitudes in American or English literature which make this possible. On the contrary, they try to make it impossible, to erase it, to pretend that it doesn't exist—as in Louis Simpson's cavalier dismissal of Gwendolyn Brooks, or in the general liberal platitudes about "the human condition" or "universals."

If the critic is half worth his salt, then he would attempt to describe what occurs in the poem and to explain—to the extent that it is possible—how the "action" takes place, i.e., how the elements of the work interact with one another to produce its effect. And if one of those elements is "Blackness"—as value, as theme, or as structure, especially the latter—then he is remiss in his duty if he does not attempt to deal with it in some logical, orderly manner. Finally, he must place some value judgment on the work, on the totality of the work—not just its theme, its sociology, or its ideology, but also its structure. And if the theme involves Blackness as value, and if the structures are Black, whether in a traditional sense or not, then the judgment must involve that Blackness as well.

Surely some structures are more distinctly Black, more recognizably Black, than others. Thus the three-line blues form is more distinctly Black than a sonnet by Claude McKay, for example. The ballad, because it is a form (in the Anglo-American tradition) which was early appropriated by Blacks—on both folk and formal levels— is also more definitely "Black" than the sonnet. But the blues, an invention of Black people, is "Blacker" than both. In fact, one may call the blues a saturated form and blues imagery, saturated structures.

This perception of a Black quality can take place on various levels of significance, thus making some poems "Blacker" than others or more significantly "Black" than others. Thus Plumpp's "Heaven Here," though saturated by its fidelity to observed event and evoking the towering model of "alcindor," weighs less in terms of meaning than, for example, Langston Hughes':

> I wish the rent
> was Heaven sent.

Or:

> I got the blues but I'm too damn mean to cry.

Both of these "poems" represent different conditions of Blackness, of saturation. This perception of Blackness, then, means that Blackness is, or can be, or should be, a value in the creation, in the description, and in the criticism of Black poetry. This is so, of course, not because I say so, but because poets say so, musicians say so, either directly, or by implication. Now, I know that this is an unpopular view, especially with those artists and those critics who think that they live in a color-blind, homogeneous United States of America. I can in all honesty merely give them my respect as writers and my pity as Black people.

At this point we begin discussing saturation as a function or condition of structure. And we may say briefly that certain characteristics of Black speech and music may so imbue the poetry as to warrant our calling certain poems or features of poems "structurally saturated." The musical referents themselves are quite clear: boogie-woogie style, blues tonality and changes, the pulse of jazz. So also are those of speech. Moreover, if we look at the broad structural categories of literature—prose, fiction, drama, and poetry—and if we further divide these, we will produce a kind of spectrum of concreteness which will parallel the forms of saturation which I have described as "a sense of fidelity to the observed and intuited truth of the Black Experience." One may arrange the categories in this way:

Science←OBSERVATION			INTUITION→Music
Factual Writing	*Fiction*	*Drama*	*Poetry*
History	Novel	Tragedy	Epic
Sociology	Novella	Comedy	Ballad
Anthropology	Short story	Tragicomedy	Ode
Economics	Parable		Personal lyric
Geography	Fable		
Journalism, *etc.*			

In Black writing, the form which would depend most on the sustained observed factual truth of the Black Experience would be the novel; the form which would depend least on factual truth and most on the intuited truth would be the lyric. Yet both of these forms can be "saturated," the novel because it approaches the quality, the nature, the character of history; the lyric, because it approaches the condition of music, with all of the special advantages and disadvantages of that medium. However diverse the spectrum, we are speaking of literature, which I define as the verbal organization of experience into beautiful forms.

The forms of Black poetry—to the extent that they are definable—can themselves be arranged into a kind of spectrum:

	History→		*Music→*	
Formal:	Literary ballads	Odes	Short formal lyrics	Free verse
				Experimental
Folk:	Worksongs	Blues	Seculars	Spirituals
	Ballads			Blues
				Worksongs
				Ballads

It is interesting to note that the folk forms are all basically involved with music, i.e., they are also songs, or primarily songs. The formal poetry based on these types can be measured against them, in a conscious act of criticism. If one knows them, then of course this measurement takes place automatically—as saturation, or degree of saturation.

Degree of saturation is a concept of meteorology which is useful to us. For example, just as the atmosphere may be 70 percent saturated with moisture, so theoretically may a poem be 70 percent or more, or less, saturated with Blackness, with the referent being on one hand fidelity to the "observed," i.e., personal and historical truth of the Black Experience; and on the other, to the intuited truth as embodied in the cultural forms, especially the music, of the folk life. This is not to say that saturation or fidelity is perceived as imitation of folk forms. To the contrary, it is perceived as logical and spiritual extensions of those forms. The following comment by James Weldon Johnson on the poetry of Sterling Brown is an elaboration and a particularization of what I mean:

> He infused his poetry with genuine characteristic flavor by adopting as his medium the common, racy, living speech of the Negro in certain phases of *real* life. For his raw material he dug down into the deep mine of Negro folk poetry. He found the unfailing sources from which sprang the Negro folk epics and ballads such as "Stagolee," "John Henry," "Casey Jones," "Long Gone John" and others.
>
> But, as I said in commenting on his work in *The Book of American Negro Poetry*: he has made more than mere transcriptions of folk poetry, and he has done more than bring to it mere artistry; he has deepened its meanings and multiplied its implications. He has actually absorbed the spirit of his material, made it his own; and without diluting its primitive frankness and raciness, truly re-expressed it with artistry and magnified power. In a word, he has taken this raw material and worked it into original and authentic poetry. (Preface, *Southern Road*, xiv, xv)

Sometimes those extensions embody parts of larger forms—quotes from a song or allusions. The most powerful of these I have called "mascons," a term which I borrowed from NASA to signify "the massive concentration of Black experiential energy." These concentrations themselves can be manipulated for special effect in a manner suggestive of chords or other tonal clusters in music. However, the evocation is not so abstract, for the structures are deeply rooted in the specific social and spiritual history of the people.

Specificity of evocation and the notion of degree of saturation lead us logically to the idea of incomplete saturation. This idea is also useful us a critical tool, for if "saturation" is incomplete in a given work, and the poem is presumably complete (i.e., it makes sense), then it is somehow complete outside of the tradition, or the framework of Blackness. What, then, do we call such a work? Hybrid? Incomplete? A failure? A new creation? Whatever we call it, it is usually completed by extensions into and reliance upon the Euro-American poetic tradition. And it must, to the extent which is apparent, be judged by the standards of that tradition. And, it should be emphasized that this applies not only to the poems of Phillis Wheatley and Alberry Whitman, who consciously accepted those standards, but also to the popular songs, the gospel songs, and the formal Black poetry, new and old, which either consciously or unconsciously accepted those standards.

With this in mind, it becomes apparent that much of what is bad technically in Black poetry and in popular song is the imperfect assimilation and mastery of vocabulary and other stylistic features of the Euro-American tradition. This often shows itself in "purple passages," or in the unconscious use of arty clichés and, at times, just plain literary detritus.

It should also be apparent that when the writer consciously or unconsciously employs material from the folk tradition he may also fail to transform the material into art. On certain technical levels, this failure can easily be demonstrated. One example, from a white novelist, is Styron's *The Confessions of Nat Turner*; one example from a white poet is Yevtushenko's poem on the death of Dr. Martin Luther King Jr., which appeared in BLACK WORLD.

For poetry, I take two examples from two fine poets, since their reputations are secure. First, my good friend Keorepetse Kgositsile. Here is his poem "Origins."

> deep in your cheeks
> your specific laughter owns
> all things south of the ghosts
> we once were, straight ahead
> the memory beckons from the future
> You and I a tribe of colors
> this song that dances
> godlike rhythms to birth
> footsteps of memory
> the very soul aspires to songs
> of origins songs of constant beginnings
> what is this thing called
> love

Here the poet's usually precise rendering of experience degenerates, in the last line, into bathos. "What is this thing called/love." The referent here is probably not the pop song but a jazz version. At any rate, the poem verbalizes it in a manner indistinct from the original pop.

The second example is from Amiri Baraka. Here we go to the rough aspect of the tradition, but even here we can make value judgments based on technique and structure. Here is Baraka's takeoff on the dozens in "T. T. Jackson Sings":

> I fucked your mother
> On top of a house
> When I got through
> She thought she was
> Mickey Mouse

The version recorded by Roger Abrahams is less halting, smooth yet tough. The couplet form is appropriate for the punch ending.

> I fucked your mother from house to house
> Out came a baby named Minnie Mouse,

These, of course, are brief examples, but the poetry of the Sixties, and earlier as well, is replete with others, both clean and dirty.

The question must now be raised precisely. What constitutes effective or successful rendering of Black poetic structure? Are there any models, or guidelines?

I say, yes. There is the example of established writers like Robert Hayden, Gwendolyn Brooks, Sterling Brown and Langston Hughes. There is the standard of observation—of fidelity to the observed truth of the Black Experience. There is also the standard of intuition—of fidelity to the intuited truth of the Black Experience.

Some people—critics, white and Black—have difficulty with this last standard. They call it mysterious, mystical, chauvinistic, and even (in a slightly different context) a "curious metaphysical argument" (Saunders Redding). I call it saturation. I authenticate it from personal experience. To those critics I say: Remember Keats did the same, proving poetic experience by his pulse and "the holiness of the imagination." Remember Norbert Wiener, the father of cybernetics, who habitually went to bed with a notebook nearby so that he could jot down the solutions to problems which intuitively came to him during sleep. Remember Stephen Spender's description of the proverbial singing of the poetic line, the nugging at his mind before the words came. Remember A. E. Housman, whose poetry came to him when he was in a state of depression similar to that produced by illness. Remember T. S. Eliot's "objective correlative," despite current skepticism about its usefulness. Remember Matthew Arnold's "touchstone" theory of criticism. At any rate, what these various and famous people did was to admit that on the deepest levels of experience there is something about the nature of art—about the nature of creativity (and that includes scientific thought as well)—that there is something which eludes analysis, something which is experienced as a whole, as complete, and as valuable. Thus the mathematician J. W. N. Sullivan, in his brilliant study, *Beethoven: His Spiritual Development,* speaks of the capacity of the music to organize experience into meaningful "wholes." Thus Matthew Arnold's famous "touchstone" theory, which says that passages of great literature should be carried about in the mind to measure other literature against. And thus in other areas of experience we find William James speaking of the "oceanic sense" in religious experience, and Wordsworth's transcendental "spots of time." And thus, too, the Christian confronted by unbelief in the risen Christ: "I know that my Redeemer liveth."

But these are all analogues to the condition of saturation and the perception of saturation, to the embodiment and experiencing of Blackness as a valuable artistic (aesthetic) whole. For the real thing, we must go to the experience itself. I cite two examples, one of which explains itself and is from Sterling Brown's "Ma Rainey":

> O Ma Rainey,
> Sing yo' song;
> Now you's back
> Whah you belong,
> Git way inside us,
> Keep us strong. . . .
> O Ma Rainey,
> Li'l an' low;
> Sing us 'bout de hard luck
> Roun' our do';
> Sing us 'bout de lonesome road
> We mus' go. . . .

I talked to a fellow, an' the fellow say
"She jes' cutch hold of us, somekindaway.
She sang Backwater Blues one day:

> 'It rained fo' days an' de skies was dark as night,
> Trouble taken place in de lowlands at night.

> 'Thundered an' lightened an' the storm begin to roll
> Thousan's of people ain't got no place to go.

> 'Den I went an' stood upon some high ol lonesome hill,
> An' looked down on the place where I used to live.'

An' den de folks, dey natchally bowed dey heads an' cried,
Bowed dey heavy heads, shet dey moufs up tight an' cried,
An' Ma lef' de stage, an' followed some de folks outside."

Dere wasn't much more de fellow say:
She jes' gits hold of us dataway.

The other example is a review of Aretha Franklin's gospel album, *Amazing Grace*, by Carman Moore, the Black composer and music critic. He calls it "all perfect musical experience." And he says:

You can hear Aretha as she hits upon an idea and turns it into a triumph—as in "Amazing Grace" where she turns the line "and grace will lead me home" into "and grace will lead me right on" (echoed by the choir, of course), "right on home." And in the early part of the same hymn we go with her as she vainly tries to call the spirit into her singing, first by moaning, then by singing a verse, and we exult with her as finally over the next two verses she goes out after that spirit and seizes it or is seized by it on a thrilling high A. A special moment, too, for me is all of "Precious Memories," a great big firm three-four tune that is more than a waltz, with James Cleveland joining Aretha to serve up what could only be called a succulent Baptist meal of soul. But the most memorable and telling passage on the album occurs on the tag end of one of the hymns when Aretha breaks out and does what a gospel singer is supposed to do in the first place—testify out loud and inspire the congregation to do likewise. She suddenly begins fervently, and over and over, to sing "I'm so glad I got re-lig-ion . . . My soul is satisfied." And contained in that one outburst are the reasons why AM radio soul music can never be the real thing, why those Blacks who insist on breaking the back of the church before starting the revolution in their lifetimes, and why any government or mystic klan that expects someday to crush the spirit of Black America can forget it. Aretha, James Cleveland and yes Wilson Pickett, and Patti LaBelle, and the rest are not keepers of that spirit: they only show where it comes from, like swaying trees show the presence of wind. The mysteries may not be grace, but they sure are amazing. (*The Village Voice*, July 6, 1972, p. 31)

What Brother Moore has described is saturation—as experience. He has also employed it as a criterion of Black art. The link with the new Black poetry has been eloquently made by many poets, but by none more succinctly than Larry Neal, in his description of James Brown as "the best poet we got, baby." A link with the old can be seen in the hymn from the Georgia Sea Islands, "I Heard the Angels Singin' ":

Ah heard the angels singin' Lawd
Ah heard the angels singin'
Ah heard the angels singin' Lawd
Ah heard the angels singin'
Well, there's no weepin' there

    No weepin' there
    No weepin' there
Ah heard the angels singin'.

Lawd, it wuz all 'roun' me shine
    All 'roun' me shine
    All 'roun' me shine
Ah heard the angels singin'.

Lawd, it wuz all over my head
    All over my head
    All over my head
Ah heard the angels singin'.

Lawd, it wuz all aroun' my feet
    All aroun' my feet
    All aroun' my feet
Ah heard the angels singin'.

That, of course, is ultimate experience of Blackness—saturation, as value, as perception of Black structures, Black themes. That can stand, too, for Black Transcendence. Below that height, however, there are many significant gradations. It is the task of the present generation of critics to make these explicit and to use them, so that our creative Brothers and Sisters can "move on up a little higher."

16 On the Criticism of Black American Literature

One View of the Black Aesthetic

Houston A. Baker, Jr.

(1976)

> Words' meanings, but also the rhythm and syntax that frame and propel their concatenation, seek their culture as the final reference for what they are describing of the world. An A flat played twice on the same saxophone by two different men does not have to sound the same.
>
> —Imamu Baraka

I

The corpus of Black American literature might be defined as that body of written works crafted by authors consciously (even, at times, self-consciously) aware of the longstanding values and significant experiences of their culture. By embodying these experiences and values in expressive form, the writer provides one means through which those who share the same culture can recognize themselves and move toward fruitful self-definition. The literature contains deep aspects of the culture, and its Black audience actively benefits from its reflection of the most humane values of a singular whole way of life.

It is, perhaps, easier (as with most definitions) to specify what would not be included here than vice versa. But certain things are clear. First, the corpus of Black American literature is predicated upon culturally specific values and experiences. Second, the literature must be viewed in a historical spectrum since it serves as a cultural mirror. These considerations seem to place the original definition within the framework of the "Black aesthetic." And insofar as that term indicates a theory that generates a particular conception of Black literature, I am willing to accept it. Theories of literature are essential if one is to have individualizing definitions of the object. It is difficult to speak meaningfully of literature independent of a theoretical context without reducing (or hopelessly expanding) our understanding to such vagaries as: a

113

body of writing in prose or verse, imaginative or creative writings, belles-lettres. While recognizing the need for theories, however, one might raise objections to the insistence of Imamu Baraka that literature is composed exclusively of propagandistic works. And one might shy away from the injunctions of Don L. Lee (Haki Madhubuti) and Larry Neal that writings can only be classified as Black American literature if they demonstrate an affinity with the Black Power concept and with the idiom of the Black urban community.[1]

Despite these reservations, one might recognize the timeliness of a theoretical perspective that treats Black American literature as a distinctive body of writings. With all its authoritarianism, stridency, and downright mistakes, the Black aesthetic is till a positive, transitional point of view that attempts to move the treatment of Black literature away from the ideational and critical frames of reference that have beset it in the past. Moreover, any abuses that have been committed in its name should come as no surprise to the individual who has read the prolific commentary on Aristotle's *Poetics*, or perused the vituperative attacks on Victor Hugo for his violation of the classical unities, or perceived the overwhelming stubbornness and subjectivity of Samuel Johnson.

Literature and criticism exist in the *Lebenswelt*. Firmly rooted in the human condition by their medium, they reflect the glories and shortcomings of their origin. Any new critical perspective, such as the Black aesthetic, is destined to attract both zealous adherents and committed opponents. The battles between the two often lead to vagueness, overstatement, and confusion.

To assert that the time for a new critical theory has arrived and to offer an apology for its more obvious failings, though, is to leap ahead in the argument. There are prior conditions that call for exploration, and certain theoretical considerations must be set forth before one can justify such a course. It will be helpful, I think, to discuss some of the ideational frames that have influenced the criticism of Black literature in America before moving to a treatment of linguistic and historical factors that play an important role in any discussion of the Black aesthetic.

II

The complexity of the American mind in regard to literature is an established fact. Vernon Parrington, D. H. Lawrence, and Van Wyck Brooks demolished the image of the innocent Yankee bumpkin turning out doggerel stanzas. And in recent years, Tony Tanner, Harry Levin, Leslie Fiedler, and Richard Chase have deepened our sense of a serious and brooding intellect behind the body of American literature. It is not, however, the overall picture of the American mind as reflected in literature that is of concern here. Rather, the output—the ideation—of that mind in regard to Black American artistry provides that focus. The responses of eminent or influential white Americans—both literary critics and others—to the creativity of Black Americans reflect certain patterns of ideas that make a number of the judgments rendered on Black American literature understandable. Realizing the diversity and intricacy of

American intellectual history, it would be absurd to attempt an exhaustive classification, but three broad categories can be set forth.

It is fitting that a view of these ideational frames begin with Thomas Jefferson. Not only was he eminent among the founding fathers, but also representative. Both his biographers and a recent literary critic, Jean Fagin Yellin, have illustrated the seminal place of his thought in colonial America. Professor Yellin has shown how his view of the Black American in *Notes on the State of Virginia* acts as a paradigm for such later writers as John Pendleton Kennedy, William Gilmore Simms, and Herman Melville.[2] It is the critical component of Jefferson's *Notes* that deserves treatment here.

After lauding Native Americans (Indians) for their simple art work, Jefferson says: "But never yet could I find that a Black had uttered a thought above the level of plain narration; never see even an elementary trait of painting or sculpture."[3] A brief and condescending nod to Black music is followed by his well-known remarks on the first Black American woman (and the second woman in America) to produce a volume of poetry:

> Religion indeed has produced a Phyllis Whately [sic.]; but it could not produce a poet. The compositions published under her name are below the dignity of criticism. The heroes of the *Dunciad* are to her, as Hercules to the author of that poem.

He continues his censure of Black writers with his less-quoted, but more interesting, tirade against Ignatius Sancho, whose letters were published in England in 1782.

> [H]is imagination is wild and extravagant, escapes incessantly from every restraint of reason and taste, and, in the course of its vagaries, leaves a tract of thought as incoherent and eccentric, as is the course of a meteor through the sky. His subjects should have led him to a process of sober reasoning: yet we find him always substituting sentiment for demonstration.

While he feels Sancho can be admitted "to the first place among those of his own colour who have presented themselves to the public judgement," he sets him at the bottom of the column when compared to white epistolers.

Jefferson's remarks are in accord with the Humean consensus. David Hume, and a host of others in Britain and America during the eighteenth century, felt that the taste of an intelligent man was sufficient to judge a literary work. The light of common reason guided the man of wit and propriety to those works that best clothed "nature" and felicitously captured what was often thought. Given this milieu, it is not surprising that Jefferson, who felt a sense of moral culpability regarding his Black slaves, was unable to appreciate the folksongs of Black America. They certainly did not satisfy Popean criteria of "What oft was thought, but ne'er so well expressed." Moreover, it is hardly striking that he reduces the singers to creatures of mere passion. First, he was concerned to show French naturalists such as Buffon that white Americans stood above many species in the human order. That process of "negative identification," considered so important for American racial attitudes by Winthrop Jordan, was at work. Second, if Black slaves were indeed sentient beings infused with common reason, how could they justifiably be enslaved? How could those clauses in the constitution Jefferson helped to formulate, those pithy statements assuring slavery in America, be sanctioned? Thus, Phillis Wheatley's verses, the products of a remarkable slave, are ranked far below those of Alexander Pope.

Sancho's letters, however, occasion more difficulty. They are the work of a man who was born on a slave ship from Africa but who, as a child, entered the household of the Duke of Montagu. He was one of the most assimilated products of a dark system: tutored by royalty, a friend of Garrick, and a subject for Gainsborough. If any Black man deserved a place in the consensus, it was Sancho, and Jefferson knew it. He, therefore, damns his work with faint praise: he is the first of his race but last in the general lists. Further, he casts doubt on the genuineness of the letters and asserts that it would be difficult to prove "they have received amendment from no other hand." The *coup de grace* is the argument from blood: "The improvement of the blacks in body and mind, in the first instance of their mixture with the whites, has been observed by every one, and proves that their inferiority is not the effect merely of their condition of life." Though Sancho's "condition of life," according to Humean standards, has fitted him for a writer, without Anglo-Saxon blood in his veins he scarcely stands a chance. Both Jefferson's slaveholding and his critical responses to Black authors are proved upon the pulses.

To label Jefferson a simple "no" man vis-à-vis Black American literature would be meaningless. The reason his views deserve notice is that they capture a prevailing American attitude. One is not only dealing with a Humean consensus, but also with a consensus about the human. Jefferson insists that Blacks do not possess that initial seed of hope which elevates Native Americans above them; they lack "a germ in their mind which only wants cultivation." Hedged round by scientific, religious, and political theories that placed the Anglo-Saxon (particularly the European Anglo-Saxon) on the highest rung of the human ladder, Jefferson was capable of articulating only the harshest judgments on works by individuals who could barely approach the ladder, much less scale it. There were, of course, theories of chronological primitivism. They categorized certain British washerwomen and South Sea islanders as noble savages, uncorrupted by the institutions of society. But Jefferson's concession to this point of view was recognition of the Indians. As an empirical observer who believed that human talent would show through regardless of the "condition of life," he found the evidence of the Black man's humanity insufficient. When Benjamin Banneker— the Black mathematician, surveyor, and compiler of almanacs—sent him examples of his work, Jefferson responded with the hope that more evidence of a similar nature would be forthcoming. The irony, of course, is that Banneker thought it necessary to convince a man whose responses were so deeply grounded in his age. The proposition runs as follows: Blacks are not as human (if human at all) as whites, hence one does not expect from them expressions of the human order, e.g., noteworthy creative works.

To move from the colonial to the middle period of American history brings a shift from one proposition to another which is less rigorous in its exclusions. The abolitionists and the pro-slavery advocates of the nineteenth century both endorsed this ideational frame—the former conditionally, the latter determinately. It would be folly for a Black American to lay critical siege to the abolitionists. Yet to turn to two representative white Americans from that group is to come away less than jubilant. William Lloyd Garrison speaks as follows about one of the most significant narratives written by a Black American:

> Mr. Douglass has very properly chosen to write his own narrative, in his own style, and according to the best of his ability, rather than to employ some one else. . . . I am confident that it is essentially true in all its statements; that nothing has been set down in malice, nothing exaggerated, nothing drawn from the imagination.[4]

These words from Garrison's preface to *Narrative of the Life of Frederick Douglass* do serve as an affadavit to the work's authenticity, and the act of prefacing an unknown author's creation is still a common practice. But Garrison's tone implies dominance or control. Since Douglass had indeed written the work himself and had assured Garrison long since of his integrity and imagination, why did the publisher of *The Liberator* feel it necessary to assume the tone of the kindly, leading father? Perhaps, for the same reason he tried (first confidently, then bitterly) to keep Douglass from founding *The North Star*. (One notices, incidentally, the differing intentions of the two publishers in the titles of their newspapers.) When he cried out against the Black publisher's changed and anti-Garrisonian stance in 1851, "There is roguery somewhere," he clarified his earlier paternalism. As long as Douglass was willing to support the Garrisonian point of view and to be guided by the man who would not "retreat a single inch," all was well. But when he manifested that power of reason properly belonging to a human being, Garrison's wrath was unequivocal. Operating on the assumption that slaves needed the direction of whites if they were to move up the scale of civilization, the abolitionist recoiled sharply before the Black man's opinions.

One suspects that Harriet Beecher Stowe would have reacted similarly. Her novel sold over 300,000 copies during its first year, and J. R. Thompson, editor of the *Southern Literary Messenger*, was all the while beseeching Frederick Holmes to blast and sear the reputation of the "vile wench in petticoats who could write such a volume." But reading *Uncle Tom's Cabin* today is often like scanning a tract by a mild racial theorizer. Blacks are impressionable, susceptible to religion, affectionate, fond of the domestic virtues, lyrical, and educable. They are (without a healthy admixture of Saxon blood) like wily children—human, to be sure, but wanting in the white advantages that ensure survival. Their "tropical fervor" and moral sensibility can contribute to the world, but only after they have been converted to Christianity and received a sound Western education, including a course in New England conscientiousness.

Both Garrison and Stowe left firmly in its place that question mark behind the query on Wedgewood's cameo: "Am I not a man and your brother?" They were willing to concede brotherhood, reserving the role of the young and inexperienced sibling for Black Americans. The shift from the colonial to the middle period, therefore, involves reclassification of the Black man as a child, one capable of full, adult, human development. During the years of fervent abolitionism and Civil War, all evidence of Black creative ability was welcomed and praised as a boon to the antislavery cause. Slave songs, narratives, verses, and orations offered affecting proof to an evangelical and sentimental age that Blacks were, after all, human.

On one hand, what is described above amounts to revisionism. On the other hand, it simply specifies the form American racial theorizing took during a particular era and in relationship to a select area of the Black experience. Slave narratives sold by the thousands, and the spirituals and work songs were suddenly of interest. But the dominating, condescending tone of the abolitionists is prevalent in even the most sympathetic critiques. After all, one is not expected to devote a great deal of scholarly concern to children, particularly in an age when youngsters are expected to observe the strictest rules when (and if) they are heard.

C. L. R. James has said of the American abolitionist movement:

> History really moves when the traditionally most civilized section of the population—in this case New Englanders representing the longest American line of continuity with the English tradition of lawful sovereignty—joins as coequals with those without whose labor society could not exist for a day—in this case the plantation chattel. Otherwise, history stays pretty much the same, or worse yet, repeats itself.

This may be true of American history in general, but the characteristic relationship between white New Englanders and Black "chattel" in this evolving pattern remained one of the adult prince of civilization to the childlike pauper of the tropics. Arna Bontemps, for example, identifies the appeal of nineteenth-century Black American slave narratives as "not unlike the vogue of the Western story in the twentieth [century]."[5] And William McFeely has spoken of the voyeuristic impulse that led whites to attend abolitionist meetings and to read slave narratives.[6] Considered good and racy adventure stories produced by lowly fugitives, even the best of these narratives (Douglass's, for example) were allowed to go out of print within a few decades after the Civil War. When Lerone Bennett speaks of the "Negro exhibit" at abolitionist meetings, therefore it comes as no surprise that he means the escaped slave himself.[7]

The reason it is absurd to berate the abolitionists, however, is that they applied a dominant point of view in a manner favorable to Black Americans. If the effects were not salutary for literature, they were for body and soul. The pro-slavery faction, by contrast, not only wanted to sear Mrs. Stowe, but also any Black "children" who entertained the idea that they could match strides with the white patriarchs. While the abolitionists endorsed a conditional Black puerility, pro-slavery advocates argued a determinate puerility. According to the latter, Blacks were the intermediate link between man and animal; they could move in one direction only—toward the bestial. As eternal and ebullient children, they demanded the protection of kind and longsuffering masters. The countless doubts about the authenticity of the slave narratives expressed by this group indicate how it reacted to the idea of creative Black Americans. And since its opinions carried the day in American letters during the post-bellum period, perhaps it is fitting to cite a later illustration of its codes. In 1877, William Owens wrote:

> Travellers and missionaries tell us that the same sweet airs which are so often heard in religious meetings in America, set to Christian hymns, are to be recognized in the boats and palm-roofed houses of Africa, set to heathen words and that the same wild stories of Buh Rabbit, Buh Wolf, and other *Buhs* that are so charming to the ears of American children, are to be heard to this day in Africa, differing only in drapery necessary to the change of scene.[8]

The quotation not only condemns American Blacks, but an entire continent to the prelapserian. Joel Chandler Harris, who was motivated by Owens to begin collecting Black animal tales, simply makes Uncle Remus a childlike figure and designates plantation children as his appropriate audience. Bernard Wolfe surely had the pro-slavery faction and its post-bellum followers in mind when he wrote: "Uncle Remus— a kind of blackface Will Rogers complete with standard minstrel dialect and planta-tion shuffle—has had remarkable staying power in our popular culture."[9] He might have added "and our literary culture." Regardless of one's angle of vision, the Black American emerges from the nineteenth-century white perspective as a child-like, lesser member of the human family, an individual whose creative efforts must be judged by standards set for juveniles. From non-being to puerility, from total exclusion to a conditional acceptance is not an overwhelming distance.

One recent writer has skillfully demonstrated that the temper of an age conditions its judicial decisions; he speaks of "racial prejudices which judges share with their fellow men."[10] By changing the phrasing, one could talk of the ideational sets literary critics share with their cultures. The first literary history of America, Moses Coit Tyler's *The Literary History of the American Revolution*, offers an illustration. Here one encounters a denunciation of Phillis Wheatley less scathing than Jefferson's:

> The other prominent representative of the town of Boston in the poetry of this period 1763–1776 is Phillis Wheatly [*sic*], a gentle-minded and intelligent slave girl, whose name still survives among us in the shape of a traditional [*sic*] vaguely testifying to the existence of poetic talent in this particular member of the African race. Unfortunately, a glance at what she wrote will show that there is no adequate basis for such tradi-tion, and that the significance of her career belongs rather to the domain of anthropol-ogy, or of hagiology, than to that of poetry—whether American or African. Her verses, which were first published in a collected form in London in 1773, under the title "Poems on Various Subjects, Religious and Moral," attracted for a time consider-able curiosity, both in England and in America,—not at all, however, because the verses were good, but because they were written by one from whom even bad verses were too good to be expected.[11]

Tyler's comments are interesting in several respects. They include the Black poet among the representatives of a particular region, and since they follow a condemna-tion of all New England for its "poetic poverty," their indictment of Wheatley is predictable. There is a kind of gamesmanship, however, in which the left hand takes away what the right has given. Tyler is republican enough to view the abolition of slavery as an absolute moral good, but he doesn't know what to make of those "human brethren" who have been released. His ironical tone—an almost whimsical detachment from the camp that debates whether Africans are capable of artistic expression—cuts two ways. He can be charged with deriding a "tradition vaguely testifying" to the Black's ability, or he can be praised for recognizing the folly that necessitates such a tradition. He seems certain that Wheatley's poems are valueless, but he doesn't know why. Assuredly, Africans are human, but can they produce worthy verse? Tyler is not prepared to answer, and his reference to anthropology almost forces one to see him as a product of the post-bellum period. Blacks are lower and somewhat curious specimen for Tyler. Only the Declaration of Independence stands in the way of those who would easily keep them down. Republicanism can, thus, accommodate Phillis Wheatley, but it can not view her as an important poet.

Of course, the author of *The Literary History* does not stand alone. White American critics from Barrett Wendell to the latest issue of *Saturday Review* have oscillated between the poles of an overall exclusion of Blacks and an acceptance of them as puerile human beings. At the turn of the century, both Barrett Wendell and William Dean Howells turned a critical eye on the Black American. A quotation from Wendell makes his point of view abundantly clear:

> However human, native Africans are still savage; and although, long before the Civil War, the Southern slaves had shown such sensitiveness to comparatively civilized conditions as to have lost their superficial savagery, and indeed as still to warrant, in many hopeful minds, even the franchise which was ultimately granted them, the spectre of darkest Africa loomed behind them all.[12]

This is a violent yoking together of the ideational frames of Jefferson and the pro-slavery faction. And the effect—no matter how emphatically one points to the Declaration of Independence or to the Social Darwinists and outright bigots of the critic's day—is devastating. A contrasting contemporary opinion is offered by Howells's conditional puerility. He felt Paul Laurence Dunbar's dialect pieces and Charles Chestnutt's [sic] *The Conjure Woman* were superb because they captured the humor and the limitations of Black America. He would not have understood the Black poet's lament to James Weldon Johnson:

> You know, of course, that I didn't start as a dialect poet. I simply came to the conclusion that I could write it as well, if not better, than anybody else I knew of, and that by doing so I should gain a hearing. I gained the hearing, and now they don't want me to write anything but dialect.[13]

For Howells, a sanguine metaphysics and an optimistic critical stance could be wedded. While the results were often beneficial to Black artists, they were frequently disastrous. Dunbar's poems in literary English—many of them extremely pessimistic—

receive only passing notice. Chesnutt's telling analysis of Southern racial prejudice earns the following comment:

> The book [*The Marrow of Tradition*] is, in fact, bitter, bitter. There is no reason in history why it should not be so, if wrong is to be repaid with hate, and yet it would be better if it were not so bitter.[14]

Believing that truth could only be extracted from the "large cheerful average of health and success and happy life," Howells hardly expected the Black man to lament or to turn bitter. Morality, for him, penetrated all things, and if those whose range of existence spanned "appetite and emotion"[15] could not reflect this point of view, something was amiss. So the man whom Mark Twain described as like himself—an old derelict—floated on in the strange seas of a complex and racist time, his mind thoroughly shaped by the tenets of an earlier age. He was incapable of raising life itself above the "eternal amenities." How could one expect him to elevate Blacks above the level of an aspiring childhood?

The twentieth century has, for the most part, offered critical responses in harmony with the three ideational patterns treated above. The new critics, for example, have been so mired in lexis (the word as meaning) and so distrustful of the world of common men that they have usually excluded Black artists. When they have turned an occasional gaze on the Black artifact, they have been so far above its praxis (the word as action) that they have committed almost comic offenses. Robert Bone has been the "new critical" whipping boy of contemporary, outraged Black writers, and Theodore Gross and David Littlejohn have run close seconds.

The political progressives (usually Marxists or Marxist-Leninists) have frequently chosen the domineering, condescending stance of certain abolitionists. Realizing the necessity for a Black advance guard if American social change is to be meaningful, they have enlisted Black artists under their banners. Like the abolitionists, however, these activists have been stung to fierce retorts when the Black man has become too energetic in his own behalf. In *Black Writers of the Thirties*, James O. Young discusses the shifting reactions of the Communist Party to the writings of Langston Hughes and Richard Wright. And Harold Cruse, in *The Crisis of the Negro Intellectual*, gives an even more telling account. Irving Howe's treatment of *Native Son* offers a case in point. In "Black Boys and Native Sons," Howe sees Wright as a paradigm for the Black artist. Ralph Ellison and James Baldwin, by comparison, have adopted false ideals. The critic's article "At Ease With Apocalypse," however, reveals an altered perspective. Here, *Native Son* is labelled a crude book. (One almost hears the cry go up: "There is roguery somewhere.") When it became apparent to Howe (through the responses of Ellison and Baldwin) that Blacks would not tolerate his prescriptive, political formulas, he seems to have turned against even his model Black artist.

There have also been a host of twentieth-century advocates for the determinate puerility of Blacks. Critics such as John Nelson, Louis Simpson, and John Leonard seem agreed on Nelson's list of characteristics: "[the Black man's] irrepressible spirits, his complete absorption in the present moment, his whimsicality, his irresponsibility, his intense superstition, his freedom from resentment." Defined in this manner, the Black writer is expected to provide easy, exotic fare for his white readers. If his work transcends such stuff, he is promoted to a conditional stage where he has a chance of reaching full civilization in his life and "universality" in his writing.

The origins of white responses to Black creativity may be obscured by a plethora of theoretical issues and by endless pages of analysis. Behind these tangible boundaries, however, lie basic ideational, or pre-shaping, patterns that condition what has been a felt rejection. W. E. B. Du Bois speaks of that "other world which does not know and does not want to know our power." There is another dimension: a world that *can not* know the Black man's expressive power because it is locked into a narrow trinity of ideation. Van Wyck Brooks divides American literature into three categories: high, low, and middle brow. Analogically, one can compare white American ideational patterns to an amplitude with three stops: exclusion, conditional and determinate puerility. Because the white critic shares this limiting range with his culture, he has seldom been able to enunciate the loud and clear praise of Black creativity that he has bestowed upon white artifacts.

But what if the objects of criticism are located, linguistically and historically, outside this compass? What if Black creativity is the result of a context—a web of meanings—different in kind and degree from that of white commentators? A view of the development of Black American language and a consideration of certain historiographical factors suggest such an eventuality.

III

"Nominalists," writes one philosopher, "make the mistake of interpreting all words as *names*, and so of not really describing their use, but only, so to speak, giving a paper draft on such a description."[16] The reason for such paper drafts, according to Ludwig Wittgenstein, is the belief that there is a determinate standard of knowledge because every word has an essential meaning. If such were the case, words would be "names" referring to an objective (but not necessarily present) essence. The counter argument he proposes is that no determinate standard of knowledge exists. Philosophy, like being itself, originates in a "speaking situation." When one arrives at a speaking situation, the origins of the conjunction between word and object are already obscured. To discuss "meaning," therefore, is to find oneself, at the outset, detailing an event dominated by language usage, by the user and his physical behavior.

The case of the baby crying, as it is presented in the *Philosophical Investigations*, makes this clearer. Jeffrey Price explains that:

Wittgenstein finds the question of the relationship of language and its object to be the same as the question of the origin of speaking. By asserting that in an infant the expression of pain replaces a situation of unbroken conjunction of certain movements and the condition of the body, Wittgenstein reveals his insistence that the original moments of expression issue in the determinations that form their content. He is grieved that this originality is obscured in our normal thinking, for if we lose sight of the origin and possibilities of speech, its deep aspect will elude us.[17]

In other words, at the original moments of expression, undifferentiated movement and words as instances of absolute separation or distinctiveness are complicated in a way that pervades all we know. Edward Sapir states the same when he says: "it may be that originally the primal cries or other types of symbols developed by man had some connection with certain emotions or attitudes or notions. But a connection is no longer directly traceable between words, or combinations of words, and what they refer to."[18] The apparent gulf between the pre-verbal moment—as a complex of physical and, perhaps, emotional "activity"—and speech raises, of course, an ancient linguistic issue: the origin of speech.

Noam Chomsky and a number of others espouse a position closer to Leibniz than to Locke, believing that only on the assumption that human beings possess specific mental faculties and innate ideas can one "understand the science of linguistics or the wondrous ability of the child of tender years to learn how to speak."[19] Opposing this view are the early works of Sapir and Benjamin Lee Whorf and the more recent efforts of Dell Hymes and William Labov, who feel that language is an essentially social phenomenon reflecting the accumulated experience of a group and determining to a great extent its world view.[20] Sidney Hook states the dichotomy as follows: "The facts [language as species-specific, manifesting a similarity of development, regardless of the particular linguistic system] are not in dispute but their interpretations are."[21] Chomsky believes the "innateness" determining linguistic competence resides in the individual speaker, while sociolinguists seem to feel that communicative competence is somehow invested by language and society. What one has is idealists facing empiricists with cognitive psychology and countless chimpanzees in the middle attempting to provide sufficient data to decide the issue.

For the moment, however, and for the sake of the present discussion, it seems enough to acknowledge that a gap exists in our understanding of the connection between the pre-expressive instant and the spoken word. This synapse is of adequate proportion to have triggered some recent concern with the whole issue of "privacy" or "private language." It is the "private," or "Black Public" (if you prefer), domain that is of greatest importance for a criticism of Black American literature. LeRoi Jones's Walker Vessels captures this with a fine brevity in *The Slave:* "But listen now. . . . Brown is not brown except when used as an intimate description of personal phenomenological fields. As your brown is not my brown, et cetera, that is, we need, ahem, a meta-language. We need some thing not included here." The experiences of Black and white speakers of English are so bifurcated that it is hard to conceive of a criticism that does not deal with the fundamental distinctions raised by a concern with language.

Coming into English in a trading situation, making contact with the language through restless vagabonds and adventurers in search of wealth, native Africans moved toward a pidgin English. Some indications of a specifically West African pidgin date back to the sixteenth century. This language was comprised of vocabulary items from various European languages, and it was so regular that syntactic rules generating an infinite number of sentences could be written.[22] But grammatical rules are not the most interesting considerations here. The social and psychological situations of the Africans and their vocabulary borrowings offer more interesting speculations. As they watched whites destroy their internal trade (both slave and other), viewed the introduction of firearms, witnessed Europeans struggling bloodily for commercial advantage, and felt themselves driven from a stable system of social organization to enthrallment in a vast pattern of trade that was to claim millions of African lives, what conjunctions existed between the pre-English instant and the employemnt of English lexical items?

One cannot compare the moments of original significance for an infant and the language contact phenomena that result in West African pidgin English. But one might assume that words like "white," "slave," "freedom" and a host of others had a significance for their Black borrowers that was firmly tied to their psycho-physical circumstances. Since language is never value-neutral, and since the situation and the values of the African were substantially different from those of the white European, the pidgin English of African (and later, Afro-American) speakers must have carried meanings (semantic levels of the lexicon) quite different from those held by Europeans. As a second language, adopted or learned for the purpose of trade, the vocabulary of the two groups who came in contact would have been almost identical. The origin of the distinctiveness between word and object, however, would have been quite different. In the public intercourse between Europeans and Africans, the speaking situation determined meaning. Behind this realm, though, stretched the vistas of origins—deep, only vaguely understood. And along this axis value first attaches itself, a phenomenon that can certainly be observed where language is learned by the adult members of a society.

Recognizing the irony/absurdity between the words (concepts) they were borrowing and the brutal realities of the slave trade, Africans were scarcely prepared to adopt in toto the "rules" of the language games of their white exploiters. It becomes clearer with each new critique of the "Sapir-Whorf hypothesis" that language is not an invisible garment that drapes itself about the spirit of a person, giving a predetermined form to all its (the spirit's) symbolic expression; hence, the Africans were, indeed, free to reverse the rules.

Wittgenstein, of course, accounted for the possibility of such linguistic behavior. Even though he felt that usage—a speaking situation—gave meaning to words and coherence to human society, he also knew that people were not trapped in a hopeless continuum of language games. They could transcend custom/rules through the act of negation. "Freedom," therefore, can become "not freedom." Another approach here is the poetical one. Langston Hughes says:

> There are words like *Freedom*
> Sweet and wonderful to say.

On my heartstrings freedom sings
All day everyday.

There are words like *Liberty*
That almost make me cry.
If you had known what I know
You would know why.[23]

If one commences with the answer Wittgenstein gives to his hypothetical questioner, a perspective totally different from the one that emerges from a discussion of American ideational frames is necessary:

"But doesn't what you say come to this: that there is no pain, for example, without pain-behavior?"—It comes to this, only of a living human being and what resembles (behaves like) a living human being can one say: it has sensations; it sees; is blind; hears; is deaf; is conscious or unconscious.

If the Black man entered the speaking situation with values antithetical to those of the white externality surrounding him, then his vocabulary and the standard forms into which it enters are less important than an attempt to hold the moments of Black, original significance in mind. What I am positing, or speculating on, of course, is the distinct possibility that whites—moving exclusively in a white public realm and unable to move beyond the ideational veil obscuring origins—have taken the Black creative work at its face value, or worse, at a value assigned by their own preconceptions.

Since everyone's reading time is limited, however, (everyone, that is, who has pursued the argument thus far), let me give just two brief examples. The first is offered by Charles Chesnutt's *The Conjure Woman*. Published as a volume of framework tales in 1899, the work's success seemed assured by the earlier reactions to one of its stories. "The Goophered Grapevine" had appeared to white critical acclaim in an 1896 issue of the *Atlantic*. Few readers were aware of Chesnutt's race, and in the heyday of the Plantation School, who would expect a Black American writer to go against the weave of what Oscar Handlin calls the "Linnaean Web."[24] Chesnutt's creation simply seemed one in a long line of opuses dedicated to portraying the Black man as a predial and loveable creature who devoted himself to strumming and a-humming all day in the antebellum South. Howells and other white critics praised the story with these assumptions as their base. Why? Is there an absence of guideposts to a different explication? On the contrary, the very title of Chesnutt's group of stories speaks of the author's intention. It holds a clue to the origins of *The Conjure Woman's* language as a whole.

John Blassingame writes:

In addition to these activities [religious and recreational], several other customs prevented the slaves from identifying with the ideals of their masters. Because of their superstitions and belief in fortune tellers, witches, magic and conjurers, many of the slaves constructed a psychological defense against total dependence on and submission to their masters. Whatever his power, the master was a puny man compared to the supernatural. Often the most powerful and significant individual on the plantation was the conjurer.[25]

The historian goes on to point out that by shrewdness and an industrious countermanding of the slave system the plantation conjurer gained control over both Blacks and whites. The real Black protagonist—the motivating force behind the action of all the tales in Chesnutt's volume—is the conjurer. By shaping the life of the entire plantation, a single Black man or woman dictates the ultimate norms and actions of secondary figures in the stories. Such conclusions, of course, can not be drawn simply from the title of the book. They indicate, though, that white critics unimbued with the Black "meaning," of the word "conjurer" were ill-prepared to evaluate Chesnutt's stories. Their referents were all grounded outside that almost exclusively Black domain that assured autonomy, obverse value, a sense of the Black self different from that held by members, or champions, of the Plantation School.

If this seems an example of "justification by the little-known work," one can turn to a later example—Richard Wright's *Native Son*. Having already set forth my own sense of the infrastructure of the novel,[26] I wish to introduce here James Emanuel's all but ignored article on the metaphorical aspects of Wright's classic.[27] Insisting that the book is rooted in a unique experience, Emanual points out a host of recurrent images that accompany Bigger Thomas's progress. Images of crucifixion, confinement, claustrophobia, heat, light all speak of a protagonist hemmed in by a world oblivious to his most pressing drives. The rhetorical structures and vocabulary of the novel are often those of the proletarian tradition of the 1930's and 1940's, but the overall effect produced by a close attention to the work's metaphorical clusters outstrips the responses of the rigidly Marxist critic. The images carry one to the folk level, to the "forms of things unknown," on which Wright's story is based. Grasping only, the bare words "furnace," "flight," "snow," "curtain," etc., the white critic has often missed the point rather than lent point to the novelist's creation. The negation of custom that rumbles mightily through most of the work's pages has been repeatedly misinterpreted by the unaware.

To stop at this point would be to risk the charge that I am setting forth only a linguistic perspective. But while the case presented here stresses the primacy of being/language/meaning, it also pushes toward a concern for the historical aspects of the critical process. If the quotation from Wittgenstein that speaks of "a living human being" is relevant, so too is R. G. Collingwood's evaluation of Toynbee's philosophy of history:

> [H]is general conception of history is ultimately naturalistic; he regards the life of a society as a natural and not a mental life, something at bottom merely biological and best understood on biological analogies. And this is connected with the fact that he never reaches the conception of historical knowledge as the reenactment of the past in the historian's mind.[28]

For the idealistic historian like Collingwood, the stress is on that mental life which makes historical inquiry possible. Events are intelligible because they have an inside, a thought side, that comes from human agents who think about what they are doing before they act. Obviously, American ideation vis-à-vis the Black man virtually excludes him from history. That which has been considered distinctively Black by white Americans has seldom included the rational, or thought side, of Black American culture. Critics have not felt it necessary to rethink the thoughts of Black historical agents. William Dray's analysis of Collingwood helps to clarify the preceding statement:

> In insisting that the historian must re-think the agent's thoughts, what Collingwood is claiming is that the point of his [the agent's] action cannot be grasped without a piece of vicarious practical reasoning on the part of the historian. The latter, on considering the agent's thoughts, must see that, from the agent's own point of view, what he did really was *the thing to do*.[29]

The historian begins with evidence, those tangible manifestations of a historical event that exist in the present:

> The whole perceptible world, then, is potentially and in principle evidence to the historian. It becomes actual evidence in so far as he can use it. And he cannot use it unless he comes to it with the right kind of historical knowledge. The more historical knowledge we have, the more we can learn from any given piece of evidence; if we had none, we could learn nothing. Evidence is evidence only when someone contemplates it historically.[30]

The Black literary text stands "historically dumb" before the critic who possesses no historical knowledge, who is incapable of realizing that the creator of the text was firmly based in a *sui generis* culture that invested what seems a common language (English) with particular value. Of course, the critic who believes the author of the Black text has been motivated to write by a kind of pure, primitive instinct is lost from the outset. But the man who fails to attempt the depths of the Black author's language—no matter how liberal he might feel himself to be—will prove equally inept. He will not be able to get at the inside to the event constituted by the creation of the text. A sympathetic and insightful act of "vicarious practical reasoning" is scarcely to be expected from the individual who sees the Black artifact not as evidence of a singular past, but as one object in that vast panoply of world creativity which he must circle in order to prove his catholicity.

The Black text is historical evidence because it is a present, palpable component of the past that formed it. Its creation—despite the mysteries of the artistic imagination—was governed by a thinking agent, by the mental life of a culture. The *sine qua non* that draws the linguistic and historiographical considerations together is the Black person as a thinking human being who possesses the supports, values, and stays of a unique culture. Wittgenstein writes: "When I think in language there aren't 'meanings' going through my mind in addition to the verbal expressions: the language is itself the vehicle of thought."

To grasp fully the significance of the Black text, however, the critic must recognize that the situation of the author was substantially different from that of the white

American. He must reach beyond the obscuring veil and seek the origins of the Black word. In order to do this, he must view the text as historical evidence. Set in language, the text is also the vehicle of thought—that source from which the tides of history flow. The proposition governing this section, therefore, might read as follows: the private sector (condition of the body, origins) leads in unbroken conjunction to the word, which is not value-neutral when it is formed. Meaning and its expression are one; hence, in the Black word resides the culturally specific meaning that grows out of the physical circumstances where language begins. As the vehicle of a rational agent's thought, the language of the Black author (as embodied in a literary text) can be taken as historical evidence. The critic must realize that behind the purely public cast of the Black author's language lie its unique origins and meanings. His evaluation remains a superficial glance at large general properties unless he follows the thread of a Black web of meaning to where it had its spinning.

IV

The significance of the Black aesthetic is that it moves beyond those white American ideational frames discussed earlier. By accepting Black American culture as a sui generis way of life, it is capable of extricating from the Black text composed in English those meanings that grow out of a particular cultural situation. The critical work of the Black aesthetician is not rooted in some mysterious affinity between the critic and the text. It does not insist upon the possession of a vaguely defined "soul." Its realization of the origins of the Black author's language and its willingness to view his created text as historical evidence are grounded on a recognition of the Black man as a fully rational agent. Since white American ideational frames have precluded such considerations, it is not surprising that a perspective—endorsed primarily by Blacks and capable of generating an accurate conception of Black American literature—has come to the fore.

What is the function of those who will champion and develop such a perspective? First, they must steep themselves in manifold historical evidence that has been too long ignored. The literary text is most revealing to the critic who possesses a high degree of historical knowledge. Second, those who would contribute to a just view of Black American literature must be able to move from the broad historical plane to the distinctive Black word. If an altruistic relationship exists between the author and his reader, the latter can not simply lead a work into being. He must lend a conscious-ness that reveals the text's most important meanings and values. In order to achieve this, he must journey, using all available signs, toward those moments of original significance when the Black word became a discrete entity. The discussion of *Native Son* and *The Conjure Woman* raises issues that fit this second prerequisite.

Third, the critic must attempt to free himself from slavish adherence to the idea-tional pulls of the critical moment (the time in which his evaluation occurs). The challenge for the critic who endorses a Black aesthetic is to go first to the evidence that is the literary text. Its words and metaphors can carry the historically aware individual toward understanding and insight. "Historically aware" does not mean engagedly activist. The events of the last decade offer ample evidence that the most abysmally unaware are often the most stridently active. The politician (or the active revolutionary) and the literary critic may require the same type of historical cognizance, but their roles should not be conflated. The rhetorical strategies of the militant warrior are usually a hindrance to the critic, whose function is predicated upon a clear grasp and explication of the deep aspects of a culture. A full analysis of *Native Son* may, finally, be more revolutionary in its implications (because it makes clear the whole way of life that is Black America) than an ill-advised injunction to revolt, a hastily tossed grenade, or a spuriously utopian social philosophy that is actually a new totalitarianism. Simply stated, one must beware of saying "right on" or "solid on that" to each voice insisting it is the most committed.

Fourth, the critic who moves toward a Black aesthetic should, indeed, number the stripes on the tulip. When told by authoritarians that only one community of Black folk and its idiom must hold his attention, he might simply point out that the boundaries of Black America are wide. The focus of those championing a Black aesthetic has been the inner city because they inhabit cities and because literature and criticism (since the eighteenth century, at any rate) have been based in urban areas. Is Barry Beckham's *My Main Mother* to be ignored or labelled an inexact representation of Black America because it is set in a small New England town? Those who claim to have their fingers on the pulse of a culture have often mistaken the thudding of their own voices for the pumping of the Black heart.

Obviously, the four points stressed include a fuller statement of the reservations mentioned at the beginning of this discussion. They do not speak as forcefully as they might about the timeliness of the Black aesthetic. That should be apparent at this point. To step outside the constricting patterns of ideation that have left a culture unknown and to move back, through language and history, to origins and values is the aim of this new theoretical stance. To generate an informed view of a body of creative works rooted in these beginnings is its most essential work. There are cultural imperatives, then, at the center of its endeavors. While the future of the Black aesthetic is beyond historical ken, one might speculate that the nature of its enterprise makes the Black scholar its most likely practitioner. The furor of contemporary white detractors and the continued appearance of white critical works governed by traditional ideational frames indicate that the Black aesthetic is, at present, a unique possession of the Black American. As it develops and moves beyond the pitfalls that endanger the life of a new theoretical framework, it will be endorsed by all scholars who hope to grasp Black American literature.

One must reiterate Wittgenstein's point, though, that words are not names. In the future, there may be no mention of a "Black aesthetic," but surely there will be individuals dedicated to a theory of Black American literature that stresses the primacy of the Black word and views the Black text as evidence of a people's singular and accomplished history. A prolegomenon for the future would call for the critic's acceptance of the Black man as the thoughtful agent of his own destiny, an individual who has invested his words with value and his creations with a significance that awaits the discerning investigator.

NOTES

1. Books, collections and articles that move toward a statement of the Black aesthetic are: the essays on literature and language in Baraka's (LeRoi Jones's) *Home: Social Essays*, New York: William Morrow, 1966; Neal's "The Black Arts Movement," *Tulane Drama Review* (Summer, 1968), pp. 29–39; Lee's (now Haki Madhubuti's) *Dynamite Voices*, Broadside Press: Detroit, 1971; Neal and Baraka's *Black Fire*, New York: William Morrow, 1968; Addison Gayle's *The Black Aesthetic*, New York: Doubleday, 1971; Stephen Henderson's *Understanding the New Black Poetry*, New York: William Morrow, 1973; and a number of articles in *Black World* (formerly *Negro Digest*).

2. *The Intricate Knot*, New York: New York University Press, 1972.

3. *Notes on the State of Virginia*, ed. William Peden (Chapel Hill: University of North Carolina Press, 1955), p. 140. The other quotations from *Notes* in my text refer to this edition and can be found between p. 137 and p. 141.

4. *Narrative of the Life of Frederick Douglass* (New York: Signet, 1968), pp. ix–x.

5. *Great Slave Narratives* (Boston: Beacon Press, 1969), p. xviii.

6. McFeely is the author of *Yankee Stepfather*, a biography of General O. O. Howard. After his helpful reading of an essay I had written on Frederick Douglass, we discussed the genre of the slave narrative at length.

7. *Before the Mayflower* (Baltimore: Penguin Books, 1964), p. 137.

8. Quoted from Bruce Jackson, ed., *The Negro and His Folklore in Nineteenth-Century Periodicals* (Austin: University of Texas Press, 1967), pp. 147–148. Owen's remark appeared first in *Lippincott Magazine*.

9. "Uncle Remus and the Malevolent Rabbit," *Commentary*, VII (July, 1969), 31.

10. Unpublished manuscript in progress on racial justice in America by The Honorable Leon Higginbotham.

11. *The Literary History of the American Revolution 1763–1783*, I (New York: Frederick Ungar, 1957), pp. 186–187.

12. *A Literary History of America* (New York: Charles Scribner's, 1900), p. 482.

13. Quoted from James Weldon Johnson, *Along This Way* (New York: The Viking Press, 1968), p. 160.

14. Quoted from Helen M. Chesnutt, *Charles Waddell Chesnutt: Pioneer of the Color Line* (Chapel Hill: University of North Carolina Press, 1952), p. 177. Howells's comment originally appeared in "A Psychological Counter-Current in Recent Fiction," *North American Review*, December, 1901.

15. Howells sets this range in his introduction to Dunbar's *Lyrics of Lowly Life*.

16. *Philosophical Investigations*, trans. G. E. M. Anscombe (New York: Macmillan, 1953), p. 118e. My discussion of Wittgenstein's point of view covers sections 243–415.

17. *Language and Being in Wittgenstein's 'Philosophical Investigations'* (The Hague: Mouton, 1973), pp. 106–107.

18. "The Status of Linguistics as a Science," in *Culture, Language and Personality: Selected Essays*, ed. David Mendelbaum (Los Angeles: University of California Press, 1953), p. 73.

19. Sidney Hook, ed., *Language and Philosophy* (New York: New York University Press, 1969), p. x. The first section of this volume, "Language and Culture," contains extremely interesting commentaries on the work of Sapir and Whorf. It is at this point that I should add a comment—a note of thanks—of my own on the very careful reading of an earlier draft of the present essay by Professor Barbara H. Smith. Professor Smith not only called the works of the sociolinguists to my attention but also discussed their hypotheses at some length. I would also like to express my gratitude to Professor Michael Peinovich, who read the earlier draft and provided helpful suggestions.

20. See: Sapir, *Language*; Whorf, *Language, Thought and Reality*; Hymes, *Foundations in Sociolinguistics* and *Language in Culture*; Labov, *Sociolinguistic Patterns*.

21. Hook, p. x.

22. Books, articles, and sections of texts dealing with the language of Black Americans include: Juanita Williamson's "Selected Features of Speech: Black and White," *CLA Journal*, June, 1970; Kirkland Jones's "The Language of the Black 'In-Crowd': Some Observations on Intra-Group Communication," *CLA Journal*, September, 1971; J. L. Dillard, *Black English*, New York: Random House, 1972; Orlando Taylor's "Historical Development of Black English and Implications for American Education," *Speech and Language of the Urban and Rural Poor*, eds. Ronald Williams and Richard Ham (Collection of papers presented at the Summer Institute on Speech and Language of the Urban and Rural Poor—July 14–18, 1969—Ohio University, Athens, Ohio); Philip S. Dale, *Language Development* (Hinsdale, Illinois: Dryden Press, 1972), pp. 244–254; Victoria Fromkin and Robert Rodman, *An Introduction to Language* (New York: Holt, Rinehart, and Winston, 1974), pp. 258–269. Of course, one of the pioneering studies in this area was Lorenzo Turner's *Africanisms in the Gallah Dialect*.

23. "Refugee in America," in *Selected Poems of Langston Hughes* (New York: Alfred A. Knopf, 1969), p. 290.

24. *Race and Nationality in American Life* (Boston: Little, Brown, 1957), pp. 71–92.

25. *The Slave Community* (New York: Oxford University Press, 1972), p. 45.

26. *Long Black Song* (Charlottesville: University Press of Virginia, 1972), pp. 122–141.

27. "Fever and Feeling: Notes on the Imagery of *Native Son*," *Negro Digest*, XVIII (1968), pp. 16–26.

28. *The Idea of History* (New York: Oxford University Press, 1970), p. 163.

29. *Philosophy of History* (Englewood Cliffs, N.J.: Prentice-Hall, 1964), p. 12.

30. Collingwood, p. 247.

17 | Toward a Black Feminist Criticism

Barbara Smith

(1977)

I do not know where to begin. Long before I tried to write this I realized that I was attempting something unprecedented, something dangerous, merely by writing about Black women writers from a feminist perspective and about Black lesbian writers from any perspective at all. These things have not been done. Not by white male critics, expectedly. Not by Black male critics. Not by white women critics who think of themselves as feminists. And most crucially not by Black women critics, who, although they pay the most attention to Black women writers as a group, seldom use a consistent feminist analysis or write about Black lesbian literature. All segments of the literary world—whether establishment, progressive, Black, female, or lesbian— do not know, or at least act as if they do not know, that Black women writers and Black lesbian writers exist.

For whites, this specialized lack of knowledge is inextricably connected to their not knowing in any concrete or politically transforming way that Black women of any description dwell in this place. Black women's existence, experience, and culture and the brutally complex systems of oppression which shape these are in the "real world" of white and/or male consciousness beneath consideration, invisible, unknown.

This invisibility, which goes beyond anything that either Black men or white women experience and tell about in their writing, is one reason it is so difficult for me to know where to start. It seems overwhelming to break such a massive silence. Even more numbing, however, is the realization that so many of the women who will read this have not yet noticed us missing either from their reading matter, their politics, or their lives. It is galling that ostensible feminists and acknowledged lesbians have been so blinded to the implications of any womanhood that is not white womanhood and that they have yet to struggle with the deep racism in themselves that is at the source of this blindness.

I think of the thousands and thousands of books, magazines, and articles which

132

have been devoted, by this time, to the subject of women's writing and I am filled with rage at the fraction of those pages that mention Black and other Third World women. I finally do not know how to begin because in 1977 I want to be writing this for a Black feminist publication, for Black women who know and love these writers as I do and who, if they do not yet know their names, have at least profoundly felt the pain of their absence.

The conditions that coalesce into the impossibilities of this essay have as much to do with politics as with the practice of literature. Any discussion of Afro-American writers can rightfully begin with the fact that for most of the time we have been in this country we have been categorically denied not only literacy but the most minimal possibility of a decent human life. In her landmark essay, "In Search of Our Mothers' Gardens," Alice Walker discloses how the political, economic, and social restrictions of slavery and racism have historically stunted the creative lives of Black women.[1]

At the present time I feel that the politics of feminism have a direct relationship to the state of Black women's literature. A viable, autonomous Black feminist movement in this country would open up the space needed for the exploration of Black women's lives and the creation of consciously Black woman–identified art. At the same time a redefinition of the goals and strategies of the white feminist movement would lead to much-needed change in the focus and content of what is now generally accepted as women's culture.

I want to make in this essay some connections between the politics of Black women's lives, what we write about, and our situation as artists. In order to do this I will look at how Black women have been viewed critically by outsiders, demonstrate the necessity for Black feminist criticism, and try to understand what the existence or nonexistence of Black lesbian writing reveals about the state of Black women's culture and the intensity of all Black women's oppression.

The role that criticism plays in making a body of literature recognizable and real hardly needs to be explained here. The necessity for nonhostile and perceptive analysis of works written by persons outside the "mainstream" of white/male cultural rule has been proven by the Black cultural resurgence of the 1960s and 1970s and by the even more recent growth of feminist literary scholarship. For books to be real and remembered they have to be talked about. For books to be understood they must be examined in such a way that the basic intentions of the writers are at least considered. Because of racism, Black literature has usually been viewed as a discrete subcategory of American literature, and there have been Black critics of Black literature who did much to keep it alive long before it caught the attention of whites. Before the advent of specifically feminist criticism in this decade, books by white women, on the other hand, were not clearly perceived as the cultural manifestation of an oppressed people. It took the surfacing of the second wave of the North American feminist movement to expose the fact that these works contain a stunningly accurate record of the impact of patriarchal values and practice upon the lives of women, and, more significantly, that literature by women provides essential insights into female experience.

In speaking about the current situation of Black women writers, it is important to remember that the existence of a feminist movement was an essential precondition to the growth of feminist literature, criticism, and women's studies, which focused at the beginning almost entirely upon investigations of literature. The fact that a parallel Black feminist movement has been much slower in evolving cannot help but have impact upon the situation of Black women writers and artists and explains in part why during this very same period we have been so ignored.

There is no political movement to give power or support to those who want to examine Black women's experience through studying our history, literature, and culture. There is no political presence that demands a minimal level of consciousness and respect from those who write or talk about our lives. Finally, there is not a developed body of Black feminist political theory whose assumptions could be used in the study of Black women's art. When Black women's books are dealt with at all, it is usually in the context of Black literature, which largely ignores the implications of sexual politics. When white women look at Black women's works they are of course ill equipped to deal with the subtleties of racial politics. A Black feminist approach to literature that embodies the realization that the politics of sex as well as the politics of race and class are crucially interlocking factors in the works of Black women writers is an absolute necessity. Until a Black feminist criticism exists we will not even know what these writers mean. The citations from a variety of critics which follow prove that without a Black feminist critical perspective not only are books by Black women misunderstood, they are destroyed in the process.

Jerry H. Bryant, *The Nation*'s white male reviewer of Alice Walker's *In Love and Trouble: Stories of Black Women*, wrote in 1973:

> The subtitle of the collection, "Stories of Black Women," is probably an attempt by the publisher to exploit not only black subjects but feminine ones. There is nothing feminist about these stories, however.[2]

Blackness and feminism are to his mind mutually exclusive and peripheral to the act of writing fiction. Bryant of course does not consider that Walker might have titled the work herself, nor did he apparently read the book, which unequivocally reveals the author's feminist consciousness.

In *The Negro Novel in America*, a book that Black critics recognize as one of the worst examples of white racist pseudoscholarship, Robert Bone cavalierly dismisses Ann Petry's classic, *The Street*. He perceives it to be "a superficial social analysis" of how slums victimize their Black inhabitants. He further objects:

> It is an attempt to interpret slum life in terms of Negro experience, when a larger frame of reference is required. As Alain Locke has observed, "*Knock on Any Door* is superior to *The Street* because it designates class and environment, rather than mere race and environment, as its antagonist."[3]

Neither Robert Bone nor Alain Locke, the Black male critic he cites, can recognize that *The Street* is one of the best delineations in literature of how sex, race, and class interact to oppress Black women.

In her review of Toni Morrison's *Sula* for the *New York Times Book Review* in 1973, putative feminist Sara Blackburn makes similarly racist comments:

> Toni Morrison is far too talented to remain only a marvelous recorder of the black side of provincial American life. If she is to maintain the large and serious audience she deserves, she is going to have to address a riskier contemporary reality than this beautiful but nevertheless distanced novel. *And if she does this, it seems to me that she might easily transcend that early and unintentionally limiting classification "black woman writer" and take her place among the most serious, important and talented American novelists now working.*[4] [Italics mine]

Recognizing Morrison's exquisite gift, Blackburn unashamedly asserts that Morrison is "too talented" to deal with mere Black folk, particularly those double nonentities, Black women. In order to be accepted as "serious," "important," "talented," and "American," she must obviously focus her efforts upon chronicling the doings of white men.

The mishandling of Black women writers by whites is paralleled more often by their not being handled at all, particularly in feminist criticism. Although Elaine Showalter in her review essay on literary criticism for *Signs* states that "the best work being produced today [in feminist criticism] is exacting and cosmopolitan," her essay is neither. If it were, she would not have failed to mention a single Black or Third World woman writer, whether "major" or "minor," to cite her questionable categories. That she also does not even hint that lesbian writers of any color exist renders her purported overview virtually meaningless. Showalter obviously thinks that the identities of being Black and female are mutually exclusive, as this statement illustrates:

> Furthermore, there are other literary subcultures (black American novelists, for example) whose history offers a precedent for feminist scholarship to use.[5]

The idea of critics like Showalter using Black literature is chilling, a case of barely disguised cultural imperialism. The final insult is that she footnotes the preceding remark by pointing readers to works on Black literature by white males Robert Bone and Roger Rosenblatt!

Two recent works by white women, Ellen Moers's *Literary Women: The Great Writers* and Patricia Meyer Spacks's *The Female Imagination*, evidence the same racist flaw.[6] Moers includes the names of four Black and one Puertorriqueña writer in her seventy pages of bibliographical notes and does not deal at all with Third World women in the body of her book. Spacks refers to a comparison between Negroes *(sic)* and women in Mary Ellmann's *Thinking About Women* under the index entry "blacks, women and." "*Black Boy* (Wright)" is the preceding entry. Nothing follows. Again there is absolutely no recognition that Black and female identity ever coexist, specifically in a group of Black women writers. Perhaps one can assume that these women do not know who Black women writers are, that like most Americans they have little opportunity to learn about them. Perhaps. Their ignorance seems suspiciously selective, however, particularly in the light of the dozens of truly obscure white women writers they are able to unearth. Spacks was herself employed at Wellesley College at the same time that Alice Walker was there teaching one of the first courses on Black women writers in the country.

I am not trying to encourage racist criticism of Black women writers like that of Sara Blackburn, to cite only one example. As a beginning, I would at least like to see in print while women's acknowledgment of the contradictions of who and what are being left out of their research and writing.[7]

Black male critics can also act as if they do not know that Black women writers exist and are, of course, hampered by an inability to comprehend Black women's experience in sexual as well as racial terms. Unfortunately, there are also those who are as virulently sexist in their treatment of Black women writers as their white male counterparts. Darwin Turner's discussion of Zora Neale Hurston in his *In a Minor Chord: Three Afro-American Writers and Their Search for Identity* is a frightening example of the near assassination of a great Black woman writer.[8] His descriptions of her and her work as "artful," "coy," "irrational," "superficial," and "shallow" bear no relationship to the actual quality of her achievements. Turner is completely insensitive to the sexual political dynamics of Hurston's life and writing.

In a recent interview the notoriously misogynist writer Ishmael Reed comments in this way upon the low sales of his newest novel:

> but the book only sold 8000 copies. I don't mind giving out the figure: 8000. Maybe if I was one of those young *female* Afro-American writers that are so hot now, I'd sell more. You know, fill my books with ghetto women who can *do no wrong*. . . . But come on, I think I could have sold 8000 copies by myself.[9]

The politics of the situation of Black women are glaringly illuminated by this statement. Neither Reed nor his white male interviewer has the slightest compunction about attacking Black women in print. They need not fear widespread public denunciation since Reed's statement is in perfect agreement with the values of a society that hates Black people, women, and Black women. Finally the two of them feel free to base their actions on the premise that Black women are powerless to alter either their political or their cultural oppression.

In her introduction to "A Bibliography of Works Written by American Black Women" Ora Williams quotes some of the reactions of her colleagues toward her efforts to do research on Black women:

> Others have reacted negatively with such statements as, "I really don't think you are going to find very much written," "Have 'they' written anything that is any good?" and, "I wouldn't go overboard with this woman's lib thing." When discussions touched on the possibility of teaching a course in which emphasis would be on the literature by Black women, one response was, "Ha, ha. That will certainly be the most nothing course ever offered!"[10]

A remark by Alice Walker capsulizes what all the preceding examples indicate about the position of Black women writers and the reasons for the damaging criticism about them. She responds to her interviewer's question, "Why do you think that the black woman writers has been so ignored in America? Does she have even more difficulty than the black male writer, who perhaps has just begun to gain recognition?" Walker replies:

> There are two reasons why the black woman writer is not taken as seriously as the black male writer. One is that she's a woman. Critics seem unusually ill-equipped to intelligently discuss and analyze the works of black women. Generally, they do not even make the attempt; they prefer, rather, to talk about the lives of black women writers, not about what they write. And, since black women writers are not—it would seem—very likable—until recently they were the least willing worshippers of male supremacy—comments about them tend to be cruel.[11]

A convincing case for Black feminist criticism can obviously be built solely upon the basis of the negativity of what already exists. It is far more gratifying, however, to demonstrate its necessity by showing how it can serve to reveal for the first time the profound subtleties of this particular body of literature.

Before suggesting how a Black feminist approach might be used to examine a specific work, I will outline some of the principles that I think a Black feminist critic could use. Beginning with a primary commitment to exploring how both sexual and racial politics and Black and female identity are inextricable elements in Black women's writings, she would also work from the assumption that Black women writers constitute an identifiable literary tradition. The breadth of her familiarity with these writers would have shown her that not only is theirs a verifiable historical tradition that parallels in time the tradition of Black men and white women writing in this country, but that thematically, stylistically, aesthetically, and conceptually Black women writers manifest common approaches to the act of creating literature as a direct result of the specific political, social, and economic experience they have been obliged to share. The way, for example, that Zora Neale Hurston, Margaret Walker, Toni Morrison, and Alice Walker incorporate the traditional Black female activities of rootworking, herbal medicine, conjure, and midwifery into the fabric of their stories is not mere coincidence, nor is their use of specifically Black female language to express their own and their characters' thoughts accidental. The use of Black women's language and cultural experience in books by Black women about Black women results in a miraculously rich coalescing of form and content and also takes their writing far beyond the confines of white/male literary structures. The Black feminist critic would find innumerable commonalities in works by Black women.

Another principle which grows out of the concept of a tradition and which would also help to strengthen this tradition would be for the critic to look first for precedents and insights in interpretation within the works of other Black women. In other words she would think and write out of her own identity and not try to graft the ideas or methodology of white/male literary thought upon the precious materials of Black women's art. Black feminist criticism would by definition be highly innovative, embodying the daring spirit of the works themselves. The Black feminist critic would be constantly aware of the political implications of her work and would assert the connections between it and the political situation of all Black women. Logically developed, Black feminist criticism would owe its existence to a Black feminist movement while at the same time contributing ideas that women in the movement could use.

Black feminist criticism applied to a particular work can overturn previous assumptions about it and expose for the first time its actual dimensions. At the "Lesbians and Literature" discussion at the 1976 Modern Language Association convention Bertha Harris suggested that if in a woman writer's work a sentence refuses to do what it is supposed to do, if there are strong images of women and if there is a refusal to be linear, the result is innately lesbian literature. As usual, I wanted to see if these ideas might be applied to the Black women writers that I know and quickly realized that many of their works were, in Harris's sense, lesbian. Not because women are "lovers," but because they are the central figures, are positively portrayed and have pivotal relationships with one another. The form and language of these works are also nothing like what white patriarchal culture requires or expects.

I was particularly struck by the way in which Toni Morrison's novels *The Bluest Eye* and *Sula* could be explored from this new perspective.[12] In both works the relationships between girls and women are essential, yet at the same time physical sexuality is overtly expressed only between men and women. Despite the apparent heterosexuality of the female characters, I discovered in rereading *Sula* that it works as a lesbian novel not only because of the passionate friendship between Sula and Nel but because of Morrison's consistently critical stance toward the heterosexual institutions of male-female relationships, marriage, and the family. Consciously or not, Morrison's work poses both lesbian and feminist questions about Black women's autonomy and their impact upon each other's lives.

Sula and Nel find each other in 1922 when each of them is twelve, on the brink of puberty and the discovery of boys. Even as awakening sexuality "clotted their dreams," each girl desires "a someone" obviously female with whom to share her feelings. Morrison writes:

> for it was in dreams that the two girls had met. Long before Edna Finch's Mellow House opened, even before they marched through the chocolate halls of Garfield Primary School . . . they had already made each other's acquaintance in the delirium of their noon dreams. They were solitary little girls whose loneliness was so profound it intoxicated them and sent them stumbling into Technicolored visions that always included a presence, a someone who, quite like the dreamer, shared the delight of the dream. When Nel, an only child, sat on the steps of her back porch surrounded by the high silence of her mother's incredibly orderly house, feeling the neatness pointing at her back, she studied the poplars and fell easily into a picture of herself lying on a flower bed, tangled in her own hair, waiting for some fiery prince. He approached but never quite arrived. But always, watching the dream along with her, were some smiling sympathetic eyes. Someone as interested as she herself in the flow of her imagined

hair, the thickness of the mattress of flowers, the voile sleeves that closed below her elbows in gold-threaded cuffs.

Similarly, Sula, also an only child, but wedged into a household of throbbing disorder constantly awry with things, people, voices and the slamming of doors, spent hours in the attic behind a roll of linoleum galloping through her own mind on a gray-and-white horse tasting sugar and smelling roses in full view of someone who shared both the taste and the speed.

So when they met, first in those chocolate halls and next through the ropes of the swing, they felt the ease and comfort of old friends. Because each had discovered years before that they were neither white nor male, and that all freedom and triumph was forbidden to them, they had set about creating something else to be. Their meeting was fortunate, for it let them use each other to grow on. Daughters of distant mothers and incomprehensible fathers (Sula's because he was dead; Nel's because he wasn't), they found in each other's eyes the intimacy they were looking for. (Pp. 51–52)

As this beautiful passage shows, their relationship, from the very beginning, is suffused with an erotic romanticism. The dreams in which they are initially drawn to each other are actually complementary aspects of the same sensuous fairy tale. Nel imagines a "fiery prince" who never quite arrives, while Sula gallops like a prince "on a gray-and-white horse."[13] The "real world" of patriarchy requires, however, that they channel this energy away from each other to the opposite sex. Lorraine Bethel explains this dynamic in her essay "Conversations with Ourselves: Black Female Relationships in Toni Cade Bambara's *Gorilla, My Love* and Toni Morrison's *Sula*":

> I am not suggesting that Sula and Nel are being consciously sexual, or that their relationship has an overt lesbian nature. I am suggesting, however, that there is a certain sensuality in their interactions that is reinforced by the mirror-like nature of their relationship. Sexual exploration and coming of age is a natural part of adolescence. Sula and Nel discover men together, and though their flirtations with males are an important part of their sexual exploration, the sensuality that they experience in each other's company is equally important.[14]

Sula and Nel must also struggle with the constrictions of racism upon their lives. The knowledge that "they were neither white nor male" is the inherent explanation of their need for each other. Morrison depicts in literature the necessary bonding that has always taken place between Black women for the sake of barest survival. Together the two girls can find the courage to create themselves.

Their relationship is severed only when Nel marries Jude, an unexceptional young man who thinks of her as "the hem—the tuck and fold that hid his raveling edges" (p. 83). Sula's inventive wildness cannot overcome social pressure or the influence of Nel's parents who "had succeeded in rubbing down to a dull glow any sparkle or splutter she had" (p. 83). Nel falls prey to convention while Sula escapes it. Yet at the wedding which ends the first phase of their relationship, Nel's final action is to look past her husband toward Sula, a slim figure in blue, gliding, with just a hint of a strut, down the path towards the road. . . . Even from the rear Nel could tell that it was Sula and that she was smiling; that something deep down in that litheness was amused. (P. 85)

When Sula returns ten years later, her rebelliousness full-blown, a major source of the town's suspicions stems from the fact that although she is almost thirty, she is still unmarried. Sula's grandmother, Eva, does not hesitate to bring up the matter as soon as she arrives. She asks:

When you gone to get married? You need to have some babies. It'll settle you. . . .
Ain't no woman got no business floatin' around without no man. (P. 92)

Sula replies: "I don't want to make somebody else. I want to make myself" (p. 92). Self-definition is a dangerous activity for any woman to engage in, especially a Black one, and it expectedly earns Sula pariah status in Medallion.

Morrison clearly points out that it is the fact that Sula has not been tamed or broken by the exigencies of heterosexual family life which most galls the others:

Among the weighty evidence piling up was the fact that Sula did not look her age. She was near thirty and, unlike them, had lost no teeth, suffered no bruises, developed no ring of fat at the waist or pocket at the back of her neck. (P. 115)

In other words she is not a domestic serf, a woman run down by obligatory child-bearing or a victim of battering. Sula also sleeps with the husbands of the town once and then discards them, needing them even less than her own mother did for sexual gratification and affection. The town reacts to her disavowal of patriarchal values by becoming fanatically serious about their own family obligations, as if in this way they might counteract Sula's radical criticism of their lives.

Sula's presence in her community functions much like the presence of lesbians everywhere to expose the contradictions of supposedly "normal" life. The opening paragraph of the essay "The Woman-Identified Woman" has amazing relevance as an explanation of Sula's position and character in the novel. It asks:

What is a lesbian? A lesbian is the rage of all women condensed to the point of explosion. She is the woman who, often beginning at an extremely early age, acts in accordance with her inner compulsion to be a more complete and freer human being than her society—perhaps then, but certainly later—cares to allow her. These needs and actions, over a period of years, bring her into painful conflict with people, situations, the accepted ways of thinking, feeling and behaving, until she is in a state of continual war with everything around her, and usually with herself. She may not be fully conscious of the political implications of what for her began as personal necessity, but on some level she has not been able to accept the limitations and oppression laid on her by the most basic role of her society—the female role.[15]

The limitations of the *Black* female role are even greater in a racist and sexist society, as is the amount of courage it takes to challenge them. It is no wonder that the townspeople see Sula's independence as imminently dangerous.

Morrison is also careful to show the reader that despite their years of separation and their opposing paths, Nel and Sula's relationship retains its primacy for each of them. Nell feels transformed when Sula returns and thinks:

> It was like getting the use of an eye back, having a cataract removed. Her old friend had come home. Sula. Who made her laugh, who made her see old things with new eyes, in whose presence she felt clever, gentle and a little raunchy. (P. 95)

Laughing together in the familiar "rib-scraping" way, Nel feels "new, soft and new" (p. 98). Morrison uses here the visual imagery which symbolizes the women's closeness throughout the novel.

Sula fractures this closeness, however, by sleeping with Nel's husband, an act of little import according to her system of values. Nel, of course, cannot understand. Sula thinks ruefully:

> Nel was the one person who had wanted nothing from her, who had accepted all aspects of her. Now she wanted everything, and all because of *that*. Nel was the first person who had been real to her, whose name she knew, who had seen as she had the slant of life that made it possible to stretch it to its limits. Now Nel was one of *them*. (Pp. 119–20)

Sula also thinks at the realization of losing Nel about how unsatisfactory her relationships with men have been and admits:

> She had been looking all along for a friend, and it took her a while to discover that a lover was not a comrade and could never be—for a woman. (P. 121)

The nearest that Sula comes to actually loving a man is in a brief affair with Ajax, and what she values most about him is the intellectual companionship he provides, the brilliance he "allows" her to show.

Sula's feelings about sex with men are also consistent with a lesbian interpretation of the novel. Morrison writes:

> She went to bed with men as frequently as she could. It was the only place where she could find what she was looking for: *misery and the ability to feel deep sorrow.* . . . During the lovemaking she found and needed to find the cutting edge. When she left off cooperating with her body and began to assert herself in the act, particles of strength gathered in her like steel shavings drawn to a spacious magnetic center, forming a tight cluster that nothing, it seemed, could break. *And there was utmost irony and outrage in lying under someone, in a position of surrender, feeling her own abiding strength and limitless power.* . . . When her partner disengaged himself, she looked up at him in wonder trying to recall his name . . . waiting impatiently for him to turn away . . . leaving her to the postcoital privateness in which she met herself, welcomed herself, and joined herself in matchless harmony. (Pp. 122–23; italics mine)

Sula uses men for sex which results, not in communion with them, but in her further delving into self.

Ultimately the deepest communion and communication in the novel occurs between two women who love each other. After their last painful meeting, which does not bring reconciliation, Sula thinks as Nel leaves her:

"So she will walk on down that road, her back so straight in that old green coat . . . thinking how much I have cost her and never remember the days when we were two throats and one eye and we had no price." (P. 147)

It is difficult to imagine a more evocative metaphor for what women can be to each other, the "pricelessness" they achieve in refusing to sell themselves for male approval, the total worth that they can only find in each other's eyes.

Decades later the novel concludes with Nel's final comprehension of the source of the grief that has plagued her from the time her husband walked out:

"All that time, all that time, I thought I was missing Jude." And the loss pressed down on her chest and came up into her throat. "We was girls together," she said as though explaining something. "O Lord, Sula," she cried, "girl, girl, girlgirlgirl."

It was a fine cry—loud and long—but it had no bottom and it had no top, just circles and circles of sorrow. (P. 174)

Again Morrison exquisitely conveys what women, Black women, mean to each other. This final passage verifies the depth of Sula and Nel's relationship and its centrality to an accurate interpretation of the work.

Sula is an exceedingly lesbian novel in the emotions expressed, in the definition of female character, and in the way that the politics of heterosexuality are portrayed. The very meaning of lesbianism is being expanded in literature, just as it is being redefined through politics. The confusion that many readers have felt about *Sula* may well have a lesbian explanation. If one sees Sula's inexplicable "evil" and noncon-formity as the evil of not being male-identified, many elements in the novel become clear. The work might be clearer still if Morrison had approached her subject with the consciousness that a lesbian relationship was at least a possibility for her charac-ters. Obviously Morrison did not *intend* the reader to perceive Sula and Nel's rela-tionship as inherently lesbian. However, this lack of intention only shows the way in which heterosexist assumptions can veil what may logically be expected to occur in a work. What I have tried to do here is not to prove that Morrison wrote something that she did not, but to point out how a Black feminist critical perspective at least allows consideration of this level of the novel's meaning.

In her interview in *Conditions: One*, Adrienne Rich talks about unconsummated relationships and the need to reevaluate the meaning of intense yet supposedly non-erotic connections between women. She asserts:

We need a lot more documentation about what actually happened: I think we can also imagine it, because we know it happened—we know it out of our own lives.[16]

Black women are still in the position of having to "imagine," discover, and verify Black lesbian literature because so little has been written from an avowedly lesbian perspective. The near nonexistence of Black lesbian literature which other Black lesbians and I so deeply feel has everything to do with the politics of our lives, the total suppression of identity that all Black women, lesbian or not, must face. This literary silence is again intensified by the unavailability of an autonomous Black feminist movement through which we could fight our oppression and also begin to name ourselves.

In a speech, "The Autonomy of Black Lesbian Women," Wilmette Brown comments upon the connection between our political reality and the literature we must invent:

> Because the isolation of Black lesbian women, given that we are superfreaks, given that our lesbianism defies both the sexual identity that capital gives us and the racial identity that capital gives us, the isolation of Black lesbian women from heterosexual Black women is very profound. Very profound. I have searched throughout Black history, Black literature, whatever, looking for some women that I could see were somehow lesbian. Now I know that in a certain sense they were all lesbian. But that was a very painful search.[17]

Heterosexual privilege is usually the only privilege that Black women have. None of us have racial or sexual privilege, almost none of us have class privilege; maintaining "straightness" is our last resort. Being out, particularly out in print, is the final renunciation of any claim to the crumbs of "tolerance" that nonthreatening "lady-like" Black women are sometimes fed. I am convinced that it is our lack of privilege and power in every other sphere that allows so few Black women to make the leap that many white women, particularly writers, have been able to make in this decade, not merely because they are white or have economic leverage, but because they have had the strength and support of a movement behind them.

As Black lesbians we must be out not only in white society but in the Black community as well, which is at least as homophobic. That the sanctions against Black lesbians are extremely high is well illustrated in this comment by Black male writer Ishmael Reed. Speaking about the inroads that whites make into Black culture, he asserts:

> In Manhattan you find people actively trying to impede intellectual debate among Afro-Americans. The powerful "liberal/radical/existentialist" influences of the Manhattan literary and drama establishment speak through tokens, like for example that ancient notion of the *one* black ideologue (who's usually a Communist), the *one* black poetess (who's usually a feminist lesbian).[18]

To Reed, "feminist" and "lesbian" are the most pejorative terms he can hurl at a Black woman and totally invalidate anything she might say, regardless of her actual politics or sexual identity. Such accusations are quite effective for keeping in line Black women writers who are writing with integrity and strength from any conceivable perspective, but especially ones who are actually feminist and lesbian. Unfortunately Reed's reactionary attitude is all too typical. A community which has not confronted sexism, because a widespread Black feminist movement has not required it to, has likewise not been challenged to examine its heterosexism. Even at this moment I am not convinced that one can write explicitly as a Black lesbian and live to tell about it.

Yet there are a handful of Black women who have risked everything for truth. Audre Lorde, Pat Parker, and Ann Allen Shockley have at least broken ground in the vast wilderness of works that do not exist.[19] Black feminist criticism will again have an essential role not only in creating a climate in which Black lesbian writers can survive, but in undertaking the total reassessment of Black literature and literary history needed to reveal the Black woman-identified women that Wilmette Brown and so many of us are looking for.

Although I have concentrated here upon what does not exist and what needs to be done, a few Black feminist critics have already begun this work. Gloria T. Hull at the University of Delaware has discovered in her research on Black women poets of the Harlem Renaissance that many of the women who are considered "minor" writers of the period were in constant contact with each other and provided both intellectual stimulation and psychological support for each other's work. At least one of these writers, Angelina Weld Grimké, wrote many unpublished love poems to women. Lorraine Bethel, a recent graduate of Yale College, has done substantial work on Black women writers, particularly in her senior essay, "This Infinity of Conscious Pain: Blues Lyricism and Hurston's Black Female Folk Aesthetic and Cultural Sensibility in *Their Eyes Were Watching God*," in which she brilliantly defines and uses the principles of Black feminist criticism. Elaine Scott at the State University of New York at Old Westbury is also involved in highly creative and politically resonant research on Hurston and other writers.

The fact that these critics are young and, except for Hull, unpublished merely indicates the impediments we face. Undoubtedly there are other women working and writing whom I do not even know, simply because there is no place to read them. As Michele Wallace states in her article "A Black Feminist's Search for Sisterhood":

> We exist as women who are Black who are feminists, each stranded for the moment, working independently because there is not yet an environment in this society remotely congenial to our struggle—[or our thoughts].[20]

I only hope that this essay is one way of breaking our silence and our isolation, of helping us to know each other.

Just as I did not know where to start, I am not sure how to end. I feel that I have tried to say too much and at the same time have left too much unsaid. What I want this essay to do is lead everyone who reads it to examine *everything* that they have ever thought and believed about feminist culture and to ask themselves how their thoughts connect to the reality of Black women's writing and lives. I want to encourage in white women, as a first step, a sane accountability to all the women who write and live on this soil. I want most of all for Black women and Black lesbians somehow not to be so alone. This last will require the most expansive of revolutions as well as many new words to tell us how to make this revolution real. I finally want to express how much easier both my waking and my sleeping hours would be if there were one book in existence that would tell me something specific about my life. One book based in Black feminist and Black lesbian experience, fiction or nonfiction. Just one work to reflect the reality that I and the Black women whom I love are trying to create. When such a book exists then each of us will not only know better how to live, but how to dream.

NOTES

1. Alice Walker, "In Search of Our Mothers' Gardens," in *Ms.*, May 1974, and in *Southern Exposure* 4, no. 4, *Generations: Women in the South* (Winter 1977): 60–64.

2. Jerry H. Bryant, "The Outskirts of a New City," *The Nation*, November 12, 1973, p. 502.

3. Robert Bone, *The Negro Novel in America* (New Haven, Conn.: Yale University Press, 1958), p. 180. *Knock on Any Door* is a novel by Black writer Willard Motley.

4. Sara Blackburn, "You Still Can't Go Home Again," *New York Times Book Review*, December 30, 1973, p. 3.

5. Elaine Showalter, "Literary Criticism," Review Essay, *Signs* 1 (Winter 1975): 460, 445.

6. Ellen Moers, *Literary Women: The Great Writers* (Garden City, N.Y.: Anchor Books, 1977); Patricia Meyer Spacks, *The Female Imagination* (New York: Avon Books, 1976).

7. An article by Nancy Hoffman, "White Women, Black Women: Inventing an Adequate Pedagogy," *Women's Studies Newsletter* 5 (Spring 1977): 21–24, gives valuable insights into how white women can approach the writing of Black women.

8. Darwin T. Turner, *In a Minor Chord: Three Afro-American Writers and Their Search for Identity* (Carbondale and Edwardsville: Southern Illinois University Press, 1971).

9. John Domini, "Roots and Racism: An Interview with Ishmael Reed," *Boston Phoenix*, April 5, 1977, p. 20.

10. Ora Williams, "A Bibliography of Works Written by American Black Women," *College Language Association Journal* 15 (March 1972): 355. There is an expanded book-length version of this bibliography: *American Black Women in the Arts and Social Sciences: A Bibliographic Survey* (Metuchen, N.J.: Scarecrow Press, 1973; rev. and expanded ed., 1978).

11. John O'Brien, ed., *Interviews with Black Writers* (New York: Liveright, 1973), p. 201.

12. Toni Morrison, *The Bluest Eye* (1970; reprint ed., New York: Pocket Books, 1972, 1976) and *Sula* (New York: Alfred A. Knopf, 1974). All subsequent references to this work will be designated in the text.

13. My sister, Beverly Smith, pointed out this connection to me.

14. Lorraine Bethel, "Conversations with Ourselves: Black Female Relationships in Toni Cade Bambara's *Gorilla, My Love* and Toni Morrison's *Sula*," unpublished paper written at Yale University, 1976, 47 pp. Bethel has worked from a premise similar to mine in a much more developed treatment of the novel.

15. New York Radicalesbians, "The Woman-Identified Woman," in *Lesbians Speak Out* (Oakland, Calif.: Women's Press Collective, 1974), p. 87.

16. Elly Bulkin, "An Interview with Adrienne Rich: Part 1," *Conditions: One* 1 (April 1977): 62.

17. Wilmette Brown, "The Autonomy of Black Lesbian Women," manuscript of speech delivered July 24, 1976, in Toronto, Canada, p. 7.

18. Domini, "Roots and Racism," p. 18.

19. Audre Lorde, *New York Head Shop and Museum* (Detroit: Broadside Press, 1974); *Coal* (New York: W. W. Norton, 1976); *Between Our Selves* (Point Reyes, Calif.: Eidolon Editions, 1976); *The Black Unicorn* (New York: W. W. Norton, 1978).

Pat Parker, *Child of Myself* (Oakland, Calif.: Women's Press Collective, 1972 and 1974); *Pit Stop* (Oakland, Calif.: Women's Press Collective, 1973); *Womanslaughter* (Oakland, Calif.: Diana Press, 1978); *Movement in Black* (Oakland, Calif.: Diane Press, 1978).

Ann Allen Shockley, *Loving Her* (Indianapolis: Bobbs-Merrill, 1974).

There is at least one Black lesbian writers' collective, Jemima, in New York. They do public readings and have available a collection of their poems. They can be contacted c/o Boyce, 41-11 Parsons Boulevard, Flushing, N.Y. 11355.

20. Michele Wallace, "A Black Feminist's Search for Sisterhood," *Village Voice*, July 28, 1975, p. 7.

18 Preface to Blackness

Text and Pretext

Henry Louis Gates, Jr.

(1979)

For Soule is forme, and doth the bodie make.
—Edmund Spenser, 1596

Music is a world within itself, with a language we all understand.
—Stevie Wonder, 1976

I

The idea of a determining formal relation between literature and social institutions does not in itself explain the sense of urgency that has, at least since the publication in 1760 of *A Narrative of the Uncommon Sufferings and Surprising Deliverance of Briton Hammon, a Negro Man,*[1] characterized nearly the whole of Afro-American writing. This idea has often encouraged a posture that belabors the social and documentary status of black art, and indeed the earliest discrete examples of written discourse by slave and ex-slave came under a scrutiny not primarily literary. Formal writing, beginning with the four autobiographical slave narratives published in English between 1760 and 1798, was taken to be collective as well as functional. Because narratives documented the potential for "culture," that is, for manners and morals, the command of written English virtually separated the African from the Afro-American, the slave from the ex-slave, titled property from fledgling human being. Well-meaning abolitionists cited these texts as proof of the common humanity of bondsman and lord; yet these same texts also demonstrated the contrary for proponents of the antebellum world view—that the African imagination was merely derivative. The command of a written language, then, could be no mean thing in the life of the slave: Learning to read, the slave narratives repeat again and again, was a decisive political act; learning to write, as measured by an eighteenth-century scale of culture and society, was an irreversible step away from the cotton field toward a freedom even larger than physical manumission. What the use of language entailed for personal social mobility and what it implied about the public Negro mind made

147

for the onerous burden of literacy, a burden having very little to do with the use of language as such, a burden so pervasive that the nineteenth-century quest for literacy and the twentieth-century quest for form became the central, indeed controlling, metaphors (if not mythical matrices) in Afro-American narrative. Once the private dream fused with a public, and therefore political, imperative, the Negro arts were committed; the pervasive sense of fundamental urgency and unity in the black arts became a millennial, if not precisely apocalyptic, force.

I do not mean to suggest that these ideas were peculiar to eighteenth-century American criticism. For example, we learn from Herder's Prize Essay of 1773 on the *Causes of the Decline of Taste in Different Nations* that in Germany "the appreciation of various folk and Gothic literatures and the comparative study of ancient, eastern, and modern foreign literatures (the criticism of literature by age and race) were strongly established, and these interests profoundly affected theories about the nature of literature as the expression of, or the power that shaped, human cultures or human nature in general." William K. Wimsatt also remarks that Friedrick Schlegel "only accented an already pervasive view when he called poetry the most specifically human energy, the central document of any culture."[2] It should not surprise us, then, that *Poems on Various Subjects, Religious and Moral, by Phillis Wheatley, Negro Servant to Mr. Wheatley of Boston*, the first book of poems published by an African in English,[3] became, almost immediately after its publication in London in 1773, the international antislavery movement's most salient argument for the African's innate mental equality. That the book went to five printings before 1800 testified far more to its acceptance as a "legitimate" product of "the African muse," writes Henri Grégoire[4] in 1808, than to the merit of its sometimes vapid elegiac verse. The no fewer than eighteen "certificates of authenticity" that preface the book, including one by John Hancock and another by the Governor of Massachusetts, Thomas Hutchinson, meant to "leave no doubt, that she is its author."[5] Literally scores of public figures—from Voltaire to George Washington, from Benjamin Rush to Benjamin Franklin—reviewed Wheatley's book, yet virtually no one discussed the book as poetry. It was an unequal contest: The documentary status of black art assumed priority over mere literary judgment; criticism rehearsed content to justify one notion of origins or another. Of these discussions, it was Thomas Jefferson's that proved most seminal to the shaping of the Afro-American critical activity.

Asserted primarily to debunk the exaggerated claims of the abolitionists, Thomas Jefferson's remarks on Phillis Wheatley's poetry, as well as on Ignatius Sancho's *Letters*,[6] exerted a prescriptive influence over the criticism of the writing of blacks for the next 150 years. "Never yet," Jefferson prefaces his discussion of Wheatley, "could I find a Black that had uttered a thought above the level of plain narration; never seen even an elementary trait of painting or sculpture." As a specimen of the human mind, Jefferson continued, Wheatley's poems as poetry did not merit discussion. "Religion," he writes, "indeed has produced a Phillis Whately [*sic*] but it could not produce a poet." "The compositions published under her name," Jefferson concludes, "are below the dignity of criticism. The heroes of the *Dunciad* are to her, as Hercules to the author of the poem." As to Sancho's *Letters*, Jefferson says:

[H]is imagination is wild and extravagant, escapes incessantly from every restraint of reason and taste, and, in the course of its vagaries, leaves a tract of thought as incoherent and eccentric, as is the course of a meteor through the sky. His subjects should have led him to a process of sober reasoning: yet we find him always substituting sentiment for demonstration.[7]

Jefferson's stature demanded response: from black writers, refutations of his doubts about their very capacity to imagine great art and hence to take a few giant steps up the Great Chain of Being; from would-be-critics, encyclopaedic and often hyperbolic replies to Jefferson's disparaging generalizations. The critical responses included Thomas Clarkson's Prize Essay, written in Latin at Cambridge in 1785 and published as *An Essay on the Slavery and Commerce of the Human Species, Particularly the African* (1788), and the following, rather remarkable, volumes: Gilbert Imlay's *A Topographical Description of the Western Territory of North America* (1793); the Marquis de Bois-Robert's two-volume *The Negro Equalled by Few Europeans* (1791); Thomas Branagan's *Preliminary Essay on the Oppression of the Exiled Sons of Africa* (1804); the Abbé Grégoire's *An Enquiry concerning the Intellectual and Moral Faculties, and Literature of Negroes* . . . (1808); Samuel Stanhope Smith's *An Essay on the Causes of the Variety of the Human Complexion and Figure in the Human Species* (1810); Lydia Child's *An Appeal in favor of That Class of Americans Called Africans* (1833); B. B. Thatcher's *Memoir of Phillis Wheatley, a Native American and a Slave* (1834); Abigail Mott's *Biographical Sketches and Interesting Anecdotes of Persons of Color* (1838); R. B. Lewis' *Light and Truth* (1844); Theodore Hally's *A Vindication of the Capacity of the Negro Race* (1851); R. T. Greener's urbane long essay in *The National Quarterly Review* (1880); Joseph Wilson's rather ambitious *Emancipation: Its Course and Progress from 1481 B.C. to A.D. 1875* (1882); William Simmon's *Men of Mark* (1887); Benjamin Brawley's *The Negro in Literature and Art* (1918); and Joel A. Rodgers' two-volume *The World's Great Men of Color* (1946).

Even more telling, for our purposes here, is that the almost quaint authenticating signatures and statements that prefaced Wheatley's book became, certainly through the period of Dunbar and Chesnutt and even until the middle of the Harlem Renaissance, fixed attestations of the "specimen" author's physical blackness. This sort of authenticating color description was so common to these prefaces that many late nineteenth- and early twentieth-century black reviewers, particularly in the *African Methodist Episcopal Church Review*, the *Southern Workman*, the *Voice of the Negro, Alexander's Magazine*, and *The Colored American*, adopted it as a political as well as rhetorical strategy to counter the intense and bitter allegations of African inferiority popularized by journalistic accounts and "colorations" of social Darwinism. Through an examination of a few of these prefaces, I propose to sketch an ironic circular thread of interpretation that commences in the eighteenth century but does not reach its fullest philosophical form until the decade between 1965 and 1975: the movement from blackness as a physical concept to blackness as a metaphysical concept. Indeed, this movement became the very text and pretext of the "Blackness" of the recent Black Arts movement, a solidly traced hermeneutical circle into which all of us find ourselves drawn.

II

Even before Jefferson allowed himself the outrageous remark that "the improvement of the blacks in body and mind, in the first instance of their mixture with the whites, has been observed by every one, and proves that their inferiority is not the effect merely of their condition of life,"[8] advocates of the unity of the human species had forged a union of literary tradition, individual talent, and innate racial capacity. Phillis Wheatley's "authenticators," for instance, announced that:

> We whose Names are under-written, do assure the world, that the POEMS specified in the following Page, were (as we verily believe) written by *Phillis*, a young Negro Girl, who was but a few years since, brought an uncultured Barbarian from Africa, and has ever since been and now is, under the Disadvantage of serving as a Slave of a Family in this Town. She has been examined by some of the best Judges, and is thought qualified to write them.[9]

Further, Wheatley herself asks indulgence of the critic, considering the occasion of her verse. "As her Attempts in Poetry are now sent into the World, it is hoped the critic will not severely censure their Defects; and we presume they have too much Merit to be cast aside with contempt, as worthless and trifling effusions." "With all their imperfections," she concludes, "the poems are now humbly submitted to the Perusal of the Public."[10] Other than the tone of the author's preface, there was little here that was "humbly submitted" to Wheatley's public. Her volume garnered immense interest as to the nature of the African imagination. So compelling did evidence of the African's artistic abilities prove to be to Enlightenment speculation on the idea of progress and the scala naturae that just nine years after Wheatley's *Poems* appeared, over one thousand British lords and ladies subscribed to have published Ignatius Sancho's collected letters. Even more pertinent in our context, Joseph Jekyll, M.P., prefaced the volume with a full biographical account of the colorful Sancho's life, structured curiously about the received relation between "genius" and "species."

People were also fascinated by the "African mind" presented in the collected letters of Ignatius Sancho. Named "from a fancied resemblance to the Squire of Don Quixote,"[11] Sancho had his portrait painted by Gainsborough and engraved by Bartolozzi. He was a correspondent of Garrick and Sterne and, apparently, something of a poet as well: "A commerce with the Muses was supported amid the trivial and momentary interruptions of a shop," Jekyll writes. Indeed, not only were "the Poets studied, and even imitated with some success," but "two pieces were constructed for the stage." In addition to his creative endeavors, Sancho was a critic—perhaps the first African critic of the arts to write in English. His "theory of Music was discussed, published, and dedicated to the Princess Royal, and Painting was so much within the circle of

Ignatius Sancho's judgment and criticism," Jekyll observes, "that several artists paid great *deference* to his opinion."

Jekyll's rather involved biography is a pretext to display the artifacts of the sable mind, as was the very publication of the *Letters* themselves. "Her motives for laying them before the publick were," the publisher admits, "the desire of showing that an untutored African may possess abilities equal to an European." Sancho was an "extraordinary Negro," his biographer relates, although he was a bit better for being a bit bad. "Freedom, riches, and leisure, naturally led to a disposition of African tendencies into indulgences; and that which dissipated the mind of Ignatius completely drained the purse," Jekyll puns. "In his attachment to women, he displayed a profuseness which not unusually characterizes the excess of the passion." "Cards had formerly seduced him," we are told, "but an unsuccessful contest at cribbage with a Jew, who won his cloaths, had determined to abjure the propensity which appears to be innate among his countrymen." Here, again, we see drawn the thread between phylogeny and ontogeny: "a French writer relates," Jekyll explains, "that in the kingdoms of Ardrah, Whydah, and Benin, a Negro will stake at play his fortune, his children, and his liberty." Thus driven to distraction, Sancho was "induced to consider the stage" since "his complexion suggested an offer to the manager of attempting Othello and Oroonoko; but a defective and incorrigible articulation rendered it abortive."

Colorful though Jekyll's anecdotes are, they are a mere pretext for the crux of his argument: a disquisition on cranial capacity, regional variation, skin color, and intelligence. The example of Sancho, made particularly human by the citation of his foibles, is meant to put to rest any suspicion as to the native abilities of the Negro:

> Such was the man whose species philosophers and anatomists have endeavored to degrade as a deterioration of the human; and such was the man whom Fuller, with a benevolence and quaintness of phrase peculiarly his own, accounted "God's Image, though cut in Ebony." To the harsh definition of the naturalist, oppressions political and legislative have been added; and such are hourly aggravated towards this unhappy race of men by vulgar prejudice and popular insult. To combat these on commercial principles, has been the labour of [others]—such an effort here, [he concludes ironically] would be an impertinent digression.

That Sancho's attainments are not merely isolated exceptions to the general morass is indicated by the state of civilization on the African "slave-coast." Jekyll continues:

> Of those who have speculatively visited and described the slave-coast, there are not wanting some who extol the mental abilities of the natives. [Some] speak highly of their mechanical powers and indefatigable industry. [Another] does not scruple to affirm, that their ingenuity rivals the Chinese.

What is more, these marks of culture and capacity signify an even more telling body of data, since the logical extensions of mechanical powers and industry are sublime arts and stable polity:

He who could penetrate the interior of Africa, might not improbably discover negro arts and polity, which could bear little analogy to the ignorance and grossness of slaves in the sugar-islands, expatriated in infamy; and brutalized under the whip and the task-master.

"And he," Jekyll summarizes, "who surveys the extent of intellect to which Ignatius Sancho had attained self-education, will perhaps conclude, that the perfection of the reasoning faculties does not depend on the colour of a common integument."[12]

Jekyll's preface became a touchstone for the literary anthropologists who saw in black art a categorical repository for the African's potential to deserve inclusion in the human community. Echoes of Jekyll's language resound throughout the prefaces to slave testimony. Gustavus Vassa's own claim in 1789 that the African's contacts with "liberal sentiments" and "the Christian religion" have "exalted human nature" is vouched for by more than one hundred Irish subscribers. Charles Ball's editor asserts in 1836 that Ball is "a common negro slave, embued by nature with a tolerable portion of intellectual capacity."[13] Both Garrison's and Phillip's prefaces to *The Narrative of the Life of Frederick Douglass* (1845) and James McCune Smith's introduction to Douglass' *My Bondage and My Freedom* (1855)[14] attest to Douglass' African heritage and former bestial status. McCune Smith proffers the additional claims for literary excellence demanded by the intensity of doubt toward the black African's mental abilities:

[T]he Negro, for the first time in the world's history brought in full contact with high civilization, must prove his title first to all that is demanded for him; in the teeth of unequal chances, he must prove himself equal to the mass of those who oppress him—therefore, absolutely superior to his apparent fate, and to their relative ability. And it is most cheering to the friends of freedom, to-day, that evidence of this equality is rapidly accumulating, not from the ranks of the half-freed colored people of the free states, but from the very depths of slavery itself; the indestructible equality of man to man is demonstrated by the ease with which black men, scarce one remove from barbarism—If slavery can be honored with such a distinction—vault into the high places of the most advanced and painfully acquired civilization.

What is more germane is a review of Douglass' *Narrative* that emphasizes the relevance of each "product" of the African mind almost as another primary argument in the abolitionists' brief against slavery:

Considered merely as a narrative, we have never read one more simple, true, coherent, and warm with genuine feeling. It is an excellent piece of writing, and on that score to be prized as a specimen of the powers of the black race, which prejudice persists in disputing. We prize highly all evidence of this kind, and it is becoming more abundant.[15]

These readings of blackness discuss the very properties of property. In fact, what we discover here is a correlation between property and properties and between character and characteristics, which proved so pervasive in the latter half of the nineteenth century that Booker T. Washington's *Up from Slavery*, for example, be-comes, after its seventh chapter, the autobiography of an institution, thereby detach-ing itself somewhat from the slave narrative tradition, where the structural movement was from institution and property to man.

This relation between essence and value, between ethics and aesthetics, became, at least as early as William Dean Howells' 1896 review of Paul Laurence Dunbar's "Majors and Minors,"[16] a correlation between a metaphysical blackness and a phys-ical blackness. Howells emphasizes almost immediately Dunbar's appearance:

> the face of a young negro, with the race's traits strangely accented: the black skin, the wooly hair, the thick, out-rolling lips, and the mild, soft eyes of the pure African type. One cannot be very sure, ever, about the age of those people, but I should have thought that this poet was about twenty years old; and I suppose that a generation ago he would have been worth, apart from his literary gift, twelve or fifteen hundred dollars, under the hammer.

Howells makes a subtle shift here from properties to property. Moreover, he outlines the still prevalent notion that treats art as artifact:

> He is, so far as I know, the first man of his color to study his race objectively, to analyze it to himself, and then to represent it in art as he felt it and found it to be; to represent it humorously, yet tenderly, and above all so faithfully that we know the portrait to be undeniably like. A race which has reached this effect in any of its members can no longer be held wholly uncivilized; and intellectually Mr. Dunbar makes a stronger claim for the negro than the negro yet has done.

Howells then makes that leap so crucial to this discussion, and so crucial to the aesthetics of the Black Arts movement:

> If his Minors [the dialect pieces] had been written by a white man, I should have been struck by their very uncommon quality; I should have said that they were wonderful divinations. But since they are expressions of a race-life from within the race, they seem to me infinitely more valuable and significant. I have sometimes fancied that perhaps the negroes *thought* black, and *felt* black: that they were racially so utterly alien and distinct from ourselves that there never could be common intellectual and emotional ground between us, and that whatever eternity might do to reconcile us, the end of time would find us far asunder as ever. But this little book, has given me pause in my speculation. Here in the artistic effect at least, is white thinking and white feeling in a black man, and perhaps the human unity, and not the race unity, is the precious thing, the divine thing, after all. God hath made of one blood all nations of men: perhaps the proof of this saying is to appear in the arts, and our hostilities and prejudices are to vanish in them.

Here in Howells we find suggestions of imperatives for the cultural renaissance that Du Bois would outline in the *Crisis* just fifteen years later. Here in Howells we find the premise that would assume a shape in the fiction of a "New Negro." Here we find the sustained apocalyptic notion of the Negro arts, about which Carl Van

Vechten and James Weldon Johnson would correspond at length. Here we find the supposition, elaborated on at length by Du Bois and even William Stanley Braithwaite, by Langston Hughes and Claude McKay, that, while blacks and whites are in essence different, that difference can be mediated through the media of art. The Black Christ would be a poetaster. And the physical blackness to which would testify critics as unalike as I. A. Richards at Cambridge and Max Eastman at the *Liberator*, referred to in separate prefaces to different volumes by Claude McKay in 1919 and 1922, would resurface in subtler form in Allen Tate and Irving Howe. Tate and Howe, the ideological counterparts of Richards and Eastman, would in 1950 and 1963 reassert a metaphysical blackness to which they were somehow privy, Tate's New Critical "extrinsic" fallacies notwithstanding. Yet if we see this remarkably persistent idea become Don L. Lee's pernicious preface to Gwendolyn Brooks's *Report from Part One*, we can perhaps take comfort in Black Arts poet Larry Neal's sensitive authenticating preface to Kimberly Benston's subtle readings of the plays of Imamu Baraka. As blind men, we have traced the circle.

III

The confusion of realms, of art with propaganda, plagued the Harlem Renaissance in the 1920s. A critical determination—a mutation of principles set in motion by Matthew Arnold's *Culture and Anarchy*, simplified thirty years later into Booker Washington's "toothbrush and bar of soap," and derived from Victorian notions of "uplifting" spiritual and moral ideals that separated the savage (noble or not) from the realm of culture and the civilized mind—meant that only certain literary treatments of black people could escape community censure. The race against Social Darwinism and the psychological remnants of slavery meant that each piece of creative writing became a political statement. Each particular manifestation served as a polemic: "Another bombshell fired into the heart of bourgeois culture," as *The World Tomorrow* editorialized in 1921. "The black writer," said Richard Wright, "approached the critical community dressed in knee pants of servility, curtseying to show that the Negro was not inferior, that he was human, and that he had a gift comparable to other men."[17] As early as 1921, W. E. B. Du Bois wrote of this in the *Crisis*:

> Negro art is today plowing a difficult row. We want everything that is said about us to tell of the best and highest and noblest in us. We insist that our Art and Propaganda be one. We fear that evil in us will be called racial, while in others it is viewed as individual. We fear that our shortcomings are not merely human.[18]

And, as late as 1925, even as sedate an observer as Heywood Broun argued that only through Art would the Negro gain his freedom: "A supremely great negro artist," he told the New York Urban League, "who could catch the imagination of the world, would do more than any other agency to remove the disabilities against which the negro now labors."[19] Further, Broun remarked that this artist-redeemer could come at any time, and he asked his audience to remain silent for ten seconds to imagine that coming! Ambiguity in language, then, and "feelings that are general" (argued for as early as 1861 by Frances E. W. Harper) garnered hostility and suspicion from the critical minority; ambiguity was a threat to "knowing the lines." The results on a growing black literature were disastrous, these perorations themselves dubious. Black literature came to be seen as a cultural artifact (the product of unique historical forces) or as a document and witness to the political and emotional tendencies of the Negro victim of white racism. Literary theory became the application of a social attitude.

By the apex of the Harlem Renaissance, then, certain latent assumptions about the relationships between "art" and "life" had become prescriptive canon. In 1925, Du Bois outlined what he called "the social compulsion" of black literature, built as it was, he contended, on "the sorrow and strain inherent in American slavery, on the difficulties that sprang from emancipation, on the feelings of revenge, despair, aspiration, and hatred which arose as the Negro struggled and fought his way upward."[20] Further, he made formal the mechanistic distinction between "method" and "content," the same distinction that allowed James Weldon Johnson to declare with glee that, sixty years after slavery, all that separated the black poet from the white was "mere technique"! Structure, by now, was atomized: "Form" was merely a surface for a reflection of the world, the "world" here being an attitude toward race; form was a repository for the disposal of ideas; message was not only meaning but value; poetic discourse was taken to be literal, or once removed; language lost its capacity to be metaphorical in the eyes of the critic; the poem approached the essay, with referents immediately perceivable; literalness precluded the view of life as "allegorical"; and black critics forgot that writers approached things through words, not the other way around. The functional and didactic aspects of formal discourse assumed primacy in normative analysis. The confusion of realms was complete: The critic became social reformer, and literature became an instrument for the social and ethical betterment of the black man.

So, while certain rather conservative notions of art and culture wove themselves into F. R. Leavis' *Scrutiny* in Cambridge in the 1930s, blacks borrowed whole the Marxist notion of base and superstructure and made of it, if you will, race and superstructure. Here, as in Wright's "Blueprint for Negro Literature," for example, "race" in American society was held to determine the social relations that determine consciousness, which, in turn, determines actual ideas and creative works. "In the beginning was the deed," said Trotsky in an attack on the Formalists; now, the deed was *black*.

This notion of race and superstructure became, during the 1940s and 1950s, in one form or another the mode of criticism of black literature. As would be expected, critics urged the supremacy of one extraliterary idea after another, as Ralph Ellison "challenged" Richard Wright on one front and James Baldwin on another. But race as the controlling "mechanism" in critical theory reached its zenith of influence and mystification when LeRoi Jones metamorphosed himself into Imamu Baraka, and his daishiki-clad, Swahili-named "harbari gani" disciples "discovered" they were black.

With virtually no exceptions, black critics employed "blackness"-as-theme to forward one argument or another for the amelioration of the Afro-American's social dilemma. Yet, the critical activity altered little, whether that "message" was integration or whether it was militant separation. Message was the medium; message reigned supreme; form became a mere convenience or, worse, a contrivance.

The commonplace observation that black literature with very few exceptions has failed to match pace with a sublime black music stems in large measure from this concern with statement. Black music, by definition, could never utilize the schism between form and content, because of the nature of music. Black music, alone of the black arts, has developed free of the imperative, the compulsion, to make an explicit political statement. Black musicians, of course, had no choice: Music groups shape masses of nonrepresentational material into significant form; it is the audible embodiment of form. All this, however, requires a specific mastery of technique, which cannot be separated from "poetic insight." There could be no "knowing the lines" in the creation of black music, especially since the Afro-American listening audience had such a refined and critical aesthetic sense. Thus, Afro-America has a tradition of masters, from Bessie Smith through John Coltrane, unequalled, perhaps, in all of modern music. In literature, however, we have no similar development, no sustained poignancy in writing. In poetry, where the command of language is indispensable if only because poetry thickens language and thus draws attention from its referential aspect, we have seen the growth of what the poet Ted Joans calls the "Hand-Grenade" poets,[21] who concern themselves with futile attempts to make poetry preach, which poetry is not capable of doing so well. And the glorification of this poetry (especially the glorification of Baraka and Don Lee's largely insipid rhetoric), in which we feel the unrelenting vise of the poet's grip upon our shoulders, has become the principal activity of the "New Black" critic. The suppositions on which this theory of criticism rests are best explicated through a close reading of four texts that, conveniently, treat poetry, literary history, and the novel.

Stephen Henderson's *Understanding the New Black Poetry* is the first attempt at a quasi-formalistic analysis of black poetry.[22] It is of the utmost importance to the history of race and superstructure criticism because it attempts to map a black poetic landscape, identifying inductively those unique cultural artifacts that critics, "especially white critics," have "widely misunderstood, misinterpreted, and undervalued for a variety of reasons—aesthetic, cultural, and political." Henderson's work is seminal insofar as he is concerned with the uses of language, but in the course of his study he succumbs to the old idea of advancing specific ideological prerequisites.

Henderson readily admits his bias: He equates aesthetics and ethics. "Ultimately," he says, "the 'beautiful' is bound up with the truth of a people's history, as they perceive it themselves." This absolute of truth Henderson defines in his fifth definition of what "Black poetry is chiefly": "Poetry by any identifiably Black person whose ideological stance vis-à-vis the history and aspirations of his people since slavery [is] adjudged by them to be 'correct.' " Hence, an ideal of truth, which exists in fact for the black poet to "find," is a "Black" truth. And "Black" is integral to the poetic equation, since "if there is such a commodity as 'blackness' in literature (and I assume that there is), it should somehow be found in concentrated or in residual form in the poetry."

Had Henderson elaborated on "residual form" in literary language, measured formally, structurally, or linguistically, he would have revolutionized black literary criticism and brought it into the twentieth century. But his theory of poetry is based on three sometimes jumbled "broad categories" that allow the black critic to define "norms" of "blackness." The first of these is an oversimplified conception of "theme": "that which is spoken of, whether the specific subject matter, the emotional response to it, or its intellectual formulation." The second is "structure," by which Henderson intends "chiefly some aspect of the poem such as diction, rhythm, figurative language, which goes into the total makeup." (At times, he notes, "I use the word in an extended sense to include what is usually called genre.") His third critical tool, the scale by which he measures the "commodity" he calls "Blackness," is "saturation." He means by this "several things, chiefly the communication of 'Blackness' and fidelity to the observed or intuited truth of the Black Experience in the United States."

Now, the textual critic has problems with Henderson's schema not only because it represents an artificial segmentation of poetic structure (which can never, in fact, be discussed as if one element existed independently of the rest) but also because that same schema tends to be defined in terms of itself, and hence is tautological. Henderson defines "theme," for example, as "perhaps the simplest and most apparent" of the three. By theme, however, he means a poem's paraphrased level of "meaning." To illustrate this, he contrasts a George Moses Horton quatrain with a couplet from Countée Cullen. The "ambiguity" of the former lines, he concludes, defined for us insofar as "it might evoke a sympathetic tear from the eye of a white [Jewish] New York professor meditating upon his people's enslavement in ancient Egypt, does make it a less precise kind of ['Black'] statement than Cullen's, because in the latter the irony cannot be appreciated without understanding the actual historical debasement of the African psyche in America." Thus, the principal corollary to the theorem of "black themes" is that the closer a "theme" approaches cultural exclusivity, the closer it comes to a higher "fidelity." Moreover, he allows himself to say, had Shakespeare's Sonnet 130 "been written by an African at Elizabeth's court, would not the thematic meaning change?" That leap of logic is difficult to comprehend, for a poem is above all atemporal and must cohere at a symbolic level, if it coheres at all. In some fairness to Stephen Henderson, much of the poetry from which he is extracting his theory is used in the language game of giving information. Stephen Henderson's problem is, in short, the "poetry" prompting his theory; he has only followed that poetry's lead and in that way left himself open to Wittgenstein's remonstration: "Do not forget that a poem, even though it is composed in the language of information, is not used in the language of giving information."

The most promising of Henderson's categories is "structure," and yet it is perhaps the most disappointing. By "structure," he means that "Black poetry is most distinctively Black" whenever "it derives its form from two basic sources, Black speech and Black music." At first glance, this idea seems exciting, since it implies a unique, almost intangible use of language peculiar to Afro-Americans. On this one could build, nay one must build, that elusive "Black Aesthetic" the race and superstructure critics have sought in vain. But Henderson's understanding of speech as referent is not linguistic; he means a literal referent to nonpoetic discourse and makes, unfortunately, no allowances for the manner in which poetic discourse differs from prosaic discourse or "instances" of speech. He provides us with an elaborate and complicated taxonomy of referents to speech and to music, yet unaccountably ignores the fact that the "meaning" of a word in a poem is derived from its context within that poem, as well as from its context in our actual, historical consciousness. But a taxonomy is a tool to knowledge, not knowledge itself. The use of language is not a stockpile of referents or forms, but an activity.

Henderson remarks with some astonishment that "Black speech in this country" is remarkable in that "certain words and constructions seem to carry an inordinate charge of emotional and psychological weight." These, he calls "mascon" words, borrowing the acronym from N.A.S.A., where it is employed to describe a "massive concentration" of matter beneath the lunar surface. What he is describing, of course, is not unique to black poetic discourse; it is common to all poetic uses of language in all literatures and is what helps to create ambiguity, paradox, and irony. This, of course, has been stated adamantly by the "practical critics" since the 1920s—those same "New" critics Henderson disparages. These usages, however, do make black poetic language unique and argue strongly for a compilation of a "black" dictionary of discrete examples of specific signification, where "Black English" departs from "general usage." They are not, I am afraid, found only in the language of black folks in this country. Had Henderson identified some criteria by which we could define an oral tradition in terms of the "grammar" it superimposes on nonliterary discourse, then shown how this comes to bear on literary discourse, and further shown such "grammars" to be distinctly black, then his contribution to our understanding of language and literature would have been no mean thing indeed.

His final category, "saturation," is the ultimate tautology: Poetry is "Black" when it communicates "Blackness." The more a text is "saturated," the "Blacker" the text. One imagines a daishiki-clad Dionysus weighing the saturated, mascon lines of Countée Cullen against those of Langston Hughes, as Paul Laurence Dunbar and Jean Toomer are silhouetted by the flames of Nigger Hell. The blacker the berry, the sweeter the juice.

Should it appear that I have belabored my reading of this theory, it is not because it is the weakest of the three theories of black literature. In fact, as I will try to show, Henderson's is by far the most imaginative of the three and has, at least, touched on areas critical to the explication of black literature. His examination of form is the first in a "race and superstructure" study and will most certainly give birth to more systematic and less polemical studies. But the notions implicit and explicit in Henderson's ideas are shared by Houston A. Baker, Jr., and Addison Gayle as well.

In the first essay of *Long Black Song, Essays in Black American Literature and Culture*,[23] Houston Baker proffers the considerable claim that black culture, particularly as "measured" through black folklore and literature, serves in intent and effect as an "index" of repudiation not only of white Western values and white Western culture but of white Western literature as well. "In fact," he writes, "it is to a great extent the culture theorizing of whites that has made for a separate and distinctive black American culture. That is to say, one index of the distinctiveness of black American culture is the extent to which it repudiates the culture theorizing of the white Western world." Repudiation, he continues, "is characteristic of black American folklore; and this is one of the most important factors in setting black American literature apart from white American literature." Further, "Black folklore and the black American literary tradition that grew out of it reflect a culture that is distinctive both of white American and of African culture, and therefore neither can provide valid standards by which black American folklore and literature may be judged." A text becomes "blacker," it surely follows, to the extent that it serves as an "index of repudiation." Here we find an ironic response to Harold Bloom's *Anxiety of Influence* in what we could characterize as an "Animosity of Influence."

Baker discusses this notion of influence between black and white American culture at length. "Call it black, Afro-American, Negro," he writes, "the fact remains that there is a fundamental, qualitative difference between it and white American culture." The bases of this "fundamental, qualitative difference" are, first, that "black American culture was developed orally or musically for many years"; second, that "black American culture was never characterized by a collective ethos"; and, finally, that "one of [black American culture's] most salient characteristics is an index of repudiation." Oral, collectivistic, and repudiative, he concludes, "each of these aspects helps to distinguish black American culture from white American culture."

These tenets suggest that there must be an arbitrary relation between a sign and its referent; indeed, that all meaning is culture-bound. Yet what we find elaborated here are rather oversimplified, basically political, criteria, which are difficult to verify, partly because they are not subject to verbal analysis (that is, can this sense of difference be measured through the literary uses of language?), partly because the thematic analytical tools employed seem to be useful primarily for black naturalist novels or for the mere paraphrasing of poetry, partly because the matter of influence is almost certainly too subtle to be traced in other than close textual readings, and finally because his three bases of "fundamental, qualitative difference" seem to me too unqualified. There is so much more to Jean Toomer, Zora Hurston, Langston Hughes, Sterling Brown, Ralph Ellison, Leon Forrest, Ishmael Reed, Toni Morrison, and Alice Walker than their "index of repudiation," whatever that is. Besides, at least Toomer, Ellison, and Reed have taken care to discuss the complex matter of literary ancestry, in print and without. It is one of the ironies of the study of black literature that our critical activity is, almost by definition, a comparative one, since many of our writers seem to be influenced by Western masters, writing in English as well as outside it, as they are by indigenous, Afro-American oral or even written forms. That the base for our literature is an oral one is certainly true; but, as Millman Parry and Albert Lord have amply demonstrated,[24] so is the base of the whole of Western literature, commencing with the Hebrews and the Greeks. Nevertheless, Baker does not suggest any critical tools for explicating the oral tradition in our literature, such as the formulaic studies so common to the subject. Nor does he suggest how folklore is displaced in literature, even though, like Henderson, he does see it at "the base of the black literary tradition." That black culture is characterized by a collective ethos most definitely demands some qualification, since our history, literary and extraliterary, often turns on a tension, a dialectic, between the private perceptions of the individual and the white public perceptions of that same individual.

Nor does Baker's thought-provoking contention of the deprivation of the American frontier stand to prove this thesis:

> When the black American reads Frederick Jackson Turner's *The Frontier in American History*, he feels no regret over the end of the Western frontier. To black America, *frontier* is an alien word; for, in essence, all frontiers established by the white psyche have been closed to the black man. Heretofore, later, few have been willing to look steadily at America's past and acknowledge that the black man was denied his part in the frontier and his share of the nation's wealth.

Yet, at least Ralph Ellison has written extensively on the fact of the frontier (physical and metaphysical) and its centrality to his sensibility. Further, Ishmael Reed uses the frontier again and again as a central trope.

Part of the problem here is not only Baker's exclusive use of thematic analysis to attempt to delineate a literary tradition but also his implicit stance that literature functions primarily as a cultural artifact, as a repository for ideas. "It is impossible to comprehend the process of transcribing cultural values," he says (in his essay "Racial Wisdom and Richard Wright's *Native Son*"), "without an understanding of the changes that have characterized both the culture as a whole and the lives of its individual transcribers." Further, "Black American literature has a human immediacy and a pointed relevance which are obscured by the overingenious methods of the New Criticism, or any other school that attempts to talk of works of art as though they had no creators or of sociohistorical factors as though they did not filter through the lives of individual human beings." Here we find the implicit thesis in *Long Black Song*, the rather Herderian notion of literature as primarily the reflection of ideas and experiences outside of it. It is not, of course, that literature is unrelated to culture, to other disciplines, or even to other arts; it is not that words and usage somehow exist in a vacuum or that the literary work of art occupies an ideal or reified, privileged status, the province of some elite cult of culture. It is just that the literary work of art is a system of signs that may be decoded with various methods, all of which assume the fundamental unity of form and content and all of which demand close reading. Only the rare critic, such as Michael G. Cooke, Nathan A. Scott, or Sherley Williams, has made of thematic analysis the subtle tool that intelligent, sensitive reading requires. Baker seems to be reading black texts in a particular fashion for other than literary purposes. In *Singers of Daybreak: Studies in Black American Literature*,[25] he suggests these purposes. "What lies behind the neglect of black American literature," he asserts, "is not a supportable body of critical criteria that includes a meaningful definition of *utile* and *dulce*, but a refusal to believe that blacks possess the humanity requisite for the production of works of art." Baker finds himself shadowboxing with the ghostly judgments of Jefferson on Phillis Wheatley and Ignatius Sancho; his blows are often telling, but his opponent's feint is deadly.

If Houston Baker's criticism teaches us more about his attitude toward being black in white America than it does about black literature, then Addison Gayle, Jr.'s *The Way of the New World* teaches us even less.[26] Gayle makes no bones about his premises:

> To evaluate the life and culture of black people, it is necessary that one live the black experience in a world where substance is more important than form, where the social takes precedence over the aesthetic, where each act, gesture, and movement is political, and where continual rebellion separates the insane from the sane, the robot from the revolutionary.

Gayle's view of America, and of the critic, means that he can base his "literary judgments" on some measure of ideology; and he does. Regrettably, he accuses James Baldwin of "ignorance of black culture." His praise of John A. Williams seems predicated on an affinity of ideology. He praises John Killens' *And Then We Heard the Thunder* because he "creates no images of racial degradation." For him, the "central flaw" of the protagonist in *Invisible Man* ("an otherwise superb novel") is "attributable more to Ellison's political beliefs than to artistic deficiency." In Addison Gayle, we see race and superstructure criticism at its basest: Not only is his approach to literature deterministic, but his treatment of the critical activity itself demonstrates an alarming disrespect for qualified scholarship.

What is wrong with employing race and superstructure as critical premises? This critical activity sees language and literature as reflections of "Blackness." It postulates "Blackness" as an entity, rather than as metaphor or sign. Thus, the notion of a signified *black* element in literature retains a certain impressiveness insofar as it exists in some mystical kingdom halfway between a fusion of psychology and religion on the one hand and the Platonic Theory of Ideas on the other. Reflections of this "Blackness" are more or less "literary" according to the ideological posture of the critic. Content is primary over form and indeed is either divorced completely from form, in terms of genesis and normative value, or else is merely facilitated by form as a means to an end. In this criticism, rhetorical value judgments are closely related to social values. This method reconstitutes "message," when what is demanded is a deconstruction of a literary system.

The race and superstructure critics would have us believe that the function of the critic is to achieve an intimate knowledge of a literary text by re-creating it from the inside: Critical thought must become the thought criticized. Only a black man, therefore, can think (hence, rethink) a "black thought." Consciousness is predetermined by culture and color. These critics, in Todorov's phrase, "re-create" a text either by repeating its own words in their own order or by establishing a relationship between the work and some system of ideas outside it. They leave no room for the idea of literature as a system. Normative judgments stem from how readily a text yields its secrets or is made to confess falsely on the rack of "black reality."

Yet, perceptions of reality are in no sense absolute; reality is a function of our senses. Writers present models of reality, rather than a description of it, though obviously the two may be related variously. In fact, fiction often contributes to cognition by providing models that highlight the nature of things precisely by their failure to coincide with it. Such, certainly, is the case in science fiction. Too, the thematic studies so common to black criticism suffer from a similar fallacy. Themes in poetry, for instance, are rarely reducible to literal statement; literature approaches its richest development when its "presentational symbolism" (as opposed by Suzanne Langer to its "literal discourse") cannot be reduced to the form of a literal proposition. Passages for creative discourse cannot be excerpted and their "meaning" presented independent of context. For Ralph Ellison, invisibility was not a matter of being seen but rather a refusal to run the gamut of one's own humanity.

"Blackness," as these critics understand it, is weak in just the decisive area where practical criticism is strong: in its capacity to give precise accounts of actual consciousness, rather than a scheme or a generalization. And the reason for the corresponding weakness is not difficult to find: It lies in the received formula of race and superstructure, which converts far too readily to the simple repetition of ideology. The critical method, then, is reductionist; literary discourse is described mechanically by classifications that find their ultimate meaning and significance somewhere else.

Ultimately, black literature is a verbal art like other verbal arts. "Blackness" is not a material object or an event but a metaphor; it does not have an "essence" as such but is defined by a network of relations that form a particular aesthetic unity. Even the slave narratives offer the text as a world, as a system of signs. The black writer is the point of consciousness of his language. If he does embody a "Black Aesthetic," then it can be measured not by "content," but by a complex structure of meanings. The correspondence of content between a writer and his world is less significant to literary criticism than is a correspondence of organization or structure, for a relation of content may be a mere reflection of prescriptive, scriptural canon, such as those argued for by Baker, Gayle, and Henderson. A relation of structure, on the other hand, according to Raymond Williams, "can show us the organizing principles by which a particular view of the world, and from that the coherence of the social group which maintains it, really operates in consciousness."[27] If there is a relationship between social and literary "facts," it must be found here.

To paraphrase René Wellek, black literature may well be dark, mysterious, and foreboding, but it is certainly not beyond careful scrutiny and fuller understanding. The tendency toward thematic criticism implies a marked inferiority complex: Afraid that our literature cannot sustain sophisticated verbal analysis, we view it from the surface merely and treat it as if it were a Chinese lantern with an elaborately wrought surface, parchment-thin but full of hot air. Black critics have enjoyed such freedom in their "discipline" that we find ourselves with no discipline at all. The present set of preconceptions has brought readers and writers into a blind alley. Literary images, even black ones, are combinations of words, not of absolute or fixed things. The tendency of black criticism toward an ideological absolutism, with its attendant

Inquisition, must come to an end. A literary text is a linguistic event; its explication must be an activity of close textual analysis. Simply because Bigger Thomas kills Mary Dalton and tosses her body into a furnace, *Native Son* is not necessarily a "blacker" novel than *Invisible Man*—Gayle notwithstanding. We urgently need to direct our attention to the nature of black figurative language, to the nature of black narrative forms, to the history and theory of Afro-American literary criticism, to the fundamental unity and form of content, and to the arbitrary relations between the sign and its referent. Finally, we must begin to understand the nature of intertextuality, that is, the nonthematic manner by which texts—poems and novels—respond to other texts. All cats may be black at night, but not to other cats.

NOTES

1. Briton Hammon, *A Narrative of the Uncommon Sufferings and Surprising Deliverance of Briton Hammon, a Negro Man* (Boston, 1760).

2. William Wimsatt and Cleanth Brooks, *Literary Criticism: A Short History* (New York: Knopf, 1969), p. 366.

3. Phillis Wheatley, *Poems* (Philadelphia: A. Bell, 1773), p. vii.

4. *De la littérature des nègres, ou recherches sur leurs facultés intellectuelles, leurs qualités morales, et leur littérature* (Paris: Maradan, 1808), p. 140.

5. Eugene Parker Chase, *Our Revolutionary Forefathers, The Letters of François, Marquis de Barbé-Marbois during His Residence in the United States as Secretary of the French Legation, 1779–1884* (New York: Duffield, 1929), pp. 84–85.

6. *Letters of the Late Ignatius Sancho, an African* (London: J. Nichols and C. Dilly, 1783), p. vi.

7. *Notes on the State of Virginia* (London: Stockdale, 1787), Bk. II, p. 196.

8. Jefferson, p. 196.

9. Wheatley, p. vii.

10. Wheatley, p. vi.

11. Sancho, p. vi.

12. Sancho, pp. xiv–xvi.

13. Charles Bail, *Fifty Years in Chains; Or, The Life of an American Slave* (New York: H. Dayton, 1858), p. 3.

14. Introd., *My Bondage and My Freedom* (New York: Miller, Orton, and Mulligan, 1855), pp. xvii–xxxi.

15. *New York Tribune*, 10 June 1845, p. 1, col. 1. Rpt. In *Liberator*, 30 May 1845, p. 97.

16. "Majors and Minors," *North American Review*, 27 June 1896, p. 630.

17. "Blueprint for Negro Writing," *New Challenge*, 2 (Fall 1937), 55.

18. "Negro Art," *Crisis*, 22 (June 1921), 55–56.

19. *New York Times*, 26 Jan. 1925, p. 3.

20. "The Social Origins of American Negro Art," *Modern Quarterly*, 3 (Autumn 1925), 53.

21. "Ted Joans: Tri-Continental Poet," *Transition*, 48 (1975), 4–12.

22. *Understanding the New Black Poetry* (New York: Morrow, 1972). All subsequent quotes are from pp. 3–69.

23. *Long Black Song* (Charlottesville: Univ. of Virginia Press, 1972).

24. Lord, *The Singer of Tales* (Cambridge: Harvard Univ. Press, 1960).

25. *Singers of Daybreak: Studies in Black American Literature* (Washington, D.C.: Howard Univ. Press, 1974).

26. *The Way of the New World* (Garden City, N.Y.: Doubleday, 1975).

27. "Base and Superstructure in Marxist Cultural Theory," *New Left Review*, 82 (Dec., 1973), 3–16.

3

The 1980s

Poststructuralism and the Growth of Feminist Theory

19 New Directions for Black Feminist Criticism

Deborah E. McDowell

(1980)

"What is commonly called literary history," writes Louise Bernikow, "is actually a record of choices. Which writers have survived their times and which have not depends upon who noticed them and chose to record their notice."[1] Women writers have fallen victim to arbitrary selection. Their writings have been "patronized, slighted, and misunderstood by a cultural establishment operating according to male norms out of male perceptions."[2] Both literary history's "sins of omission" and literary criticism's inaccurate and partisan judgments of women writers have come under attack since the early 1970s by feminist critics.[3] To date, no one has formulated a precise or complete definition of feminist criticism, but since its inception, its theorists and practitioners have agreed that it is a "corrective, unmasking the omissions and distortions of the past—the errors of a literary critical tradition that arise from and reflect a culture creature, perpetuated, and dominated by men."[4]

These early theorists and practitioners of feminist literary criticism were largely white females who, wittingly or not, perpetrated against the Black woman writer the same exclusive practices they so vehemently decried in white male scholars. Seeing the experiences of white women, particularly white middle-class women, as normative, white female scholars proceeded blindly to exclude the work of Black women writers from literary anthologies and critical studies. Among the most flagrant examples of this chauvinism is Patricia Meyer Spacks's *The Female Imagination*. In a weak defense of her book's exclusive focus on women in the Anglo-American literary tradition, Spacks quotes Phyllis Chesler (a white female psychologist): "I have no theory to offer of Third World female psychology in America. . . . As a white woman, I'm reluctant and unable to construct theories about experiences I haven't had."[5] But, as Alice Walker observes, "Spacks never lived in nineteenth-century Yorkshire, so why theorize about the Brontës?"[6]

Not only have Black women writers been "disenfranchised" from critical works by

167

white women scholars on the "female tradition," but they have also been frequently excised from those on the Afro-American literary tradition by Black scholars, most of whom are males. For example, Robert Stepto's *From Behind the Veil: A Study of Afro-American Narrative* purports to be "a history . . . of the historical consciousness of an Afro-American art form—namely, the Afro-American written narrative."[7] Yet, Black women writers are conspicuously absent from the table of contents. Though Stepto does have a token two-page discussion of Zora Neale Hurston's *Their Eyes Were Watching God* in which he refers to it as a "seminal narrative in Afro-American letters,"[8] he did not feel that the novel merited its own chapter or the thorough analysis accorded the other works he discusses.

When Black women writers are neither ignored altogether nor merely given honorable mention, they are critically misunderstood and summarily dismissed. In *The Negro Novel in America*, for example, Robert Bone's reading of Jessie Fauset's novels is both partisan and superficial and might explain the reasons Fauset remains obscure. Bone argues that Fauset is the foremost member of the "Rear Guard" of writers "who lagged behind," clinging to established literary traditions. The "Rear Guard" drew their source material from the Negro middle class in their efforts "to orient Negro art toward white opinion," and "to apprise educated whites of the existence of respectable Negroes." Bone adds that Fauset's emphasis on the Black middle class results in novels that are "uniformly sophomoric, trivial and dull."[9]

While David Littlejohn praises Black fiction since 1940, he denigrates the work of Fauset and Nella Larsen. He maintains that "the newer writers are obviously writing as men, for men," and are avoiding the "very close and steamy" writing that is the result of "any subculture's taking itself too seriously, defining the world and its values exclusively in the terms of its own restrictive norms and concerns."[10] This "phallic criticism,"[11] to use Mary Ellman's term, is based on masculine-centered values and definitions. It has dominated the criticism of Black women writers and has done much to guarantee that most would be, in Alice Walker's words, "casually pilloried and consigned to a sneering oblivion."[12]

Suffice it to say that the critical community has not favored Black women writers. The recognition among Black female critics and writers that white women, white men, and Black men consider their experiences as normative and Black women's experiences as deviant has given rise to Black feminist criticism. Much as in white feminist criticism, the critical postulates of Black women's literature are only skeletally defined. Although there is no concrete definition of Black feminist criticism, a handful of Black female scholars have begun the necessary enterprise of resurrecting forgotten Black women writers and revising misinformed critical opinions of them. Justifiably enraged by the critical establishment's neglect and mishandling of Black women writers, these critics are calling for, in the words of Barbara Smith, "nonhostile and perceptive analysis of works written by persons outside the 'mainstream' of white/male cultural rule."[13]

Despite the urgency and timeliness of the enterprise, however, no substantial body of Black feminist criticism—either in theory or practice—exists, a fact which might be explained partially by our limited access to and control of the media.[14] Another explanation for the paucity of Black feminist criticism, notes Barbara Smith, is the lack of a "developed body of Black feminist political theory whose assumptions could be used in the study of Black women's art."

Despite the strained circumstances under which Black feminist critics labor, a few committed Black female scholars have broken necessary ground. For the remainder of this essay I would like to focus on selected writings of Black feminist critics, discussing their strengths and weaknesses and suggesting new directions toward which the criticism might move and pitfalls that it might avoid.

Unfortunately, Black feminist scholarship has been decidedly more practical than theoretical, and the theories developed thus far have often lacked sophistication and have been marred by slogans, rhetoric, and idealism. The articles that attempt to apply these theoretical tenets often lack precision and detail. These limitations are not without reason. As Dorin Schumacher observes, "the feminist critic has few philosophical shelters, pillars, or guideposts," and thus "feminist criticism is fraught with intellectual and professional risks, offering more opportunity for creativity, yet greater possibility of errors."[15]

The earliest theoretical statement on Black feminist criticism is Barbara Smith's "Toward a Black Feminist Criticism." Though its importance as a groundbreaking piece of scholarship cannot be denied, it suffers from lack of precision and detail. In justifying the need for a Black feminist aesthetic, Smith argues that "a Black feminist approach to literature that embodies the realization that the politics of sex as well as the politics of race and class are crucially interlocking factors in the works of Black women writers is an absolute necessity." Until such an approach exists, she continues, "we will not even know what these writers mean."

Smith points out that "thematically, stylistically, aesthetically, and conceptually Black women writers manifest common approaches to the act of creating literature as a direct result of the specific political, social, and economic experience they have been obliged to share." She offers, as an example, the incorporation of rootworking, herbal medicine, conjure, and midwifery in the stories of Zora Neale Hurston, Margaret Walker, Toni Morrison, and Alice Walker. While these folk elements certainly do appear in the work of the writers, they also appear in the works of certain Black male writers, a fact that Smith omits. If Black women writers use these elements differently from Black male writers, such a distinction must be made before one can effectively articulate the basis of a Black feminist aesthetic.

Smith maintains further that Zora Neale Hurston, Margaret Walker, Toni Morrison, and Alice Walker use a "specifically black female language to express their own and their characters' thoughts," but she fails to describe or to provide examples of this unique language. Of course, we have come recently to acknowledge that "many of our habits of language usage are sex-derived, sex-associated, and/or sex-distinctive," that "the ways in which men and women internalize and manipulate language" are undeniably sex-related.[16] But this realization in itself simply paves the way for further investigation that can begin by exploring some critical questions. For example, is there a monolithic Black female language? Do Black female high school dropouts, welfare mothers, college graduates, and Ph.D.s share a common language?

Are there regional variations in this common language? Further, some Black male critics have tried to describe the uniquely "Black linguistic elegance"[17] that characterizes Black poetry. Are there noticeable differences between the languages of Black females and Black males? These and other questions must be addressed with precision if current feminist terminology is to function beyond mere critical jargon.

Smith turns from her discussion of the commonalities among Black women writers to describe the nature of her critical enterprise. "Black feminist criticism would by definition be highly innovative," she maintains. "Applied to a particular work [it] can overturn previous assumptions about [the work] and expose for the first time its actual dimensions." Smith then proceeds to demonstrate this critical postulate by interpreting Toni Morrison's *Sula* as a lesbian novel, an interpretation she believes is maintained in "the emotions expressed, in the definition of female character and in the way that the politics of heterosexuality are portrayed." Smith vacillates between arguing forthrightly for the validity of her interpretation and recanting or overqualifying it in a way that undercuts her own credibility.

According to Smith, "if in a woman writer's work a sentence refuses to do what it is supposed to do, if there are strong images of women and if there is a refusal to be linear, the result is innately lesbian literature." She adds, "because of Morrison's consistently critical stance toward the heterosexual institutions of male-female relationships, marriage, and the family," *Sula* works as a lesbian novel. This definition of lesbianism is vague and imprecise; it subsumes far more Black women writers, particularly contemporary ones, than not into the canon of Lesbian writers. For example, Jessie Fauset, Nella Larsen, and Zora Neale Hurston all criticize major socializing institutions, as do Gwendolyn Brooks, Alice Walker, and Toni Cade Bambara. Further, if we apply Smith's definition of lesbianism, there are probably a few Black male writers who qualify as well. All of this is to say that Smith has simultaneously oversimplified and obscured the issue of lesbianism. Obviously aware of the delicacy of her position, she interjects that "the very meaning of lesbianism is being expanded in literature." Unfortunately, her qualification does not strengthen her argument. One of the major tasks ahead of Black feminist critics who write from a lesbian perspective, then, is to define lesbianism and lesbian literature precisely. Until they can offer a definition which is not vacuous, their attempts to distinguish Black lesbian writers from those who are not will be hindered.[18]

Even as I call for firmer definitions of lesbianism and lesbian literature, I question whether a lesbian aesthetic is not finally a reductive approach to the study of Black women's literature which possibly ignores other equally important aspects of the literature. For example, reading *Sula* solely from a lesbian perspective overlooks the novel's density and complexity, its skillful blend of folklore, omens, and dreams, its metaphorical and symbolic richness. Although I do not quarrel with Smith's appeal for fresher, more innovative approaches to Black women's literature, I suspect that "innovative" analysis is pressed to the service of an individual political persuasion. One's personal and political presuppositions enter into one's critical judgments. Nevertheless, we should heed Annette Kolodny's warning for feminist critics to be wary of reading literature as though it were polemic . . . If when using literary materials to make what is essentially a political point, we find ourselves virtually rewriting a text, ignoring certain aspects of plot or characterization, or over-simplifying the action to fit our "political" thesis, then we are neither practicing an honest criticism nor saying anything useful about the nature of art (or about the art of political persuasion, for that matter).[19]

Alerting feminist critics to the dangers of political ideology yoked with aesthetic judgment is not synonymous with denying that feminist criticism is a valid and necessary cultural and political enterprise. Indeed, it is both possible and useful to translate ideological positions into aesthetic ones, but if the criticism is to be responsible, the two must be balanced.

Because it is a cultural and political enterprise, feminist critics, in the main, believe that their criticism can effect social change. Smith certainly argues for socially relevant criticism in her conclusion that "Black feminist criticism would owe its existence to a Black feminist movement while at the same time contributing ideas that women in the movement could use." This is an exciting idea in itself, but we should ask: What ideas, specifically, would Black feminist criticism contribute to the movement? Further, even though the proposition of a fruitful relationship between political activism and the academy is an interesting (and necessary) one, I doubt its feasibility. I am not sure that either in theory or in practice Black feminist criticism will be able to alter significantly circumstances that have led to the oppression of Black women. Moreover, as Lillian Robinson pointedly remarks, there is no assurance that feminist aesthetics "will be productive of a vision of art or of social relations that is of the slightest use to the masses of women, or even one that acknowledges the existence and struggle of such women."[20] I agree with Robinson that "ideological criticism must take place in the context of a political movement that can put it to work. The revolution is simply not going to be made by literary journals."[21] I should say that I am not arguing a defeatist position with respect to the social and political uses to which feminist criticism can be put. Just as it is both possible and useful to translate ideological positions into aesthetic ones, it must likewise be possible and useful to translate aesthetic positions into the machinery for social change.

Despite the shortcomings of Smith's article, she raises critical issues on which Black feminist critics can build. There are many tasks ahead of these critics, not the least of which is to attempt to formulate some clear definitions of what Black feminist criticism is. I use the term here simply to refer to Black female critics who analyze the works of Black female writers from a feminist or political perspective. But the term can also apply to any criticism written by a Black woman regardless of her subject or perspective—a book written by a male from a feminist or political perspective, a book written by a Black woman or about Black women authors in general, or any writings by women.[22]

In addition to defining the methodology, Black feminist critics need to determine the extent to which their criticism intersects with that of white feminist critics.

Barbara Smith and others have rightfully challenged white women scholars to become more accountable to Black and Third World women writers, but will that require white women to use a different set of critical tools when studying Black women writers? Are white women's theories predicated upon culturally specific values and assumptions? Andrea Benton Rushing has attempted to answer these questions in her series of articles on images of Black women in literature. She maintains, for example, that critical categories of women, based on analyses of white women characters, are Euro-American in derivation and hence inappropriate to a consideration of Black women characters.[23] Such distinctions are necessary and, if held uniformly, can materially alter the shape of Black feminist scholarship.

Regardless of which theoretical framework Black feminist critics choose, they must have an informed handle on Black literature and Black culture in general. Such a grounding can give this scholarship more texture and completeness and perhaps prevent some of the problems that have had a vitiating effect on the criticism.

This footing in Black history and culture serves as a basis for the study of the literature. Termed "contextual" by theoreticians, this approach is often frowned upon if not dismissed entirely by critics who insist exclusively upon textual and linguistic analysis. Its limitations notwithstanding, I firmly believe that the contextual approach to Black women's literature exposes the conditions under which literature is produced, published, and reviewed. This approach is not only useful but necessary to Black feminist critics.

To those working with Black women writers prior to 1940, the contextual approach is especially useful. In researching Jessie Fauset, Nella Larsen, and Zora Neale Hurston, for example, it is useful to determine what the prevalent attitudes about Black women were during the time that they wrote. There is much information in the Black "little" magazines published during the Harlem Renaissance. An examination of *The Messenger*, for instance, reveals that the dominant social attitudes about Black women were strikingly consistent with traditional middle-class expectations of women. *The Messenger* ran a monthly symposium for some time entitled "Negro Womanhood's Greatest Needs." While a few female contributors stressed the importance of women being equal to men socially, professionally, and economically, the majority emphasized that a woman's place was in the home. It was her duty "to cling to the home [since] great men and women evolve from the environment of the hearthstone."[24]

One of the most startling entries came from a woman who wrote:

The New Negro Woman, with her head erect and spirit undaunted, is resolutely marching forward, ever conscious of her historic and noble mission of doing her bit toward the liberation of her people in particular and the human race in general. Upon her shoulders rests the big task to create and keep alive, in the breast of black men, a holy and consuming passion to break with the slave traditions of the past; to spurn and overcome the fatal, insidious inferiority complex of the present, which . . . bobs up ever and anon, to arrest the progress of the New Negro Manhood Movement; and to fight with increasing vigor, with dauntless courage, unrelenting zeal and intelligent vision for the attainment of the stature of a full man, a free race and a new world.[25]

Not only does the contributor charge the Black woman with a formidable task, but she also sees her solely in relation to Black men.

This information enhances our understanding of what Fauset, Larsen, and Hurston confronted in attempting to offer alternative images of Black women. Moreover, it helps to clarify certain textual problems and ambiguities of their work. Though Fauset and Hurston, for example, explored feminist concerns, they leaned toward ambivalence. Fauset especially is alternately forthright and cagey, radical and traditional, on issues that confront women. Her first novel, *There Is Confusion* (1924), is flawed by an unanticipated and abrupt reversal in characterization that brings the central female character more in line with a feminine norm. Similarly, in her last novel, *Seraph on the Suwanee* (1948), Zora Neale Hurston depicts a female character who shows promise for growth and change, for a departure from the conventional expectations of womanhood, but who in the end apotheosizes marriage, motherhood, and domestic servitude.

These two examples alone clearly capture the tension between social pressure and artistic integrity which is felt, to some extent, by all women writers. As Tillie Olsen points out, the fear of reprisal from the publishing and critical arenas is a looming obstacle to the woman writer's coming into her own authentic voice. "Fear—the need to please, to be safe—in the literary realm too. Founded fear. Power is still in the hands of men. Power of validation, publication, approval, reputation . . ."[26]

While insisting on the validity, usefulness, and necessity of contextual approaches to Black women's literature, the Black feminist critic must not ignore the importance of rigorous textual analysis. I am aware of many feminist critics' stubborn resistance to the critical methodology handed down by white men. Although the resistance is certainly politically consistent and logical, I agree with Annette Kolodny that feminist criticism would be "short-sighted if it summarily rejected all the inherited tools of critical analysis simply because they are male and western." We should, rather, salvage what we find useful in past methodologies, reject what we do not, and, where necessary, move toward "inventing new methods of analysis."[27] Particularly useful is Lillian Robinson's suggestion that "a radical kind of textual criticism . . . could usefully study the way the texture of sentences, choice of metaphors, patterns of exposition and narrative relate to [feminist] ideology."[28]

This rigorous textual analysis involves, as Barbara Smith recommends, isolating as many thematic, stylistic, and linguistic commonalities among Black women writers as possible. Among contemporary Black female novelists, the thematic parallels are legion. In Alice Walker and Toni Morrison, for example, the theme of the thwarted female artist figures prominently.[29] Pauline Breedlove in Morrison's *The Bluest Eye*, for example, is obsessed with ordering things:

Jars on shelves at canning, peach pits on the step, sticks, stones, leaves. . . . Whatever portable plurality she found, she organized into neat lines, according to their size, shape or gradations of color. . . . she missed without knowing what she missed—paints and crayons.[30]

Similarly, Eva Peace in *Sula* is forever ordering the pleats in her dress. And Sula's strange and destructive behavior is explained as "the consequence of an idle imagination."

> Had she paints, clay, or knew the discipline of the dance, or strings; had she anything to engage her tremendous curiosity and her gift for metaphor, she might have exchanged the restlessness and preoccupation with whim for an activity that provided her with all she yearned for. And like any artist with no form, she became dangerous.[31]

Likewise, Meridian's mother in Alice Walker's novel *Meridian* makes artificial flowers and prayer pillows too small for kneeling.

The use of "clothing as iconography"[32] is central to writings by Black women. For example, in one of Jessie Fauset's early short stories, "The Sleeper Wakes" (1920), Amy, the protagonist, is associated with pink clothing (suggesting innocence and immaturity) while she is blinded by fairy-tale notions of love and marriage. However, after she declares her independence from her racist and sexist husband, Amy no longer wears pink. The imagery of clothing is abundant in Zora Neale Hurston's *Their Eyes Were Watching God* (1937). Janie's apron, her silks and satins, her head scarves, and finally her overalls all symbolize various stages of her journey from captivity to liberation. Finally, in Alice Walker's *Meridian*, Meridian's railroad cap and dungarees are emblems of her rejection of conventional images and expectations of womanhood.

A final theme that recurs in the novels of Black women writers is the motif of the journey. Though one can also find this same motif in the works of Black male writers, they do not use it in the same way as do Black female writers.[33] For example, the journey of the Black male character in works by Black men takes him underground. It is a "descent into the underworld,"[34] and is primarily political and social in its implications. Ralph Ellison's *Invisible Man*, Imamu Amiri Baraka's *The System of Dante's Hell*, and Richard Wright's "The Man Who Lived Underground" exemplify this quest. The Black female's journey, on the other hand, though at times touching the political and social, is basically a personal and psychological journey. The female character in the works of Black women is in a state of becoming "part of an evolutionary spiral, moving from victimization to consciousness."[35] The heroines in Zora Neale Hurston's *Their Eyes Were Watching God*, in Alice Walker's *Meridian*, and in Toni Cade Bambara's *The Salt Eaters* are emblematic of this distinction.

Even though isolating such thematic and imagistic commonalities should continue to be one of the Black feminist critic's most urgent tasks, she should beware of generalizing on the basis of too few examples. If one argues authoritatively for the existence of a Black female "consciousness" or "vision" or "literary tradition," one must be sure that the parallels found recur with enough consistency to support these generalizations. Further, Black feminist critics should not become obsessed in searching for common themes and images in Black women's works. As I pointed out earlier, investigating the question of "female" language is critical and may well be among the most challenging jobs awaiting the Black feminist critic. The growing body of research on gender-specific uses of language might aid these critics. In fact, wherever possible, feminist critics should draw on the scholarship of feminists in other disciplines.

An equally challenging and necessary task ahead of the Black feminist critic is a thoroughgoing examination of the works of Black male writers. In her introduction to *Midnight Birds*, Mary Helen Washington argues for the importance of giving Black women writers their due first:

> Black women are searching for a specific language, specific symbols, specific images with which to record their lives, and, even though they can claim a rightful place in the Afro-American tradition and the feminist tradition of women writers, it is also clear that, for purposes of liberation, black women writers will first insist on their own name, their own space.[36]

I likewise believe that the immediate concern of Black feminist critics must be to develop a fuller understanding of Black women writers who have not received the critical attention Black male writers have. Yet, I cannot advocate indefinitely such a separatist position, for the countless thematic, stylistic, and imagistic parallels between Black male and female writers must be examined. Black feminist critics should explore these parallels in an effort to determine the ways in which these commonalities are manifested differently in Black women's writing and the ways in which they coincide with writings by Black men.

Of course, there are feminist critics who are already examining Black male writers, but much of the scholarship has been limited to discussions of the negative images of Black women found in the works of these authors.[37] Although this scholarship served an important function in pioneering Black feminist critics, it has virtually run its course. Feminist critics run the risk of plunging their work into cliché and triviality if they continue merely to focus on how Black men treat Black women in literature. Hortense Spillers offers a more sophisticated approach to this issue in her discussion of the power of language and myth in female relations in James Baldwin's *If Beale Street Could Talk*. One of Spillers's most cogent points is that "woman-freedom, or its negation, is tied to the assertions of myth, or ways of saying things."[38]

Black feminist criticism is a knotty issue, and while I have attempted to describe it, to call for clearer definitions of its methodology, to offer warnings of its limitations, I await the day when Black feminist criticism will expand to embrace other modes of critical inquiry. In other words, I am philosophically opposed to what Annis Pratt calls "methodolatry." Wole Soyinka has offered one of the most cogent defenses against critical absolutism. He explains:

> The danger which a literary ideology poses is the act of consecration—and of course excommunication. Thanks to the tendency of the modern consumer-mind to facilitate digestion by putting in strict categories what are essentially fluid operations of the creative mind upon social and natural phenomena, the formulation of a literary ideol-

ogy tends to congeal sooner or later into instant capsules which, administered also to the writer, may end by asphyxiating the creative process.[39]

Whether Black feminist criticism will or should remain a separatist enterprise is a debatable point. Black feminist critics ought to move from this issue to consider the specific language of Black women's literature, to describe the ways Black women writers employ literary devices in a distinct way, and to compare the way Black women writers create their own mythic structures. If they focus on these and other pertinent issues, Black feminist critics will have laid the cornerstone for a sound, thorough articulation of the Black feminist aesthetic.

NOTES

1. Louise Bernikow, *The World Split Open: Four Centuries of Women Poets in England and America, 1552–1950* (New York, 1974), 3.

2. William Morgan, "Feminism and Literary Study: A Reply to Annette Kolodny," *Critical Inquiry*, 2 (Summer 1976), B11.

3. The year 1970 was the beginning of the Modern Language Association's Commission on the Status of Women, which offered panels and workshops that were feminist in approach.

4. Statement by Barbara Desmarais quoted in Annis Pratt, "The New Feminist Criticisms: Exploring the History of the New Space," in *Beyond Intellectual Sexism: A New Woman, A New Reality*, ed. Joan I. Roberts (New York, 1976), 176.

5. Patricia Meyer Spacks. *The Female Imagination* (New York, 1976), 5. Ellen Moers, *Literary Women: The Great Writers* (Garden City, N.Y., 1977) is another example of what Alice Walker terms "white female chauvinism."

6. Alice Walker, "One Child of One's Own—An Essay on Creativity," *Ms.*, August 1979, 50.

7. Robert Stepto, *From Behind the Veil: A Study of Afro-American Narrative* (Urbana, Ill., 1979). x. Other sexist critical works include Donald B. Gibson, ed., *Five Black Writers* (New York, 1970), a collection of essays on Wright, Ellison, Baldwin, Hughes, and Leroi Jones, and Jean Wagner, *Black Poets of the United States: From Paul Lawrence Dunbar to Langston Hughes*, trans. Kenneth Douglas (Urbana, Ill., 1973).

8. Stepto, *From Behind the Veil*, 166.

9. Robert Bone, *The Negro Novel in America* (1958: reprint, New Haven, Conn., 1972), 97, 101.

10. David Littlejohn, *Black on White: A Critical Survey of Writing by American Negroes* (New York, 1966), 48–49.

11. Ellman's concept of "phallic criticism" is discussed in a chapter of the same name in her *Thinking About Women* (New York, 1968), 28–54.

12. Introduction to *Zora Neale Hurston: A Literary Biography* by Robert Hemenway (Urbana, Ill., 1976), xiv. Although Walker makes this observation specifically about Hurston, it is one that can apply to a number of Black women writers.

13. Barbara Smith, "Toward a Black Feminist Criticism," *Black American Literature Forum* 14 (1980): 411–12.

14. See Evelyn Hammonds, "Toward a Black Feminist Aesthetic," *Sojourner*, October 1980, 7, for a discussion of the limitations on Black feminist critics. She correctly points out that

Black feminist critics "have no newspapers, no mass-marketed magazines or journals that are explicitly oriented toward the involvement of women of color in the feminist movement."

15. Dorin Schumacher. "Subjectives: A Theory of the Critical Process," in *Feminist Literary Criticism: Explorations in Theory*, ed. Josephine Donovan (Lexington, Kent. 1979), 34.

16. Annette Kolodny, "The Feminist as Literary Critic," Critical Response, *Critical Inquiry*, 2 (Summer 1976), 824–25. See also Cheris Kramer, Barrie Thorne, and Nancy Henley, "Perspectives on Language and Communication," *Signs*, 3 (Spring 1978), 638–51, and Nelly Farman, "The Study of Women and Language: Comment on Vol. 3. no. 3," *Signs*, 4 (Fall 1978), 152–85.

17. Stephen Henderson, *Understanding the New Black Poetry: Black Speech and Black Music as Poetic References* (New York, 1973), 31–46.

18. Some attempts have been made to define or at least discuss lesbianism. See Adrienne Rich's two essays, "It is the Lesbian in Us . . ." and "The Meaning of Our Love for Woman is What We Have," in *On Lies, Secrets and Silence* (New York, 1979), 199–202 and 223–30, respectively. See also Bertha Harris's "*What We Mean to Say*: Notes Toward Defining the Nature of Lesbian Literature," *Heresies*, 1 (Fall 1977), 5–8, and Blanche Cook's " 'Women Alone Stir My imagination': Lesbianism and the Cultural Tradition," *Signs*, 4 (Sumner 1979): 718–39. Also, at least one bibliography of Black lesbian writers has been compiled. See Ann Allen Shockley's "The Black Lesbian in American Literature: An Overview," *Conditions. Five*, 2 (Fall 1979):133–42.

19. Annette Kolodny, "Some Notes on Defining a 'Feminist Literary Criticism,' " *Critical Inquiry*, 2 (Fall 1975), 90.

20. Lillian S. Robinson, "Working Women Writing," *Sex, Class, and Culture* (Bloomington, Ind., 1978), 226.

21. Robinson, "The Critical Task," *Sex, Class, and Culture*, 52.

22. I am borrowing here from Kolodny, who makes similar statements in "Some Notes on Defining a 'Feminist Literary Criticism,' " 75.

23. Andrea Benton Rushing, "Images of Black Women in Afro-American Poetry," in *The Afro-American Woman: Struggles and Images*, ed. Sharon Harley and Rosalyn Terborg-Penn (Port Washington, N.Y., 1978), 74–84. She argues that few of the stereotypic traits which Mary Ellman describes in *Thinking About Women* "seem appropriate to Afro-American images of black women." See also her "Images of Black Women in Modern African Poetry: An Overview," in *Sturdy Black Bridges: Visions of Black Women in Literature*, ed. Roseann P. Bell et al. (New York, 1979), 18–24. Rushing argues similarly that Mary Ann Ferguson's categories of women (the submissive wife, the mother angel or "mom," the woman on a pedestal, for example) cannot be applied to Black women characters, whose cultural imperatives are different from white women's.

24. *The Messenger*, 9 (April 1927), 109.

25. *The Messenger*, 5 (July 1923), 757.

26. Tillie Olsen, *Silences* (New York, 1978), 257.

27. Kolodny, "Some Notes on Defining a 'Feminist Literary Criticism,' " 89.

28. Lillian S. Robinson, "Dwelling in Decencies: Radical Criticism and Feminist Perspectives," in *Feminist Criticism*, ed. Cheryl Brown and Karen Olsen (Metuchen, N.J., 1978), 34.

29. For a discussion of Toni Morrison's frustrated female artists see Renita Weems, "Artists Without Art Form: A Look at One Black Woman's World of Unrevered Black Women," *Conditions: Five*, 2 (Fall 1979), 48–58. See also Alice Walker's classic essay, "In Search of Our Mothers' Gardens" for a discussion of Black women's creativity in general.

30. Toni Morrison, *The Bluest Eye* (New York, 1970), 88–89.

31. Toni Morrison, *Sula* (New York, 1980), 105.

32. Kolodny, "Some Notes on Defining a 'Feminist Literary Criticism,' " 86.

33. In an NEH Summer Seminar at Yale University in the summer of 1980, Carolyn Naylor of Santa Clara University suggested this to me.

34. For a discussion of this idea see Michael G. Cooke, "The Descent into the Underworld and Modern Black Fiction," *Iowa Review*, 5 (Fall 1974), 72–90.

35. Mary Helen Washington, *Midnight Birds: Stories of Contemporary Black Women Writers* (Garden City, N.Y., 1980), 43.

36. Ibid., xvii.

37. See Saundra Towns, "The Black Woman as Whore: Genesis of the Myth," *The Black Position* 3 (1974), 39–59, and Sylvia Keady, "Richard Wright's Women Characters and Inequality," *Black American Literature Forum* 10 (1976), 124–28, for example.

38. Hostense Spillers, "The Politics of Intimacy: A Discussion," in Bell et al., eds., *Sturdy Black Bridges*, 88.

39. Wole Soyinka, *Myth, Literature and the African World* (London, 1976), 61.

20 | Generational Shifts and the Recent Criticism of Afro-American Literature

Houston A. Baker, Jr.

(1981)

I

There exist any number of possible ways to describe changes that have occurred in Afro-American literary criticism during the past four decades. If one assumes a philosophical orientation, one can trace a movement from democratic pluralism ("integrationist poetics") through romantic Marxism (the "Black Aesthetic") to a version of Aristotelian metaphysics (the "Reconstruction of Instruction"). From another perspective, one can describe the ascendant class interests that have characterized Afro-America since World War II, forcing scholars, in one instance, to assess Afro-American expressive culture at a mass level and, in another instance, to engage in a kind of critical "professionalism" that seems contrary to mass interests. One can survey, on yet another level, transformations in the recent criticism of Afro-American literature from a perspective in the philosophy of science; from this vantage point, one can explore conceptual, or "paradigm," changes that have marked the critical enterprise in recent years. These various levels of analysis can be combined, I think, in the notion of the "generational shift."

A "generational shift" can be defined as an ideologically motivated movement overseen by young or newly-emergent intellectuals who are dedicated to refuting the work of their intellectual predecessors and to establishing a new framework of intellectual inquiry. The effective component of such shifts is described by Lewis Feuer: "Every birth or revival of an ideology is borne by a new generational wave: in its experience, each such new intellectual generation feels everything is being born anew, that the past is meaningless, or irrelevant, or nonexistent."[1] The new generation's break with the past is normally signaled by its adoption of what the philosopher of science Thomas S. Kuhn (to whose work I shall return later) designates a

179

new "paradigm"; i.e., a new set of guiding assumptions that unifies the intellectual community.[2]

In the recent criticism of Afro-American literature, there have been two distinct generational shifts. Both have involved ideological and aesthetic reorientations, and both have been accompanied by shifts in literary-critical and literary-theoretical paradigms. The first such shift occurred during the mid-1960s. It led to the displacement of what might be described as integrationist poetics and gave birth to a new object of scholarly investigation.

II

The dominant critical perspective on Afro-American literature during the late 1950s and early 1960s might be called the poetics of integrationism. Richard Wright's essay "The Literature of the Negro in the United States," which appears in his 1957 collection entitled *White Man, Listen!*, offers an illustration of integrationist poetics.[3] Wright optimistically predicts that Afro-American literature may soon be indistinguishable from the mainstream of American arts and letters. The basis for his optimism is the Supreme Court's decision in *Brown* vs. *Topeka Board of Education* (1954), in which the Court ruled that the doctrine "separate but equal" was inherently unequal. According to Wright, this ruling ensures a future "equality" in the experiences of black and white Americans, and this equality of *social* experience will translate in the literary domain as a homogeneity of represented experience (pp. 103–105). When Afro-American writers have achieved such equality and homogeneity, they will stand at one with the majority culture—in a relationship that Wright terms "entity" (p. 72).

But the foregoing stipulations apply only to what Wright calls the "Narcissistic Level"—i.e., the self-consciously literate level—of Afro-American culture (pp. 84–85). At the folk, or mass, level the relationship between Afro-American and the majority culture has always been one of "identity" (as in "the black person's quest for identity"), or separateness (p. 72). And though Wright argues that the self-consciously literate products of Afro-America that signify a division between cultures (e.g., "protest" poems and novels) may disappear relatively quickly under the influence of the Brown decision, he is not so optimistic with regard to the "Forms of Things Unknown" (p. 83)—i.e., the expressive products of the black American masses. For blues, jazz, work songs, and verbal forms such as folktales, boasts, toasts, and dozens are functions of the black masses' relationship of "identity" with the mainstream culture. They signal, that is to say, an absence of equality and represent a *sensualization* of the masses' ongoing suffering (p. 83). They are, according to Wright, improvisational forms filled "with a content wrung from a bleak and barren environment, an environment that stung, crushed, all but killed" (p. 84). Only when the "Forms of Things Unknown" have disappeared altogether, or when conditions have been realized that enable them to be raised to a level of self-conscious art, will one be able to argue that an egalitarian ideal has been achieved in American life and art. The only course leading to such a positive goal, Wright implies, is momentous social action like that represented by the 1954 Supreme Court decision.

Hence, the black spokesman who champions a poetics of integrationism is constantly in search of social indicators (such as the Brown decision) that signal a democratic pluralism in American life. The implicit goal of this philosophical orientation is a raceless, classless community of men and women living in perfect harmony (p. 105). The integrationist critic, as Wright demonstrates, founds his predictions of a future, homogeneous body of American creative expression on such social evidence as the Emancipation Proclamation, Constitutional amendments, Supreme Court decisions, or any one of many other documented claims that suggest that America is moving toward a pluralistic ideal. The tone that such critics adopt is always one of optimism.

Arthur P. Davis offers a striking example of an Afro-American critic who has repeatedly sought to discover evidence to support his arguments that a oneness of all Americans and a harmonious merger of disparate forms of American creative expression are impending American social realities. What seems implicit in Davis's critical formulations is a call for Afro-American writers to speed the emergence of such realities by offering genuine, artistic contributions to the kind of classless, raceless literature that he and other integrationist critics assume will carry the future. An injunction of this type can be inferred, for example, from the 1941 "Introduction" to *The Negro Caravan*, the influential anthology of Afro-American expression that Davis coedited with Sterling Brown and Ulysses Lee:

> The editors . . . do not believe that the expression "Negro literature" is an accurate one, and in spite of its convenient brevity, they have avoided using it. "Negro literature" has no application if it means *structural peculiarity*, or a Negro school of writing. The Negro writes in the forms evolved in English and American literature. . . . The editors consider Negro writers to be American writers, and literature by American Negroes to be a segment of American literature. . . . The chief cause for objection to the term is that "Negro literature" is too easily placed by certain critics, white and Negro, in an alcove apart. The next step is a double standard of judgment, which in dangerous for the future of Negro writers. (My italics)[4]

In the 1950s and 1960s, Davis continued to champion the poetics implicit in such earlier work as *The Negro Caravan*. His essay "Integration and Race Literature," which he presented to the first conference of Afro-American writers sponsored by the American Society of African Culture in 1959, states:

> The course of Negro American literature has been highlighted by a series of social and political crises over the Negro's position in America. The Abolition Movement, the Civil War, Reconstruction, World War I, and the riot-lynching period of the twenties all radically influenced Negro writing. Each crisis in turn produced a new tradition in our literature; and as each crisis has passed, the Negro writer has dropped the social tradition which the occasion demanded and moved towards the mainstream of American literature. The integration controversy is another crisis, and from it we hope that

the Negro will move permanently into full participation in American life—social, economic, political, and literary.[5]

The stirring drama implied here of black writers finding their way through various "little" traditions to the glory of the "great" mainstream is a function of Davis's solid faith in American pluralistic ideals. He regards history and society from a specific philosophical and ideological standpoint: Afro-Americans and their expressive traditions, like other minority cultures, have always moved unceasingly toward a unity with American majority culture. He thus predicts—like Wright—the eventual disappearance of social conditions that produce literary works of art that are identifiable (in terms of "structural peculiarity") as "Negro" or "Afro-American" literature.

Wright and Davis represent a generation whose philosophy, ideology, and attendant poetics support the vanishing of Afro-American literature qua Afro-American literature. I shall examine this proposition at greater length in the next section. At this point, I simply want to suggest that the consequences of this generational position for literary-critical axiology can be inferred from the "Introduction" to *The Negro Caravan*. The editors of that work assert: "They [Afro-American writers] must ask that their books be judged as books, without sentimental allowances. In their own defense they must demand a single standard of criticism" (p. 7). This assertion suggests that black writers should construct their works in ways that make them acceptable in the sight of those who mold a "single standard of criticism" in America. These standard bearers were for many years, however, a small, exclusive community of individuals labelled by black spokesmen of the sixties as the "white, literary-critical establishment." And only a poetics buttressed by a philosophical viewpoint that augured the eventual unification of all talented creative men and women as judges could have prompted such able spokesmen as Wright, Brown, and Davis to consider that works of Afro-American literature and verbal art be subjected to a "single standard" of American literary-critical judgment.

III

The generational shift that displaced the integrationist poetics just described brought forth a group of intellectuals most clearly distinguished from its predecessors by its different ideological and philosophical posture vis-à-vis American egalitarian ideals. After the arrests, bombings, and assassinations that comprised the white South's reaction to non-violent, direct-action protests by hundreds of thousands of civil rights workers from the late fifties to the mid-sixties, it was difficult for even the most committed optimist to feel that integration was an impending American social reality.[6] Rather than searching for documentary evidence and the indelible faith necessary to argue for an undemonstrated American egalitarianism, the emerging generation set itself the task of analyzing the nature, aims, ends, and arts of those hundreds of thousands of their own people who were assaulting America's manifest structures of exclusion.

The Afro-American masses demonstrated through their violent acts ("urban riots") in Harlem, Watts, and other communities throughout the nation that they were intent on black social and political sovereignty in America. Their acts signaled the birth of a new ideology, one that received its proper name in 1966,[7] when Stokely Carmichael designated it "Black Power":

> [Black Power] is a call for black people in this country to unite, to recognize their heritage, to build a sense of community. It is a call for black people to begin to define their own goals, to lead their own organizations and to support those organizations. It is a call to reject the racist institutions and values of [American] society.[8]

This definition, drawn from Carmichael and Charles Hamilton's work entitled *Black Power*, expresses a clear imperative for Afro-Americans to focus their social efforts and political vision on their own self-interests. This particularity of Black Power— its sharp emphasis on the immediate concerns of Afro-Americans themselves—was a direct counterthrust by an emergent generation to the call for a general, raceless, classless community of men and women central to an earlier integrationist framework. The community that was of interest to the emergent generation was not a future generation of integrated Americans, but rather a present, vibrant group of men and women who constituted the heart of Afro-America. The Afro-American masses became, in the late sixties and early seventies, both subject and audience for the utterances of black political spokesmen moved by a new ideology.

The poetics accompanying the new ideological orientation were first suggested by Amiri Baraka (LeRoi Jones) in an address entitled "The Myth of a 'Negro Literature,' " which he presented to the American Society of American Culture in 1962:

> Where is the Negro-ness of a literature written in imitation of the meanest of social intelligences to be found in American culture, i.e., the white middle class? How can it even begin to express the emotional predicament of black Western men? Such a literature, even if its "characters" are black, takes on the emotional barrenness of its model, and the blackness of the characters is like the blackness of Al Jolson, an unconvincing device. It is like using black checkers instead of white. They are still checkers.[9]

At the self-consciously literate level of Afro-American expression, the passage implies, black spokesmen have deserted the genuine emotional referents and the authentic experiential categories of black life in America. The homogeneity between their representations of experience and those of the white mainstream are a cause for disgust rather than an occasion for rejoicing. Finally, the quoted passage implies that the enervating merger of black and white expression at the "Narcissistic" level (to use Wright's phrase) of Afro-American life is a result of the black writer's acceptance of a "single standard of criticism" molded by white America. Baraka, thus, inverts the literary-critical optimism and axiology of an earlier generation, rejecting entirely the notion that "Negro Literature" should not stand apart as a unique body of expression. It is precisely the desertion by black writers of those aspects of Afro-American life that foster the uniqueness and authenticity of black expression that Baraka condemns most severely in his essay.

But where, then, does one discover in Afro-America genuine reflections of the true emotional referents and experiential categories of black life if not in its self-consciously literate works of art? Like the more avowedly political spokesmen of his day, Baraka turned to the world of the masses, and there he discovered the "forms of things unknown" (Wright's designation for black, folk expressive forms):

> Negro music alone, because it drew its strengths and beauties out of the depth of the black man's soul, and because to a large extent its traditions could be carried on by the lowest classes of Negroes, has been able to survive the constant and willful dilutions of the black middle class. Blues and jazz have been the only consistent exhibitors of "Negritude" in formal American culture simply because the bearers of its tradition maintained their essential identities as Negroes; in no other art (and I will persist in calling Negro music Art) has this been possible. (P. 107)

In this statement, Baraka seems to parallel the Richard Wright of an earlier generation. But while Wright felt that the disappearance of the "forms of things unknown" would signal a positive stage in the integration of American life and art, Baraka established the Harlem Black Arts Repertory Theatre/School in 1965 as an enterprise devoted to the continuance, development, and strengthening of the "coon shout," blues, jazz, holler, and other expressive forms of the "lowest classes of Negroes."[10] He, and other artists who contributed to the establishment of the school, felt that the perpetuation of such forms would help give birth to a new black nation. Larry Neal, who worked with Baraka during the mid-sixties, delineates both the complementarity of the Black Arts and Black Power movements and the affective component of a generational shift in his often-quoted essay "The Black Arts Movement":

> Black Art is the aesthetic and spiritual sister of the Black Power concept. As such, it envisions an art that speaks directly to the needs and aspirations of Black America. In order to perform this task, the Black Arts Movement proposes a radical reordering of the western cultural aesthetic. It proposes a separate symbolism, mythology, critique, and iconology.[11]

The Black Arts Movement, therefore, like its ideological counterpart Black Power, was concerned with the articulation of experiences (and the satisfaction of audience demands) that found their essential character among the black urban masses. The guiding assumption of the movement was that if a literary-critical investigator looked to the characteristic musical and verbal forms of the masses, he would discover unique aspects of Afro-American creative expression—aspects of form and performance—that lay closest to the veritable emotional referents and experiential categories of Afro-American culture. The result of such critical investigations, according to Neal and other spokesmen such as Baraka and Addison Gayle, Jr. (to name but three prominent advocates for the Black Arts), would be the discovery of a "Black Aesthetic"—i.e., a distinctive code for the creation and evaluation of black art. From an assumed "structural peculiarity" of Afro-American expressive culture, the emergent generation of intellectuals proceeded to assert a *sui generis* tradition of Afro-American art and a unique "standard of criticism" suitable for its elucidation.

Stephen Henderson's essay entitled "The Forms of Things Unknown," which stands as the introduction to his anthology *Understanding the New Black Poetry*, offers one of the most suggestive illustrations of this discovery process at work.[12] Henderson's formulations mark a high point in the first generational shift in the recent criticism of Afro-American literature because he is a spokesman *par excellence* for what emerged from his generation as a new object of literary-critical and literary-theoretical investigation. Before turning to the specifics of his arguments, however, I want to focus for a moment on the work of Thomas Kuhn to clarify what I mean by a "new object" of investigation.

IV

In his work *The Structure of Scientific Revolutions*, Kuhn sets out to define the nature of a scientific "revolution," or shift in the fundamental ways in which the scientific community perceives and accounts for phenomena. He first postulates that the guiding construct in the practice of normal science is what he defines as the "paradigm"; i.e., a constellation of "beliefs, values, techniques and so on shared by the members of a given community."[13] He further defines a paradigm as the "universally recognized scientific achievements that for a time provide model problems and solutions to a community of practitioners [of normal science]" (p. viii). A paradigm, thus, sets the parameters of scholarly investigation, constraining both the boundaries of an investigator's perception and the degree of legitimacy attributed to various problems and methodologies. A forceful example of a scientific revolution and its enabling paradigm shift was the displacement of geocentricism by a Copernican cosmology. Kuhn writes: "The Copernicans who denied its traditional title 'planet' to the sun were not only learning what 'planet' meant or what the sun was. Instead, they were changing the meaning of 'planet' so that it could continue to make useful distinctions in a world where all celestial bodies, not just the sun, were seen differently from the way they had been seen before" (pp. 128–29).

The effects of this kind of paradigmatic shift on the assumptions and higher-order rules of a scholarly community are additionally clarified when Kuhn says:

> Led by a new paradigm, scientists adopt new instruments and look in new places. Even more important, during revolutions scientists see new and different things when looking with familiar instruments in places they have looked before. It is rather as if the professional community had been suddenly transported to another planet where *familiar objects are seen in a different light and are joined by unfamiliar ones as well* . . . paradigm changes . . . cause scientists to see the world of their research-engagement differently. In so far as their only recourse to that world is through what they see and do, we may want to say that after a revolution scientists are responding to a different world. (My italics, p. 111)

Kuhn cites as an experimental instance of such changes in perception the classic work of George M. Stratton. Stratton fitted his subjects with goggles that contained inverting lenses. Initially, these subjects saw the world upside down and existed in a state of extreme disorientation. Eventually, though, their entire visual field flipped over, and:

> Thereafter, objects are again seen as they had been before the goggles were put on. The assimilation of a previously anomalous visual field . . . reacted upon and changed the field itself. Literally as well as metaphorically . . . [the subject] accustomed to inverting lenses . . . [underwent] a *revolutionary transformation of vision*. (My italics, p. 112)

In terms of the present discussion of Afro-American literary criticism, I want to suggest that Stephen Henderson and other Afro-American intellectuals of his generation fomented a change in the perceptual field of Afro-American literary study that amounted, finally, to a "revolutionary transformation" of literary-critical and literary-theoretical vision vis-à-vis black expressive culture. Before the mid-sixties scholars were led by an integrationist paradigm that permitted them to perceive as "literature" or "art" only those Afro-American expressive works that approached or conformed to the "single standard of criticism" advocated by the editors of *The Negro Caravan*. In adopting such a "standard," an integrationist poetics bound its perceptual field and constrained its domain of legitimate investigative problems to Afro-American expressive objects and events that came nearest this standard. Under the old paradigm, therefore, a scholar could not see that "Negro music" qua "Negro music" or "Negro Poetry" qua "Negro poetry" constituted art. For "Negro-ness" was viewed by the old paradigm as a condition (a set of properties of "structural peculiarities") that excluded such a phenomenon as "*Negro* poetry" from the artworld.[14] The integrationists held it as a first law that art was an American area of achievement in which race and class did not comprise significant variables. To discover, assert, or label the "Negro-ness" or "Blackness" of an expressive work as a fundamental condition of its "artistic-ness" was, thus, for the new generation to "flip over" the integrationist field of vision. And this revised perceptual orientation is precisely what Henderson and his contemporaries achieved. Their efforts made it possible for literary-critical and literary-theoretical investigators to see "familiar objects" in a different light and to include previously "unfamiliar" objects in an expanded (and sharply modified) American artworld. In "The Forms of Things Unknown," Henderson masterfully outlines the hypotheses, boundaries, and legitimate problems of the new paradigmatic framework called the "Black Aesthetic."

V

Henderson's assumption is that in literature there exists "such a commodity as 'blackness'" (p. 3). He further argues that this "commodity" should be most easily located in poetry "since poetry is the most concentrated and the most allusive of the verbal arts" (p. 3). Implicit in these statements is Henderson's claim that an enabling condition for art (and particularly for "poetry") in Afro-American culture is the possession of blackness by an expressive object or event. The ontological status—the very condition of being—of Afro-American poetic expression is, in fact, a function of this commodity of blackness. The most legitimate paradigmatic question that a literary-critical investigator or a literary theorist can pose, therefore, is: In what place and by what means does the commodity "blackness" achieve form and substance?

The title of Henderson's essay suggests the answer he provides to this question. He states that blackness must be defined, at a *structural* level of expressive objects and events, as an "interior dynamism" that derives its force from the "inner life" of the Afro-American folk (pp. 5–6). And he is quite explicit that what he intends by "inner life" is, in fact, the constellation of cultural values and beliefs that characterizes what the philosopher Albert Hofstadter calls a "reference public." Hofstadter writes:

> Predication of "good" . . . tends to lose meaningful direction when the public whose valuations are considered in judging the object is not specified. I do not see how we can hope to speak sensibly about the aesthetic goodness of objects unless we think of them in the context of reception and valuation by persons, the so-called "context of consumption." Properties by virtue of which we value objects aesthetically—e.g., beauty, grace, charm, the tragic, the comic, balance, proportion, expressive symbolism, versimilitude, propriety—always require some reference to the apprehending and valuing person. . . . Any public taken as the public referred to in a normative esthetic judgment I shall call the judgment's *reference public.* The reference public is the group whose appreciations or valuations are used as data on which to base the judgment. It is the group to which universality of appeal may or may not appertain.[15]

Henderson says that the existence of black poetry is a function of a black audience's concurrence that a particular verbal performance (whether written or oral) by some person of "known Black African ancestry" is, in fact, poetry (p. 7). The array of values and beliefs—the cultural codes—that allows a black reference public to make such a normative judgment constitutes the inner life of the folk. "Inner life," then—on the assumption that the operative codes of a culture are historically conditioned and are maintaned at a level of interacting cultural systems—is translated as "ethnic roots." Questions of the ontology and valuation of a black poem, according to Henderson, "can not be resolved without considering the ethnic roots of Black poetry, which I insist are ultimately understood only by Black people themselves" (pp. 7–8). What he seeks to establish, or to support, with this claim, I think, is a kind of cultural holism—an interconnectedness (temporally determined) of a cultural discourse—that can only be successfully apprehended through a set of theoretical concepts and critical categories arrived at by in-depth investigation of the fundamental expressive manifestations of a culture.

In order to achieve such apprehension, the literary investigator (like the cultural anthropologist) must go to the best available informants; i.e., to natives of the culture, or to the "reference public." "One must not consider the poem in isolation," writes Henderson, "but in relationship to the reader/audience, and the reader to the wider context of the phenomenon which we call, for the sake of convenience, the Black Experience" (p. 62). His tone approximates even more closely that of cultural anthropology in the following stipulations on literary-critical axiology:

[T]he recognition of Blackness in poetry is a value judgment which on certain levels and in certain instances, notably in matters of meanings that go beyond questions of structure and theme, must rest upon one's immersion in the totality of the Black Experience. It means that the ultimate criteria for critical evaluation must be found in the sources of the creation, that is, in the Black Community itself. (Pp. 65–66)

The notion that a conditioning cultural holism is a necessary consideration in the investigation of a culture's works of verbal art receives yet another designation that has anthropological parallels when Henderson talks of a "Soul Field." Field theory in anthropology stresses the continuous nature of conceptual structures that make up various areas, or "fields," of a culture, e.g., kinship or color terms and their attendant connotations or sense. For Henderson, the "Soul Field" of Afro-American culture is "the complex galaxy of personal, social, institutional, historical, religious, and myth-ical meanings that affect everything we say or do as Black people sharing a common heritage" (p. 41). In this definition, "meanings" is the operative term, and it situates the author's designation of "field" decisively within the realm of semantics. Hender-son's "Soul Field" is, thus, similar to J. Trier's *Sinnfeld*, or conceptual field; i.e., the area of a culture's linguistic system that contains the encyclopedia or mappings of various "senses" of lexical items drawn from the same culture's *Wortfeld*, or lexicon.[16]

The theoretical concepts and critical categories for analyzing black poetry that Henderson sets forth in "The Forms of Things Unknown" are coextensive with the case he makes for the holism and continuity of Afro-American culture. His three major categories are theme, structure, and saturation. And in dividing each category into analytic subsets, he never loses sight of the "inner life" of the folk, of that interconnected "field" of uniquely black meanings and values that he postulates as the essential determinants of these subsets. He, thus, seeks to ensure a relationship of identity between his own critical categories and the "real," experiential categories of Afro-American life. For example, he identifies "theme" with what he perceives as the *actual* guiding concern of the collective, evolving consciousness of Afro-America.

He finds that the most significant concern of that consciousness has always been "the idea of liberation" (p. 18) and suggests that the "old word, 'freedom,' " might be substituted for this phrase to denote the overriding theme (i.e., that which is "being spoken of") of Afro-American expressive culture. Hence, a "real" lexical category ("freedom") and its complex conceptual mappings in Afro-American culture are identified as one subset of the critical category "theme." Similarly, the actual speech and music of Afro-American culture and their various forms, techniques, devices, nuances, rules, and so on are identified as fundamental structural referents in the continuum of black expressive culture:

Structurally speaking . . . whenever Black poetry is most distinctively and effectively *Black*, it derives its form from two basic sources, Black speech and Black music. . . .

By Black speech I mean the speech of the majority of Black people in this country. . . .
This includes the techniques and timbres of the sermon and other forms of oratory, the
dozens, the rap, the signifying, and the oral folktale. . . . By Black music I mean essentially the vast fluid body of Black song—spirituals, shouts, jubilees, gospel songs, field
cries, blues, pop songs by Blacks, and, in addition, jazz (by whatever name one calls it)
and non-jazz by Black composers who *consciously* or *unconsciously* draw upon the
Black musical tradition. (Pp. 30–31)

Here, Henderson effectively delineates a continuum of Afro-American verbal and
musical expressive behavior that begins with everyday speech and popular music and
extends to works of "high art."

Finally, "saturation" is a category in harmony with the assumed uniqueness of both
the Afro-American *Sinnfeld* and *Wortfeld*. For Henderson insists that "saturation" is
a perceptual category that has to do with a distinctive semantics:

Certain words and constructions [e.g., *rock, jelly, jook*] seem to carry an inordinate
charge of emotional and psychological weight [in Afro-American culture], so that
whenever they are used they set all kinds of bells ringing, all kinds of synapses snapping, on all kinds of levels. . . . I call such words 'mascon' words. . . . to mean a *massive concentration of Black experiential energy* which powerfully affects the meaning
of Black speech, Black song, and Black poetry—if one, indeed, has to make such
distinctions. (P. 43)

From an assumed "particularity," wholeness, and continuity of Afro-American
culture—characteristics that manifest themselves most clearly among the Afro-
American folk or masses—Henderson, thus, moves to the articulation of theoretical
concepts and critical categories that provide what he calls "a way of speaking about
all kinds of Black poetry despite the kinds of questions that can be raised" (p. 10).
He proposes, in short, a theory to account for the continuity—the unity in theme,
structure, and semantics—of black speech, music, and poetry (both oral and written).
He refuses, from the outset, to follow a traditional literary-critical path; i.e., predi-
cating this continuity on history or chronology alone. Instead, he observes the contemporary scene in Afro-American poetry (i.e., the state of the art of black poetry in
the 1960s and early 1970s) and realizes that the oral tradition of the urban masses is
the dominant force shaping the work of Afro-American poets. From this modern
instantiation of the reciprocity between expressive folk culture and self-conscious,
literary expression, he proposes that all black "poetic" expression can be understood
in terms of such a reciprocal pattern. "Understanding" the "new black poetry" in its
relationship to black urban folk culture, therefore, provides direction and definition
in the larger enterprise of understanding the artistic codes—or the cultural system
that is "art"—in black American culture. A comprehension of the "forms of things
unknown" and the cultural anthropological assumptions that it presupposes lead to
the discovery of a unique artistic tradition, one embodying peculiar themes, structures, and meanings.

The "Black Aesthetic" signaled for Henderson and his contemporaries the codes that determine this tradition as well as the theoretical standpoint (one marked by appropriate categories) that would enable one to see, to "speak about," this tradition. And like all new paradigms, the "Black Aesthetic" had distinctive perceptual and semantic ramifications. It changed the meaning of both "black" and "aesthetic" in the American literary-critical universe of discourse so that these terms could continue to make "useful distinctions" in a world where works of Afro-American expressive art had come to be seen quite differently from the manner in which they were viewed by an older integrationist paradigm.

VI

Earlier, I referred to the philosophical orientation of the Black Aesthetic as romantic Marxism. Having discussed Henderson's work, perhaps I can now clarify this designation. For me, the fact that the aesthetics of the Black Arts movement were idealistically centered in the imagination of the black critical observer makes them "romantic."[17] This critical centrality of the Afro-American mind is illustrated by Henderson's assumption that "Blackness" is not a theoretical reification, but a reality, accessible only to those who can "imagine" in uniquely black ways. From this perspective, the word "understanding" in the title of his anthology is a sign for spiritual journey in which what the black imagination seizes upon as black must be black, whether it existed before or not.

The notion of a "reference public" gives way, therefore, at a lower level of the Black Aesthetic's argument, to a kind of impressionistic chauvinism. For it is, finally, *only* the black imagination that can experience blackness, in poetry, or in life. As a result, the creative and critical framework suggested by Henderson resembles, at times, a closed circle:

> [F]or one who is totally immersed, as it were, or saturated in the Black Experience the slightest formulation of the typical or true-to-life [Black] experience, whether positive or negative, is enough to bring on at least subliminal recognition [of the "formulation" of the experience as "Black"]. . . . I have tried to postulate a concept that would be useful in talking about what Black people feel is their distinctiveness, without being presumptuous enough to attempt a description or definition of it. This quality or condition of Black awareness I call *saturation*. I intend it as a sign, like the mathematical symbol *infinity*, or the term "Soul." It allows us to talk about the thing [a "distinctive" feeling of "Blackness"], even to some extent to use it, though we can't, thank God! ultimately abstract and analyze it: it must be experienced. (Pp. 63, 68)

"Saturation" also gives way, then, at a lower level of the argument to cultural xenophobia. Rather than an indicator for a *sui generis* semantics, it becomes a mysterious trait of consciousness. In "Saturation: Progress Report on a Theory of Black Poetry," an article that appeared two years after his anthology, Henderson comments on the critical reactions that his romantic specifications evoked:

Some people—critics, white and Black—have difficulty with this last standard [i.e., the critical standard of "intuition" for judging the successful rendering of "Black poetic structure"]. They call it mysterious, mystical, chauvinistic, and even (in a slightly different context) a "curious metaphysical argument" (Saunders Redding). I call it *saturation*. I authenticate it from personal experience. To those critics I say: Remember Keats did the same, proving poetic experience by his pulse and the "holiness of the imagination."[18]

But if Henderson's romanticism led him to chauvinistically posit an "intuitive sense," a "condition" of "Blackness" that can only be grasped by the "saturated" or "immersed" black imagination, it also led him to suggest the kind of higher-order, cultural-anthropological argument that I have extrapolated from his work and discussed in the preceding section. I think the romanticism of Henderson and his contemporaries—like that of romantics gone before who believed they were compelled to "create a system or be enslav'd by another Man's"—lay in their metaphysical rebelliousness, their willingness to postulate a positive and distinctive category of existence ("Blackness") and then to read the universe in terms of that category.[19] The predication of such a category was not only a radical political act designed to effect the liberation struggles of Afro-America, but also a bold critical act designed to break the interpretive monopoly on Afro-American expressive culture that had been held from time immemorial by a white, literary-critical establishment that set a "single standard of criticism":

> If the critic is half worth his salt, then he would attempt to describe what occurs in the poem and to *explain*—to the extent that it is possible—how the "action" takes place, i.e., how the elements of the work interact with one another to produce its effect. And if one of those elements is "Blackness"—as value, as theme, or as structure, especially the latter—then he is remiss in his duty if he does not attempt to deal with it in some logical, orderly manner.[20]

Given Henderson's arguments for the black person's own intuitive sense of experience as the only valid guide to the recognition of "Blackness" as an "element," it seems unlikely that many white critics would prove "worth their salt" vis-à-vis Afro-American literature and criticism. And there is a kind of implicit antinomianism in the following assertion from his essay "The Question of Form and Judgment in Contemporary Black American Poetry: 1962–1977": "Historically, the question of what constitutes a Black poem or how to judge one does not really come to a head until the 1960s and the promulgation of the Black Aesthetic in literature and the other arts. In a special sense . . . 'Black' poetry was invented in the 1960s along with the radicalization of the word 'Black' and the emergence of the Black Power philosophy."[21] Here, the faith that postulated "Blackness" as a distinctive category of existence is seen as the generative source of a new art, politics, and criticism nullifying the interpretive authority of a white, critical orthodoxy.

The rebelliousness that seemed to close the circle of Afro-American criticism to white participants, however, was not only romantic, it was also Marxist. Henderson and his contemporaries attempted to base their arguments for an Afro-American intuitive sense of "Blackness" on the notion that such a sense was a function of the continuity of Afro-American culture. The distinctive cultural circumstances that comprised the material bases of Afro-American culture—i.e., the means and instrumentalities of production, distribution, and consumption that marked the formation and growth of an African culture in America—were always seen by spokesmen for the Black Aesthetic as determinants of a consciousness that was distinctively "Black." And the most accurate reflection of the economics of slavery (and their subsequent forms) in the American economy was held to take place at a mass or folk level. Hence, the expressive forms of black folk consciousness were defined by Black Aestheticians as underdetermined by material circumstances that vary within a narrow range. To take up such forms is to find oneself involved with the "authentic" or basic (as in the "material base") categories of Afro-American existence. "Culture determines consciousness" became a watchword for the Black Aesthetic, and by "culture" its spokesmen meant a complex of material and expressive components that could only be discovered at a mass level of Afro-American experience. It was their emphasis on this level—an emphasis motivated by a paradoxical desire to ground an idealistic rebelliousness in a materialist reading of history—that led to a deepened scholarly interest during the sixties and early seventies in both Afro-American folklore and other black expressive forms that had long been (in Henderson's words) "under siege" by "white critical condescension and snobbery, and more recently, outright pathological ignorance and fear."[22] And through their investigation of the "forms of things unknown" in recent years, some white critics were able to reenter the critical circle.[23] They reentered, however, not as superordinate authorities, but as serious scholars working in harmony with some of the fundamental postulates of the Black Aesthetic.

There is also a more clichéd sense in which the Black Aesthetic was Marxist, and it finds its best illustration in the insistence by spokesmen for the new paradigm that expressive culture has a "social function." Black Aestheticians were quick to assert that works of verbal art have direct effects in the solution of social problems and in the shaping of social consciousness. The prescriptive formulations of a spokesman like Ron Karenga demonstrate this aspect of the Black Aesthetic: "All black art, irregardless of any technical requirements, must have three basic characteristics which make it revolutionary. In brief, it must be functional, collective and committing."[24] Like Mao Tse-Tung, whom he is paraphrasing, Karenga and other spokesmen for the Black Arts felt that poems and novels could (and should) be designed to move audiences to revolutionary action.

It should be clear at this point that there were blatant weaknesses in the critical framework that actually accompanied the postulates of the Black Aesthetic. Too often in their attempts to locate the parameters of Afro-American culture, spokesmen for the new paradigm settled instead for a romantically conceived domain of "race." And their claims to have achieved a scholarly consensus on "culture" sometimes revealed themselves as functions of a defensive chauvinism on the part of spokesmen who had gained the limelight. What is encouraging, though in, any evaluation of the Afro-American intellectual milieu during the late stages of the Black Arts movement is that Black Aesthetic spokesmen themselves first pointed out (and suggested ways beyond) such critical and theoretical weaknesses.

In his essay "The Black Contribution to American Letters: The Writer as Activist—1960 and After," Larry Neal identifies the Black Aesthetic's interest in an African past and in African-American folklore as a species of Herderian nationalism and goes on to say: "Nationalism, wherever it occurs in the modern world, must legitimize itself by evoking the muse of history. This is an especially necessary step where the nation or group feels that its social oppression is inextricably bound up with the destruction of its traditional culture and with the suppression of that culture's achievements in the intellectual sphere."[25] A social group's reaction in such nationalistic instances, according to Neal, is understandably (though also, regrettably) one of total introspection—i.e., drawing in unto itself and labeling the historically oppressive culture as "the enemy" (p. 782). A fear of the destruction of Afro-American culture by an "aggressive and alien" West, for example, prompted Black Aesthetic spokesmen to think only in racial terms and to speak only in "strident" tones as a means of defending their culture against what they perceived as threats from the West. Such a strategy, however, in Neal's view, represents a confusion of politics and art, an undesirable conflation of the "public" domain of social activism and the "private" field of language reserved for artistic creation and literary-theoretical investigation.

Such a response is, in his estimation, finally a form of distorted "Marxist literary theory in which the concept of race is substituted for the Marxist idea of class" (p. 783). The attempt to apply the "ideology of race to artistic creation" (p. 784), he says, is simply a contemporary manifestation of Afro-American literature's (and, by implication, literary criticism's) historical dilemma:

> The historical problem of black literature is that it has in a sense been perpetually hamstrung by its need to address itself to the question of racism in America. Unlike black music, it has rarely been allowed to exist on its own terms, but rather [has] been utilized as a means of public relations in the struggle for human rights. Literature can indeed make excellent propaganda, but through propaganda alone the black writer can never perform the highest function of his art: that of revealing to man his most enduring human possibilities and limitations. (P. 784)

In order to perform the "highest function" of artistic creation and criticism the black spokesman must concentrate his attention and efforts on "method"—on "form, structure, and genre"—rather than on "experience" or "content" (pp. 783–84). Neal, therefore, who called in the sixties for a literature and a criticism that spoke "directly to the needs and aspirations of black people," ends his later essay by calling for a creativity that projects "the accumulated weight of the world's aesthetic, intellectual, and historical experience" as a function of its mastery of "form." His revised formalist position leads not only to a condemnation of the critical weaknesses of former allies in the Black Aesthetic camp, but also to a valorization of the theoretical formulations of such celebrated "Western" theoreticians as Northrop Frye and Kenneth Burke (pp. 783–84).

A new order of literary-critical and literary-theoretical thought—one that sought to situate the higher-order rules of the Black Aesthetic within a contemporary universe of literary-theoretical discourse—was signaled during the mid-seventies not only by Neal's essay, but also by symposia and conferences on the Black Arts that occurred throughout the United States.[26] It was at one such symposium that Henderson presented his essay "The Question of Form and Judgment," which I have previously cited.[27] Like Neal, Henderson is drawn to a more formalist critique in his 1977 essay. For example, he implicitly rejects an intuitive "saturation" in favor of a more empirical approach to literary study: "in criticism, intuition, though vital, is not enough. The canons, the categories, the dynamics must be as clear and reasoned as possible. These must rest on a sound empirical base" (p. 36). This "sound empirical base" is, in the final analysis, a data base acquired through the kind of cultural-anthropological investigation that I suggested when discussing "The Forms of Things Unknown." "Black poetry," Henderson continues, "can and should be judged by the same standards that any other poetry is judged by—by those standards which validly arise out of the culture" (p. 33). And the primary and secondary sources that he takes up in his 1977 discussion indicate that he has a very clear notion of "culture" as a category in literary study.

I think it would be incorrect to assert that the mid- and later-seventies witnessed a total revisionism on the part of former advocates for the Black Aesthetic. It seems fair, however, to say that some early spokesmen had by this time begun to point out weaknesses of the structure they had raised on the ideological foundations of Black Power. The defensive inwardness of the Black Aesthetic—its manifest appeal to a racially conditioned, revolutionary, and intuitive standard of critical judgment—made the new paradigm an ideal instrument of vision for those who wished to usher into the world new and *sui generis* Afro-American objects of investigation. Ultimately, though, such introspection could not answer the kinds of theoretical questions occasioned by the entry of these objects into the world. In a sense, the Afro-American literary-critical investigator had been given—through a bold act of the critical imagination—a unique literary tradition but no distinctive theoretical vocabulary with which to discuss this tradition. He had been given linguistic forms of power and beauty, but the language meted out by Karenga and others of his ilk was, sometimes, little more than a curse. A new paradigm (one coextensive with a contemporary universe whose participants were attempting to formulate adequate, theoretical ways of discussing art) was in order.

VII

Discussing the manner of progression of a new philosophical posture born of a generational shift, Feuer comments:

[F]rom its point of origin with an insurgent generational group, the new emotional standpoint, the new perspective, the new imagery, the new metaphors and idioms spread to the more conventional sections of their own generation, then to their slightly older opponents and their relative elders. Thus, by the time that conservative Americans spoke of themselves as "pragmatic," and virtually every American politician defined himself as a "pragmatist," the word "pragmatist" had become a cliché, and its span as a movement was done. A new insurgent generation would perforce have to explore novel emotions, images, and idioms in order to define its own independent character, its own "revolutionary" aims against the elders.[28]

One might substitute "Black Aesthetic" and "Black Aesthetic" for the implied "pragmatism" and the explicit "pragmatist" of the foregoing remarks. For by the end of the 1970s, the notion of a uniquely Afro-American field of aesthetic experience marked by unique works of verbal and literary art had become a commonplace in American literary criticism. The philosophical tenets that supported early manifestations of this notion, however, had been discredited by the failure of revolutionary black social and political groups to achieve their desired ends. "Black Power," that is to say, as a motivating philosophy for the Black Aesthetic, was deemed an ideological failure by the mid-seventies because it had failed to give birth to a sovereign Afro-American state within the United States. Hence, those who adopted fundamental postulates of the Black Aesthetic as givens in the late seventies did so without a corresponding acceptance of its initial philosophical buttresses.

The "imagery" of a new and resplendent nation of Afro-Americans invested with Black Power, like the "emotional standpoint" which insisted that this hypothetical nation should have a collective and functional literature and criticism, gave way in the late seventies to a new idiom. In defining its independent character, a new group of intellectuals found it *de rigueur* to separate the language of criticism from the vocabulary of political ideology. Their supporting philosophical posture for this separation was a dualism predicated on a distinction between "literary" and "extra-literary" realms of human behavior. Their proclaimed mission was to "reconstruct" the pedagogy and study of Afro-American literature so that it would reflect the most advanced thinking of a contemporary universe of literary-theoretical discourse. This goal was similar in some respects to the revisionist efforts of Neal and Henderson discussed in the preceding section. Like their immediate forerunners, the "reconstructionists" were interested in establishing a sound theoretical framework for the future study of Afro-American literature. In their attempts to achieve this goal, however, some spokesmen for the new generation (whose work I shall discuss shortly) were hampered by a literary-critical "professionalism" that was a function of their emergent class interests.

At the outset of the present essay, I implied that the notion "generational shifts" was sufficient to offer some account of the "ascendant class interests that have characterized Afro-America since World War II." The emergence of a mass, black audience, which was so important for the Black Power and Black Arts movements, was the first instance that I had in mind.[29] But the vertical mobility of Afro-Americans prompted by black political activism during the sixties and early seventies also resulted in the emergence during the 1970s of what has been called a "new black middle class."[30] The opening of the doors, personnel rosters, and coffers of the white academy to minority groups effected by the radical politics of the past two decades provided the conditions of possibility for the appearance of Afro-American critics who have adopted postures, standards, and vocabularies of their white compeers. The disappearance of a mass black audience for both literary-critical and revolutionary-political discourse brought about by the billions of dollars and countless man-hours spent to suppress the American radical left in recent years has been ironically accompanied, therefore, by the emergence of Afro-American spokesmen whose class status (new, black middle-class) and privileges are, in fact, contingent upon their adherence to accepted (i.e., white) standards of their profession. Bernard Anderson's reflections on the situation of black corporate middle-managers who assumed positions in the late sixties and early seventies serve as well to describe the situation of a new group of Afro-American literary critics:

> As pioneers in a career-development process, these [black] managers face challenges and uncertainties unknown to most white managers. Many feel an extra responsibility to maintain high performance levels, and most recognize an environment of competition that will tolerate only slight failure. . . . Some black middle managers feel the need to conform to a value system alien to the experience of most black Americans but essential for success in professional management.[31]

One result of a class-oriented professionalism among Afro-American literary critics has been a sometimes uncritical imposition upon Afro-American culture of literary theories borrowed from prominent white scholars.

When such borrowings have occurred among the generation that displaced the Black Aesthetic, the outcome has sometimes been disastrous for the course of Afro-American literary study. For instead of developing the mode of analysis suggested by the higher-order arguments of a previous generation, the emergent generation has chosen to distinguish Afro-American literature as an autonomous cultural domain and to criticize it in terms "alien" to the implied cultural-anthropological approach of the Black Aesthetic. Rather than attempting to assess the merits of the Black Aesthetic's methodological assumptions, that is to say, the new generation has adopted the "professional" assumptions (and attendant jargon) that mark the world of white academic literary critics. A positive outcome to the emergent generation's endeavors has been a strong and continuing emphasis on the necessity for an adequate theoretical framework for the study of Afro-American literature. The negative results of their efforts have been an unfortunate burdening of the universe of discourse surrounding Afro-American culture with meaningless jargon and the articulation of a variety of lamentably confused utterances on language, literature, and culture. The emergent generation is fundamentally correct, I feel, in its call for serious literary study of Afro-American literature. But it is misguided, I believe, in its wholesale adoption of terminology and implicit assumptions of white, "professional" critics. A view of essays by principal spokesmen for the new theoretical prospect will serve to clarify these judgments. The essays appear in the handbook of the new generation entitled *Afro-American Literature: The Reconstruction of Instruction* (1979).[32]

Edited by Dexter Fisher and Robert B. Stepto, *Afro-American Literature* "grew out of the lectures and course design workshops of the 1977 Modern Language Association/National Endowment for the Humanities Summer Seminar on Afro-American Literature" (p. 1). The volume sets forth basic tenets of a new paradigm. The guiding assumption—i.e., that a literature known as "Afro-American" exists in the world—is stated as follows by Stepto in his "Introduction": "[Afro-American] literature fills bookstore shelves and, increasingly, the stacks of libraries; symposia and seminars on the literature are regularly held; prominent contemporary black writers give scores of readings; and so the question of the literature's existence, at this juncture in literary studies, is not at issue" (p. 1). The second, fundamental assumption—i.e., that literature consists in "written art" (p. 3)—is implied by Stepto later in the same "Introduction" when he is describing the unit of *Afro-American Literature* devoted to "Afro-American folklore *and* Afro-American literature as well as Afro-American folklore *in* Afro-American literature" (pp. 3–4). According to the editor, folklore can be transformed into a "written art" that may, in turn, comprise "fiction" (p. 4). Further, he suggests that the "folk" roots of a work like Frederick Douglass's *Narrative of the Life of Frederick Douglass* are to be distinguished from its "literary roots" (p. 5). The condition signaled by "written" seems at first glance, therefore, a necessary one for "literary" and "literature" in Stepto's thinking.

There is, however, some indication in the "Introduction" that the new generation does not wish to confine its definition of the "literary" exclusively to what is "written." At the midpoint of his opening remarks, Stepto asserts that there are "discrete literary texts that are inherently interdisciplinary (e.g., blues) and often multigeneric (dialect voicings in all written art forms)" (p. 3). If "blues" and "dialect voicings" constitute, respectively, a literary text and a genre, then it would appear to follow that any distinctly Afro-American expressive form (not merely written ones) can be encompassed by the "literary" domain. The boundaries of the new generation's theoretical inquiries, therefore, can apparently be expanded at will to include whatever seems distinctly expressive in Afro-America. Stepto suggests, for example, that "a methodology for an integrated study of Afro-American folklore and literature" (p. 4) should form part of the scholar-teacher's tools. And he goes on to propose that there are "various ways in which an instructor . . . can present a collection of art forms and still respond to the literary qualities of many of those forms in the course of the presentation" (p. 3). On one hand, then, the new prospect implies a rejection of modes of inquiry that are sociological in character or that seek to explore ranges of experience lying beyond the transactions of an exclusive sphere of written art: "central . . . to this volume as a whole" is a rejection of "extraliterary values, ideas, and pedagogical constructions that have plagued the teaching of . . . [Afro-American] literature" (p. 2). On the other hand, the new prospect attempts to preserve a concern for the "forms of things unknown" (e.g., blues) by reading them under the aspect of a Procrustean definition of "literary." Similarly, it attempts to maintain certain manifestations of Afro-American ordinary discourse (e.g., dialect voicings) as legitimate areas of study by reading them as literary genre. Finally, the new prospect, as defined by Stepto, implies that the entire realm of the Afro-American arts can be subsumed by the "literary" since any collection of black art forms can be explicated in terms of its "literary qualities." Such qualities, under the terms of the new prospect, take on the character of sacrosanct, cultural universals (a point to which I shall return shortly).

Kuhn points out that a paradigmatic shift in a community's conception of the physical world results in "the whole conceptual web whose strands are space, time, matter, force and so on" being shifted and "laid down again on nature whole" (p. 149). While the earlier Black Aesthetic was concerned to determine how the commodity of "blackness" shaped the Afro-American artistic domain, the emergent theoretical prospect attempts to discover how the qualities of a "literary" domain shape Afro-American life as a whole. There is, thus, a movement from the whole of culture to the part signaled by the most recent generational shift in Afro-American literary criticism. For what the new group seeks to specify is a new "literary" conceptual scheme for apprehending Afro-American culture. This project constitutes its main theoretical goal. Two of *Afro-American Literature*'s most important essays—Stepto's "Teaching Afro-American Literature: Survey or Tradition: The Reconstruction of Instruction" and Henry Louis Gates, Jr.'s "Preface to Blackness: Text and Pretext"—are devoted to this goal.

Stepto's basic premise in "Teaching Afro-American Literature" is that the typical (i.e., normative) teacher of Afro-American literature is a harried, irresponsible pedagogue ignorant of the "inner" workings of the Afro-American literary domain. It follows from this proposition that pedagogy surrounding the literature must be reconstructed on a sound basis by someone familiar with the "myriad cultural metaphors," "coded structures," and "poetic rhetoric" of Afro-America (p. 9). Stepto asserts that only a person who has learned to read the discrete literary texts of Afro-America in ways that ensure a proximity and "intimacy, with writers and texts outside the normal boundaries of nonliterary structures" (p. 16) can achieve this required familiarity. According to the author, moreover, it is a specific form of "literacy"—of proficient reading—that leads to the reconstruction of instruction.

Understandably, given the author's earlier claims, this literacy is not based on a comprehension or study of "extraliterary" structures. Its epistemological foundation is, instead, the instructor's apprehension and comprehension of what Stepto calls the "Afro-American canonical story or pregeneric myth, the particular historicity of the Afro-American literary tradition, and the Afro-American landscape or *genius loci*" (p. 18). This "pregeneric myth," according to Stepto, is "the quest for freedom and literacy" (p. 18), and he further asserts that the myth is an "aesthetic and rhetorical principle" that can serve as the basis for constructing a proper course in Afro-American literature (p. 17). The Afro-American "pregeneric myth" is, therefore, (at one and the same instant) somehow a prelinguistic reality, a quest, and a pedagogical discovery principle.

It is at this point in Stepto's specifications that what I earlier referred to as an "unfortunate burdening" of the universe of discourse surrounding Afro-American culture with jargon becomes apparent. For the author's formulations on a "pregeneric myth" reflect his metaphysical leanings far more clearly than they project a desirable methodological competence. They signal, in fact, what I called at the outset of this essay a "version, of Aristotelian metaphysics." Stepto's pregeneric myth has the character of prime matter capable of assuming an unceasing variety of forms. Just as for Aristotle "the elements are the simplest physical things, and within them the distinction of matter and form can only be made by an abstraction of thought,"[33] so for Stepto the pregeneric myth is informed matter that serves as the core and essence of that which is "literary" in Afro-America. It is the substance out of which all black expression molds itself: "The quest for freedom and literacy is found in every major text . . ." (p. 18). Further: "If an Afro-American literary tradition exists, it does so not because there is a sizeable chronology of authors and texts but because those authors and texts seek collectively their own literary forms—their own admixture of genre—bound historically and linguistically to a shared pregeneric myth" (p. 19).

A simplified statement of the conceptual scheme implied by Stepto's notion of cultural evolution would be: The various structures of a culture derive from the informed matter of myth. The principal difficulty with this notion is that the author fails to make clear the mode of being of a "myth" that is not only pregeneric, but also, it would seem, prelinguistic. "Nonliterary structures," Stepto tells us, evolve "almost exclusively from freedom myths devoid of linguistic properties" (p. 18). Such structures, we are further told, "speak rarely to questions of freedom and literacy" (p. 18). The question one must pose in light of such assertions is: Are "nonliterary structures" indeed devoid of linguistic properties? If so, then "literacy" and "freedom" can scarcely function as dependent variables in a single, generative myth. For under conditions of mutual inclusiveness (where the variables are *ab initio*, functions of one another) the structures generated from the myth could not logically be devoid of that which is essential to literacy; i.e., linguistic properties. It is important to note, for example, that the "nonliterary" structure known as the African Methodist Episcopal Church preserves in its name, and particularly in the linguistic sign "African," a marker of the structure's cultural origin and orientation. And it is difficult to imagine the kind of cognition that would be required to summon to consciousness cultural structures devoid of all linguistic properties such as a name, a written history, or a controlling interest in the semantic field of a culture's language. But, perhaps, what Stepto actually meant to suggest by his statement was that "freedom myths" are devoid of linguistic properties. Under this interpretation of his statement, however, one would have to adopt a philosophically idealistic conception of myth that seems contrary to the larger enterprise of the reconstructionists. For Stepto insists that the "reconstruction" of Afro-American literary instruction is contingent upon the discoverability through "literacy" (a process of linguistic transaction) of the Afro-American pregeneric myth. And how could such a goal be achieved if myths existed only as prelinguistic, philosophical ideals? In sum, Stepto seems to have adopted a critical rhetoric that plays him false. Having assumed some intrinsic merit and inherent clarity in the notion "pregeneric myth," he fails to analytically delineate the mode of existence of such a myth or to clarify the manner in which it is capable of generating two distinct kinds of cultural structures.

One sign of the problematical status of this myth in Stepto's formulations is the apparent "agentlessness." of its operations. According to the author, the pregeneric myth is simply "set in motion" (p. 20), and one can observe its "motion through both chronological and linguistic time" (p. 19). Yet, the efficacy of motion suggested here seems to have no historically based community of agents or agencies for its origination or perpetuation. The myth and its operations, therefore, are finally reduced in Stepto's thinking to an aberrant version of Aristotle's "unmoved mover." For Aristotle specifies that the force which moves the "first heaven" has "no contingency; it is not subject even to minimal change (spatial motion in a circle), since that is what it originates."[34] Stepto, however, wants both to posit an "unmoved" substance as his pregeneric myth and to claim that this myth moves as "literary history." In fact, he designates the shape of its literary-historical movement as a circle—a "magic circle" or *temenos*—representing one kind of ideal harmony, or perfection of motion.

At this point in his description, Stepto (not surprisingly) feels compelled to illustrate his formulations with examples drawn from the Afro-American literary tradition. He first asserts that the phrase "the black belt" is one of Afro-America's metaphors for the *genius loci* (a term borrowed from Geoffrey Hartman signifying "spirit of place") that resides within the interior of the "magic circle" previously mentioned (p. 20). Employing this metaphor, the late-nineteenth-century founder and president of Tuskegee Institute, Booker T. Washington, wrote:

> So far as I can learn the term was first used to designate a part of the country which was distinguished by the colour of the soil. The part of the country possessing this thick, dark soil was, of course, the part of the south where the slaves were most profitable, and consequently they were taken there in the largest numbers. Later, and especially since the war, the term seems to be used wholly in a political sense—that is, to designate the counties where the black people out number the white.[35]

Stepto feels that this description comprises an act of disingenuity on Washington's part. However, when he proceeds to demonstrate that Washington's statement is a "literary offense" (something akin to a sin of shallowness in the reading of metaphor) vis-à-vis the metaphor "the black belt," Stepto does not summon logical, rhetorical, or linguistic criteria. In condemning Washington for describing only geological and political dimensions of the black belt rather than historical and symbolic dimensions, Stepto summons "extraliterary" criteria, insisting that the turn-of-the-century black leader's "offense" was committed in order to insure his success in soliciting philanthropic funds for Tuskegee. The author of *Up From Slavery*, in Stepto's view, merely glossed the metaphor "the black belt" in order to keep his white, potential benefactors happy.

We, thus, find ourselves thrust into the historical dust and heat of turn-of-the-century white philanthropy in America. And what Stepto calls a "geographical metaphor" (i.e., "the black belt") becomes, in his own reading, simply a sign for one American region where such philanthropy had its greatest impact. Contrary to his earlier injunction, therefore, Stepto allows a "nonliterary structure" to become central to his own "reading of art" (p. 20). He assumes, however, that he has achieved his interpretation of Washington solely on the basis of his own "literacy" in regard to the black leader's employment of metaphor. He further assumes that when he contrasts W. E. B. Du Bois's employment of "the black belt" with Washington's usage that he is engaged in a purely "literary" act of "reading within tradition" (p. 21). But if the "tradition" that he has in mind requires a comprehension of turn-of-the-century white philanthropy where Washington is concerned, then surely Stepto does his reader a disservice when he fails to reveal that Du Bois's "rhetorical journey into the soul of a race" (p. 21) in fact curtailed white philanthropy to Atlanta University, cost Du Bois his teaching position at the same university, and led the author of *The Souls of Black Folk* to an even deeper engagement with the metaphor "the black belt."

In his attempt to maintain the exclusively "literary" affiliations of a pregeneric myth and its operations, Stepto introduces historical and sociological structures into his reading only where they will not seem to conflict dramatically with his claim that all necessary keys for literacy in the tradition generated by the pregeneric myth are linguistically situated within the texts of black authors themselves. Such reading is, at best, an exercise in the positing of cultural metaphors followed by attempts to fit such metaphors into a needlessly narrow framework of interpretation. Yet, Stepto asserts "it is reading of this sort that our instructor's new pedagogy should both emulate and promote" (p. 21).

Rather than offering additional examples of such reading, Stepto turns to a consideration of what one early-twentieth-century critic called the relationship between "tradition and the individual talent."[36] For Stepto, this relationship is described as the tension between "Genius and *genius loci*" and between *temenos* and *genius loci*. And the mediation between these facets of Afro-American culture constitutes what the author calls "modal improvisation." Although his borrowed terminology is almost hopelessly confusing here, what Stepto seems to suggest is that the Afro-American literature instructor must engage in "literate" communion with the inner dynamics of the region of Afro-America comprised by a pregeneric myth and its myriad forms and operations. The instructor's pedagogical "genius" consists in his ability to comprehend the "eternal landscape" (p. 22) that is the pregeneric myth—i.e., the sacred domain of the "literary" in Afro-American culture.

An "eternal landscape" (without beginning or end and agentless in its creation and motions) is but another means of denoting for Stepto what he describes earlier in his essay as the "various dimensions of literacy achieved within the deeper recesses of the art form" (p. 13). At another point in "Teaching Afro American Literature," the author speaks of an "immersion in the multiple images and landscapes of metaphor" (p. 15). This cumulative employment of images of a sacred interiority seems to suggest that Stepto believes there is an inner sanctum of pregeneric, mythic, literary "intimacy" resident in works of Afro-American art. Further, he seems to feel that entrance to this sanctum can be gained only by the initiated. One might posit, therefore, that what is presented by "Teaching Afro-American literature" is a scheme of mystical literacy that finally comprises what might be called a theology of literacy.

For the "conceptual web" laid upon Afro-America by Stepto's essay asserts the primacy and sacredness among cultural activities of the literary-critical and literary-theoretical enterprise. The argument of the essay is, in the end, a religious interpretation manqué, complete with an unmoved mover, a priestly class of "literate" initiates, and an eternal landscape of cultural metaphor that can be obtained by those who are free of literary "offense." And the "qualities" that derive from such a landscape (since they are coextensive with the generation of cultural structure) operate as "universals."

The articulation of such a literary-critical orthodoxy is scarcely a new departure in the history of literary criticism. In his "General Introduction" to *The English Poets* published in 1880, Matthew Arnold wrote: "More and more mankind will discover that we have to turn to poetry to interpret life for us, to console us, to sustain us. Without poetry, our science will appear incomplete; and most of what now passes for religion and philosophy will be replaced by poetry."[37] As a function of this conceptualization of the "higher uses" of poetry, Arnold confidently proclaimed: "In poetry, which is thought and art in one, it is the glory, the eternal honour, that charlatanism shall have no entrance; that this noble sphere be kept inviolate and inviolable" (p. 3). Stepto's assumption that his "reconstructed" scheme for teaching Afro-American literature may "nurture literacy in the academy" (p. 23) is certainly akin to Arnold's formulations on the exalted mission of poetry. And his zeal in preserving "inviolate" the sacred domain of the literary surely constitutes a modern, Arnoldian instance of a theology of literary. As a function of this zeal, Stepto condemns with fierce self-righteousness any pedagogical contextualization of Afro-American literature that might lead a student to ascribe to, say, a Langston Hughes poem, a use-value, or meaning, in opposition to the kind of linguistic and rhetorical values made available by the reconstruction of instruction.

The author of "Teaching Afro-American Literature" emerges as a person incapable of acknowledging that the decision to investigate the material bases of the society that provided enabling conditions for Hughes's metaphors is a sound literary-theoretical decision. Semantic and pragmatic considerations of metaphor suggest that the information communicated by metaphor is hardly localized in a given image on a given page (or, exclusively within the confines of a "magical" literary circle). Rather, the communication process is a function of myriad factors; e.g., a native speaker's ability to recognize ungrammatical sentences, the vast store of encyclopedic knowledge constituting a speech community's common knowledge of objects and concepts, relevant information supplied by the verbal context of a specific metaphoric text, and, finally, the relevant knowledge brought to bear by an "introjecting" listener or reader.[38] Conceived under these terms, metaphoric communication may actually be more fittingly comprehended by an investigation of the material bases of society than by an initiate's passage "from metaphor to metaphor and from image to image of the same metaphor in order to locate the Afro-American *genius loci*" (p. 21). Hughes is, perhaps, more comprehensible, for example, within the framework of Afro-American verbal and musical performance than within the borrowed framework for the description of written inscriptions of cultural metaphor adduced by Stepto. Only a full investigation of Afro-American metaphor—an analysis based on the best theoretical models available—will enable a student to decide.

The zeal that forced Stepto to adopt a narrow, "literary" conception of metaphor should not be totally condemned. For it is correct (and fair) to point out that a kind of sacred crusade did seem in order by the mid-seventies to modify or "reconstruct" the instruction and study of Afro-American literature that were not then based on sound theoretical foundations. While I do not think the type of mediocre instruction and misguided criticism that Stepto describes were, in fact, as prevalent as he assumes, I do feel that there were enough charlatans about in the mid-seventies to justify renewed vigilance and effort. But though one comes away from "Teaching Afro-American Literature" with a fine sense of these villains, one does not depart the essay (or others in *Afro-American Literature*) with a sense that the reconstructionists are either broad-minded or well-informed in their preachments. In fact, I think the instructor who seeks to model his course on the formulations of Stepto might find himself as nonplused as the critic who attempts to pattern his investigative strategies on the model implicit in Gates's "Preface to Blackness: Text and Pretext."

Just as Stepto's work begins with the assumption that the pedagogy surrounding Afro-American literature rests on a mistake, so Gates's essay commences with the notion that the criticism of Afro-American literature (prior to 1975) rested upon a mistake. This mistake, according to Gates, consisted in the assumption by past critics that a "determining formal relation" exists between "literature" and "social institutions."

> The idea of a determining formal relation between literature and social institutions does not in itself explain the sense of urgency that has, at least since the publication in 1760 of *A Narrative of the Uncommon Sufferings and Surprising Deliverance of Briton Hammon, a Negro Man*, characterized nearly the whole of Afro-American writing. This idea has often encouraged a posture that belabors the social and documentary status of black art, and indeed the earliest discrete examples of writtern discourse by slave and ex-slave came under a scrutiny not primarily literary. (P. 44)

For Gates, "social institutions" is an omnibus category equivalent to Stepto's "nonliterary structures." Such institutions include: the philosophical musings of the Enlightenment on the "African Mind," eighteenth-century debates concerning the African's place in the great chain of being, the politics of abolitionism, or (more recently) the economics, politics, and sociology of the Afro-American liberation struggle in the twentieth century. Gates contends that Afro-American literature has repeatedly been interpreted and evaluated according to criteria derived from such "institutions."

As a case in point, he surveys the critical response that marked the publication of Phillis Wheatley's *Poems on Various Subjects, Religious and Moral*, discovering that "almost immediately after its publication in London in 1773," the black Boston poet's collection became "the international antislavery movement's most salient argument for the African's innate mental equality" (p. 46). Gates goes on to point out that "literally scores of public figures" provided prefatory signatures, polemical reviews, or "authenticating" remarks dedicated to proving that Wheatley's verse was (or was not, as the case may be) truly the product of an African imagination. Such responses were useless in the office of criticism, however, because "virtually no one," according to Gates, "discusses . . . [Wheatley's collection] as poetry" (p. 46). Hence: "The documentary status of black art assumed priority over mere literary judgment; criticism rehearsed content to justify one notion of origins or another" (p. 46).

Thomas Jefferson's condemnation (on "extraliterary" grounds) of Wheatley and of the black eighteenth-century epistler Ignatius Sancho set an influential model for the discussion of Afro-American literature that, in Gates's view, "exerted a prescriptive influence over the criticism of the writings of blacks for the next 150 years" (p. 46). Jefferson's recourse to philosophical, political, religious, economic and other cultural systems for descriptive and evaluative terms in which to discuss black writing was, in short, a mistake that has been replicated through the decades by both white and Afro-American commentators. William Dean Howells, the writers of the Harlem Renaissance, and, most recently, according to Gates, spokesmen for the Black Aesthetic have repeated the critical offense of Jefferson. They have assumed that there is, in fact, a determining formal relation between literature and other cultural institutions and that various dimensions of these other institutions constitute areas of knowledge relevant to literary criticism. Gates says, "No," in thunder, to such assumptions. For as he reviews the "prefaces" affixed to various Afro-American texts through the decades, he finds no useful criteria for the practice of literary criticism. He discovers only introductory remarks that are "pretexts" for discussing African humanity, or for displaying "artifacts of the sable mind" (p. 49), or for chronicling the prefacer's own "attitude toward being black in white America" (p. 65).

Like Larry Neal,[39] Gates concludes that such "pretexts" and the lamentable critical situation that they imply are functions of the powerful influence of "race" as a variable in all spheres of American intellectual endeavor related to Afro-America. And like Neal, he states that racial considerations have been substituted for "class" as a category in the thinking of those who have attempted to criticize Afro-American literature, resulting in what he calls "race and superstructure" criticism: "blacks borrowed whole the Marxist notion of base and superstructure and made of it, if you will, race and superstructure" (p. 56). Gates also believes that Afro-American creative writers have fallen prey to the mode of thought that marks "race and superstructure" criticism. For these writers have shaped their work on polemical, documentary lines designed to prove the equality of Afro-Americans or to argue a case for their humanity. And in the process, they have neglected the "literary" engagement that results in true art.

What, then, is the path that leads beyond the critical and creative failings of the past? According to Gates, it lies in a semiotic understanding of literature as a "system" of signs that stand in an "arbitrary" relationship to social reality (pp. 64–68). Having drawn a semiotic circle around literature, however, he moves rapidly to disclaim the notion that literature as a "system" is radically distinct from other domains of culture:

It is not, of course, that literature is unrelated to culture, to other disciplines, or even to other arts; it is not that words and usage somehow exist in a vacuum or that the literary work of art occupies an ideal or reified, privileged status, the province of some elite cult of culture. It is just that the literary work of art is a system of signs that may be decoded with various methods, all of which assume the fundamental unity of form and content and all of which demand close reading. (P. 64)

The epistemology on which this description rests is stated as follows:

[P]erceptions of reality are in no sense absolute; reality is a function of our senses. Writers present models of reality, rather than a description of it, though obviously the two may be related variously. In fact, fiction often contributes to cognition by providing models that highlight the nature of things precisely by their failure to coincide with it. Such certainly is the case in science fiction. (P. 66)

The semiotic notion of literature and culture implied by Gates seems to combine empiricism (reality as a "function of our senses") with an ontology of the sign that suggests that signs are somehow "natural" or "inherent" to human beings. For if "reality" is, indeed, a function of our senses, then observation and study of these physiological capacities should yield some comprehension of a subject's "reality." In truth, however, it is not these physiological processes in themselves that interest Gates, but rather the operation of such processes under the conditions of "models" of cognition, which, of course, is a very different thing. For if one begins not with the senses, but with cognition, then one is required to ask: How are "models" of cognition conceived, articulated, and transmitted in human cultures? Certainly, one of the obvious answers here is *not* that human beings are endowed at birth with a "system of signs," but rather that models of cognition are conceived in, articulated through, and transmitted by language. And like other systems of culture, language *is* a "social institution." Hence, if cognitive "models" of "fiction" differ from those of other spheres of human behavior, they do not do so because fiction is somehow discontinuous with social institutions. In fact, it is the attempt to understand the coextensiveness of language as a social institution and literature *as a system within* it that constitutes what is, perhaps, the defining process of literary-theoretical study in our day.

When, therefore, Gates proposes metaphysical and behavioral models that suggest that a literature, or even a single text (p. 67), exists as a structured "world" ("a system of signs") that can be comprehended without reference to "social institutions," he seems misguided in his claims and only vaguely aware of recent developments in literary study, symbolic anthropology, linguistics, the psychology of perception, and other related areas of intellectual inquiry. He seems, in fact, to have adopted, without qualification, a theory of the literary sign (of the "word" in a literary text) that presupposes a privileged status for the creative writer: "The black writer is the point of consciousness of his language" (p. 67). What this assertion means to Gates is that a writer is more capable than others in society of producing a "complex structure of meanings"—a linguistic structure that (presumably) corresponds more closely than those produced by non-writers—to the organizing principles by which a group's world view operates in consciousness (p. 67).

One might be at a loss to understand how a writer can achieve this end unless he is fully aware of language as a social institution and of the relationship that language bears to other institutions that create, shape, maintain, and transmit a society's "organizing principles." Surely, Gates does not mean to suggest that the mind of the writer is an autonomous semantic domain where complex structures are conceived and maintained "non-linguistically." On the other hand, if such structures of meaning are, in fact, "complex" because they are linguistically maintained, then so, too, are similar structures that are conceived by non-writers.

That is to say, Gates renders but small service to the office of theoretical distinction when he states that "a poem is above all atemporal and must cohere at a symbolic level, if it coheres at all" (p. 60), or when he posits that "literature approaches its richest development when its 'presentational symbolism' (as opposed by Suzanne Langer to its 'literal discourse') cannot be reduced to the form of a literal proposition" (p. 66). The reason such sober generalities contribute little to our understanding of literature, of course, is that Gates provides no just notion of the nature of "literal discourse," failing to admit both its social-institutional status and its fundamental existence as a symbolic system. On what basis, then, except a somewhat naive belief in the explanatory power of semiotics can he suggest a radical disjunction between literature and other modes of linguistic behavior in a culture? The critic who attempted to pattern his work on Gates's model would find himself confronted by a theory of language, literature, and culture that suggests that "literary" meanings are conceived in a non-social, non-institutional manner by the "point of consciousness" of a language and are maintained and transmitted in an agentless fashion within a closed circle of "intertextuality" (p. 68). It does seem, therefore, that despite his disclaimer, Gates feels that "literature is unrelated to culture." For culture consists in the interplay of various human symbolic systems, an interplay that is essential to the production and comprehension of meaning. Gates's independent literary domain, which produces meanings from some mysteriously non-social, non-institutional medium, bears no relationship to such a process.

One reason Gates fails to articulate an adequate theory of literary semantics in his essay, I think, is that he allots an inordinate amount of space to the castigation of his critical forebears. And his attacks are often restatements of shortcomings that his predecessors had recognized and discussed by the later seventies. Yet Gates provides elaborate detail in, for example, his analysis of the Black Aesthetic.

Among the many charges that he levels against Stephen Henderson, Addison Gayle, Jr., and the present author is the accusation that the spokesmen for a Black Aesthetic assumed they could "achieve an intimate knowledge of a literary text by recreating it from the inside: Critical thought must become the thought criticized" (p. 66). Though Gates employs familiar terminology here,[40] what he seems to object to in the work of Black Aesthetic spokesmen is their treatment of the text as subject. He levels the charge, in short, that these spokesmen postulated a tautological, literary-critical circle, assuming that the thought of an Afro-American literary text was "black thought" and, hence, could be "re-thought" only by a black critic. And while there is some merit in this charge (as Henderson's and Neal's previously mentioned re-considerations of their initial critical postures make clear), it is scarcely true, as Gates argues, that Black Aestheticians did nothing in their work but reiterate presuppositions about "black thought" and then interpret Afro-American writing in accord with the entailments of such presuppositions. For the insular vision that would have resulted from this strategy would not have enabled Black Aestheticians to discuss and interpret Afro-American verbal behavior in the holistic ways conceived by Henderson, Neal, Gayle, and the present author. Spokesmen for the Black Aesthetic seldom conceived of the "text" as a closed enterprise. Instead, they normally thought (at the higher level of their arguments) of the text as an occasion for transactions between writer and reader, between performer and audience. And far from insisting that the written text is, in itself, a repository of inviolable "black thought" to be preserved at all costs, they called for the "destruction of the text"—for an open-endedness of performance and response that created conditions of possibility for the emergence of both new meanings and new strategies of verbal transaction.[41] True, such spokesmen never saw the text as discontinuous with its social origins, but then they also never conceived of these "origins" as somehow divorced from the semantics of the metaphorical instances represented in black "artistic" texts. In short, they never thought of culture under the terms of a semiotic analysis that restricted its formulations to the literary domain alone.

On the other hand, they were certainly never so innocent as Gates would have one believe. Their semantics were never so crude as to permit them to accept the notion that the words of a literary text stand in a one-to-one relationship to the "things" of Afro-American culture. In fact, they were so intent on discovering the full dimensions of the artistic "word" that they attempted to situate its various manifestations within a continuum of verbal behavior in Afro-American culture as a whole. Further, they sought to understand this continuum within the complex webs of interacting cultural systems that ultimately gave meaning to such words.

Rather than a referential semantics, therefore, what was implicit in the higher-order arguments of Black Aesthetic spokesmen (as I have attempted to demonstrate in my earlier discussions) was an anthropological approach to Afro-American art. I think, in fact, that Gates recognizes this and is, finally, unwilling to accept the kind of critical responsibilities signaled by such an enterprise. For though he spends a great deal of energy arguing with Henderson's and my own assumptions on Afro-American culture, he refuses (not without some disingenuity) to acknowledge our actual readings of Afro-American texts. The reason for this refusal, I think, is that our readings bring together, in what one hopes are useful ways, our knowledge of various social institutions, or cultural systems (including language), in our attempts to reveal the *sui generis* character of Afro-American artistic texts. Gates's formulations, however, imply an ideal critic whose readings would summon knowledge only from the literary system of Afro-America. The semantics endorsed by his ideal critic would not be those of a culture. They would constitute, instead, the specially consecrated meanings of an intertextual world of "written art."

The emphasis on "close reading" (p. 64) in Gates's formulations, therefore, might justifiably be designated a call for a "closed" reading of selected Afro-American written texts. In fact, the author implies that the very defining criteria of a culture may be extrapolated from selected written, literary texts rather than vice-versa. For example, if any Afro-American literary artists has entertained the notion of "frontier," then Gates feels the notion must have defining force in Afro-American culture. Only by ignoring the mass level of Afro-America and holding up the "message" of literary works of art by Ralph Ellison and Ishmael Reed as "normative" utterances in Afro-American culture can Gates support such a claim. His claim is, thus, a function of the privileged status he grants to the writer and the elitist status that he bestows on "literary uses of language."

But if it is true that scholarly investigations of an Afro-American expressive tradition must begin at a mass level—at the level of the "forms of things unknown"—then Gates's claim that the notion of "frontier" has defining force in Afro-America would have to be supported by the testimony of, say, the blues, work songs, or early folktales of Afro-America. And I think that an emphasis on frontier, in the sense intended by Frederick Jackson Turner, is scarcely to be discerned in these cultural manifests.

Gates, however, is interested only in what writers (as "points of consciousness") have to say, and he seems to feel no obligation to turn to Afro-American folklore. In fact, when he comments on Henderson's formulations on Afro-American folk language, or vernacular, he reveals not only a lack of interest in folk processes, but also some profound misconceptions about the nature of Afro-American language.

Henderson attempts to establish a verbal and musical continuum of expressive behavior in Afro-American culture as an analytical category. In this process, he encounters certain verbal items that seem to claim (through usage) expansive territory in the Afro-American "sign field." Gates mistakenly assumes that Henderson is setting such items (e.g., "jook," "jelly") apart from a canon of "ordinary" usage as "poetic discourse." This assumption is a function of Gates's critical methodology, which is predicated on a distinction between ordinary and poetic discourse. And the assumption compels him to cast aspersions on the originality of Henderson's work by asserting that "practical critics" since the 1920s have been engaged in actions similar to those of the Black Aesthetic spokesman.

The fault here is that Gates fails to recognize that Henderson is not seeking to isolate a lexicon of Afro-American "poetic" usages, nor to demonstrate how such usages "superimpose" a "grammar" (Gates's notion) on "nonliterary discourse." Henderson is concerned, instead, to demonstrate that Afro-American ordinary discourse is, in fact, continuous with Afro-American artistic discourse and that an investigation of the black oral tradition would finally concern itself not simply with a lexicon, but also with a "grammar" adequate to describe the syntax and phonology of all Afro-American speech.

Gates is incapable of understanding this notion, however, because he believes that the artistic domain is unrelated to ordinary, "social" modes of behavior. Hence, he is enamored of the written, literary work, suggesting that a mere dictionary of black "poetic" words and their "specific signification" would lead to an understanding of how "Black English" departs from "general usage." This view of language is coextensive with his views of literature and culture. For it concentrates solely on words as "artistic" words and ignores the complexities of the syntax and phonology that give resonance to such words. "A literary text," Gates writes, "is a linguistic event; its explication must be an activity of close textual analysis" (p. 68).

It is not, however, the "text" that constitutes an "event" (if by this Gates means a process of linguistic transaction). It is rather the reading or performance by human beings of a kind of score, or graphemic record, if you will, that constitutes the event and, in the process, produces (or reproduces) the meaningful text. And the observer or critic who wishes to "analyze" such a text must have a knowledge of far more than the mere words of the performers. He should, it seems to me, have some theoretically adequate notions of the entire array of cultural forces which shape the performers' or readers' cognition and allow them to actualize the text as an instance of a distinctive cultural semantics. Gates has no such notions to bring to bear. And his later essay in *Afro-American Literature* entitled "Dis and Dat: Dialect and the Descent" reveals some confusion on issues of both language and culture.

Briefly, we are told by Gates that "culture is imprisoned in a linguistic contour that no longer matches . . . the changing landscape of fact" (p. 92). This appears a mild form of Whorfianism[42] until one asks: How do "facts" achieve a non-linguistic existence? The answer is that they do not achieve such an existence. Placed in proper perspective, Gates's statement simply means that different communities of speakers of the same language have differential access to "modern" ideas. But in his efforts to preserve language apart from other social institutions, Gates ignores agents or speakers until he wishes to add further mystery and distinctiveness to his own conceptions of language. When he finally comes to reflect on speakers, he invokes the notion of "privacy," insisting that lying and remaining silent both offer instances of the employment of a "personal" thesaurus by a speaker (p. 93). Now, this conception stands in contrast to Gates's earlier Whorfianism.[43] And, to my knowledge, it possesses little support in the literature of linguistics or semiotics.

The notions that Gates advocates presuppose uniquely "personal" meanings for lexical items that form part of a culture's "public discourse." But what is unique, or personal, about these items is surely their difference from public discourse; their very identity, that is to say, is a function of public discourse. Further, the ability to use such lexical items to lie, or to misinform, scarcely constitutes an argument for privacy. Umberto Eco, for example, writes:

A sign is everything which can be taken as significantly substituting for something else. This something else does not necessarily have to exist or to actually be somewhere at the moment in which a sign stands for it. Thus *semiotics is in principle the discipline studying everything which can be used in order to lie.* If something cannot be used to tell a lie, conversely it cannot be used to tell the truth: it cannot in fact be used "to tell" at all.[44]

The word, in short, becomes a sign by being able to tell, and unless Gates means to propose the idealistic notion that each human mind generates its own system of meaningful, non-public signs, it is difficult to understand how he conceives of sign usage in lying as an instance of "private" usage of language. His goal in "Dis and Dat" (an unfortunate choice of lexical items for his title since the phonological feature *d* for *th* is not unique to Black English Vernacular, but rather can be found in other non-standard language varieties) is to define Afro-American "dialect" as a kind of "private," subconscious code signifying a "hermetic closed world" (p. 94). The problem with this very suggestive notion, however, is that Gates not only seems to misunderstand the issue of privacy in language and philosophy, but also seems to fail to comprehend the nature of Black English Vernacular as a natural language.

He bases his understanding of this language on a nineteenth-century magazine article by a writer named James A. Harrison, who asserted that "the poetic and multiform messages which nature sends him [the Afro-American] through his auditory nerve" are reproduced, in words, by the Afro-American (p. 95). Gates takes Harrison's claims seriously, assuming that there is a fundamental physiological difference between the linguistic behavior of Afro-Americans and other human beings: "One did not believe one's eyes, were one black; one believed [presumably on the basis of the Afro-American's direct auditory contact with nature] . . . one's ears" (p. 109). On the basis of such problematical linguistic and cultural assumptions as the foregoing, Gates proposes that Black English Vernacular was essentially musical, poetical, spoken discourse generated by means other than those employed to generate standard English and maintained by Afro-Americans as a code of symbolic inversion.

There are reasons for studying the process of symbolic, linguistic inversion in Afro-American culture, and, indeed, for studying the relationship between the tonal characteristics of African languages (which is what both Harrison and Gates have in mind when they say "musical") in relationship to Afro-American speech. Such study, however, should not be grounded on the assertions of Wole Soyinka, Derek Walcott, or James A. Harrison (Gates's sources). It should be a matter of careful, holistic cultural analysis that summons as evidence a large, historical body of informed comment and scholarship on Black English Vernacular. A beginning has been made in this direction by Henderson in his previously mentioned essay "The Question of Form and Judgment," which commences with the assumption that a discussion of Afro-American poetry (whether written in "dialect" or in standard English) must be based on sound historical notions of Black English Vernacular resulting from detailed research.[45]

Neither Gates nor Stepto, who are the principal spokesmen for the new theoretical prospect in *Afro-American Literature*, has undertaken the detailed research in various domains of Afro-American culture that leads to adequate theoretical formulations. Stepto's stipulations on the ontology of a pregeneric myth from which all Afro-American cultural "structures" originate are just as problematical as Gates's notions of a generative, artistic "point of consciousness" whose "literary uses of language" are independent of "social institutions." The narrowness of Stepto's conception of the "literary" forces him to adopt "nonliterary" criteria in his reading of *Up From Slavery*. And the instability of Gates's views of language and culture forces him to relinquish his advocacy for a synchronic, close reading of literary utterances when he comes to discuss Afro-American dialect poetry. Social institutions, and far more than "literary" criteria, are implied when he asserts:

When using a word we wake into resonance, as it were, its entire previous history. A text is embedded in specific historical time; it has what linguists call a diachronic structure. To read fully is to restore all that one can of the immediacies of value and intent in which speech actually occurs. (P. 114)

Here, contextualization, rethinking the "intent" of the speaker, and "institutional" considerations are all advocated in a way that hardly seems opposed to the critical strategies of the Black Aesthetic.

To concentrate exclusively on the shortcomings and contradictions of Stepto and Gates, however, is to minimize their achievements. For both writers have suggested, in stimulating ways, that Afro-American literature can be incorporated into a contemporary universe of literary-theoretical discourse. True, the terms on which they propose incorporation amount in one instance to a theology of literacy and, in another, to a mysterious semiotics of literary consciousness. Nonetheless, the very act of proposing that a sound, theoretical orientation toward an Afro-American literary tradition is necessary constitutes a logical second step after the paradigmatic establishment of that tradition by the Black Aesthetic.

Furthermore, Stepto and Gates are both better critics than theoreticians. Hence, they provide interpretations of texts that are, at times, quite striking. (Gates's reflections on structuralism and his structuralist reading of the *Narrative of the Life of Frederick Douglass* are quite provocative.) In addition, neither is so imprisoned by his theoretical claims that he refuses to acknowledge the claims of radically competing theories. For example, the essay by Sherley Anne Williams entitled "The Blues Roots of Contemporary Afro-American Poetry" (pp. 72–87) that appears in *Afro-American Literature* is based on the work of Henderson and stands in direct contrast in its methodology to the stipulations on written, noninstitutional, literary art adduced by Stepto and Gates. And although Robert Hemenway, in his fine essay on Zora Neale Hurston's relationship to Afro-American folk processes (pp. 122–52), makes a gallant attempt to join the camp of Stepto and Gates, his work finally suggests the type of linguistic, expressive continuum implied by Henderson rather than the segmented model of Gates. Finally, Robert O'Meally's brilliant essay on Frederick Douglass's *Narrative* (pp. 192–211) is antithetical at every turn to Stepto's notion that critical "literacy" is a function of the reader's understanding of written "metaphor," or inscribed instances of "poetic rhetoric *in isolatio*" (p. 9). For it is O'Meally's agile contextualizing of Douglass's work within the continuum of Afro-American verbal behavior that enables him to provide a reading of the work that suggests "intertextual" possibilities that are far more engaging than those suggested by Stepto's own reading of the *Narrative* (pp. 178–91).

In his editorial capacity, therefore, Stepto has rendered a service to the scholarly community by refusing to allow his theory of the "literary" to foreclose the inclusion of essays that contradict, or sharply qualify, his own explicit claims. Unfortunately, he and his coeditor did not work as effectively in their choice of course designs—the models of "reconstructed" instruction toward which the whole of *Afro-American Literature* is directed (if we are to believe the volume's title). Briefly, the section entitled "Afro-American Literature Course Designs" reflects all of the theoretical confusions that have been surveyed heretofore. There are models for courses based on weak distinctions between "literary" and "socio-historical" principles (p. 237); the assumption that literature is an "act of language" (p. 234); the notion that the "oral tradition is . . . a language with a grammar, a syntax, and standards of eloquence of its own" (p. 237); the idea that folk forms are "literary" genres (p. 246); and, finally, the assumption that "interdisciplinary" status can be achieved merely by bringing together different forms of art rather than by summoning methods and models from an array of intellectual disciplines (pp. 250–55). The concluding course designs, thus, capture the novelty and promise, as well as the shortcomings, of the new theoretical prospect. The types of distinctions, concerns, and endeavors they suggest are, indeed, significant for the future study of Afro-American literature and verbal art. What they lack—i.e., sound theories of ordinary and literary discourse, an adequate theory of semantics, and a comprehensive theory of reading—will, one hopes, be provided in time by scholars of Afro-American literature who are as persuaded as the reconstructionists that the Afro-American literary tradition can, indeed, withstand sharp critical scrutiny and can survive (as a subject of study) the limitations of early attempts at its literary-theoretical comprehension.

VIII

In *Ideology and Utopia*, Karl Mannheim writes:

> To-day we have arrived at the point where we can see clearly that there are differences in modes of thought, not only in different historical periods but also in different cultures. Slowly it dawns upon us that not only does the content of thought change but also its categorical structure. Only very recently has it become possible to investigate the hypothesis that, in the past as well as the present, the dominant modes of thought are supplanted by new categories when the social basis of the group of which these thought-forms are characteristic disintegrates or is transformed under the impact of social change.[46]

The generational shifts discussed in the preceding pages attest the accuracy of Mannheim's observation. The notion of "generational shift," as I have defined it, begins with the assumption that changes in the "categorical structure" of thought are coextensive with social change. The literary-theoretical goal of an analysis deriving from the concept of generational shifts is a "systematic and total formulation" of problems of Afro-American literary study. For only by investigating the guiding assumptions (the "categories" of thought, as it were) of recent Afro-American literary criticism can one gain a sense of the virtues and limitations of what have stood during the past four decades as opposing generational paradigms. What emerges from such an investigation is, first, a realization of the socially and generationally conditioned selectivity, or partiality, of such paradigms. They can be as meetly defined by their exclusions as by their manifest content. The quasi-political rhetoric of the Black Aesthetic seems to compete (at its weakest points) with the quasi-religious and semiotic jargon of the reconstructionists for a kind of flawed critical ascendancy.

Yet what also emerges from an investigation of generational shifts in recent Afro-American literary criticism is the sense that this criticism has progressed during the past forty years to a point where some "systematic" formulation of theoretical problems is possible. The extremism and shortsightedness of recent generations have been counterbalanced, that is to say, by their serious dedication to the analysis of an object that did not even exist in the world prior to the mid-sixties. The perceptual reorientations of recent generations have served as enabling conditions for a "mode of thought" that takes the theoretical investigation of a unique tradition of *Afro-American literature* as a normative enterprise.

Given the foregoing discussion, it is perhaps clear that my own preference where such theoretical investigation is concerned is the kind of holistic, cultural-anthropological approach that is implicit in the work of Henderson and other spokesmen for the Black Aesthetic. This does not mean, however, that I seek to minimize the importance of the necessary and forceful call that the reconstructionists have issued for serious literary-theoretical endeavors on the part of Afro-Americanists. Still, I am persuaded that at this juncture in the progress of critical generations the theoretical prospect that I call the "anthropology of art" is the most realistic and fruitful approach to the future study of Afro-American literature and culture.[47] The guiding assumption of the anthropology of art is coextensive with basic tenets of the Black Aesthetic insofar as both prospects assert that works of Afro-American literature and verbal art can not be adequately understood unless they are contextualized within the interdependent systems of Afro-American culture. But the anthropology of art departs from both the Black Aesthetic and the reconstructionist prospects in its assumption that art can not be studied without serious attention to the methods and models of many disciplines. The contextualization of a work of literary or verbal art, from the perspective of the anthropology of art, is an "interdisciplinary" enterprise in the most contemporary sense of that word. Rather than ignoring (or denigrating) the research and insights of scholars in the nature, social, and behavioral sciences, the anthropology of art views such efforts as positive, rational attempts to comprehend the full dimensions of human behavior. And such efforts serve the literary-theoretical investigator as guides and contributions to an understanding of the symbolic dimensions of human behavior that comprise Afro-American literature and verbal art.

In his essay "Ideology as a Cultural System," Clifford Geertz writes: "The sociology of knowledge ought to be called the sociology of meaning, for what is socially determined is not the nature of conception but the vehicles of conception."[48] I think the anthropology of art stands today not only as a "vehicle of conception" rich in theoretical possibilities, but also as a "categorical structure" that may signal a next generational shift in the criticism of Afro-American literature.

NOTES

1. Lewis S. Feuer, *Ideology and Ideologists* (Oxford: Basil Blackwell, 1975). p. 70. Professor Chester Fontenot was kind enough to remind me that T. S. Eliot's "Tradition and the Individual Talent" and Harold Bloom's *The Anxiety of Influence* also offer approaches to questions of the relationships between old and new generations of intellectuals or writers.

2. Thomas S. Kuhn, *The Structure of Scientific Revolutions* (Chicago: University of Chicago Press, 1970).

3. Richard Wright, "The Literature of the Negro in the United States," in *White Man, Listen!* (Garden City, NY: Anchor Books, 1964), pp. 69–105. All citations from Wright's essay refer to this edition and are hereafter marked by page numbers in parentheses.

4. Brown, Davis, and Lee, eds., *The Negro Caravan* (New York: Dryden Press, 1941; Arno repr. 1969), p. 7. All citations from the work refer to this edition and are hereafter marked by page numbers in parentheses.

5. In *The American Negro Writer and His Roots, Selected Papers from the First Conference of Negro Writers, March, 1959* (New York: American Society of African Culture, 1960), pp. 39–40.

6. For historical details on the events of this period, the reader may wish to consult John Hope Franklin, "A Brief History," in *The Black American Reference Book*, ed. Mabel M. Smythe (Englewood Cliffs, NJ: Prentice-Hall, 1976), pp. 1–89.

7. The phrase was originally uttered as part of a call-and-response chant between Carmichael and his audience during the course of a several-day protest march in Mississippi.

8. From Stokely Carmichael and Charles V. Hamilton, *Black Power: The Politics of Liberation in America* (New York: Vintage, 1967), pp. 43–44.

9. In *Home, Social Essays* (New York: Morrow, 1966), p. 110. All citations of the essay refer to this edition and are hereafter marked by page numbers in parentheses.

10. For an account of this enterprise, the reader may consult Theodore R. Hudson, *From LeRoi Jones to Amiri Baraka: The Literary Works* (Durham, NC: Duke University Press, 1973), pp. 20–25.

11. In *The Black Aesthetic*, ed. Addison Gayle, Jr. (New York: Doubleday, 1971), p. 272.

12. *Understanding the New Black Poetry: Black Speech and Black Music as Poetic References* (New York: Morrow, 1973), pp. 1–69. All citations refer to this edition and are hereafter marked by page numbers in parentheses.

13. Kuhn, *Structure* (Chicago: University of Chicago Press, 1970), p. 175. All citations refer to this edition and are hereafter marked by page numbers in parentheses.

14. In "The Artworld," in *Philosophy Looks at the Arts*, ed. Joseph Margolis (Philadelphia: Temple University Press, 1978), pp. 132–45, Arthur Danto writes, "terrain is constituted artistic in virtue of artistic theories, so that one use of theories, in addition to helping us discriminate art from the rest, consists in making art possible." The theoretical constraints of the integrationist paradigm excluded "Negro" expressive works from the American, literary artworld.

15. Albert Hofstadter, "On the Grounds of Aesthetic Judgment," in *Contemporary Aesthetics*, ed. Matthew Lipman (Boston: Allyn and Bacon, 1973), pp. 473–74. In both the concept "artworld" and "reference public," I have interpreted the Black Aesthetic as an institutional theory of art. For a recent critique of such theories, the reader may consult Marx W. Wartofsky, "Art, Artworlds, and Ideology," *Journal of Aesthetics and Art Criticism*, 38 (1980), 239–

47. In contrast to the "institutional" dimensions of the Black Aesthetic are its idealistic assumptions.

16. For reflections on field theory and on the work of Trier, see John Lyons, *Semantics*, I (Cambridge: Cambridge University Press, 1977), pp. 250–61.

17. I have discussed the romantic idealism of the Black Aesthetic in "The Black Spokesman as Critic: Reflections on the Black Aesthetic," the fifth chapter of my book entitled *The Journey Back: Issues in Black Literature and Criticism* (Chicago: University of Chicago Press, 1980), pp. 132–43.

18. Stephen Henderson, "Saturation: Progress Report on a Theory of Black Poetry," *Black World*, 24 (1975), 14.

19. The words on the creation of system are, of course, those of William Blake's Los, drawn from *Jerusalem*. Los, like the Black Aestheticians, also refused at points to "reason" or "compare," feeling that the imperative "business" was "to create."

20. Henderson, "Saturation," p. 9.

21. Henderson, "The Question of Form," in *A Dark and Sudden Beauty: Two Essays in Black American Poetry by George Kent and Stephen Henderson*, ed. Houston A. Baker, Jr. (Philadelphia: Afro-American Studies Program of the University of Pennsylvania, 1977), p. 24.

22. Henderson, "Question of Form," p. 32.

23. I have in mind Robert E. Hemenway, author of the superb scholarly effort *Zora Neale Hurston: A Literary Biography* (Urbana: University of Illinois Press, 1977) and Lawrence W. Levine, author of the important book *Black Culture and Black Consciousness: Afro-American Folk Thought from Slavery to Freedom* (New York: Oxford University Press, 1977).

24. "Black Cultural Nationalism," in *The Black Aesthetic*, p. 33.

25. Neal, "The Black Contribution to American Letters: Part II, The Writer as Activist— 1960 and After," in *The Black American Reference Book*, ed. Mable M. Smythe (Englewood Cliffs, NJ: Prentice-Hall, 1976), pp. 781–82. All citations refer to this edition and are hereafter marked by page numbers in parentheses.

26. I have in mind the conferences of black writers sponsored by the Howard University Institute for the Arts and the Humanities. Also important, I think, were the symposia held at the University of Pennsylvania in 1975 and 1977. Proceedings of these national gatherings can be found in *The Image of Black Folk in American Literature* (Washington, DC: Howard University Institute for the Arts and the Humanities, 1976) and in *Reading Black: Essays in the Criticism of African, Caribbean, and Afro-American Literature* (Ithaca, NY: Cornell University, Africana Studies and Research Center, Monograph Series No. 4, 1976).

27. The symposium was entitled "The Function of Black American Poetry, 1760–1977," and it was sponsored by the Afro-American Studies Program at the University of Pennsylvania, March 24–26, 1977. Selected proceedings of this symposium appeared in *A Dark and Sudden Beauty*.

28. Feuer, *Ideology and Ideologists*, p. 57.

29. I have discussed this phenomenon at length in *The Journey Back*, pp. 126–31.

30. It is difficult to date the first, contemporary usage of this term. Ben J. Wattenberg and Richard Scammon's article entitled "Black Progress and Liberal Rhetoric" (*Commentary*, April 1973, pp. 35–44), which proclaimed that 52 percent of Black Americans could be defined as "middle class," certainly gave life to ongoing attempts to define what E. Franklin Frazier designated the "Black Bourgeoisie" in his seminal study *Black Bourgeoisie* (1957). The special issue of *Ebony* magazine entitled "The Black Middle Class" (August 1973) seems to have been prompted as much by the necessity to answer Wattenberg and Scammon as by a desire to

"update" Frazier at a time when (between 1960 and 1970) the number of blacks employed in professional and technical operations had increased by 131 percent and the number of blacks in the clerical force had grown by 121 percent. Some of the major investigative issues that are signalled by the employment of the term "new black middle class" are addressed by William Julius Wilson in his study *The Declining Significance of Race: Blacks and Changing American Institutions* (Chicago: University of Chicago Press, 1978). In 1979 and 1980, the Afro-American Studies Program of the University of Pennsylvania took up the issues raised by Wilson and by the concept of a "new black middle class" in its annual spring symposia. The proceedings of those symposia can be found in: *The Declining Significance of Race?: A Dialogue Among Black and White Social Scientists*, ed. Joseph R. Washington, Jr. (Philadelphia: Afro-American Studies Program of the University of Pennsylvania, 1979) and *Dilemmas of the New Black Middle Class*, ed. Joseph R. Washington, Jr., in manuscript. Essentially, the term "new black middle class" seems to denote a stratum of Afro-American professionals whose education, occupations, and income place them on a level near that of their similarly employed white counterparts.

31. Quoted from William Julius Wilson, "The Declining Significance of Race: Myth or Reality," in *The Declining Significance of Race?* ed. Joseph R. Washington, Jr., p. 15.

32. Dexter Fisher and Robert B. Stepto, eds., *Afro-American Literature: The Reconstruction of Instruction* (New York: Modern Language Association of America, 1979). All citations refer to this edition and are hereafter marked by page numbers in parentheses.

33. Sir David Ross, *Aristotle* (London: Methuen, 1923), pp. 73–74. "Prime" matter is unlike "secondary matter" since the latter can not only "exist apart" (e.g., "tissues" may or may not be combined into organs) but can also be severed in reality (i.e., organs may be broken up into their component tissues). It is the inseparability of "form" and "matter" where Stepto is concerned (his "myth" is both structured and structuring) that gives his pregeneric myth the character of "prime" or "informed" matter (see Ross, p. 71).

34. *Metaphysics*, in *Aristotle's Metaphysics*, ed. John Warrington (London: J. M. Dent, 1956), p. 346. When Aristotle discusses "The Prime Mover" in one of the books of the *Metaphysics*, he sets forth what according to Sir David Ross is his only "systemic essay in theology" (Warrington, p. 331). Stepto, in adducing the agentless operation of his pregeneric myth, is on similar theological ground, attempting to find some thing that is "eternal, substance, and actuality" (Warrington, p. 345) to move the great sphere of Afro-American literary lights.

35. Quoted from *Afro-American Literature*, pp. 20–21.

36. T. S. Eliot, "Tradition and the Individual Talent," in *Selected Essays* (New York: Harcourt, Brace, 1950), pp. 3–11. According to Eliot, the poet can not know what valuable poetic "work" is to be done "unless he lives in what is not merely the present, but the present moment of the past, unless he is conscious, not of what is dead, but of what is already living" (p. 11).

37. Matthew Arnold, "The Study of Poetry," in *The Works of Matthew Arnold*, IV (New York: AMS Press, 1970), p. 2. All citations refer to this edition and are hereafter marked by page numbers in parentheses.

38. These "factors" are treated in detail by Samuel R. Levin in *The Semantics of Metaphor* (Baltimore: The Johns Hopkins University Press, 1977) and by Robert Rogers in *Metaphor: A Psychoanalytic View* (Berkeley: University of California Press, 1978). Additional theoretical discussion of metaphor can be found in the stimulating issue of *Critical Inquiry*, 5 (Autumn 1978) devoted to the subject.

39. I refer to Neal's "The Black Contribution to American Letters," which I discussed in an earlier section of this essay.

40. Gerard Genette defines the text as "subject" in *Figures* (Paris: Editions du Seuil, 1966). Georges Poulet and Paul Ricoeur have also entered reflections on the process whereby "critical thought *becomes* the thought criticized." The quotation here is from Maria Corti's *An Introduction to Literary Semiotics* (Bloomington: Indiana University Press, 1978), p. 43.

41. I have discussed the concept of "the destruction of the text" in *The Journey Back*, pp. 127–28. In his essay "And Shine Swam On," which serves as the "Afterword" for the anthology *Black Fire*, eds. Larry Neal and LeRoi Jones (New York: Morrow, 1968), Neal says that true Afro-American poetry lies in verbal and musical performance, not in written texts: "The text could be destroyed and no one would be hurt in the least by it" (p. 653).

42. By "Whorfianism" I mean the scholarly position assumed by Benjamin Lee Whorf. Whorf, in his studies of the Hopi Indiana, emphasized the interpenetration of language and reality; the worldview of the Hopi, according to Whorf, is coded into their language. Hence, language and worldview are coextensive (mild Whorfianism) or coterminous (strong Whorfianism), and this makes for a kind of linguistic determinism in human affairs. For a more detailed view of Whorf's thought, consult *Language, Thought and Reality*, ed. John B. Carroll, a collection of Whorf's essays published by the MIT Press in 1956.

43. Instead of language determining worldview, the individual worldview (under the aspect of "privacy") determines, or fashions, its own peculiar language.

44. Umberto Eco, *A Theory of Semiotics* (Bloomington: Indiana University Press, 1976), pp. 6–7.

45. This is not, however, an injunction to regard Henderson as an expert on Black English Vernacular as a subject of study in itself. For such expert testimony one must turn to the work of Geneva Smitherman, William Labov, and others. A good beginning, of course, is Lorenzo Turner's pioneering study *Africanisms in the Gullah Dialect*.

46. *Ideology and Utopia: An Introduction to the Sociology of Knowledge* (New York: Harcourt, Brace, 1936), pp. 82–89. My reading in "ideology" and the "sociology of knowledge" prompted this essay on generational shifts. It seemed appropriate to situate the discussion within its proper ambit as a means of concluding.

47. In *The Journey Back: Issues in Black Literature and Criticism*, I discuss the assumptions and methodology of this approach to literary study.

48. In *The Interpretation of Cultures: Selected Essays by Clifford Geertz* (New York: Basic Books, 1973), p. 212.

21 Some Implications of Womanist Theory

Sherley Anne Williams

(1986)

I am an Afro-Americanist and enough of an Africanist to know something of the enormous differences between African literatures and Afro-American literature, and something, too, of the remarkable parallels and similarities between them. We do in English, after all, trace our literary roots back to the same foreparents, the Senegalese-American, Phillis Wheatley and the Nigerian-American, Gustavas Vassa or Olaudah Equiano, the African. So you must make your own analogies with what follows here; I am assuming that feminist criticism receives much the same reception it has met with among Afro-American critics, male and female. Often, feminist concerns are seen as a divisive, white importation that further fragments an already divided and embattled race, as trivial mind games unworthy of response while black people everywhere confront massive economic and social problems. I don't deny feminism's potential for divisiveness, but the concerns of women are neither trivial nor petty. The relation between male and female is the very foundation of human society. If black men refuse to engage the unease at the race's heart, they cannot speak or even see truthfully anywhere else.

Feminist readings can lead to misapprehensions of particular texts or even of a whole tradition, but certain of its formulations offer us a vocabulary that can be made meaningful in terms of our own experience. Feminist theory, like black aesthetics, offers us not only the possibility of changing one's *reading* of the world, but of changing the world itself. And like black aesthetics, it is far more egalitarian than the prevailing mode. What follows, then, is both a critique of feminist theory and an application of that branch of it Alice Walker has called "womanist."[1] It is as much *bolekaja* criticism as "feminist" theory, for black women writers have been urging black men not so much to "come down [and] fight," as to come down and talk, even before Chinweizu, Jemie, and Madubuike coined a critical term to describe our challenge.[2]

218

Feminist criticism, to paraphrase Elaine Showalter's words in the "Introduction" to *The New Feminist Criticism*,[3] challenges the fundamental theoretical assumptions of literary history and criticism by demanding a radical rethinking and revisioning of the conceptual grounds of literary study that have been based almost entirely on male literary experiences. Some of the implications of this radical revisioning have already been realized in Afro-American literature. The works of forgotten black women writers are being resurrected and critics are at work revising the slighting, often misinformed critical opinions of their works. We have a fuller understanding of these writers because feminist criticism has begun to eliminate much of the phallocentrism from our readings of their work and to recover the female aesthetics said to distinguish female creativity from male. We can see the results of this inquiry in the numerous monographs and articles that have appeared in the nine years since the publication of Barbara Smith's ground-breaking essay, "Toward a Black Feminist Criticism" and in the fact that some black male critics are now numbered among the ranks of feminist critics.

Much of the present interest in black feminist criticism is rooted in the fact that black women writers are among the most exciting writers on the contemporary American literary scene, but the interest began in the confrontation of black women readers in the early seventies with black female portraiture (or its lack) in fiction by black male writers. Deborah E. McDowell, in "New Directions for Black Feminist Theory,"[4] values these pioneering studies of negative and derogatory female portraiture as an impetus to early black feminist inquiry and acknowledges that a black feminist criticism must do more than "merely focus on how black men have treated black women in literature." McDowell's major concern is with encouraging the development of theories that will help us to properly see and understand the themes, motifs, and idioms used by black women writers, but she raises other important issues as well. She touches upon one of the most disturbing aspects of current black feminist criticism, its separatism—its tendency to see not only a distinct black female culture but to see that culture as a separate cultural form having more in common with white female experience than with the facticity of Afro-American life. This proposition is problematic, even as a theoretical conjecture, especially since even its adherents have conceded that, until quite recently, black women's literary experiences were excluded from consideration in the literature of white feminists. For this reason, I prefer Alice Walker's term, womanist, as the referent for what I attempt here. Womanist theory is, by definition, "committed to the survival and wholeness of entire people," female and male, as well as to a valorization of women's works in all their varieties and multitudes. That commitment places it squarely within the challenge of engagement implicit in *bolekaja* criticism.

McDowell also calls for black feminist critics to turn their attention to the "challenging and necessary task" of a thoroughgoing examination of the works of black male writers, and suggests a line of inquiry that implicitly affirms kinship among Afro-American writers, "the countless thematic, stylistic, and imagistic parallels between black male and black female writing." Her call, however, does not go far enough. By limiting the studies of writings by black males to efforts "to determine the ways in which these commonalities are manifested differently in black women's writings and the ways in which they coincide with writings by black men," she seems to imply that feminist inquiry can only illuminate works by women and works that include female portraiture, that our rereadings of female image will not also change our readings of men. Womanist inquiry, on the other hand, assumes that it can talk both effectively and productively about men. This is a necessary assumption because the negative, stereotyped images of black women are only a part of the problem of phallocentric writings by black males. In order to understand that problem more fully, we must turn to what black men have written about themselves.

Much literature, classic and popular, by white American males valorizes the white patriarchal ideals of physical aggression, heroic conquest, and intellectual domination. A conventional feminist reading of black male literature, recognizing that a difference in actual circumstances forced distinguishing and different characteristics on would-be black patriarchs, would see these ideals only partially "encoded" in writings by black American males. Even so, such ideals would be the desired ones and deviation from them taken as signs of diminished masculine self-esteem. That is, explicit social protest about racial prohibitions that restrict black men from exercising patriarchal authority is part of their "heroic quest" because they don't possess all the privileges of white men. Such a reading, of course, tends to reduce the black struggle for justice and equal opportunity to the right to beat one's wife and daughter. Many black men refused to exercise such "rights" and many black women resisted those who tried.[5] Nor was physical aggression really a value in the literature of black males before 1940. Physical force, even when used by non-heroic black men, was almost always defensive, especially against white people, and, when used against other blacks, generally symbolized the corruption wrought by slavery. The initial formulation, however, does serve to illuminate some instances of black male self-portraiture, particularly in nineteenth-century narrative and fiction.

Nineteenth-century black men, confronted with the impossibility of being the (white) patriarch, began to subvert certain of patriarchy's ideals and values to conform to their own images. Thus, the degree to which, and the basis on which, the hero avoids physical aggression was one means of establishing the hero's noble stature and contributed to the hero's intellectual equality with—not dominance over—the collective white man. Frederick Douglass's 1845 autobiography, *Narrative of the Life of Frederick Douglass, An American Slave*,[6] offers several instances of this subversion and redefinition of white patriarchal ideals. I focus on what he will later call "The Fight."[7] Douglass, an "uppity" slave, is hired out to Covey, a "nigger-breaker," to have his spirit curbed. Douglass's "fight" with Covey marks the turning point in his development from slave to free man. In the instant he refuses to be whipped, Douglass ceases "to be a slave in fact." Yet Douglass is not the aggressor. Douglass seizes Covey by the throat when the latter tries to tie him up and holds him "uneasy"; though Douglass does draw Covey's blood, he actually touches him only with the ends of his fingers. Douglass brings the white man to the ground but never lays violent hands on him; rather, he "seizes him by the collar." Douglass is thus able to dominate Covey by his own self-restraint and self-control rather than by force major. Douglass takes a great delight in having bested Covey while conforming to a semblance of the master-slave relationship. In the later retelling of the episode he returns "a polite, 'Yes, sir,'" to Covey's outraged, "Are you going to continue to resist?" and concludes, "I was victorious because my aim had not been to injure him but to prevent his injuring me."

Robert B. Stepto, in *From Behind the Veil*[8] (itself a brilliant example of the use to which genre studies can be put), details the brilliant strokes by which, "Douglass reinforces his posture as an articulate hero"—that is, the intellectual equal of the white men who introduce and thus vouch for the authenticity of Douglass and his narrative before the white world. In "supplant[ing the white men] as the definitive historian[s] of his past," Douglass self-consciously reverses the usual patterns of authentication in black texts; this manifestation of his intellectual independence is characterized by the same restraint and subtlety as his description of his successful psychological rite of passage.

The pattern of self-restraint, of physical self-control as an avenue to moral superiority and intellectual equality vis-à-vis white society, dominates male self-portraiture in the nineteenth century, where achieving heroic stature is most often the means by which the black male hero also assumes the mantle of the "patriarch." But the black patriarch in the nineteenth century has more to do with providing for and protecting his "dependents" than with wielding authority or exploiting their dependency so as to achieve his own privilege. Once free, Douglass marries, takes a job, becomes a leader in the struggle for the abolition of slavery; Josiah Henson, the model for Harriet Beecher Stowe's *Uncle Tom*,[9] escapes from slavery with his wife beside him and two children on his back, works on the Underground Railroad, and founds a black township in Canada. Dr. Miller, the hero of Charles Chesnutt's turn-of-the-century novel, *The Marrow of Tradition*,[10] is a husband, father, son, and founder of a hospital and school for blacks. Black male heroic stature was most often achieved within the context of marriage, family, and black community—all of which depend on a relationship with, if not a black woman, at least other black people.

The nature of the black male character's heroic quest and the means by which the hero achieves intellectual parity begin to change in the twentieth century. The heroic quest through the early thirties was a largely introspective one whose goal was the reintegration of the educated hero with the unlettered black masses who symbolized his negro-ness.[11] But the valuation of black community and black family (often an extended family) continues until 1940. Richard Wright's *Native Son* began a period in which the black heroic quest was increasingly externalized. A perceptive, though not necessarily articulate or educated, protagonist seeks recognition from the white power structure and in the process comes to recognize—and realize—himself. By the mid-1960s, white society was typically characterized by physically frail and cowardly, morally weak, sexually impotent, effeminate white men and superfeminine white women who personified the official standard of feminine beauty—delicate, dainty, sexually inhibited until liberated by a hyperpotent black man.[12] The goal of the black hero's quest was to dominate the one and marry the other. Black community, once the object of heroic quest, was, in these works, an impediment to its success;

black female portraiture, when present, was often no more than demeaning stereo-types used to justify what even the hero sometimes recognized as a pathological obsession with the white woman. This kind of heroic quest is a dominant feature in some important contemporary texts; however, black male self-portraiture, by the late 1970s, was presented within a broader spectrum of themes—patriarchal responsibility, sibling relations, and male bonding—that were self-questioning rather than self-satisfied or self-righteous.[13] These few texts can be construed as a positive response to the black feminist criticism of the early seventies. Yet they are largely neglected by the Afro-American critical establishment which, by and large, leaves to *The New York Times* the task of canonizing our literature. The present interest in black women's writing arose outside that hegemony, as had the interest in black poetry in the late sixties. And, like the black aesthetics that arose as a response to black arts poetry, black feminist criticism runs the risk of being narrowly proscriptive rather than broadly analytic.

Michele Wallace, using a combination of fiction and nonfiction prose—the novels of Richard Wright, Ralph Ellison, and James Baldwin, the essays of Baldwin, Norman Mailer, and Eldridge Cleaver—suggests, in *Black Macho and the Myth of the Superwoman*,[14] a black feminist reading of the development of modern black male self-image that is similar to what I have said here. Wallace was roundly damned and told by sister feminists "to read it again," as though we ourselves had not suspected, even suggested, these things before. And no one has quite dared since then to hold up the record black men have written of themselves. Rather, since black men gave little evidence of talking to us, we talked to each other.

Having confronted what black men have said about us, it is now time for black feminist critics to confront black male writers with what they have said about themselves. What is needed is a thoroughgoing examination of male images in the works of black male writers. This is a necessary step in ending the separatist tendency in Afro-American criticism and in achieving in Afro-American literature feminist's theory's avowed aim of "challenging the fundamental theoretical assumptions of traditional literary history and criticism." Black women as readers and writers have been kept out of literary endeavor, so we had, and have, a lot to say. But to focus solely on ourselves is to fall into the same hole The Brother has dug for himself—narcissism, isolation, inarticulation, obscurity. Of course we must keep talking to and about ourselves, but literature, as Chinweizu and Walker remind us, is about community and dialogue; theories or ways of reading ought actively to promote the enlargement of both.

NOTES

1. Alice Walker, *In Search of Our Mothers' Gardens* (San Diego: Harcourt Brace/Jovanovich, 1984), xi.

2. Onwuchekwa Jemie, Chinweizu, Ihechukwu Madbuike, *Toward the Decolonization of African Literature* (Washington: Howard University Press, 1983), xii.

3. Elaine Showalter, ed., *The New Feminist Criticism: Essays on Women, Literature and Theory* (New York: Pantheon Books, 1985), 8.

4. Deborah McDowell, "New Directions for Black Feminist Criticism," *op. cit.*, 196.

5. Further research in both traditional and contemporary Afro-American orature just might document that the community valued going "upside" anyone's head as a *last*, rather than the first, resort at least as much as they admired the ability or will to do so.

6. Frederick Douglass, *Narrative of the Life of an American Slave Written by Himself*, ed. Benjamin Quarles (1845; reprint, Cambridge, Mass.: Harvard University Press, 1960), 103–104.

7. Frederick Douglass, *My Bondage and My Freedom* 1855 (reprint, New York: Arno Press, 1969), 243.

8. Robert B. Stepto, *From Behind the Veil* (Urbana, Ill.: 1979), 16–26.

9. Josiah Henson, *Father Henson's Own Story* (reprint, Upper Saddle River, N.J.: 1849; Literature House rep, 1970).

10. Charles Chesnutt, *The Marrow of Tradition* (1901; reprint, Ann Arbor, Mich.: University of Michigan Press, 1969).

11. The key texts include James Weldon Johnson's *The Autobiography of an Ex-Colored Man* (1912), Jean Toomer's *Cane* (1923), and Langston Hughes's *Not Without Laughter* (1930).

12. The terminology is drawn from Eldridge Cleaver's *Soul on Ice* (New York: McGraw-Hill, Inc., 1968), but the portrayal can be found in the works of black male writers from Richard Wright and Ralph Ellison to Ishmael Reed.

13. Ernest J. Gaines's *In My Father's House* (New York: W. W. Norton Co., 1978) and Wesley Brown's *Tragic Magic* (New York: Random House, 1978) come most readily to mind; however, the works of William Melvin Kelley, John McCluskey, and John A. Williams present a range of black male characters that still awaits close discussion.

14. Michelle Wallace, *Black Macho and the Myth of the Superwoman* (New York: The Dial Press, 1978).

22 Belief, Theory, and Blues

Notes for a Post-Structuralist Criticism of Afro-American Literature

Houston A. Baker, Jr.

(1986)

I

Faith may be conceived, I think, as an affective disposition toward the symbolic that serves as a ground for belief. If faith is indeed the evidence of things hoped for, the essence of things unseen, it is still not without symbolic resources for holding the "unseen" in the mind's eye of the believer. Belief and theory meet precisely at the place of such symbolic resources. Metaphor is the ground, that is to say, on which theory and belief meet. The universe of intellectual discourse that has experienced the entry of Thomas Kuhn's *The Structure of Scientific Revolutions* and that has absorbed the debates attendant upon that work's formulations surely contains ample support for the notion that all theories are but "paradigms" conceived and supported by a select community of scholars. And a paradigm is best thought of as a model or a picture—a *metaphorical* mode of appropriating masses of data to ourselves as "reality." Paradigms, like faith, are in a sense the essence of things hoped for, the evidence of things unseen. "Faith," wrote H. L. Mencken, "may be defined briefly as an illogical belief in the occurrence of the improbable." Both the "illogical" and the "improbable" signal the worlds of faith, belief, theory—and metaphor.

In a sense too complex to enter fully into here, the movement of Afro-American literary study during the past several decades has represented a journey from belief to theory over the shifty terrain of metaphor and in the regions of increasing metaphorical sophistication. Some years ago, I proposed the argument that the Black Aesthetic (a dominant critical and theoretical posture among black spokespersons of the 1960s and the 1970s), in its conative assertiveness, was but a continuation of a critical line founded on idealism. The thing most needed for the realization—the wish-fulfillment, as it were—of the Afro-American critic who predicted a glorious future for the works of art that he or she studied was always absent—always merely

224

an ideal. Only in a pluralistic and genuinely democratic society could the demands and dreams of both black writers and critics become lived realities. And that society remained but a metaphor, something hoped for and unseen. During the 1960s and 1970s, black spokespersons substituted a darker metaphor for an American democratic ideal. They conceived a Black Nation as the world in which Afro-American works of art would have successful and perdurable effects. The new metaphor and its attendant patterns of belief proved perhaps more effective for the progress of Afro-American criticism than earlier paradigms, but once the faith (which Adam Powell so adamantly urged us to keep) was lost in "blackness," little of a theoretical cast remained.

Rather than "probability," in the sense implied by Mencken, perhaps the faith that has traditionally characterized Afro-American literary study is a matter of possibility. What founders of our critical line and their successors in the Black Aesthetic most decisively bequeathed was a belief in the possibility of a strong tradition of Afro-American art and critical reflection, a tradition invulnerable to the scathing derogation of a racist society, and in tracing its lineage to sounds, rhythms, and behaviors far older than those of the verdant shores of a New World.

The master of metaphor in the Afro-American community, of course, has long since been acknowledged as the preacher, and James Weldon Johnson's preacher-as-Creator in "The Creation" captures the sense of metaphorical possibility I have in mind when he says, "I'll make me a world." Stepping out on space and conatively declaring the possibility of a signal and accomplished world of Afro-American literary art amenable to advanced modes of study and interpretation constitutes an act equivalent to that of Johnson's speaker. The movement from metaphors of possibility to possible explanatory metaphors is a journey from belief to theory. Having seized the possibility of a signal world, the task of the scholar of Afro-American literature is to elaborate metaphors that supply appropriate and adequate characterizations of the world. After idealism has willed a world into existence and secured its acknowledgement, the scholar's job is to persuasively isolate and describe features of this world by suggesting what he or she deems an adequate paradigm. Having arrived at such an articulation, however, the scholar has not left behind belief in any extended, metaphorical sense of the term.

The scholar does not take his or her paradigm as a map of reality, but as a possible guide to phenomena that he or she both perceives and half-creates. A paradigm is the most persuasively complete account available for what its proposer believes is to be seen. Like the particle physicist, the scholar is not privileged to conduct an on-site reality check vis-à-vis the phenomena that are of most interest, nor is one required to do so under the conditions of metaphorical persuasiveness that I have implied.

While the paradigm is, indeed, a model, it should not be conceived in the stick-and-colored-ball terms through which so many of us received our first instruction in molecules. Rather, the paradigm should be conceived as a trope, an unusual and defamiliarizing figure of language. The figure of the preacher is again suggestive. As he weaves his sermon, the Afro-American minister is likely to "fire arrows from God's quiver of truth" or to use a "mighty truth to break the heart of stone." He will evoke a celestial railway running from the Garden of Creation to the burning of the Last Judgment. His hand raised perilously above the heads of occupants of the mourner's bench, he will tell of the locomotive's cow-catcher wounding King Jesus in the side and releasing redemptive blood like a bold creek rising. The symbolic grounds of belief are, thus, resonantly and persuasively woven by the religious man of words. He is one who can miraculously transform a Southern landscape by interweaving a baseball pennant race with shards of Martin Luther King's orations and American patriotic gore. The mix is a heady one: "Land where my fathers died, land of the Pilgrims' pride! Land where all men have a dream, as Dr. King told us! Land of the world-famous Atlanta Braves!" When skillfully wrought, the preacher's metaphors for belief yield restless "Amens!" of assent.

Similarly, when the scholar's paradigmatic metaphors, or tropes, are appropriately wrought, assent is guaranteed. What the scholar achieves by using successful theoretical tropes—i.e., striking linguistic figures, extended and detailed to provide accounts of, say, literary works of art—is a view of "reality" in which subject and object fruitfully unite in a metaphorical bond. Scholars construct self-consistent, coherent models that both they and their audiences agree upon as the way "things" indisputably are. A disconcerting aspect of such tropological work is that what are normally regarded as "things" may, indeed, cease to exist in an empirical and observable simplicity. Bertrand Russell once wryly commented on the entailments of modern physics as follows: "The observer, when he seems to himself to be observing a stone, is really, if physics is to be believed, observing the effects of the stone upon himself." Relativistic, fluid, demanding artful interpretation—such is the world implied by Russell's observation. And such, as well, is the world of Afro-American literary art willed into existence by the metaphorical beliefs and theoretical metaphors of those who have brought us to the present, enormously exciting moment in the study of Afro-American literature and culture.

The metaphors likely to prevail in a universe of Afro-American literary-theoretical discourse are metaphors drawn from the vernacular. By the vernacular I want to suggest not only the majority of Afro-Americans, but, in both an economic and a political sense, the American majority. An image from a resonantly vernacular tradition of Afro-American expression serves to capture my notion of the vernacular. The picture is drawn from the black blues and sung as follows by Howlin' Wolf: "I'm a poor boy, a long way from home/well, Lawd, I'm a poor boy, a long way from home/ No spending money in my pocket, no spare meat on my bones." Citizens of the vernacular are those not numbered among the 44/100ths percent of the world that controls the major share of its capital resources. They are people like me whose epic drama is getting out of bed in the morning and making it from stormy Monday to "just one more Saturday night." By vernacular metaphors, then, I want to suggest paradigmatic explanations that account for human behavior at an "ordinary" level, if such a term can be invoked without setting off all kinds of judgmental bells. By "ordinary," I want to signal "most of us," and my dichotomy would be similar to that of a writer like Chinweizu who separates "the West" and "the rest of us." Hence, what I am after, and what I think Afro-American literary study in general must seek, are explanatory models that answer questions like: What are the nature and function of human symbolic behavior? How do various symbolic systems combine and diverge to produce expressive behavior? How do axiological constraints operate in human communities to privilege certain forms of expressive behavior? My own first model for arriving at adequate answers to such questions was drawn from the realm of symbolic anthropology. I believed that an interdisciplinary account predicated on the assumption of "Man as Speaking Subject" and employing resources of contemporary linguistic theory would illuminate the way in which Afro-American literary works of art functioned as uniquely expressive behavior that received the positive judgment of the Afro-American community. In more recent work, my metaphorical grounding has shifted from man as speaker to the text conceived of as an always/already spoken. The most adequate way, perhaps, of representing the nature of my current tropological energies is to turn now to reflections drawn from the "introduction" to my recently-completed critical study entitled *Blues, Ideology, and Afro-American Literature.*[1] Some of the more general assertions of the foregoing prefatory remarks will surely be clarified and, I hope, profitably extended by the following discussions, which begin with a rather-too-autobiographical account of my shift from a symbolic to a more materialistically-oriented critical prospect.

II

Standing at the crossroads, tried to flag a ride,
Standing at the crossroads, tried to flag a ride,
Ain't nobody seem to know me, everybody passed me by.

—"CROSSROAD BLUES"

In every case the result of an untrue mode of knowledge must not be allowed to run away into an empty nothing, but must necessarily be grasped as the nothing *of that from which it results*—a result which contains what was true in the preceding knowledge. —HEGEL, *PHENOMENOLOGY OF SPIRIT*

So perhaps we shy from confronting our cultural wholeness because it offers no easily recognizable points of rest, no facile certainties as to who, what, or where (culturally or historically) we are. Instead, the whole is always in cacophonic motion.

—RALPH ELLISON, "THE LITTLE MAN AT THE CHEHAW STATION"

[M]aybe one day, you'll find they actually do understand exactly what you are talking about, all these fantasy people. All these blues people.

—AMIRI BARAKA, *DUTCHMAN*

FROM SYMBOL TO IDEOLOGY

In my book *The Journey Back: Issues in Black Literature and Criticism* (Chicago: University of Chicago Press, 1980), I envisioned the "speaking subject" creating language (a code) to be deciphered by the present-day commentator. In my current study, I envision language (the code) "speaking" the subject. The subject is "de-centered." My quest during the past decade has been for the distinctive, the culturally-specific aspects of Afro-American literature and culture. Convinced that I had found such specificity in a peculiar subjectivity, the objectivity of economics and the sound lessons of post-structuralism arose to re-orient my thinking. I was convinced that the symbolic and, quite specifically, the symbolically-anthropological offered avenues to the comprehension of Afro-American expressive culture in its plenitude.[2] I discovered that the symbolic's antithesis—i.e., practical reason or the material—is as necessary for understanding Afro-American discourse as the cultural-in-itself.

My shift from a centered to a de-centered subject, from an exclusively symbolic to a more inclusively expressive perspective was prompted by the curious force of dialectical thought. My access to the study of such thought came from attentive readings of Fredric Jameson, Hayden White, Marshall Sahlins, and others. While profiting from the observations of these scholars, I also began to attend meetings of a study group devoted to Hegel's *Phenomenology of Spirit*.

Having journeyed, with the aid of symbolic anthropology, to what appeared the soundest possible observations on Afro-American art, I found myself confronted suddenly by a figure-to-ground reversal. A fitting image for the effect of my re-orientation toward the material is the gestalt illustration of the Greek hydria (a water vase with curved handles) that transforms itself into the face of an older woman. John Keats' "Ode on a Grecian Urn," with its familiar detailings of the economies of "art" and human emotions, might be considered one moment in the gestalt shift that I have in mind. Contrasting with these romantic figurations is the emergent face of a venerable ancestry. The shift from Greek hydrias to ancestral faces is a shift from high art to vernacular expression in America.

The "vernacular," in relation to human beings, signals, "a slave born on his master's estate." In expressive terms, vernacular indicates "arts native or peculiar to a particular country or locale." The material conditions of slavery in the United States and the rhythms of Afro-American blues combined and emerged from my revised materialistic perspective as an ancestral matrix that has produced a forceful and indigenous American creativity. The moment of emergence of economic and vernacular concerns left me, as the French say, *entre les deux*: suspended somewhere between anthropology and analytical strategies that Fredric Jameson calls the "ideology of form."[3]

IDEOLOGY, SEMIOTICS, AND THE MATERIAL

I do not want to imply, however, in acknowledging a concern for the ideology of form, that may symbolic-anthropological orientation was untrue, in the sense of deluded or deceived. This symbolic orientation was simply one moment in my experiencing of Afro-American culture—a moment superseded now by a prospect that constitutes its determinate negation.[4] What was true in my prior framework remains so in my current concern for the ideology of form. Certainly, the mode of ideological investigation proposed by Jameson is an analysis that escapes all hints of "vulgar Marxism" through its studious attention to modern critiques of political economy, and also through its shrewd incorporation of post-structuralist thought.[5]

In the chapters of *Blues, Ideology, and Afro-American Literature*, I too attempt to avoid a naive Marxism. I do not believe, for example, that a fruitful correlation exists when one merely claims that certain black folk seculars are determinate results of agricultural gang labor. Such attributions simply privilege the material as a substrate while failing to provide detailed accounts of the processes leading from an apparent substrate to a peculiar expressive form. A faith of enormous magnitude is required to accept such crude formulations as adequate explanatory statements. The "material" is shifty ground. And current-critiques of political economy suggest that postulates based on this ground can be appropriately understood only in "semiotic" terms. Hence, the employment of ideology as an analytical category begins with the awareness that "production" as well as "modes of production" must be grasped in terms of the sign. Jean Baudrillard, for example, argues a persuasive case for "political economy" as a code existing in a relationship of identity with language.[6] To read economics as a semiotic process leads to the realization that ideological analyses may be as decidedly intertextual as, say, analyses of the relationship between Afro-American vernacular expression and more sophisticated forms of verbal art. For if what is normally categorized as material (e.g., "raw material," "consumer goods") can be semiotically interpreted, then any collection of such entities and their defining interrelationships may be defined as a text.

In *Blues, Ideology, and Afro-American Literature*, however, I do not write or interpret the *material* in exclusively semiotic terms. Although fully aware of insights to be gained from semiotics, my analyses focus directly on the living and laboring conditions of people designated as "the desperate class" by James Weldon Johnson's narrator in *The Autobiography of an Ex-Coloured Man*. Such people constitute the vernacular in the United States. Their lives have always been sharply conditioned by an "economics of slavery" as they worked agricultural rows, searing furnaces, rolling levees, bustling roundhouses, and piney-woods' logging camps in America. The sense of "production" and "modes of production" that foregrounds this Afro-American labor in the United States seems an appropriate inscription of the material.

THE MATRIX AS BLUES

The guiding presupposition of my new book is that Afro-American culture is a complex, reflexive enterprise which finds its proper figuration in blues conceived of as a matrix. A matrix is a womb, a network, a rock bearing embedded fossils, a rocky trace of a gemstone's removal, a principal metal in an alloy, a mat or plate for reproducing print or phonograph records respectively. The matrix is a point of ceaseless input and output, a web of intersecting, crisscrossing impulses always in productive transit. Afro-American blues constitute such a vibrant network. They are what the French philosopher Jacques Derrida might describe as the "always already" of Afro-American culture.[7] They are the multiplex, enabling script in which Afro-American cultural discourse is inscribed.

First arranged, scored, and published for commercial distribution early in the twentieth century when Hart Wand, Arthur "Baby" Seals, and W. C. Handy released their first compositions, the blues defy narrow definition. For they exist not as a function of formal inscription, but as a forceful condition of Afro-American inscription itself. They were for Handy a "found" folk signified, awakening him from (perhaps) a dream of American form in Tutwiler, Mississippi, in 1903.[8] At a railroad juncture deep in the Southern night Handy dozed restlessly as he awaited the arrival of a much-delayed train. A guitar's bottle-neck resonance suddenly jolted him to consciousness, as a lean, loose-jointed, shabbily-clad black man sang:

> Goin' where the Southern cross the Dog.
> Goin' where the Southern cross the Dog.
> Goin' where the Southern cross the Dog.

This haunting invocation of railroad crossings in bottle-neck tones left Handy stupified and motivated. In 1914, he published his own "Yellow Dog Blues."

But the autobiographical account of the man called "Father of the Blues" offers only a simplistic detailing of a progress, describing, as it were, the elevation of a "primitive" folk ditty to the status of "art" in America. Handy's rendering leaves unexamined, therefore, myriad corridors, mainroads, and way-stations of an extraordinary and elusive Afro-American cultural phenomenon.

DEFINING BLUES

The task of adequately describing the blues is equivalent to the labor of describing a world-class athlete's awesome gymnastics. Adequate appreciation demands comprehensive attention. An investigator has to be there, following a course recommended by one of the African writer Wole Soyinka's ironic narrators to a London landlord to "see for yourself."

The elaborations of the blues may begin in an austere self-accusation: "Now this trouble I'm having, I brought it all on myself." But the accusation seamlessly fades into humorous acknowledgment of duplicity's always-duplicitious triumph: "You know the woman that I love, I stoled her from my best friend,/But you know that fool done got lucky and stole her back again." Simple provisos for the troubled mind are commonplace, and drear exactions of crushing manual labor are objects of wry, in situ commentary. Numinous invocation punctuates a guitar's resonant back beat with: "Lawd, Lawd, Lawd . . . have mercy on me/Please send me someone, to end this misery." Existential declarations of lack combine with lustily macabre prophecies of the subject's demise. If a "match box" will hold his clothes, surely the roadside of much-travelled highways will be his memorial plot: "You can bury my body down by the highway side/So my old devil spirit can catch a Greyhound bus and ride." Conative formulations of a brighter future (sun shining in the back door some day, wind rising to blow the blues away) join with a slow moving *askesis* of present, amorous imprisonment: "You leavin' now, baby, but you hangin' crepe on my door," or, "She got a mortgage on my body, and lien on my soul." Deprecating confessionals and slack-strumming growls of violent solutions combine: "My lead mule's cripple, you know my off mule's blind/You know I can't drive nobody/Bring me a loaded .39 (I'm go'n pop him, pop that mule!)." The wish for a river of whiskey where if one were a "divin' duck" he would submerge himself and never "come up" is a function of a world in which: "When you lose yo' eyesight, yo' best friend's gone/Sometimes yo' own dear people don't want to fool with you long."

Like a streamlined athlete's awesomely dazzling explosions of prowess, the blues song erupts, creating a veritable playful festival of meaning. Rather than a rigidly personalized form, the blues offer a phylogenetic recapitulation—a non-linear, freely-associative, non-sequential meditation—of species experience. What emerges is not a filled subject, but an anonymous (nameless) voice issuing from the black (w)hole.[9] The blues singer's signatory coda is always atopic, placeless: "If anybody ask you who sang this song/Tell 'em X done been here and gone." The "signature" is a space already "X" (ed), a trace of the already "gone"—a fissure rejoined. Nevertheless, the "you" (audience) addressed is always free to invoke the X(ed) spot in the body's absence.[10] For the signature comprises a scripted authentication of "your" feelings. Its mark is an invitation to energizing intersubjectivity. Its implied (in)junction reads: Here is my body meant for (a phylogenetically conceived) you.

The blues are a synthesis (albeit one always synthesizing rather than one already hypostatized). Combining work songs, group seculars, field hollers, sacred harmonies, proverbial wisdom, folk philosophy, political commentary, ribald humor, elegiac lament, and much more, they constitute an amalgam that seems always to have been in motion in America—always becoming, shaping, transforming, displacing the peculiar experience of Africans in the New World.

BLUES AS CODE AND FORCE

One way of describing the blues is to claim their amalgam as a code radically conditioning Afro-America's cultural signifying. Such a description implies a prospect in which any aspect of the blues—a guitar's growling vamp or a stanza's sardonic boast of heroically back-breaking labor—"stands," in Umberto Eco's words, "for something else" by virtue of a systematic set of conventional procedures.[11] The materiality of any blues manifestation such as a guitar's walking bass, or a French harp's "whoop" of motion-seen, is, one might say, enciphered in ways that enable the material to escape into a named or coded blues signification. The material, thus, slips into irreversible difference. And as phenomena named and set in a meaningful relation by a blues code, both the harmonica's whoop and the guitar's bass can recapitulate vast dimensions of experience, for such discrete blues instances are always intertextually related by the blues code as a whole. Moreover, they are involved in the code's manifold interconnections with other codes of Afro-American culture.

A further characterization of blues suggests that they are equivalent to Hegelian "force."[12] In the *Phenomenology*, Hegel speaks of a flux in which there is "only *difference* as a *universal* difference, or as a difference into which the many antitheses have been resolved. This difference, as a *universal* difference, is consequently the *simple element in the play of Force itself* and what is true in it. It is the *law of Force*" (p. 90). Force is thus defined as a relational matrix wherein difference is the law. Finally the blues, employed as an image for the investigation of culture, represent a force not unlike electricity. Hegel writes:

> Of course, given *positive* electricity, negative too is given *in principle*; for the positive is, only as related to a negative, or, the positive is in *its own self* the difference from itself; and similarly with the negative. But that electricity as such should divide itself in this way is not in itself a necessity. Electricity, as *simple Force*, is indifferent to its law— *to be* positive and negative; and if we call the former its *Notion* but the latter its being, then its Notion is indifferent to its being. It merely has this property, which just means that this property is not *in itself* necessary to it . . . It is only with law as law that we are to compare its *Notion* as Notion, or its necessity. But in all these forms, necessity has shown itself to be only an empty word. (P. 93)

Metaphorically extending Hegel's formulation vis-à-vis electricity, one might say that a traditional property of cultural study may well be the kind of dichotomies inscribed in terms like "culture" and "practical reason." But even if such dichotomies are raised to the status of law, they never constitute the necessity or "determinant instances" of cultural study and explanation conceived in terms of force—envisioned, that is, in the analytic notion of a blues matrix as force. The blues, therefore, comprise a mediational site at which familiar antinomies are resolved (or dissolved) in the office of adequate cultural understanding.

BLUES TRANSLATION AT THE JUNCTION

To suggest a trope for the blues as a forceful matrix in cultural understanding is to summon an image of the black blues singer at the railway junction lustily transforming experiences of a durative (unceasingly oppressive) landscape into the extraordinary energies of rhythmic song. The railway juncture is marked by transience. Its inhabitants are always travelers—a multifarious assembly in transit. The "X" of crossing roadbeds signals the multidirectionality of the juncture and is simply a single instance in a boundless network that redoubles and circles, makes sidings and ladders, forms Ys and branches over the vastness of hundreds of thousands of American miles. Polymorphous and multidirectional, scene of arrivals and departures, place betwixt and between (ever *entre les deux*), the juncture is the way-station of the blues.

The singer and his production are always at this intersection, this crossing, codifying force, providing resonance for experience's multiplicities. Singer and song never arrest transience—fix it in "transcendent form." Instead, they provide expressive equivalence for the juncture's ceaseless flux. Hence, they may be conceived of as translators.[13]

Like translators of written texts, blues and their sundry performers offer interpretations of the experiencing of experience. To experience the juncture's ever-changing scenes, like successive readings of ever-varying texts by conventional translators, is to produce vibrantly polyvalent interpretations encoded as blues. The singer's product, like the railway juncture itself (or a successful translator's original), constitutes a lively scene, a robust matrix, in which endless antinomies are mediated and understanding and explanation find conditions of possibility.

The durative—transliterated as lyrical statements of injustice, despair, loss, absence, denial, and so forth—is complemented in blues performance by an instrumental energy (guitar, harmonica, fiddle, gut-bucket bass, molasses jug, washboard) that employs locomotive rhythms, train bells and whistles, as onomatopoeic references. In *A Theory of Semiotics*, Eco writes:

> Music presents, on the one hand, the problem of a semiotic system without a semantic level (or a content plane): on the other hand, however, there are musical "signs" (or syntagms) with an explicit denotative value (trumpet signals in the army) and there are syntagms or entire "texts" possessing pre-culturalized connotative value ("pastoral" or "thrilling" music, etc.). (P. 111)

The absence of what Eco calls a content plane implies what is commonly referred to as the "abstractness" of instrumental music. The "musical sign," on the other hand, suggests cultural signals that function onomatopoetically by calling to mind "natural" sounds, or sounds "naturally" associated with common human situations. Surely, though, it would be a mistake to claim that onomatopoeia is, in any sense, "natural"; for different cultures encode even the "same" natural sounds in varying ways. (A rooster onomatopoetically sounded in Puerto Rican Spanish is phonically unrecognizable in United States English, as a classic Puerto Rican short story makes hilariously clear.)

If onomatopoeia is taken as cultural mimesis, however, it is possible to apply the semiotician's observations to blues by pointing out that the dominant blues syntagm in America is an instrumental imitation of *train-wheels-over-track-junctures*. This sound is the "sign," as it were, of the blues, and it combines an intriguing melange of phonics: rattling gondolas, clattering flatbeds, quilling whistles, clanging bells, rumbling box-cars, and other railroad sounds. A blues text may, thus, announce itself by the onomatopoeia of the train's whistle sounded on the indrawn breath of a harmonica or a train's bell tinkled on the high keys of an upright piano. The blues stanzas may then roll through an extended meditative repertoire with a steady train-wheels-over-track-junctures guitar backbeat as a traditional, syntagmatic complement. If desire and absence are driving conditions of blues performances, the amelioration of such conditions is implied by the onomatopoeic training of blues voice and instrument. Only a trained voice can sing the blues.[14]

At the junctures, the intersections of experience where roads cross and diverge, the blues singer and his performance serve as codifiers, absorbing and transforming discontinuous experience into formal expressive instances that bear only the trace of origins, refusing to be pinned down to any final, dualistic significance. Even as they speak of paralyzing absence and ineradicable desire, their instrumental rhythms suggest change, movement, action, continuance, unlimited and unending possibility. Like signification itself, blues are always nomadically wandering. Like the freight-hopping hobo, they are ever on the move, ceaselessly summing novel experience.

ANTINOMIES AND BLUES MEDIATION

The blues performance is further suggestive if economic conditions of Afro-American existence are brought to mind. Standing at the juncture, or railhead, the singer draws into his repertoire hollers, cries, whoops, and moans of black men and women working in fields without recompense. The performance can be cryptically conceived, therefore, in terms suggested by the bluesman Booker White, who has said: "The foundation of the blues is working behind a mule way back in slavery time."[15] As a force, the blues matrix defines itself as a network mediating poverty and abundance in much the same manner that it reconciles durative and kinetic. Many instances of the blues performance contain lyrical inscriptions of both existential lack and commercial possibility. The performance that sings of abysmal poverty and deprivation may be recompenced by sumptuous food and stimulating beverage at a country picnic, amorous favors from an attentive listener, enhanced Afro-American communality, or Yankee dollars from representatives of record companies traveling the South in search of blues as commodifiable entertainment. The performance, therefore, mediates one of the most prevalent of all antinomies in cultural investigation—creativity and commerce.

As driving force, the blues matrix, thus, avoids simple dualities. It perpetually achieves its effects as a fluid and multivalent network. It is only when "understanding"—i.e., the analytical work of a translator who translates the infinite changes of the blues—converges with such blues "force" that adequate explanatory perception (and half-creation) occurs. The matrix effectively functions toward cultural understanding, that is, only when an investigator brings an inventive attention to bear.

THE INVESTIGATOR, RELATIVELY, AND BLUES EFFECT

The blues matrix is a "cultural invention"; i.e., a "negative symbol" that generates (or obliges one to invent) its own referents.[16] As an inventive trope, this matrix provides the type of image or model that is always present in accounts of culture and cultural products. If the analyses that I provide in my new book prove successful, the blues matrix will have taken effect (and affect) through me.

To "take effect," of course, is not identical with to "come into existence" or to "demonstrate serviceability for the first time." Since what I have defined as a blues matrix is so demonstrably anterior to any single instance of its cultural-explanatory employment, then my predecessors are obviously legion. "Take effect," therefore, does not herald discovery in the traditional sense of that word. Rather, it signals the tropological nature of my uses of an already extant matrix.

Accounts of art, literature, and culture ordinarily fail to acknowledge their governing theories; further, they almost invariably conceal the inventive character of such theories. Nevertheless, all accounts of art, expressive culture, or culture in general are indisputably functions of their creators' tropological energies. When such creators talk of "art," for example, they are never dealing with existential givens. Rather, they are summoning objects, processes, or events defined by a model that they have created (by and for themselves) as a picture of art. Such models, or tropes, are continually invoked to constitute and explain phenomena unseen and unheard by the senses. Any single model, or any complementary set of inventive tropes, therefore, will offer only a selective account of experience—a partial reading, as it were, of the world. While the single account temporarily reduces chaos to ordered plan, all such accounts are eternally troubled by "remainders."

Where literary art is concerned, for example, a single, ordering, investigative model or trope will necessarily exclude phenomena that an alternative model or trope privileges as a definitive artistic instance. Recognizing the determinacy of "invention" in cultural explanation entails the acknowledgment of what might be called normative relativity. To acknowledge relativity in our post-Heisenbergian universe is, of course, far from original. Nor is it an invitation to the skeptics or the conservatives to heroically assume the critical stage.

The assumption of normative relativity, far from being a call to abandonment or retrenchment in the critical arena, constitutes an invitation to speculative explorations that are aware both of their own partiality and their heuristic translations from suggestive (sometimes dramatic) images to inscribed concepts. The openness implied by relativity enables, say, the literary critic to re-cognize his endeavors, presupposing from the outset that such labors are not directed toward independent, observable, empirical phenomena, but rather toward processes, objects, and events that he or she half-creates (and privileges as "art") through his or her own speculative, inventive energies and interests.

One axiological extrapolation from these observations on invention and relativity is that no object, process, or signal element possesses intrinsic aesthetic value. The "art object" as well as its value are selective constructions of the critic's tropes and models. A radicalizing uncertainty may, thus, be said to mark cultural explanation. This uncertainty is similar in kind to the always selective endeavors of, say, the particle physicist.[17]

The physicist is always compelled to choose between velocity and position.[18] Similarly, an investigator of, say, Afro-American expressive culture is ceaselessly compelled to forgo manifold variables in order to apply intensive energy to a selected array.

Continuing the metaphor, one might say that if the investigator's efforts are sufficiently charged with blues energy,[19] he is almost certain to re-model elements and events appearing in traditional, Anglo-American space-time in ways that make them "jump" several rings toward blackness and the vernacular. The blues-oriented observer (the *trained* critic) necessarily "heats up" the observational space by his or her very presence.[20]

The entailments of an inventive, tropological, investigative model such as that proposed by *Blues, Ideology, and Afro-American Literature* include not only awareness of the metaphorical nature of the blues matrix, but also a willingness on my own part to do more than merely hear, read, or see the blues. I must also play (with and on) them. Since the explanatory possibilities of a blues matrix—like analytical possibilities of a delimited set of forces in unified field theory—are hypothetically unbounded, the blues challenge investigative understanding to an unlimited play.

BLUES AND VERNACULAR EXPRESSION IN AMERICA

The blues should be privileged in the study of American culture to precisely the extent that inventive understanding successfully converges with blues force to yield accounts that persuasively and playfully refigure expressive geographies in the United States. My own ludic uses of the blues are various, and each figuration implies the valorization of vernacular facets of American culture. The Afro-American writer James Alan McPherson is, I think, the commentator who most brilliantly and encouragingly coalesces blues, vernacular, and cultural geographies of the United States in his introduction to *Railroad: Trains and Train People in American Culture.*[21]

Having described a fiduciary reaction to the steam locomotive by nineteenth-century financiers and an adverse artistic response by such traditional American writers as Melville, Hawthorne, and Thoreau, McPherson details the reaction of another sector of the United States population to the railroad:

> To a third group of people, those not bound by the assumptions of either business or classical traditions in art, the shrill whistle might have spoken of new possibilities. These were the backwoodsmen and Africans and recent immigrants—the people who comprised the vernacular level of American society. To them the machine might have been loud and frightening, but its whistle and its wheels promised movement. And since a commitment to both freedom and movement was the basic promise of democracy, it was probable that such people would view the locomotive as a challenge to the integrative powers of their imaginations. (P. 6)

Afro-Americans—at the bottom even of the vernacular ladder in America—responded to the railroad as a "meaningful symbol offering both economic progress and the possibility of aesthetic expression" (p. 9). This possibility came from the locomotive's drive and thrust, its promise of unrestrained mobility and unlimited freedom. The blues musician at the crossing, as I have already suggested, became an expert at reproducing or translating these locomotive energies. With the birth of the blues, the vernacular realm of American culture acquired a music that, in McPherson's words, had "wide appeal because it expressed a toughness of spirit and resilience, a willingness to transcend difficulties which was strikingly familiar to those whites who remembered their own history" (p. 16). The signal expressive achievement of blues, then, lay in their translation of extraordinary technological innovativeness, unsettling demographic fluidity, and boundless frontier energy into expression which attracted avid interest from the American masses. By the 1920s, American financiers had become aware of commercial possibilities not only of railroads, but also of the black music deriving from them.

A "race record" market flourished during the Twenties. Major companies issued blues releases under labels such as Columbia, Vocalion, Okeh, Gennett, and Victor. Sometimes as many as ten blues releases appeared in a single week; their sales (aided by radio's dissemination of the music) climbed to hundreds of thousands. The onset of the Great Depression ended this phenomenal boom. During their heyday, however, the blues unequivocally signified a ludic predominance of the vernacular with that sassy, growling, moaning, whooping confidence that marks their finest performances.

McPherson's assessment seems fully justified. It serves, in fact, as a suggestive play in the overall project of refiguring American expressive geographies. Resonantly complementing the insights of such astute commentators as Albert Murray, Paul Oliver, Samuel Charters, Amiri Baraka, and others,[22] McPherson's judgments highlight the value of the blues matrix for cultural analysis in the United States.

In harmony with other brilliant commentators on the blues already noted, Ralph Ellison selects the railroad way-station (the "Chehaw Station") as his topos for the American "little man."[23] In "The Little Man at the Chehaw Station," he autobiographically details his own confirmation of his Tuskegee music teacher's observation that in the United States:

> You must *always* play your best, even if it's only in the waiting room at Chehaw
> Station, because in this country there'll always be a little man hidden behind the stove
> . . . and he'll know the *music*, and the *tradition*, and the standards of *musicianship*
> required for whatever you set out to perform. (P. 25)

When Hazel Harrison made this statement to a young Ellison, he felt that she was joking. But as he matured and moved through a diversity of American scenes, Ellison realized that the inhabitants of the "drab, utilitarian structure" of the American vernacular do far more than respond in expressive ways to "blues-echoing, train-whistle rhapsodies blared by fast express trains" thundering past the junction. At the vernacular level, according to Ellison, people possess a "cultivated taste" that asserts its "authority out of obscurity" (p. 26). The "little man" finally comes to represent, therefore, "that unknown quality which renders the American audience far more than a receptive instrument that may be dominated through a skillful exercise of the sheerly 'rhetorical' elements—the flash and filigree—of the artist's craft" (p. 26).

From Ellison's opening gambit and wonderfully illustrative succeeding examples, I infer that the vernacular (in its expressive adequacy and adept critical facility) always absorbs "classical" elements of American life and art. Indeed, Ellison seems to imply that expressive performers in America who ignore the judgments of the vernacular are destined to failure.

Although his injunctions are intended principally to advocate a traditional "melting pot" ideal in American "high art," Ellison's observations ultimately valorize a comprehensive, vernacular expressiveness in America. Though he seldom loses sight of the possibilities of a classically "transcendent" American high art, he derives his most forceful examples from the vernacular: Blues seem implicitly to comprise the All of American culture.

BLUES MOMENTS IN AFRO-AMERICAN EXPRESSION

In *Blues, Ideology, and Afro-American Literature,* I attempt to provide suggestive accounts of moments in Afro-American discourse when personae, protagonists, autobiographical narrators, or literary critics successfully negotiate an obdurate "economics of slavery" and achieve a resonant, improvisational, expressive dignity. Such moments and their successful analysis provide cogent examples of the blues matrix at work.

The expressive instances that I have in mind occur in passages such as the conclusion of the *Narrative of the Life of Frederick Douglass.* Standing at a Nantucket convention, riffing (in the "break" suddenly confronting him) on the personal troubles he has seen and successfully negotiated in a "prisonhouse of American bondage," Douglass achieves a profoundly dignified blues voice. Zora Neale Hurston's protagonist Janie in the novel *Their Eyes Were Watching God*—as she lyrically and idiomatically relates a tale of personal suffering and triumph that begins in the sexual exploitations of slavery—is a blues artist par excellence. Her wisdom might well be joined to that of Amiri Baraka's Walker Vessels (a "locomotive container" of blues?), whose chameleon code-switching from academic philosophy to blues insight makes him a veritable incarnation of the absorptively vernacular. The narrator of Richard Wright's *Black Boy* inscribes a black blues life's lean desire and suggests yet further instance of the blues matrix's expressive energies. Ellison's invisible man and Baraka's narrator in *The System of Dante's Hell* (whose blues book produces dance) provide additional examples. Finally, Toni Morrison's Milkman Dead in *Song of Solomon* discovers through "Sugarman's" song that an awesomely expressive blues response may well consist of improvisational and serendipitous surrender to the air:

> As fleet and bright as a lodestar he wheeled toward Guitar and it did not matter which one of them would give up his ghost in the killing arms of his brother. For now he knew what Shalimar knew: If you surrendered to the air, you could *ride* it.[24]

Such blues moments are but random instances of the blues matrix at work in Afro-American cultural expression. In my study as a whole, I attempt persuasively to demonstrate that a blues matrix (as a vernacular trope for American cultural explanation in general) possesses enormous force for the study of literature, criticism, and culture. I know that I have appropriated the vastness of the vernacular in the United States to a single matrix. But I trust that my necessary selectivity will be interpreted not as a sign of myopic exclusiveness, but as an invitation to inventive play. The success of my efforts would be effectively signaled, I think, by the transformation of my "I" into a juncture at which readers of my book could freely improvise their own distinctive tropes for cultural explanation. A closing that in fact opened on such inventive possibilities (like the close of these remarks) would be appropriately marked by the crossing sign's inviting "X." That deconstructive "X" might mark a middle ground on which belief and theory converge in productive and creditable explanations of America.

NOTES

1. (Chicago: University of Chicago Press, 1984).

2. Though a great many sources were involved in my re-oriented cultural thinking, certainly the terminology employed in my discussion at this point derives from Marshall Sahlins's wonderfully lucid *Culture and Practical Reason* (Chicago: University of Chicago Press, 1976). Sahlins delineates two modes of thinking that have characterized anthropology from its inception. These two poles are: "symbolic" and "functionalist." Sahlins resolves the dichotomy suggested by these terms through the middle term "cultural proposition," a phrase that he defines as a cultural mediating ground on which the material and symbolic, the useful and the ineffable, ceaselessly converge and depart.

3. The "ideology of form" as a description of Jameson's project derives from the essay "The Symbolic Inference; or, Kenneth Burke and Ideological Analysis," *Critical Inquiry*, 4 (1978), 507–523. Surely, though, Jameson's most recent study, *The Political Unconscious: Narrative as a Socially Symbolic Act* (Ithaca, New York: Cornell University Press, 1981), offers the fullest description of his views on ways in which cultural texts formally inscribe material/ historical condition of their production, distribution, and consumption.

4. The Hegelian epigraph that marks the beginning of these remarks, taken from the *Phenomenology of Spirit*, offers the best definition I know of "determinate negation."

5. I have in mind Louis Althusser's and Etienne Balibar's *Reading Capital* (London: NLB, 1977), as well as Jean Baudrillard's *For a Critique of the Political Economy of the Sign* (1972; trans. St. Louis, Missouri: Telos Press, 1981) and *The Mirror of Production* (1973; trans. St. Louis, Missouri: Telos Press, 1975). By "post-structuralist" thought, I have in mind the universe of discourse constituted by *deconstruction*. Jacques Derrida's *Of Grammatology* (1967; trans. Baltimore, Maryland: The Johns Hopkins Press, 1976) is, perhaps, the locus classicus of the deconstructionist project. One of the more helpful accounts of deconstruction is Christopher Norris's *Deconstruction: Theory and Practice* (London: Methuen, 1982). Of course, there is a certain collapsing of post-structuralism and political economy in the sources cited previously.

6. See *For a Critique of the Political Economy of the Sign*.

7. In *Of Grammatology*, Derrida defines a problematic in which writing conceived as an iterable differe(a)nce, is held to be *always already* instituted (or, in motion) when a traditionally designated *Man* begins to speak. Hence, script is anterior to speech, and absence and differe(a)nce displace presence and identity (conceived of as "Intention") in philosophical discourse.

8. The story appears in Handy's *Father of the Blues*, ed. Arna Bontemps (New York: Macmillan, 1941), p. 78. Other defining sources of blues include: Paul Oliver, *The Story of the Blues* (London: Chilton, 1969); Samuel B. Charters, *The Country Blues* (New York: Rinehart, 1959); Giles Oakley, *The Devil's Music: A History of the Country Blues* (New York: Harcourt

Brace Jovanovich, 1976); Amiri Baraka, *Blues People: Negro Music in White America* (New York: Morrow, 1963); Albert Murray, *Stomping the Blues* (New York: McGraw-Hill, 1976); and William Ferris, *Blues From the Delta* (Garden City, New York: Anchor, 1979).

9. The description at this point is coextensive with the "de-centering" of the subject mentioned earlier. What I wish to effect by noting a "subject" who is not filled is a displacement of the notion that knowledge, or "art," or "song," is a manifestation of an ever-more-clearly-defined individual consciousness of *Man*. In accord with Michel Foucault's explorations in his *Archaeology of Knowledge* (1969; trans. New York: Harper and Row, 1972), I want to claim that blues are like a discourse that comprise the "already said" of Afro-America. Blues' governing statements and sites are, thus, vastly more interesting in the process of cultural investigation than either a history of ideas or a history of individual, subjective consciousness, vis-à-vis blues. When I move to the "X" of the trace and the body as host, I am invoking Mark Taylor's formulations in a suggestive deconstructive essay toward radical Christology called "The Text as Victim," in *Deconstruction and Theology* (New York: Crossroad, 1982), pp. 58–78.

10. The terms used in "The Text as Victim" are "host" and "parasite." The words of the blues are host-like in the sense of a Christological/Logos-as-Host. But without the dialogical action of the parasite, of course, there could be no host. Host is, thus, parasitic upon a parasite's citation. Both, in Taylor's statement of the matter, are *para-sites*.

11. The definition of "code" is drawn from *A Theory of Semiotics* (Bloomington: Indiana University Press, 1976). All references to Eco refer to this work and are hereafter marked by page numbers in parentheses.

12. *Phenomenology of the Spirit*, trans. A. V. Miller (New York: Oxford University Press, 1977). While it is true that the material dimensions of the dialectic are of primary importance in my current study, it is also true that the locus classicus of the dialectic, in and for itself, is the *Phenomenology*. Marx may well have stood Hegel on his head through a materialist inversion of the *Phenomenology*, but subsequent generations have always looked at that uprighted figure—Hegel himself—as an authentic host.

13. Having heard Professor John Felstiner in a session of the 1982 Modern Language Association Convention present a masterful paper defining "translation" as a process of preserving "something of value" by keeping it in motion, I decided that the blues were apt translators of experience. Felstiner, it seemed to me, sought to demonstrate that translation was a process equivalent to gift-giving in Mauss's classic definition of that activity. The value of the gift of translation is never fixed because, say, the poem is always in a transliteral motion, moving from one alphabet to another, always renewing and being renewed in the process. Translation forestalls fixity. It calls attention always to the translated's excess—to its complex multivalence.

14. One of the most inspiring and intriguing descriptions of the relationship between blues voice and the sounds of the railroad is Albert Murray's lyrical exposition in *Stomping the Blues*.

15. Quoted in Oakley, *The Devil's Music*, p. 7.

16. I have appropriated the term "negative symbol" from Roy Wagner's monograph *The Invention of Culture* (Chicago: University of Chicago Press, 1975), p. xvi.

17. My references to a "post-Heisenbergian universe" and to the "particle physicist" were made possible by a joyful reading of Gary Zukav's *The Dancing Wu Li Masters: An Overview of the New Physics* (New York: Morrow, 1979).

18. Zukav writes: "According to the uncertainty principle, we cannot measure accurately,

at the same time, both the position and the momentum of a moving particle. The more precisely we determine one of these properties, the less we know about the other. If we precisely determine the position of the particle, then, strange as it sounds, there is nothing that we can know about its momentum. If we precisely determine the momentum of the particle, there is no way to determine its position" (p. 111). Briefly, if we bring to bear enough energy to actually "see" the imagined "particle," that energy has always already moved the particle from its position (which is one of the aspects of its existence that one attempts to determine) when we take our measurement. Indeterminacy thus becomes normative.

19. The "blues force" is my translational equivalent in investigative "energy" for the investigative energy delineated by Heisenberg's formulations.

20. Eco employs the metaphor of "ecological variation" in his discussions of the semiotic investigation of culture to describe observer effect in the mapping of experience (see *A Theory of Semiotics*, p. 29).

21. (New York: Random House, 1976). All citations refer to this edition and are hereafter marked by page numbers in parentheses.

22. See fn. 8 above.

23. The Chehaw Station is a whistle-stop near Tuskegee, Alabama. It was a feature of the landscape of Tuskegee Institute where Ellison studied music (and much else). His essay "The Little Man at the Chehaw Station" appears in *American Scholar*, 47 (1978), 24–48. All citations refer to this version and are hereafter marked by page numbers in parentheses.

24. *Song of Solomon* (New York: Knopf, 1977), p. 337.

"Woman's Era"

Rethinking Black Feminist Theory

Hazel V. Carby

(1987)

On May, 20, 1893, Frances Harper addressed the World's Congress of Representative Women assembled as part of the Columbian Exposition in Chicago. She encouraged her audience to see themselves standing "on the threshold of woman's era" and urged that they be prepared to receive the "responsibility of political power."[1] Harper was the last of six black women to address the delegates; on the previous two days Fannie Barrier Williams, Anna Julia Cooper, Fannie Jackson Coppin, Sarah J. Early, and Hallie Quinn Brown had been the black spokeswomen at this international but overwhelmingly white women's forum. Williams spoke of the women "for whom real ability, virtue, and special talents count for nothing when they become applicants for respectable employment" and asserted that black women were increasingly "a part of the social forces that must help to determine the questions that so concern women generally."[2] Anna Julia Cooper described the black woman's struggle for sexual autonomy as "a struggle against fearful and overwhelming odds, that often ended in a horrible death. . . . The painful, patient, and silent toil of mothers to gain a fee simple title to the bodies of their daughters, the despairing fight . . . to keep hallow their own persons." She contrasted the white woman who "could at least plead for her own emancipation" to the black women of the South who have to "suffer and struggle and be silent" and made her concluding appeal to "the solidarity of humanity, the oneness of life, and the unnaturalness and injustice of all special favoritisms, whether of sex, race, country, or condition."[3] Fannie Jackson Coppin declared that the conference should not be "indifferent to the history of the colored women of America," for their fight could only aid all women in their struggle against oppression, and Sarah J. Early and Hallie Quinn Brown gave detailed accounts of the organizations that black women had established.[4]

It appeared that the Columbian Exposition had provided the occasion for women in general and black women in particular to gain a space for themselves in which they could exert a political presence. However, for black women the preparations for the World's Congress had been a disheartening experience, and the World's Congress itself proved to be a significant moment in the history of the uneasy relations between organized black and white women. Since emancipation black women had been active within the black community in the formation of mutual-aid societies, benevolent associations, local literary societies, and the many organizations of the various black churches, but they had also looked toward the nationally organized suffrage and temperance movements, dominated by white women, to provide an avenue for the expression of their particular concerns as women and as feminists. The struggle of black women to achieve adequate representation within the women's suffrage and temperance movements had been continually undermined by a pernicious and persistent racism, and the World's Congress was no exception. While Harper, Williams, Cooper, Coppin, Early, and Brown were on the women's platform, Ida B. Wells was in the Haitian pavilion protesting the virtual exclusion of Afro-Americans from the exposition, circulating the pamphlet she had edited, *The Reason Why: The Colored American Is Not in the World's Columbian Exposition.*[5]

The fight for black representation had begun at the presidential level with an attempt to persuade Benjamin Harrison to appoint a black member to the National Board of Commissioners for the exposition. The president's intransigent refusal to act led the black community to focus their hopes on the Board of Lady Managers appointed to be "the channel of communication through which all women may be brought into relation with the exposition, and through which all applications for space for the use of women or their exhibits in the buildings shall be made."[6] Two organizations of black women were formed, the Woman's Columbian Association and the Women's Columbian Auxiliary Association, and both unsuccessfully petitioned the Board of Lady Managers to establish mechanisms of representation for black Americans. Sympathetic sentiments were expressed by a few members of the board, but no appointment was made, and some members of the board threatened to resign rather than work with a black representative. Indeed, the general belief of the board members was that black women were incapable of any organized critique of their committee and that a white women must be behind such "articulate and sustained protests."[7] The fact that six black women eventually addressed the World's Congress was not the result of a practice of sisterhood or evidence of a concern to provide a black political presence but part of a discourse of exoticism that pervaded the fair. Black Americans were included in a highly selective manner as part of exhibits with other ethnic groups which reinforced conventional racist attitudes of the American imagination. The accommodation of racial diversity in ethnic villages at the fair was an attempt to scientifically legitimate racist assumptions, and, as one historian notes, "the results were devastating not only for American blacks, Native Americans, and the Chinese, but also for other non-white peoples of the world."[8]

The Columbian Exposition was widely regarded as "the greatest fair in history."[9] The "White City," symbol of American progress, was built to house the exposition in Jackson Park on the shores of Lake Michigan in Chicago. It has been characterized by a contemporary cultural critic as simultaneously "a fitting conclusion of an age" and the inauguration of another. "It lays bare a plan for a future. Like the Gilded Age, White City straddles a divide: a consummation and a new beginning."[10] For black Americans it was "literally and figuratively a White City" which symbolized "not the material progress of America, but a moral regression—the reconciliation of the North and South at the expense of Negroes."[11] At the time, black visitors expressed their resentment at their virtual exclusion by renaming the fair "the great American white elephant" and "the white American's World's Fair"; Frederick Douglass, attending the fair as commissioner from Haiti, called the exposition "a whited sepulcher."[12] The Columbian Exposition embodied the definitive failure of the hopes of emancipation and reconstruction and inaugurated an age that was to be dominated by "the problem of the color-line."[13]

To appear as a black woman on the platform of the Congress of Representative Women was to be placed in a highly contradictory position, at once part of and excluded from the dominant discourse of white women's politics. . . . The arguments are theoretical and political, responding to contemporary black and white feminist cultural politics. The historical and literary analyses are materialist, interpreting individual texts in relation to the dominant ideological and social formations in which they were produced. . . .

First, in order to gain a public voice as orators or published writers, black women had to confront the dominant domestic ideologies and literary conventions of womanhood which excluded them from the definition "woman." . . . These ideologies of womanhood . . . were adopted, adapted, and transformed to effectively represent the material conditions of black women, and . . . black women intellectuals reconstructed the sexual ideologies of the nineteenth century to produce an alternative discourse of black womanhood.

Second, [a] historical account questions those strands of contemporary feminist historiography and literary criticism which seek to establish the existence of an American sisterhood between black and white women. Considering the history of the failure of any significant political alliances between black and white women in the nineteenth century, I challenge the impulse in the contemporary women's movement to discover a lost sisterhood and to reestablish feminist solidarity. Individual white women helped publish and promote individual black women, but the texts of black women from ex-slave Harriet Jacobs to educator Anna Julia Cooper are testaments to the racist practices of the suffrage and temperance movements and indictments of the ways in which white women allied themselves not with black women but with a racist patriarchal order against all black people. Only by confronting this history of difference can we hope to understand the boundaries that separate white feminists from all women of color.[14]

Third, though Afro-American cultural and literary history commonly regards the late nineteenth and early twentieth centuries in terms of great men, as the Age of Washington and Du Bois, marginalizing the political contributions of black women, these were the years of the first flowering of black women's autonomous organizations and a period of intense intellectual activity and productivity. An examination of the literary contributions of Frances Harper and Pauline Hopkins and the political writings of Anna Julia Cooper and Ida B. Wells will reconstruct our view of this period. Writing in the midst of a new "black women's renaissance," the contemporary discovery and recognition of black women by the corporate world of academia, publishing, and Hollywood—marked by the celebrity of Alice Walker and Toni Morrison—I try to establish the existence of an earlier and perhaps more politically resonant renaissance so we may rethink the cultural politics of black women.

Fourth, . . . to understand the first novels which were written at the end of the nineteenth century, one has to understand not only the discourse and context in which they were produced but also the intellectual forms and practices of black women that preceded them [by examining] narratives of slave and free women, the relation of political lecturing to the politics of fiction, and a variety of essay, journalistic, and magazine writing. . . .

. . . [T]wo fields of academic inquiry [have] emerged: black feminist literary criticism and black women's history. As a first step toward assessing what has come to be called black feminist theory, I want to consider its history and to analyze its major tendencies.

It is now a decade since Barbara Smith published "Toward a Black Feminist Criticism" (1977), addressing the conditions of both politics and literature that she felt could provide the necessary basis for an adequate consideration of black women's literature.[15] Smith argued that since the "feminist movement was an essential precondition to the growth of feminist literature, criticism, and women's studies," the lack of an autonomous black feminist movement contributed to the neglect of black women writers and artists, there being no "political movement to give power or support to those who want to examine Black women's experience." Hence, without a political movement there was no black feminist political theory to form a basis for a critical approach to the art of black women. Smith argued for the development of both the political movement and the political theory so that a black feminist literary criticism would embody "the realization that the politics of sex as well as the politics of race and class are crucially interlocking factors in the works of Black women writers" (170). To support her argument, Smith indicted a variety of male critics and white feminist critics for their sexist and racist assumptions which prevented the critical recognition of the importance of the work of black women writers.

In many ways, "Toward a Black Feminist Criticism" acted as a manifesto for black feminist critics, stating both the principles and the conditions of their work. Smith argued that a black feminist approach should have a primary commitment to the exploration of the interrelation of sexual and racial politics and that black and female identities were "inextricable elements in Black women's writings." Smith also asserted that a black feminist critic should "work from the assumption that Black women writers constitute an identifiable literary tradition" (174). Smith was convinced that it was possible to reveal a verifiable literary tradition because of the common experience of the writers and the shared use of a black female language.

The use of Black women's language and cultural experience in books *by* Black women *about* Black women results in a miraculously rich coalescing of form and content and also takes their writing far beyond the confines of white/male literary structures. The Black feminist critic would find innumerable commonalities in works by Black women. (174)

A second principle that Smith proposed to govern black feminist critical practice was the establishment of precedents and insights in interpretation within the works of other black women. The critic should write and think "out of her own identity," asserted Smith, the implication being that the identity of the critic would be synonymous with that of the author under scrutiny. The identities that most concerned Smith were those of a black feminist and a black lesbian. The principles of interpretation that she employed, she hoped, would combine to produce a new methodology, a criticism that was innovative and constantly self-conscious of the relationship between its own perspective and the political situation of all black women. Black feminist criticism, in Smith's terms, was defined as being both dependent on and contributing to a black feminist political movement (175). Convinced of the possibilities for a radical change, Smith concluded that it was possible to undertake a "total reassessment of Black literature and literary history needed to reveal the Black woman-identified woman" (182–83).

Smith's essay was an important statement that made visible the intense repression of the black female and lesbian voice. As a critical manifesto it represented a radical departure from the earlier work of Mary Helen Washington, who had edited the first contemporary anthology of black women's fiction, *Black-Eyed Susans*, two years earlier.[16] Washington did not attempt to define, explicitly, a black feminist critical perspective but concentrated on recovering and situating the neglected fiction of black women writers and establishing the major themes and images for use in a teaching situation.[17] However, there are major problems with Smith's essay as a critical manifesto, particularly in its assertion of the existence of an essential black female experience and an exclusive black female language in which this experience is embodied. Smith's essay assumes a very simple one-to-one correspondence between fiction and reality, and her model of a black feminist critical perspective is undermined as a political practice by being dependent on those who are, biologically, black and female. For Smith, her reliance on common experiences confines black feminist criticism to black women critics of black women artists depicting black women. This position can lead to the political cul de sac identified by Alice Walker as a problem of white feminist criticism in her essay "One Child of One's Own."[18] Walker criticized the position taken by Patricia Meyer Spacks, in the introduction to her book *The Female Imagination*, where she justified her concentration on the lives of white middle-class women by reiterating Phyllis Chesler's comment: "I have no theory to offer to Third World female psychology in America . . . As a white woman, I'm reluctant and unable to construct theories about experiences I haven't had." To which Spacks added. "So am I." Walker challenged Spacks's exclusive concentration on white middle-class writers by asking:

Why only these? Because they are white, and middle class, and because, to Spacks, female imagination is only that. Perhaps, however, this is the white female imagination, one that is "reluctant and unable to construct theories about experiences I haven't had." (Yet Spacks never lived in nineteenth-century Yorkshire, so why theorize about the Brontës?)[19]

Walker's point should be seriously considered, for a black feminist criticism cannot afford to be essentialist and ahistorical, reducing the experience of all black women to a common denominator and limiting black feminist critics to an exposition of an equivalent black "female imagination."

In 1982, Smith's manifesto was reprinted in a text which attempted to realize its project.[20] *All the Women Are White, All the Blacks Are Men, But Some of Us Are Brave*, edited by Gloria T. Hull, Patricia Bell Scott, and Barbara Smith, was a text dedicated to the establishment of black women's studies in the academy.

> Merely to use the term "Black women's studies" is an act charged with political significance. At the very least, the combining of these words to name a discipline means taking the stance that Black women exist—and exist positively—a stance that is in direct opposition to most of what passes for culture and thought on the North American continent. To use the term and to act on it in a white-male world is an act of political courage.[21]

To state unequivocally, as the editors do, that black women's studies is a discipline is a culminating act of the strand of black feminist theory committed to autonomy. The four issues that the editors see as being most important in relation to black women's studies acknowledge no allies or alliances:

> (1) the general political situation of Afro-American women and the bearing this has had upon the implementation of Black women's studies; (2) the relationship of Black women's studies to Black feminist politics and the Black feminist movement; (3) the necessity for Black women's studies to be feminist, radical, and analytical; and (4) the need for teachers of Black women's studies to be aware of our problematic political positions in the academy and of the potentially antagonistic conditions under which we must work.[22]

However, in the foreword to the book, Mary Berry, while criticizing women's studies for not focusing on black women, recognized that women's studies exists on the "periphery of academic life, like Black Studies."[23] Where, then, we can ask, lie black women's studies? On the periphery of the already marginalized, we could assume, a very precarious and dangerous position from which to assert total independence. For, as Berry acknowledged, pioneering work on black women was undertaken by white as well as black women historians, and black women's studies has a crucial contribution to make to the understanding of the oppression of the whole of the black community. Berry, then, implicitly understood that work on black women should be engaged with women's studies and Afro-American studies. The editors acknowledged the contributions to the volume made by white female scholars but were unclear about the relation of their work to a black feminism. They constantly engaged, as teachers and writers, with women's studies and Afro-American studies, yet it is unclear how or whether black women's studies should transform either or both of the former.[24] The editors acknowledged with dismay that "much of the current teaching and writing about Black women is not feminist, is not radical, and unfortunately is not always even analytical" and were aggressively aware of the pitfalls of mimicking a male-centered canonical structure of "great black women." In opposition to teaching about exceptional black women, the editors were committed to teaching as an act that furthered liberation in its exploration of "the experience of supposedly 'ordinary' Black women whose 'unexceptional' actions enabled us and the race to survive."[25] *But Some of Us Are Brave* was a collective attempt to produce a book that could be a pedagogical tool in this process.

An alternative approach to black feminist politics is embodied in Deborah McDowell's 1980 essay, "New Directions for Black Feminist Criticism," and in Barbara Christian's *Black Feminist Criticism: Perspectives on Black Women Writers.*[26] McDowell, like Smith, showed that white female critics continued to perpetrate against black women the exclusive practices they condemned in white male scholarship by establishing the experience of white middle-class women as normative within the feminist arena. She also attacked male critics for the way in which their masculine-centered values dominated their criticism of the work of black women writers (186–87). However, the main concern of McDowell's essay was to look back at "Toward a Black Feminist Criticism" in order to assess the development of black feminist scholarship.

While acknowledging the lack of a concrete definition for or substantial body of black feminist criticism, McDowell argued that "the theories developed thus far have often lacked sophistication and have been marred by slogans, rhetoric, and idealism" (188). Two very important critiques of Smith's position were made by McDowell. She questioned the existence of a monolithic black female language (189) and problematized what she saw to be Smith's oversimplification and obscuring of the issue of lesbianism. McDowell called for a firmer definition of what constituted lesbianism and lesbian literature and questioned "whether a lesbian aesthetic is not finally a reductive approach to the study of Black women's literature" (190).

Moreover, unlike Smith's asserting the close and necessary links between a black feminist political framework and a black feminist criticism, McDowell was concerned to warn feminist critics of "the dangers of political ideology yoked with aesthetic judgment" and worried that Smith's "innovative analysis is pressed to the service of an individual political persuasion" (190). McDowell made more complex the relationship between fiction and criticism on the one hand and the possibilities of social change in the lives of the masses of black women on the other and also doubted the feasibility of a productive relationship between the academy and political activism.

McDowell's project was to establish the parameters for a clearer definition of black feminist criticism. Like Smith, McDowell applied the term to "Black female critics who analyze the works of Black female writers from a feminist or political perspective" but also departed from Smith's definitions when she extended her argument to state that the term can also apply to any criticism written by a Black woman regardless of her subject or perspective—a book written by a male from a feminist or political perspective, a book written by a Black woman or about Black women authors in general, or any writings by women. (191)

Thus, McDowell identified the need for a specific methodology while at the same time producing a very mystifying definition of her own. The semantic confusion of the statement gives cause to wonder at the possibility that an antifeminist celebration of a racist tract could be called black feminist as long as it was written by a black woman! Surely black feminist theory is emptied of its feminist content if the perspective of the critic doesn't matter.

Nevertheless, McDowell posed very pertinent questions that have yet to be adequately answered regarding the extent to which black and white feminist critics have intersecting interests and the necessity for being able to discern culturally specific analytic strategies that may distinguish black from white feminist criticism. McDowell also argued for a contextual awareness of the conditions under which black women's literature was produced, published, and reviewed, accompanied by a rigorous textual analysis which revealed any stylistic and linguistic commonalities across the texts of black women. She regarded the parameters of a tradition as an issue to be argued and established, not assumed, and warned against an easy reliance on generalities, especially in relation to the existence of a black female "consciousness" or "vision" (196). Like Washington, McDowell stressed that the "immediate concern of Black feminist critics must be to develop a fuller understanding of Black women writers" but did not support a "separatist position" as a long-term strategy and argued for an exploration of parallels between the texts of black women and those of black men. However, McDowell did not include the possibility of a black feminist reading of literature written by either white male or female authors, and while she called for black feminist criticism to ultimately "expand to embrace other modes of critical inquiry," these modes remain unspecified. In an attack against "critical absolutism," McDowell concluded by making an analogy between Marxism as dogma and black feminist criticism as a separatist enterprise, an analogy which did not clarify her political or theoretical position and confused her appeal for a "sound, thorough articulation of the Black feminist aesthetic" (196–97).

As opposed to the collective act of *But Some of Us Are Brave*, Christian has collected together her own essays written between 1975 and 1984. The introduction, "Black Feminist Process: In the Midst of . . . ," reflects the structure of the collection as a whole as the essays cover the period of the development of contemporary black feminist criticism. However, the book does not exemplify the history of the development of contemporary black feminist criticism but rather concentrates on situating the contributions of an individual critic over the period of a decade. Christian's work has been concerned with establishing a literary history of black women's writing and has depended very heavily on the conceptual apparatus of stereotypes and images.[27] However, it is necessary to confront Christian's assertions that the prime motivation for nineteenth- and early-twentieth-century black writers was to confront the negative images of blacks held by whites and to dispute the simplistic model of the literary development of black women writers indicated by such titles as "From Stereotype to Character."[28] Christian's work represents a significant strand of black feminist criticism that has concentrated on the explication of stereotypes at the expense of engaging in the theoretical and historical questions raised by the construction of a tradition of black women writing. Indeed, in the introduction to *Black Feminist Criticism*, Christian herself raises some of the questions that are left unanswered in the body of her work so far but which are crucial to understanding or defining a black feminist critical practice:

> What is a literary critic, a black woman critic, a black feminist literary critic, a black feminist social literary critic? The adjectives mount up, defining, qualifying, the activity. How does one distinguish them? The need to articulate a theory, to categorize the activities is a good part of the activity itself to the point where I wonder how we ever get around to doing anything else. What do these categories tell anyone about my method? Do I do formalist criticism, operative or expressive criticism, mimetic or structuralist criticism? . . . Can one theorize effectively about an evolving process? Are the labels informative or primarily a way of nipping questions in the bud? What are the philosophical questions behind my praxis? (x–xi)

Christian, unlike many feminist critics, divorces what she considers to be sound critical practice from political practice when she states that what irks her about "much literary criticism today" is that "so often the text is but an occasion for espousing [the critic's] philosophical point of view—revolutionary black, feminist, or socialist program."[29] Thus, ten years after the term black feminist criticism was coined, it is used as the title of a book as if a readership would recognize and identify its parameters; yet, in the very attempt to define itself, even in the work of one individual critic, the contradictory impulses of black feminist criticism are clear. In a review of Christian's book, Hortense Spillers points to the ideological nature of the apparent separation between the critical project and its political dimensions:

> The critical projects that relate to the African-American community point to a crucial aspect of the entire theme of liberation. The same might be said for the career of feminist inquiry and its impact on the community: in other words, the various critical projects that intersect with African-American life and thought in the United States complement the actualities of an objective and historic situation, even if, in the name of the dominant ruling discourses, and in the interests of the ruling cultural and political apparatus, the convergence between intellectual and political life remains masked.[30]

What I want to advocate is that black feminist criticism be regarded critically as a problem, not a solution, as a sign that should be interrogated, a locus of contradictions. Black feminist criticism has its source and its primary motivation in academic legitimation, placement within a framework of bourgeois humanistic discourse. But, as Cornel West has argued in a wider context, the dilemma of black intellectuals seeking legitimation through the academy is that

> it is existentially and intellectually stultifying for black intellectuals. It is existentially debilitating because it not only generates anxieties of defensiveness on the part of black intellectuals; it also thrives on them. The need for hierarchical ranking and the deep-seated racism shot through bourgeois humanistic scholarship cannot provide black intellectuals with either the proper ethos or conceptual framework to overcome a defensive posture. And charges of intellectual inferiority can never be met upon the opponent's terrain—to try to do so only intensifies one's anxieties. Rather the terrain itself must be viewed as part and parcel of an antiquated form of life unworthy of setting the terms of contemporary discourse.[31]

This critique is applicable for a number of reasons. Black feminist criticism for the main part accepts the prevailing paradigms predominant in the academy, as has women's studies and Afro-American studies, and seeks to organize itself as a discipline in the same way. Also, it is overwhelmingly defensive in its posture, attempting to discover, prove, and legitimate the intellectual worthiness of black women so that they may claim their rightful placement as both subjects and creators of the curriculum.

Black feminist theory continues to be shaped by the tensions apparent in feminist theory in general that have been characterized by Elaine Showalter as three phases of development. To paraphrase and adapt her model, these would be (1) the concentration on the mysogyny (and racism) of literary practice; (2) the discovery that (black) women writers had a literature of their own (previously hidden by patriarchal [and racist] values) and the development of a (black) female aesthetic; and (3) a challenge to and rethinking of the conceptual grounds of literary study and an increased concern with theory.[32] Though it is not possible to argue that these different approaches appear chronologically over the last ten years in black feminist work, it is important to recognize that in addition to the specific concerns of black feminist theory it shares a structural and conceptual pattern of questions and issues with other modes of feminist inquiry.

Black feminist criticism has too frequently been reduced to an experiential relationship that exists between black women as critics and black women as writers who represent black women's reality. Theoretically this reliance on a common, or shared, experience is essentialist and ahistorical. Following the methodologies of mainstream literary criticism and feminist literary criticism, black feminist criticism presupposes the existence of a tradition and has concentrated on establishing a narrative of that tradition. This narrative constitutes a canon from these essentialist views of experience which is then placed alongside, though unrelated to, traditional and feminist canons. This book does not assume the existence of a tradition or traditions of black women writing and, indeed, is critical of traditions of Afro-American intellectual thought that have been constructed as paradigmatic of Afro-American history.

One other essentialist aspect of black feminist criticism should be considered: the search for or assumption of the existence of a black female language. The theoretical perspective of the book is that no language or experience is divorced from the shared context in which different groups that share a language express their differing group interests. Language is accented differently by competing groups, and therefore the terrain of language is a terrain of power relations.[33] This struggle within and over language reveals the nature of the structure of social relations and the hierarchy of power, not the nature of one particular group. The sign, then, is an arena of struggle and a construct between socially organized persons in the process of their interaction; the forms that signs take are conditioned by the social organization of the partici-pants involved and also by the immediate conditions of their interactions. Hence, . . . we must be historically specific and aware of the differently oriented social interests within one and the same sign community. In these terms, black and feminist cannot be absolute, transhistorical forms (or form) of identity.

. . . [F]eminist critical practice . . . pays particular attention to the articulation of gender, race, and class.[34] Social, political, and economic analyses that use class as a fundamental category often assert the necessity for white and black to sink their differences and unite in a common and general class struggle. The call for class solidarity is paralleled within contemporary feminist practice by the concept of sister-hood. This appeal to sisterhood has two political consequences that should be ques-tioned. First, in order to establish the common grounds for a unified women's move-ment, material differences in the lives of working-class and middle-class women or white and black women have been dismissed. The search to establish that these bonds of sisterhood have always existed has led to a feminist historiography and criticism which denies the hierarchical structuring of the relations between black and white women and often takes the concerns of middle-class, articulate white women as a norm.

[Criticism must work] within the theoretical premises of societies "structured in dominance" by class, by race, and by gender and [offer] a materialist account of the cultural production of black women intellectuals within the social relations that inscribed them.[35] It delineates the sexual ideologies that defined the ways in which white and black women "lived" their relation to their material conditions of exis-tence. Ideologies of white womanhood were the sites of racial and class struggle which enabled white women to negotiate their subordinate role in relation to patri-archy and at the same time to ally their class interests with men and against establish-ing an alliance with black women. We need more feminist work that interrogates sexual ideologies for their racial specificity and acknowledges whiteness, not just blackness, as a racial categorization. Work that uses race as a central category does not necessarily need to be about black women.

An emphasis on the importance of establishing historically specific forms of racism should also apply to gender oppression. It is not enough to use the feminist theoreti-cal back door to assert that because racism and sexism predate capitalism there is no further need to specify their particular articulation with economic systems of oppres-sion. On the contrary, racisms and sexisms need to be regarded as particular historical practices articulated with each other and with other practices in a social formation.

For example, the institutionalized rape of black women as slaves needs to be distinguished from the institutionalized rape of black women as an instrument of political terror, alongside lynching, in the South. Rape itself should not be regarded as a transhistorical mechanism of women's oppression but as one that acquires specific political or economic meanings at different moments in history.

For feminist historiography and critical practice the inclusion of the analytic categories of race and class means having to acknowledge that women were not only the subjects but also the perpetrators of oppression. The hegemonic control of dominant classes has been secured at the expense of sisterhood. Hegemony is never finally and utterly won but needs to be continually worked on and reconstructed, and sexual and racial ideologies are crucial mechanisms in the maintenance of power. For women this has meant that many of their representative organizations have been disabled by strategies and struggles which have been race-specific, leading to racially divided movements like the temperance and suffrage campaigns. No history should blandly label these organizations "women's movements," for we have to understand the importance of the different issues around which white and black women organized and how this related to their differing material circumstances. A revision of contemporary feminist historiography should investigate the different ways in which racist ideologies have been constructed and made operative under different historical conditions. But, like sexual ideologies, racism, in its appeal to the natural order of things, appears as a transhistorical, essentialist category, and critiques of racism can imitate this appearance.

. . . [T]he contradictions faced by the black women intellectuals at the Columbian Exposition continue to haunt the contemporary women's movement.

NOTES

1. Frances Harper, "Woman's Political Future," in May Wright Sewell, ed., *World's Congress of Representative Women* (Chicago: Rand McNally, 1894), pp. 433–37.

2. Fannie Barrier Williams, "The Intellectual Progress of the Colored Women of the United States since the Emancipation Proclamation," in Sewell, *World's Congress*, pp. 696–711.

3. Anna Julia Cooper, "The Intellectual Progress of the Colored Women of the United States since the Emancipation Proclamation," in Sewell, *World's Congress*, pp. 711–15.

4. Fannie Jackson Coppin, and Sarah J. Early and Hallie Quinn Brown, "The Organized Efforts of the Colored Women of the South to Improve Their Condition," in Sewell, *World's Congress*, pp. 715–17, 718–29.

5. Ida B. Wells, ed., *The Reason Why: The Colored American Is Not in the World's Columbian Exposition* (Chicago: by the author, 1893).

6. Report of Mrs. Potter Palmer, President, to the Board of Lady Managers, September 2, 1891 (Chicago), cited in Ann Massa, "Black Women in the 'White City,'" *Journal of American Studies* 8 (December 1974): 320.

7. Ibid., p. 329.

8. Robert W. Rydell, "The World's Columbian Exposition of 1893: Racist Underpinnings of a Utopian Artifact," *Journal of American Culture* 1 (Summer 1978), 257–75.

9. David F. Burg, *Chicago's White City of 1893* (Lexington: University of Kentucky Press, 1976), p. 75.

10. Alan Trachtenberg, *The Incorporation of America: Culture and Society in the Gilded Age* (New York: Hill and Wang, 1982), p. 209.

11. F. L. Barnett, "The Reason Why," in Wells, *The Reason Why*, p. 79. Elliot M. Rudwick and August Meier, "Black Man in the 'White City': Negroes and the Columbian Exposition, 1893," *Phylon* 26 (Winter 1965): 361.

12. Rudwick and Meier, "Black Man in the 'White City,'" p. 354; Frederick Douglass, "Introduction," in Wells, *The Reason Why*, p. 4.

13. W. E. B. Du Bois, *The Souls of Black Folk* (1903; reprint New York: Fawcett World Library, 1961), p. 23.

14. Hazel V. Carby, "White Woman Listen: Black Feminism and the Boundaries of Sisterhood," in Centre for Contemporary Cultural Studies. *The Empire Strikes Back: Race and Racism in Seventies Britain* (London: Hutchinson, 1982), pp. 212–35.

15. Barbara Smith, "Toward a Black Feminist Criticism," *Conditions: Two* 1 (October 1977), reprinted in Elaine Showalter, ed., *The New Feminist Criticism: Essays on Women, Literature, and Theory* (New York: Pantheon, 1985), pp. 168–85. References are to this edition; page numbers will be given parenthetically in the text.

16. Mary Helen Washington, ed., *Black-Eyed Susans* (New York: Anchor Press, 1975). The first contemporary anthology of black women's writings, fiction and nonfiction, was Toni Cade, ed., *The Black Woman* (New York: New American Library, 1970).

17. See also Mary Helen Washington, "Teaching Black-Eyed Susans: An Approach to the Study of Black Women Writers," in Gloria T. Hull, Patricia Bell Scott, and Barbara Smith, eds., *All the Women Are White, All the Blacks Are Men, But Some of Us Are Brave* (Old Westbury, N.Y.: Feminist Press, 1982), pp. 208–17.

18. Alice Walker, "One Child of One's Own: A Meaningful Digression within the Work(s)," *In Search of Our Mothers' Gardens* (New York: Harcourt Brace Jovanovitch, 1983), pp. 361–83.

19. Ibid., p. 372.

20. See also the introduction to Barbara Smith, ed., *Home Girls: A Black Feminist Anthology* (New York: Kitchen Table, Women of Color Press, 1983).

21. Hull et. al., "The Politics of Black Women's Studies," in *But Some of Us Are are Brave*, p. xvii.

22. Ibid.

23. Mary Berry, "Foreword," Hull et al., *But Some of Us Are Brave*, p. xv.

24. My position is that cultural studies is not disciplinary, nor does it seek to be a discipline even in the sense that American studies, Afro-American studies, or women's studies are interdisciplinary; rather it is a critical position which interrogates the assumptions of and principles of critical practice of all three modes of inquiry. As a practitioner of cultural studies notes: "The relation of cultural studies to the other disciplines is rather one of critique: of their historical construction, of their claims, of their omissions, and particularly of the forms of their separation. At the same time, a critical relationship to the disciplines is also a critical stance to their forms of knowledge production—to the prevalent social relations of research, the labor process of higher education." Michael Green, "The Centre for Contemporary Cultural Studies," in Peter Widdowson, ed., *Re-Reading English* (London: Methuen, 1982), p. 84.

25. Hull et al., "Politics of Black Women's Studies," *But Some of Us Are Brave*, pp. xxi-xxii.

26. Deborah McDowell, "New Directions for Black Feminist Criticism," *Black American Literature Forum* 14 (1980), reprinted in Showalter, *The New Feminist Criticism*, pp. 186–99. References are to this edition; page numbers will be given parenthetically in the text. Barbara Christian, *Black Feminist Criticism: Perspectives on Black Women Writers* (New York: Pergamon Press, 1985).

27. See also Barbara Christian, *Black Women Novelists: The Development of a Tradition, 1892–1976* (Westport, Conn.: Greenwood Press, 1980).

28. Christian, *Black Feminist Criticism*, pp. 1–30.

29. Ibid., pp. x–xi.

30. Hortense Spillers, "Black/Female/Critic," *Women's Review of Books* 2 (September 1985): 9–10.

31. Cornel West, "The Dilemma of the Black Intellectual," *Cultural Critique* 1 (Fall 1985): 116–17.

32. Showalter, "The Feminist Critical Revolution," in *The New Feminist Criticism*, pp. 3–17.

33. This argument is drawn from V. N. Volosinov, *Marxism and the Philosophy of Language* (New York: Seminar Press, 1973). Volosinov was a Soviet theorist associated with the circle of Mikhail Bakhtin.

34. I am particularly drawing on that aspect of cultural studies which has analyzed issues of race and the study of black culture. A key figure is Stuart Hall. For many years the director of the Centre for Contemporary Cultural Studies, he has written a number of major theoretical essays on culture and ideology, including: "Cultural Studies: Two Paradigms," *Media, Culture, and Society* 2 (1980): 57–72; "The Rediscovery of 'Ideology': Return of the Repressed in Media Studies," in Michael Gurevitch, Tony Bennett, James Curran, and Janet Woolacott, eds., *Culture, Society, and the Media* (New York: Methuen, 1982), pp. 56–90; "Culture, the Media, and the 'Ideological' Effect," in James Curran, Michael Gurevitch, and Janet Woolacott, eds., *Mass Communications and Society* (London: Edward Arnold, 1977), pp. 315–48; "Notes on Deconstructing 'The Popular,'" in Ralph Samuel, ed., *People's History and Socialist Theory*, History Workshop Series (London: Routledge and Kegan Paul, 1981); "A 'Reading' of Marx's *1857* Introduction to the Grundrisse," *CCCS Stencilled Papers* I (1973); "Rethinking the Base/Superstructure Metaphor," in John Bloomfield, ed., *Class, Party, and Hegemony* (London: Lawrence and Wishart, 1977), pp. 43–72. Hall's work on race that has been particularly influential includes: *Policing the Crisis: Mugging, the State, and Law and Order* (London: Macmillan, 1978); "Pluralism, Race, and Class in Caribbean Society," in *Race and Class in Post-Colonial Society* (Paris: UNESCO, 1977), pp. 150–82; "Racism and Reaction," in *Five Views of Multi-Racial Britain* (London: Commission for Racial Equality, 1978), pp. 23–35; "Race, Articulation and Societies Structured in Dominance," in *Sociological Theories: Race and Colonialism* (Paris: UNESCO, 1980), pp. 305–45; "The Whites of Their Eyes: Racist Ideologies and the Media," in George Bridges and Rosalind Brunt, eds., *Silver Linings: Some Strategies for the Eighties* (London: Lawrence and Wishart, 1981), pp. 28–52. Younger scholars influenced by Hall and the work of C. L. R. James include the authors of *The Empire Strikes Back* (see note 14 above) and Paul Gilroy, "Managing the 'Underclass': A Further Note on the Sociology of Race Relations in Britain," *Race and Class* 22 (Summer 1980): 47–62; Paul Gilroy, "You Can't Fool the Youths . . . Race and Class Formation in the 1980s," *Race and Class* 23 (Autumn 1981/Winter 1982): 207–22; and Paul Gilroy, *There Ain't No Black In The Union Jack* (London: Hutchinson, 1987). For collections of essays by C. L. R. James, see *The Future in the Present* (London: Allison and Busby, 1977); *Spheres of Existence* (London:

Allison and Busby, 1980); *At the Rendezvous of Victory* (London: Allison and Busby, 1984); and his cultural history of cricket in the West Indies, *Beyond a Boundary* (1963; reprint London: Stanley Paul, 1980). In the United States there is the related work of Cedric J. Robinson, *Black Marxism: The Making of the Black Radical Tradition* (London: Zed Press, 1983); Cornel West, *Prophesy Deliverance! An Afro-American Revolutionary Christianity* (Philadelphia: Westminster Press, 1982); and Cornel West, "The Dilemma of the Black Intellectual," see note 31; John Brown Childs, "Afro-American Intellectuals and the People's Culture," *Theory and Society* 13 (1984): 69–90; John Brown Childs, "Concepts of Culture in Afro-American Political Thought, 1890–1920," *Social Text* 4 (Fall 1981): 28–43; and Ronald Takaki, *Iron Cages: Race and Culture in 19th-Century America* (Seattle: University of Washington Press, 1979), which fuses black intellectual tradition, cultural studies, and western Marxism.

35. The phrase is taken from Hall, "Race, Articulation, and Societies Structured in Dominance."

24 Mama's Baby, Papa's Maybe

An American Grammar Book

Hortense J. Spillers

(1987)

1

Let's face it. I am a marked woman, but not everybody knows my name. "Peaches" and "Brown Sugar," "Sapphire" and "Earth Mother," "Aunty," "Granny," God's "Holy Fool," a "Miss Ebony First," or "Black Woman at the Podium": I describe a locus of confounded identities, a meeting ground of investments and privations in the national treasury of rhetorical wealth. My country needs me, and if I were not here, I would have to be invented.

W. E. B. Du Bois predicted as early as 1903 that the twentieth century would be the century of the "color line." We could add to this spatiotemporal configuration another thematic of analogously terrible weight: if the "black woman" can be seen as a particular figuration of the split subject that psychoanalytic theory posits, then this century marks the site of "its" profoundest revelation. The problem before us is deceptively simple: the terms enclosed in quotation marks in the preceding paragraph isolate overdetermined nominative properties. Embedded in bizarre axiological ground, they demonstrate a sort of telegraphic coding; they are markers so loaded with mythical prepossession that there is no easy way for the agents buried beneath them to come clean. In that regard, the names by which I am called in the public place render an example of signifying property plus. In order for me to speak a truer word concerning myself, I must strip down through layers of attenuated meanings, made an excess in time, over time, assigned by a particular historical order, and there await whatever marvels of my own inventiveness. The personal pronouns are offered in the service of a collective function.

In certain human societies, a child's identity is determined through the line of the Mother, but the United States, from at least one author's point of view, is not one of them: "In essence, the Negro community has been forced into a matriarchal structure

257

which, because it is so far out of line with the rest of American society, seriously retards the progress of the group as a whole, and imposes a crushing burden on the Negro male and, in consequence, on a great many Negro women as well" [Moynihan 75].

The notorious bastard, from Vico's banished Roman mothers of such sons, to Caliban, to Heathcliff, and Joe Christmas, has no official female equivalent. Because the traditional rites and laws of inheritance rarely pertain to the female child, bastard status signals to those who need to know which son of the Father's is the legitimate heir and which one the impostor. For that reason, property seems wholly the business of the male. A "she" cannot, therefore, qualify for bastard, or "natural son" status, and that she cannot provides further insight into the coils and recoils of patriarchal wealth and fortune. According to Daniel Patrick Moynihan's celebrated "Report" of the late sixties, the "Negro Family" has no Father to speak of—his Name, his Law, his Symbolic function mark the impressive missing agencies in the essential life of the black community, the "Report" maintains, and it is, surprisingly, the fault of the Daughter, or the female line. This stunning reversal of the castration thematic, displacing the Name and the Law of the Father to the territory of the Mother and Daughter, becomes an aspect of the African-American female's misnaming. We attempt to undo this misnaming in order to reclaim the relationship between Fathers and Daughters within this social matrix for a quite different structure of cultural fictions. For Daughters and Fathers are here made to manifest the very same rhetorical symptoms of absence and denial, to embody the double and contrastive agencies of a prescribed internecine degradation. "Sapphire" enacts her "Old Man" in drag, just as her "Old Man" becomes "Sapphire" in outrageous caricature.

In other words, in the historic outline of dominance, the respective subject-positions of "female" and "male" adhere to no symbolic integrity. At a time when current critical discourses appear to compel us more and more decidedly toward gender "undecidability," it would appear reactionary, if not dumb, to insist on the integrity of female/male gender. But undressing these conflations of meaning, as they appear under the rule of dominance, would restore, as figurative possibility, not only Power to the Female (for Maternity), but also Power to the Male (for Paternity). We would gain, in short, the potential for gender differentiation as it might express itself along a range of stress points, including human biology in its intersection with the project of culture.

Though among the most readily available "whipping boys" of fairly recent public discourse concerning African-Americans and national policy, "The Moynihan Report" is by no means unprecedented in its conclusions; it belongs, rather, to a class of symbolic paradigms that 1) inscribe "ethnicity" as a scene of negation and 2) confirm the human body as a metonymic figure for an entire repertoire of human and social arrangements. In that regard, the "Report" pursues a behavioral rule of public documentary. Under the Moynihan rule, "ethnicity" itself identifies a total objectification of human and cultural motives—the "white" family, by implication, and the "Negro Family," by outright assertion, in a constant opposition of binary meanings. Apparently spontaneous, these "actants" are wholly generated, with neither past nor future, as tribal currents moving out of time. Moynihan's "Families" are pure present and always tense. "Ethnicity" in this case freezes in meaning, takes on constancy, assumes the look and the affects of the Eternal. We could say, then, that in its powerful stillness, "ethnicity," from the point of view of the "Report," embodies nothing more than a mode of memorial time, as Roland Barthes outlines the dynamics of myth [see "Myth Today" 109–59; esp. 122–23]. As a signifier that has no movement in the field of signification, the use of "ethnicity" for the living becomes purely appreciative, although one would be unwise not to concede its dangerous and fatal effects.

"Ethnicity" perceived as mythical time enables a writer to perform a variety of conceptual moves all at once. Under its hegemony, the human body becomes a defenseless target for rape and veneration, and the body, in its material and abstract phase, a resource for metaphor. For example, Moynihan's "tangle of pathology" provides the descriptive strategy for the work's fourth chapter, which suggests that "underachievement" in black males of the lower classes is primarily the fault of black females, who achieve out of all proportion, both to their numbers in the community and to the paradigmatic example before the nation: "Ours is a society which presumes male leadership in private and public affairs. . . . A subculture, such as that of the Negro American, in which this is not the pattern, is placed at a distinct disadvantage" [75]. Between charts and diagrams, we are asked to consider the impact of qualitative measure on the black male's performance on standardized examinations, matriculation in schools of higher and professional training, etc. Even though Moynihan sounds a critique on his own argument here, he quickly withdraws from its possibilities, suggesting that black males should reign because that is the way the majority culture carries things out: "It is clearly a disadvantage for a minority group to be operating under one principle, while the great majority of the population . . . is operating on another" [75]. Those persons living according to the perceived "matriarchal" pattern are, therefore, caught in a state of social "pathology."

Even though Daughters have their own agenda with reference to this order of Fathers (imagining for the moment that Moynihan's fiction—and others like it—does not represent an adequate one and that there *is*, once we dis-cover him, a Father here), my contention that these social and cultural subjects make doubles, unstable in their respective identities, in effect transports us to a common historical ground, the socio-political order of the New Work. That order, with its human sequence written in blood, represents for its African and indigenous peoples a scene of actual mutilation, dismemberment, and exile. First of all, the New-World, diasporic plight marked a theft of the body—a willful and violent (and unimaginable from this distance) severing of the captive body from its motive will, its active desire. Under these conditions, we lose at least gender difference in the outcome, and the female body and the male body become a territory of cultural and political maneuver, not at all gender-related, gender-specific. But this body, at least from the point of view of the captive community, focuses a private and particular space, at which point of convergence biological, sexual, social, cultural, linguistic, ritualistic, and psychological fortunes join. This profound intimacy of interlocking detail is disrupted, however, by externally imposed meanings and uses: 1) the captive body becomes the source of an irresistible, destructive sensuality; 2) at the same time—in stunning contradiction—the captive body reduces to a thing becoming *being for* the captor; 3) in this absence *from* a subject position, the captured sexualities provide a physical and biological expression of "otherness"; 4) as a category of "otherness," the captive body translates into a potential for pornotroping and embodies sheer physical powerlessness that slides into a more general "powerlessness," resonating through various centers of human and social meaning.

But I would make a distinction in this case between "body" and "flesh" and impose that distinction as the central one between captive and liberated subject-positions. In that sense, before the "body" there is the "flesh," that zero degree of social conceptualization that does not escape concealment under the brush of discourse, or the reflexes of iconography. Even though the European hegemonies stole bodies—some of them female—out of West African communities in concert with the African "middleman," we regard this human and social irreparability as high crimes against the flesh, as the person of African females and African males registered the wounding. If we think of the "flesh" as a primary narrative, then we mean its seared, divided, ripped-apartness, riveted to the ship's hole, fallen, or escaped overboard.

One of the most poignant aspects of William Goodell's contemporaneous study of the North American slave codes gives precise expression to the tortures and instruments of captivity. Reporting an instance of Jonathan Edwards's observations on the tortures of enslavement, Goodell narrates: "The smack of the whip is all day long in the ears of those who are on the plantation, or in the vicinity; and it is used with such dexterity and severity as not only to lacerate the skin, but to tear, out small portions of the flesh at almost every stake" [221]. The anatomical specifications of rupture, of altered human tissue, take on the objective description of laboratory prose—eyes beaten out, arms, backs, skulls branded, a left jaw, a right ankle, punctured; teeth missing, as the calculated work of iron, whips, chains, knives, the canine patrol, the bullet.

These undecipherable markings on the captive body render a kind of hieroglyphics of the flesh whose severe disjunctures come to be hidden to the cultural seeing by skin color. We might well ask if this phenomenon of marking and branding actually "transfers" from one generation to another, finding its various symbolic substitutions in an efficacy of meanings that repeat the initiating moments? As Elaine Scarry describes the mechanisms of torture [Scarry 27–59], these lacerations, woundings, fissures, tears, scars, openings, ruptures, lesions, rendings, punctures of the flesh create the distance between what I would designate a cultural vestibularity and the culture, whose state apparatus, including judges, attorneys, "owners," "soul-drivers," "overseers," and "men of God," apparently colludes with a protocol of "search and destroy." This body whose flesh carries the female and the male to the frontiers of survival bears in person the marks of a cultural text whose inside has been turned outside.

The flesh is the concentration of "ethnicity" that contemporary critical discourses neither acknowledge nor discourse away. It is this "flesh and blood" entity, in the vestibule (or "pre-view") of a colonized North America that is essentially ejected from "The Female Body in Western Culture" [see Suleiman, ed.], but it makes good theory, or commemorative violation of body and mind—but also the topic of specifically externalized acts of torture and prostration that we imagine as the peculiar province of male brutality and torture inflicted by other males. A female body strung from a tree limb, or bleeding from the breast on any given day of field work because the "overseer," standing the length of a whip, has popped her flesh open, adds a lexical and living dimension to the narratives of women in culture and society [Davis 9]. This materialized scene of unprotected female flesh—of female flesh "ungendered"—offers a praxis and a theory, a text for living and for dying, and a method for reading both through their diverse mediations.

Among the myriad uses to which the enslaved community was put, Goodell identifies its value for medical research: "Assortments of diseased, damaged, and disabled Negroes, deemed incurable and otherwise worthless are bought up, it seems . . . by medical institutions, to be experimented and operated upon, for purposes of 'medical education' and the interest of medical science" [86–87; Goodell's emphasis]. From the *Charleston Mercury* for October 12, 1838, Goodell notes this advertisement:

'To planters and others—Wanted, fifty Negroes, any person, having sick Negroes, considered incurable by their respective physicians, and wishing to dispose of them, Dr. S. will pay cash for Negroes affected with scrofula, or king's evil, confirmed hypochondriasm, apoplexy, diseases of the liver, kidneys, spleen, stomach and intestines, bladder and its appendages, diarrhea, dysentery, etc. The highest *cash* price will be paid, on application as above at No. 110 Church Street, Charleston. [87; Goodell's emphasis]

This profitable "atomizing" of the captive body provides another angle on the divided flesh: we lose any hint or suggestion of a dimension of ethics, of relatedness between human personality and its anatomical features, between one human personality and another, between human personality and cultural institutions. To that extent, the procedures adopted for the captive flesh demarcate a total objectification, as the entire captive community becomes a living laboratory.

The captive body, then, brings into focus a gathering of social realities as well as a metaphor for value so thoroughly interwoven in their literal and figurative emphases that distinctions between them are virtually useless. Even though the captive flesh/body has been "liberated," and no one need pretend that even the quotation marks do not matter, dominant symbolic activity, the ruling episteme that releases the dynamics of naming and valuation, remains grounded in the originating metaphors of captivity and mutilation so that it is as if neither time nor history, nor historiography and its topics, shows movement, as the human subject is "murdered" over and over again by the passions of a bloodless and anonymous archaism, showing itself in endless disguise. Faulkner's young Chick Mallison in *The Mansion* calls "it" by other names—"the ancient subterrene atavistic fear" [227]. And I would call it the Great

Long National Shame. But people do not talk like that anymore—it is "embarrass-ing." Just as the retrieval of mutilated female bodies will likely be "backward" for some people. Neither the shameface of the embarrassed, nor the not-looking-back of the self-assured is of much interest to us, and will not help at all if rigor is our dream. We might concede, at the very least, that sticks and bricks *might* break our bones, but words will most certainly *kill* us.

The symbolic order that I wish to trace in this writing, calling it an "American grammar," begins at the "beginning," which is really a rupture and a radically different kind of cultural continuation. The massive demographic shifts, the violent formation of a modern African consciousness, that take place on the subsaharan Continent during the initiative strikes which open the Atlantic Slave Trade in the fifteenth century of our Christ, interrupted hundreds of years of black African culture. We write and think, then, about an outcome of aspects of African-American life in the United States under the pressure of those events. I might as well add that the familiarity of this narrative does nothing to appease the hunger of recorded memory, nor does the persistence of the repeated rob these well-known, oft-told events of their power, even now, to startle. In a very real sense, every writing as revision makes the "discovery" all over again.

2

The narratives by African peoples and their descendants, though not as numerous from those early centuries of the "execrable trade" as the researcher would wish, suggest in their rare occurrence, that the visual shock waves touched off when African and European "met" reverberated on both sides of the encounter. The narrative of the "Life of Olaudah Equiano, or Gustavus Vassa, the African. Written by Himself," first published in London in 1789, makes it quite clear that the first Europeans Equiano observed on what is now Nigerian soil were as unreal for him as he and others must have been for the European captors. The cruelty of "these white men with horrible looks, red faces, and long hair," of these "spirits," as the narrator would have it, occupies several pages of Equjano's attention, alongside a firsthand account of Nigerian interior life [27 ff.]. We are justified in regarding the outcome of Equi-ano's experience in the same light as he himself might have—as a "fall," as a veritable descent into the loss of communicative force.

If, as Todorov points out, the Mayan and Aztec peoples "lost control of commu-nication" [61] in light of Spanish Intervention, we could observe, similarly, that Vassa falls among men whose language is not only strange to him, but whose habits and practices strike him as "astonishing":

[The sea, the slave ship] filled me with astonishment, which was soon converted into terror, when I was carried on board. I was immediately handled, and tossed up to see if I were sound, by some of the crew; and I was now persuaded that I had gotten into a world of bad spirits, and that they were going to kill me. Their complexions, too, differing so much from ours, their long hair, and the language they spoke (which was different from any I had ever heard), united to confirm me in this belief. [Equiano 27]

The captivating party does not only "earn" the right to dispose of the captive body as it sees fit, but gains, consequently, the right to name and "name" it: Equiano, for instance, identifies at least three different names that he is given in numerous passages between his Benin homeland and the Virginia colony, the latter and England— "Michael," "Jacob," "Gustavus Vassa" [35; 36].

The nicknames by which African-American women have been called, or regarded; or imagined on the New World scene—the opening lines of this essay provide examples—demonstrate the powers of distortion that the dominant community seizes as its unlawful prerogative: Moynihan's, "Negro Family," then, borrows its narrative energies from the grid of associations, from the semantic and iconic folds buried deep in the collective past, that come to surround and signify the captive person. Though there is no absolute point of chronological initiation, we might repeat certain familiar impression points that lend shape to the business of dehumanized naming. Expecting to find direct and amplified reference to African women during the opening years of the Trade, the observer is disappointed time and again that this cultural subject is concealed beneath the mighty debris of the itemized account, between the lines of the massive logs of commercial enterprise that overrun the sense of clarity we believed we had gained concerning this collective humiliation. Elizabeth Donnan's enormous, four-volume documentation becomes a case in point.

Turning directly to this source, we discover what we had not expected to find— that this aspect of the search is rendered problematic and that observations of a field of manners and its related sociometries are an outgrowth of the industry of the "exterior other" [Todorov 3], called "anthropology" later on. The European males who laded and captained these galleys and who policed and corralled these human beings in hundreds of vessels from Liverpool to Elmina, to Jamaica; from the Cayenne Islands, to the ports at Charleston and Salem, and for three centuries of human life, were not curious about this "cargo" that bled, packed like so many live sardines among the immovable objects. Such inveterate obscene blindness might be denied, point blank, as a possibility for anyone, except that we know it happened.

Donnan's first volume covers three centuries of European "discovery" and "conquest," beginning 50 years before pious Cristobal, Christum Ferens, the bearer of Christ, laid claim to what he thought was the "Indies." From Gomes Eannes de Azurara's "Chronicle of the Discovery and Conquest of Guinea, 1441–1448" [Donnan 1:18–41], we learn that the Portuguese probably gain the dubious distinction of having introduced black Africans to the European market of servitude. We are also reminded that "Geography" is not a divine gift. Quite to the contrary, its boundaries were shifted during the European "Age of Conquest" in giddy desperation, according to the dictates of conquering armies, the edicts of prelates, the peculiar myopia of the medieval Christian mind. Looking for the "Nile River," for example, according to the fifteenth-century Portuguese notion, is someone's joke. For all that the pre-Columbian "explorers" knew about the sciences of navigation and geography, we are surprised that more parties of them did not end up "discovering" Europe. Perhaps, from a certain angle, that is precisely all that they found—an alternative reading of ego. The Portuguese, having little idea where the Nile ran, at least understood right away that there were men and women darker-skinned than themselves, but they were not specifically knowledgeable, or ingenious, about the various families and groupings represented by them. De Azurara records encounters with "Moors," "Mooresses," "Mulattoes," and people "black as Ethiops" [1:28], but it seems that the "Land of Guinea," or of "Black Men," or of "The Negroes" [1:35] was located anywhere southeast of Cape Verde, the Canaries, and the River Senegal, looking at an eighteenth-century European version of the subsaharan Continent along the West African coast [1:frontispiece].

Three genetic distinctions are available to the Portuguese eye, all along the riffs of melanin in the skin: In a field of captives, some of the observed are "white enough, fair to look upon, and well-proportioned." Others are less "white like mulattoes," and still others "black as Ethiops, and so ugly, both in features and in body, as almost to appear (to those who saw them) the images of a lower hemisphere" [1:28]. By implication, this "third man," standing for the most aberrant phenotype to the observing eye, embodies the linguistic community most unknown to the European. Arabic translators among the Europeans could at least "talk" to the "Moors" and instruct them to ransom themselves, or else. . . .

Typically, there is in this grammar of description the perspective of "declension," not of simultaneity, and its point of initiation is solipsistic—it begins with a narrative self, in an apparent unity of feeling, and unlike Equiano, who also saw "ugly" when he looked out, this collective self uncovers the means by which to subjugate the "foreign code of conscience," whose most easily remarkable and irremediable difference is perceived in skin color. By the time of De Azurara's mid-fifteenth century narrative and a century and a half before Shakespeare's "old black ram" of an Othello "tups" that "white ewe" of a Desdemona, the magic of skin color is already installed as a decisive factor in human dealings.

In De Azurara's narrative, we observe males looking at other males, as "female" is subsumed here under the general category of estrangement. Few places in these excerpts carve out a distinct female space, though there are moments of portrayal that perceive female captives in the implications of socio-cultural function. When the field of captives (referred to above) is divided among the spoilers, no heed is paid to relations, as fathers are separated from sons, husbands from wives, brothers from sisters and brothers, mothers from children—male and female. It seems clear that the political program of European Christianity promotes this hierarchical view among males, although it remains puzzling to us exactly how this version of Christianity transforms the "pagan" also into the "ugly." It appears that human beings came up with degrees of "fair" and then the "hideous," in its overtones of bestiality, as the opposite of "fair," all by themselves, without stage direction, even though there is the curious and blazing exception of Nietzsche's Socrates, who was Athens's ugliest and wisest and best citizen. The intimate choreography that the Portuguese narrator sets going between the "faithless" and the "ugly" transforms a partnership of dancers into a single figure. Once the "faithless," indiscriminate of the three stops of Portuguese skin color, are transported to Europe, they become an altered, human factor:

> And so their lot was now quite contrary to what it had been, since before they had lived in perdition of soul and body; of their souls, in that they were yet pagans, without the clearness and the light of the Holy Faith; and of their bodies, in that they lived like beasts, without any custom of reasonable beings-for they had no knowledge of bread and wine, and they were without covering of clothes, or the lodgment of houses; and worse than all, through the great ignorance that was in them, in that they had no understanding of good, but only knew how to live in bestial sloth. [1:30]

The altered human factor renders an alterity of European ego, an invention, or "discovery" as decisive in the full range of its social implications as the birth of a newborn. According to the semantic alignments of the excerpted passage, person-hood, for this European observer, locates an immediately outward and superficial determination, gauged by quite arbitrarily opposed and specular categories: that these "pagans" did not have "bread" and "wine" did not mean that they were feastless, as Equiano observes about the Benin diet, c. 1745, in the province of Essaka:

> Our manner of living is entirely plain; for as yet the natives are unacquainted with those refinements in cookery which debauch the taste; bullocks, goats, and poultry supply the greatest part of their food. (These constitute likewise the principal wealth of the country, and the chief articles of its commerce.) The flesh is usually stewed in a pan; to make it savory we sometimes use pepper, and other spices, and we have salt made of wood ashes. Our vegetables are mostly plaintains, eadas, yams, beans and Indian corn. The head of the family usually eats alone; his wives and slaves have also their separate tables. [Equiano 8].

Just as fufu serves the Ghanaian diet today as a starch-and-bread-substitute, palm wine (an item by the same name in the eighteenth-century palate of the Benin community) need not be Heitz Cellars' Martha's Vineyard and vice-versa in order for a guest, say, to imagine that she has enjoyed. That African housing arrangements of the fifteenth century did not resemble those familiar to De Azurara's narrator need not have meant that the African communities he encountered were without dwellings. Again, Equiano's narrative suggests that by the middle of the eighteenth century, at least, African living patterns were not only quite distinct in their sociometrical implications, but that also their architectonics accurately reflected the climate and availability of resources in the local circumstance: "These houses never exceed one story in height; they are always built of wood, or stakes driven into the ground, crossed with wattles, and neatly plastered within and without" [9]. Hierarchical impulse in both De Azurara's and Equiano's narratives translates all perceived difference as a fundamental degradation or transcendence, but at least in Equiano's case, cultural practices are not observed in any intimate connection with skin color. For all intents and purposes, the politics of melanin, not isolated in its strange powers from the imperatives of a mercantile and competitive economics of European nation-states, will make of "transcendence" and "degradation" the basis of a historic violence that will rewrite

the histories of modern Europe and black Africa. These mutually exclusive nominative elements come to rest on the same governing semantics—the ahistorical, or
symptoms of the "sacred."

By August 1518, the Spanish king, Francisco de Los Covos, under the aegis of a
powerful negation, could order "4000 negro slaves both male and female, provided
they be Christians" to be taken to the Caribbean, "the islands and the mainland of
the ocean sea already discovered or to be discovered" [Donnan 1:42]. Though the
notorious "Middle Passage" appears to the investigator as a vast background without
boundaries in time and space, we see it related in Donnan's accounts to the opening
up of the entire Western hemisphere for the specific purposes of enslavement and
colonization. De Azurara's narrative belongs, then, to a discourse of appropriation
whose strategies will prove fatal to communities along the coastline of West Africa,
stretching, according to Olaudah Equiano, "3400 miles, from Senegal to Angola, and
[will include] a variety of kingdoms" [Equiano 5].

The conditions of "Middle Passage" are among the most incredible narratives
available to the student, as it remains not easily imaginable. Late in the chronicles of
the Atlantic Slave Trade, Britain's Parliament entertained discussions concerning possible "regulations" for slave vessels. A Captain Perry visited the Liverpool port, and
among the ships that he inspected was "The Brookes," probably the most well-known
image of the slave galley with its representative personae etched into the drawing like
so many cartoon figures. Elizabeth Donnan's second volume carries the "Brookes
Plan," along with an elaborate delineation of its dimensions from the investigative
reporting of Perry himself: "Let it now be supposed . . . further, that every man slave
is to be allowed six feet by one foot four inches for room, every woman five feet ten
by one foot four, every boy five feet by one foot two, and every girl four feet six by
one foot . . ." [2:592, n]. The owner of "The Brookes," James Jones, had recommended that "five females be reckoned as four males, and three boys or girls as equal
to two grown persons"[2:592].

These scaled inequalities complement the commanding terms of the dehumanizing,
ungendering, and defacing project of African persons that De Azurara's narrator
might have recognized. It has been pointed out to me that these measurements do
reveal the application of the gender rule to the material conditions of passage, but I
would suggest that "gendering" takes place within the confines of the domestic, an
essential metaphor that then spreads its tentacles for male and female subject over a
wider ground of human and social purposes. Domesticity appears to gain its power
by way of a common origin of cultural fictions that are grounded in the specificity of
proper names, more exactly, a patronymic, which, in turn, situates those persons it
"covers" in a particular place. Contrarily, the cargo of a ship might not be regarded
as elements of the domestic, even though the vessel that carries it is sometimes
romantically (ironically?) personified as "she." The human cargo of a slave vessel—
in the fundamental effacement and remission of African family and proper names—
offers a counter-narrative to notions of the domestic.

Those African persons in "Middle Passage" were literally suspended in the "oceanic," if we think of the latter in its Freudian orientation as an analogy for undiffer-

entiated identity: removed from the indigenous land and culture, and not-yet "American" either, these captive persons, without names that their captors would recognize, were in movement across the Atlantic, but they were also nowhere at all. Inasmuch as, on any given day, we might imagine, the captive personality did not know where s/he was, we could say that they were the culturally "unmade," thrown in the midst of a figurative darkness that "exposed" their destinies to an unknown course. Often enough for the captains of these galleys, navigational science of the day was not sufficient to guarantee the intended destination. We might say that the slave ship, its crew, and its human-as-cargo stand for a wild and unclaimed richness of possibility that is not interrupted, not "counted"/"accounted," or differentiated, until its movement gains the land thousands of miles away from the point of departure. Under these conditions, one is neither female, nor male, as both subjects are taken into "account" as quantities: The female in "Middle Passage," as the apparently smaller physical mass, occupies "less room" in a directly translatable money economy. But she is, nevertheless, quantifiable by the same rules of accounting as her male counterpart.

It is not only difficult for the student to find "female" in "Middle Passage," but also, as Herbert S. Klein observes, "African women did not enter the Atlantic slave trade in anything like the numbers of African men. At all ages, men outnumbered women on the slave ships bound for America from Africa" [Klein 29]. Though this observation does not change the reality of African women's captivity and servitude in New World communities, it does provide a perspective from which to contemplate the internal African slave trade, which, according to Africanists, remained a predominantly female market. Klein nevertheless affirms that those females forced into the trade were segregated "from men for policing purposes" [35]. He claims that both "were allotted the same space between decks . . . and both were fed the same food" [35]. It is not altogether clear from Klein's observations for whom the "police" kept vigil. It is certainly known from evidence presented in Donnan's third volume ("New England and the Middle Colonies") that insurrection was both frequent and feared in passage, and we have not yet found a great deal of evidence to support a thesis that female captives participated in insurrectionary activity [see White 63–64]. Because it was the rule, however—not the exception—that the African female, in both indigenous African cultures and in what becomes her "home," performed tasks of hard physical labor—so much so that the quintessential "slave" is not a male, but a female, we wonder at the seeming docility of the subject, granting her a "feminization" that enslavement kept at bay. Indeed, across the spate of discourse that I examined for this writing, the acts of enslavement and responses to it comprise a more or less agonistic engagement of confrontational hostilities among males. The visual and historical evidence betrays the dominant discourse on the matter as incomplete, but counter-evidence is inadequate as well: the sexual violation of captive females and their own express rage against their oppressors did not constitute events that captains and their crews rushed to record in letters to their sponsoring companies, or sons on board in letters home to their New England mamas.

One suspects that there are several ways to snare a mockingbird, so that insurrection might have involved, from time to time, rather more subtle means than mutiny on the "Felicity," for instance. At any rate, we get very little notion in the written record of the life of women, children, and infants in "Middle Passage," and no idea of the fate of the pregnant female captive and the unborn, which startling thematic Bell Hooks addresses in the opening chapter of her pathfinding work [see Hooks 15–49]. From Hooks's lead, however, we might guess that the "reproduction of mothering" in this historic instance carries few of the benefits of a patriarchilized female gender, which, from one point of view, is the only female gender there is.

The relative silence of the record on this point constitutes a portion of the disquieting lacunae that feminist investigation seeks to fill. Such silence is the nickname of distortion, of the unknown human factor that a revised public discourse would both undo and reveal. This cultural subject is inscribed historically as anonymity/anomie in various public documents of European-American mal(e)venture, from Portuguese De Azurara in the middle of the fifteenth century, to South Carolina's Henry Laurens in the eighteenth.

What confuses and enriches the picture is precisely the sameness of anonymous portrayal that adheres tenaciously across the division of gender. In the vertical columns of accounts and ledgers that comprise Donnan's work, the terms "Negroes" and "Slaves" denote a common status. For instance, entries in one account, from September 1700 through September 1702, are specifically descriptive of the names of ships and the private traders in Barbados who will receive the stipulated goods, but "No. Negroes" and "Sum sold for per head" are so exactly arithmetical that it is as if these additions and multiplications belong to the other side of an equation [Donnan 2:25]. One is struck by the detail and precision that characterize these accounts, as a narrative, or story, is always implied by a man or woman's name: "Wm. Webster," "John Dunn," "Thos. Brownbill," "Robt. Knowles." But the "other" side of the page, as it were, equally precise, throws no face in view. It seems that nothing breaks the uniformity in this guise. If in no other way, the destruction of the African name, of kin, of linguistic, and ritual connections is so obvious in the vital stats sheet that we tend to overlook it. Quite naturally, the trader is not interested, in any semantic sense, in this "baggage" that he must deliver, but that he is not is all the more reason to search out the metaphorical implications of naming as one of the key sources of a bitter Americanizing for African persons.

The loss of the indigenous name/land provides a metaphor of displacement for other human and cultural features and relations, including the displacement of the genitalia, the female's and the male's desire that engenders future. The fact that the enslaved person's access to the issue of his/her own body is not entirely clear in this historic period throws in crisis all aspects of the blood relations, as captors apparently felt no obligation to acknowledge them. Actually trying to understand how the confusions of consanguinity worked becomes the project, because the outcome goes far to explain the rule of gender and its application to the African female in captivity.

3

Even though the essays in Claire C. Robertson's and Martin A. Klein's *Women and Slavery In Africa* have specifically to do with aspects of the internal African slave trade, some of their observations shed light on the captivities of the Diaspora. At least these observations have the benefit of altering the kind of questions we might ask of these silent chapters. For example, Robertson's essay, which opens the volume, discusses the term "slavery" in a wide variety of relationships. The enslaved person as property identifies the most familiar element of a most startling proposition. But to overlap kinlessness on the requirements of property might enlarge our view of the conditions of enslavement. Looking specifically at documents from the West African societies of Songhay and Dahomey, Claude Meillassoux elaborates several features of the property/kinless constellation that are highly suggestive for our own quite different purposes.

Meillassoux argues that "slavery creates an economic and social agent whose virtue lies in being outside the kinship system" ["Female Slavery," Robertson and Klein, 50]. Because the Atlantic trade involved heterogeneous social and ethnic formations in an explicit power relationship, we certainly cannot mean "kinship system" in precisely the same way that Meillassoux observes at work within the intricate calculus of descent among West African societies. However, the idea becomes useful as a point of contemplation when we try to sharpen our own sense of the African female's reproductive uses within the diasporic enterprise of enslavement and the genetic reproduction of the enslaved. In effect, under conditions of captivity, the offspring of the female does not "belong" to the Mother, nor is s/he "related" to the "owner," though the latter "possesses" it, and in the African-American instance, often fathered it, and, as often, without whatever benefit of patrimony. In the social outline that Meillassoux is pursuing, the offspring of the enslaved, "being unrelated both to their begetters and to their owners . . . , find themselves in the situation of being orphans" [50].

In the context of the United States, we could not say that the enslaved offspring was "orphaned," but the child does become, under the press of a patronymic, patrifocal, patrilineal, and patriarchal order, the man/woman on the boundary, whose human and familial status, by the very nature of the case, had yet to be defined. I would call this enforced state of breach another instance of vestibular cultural formation where "kinship" loses meaning, since it can be invaded at any given and arbitrary moment by the property relations. I certainly do not mean to say that African peoples in the New World did not maintain the powerful ties of sympathy that bind blood-relations in a network of feeling, of continuity. It is precisely that relationship—not customarily recognized by the code of slavery—that historians have long identified as the inviolable "Black Family" and further suggest that this structure remains one of the supreme social achievements of African-Americans under conditions of enslavement [see John Blassingame 79 ff.].

Indeed, the revised "Black Family" of enslavement has engendered an older tradition of historiographical and sociological writings than we usually think. Ironically enough, E. Franklin Frazier's *Negro Family in the United States* likely provides the closest contemporary narrative of conceptualization for the "Moynihan Report." Originally published in 1939, Frazier's work underwent two redactions in 1948 and 1966. Even though Frazier's outlook on his familial configuration remains basically sanguine, I would support Angela Davis's skeptical reading of Frazier's "Black Matriarchate" [Davis 14]. "Except where the master's will was concerned," Frazier contends, this matriarchal figure "developed a spirit of independence and a keen sense of her personal rights" [1966:47]. The "exception" in this instance tends to be overwhelming as the African-American female's "dominance" and "strength" come to be interpreted by later generations—both black and white, oddly enough—as a "pathology," as an instrument of castration. Frazier's larger point, we might suppose, is that African-Americans developed such resourcefulness under conditions of captivity that "family" must be conceded as one of their redoubtable social attainments. This line of interpretation is pursued by Blassingame and Eugene Genovese [*Roll, Jordan, Roll* 70–75], among other U.S. historians, and indeed assumes a centrality of focus in our own thinking about the impact and outcome of captivity.

It seems clear, however, that "Family," as we practice and understand it "in the West"—the vertical transfer of a bloodline, of a patronymic, of titles and entitlements, of real estate and the prerogatives of "cold cash," from fathers to sons and in the supposedly free exchange of affectional ties between a male and a female of his choice—becomes the mythically revered privilege of a free and freed community. In that sense, African peoples in the historic Diaspora had nothing to prove if the point had been that they were not capable of "family" (read "civilization"), since it is stunningly evident, in Equlano's narrative, for instance, that Africans were not only capable of the concept and the practice of "family" including "slaves," but in modes of elaboration and naming that were at least as complex as those of the "nuclear family" "in the West."

Whether or not we decide that the support systems that African-Americans derived under conditions of captivity should be called "family," or something else, strikes me as supremely impertinent. The point remains that captive persons were forced into patterns of dispersal, beginning with the Trade itself, into the horizontal relatedness of language groups, discourse formations, bloodlines, names, and properties by the legal arrangements of enslavement. It is true that the most "well-meaning" of "masters" (and there must have been some) could not, did not alter the ideological and hegemonic mandates of dominance. It must be conceded that African-Americans, under the press of a hostile and compulsory patriarchal order, bound and determined to destroy them, or to preserve them only in the service and at the behest of the "master" class, exercised a degree of courage and will to survive that startles the imagination even now. Although it makes good revisionist history to read this tale liberally, it is probably truer than we know at this distance (and truer than contemporary social practice in the community would suggest on occasion) that the captive person developed, time and again, certain ethical and sentimental features that tied her and him, across the landscape to others, often sold from hand to hand, of the same and different blood in a common fabric of memory and inspiration.

We might choose to call this connectedness "family," or "support structure," but that is a rather different case from the moves of a dominant symbolic order, pledged to maintain the supremacy of race. It is that order that forces "family" to modify itself when it does not mean family of the "master," or dominant enclave. It is this rhetorical and symbolic move that declares primacy over any other human and social claim, and in that political order of things, "kin," just as gender formation, has no decisive legal or social efficacy.

We return frequently to Frederick Douglass's careful elaborations of the arrangements of captivity, and we are astonished each reading by two dispersed, yet poignantly related, familial enactments that suggest a connection between "kinship" and "property." Douglass tells us early in the opening chapter of the 1845 *Narrative* that he was separated in infancy from his mother: "For what this separation is [*sic*] done, I do not know, unless it be to hinder the development of the child's affection toward its mother, and to blunt and destroy the natural affection of the mother for the child. This is the inevitable result" [22].

Perhaps one of the assertions that Meillassoux advances concerning indigenous African formations of enslavement might be turned as a question, against the perspective of Douglass's witness: is the genetic reproduction of the slave and the recognition of the rights of the slave to his or her offspring a check on the profitability of slavery? And how so, if so? We see vaguely the route to framing a response, especially to the question's second half and perhaps to the first: the enslaved must not be permitted to perceive that he or she has any human rights that matter. Certainly if "kinship" were possible, the property relations would be undermined, since the offspring would then "belong" to a mother and a father. In the system that Douglass articulates, genetic reproduction becomes, then, not an elaboration of the life-principle in its cultural overlap, but an extension of the boundaries of proliferating properties. Meillassoux goes so far as to argue that "slavery exists where the slave class is reproduced through institutional apparatus: war and market" [50]. Since, in the United States, the market of slavery identified the chief institutional means for maintaining a class of enforced servile labor, it seems that the biological reproduction of the enslaved was not alone sufficient to reenforce the estate of slavery. If, as Meillassoux contends, "femininity loses its sacredness in slavery" [64], then so does "motherhood" as female blood-rite/right. To that extent, the captive female body locates precisely a moment of converging political and social vectors that mark the flesh as a prime commodity of exchange. While this proposition is open to further exploration, suffice it to say now that this open exchange of female bodies in the raw offers a kind of Ur-text to the dynamics of signification and representation that the gendered female would unravel.

For Douglass, the loss of his mother eventuates in alienation from his brother and sisters, who live in the same house with him: "The early separation of us from our mother had well nigh blotted the fact of our relationship from our memories" [45]. What could this mean? The physical proximity of the siblings survives the mother's death. They grasp their connection in the physical sense, but Douglass appears to mean a psychological bonding whose success mandates the mother's presence. Could we say, then, that the feeling of kinship is not inevitable? That it describes a relationship that appears "natural," but must be "cultivated" under actual material conditions? If the child's humanity is mirrored initially in the eyes of its mother, or the maternal function, then we might be able to guess that the social subject grasps the whole dynamic of resemblance and kinship by way of the same source.

There is an amazing thematic synonymity on this point between aspects of Douglass's *Narrative* and Malcolm El-Hajj Malik El Shabazz's *Autobiography of Malcolm X* [21 ff.]. Through the loss of the mother, in the latter contemporary instance, to the institution of "insanity" and the state—a full century after Douglass's writing and under social conditions that might be designated a post-emancipation neo-enslavement—Malcolm and his siblings, robbed of their activist father in a kkk-like ambush, are not only widely dispersed across a makeshift social terrain, but also show symptoms of estrangement and "disremembering" that require many years to heal, and even then, only by way of Malcolm's prison ordeal turned, eventually, into a redemptive occurrence.

The destructive loss of the natural mother, whose biological/genetic relationship to the child remains unique and unambiguous, opens the enslaved young to social ambiguity and chaos: the ambiguity of his/her fatherhood and to a structure of other relational elements, now threatened, that would declare the young's connection to a genetic and historic future by way of their own siblings. That the father in Douglass's case was most likely the "master," not by any means special to Douglass, involves a hideous paradox. Fatherhood, at best a supreme cultural courtesy, attenuates here on the one hand into a monstrous accumulation of power on the other. One has been "made" and "bought" by disparate currencies, linking back to a common origin of exchange and domination. The denied genetic link becomes the chief strategy of an undenied ownership, as if the interrogation into the father's identity—the blank space where his proper name will fit—were answered by the fact, de jure of a material possession. "And this is done," Douglass asserts, "too obviously to administer to the [masters'] own lusts, and make a gratification of their wicked desires profitable as well as pleasurable" [23].

Whether or not the captive female and/or her sexual oppressor derived "pleasure" from their seductions and couplings is not a question we can politely ask. Whether or not "pleasure" is possible at all under conditions that I would aver as non-freedom for both or either of the parties has not been settled. Indeed, we could go so far as to entertain the very real possibility that "sexuality," as a term of implied relationship and desire, is dubiously appropriate, manageable, or accurate to any of the familial arrangements under a system of enslavement, from the master's family to the captive enclave. Under these arrangements, the customary lexis of sexuality, including "reproduction," "motherhood," "pleasure," and "desire" are thrown into unrelieved crisis.

If the testimony of Linda Brent/Harriet Jacobs is to be believed, the official mistresses of slavery's "masters" constitute a privileged class of the tormented, if such contradiction can be entertained [Brent 29–35]. Linda Brent/Harriet Jacobs recounts in the course of her narrative scenes from a "psychodrama," opposing herself and "Mrs. Flint," in what we have come to consider the classic alignment between captive woman and free. Suspecting that her husband, Dr. Flint, has sexual designs on the young Linda (and the doctor is nearly humorously incompetent at it, according to the story line), Mrs. Flint assumes the role of a perambulatory nightmare who visits the captive woman in the spirit of a veiled seduction. Mrs. Flint imitates the incubus who "rides" its victim in order to exact confession, expiation, and anything else that the immaterial power might want. (Gayl Jones's *Corregidora* [1975] weaves a contemporary fictional situation around the historic motif of entangled female sexualities.) This narrative scene from Brent's work, dictated to Lydia Maria Child, provides an instance of a repeated sequence, purportedly based on "real" life. But the scene in question appears to so commingle its signals with the fictive, with casebook narratives from psychoanalysis, that we are certain that the narrator has her hands on an explosive moment of New-World/U.S. history that feminist investigation is beginning to unravel. The narrator recalls:

> Sometimes I woke up, and found her Bending over me. At other times, she whispered in my ear, as though it were her husband who was speaking to me, and listened to hear what I would answer. If she startled me, on such occasion, she would glide stealthily away; and the next morning she would tell me I had been talking in my sleep, and ask who I was talking to. At last, I began to be fearful for my life. [Brent 33]

The "jealous mistress" here (but "jealous" for whom?) forms an analogy with the "master" to the extent that male dominative modes give the male the material means to fully act out what the female might only wish. The mistress in the case of Brent's narrative becomes a metaphor for his madness that arises in the ecstasy of unchecked power. Mrs. Flint enacts a male alibi and prosthetic motion that is mobilized at night, at the material place of the dream work. In both male and female instances, the subject attempts to *inculcate* his or her will into the vulnerable, supine body. Though this is barely hinted on the surface of the text, we might say that Brent, between the lines of her narrative, demarcates a sexuality that is neuter-bound, inasmuch as it represents an open vulnerability to a gigantic sexualized repertoire that may be alternately expressed as male/female. Since the gendered female exists for the male, we might suggest that the ungendered female—in an amazing stroke of pansexual potential—might be invaded/raided by another woman or man.

If *Incidents in the Life of a Slave Girl* were a novel, and not the memoirs of an escaped female captive, then we might say that "Mrs. Flint" is also the narrator's projection, her creation, so that for all her pious and correct umbrage toward the outrage of her captivity, some aspect of Linda Brent is released in a manifold repetition crisis that the doctor's wife comes to stand in for. In the case of both an imagined fiction and the narrative we have from Brent/Jacobs/Child, published only four years before the official proclamations of Freedom, we could say that African-American women's community and Anglo-American women's community, under certain shared cultural conditions, were the twin actants on a common psychic landscape, were subject to the same fabric of dread and humiliation. Neither could claim her body and its various productions—for quite different reasons, albeit—as her own, and in the case of the doctor's wife, she appears not to have wanted her body at all, but to desire to enter someone else's, specifically, Linda Brent's, in an apparently classic instance of sexual "jealousy" and appropriation. In fact, from one point of view, we cannot unravel one female's narrative from the other's, cannot decipher one without tripping over the other. In that sense, these "threads cable-strong" of an incestuous, interracial genealogy uncover slavery in the United States as one of the richest displays of the psychoanalytic dimensions of culture before the science of European psychoanalysis takes hold.

4

But just as we duly regard similarities between life conditions of American women— captive and free—we must observe those undeniable contrasts and differences so decisive that the African-American female's historic claim to the territory of woman- hood and "femininity" still tends to rest too solidly on the subtle and shifting calibra- tions of a liberal ideology. Valerie Smith's reading of the tale of Linda Brent as a tale of "garreting" enables our notion that female gender for captive women's community is the tale writ between the lines and in the not-quite spaces of an American domes- ticity. It is this tale that we try to make clearer, or, keeping with the metaphor, "bring on line."

If the point is that the historic conditions of African-American women might be read as an unprecedented occasion in the national context, then gender and the arrangements of gender are both crucial and evasive. Holding, however, to a special- ized reading of female gender as an outcome of a certain political, socio-cultural empowerment within the context of the United States, we would regard dispossession as the *loss* of gender, or one of the chief elements in an altered reading of gender: "Women are considered of no value, unless they continually increase their owner's stock. They were put on par with animals" [Brent 49]. Linda Brent's witness appears to contradict the point I would make, but I am suggesting that even though the enslaved female reproduced other enslaved persons, we do not read "birth" in this instance as a reproduction of mothering precisely because the female, like the male, has been robbed of the parental right, the parental function. One treads dangerous ground in suggesting an equation between gender and mothering; in fact, feminist inquiry/praxis and the actual day-to-day living of numberless American women— black and white—have gone far to break the enthrallment of a female subject- position to the theoretical and actual situation of maternity. Our task here would be lightened considerably if we could simply slide over the powerful "No," the signifi- cant exception. In the historic formation to which I point, however, motherhood and female gendering/ungendering appear so intimately aligned that they seem to speak the same language. At least it is plausible to say that motherhood, while it does not exhaust the problematics of female gender, offers one prominent line of approach to it. I would go farther: Because African-American women experienced uncertainty regarding their infants' lives in the historic situation, gendering, in its coeval reference to African-American women, insinuates an implicit and unresolved puzzle both within current feminist discourse and within those discursive communities that investigate the entire problematic of culture. Are we mistaken to suspect that history— at least in this instance—repeats itself yet again?

Every feature of social and human differentiation disappears in public discourses regarding the African-American person, as we encounter, in the juridical codes of slavery, personality reified. William Goodell's study not only demonstrates the rhetorical and moral passions of the abolitionist project, but also lends insight into the corpus of law that underwrites enslavement. If "slave" is perceived as the essence of stillness (an early version of "ethnicity"), or of an undynamic human state, fixed in time and space, then the law articulates this impossibility as its inherent feature. "Slaves shall be deemed, sold, taken, reputed and adjudged in law to be chattels personal, in the hands of their owners and possessors, and their executors, administrators, and assigns, to all intents, constructions, and purposes whatsoever" [23].

Even though we tend to parody and simplify matters to behave as if the various civil codes of the slave-holding United States were monolithically informed, unified, and executed in their application, or that the "code" itself is spontaneously generated in an undivided historic moment, we read it nevertheless as exactly this—the peak points, the salient and characteristic features of a human and social procedure that evolves over a natural historical sequence and represents, consequently, the narrative shorthand of a transaction that is riddled, in practice, with contradictions, accident, and surprise. We could suppose that the legal encodations of enslavement stand for the statistically average case, that the legal code provides the topics of a project increasingly threatened and self-conscious: it is, perhaps, not by chance that the laws regarding slavery appear to crystallize in the precise moment when agitation against the arrangement becomes articulate in certain European and New-World communities. In that regard, the slave codes that Goodell describes are themselves an instance of the counter and isolated text that seeks to silence the contradictions and antitheses engendered by it. For example, aspects of Article 461 of the South Carolina Civil Code call attention to just the sort of uneasy oxymoronic character that the "peculiar institution" attempts to sustain in transforming personality into property.

1) The "slave" is movable by nature, but "immovable by the operation of law" [Goodell 24]. As I read this, law itself is compelled to a point of saturation, or a reverse zero degree, beyond which it cannot move in the behalf of the enslaved or the free. We recall, too, that the "master," under these perversions of judicial power, is impelled to treat the enslaved as property, and not as person. These laws stand for the kind of social formulation that armed forces will help excise from a living context in the campaigns of civil war. They also embody the untenable human relationship that Henry David Thoreau believed occasioned acts of "civil disobedience," the moral philosophy to which Martin Luther King, Jr. would subscribe in the latter half of the twentieth century.

2) Slaves shall be reputed and considered real estate, "subject to be mortgaged according to the rules prescribed by law" [Goodell 24]. I emphasize "reputed," and "considered" as predicate adjectives that invite attention because they denote a con-

trivance, not an intransitive "is," or the transfer of nominative property from one syntactic point to another by way of a weakened copulative. The status of the "reputed" can change, as it will significantly before the nineteenth century closes. The mood here—the "shall be"—is pointedly subjunctive, or the situation devoutly to be wished. That the slave-holding class is forced, in time, to think and do something else is the narrative of violence that enslavement itself has been preparing for a couple of centuries.

Louisiana's and South Carolina's written codes offer a paradigm for praxis in those instances where a written text is missing. In that case, the "chattel principle has . . . been affirmed and maintained by the courts, and involved in legislative acts" [Goodell 25]. In Maryland, a legislative enactment of 1798 shows so forceful a synonymity of motives between branches of comparable governance that a line between "judicial" and "legislative" functions is useless to draw: "In case the personal property of a ward shall consist of specific articles, such as slaves, working beasts, animals of any kind, stock, furniture, plates, books, and so forth, the Court if it shall deem it advantageous to the ward, may at any time, pass an order for the sale thereof" [56]. This inanimate and corporate ownership—the voting district of a ward—is here spoken for, or might be, as a single slave-holding male in determinations concerning property.

The eye pauses, however, not so much at the provisions of this enactment as at the details of its delineation. Everywhere in the descriptive document, we are stunned by the simultaneity of disparate items in a grammatical series: "Slave" appears in the same context with beasts of burden, *all* and any animal(s), various livestock, and a virtually endless profusion of domestic content from the culinary item to the book. Unlike the taxonomy of Borges's "Certain Chinese encyclopedia," whose contemplation opens Foucault's *Order of Things*, these items from a certain American encyclopedia do not sustain discrete and localized "powers of contagion," nor has the ground of their concatenation been dessicated beneath them. That imposed uniformity comprises the shock, that somehow this mix of named things, live and inanimate, collapsed by contiguity to the same text of "realism," carries a disturbingly prominent item of misplacement. To that extent, the project of liberation for African-Americans has found urgency in two passionate motivations that are twinned—1) to break apart, to rupture violently the laws of American behavior that make such syntax possible; 2) to introduce a new semantic field/fold more appropriate to his/her own historic movement. I regard this twin compulsion as distinct, though related, moments of the very same narrative process that might appear as a concentration or a dispersal. The narratives of Linda Brent, Frederick Douglass, and Malcolm El-Hajj Malik El-Shabazz (aspects of which are examined in this essay) each represent both narrative ambitions as they occur under the auspices of "author."

Relatedly, we might interpret the whole career of African-Americans, a decisive factor in national political life since the mid-seventeenth century, in light of the intervening, intruding tale, or the tale—like Brent's "garret" space—"between the lines," which are already inscribed, as a metaphor of social and cultural management.

According to this reading, gender, or sex-rule assignation, or the clear differentiation of sexual stuff, sustained elsewhere in the culture, does not emerge for the African-American female in this historic instance, except indirectly, except as a way to reenforce through the process of birthing, "the reproduction of the relations of production" that involves "the reproduction of the values and behavior patterns necessary to maintain the system of hierarchy in its various aspects of gender, class, and race or ethnicity" [Margaret Strobel, "Slavery and Reproductive Labor in Mombasa," Robertson and Klein 121]: Following, Strobel's lead, I would suggest that the foregoing identifies one of the three categories of reproductive labor that African-American females carry out under the regime of captivity. But this replication of ideology is never simple in the case of female subject-positions, and it appears to acquire a thickened layer of motives in the case of African-American females.

If we can account for an originary narrative and judicial principle that might have engendered a "Moynihan Report," many years into the twentieth century, we cannot do much better than look at Goodell's reading of the *partus sequitur ventrem*: the condition of the slave mother is "forever entailed on all her remotest posterity." This maxim of civil law, in Goodell's view, the "genuine and degrading principle of slavery, inasmuch as it places the slave upon a level with brute animals, prevails universally in the slave-holding states" [Goodell 27]. But what is the "condition" of the mother? Is it the "condition" of enslavement the writer means, or does he mean the "mark" and the "knowledge" of the mother upon the child that here translates into the culturally forbidden and impure? In an elision of terms, mother and enslavement are indistinct categories of the illegitimate inasmuch as each of these synonymous elements defines, in effect, a cultural situation that is father-lacking. Goodell, who does not only report this maxim of law as an aspect of his own factuality, but also regards it, as does Douglass, as a fundamental degradation, supposes descent and identity through the female line as comparable to a brute animality. Knowing already that there are human communities that align social reproductive procedure according to the line of the mother, and Goodell himself might have known it some years later, we can only conclude that the provisions of patriarchy, here exacerbated by the preponderant powers of an enslaving class, declare Mother Right, by definition, a negating feature of human community.

Even though we are not even talking about any of the matriarchal features of social production/reproduction—matrifocality, matrilinearity, matriarchy—when we speak of the enslaved person, we perceive that the dominant culture, in a fatal misunderstanding, assigns a matriarchist value where it does not belong; actually misnames the power of the female regarding the enslaved community. Such naming is false because the female could not, in fact, claim her child, and false, once again, because "motherhood" is not perceived in the prevailing social climate as a legitimate procedure of cultural inheritance.

The African-American male has been touched, therefore, by the mother, handed by her in ways that he cannot escape, and in ways that the white American male is allowed to temporize by a fatherly reprieve. This human and historic development—

the text that has been inscribed on the benighted heart of the continent—takes us to the center of an inexorable difference in the depths of American women's community: the African-American woman, the mother, the daughter, becomes historically the powerful and shadowy evocation of a cultural synthesis long evaporated—the law of the Mother—only and precisely because legal enslavement removed the African-American male not so much from sight as from mimetic view as a partner in the prevailing social fiction of the Father's name, the Father's law.

Therefore, the female, in this order of things, breaks in upon the imagination with a forcefulness that marks both a denial and an "illegitimacy." Because of this peculiar American denial, the black American male embodies the *only* American community of males which has had the specific occasion to learn *who* the female is within itself, the infant child who bears the life against the could-be fateful gamble, against the odds of pulverization and murder, including her own. It is the heritage of the mother that the African-American male must regain as an aspect of his own personhood—the power of "yes" to the "female" within.

This different cultural text actually reconfigures, in historically ordained discourse, certain *representational* potentialities for African-Americans: 1) motherhood as female blood rite is outraged, is denied, at the very same time that it becomes the founding term of a human and social enactment; 2) a dual fatherhood is set in motion, comprised of the African father's banished name and body and the captor father's mocking presence. In this play of paradox, only the female stands in the *flesh*, both mother and mother-dispossessed. This problematizing of gender places her, in my view, out of the traditional symbolics of female gender, and it is our task to make a place for this different social subject. In doing so, we are less interested in joining the ranks of gendered femaleness than gaining the *insurgent* ground as female social subject. Actually *claiming* the monstrosity (of a female with the potential to "name"), which her culture imposes in blindness, "Sapphire" might rewrite after all a radically different text for a female empowerment.

WORKS CITED

Barthes, Roland. *Mythologies*. Trans. Annette Lavers. New York: Hill and Wang, 1972.

Blassingame, John. *The Slave Community: Plantation Life in the Antebellum South*. New York: Oxford UP, 1972.

Brent, Linda. *Incidents in the Life of a Slave Girl*. Ed. L. Maria Child. Introduced by Walter Teller. Rpt. New York: Harvest/HBJ Book, 1973.

Davis, Angela Y. *Women, Race and Class*. New York: Random House 1981.

de Azurara, Gomes Eannes. "The Chronicle of the Discovery and Conquest of Guinea 1441–1448." Trans. C. Raymond Beazley and Edgar Prestage. London: Hakluyt Society, 1896, 1897, in Elizabeth Donnan, *Documents Illustrative of the History of the Slave Trade to America*. Washington, 1932, 1:18–41.

Donnan, Elizabeth. *Documents Illustrative of the History of the Slave Trade to America*: 4 vols. Washington, D.C.: The Carnegie Institution of Washington, 1932.

Douglass, Frederick. *Narrative of the Life of Frederick Douglass An American Slave. Written by Himself*. Rpt. New York: Signet Books, 1968.

El Shabazz, Malcolm El-Hajj Malik. *Autobiography of Malcolm X*. With Alex Haley. Introduced by M. S. Handler. New York: Grove Press, 1966.

Equiano, Olaudah. "The Life of Olaudah Equiano, or Gustavus Vassa, The African, Written by Himself," in *Great Slave Narratives*. Introduced and selected by Arna Bontemps. Boston: Beacon Press, 1969. 1–192.

Faulkner, William. *The Mansion*. New York: Vintage Books, 1965.

Frazier, E. Franklin. *The Negro Family in the United States*. Rev. with foreword by Nathan Glazer. Chicago: The U of Chicago P. 1966.

Genovese, Eugene. *Roll, Jordan, Roll: The World the Slaves Made*. New York: Pantheon Books, 1974.

Goodell, William. *The American Slave Code In Theory and Practice Shown By Its Statutes, Judicial Decisions, and Illustrative Facts*; 3rd ed. New York: American and Foreign Anti-Slavery Society, 1853.

Hooks, Bell. *Ain't I a Woman: Black Women and Feminism*. Boston: South End Press, 1981.

Klein, Herbert S. "African Women in the Atlantic Slave Trade." Robertson and Klein 29–39.

Meilassoux, Claude. "Female Slavery." Robertson and Klein 49–67.

Moynihan, Daniel P. "The Moynihan Report" [*The Negro Family: The Case for National Action*. Washington, D.C.: U.S. Department of Labor, 1965]. *The Moynihan Report and the Politics of Controversy: A Transaction Social Science and Public Policy Report*. Ed. Lee Rainwater and William L. Yancey. Cambridge: MIT Press, 1967. 47–94.

Robertson, Claire C., and Martin A. Klein, eds. *Women and Slavery in Africa*. Madison: U of Wisconsin P. 1983.

Scarry, Elaine. *The Body in Pain: The Making and Unmaking of the World*. New York: Oxford UP, 1985.

Smith, Valerie, "Loopholes of Retreat: Architecture and Ideology in Harriet Jacobs's *Incidents in the Life of a Slave Girl*." Paper presented at the 1985 American Studies Association Meeting, San Diego. Cited in Henry Louis Gates, Jr., "What's Love Got to Do With It?" *New Literary History* 18.2 (Winter 1987): 360.

Strobel, Margaret. "Slavery and Reproductive Labor In Mombasa." Robertson and Klein 111–30.

Suleiman, Susan Rubin, ed. *The Female Body in Western Culture*. Cambridge: Harvard UP, 1986.

Todorov, Tzvetan. *The Conquest of America: The Question of the Other*. Trans. Richard Howard. New York: Harper Colophon Books, 1984.

White, Deborah Grey. *Ar'n't I A Woman? Female Slaves in the Plantation South*. New York: Norton, 1985.

25 | The Race for Theory

Barbara Christian

(1987)

I have seized this occasion to break the silence among those of us, critics, as we are now called, who have been intimidated, devalued by what I call the race for theory. I have become convinced that there has been a takeover in the literary world by Western philosophers from the old literary elite, the neutral humanists. Philosophers have been able to effect such a takeover because so much of the literature of the West has become pallid, laden with despair, self-indulgent, and disconnected. The New Philosophers, eager to understand a world that is today fast escaping their political control, have redefined literature so that the distinctions implied by that term, that is, the distinctions between everything written and those things written to evoke feeling as well as to express thought, have been blurred. They have changed literary critical language to suit their own purposes as philosophers, and they have reinvented the meaning of theory.

My first response to this realization was to ignore it. Perhaps, in spite of the egocentrism of this trend, some good might come of it. I had, I felt, more pressing and interesting things to do, such as reading and studying the history and literature of black women, a history that had been totally ignored, a contemporary literature bursting with originality, passion, insight, and beauty. But, unfortunately, it is difficult to ignore this new takeover, because theory has become a commodity that helps determine whether we are hired or promoted in academic institutions—worse, whether we are heard at all. Due to this new orientation works (a word that evokes labor) have become texts. Critics are no longer concerned with literature but with other critics' texts, for the critic yearning for attention has displaced the writer and has conceived of herself or himself as the center. Interestingly, in the first part of this century, at least in England and America, the critic was usually also a writer of poetry, plays, or novels. But today, as a new generation of professionals develops, she or he is increasingly an academic. Activities such as teaching or writing one's response

280

to specific works of literature have, among this group, become subordinated to one primary thrust—that moment when one creates a theory, thus fixing a constellation of ideas for a time at least, a fixing which no doubt will be replaced in another month or so by somebody else's competing theory as the race accelerates. Perhaps because those who have effected the takeover have the power (although they deny it) first of all to be published, and thereby to determine the ideas that are deemed valuable, some of our most daring and potentially radical critics (and by *our* I mean black, women, Third World) have been influenced, even co-opted into speaking a language and defining their discussion in terms alien to and opposed to our needs and orientation. At least so far, the creative writers I study have resisted this language.

For people of color have always theorized—but in forms quite different from the Western form of abstract logic. And I am inclined to say that our theorizing (and I intentionally use the verb rather than the noun) is often in narrative forms, in the stories we create, in riddles and proverbs, in the play with language, because *dynamic* rather than fixed ideas seem more to our liking. How else have we managed to survive with such spiritedness the assault on our bodies, social institutions, countries, our very humanity? And "women," at least the women I grew up around, continuously speculated about the nature of life through pithy language that unmasked the power relations of their world. It is this language, and the grace and pleasure with which they played with it, that I find celebrated, refined, critiqued in the works of writers like Toni Morrison and Alice Walker. My folk, in other words, have always been a race for theory—though more in the form of the hieroglyph, a written figure that is both sensual and abstract, both beautiful and communicative. In my own work I try to illuminate and explain these hieroglyphs, which is, I think, an activity quite different from the creating of the hieroglyphs themselves. As the Buddhists would say, the finger pointing at the moon is not the moon.

In this discussion, however, I am more concerned with the issue raised by my first use of the term, the race for theory, in relation to its academic hegemony, and possibly of its inappropriateness to the energetic emerging literatures in the world today. The pervasiveness of this academic hegemony is an issue continually spoken about—but usually in hidden groups, lest we, who are disturbed by it, appear ignorant to the reigning academic elite. Among the folk who speak in muted tones are people of color, feminists, radical critics, creative writers, who have struggled for much longer than a decade to make their voices, their various voices heard, and for whom literature is not an occasion for discourse among critics but is necessary nourishment for their people and one way by which they come to understand their lives better. Clichéd though this may be, it bears, I think, repeating here.

The race for theory—with its linguistic jargon; its emphasis on quoting its prophets; its tendency toward "biblical" exegesis; its refusal even to mention specific works of creative writers, far less contemporary ones; its preoccupations with mechanical analyses of language; graphs; algebraic equations; its gross generalizations about culture—has silenced many of us to the extent that some of us feel we can no longer discuss our own literature, and others have developed intense writing blocks and are puzzled by the incomprehensibility of the language set adrift in literary circles. There have been, in the last year, any number of occasions on which I had to convince literary critics who have pioneered entire new areas of critical inquiry that they did have something to say. Some of us are continually harassed to invent wholesale theories regardless of the complexity of the literature we study. I, for one, am tired of being asked to produce a black feminist literary theory as if I were a mechanical man. For I believe such theory is prescriptive—it ought to have some relationship to practice. Because I can count on one hand the number of people attempting to be black feminist literary critics in the world today, I consider it presumptuous of me to invent a theory of how we ought to read. Instead, I think we need to read the works of our writers in our various ways and remain open to the intricacies of the intersection of language, class, race and gender in the literature. And it would help if we share our process, that is, our practice, as much as possible because, finally, our work is a collective endeavor.

The insidious quality of this race for theory is symbolized for me by a term like "minority discourse," a label that is borrowed from the reigning theory of the day but which is untrue to the literatures being produced by our writers, for many of our literatures (certainly Afro-American literature) are central, not minor. I have used the passive voice in my last sentence construction, contrary to the rules of black English, which like all languages has a particular value system, because I have not placed responsibility on any particular person or group. But that is precisely because this new ideology has become so prevalent among us that it behaves like so many of the other ideologies with which we have had to contend. It appears to have neither head nor center. At the least, though, we can say that the terms "minority" and "discourse" are located firmly in a Western dualistic or "binary" frame which sees the rest of the world as minor and tries to convince the rest of the world that it is major, usually through force and then through language, even as it claims many of the ideas that we, its "historical" other, have known and spoken about for so long. For many of us have never conceived of ourselves only as somebody's other.

Let me not give the impression that by objecting to the race for theory I ally myself with or agree with the neutral humanists who see literature as pure expression and will not admit to the obvious control of its production, value, and distribution by those who have power, who deny, in other words, that literature is, of necessity, political. I am studying an entire body of literature that has been denigrated for centuries by such terms as *political*. For an entire century Afro-American writers, from Charles Chesnutt in the nineteenth century through Richard Wright in the 1930s, Imamu Baraka in the 1960s, Alice Walker in the 1970s, have protested the literary hierarchy of dominance, which declares when literature is literature, when literature is great, depending on what it thinks is to its advantage. The black arts movement of the 1960s, out of which black studies, the feminist literary movement of the 1970s, and women's studies grew, articulated precisely those issues, which came *not* from the declarations of the New Western Philosophers but from these groups' reflections on their own lives. That Western scholars have long believed their ideas to be universal has been strongly opposed by many such groups. Some of my colleagues do not see black critical writers of previous decades as eloquent enough.

Clearly they have not read Richard Wright's "Blueprint for Negro Writing," Ralph Ellison's *Shadow and Act*, Charles Chesnutt's resignation from being a writer, or Alice for this general ignorance of what our writer-critics have said. One is that black writing has been generally ignored in this country. Because we, as Toni Morrison has put it, are seen as a discredited people, it is no surprise, then, that our creations are also discredited. But this is also due to the fact that, until recently, dominant critics in the Western world have also been creative writers who have had access to the upper-middle-class institutions of education, and, until recently, our writers have decidedly been excluded from these institutions and in fact have often been opposed to them. Because of the academic world's general ignorance about the literature of black people, and of women, whose work too has been discredited, it is not surprising that so many of our critics think that the position arguing that literature is political begins with these New Philosophers. Unfortunately, many of our young critics do not investigate the reasons *why* that statement—literature is political—is now acceptable when before it was not; nor do we look to our own antecedents for the sophisticated arguments upon which we can build in order to change the tendency of any established Western idea to become hegemonic.

For I feel that the new emphasis on literary critical theory is as hegemonic as the world it attacks. I see the language it creates as one that mystifies rather than clarifies our condition, making it possible for a few people who know that particular language to control the critical scene. That language surfaced, interestingly enough, just when the literature of peoples of color, black women, Latin Americans, and Africans began to move to "the center." Such words as *center* and *periphery* are themselves instructive. *Discourse, canon, texts,* words as Latinate as the tradition from which they come, are quite familiar to me. Because I went to a Catholic mission school in the West Indies I must confess that I cannot hear the word "canon" without smelling incense, that the word "text" immediately brings back agonizing memories of biblical exegesis, that "discourse" reeks for me of metaphysics forced down my throat in those courses that traced *world* philosophy from Aristotle through Aquinus to Heidegger. "Periphery" too is a word I heard throughout my childhood, for if anything was seen as being at the periphery, it was those small Caribbean islands that had neither land mass nor military power. Still I noted how intensely important this periphery was, for U.S. troups were continually invading to be occurring. As I lived among folk for whom language was an absolutely necessary way of validating our existence, I was told that the minds of the world lived only in the small continent of Europe. The metaphysical language of the New Philosophy, then, I must admit, is repulsive to me and is one reason why I raced from philosophy to literature, because the latter seemed to me to have the possibilities of rendering the world as large and as complicated as I experienced it, as sensual as I knew it was. In literature I sensed the possibility of the integration of feeling/knowledge, rather than the split between the abstract and the emotional in which Western philosophy inevitably indulged.

Now I am being told that philosophers are the ones who write literature; that authors are dead, irrelevant, mere vessels through which their narratives ooze; that they do not work nor have they the faintest idea what they are doing—rather, they produce texts as disembodied as the angels. I am frankly astonished that scholars who call themselves Marxists or post-Marxists could seriously use such metaphysical language even as they attempt to deconstruct the philosophical tradition from which their language comes. And as a student of literature, I am appalled by the sheer ugliness of the language, its lack of clarity, its unnecessarily complicated sentence constructions, its lack of pleasurableness, its alienating quality. It is the kind of writing for which composition teachers would give a first-year student a resounding F.

Because I am a curious person, however, I postponed readings of black women writers I was working on and read some of the prophets of this new literary orientation. These writers did announce their dissatisfaction with some of the cornerstone ideas of their own tradition, a dissatisfaction with which I was born. But in their attempt to change the orientation of Western scholarship, they, as usual, concentrated on themselves and were not in the slightest interested in the worlds they had ignored or controlled. Again I was supposed to know them, while they were not at all interested in knowing me. Instead, they sought to "deconstruct" the tradition to which they belonged even as they used the same forms, style, and language of that tradition, forms that necessarily embody its values. And increasingly as I read them and saw their substitution of their philosophical writings for literary ones, I began to have the uneasy feeling that their folk were not producing any literature worth mentioning. For they always harkened back to the masterpieces of the past, again reifying the very texts they said they were deconstructing. Increasingly, as their way, their terms, their approaches remained central and became the means by which one defined literary critics, many of my own peers who had previously been concentrating on dealing with the other side of the equation—the reclamation and discussion of past and present Third World literatures—were diverted into continually discussing the new literary theory.

From my point of view as a critic of contemporary Afro-American women's writing, this orientation is extremely problematic. In attempting to find the deep structures in the literary tradition, a major preoccupation of the new New Criticism, many of us have become obsessed with the nature of reading itself to the extent that we have stopped writing about literature being written today. Since I am slightly paranoid, it has begun to occur to me that the literature being produced *is* precisely one of the reasons why this new philosophical-literary-critical theory of relativity is so prominent. In other words, the literature of blacks, women of South America and Africa, and so forth, as overtly "political" literature was being preempted by a new Western concept which proclaimed that reality does not exist, that everything is relative, and that every text is silent about something—which indeed it must necessarily be.

There is, of course, much to be learned from exploring how we know what we know, how we read what we read, an exploration which, of necessity, can have no end. But there also has to be a "what," and that "what," when it is even mentioned by the New Philosophers, are texts of the past, primarily Western male texts, whose norms are again being transferred onto Third World and female texts as theories of reading proliferate. Inevitably a hierarchy has now developed between what is called theoretical criticism and practical criticism, as mind is deemed superior to matter. I have no quarrel with those who wish to philosophize about how we know what we know. But I do resent the fact that this particular orientation is so privileged, and has diverted so many of us from doing the first readings of the literature being written today as well as of past works about which nothing has been written. I note, for example, that there is little work done on Gloria Naylor, that most of Alice Walker's works have not been commented on—despite the rage around *The Color Purple*— that there has yet to be an in-depth study of Frances Harper, the nineteenth-century abolitionist poet and novelist. If our emphasis on theoretical criticism continues, critics of the future may have to reclaim the writers we are now ignoring, that is, if they are even aware these artists exist.

I am particularly perturbed by the movement to exalt theory, as well, because of my own adult history. I was an active member of the black arts movement of the sixties and know how dangerous theory can become. Many today may not be aware of this, but the black arts movement tried to create black literary theory and in doing so became prescriptive. My fear is that when theory is not rooted in practice, it becomes prescriptive, exclusive, elitish.

An example of this prescriptiveness is the approach the black arts movement took toward language. For it, blackness resided in the use of black talk which they defined as hip urban language. So that when Nikki Giovanni reviewed Paule Marshall's *Chosen Place, Timeless People*, she criticized the novel on the grounds that it was not black, for the language was too elegant, too white. Blacks, she said, did not speak that way. Having come from the West Indies where we do, some of the time, speak that way, I was amazed by the narrowness of her vision. The emphasis on one way to be black resulted in the works of Southern writers being seen as nonblack because the black talk of Georgia does not sound like the black talk of Philadelphia. Because the ideologues, like Baraka, came from the urban centers, they tended to privilege their way of speaking, thinking, writing, and to condemn other kinds of writing as not being black enough. Whole areas of the canon were assessed according to the dictum of the black arts nationalist point of view, as in Addison Gayle's *The Way of the New World*, and other works were ignored because they did not fit the scheme of cultural nationalism. Older writers like Ralph Ellison and James Baldwin were condemned because they saw that the intersection of Western and African influences resulted in a new Afro-American culture, a position with which many of the black nationalist idealogues disagreed. Writers were told that writing love poems was not being black. Further examples abound.

It is this tendency toward the monolithic, monotheistic, and so on, that worries me about the race for theory. Constructs like the *center* and the *periphery* reveal that tendency to want to make the world less complex by organizing it according to one principle, to fix it through an idea which is really an ideal. Many of us are particularly sensitive to monolithism because one major element of ideologies of dominance, such as sexism and racism, is to dehumanize people by stereotyping them, by denying them their variousness and complexity. Inevitably, monolithism becomes a meta-system, in which there is a controlling ideal, especially in relation to pleasure. Language as one form of pleasure is immediately restricted and becomes heavy, abstract, prescriptive, monotonous.

Variety, multiplicity, eroticism are difficult to control. And it may very well be that these are the reasons why writers are often seen as persona non grata by political states, whatever form they take, because writers/artists have a tendency to refuse to give up their way of seeing the world and of playing with possibilities; in fact, their very expression relies on that insistence. Perhaps that is why creative literature, even when written by politically reactionary people, can be so freeing, for in having to embody ideas and recreate the world, writers cannot merely produce "one way."

The characteristics of the black arts movement are, I am afraid, being repeated again today, certainly in the other area to which I am especially tuned. In the race for theory, feminists, eager to enter the halls of power, have attempted their own prescriptions. So often I have read books on feminist literary theory that restrict the definition of what *feminist* means and overgeneralize about so much of the world that most women as well as men are excluded. And seldom do feminist theorists take into account the complexity of life—that women are of many races and ethnic backgrounds with different histories and cultures and that as a rule women belong to different classes that have different concerns. Seldom do they note these distinctions, because if they did they could not articulate a theory. Often as a way of clearing themselves they do acknowledge that women of color, for example, do exist, then go on to do what they were going to do anyway, which is to invent a theory that has little relevance for us.

That tendency toward monolithism is precisely how I see the means to creating a female language, because language, they say, is male and necessarily conceives of woman as other. Clearly many of them have been irritated by the theories of Lacan for whom language is phallic. But suppose there are peoples in the world whose language was invented primarily in relation to women, who after all are the ones who relate to children and teach language. Some native American languages, for example, use female pronouns when speaking about non-gender-specific activity. Who knows who, according to gender, created languages? Further, by positing the body as the source of everything, French feminists return to the old myth that biology determines everything and ignore the fact that gender is a social rather than a biological construct.

I could go on critiquing the positions of French feminists who are themselves more various in their points of view than the label used to describe them, but that is not my point. What I am concerned about is the authority this school now has in feminist scholarship—the way it has become authoritative discourse, monologic, which occurs precisely because it does have access to the means of promulgating its ideas. The black arts movement was able to do this for a time because of the political movements of the 1960s—so too with the French feminists who could not be inventing "theory" if a space had not been created by the women's movement. In both cases, both groups posited a theory that excluded many of the people who made that space possible. Hence, one of the reasons for the surge of Afro-American women's writing during the 1970s and its emphasis on sexism in the black community is precisely that when the ideologues of the 1960s said black, they meant black male.

I and many of my sisters do not see the world as being so simple. And perhaps that is why we have not rushed to create abstract theories. For we know there are countless women of color, both in America and in the rest of the world, to whom our singular ideas would be applied. There is, therefore, a caution we feel about pronouncing black feminist theory that might be seen as a decisive statement about Third World women. This is not to say we are not theorizing. Certainly our literature is an indication of the ways in which our theorizing, of necessity, is based on our multiplicity of experiences.

There is at least one other lesson I learned from the black arts movement. One reason for its monolithic approach had to do with its desire to destroy the power that controlled black people, but it was a power that many of its ideologues wished to achieve. The nature of our context today is such that an approach which desires power single-mindedly must of necessity become like that which it wishes to destroy. Rather than wanting to change the whole model, many of us want to be all the center. It is this point of view that writers like June Jordan and Audre Lorde continually critique even as they call for empowerment, as they emphasize the fear of difference among us and our need for leaders rather than a reliance on ourselves.

For one must distinguish the desire for power from the need to become empowered—that is, seeing oneself as capable of and having the right to determine one's life. Such empowerment is partially derived from a knowledge of history. The black arts movement did result in the creation of Afro-American studies as a concept, thus giving it a place in the university where one might engage in the reclamation of Afro-American history and culture and pass it on to others. I am particularly concerned that institutions such as black studies and women's studies, fought for with such vigor and at some sacrifice, are not often seen as important by many of our black or women scholars precisely because the old hierarchy of traditional departments is seen as superior to these "marginal" groups. Yet, it is in this context that many others of us are discovering the extent of our complexity, the interrelationships of different areas of knowledge in relation to a distinctly Afro-American or female experience. Rather than having to view our world as subordinate to others, or rather than having to work as if we were hybrids, we can pursue ourselves as subjects.

My major objection to the race for theory, as some readers have probably guessed by now, really hinges on the question, "For whom are we doing what we are doing when we do literary criticism?" It is, I think, the central question today, especially for the few of us who have infiltrated the academy enough to be wooed by it. The answer to that question determines what orientation we take in our work, the language we use, the purposes for which it is intended.

I can only speak for myself. But what I write and how I write is done in order to save my own life. And I mean that literally. For me, literature is a way of knowing that I am not hallucinating, that whatever I feel/know is. It is an affirmation that sensuality is intelligence, that sensual language is language that makes sense. My response, then, is directed to those who write what I read and to those who read what I read—put concretely—to Toni Morrison and to people who read Toni Morrison (among whom I would count few academics). That number is increasing, as is the readership of Alice Walker and Paule Marshall. But in no way is the literature Morrison, Marshall, or Walker create supported by the academic world. And, given the political context of our society, I do not expect that to change soon. For there is no reason, given who controls these institutions, for them to be anything other than threatened by these writers.

My readings do presuppose a need, a desire among folk who, like me, also want to save their own lives. My concern, then, is a passionate one, for the literature of people who are not in power has always been in danger of extinction or of co-optation, not because we do not theorize but because what we can even imagine, far less who we can reach, is constantly limited by societal structures. For me, literary criticism is promotion as well as understanding, a response to the writer to whom there is often no response, to folk who need the writing as much as they need anything. I know, from literary history, that writing disappears unless there is a response to it. Because I write about writers who are now writing, I hope to help ensure that their tradition has continuity and survives.

So my "method," to use a new "lit. crit." word, is not fixed but relates to what I read and to the historical context of the writers I read and to the many critical activities in which I am engaged, which may or may not involve writing. It is a learning from the language of creative writers, which is one of surprise, so that I might discover what language I might use. For my language is very much based on what I read and how it affects me, that is, on the surprise that comes from reading something that compels you to read differently, as I believe literature does. I, therefore, have no set method, another prerequisite of the new theory, since for me every work suggests a new approach. As risky as that might seem, it is, I believe, what intelligence means—a tuned sensitivity to that which is alive and therefore cannot be known until it is known. Audre Lorde puts it in a far more succinct and sensual way in her essay, "Poetry Is Not a Luxury."

As they become known to and accepted by us, our feelings and the honest exploration of them become sanctuaries and spawning grounds for the most radical and daring of ideas. They become a safe-house for that difference so necessary to change and the conceptualization of any meaningful action. Right now, I could name at least ten ideas I would have found intolerable or incomprehensible and frightening, except as they came after dreams and poems. This is not idle fantasy, but a disciplined attention to the true meaning of "it feels right to me." We can train ourselves to respect our feelings and to transpose them into a language so they can be shared. And where that language does not yet exist, it is our poetry which helps to fashion it. Poetry is not only dream and vision; it is the skeleton architecture of our lives. It lays the foundations for a future of change, a bridge across our fears of what has never been before.[1]

NOTE

1. Audre Lorde, "Poetry Is Not a Luxury," in Audre Lorde, *Sister Outsider* (Trumansburg, N.Y.: Crossing Press, 1984), 37.

26

The Black Canon

Reconstructing Black American Literary Criticism

Joyce A. Joyce

(1987)

In April 1984 a former student of mine came to my office specifically to discuss James Baldwin's essay "On Being 'White' . . . And Other Lies," which appeared in the April 1984 issue of *Essence* magazine.[1] This very bright young woman was bothered because she knew that if she only marginally understood the essay, then many of "our people"—to use her phraseology—the ones who read *Essence* but who have not read some of Baldwin's other works, would not understand the essay. I still have trouble believing that the response I gave this young woman came from my mouth as I heard myself say that James Baldwin writes like James Baldwin. "How is he supposed to write?" I asked the student, whom my emotions told me I was failing. Her response was simple. She said, "He is supposed to be clear."

I realized that I was trapped by my own contradictions and elitism, while I agreed that if a reader is familiar with Baldwin's previous essays, particularly his "Down at the Cross: Letter from a Region in My Mind," the major piece in *The Fire Next Time*, he or she would better understand how Baldwin thinks, how he shapes his ideas, his thought and feeling patterns—his Baldwinian sensibility. As the student stared at me, I realized that she and I—the student and the teacher—had exchanged places. For she was teaching me—implicitly reminding me of all those times when I cajoled and coerced her away from narrow and provincial interpretations of the literary work and preached of the responsibility of the writer to his or her audience.

As we discussed the contents of Baldwin's essay, I was intellectually paralyzed by thoughts of the intricacies of the relationship of the writer to the audience, by the historical interrelationship between literature, class, values and the literary canon, and finally by my frustration as to how all these complexities augment ad finitum when the writer is a Black American. For in the first works of Black American literature the responsibility of the writers to their audience was as easy to deduce as it was to identify their audience. The slave narratives, most of the poetry, *Clotel*, and *Our Nig* were all addressed to white audiences with the explicit aim of denouncing slavery. This concentration on the relationship of Black Americans to the hegemony, to mainstream society, continues to this day to be the predominant issue in Black American literature, despite the change in focus we find in some of the works of Black women writers.

With Black American literature particularly, the issue of the responsibility of the creative writer is directly related to the responsibility of the literary critic. As is the case with James Baldwin, the most influential critics of Black literature have been the creative writers themselves, as evidenced also by W. E. B. Du Bois, Langston Hughes, Richard Wright, Ralph Ellison, Amiri Baraka, and Ishmael Reed. In his essay "Afro-American Literary Critics: An Introduction," found in Addison Gayle's landmark edition of *The Black Aesthetic*, Darwin Turner pinpoints why up to the 1960s a number of Black literary artists were also critics. Turner explains, "When a white publisher has wanted a black man to write about Afro-American literature, the publisher generally has turned to a famous creative writer. The reason is obvious. White publishers and readers have not been, and are not, familiar with the names and work of black scholars—the academic critics. Therefore, publishers have called upon the only blacks they have known—the famous writers."[2] After the 1960s, however, a group of literary scholars who had not begun their careers as creative artists emerged.

The 1960s mark a subtly contradictory change in Black academia reflective of the same contradictions inherent in the social, economic, and political strife that affected the lives of all Black Americans. Organizations like SNCC and CORE; the work of political figures like Stokely Carmichael, H. Rap Brown, Julian Bond, Huey Newton, Medgar Evers, Martin Luther King, Malcolm X, and Elijah Muhammad; the intense activity of voter registration drives, sit-ins, boycotts, and riots, the Black Arts Movement; and the work of Black innovative jazz musicians together constituted a Black social force that elicited affirmative action programs and the merger of a select number of Blacks into American mainstream society. This merger embodies the same shift in Black consciousness that Alain Locke described in 1925 in *The New Negro* where he suggested that the mass movement of Blacks from a rural to an urban environment thrust a large number of Blacks into contact with mainstream values. He wrote:

A main change has been, of course, that shifting of the Negro population which has made the Negro problem no longer exclusively or even predominately Southern . . . Then the trend of migration has not only been toward the North and the Central Midwest, but cityward and to the great centers of industry—the problems of adjustment are new, practical, local and not peculiarly racial. Rather they are an integral part of the large industrial and social problems of our present-day democracy. And finally, with the Negro rapidly in process of class differentiation, if it ever was warrantable to regard and treat the Negro *en masse* it is becoming with every day less possible, more unjust and more ridiculous.[3]

Professor Locke's comments here manifest the same social and ideological paradoxes that describe the relationship between the contemporary Black literary critic and his exogamic, elitist, epistemological adaptations.

For Professor Locke's assertion that to regard and treat the Negro en masse is becoming "every day less possible, more unjust and more ridiculous" is the historical prototype for Henry Louis Gates, Jr.'s denial of blackness or race as an important element of literary analysis of Black literature. Immersed in poststructuralist critical theory, Gates writes:

> Ultimately, black literature is a verbal art like other verbal arts. "Blackness" is not a material object or an event but a metaphor; it does not have an "essence" as such but is defined by a network of relations that form a particular aesthetic unity. . . . The black writer is the point of consciousness of his language. If he does embody a "Black Aesthetic," then it can be measured not by "content," but by a complex structure of meanings. The correspondence of content between a writer and his world is less significant to literary criticism than is a correspondence of organization or structure, for a relation of content may be a mere reflection of prescriptive, scriptural canon, such as those argued for by Baker, Gayle, and Henderson.[4]

Interestingly enough, Locke's attenuation of race as a dominant issue in the lives of Blacks in the 1920s and Gates's rejection of race, reflecting periods of intense critical change for Black Americans, point to their own class orientation that ironically results from social changes provoked by racial issues.

In their succinct but thorough histories of Black American literary criticism, Houston Baker, Jr. in "Generational Shifts and the Recent Criticism of Afro-American Literature"[5] and Darwin Turner in the already cited "Afro-American Literary Critics: An Introduction" inadvertently corroborate Richard Wright's assertion that "expression springs out of an environment." Prophetically describing the direction of Black literary expression, Wright predicted in 1957

> an understanding of Negro expression cannot be arrived at without a constant reference to the environment which cradles it. Directly after World War II, the United States and Soviet Russia emerged as the two dominant world powers. This meant a lessening of the influence of the ideology of Marxism in America and a frantic attempt on the part of white Americans to set their racial house somewhat in order in the face of world criticism. . . . The recent decision of the United States Supreme Court to integrate the schools of America on a basis of racial equality is one, but by no means the chief, change that has come over the American outlook. Naturally this effort on the part of the American nation to assimilate the Negro has had its effect upon Negro literary expression. . . . the mode and pitch of Negro literary expression would alter as soon as the attitude of the nation toward the Negro changed.[6]

The idea that white America has changed its attitude toward the Negro is quite dubious. However, what appears to have changed or grown is the intensity of the Black American's adoption of mainstream lifestyles and ideology, particularly the middle-class Black man's.

Up to the appearance of Dexter Fisher and Robert Stepto's *Afro-American Literature: The Reconstruction of Instruction* in 1979 and Michael Harper and Robert Stepto's edition of *Chant of Saints: A Gathering of Afro-American Literature, Art, and Scholarship*, also in 1979,[7] the Black American literary critic saw his role not as a point of consciousness for his or her people. This role was not one the critic had to contrive. A mere glance at the representative works from the Black literary canon chosen by any means of selection reveals that the most predominant, recurring, persistent, and obvious theme in Black American literature is that of liberation from the oppressive economic, social, political, and psychological strictures imposed on the Black man by white America. As characteristic, then, of the relationship between the critic and the work he or she analyzes, the critic takes his or her cues from the literary work itself as well as from the historical context of which that work is a part.

Consequently, Black American literary critics, like Black creative writers, saw a direct relationship between Black lives—Black realities—and Black literature. The function of the creative writer and the literary scholar was to guide, to serve as an intermediary in explaining the relationship between Black people and those forces that attempt to subdue them. The denial or rejection of this role as go-between in some contemporary Black literary criticism reflects the paradoxical elements of Alain Locke's assertions and the implicit paradoxes inherent in Black poststructuralist criticism: for the problem is that no matter how the Black man merges into American mainstream society, he or she looks at himself from an individualistic perspective that enables him or her to accept elitist American values and thus widen the chasm between his or her worldview and that of those masses of Blacks whose lives are still stifled by oppressive environmental, intellectual phenomena. When Professor Gates denies that consciousness is predetermined by culture and color (66), he manifests a sharp break with traditional Black literary criticism and strikingly bears out another of Wright's prophetic pronouncements made in 1957 when he said, ". . . the Negro, as he learns to stand on his own feet and expresses himself not in purely racial, but human terms, will launch criticism upon his native land which made him feel a sense of estrangement that he never wanted. This new attitude could have a healthy effect upon the culture of the United States. At long last, maybe a merging of Negro expression with American expression will take place" (104–5).

If we look at the most recently published works of Black literary criticism and theory—Joe Weixlmann and Chester Fontenot's edition of *Studies in Black American Literature: Black American Prose Theory, Volume 1* (1984), Henry Louis Gates, Jr.'s edition of *Black Literature & Literary Theory* (1984), Houston A. Baker, Jr.'s *Blues, Ideology, and Afro-American Literature: A Vernacular Theory* (1984), and even Michael Cooke's most recent *Afro-American Literature in the Twentieth Century: The Achievement of Intimacy* (1984)—we witness the merger of Negro expression with Euro-American expression. For the modes of execution in all these works, with the exception of Professor Cooke's ground-breaking study, prompt the same response that my student felt when reading Baldwin's essay in *Essence*.

Following the same methodological strategies characteristic of the works of Northrop Frye and poststructuralist critics like Roland Barthes, Paul de Man, Jacques

Derrida, and Geoffrey Hartman, Black poststructuralist critics have adopted a linguistic system and an accompanying world view that communicate to a small, isolated audience. Their pseudoscientific language is distant and sterile. These writers evince their powers of ratiocination with an overwhelming denial of most, if not all, the senses. Ironically, they challenge the intellect, "dulling" themselves to the realities of the sensual, communicative function of language. As Wright predicted, this merger of Black expression into the mainstream estranges the Black poststructuralist in a manner that he perhaps "never wanted," in a way which contradicts his primary goal in adopting poststructuralist methodology.

Although the paradox embodied in this estrangement holds quite true for the white poststructuralist critic as well, its negative effects are more severe for the Black scholar. Structuralism in mainstream culture is a reaction to the alienation and despair of late nineteenth and early twentieth-century existentialism which "spoke of isolated man, cut off from objects and even from other men, in an absurd condition of being."[8] In order to demonstrate the common bond that unites all human beings, structuralist thinkers—philosophers, linguists, psychoanalysts, anthropologists, and literary critics—use a complex linguistic system to illuminate "the configurations of human mentality itself" (79). Structuralism, then, "is a way of looking for reality not in individual things [in man isolated] but in the relationships among them" (4), that is, in the linguistic patterns that bind men together. Yet, ironically, the idea that the words on the page have no relationship to an external world and the language used— the unique meanings of words like *code, encode, sign, signifier, signified, difference, discourse, narratology,* and *text*—create the very alienation and estrangement that structuralists and poststructuralists attempt to defeat. Hence I see an inherent contradiction between those values postmodernists intend to transmit and those perceived by many readers.

In the September 1983 special issue of *Critical Inquiry*, Professor Barbara H. Smith's comments on the classic canonical author can analogously illuminate how values are transmitted through literary theory as well. She says simply, "The endurance of a classic canonical author such as Homer . . . owes not to the alleged transcultural or universal value of his works but, on the contrary, to the continuity of their circulation in a particular culture."[9] Thus, in adopting a critical methodology, the Black literary critic must ask himself or herself: "How does a Black literary theorist/critic gain a voice in the white literary establishment?" Moreover, despite Professor Smith's and the poststructuralists' attenuation of values, the Black literary critic should question the values that will be transmitted through his or her work. The Black critic must be ever cognizant of the fact that not only what he or she says, but also how he or she writes will determine the values to be circulated and preserved over time once he or she is accepted by mainstream society, if this acceptance is his or her primary goal. Despite writers like John Oliver Killens, John Williams, Gayl Jones, Naomi Long Madgett, and Ann Petry, who are seriously overlooked by the white mainstream, the most neglected aspect of Black American literature concerns the issue of form or structure. I agree fully with Professor Gates when he says that social and polemical functions of Black literature have overwhelmingly superseded or, to use his word, "repressed" the structure of Black literature.[10] But I must part ways with him when he outlines the methodology he uses to call attention to what he refers to as "the language of the black text." He says, "A study of the so-called arbitrariness, and of the relation between a sign, of the ways in which concepts divide reality arbitrarily, and of the relation between a sign, such as blackness, and its referent, such as absence, can help us to engage in more sophisticated readings of black texts."[11] It is insidious for the Black literary critic to adopt any kind of strategy that diminishes or in this case—through an allusion to binary oppositions—negates his blackness. It is not a fortuitous occurrence that Black creative writers for nearly two hundred years have consistently addressed the ramifications of slavery and racism. One such ramification that underpins W. E. B. Du Bois's essays and Langston Hughes's poetry and that emerged undisguised in the 1960s is the issue of Black pride, self-respect as opposed to self-abnegation or even self-veiling.

The Black creative writer has continuously struggled to assert his or her real self and to establish a connection between the self and the people outside that self. The Black creative writer understands that it is not yet time—and it might not ever be possible—for a people with hundreds of years of disenfranchisement and who since slavery have venerated the intellect and the written word to view language as merely a system of codes or as mere play. Language has been an essential medium for the evolution of Black pride and the dissolution of the double consciousness. For as evidenced by David Walker's *Appeal*, Claude McKay's "If We Must Die," Richard Wright's *Native Son*, the poetry of Sonia Sanchez and Amiri Baraka, and most recently by Toni Morrison's *Tar Baby*, the Black writer recognizes that the way in which we interpret our world is more than a function of the languages we have at our disposal, as Terry Eagleton asserts.[12] Even though Innis Brown in Margaret Walker's *Jubilee* cannot read or write, he understands clearly—he interprets quite accurately—that he has been wronged when his white landlord attempts to collect from Innis money for services Innis has not received. And though he too cannot read or write, Jake, Milkman's grandfather in Morrison's *Song of Solomon*, dies rather than surrender his land to the whites who shoot him. Shared experiences like these can bond a people together in ways that far exceed language. Hence what I refer to as the "poststructuralist sensibility" does not aptly apply to Black American literary works. In explaining that an essential difference between structuralism and poststructuralism is the radical separation of the signifier from the signified, Terry Eagleton presents what I see as the "poststructuralist sensibility." He writes, ". . . nothing is ever fully present in signs: it is an illusion for me to believe that I can even be fully present to you in what I say or write, because to use signs at all entails that my meaning is always somehow dispersed, divided and never quite at one with itself. Not only my meaning, indeed, but *me:* since language is something I am made out of, rather than merely a convenient tool I use, the whole idea that I am a stable, unified entity must also be a fiction" (129–30). For the Black American—even the Black intellectual—to maintain that meaningful or real communication between human beings is impossible because we cannot know each other through language would be to erase or ignore the continuity embodied in Black American history.

Pushed to its extreme, poststructuralist thinking perhaps helps to explain why it has become increasingly difficult for members of contemporary society to sustain commitments, to assume responsibility, to admit to a clear right and an obvious wrong.

Yet we can only reluctantly find fault with any ideology or critical methodology that seeks to heighten our awareness and cure us of the political, elitist, and narrow pedagogical and intellectual biases that have long dictated what we teach as well as how we teach. Interestingly enough, discussions such as Barbara Smith's "Contingencies of Value" and Richard Ohmann's "The Shaping of a Canon: U.S. Fiction, 1960–1975,"[13] and even Robert E. Scholes's "The Humanities, Criticism and Semiotics"[14] all echo some of the ideas espoused at length by the Black theoretician Larry Neal, by poets like Sonia Sanchez, Amiri Baraka, and Haki Madhubuti, and by scholars like Addison Gayle and Stephen Henderson. All of these writers have given continuous attention to how the needs and values of the hegemony have attempted to dictate the subject matter of the Black American writer and to determine whether a writer is published at all. To my knowledge only Sonia Sanchez and perhaps Gwendolyn Brooks have met this dilemma by having their works published exclusively by Black presses. This act implicitly suggests their response to the issue of their intended audience and to the question of their attitude toward their acceptance by the intellectual mainstream.

It is no accident that the Black poststructuralist methodology has so far been applied to fiction, the trickster tale, and the slave narrative. Black poetry—particularly that written during and after the 1960s—defies both linguistically and ideologically the "poststructuralist sensibility." According to Terry Eagleton, "most literary theories . . . unconsciously 'foreground' a particular literary genre, and derive their general pronouncements from this" (51). Equally as telling as their avoidance of Black poetry is the unsettling fact that Black American literary criticism has skipped a whole phase in the evolution of literary theory. The natural cycle organically requires that one school of literary thought be created from the one that goes before. For just as structuralism is a reaction to the despair of existentialism, poststructuralism is a reaction to the limitations of the concepts of the sign. "The poststructuralist attitude is therefore literally unthinkable without structuralism."[15] Consequently, the move in Black American literature from polemical, biographical criticism to poststructuralist theories means that these principles are being applied in a historical vacuum.

Since the Black creative writer has always used language as a means of communication to bind people together, the job of the Black literary critic should be to find a point of merger between the communal, utilitarian, phenomenal nature of Black literature and the aesthetic or linguistic—if you will—analyses that illuminate the "universality" of a literary text. Rather than being a "linguistic event" or a complex network of linguistic systems that embody the union of the signified and the signifier independent of phenomenal reality, Black creative art is an act of love which attempts to destroy estrangement and elitism by demonstrating a strong fondness or enthusiasm for freedom and an affectionate concern for the lives of people, especially Black people. Black creative art addresses the benevolence, kindness, and the brotherhood that men should feel toward each other. Just as language has no function without man, the Black literary critic is free to go beyond the bonds of the creative writer. For we have many thoughts that we have yet no words for, particularly those thoughts that remain in an inchoate state. It should be the job of the Black literary critic to force ideas to the surface, to give them force in order to affect, to guide, to animate, and to arouse the minds and emotions of Black people.

NOTES

1. James Baldwin, "On Being 'White' . . . And Other Lies," *Essence*, April 1984, pp. 90–92.

2. Darwin Turner, "Afro-American Literary Critics: An Introduction," in *The Black Aesthetic*, ed. Addison Gayle (Garden City, N.Y., 1971), p. 66.

3. Alain Locke, "The New Negro," in *Cavalcade: Negro American Writing from 1760 to the Present*, ed. Arthur P. Davis and Saunders Redding (Boston, 1971), p. 276.

4. Henry Louis Gates, Jr., "Preface to Blackness: Text and Pretext," in *Afro-American Literature: The Reconstruction of Instruction*, ed. Dexter Fisher and Robert B. Stepto (New York, 1979), p. 67; hereafter cited in text.

5. Houston A. Baker, Jr., "Generational Shifts and the Recent Criticism of Afro-American Literature," *Black American Literature Forum*, 15, No. 11 (Spring 1981), 3–21.

6. Richard Wright, "The Literature of the Negro in the United States," in *White Man, Listen!* (Garden City, N.Y., 1964), pp. 103–4; hereafter cited in text.

7. *Chant of Saints: A Gathering of Afro-American Literature, Art, and Scholarship*, ed. Michael S. Harper and Robert B. Stepto (Urbana, Ill., 1979).

8. Robert E. Scholes, *Structuralism in Literature: An Introduction* (New Haven, 1974), p. 1; hereafter cited in text.

9. Barbara H. Smith, "Contingencies of Value," *Critical Inquiry*, 10, No. 1 (Sept. 1983), 30.

10. Henry Louis Gates, Jr., "Criticism in the Jungle," in *Black Literature and Literary Theory*, ed. Henry Louis Gates, Jr. (New York, 1984), pp. 5–6.

11. Gates, "Criticism in the Jungle," p. 7.

12. Terry Eagleton, *Literary Theory: An Introduction* (Minneapolis, 1983), p. 107; hereafter cited in text.

13. Richard Ohmann, "The Shaping of a Canon: U.S. Fiction, 1960–1975," *Critical Inquiry*, 10, No. 1 (Sept. 1983), 199–223.

14. Robert E. Scholes, *Semiotics and Interpretation* (New Haven, 1982).

15. Josué V. Harari, "Critical Factions/Critical Fictions," in *Textual Strategies: Perspectives in Post-Structuralist Criticism*, ed. Josué V. Harari (New York, 1979), p. 30.

27 "What's Love Got to Do with It?"

Critical Theory, Integrity, and the Black Idiom

Henry Louis Gates, Jr.

(1987)

> Rather than being a "linguistic event" or a complex network of
> linguistic systems that embody the union of the signified and the
> signifier independent of phenomenal reality, Black creative art is an
> act of love which attempts to destroy estrangement and elitism by
> demonstrating a strong fondness or enthusiasm for freedom and an
> affectionate concern for the lives of people, especially Black people.
> —Joyce A. Joyce

> It may seem to you that I'm acting confused
> When you're close to me.
> If I tend to look dazed
> I read it someplace, I've got cause to be.
> There's a name for it,
> There's a phrase that fits.
> But whatever the reason
> You do it for me—oh, oh, oh
> What's love got to do, got to do with it?
> What's love but a secondhand emotion?
> What's love got to do, got to do with it?
> Who needs a heart when a heart can be broken?
> —Tina Turner, "What's Love Got to Do with It?"
> lyrics by Terry Britten and Graham Lyle

I have structured my response to Joyce Joyce's "The Black Canon" in two parts. The first section of this essay attempts to account for the prevalence among Afro-Americans of what Paul de Man called the "resistance to theory."[1] The second section of this essay attempts to respond directly to the salient parts of Professor Joyce's argument. While the first part of my essay is historical, it also explains why literary theory has been useful in my work, in an attempt to defamiliarize a black text from

298

this black reader's experiences as an African-American. This section of my essay, then, is something of an auto-critography, generated by what I take to be the curiously personal terms of Joyce Joyce's critique of the remarkably vague, yet allegedly antiblack, thing that she calls, variously, "structuralism" or "poststructuralism." Apparently for Joyce Joyce, and for several other critics, my name and my work have become metonyms for "structuralism," "poststructuralism," and/or "deconstructionism" in the black tradition, even when these terms are not defined at all or, perhaps worse, not adequately understood. (While Houston Baker generously acknowledges my influence in his remarkable work *Blues, Ideology, and Afro-American Literature,*[2] let me state clearly that our relation of influence is a reciprocal one, in which each stands as "ideal reader" for the other.) These terms become epithets where used as in Joyce Joyce's essay, and mostly opprobrious epithets at that. Just imagine: if Richard Pryor (and his all-too-eager convert Michael Cooke) have their way and abolish the use of the word nigger even among ourselves, and black feminists abolish m_____, perhaps the worst thing a black person will be able to call another black person will be: "You black poststructuralist, you!" What would Du Bois have said?!

I must confess that I am bewildered by Joyce Joyce's implied claim that to engage in black critical theory is to be, somehow, antiblack. In fact, I find this sort of claim to be both false and a potentially dangerous—and dishonest—form of witch-hunting or nigger-baiting. While it is one thing to say that someone is wrong in their premises or their conclusions, it is quite another to ascertain (on that person's behalf) their motivations, their intentions, their affect; and then to imply that they do not love their culture, or that they seek to deny their heritage, or that they are alienated from their "race," appealing all the while to an undefined transcendant essence called "the Black Experience," from which Houston Baker and I have somehow strayed. This is silliness.

Who can disagree that there is more energy being manifested and good work being brought to bear on black texts by black critics today than at any other time in our history, and that a large part of the explanation for this wonderful phenomenon is the growing critical sophistication of black readers of literature? Or that this sophistication is not directly related to the fact that we are taking our work—the close reading, interpretation, and preservation of the texts and authors of our tradition— with the utmost seriousness? What else is there for a critic to do? *What's love got to do with it,* Joyce Joyce? Precisely this: it is an act of love of the tradition—by which I mean our tradition—to bring to bear upon it honesty, insight, and skepticism, as well as praise, enthusiasm, and dedication; all values fundamental to the blues and to signifying, those two canonical black discourses in which Houston and I locate the black critical difference. It is merely a mode of critical masturbation to praise a black text simply because it is somehow "black," and it is irresponsible to act as if we are not all fellow citizens of literature for whom developments in other sections of the republic of letters have no bearing or relevance. To do either is most certainly not to manifest "love" for our tradition.

Before I can respond more directly to Joyce Joyce's essay, however, I want to examine the larger resistance to (white) theory in the (black) tradition.[3]

I

Unlike almost every other literary tradition, the Afro-American literary tradition was generated as a response to allegations that its authors did not, and could not, create "literature." Philosophers and literary critics, such as Hume, Kant, Jefferson, and Hegel, seemed to decide that the presence of a written literature was the signal measure of the potential, innate "humanity" of a race. The African living in Europe or in the New World seems to have felt compelled to create a literature both to demonstrate, implicitly, that blacks did indeed possess the intellectual ability to create a written art, but also to indict the several social and economic institutions that delimited the "humanity" of all black people in Western cultures.

So insistent did these racist allegations prove to be, at least from the eighteenth to the early twentieth centuries, that it is fair to describe the subtext of the history of black letters as this urge to refute the claim that because blacks had no written traditions, they were bearers of an "inferior" culture. The relation between European and American critical theory, then, and the development of the African and Afro-American literary traditions, can readily be seen to have been ironic, indeed. Even as late as 1911, when J. E. Casely Hayford published *Ethiopia Unbound* (the "first" African novel), that pioneering author felt compelled to address this matter in the first two paragraphs of his text. "At the dawn of the twentieth century," the novel opens, "men of light and leading both in Europe and in America had not yet made up their minds as to what place to assign to the spiritual aspirations of the black man; . . . Before this time," the narrative continues, "it had been discovered that the black man was not necessarily the missing link between man and ape. It had even been granted that for intellectual endowments he had nothing to be ashamed of in an *open* competition with the Aryan or any other type."[4] *Ethiopia Unbound*, it seems obvious, was concerned to settle the matter of black mental equality, which had remained something of an open question in European discourse for two hundred years. Concluding this curiously polemical exposition of three paragraphs, which precedes the introduction of the novel's protagonist, Casely Hayford points to "the names of men like [W. E. B.] Du Bois, Booker T. Washington, [Wilmot E.] Blyden, [Paul Laurence] Dunbar, [Samuel] Coleridge-Taylor, and others" (2) as prima facie evidence of the sheer saliency of what Carter G. Woodson once termed "the public [Negro] mind."[5] These were men, the narrative concludes, "who had distinguished themselves in the fields of activity and intellectuality" (2), men who had demonstrated conclusively that the African's first cousin was indeed the European, rather than the ape.

That the presence of a written literature could assume such large proportions in several Western cultures from the Enlightenment to this century is even more curious than is the fact that blacks themselves, as late as 1911, felt moved to respond to this stimulus, indeed felt the need to speak the matter silent, to end the argument by producing literature. Few literary traditions have begun or been sustained by such a complex and curious relation to its criticism: allegations of an absence led directly to a presence, a literature often inextricably bound in a dialogue with its potentially harshest critics.[6]

Black literature and its criticism, then, have been put to uses that were not primarily aesthetic; rather, they have formed part of a larger discourse on the nature of the black and his or her role in the order of things. The integral relation between theory and a literary text, therefore, which so very often in other traditions has been a sustaining relation, in our tradition has been an extraordinarily problematical one. The relation among theory, tradition, and integrity within the black literary tradition has not been, and perhaps cannot be, a straightforward matter.

Let us consider the etymology of the word integrity, which I take to be the keyword implied in Dr. Joyce's essay. Integrity is a curious keyword to address in a period of bold and sometimes exhilarating speculation and experimentation, two other words which aptly characterize literary criticism, generally, and Afro-American criticism, specifically, at the present time. The Latin origin of the English word *integritas* connotes wholeness, entireness, completeness, chastity, and purity; most of which are descriptive terms that made their way frequently into the writings of the American New Critics, critics who seem not to have cared particularly for, or about, the literature of Afro-Americans. Two of the most common definitions of integrity elaborate upon the sense of wholeness derived from the Latin original. Let me cite these here, as taken from the *Oxford English Dictionary*: "1. The condition of having no part or element taken away or wanting; undivided or unbroken state; material wholeness, completeness, entirety; something undivided; an integral whole; 2. The condition of not being marred or violated; unimpaired or uncorrupted condition; original perfect state; soundness." It is the second definition of integrity—that is to say, the one connoting the absence of violation and corruption, the preservation of an initial wholeness or soundness—which I would like to consider in this deliberation upon "Theory and Integrity," or more precisely upon that relationship which ideally should obtain between African or Afro-American literature and the theories we borrow, revise, or fabricate to account for the precise nature and shape of our literature and its "being" in the world.

It is probably true that critics of Afro-American literature (which, by the way, I employ as a less ethnocentric designation than "the Black Critic") are more concerned with the complex relation between literature and literary theory than we have ever been before. There are many reasons for this, not the least of which is our increasingly central role in "the profession," precisely when our colleagues in other literatures are engulfed in their own extensive debates about the intellectual merit of so very much theorizing. Theory, as a second-order reflection upon a primary gesture such as "literature," has always been viewed with deep mistrust and suspicion by those scholars who find it presumptuous and perhaps even decadent when criticism claims the right to stand, as discourse, on its own, as parallel textual universe to literature. Theoretical texts breed other, equally "decadent," theoretical responses in a creative process that can be remarkably far removed from a poem or a novel.

For the critic of Afro-American literature, this process is even more perilous precisely because the largest part of contemporary literary theory derives from critics of Western European languages and literatures. Is the use of theory to write about Afro-American literature, we might ask rhetorically, merely another form of intellectual indenture, a form of servitude of the mind as pernicious in its intellectual implications as any other form of enslavement? This is the issue raised, for me at least, by the implied presence of the word *integrity* in Joyce Joyce's essay, but also by my own work over the past decade. Does the propensity to theorize about a text or a literary tradition "mar," "violate," "impair," or "corrupt" the "soundness" of a purported "original perfect state" of a black text or of the black tradition? To argue the affirmative is to align one's position with the New Critical position that texts are "wholes" in the first place.

To be sure, this matter of criticism and integrity has a long and rather tortured history in black letters. It was David Hume, after all, who called the Jamaican poet of Latin verse, Francis Williams, "a parrot who merely speaks a few words plainly";[7] and Phillis Wheatley has for far too long suffered from the spurious attacks of black and white critics alike for being the original *rara avis* of a school of so-called "mockingbird poets," whose use and imitation of received European and American literary conventions have been regarded, simply put, as a corruption itself of a "purer" black expression, privileged somehow in black artistic forms such as the blues, signifying, the spirituals, and the Afro-American dance. Can we, as critics, escape a "mockingbird" relation to theory, one destined to be derivative, often to the point of parody? Can we, moreover, escape the racism of so many critical theorists, from Hume and Kant through the Southern Agrarians and the Frankfurt School?

As I have argued elsewhere, there are complex historical reasons for the resistance to theory among critics of comparative black literature, which stem in part from healthy reactions against the marriage of logocentrism and ethnocentrism in much of post-Renaissance Western aesthetic discourse. Although there have been a few notable exceptions, theory as a subject of inquiry has only in the past decade begun to sneak into the discourse of Afro-American literature. The implicit racism of some of the Southern Agrarians who became the New Critics and Adorno's bizarre thoughts about something he calls "jazz" did not serve to speed this process along at all. Sterling A. Brown has summed up the relation of the black tradition to the Western critical tradition. In response to Robert Penn Warren's line from "Pondy Woods" (1945), "Nigger, your breed ain't metaphysical," Brown replies, "Cracker, your breed ain't exegetical."[8] No tradition is "naturally" metaphysical or exegetical, of course. Only recently have some scholars attempted to convince critics of black literature that the racism of the Western critical tradition was not a sufficient reason for us to fail to theorize about our own endeavor, or even to make use of contemporary theoretical innovations when this seemed either useful or appropriate. Perhaps predictably, a number of these attempts share a concern with that which, in the received tradition of Afro-American criticism, has been most repressed: that is, with close readings of the text itself. This return of the repressed—the very language of the black text—has generated a new interest among our critics in theory. My charged advocacy of the relevance of contemporary theory to reading Afro-American and

African literature closely has been designed as the prelude to the definition of principles of literary criticism peculiar to the black literary traditions themselves, related to and compatible with contemporary critical theory generally, yet "indelibly black," as Robert Farris Thompson puts it.[9] All theory is text-specific, and ours must be as well. Lest I be misunderstood, I have tried to work through contemporary theories of literature not to "apply" them to black texts, but rather to transform by translating them into a new rhetorical realm. These attempts have been successful in varying degrees; nevertheless, I have tried to make them at all times interesting episodes in one critic's reflection on the black "text-milieu," what he means by "the tradition," and from which he extracts his "canon."

It is only through this critical activity that the profession, in a world of dramatically fluid relations of knowledge and power, and of the reemerging presence of the tongues of Babel, can redefine itself away from a Eurocentric notion of a hierarchical canon of texts, mostly white, Western, and male, and encourage and sustain a truly comparative and pluralistic notion of the institution of literature. What all students of literature share in common is the art of interpretation, even where we do not share in common the same texts. The hegemony implicit in the phrase "the Western tradition" reflects material relationships primarily, and not so-called universal, transcendant normative judgments. Judgment is specific, both culturally and temporally. The sometimes vulgar nationalism implicit in would-be literary categories such as "American Literature," or the not-so-latent imperialism implied by the vulgar phrase "Commonwealth literature," are extraliterary designations of control, symbolic of material and concomitant political relations, rather than literary ones. We, the scholars of our profession, must eschew these categories of domination and ideology and insist upon the fundamental redefinition of what it is to speak of "the canon."

Whether we realize it or not, each of us brings to a text an implicit theory of literature, or even an unwitting hybrid of theories, a critical gumbo as it were. To become aware of contemporary theory is to become aware of one's presuppositions, those ideological and aesthetic assumptions which we bring to a text unwittingly. It is incumbent upon us, those of us who respect the sheer integrity of the black tradition, to turn to this very tradition to create self-generated theories about the black literary endeavor. We must, above all, respect the integrity, the wholeness, of the black work of art, by bringing to bear upon the explication of its meanings all of the attention to language that we may learn from several developments in contemporary theory. By the very process of "application," as it were, we recreate, through revision, the critical theory at hand. As our familiarity with the black tradition and with literary theory expands, we shall invent our own theories, as some of us have begun to do—black, text-specific theories.

I have tried to utilize contemporary theory to defamiliarize the texts of the black tradition, to create a distance between this black reader and our black texts, so that I may more readily see the formal workings of those texts. Wilhelm von Humboldt describes this phenomenon in the following way: "Man lives with things mainly, even exclusively—since sentiment and action in him depend upon his mental representations—as they are conveyed to him by language. Through the same act by which he spins language out of himself he weaves himself into it, and every language draws a circle around the people to which it belongs, a circle that can only be transcended in so far as one at the same time enters another one." I have turned to literary theory as a "second circle." I have done this to preserve the integrity of these texts, by trying to avoid confusing my experience as an Afro-American with the black act of language which defines a text. On the other hand, by learning to read a black text within a black formal cultural matrix, and explicating it with the principles of criticism at work in both the Euro-American and Afro-American traditions, I believe that we critics can produce richer structures of meaning than are possible otherwise.

This is the challenge of the critic of black literature in the 1980s: not to shy away from literary theory; rather, to translate it into the black idiom, renaming principles of criticism where appropriate, but especially naming indigenous black principles of criticism and applying these to explicate our own texts. It is incumbent upon us to protect the integrity of our tradition by bringing to bear upon its criticism any tool of sensitivity to language that is appropriate. And what do I mean by "appropriate"? Simply this: any tool that enables the critic to explain the complex workings of the language of a text is an "appropriate" tool. For it is language, the black language of black texts, which expresses the distinctive quality of our literary tradition. A literary tradition, like an individual, is to a large extent defined by its past, its received traditions. We critics in the 1980s have the especial privilege of explicating the black tradition in ever closer detail. We shall not meet this challenge by remaining afraid of, or naive about, literary theory; rather, we will only inflict upon our literary tradition the violation of the uninformed reading. We are the keepers of the black literary tradition. No matter what theories we seem to embrace, we have more in common with each other than we do with any other critic of any other literature. We write for each other, and for our own contemporary writers. This relation is a sacred trust.

Let me end this section of my essay with a historical anecdote. In 1915, Edmond Laforest, a prominent member of the Haitian literary movement called "La Ronde," made of his death a symbolic, if ironic, statement of the curious relation of the "non-Western" writer to the act of writing in a modern language. M. Laforest, with an inimitable, if fatal, flair for the grand gesture, calmly tied a Larousse dictionary around his neck, then proceeded to commit suicide by drowning. While other black writers, before and after M. Laforest, have suffocated as artists beneath the weight of various modern languages, Laforest chose to make his death an emblem of this relation of indenture. We commit intellectual suicide by binding ourselves too tightly to nonblack theory; but we drown just as surely as did Laforest if we pretend that "theory" is "white," or worse—that it is "antiblack." Let scores of black theories proliferate, and let us encourage speculation among ourselves about our own literature. And let us, finally, realize that we must be each other's allies, even when we most disagree, because those who would dismiss both black literature and black criticism will no doubt increase in numbers in this period of profound economic fear and scarcity unless we meet their challenge head-on.

II

That said, let me respond to the salient points in Joyce Joyce's essay. Joyce Joyce's anecdote about the student who could not understand Jimmy Baldwin's essay "On Being 'White' . . . and Other Lies" is only remarkable for what it reveals about her student's lack of reading skills and/or training. Let me cite a typical paragraph of Baldwin's text, since so very much of Joyce Joyce's argument turns upon the idea of critical language as a barrier of alienation between black critics and "our people":

> Without further pursuing the implication of this mutual act of faith, one is neverthe-less aware that the Jewish translation into a white American can sustain the state of Israel in a way that the Black presence, here, can scarcely hope—at least, not yet—to halt the slaughter in South Africa.
>   And there is a reason for that.
>   America became white—the people who, as they claim, "settled" in the country became white—because of the necessity of denying the Black presence, and justifying the Black subjugation. No community can be based on such a principle—or, in other words, no community can be established on so genocidal a lie. White men—from Norway, for example, where they were *Norwegians*—became white: by slaughtering the cattle, poisoning the wells, torching the houses, massacring Native Americans, raping Black women.[10]

We are not exactly talking about the obscure or difficult language of Fanon or Hegel or Heidegger or Wittgenstein here, now are we? Rather than being "trapped by [her] own contradiction and elitism," as Joyce Joyce claims she was, and granting this student her point, Joyce Joyce should have done what Anna Julia Cooper or Du Bois would have done: sent the student back to the text and told her to read it again—and again, until she got it right. Then, she, a teacher in training, I presume, must serve as an interpreter, as mediator, between Baldwin's text and "our people" out there. (Would the superb and thoughtful editors of *Essence*, by the way, publish an essay their readers could not understand? Perhaps the anecdote is merely apocryphal, after all.) Next time, give the child a dictionary, Joyce, and make her come back in a week.

To use this anecdote to conclude that Baldwin (and, of course, we blankety-blank poststructuralists) has abnegated "the responsibility of the writer to his or her audi-ence" is for a university professor to fail to understand or satisfy our most fundamen-tal charge as teachers of literature: to preach the responsibility of the reader to his or her writers. Joyce Joyce, rather regrettably, has forgotten that the two propositions are inseparable and that the latter is the basic charge that any professor of literature accepts when he or she walks into a classroom or opens a text. That's what love's got to do, got to do with it, Joyce Joyce. How hard are we willing to work to meet our responsibilities to our writers? What would you have Jimmy Baldwin do: rewrite that paragraph, reduce his level of diction to a lower common denominator, then poll the readers of *Essence* to see if they understood the essay? What insolence; what arrogance! What's love got to do with your student's relation to Baldwin and his text? We should beg our writers to publish in *Essence* and in every other black publication, from *Ebony* and *Jet* to the *Black American Literature Forum* and the *CLA Journal.*

The relationship between writer and reader is a reciprocal relationship, and one sells our authors short if one insists that their "responsibility," as you put it, is "to be clear." Clear to whom, or to what? Their "responsibility" is to write. Our responsibility, as critics, to our writers, is to work at understanding them, not to demand that they write at such a level that every one of "our people" understands every word of every black writer without working at it. Your assertion that "the first works of black American literature" were "addressed to white audiences" is not strictly true. The author of *Our Nig*, for example, writes that "I appeal to my colored brethren universally for patronage, hoping they will not condemn this attempt of their sister to be erudite, but rally around me a faithful band of supporters and defenders."[11] How much "blacker" can an author get? No, even at the beginning of the tradition, black writers wrote for a double or mulatto audience, one black and white. Even Phillis Wheatley, whose poetry was the object of severe scrutiny for those who would deny us membership in the human community, wrote "for" Arbour Tanner, Scipio Moorehead, and Jupiter Hammon, just as black critics today write "for" each other and "for" our writers, and not "for" Derrida, Jameson, Said, or Bloom.

It is just not true that "the most influential critics of black literature have been the creative writers themselves." Rather, I believe that our "most influential critics" have been academic critics, such as W. S. Scarborough, Alain Locke, Sterling A. Brown, Du Bois (a mediocre poet and terrible novelist), J. Saunders Redding, Darwin T. Turner, and Houston A. Baker, among others (though both Brown and Baker are also poets). "Most influential" does not necessarily mean whom a white publisher publishes; most influential, to me, means who has generated a critical legacy, a critical tradition upon which other critics have built or can build. Among the writers that Joyce Joyce lists, Ralph Ellison has been "most influential" in the sense that I am defining it, while Hughes is cited mainly for "The Negro Artist and the Racial Mountain," Wright mostly for his two major pieces, "The Literature of the Negro in the United States" and "Blueprint for Negro Literature," while almost none of us cites Du Bois at all, despite the fact that Du Bois was probably the very first systematic literary and cultural theorist in the tradition. Rather, we genuflect to Du Bois.

I am not attempting to deny that creative writers such as Amiri Baraka and Ishmael Reed have been remarkably important. Rather, I deny Joyce Joyce's claim that a new generation of academic critics has usurped the place of influence in the black tradition which creative writers occupied before "the 1960s." The matter is just not as simple as a "shift in black consciousness" in the 1960s, similar to that caused by migration in the 1920s, which Joyce Joyce maintains led to "the merger of a select number of blacks into American mainstream society" and, accordingly, to our "exogamic, elitist, epistemological adaptations." No, I learned my trade as a critic of black literature from a black academic critic, Charles Davis, who made me read Scarborough, Locke, Redding, Ellison, Turner, and Houston Baker as a matter of course.

This is a crucial matter in Joyce Joyce's argument, though it is muddled. For she implies (1) that larger sociopolitical changes in the 1960s led to the crossover of blacks into white institutions (true), and (2) that the critical language that I use, and my firm belief that "race" is not an essence but a trope for ethnicity or culture, both result from being trained into a "class orientation that ironically result[s] from social changes provoked by racial issues."

There are several false leaps being made here. In the first place, what Joyce Joyce erroneously thinks of as our "race" is our culture. Of course I "believe in" Afro-American culture; indeed, I celebrate it every day. But I also believe that to know it, to find it, to touch it, one must locate it in its manifestations (texts, expressive culture, music, the dance, language, and so forth) and not in the realm of the abstract or the a priori. Who can argue with that? The point of my passage about our language with which Joyce Joyce takes such issue is that for a literary critic to discuss "the black aesthetic," he or she must "find" it in language use. What is so controversial, or aristocratic, about that? As for my "class orientation," the history of my family, whether or not we were slaves or free, black or mulatto, property owners or share-croppers, Howard M.D.s or janitors, is really none of Joyce Joyce's business. To say, moreover, that, because I matriculated at Yale (when Arna Bontemps and Houston Baker taught black literature there, by the way) and at the University of Cambridge, I became a "poststructuralist" is simply illogical.

This claim is crucial to Joyce Joyce's argument, however, because of her assertion that "middle-class black men" adopted "mainstream [white] lifestyles and ideology" with great intensity after the "integration" of the 1960s. This dangerous tendency, her argument runs, culminated in 1979 with my oft-cited statement about a black writer or critic being the point of consciousness of our language. I am delighted that Joyce Joyce points to the significance of this statement, because I think that it is of crucial importance to the black critical activity, and especially to the subsequent attention to actual black language use that is apparent in much of our criticism since 1979.

Why has that statement been such an important one in the development of Afro-American literary criticism? Precisely because if our literary critics saw her or his central function as that of a "guide," as Joyce Joyce puts it, or as "an intermediary in explaining the relationship between black people and those forces that attempt to subdue them," she or he tended to fail at both tasks: neither were we as critics in a position to "lead" our people to "freedom," nor did we do justice to the texts created by our writers. Since when have black people turned to our critics to lead us out of the wilderness of Western racism into the promised land of freedom? If black readers turn to black critics, I would imagine they do so to learn about the wondrous workings of literature, our literature, or how our artists have represented the complex encounter of every aspect of black culture with itself and with the Other in formal literary language. Who reads our books anyway? Who can doubt that *Black Fire*, the splendid anthology of the Black Arts edited by Larry Neal and LeRoi Jones, has sold vastly more copies to black intellectuals than to "our people"?[12] Let us not deceive ourselves about our readership.

Joyce Joyce makes a monumental error here, when she offers the following "syllogism":

1. The sixties led to the "integration" of a few black people into historically white institutions.
2. Such exposure to mainstream culture led to the imitation by blacks of white values, habits, and so on.
3. Therefore, black people so educated or exposed suffer from "an individualistic perspective that enables him or her to accept elitist American values and thus widen the chasm between his or her worldview and that of those masses of Blacks whose lives are still stifled by oppressive environmental, intellectual phenomena."

Joyce Joyce arrives at this syllogism all because, I think, we can see important structures of meaning in black texts using sophisticated tools of literary analysis! As my friend Ernie Wilson used to say in the late sixties, "Yeah, but compared to what?"

Let me state clearly that I have no fantasy about my readership: I write for our writers and for our critics. If I write a book review, say, for a popular Afro-American newspaper, I write in one voice; if I write a close analysis of a black text and publish it in a specialist journal, I choose another voice, or voices. Is not that my "responsibility," to use Joyce Joyce's word, and my privilege as a writer? But no, I do not think that my task as a critic is to lead black people to "freedom." My task is to explicate black texts. That's why I became a critic. In 1984, I voted for Jesse Jackson for President: if he stays out of literary criticism, I shall let him continue to speak for me in the political realm. (He did not, by the way, return the donation that Sharon Adams and I sent him, so I suppose that being a "poststructuralist" is okay with Jesse.)

And who is to say that Baker's work or mine is not implicitly political because it is "poststructuralist"? How can the demonstration that our texts sustain ever closer and sophisticated readings not be political, at a time in the academy when all sorts of so-called canonical critics mediate their racism through calls for "purity" of "the tradition," demands as implicitly racist as anything the Southern Agrarians said? How can the deconstruction, as it were, of the forms of racism itself (as carried out, for example, in a recent issue of *Critical Inquiry* by black and nonblack poststructuralists) not be political?[13] How can the use of literary analysis to explicate the racist social text in which we still find ourselves be anything but political? To be political, however, does not mean that I have to write at the level of diction of a Marvel comic book. No, my task—as I see it—is to train university graduate and undergraduate students to think, to read, and, yes Joyce, even to *write* clearly, helping them to expose false uses of language, fraudulent claims and muddled argument, propaganda and vicious lies from all of which our people have suffered just as surely as we have from an economic order in which we were zeroes and a metaphysical order in which we were absences. These are the "values," as Joyce Joyce puts it, which I hope "will be transmitted through [my] work."

Does my work "negate [my] blackness," as Joyce Joyce claims? I would challenge

Joyce Joyce to demonstrate anywhere in my entire work how I have, even once, negated my blackness. Simply because I have attacked an error in logic in the work of certain Black Aestheticians does not mean that I am antiblack, or that I do not love black art or music, or that I feel alienated from black people, or that I am trying to pass like some poststructural ex-colored man. My feelings about black culture and black people are everywhere manifested in my work and in the way that I define my role in the profession, which is as a critic who would like to think that history will regard him as having been a solid "race man," as we put it. My association with Black Studies departments is by choice, just as is my choice of subject matter. (Believe me, Joyce, almost no one at Cambridge wanted me to write about black literature!)

No, Joyce Joyce, I am as black as I ever was, which is just as black as I ever want to be. And I am asserting my "real self," as you put it so glibly, and whatever influence that my work has had or might have on readers of black literature establishes a connection between the self and the people outside the self, as you put it. And for the record, let me add here that only a black person alienated from black language use could fail to understand that we have been deconstructing white people's languages—as "a system of codes or as mere play"—since 1619. That's what signifying is all about. (If you don't believe me, by the way, ask your grandparents, or your parents, especially your mother.)

But enough, Joyce Joyce. Let me respond to your two final points: first, your claim that "the poststructuralist sensibility" does not "aptly apply to black American literary work." I challenge you to refute any of Houston Baker's readings, or my own, to justify such a strange claim. Argue with our readings, not with your idea of who or what we are as black people, or with your idea of how so very many social ills can be traced, by fits and starts, to "poststructuralist thinking."

Finally, to your curious claims that "black American literary criticism has skipped a whole phase in the evolution of literary theory," that "one school of literary thought [must] be created from the one that goes before," and that "the move in black American literature from polemical, biographical criticism to poststructuralist theories mean[s] that these principles are being applied in a historical vacuum," let me respond by saying that my work arose as a direct response to the theories of the Black Arts Movement, as Houston Baker demonstrates so very well in the essay that you cite. Let me also point out politely that my work with binary oppositions which you cite (such as my earlier Frederick Douglass essay)[14] is structuralist as is the work of several other critics of black literature in the seventies (Sunday Anozie, O. A. Ladimeji, Jay Edwards, and the essays in the black journal *The Conch*) and that my work as a poststructuralist emerged directly from my experiments as a structuralist, as Houston Baker also makes clear. No vacuum here; I am acutely aware of the tradition in which I write.

Was it Keynes who said that those who are "against theory" and believe in common sense are merely in the grip of another theory? Joyce Joyce makes a false opposition between theory and humanism, or theory and black men. She also has failed to realize that lucidity through oversimplification is easy enough to achieve; however, it is the lucidity of command which is the challenge posed before any critic of any literature. The use of fashionable critical language without the pressure of that language is as foolish as is the implied allegation that Houston and I are nouveau ideological Uncle Toms because we read and write theory.

CODA

Neither ideology nor blackness can exist as an entity in itself, outside of its forms, or its texts. This is the central theme of *Mumbo Jumbo*, for example. But how can we read the text of black ideology? What language(s) do black people use to represent or to contain their ideological positions? In what forms of language do we speak, or write, or rewrite? These are the issues at the heart of Joyce Joyce's essay.

Can we derive a valid, integral "black" text of ideology from borrowed or appropriated forms? That is, can an authentic black text emerge in the forms of language inherited from the master's class, whether that be, for instance, the realistic novel or poststructuralist theory? Can a black woman's text emerge authentically as borrowed, or "liberated," or revised, from the patriarchal forms of the slave narratives, on one hand, or from the white matriarchal forms of the sentimental novel, on the other, as Harriet Jacobs and Harriet Wilson attempted to do in *Incidents in the Life of a Slave Girl* (1861) and *Our Nig* (1859)?

How much space is there between these two forms through which to maneuver, to maneuver without a certain preordained confinement or "garroting," such as that to which Valerie Smith alludes so pregnantly in her superb poststructural reading of Jacobs's *Incidents in the Life of a Slave Girl?*[15] Is to revise, in this sense, to exist within the confines of the garrot, to extend the metaphor, only to learn to manipulate the representation of black structures of feeling between the cracks, the dark spaces, provided for us by the white masters? Can we write true texts of our ideological selves by the appropriation of received forms of the oppressor—be that oppressor patriarchy or racism—forms in which we see no reflection of our own faces, and through which we hear no true resonances of our own voices? Where lies the liberation in revision, where lies the ideological integrity of defining freedom in the modes and forms of difference charted so cogently by so many poststructural critics of black literature?

It is in these spaces, or garrots, of difference that black literature has dwelled. And while it is crucial to read closely these patterns of formal difference, it is incumbent upon us as well to understand that the quest was lost, in a major sense, before it had even begun simply because the terms of our own self-representation have been provided by the master. Are our choices only to dwell in the quicksand or the garrot of refutation, or negation, or revision? The ideological critique of revision must follow, for us as critics, our detailed and ever closer readings of these very modes of revision. It is not enough for us to show that these exist, and to define these as satisfactory gestures of ideological independence. In this sense, our next set of concerns must be to address the black political signified, and to urge for our writers the fullest and most ironic explorations of manner and matter, of content and form, of structure and sensibility so familiar and poignant to us in our most sublime forms of art, verbal and nonverbal black music, where ideology and art are one, whether we listen to Bessie Smith or to postmodern and poststructural Coltrane.

But what of the ideology of the black critical text? And what of our own critical discourse? In whose voices do we speak? Have we merely renamed the terms of the Other?

Just as we must urge of our writers the meeting of this challenge, we as critics must turn to our own peculiarly black structures of thought and language to develop our own language of criticism, or else we will surely sink in the mire of Nella Larsen's quicksand, remain alienated in the isolation of Harriet Jacobs's garrot, or masked in the received stereotype of the Black Other helping Huck Honey to return to the Raft again, singing "China Gate" with Nat King Cole under the Da Nang moon, standing with the Incredible Hulk as the monstrous split doubled selves of mild mannered white people, or as Rocky's too-devoted trainer Apollo Creed, or reflecting our balded heads in the shining flash of Mr. T's signifying gold chains.

As Tina Turner puts it:

> I've been taking on a new direction,
> But I have to say
> I've been thinking about my own protection
> It scares me to feel this way.
> Oh, oh, oh,
> What's love got to do, got to do with it?
> What's love but a sweet old-fashioned notion. . . .

NOTES

1. See Paul de Man, "The Resistance to Theory," *Yale French Studies*, No. 63 (1982), 3–20.

2. Houston A. Baker, Jr., *Blues, Ideology, and Afro-American Literature: A Vernacular Theory* (Chicago, 1984).

3. Fuller versions of this section of my essay appear in my "Criticism in the Jungle," in *Black Literature and Literary Theory*, ed. Henry Louis Gates, Jr. (New York, 1985), pp. 1–24 and "Writing 'Race' and the Difference It Makes," *Critical Inquiry*, 12, No. 1 (Autumn 1985), 1–20.

4. J. E. Casely Hayford, *Ethiopia Unbound: Studies in Race Emancipation* (London, 1911), pp. 1–2; hereafter cited in text.

5. Carter G. Woodson, "Introduction," *The Mind of the Negro as Reflected in Letters Written During the Crisis, 1800–1860* (New York, 1969), p. v.

6. I have traced the history and theory of this critical debate in my *Black Letters and the Enlightenment*, forthcoming from Oxford University Press.

7. David Hume, "Of National Character," in *The Philosophical Works*, ed. Thomas Hill Green and Thomas Hodge Grose (Darmstadt, 1964), III, 252 n. 1.

8. Sterling A. Brown, Lecture, Yale University, 17 April 1979.

9. Robert Farris Thompson, *Indelibly Black: Essays on African and Afro-American Art* (forthcoming).

10. James Baldwin, "On Being 'White' . . . and Other Lies," *Essence*, April 1984, pp. 90–92.

11. Harriet Wilson, *Our Nig* (Boston, 1859), p. i.

12. *Black Fire: An Anthology of Afro-American Writing*, ed. LeRoi Jones and Larry Neal (New York, 1968).

13. See *Critical Inquiry*, 12, No. 1 (Autumn 1985).

14. Henry Louis Gates, Jr., "Binary Oppositions in Chapter One of *Narrative of the Life of Frederick Douglass, an American Slave. Written by Himself*," in *Afro-American Literature: The Reconstruction of Instruction*, ed. Dexter Fisher and Robert B. Stepto (New York, 1979), pp. 212–33.

15. Valerie Smith, " 'Loopholes of Retreat': Architecture and Ideology in Harriet Jacobs's *Incidents in the Life of a Slave Girl*," paper presented at the 1985 American Studies Association meeting, San Diego.

28 In Dubious Battle

Houston A. Baker, Jr

(1987)

While it may be true that one sometimes has a choice of weapons (even if they are forged or invented on the spot), it is also true that one seldom has the luxury of choosing where one's battles are going to be fought. In the realm of Afro-American literary criticism there seems recently to have occurred a correlation between an increase in available weapons and nonce embattlement. Within the past month (August/September, 1985), for example, I have found myself in conflict with other Afro-American critics. (The fact that both were Afro-American women may be altogether fortuitous. In any case, my response is not directed toward a group. It is directed against specific conservatisms, misjudgments, and errors.) The grounds on which these recent conflicts occurred did not seem to me particularly appropriate for battle, and I found myself, ironically, defending what I have considered a desirable expansiveness, diversity, originality, and, yes, complexity in the Afro-American critical and theoretical arsenal.

The first instance of unexpected embattlement occurred at a conference in August of 1985 when a black woman suggested that everything I had just said about the need for a new problematic surrounding investigations of the Harlem Renaissance was misconceived. Refusing to grant my claim that traditional definitions were inadequate, she insisted that we should confine the Harlem Renaissance to four years (1925–1929) and allow the significance of these years to be evaluated only through study of what she called "the artists," meaning, in her case, self-declared poets, playwrights, and novelists and *not* blues singers, dancers, musicians, graphic artists, painters, sculptors, book illustrators, intellectuals, popular political leaders of genius, and the like. Well, there we were—before an almost exclusively white audience with a black speaker (myself) who was urging a view of Afro-American modernism directly in opposition to traditional claims about the "failures" of the Harlem Renaissance and the "limitations" of black artists—under attack by a black woman who

313

wanted traditionally defined contours and contents of what she thought of as Afro-American "art" left intact.

Now what was especially surprising about this embattled moment was the fact that just a year prior to my presentation, the questioner herself had set forth an explication of a well-known Harlem Renaissance novel that flew directly in the face of traditional definitions. Implicitly, she suggested at a 1984 session of the English Institute that no one could comprehend the Harlem Renaissance if his or her critical orientation remained narrowly "artistic" and if his or her political focus remained exclusively assimilationist. Why, then, were we in dubious battle? I think the explanation becomes apparent after a survey of the second embattlement.

The day before I left to deliver my "Harlem Renaissance Revised" lecture at the English Institute, I received a note from the editor of *New Literary History* informing me that he had accepted an essay on Afro-American literary criticism by a black woman critic who "mentioned" both my work and that of Henry Louis Gates, Jr.: Would I care to respond? My first reaction was pleasure on discovering that the journal had opened its pages willingly to Afro-American critical concerns. My second reaction was bafflement. I could not fathom why I was being told by the editor of a journal that has, throughout its history, been relentlessly Euro-American that both mine and Professor Gates's critical positions were under siege in the same essay by an Afro-American woman whose work *New Literary History* had endorsed through the act of acceptance.

I knew that if I chose (as, obviously, I did) to comment on the essay, I would perforce, occupy a surprising and totally unanticipated battlefield—one that could not possibly have been dreamed of, say, five years ago. After reading Professor Joyce's "The Black Canon: Reconstructing Black American Literary Criticism" on my return from Cambridge, however, I realized there was scarcely any choice but to take up arms. For on reading the work, I found the following errors and misstatements:

1. Alain Locke's *The New Negro* (1925) is a critical document that calls for an "attenuation of race" as a criterion in the growth, development, and progress of Afro-American culture. ("Race" is, of course, the signal criterion for Locke in both his introduction to *The New Negro* and in many of the essays by the more than thirty contributors to the volume.)

2. Richard Wright's "The Literature of the Negro in the United States" (1957) is "prophetic" in its suggestion that "Negro" expression and general American expression will soon merge. (It is, on the contrary, Wright's second prediction in his essay—that is, that there may occur a "sharp turn toward strictly racial themes" in Negro expression—that is prophetic of Afro-American literary and critical concerns of the 1960s and 1970s.)

3. *Our Nig* (1859) is a work that addresses itself to "slavery." (The novel is set in the North and concerns itself, to be sure, with the brutal conditions of labor—but not with slavery.)

4. The "first" works of Afro-American literary creation are "slave" novels and narratives. (Ah, alas poor Phillis Wheatley and the 150 years of Afro-American expression preceding *Clotel*!)

5. *Structuralism* is a movement that originated to combat the alienation and despair of existentialism. (Surely, there is ample reason to think of, say, Marx, who is scarcely postexistentialist, as a structuralist if the structuralist position is conceived of in its generally accepted linguistic orientation. Structures of "mind" are not invented ab nihilo as a solace for alienation. Rather, they are posited on the basis of a prior linguistic model that augurs such structures. If one perceives the possibility of adequately explaining complex phenomena—such as language—in systematic ways on the basis of a minimal set of clear and distinct units, then one would seem to have a powerful theory in harmony with Occam's razor. Structuralism thought it had achieved such a theory.)

6. The "phases" of literary criticism are "organic" and "evolutionary." Hence, Afro-American critical ontogeny must recapitulate Euro-American critical phylogeny. (How strange to assert that Afro-American criticism should return, first, to the limited province of structuralism before its practitioners "advance" to the liberating vision of poststructuralism.)

7. There is a "mainstream" of American culture defined exclusively by white American norms, standards, practices, criteria, institutions, and so on. The counterpart to this "mainstream" is—to invoke Chinweizu's formula in *The West and the Rest of Us*—"the rest of us." (Like myths of "self and other," redeemed "master" and irredeemable "slave," the myth of an exclusively white mainstream into which Afro-Americans can "merge" by choice is utter and patent nonsense—a fiction perpetrated by rich Anglo-American males and rejected out of hand by most Afro-Americans from 1619 to our multi-ethnic, multidimensional, and complex present.)

8. The "primary goal" of "poststructuralist" Afro-American literary critics is to gain a voice in "mainstream" institutions, and, hence, to merge "nonracially" with a majority culture. This "goal" is in harmony with Locke's "attenuations of race," Wright's prophecies, and structural realities (mainstream vs. "other") in the United States. (The compounded errors of Professor Joyce noted so far reduce the terms of her "goal" ascription to a misleading and erroneous assertion that no serious journal or scholar would ponder for more than an instant.)

The list of errors could be multiplied. (Professor Joyce, for example, suggests that the intended "audience" for *Our Nig* was white. Harriet Wilson, author of the novel, quite explicitly directs her work to "my colored brethren universally.") Rather than continue the list of errors, however, I want to suggest, quite simply, that the embattled moment that has produced my foregoing selected list should never have occurred. The battle is altogether dubious and unprofitable. For it is impossible to believe that an essay focused on Anglo-American criticism as dreadfully flawed by factual mistakes as Professor Joyce's work on Afro-American criticism would have been accepted or printed by a major critical or theoretical journal. Why, then, was her essay accepted and published by *New Literary History*?

The most charitable explanation is that the journal's editors were victims of a too casual reader's report. A less charitable, and, I think, more accurate view, is that many people share Professor Joyce's essential animosity toward recent modes of critical and theoretical discussion that have enlarged the universe of discourse surrounding Afro-American expressive culture. Their animosity springs from the fact that the new critical and theoretical modes marking investigations of black expressive culture so clearly escape the minstrel simplicity that Anglo-Americans have traditionally imagined and assigned (and that some Afro-Americans have willingly provided and accepted) as the farthest reaches of the black voice in the United States.

What Professor Joyce calls "poststructuralist" critics are, in reality, a group of spokespersons who move across both ethnic and gender boundaries and who have decisively relinquished the role of simple-minded, conservative spokespersons on behalf of a putatively simple-minded expressive culture. They have seized initiative by formulating suggestive theories of Afro-American expressive culture that bring their work into harmony not with a mainstream, nor with an academic majority (both of which remain wedded to an old literary history), but with an avant garde in contemporary world literary study.

What Professor Joyce seems to object to most vehemently is a new sound, one that seems to her "unclear." She is joined in her distress, I am sure, by many would-be masters and aspiring mistresses of the "good old days" when a profound black critical utterance was held to sound like the following revelation: "For the negro, reality is real (reality: whatever controls yr/thought processes; controls yr/pure & unpure actions). Blackpeople's reality is controlled by alien forces."

Alas, the days when such injunctions were predominant (and very much needed) are past. Life has become more complex in a decade of rabid conservatism, reduced material resources, actual starvation, and religiously inspired bigotry. Fortunately, critics and theorists of Afro-American expressive culture have, likewise, become more complex, realizing that assertions of a "noble savagery," sensually humanistic delightfulness, and monosyllabic clarity of Afro-American expressive culture achieve nothing but a pat on the head and a reinforcement of a Howellsian minstrel sensibility in the academy. William Dean Howells, of course, wrote at the turn of the century that "appetite" and "emotion" (the only ethnic variables he could discover in Paul Laurence Dunbar's work) marked the range of the Afro-American mind.

In the context created by the foregoing remarks, let me focus for a moment on Professor Joyce's essay and on the question posed by Professor Deborah McDowell at the 1985 English Institute. Both responses to the sound of my criticism and theory—which are, admittedly, informed by poststructuralism but scarcely confined to that province alone—seem to me to represent what I can only call a new black conservatism, one that ironically derives from black women critics. I say "ironically" because in the world of avant-garde literary study today, it is possible to think that black women, above all others perhaps, should be in the vanguard of one of the most exciting areas of literary criticism and theory in the United States.

I refer, of course, to the conjunction between the concerns of feminist criticism and Afro-American literary and expressive cultural study marked by the attention that such authors as Alice Walker, Toni Morrison, Gloria Naylor, Zora Neale Hurston and others have recently received. How, one might ask, in a day when there is such an abundance of opportunity for theoretical daring and critical inventiveness by black women critics can one such critic urge or suggest to anyone that the Harlem Renaissance comprised a period of four years' duration? And how, in an era when all conventional myths of an unequivocal division between fictive and ordinary discourse, between "metaphors of everyday life" and "artistic metaphors," are being exploded can a black woman critic suggest that evaluations of the Harlem Renaissance should be based only on the work of literary "artists"? Further, how can a black woman critic like Professor Joyce be (in her words) "intellectually paralyzed" by questions of the relationship between writers and their audiences in an era that has witnessed the production of more high caliber critical and theoretical work on this topic than on perhaps any other? And why should she *fail* to realize that it is precisely because there has been such high caliber work and because critics and theoreticians whom she labels "poststructuralist" Afro-Americanists have read so very much of it and applied it to Afro-American expressive culture that she should have been able to offer a much better and far more informed response to the student who asked her about Baldwin? All that was required for an adequate response—one rendered without tears, shame, or recourse to ethnic ratiocination—was reading. She had only to be well read in contemporary literary criticism and theory. (Incidentally, one might say as a purely readerly aside that if there is a single Afro-American writer who has made himself indisputably clear on the question of the black writer's "social responsibility" to communicate with the masses, or to be limpidly "clear" in his creative writing, it is James Baldwin. Professor Joyce might simply have referred the student to the Cleaver/Baldwin exchange of a few years back and then gone on to point out that in his role as a concerned citizen and Afro-American activist Baldwin served as a principal spokesperson of the civil rights movement in America.) Now, there is no evidence in "The Black Canon: Reconstructing Black American Literary Criticism" that Professor Joyce has read either European and American poststructuralists, or Afro-American poststructuralists. The only hint that she has taken up the current universe of discourse surrounding Afro-American expressive culture is her misappropriated quotation from Gates's "Criticism in the Jungle," which she thinks is a denial of race, but which is, in reality, a statement of the difficulties encountered by non-Western spokespersons who utilize Western languages.

The nonce appearance of battlefields is the result of a combination of white ignorance, black willingness to tread conservative/minstrel paths, and a multi-ethnic fear in the academy of new and difficult modes of critical and theoretical study. The rewards of dubious battles that occur on such fields are scant. They are scant, that is to say, for Afro-Americans and Afro-Americanists who are dedicated to the comprehension of an enduring, salvific, and structurally unique African sound in the Americas. The spoils of such skirmishes are, however, more profitable for those who possess no such dedication.

For example, to execute voluntarily an about-face and pronounce Afro-American expressivity of short duration and limited "artistic" success may result in favors from those in power. Further, to publish a grossly erroneous attack on Afro-American literary criticism in a journal traditionally devoted to Afro-American points of view and directed to a white audience could, I suppose, be profitable in an academic world where any attack whatsoever on anything Afro-American whatsoever is taken as a valuable sortie.

White ignorance was signaled (in the skirmishes described in the present discussion) by all of those blank white faces at the English Institute. Those faces showed no trace of understanding about the Harlem Renaissance not only because they were ignorant of the avant-garde secondary sources and critical methods invoked, but also because they did not have a clue about the primary sounds, voices, and Afro-American expressive products being analyzed. Further white ignorance is signalled by the acceptance of an essay on Afro-American literary criticism replete with misstatements, errors of fact, and misinterpretations by a quite fine, "white" journal in literary criticism and theory.

Finally, there are the disciplinary fears of the "new" to be contended with in the dubious battles of August/September, 1985. I do feel that conservatives—black and white alike—are right to feel animosity and apprehension before what is so glibly (and, so often, without even the barest modicum of reading) labelled "obscurantist," "murky," or "pretentious" poststructuralism. My understanding of the finer work of poststructuralism traces its inception to a French Hegelianism that provokes a thoroughgoing critique of Western philosophy and its privileges (such as colonialism, slavery, racism, and so on) and privilegings. Indeed, the towers of an old mastery are more resonantly toppled by a poststructuralist critique—which discounts notions of God, Self, History, and the Book in the service of a new interpretive economy—than by any other operative intellectual position (in the 1980s) that I can readily call to mind. It seems to me that a reading and appropriation of the efforts in philosophy, political economy, psychology, and popular culture of poststructuralist thinkers such as Derrida, Althusser, Lacan, and Baudrillard could well lead one to hear the sound of poststructuralism as a note in clear harmony with, say, the freedom cries of millions of blacks in South Africa bent on a new and revolutionary existence. If critics and theorists would hear this sound as such where Afro-American expressive culture is concerned, however, there is no recourse for them but the willing relinquishment of an old minstrelsy and the abandonment of an all too prevalent laziness and complacency. Frankly, I believe the sound is worth hearing. It has been, and will continue to be (if we are not undone in dubious and time-consuming battle with compradors) the political and academic heralding note of a new and liberating future.

29

"Who the Cap Fit"

Unconsciousness and Unconscionableness in the Criticism of Houston A. Baker, Jr., and Henry Louis Gates, Jr.

Joyce A. Joyce

(1987)

WHAT LIFE HAS TAUGHT ME
I WOULD LIKE TO SHARE WITH
THOSE WHO WANT TO LEARN. . . .

UNTIL THE PHILOSOPHY WHICH HOLDS
ONE RACE SUPERIOR AND ANOTHER INFERIOR
IS FINALLY AND PERMANENTLY DISCREDITED
AND ABANDONED
. . . UNTIL THERE ARE NO LONGER
FIRST CLASS AND SECOND CLASS CITIZENS
OF ANY NATION
UNTIL THE COLOUR OF A MAN'S SKIN
IS OF NO MORE SIGNIFICANCE THAN
THE COLOUR OF HIS EYES
. . . UNTIL THEIR BASIC HUMAN RIGHTS
ARE EQUALLY GUARANTEED TO ALL,
WITHOUT REGARD TO RACE
. . . UNTIL THAT DAY,
THE DREAM OF LASTING PEACE, WORLD
CITIZENSHIP AND THE RULE OF INTER-
NATIONAL MORALITY
WILL REMAIN BUT A FLEETING ILLUSION
TO BE PURSUED, BUT NEVER ATTAINED—
AND UNTIL THE IGNOBLE AND UNHAPPY
REGIMES THAT NOW HOLD OUR BROTHERS
IN ANGOLA, IN MOZAMBIQUE, SOUTH AFRICA
IN SUBHUMAN BONDAGE, HAVE BEEN
TOPPLED, UTTERLY DESTROYED,
UNTIL THAT DAY THE AFRICAN CONTINENT

WILL NOT KNOW PEACE.
WE AFRICANS WILL FIGHT, IF NECESSARY,
AND WE KNOW WE SHALL WIN
AS WE ARE CONFIDENT IN THE VICTORY OF
GOOD OVER EVIL, OF GOOD OVER EVIL.

—Speech by HIM Haile Selassie I,
sung by Bob Marley and the Wailers
on *Rastaman Vibration*

In the fall of 1985 when Professor Ralph Cohen, editor of *New Literary History*, wrote to me explaining that he had invited Professors Baker and Gates to respond to my essay "The Black Cannon: Reconstructing Black American Literary Criticism," I knew that my two Black colleagues would not respond with either geniality or comradeship. Yet, I must say—to use E. M. Forster's words from *Howards End*—"premonition is not preparation." Although I was quite aware that Baker and Gates assume positions as vanguards of Afro-American literary criticism, I would never have guessed that their "dubious" and "honest" replies would respond with misogynist, paranoid, elitist, and paternalistic signs. Nonetheless, rather than engage in a defensive battle ("nonce embattlement," to use Baker's term), I choose here (as in the essay itself) to respond to the real issues at hand—most of which were left undeveloped previously. For I believe strongly that the words of Haile Selassie's speech, as they are sung by Bob Marley and the Wailers, embody the philosophy and the power needed for an overall, orchestrated surge of energy—economic, political, social, personal, and intellectual—to counteract the abusive, binding, numbing effect of the historical oppression of Blacks around the world.

Perhaps nothing better illustrates the spiritually impoverished predicament in which Black America finds itself than Tina Turner's song "What's Love Got to Do with It?" and its accompanying video. This song represents the denial of love and the degeneration of values that begin with self-love and are reflected in the way one human being responds to another. This song suggests to our young people not only that sex for sex's sake (like writing for writing's sake or "the 'free movement' of writing itself") is a legitimate or healthy attitude, but also that the biological satisfaction the sex act brings is the ultimate fulfillment, the most they should hope for in an intimate relationship with another person. And equally insidious is the video that flaunts the Black woman as sex object for Black men *and* white men, as Turner, with bleached stylishly unkempt hair suggestive of the white blond (all signifying aside) and wearing a tight leather skirt and jacket and very high heels that accentuate her shapely legs, struts down the street. This video and the song lure our young people into the world of glamour, rapacity, and ignorance. Unaware that they are being manipulated, the young Black women who imitate Tina Turner manifest the self-hatred and self-denial widespread among contemporary Black Americans. The philosophy of which Marley sings urges Blacks around the world—not just Rastafarians—to bond in a concentrated effort to destroy the effects of mental slavery, the evidence of which is reflected in Turner's song and video. It is this idea of bonding together that meets the most resistance, embodied in such comments as "Why do I have to call myself Black?" and "Why can't I just be a person?" Amusingly enough, in his editor's introduction to the *Critical Inquiry* issue *"Race," Writing and Difference*, Gates provides the intellectual, quasi-scientific, literary counterpart to these questions when he says, "Race, as a meaningful criterion within the biological sciences, has long been recognized to be a fiction. When we speak of 'the white race' or 'the black race,' 'the Jewish race' or 'the Aryan race,' we speak in biological misnomers and, more generally, in metaphors."[1] He might as well have said, like Turner, "What's Race Got to Do with It?" Turner's song and video and the Gates passage attest to the prevalent, malevolent, unconscionable, illusionary idea that race and (it goes unsaid) racism have ceased to be the leading impediments that thwart the mental and physical lives of Black people at all levels of human endeavor.

Turner's song and Gates's use of it as an epigraph and referent fasten on the lack of commitment suggested by the song and also typify the poststructuralist sensibility. The salient contradictions and distortions inherent in Gates's and Baker's responses to my essay beg the question—not of the nature of their critical discourse, but of its purpose. A close reading of their responses reveals that neither of these men can read. For they both—and Baker embarrassingly so—overstate their cases against what they see as my errors and misjudgments. Perhaps, in the past few years, they have used the obfuscating language and ideas of Derrida, Barthes, Paul de Man, Foucault, Kristeva, Althusser, Bakhtin, and others to cloak their difficulties. In Baker's case, I fear, the problem is much worse than an inability to read. His distortions of what I wrote and his more serious warping of what took place at the English Institute are, simply put, unethical. After a number of inquiries, I learned that the question posed was *not* directed to Baker, but to any one of the three panelists—Baker himself, Eleanor Traylor, and Arnold Rampersad—during the question and answer session (see the second paragraph of Baker's "In Dubious Battle"). Therefore, the question was not a direct response to Baker's assertion of a "need for a new problematic surrounding investigation of the Harlem Renaissance," nor was the question aimed at refuting his "claim that traditional definitions [of the Harlem Renaissance] were inadequate." Since the three panelists all had presented various definitions of the Harlem Renaissance, set its boundaries at different places, and chosen to talk only about the male writers of the Renaissance, Professor Deborah McDowell asked any member of the panel to address the implications of their definitions of that Renaissance and of modernism in relation to the study of Black women writers, some of whom were among the most prolific of the period. Baker, in this case the self-appointed vanguard of the panelists, took it upon himself to respond first to McDowell's question. Her question—like my essay—was not intended as a personal attack on Baker.

His distortion of this incident follows the same pattern as his warping of the issues in my essay. In his paraphrasing of my comments on Alain Locke, he completely ignores the quotation I use wherein Locke himself addresses the Negro's ascent into the middle class and the effects of this upward mobility in society's treating "the Negro en masse," in other words of looking at the entire group as a race of people who identify with each other and respond to the world in much the same way. Moreover, I am sure Baker is familiar with Zora Neale Hurston's castigation of Alain Locke's middle-class notions, with the class and ideological conflict between Du Bois and Garvey, and with the sexist conflict between Langston Hughes and Hurston, all of which serve as prototypes and historical references for the interchange that now takes place between him, Gates, and myself. I am amused that both Baker and Gates cite what they see as a factual error in my saying that *Our Nig* concerns itself with slavery and that it was addressed to a white audience. Although I clearly grouped *Our Nig* with the slave narratives, most of the poetry, and with *Clotel* in referring to the intended audience for Black American literature at its beginnings, I see no essential reason for taking issue with the inclusion of *Our Nig*, nor the exclusion of Phillis Wheatley. What emerges here is that Gates and Baker have two standards for judgment, one by which they judge and adopt the ideas of European and American white males and the other by which they adjudicate the work of Black women. They allow the one group greater latitude for metaphorical language than they do the other.

Their trivializing retorts and their total neglect of the real issue surrounding my reference to *Our Nig, Clotel,* and the slave narratives—"the issue of the historical interrelationship between literature, class, and values" and of "how all these complexities augment ad infinitum where the writer is a Black American"—are akin to the tone of their unconscionable contortion of my opening anecdote about my student's confusion with Baldwin's article in *Essence* magazine. My student would never have responded by skirting the central issue. Contrary to what Gates writes, the emphasis in my recounting of the conversation about Baldwin between me and my student was not on Baldwin's abnegation of his responsibility to his audience, but rather on my responsibility to the student. This peculiar warping that characterizes Gates's paraphrasing typifies the strategy he employs throughout his response. My emphasis was not on Baldwin's relationship to poststructuralist obscurantism, but on my own evasiveness and elitism, which shared a kinship with poststructuralist methodology. Thus Gates's question "What would you [meaning me] have Jimmy Baldwin do?" is a willful contortion of my point. What I wrote clearly suggested that if my student were having trouble with Baldwin, then it was indeed my responsibility—the responsibility of the critic/teacher—not to ask an elitist question, but to elucidate Baldwin for her and to refer her to further readings as Gates and Baker are corroboratively quick to point out.

Gates not only contrives his retort, but he also unnecessarily dilates it, still failing to give attention to the connections among literature, class, and values, the triad that obviously spurred my use of the anecdote. Instead of responding forthrightly to this question which has a direct bearing on the future of Black literary critical discourse (and perhaps on all critical discourse), he imagines that my argument is with Baldwin. Gates says, "The relationship between writer and reader is a reciprocal relationship, and one sells our authors short if one insists that their 'responsibility,' as you [meaning me] put it, is 'to be clear.' " He continues, "Our responsibility, as critics, to our writers, is to work at understanding them, not to demand that they write at such a level that every one of 'our people' understands every word of every black writer without working at it." Again quite amusingly, this comment contradicts Gates's later assertion that "if I [Gates] write a book review, say, for a popular Afro-American newspaper, I write in one voice; if I write a close analysis of a black text and publish it in a specialist journal, I choose another voice, or voices." Perhaps Gates needs to elaborate upon a definition of voice and upon the need for a change of voice if, as he stated earlier, the reader's responsibility is to work at understanding our writers and if we should not demand that a writer write at "such a level that every one of 'our people' understands every word." What Gates stumbles on here is the most forbidden fruit of poststructuralist thinking—the truth of the matter.

Of course, it is necessary that a writer address his or her words to an audience and that he should have a clear understanding of that audience's sensibility or history. If the relationship between the writer and reader is reciprocal, as Gates says, why does he then avoid elaborating upon the relationship between the critic and the reader? Unfortunately, Gates stops at maintaining that the responsibility of the writer is to write, that his task is to explicate Black texts, and that he is not deceived about his readership. Again the pertinent issue that Gates avoids involves two questions: For what reason does the critic write? And who exactly is his readership? By referring to Larry Neal and LeRoi Jones's "splendid" anthology *Black Fire*, Gates cunningly leads us "black intellectuals" to believe that his own work shares the spirit, ideology, and purpose of *Black Fire*. However, those of us (Black and white) who understand that Larry Neal's lifelong work was to destroy that "white thing" within us can only be taken aback at any hint of a comparison between the works in *Black Fire* and Gates's "The Blackness of Blackness: A Critique of the Sign and the Signifying Monkey," "Preface to Blackness: Text and Pretext," and "Editor's Introduction: Writing 'Race' and the Difference It Makes."[2]   To illustrate, I shall contrast a passage from Neal's "And Shine Swam On" at the end of *Black Fire* to one from Anthony Appiah's "The Uncompleted Argument: Du Bois and the Illusion of Race" (which Gates as editor endorses by inclusion in *"Race," Writing, and Difference*). The juxtaposition of the passages illustrates the vastly different attitudes toward the issue of race and the purpose of Black literary discourse that separate contemporary, quasi-scientific, alienating analyses from the best earlier Black literary criticism. Neal writes,

Our music has always been the most dominant manifestation of what we are and feel, literature was just an afterthought, the step taken by the Negro bourgeoisie who desired acceptance on the white man's terms. And that is precisely why the literature has failed. It was the case of one elite addressing another elite.

But our music is something else. The best of it has always operated at the core of our lives, forcing itself upon us as in a ritual. It has always, somehow, represented the collective psyche. Black literature must attempt to achieve that same sense of collective ritual, but ritual directed at the destruction of useless, dead ideas. . . .

Finally, the black artist must link his work to the struggle for his liberation and the

liberation of his brothers and sisters . . . He will be furthering the psychological liberation of his people, without which, no change is even possible.

The artist and the political activist are one. They are both shapers of the future
reality. Both understand and manipulate the collective myths of the race.[3]

A philosophy professor at Yale University, Anthony Appiah very painstakingly writes,

I can now express simply one measure of the extent to which members of these human
populations we call races differ more from each other than they do from members of
the same race. For example, the value of the J [a genetic variable] for Caucasoids
based largely on samples from the English population—is estimated to be about
0.857, while that for the whole human population is estimated at 0.852. The chances,
in other words, that two people taken at random from the human population will
have the same characteristic at a locus, are about 85.2 percent, while the chances for
two (white) people taken from the population of England are about 85.7 percent. And
since 85.2 is 100 minus 14.8 and 85.7 is 100 minus 14.3, this is equivalent to what I
said in the introduction: the chances of two people who are both Caucasoid differing
in genetic constitution at one site on a given chromosome are about 14.3 percent,
while, for any two people taken at random from the human population, they are
about 14.8 percent. The conclusion is obvious: given only a person's race, it is hard to
say what his or her biological characteristic will be, except in respect of the "grosser"
features of color, hair, and bone.[4]

After getting through this passage, we can only breathe a thankful sigh of relief. In
fact, we are so appreciative at having come through the experience that we do not
become angry about being told, in such a dilated fashion, what most Black people
have always known: that the division of mankind into races is a biologically unsound
contrivance.

Certainly, W. E. B. Du Bois was aware of this fact. Yet, Du Bois, like Larry Neal,
Sonia Sanchez, Audre Lorde, June Jordan, Amiri Baraka, and others, grapples with
various strategies in combating the inane, illogical concept and ramifications of race.
Not one of them uses his or her intellectual energy to rationalize him or herself out
of what is dubbed "the Negro race." Instead they use their energies—in different
ways—attempting to bring out the psychological and economic liberation of Black
people. Their lives and the nature of their work answer Gates's question as to what I
would have the Black critic/teacher do: merge the roles of critic and political activist,
as stated by Neal in the passage cited above and by Sonia Sanchez in "The Poet as
Creator of Social Values."[5] This goal does not necessarily have to be accomplished
by marching in front of the South African Embassy in Washington, D.C. It certainly
cannot be achieved by the casual, gratuitous mentioning of South Africa at the end
of Baker's response, nor by Gates's wasting a vote on Jesse Jackson, knowing that he
was neither the Democratic nor the Republican nominee.

Meaningful political involvement, in the case of the Black critic especially, demands
that we give "presence" to the text, that we deal with the question of values, that we
distinguish clearly between indigenous values (those that serve our own best interests)

and alien ones (those that do not serve our best interests), and that we remain mindful, as Eugene Goodheart puts it, that "the value and interests [which] determine discourse (in its possible variety) emerge from a combination of character (temperament, disposition) and history (circumstance, experience)."[6] In other words, the literary critical activity is not free of personality and history, as the deconstructionists would have us believe. Neither should literary critical involvement be free of commitment, especially in the case of the Black critic. The poststructuralist sensibility in its claim that to acquire knowledge is impossible, its emphases on fragmentation, plurality of meaning, selflessness, and indeterminacy only exacerbate the Black critic's estrangement from the important social, political, economic, and, maybe most importantly, the psychological forces that shape Black culture and that are responsible for what Neal refers to as a collective psyche. Gates is absolutely incorrect when he implies that the Black critic writes for the Black intellectual, not for our people. The young (and old) Black intellectuals in my graduate and undergraduate classes, whose psyches I play a role in shaping, are indeed our people. They, in turn, are raising children (our people) whose consciousness these students shape and who may some day read and be influenced by our work. Significantly, our Black colleagues around the country are also our people.

Black critics then have the opportunity to influence the very complicated human network that makes for change. They do this by using their skills to show the need for political bonding between Black people around the world. Instead of inundating our works with superfluous, contrived references to fashionable scholars and philosophers who have decided that literature and life no longer have meaning and thus that existence is a game, the Black American critic—merely and significantly because he or she lives in a powerful country—should be at the vanguard of a worldwide Black intellectual movement in much the same way as Du Bois, Wright, and C. L. R. James were. Aimed at showing the shared experiences of Black peoples, the Black creative process could link the critic's vision to the world outside. Critics could, for instance, use the South African social worker Ellen Kuzwayo's autobiography *Call Me Woman* and Bessie Head's novel *A Question of Power* as "signifiers" for "signified" cultural, political, sexist, and mental conditions that work as "signs" to connect the lives of South African and American Black women.[7] Such an endeavor would be far less contrived and far less farfetched than Baker's legion of superfluous allusions and Gates's glorification of nothingness in "The Signifying Monkey."

Because I do not "defamiliarize" myself from a piece of Black literature by using postmodern or poststructuralist jargon, and because I fancy that I can think for myself, Gates and Baker suggest that I do not know the differences among structuralism, poststructuralism, and desconstruction and that my knowledge appears at best "murky," "muddled," and "pretentious." Although the appearance of *Afro-American Literature: The Reconstruction of Instruction* and *Chant of Saints* stimulated my interest in contemporary literary theory, ironically it was the 1984 publication of Gates's *Black Literature and Theory* which recharged my energies, motivating me to read persistently and widely.[8] The more I read, the more dismayed I became. For I do not understand how a Black critic aware of the implantations of racist structures in the consciousness of Blacks and whites could accept poststructuralist ideas and practices. This dilemma reveals an unsettling paradox. Both Gates and Baker maintain that Black literature is as viable a literature as that of any other group and thus that Black literature also merits close readings. Yet the peculiar dilemma is that the reason Black literature has not received the benefits of close analyses lies in the inferior status given Black Americans and anything we produce. Our literature confronts this issue of imposed inferiority quite aggressively on a multitude of levels. Baker and Gates skirt the issue in different ways, but achieve the same results. Gates implies that he, like the monkey in the tree, signifies upon his readers and thus subverts their ideas. The question arises, however, as to the need to subvert the Black intellectuals, especially those who bought *Black Fire*, "a radical"/ "antiwhite" Black text for its time and ours. Baker, on the other hand, in his conclusion to *Blues, Ideology, and Afro-American Literature* says, "My project is a minute beginning in the labor of writing/righting American history and literary history."[9] We can only question then the reasons for the contradiction between the intended aim of *Blues, Ideology* and the semantic disjunction that typify the essays in the text. In fact, I cannot fathom why a Black critic would trust that the master would provide him or her with tools with which he or she can seek independence. For, to use Audre Lorde's phraseology, "the master's tools will never dismantle the master's house."[10]

Although I am well aware that I have in no way addressed all of the charges of ignorance and ineptness made against me by Gates and Baker, I would like for the remainder of this response to attend to the idea that I am hostile toward or resistant to theory and to answer the question "What's Love Got to Do with It?" I hope to show that my views of Black literary criticism are inextricably and unembarrassingly tied to my identity as a Black person and that Gates's and Baker's responses are, by nature, inextricably related to an absence of identity. Thus, the central issue here is identity. In his "In Dubious Battle," Baker questions why a journal like *New Literary History* would begin its attention to Black literary criticism with such a "dreadfully flawed" essay as my own. His answer is that the "journal's editors were victims of a too casual reader's report" and that "many people share Professor Joyce's essential animosity toward recent modes of critical and theoretical discussion that have enlarged the universe of discourse surrounding Afro-American expressive culture." Again, a contradiction emerges. If *New Literary History* has not previously opened its pages to issues of Black critical discourse, is it not now time that its editors do so, since "critics and theorists of Afro-American expressive culture have, likewise, become more complex," to use Baker's own words? The truth of the matter is that, as I have shown from the outset, Baker continuously distorts issues and unscrupulously overstates his case. Black American critics are not by any means the only scholars who question the usefulness of poststructuralist thinking and methodology. I refer Baker to Eugene Goodheart's *The Skeptic Disposition in Contemporary Criticism* and to Howard Felperin's *Beyond Deconstruction: The Uses and Abuses of Literary Theory*. Felperin writes:

[I]t is deeply ironic, to say the least, that the yearnings for a quasi- or pseudo-scientific discourse, which we have seen at work in all the dominant theoretical discourses, and which aim at attracting to themselves some of the supposed cultural prestige and centrality of science and technology—as a result of the disastrous side-effects of their long cultural hegemony—are themselves losing the prestige and centrality they have so long enjoyed. And it is no less ironic that the search for a quasi-scientific or theoretical "ground" in which the various schools hope to found their practice seems to turn up only an infinitely varied groundlessness.[11]

Of course, the most obvious weakness in Baker's and Gates's charges of my hostility to theory is the illogical position that to refuse to accept poststructuralist meaninglessness is to be resistant to theory. I must admit straightforwardly at this point that I question whether Baker and Gates really believe what they write. For instance, in *Blues, Ideology*, in which Baker revises the commonly cited "Generational Shifts and the Recent Criticism of Afro-American Literature," Baker says, "The negative results of reconstructionism include an unfortunate burdening of the universe of discourse surrounding Afro-American expressive culture with meaningless jargon and the articulation of a variety of lamentably confused utterances on language, literature, and culture" (90). This comment proves to be quite startling to any reader who even glances at the pages of *Blues, Ideology*. The entire collection is suffused with poststructuralist jargon in its use of words like *code, binary opposition, decentering, signifying, absence, intertextual*, and *difference*. Moreover, the strategy Baker employs throughout the volume heavily embodies—despite what he refers to as his "interdisciplinary" approach—a poststructuralist methodology. Obviously then, it is rather difficult to discern Baker's position toward Black literary criticism from what he says. We can depend only upon our analyses of the unmistakeable patterns that emerge.

I would like now to move to Gates's charge of my resistance to theory, and then end with my own theory on the merger between love and the Black literary critic. As I have already said, Gates too overstates his case to the point of being illogical. A glaring leap in logic accompanies the comment "I must confess that I am bewildered by Joyce Joyce's implied claim that to engage in black critical theory is to be, somehow, antiblack." Consistent with the air of superiority which pervades his "Critical Theory, Integrity, and the Black Idiom," Gates makes at least two errors in logic here. The first is to maintain that his mode of critical theory is Black critical theory and the other is to maintain that my objections to his analysis of Black literature suggest that he is antiblack. A significant difference exists between being "not" Black and being antiblack. Of course, the real issue, the one that Gates refuses to let surface, and I might add a very old one, concerns whether being a Black person who writes about Black literature makes one a Black critic, especially if blackness is a trope, as Gates would surely argue. He clearly understands that my answer to this question is an emphatic "No." Rather than grapple with this issue (that is almost as old as Black literature itself), Gates attempts to distort it. If we know that the idea of race divisions is ludicrous, then we understand that to refer to a craftswoman or man as a Black critic begins with, but extends *far* beyond (or beneath), skin color. For the Black writer/critic, blackness has always been—until very recently and except for the few exceptions that can always be expected—a matter of perspective, commitment, involvement, and love-bonding.

My argument, then, is not with Gates's "propensity to theorize," but with the nature of his theorizing. Although literary theory by nature is esoteric and thus removed from the mundane functions of our daily lives, a serious need for purpose underscores much of what is presently being published. My call in "The Black Canon" is not one that I cloaked behind terms such as "ontogeny" and "phylogeny," but one that questions this move of Black criticism away from transcendence and interiority and, consequently, purpose. Neither Gates nor Baker elaborates upon my point that a natural, integral relationship does exist between Euro-American literature—Eliot's and Stevens's poetry as well as Beckett's plays and Barth's fiction— and Euro-American critical theory. Among the most modern of the novels written by Black writers—works like *!Click Song, The Salt Eaters,* and *Tar Baby*—only Reed's relatively early *Mumbo Jumbo* shares a striking "decentering," "playful" affinity with Beckett and Barth. Stated again, poststructuralist methodology imposes a strategy upon Black literature from the outside while a direct relationship exists between Euro-American literature and its criticism. How can the extraneous, alien poststructuralist practices serve as the "prelude to the definition of principles of literary criticism peculiar to the black literary traditions"? What is the source of this relationship that makes Black literary traditions "related to and compatible with contemporary critical theory"? I have so far nowhere come across the answers to these questions.

Finally, Gates and Baker agree (since they are "ideal readers" for each other) that they are "spokespersons who move across ethnic and gender boundaries and who have decisively relinquished the role of simpleminded conservative spokespersons on behalf of a putatively simpleminded expressive culture." These embarrassing words imply that those Black literary critics who worked to provide what is now the foundation of Afro-American literary criticism and whose ideas have been subsumed and reshaped by Gates and Baker are simpleminded. These final comments water the seeds that I have planted throughout this essay: While Black American literature and its criticism are rooted in an allegiance to Black people, Baker and Gates have "relinquished" that allegiance. The first sign manifests itself in the hostile, warlike, ungracious nature of their responses to my essay. Although Baker goes so far as to suggest that Deborah McDowell should not have challenged him (the vanguard) in a "mixed" audience, he has, as we can deduce from his language, no hesitation in attempting to make me appear mindless and backwards in the eyes of white society. He himself brings up the issue of the readership of *New Literary History.* Both he and Gates broke the most important code of the signifying tradition: they failed to attack by subversion (to speak in such a way that the master does not grasp their meaning). They failed to demonstrate love and respect for a Black sister. They do not understand that Black political involvement can be achieved even in the ivory towers of academe as well as on the streets and that an interrelationship exists between the two. Political involvement, the commitment to struggle for the movement of Blacks into all strata of society, means that neither should have censured *New Literary History* for accepting the work of a Black sister. They should have been committed to strategies for revision rather than to the proliferation of their individual ideas and to the protection of their egos. As literary critics, they should have been committed to the future of a Black American criticism that gains its strengths through challenges and trials rather than through censorship and bravado.

This critical skirmish, I fear, shares a relationship with the fight that took place during one of this year's 1986 NBA Championship games. When Ralph Sampson, a Black player for the Houston Rockets, threw a few punches at white Celtics player Jerry Sichting, Dennis Johnson, a Black player for the Celtics, interceded and began to punch Sampson and pull on his jersey. What might be even more important than Johnson's reasons for exacerbating an already terrible situation is the picture that highlighted the event in *The Washington Post* the following day (June 6, 1986). The picture shows Dennis Johnson and Ralph Sampson—the two Blacks—scowling and perhaps even growling at each other ferociously. This photograph totally distorts the nature of the situation (the real issue) which caused the fight. Analogously, Baker and Gates not only distorted my ideas, but responded as if the ideas had no foundation in Black American literature, criticism, or history. Eugene Goodheart's comments on deconstructive play relates metaphorically to the analogy between Dennis Johnson, Baker, and Gates: "An overflowing play that expresses the fullness of life is the freedom beyond the rules of the game. When the conviction disappears the game ceases to be an occasion for personal expression, it becomes instead a mechanism to be disassembled and examined with detachment" (162). It is the power of language that we should depend upon in literary discourse to maintain a balance between play and game. If the game requires conviction and that we remain ever mindful of our interaction with others and of the effect language has on us, then the critic has the same responsibility in the literary game as the referee in an athletic competition. For the power of the critic's language has the same effect as the authority and integrity of the referee: to attempt to influence and interpret experience in a direction that leads to the brotherhood of man (as Bob Marley sings). And, of course, the cap of responsibility is all the heavier if the referee/critic is Black.

NOTES

1. Henry Louis Gates, Jr., "Writing 'Race' and the Difference It Makes," *Critical Inquiry*, 12, No. 1 (Autumn 1985), 4; hereafter cited in text.

2. Henry Louis Gates, Jr., "The 'Blackness of Blackness': A Critique of the Sign and the Signifying Monkey," in *Black Literature and Literary Theory* (New York, 1984), pp. 285–321, and "Preface to Blackness: Text and Pretext," in *Afro-American Literature: The Reconstruction of Instruction*, ed. Dexter Fisher and Robert B. Stepto (New York, 1979), pp. 44–69.

3. Larry Neal, "And Shine Swam On," in *Black Fire: An Anthology of Afro-American Writing*, ed. LeRoi Jones and Larry Neal (New York, 1968), pp. 654–56.

4. Anthony Appiah, "The Uncompleted Argument: Du Bois and the Illusion of Race," *Critical Inquiry*, 12, No. 1 (Autumn 1985), 31.

5. Sonia Sanchez, "The Poet as Creator of Social Values," in *Crises and Culture* (New York, 1983), pp. 1–4.

6. Eugene Goodheart, *The Skeptic Disposition in Contemporary Criticism* (Princeton, 1984), p. 175; hereafter cited in text.

7. Ellen Kuzwayo, *Call Me Woman* (London, 1985) and Bessie Head, *A Question of Power* (London, 1973).

8. Henry Louis Gates, Jr., *Black Literature and Theory* (New York, 1984).

9. Houston A. Baker, Jr., *Blues, Ideology, and Afro-American Literature: A Vernacular Theory* (Chicago, 1984), p. 200; hereafter cited in text.

10. Audre Lorde, "The Master's Tools Will Never Dismantle the Master's House," in her *Sister Outsider: Essays and Speeches by Audre Lorde* (Trumansburg, N.Y., 1984), pp. 110–13.

11. Howard Felperin, *Beyond Deconstruction: The Uses and Abuses of Literary Theory* (Oxford, 1985), pp. 203–4.

30 Appropriative Gestures

Theory and Afro-American Literary Criticism

Michael Awkward

(1988)

Barbara Christian's "The Race for Theory" leaves no doubt in the mind of its readers that the esteemed black feminist critic is—in the words of the controversial Steven Knapp and Walter Benn Michaels essay—against theory. Christian's reaction to theory, however, differs from that of Knapp and Michaels, who seek to discredit theory by discussing what they argue are its fallacious oppositions—meaning/intent, knowledge/belief. She also differs from Afro-American critic Joyce Joyce, who discusses what she views as the ideologically deficient theoretical practice of several black critics in order to demonstrate an incompatibility between practical Afrocentric criticism and contemporary literary theory.[1] For Christian neither systematically attacks what she believes are the inadequacies of its most basic tenets nor attempts to address in specific ways what she holds are the flawed critical practices of Afro-Americanist uses of theory. Instead, Christian asserts that theory is a putatively radical enterprise which has done little to change the status quo or advance our comprehension of the processes of literary production, and that its ideologically radical practitioners have been "co-opted into speaking a language and defining their discussion in terms alien to and opposed to our needs and orientation."

The particulars of Christian's attacks on theory certainly are not original, nor are they, I believe, particularly persuasive. By condemning the discourse of literary theory, calling those who employ theoretical paradigms "critic[s] yearning for attention," and implying that literary theory has gained a significant hold on our attention primarily because "so much of the literature of the West has become pallid, laden with despair, self-indulgent and disconnected," Christian rehearses old arguments which, frankly, I am not interested in addressing. I am aware of no evidence which convincingly suggests that today's literary critics are, as a group, any more egotistical than their predecessors, or that figurations of despair historically have proven any less analytically provocative than those of any other psychological/emotional state.

331

What I am interested in exploring—and arguing against—are Christian's specific reasons for viewing as counterproductive the theoretical practice of black feminist criticism and other non-hegemonic—non-white male—schools of literary analysis. For I believe that the strategies of reading which she deplores offer the Afrocentric critic a means of more fully and adequately decoding the black literary text and canon than what the critic Daniel O'Hara might call the "fly-by-the-seat-of-one's-pants"[2] approach Christian advances at the end of her essay as a corrective to "the race for theory."

Christian characterizes her own critical practice as an effort to save the emerging, under-appreciated Afro-American woman's text from the types of critical marginality and canonical oblivion that had previously been the fate of early-and-mid-twentieth century products of black female imaginations. Clearly, Christian's preservatory impulses are commendable and historically well founded. Despite the inroads some Afro-American women's texts have made in small areas in the canon, black women's literature still does not assume the prominent place in courses and criticism that those who devote a great deal of scholarly attention to it feel it merits. I do not, then, object to the tenets which inform Christian's critical practice, nor do I feel that it is correct to dismiss out of hand the works of those scholars in the field which are not obviously informed by post-structuralist theories. The types of re-readings of neglected black women's texts and "first readings" of new works to which Christian has devoted herself can be, when performed in the energetic manner with which she approaches her work, quite helpful to our understanding of what she has called "the development of the tradition" of black women's literature. What I do object to where Christian's discussion of Afro-American critical engagement of literary theory is concerned is her consistent refusal to acknowledge that its employment by several clearly Afrocentric critics has indeed deepened our received knowledge of the textual production of black writers.

Christian sees literary theory as a coercive hegemonic force which has begun to poison the discourse of "some of our most daring and potentially radical critics (and by *our* I mean black, women, Third World)" whose adoption of post-structuralist modes of reading suggests that they "have been influenced, even co-opted" by a hegemonic critical discourse. While here, as at most points in her essay, she is unwilling to name victims or villains, Christian suggests that, as an enterprise, literary theory has corrupted a previously methodologically sound black feminist criticism, forcing its practitioners either into silence or into the defensive postures of black female natives invaded by an alien, white, phallocentric critical discourse that they employ against their will and better judgment. While the imagery she uses resonates with historically significant indignation—the black female critic as pure Afrocentric maiden corrupted by an institutionally all-powerful white male post-structuralist theory—Christian's representation of theoretically informed black female (and other non-caucasian and/or male) critics as "co-opted" can only be read as an attack on their personal integrity and recent work. She apparently cannot even conceive of the possibility that these critics choose to employ theory because they believe it offers provocative means of discussing the texts of non-hegemonic groups, that theory indeed is viewed by them as useful in the critical analysis of the literary products of "the other."

Further, Christian's "resistance to theory" leads her to overstate her claims about a purely descriptive, non-theoretical stage of black feminist criticism. One of its earlier and most eloquent statements, Barbara Smith's groundbreaking essay "Toward a Black Feminist Criticism," is essentially a theoretical—if not post-structuralist— discussion of critical practice and textual production. In this much-anthologized essay, Smith—like all theorists—prescriptively asserts what she believes ought to be the informing principles of the critics she wants to persuade. She defines the limits of the black feminist interpretive project, telling aspiring black feminist critics how Afro-American women's texts ought to be read and suggesting what sorts of findings such readings ought to uncover. Smith says: "Beginning with a primary commitment to exploring how both sexual and racial politics and Black and female identity are inextricable elements in Black women's writings, she would also work from the assumption that Black women writers constitute an identifiable literary tradition. . . . [S]he would think and write out of her own identity and not try to graft the ideas or methodology of white/male literary thought upon the precise materials of Black women's art" (pp. 174–5).

While post-structuralist theorists might intervene here and censure Smith's over-determined collision of biology and ideology—Smith assumes that the black feminist critic will necessarily be a black woman, that whites and black men are incapable of offering the types of analyses she advocates because they "are of course ill-equipped to deal [simultaneously] with the subtleties of racial [and sexual] politics" (p. 170)[3]— it is in her move from theory to practice that contemporary critical theory could be most helpful to her project. For Smith problematically believes that her (now generally accepted) theoretical suggestions—that one analyze in black women's texts figurations of the relationships between race, gender and class, as well as demonstrate the contours of the black woman's literary tradition—will lead necessarily to critical acts such as her still-controversial reading of Toni Morrison's *Sula* as a lesbian novel. Unlike Deborah McDowell, who in "New Directions for Black Feminist Criticism" argues that the problems with Smith's analysis result from a lack of a precise definition of the term "lesbian" and from the fact that Smith's " 'innovative' analysis is pressed to the service of an individual political persuasion" (p. 190), I feel that the problems with Smith's critical manuevers lie in her lack of awareness of the contemporary literary theories that Christian devalues. Combined with her own convincingly articulated black feminist approach, an engagement of reader-response theory and theories about the textual construction of gendered/ideological readers might have led Smith to be even more innovative. Rather than arguing that Morrison's is a black lesbian text (a reading to which Morrison herself forcefully objected in a recent interview),[4] she might instead have offered a theory of a black lesbian reader. Rather than involving herself needlessly and unprofitably in discussions of authorial intent,[5] Smith might have focused on the (effects on the reader) of *Sula's* clear and consistent critique of heterosexual institutions, on the text's progressive "lesbianization" of the reader. Whether Morrison intends this is, to a certain extent, beside the point; the point of Smith's theorizing is that such a process does—or at least can—indeed occur as a necessary function of careful, ideologically informed reading of Morrison's novel. The problem with the move from practical theory to theoretical practice in "Toward a Black Feminist Criticism" is not, as Christian's perspectives suggest, Smith's attempt to "overgeneralize," to theorize, about the process of reading, but her insufficient awareness of advances in reader-response theory that would have allowed her to discuss in a more convincing manner her perceptions of the effects of reading Morrison's novel.

My own intent here is not to discredit Smith's essay, which I believe remains the most influential work in the area of black feminist criticism. Rather, it is to suggest the misconceptions that mar Christian's three most forcefully articulated arguments against a black feminist engagement of literary theory: 1) that black feminist criticism and literary theory are essentially incompatible enterprises; 2) that post-structuralism is the cause of (premature) attempts at black feminist literary theory; and 3) that black feminist literary theory has not—and should not have—emerged before the practice of reading black women's texts is more firmly established. Clearly, Smith's essay—and its careful analysis—serves to challenge the general applicability to black feminist criticism of Christian's suppositions. For Smith's 1977 essay (reprinted in 1985) (however problematically) theorizes despite its lack of a clearly informed awareness of deconstruction, reader-response theory, semiotics, or any of what Smith terms "the ideas or methodology of white/male literary thought," and does so while bemoaning the paucity of black feminist critical acts. Despite an obviously antagonistic relationship to white/male hegemony, Smith believes, like the villainous post-structuralist theorists of Christian's essay, that she can offer a prescription, a theory, of how most profitably to read literary texts.

Unlike Smith, Christian is concerned primarily not with theorizing about profitable means by which to approach Afro-American women's literature, but with "help[ing to] ensure that [the black woman's literary] tradition has continuity and survives" by offering "first readings" of new works by Afro-American women. As a consequence, she perceives as quite problematic the insistence that black feminist critics devise theoretical ways of approaching the Afro-American woman's literary tradition. She says:

> Some of us are continually harassed to invent wholesale theories regardless of the complexity of the literature we study. I, for one, am tired of being asked to produce a black feminist literary theory as if I were a mechanical man. For I believe such theory is prescriptive—it ought to have some relationship to practice. Since I can count on one hand the number of people attempting to be black feminist literary critics in the world today, I consider it presumptuous of me to invent a theory of how we ought to read.

Certainly Christian's anger is justified if, as she suggests, the requests she has received to offer theoretical models adequate to a discussion of black women's literature have indeed taken the form of intellectual harassment. But she can argue that critical practice in the last fifteen years has not adequately prepared the way for new theories of black women's textual production only by being as restrictive in her definition of "black feminist literary critics" as she accuses feminist literary theorists of being when they define the term "feminist." (Are black feminist critics only black women? If so, they number much more than a handful. Can a gendered and/or racial other learn the ideology, speak the discourse, of "black feminist literary critics"? If not, how should we label such essential works on black women writers as Robert Hemenway's biography of Zora Neale Hurston, Barbara Johnson's essays on Hurston, Calvin Hernton's *The Sexual Mountain and Black Women Writers?*) A multitude of readings—by black and white women and men—have appeared in journals, collections of essays, and books that analyze black women's texts in terms of "the intricacies of the intersection of language, class, race, and gender," enough at least to suggest to Christian, as it has to other black female critics, that black feminist criticism has reached an appropriate time in its history to begin theorizing about its practice and the literary production of Afro-American woman writers.

In *The Resistance to Theory*, Paul de Man suggests:

> Literary theory can be said to come into being when the approach to literary texts is no longer based on non-linguistic, that is to say historical and aesthetic, considerations or, to put it somewhat less crudely, when the object of discussion is no longer the meaning or the value but the modalities of production and of reception of meaning and of value prior to their establishment. (P. 7)

I believe that the time has indeed arrived for the black feminist critical move beyond simply "non-linguistic" analyses of the texts of black women writers. As illuminating as a Barbara Christian "first reading" of Toni Morrison's *Beloved* or of new works by Gloria Naylor, Paule Marshall, Alice Walker, Ntozake Shange and Toni Cade Bambara would undoubtedly prove, such readings will do little to insure the survival of the black women's literary tradition. I firmly believe that the tradition's critical establishment has in the past required, and still requires, such self-consciously preservatory acts. But if the literature of black women is to continue to make inroads in the canon, if it is to gain the respect it doubtlessly deserves as an ideologically and aesthetically complex, analytically rich literary tradition within an increasingly theoretical academy, it will require that its critics continue to move beyond description and master the discourse of contemporary literary theory.

I do not mean that Christian must herself undergo a miraculous change in perspective and become a Derridean, Foucauldian or Barthesian post-structuralist critic. I do believe, however, that literary theory provides Afro-Americans and other non-hegemonic groups with a means by which to begin to offer other, currently even more essential, types of responses: text-specific theories of the modalities of black textual production. Whatever the strictly personal or specifically "tribal" uses to which members of oppressed groups put their writers' texts, I believe it is the literary critic's responsibility—whenever he or she acts in the role of critic—to discuss such works in as full, complex, and sophisticated ways as possible. Henry Louis Gates states his view of this responsibility in the following way:

This is the challenge of the critic of black literature in the 1980s: not to shy away from literary theory; rather, to translate it into the black idiom, *renaming* principles of criticism where appropriate, but especially *naming* indigenous black principles of criticism and applying these to explicate our own texts. It is incumbent upon us to protect the integrity of our tradition by bringing to bear upon its criticism any tool of sensitivity to language that is appropriate . . . *any* tool that enables the critic to explain the complex workings of the language of a text. (*Figures in Black*, p. xxi)[6]

Zora Neale Hurston has argued that the Afro-American is an "appropriative" creature, that "while he lives and moves in the midst of a white civilization, everything he touches is re-interpreted for his own use" (p. 28). Certainly one of the means by which Afro-Americans have, in Christian's words, "managed to survive with such spiritedness the assault on our bodies, social institutions, countries, our very humanity" has been by successfully appropriating putatively superior Western cultural and expressive systems—Christianity, the English language, Western literary genres—and transferring them into forms through which we expressed our culturally distinct black souls. It is this history that suggests that we need not stand before even the most apparently obscure literary theories as silenced, confused, and discursively "blocked" victims of recent developments in the study of literary texts. Literary theory is, despite its origins and white androcentric uses to which it has generally been put, a tool that Afro-American critics can—and have begun to—successfully employ in explications of our own traditions' texts and intertexts. To continue to assert, despite its wonderfully provocative and useful employment by figures such as Gates, Hortense Spillers, Houston Baker, and Mary Helen Washington, that literary theory cannot serve the best, blackest interests of our literary tradition is to devalue in significant ways these critics' recent contributions to our understanding of black textual production. Such critics have demonstrated irrefutably that theory can be appropriated in ways that will allow us to continue to further our comprehension of Afro-American texts, and to insure both their survival and their impact.

NOTES

1. See Knapp and Michaels 1985, and Joyce 1987.
2. In Mitchell 1985: 37
3. For a fuller discussion of this collision of biology and ideology in black feminist criticism, see my 1988 essay 'Race, gender, and the politics of reading.'
4. In her interview collected in Tate 1983, Morrison asserts—obviously with Smith's comments in mind: "Nobody ever talked about friendship between women unless it was homosexual, and there is no homosexuality in *Sula*" (p. 118).
5. The problems with Smith's discussion of *Sula* are most glaringly manifested in her attempts to distinguish between textual meaning and authorial intent. She argues that despite the novel's "consistently critical stance toward the heterosexual institutions of male-female relationships, marriage, and the family" (p. 175), Morrison's failure to "approach . . . her

subject with the consciousness that a lesbian relationship was at least a possibility for her characters" results from the novelist's overdetermined "heterosexual assumptions [that] can veil what may logically be expected to occur in a work" (p. 181).

    6. Gates 1987.

REFERENCES

Awkward, Michael 1988. "Race, gender, and the politics of reading," *Black American Literature Forum* 22:1:5–27.

Baker, Houston A., Jr. 1980. *The Journey Back*. Chicago: University of Chicago Press.

Baker, Houston A., Jr. 1984. *Blues, Ideology, and Afro-American Literature*. Chicago: University of Chicago Press.

Christian, Barbara. "The race for theory," chapter 25 in this volume.

Gates, Henry Louis, Jr. (ed.) 1984. *Black Literature and Literary Theory*. New York: Methuen.

Gates, Henry Louis, Jr. 1987. *Figures in Black*. New York: Oxford University Press.

Gates, Henry Louis, Jr. 1987. " 'What's love got to do with it?' Critical theory, integrity; and the black idiom," *New Literary History* 18:2 (Winter): 345–62.

Hemenway, Robert 1977. *Zora Neale Hurston: A Literary Biography*. Urbana: University of Illinois Press.

Hernton, Calvin 1987. *The Sexual Mountain and Black Women Writers*. New York: Doubleday.

Hurston, Zora Neale 1934. "Characteristics of negro expression," in *Negro: An Anthology*, ed. Nancy Cunard. Repr. London: Negro University Press, 1969: 24–31.

Johnson, Barbara 1984. "Metaphor, metonymy and voice in *Their Eyes Were Watching God*," in Gates 1987: 205–19.

Johnson, Barbara 1986. "Thresholds of difference: structures of address in Zora Neale Hurston," *"Race," Writing, and Difference*, ed. Henry Louis Gates. Chicago: University of Chicago Press.

Joyce, Joyce A. 1987. "The black canon: Reconstructing black American literary criticism," *New Literary History* 18.2:335–44.

Knapp, Steven and Michaels, Walter Benn 1985. "Against theory," in Mitchell 1985: 11–30.

McDowell, Deborah 1987. " 'The Changing Same': Generational connections and black women novelists," *New Literary History* 18.2:281–302.

McDowell, Deborah 1985. "New directions for black feminist criticism," in *The New Feminist Criticism*, ed. Elaine Showalter. New York: Pantheon: 186–99.

Man, Paul de 1986. *The Resistance to Theory*. Minneapolis: Minnesota University Press.

Mitchell, W. J. T. (ed.) 1985. *Against Theory: Literary Studies and the New Pragmatism*. Chicago: University of Chicago Press.

Morrison, Toni 1974. *Sula*. New York: Knopf.

Morrison, Toni 1987. *Beloved*. New York: Knopf.

O'Hara, Daniel 1985 "Revisionary madness: The prospects of American literary theory at the present time," in Mitchell 1985: 31–47.

Smith, Barbara 1985. "Toward a black feminist criticism," in *The New Feminist Criticism*, ed. Elaine Showalter. New York: Pantheon: 168–85.

Spillers, Hortense 1985. "Cross-currents, discontinuities: black women's fiction," in *Conjuring:*

Black Women, Fiction, and Literary Tradition, ed. Marjorie Pryse and Spillers. Bloomington: Indiana University Press: 249–61.

Tate, Claudia (ed.) 1983. *Black Women Writers at Work*. New York: Continuum.

Washington, Mary Helen 1984. " 'Taming all that anger down': Rage and silence in Gwendolyn Brooks's *Maud Martha*," in Gates 1984: 249–62.

31 | Introduction to *The Signifying Monkey: A Theory of Afro-American Literary Criticism*

Henry Louis Gates, Jr.

(1988)

I

Black English vernacular, according to William Labov's three-year National Science Foundation study released in 1985, "is a healthy, living form of language," one which "shows the signs of people developing their own grammar" and one which manifests various linguistic signs of "separate development." Labov's extensive research leads him to conclude that "There is evidence that, far from getting more similar [to standard English], the black vernacular is going its own way." The black vernacular, he continues, "is reflecting [a larger social] picture [of segregated speech communities]. The blacks' own grammar, which is very rich and complicated, is developing its own way. It looks as if new things are happening in black grammar." The black vernacular, in other words, is thriving despite predictions during the civil rights era that it would soon be a necessary casualty of school desegregation and the larger socioeconomic integration of black people into mainstream American institutions. Because de facto segregation of black and white schoolchildren has replaced de jure segregation, and because black unemployment in 1988 is much higher than it was in 1968, it is impossible for us to determine if black vernacular English would have disappeared under certain ideal social conditions. It has not, however, disappeared; as Labov's study shows, the black vernacular has assumed the singular role as the black person's ultimate sign of difference, a blackness of the tongue. It is in the vernacular that, since slavery, the black person has encoded private yet communal cultural rituals.

The Signifying Monkey explores the relation of the black vernacular tradition to the Afro-American literary tradition. The book attempts to identify a theory of criticism that is inscribed within the black vernacular tradition and that in turn informs the shape of the Afro-American literary tradition. My desire has been to allow the black tradition to speak for itself about its nature and various functions, rather than to read it, or analyze it, in terms of literary theories borrowed whole from other traditions, appropriated from without. While this latter mode of literary analysis can be a revealing and rewarding exercise, each literary tradition, at least implicitly, contains within it an argument for how it can be read. It is one such implicit argument or theory about the black tradition that I wish to discuss in this book.

At a time when the study of literature is characterized by what many scholars feel to be an undue concern with literary theory, why bother to elaborate more theory, risking further distance from the primary texts that should be, indeed must be, the critic's primary concern? This question is not idle, because theorizing can take us rather far afield from the literature that a tradition comprises. Theory can serve to mystify what strike some readers as fairly straightforward matters of taste and application, of representation and reference, of denotation and meaning. I have tried to define a theory of Afro-American criticism not to mystify black literature, or to obscure its several delightful modes of creating meaning, but to begin to suggest how richly textured and layered that black literary artistry indeed is. By discussing explicitly that which is implicit in what we might think of as the logic of the tradition, I hope to enhance the reader's experience of black texts by identifying levels of meaning and expression that might otherwise remain mediated, or buried beneath the surface. If anything, my desire here has been to demystify the curious notion that theory is the province of the Western tradition, something alien or removed from a so-called noncanonical tradition such as that of the Afro-American.

I have also taken to heart Paulin J. Hountondji's perceptive admonition that "if theoretical discourse is to be meaningful in modern Africa, it must promote within African society itself a theoretical debate of its own that is capable of developing its themes and problems autonomously instead of remaining a remote appendix to European theoretical and scientific debates." The same caution about the uses and abuses of critical discourse in philosophy applies to literature. Our goal must not be to embed, as it were, Europe within Africa or Africa within Europe, which Anthony Appiah has called "the Naipaul fallacy": "the post-colonial legacy which requires us to show that African literature is worthy of study precisely (but only) because it is fundamentally the same as European literature." Nor, Appiah continues, does African literature need "justification" to Western readers in order to overcome their tendency to ignore it. Moreover, the turn to theory is not intended, as Hountondji rightly says, "to prove that blacks could sometimes be as intelligent, moral and artistic as whites," or "to persuade people that blacks can be good philosophers too," or to "try to win certificates of humanity from whites or to display the splendours of African civilizations to them." Rather, I have written this book to analyze a theory of reading that is there, that has been generated from within the black tradition itself, autonomously. At the very least, certainly, theoretical traditions are related by analogy, but it seemed to me that an ideal way to confound a Eurocentric bias in this project was to explore the black vernacular.

To do so, I have turned to two signal trickster figures, Esu-Elegbara and the

Signifying Monkey, in whose myths are registered certain principles of both formal language use and its interpretation. These two separate but related trickster figures serve in their respective traditions as points of conscious articulation of language traditions aware of themselves as traditions, complete with a history, patterns of development and revision, and internal principles of patterning and organization. Theirs is a meta-discourse, a discourse about itself. These admittedly complex matters are addressed, in the black tradition, in the vernacular, far away from the eyes and ears of outsiders, those who do not speak the language of tradition. While I shall suggest reasons for this penchant of the black tradition to theorize about itself in the vernacular, it should be apparent that this protective tendency is not generally re-marked upon in studies of the literary theory of sustained literate traditions such as the European or American. My attempt to disclose the closed black vernacular tradition is meant to enrich the reader's experience of reference and representation, of connotation and denotation, of truth and understanding, as these configure in the black formal literary traditions and in the antics of two tricksters found in black myths.

At first glance, these two tricksters would seem to have little in common. Esu, both a trickster and the messenger of the gods, figures prominently in the mythologies of Yoruba cultures found in Nigeria, Benin, Brazil, Cuba, and Haiti, among others. The Signifying Monkey, it seems, is distinctly Afro-American. Nevertheless, the central place of both figures in their traditions is determined by their curious tendency to reflect on the uses of formal language. The theory of Signifyin(g) arises from these moments of self-reflexiveness.

Whereas Esu serves as a figure for the nature and function of interpretation and double-voiced utterance, the Signifying Monkey serves as the figure-of-figures, as the trope in which are encoded several other peculiarly black rhetorical tropes. While both tricksters stand for certain principles of verbal expression, I am concerned to explore the place each accords forms of language use in the production of meaning in literature. I am equally concerned to demonstrate that the Monkey's language of Signifyin(g) functions as a metaphor for formal revision, or intertextuality, within the Afro-American literary tradition. Finally, I attempt to show through their functional equivalency that the two figures are related historically and are distinct aspects of a larger, unified phenomenon. Together, the two tricksters articulate the black tradi-tion's theory of its literature.

This book is not an attempt to chart through practical criticism the precise rela-tions that obtain among our canonical texts. That sort of detailed account most properly should occupy a book of its own, as a sequel to this book of theory. To illustrate my initial three theoretical chapters, however, I have selected a fair sample of canonical texts to read closely. Four chapters of close readings follow, then, to explain different modes of Signifyin(g) revisions at work in the Afro-American liter-ary tradition. I make no claim for inclusiveness in the selection of these texts; rather, they were settled on primarily for the range of concerns they demonstrate about this book's theoretical assumptions. My triangles of influence and my tracings of the intricacies of metaphors of voice from antecedent text to revised text are illustrative;

other texts could just as easily have been chosen. Rather than a selective history of Afro-American literature, then, *The Signifying Monkey* is an attempt to arrive at a theory of this tradition. Precisely because I could have selected numerous other texts as exempla, I hope to draw on the premises of this book to write a detailed account of the Afro-American literary tradition. *The Signifying Monkey* is a theoretical prologue to that work.

A vernacular tradition's relation to a formal literary tradition is that of a parallel discursive universe. By explicating two seemingly distinct bodies of myths, one common to several black traditions and the other an American phenomenon, I have tried to show how the vernacular informs and becomes the foundation for formal black literature. While the history of the criticism of black texts is a subject of considerable interest to me, a truly indigenous black literary criticism is to be found in the vernacular. What's more, I believe that black writers, both explicitly and implicitly, turn to the vernacular in various formal ways to inform their creation of written fictions. To do so, it seems to me, is to ground one's literary practice outside the Western tradition. Whereas black writers most certainly revise texts in the Western tradition, they often seek to do so "authentically," with a black difference, a compelling sense of difference based on the black vernacular.

Black writers also read each other, and seem intent on refiguring what we might think of as key canonical topoi and tropes received from the black tradition itself. The editors of *The Negro Caravan*—Sterling A. Brown, Arthur P. Davis, and Ulysses Lee—noted this fact as early as 1941, when discussing the formal relation of Frances E. W. Harper's novel, *Iola Leroy* (1892), to William Wells Brown's novel, *Clotel* (1853): "There are repetitions of situations from Brown's *Clotel*, something of a forecast of a sort of literary inbreeding which causes Negro writers to be influenced by other Negroes more than should ordinarily be expected." Regardless of what should obtain in a tradition, by 1941 it was apparent to these seminal scholars that black writers read, repeated, imitated, and revised each other's texts to a remarkable extent. This web of filiation makes theorizing about black principles of interpretation and revision an obvious project for critics who have undertaken close readings of black canonical texts. This I attempt to do in *The Signifying Monkey*.

It is probably true that critics of African and Afro-American literature were trained to think of the institution of literature essentially as a set of Western texts. The methods devised to read these texts are culture-specific and temporal-specific, and they are text-specific as well. We learn to read the text at hand. And texts have a curious habit of generating other texts that resemble themselves.

Black writers, like critics of black literature, learn to write by reading literature, especially the canonical texts of the Western tradition. Consequently, black texts resemble other, Western texts. These black texts employ many of the conventions of literacy form that comprise the Western tradition. Black literature shares much with, far more than it differs from, the Western textual tradition, primarily as registered in English, Spanish, Portuguese, and French. But black formal repetition always repeats with a difference, a black difference that manifests itself in specific language use. And the repository that contains the language that is the source—and the reflection—of black difference is the black English vernacular tradition.

A novelist such as Ralph Ellison or Ishmael Reed creates texts that are double-voiced in the sense that their literary antecedents are both white and black novels, but also modes of figuration lifted from the black vernacular tradition. One can readily agree with Susan Willis that black texts are "mulattoes" (or "mulatas"), with a two-toned heritage: these texts speak in standard Romance or Germanic languages and literary structures, but almost always speak with a distinct and resonant accent, an accent that Signifies (upon) the various black vernacular literary traditions, which are still being written down. To locate, and then to theorize about, this formal difference is to utilize certain tools of close reading that facilitate explication. It is also to explain what we might think of as the discrete black difference, and to reveal its workings. It is not to be expected that we shall reinvent literature; nor shall we reinvent criticism. We shall, however, have to name the discrete seemingly disparate elements that compose the structures of which our vernacular literary traditions consist.

The black tradition has theorized about itself, explicitly. Melville Herskovits was quick to point out that the Fon of Dahomey named and could specify their philosophical system; he did not need to read into its parts metaphorical meanings analogous to Western philosophy. The tradition named its own assumptions. "[In] no sense," Herskovits contends, is the metaphysical system of the Fon "to be regarded as a kind of synthesis arrived at by the ethnographer from however implicit manifestations of the religious life he has observed in the field." Rather, the Fon themselves are characterized by "long and considered speculation," by "the systematisation of belief," by "the development of a complex philosophy of the Universe." Moreover, Herskovits concludes, "The upper-class Dahomean does not need to restrict himself to describing concrete instances when discussing the larger concepts underlying his everyday religious practice; he is not at a loss when questioned of the nature of the world as a whole, or abstract principles such as justice, or destiny, or accident are asked him." For the Yoruba, the several myths of Esu stand as the tradition's repository of its own theory of interpretation. The Fon, once removed from the Yoruba antecedent, even more extensively employ the figure of writing to name the nature and function of interpretation, of both secular and sacred interpretation.

Naming the black tradition's own theory of itself is to echo and rename other theories of literary criticism. Our task is not to reinvent our traditions as if they bore no relation to that tradition created and borne, in the main, by white men. Our writers used that impressive tradition to define themselves, both with and against their concept of received order. We must do the same, with or against the Western critical canon. To name our tradition is to rename each of its antecedents, no matter how pale they might seem. To rename is to revise, and to revise is to Signify.

The black tradition has inscribed within it the very principles by which it can be read. Ours is an extraordinarily self-reflexive tradition, a tradition exceptionally conscious of its history and of the simultaneity of its canonical texts, which tend to be taken as verbal models of the Afro-American social condition, to be revised. Because of the experience of diaspora, the fragments that contain the traces of a coherent system of order must be reassembled. These fragments embody aspects of a theory of critical principles around which the discrete texts of the tradition configure, in the critic's reading of the textual past. To reassemble fragments, of course, is to engage in an act of speculation, to attempt to weave a fiction of origins and subgeneration. It is to render the implicit as explicit, and at times to imagine the whole from the part.

Literary theory has rarely been as widely discussed in literature departments as it is today. Like every other critic of black literature, I have been trained to read using one or several of the generally accepted theories of criticism. In my first book of criticism, *Figures in Black: Words, Signs, and the "Racial" Self*, I sought to chart one noncanonical critic's experiments with these theories of criticism, which I drew on to read black texts, as if on safari through the jungle of criticism. This gesture has been crucial to the development of my thinking about the "proper work" for a black criticism: to define itself with—and against—other theoretical activities. While this sort of criticism has helped to demonstrate that distinct literary canons need not necessarily segregate critics—indeed, that shared critical approaches can define a canon of criticism—I believe it necessary to draw on the black tradition itself to define a theory of its nature and function.

Whereas various poststructural theories provide points of departure for the chapters of *Figures in Black*, in this book they surface primarily as analogies. Analogies, of course, serve to suggest moments of similarity, identity, and even difference within a shared framework of presupposition. My use of this sort of analogy is designed to show the many-faceted nature of contemporary criticism, and not to suggest limitations or lucunae in black theory. While I delight in the sense of difference that our literary tradition yields upon careful explication, I also delight in the sense of similarity that discrete literary traditions yield in comparative literary criticism. Anyone who analyzes black literature must do so as a comparativist, by definition, because our canonical texts have complex double formal antecedents, the Western and the black.

Free of the white person's gaze, black people created their own unique vernacular structures and relished in the double play that these forms bore to white forms. Repetition and revision are fundamental to black artistic forms, from painting and sculpture to music and language use. I decided to analyze the nature and function of Signifyin(g) precisely because it *is* repetition and revision, or repetition with a signal difference. Whatever is black about black American literature is to be found in this identifiable black Signifyin(g) difference. That, most succinctly if ambiguously, describes the premise of this book. Lest this theory of criticism, however, be thought of as only black, let me admit that the implicit premise of this study is that all texts Signify upon other texts, in motivated and unmotivated ways. Perhaps critics of other literatures will find this theory useful as they attempt to account for the configuration of the texts in their traditions. Comparative literature, ultimately, embraces a vastly richer field than the study of French, German, and English literature, no matter how fertile these fields admittedly are. That the myths of black slaves and ex-slaves embody theories of their own status within a tradition is only one of the more striking instances of what Ralph Ellison calls the "complexity" of the Negro's existence in Western culture.

II

The black tradition is double-voiced. The trope of the Talking Book, of double-voiced texts that talk to other texts, is the unifying metaphor within this book. Signifyin(g) is the figure of the double-voiced, epitomized by Esu's depictions in sculpture as possessing two mouths. There are four sorts of double-voiced textual relations that I wish to define.

TROPOLOGICAL REVISION

By tropological revision I mean the manner in which a specific trope is repeated, with differences, between two or more texts. The revision of specific tropes recurs with surprising frequency in the Afro-American literary tradition. The descent underground, the vertical "ascent" from South to North, myriad figures of the double, and especially double consciousness all come readily to mind. But there are other tropes that would seem to preoccupy the texts of the black tradition. The first trope shared in the black narrative tradition is what I shall call the Talking Book. This compelling trope appears in James Gronniosaw's 1770 slave narrative, and then is revised in at least four other texts published between 1785 and 1815. We might think of this as the ur-trope of the tradition. The form that repetition and difference take among these texts is the first example of Signifyin(g) as repetition and difference in the Anglo-African narrative tradition.

THE SPEAKERLY TEXT

The second mode of Signifyin(g) that I have chosen to represent in this text is exemplified in the peculiar play of "voices" at work in the use of "free indirect discourse" in Zora Neale Hurstson's *Their Eyes Were Watching God*. Above all else, Hurston's narrative strategy seems to concern itself with the possibilities of representation of the speaking black voice in writing. Hurston's text, I shall claim, seems to aspire to the status of what she and, later, Ishmael Reed call the Talking Book. It is striking that this figure echoes the first figure repeated and revised in the tradition. Hurston's use is remarkably complex, and accomplished. Free indirect discourse is represented in this canonical text as if it were a dynamic character, with shifts in its level of diction drawn upon to reflect a certain development of self-consciousness in a hybrid character, a character who is neither the novel's protagonist nor the text's disembodied narrator, but a blend of both, an emergent and merging moment of consciousness. The direct discourse of the novel's black speech community and the initial standard English of the narrator come together to form a third term, a truly double-voiced narrative mode. That element of narration that the Russian Formalists called *skaz*—when a text seems to be aspiring to the status of oral narration—is most clearly the closest analogue of Hurston's rhetorical strategy. The attendant ramifications of this device upon received modes of mimesis and diegesis occupy my attention in this chapter. Finally, I shall use Hurston's own theory of Signifyin(g) to analyze her narrative strategy, including the identification of Signifyin(g) rituals in the body of her text.

TALKING TEXTS

Chapter 5 explores one instance of a black form of intertextuality. Within the limits of the metaphor of the double-voiced that I am tracing from Esu-Elegbara to Alice Walker's novel *The Color Purple*, I have chosen to explicate Reed's novel *Mumbo Jumbo* to show how black texts "talk" to other black texts. Since *Mumbo Jumbo* would seem to be a signal text of revision and critique, cast in a so-called postmodern narrative, the implicit relation among modernism, realism, and postmodernism comes to bear here in the texts of *Invisible Man, Native Son, Black Boy*, and *Mumbo Jumbo*. Again, the relation of mimesis to diegesis shall occupy my attention in *Mumbo Jumbo*'s foregrounded double voices.

REWARDING THE SPEAKERLY

If Hurston's novel seems to have been designed to declare that, indeed, a text could be written in black dialect, then it seems to me that Walker's *The Color Purple* aims to do just that, as a direct revision of Hurston's explicit and implicit strategies of narration. Walker, whose preoccupation with Hurston as a deeply admired antecedent has been the subject of several of her critical comments, revises and echoes Hurston in a number of ways. Her use of the epistolary form to write a novel in the language seemingly spoken by Hurston's protagonist is perhaps the most stunning instance of revision in the tradition of the black novel. Here, let me introduce a distinction: Reed's use of parody would seem to be fittingly described as motivated Signifyin(g), in which the text Signifies upon other black texts, in the manner of the vernacular ritual of "close reading." Walker's use of pastiche, on the other hand, corresponds to unmotivated Signifyin(g), by which I mean to suggest not the absence of a profound intention but the absence of a negative critique. The relation between parody and pastiche is that between motivated and unmotivated Signifyin(g).

Whereas Reed seems to be about the clearing of a space of narration, Walker seems to be intent on underscoring the relation of her text to Hurston's, in a joyous proclamation of antecedent and descendant texts. The most salient analogue for this unmotivated mode of revision in the broader black cultural tradition might be that between black jazz musicians who perform each other's standards on a joint album, not to critique these but to engage in refiguration as an act of homage. Such an instance, one of hundreds, is the relationship between two jazz greats on the album they made together, *Duke Ellington and John Coltrane*. This form of the double-voiced implies unity and resemblance rather than critique and difference.

The premise of this book is that the literary discourse that is most consistently "black," as read against our tradition's own theory of itself, is the most figurative, and that the modes of interpretation most in accord with the vernacular tradition's theory of criticism are those that direct attention to the manner in which language is used. Black texts Signify upon other black texts in the tradition by engaging in what Ellison has defined as implicit formal critiques of language use, of rhetorical strategy. Literary Signification, then, is similar to parody and pastiche, wherein parody corresponds to what I am calling motivated Signification while pastiche would correspond roughly to unmotivated Signification. By motivation I do not mean to suggest the lack of intention, for parody and pastiche imply intention, ranging from severe critique to acknowledgment and placement within a literary tradition. Pastiche can imply either homage to an antecedent text or futility in the face of a seemingly indomitable mode of representation. Black writers Signify on each other's texts for all of these reasons, and the relations of Signification that obtain between and among black texts serve as a basis for a theory of formal revision in the Afro-American tradition. Literary echoes, or pastiche, as found in Ellison's *Invisible Man*, of signal tropes found in Emerson, Eliot, Joyce, Crane, or Melville (among others) constitute one mode of Signifyin(g).

But so does Ellison's implicit rhetorical critique of the conventions of realism found in Richard Wright's *Native Son, The Man Who Lived Underground*, and *Black Boy*. Reed's parodies of Wright and Ellison constitute a Signification of a profoundly motivated order, especially as found in the text of *Mumbo Jumbo*. Hurston's multi-leveled use of voice in *Their Eyes Were Watching God* represents a Signification upon the entire tradition of dialect poetry as well as a brilliant and subtle critique of received notions of voice in the realistic novel, amounting to a remarkably novel critique and extension of Henry James's use of point-of-view as point-of-consciousness. Hurston's novel, like Sterling A. Brown's *Southern Road*, amounts to a refutation of critics such as James Welson Johnson, who argued just six years before the publication of *Their Eyes* that the passing of dialect as a literary device among black authors was complete. Moreover, by representing her protagonist as a mulatto, who eschews the bourgeois life and marries a dark-complexioned migrant worker, Hurston Signifies upon the female novel of passing, an ironic form of fantasy that she inherited from Nella Larsen and Jessie Fauset. Finally, Walker's decision to place *The Color Purple* in a line of descent that runs directly from *Their Eyes* by engaging in a narrative strategy that tropes Hurston's concept of voice (by shifting it into the form of the epistolary novel and a written rather than a spoken vernacular) both extends dramatically the modes of revision available to writers in the tradition and reveals that acts of formal revision can be loving acts of bonding rather than ritual slayings at Esu's crossroads.

32 Speaking in Tongues

Dialogics, Dialectics, and the Black Woman Writer's Literary Tradition

Mae Gwendolyn Henderson

(1989)

> I am who I am, doing what I came to do, acting upon you like a drug or a chisel to remind you of your me-ness as I discover you in myself.
>
> —Audre Lorde, *Sister Outsider*

> There's a noisy feelin' near the cracks
> crowdin' me . . . slips into those long, loopin' "B's"
> There's a noisy feelin' near the cracks
> crowdin' me . . . slips into those long, loopin' "B's"
> of Miss Garrison's handwritin' class;
> they become the wire hoops I must jump through.
> It spooks my alley, it spooks my play,
> more nosey now than noisy,
>   lookin' for a tongue
>   lookin' for a tongue
>   to get holy in.
> Who can tell this feelin' where to set up church?
> Who can tell this noise where to go?
> A root woman workin' . . . a mo-jo,
> just to the left of my ear.
>
> —Cherry Muhanji, *Tight Spaces*

Some years ago, three black feminist critics and scholars edited an anthology entitled *All the Women Are White, All the Blacks Are Men, But Some of Us Are Brave,*[1] suggesting in the title the unique and peculiar dilemma of black women. Since then it has perhaps become almost commonplace for literary critics, male and female, black and white, to note that black women have been discounted or unaccounted for in the "traditions" of black, women's, and American literature as well as in the

348

contemporary literary-critical dialogue. More recently, black women writers have begun to receive token recognition as they are subsumed under the category of woman in the feminist critique and the category of black in the racial critique. Certainly these "gendered" and "racial" decodings of black women authors present strong and revisionary methods of reading, focusing as they do on literary discourses regarded as marginal to the dominant literary-critical tradition. Yet the "critical insights" of one reading might well become the "blind spots" of another reading. That is, by privileging one category of analysis at the expense of the other, each of these methods risks setting up what Fredric Jameson describes as "strategies of containment," which restrict or repress different or alternative readings.[2] More specifically, blindness to what Nancy Fraser describes as "the gender subtext" can be just as occluding as blindness to the racial subtext in the works of black women writers.[3]

Such approaches can result in exclusion at worst and, at best, a reading of part of the text as the whole—a strategy that threatens to replicate (if not valorize) the reification against which black women struggle in life and literature. What I propose is a theory of interpretation based on what I refer to as the "simultaneity of discourse," a term inspired by Barbara Smith's seminal work on black feminist criticism.[4] This concept is meant to signify a mode of reading which examines the ways in which the perspectives of race and gender, and their interrelationships, structure the discourse of black women writers. Such an approach is intended to acknowledge and overcome the limitations imposed by assumptions of internal identity (homogeneity) and the repression of internal differences (heterogeneity) in racial and gendered readings of works by black women writers. In other words, I propose a model that seeks to account for racial difference within gender identity and gender difference within racial identity. This approach represents my effort to avoid what one critic describes as the presumed "absolute and self-sufficient" otherness of the critical stance in order to allow the complex representations of black women writers to steer us away from "a simple and reductive paradigm of 'otherness.'"[5]

DISCURSIVE DIVERSITY: SPEAKING IN TONGUES

What is at once characteristic and suggestive about black women's writing is its interlocutory, or dialogic, character, reflecting not only a relationship with the "other(s)," but an internal dialogue with the plural aspects of self that constitute the matrix of black female subjectivity. The interlocutory character of black women's writing is, thus, not only a consequence of a dialogic relationship with an imaginary or "generalized Other," but a dialogue with the aspects of "otherness" within the self. The complex situatedness of the black woman as not only the "Other" of the Same, but also as the "other" of the other(s) implies, as we shall see, a relationship of difference and identification with the "other(s)."

It is Mikhail Bakhtin's notion of dialogism and consciousness that provides the primary model for this approach. According to Bakhtin, each social group speaks in its own "social dialect"—possesses its own unique language—expressing shared values, perspectives, ideology, and norms. These social dialects become the "languages" of heteroglossia "intersect[ing] with each other in many different ways. . . . As such they all may be juxtaposed to one another, mutually supplement one another, contradict one another and be interrelated dialogically."[6] Yet if language, for Bakhtin, is an expression of social identity, then subjectivity (subjecthood) is constituted as a social entity through the "role of [the] word as medium of consciousness." Consciousness, then, like language, is shaped by the social environment. ("Consciousness, becomes consciousness only . . . in the process of social interaction.") Moreover, "the semiotic material of the psyche is preeminently the word—*inner speech*." Bakhtin in fact defines the relationship between consciousness and inner speech even more precisely: "Analysis would show that the units of which inner speech is constituted are certain *whole entities . . . [resembling] the alternating lines of a dialogue.* There was good reason why thinkers in ancient times should have conceived of inner speech as *inner dialogue*."[7] Thus consciousness becomes a kind of "inner speech" reflecting "the outer word" in a process that links the psyche, language, and social interaction.

It is the process by which these heteroglossic voices of the other(s) "encounter one another and coexist in the consciousness of real people—first and foremost in the creative consciousness of people who write novels,"[8] that speaks to the situation of black women writers in particular, "privileged" by a social positionality that enables them to speak in dialogically racial and gendered voices to the other(s) both within and without. If the psyche functions as an internalization of heterogeneous social voices, black women's speech/writing becomes at once a dialogue between self and society and between self and psyche. Writing as inner speech, then, becomes what Bakhtin would describe as "a unique form of collaboration with oneself" in the works of these writers.[9]

Revising and expanding Teresa de Lauretis's formulation of the "social subject and the relations of subjectivity to sociality," I propose a model that is intended not only to address "a subject en-gendered in the experiencing of race," but also what I submit is a subject "racialized" in the experiencing of gender.[10] Speaking both to and from the position of the other(s), black women writers must, in the words of Audre Lorde, deal not only with "the external manifestations of racism and sexism," but also "with the results of those distortions internalized within our consciousness of ourselves and one another."[11]

What distinguishes black women's writing, then, is the privileging (rather than repressing) of "the other in ourselves." Writing of Lorde's notion of self and otherness, black feminist critic Barbara Christian observes of Lorde what I argue is true to a greater or lesser degree in the discourse of black women writers: "As a black, lesbian, feminist, poet, mother, Lorde has, in her own life, had to search long and hard for *her* people. In responding to each of these audiences, in which a part of her identity lies, she refuses to give up her differences. In fact she uses them, as woman to man, black to white, lesbian to heterosexual, as a means of conducting creative dialogue."[12]

If black women speak from a multiple and complex social, historical, and cultural positionality which, in effect, constitutes black female subjectivity, Christian's term "creative dialogue" then refers to the expression of a multiple dialogic of differences based on this complex subjectivity. At the same time, however, black women enter into a dialectic of identity with those aspects of self shared with others. It is Hans-Georg Gadamer's "dialectical model of conversation," rather than Bakhtin's dialogics of discourse, that provides an appropriate model for articulating a relation of mutuality and reciprocity with the "Thou"—or intimate other(s). Whatever the critic thinks of Gadamer's views concerning history, tradition, and the like, one can still find Gadamer's emphases—especially as they complement Bakhtin's—to be useful and productive. If the Bakhtinian model is primarily adversarial, assuming that verbal communication (and social interaction) is characterized by contestation with the other(s), then the Gadamerian model presupposes as its goal a language of consensus, communality, and even identification, in which "one claims to express the other's claim and even to understand the other better than the other understands [him or herself]." In the "I-Thou" relationship proposed by Gadamer, "the important thing is . . . to experience the 'Thou' truly as a 'Thou,' that is, not to overlook [the other's] claim and to listen to what [s/he] has to say to us." Gadamer's dialectic, based on a typology of the "hermeneutical experience," privileges tradition as "a genuine partner in communication, with which we have fellowship as does the 'I' with a 'Thou.' " For black and women writers, such an avowal of tradition in the subdominant order, of course, constitutes an operative challenge to the dominant order. It is this rereading of the notion of tradition within a field of gender and ethnicity that supports and enables the notion of community among those who share a common history, language, and culture. If Bakhtin's dialogic engagement with the Other signifies conflict, Gadamer's monologic acknowledgment of the Thou signifies the potential of agreement. If the Bakhtinian dialogic model speaks to the other within, then Gadamer's speaks to the same within. Thus, "the [dialectic] understanding of the [Thou]" (like the dialogic understanding of the other[s]) becomes "a form of self-relatedness."[13]

It is this notion of discursive difference and identity underlying the simultaneity of discourse which typically characterizes black women's writing. Through the multiple voices that enunciate her complex subjectivity, the black woman writer not only speaks familiarly in the discourse of the other(s), but as Other she is in contestorial dialogue with the hegemonic dominant and subdominant or "ambiguously (non)hegemonic" discourses.[14] These writers enter simultaneously into familial, or testimonial and public, or competitive discourses—discourses that both affirm and challenge the values and expectations of the reader. As such, black women writers enter into testimonial discourse with black men as blacks, with white women as women, and with black women as black women.[15] At the same time, they enter into a competitive discourse with black men as women, with white women as blacks, and with white men as black women. If black women speak a discourse of racial and gendered difference in the dominant or hegemonic discursive order, they speak a discourse of racial and gender identity and difference in the subdominant discursive order. This dialogic of difference and dialectic of identity characterize both black women's subjectivity and black women's discourse. It is the complexity of these simultaneously homogeneous and heterogeneous social and discursive domains out of which black women write and construct themselves (as blacks and women and, often, as poor, black women) that enables black women writers authoritatively to speak to and engage both hegemonic and ambiguously (non)hegemonic discourse.

Janie, the protagonist in Zora Neale Hurston's *Their Eyes Were Watching God*, demonstrates how the dialectics/dialogics of black and female subjectivity structure black women's discourse.[16] Combining personal and public forms of discourse in the court scene where she is on trial and fighting not only for her life but against "lying thoughts" and "misunderstanding," Janie addresses the judge, a jury composed of "twelve more white men," and spectators ("eight or ten white women" and "all the Negroes [men] for miles around" [274]). The challenge of Hurston's character is that of the black woman writer—to speak at once to a diverse audience about her experience in a racist and sexist society where to be black and female is to be, so to speak, "on trial." Janie not only speaks in a discourse of gender and racial difference to the white male judge and jurors, but also in a discourse of gender difference (and racial identity) to the black male spectators and a discourse of racial difference (and gender identity) to the white women spectators. Significantly, it is the white men who constitute both judge and jury, and, by virtue of their control of power and discourse, possess the authority of life and death over the black woman. In contrast, the black men (who are convinced that the "nigger [woman] kin kill . . . jus' as many niggers as she please") and white women (who "didn't seem too mad") read and witness/ oppose a situation over which they exercise neither power nor discourse (225, 280).

Janie's courtroom discourse also emblematizes the way in which the categories of public and private break down in black women's discourse. In the context of Janie's courtroom scene, testimonial discourse takes on an expanded meaning, referring to both juridical, public, and dominant discourse as well as familial, private, and non-dominant discourse. Testimonial, in this sense, derives its meaning from both "testimony" as an official discursive mode and "testifying," defined by Geneva Smitherman as "a ritualized form of . . . communication in which the speaker gives verbal witness to the efficacy, truth, and power of some experience in which [the group has] shared." The latter connotation suggests an additional meaning in the context of theological discourse where testifying refers to a "spontaneous expression to the church community [by whomever] feels the spirit."[17]

Like Janie, black women must speak in a plurality of voices as well as in a multiplicity of discourses. This discursive diversity, or simultaneity of discourse, I call "speaking in tongues." Significantly, glossolalia, or speaking in tongues, is a practice associated with black women in the Pentecostal Holiness church, the church of my childhood and the church of my mother. In the Holiness church (or as we called it, the Sanctified church), speaking unknown tongues (tongues known only to God) is in fact a sign of election, or holiness. As a trope it is also intended to remind us of Alice Walker's characterization of black women as artists, as "Creators," intensely rich in that spirituality which Walker sees as "the basis of Art." [18]

Glossolalia is perhaps the meaning most frequently associated with speaking in tongues. It is this connotation which emphasizes the particular, private, closed, and privileged communication between the congregant and the divinity. Inaccessible to the general congregation, this mode of communication is outside the realm of public discourse and foreign to the known tongues of humankind.

But there is a second connotation to the notion of speaking in tongues—one that suggests not glossolalia, but heteroglossia, the ability to speak in diverse known languages. While glossolalia refers to the ability to "utter the mysteries of the spirit," heteroglossia describes the ability to speak in the multiple languages of public discourse. If glossolalia suggests private, nonmediated, nondifferentiated univocality, heteroglossia connotes public, differentiated, social, mediated, dialogic discourse. Returning from the trope to the act of reading, perhaps we can say that speaking in tongues connotes both the semiotic, presymbolic babble (baby talk), as between mother and child—which Julia Kristeva postulates as the "mother tongue"—as well as the diversity of voices, discourses, and languages described by Mikhail Bakhtin.

Speaking in tongues, my trope for both glossolalia and heteroglossia, has a precise genealogical evolution in the Scriptures. In Genesis 11, God confounded the world's language when the city of Babel built a tower in an attempt to reach the heavens. Speaking in many and different tongues, the dwellers of Babel, unable to understand each other, fell into confusion, discord, and strife, and had to abandon the project. Etymologically, the name of the city Babel sounds much like the Hebrew word for "babble"—meaning confused, as in baby talk. Babel, then, suggests the two related, but distinctly different, meanings of speaking in tongues, meanings borne out in other parts of the Scriptures. The most common is that implied in 1 Corinthians 14—the ability to speak in unknown tongues. According to this interpretation, speaking in tongues suggests the ability to speak in and through the spirit. Associated with glossolalia—speech in unknown tongues—it is ecstatic, rapturous, inspired speech, based on a relation of intimacy and identification between the individual and God.

If Genesis tells of the disempowerment of a people by the introduction of different tongues, then Acts 2 suggests the empowerment of the disciples who, assembled on the day of Pentecost in the upper room of the temple in Jerusalem, "were filled with the Holy Spirit and began to speak in other tongues." Although the people thought the disciples had "imbibed a strange and unknown wine," it was the Holy Spirit which had driven them, filled with ecstasy, from the upper room to speak among the five thousand Jews surrounding the temple. The Scriptures tell us that the tribes of Israel all understood them, each in his own tongue. The Old Testament then, suggests the dialogics of difference in its diversity of discourse, while the New Testament, in its unifying language of the spirit, suggests the dialectics of identity. If the Bakhtinian model suggests the multiplicity of speech as suggested in the dialogics of difference, then Gadamer's model moves toward a unity of understanding in its dialectics of identity.

It is the first as well as the second meaning which we privilege in speaking of black women writers: the first connoting polyphony, multivocality, and plurality of voices, and the second signifying intimate, private, inspired utterances. Through their intimacy with the discourse of the other(s), black women writers weave into their work competing and complementary discourses—discourses that seek both to adjudicate competing claims and witness common concerns.[19]

Also interesting is the link between the gift of tongues, the gift of prophecy, and the gift of interpretation. While distinguishing between these three gifts, the Scriptures frequently conflate or conjoin them. If to speak in tongues is to utter mysteries in and through the Spirit, to prophesy is to speak to others in a (diversity of) language(s) which the congregation can understand. The Scriptures would suggest that the disciples were able to perform both. I propose, at this juncture, an enabling critical fiction—that it is black women writers who are the modern day apostles, empowered by experience to speak as poets and prophets in many tongues. With this critical gesture, I also intend to signify a deliberate intervention by black women writers into the canonic tradition of sacred/literary texts.[20]

A DISCURSIVE DILEMMA

In their works, black women writers have encoded oppression as a discursive dilemma, that is, their works have consistently raised the problem of the black woman's relationship to power and discourse. Silence is an important element of this code. The classic black woman's text *Their Eyes Were Watching God* charts the female protagonist's development from voicelessness to voice, from silence to tongues. Yet this movement does not exist without intervention by the other(s)—who speak for and about black women. In other words, it is not that black women, in the past, have had nothing to say, but rather that they have had no say. The absence of black female voices has allowed others to inscribe, or write, and ascribe to, or read, them. The notion of speaking in tongues, however, leads us away from an examination of how the Other has written/read black women and toward an examination of how black women have written the other(s)' writing/reading black women.

Using the notion of "speaking in tongues" as our model, let us offer a kind of paradigmatic reading of two works which encode and resist the material and discursive dilemma of the black woman writer. Sherley Anne Williams's *Dessa Rose* and Toni Morrison's *Sula* are novels that emphasize respectively the intercultural/racial and intracultural/racial sites from which black women speak, as well as the signs under which they speak in both these milieus.[21] Artificial though this separation may be—since, as we have seen, black women are located simultaneously within both these discursive domains—such a distinction makes possible an examination of black women's literary relations to both dominant and subdominant discourse. These works also allow us to compare the suppression of the black female voice in the dominant discourse with its repression in the subdominant discourse.[22] Finally, they provide models for the disruption of the dominant and subdominant discourse by black and female expression, as well as for the appropriation and transformation of these discourses.

The heroine of Sherley Anne Williams's first novel, *Dessa Rose*, is a fugitive slave woman introduced to the reader as "the Darky" by Adam Nehemiah, a white male writer interviewing her in preparation for a forthcoming book, *The Roots of Rebellion in the Slave Population and some Means of Eradicating Them* (or, more simply,

The Work). The opening section of the novel is structured primarily by notations from Nehemiah's journal, based on his interactions with the slave woman during her confinement in a root cellar while awaiting her fate at the gallows. The latter section, describing her adventures as a fugitive involved in a scam against unsuspecting slaveholders and traders, is narrated primarily in the voice of Dessa (as the slave woman calls herself) after she has managed, with the assistance of fellow slaves, to escape the root cellar. At the end of the novel, the writer-interviewer, Adam Nehemiah, still carrying around his notes for *The Work*, espies the fugitive Dessa.

Brandishing a poster advertising a reward for her recapture, and a physical description of her identifying markings (an R branded on the thigh and whip-scarred hips), Adam Nehemiah coerces the local sheriff into detaining Dessa for identification. Significantly, Adam Nehemiah, named after his precursor—the archetypal white male namer, creator, and interpreter—attempts not only to remand Dessa into slavery but to inscribe her experiences as a slave woman through a discourse that suppresses her voice. Like the Adam of Genesis, Nehemiah asserts the right of ownership through the privilege of naming. Not only is his claim of discursive and material power held together symbolically in his name, but his acts and his words conflate: Nehemiah not only wishes to capture Odessa (as he calls her) in words that are instructive in the preservation of slavery, but he wishes to confine her in material slavery. Just as the biblical Nehemiah constructed the wall to protect the Israelites against attack by their enemies, so Williams's Nehemiah sets out to write a manual designed to protect the American South against insurrection by the slaves. Ironically, the character of Nehemiah, a patriot and leader of the Jews after the years of Babylonian captivity, is reread in the context of the Old South as a racist and expert on the "sound management" of the slaves.[23]

Dessa fears that exposure of her scars/branding will confirm her slave status. As she awaits the arrival of Ruth, the white woman who abets in the perpetration of the scam, Dessa thinks to herself, "I could feel everyone of them scars, the one roped partway to my navel that the waist of my draws itched, the corduroyed welts across my hips, and R on my thighs" (223). What interests me here is the literal inscription of Dessa's body, signified by the whip marks and, more specifically, the branded R, as well as the white male writer-cum-reader's attempt to exercise discursive domination over Dessa. Seeking to inscribe black female subjectivity, the white male, in effect, relegates the black woman to the status of discursive object, or spoken subject. The location of the inscriptions—in the area of the genitalia—moreover, signals an attempt to inscribe the sign *slave* in an area that marks her as woman ("Scar tissue plowed through her pubic hair region so no hair would ever grow there again" [154]). The effect is to attempt to deprive the slave woman of her femininity and render the surface of her skin a parchment upon which meaning is etched by the whip (pen) of white patriarchal authority and sealed by the firebrand. Together, these inscriptions produce the meaning of black female subjectivity in the discursive domain of slavery.[24] Importantly, the literal inscription of the flesh emphasizes what Monique Wittig, insisting on "the *material* oppression of individuals by discourses," describes as the "unrelenting tyranny that [male discourses] exert upon our *physical* and *mental* selves" (emphasis mine).[25] Dessa is ordered by the sheriff to lift her skirt so that these inscriptions can be "read" by her potential captors. (Perhaps we should read the R on Dessa's thigh as part of an acrostic for *Read*.) The signifying function of her scars is reinforced when Dessa recognizes that "[Nehemiah] wouldn't have to say nothing. Sheriff would see [i.e., read] that for himself" (223). Her remarks also suggest the mortal consequence of such a reading, or misreading.[26] "This [the scars] was what would betray me . . . these white mens would kill me" (223).

If Williams's *Dessa Rose* contains a representation of the inscription of black female in the dominative white and male discourse, then Morrison's *Sula* contains a representation of female ascription in black subdominative discourse. If in the context of the white community's discourse Dessa is suppressed as woman and black, in the discourse of the black community she is repressed as woman.

Like Dessa, Sula is marked. Unlike Dessa, Sula is marked from birth. Here is a mark of nativity—a biological rather than cultural inscription, appropriate in this instance because it functions to mark her as a "naturally" inferior female within the black community.[27] The birthmark, "spread[ing] from the middle of the lid toward the eyebrow" (45), is associated with a series of images. For her mother, Hannah, Sula's birthmark "looked more and more like a stem and a rose" (64). Although in European and Eurocentric culture the rose is the gift of love as well as the traditional romantic symbol of female beauty and innocence (lily-white skin and rose blush), it is a symbol that has been appropriated by black women writers from Frances Harper, who uses it as a symbol of romantic love, to Alice Walker, who associates it with sexual love.[28]

Jude, the husband of Nel, Sula's best friend, refers to the birthmark as a "copper-head" and, later, as "the rattlesnake over her eye." If the image of the rose suggests female romantic love and sexuality, then the snake evokes the archetypal Garden and the story of Eve's seduction by the serpent.[29] The association is significant in light of the subsequent seduction scene between Jude and Sula, for it is Jude's perception of the snake imagery which structures his relationship with Sula, suggesting not only that the meaning he ascribes to the birthmark reflects the potential of his relationship with her, but that, on a broader level, it is the "male gaze" which constitutes female subjectivity. At the same time, Morrison redeploys the role of Other in a way that suggests how the black woman as Other is used to constitute (black) male subjectivity.

The community, "clearing up," as it thought, "the meaning of the birthmark over her eye," tells the reader that "it was not a stemmed rose, or a snake, it was Hannah's ashes marking Sula from the very beginning" (99). (That Sula had watched her mother burn to death was her grandmother's contention and the community gossip.) If Jude represents the subject constituted in relation to the black woman as Other, the community represents a culture constituted in relation to the black woman as Other:

> Their conviction of Sula's evil changed them in accountable yet mysterious ways. Once the source of their personal misfortune was identified, they had leave to protect and

love one another. They began to cherish their husbands and wives, protect their children, repair their homes and in general band together against the devil in their midst. (102)

Sula signifies, for the community, the chaos and evil against which it must define and protect itself. Convinced that she bears the mark of the devil because of her association with Shadrack, the town reprobate, the community closes ranks against one who transgresses the boundaries prescribed for women.

For Shadrack, the shell-shocked World War I veteran who has become the community pariah, Sula's birthmark represents "the mark of the fish he loved"—the tadpole (134). A symbol of the primordial beginnings of life in the sea, the tadpole represents potential, transformation, and rebirth. Such an image contrasts with the apocalyptic ending of life by fire suggested by the community's perception of Hannah's ashes.[30] As an amphibious creature, the tadpole has the capacity to live both terrestrially and aquatically. Etymologically, Sula's name is derived from the designation of a genus of seabird, again an image associated with a dual environment—aquatic and aerial. These contrasts suggestively position Sula at the crossroads or intersection of life and death, land and sea, earth and air. Thus both the mark and the designation are particularly appropriate for the black woman as one situated within two social domains (black and female) and, as such, implicated in both a racial and gendered discourse.

But it is the black community—the Bottom—which provides the setting for the action in Morrison's novel, and it is the men who have the final say in the community: "It was the men," writes the narrator, "who gave [Sula] the final label, who *finger-printed* her for all time" (emphasis mine; 197). The men in the community speak a racial discourse that reduces Sula finally to her sexuality: "The word was passed around" that "Sula slept with *white* men" (emphasis mine; 97). It is thus her sexuality, read through the race relation, which structures her subjectivity within the male-dominated discourse of the black community.

The power of male discourse and naming is also suggested in the epithet directed to the twelve-year-old Sula as she, along with her friend Nel, saunters by Edna Finch's ice cream parlor one afternoon, passing the old and young men of the Bottom:

> Pigmeat. The words were in all their minds. And one of them, one of the young ones, said it aloud. His name was Ajax, a twenty-one-year-old pool haunt of sinister beauty. Graceful and economical in every movement, he held a place of envy with men of all ages for his magnificently foul mouth. In fact he seldom cursed, and the epithets he chose were dull, even harmless. His reputation was derived from the way he handled words. When he said "hell" he hit the *h* with his lungs and the impact was greater than the achievement of the most imaginative foul mouth in town. He could say "shit" with a nastiness impossible to imitate. (43)

Not only does the language itself take on a special potency when exercised by males, but the epithet "pigmeat" which Ajax confers on Sula still has a powerful hold on her seventeen years later, when at twenty-nine, having traveled across the country and returned to the Bottom, she is greeted by the now thirty-eight-year-old Ajax at her screen door: "Sula . . . was curious. She knew nothing about him except the word he had called out to her years ago and the feeling he had excited in her then" (110).

The images associated with Sula's birthmark connote, as we have seen, a plurality of meanings. These images become not only symbols of opposition and ambiguity associated with the stemmed rose, snake, fire, and tadpole, but they evoke the qualities of permanence and mutability (nature and culture) inherent in the sign of the birthmark, the meaning and valence of which changes with the reading and the reader. At one point, Nel, Sula's complement in the novel, describes her as one who "helped others define themselves," that is, one who takes on the complementary aspect of the Other in the process of constituting subjectivity. As if to underscore Sula's signifying function as absence or mutability, Sula is described as having "no center" and "no ego," "no speck around which to grow" (103). The plurality and flux of meaning ascribed to the birthmark share some of the characteristics of the Sign or, perhaps more precisely, the Signifier. Sula's association with the birthmark gradually evolves, through synecdoche, into an identification between the subject/ object and the Sign. Thus her entry into the subdominative discursive order confers on her the status of "a free-floating signifier," open to diverse interpretations.

The inscription (writing) of Dessa and the ascription (reading) of Sula together encode the discursive dilemma of black women in hegemonic and ambiguously (non) hegemonic discursive contexts. However, these works also embody a code of resistance to the discursive and material dominance of black women. To different degrees and in different ways, Williams and Morrison fashion a counterdiscourse within their texts.

DISRUPTION AND REVISION

In negotiating the discursive dilemma of their characters, these writers accomplish two objectives: the self-inscription of black womanhood, and the establishment of a dialogue of discourses with the other(s). The self-inscription of black women requires disruption, rereading and rewriting the conventional and canonical stories, as well as revising the conventional generic forms that convey these stories. Through this interventionist, intertextual, and revisionary activity, black women writers enter into dialogue with the discourses of the other(s). Disruption—the initial response to hegemonic and ambiguously (non)hegemonic discourse—and revision (rewriting or rereading) together suggest a model for reading black and female literary expression.

Dessa's continued rejection of Adam Nehemiah's inscription suggests that we must read with some measure of credence her claims of being mis-recognized. ("I don't know this master, Mistress," she says. "They mistook me for another Dessa, Mistress" [226–227].) Ultimately, Dessa's insistence on *meconnaissance* is vindicated in the failure of Nehemiah's attempts either to confine her in the social system or define her in the dominant discourse.

Dessa not only succeeds in rupturing the narrator's discourse at the outset of the novel through a series of interventionist acts—singing, evasion, silence, nonacquiescence, and dissemblance—but she employs these strategies to effect her escape and seize discursive control of the story.[31] Moreover, Dessa's repeated use of the use of the word *track* (a term connoting both pursuit and inscription) in reference to Nehemiah takes on added significance in the context of both her inscription and revision. Tracking becomes the object of her reflections: "Why this white man *track* me down like he owned me, like a bloodhound on my *trail*," and later, "crazy white man, *tracking* me all cross the country like he owned me" (emphasis mine; 225). In other words, Nehemiah *tracks* Dessa in an attempt to establish ownership—that is, the colonization—of her body. Yet tracking also suggests that Dessa's flight becomes a text that she writes and Nehemiah reads. His tracking (i.e., reading of Dessa's text) thus becomes the means by which he attempts to capture her (i.e., suppress her voice in the production of his own text).

If the pursuit/flight pattern emblematizes a strategic engagement for discursive control, Dessa's tracks also mark her emergence as narrator of her own story. It is her escape—loosely speaking, her "making tracks"—that precludes the closure/completion of Nehemiah's book. The story of Dessa's successful revolt and escape, in effect, prefigures the rewriting of *The Work*—Nehemiah's projected treatise on the control of slaves and the prevention of slave revolts. The latter part of the novel, recounted from Dessa's perspective and in her own voice, establishes her as the successful author of her own narrative. Tracking thus becomes a metaphor for writing/reading from the white male narrator's perspective, and a metaphor for revision (*re*writing/*re*reading) from Dessa's. Creating her own track therefore corresponds to Dessa's assumption of discursive control of the novel, that is, the telling of her own story. In flight, then, Dessa challenges the material and discursive elements of her oppression and, at the same time, provides a model for writing as struggle.

Nehemiah's inability to capture Dessa in print is paralleled, finally, in his failure to secure her recapture. As Dessa walks out of the sheriff's office, Nehemiah cries: "I know it's her . . . I got her down here in my book." Leaving, Dessa tells the reader, "And he reach and took out that little black-bound pad he wrote in the whole time I knowed him" (231). But the futility of his efforts is represented in the reactions of the onlookers to the unbound pages of Nehemiah's notebook as they tumble and scatter to the floor:

[Sheriff] Nemi, ain't nothing but some scribbling on here. . . . Can't no one read this.

[Ruth] And these [pages] is blank, sheriff. (232)

Finally, in two dramatic acts of self-entitlement, Dessa reaffirms her ability to name herself and her own experience. In the first instance, she challenges Nehemiah's efforts to capture her—in person and in print: "Why, he didn't even know how to call my name—talking about Odessa" (emphasis mine; 225). And in the second, after her release she informs Ruth, her white accomplice and alleged mistress, "My name Dessa, Dessa Rose. Ain't no O to it" (232). She is, of course, distinguishing between Odessa, an ascription by the white, male slave master and used by both

Nehemiah and Ruth, and Dessa, her entitlement proper. Her rejection of the O signifies her rejection of the inscription of her body by the other(s). In other words, Dessa's repudiation of the O (Otherness?) signifies her always already presence— what Ralph Ellison describes as the unquestioned humanity of the slave. She deletes nothing—except the white, male other's inscription/ascription.[32]

At the conclusion of the novel, Dessa once again affirms the importance of writing oneself and one's own history. It is a responsibility that devolves upon the next generation, privileged with a literacy Dessa herself has been denied: "My mind wanders. This is why I have it down, why I has the child say it back. I never will forget Nemi trying to read [and write] me, knowing I had put myself in his hands. Well, *this* the childrens have heard from our own lips" (236). Yet, as Walker might say, the story bears the mother's signature.[33]

While Dessa, through interventions and rewriting, rejects white, male attempts to write and read black female subjectivity, Sula, through disruption and rereading, repudiates black male readings of black female subjectivity. (Significantly, black males, like white females, lack the power to *write*, but not the power to *read* black women.) If it is her sexuality which structures Sula within the confines of black (male) discourse, it is also her sexuality which creates a rupture in that discourse. It is through the act of sexual intercourse that Sula discovers "the center of . . . silence" and a "loneliness so profound *the word itself had no meaning*" (emphasis mine; 106). The "desperate terrain" which she reaches, the "high silence of orgasm" (112), is a nodal point that locates Sula in the interstices of the closed system of (black) male signification. She has, in effect, "[leapt] from the edge" of discourse "into soundlessness" and "[gone] down howling" (106). Howling, a unary movement of nondifferentiated sound, contrasts with the phonic differentiation on which the closed system of language is based. Like the birthmark, which is the symbolic sign of life, the howl is the first sound of life—not yet broken down and differentiated to emerge as intersubjective communication, or discourse. The howl, signifying a prediscursive mode, thus becomes an act of self-reconstitution as well as an act of subversion or resistance to the "network of signification" represented by the symbolic order. The "high silence of orgasm" and the howl allow temporary retreats from or breaks in the dominant discourse. Like Dessa's evasions and interventions, Sula's silences and howls serve to disrupt or subvert the "symbolic function of the language." It is precisely these violations or transgressions of the symbolic order that allow for the expression of the suppressed or repressed aspects of black female subjectivity. The reconstitutive function of Sula's sexuality is suggested in the image of the "post-coital privateness in which she met herself, welcomed herself, and joined herself in matchless harmony" (107). The image is that of symbiosis and fusion—a stage or condition represented in psychoanalysis as pre-Oedipal and anterior to the acquisition of language or entry into the symbolic order.[34]

It is through the howl of orgasm that Sula discovers a prediscursive center of experience that positions her at a vantage point outside of the dominant discursive order. The howl is a form of speaking in tongues and a linguistic disruption that serves as the precondition for Sula's entry into language. Unless she breaks the conventional structures and associations of the dominant discourse, Sula cannot enter through the interstices.[35] (This reading of *Sula*, in effect, reverses the bibical movement from contestorial, public discourse to intimate, familial discourse.)

In contrast to the howl, of course, is the stunning language of poetic metaphor with which Sula represents her lover and the act of love:

> If I take a chamois and rub real hard on the bone, right on the ledge of your cheek bone, some of the black will disappear. It will flake away into the chamois and underneath there will be gold leaf. . . . And if I take a nail file or even Eva's old paring knife . . . and scrape away at the gold, it will fall away and there will be alabaster. . . . Then I can take a chisel and small tap hammer and tap away at the alabaster. It will crack then like ice under the pick, and through the breaks I will see the [fertile] loam. (112)

It is an eloquent passage—not of self-representation, however, but of representation of the male other. If Sula cannot find the language, the trope, the form, to embody her own "experimental" life, she "engage[s] her tremendous curiosity and her gift for metaphor" in the delineation of her lover. The poetic penetration of her lover through the layers of black, gold leaf, alabaster, and loam signals that her assumption of a "masculine" role parallels the appropriation of the male voice, prerequisite for her entry into the symbolic order. (Such an appropriation is, of course, earlier signaled by the association of the birthmark with the stemmed rose, the snake, the tadpole— a series of phallic images.)

I propose, however, in the spirit of the metaphor, to take it one step further and suggest that the imagery and mode of the prose poem form a kind of model for the deconstructive function of black feminist literary criticism—and to the extent that literature itself is always an act of interpretation, a model for the deconstructive function of black women's writing—that is, to interpret or interpenetrate the signifying structures of the dominant and subdominant discourse in order to formulate a critique and, ultimately, a transformation of the hegemonic white and male symbolic order.

If Williams's primary emphasis is on the act of rewriting, then Morrison's is on the act of rereading. Perhaps the best example of Sula's deconstructive rereading of the black male text is exemplified in her reformulation of Jude's "whiny tale" describing his victimization as a black man in a world that the "white man running":

> I don't know what the fuss is about. I mean, everything in the world loves you. White men love you. They spend so much time worrying about your penis they forget their own. The only thing they want to do is cut off a nigger's privates. And if that ain't love and respect I don't know what is. And white women? They chase you all to every corner of the earth, feel for you under every bed. . . . now ain't that love? They think rape soon's they see you, and if they don't get the rape they looking for, they scream it anyway just so the search won't be in vain. Colored women worry themselves into bad health just trying to hang on to your cuffs. Even little children—white and black,

boys and girls—spend all their childhood eating their hearts out 'cause they think you don't love them. And if that ain't enough, you love yourselves. Nothing in this world loves a black man more that another black man. (89)

Adrienne Munich points out that "Jude's real difficulties allow him to maintain his male identity, to exploit women, and not to examine himself." Sula, she argues, turns "Jude's story of powerlessness into a tale of power." Through a deconstructive reading of his story, Sula's interpretation demonstrates how Jude uses "racial politics [to masks] sexual politics."[36]

If Sula's silences and howls represent breaks in the symbolic order, then her magnificent prose poem looks to the possibilities of appropriating the male voice as a prerequisite for entry into that order. Dessa similarly moves from intervention to appropriation and revision of the dominant discourse. As the author of her own story, Dessa writes herself into the dominant discourse and, in the process, transforms it. What these two works suggest in variable, but interchangeable, strategies is that, in both dominant and subdominant discourses, the initial expression of a marginal presence takes the form of disruption—a departure or a break with conventional semantics and/or phonetics. This rupture is followed by a rewriting or rereading of the dominant story, resulting in a "delegitimation" of the prior story or a "displacement" which shifts attention "to the other side of the story."[37] Disruption—the initial response to hegemonic and ambiguously (non)hegemonic discourse—and the subsequent response, revision (rewriting or rereading), together represent a progressive model for black and female utterance. I propose, in an appropriation of a current critical paradigm, that Sula's primal scream constitutes a "womblike matrix" in which soundlessness can be transformed into utterance, unity into diversity, formlessness into form, chaos into art, silence into tongues, and glossolalia into heteroglossia.

It is this quality of speaking in tongues, that is, multivocality, I further propose, that accounts in part for the current popularity and critical success of black women's writing. The engagement of multiple others broadens the audience for black women's writing, for like the disciples of Pentecost who spoke in diverse tongues, black women, speaking out of the specificity of their racial and gender experiences, are able to communicate in a diversity of discourses. If the ability to communicate accounts for the popularity of black women writers, it also explains much of the controversy surrounding some of this writing. Black women's writing speaks with what Mikhail Bakhtin would describe as heterological or "centrifugal force" but (in a sense somewhat different from that which Bakhtin intended) also unifying or "centripetal force."[38] This literature speaks as much to the notion of commonality and universalism as it does to the sense of difference and diversity.

Yet the objective of these writers is not, as some critics suggest, to move from margin to center, but to remain on the boarders of discourse, speaking from the vantage point of the insider/outsider. As Bakhtin further suggests, fusion with the (dominant) Other can only duplicate the tragedy or misfortune of the Other's dilemma. On the other hand, as Gadamer makes clear, "there is a kind of experience of the 'Thou' that seeks to discover things that are typical in the behaviour of [the other] and is able to make predictions concerning another person on the basis of [a commonality] of experience."[39] To maintain this insider/outsider position, or perhaps what Myra Jehlen calls the "extra-terrestrial fulcrum" that Archimedes never acquired, is to see the other, but also to see what the other cannot see, and to use this insight to enrich both our own and the other's understanding.[40]

As gendered and racial subjects, black women speak/write in multiple voices—not all simultaneously or with equal weight, but with various and changing degrees of intensity, privileging one parole and then another. One discovers in these writers a kind of internal dialogue reflecting an intrasubjective engagement with the intersubjective aspects of self, a dialectic neither repressing difference nor, for that matter, privileging identity, but rather expressing engagement with the social aspects of self ("the other[s] in ourselves"). It is this subjective plurality (rather than the notion of the cohesive or fractured subject) that, finally, allows the black woman to become an expressive site for a dialectics/dialogics of identity and difference.

Unlike Bloom's "anxiety of influence" model configuring a white male poetic tradition shaped by an adversarial dialogue between literary fathers and sons (as well as the appropriation of this model by Joseph Skerrett and others to discuss black male writers), and unlike Gilbert and Gubar's "anxiety of authorship" model informed by the white woman writer's sense of "dis-ease" within a white patriarchal tradition, the present model configures a tradition of black woman writers generated less by neurotic anxiety or dis-ease than by an emancipatory impulse which freely engages both hegemonic and ambiguously (non)hegemonic discourse.[41] Summarizing Morrison's perspectives, Andrea Stuart perhaps best expresses this notion:

> I think you [Morrison] summed up the appeal of black women writers when you said that white men, quite naturally, wrote about themselves and their world; white women tended to write about white men because they were so close to them as husbands, lovers and sons; and black men wrote about white men as the oppressor or the yardstick against which they measured themselves. Only black women writers were not interested in writing about white men and therefore they freed literature to take on other concerns.[42]

In conclusion, I return to the gifts of the Holy Spirit: I Corinthians 12 tells us that "the [one] who speaks in tongues should pray that [s/he] may interpret what [s/he] says." Yet the Scriptures also speak to interpretation as a separate gift—the ninth and final gift of the spirit. Might I suggest that if black women writers speak in tongues, then it is we black feminist critics who are charged with the hermeneutical task of interpreting tongues?

NOTES

1. Gloria Hull, Patricia Bell Scott, and Barbara Smith, eds., *All the Women Are White, All the Blacks Are Men, But Some of Us Are Brave* (Old Westbury, N.Y.: Feminist Press, 1982).

2. Fredric Jameson, *The Political Unconscious: Narrative as a Socially Symbolic Act* (Ithaca N.Y.: Cornell University Press, 1981), 53.

3. The phrase "gender subtext" is used by Nancy Fraser (and attributed to Dorothy Smith) in Fraser's critique of Habermas in Nancy Fraser, "What's Critical about Critical Theory?" in Seyla Benehabib and Drucilla Cornell, eds., *Feminism as Critique* (Minneapolis: University of Minnesota Press, 1987), 42.

4. See Barbara Smith, ed., *Home Girls: A Black Feminist Anthology* (New York: Kitchen Table: Women of Color Press, 1983), xxxii.

5. John Carlos Rowe, "To Live Outside the Law, You Must Be Honest: The Authority of the Margin in Contemporary Theory," *Cultural Critique* I (2): 67–68.

6. Mikhail Bakhtin, "Discourse in the Novel," reprinted in Michael Holquist, ed., *The Dialogic Imagination: Four Essays by M. M. Bakhtin* (Austin: University of Texas Press, 1981), 292. Bakhtin's social groups are designated according to class, religion, generation, religion, and profession. The interpretative model I propose extends and rereads Bakhtin's theory from the standpoint of race and gender, categories absent in Bakhtin's original system of social and linguistic stratification.

7. V. N. Volosinov [Mikhail Bakhtin], *Marxism and the Philosophy of Language* (New York: Seminar Press, 1973), II, 29, 38. Originally published in Russian as *Marksizm I Filosofija Jazyka* (Leningrad, 1930). Notably, this concept of the "subjective psyche" constituted primarily as a "social entity" distinguishes the Bakhtinian notion of self from the Freudian notion of identity.

8. Bakhtin, "Discourse in the Novel," 292.

9. According to Bakhtin, "The processes that basically define the content of the psyche occur not inside but outside the individual organism. . . . Moreover, the psyche enjoys extra-territorial status . . . [as] a social entity that penetrates inside the organism of the individual personal" (*Marxism and Philosophy of Language* 25, 39). Explicating Caryl Emerson's position on Bakhtin, Gary Saul Morson argues that selfhood "derives from an internalization of the voices a person has heard, and each of these voices is saturated with social and ideological values." "Thought itself," he writes, "is but 'inner speech,' and inner speech is outer speech that we have learned to 'speak' in our heads while retaining the full register of conflicting social values." See Gary Saul Morson, "Dialogue, Monologue, and the Social: A Reply to Ken Hirshkop," in Morson, ed., *Bakhtin: Essays and Dialogues on His Work* (Chicago: University of Chicago Press, 1986), 85.

10. Teresa de Lauretis, *Technologies of Gender* (Bloomington: Indiana University Press, 1987), 2.

11. Audre Lorde, "Eye to Eye," included in *Sister Outsider* (Tramansburg, N.Y.: Crossing Press, 1984), 147.

12. Barbara Christian, "The Dynamics of Difference: Book Review of Audre Lorde's *Sister Outsider*," in *Black Feminist Criticism: Perspectives in Black Women Writers* (New York: Pergamon Press, 1985), 209.

13. While acknowledging the importance of historicism, I can only agree with Frank Lentricchia's conclusion that in some respects Gadamer's "historicist argument begs more questions than it answers. If we can applaud the generous intention, virtually unknown in structuralist quarters, of recapturing history for textual interpretation, then we can only be stunned by the implication of what he has uncritically to say about authority, the power of tradition, knowledge, our institutions, and our attitudes." See Frank Lentricchia, *After the New Criticism* (Chicago: University of Chicago Press, 1980), 153. Certainly, Gadamer's model privileges the

individual's relation to history and tradition in a way that might seem problematic in formulating a discursive model for the "noncanonical" or marginalized writer. However, just as the above model of dialogics is meant to extend Bakhtin's notion of class difference to encompass gender and race, so the present model revises and limits Gadamer's notion of tradition. See Hans-Georg Gadamer, *Truth and Method* (New York: Seabury Press, 1975), 321–325. My introduction to the significance of Gadamer's work for my own reading of black women writers was first suggested by Don Bialostosky's excellent paper entitled "Dialectic and Anti-Dialectic: A Bakhtinian Critique of Gadamer's Dialectical Model of Conversation," delivered at the International Association of Philosophy and Literature in May 1989 at Emory University in Atlanta, Georgia.

14. I extend Rachel Blau DuPlessis's term designating white women as a group privileged by race and oppressed by gender to black men as a group privileged by gender and oppressed by race. In this instance, I use "ambiguously (non)hegemonic" to signify the discursive status of both these groups.

15. Black women enter into dialogue with other black women in a discourse that I would characterize as primarily testimonial, resulting from a similar discursive and social positionality. It is this commonality of history, culture, and language which, finally, constitutes the basis of a tradition of black women's expressive culture. In terms of actual literary dialogue among black women, I would suggest a relatively modern provenance of such a tradition, but again, one based primarily on a dialogue of affirmation rather than contestation. As I see it, this dialogue begins with Alice Walker's response to Zora Neale Hurston. Although the present article is devoted primarily to contestorial function of black women's writing, my forthcoming work (of which the present essay constitutes only a part) deals extensively with the relationships among black women writers.

16. Zora Neale Hurston, *Their Eyes Were Watching God* (1937; rpt., Urbana: University of Illinois Press, 1978). All subsequent references in the text.

17. Geneva Smitherman, *Talkin and Testifyin: The Language of Black America* (Detroit: Wayne State University Press, 1986), 58.

18. Alice Walker, "In Search of Our Mothers' Gardens," in *In Search of Our Mothers' Gardens: Womanist Prose* (New York: Harcourt Brace Jovanovich, 1984), 232.

19. Not only does such an approach problematize conventional categories and boundaries of discourse, but, most importantly, it signals the collapse of the unifying consensus posited by the discourse of universalism and reconstructs the concept of unity in diversity implicit in the discourse of difference.

20. The arrogant and misogynistic Paul tells us, "I thank God that I speak in tongues more than all of you. But in church I would rather speak five intelligible words to instruct others [i.e., to prosphesy] than ten thousand words in a tongue." Even though we are perhaps most familiar with Paul's injunction to women in the church to keep silent, the prophet Joel, in the Old Testament, speaks to a diversity of voices that includes women: "In the last days, God says, I will pour out my Spirit on all people. Your sons and *daughters* will prophesy. . . . Even on my servants, both men and *women*, I will pour out my Spirit in those days, and they will prophesy" (emphasis mine). I am grateful to the Rev. Joseph Stephens whose vast scriptural knowledge helped guide me through these and other revelations.

21. Sherley Anne Williams, *Dessa Rose* (New York: William Morrow, 1986), and Toni Morrison, *Sula* (New York: Alfred A. Knopf, 1973; rpt., Bantam, 1975). Page references for these two works are given in the text.

22. I draw on the distinction between the political connotation of *suppression* and the

psychological connotation of *repression*. Suppression results from external pressures and censorship imposed by the dominant culture, while repression refers to the internal self-censorship and silencing emanating from the subdominative community.

23. Nehemiah, a minor prophet in the Old Testament, is best remembered for rebuilding the walls around Jerusalem in order to fortify the city against invasion by hostile neighbors of Israel. Under his governorship, Ezra and the Levites instructed the people in the law of Moses "which the Lord had commanded for Israel." He is represented as a reformer who restored the ancient ordinances regarding proper observance of the Sabbath and the collection of the tithes; he also enforced bans against intermarriage with the Gentiles. He is perhaps most noted for the reply he sent, while rebuilding the walls, to a request from his enemies, Sanballat and Gesham, to meet with him: "I am doing a great *work* and cannot go down" (emphasis mine). Williams's Nehemiah, like his prototype, is devoted to the completion of a project he calls *The Work*—in this instance a book entitled *The Roots of Rebellion in the Slave Population and Some Means of Eradicating Them*. Significantly, the name of Williams's character, Adam Nehemiah, reverses the name of Nehemiah Adams, author of *A South-side View of Slavery* (1854), and a Boston minister who wrote an account of his experiences in the South from a point of view apostate to the northern antislavery cause.

24. The mark of the whip inscribes Dessa as a slave while she remains within the discursive domain of slavery—a domain architecturally figured by the prison from which she escapes, but also a domain legally and more discursively defined by the Fugitive Slave Act, the runaway ads, and the courts and depositions of the nation. Note, however, that within the northern lecture halls and the slave narratives—the spatial and discursive domains of abolitionism—the marks do not identify an individual, but signify upon the character and nature of the institution of slavery.

25. Monique Wittig, "The Straight Mind," *Feminist Issues* I (Summer 1980): 105–106.

26. Although the status of slave is not a "misreading" within the discursive domain of slavery, it is clearly a misreading according to Dessa's self-identification.

27. One might describe Sula's birthmark as an iconicized representation rather than, strictly speaking, an inscription. For our purposes, however, it has the force of a sign marking her birth or entry into black discourse.

28. Morrison's epigram to the novel highlights the cultural significance of the birthmark by quoting from Tennessee Williams's *The Rose Tattoo*: "Nobody knew my rose of the world but me. . . . I had too much glory. They don't want glory like that in nobody's heart." In "The Mission of the Flowers," Harper describes the rose as "a thing of joy and beauty" whose mission is to "lay her fairest buds and flowers upon the altars of love." Walker's protagonist Celie compares her own sex to the "inside of a wet rose." See Frances E. W. Harper, *Idylls of the Bible* (Philadelphia: George S. Ferguson, 1901), quoted in Erlene Stetson, ed., *Black Sister* (Bloomington: Indiana University Press, 1981), 34–6, and Alice Walker, *The Color Purple* (New York: Harcourt Brace Jovanovich, 1982), 69. In naming her own character Dessa Rose Williams not only plays on the above connotations, but links them, at the same time, to the transcendence implicit in "arising" and the insurgence suggested in "uprising."

29. Signifying perhaps on Hawthorne's short story "The Birthmark," Sula's mark can be reread as a sign of human imperfection and mortality, a consequence of Eve's seduction by the serpent in the Garden.

30. The fire and water image, associated with the tadpole and ashes, respectively complement and contrast with that of the snake—a symbol of death and renewal—and that of the

stemmed rose—an image suggesting not only love and sexuality, but the beauty and brevity of life as a temporal experience.

31. I do not develop here the interviewer's misreadings of Dessa in the early part of the novel, nor the specific insurgent strategies with which Dessa continually outwits him. These details are treated extensively, however, in my article on Williams's "Meditations on History," the short story on which the novel is based. It appears in Linda Kauffman, ed., *Gender and Theory: A Dialogue between the Sexes*, vol. 2 (London: Basil Blackwell, 1989).

32. Williams also uses onomastics to signify upon a less rebellious female heroine, somewhat more complicitous with female ascription by the Other. See Kaja Silverman's excellent discussion of Pauline Réage's *The Story of O*, in her article "Histoire d'O: The Construction of a Female Subject," in Carole S. Vance, ed., *Pleasure and Danger: Exploring Female Sexuality* (Boston: Routledge and Kegan Paul, 1984).

33. Williams, in her earlier version of this story, "Meditations on History," privileges orality (rather than writing)—as I attempt to demonstrate in my article "W(R)iting *The Work* and Working the Rites," in Kauffman, *Gender and Theory*, vol. 2.

34. Positing a kind of "mother tongue," Julia Kristeva argues that "language as symbolic function constitutes itself at the the cost of repressing instinctual drive and continuous relation to the mother." This order of expression, she contends, is presymbolic and linked with the mother tongue. According to Nelly Furman's interpretation, the existence of this order "does not refute the symbolic but is anterior to it, and associated with the maternal aspects of language. This order, which [Kristeva] calls 'semiotic,' is not a separate entity from the symbolic, on the contrary, it is the system which supports symbolic coherence." Continuing, Furman quotes Josette Feral in establishing a dialogical relationship between the semiotic and symbolic orders "which places the semiotic *inside* the symbolic as a condition of the symbolic, while positing the symbolic as a condition of the semiotic and founded on its repression. Now it happens that the Name-of-the-Father, in order to establish itself, needs the repression of the mother. It needs this otherness in order to reassure itself about its unity and identity, but is unwittingly affected by this otherness that is working within it." Nelly Furman, "The Politics of Language: Beyond the Gender Principle?" in Gayle Greene and Coppelia Kahn, eds., *Making A Difference: Feminist Literary Criticism* (London and New York: Methuen, 1985), 72–73.

35. In contrast to Dessa, who disrupts the dominant discourse, Sula would seem to disrupt not only discourse but, indeed, language itself.

36. Adrienne Munich, "Feminist Criticism and Literary Tradition," in Greene and Kahn, *Making a Difference*, 245–254.

37. Rachel Blau DuPlessis uses these terms to describe the "tactics of revisionary mythopoesis" created by women poets whose purpose is to "attack cultural hegemony." "Narrative displacement is like breaking the sentence," writes DuPlessis, "because it offers the possibility of speech to the female in the case, giving voice to the muted. Narrative delegitimation 'breaks the sequence'; a realignment that puts the last first and the first last has always ruptured conventional morality, politics, and narrative." Rachel Blau DuPlessis, *Writing beyond the Ending* (Bloomington: Indiana University Press, 1985), 108.

38. Bakhtin, "Discourse in the Novel," 271–272.

39. Gadamer, *Truth and Method*, 321.

40. Myra Jehlen, "Archimedes and the Paradox of Feminist Criticism," reprinted in Elizabeth Abel and Emily K. Abel, eds., *The Signs Reader: Women, Gender and Scholarship* (Chicago: University of Chicago Press, 1983).

41. See Harold Bloom, *The Anxiety of Influence: A Theory of Poetry* (New York: Oxford University Press, 1973); Sandra M. Gilbert and Susan Gubar, eds., *The Madwoman in the Attic: The Woman Writer and the Nineteenth-Century Literary Imagination* (New Haven: Yale University Press, 1979); and Joseph T. Skerret, "The Wright Interpretation: Ralph Ellison and the Anxiety of Influence," *Massachusetts Review* 21 (Spring 1980): 196–212.

42. Andrea Stuart in an interview with Toni Morrison, "Telling Our Story," *Sparerib* (February 1988): 12–15.

Black Feminist Theory and the Representation of the "Other"

Valerie Smith

(1989)

In her now classic review essay "Critical Cross-Dressing: Male Feminists and the Woman of the Year," Elaine Showalter considers the ways in which a number of prominent English and American male theorists—among them Wayne Booth, Robert Scholes, Jonathan Culler, and Terry Eagleton—have employed feminist criticism within their own critical positions. Although Showalter praises Culler's ability to read as a feminist and confront "what might be implied by reading as a man and questioning or [surrendering] paternal privileges," she suggests that often male theorists, specifically Eagleton, borrow the language of feminism to compete with women instead of examining "the masculinist bias of their own reading system."[1] This general direction by male theorists, she argues, resembles a parallel phenomenon in popular culture—the rise of the male heroine. Her discussion of *Tootsie* indicates that Dorothy Michaels, the woman character Dustin Hoffman impersonates in the movie, derives her power not in response to the oppression of women but from an instinctive male reaction to being treated like a woman. For a man to act/write like/as a woman is thus not necessarily a tribute to women, but more likely a suggestion that women must be taught by men how to assert themselves.

In her essay Showalter problematizes the function of feminist criticism in response to a growing tendency among Western white male theorists to incorporate feminism in their critical positions. Because the black feminist as writer of both critical and imaginative texts appears with increasing frequency in the work of male Afro-Americanists and Anglo-American feminists, I consider here the place of the black feminist in these apposite modes of inquiry. I begin by defining various stages of the black feminist enterprise within the context of changes in these other theoretical positions, and I suggest how the black feminist has been employed in relation to them. I then offer a reading of *Sarah Phillips* (1984) by Andrea Lee, a fictional text about an upper-middle-class young black woman that thematizes this issue of the status of the "other" in a text by and about someone simultaneously marginal and privileged.

It is not my intention to reclaim the black feminist project from those who are not black women; to do so would be to define the field too narrowly, emphasizing unduly the implications of a shared experience between "black women as critics and black women as writers who represent black women's reality."[2] Indeed, as the following remarks indicate, I understand the phrase *black feminist theory* to refer not only to theory written (or practiced) by black feminists, but also to a way of reading inscriptions of race (particularly but not exclusively blackness), gender (particularly but not exclusively womanhood), and class in modes of cultural expression. Rather, I examine black feminism in the context of these related theoretical positions in order to raise questions about the way the "other" is represented in oppositional discourse. This sort of question seems especially important now that modes of inquiry once considered radical are becoming increasingly institutionalized.

Feminist literary theory and Afro-Americanist literary theory have developed along parallel lines. Both arose out of reactive, polemical modes of criticism. Recognizing that the term *literature* as it was commonly understood in the academy referred to a body of texts written by and in the interest of a white male elite, feminist critics (mostly white) and Afro-Americanist (mostly male) undertook the archaeological work of locating and/or reinterpreting overlooked and misread women and black writers.

Black feminist criticism originated from a similar impulse. In reaction to critical acts of omission and condescension, the earliest practitioners identified ways in which white male, Anglo-American feminist, and male Afro-Americanist scholars and reviewers had ignored and condescended to the work of black women and undertook editorial projects to recover their writings. To mention but a few examples: Mary Helen Washington called attention to the ways in which the androcentric Afro-American literary tradition and establishment privileged the solitary, literate adventurers found in texts by male authors such as Frederick Douglass and Richard Wright and ignored the more muted achievements of the female protagonists featured in the work of women writers such as Harriet Jacobs, Zora Neale Hurston, and Gwendolyn Brooks.[3] Barbara Smith notes the ways in which not only Elaine Showalter, Ellen Moers, and Patricia Meyer Spacks, but also Robert Bone and Darwin Turner dismiss the writings of black women. And Deborah E. McDowell cites the omissions of Spacks, Bone, David Littlejohn, and Robert Stepto.[4] The legacy of oversights and condescension occasioned a number of editorial projects that recovered black women's writings; these much-needed projects continue to be undertaken.[5]

From the reactive impulse of these first-stage archaeological projects developed work of greater theoretical sophistication. More recent studies are less concerned with oversights in the work of others, involved instead with constructing alternative literary histories and traditions and exploring changes in assumptions about the nature of critical activity as assumptions about the nature of literature are transformed. As the kinds of questions Anglo-American feminists and male Afro-Americanists pose became increasingly self-referential—for instance, revealing the critics' own complicities and conceptualizing the links between various instances of practical criticism—they have each been drawn inevitably toward a third oppositional discourse: the discourse of deconstruction.

It should not surprise us that a number of Anglo-American feminists and Afro-Americanists have found contemporary theory compatible with the goals of their broader critical enterprise. The techniques and assumptions of deconstructive criticism destabilize the narrative relations that enshrine configurations according to genre, gender, culture, or models of behavior and personality. However, the alliances between contemporary theory on the one hand, and Anglo-American feminists or Afro-Americanists on the other, have raised inevitable questions about the institutionalization of each of these putatively marginal modes of inquiry. Anglo-American feminists as well as male Afro-Americanists are being asked to consider the extent to which their own adherence to a deconstructive practice, which by now has been adopted into the academy, undermines the fundamental assumptions of their broader, more profoundly oppositional enterprise.

The question of the place of feminist critical practice in the institution, for instance, prompted the 1982 dialogue in *Diacritics* between Peggy Kamuf and Nancy K. Miller. Kamuf argues that as long as mainstream feminists install writing by and about women at the center of their modes of inquiry and attempt to locate knowledge about women within an institutionalized humanistic discourse, they sustain the very ways of knowing that have historically excluded women's work:

> If feminist theory lets itself be guided by questions such as what is women's language, literature, style or experience, from where does it get its faith in the form of these questions to get at truth, if not from the central store that supplies humanism with its faith in the universal truth of man?[6]

In turn, Miller addresses what she perceives to be Kamuf's overinvestment in deconstructive operations. Reasserting the significance of women as historical and material subjects, she suggests that the destabilization of all categories of identity, including the category "woman," may well serve the interests of a male hegemony whose own power is under siege. As she argues,

> What bothers me about the metalogically "correct" position is what I take to be its necessary implications for practice: that by glossing "woman" as an archaic signifier, it glosses over the *referential* suffering of women. . . . It may also be the case that having been killed off with "man," the author can now be rethought beyond traditional notions of biography, now that through feminist rewritings of literary history the security of a masculine identity, the hegemony of homogeneity, has been radically problematized.[7]

Some of the most provocative and progressive work in Anglo-American feminist theory seeks to mediate these two positions. In *Crossing the Double-Cross: The Practice of Feminist Criticism*, Elizabeth A. Meese explores the possibilities of an interactive relation between feminist literary criticism and deconstruction. She argues for and illustrates a mode of feminist inquiry that employs the power of deconstruc-

372 / *Valerie Smith*

tion's critique of difference even as it seeks to challenge and politicize the enterprise of critical theory.[8] Likewise, Teresa de Lauretis situates her collection of essays entitled *Feminists Studies/Critical Studies* as a juncture in which "feminism is being both integrated and quietly suffocated within the institutions."[9] She urges a feminist model of identity that is "multiple, shifting, and often self-contradictory . . . an identity made up of heterogeneous and heteronomous representations of gender, race, and class, and often indeed across languages and cultures":[10]

> Here is where . . . feminism differs from other contemporary modes of radical, critical or creative thinking, such as post-modernism and philosophical antihumanism: feminism defines itself as a political instance, not merely a sexual politics but a politics of experience, of everyday life, which later then in turn enters the public sphere of expression and creative practice, displacing aesthetic hierarchies and generic categories, and which thus establishes the semiotic ground for a different production of reference and meaning.[11]

Recent work in Afro-American literary theory has occasioned a similar anxiety about institutionalization. Robert B. Stepto, Henry Louis Gates, and Houston A. Baker have been accused of dismantling the black subject when they bring contemporary theory to bear on their readings of black texts. In his 1984 study, *Blues, Ideology, and Afro-American Literature: A Vernacular Theory*, Baker himself argues that the presence of Afro-American critics in historically white academic institutions of higher learning has spawned a generation of scholars whose work is overly dependent on their white colleagues' assumptions and rhetoric.[12] To his mind, Stepto and Gates, two self-styled Reconstructionists, fall victim to this kind of co-optation in their early work. Both Stepto's "Teaching Afro-American Literature: Survey or Tradition: The Reconstruction of Instruction" and Gates's "Preface to Blackness: Text and Pretext" seek to explore the figurative power and complexity not only of Afro-American written art, but indeed of Afro-American cultural life more broadly defined.[13] Stepto's essay, like his book, *From Behind the Veil: A Study of Afro-American Narrative*, argues for the primacy of a pregeneric myth, the quest for freedom and literacy, in the Afro-American literary tradition.[14] But as Baker argues, Stepto's articulation of this myth underscores its apparent "agentlessness." According to Stepto, the pregeneric myth is simply "set in motion." Writes Baker, "the efficacy of motion suggested here seems to have no historically based community or agency or agencies for its origination or perpetuation."[15]

Gates's "Preface to Blackness" explores the extent to which social institutions and extraliterary considerations have intruded into the critical discourse about Afro-American literature. In order to reaffirm the textuality of instances of black written art, he argues for a semiotic understanding of literature as a system of signs that stand in an arbitrary relation to social reality. For Baker, such a theory of language, literature, and culture suggests that " 'literary' meanings are conceived in a nonsocial, noninstitutional manner by the 'point of consciousness' of a language and maintained and transmitted, without an agent, within a closed circle of 'intertextuality.' "[16] Baker's position indicates his concern that in their efforts to align the aims of Afro-

American critical activity with the goals and assumptions of prevailing theoretical discourses, both Stepto and Gates extract black writers from their relationship to their audience and from the circumstances in which they wrote and were read.

Interestingly, Baker's critique of Stepto and Gates appears in revised form within the same work in which he develops his own considerations about ways in which contemporary theory may be used to explore the workings of the vernacular in black expressive culture. Whether he succeeds in his effort to adjust the terms of poststructuralist theory to accommodate the nuances of black vernacular culture remains debatable. For Joyce Ann Joyce, however, Gates, Stepto, and Baker have all adopted a critical "linguistic system" that reflects their connection to an elite academic community of theoreticians and denies the significance of race for critic and writer alike. The intensity of this debate among Afro-Americanists is underscored by the fact that Joyce's essay occasions strikingly acrimonious responses from both Gates and Baker.

At these analogous points of self-scrutiny, then, feminists and Afro-Americanists alike have considered the extent to which they may betray the origins of their respective modes of inquiry when they seek to employ the discourse of contemporary theory. When Anglo-American feminists have argued for the inclusion of Anne Bradstreet or Kate Chopin within the literary canon, and when male Afro-Americanists have insisted on the significance of Charles Chesnutt or Jean Toomer, what they have argued is a recognition of the literary activity of those who have written despite political, cultural, economic, and social marginalization and oppression. They argue, in other words, that to exclude the work of blacks and women is to deny the historical existence of these "others" as producers of literature. If feminists and Afro-Americanists now relinquish too easily the material conditions of the lives of blacks and women, they may well relinquish the very grounds on which their respective disciplines were established.

These debates from within feminist and Afro-Americanist discourse coincided with black feminist charges that the cultural productions of black women were excluded from both modes of inquiry. Audre Lorde, bell hooks (Gloria Watkins), Angela Davis, Barbara Smith, Mary Helen Washington, and Deborah McDowell, to name but a few, have all argued that the experiences of women of color needed to be represented if these oppositional discourses were to remain radical. The eruptions of these critical voices into feminist and Afro-Americanist literary theory, like their self-contained critical and theoretical utterances, question the totalizing tendencies of mainstream as well as reactive critical practice and caution that the hope of oppositional discourse rests on its awareness of its own complicities.

These twin challenges have resulted in an impulse among Anglo-American feminists and Afro-Americanists to rematerialize the subject of their theoretical positions. Meese, as I suggested earlier, examines the contributions deconstructive method can make to feminist critical practice, but only insofar as feminist assumptions repoliticize her use of theory. De Lauretis affirms the basis of feminism in "a politics of everyday life." And similarly, in his more recent work, for instance "The Blackness of Blackness: A Critique of the Sign of the Signifying Monkey," Gates argues for a material basis of his theoretical explorations by translating them into the black idiom, renaming principles of criticism where appropriate, and naming indigenous principles of criticism.

The black woman as critic, and more broadly as the locus where gender-, class-, and race-based oppression intersect, is often invoked when Anglo-American feminists and male Afro-Americanists begin to rematerialize their discourse. This may be the case because the move away from historical specificity associated with deconstruction resembles all too closely the totalizing tendency commonly associated with androcentric criticism. In other words, when historical specificity is denied or remains implicit, all the women are presumed white, all the blacks male. The move to include black women as historical presences and as speaking subjects in critical discourse may well then be used as a defense against charges of racial hegemony on the part of white women and sexist hegemony on the part of black males.

Meese ensures that the discourse of feminism grounds her explorations into deconstructive practice by unifying her chapters around the problems of race, class, and sexual preference. She thus offers readings not only of works by Mary Wilkins Freeman, Marilynne Robinson, Tillie Olsen and Virginia Woolf, but also of the fiction of Alice Walker and Zora Neale Hurston. The politics of de Lauretis's introduction are likewise undergirded in the material conditions of working women's lives. She buttresses, for instance, her observations about the conflicting claims of different feminisms with evidence drawn from a speech by the black feminist activist, writer, and attorney Flo Kennedy. And in her critique of the (white) feminist discourse in sexuality, she cites Hortense Spillers's work on the absence of feminist perspectives on black women's sexuality. Zora Neale Hurston, Phillis Wheatley, Alice Walker, and Rebecca Cox Jackson, the black Shaker visionary, ground Gates's essay "Writing 'Race' and the Difference It Makes," just as discussions of writings by Hurston and Linda Brent are central to Baker's consideration of the economics of a new American literary history.

That the black woman appears in all of these texts as a historicizing presence testifies to the power of the insistent voices of black feminist literary and cultural critics. Yet it is striking that at precisely the moment when Anglo-American feminists and male Afro-Americanists begin to reconsider the material ground of their enterprise, they demonstrate their return to earth, as it were, by invoking the specific experiences of black women and the writings of black women. This association of black women with reembodiment resembles rather closely the association, in classic Western philosophy and in nineteenth-century cultural constructions of womanhood, of women of color with the body and therefore with animal passions and slave labor. Although in these theoretical contexts the impulse to rehistoricize produces insightful readings and illuminating theories, and is politically progressive and long overdue, nevertheless the link between black women's experiences and "the material" seems conceptually problematic.

If *Tootsie* can help us understand the white male theorists' use of feminism, I suggest that Amy Jones's 1987 film *Maid to Order* might offer a perspective on the use of the black woman or the black feminist in Anglo-American feminist or Afro-Americanist discourse. *Maid to Order* is a comic fantasy about a spoiled, rich white young woman from Beverly Hills (played by Ally Sheedy) who is sent by her fairy godmother (played by Beverly D'Angelo) to work as a maid in the home of a ludicrously nouveau riche agent and his wife in Malibu. She shares responsibilities with two other maids—one black, played by Merry Clayton, and one Latina, played by Begona Plaza. From the experience of deprivation and from her friendship with the black maid, she learns the value of love and labor; she is transformed, in other words, into a better person.

With its subtle critique of the racist policies for hiring domestic help in Southern California, *Maid to Order* seems rather progressive for a popular fantasy film. Yet even within this context, the figure of the black woman is commodified in ways that are familiar from classic cinematic narratives. From movies such as John Stahl's 1934 version of *Imitation of Life* (or Douglas Sirk's 1959 remake) and Fred Zinnemann's 1952 *Member of the Wedding* to a contemporary film such as *Maid to Order*, black women are employed, if not sacrificed, to humanize their white superordinates, to teach them something about the content of their own subject positions. When black women operate in oppositional discourse as a sign for the author's awareness of materialist concerns, then they seem to be fetishized in much the same way as they are in mass culture.

If Anglo-American feminists and male Afro-Americanists are currently in the process of rematerializing their theoretical discourse, black feminists might be said to be emerging into a theoretical phase. The early, archaeological work gave way among black feminists as well to a period in which they offered textual analyses of individual works or clusters of works. Recent, third-stage black feminist work is concerned much less with the silences in other critical traditions; rather, the writings of Susan Willis, Hazel V. Carby, Mary Helen Washington, Dianne F. Sadoff, Deborah E. McDowell, Hortense Spillers, and others have become increasingly self-conscious and self-reflexive, examining ways in which literary study—the ways in which, for instance, we understand the meaning of influence, the meaning of a tradition, the meaning of literary periods, the meaning of literature itself—changes once questions of race, class, and gender become central to the process of literary analysis. In this third stage, then, black feminist theorists might be said to challenge the conceptualizations of literary study and to concern themselves increasingly with the effect of race, class, and gender on the practice of literary criticism.

Black feminist literary theory proceeds from the assumption that black women experience a unique form of oppression in discursive and nondiscursive practices alike because they are victims at once of sexism, racism, and by extension classism. However, as Elizabeth V. Spelman and Barbara Smith demonstrate separately, one oversimplifies by saying merely that black women experience sexism and racism. "For to say merely *that*, suggests that black women experience one form of oppression, as blacks—the same thing black men experience—and that they experience another form of oppression, as women—the same thing white women experience."[17] Such a formulation erases the specificity of the black woman's experience, constituting her as the point of intersection between black men's and white women's experience.

As an alternative to this position, what Smith calls the additive analysis, black feminist theorists argue that the meaning of blackness in this country shapes profoundly the experience of gender, just as the conditions of womanhood affect ineluctably the experience of race. Precisely because the conditions of the black woman's oppression are thus specific and complex, black feminist literary theorists seek particularized methodologies that might reveal the ways in which that oppression is represented in literary texts. These methods are necessarily flexible, holding in balance the three variables of race, gender, and class and destabilizing the centrality of any one. More generally, they call into question a variety of standards of valuation that mainstream feminist and androcentric Afro-Americanist theory might naturalize.

Proceeding from a point related to but different from the centers of these other modes of inquiry, black feminist critics demonstrate that the meaning of political action, work, family, and sexuality, indeed any feature of the experience of culture, varies depending on the material circumstances that surround and define one's point of reference. And as gender and race taken separately determine the conditions not only of oppression but also of liberation, so too does the interplay between these categories give rise to its own conception of liberation.

I want to resist the temptation to define or overspecify the particular questions that a black feminist theoretical approach might pose of a text. But I would characterize black feminist literary theory more broadly by arguing that it seeks to explore representations of black women's lives through techniques of analysis which suspend the variables of race, class, and gender in mutually interrogative relation.

The fiction of tradition represents one theoretical conception to which a number of black feminist theorists return. In a persuasively argued recent essay, Deborah McDowell examines the relationship between novels of racial uplift in the 1920s and recent black fiction.[18] Although Hazel V. Carby asserts in her book, *Reconstructing Womanhood*, that she is not engaged in the process of constructing the contours of a black female literary tradition, yet she establishes a lineage of black women intellectuals engaged in the ideological debates of their time. Mary Helen Washington and Dianne Sadoff likewise consider how race, class, and gender affect, respectively, the meaning of literary influence and the politics of literary reception. I focus here for a moment on the ways in which Washington's " 'Taming All That Anger Down': Rage and Silence in Gwendolyn Brooks's *Maud Martha*" [19] and Sadoff's "Black Matrilineage: The Case of Alice Walker and Zora Neale Neale Hurston"[20] make use of these three variables in their reformulation of the fiction of literary tradition.

In this essay, as in much of her recent writing, Washington argues that the material circumstances of black women's lives require one to develop revisionist strategies for evaluating and reading their work. She demonstrates here that precisely because the early reviewers and critics failed to comprehend the significance of race and gender for both a black woman writer and a young black urban girl, they trivialized Brooks and her only novel, a text made up of vignettes which are themselves comprised of short, declarative sentences.

Contemporary reviewers likened Brooks's style "to the exquisite delicacy of a lyric poem," Washington writes. They gave it "the kind of ladylike treatment that assured its dismissal."[21] But by examining the subtext of color prejudice, racial self-hatred, sexual insecurity, and powerlessness that underlies virtually every chapter, Washington demonstrates that the structure and grammar of the novel enact not what one reviewer called the protagonist's "spunk," but rather her repressed anger. In her discussion of the historical conditions that circumscribe the lives of black women in the 1940s and 1950s, Washington suggests ways in which Maud's oppression recalls Brooks's own marginal position within the publishing industry. Brooks inscribes not only Maud Martha's frustration, then, but also her own.

Washington's discussion here considers as well Brooks's reluctance to represent black women as heroic figures as a further sign of her oppression by a racist and sexist literary establishment. She thus prompts not only new readings of the text, but also of the relation between author and character. Indeed, Washington's discussion, turning as it does on the representation of the circumstances of Maud's life, enables a redefinition of the way a range of texts in the Afro-American canon are read. In her words, "if Maud Martha is considered an integral part of the Afro-American canon, we will have to revise our conception of power and powerlessness, of heroism, of symbolic landscapes and ritual grounds."[22]

In her article, Dianne Sadoff argues that black women writers share neither the anxiety of influence Harold Bloom attributes to male writers nor the primary anxiety of authority Sandra Gilbert and Susan Gubar attribute to white women writers. Rather, she demonstrates that "race and class oppression intensify the black woman writer's need to discover an untroubled matrilineal heritage. In celebrating her literary foremothers, the contemporary black woman writer covers over more profoundly than does the white writer her ambivalence about matrilineage, her own misreading of precursors, and her link to an oral as well as a written tradition."[23]

Sadoff's examination of the relationship between Zora Neale Hurston and Alice Walker reveals a compelling tension between the explicit subjects of each author's work and the subversive material that underlies those surfaces. An ancestor claimed as significant by most recent black women writers, Zora Neale Hurston misrepresents herself within her fiction, Sadoff argues. *Their Eyes Were Watching God* may announce itself, for instance, as a celebration of heterosexual love, but Hurston manipulates narrative strategies to ensure that the male is eliminated and the female liberated. Sadoff goes on to show that Walker affirms her tie to Hurston by inscribing a similar double agenda throughout her work, problematizing the status of heterosexual love in similar ways. Moreover, while her essays document her enthusiastic pursuit of Hurston as a literary foremother, her novels display a profound anxiety about biological motherhood. Sadoff's readings demonstrate, then, that the peril of uniqueness compels an intense need on the part of black women writers to identify a literary matrilineage even as their historical circumstances occasion their ambivalence about the fact and process of mothering.

These two essays thus show that the black feminist enterprise, at this stage necessarily materialist, calls for a reconception of the politics of literary reception, the meaning of literary influence, and the content of literary tradition.

At this point in its evolution, black feminist literary theory does not yet appear to replicate the totalizing tendency I attributed to Anglo-American feminism and male Afro-Americanism earlier. No doubt because it has remained marginal, what has been primarily a heterosexual, Afro-American-centered feminist discourse has been concerned with refining its own mode of inquiry, perhaps at the expense of annexing to itself the experiences of "others" such as lesbians and other women of color.

Fiction by black women has, however, achieved significant visibility operating simultaneously as a body of texts both marginal and mainstream. Andrea Lee's *Sarah Phillips* thematizes this very issue and suggests that the very activity of conceptualizing the self as insider may occasion a fetishization of the "other."

The stories that make up Andrea Lee's *Sarah Phillips* appeared separately in *The New Yorker* magazine before they were collected and published together in 1984. This fact about the publishing history alone suggests that in at least one way this is a text of privilege; the content of the stories themselves also foregrounds the issue of class position. Each story is a vignette taken from the life of the title character, the daughter of a prosperous Baptist minister and his school-teacher wife. With the exception of the first, entitled "In France," the stories are arranged chronologically to sketch Sarah Phillips's girlhood and adolescence in private schools and progressive summer camps in and around Philadelphia, undergraduate years at Harvard, and obligatory expatriation to Europe after graduation.

In addition to their common subject, the majority of the stories share a common structure. Most of the stories establish a community of insiders, disparate voices brought into unison, poised in a continuous present. In each instance, the stasis achieved by the choice of verb tenses, imagery, and patterns of allusion is interrupted by the presence of an outsider, someone who is constituted as the "other" according to the characteristics and assumptions of the narrative community. In virtually every instance, the presence of this "other" serves to historicize a vignette that had existed for the narrator as a moment out of time. The stories thus enact a tension between the narrative of the community of privilege, posited as ahistorical, and a destabilizing eruption, posited as inescapably historical.

Contemporary reviews identified two problematic areas of the text—the significance of Sarah's class position and the ambiguous relation between narrator and protagonist. Mary Helen Washington places it in a tradition with William Wells Brown's *Clotel*, Frances E. W. Harper's *Iola Leroy*, and James Weldon Johnson's *Autobiography of an Ex-Colored Man*, all works about a privileged black narrator tenuously connected to his or her blackness who needs to escape the problematic meanings of that identity. Washington argues that in these other novels, in varying degrees the narrators recognize the complex interplay between issues of class and race. The narrator of *Sarah Phillips*, in contrast, participates in the character's capitulation to her own position. Washington writes: "By the fourth or fifth story, I felt that the privileged kid had become the privileged narrator, no longer willing to struggle over issues of race and class, unable to bear the 'alarming knowledge' that these issues must reveal."[24]

Sherley Anne Williams compares the text to Richard Wright's *Black Boy*, arguing that both works "literally and figuratively [renounce] oral culture and black traditions for personal autonomy." She remarks that *Sarah Phillips* holds up to mockery "not the pretensions of her upper middle class heroine, but the 'outworn rituals' of black community."[25]

Both reviews suggest a point of contrast between Lee on the one hand and other contemporary black women writers who construct fictional communities of privilege. Toni Morrison, like Paule Marshall, Gloria Naylor, and Ntozake Shange, to name but a few, occasionally centers her novels on middle-class black characters. But as Susan Willis has written, in Morrison's novels, black middle-class life is generally characterized by a measure of alienation from the cultural heritage of the black rural South. Her characters are saved from "the upper reaches of bourgeois reification" by "eruptions of 'funk' "—characters or experiences that invoke the characters' cultural past and repressed emotional lives.[26] The energy of the text is thus in every case with the characters who represent "funk": Sula, Pilate, Son, even Cholly Breedlove; Morrison consistently problematizes what it means to be black and privileged.

Lee's narrator, on the other hand, seems as alienated from outsiders as the protagonist does. The text is sufficiently invested in its own construction of what it means to be privileged that it marginalizes those different from the protagonist herself. Rather than disparage *Sarah Phillips* on the basis of its politics, however, I should like to consider ways in which the "other" is figured here. For it seems to me that like the examples drawn earlier from feminist and Afro-Americanist discourse, this text also equates that "other" with the historical or the material.

My argument focuses primarily on a story entitled "Gypsies," in which a family of itinerants disrupt the orderliness of Sarah's suburban girlhood and force at least a symbolic acknowledgment of her place in a broader historical reality. But I begin with a reading of "In France," the story with which the volume begins, for it establishes a perspective by means of which the other stories may be read.

"In France" violates the chronological arrangement of stories, since it recounts the most recent events in the protagonist's life. The story breaks the pattern of the other stories in the volume in yet another way, for it is the only one to situate Sarah as an alien in her environment. The reader learns at once that Sarah is an American in Paris, but her story is filtered through the account of another American living there, a girl named Kate who seems to be missing. Rumors circulate that Kate is being held hostage by her present lover and ex-boyfriend lover who were "collecting her allowance and had bought a luxurious Fiat—the same model the Pope drove—with the profits."[27]

As it is recounted here, Kate's story invokes an absent double, underscoring Sarah's isolation. Moreover, the rumor of her mistreatment at the hands of her male friends presages the abuse Sarah's lover Henri and his friends inflict on her later in the story. We learn that after the death of her father and her graduation from Harvard, Sarah "cast off kin and convention in a foreign tongue" (4) and went to study French in Switzerland. Upon meeting Henri she leaves school and moves into the Paris apartment he shares with his friends Alain and Roger. Together they spend their time in cafés, museums, their apartment, and on occasional weekend expeditions into the country. The story turns on one such trip to the island of Jersey, when ostensibly harmless banter among the four of them suddenly turns nasty.

In this exchange Henri verbally assaults Sarah with racial insults, saying:

Did you ever wonder . . . why our beautiful Sarah is such a mixture of races? . . . It's a very American tale. This *Irlandaise* was part redskin, and not only that but part Jew as well—some Americans are part Jew, aren't they? And one day this *Irlandaise* was walking through the jungle near New Orleans, when she was raped by a jazz musician as big and black as King Kong, with sexual equipment to match. And from this agreeable encounter was born our little Sarah, *notre Negresse pasteurisée*. (11)

Sarah responds in two ways. In the shock of the moment she recognizes that she cannot ignore this parody of miscegenation. Her class position notwithstanding, she plays some role in the drama of race relations from which such stereotypes derive. Several hours later, the meaning of the insult strikes her again, this time in a dream—one that impels her to return home: "I awoke with a start from a horrid dream in which I was conducting a monotonous struggle with an old woman with a dreadful spidery strength in her arms; her skin was dark and leathery, and she smelled like one of the old Philadelphia church-women who used to babysit with me" (14).

The dream prompts her to reflect more calmly on the fact that she will never be able to escape the call of her personal history. She remarks:

I had hoped to join the ranks of dreaming expatriates for whom Paris can become a self-sufficient universe, but my life there had been no more than a slight hysteria, filled with the experimental naughtiness of children reacting against their training. It was clear, much as I did not want to know it, that my days in France had a number, that for me the bright, frank, endlessly beckoning horizon of the runaway had been, at some point, transformed into a complicated return. (15)

The story thus suggests that the past is inescapable. It anticipates Sarah's return home even though that return remains undramatized. I would argue that the subsequent stories, all of which center on events from Sarah's earlier life, function symbolically as that return home. The recurrent patterns that run through these other vignettes recapitulate the tension within the first story between escape and return. They indicate that the past may elude integration into the present, but it can also never be avoided.

In "Gypsies," the narrator attributes to Franklin Place, the street on which Sarah grows up, the ubiquity of a symbol. The opening description works against historical or geographical specificity, and instead represents the neighborhood in terms of the icons of upper-middle-class suburban culture. That is to say, in the opening paragraph the narrator locates the street in her dreams and nightmares, in her patterns of associations, before she locates it in a Philadelphia suburb. In this description, the suburb is represented as an abstraction, the fulfillment of a fantasy, distinct from the conditions of the world outside its boundaries.

Franklin Place, the street that ran like a vein through most of my dreams and night-mares, the stretch of territory I automatically envisioned when someone said "neigh-borhood," lay in a Philadelphia suburb. The town was green and pretty, but had the constrained, slightly unreal atmosphere of a colony or a foreign enclave, that was because the people who owned the rambling houses behind the shrubbery were black. For them—doctors, ministers, teachers who had grown up in Philadelphia row houses—the lawns and tree-lined streets represented the fulfillment of a fantasy long deferred, and acted as a barrier against the predictable cruelty of the world. (39)

If this opening paragraph bestows a quality of unreality on the landscape against which this and several of the other stories take place, subsequent paragraphs render the world beyond the neighborhood even more ephemeral. From the narrator's per-spective, historical events and political struggle represent levels of experience with which one may engage, but only imaginatively, the songs of cicadas providing a musical transition from Franklin Place to the world of those less privileged. As the narrator remarks:

For as long as I could remember, the civil rights movement had been unrolling like a dim frieze behind the small pleasures and defeats of my childhood; it seemed dull, a necessary burden on my conscience, like good grades or hungry people in India. My occasional hair-raising reveries of venturing into the netherworld of Mississippi or Alabama only added a voluptuous edge to the pleasure of eating an ice-cream cone while seated on a shady curb of Franklin Place. (39–40)

The image of the civil rights movement as a frieze fixes and aestheticizes the process of historical change, as if the inertia of Sarah's life had afflicted the world beyond the parameters of her neighborhood.

The illusion of timelessness and unassailability is sustained additionally by the narrator's tendency to cast the particular in terms of the habitual or familiar through her use of the second-person pronoun and the English equivalent of the French imperfect tense. For even as she narrows the focus of the story to the time of her encounter with the gypsies, the narrator describes that particular day in terms that homogenize or encompass, terms that, in other words, move away from particularity. Indeed, the impulse toward generalization and away from particularity is rendered nowhere more clearly than in the description of Sarah in which she is described as if she were a twin of her best friend Lyn Yancey.

On the day in question, a battered red pickup truck bearing its load of log furniture and a family of gypsies disturbs the peace of Franklin Place, a neighborhood of sedans, station wagons, and sports cars. Neither black nor white, the gypsies defy the categories available to Sarah and Lyn: the wife's breasts swaying back and forth in a way in which "the well-contained bosoms of [their] mothers never do" (43). Despite their marginal status, the gypsies articulate the assumptions about race and class shared by the majority culture. "It's a real crime for colored to live like this," says the wife. "You are very lucky little girls, very lucky, do you understand? When my son was your age he never got to play like you girls" (43).

At dinner that evening, Sarah repeats for her family her conversation with the gypsies. The exchange that ensues disrupts the veneer of family harmony, introducing social reality into the magic of the private sphere. Her father, ordinarily a man of great restraint, loses his sense of decorum. "Most of the world despises gypsies, but a gypsy can always look down on a Negro! Heck, that fellow was right to spit! You can dress it up with trees and big houses and people who don't stink too bad, but a nigger neighborhood is still a nigger neighborhood" (44).

Sarah and Lyn later meet at the swim club. The narrator's description of the pool at night betrays if not the young girls' yearnings, then her own nostalgia for the familiar tranquility. The language thus shifts dramatically from the father's clipped vernacular speech. Their rediscovered contentment lasts only until the return home, however, for on the street they confront the gypsies again, an insistent presence that cannot be ignored. The final paragraph of the story suggests that the protagonist's life has been altered profoundly. The narrator remarks, "nothing looked different, yet everything was, and for the first time Franklin Place seemed genuinely connected to a world that was neither insulated nor serene. Throughout the rest of the summer, on the rare occasions when a truck appeared in our neighborhood, Lyn and I would dash to see it, our hearts pounding with perverse excitement and with a fresh desire for knowledge" (46). This final formulation resonates with a certain falseness; the narrator allows Sarah and Lyn the freedom to be entertained by historical events, as if the dim frieze of the civil rights movement might somehow amuse or stimulate them. Indeed, throughout the collection, stories conclude with similar ambivalence; Lee leaves unresolved the issue as to whether the insiders' acknowledgment of the other is symbolic or transformative.

The story thus constitutes a community of insiders rendered ahistorical and homogeneous by the allusions, descriptions, and grammar of the narrator. The presence of someone from outside of that community reminds the residents of Franklin Place of the contingencies on which their apparently stable lives are founded. Simultaneously, the outsider reminds the privileged community of the circumstances of their history. The exchange destabilizes the narrator's ability to totalize the experience the story describes.

Lee's persistent interest in eruptions into communities of privilege causes these stories to be useful texts within which to observe the relation between the presence of the "other" in theoretical discourse. The black woman protagonist in these stories locates herself within, rather than outside of, the normative community, be it an integrated camp for middle-class children, her neighborhood, or her family. Her very presence within these exclusionary communities suggests that the circumstances of race and gender alone protect no one from the seductions of reading her own experience as normative and fetishizing the experience of the other.

This essay offers three perspectives on the contemporary black feminist enterprise. It shows how black feminism is invoked in mainstream feminist and Afro-Americanist discourse, it presents in broad outlines the space black feminist theory occupies independently, and it suggests how one contemporary black woman novelist thematizes the relationship between those who occupy privileged discursive spaces and the "other."

I have approached the subject from three perspectives in part because of my own evident suspicion of totalizing formulations. But my approach reflects as well the black feminist skepticism about the reification of boundaries that historically have excluded the writing of black women from serious consideration within the academic and literary establishments. Since, to my mind, some of the most compelling and representative black feminist writing treads the boundary between anthology and criticism, or between cultural theory and literary theory, it seems appropriate that a consideration of this critical perspective would approach it from a variety of points of view.

NOTES

1. Elaine Showalter, "Critical Cross-Dressing: Male Feminism and the Woman of the Year," in Alice Jardine and Paul Smith, eds., *Men in Feminism* (Methuen: New York, 1987), 127.

2. Hazel V. Carby, *Reconstructing Womanhood: The Emergence of the Afro-American Woman Novelist* (New York: Oxford University Press, 1987), 9.

3. Mary Helen Washington, "Introduction," in Mary Helen Washington, ed., *Black-Eyed Susans: Classic Stories by and about Black Women* (Garden City, N.Y.: Anchor Books, 1975), x–xxxii.

4. See Barbara Smith, "Toward a Black Feminist Criticism," *Conditions Two I* (October 1977), and Deborah E. McDowell, "New Directions for Black Feminist Criticism," *Black American Literature Forum 14*. Both were reprinted in Elaine Showalter, ed., *The New Feminist Criticism; Essays on Women, Literature and Theory* (New York: Pantheon, 1985), 168–185 and 186–199, respectively.

5. See, for instance, the reprint series that McDowell edits for Beacon Press and her Rutgers University Press reprint of Nella Larsen's *Quicksand* and *Passing*; Washington's three anthologies, *Black-Eyed Susans, Midnight Birds,* and *Invented Lives* and her Feminist Press edition of Paule Marshall's *Brown Girl, Brownstones*; Nellie McKay's edition of Louise Meriwether's *Daddy Was a Number Runner*; and Gloria T. Hull's edition of Alice Dunbar-Nelson's diary, *Give Us Each Day*, to name but a few. Black women are not exclusively responsible for these kinds of editorial projects. See also William Andrews, *Sisters of the Spirit: Three Black Women's Autobiographies of the Nineteenth Century*; Henry Louis Gates's edition of Harriet E. Wilson's *Our Nig* and his Oxford University Press reprint series; and Jean Fagan Yellin's edition of Harriet Jacobs's *Incidents in the Life of a Slave Girl*.

6. Peggy Kamuf, "Replacing Feminist Criticism," *Diacritics 2* (Summer 1982): 44.

7. Nancy K. Miller, "The Text's Heroine: A Feminist Critic and Her Fictions," *Diacritics 12* (Summer 1982): 49–50.

8. Elizabeth A. Meese, *Crossing the Double-Cross: The Practice of Feminist Criticism* (Chapel Hill: University of North Carolina Press, 1986).

9. Teresa de Lauretis, "Feminist Studies/Critical Studies: Issues, Terms, and Contexts," in Teresa de Lauretis, ed., *Feminist Studies/Critical Studies* (Bloomington: Indiana University Press, 1986), 2.

10. Ibid., 9.

11. Ibid., 10.

12. Houston A. Baker, Jr., *Blues, Ideology, and Afro-American Literature* (Chicago: University of Chicago Press, 1984).

13. See Robert B. Stepto, "Teaching Afro-American Literature: Survey or Tradition: The Reconstruction of Instruction," and Henry Louis Gates, Jr., "Preface to Blackness: Text and Pretext," both in Dexter Fisher and Robert B. Stepto, eds., *Afro-American Literature: The Reconstruction of Instruction* (New York: Modern Language Association of America, 1979), 8–24 and 44–69, respectively.

14. Robert B. Stepto, *From Behind the Veil: A Study of Afro-American Narrative* (Urbana: University of Illinois Press, 1979).

15. Baker, *Blues*, 94.

16. Ibid., 101.

17. Elizabeth V. Spelman, "Theories of Race and Gender: The Erasure of Black Women," *Quest 5* (1979): 42.

18. Deborah E. McDowell, " 'The Changing Same': Generational Connections and Black Women Novelists," *New Literary History 18* (Winter 1987).

19. Mary Helen Washington, " 'Taming All That Anger Down': Rage and Silence in Gwendolyn Brooks's *Maud Martha*," in Henry Louis Gates, Jr., ed., *Black Literature and Literary Theory* (New York: Methuen, 1984), 249–262.

20. Dianne F. Sadoff, "Black Matrilineage: The Case of Alice Walker and Zora Neale Hurston," *Signs 11* (Autumn 1985): 4–26.

21. Washington, "Taming," 249.

22. Ibid., 260.

23. Sadoff, "Black Matrilineage," 5.

24. Mary Helen Washington, "Young, Gifted and Black," *Women's Review of Books 2* (March 1985): 3.

25. Sherley Anne Williams, "Roots of Privilege: New Black Fiction," *Ms. 13* (June 1985): 71.

26. See Susan Willis, "Eruptions of Funk: Historicizing Toni Morrison," in *Specifying: Black Women Writing the American Experience* (Madison: University of Wisconsin Press, 1987), 83–109.

27. Andrea Lee, *Sarah Phillips* (New York: Penguin Books, 1984), 3. Subsequent references to this edition are noted in the text by page number.

4 | The 1990s

Feminist Expansions, Queer Theory, and the
Turn to Cultural Studies

34 Revision and (Re)membrance

A Theory of Literary Structures in Literature by African-American Women Writers

Karla F. C. Holloway

(1990)

I

> There were no memories among those pieces. Certainly no memories to be cherished.
> —TONI MORRISON, *THE BLUEST EYE*

A stream of linguistic madness that merges the images of an internally fractured psyche and an externally flattened physical world is the opening and closing linguistic figuration in Toni Morrison's *The Bluest Eye*. We come to learn that the injured spirit belongs to Pecola and that the opening scene of the fictional Dick-and-Jane house that her metaphorically blued eyes see ("Here is the house. It is green and white. . . . It is very pretty. Here is the family. Mother, Father, Dick and Jane live in the green-and-white house."[7]) is the one-dimensional remnant of the illusory world that has claimed her.

This fragmented and flattened stream is just one of the shapes of language in Morrison's shifting novel. There is also the ironically poetic and visually vivid language that describes Claudia's struggle to rise above the depression in her physical world:

> She spent her days, her tendril, sap-green days, walking up and down, her head yielding to the bent of a drummer so distant only she could hear. . . . she flailed her arms like a bird in an eternal, grotesquely futile effort . . . intent on the blue void it could not reach—could not even see—but which filled the valleys of the mind. (158)

Colors and textures thicken this novel as if they are the only dimensions left of language and vision that are able to tell the story of Pecola's madness. Even though the sisters who befriend her are saved by "the greens and blues in [their] mother's voice [that] took all the grief out of the words" (24), Pecola is left with the biting

387

shards of all the grief that surrounds her. "The damage done was total" (158), her one-time friend Claudia reflects. The only language which remains for her is the internalized monologue of a narrative stream whose shape, sound, and sense contain the fractured psyche of the tragically injured Pecola. It alone can testify that her madness was framed by the recurrence of a shifting textual language. Each change in the narrative reminds the reader of another of its forms. Eventually it is this characteristic of a shifting language which frames the recursive structures (signals of textual reflexiveness) of Morrison's first novel.

My purpose in this essay is to suggest ways in which the recursive structures of language in literature by contemporary African-American women writers are signaled by what is essentially a "multiplied" text. Recursive structures accomplish a blend between figurative processes that are reflective (like a mirror) and symbolic processes whose depth and resonance make them reflexive. This combination results in texts that are at once emblematic of the culture they describe as well as interpretive of this culture. Literature that strikes this reflective/reflexive posture is characteristically polyphonic. The textual characterizations and events, the settings and symbolic systems are multiple and layered rather than individual and one-dimensional. This literature displays the gathered effects of these literary structures to the extent that, when we can identify and recognize them, we are also able to specify their relationship to thematic and stylistic emphases of the traditions illustrated in these works. Because all of the structures share complexity—features of what I refer to as both the "multiplied text" and the "layered" text—I have chosen to use the term *plurisignation* as a means of illustrating the dimensions of vision and language in the contemporary literature of writers in this tradition.[1]

Plurisignant texts are notable by their translucence. One interesting consequence of this imagery is a certain "posturing" of the textual language. This posture places the narrative language at a formative threshold rather than on an achieved and rigid structure. This is not to suggest that thesis and content are constantly *in potentia* in these texts. It means instead that these works are often characterized by the presence of a translucent flux and identified by a shifting, sometimes nebulous text. The characteristic of words and places in these works is their representation of events and ideas that revise and multiply meanings to the point that their external ambivalence is but an outward sign of internal displacement. The result for these translucent works is textural dissonance.

Whether it is gender or culture or a complication of both that has directed the works of contemporary African-American women writers toward this exploration of the state of being of its voices, the various linguistic postures within these texts are clearly intertextual. Writing in *Figures in Black*, Henry Louis Gates suggests that "shared modes of figuration result only when writers read each other's texts and seize upon topoi and tropes to revise in their own texts . . . a process of grounding [that] has served to create formal lines of continuity between the texts that together comprise the shared text of blackness" (128–29). Considerations of gender weave an additional texture into this line of continuity.

The translucence I refer to begins to have an interesting quality when viewed not only as method in literature, but as an objective dimension of the literature. It is this kind of complexity that becomes a "formal line of continuity" and that identifies the discrete aspects in the texts of African-American women's writing. One might look, for example, at how black women in the literature of these authors visualize themselves. Instead of reflections that isolate and individuate, characters such as Gwendolyn Brooks's Maud Martha or Ntozake Shange's Sassafrass see themselves surrounded by a tradition of women like them.

Sassafrass's ancestral women come "from out of a closet" and beg her to "make . . . a song . . . so high all us spirits can hold it and be in your tune" (80–81). The "Lady" that Sassafrass conjures calls to "multitudes of brown-skinned dancing girls" (81) who become Sassafrass's spirit-informants, assuring her a place in their own line of continuity as they stabilize her spiritual relationship to them. Shange's achievement is a text that recalls ancestral voices to assist her own obviously contemporary story. For example, it is when Sassafrass's living begins to echo a blues song that the text dissolves into italics and the "Lady" comes from the closet. When this ancestral "Lady sigh[s] a familiar sigh" (180). Sassafrass herself enters the italicized narrative. This is a signal that there is no level of the story, no space in this narrative that is not here:

> The Lady turned to the doorway on her right and shouted, "Come on, y'all," and multitudes of brown-skinned dancing girls with ostrich-feather headpieces and tap shoes started doing the cake-walk all around Sassafrass, who was trying to figure out the stitching pattern on their embroidered dresses. (81)

The message for Sassafrass is that the texture of their appearance (the "stitching pattern") is as important as their lineage. These ladies are there to instruct her and, even more importantly, to replace the abusive Mitch, who, Shange writes, had been "on her mind" (82). The mixture of images that Sassafrass learns to live with—the creation banner over the stove, the looms that revision her own growing-up in her mother's house, her writing and her recipes—are all fragments of the spiritual energy she will need in order to rescue her spirit from the disabling presence of Mitch.

The poignancy in Shange's writing extends from her successful mingling of languages. Poetry and music exist in the same spaces as dialogues and dreams. Women's sharing of their most intimate and creative language with each other is a significant feature of Shange's method. Part of this sharing is clearly evident in the recipes and letters from Sassafrass's, Cypress's, and Indigo's mother, but it is also an important dimension of the lesbian relationships in this novel. Some of the most generative and thickest language surrounds Shange's descriptions of the women's dance collective the Azure Bosom.

Dense in color and texture, and full and resonant in shapes and forms, this collective represents the deepest levels of the stylistic effort in *Sassafrass, Cypress & Indigo*. Here, the language is as full-bodied as the women's gender dance, "a dance of women discovering themselves in the universe" (141). In the house Cypress shares with the dancers from the Azure Bosom, she sees "herself everywhere . . . nothing different from her in essence: no thing not woman" (139). In this novel, Shange brings full circle the revelation of her dramatic choreopoem *for colored girls*. Here, the generational dimensions of womanself are explored as a variety of creative energies—Sassafrass's weaving and writing, Cypress's dance, and eventually Indigo's personification of biological creativity. She becomes a midwife—a creatrix. Because it is Indigo's vision that both opens and closes the story, she is Shange's final coalescence of the extended imaginative dimensions of the novel. Indigo represents the metaphorical bridge between African-American women and their African ancestry. She is an elemental link, embodying the qualities of air ("a moon in her mouth"), earth (" 'earth blood, filled up with the Geechees long gone' "), and water (" 'and the sea' " [1]). It is not until Sassafrass wears white and sees a vision of her "Mother" (Shange capitalizes this word, giving it a resonance and depth that extends beyond her immediate biological mother) that she finds the spirit she shares with her sister Indigo. By this time in the story, Indigo has come to embody the midwifery talents of her mentor Aunt Haydee. We are told that her place in the ancestral tradition Haydee represents is appropriate because, more than having "an interest in folklore," Indigo "was the folks" (224).

Maud Martha's vision of her place in the line of ancient folks that claim Sassafrass as one of them is vision as well as revision. Her recursive glance represents both a call from her history and a response from her own psyche:

> A procession of pioneer women strode down her imagination; strong women, bold; praiseworthy, faithful, stout-minded; with a stout light beating in the eyes. Women who could stand low temperatures. Women who would toil eminently, to improve the lot of their men. Women who cooked. She thought of herself, dying for her man. It was a beautiful thought. (200–01)

That Maud Martha's imagination shifts in this novella just enough so that she does not become the sacrificial victim of a man who would define the parameters of her own dream for her is its thesis. Instead, Maud Martha learns to include her own self as something "decently constant" to depend upon—similar to the discovery of Toni Morrison's Sethe (in *Beloved*), who learns to accept that she is her own "best thing"—and learns as well that "learning was work." Significantly, Maud Martha does not revision the procession of women from her imagination. Instead, she learns to revisualize the nature of their work. In *Maud Martha*, translucence is related to the shifting presence of Maud and her dreams. For example, her husband tells her that the place he visualizes for her, their apartment, will be her "dream." But the reader is confronted with textual structures that insist on their own dreaminess: the silences that fracture each scene and the stifling spaces of Maud's life (both the apartment and her marriage) that define her liminality. Maud's thoughts mix themselves into these structures as if they are actually translucent. In an episode that describes Maud's sparing the life of a tiny mouse which "vanishes" after her act of liberation, Brooks writes, "Suddenly, she was conscious of a new cleanness in her. A wide air walked in her. . . . In the center of [her] simple restraint was—creation" (212–13).

Equally as significant a moment and also an illustration of the revision that occurs when "modes of figuration" are shared is the moment that follows the embrace between Ciel and Mattle in Gloria Naylor's *The Women of Brewster Place*. I find in Maud's sudden translucence (the wide air that "walked" in her) a luminous quality similar to Ciel's moan, a sound so "agonizingly slow, it broke its way through [her] parched lips in a spaghetti-thin column of air that could be faintly heard in the frozen room" (103).[2] Both moments mark occasions that initiate a cleansing of psychic despair. Maud realizes that she is good, and Luciela realizes her grief.

The Women of Brewster Place is a novel where time and place (space) immediately collide. The first section. "Dawn," is an introduction to the history of Brewster Place, which Naylor characterizes as a *"bastard child"* (1). The focus in the novel is on the women of this place, whose own histories are as bastardized as their contemporary locus. Mattle, Ciel, Etta Mae, "The Two," and Kiswana are all women separated from their familial sources and are left alone to become the communal "daughters" of the place. Such spiritual dislocation, complicated by the vapid air of Brewster Place, exacts its tragic due. In the last section of the novel, "Dusk," Brewster Place "wait[s] for death, which is a second behind the expiration of its spirit in the minds of its children. . . . the colored daughters of Brewster, spread over the canvas of time, still wake up with their dreams misted on the edge of a yawn" (192).

In this work, the metaphor of a place serves as an ancestral presence. Brewster Place exists both before the women who inherit it and afterwards. Its fundamental irony, and Naylor's bitter commentary on these spiritually dispossessing city spaces, is that Brewster Place is generatively inadequate and sterile. Over and over again African-American women's texts present characters poised between a spiritual place and a place that has been defined for them, assigned by some person, or extracted from some ritual they are unable to remember.

The quality of translucence that reveals such plurisignant texts is also one that complicates the identities of the tellers of the stories. The boundaries between narrative voices and dialogue often become obscure, merging one into the other.[3] Speech that is circumvented has come to be a discrete feature of the African-American women writers' canon. The result of this frustration, this struggle towards articulation, is that voice in these writer's works is manipulated—inverted from its usual dimensions and re-placed into non-traditional spheres (layers) of the text. In this formulation, speech is often liminal, translucent, and subject to disarray, dislocation (in the Freudian sense of *Verschetbung*), and dispersion. Only the thematic emphasis on the recovery of some dimension of voice restores the balance to the text between its voices and those collected into its rearticulated universe. Such empowerment at the metaphorical level—storms and hurricanes that have psychically disruptive potentials, trees that are serene and knowledgeable, rivers whose resident ladies (goddesses) hold the promise (or denial) of fertility—provides poetic activation of the textual voices in African-American women writers' texts.

II

> Only the final section . . . raises the poetry to a sustained high level . . . recall[ing] the
> English metaphysicals . . . fus[ing] African and European elements as in the beat of
> Mr. Soyinka's early verse.   —WILLIAM RIGGAN, REVIEWING SOYINKA'S
> *MANDELA'S EARTH AND OTHER POEMS*

> Indeed, the basic difference between British and Igbo experiences and values are what
> make it necessary . . . to have to bend the English language in order to express Igbo
> experience and value in it.   —CHINWEIZU (EMPHASIS ADDED)[4]

SHIFT

I cite the Riggan review and the Chinwetzu excerpt as a means of focusing on both
the nature of textual revision and the substance of the interpretive discourse that
often follows the work of writers whose cultural sources are non-Western. Central to
my definition of metaphorical revision in the texts of African-American women
writers is an acknowledgment of the cultural sources of their (re)membered theses.
What becomes increasingly important to my consideration of the intertextual nature
of the literature produced by black women writers is the premise that the plurisignant
text has a multiple generation as well as a multiple presence. Both source and
substance are traceable through the culturally specific figurations of language that
are discrete figures in literature by black women authors. Shift happens when the
textual language "bends" in an acknowledgment of "experience and value" that are
not Western. A critical language that does not acknowledge the bend, or is itself
inflexible and monolithic, artificially submerges the multiple voices within this literature. For this reason, critical strategies that address the issues within these texts must
in one sense be mediative strategies between the traditional ideologies of the theoretical discourse and the ancestry of the text itself. Such mediation demands a shift in
the scope (if not the tone) of critical terminology—a redirection that calls attention
to different (and often contrary) ideologies. This is a task that demands a particular
kind of assertiveness. This assertiveness directs my discussion on the nature of shift
and revision.

My primary argument is this: When the interpretive spaces of the Afrocentric text
are culturally specified, and when theory attends to the dimensions of gender that are
discrete in the figurations of texts by black women writers, the tangential accomplishment of such specification and articulation is a presentation of the plurisignant text
as the ideal center of the critical discourse among the cultural etymologies of words
within the critical and textual traditions. Texts by black women writers are those
which are most likely to force apart the enclosed spaces of critical inquiry. The
ideologies especially challenged by the plurisignant text are those held by the "resident theoreticians"—those who have gerrymandered the districts of the interpretive
community to the extent that all texts and theorists who do not succumb to the
lexical tyranny of the English metaphysicals (and their descendants) are effectively

redlined. Such a community has decided upon its membership by a tacit agreement on the formal methods of interpretation and has effectively enclosed the terms of inquiry and imprisoned methodology in the lexical tyranny of Western ideologies. However, by disabling the definitions—that is, by acknowledging a textual language that is translucent and in flux—both the text and (ideally) the inquiry surrounding the text are freed from the tyranny of the West. This act of liberation is directly related to the language within black women writers' texts because their plurisignant nature models the cultural complexity of the language that would engage a "liberated" interpretive community.

In a rather serious "play" with the issues of critical theorizing, Barbara Christian's essay "The Race for Theory" identifies black women as having the historical claim as the "race" (and gender) for theory because:

> people of color have always theorized . . . in forms quite different from the Western form of abstract logic . . . in the stories we create, in riddles and proverbs, in the play with language because dynamic rather than fixed ideas seem more to our liking. . . . And women . . . continuously speculated about the nature of life through pithy language that unmasked the power relations of their world. It is this language, and the grace and pleasure with which they played with it, that I find celebrated, refined, critiqued in the works of [black women writers].(68)[5]

Christian's familiar note that the form of black women's textual language is a hieroglyph ("familiar" because it is a figure Zora Neale Hurston used to describe "Negro" Speech) that is both "sensual and abstract . . . beautiful and communicative" (68) is an appropriate metaphor as well for the activities of criticism and interpretation of these texts.

However, instead of grace and dynamism, pleasure and pithy speculation, the more likely dimensions of literary assessment have been those that reflect the sort of cultural chauvinism evident in William Riggan's assessment of Wole Soyinka's 1988 book of poetry. Riggan, who is only able to critically appreciate Soyinka's verse when the author "reaches the level of the English metaphysicals" with poetry that reflects its European ancestry, would constrict the African and African-American writer's literary domain. Such ethnocentrism is in fact responsible for disabling the relationship between African and African-American texts and their literary traditions rather than encouraging their (mediative) dialogue.

The idea that the plurisignant text calls attention to the syncretic relationship between individual novels and the novels within the cultural as well as gender-specified genre suggests that the polyphonic nature of these texts is essential not only to their internal figurations, but is also definitive of the tradition that collectively identifies them. Not only do the texts of African-American women writers articulate the dimensions of cultural pluralism in their world, but the perceptual "outsidedness" of these authors (a factor of both gender and culture) propels a revision in the critical discourse about their literature. In such a discursive space, "shift" becomes a necessary mediation between the reader and the text and encourages a dialogue among critical postures within the interpretive community. Shift positions the alternative interpretations represented by the assertions of culture and gender within the textures of this literature. The critical result is a theoretical acknowledgment of the multiplied text.

In case a shifting text and a shiftiness in critical vocabulary seem too problematic for what is generally an urge towards firmness in literary theory, let me suggest a perspective of Paul Ricoeur's as a potentially stabilizing one. In "Hermeneutics: The Approaches to Symbol," Ricoeur notes that "it is only when . . . interpretation is seen to be contained in the other that the antithetic is no longer simply the clash of opposites but the passage of each into the other" (88). Ricoeur is certain of a textural point of intersection in symbols. The concrete moments of a dialectic represent a "peak of mediation." He notes:

> In order to think in accord with symbols one must subject them to a dialectic; only then is it possible to . . . come back to living speech. In returning to the attitude of listening to language, *reflection passes into the fullness of speech . . . the fullness of language . . . that has been instructed by the whole process of meaning.* (88, emphasis added)

I suggest that it takes only a slight shift for an understanding of Ricoeur's comment regarding the "passage of each into the other" to extend to the "Others" who are the subjects and authors of African-American literature. The metaphorical figuration that results from this reformulated "other" (the symbols, the speech, the reflective language that Ricoeur includes in the processes that make meaning) is a symbolic reflection of my initial claim about the translucent nature of the plurisignant text. This refiguration brings me to a point where a reconsideration of gender and culture in what I have described as the "translucent" texts of African-American women writers is appropriate.

III

[T]he unconscious is the discourse of the Other. . . . The dimension of truth emerges only with the appearance of language.   —LACAN

(RE)MEMBRANCE

In a reflection on the use of folk material as "imagery and motif" as well as "a basic element of the inner forms" of African-American literature, Keith Byerman's conclusion is that its use "implies a fundamentally conservative [i.e., preservationist], organic vision on the part of these writers" who recognize the "wholeness, creativity, endurance[,] and concreteness" in maintaining the perspectives of the past as "vital to their own sensibilities" (276). Byerman underscores an important relationship between folk material and the perspectives of the past it recovers in his concluding chapter of *Fingering the Jagged Grain*. However, the "wholeness" and "concreteness" that he suggests are features of this (re)membrance of the past are in fact antithetical to the issue he attempts to resolve in his study. Actually, the search for wholeness is representative of the critical strategies of Western cultures. It represents a sensibility that privileges the recovery of an individual (and independent) text over its fragmented textural dimensions. Byerman's discussion is an example of the negative dialectic that can disable the relationship between interpretive effort and the textual tradition. Although he clearly understands the thematic effort of these works as an attempt to diminish the importance of "individual identity [which] does not exist separate from the community" (277), it is because the "concrete" history which engages the community and its members is a disabling (and therefore translucent) history that literature by African-American women writers actually dissembles the "wholeness" of this revived folkloric text. This is, however, not an act of textual sabotage.

Such activity in African-American women writers' texts is paradoxically an effect of *(re)membrance*—a word which cannot, in this canon where the "shared" tradition belies the scattering effects of the diaspora as well as its contradictory "gathering," simply mean "wholeness." Such an image gives a critical edge to what Morrison's Sethe calls in *Beloved* "rememory." Sethe's vision of history has a translucence akin to that described at the opening of this essay. It is "a picture floating . . . a thought picture" that has as much a place in her vision of the past as it has in the actual past. Consequently, it represents a multiplied (and seemingly contradictory) form of memory because although it achieves its presence through its translucence, its form is a consequence of Sethe's visualization. It is this kind of implicit dualism that calls attention to the cultural traditions within this literature and that begs the questions of gender. For example, it is important to acknowledge the West African ideologies represented in the narrative traditions in African-American women's literature because such tracery would assure our exploring the vestiges of folktales in the African-American text in conjunction with the historically female voices of/in the tales. The tellers, the mode of telling, the complications and sometimes obfuscations of telling become critical not only to the "folkloric" tradition, but to the larger narrative traditions as well. The specificity of voice as well as its assignation are facets of the (re)membered texts by women of the African diaspora.

In "Reshuffling the Deck," Claudia Tate comments on the canon, noting that

> unlike the black aesthetics, black feminist criticism examines not only its discursive territory but its own methodologies as well, *realizing that they are not ideologically neutral.* . . . The criticism's placement in traditional, academic, humanistic discourse gives rise to this reflexive posture because critics involved in this enterprise realize that the very terms for engaging in this discourse, that is, formulating hypotheses and evolving praxcs, inherently valorize cultural production that is white, patriarchal, and bourgeois-capitalistic. (120, emphases added)

Tate recognizes, in this essay that reviews contemporary works in Black feminist criticism, the "changing literal and figurative terms of the game," which is a tacit recognition of the quality of "shift" and the nature of (re)membrance. The figuration that is accomplished in these texts is one that reshapes the familiar structures of memory and that implicates a pre-text for African-American women's writing that would, if tapped into, address the significance of their race and culture and gender. The mythopoeic territory for these writers is a territory defined through the recon-figuration of memory. (Re)membrance does not imply the wholeness Byerman (for example) figures as a result of the folkloric traditions in Black literature. Instead, (re)membrance is activation in the face of stasis, a restoration of fluidity, translucence, and movement to the traditions of memory that become the subjects of these works. The substance of literary traditions, whether European or African or American or combinations thereof, is reconstituted in such a literary ethic.

In a recognition that the text of feminist literary studies is discrete, Lillian Robin-son calls for the "next step in the theoretical process" which will be "for the female nontext to become the text" (32).[6] Robinson identifies this nontext as the "creative incapacity" equated with silence and sees the restoration of voice as a discrete aspect of a feminist critical tradition. But it is exactly this kind of definition which, as it asserts the feminist text, simultaneously squeezes the black woman writer's literary tradition into a space too narrow to contain it. The (re)membered textural source of this gender-specified literary tradition includes a *cultural* source which is based in a collective orature. Robinson, who clearly understands that there is significant em-powerment through language, curiously reaches for restoration of "a common liter-ary heritage" within the restored "voice" of women's texts. However, such restoration may very well undermine the cultural specificity of women's language in the African-American text. The "common" heritage which Robinson concludes may be the "real thing" for feminist criticism is one she artificially simplifies to a decision that "people have to live in a house, not in a metaphor" (34). It is precisely because of this kind of formulation that critical theories of African-American women's texts must clarify the distinctiveness of the traditions those texts embody and the specificity of the heritage that resonates in the texts, lest those traditions and that heritage be sub-sumed into a feminist-inspired "commonness."

Consider my final epigraph. How can the discourse of the Other possibly be perceived as a monologue? Truth, language, and alterity (otherness) find their defini-tion within the "discursive territories" of a literary heritage that values and affirms pluralism. A consideration of the text, specifically its language, is exactly what forces critical inquiry back into a textual tradition and forward toward a theory that unequivocally addresses the source, meanings, and cultural complications represented within the textual language. Because the African-American woman's literary tradition is generated from a special relationship to words, the concerns of orature and the emergence of a textual language that acknowledges its oral generation must affect the work of the critics of this tradition.

The revised and (re)membered word is both an anomaly in and a concretizing of the traditions represented in literature by African-American women. Such seeming contradiction, rather than calling attention to a weakness, should draw attention to the need to identify, call, and specify the plurisignance within the texts of this tradition. This is a task of definition as much as it is an act of interpretation.

Interestingly, the critical task participates in the "layering" that is intrinsic to the texts of African-American women writers. I find in what the editors of *Yale French Studies* identify as the need to read "collectively, [to speak] in a plural voice" the dimension of feminist criticism that is most like the texts of the African-American woman's tradition, and it is because of this similarity that I basically agree with Lacan's judgment that it is our own "unconscious" that is the actual Other. The presence of the differing self, the "Other" is established through a recursive project, one that repeats the text in order to produce the text. As Christopher Miller effectively argues in "Theories of Africans: The Question of Literary Anthropology":

> By defining the Other's difference, one is forced to take into account, or to ignore at one's peril, the shadow cast by the self. But without some attention to the African past, some effort to describe the Other, how can we accurately read the African present? There are in fact two ways to lose identity, be it one's own or someone else's . . . by segregation in the particular or by dilution in the "universal." (300)

Miller's citation of Césaire's comment on the loss of identity is a maxim critical to the textual and accompanying critical need for a reflective (re)membrance of the textual source which is, after all, the basis of its identity. Within such a perspective, the nature of a critical language is redefined and is subsequently shifted towards the full-bodied voices of the shared traditions reflected within the literature.

NOTES

1. I use *plurisignation* in an effort to distinguish the idea of multiple meanings from a text that is (simply) ambiguous. Rather than meaning either one or the other of these terms, a plurisignant text signals the concurrent presence of multiple as well as ambiguous meanings.

2. Interestingly, "luminous" moments in this literature are often accompanied by a visual translucence that effectively includes the textual language as a factor in the shimmering quality of the metaphorical intent.

3. Zora Neale Hurston is the foremother in African-American literature of merged textual voices. *Their Eyes Were Watching God*, especially, uses this device in the blending of the poetic narrative voice and the poetic dialect of Janie's storytelling and reflective dialogues with her friend Pheoby. For further discussion of this dimension of narrative, see Holloway.

4. My preference here, and indeed the thoughtful advice of a reader of this essay, was to use citations that dealt more directly with the women writers under consideration. However, there is a compelling reason that the Riggan/Chinweizu epigraphs serve as appropriate choices for my discussion in this section. In focusing on Riggan's comment about Soyinka, I am able to draw attention to the paucity of critical response that African women writers have received outside of those theorists sympathetically interested in the traditions their gendered and encultured literature reflects. On the other hand, African male writers have managed to enter the wider critical arena (in other words, white males comment on their work). Unfortunately, this extended audience minimally (if at all) appreciates or understands the cultural traditions in the literature. The Riggan response is so striking in its ethnocentrism that it begs to be highlighted. (Carol Boyce Davies relates this issue of critical inattention to African women writers in the

thoughtful discussion of her introduction.) As a consequence of Riggan's assessment, Chinweizu's comment on the cultural dimensions within a linguistic system, especially as he directly comments on the "British" experience which Riggan celebrates, is a particularly poignant example of my point concerning the cultural sources of (re)membered theses.

5. Christian's essay bewails the lack of clarity in the critical enterprise, arguing that it underscores a central inattentiveness to text. In addition she argues that this criticism is as "hegemonic as the world it attacks." Christian's comments have the effect of reducing "valuable" critical activity to a practical criticism (similar to her own enterprise) while undermining the theoretical because it "has silenced many of us to the extent that some of us feel we can no longer discuss our own literature." Ironically, Christian's protest against writers whose criticism ignores the third world and continues to exert its control over the Western world implies the need for a textual exploration of the "center" of the literature of African and African-American women writers from the center that their texts identify.

WORKS CITED

Brooks, Gwendolyn. *Maud Martha*. 1953. *Blacks*. Chicago: David, 1957. 141–322.

Byerman, Keith. *Fingering the Jagged Grain*. Athens: U of Georgia P. 1985.

Christian, Barbara. "The Race for Theory." *Feminist-Studies* 14.1 (1988): 67–80.

Davies, Carol Boyce. *Ngambika: Studies of Women in African Literature*. Trenton: Africa World P. 1986.

Gates, Henry Louis, Jr. *Figures in Black: Words, Signs and the "Racial" Self*. New York: Oxford UP, 1987.

Holloway, Karla. *The Character of the Word: The Texts of Zora Neale Hurston*. New York: Greenwood, 1987.

Miller, Christopher. "Theories of Africans: The Question of Literary Anthropology." *"Race," Writing and Difference*. Ed. Henry Louis Gates, Jr. Chicago: U of Chicago P. 1985. 281–300.

Morrison, Toni. *The Bluest Eye*. 1970. New York: Pocket, 1972.

———. *Beloved*. New York: Knopf. 1987.

Naylor, Gloria. *The Women of Brewster Place*. New York: Viking, 1982.

Ricoeur, Paul. "Hermeneutics: The Approaches to Symbol." *Existential Phenomenology to Structuralism*. Ed. Vernon Gras. New York: Dell, 1973. 87–118.

Robinson, Lillian. "Canon Fathers and Myth Universe." *New Literary History* 19.1 (1987): 23–36.

Shange, Ntozaké. *Sassafrass, Cypress & Indigo*. New York: St. Martin's, 1982.

Tate, Claudia. "Reshuffling the Deck: Or, (Re)Reading Race and Gender in Black Women's Writing." *Tulsa Studies in Women's Literature* 7.1 (1988): 119–31.

35 Toward a Black Gay Aesthetic

Signifying in Contemporary Black Gay Literature

Charles I. Nero

(1991)

> Western literature has often posited the heterosexual white male as hero, with Gays, Blacks and women as Other. . . . The development of Black literature, women's literature, Gay literature, and now Black Gay literature is not so much a rewriting of history as an additional writing of it; together these various literatures, like our various selves, produce history. . . . Our past as Black Gay men is only now being examined.
>
> —Daniel Garrett, "Other Countries: The Importance of Difference"[1]

> Much of the Afro-American literary tradition can be read as successive attempts to create a new narrative space for representing the recurring referent of Afro-American literature, the so-called Black Experience.
>
> —Henry Louis Gates, Jr., *The Signifying Monkey*[2]

> All I can say is—if this is my time in life . . . goodbye misery.
>
> —Lorraine Hansberry, *A Raisin in the Sun*[3]

INTRODUCTION

With only a few exceptions, the intellectual writings of black Americans have been dominated by heterosexual ideologies that have resulted in the gay male experience being either excluded, marginalized, or ridiculed.[4] Because of the heterosexism among African American intellectuals and the racism in the white gay community, black gay men have been an invisible population. However, the last five years have seen a movement characterized by political activism and literary production by openly gay black men. Given their invisibility by both black heterosexism and white gay racism, two questions emerge: How have black gay men created a positive identity for themselves and how have they constructed literary texts which would render their lives visible, and therefore valid? I propose in this essay to answer the former by answering the latter, i.e., I will focus on the strategies by black men who have either identified themselves as gay or who feature black gay characters prominently in their work. The writers I examine will be Samuel Delany, George Wolfe, Billi Gordon, Larry Duplechan, Craig R. Harris, and Essex Hemphill.

The critical framework that I use is strongly influenced by my reading of Mary Helen Washington's *Invented Lives* and Henry Louis Gates, Jr.'s critical method of signifying. In *Invented Lives*, Washington brilliantly analyzes the narrative strategies ten black women have used between 1860 and 1960 to bring themselves into visibility and power in a world dominated by racism and sexism.[5] Like Washington, Gates's concern is with the paradoxical relationship of African Americans with the printed text, i.e., since Eurocentric writing defines the black as "other," how does the "other" gain authority in the text? To resolve this, Gates proposes a theory of criticism based upon the African American oral tradition of signifying. Signifying is, for Gates, "the black term for what in classical European rhetoric are called the figures of signification," or stated differently, "the indirect use of words that changes the meaning of a word or words."[6] Signifying has numerous figures which include: capping, loud-talking, the dozens, reading, going off, talking smart, sounding, joaning (jonesing), dropping lugs, snapping, woofing, styling out, and calling out of one's name.

As a rhetorical strategy, signifying assumes that there is shared knowledge between communicators and, therefore, that information can be given indirectly. Geneva Smitherman in *Talkin and Testifyin* gives the following examples of signifying:

- Stokely Carmichael, addressing a white audience at the University of California, Berkeley, 1966: "It's a privilege and an honor to be in the white intellectual ghetto of the West."
- Malcolm X on Martin Luther King, Jr.'s nonviolent revolution (referring to the common practice of singing "We Shall Overcome" at civil rights protests of the sixties): "In a revolution, you swinging, not singing."
- Reverend Jesse Jackson, merging sacred and secular siggin in a Breadbasket Saturday morning sermon: "Pimp, punk, prostitute, preacher, Ph.D.—all the P's —you still in slavery!"
- A black middle-class wife to her husband who had just arrived home several hours later than usual: "You sho got home early today for a change."[7]

Effective signifying is, Smitherman states, "to put somebody in check . . . to make them think about and, one hopes, correct their behavior."[8] Because signifying relies on indirection to give information, it requires that participants in any communicative encounter pay attention to, as Claudia Mitchell-Kernan states, "the total universe of discourse."[9]

Gates's theory of signifying focuses on black forms of talk. I believe that identifying these forms of talk in contemporary black gay literature is important for two reasons. First, the use of signifying by black gay men places their writing squarely within the African American literary tradition. Second, signifying permits black gay men to revise the "Black Experience" in African American literature and, thereby, to create a space for themselves.

The remainder of this essay is divided into two parts. The first part examines the heterosexist context in which black gay men write. Examined are heterosexism and homophobia in the writings of contemporary social scientists, scholars, and, in a longer passage, the novels of Toni Morrison. The last section discusses black gay men's attempts to revise the African American literary tradition. Specifically examined are the signifying on representations of desire, the black religious experience, and gender configurations.

HETEROSEXISM AND AFRICAN AMERICAN INTELLECTUALS

Some social scientists have claimed that homosexuality is alien to the black community. Communication scholar Molefi Asante has argued in *Afrocentricity: A Theory of Social Change* that homosexual practices among black men were initially imposed on them by their white slave owners and that the practice is maintained by the American prison institution.[10] Asante has attributed homosexuality to Greco-Roman culture, with the added assertion that "homosexuality does not represent an Afrocentric way of life."[11] Likewise, in *Black Skin, White Masks*, Frantz Fanon, the widely read Martiniquois psychiatrist and freedom-fighter, declared that "Caribbean men never experience the Oedipus complex," and therefore, in the Caribbean, "there is no homosexuality, which is, rather, an attribute of the white race, Western civilization."[12]

Other scholars and writers have contended that homosexuality is a pathology stemming from the inability of black men to cope with the complexities of manhood in a racist society. Alvin Poussaint, the noted Harvard psychiatrist and adviser to the *Cosby Show*, stated in a 1978 *Ebony* article that some black men adopt homosexuality as a maneuver to help them avoid the increasing tension developing between black men and women.[13] "Homosexuality," according to black writer and liberationist Imamu Amiri Baraka, "is the most extreme form of alienation acknowledged within white society" and it occurs among "a people who lose their self-sufficiency because they depend on their subjects to do the world's work," thus rendering them "effeminate and perverted."[14] According to Eldridge Cleaver, homosexuality among black men is a "racial death wish," and a frustrating experience because "in their sickness [black men who practice homosexuality] are unable to have a baby by a white man."[15] In *The Endangered Black Family*, Nathan Hare and Julia Hare view homosexuals as confused but worthy of compassion because, they state, "Some of them may yet be saved."[16] The Hares seem to imply that black gay and lesbian people require treatment for either illness or brainwashing: "What we must do is offer the homosexual brother or sister a proper compassion and acceptance without advocacy. We might not advocate, for instance, the religion of Mormonism, or venereal disease, laziness or gross obesity."[17]

The acclaimed writer Toni Morrison has woven into her novels these ideas of homosexuality as alien to African cultures, as forced upon black men by racist

European civilizations, and as the inability to acquire and sustain manhood. In her first novel, *The Bluest Eye*, she played on the stereotype of the "light-skinned" black man as weak, effeminate, and sexually impotent. Soaphead Church, "a cinnamon-eyed West Indian with lightly browned skin," limited his sexual interests to little girls because, Morrison wrote, "he was too diffident to confront homosexuality" and found "little boys insulting, scary, and stubborn."[18] In *Tar Baby*, black homosexual men were self-mutilating transvestites who had dumped their masculinity because they "found the whole business of being black and men at the same time too difficult."[19]

In her 1988 Pulitzer Prize-winning *Beloved*, Morrison surpassed her earlier efforts in using homophobia with the creation of the five heroic black men of the Sweet Home plantation. Sweet Home men were unlike slaves on nearby plantations, as their owner Mr. Garner bragged to other farmers: "Y'all got boys. Young boys, old boys, picky boys, stroppin boys. Now at Sweet Home, my niggers is men every one of em. Bought um thataway, raised em thataway. Men every one."[20] Although deprived of sex with women, Sweet Home men were capable of enormous restraint and for sexual relief they either masturbated or engaged in sex with farm animals. When Mr. Garner added to his plantation a new slave, the thirteen-year-old "iron-eyed" Sethe, the Sweet Home men "let the girl be" and allowed her to choose one of them despite the fact that they "were young and so sick with the absence of women they had taken to *calves*" (emphasis added).[21] Sethe took over a year to choose one of the Sweet Home men. Morrison described that year of waiting: "[It was] a long, tough year of thrashing on pallets eaten up with dreams of her. A year of yearning, when rape seemed the solitary gift of life. The restraint they had exercised possible only because they were Sweet Home men."[22]

Yet Morrison's description of the restrained Sweet Home men does a great disservice to the complexity of men's lives. Her description reinforces a false notion of a hierarchy of sexual practices in which masturbation is only a substitute for intercourse. Morrison's description is homophobic because it reveals her inability to imagine homosexual relationships among heroic characters. By implication, sex with farm animals is preferable to homoerotic sex, which is like a perverse reading of a spiritual: "Before I practice homosexuality, I'll practice bestiality, and go home to my Father and be free."

Morrison rejects from her fiction the idea that homosexual desire among slave men could actually lead to loving relationships. This, in fact, did happen. Autobiographical evidence exists that slave men in the Americas practiced and even institutionalized homosexuality. Esteban Montejo, the subject of *The Autobiography of a Runaway Slave*, twice discusses the prevalence of homosexuality among Cuban slave men in his comments on the sexual customs of the plantation. The first incident refers to physical abuse and possibly the rape of young black boys. Montejo states:

> If a boy was pretty and lively he was sent inside, to the master's house. And there they
> started softening him up . . . well, I don't know! They used to give the boy a long
> palm-leaf and make him stand at one end of the table while they ate. And they said,

"Now see that no flies get in the food." If a fly did, they scolded him severely and even whipped him.[23]

The second incident is discussed within the context of the scarcity of women on the plantation. "To have one [a woman] of your own," Montejo writes, "you had either to be over twenty-five or catch yourself one in the fields."[24] Some men, however, he states, "had sex among themselves and did not want to know anything of women."[25] Montejo's comments include observations about the economics of homosexual households. He notes that the division of labor in these households resembled male-female roles in which the "effeminate men washed the clothes and did the cooking too, if they had a husband."[26] The men in these relationships also benefited financially from the existence of the "provision grounds," lands allocated to slaves in the Caribbean to grow crops to sell in the local markets on Sunday. Montejo writes: "The [effeminate men] were good workers and occupied themselves with their plots of land, giving the produce to their husbands to sell to the white farmers."[27]

Most interesting in Montejo's narrative is the reaction of other slaves to their homosexual brethren. The older men hated homosexuality, he states, and they "would have nothing to do with queers."[28] Their hatred leads Montejo to speculate that the practice did not come from Africa. Unfortunately, Montejo limits his speculations on homosexuality to origins and not to prohibitions. Thus, another speculation could be that homosexuality was prohibited, but that the practice itself was neither unknown nor undreamt. Montejo's narrative suggests that the influence of the old men over the feelings and attitudes of other slaves about homosexuality was limited. The slaves did not have a pejorative name for those who practiced homosexuality and it was not until "after Abolition that the term [effeminate] came into use," Montejo states.[29] Montejo, himself, held the view that the practice of homosexuality was a private matter: "To tell the truth, it [homosexuality] never bothered me. I am of the opinion that a man can stick his arse where he wants."[30] Montejo's narrative challenges the heterosexist assumptions about the sexualities and the family life of blacks before abolition in the Americas. At least in Cuba, homoerotic sex and exclusively male families were not uncommon.

In the United States, accounts of homosexuality among blacks before abolition are scanty. This is because accounts of slaves' sexuality are sparse and, until recently, social customs in the United States and Great Britain proscribed public discussions of sexuality.[31] Homosexuality, however, did occur during the colonial period among black men because laws forbidding the practice were created and sentences were carried out. These laws and sentences are discussed in A. Leon Higginbotham, Jr.'s *In the Matter of Color: Race and the American Legal Process* and Jonathan Katz's two documentary works *Gay/Lesbian Almanac* and *Gay American History*. Katz documents the case of Jan Creoli, identified as a "negro," who in 1646 in New Netherland (Manhattan) was sentenced to be "choked to death, and then burnt to ashes" for committing the act of sodomy with ten-year-old Manuel Congo.[32] Congo, whose name suggests that he was black, was sentenced "to be carried to the place where Creoli is to be executed, tied to a stake, and faggots piled around him, for justice sake, and to be flogged."[33] In a second case, "Mingo alias Cocke Negro," a Massachusetts slave, was reportedly executed for "forcible Buggery," a term that Katz suggests is a male-male act, rather than bestiality.[34] Both Katz and Higginbotham discuss the development of sexual crime laws in Pennsylvania between 1700 and 1780 that carefully distinguished between blacks and whites: Life imprisonment was the penalty for whites and death was for blacks convicted of buggery, which, Katz notes, probably meant bestiality and sodomy.[35]

Although the evidence for homosexual practices among black male slaves is small, it does suggest that we do not exclude homoeroticism from life on the plantation. The gay Jewish historian Martin Bauml Duberman's words are most appropriate here:

> After all, to date we've accumulated only a tiny collection of historical materials that record the existence of *heterosexual* behavior in the past. Yet no one claims that that minuscule amount of evidence is an accurate measure of the actual amount of heterosexual activity which took place.[36]

Duberman's words and the evidence we have suggest that, at best, our understanding of the sexuality of our slave ancestors is fragmentary. We need to uncover more and to reread diaries, letters, and narratives to gain a greater understanding of the sexuality of our forebears. At the very least, we need to revise our models of the black family and of homosexuality as alien to black culture.

Morrison's homophobia, as that of so many other black intellectuals, is perhaps more closely related to Judeo-Christian beliefs than to the beliefs of her ancestors. Male homosexuality is associated with biblical ideas of weakness as effeminacy.[37] Many of these intellectuals would also argue that the Judeo-Christian tradition is a major tool of the Western-Eurocentric view of reality that furthers the oppression of blacks. Paradoxically, by their condemnation of homosexuality and lesbianism, these intellectuals contribute to upholding an oppressive Eurocentric view of reality.

ENTER BLACK GAY MEN

It should be obvious that black gay men must look at other black intellectuals with great caution and skepticism because the dominant view of reality expressed is oppressively heterosexist. Black gay men must also be cautious of looking for an image of themselves in white gay men because the United States is still a racist society. For example, even though one in five homosexual or bisexual men with AIDS is black, it can be argued that Larry Kramer's searing AIDS polemic, *The Normal Heart*, is about gay people, not black people. The characters in the drama are from the "fabled 1970s Fire Island/*After Dark* crowd," which tended to be white, middle-class, and very exclusionary on the basis of race, unless one counts the occasional presence of the reigning "disco diva"—who was usually a black woman or the wonderful African American gender-blurring singer Sylvester. In addition, Kramer makes several remarks in *The Normal Heart* that imply that he accepts certain historically racist ideas about blacks.[38] With a critical eye, one can also find occurrences of racism in works ranging from literature to visual pornography created by or aimed at gay men that employ a racist vision of reality.[39]

Partly as a reaction to racism in gay culture, but mostly in response to the heterosexism of black intellectuals and writers, African American gay men signify on many aspects of the "Black Experience" in their literature. The areas discussed in this section are representations of sexual desire, the black religious experience, and gender configurations.

REPRESENTING SEXUAL DESIRE

Because of the historical and often virulent presence of racism, black literature has frequently had as its goal the elevation of "the race" by presenting the group in its "best light." The race's "best light" often has meant depicting blacks with those values and ways that mirrored white Americans and Europeans. For black writers this has usually meant tremendous anxiety over the representation of sexuality. An excellent example of this anxiety is W. E. B. Du Bois's reaction to Claude McKay's 1920 novel *Home to Harlem*. In the novel, McKay, gay and Jamaican, wrote about much of the night life in Harlem, including one of the first descriptions of a gay and lesbian bar in an African American work of fiction. DuBois wrote:

> Claude McKay's *Home to Harlem* for the most part nauseates me, and after the dirtier parts of its filth I feel distinctly like taking a bath ... McKay has set out to cater for that prurient demand on the part of white folks for a portrayal in Negroes of that utter licentiousness ... which a certain decadent section of the white world ... wants to see written out in black and white and saddled on black Harlem. ... He has used every art and emphasis to paint drunkenness, fighting, lascivious sexual promiscuity and utter absence of restraint in as bold and bright colors as he can. ... As a picture of Harlem life or of Negro life anywhere, it is, of course, nonsense. Untrue, not so much as on account of its facts, but on account of its emphasis and glaring colors.[40]

The anxiety that Du Bois felt was as acute for black women. Mary Helen Washington comments that this anxiety about the representation of sexuality "goes back to the nineteenth century and the prescription for womanly 'virtues' which made slave women automatically immoral and less feminine than white women," as in the case of the slave woman Harriet Jacobs, who considered not publishing her 1860 narrative *Incidents in the Life of a Slave Girl* because she "bore two children as a single woman rather than submit to forced concubinage."[41] The representation of sexuality is even more problematic for black gay men than for heterosexual African Americans because of societal disapproval against impersonal sex, in which gay men frequently engage, and because gay sex is not connected in any way with the means of reproduction.

Black gay science fiction writer Samuel Delany, in his autobiography *The Motion of Light in Water*, takes particular delight in signifying on society's disapproval of impersonal homoerotic sex. His signifying is greatly aided by using the autobiographical form, a successful mode for black Americans, as Michael Cooke maintains, because "the self is the source of the system of which it is a part, creates what it discovers, and although it is nothing unto itself, it is the possibility of everything for itself."[42] By using himself as the source of the system, Delany is able to signify on ideas about impersonal sex. Delany imbues situations involving impersonal sex with social and political significance in the context of the repressive 1950s and early 1960s. Contrary to stereotypes that group sex is wild and out of control, the situation on the piers at the end of Christopher Street "with thirty-five, fifty, a hundred all-but-strangers is," Delany states, "hugely ordered, highly social, attentive, silent, and grounded in a certain care, if not community."[43] At the piers, when arrests of eight or nine men occurred and were reported in the newspapers without mentioning the hundreds who had escaped, it was a reassurance to the city fathers, the police, the men arrested, and even those who escaped "that the image of the homosexual as outside society—which is the myth that the outside of language, with all its articulation, is based on—was, somehow, despite the arrests, intact."[44] Delany's first visit to the St. Mark's Baths in 1963 produced a Foucault-like revelation that the legal and medical silences on homosexuality was "a huge and pervasive discourse" which prevented one from gaining "a clear, accurate, and extensive picture of extant public sexual institutions."[45] The result of Delany's signification is that his participation in impersonal sex in public places is given a political and social importance much like the significance given to ordinary, day-to-day acts of resistance recounted by the subjects of African American autobiographies from Frederick Douglass's *My Bondage and My Freedom* to Maya Angelou's *I Know Why the Caged Bird Sings*.

Just as Delany seeks to revise attitudes about impersonal sex, Larry Duplechan signifies on both black middle-class and gay stereotypes of interracial love and lust. On the one hand, the black middle class and the mental health professions have conspired together to label a black person's sexual attraction to a white as pathology.[46] On the other, gay men have created a host of terms to denigrate participants in black/white sexual relationships, e.g.: *dinge queen, chocolate lover*, and *snow queen*. In *Blackbird* and *Eight Days a Week*, we are introduced to Duplechan's protagonist, Johnnie Ray Rousseau, as a senior in high school in the former, and as a 22-year-old aspiring singer living in Los Angeles in the latter. In Duplechan's first novel, *Eight Days a Week*, he summarizes both the gay and the black middle-class stereotype: "I was once told by a black alto sax player named Zaz (we were in bed at the time, mind you) that my preference for white men (and blonds, the whitest of white, to boot) was the sad but understandable end result of 300 years of white male oppression."[47] Contrary to Zaz's opinion, Johnnie Ray's sexual attraction to white men is anything but the result of 300 years of white male oppression, and if it is, it allows Duplechan a major moment of signifying in African American literature: the sexual objectification of white men by a black man.

Revising our culture's ideas about male–male sexual desire and love is a major concern in Essex Hemphill's collection of poems *Conditions*.[48] In particular, "Conditions XXIV" signifies on heterosexual culture's highly celebrated "rite of passage," the marriage ceremony. Hemphill signifies on the marriage ceremony in an excellent example of "capping," a figure of speech which revises an original statement by adding new terms. Hemphill honors the bonds created from desire by capping on the exchange of wedding bands. In the opening and closing sentences, fingers are not the received place for wedding rings:

> In america
> I place my ring
> on your cock
> where it belongs . . .

> In america,
> place your ring
> on my cock
> where it belongs.

Vows are also exchanged in the poem, but they do not restrict and confine. Instead, these vows are "What the rose whispers/before blooming." The vows are:

> I give you my heart,
> a safe house.
> I give you promises other than
> milk, honey, liberty.
> I assume you will always
> be a free man with a dream.

Implicitly, "Conditions XXIV" strips away the public pomp and spectacle of the wedding ceremony to reveal its most fundamental level: desire. By capping on the wedding ceremony, Hemphill places homoerotic desire on an equal plane with heterosexuality.

SIGNIFYING ON THE CHURCH

Historically, religion has served as a liberating force in the African American community. Black slaves publicly and politically declared that Christianity and the institution of slavery were incompatible as early as 1774, according to Albert Raboteau in *Slave Religion*. "In that year," Raboteau notes, "the governor of Massachusetts received 'The Petition of a Grate Number of Blacks of this Province who by divine permission are held in a state of slavery within the bowels of a free and Christian Country.' "[49] In the petition slaves argued for their freedom by combining the political rhetoric of the Revolution with an appeal to the claims of Christian fellowship. Christian churches were some of the first institutions blacks created and owned in the United States. From 1790 to 1830 ambitious northern free black men like Richard Allen and Absalom Jones circumvented racism by creating new Christian denominations, notably the African Methodist Episcopal and the African Methodist Episcopal Zion churches.

The organized black church, however, has not been free from oppressing its constituents. Historically, the black church has practiced sexism. In her 1849 narrative, Jarena Lee, a spiritual visionary and a free black woman, reported having her desire to preach thwarted by her husband and Rev. Richard Allen.[50] Lee, however, overcame the objections of men by claiming that her instructions came directly from God; thus, those instructions superseded the sexist prohibitions of men. Some contemporary black churches and their ministers have adopted heterosexist policies and have openly made homophobic remarks. In an essay which appeared in the gay anthology *Black Men/White Men*, Leonard Patterson, a black gay minister, movingly wrote about how he was forced to leave Ebenezer Baptist Church in Atlanta, Georgia. Patterson's troubles at Ebenezer began when Reverend Joseph Roberts replaced Reverend Martin L. King, Sr. Roberts objected to the fact that Patterson's white lover also attended Ebenezer. Moreover, Patterson was guilty of not playing the game: "I was told, in effect, that as long as I played the political game and went with a person who was more easily passed off as a 'cousin,' I would be able to go far in the ministry. Perhaps I should even marry and have someone on the side. Apparently these arrangements would make me more 'respectable.' "[51] For refusing to play the political game, Patterson states that he was "attacked verbally from the pulpit, forbidden to enter the study for prayer with the other associate ministers, and had seeds of animosity planted against [him] . . . in the minds of certain members so that in meetings with them the subject of homosexuality would inevitably be brought up."[52] Patterson recounts an extremely offensive remark made to him by a church member one Sunday: "If you lie down with dogs, you get up smelling like dirt."[53] Patterson and his lover finally left Ebenezer. Although disillusioned with organized religion, Patterson writes encouragingly that what he and his lover experienced at Ebenezer has "given us more strength to love each other and others."[54]

Exorcism is a practice used to oppress gays in the church. The late Pentecostal minister and professor, Reverend James Tinney, underwent an exorcism when he came out as a gay man. Tinney briefly mentions the experience in his essay "Struggles of a Black Pentecostal," which was originally published in a 1981 issue of *Insight*. Five years later in *Blackbird* Duplechan signifies on Tinney's reflections on exorcism. It should be noted that Duplechan was probably familiar with Tinney's essay. Both that essay and Duplechan's short story "Peanuts and the Old Spice Kid" appeared in Michael Smith's anthology *Black Men/White Men*.

The events which precipitate the exorcism are similar in *Blackbird* and in Tinney's essay. Both Tinney and Duplechan's protagonist, Johnnie Ray Rousseau, are aware of their sexual identity. Tinney writes that he was aware of his homoerotic feelings "even at the age of four."[55] Johnnie Ray's exorcism is preceded by an enjoyable first sexual experience with the older bi-ethnic Marshall Two Hawks McNeil, a college student. Publicly stating and affirming their sexual identity actually causes the exorcisms. Put another way, their exorcisms are punishments for stating that they practice "the love that dares not speak its name." Tinney announced to his wife of three years that he was gay. Her reaction set into motion the events that caused the exorcism: "She immediately called the pastor and his wife and other close confidants to pray for me."[56] Johnnie Ray's exorcism was set into motion by two events. First, his confidential confession to Daniel Levine, the youth minister, that he had gay feelings. Then, Levine's betrayal of the confidential confession to Johnnie Ray's parents provoked the second event: the teenager's affirmation of his sexual identity to his parents in the presence of the minister.

Tinney does not discuss the events of his exorcism. In fact, he limits the actions of his wife, minister, and church members to one sentence: "Pray and talk and counsel they did."[57] Tinney's description of the exorcism is brief, but the event left him traumatized. The exorcism, he wrote, "was extremely painful to my own sense of worth and well-being. It was an experience I would not wish upon anyone ever."[58]

Duplechan signifies explicitly and implicitly on Tinney's remark "Pray and talk and counsel they did." Explicitly Duplechan "reads" Tinney by giving a fuller narrative description of the praying, talking, and counseling of the church people. Implicitly, Duplechan's "reading" of Tinney is a critique of the clergy and the values of the middle class. Further, Duplechan's "reading" is an example of what Smitherman calls heavy signifying, "a way of teaching or driving home a cognitive message but . . . without preaching or lecturing."[59]

Let us consider Duplechan's "read" or "heavy signifying" of each of the three terms—pray, talk, and counsel—as they occur in the confrontation between Johnnie Ray and the church people—his parents and the youth minister. The confrontation about Johnnie Ray's homosexuality happens at his home. Duplechan shows that prayer is often a means of ensuring conformity. In an emotional outburst Johnnie Ray's mother asks the teen: "Have you asked him? Have you asked the savior to help you? . . . Have you prayed every day for help? Every day?"[60] When Johnnie Ray answers no, his mother incredulously asks him, "Don't you want to be normal?"[61] Normality, which is conforming to existing value structures, is believed by the middle classes to be what will guarantee them success in the world. Johnnie Ray's mother reveals that she is less concerned with his happiness than she is with his possibilities of success. To insure his success, she and her husband must use talk to force Johnnie Ray to become normal. Talk, thus, is a means of intimidation. When Johnnie Ray claims that he has accepted it as a fact that he is gay, his mother intimidates him by "loud talking":

> You probably think you're real cute . . . going to Daniel [the youth minister] with this 'I think I'm a homosexual' crap, and now sittin' here and tellin' us you've *accepted* that you're gay . . . Lord ha' mercy today! I don't know what I coulda done to give birth to a *pervert*.[62]

While Johnnie Ray's mother uses "loud talking" to intimidate her son, his father cries. When his father finally talks, it is a mixture of intimidation and compassion: "You're no pervert," he says. "No son of mine is gonna be a pervert. You're just a little confused."[63] Finally, there is the expert, Reverend Levine, who offers counsel. Levine, however, is a scoundrel. Although he has betrayed Johnnie Ray's confidence, he sits throughout the entire family crisis "looking as holy and righteous at having done so as my parents looked utterly devastated at the news."⁶⁴ Levine is able to sit "in beatific calm" because of the family's unhappiness.⁶⁵ In other words, the family crisis that Levine has provided proves that the ministry is necessary. Levine's expert counsel to the family, which they reluctantly agree upon, is an exorcism—"a deliverance from unclean spirits."⁶⁶

By signifying on Tinney, Duplechan exposes an unholy alliance between the church and the middle classes. The church is eager to oppress gay people to prove its worth to the middle classes. For the sake of conformity which, with hope, leads to success, the middle class is willing to oppress its children. The middle class, thus, is denounced for its willingness to use the church to further its ambitions.

In the short story "Cut Off from among Their People," Craig G. Harris does a "heavy sig" on the black family which also signifies on strategies from slave narratives. The story takes place at the funeral of Jeff's lover, who has died of complications from AIDS. Both the family and the church, two major institutions in the heterosexual African American community, are allied against Jeff. The lover's biological family has "diplomatically" excluded Jeff from the decisions about the funeral. At the funeral Jeff is ignored by the family and humiliated by the church. The lover's mother stares at him contemptuously. Jeff is not allowed to sit with the family. The minister chosen by the family only adds to Jeff's humiliation. The minister is asked not to wear his ceremonial robes but instead to wear an ordinary suit.

The "heavy sig" is done by using irony. The minister is exposed as a scoundrel, similar to Levine in *Blackbird*. At the funeral he delivers a homophobic sermon from the book of Leviticus:

In Leviticus, Chapter 20, the Lord tell [sic] us: If a man lie with mankind as he lieth with a woman, both of them have committed an abomination: they shall surely be put to death; their blood shall be upon them. There's no cause to wonder why medical science could not find a cure for this man's illness. How could medicine cure temptation? What drug can exorcise Satan from a young man's soul? The only cure is to be found in the Lord. The only cure is repentance, for Leviticus clearly tells us, ". . . whoever shall commit any of these abominations, even the souls that commit them shall be cut off from among their people."⁶⁷

After the funeral Jeff is abandoned and left to his own devices to get to the burial site. His humiliation is relieved by a sympathetic undertaker who offers Jeff a ride to the burial site. Ironically, it is the undertaker, the caregiver to the dead—not the minister, who is the caregiver to the living—who offers Jeff the compassion he so desperately needs. Denouncing both the family and the church, the undertaker's remarks to Jeff become the authentic sermon in the story:

I lost my lover to AIDS three months ago. It's been very difficult—living with these memories and secrets and hurt, and with no one to share them. These people won't allow themselves to understand. If it's not preached from a pulpit and kissed up to the

Almighty, they don't want to know about it. So, I hold it in, and hold it in, and then I see us passing, one after another—tearless funerals, the widowed treated like nonentities, and these "another faggot burns in hell" sermons. My heart goes out to you brother. You gotta let your love for him keep you strong.[68]

As a result of Harris's use of ironic signifying, one is left to ponder the meaning of the story's title, "Cut Off from among Their People." Who is cut off from their people? The story immediately implies that black gays are oppressed because they are alienated from their families. The opposite, however, is also true: Black families are oppressors, are alienated from their gay children, and thus, suffer. Black families suffer because their oppression robs them of a crucial sign of humaneness: compassion. By their oppression, the family of Jeff's deceased lover has lost the ability to be compassionate.

Harris's strategy—the cost of oppression is the loss of humanity—signifies on slave narratives by authors such as Frederick Douglass. Slave owners' loss of compassion, the sign of humaneness, is a recurring theme in Frederick Douglass's 1845 narrative. Slavery, Douglass contended, placed in the hands of whites "the fatal poison of irresponsible power."[69] Douglass gives numerous grisly examples of his contention: murderous overseers, greedy urban craftsmen, and raping masters. But perhaps none of his examples is meant to be as moving as that of his slave mistress, Mrs. Auld. Originally a woman of independent means, Douglass describes her before "the fatal poison of irresponsible power" took full control of her:

> I was utterly astonished at her goodness. I scarcely knew how to behave towards her. She was entirely unlike any other white woman I had ever seen. I could not approach her as I was accustomed to approach other white ladies. My early instruction was all out of place. The crouching servility, usually so acceptable a quality in a slave, did not answer when manifested toward her. Her favor was not gained by it; she seemed to be disturbed by it. She did not deem it impudent or unmannerly for a slave to look her in the face. The meanest slave was put fully at ease in her presence, and none left without feeling better for having seen her. Her face was made of heavenly smiles, and her voice of tranquil music.[70]

Mrs. Auld even disobeyed the law and taught Douglass some rudiments of spelling. However, Douglass states, "Slavery proved as injurious to her as it did to me. . . . Under its influence, the tender heart became stone, and the lamblike disposition gave way to one of tiger-like fierceness."[71]

"Cut Off from among Their People" is an extraordinary act of "heavy signifying." By using a strategy similar to Frederick Douglass's, Harris equates heterosexism and homophobia with slavery. For upholding heterosexism and homophobia, the church and the black family are oppressors. As rendered by Harris, they are like the Mrs. Auld of Douglass's narrative. They are kind to the black gay man when he is a child, and corrupted by intolerance years later. Their oppression has robbed them of compassion. The black family and their church, thus, have lost the sign of humanity.

GENDER CONFIGURATIONS

The last section of this essay examines gay men and the problem of gender configurations. Specifically, in the black literary tradition gay men have been objects of ridicule for not possessing masculine-appearing behaviors. This ridicule was especially evident in the militant Black Power movement of the 1960s and 1970s. The militancy that characterized that movement placed an enormous emphasis on developing black "manhood." Manhood became a metaphor for the strength and potency necessary to overthrow the oppressive forces of a white racist society. Images of pathetic homosexuals were often used to show what black manhood was not or to what it could degenerate. For example, Haki Madhubuti (Don L. Lee) wrote in "Don't Cry Scream":

> swung on a faggot who politely
> scratched his ass in my presence.
> he smiled broken teeth stained from
> his over-used tongue, fisted-face.
> teeth dropped in tune with ray
> charles singing "yesterday."[72]

Concurrent with the Black Power movement's image of manhood was the development of the urban tough, loud, back-talking gay black man. This stereotype was seen on the Broadway stage in Melvin Van Peebles's *Ain't Supposed to Die a Natural Death*, but it was most clearly articulated by Antonio Fargas's character, Lindy, in the film *Car Wash*. When the black militant Abdullah accused Lindy of being another example of how the white man has corrupted the black man and robbed him of his masculinity, Lindy responded, "Honey, I'm more man than you'll ever be and more woman than you'll ever get." Lindy was a gratifying character because he was tough and articulate, yet his character was not revolutionary. Vito Russo comments in *The Celluloid Closet:* "Lindy is only a cartoon—[his] effect in the end was just that of the safe sissy who ruled the day in the topsy-turvy situations of Thirties comedies."[73] But the stereotype of the tough, loud, back-talking effeminate black gay man as an object of ridicule is revised in works by Samuel Delany, George Wolfe, and Billi Gordon.

Delany signifies on such a stereotype in a section of *The Motion of Light in Water* called "A black man . . . ? A gay man . . . ?" The section's title itself suggests the dilemma of a bifurcated identity that Julius Johnson discusses in his doctoral dissertation "Influence of Assimilation on the Psychosocial Adjustment of Black Homosexual Men."[74] Johnson documented the fact that some African American brothers become "black gay men" while others become "gay black men"; the designation often underscores painful decisions to have primary identities either in the black or in the gay community.

Delany's first memory of a gay black man was Herman, an outrageously effeminate musician who played the organ in his father's mortuary. As a child, Delany admits that he was as confused as he was amused by Herman's aggressive antics. When a casket delivery man asked Herman if he was "one of them faggots that likes men," Herman quickly signified on the man:

> "Me? Oh, chile', chile', you must be ill or something! . . . I swear, you must have been workin' out in the heat too long today. I do believe you must be sick!" Here he would feel the man's forehead, then removing his hand, look at the sweat that had come off on his own palm, touch his finger to his tongue, and declare, "Oh, my lord, you are tasty! . . . Imagine, honey! Thinkin' such nastiness like that about a woman like me! I mean, I just might faint right here, and you gonna have to carry me to a chair and fan me and bring me my smellin' salts!" Meanwhile he would be rubbing the man's chest and arms.[75]

Ultimately Delany's attitude toward Herman was one of ambivalence. Delany's sig on the stereotype was his recognition of its artifice. He recognized that there were many unanswered questions about Herman's sexual life: "Had he gone to bars? Had he gone to baths? . . . Had there been a long-term lover, waiting for him at home, unmet by, and unmentioned to, people like my father whom he worked for?"[76] Herman had played a role to survive in a heterosexist and homophobic world. In that role "Herman had a place in our social scheme," Delany wrote, "but by no means an acceptable place, and certainly not a place I wanted to fill."[77] Thus, as a teen, Delany remembered that he did not see Herman as a role model for a man. As an adult, however, Delany's opinion of Herman changed. He did not see Herman as a role model, but, he stated, "I always treasured the image of Herman's outrageous and defiant freedom to say absolutely anything. . . . Anything except, of course, I am queer, and I like men sexually better than women."[78]

In *The Colored Museum*, George Wolfe introduces Miss Roj, a black transvestite "dressed in striped patio pants, white go-go boots, a halter and cat-shaped sunglasses."[79] Wolfe makes it clear that Miss Roj is a subject most appropriate for African American literature by signifying, perhaps deliberately, on Ralph Ellison's *Invisible Man*. In particular, he signifies on its prologue, to create a powerful social comment on the alienation of the black urban poor. Wolfe's character, Miss Roj, comments that she "comes from another galaxy, as do all snap queens. That's right," she says, "I ain't just your regular oppressed American Negro. No-no-no! I am an extra-terrestrial, and I ain't talkin none of that shit you seen in the movies."[80] Compare that with the first two sentences in the prologue of *Invisible Man*: "I am an invisible man. No, I am not a spook like those who haunted Edgar Allan Poe; nor am I one of your Hollywood-movie ectoplasms."[81] Ellison's nameless protagonist lives in a hole lit by 1,369 bulbs; Miss Roj, whose real name the audience never learns, inhabits every Wednesday, Friday, and Saturday night a disco with blaring lights called the Bottomless Pit, "the watering hole for the wild and weary which asks the question, 'Is there life after Jherri-curl?' "[82] In Ellison's prologue the protagonist gets high on marijuana; Miss Roj gets drunk on Cuba libres [perhaps a veiled reference to popular drinks in the early 1950s, which is when *Invisible Man* was written] and proceeds *to snap*, that is, "when something strikes . . . [one's] fancy, when the truth comes piercing through the dark, well you just can't let it pass unnoticed. No darling. You must pronounce it with a snap [of the fingers]."[83]

Ellison's protagonist almost beats a man to death for calling him a nigger. Of course, one wonders how one can be beaten by invisibility. In a scene with a provocation and an outcome similar to Ellison's, Miss Roj "snaps" (signifies) on an assailant. She states:

> Like the time this asshole at Jones Beach decided to take issue with my culotte-sailor ensemble. This child, this muscle-bound Brooklyn thug in a skin tight bikini, very skin-tight so the whole world can see that instead of a brain, God gave him an extra-thick piece of sausage. You know the kind who beat up on their wives for breakfast. Well he decided to blurt out while I walked by, "Hey look at da monkey coon in da faggit suit." Well, I walked up to the poor dear, very calmly lifted my hand and . . . (rapid snaps). A heart attack, right there on the beach. You don't believe it?[84]

Ellison's prologue ends with the protagonist listening to Louis Armstrong's "What Did I Do to Be So Black and Blue?"; the lights fade on Miss Roj dancing to Aretha Franklin's "Respect." As white Americans must have been puzzled, outraged, and even guilt-stricken after reading Ellison's *Invisible Man*, so too is the effect Miss Roj has had on the assimilated blacks Wolfe chose to confront. During performances of *The Colored Museum*, black audience members have verbally attacked the actor playing Miss Roj and African American intellectuals have lambasted Wolfe for either not portraying blacks in their "best light" or for demeaning women.[85]

One of the oddest works to appear in black gay culture is Billi Gordon's cookbook, *You've Had Worse Things in Your Mouth*. The title itself is an act of signifying. While one may think it odd to include a cookbook here, it is important to keep in mind that that mode of presentation has been used to create social history in two other books by Afro-Americans. National Public Radio commentator and self-styled writing griot Vertamae Smart Grosvenor came to public prominence in her 1970 *Vibration Cooking; or the Travel Notes of a Geechee Girl*. The format of the book itself was signifying on the published travel narratives of eighteenth- and nineteenth-century whites such as Frederick Law Olmsted, whose observations on slavery have been treated by some historians as more reliable than artifacts actually left by the slaves. Norma Jean and Carole Darden's 1978 *Spoonbread and Strawberry Wine* was as much a family history of North Carolina middle-class blacks as it was a compendium of recipes.

Like George Wolfe, Gordon signifies repeatedly on racial stereotypes and on middle-class culture. On the cover of his cookbook, Gordon, a three-hundred-pound-plus dark-skinned black man, appears in drag. But not just any drag. He is wearing a red kerchief, a red-and-white checkered blouse, and a white apron, calling to mind some combination of Aunt Jemima and Hattie McDaniel in *Gone with the Wind*. As if that were not enough, Gordon signifies in every way imaginable on the American cultural stereotype of mammies as sexless, loyal, no-nonsense creatures. Gordon's character is lusty, vengeful, and flirtatious. Gordon appears in pictures surrounded by adoring muscled, swimsuit-clad white men; he wears bikini swimsuits, tennis outfits, long blond wigs, huge rebellious Afro-wigs, and shocking lamé evening wear. As for recipes, one is quite reluctant to try any of them, particularly those from the section called "Revenge Cooking" in which the ingredients include laxatives, seaweed, and entire bottles of Tabasco sauce. Billi Gordon signifies on the American stereotype of the mammy by reversing it and turning it upside down: His depiction of a mammy with a sex life is far from loyal, and certainly his character cannot and/ or does not want to cook.

CONCLUSION: TOWARD A BLACK GAY AESTHETIC

Restricted by racism and heterosexism, writers such as Samuel Delany, Larry Duplechan, Essex Hemphill, Craig G. Harris, George Wolfe, and Billi Gordon have begun to create a literature that validates our lives as black and as gay. My critical reading of this literature relied upon techniques based in the African American tradition of signifying. The writers discussed in this essay are some of the newest members of the African American literary tradition. Clearly, they also seek to revise the aesthetics of that tradition. Homophobia and heterosexism are oppressive forces which must be eliminated from the social, scientific, critical, and imaginative writings within the African American literary tradition.

NOTES

1. Daniel Garrett, "Other Countries: The Importance of Difference," in *Other Countries: Black Gay Voices*, ed. Cary Alan Johnson, Colin Robinson, and Terence Taylor (New York: Other Countries, 1988), p. 27.
2. Henry Louis Gates, Jr., *The Signifying Monkey: A Theory of African American Literary Criticism* (New York: Oxford University Press, 1988), p. 111.
3. Lorraine Hansberry, *A Raisin in the Sun* (New York: New American Library, 1958), p. 79.
4. Cogent discussions of homophobia among Black American intellectuals can be found in Cheryl Clarke, "The Failure to Transform: Homophobia in the Black Community," in *Home Girls: A Black Feminist Perspective*, ed. Barbara Smith (New York: Kitchen Table Press, 1983), pp. 197–208; Ann Allen Shockley, "The Illegitimates of Afro-American Literature," *Lambda Rising Book Report* 1, no. 4: 1+.
5. Mary Helen Washington, *Invented Lives* (Garden City, N.Y.: Doubleday, 1987).
6. Gates, *The Signifying Monkey*, p. 81.
7. Geneva Smitherman, *Talkin and Testifyin* (Boston: Houghton Mifflin, 1977), p. 120.
8. Smitherman, *Talkin and Testifyin*, p. 121.
9. Claudia Mitchell-Kernan, "Signifying as a Form of Verbal Art," in *Mother Wit from the Laughing Barrel: Readings in the Interpretation of Afro-American Folklore*, ed. Alan Dundes (Englewood Cliffs N.J.: Prentice-Hall, 1973), p. 314.
10. Molefi Kete Asnate, *Afrocentricity: A Theory of Social Change* (Buffalo, N.Y.: Amulefi, 1980), p. 66.

11. Asante, *Afrocentricity*, p. 64.

12. Frantz Fanon, *Black Skin, White Masks*, trans. Constance Farrington (New York: Grove Press, 1963), p. 84.

13. Alvin Poussaint, "What Makes Them Tick," *Ebony*, October 1978, p. 79.

14. Quoted in Georges-Michel Sarotte, *Like a Brother, Like a Lover: Male Homosexuality in the American Novel and Theatre from Herman Melville to James Baldwin*, trans. Richard Miller (New York: Doubleday, 1978), p. 94.

15. Eldridge Cleaver, *Soul on Ice* (New York: Random House, 1969), p. 174.

16. Nathan Hare and Julia Hare, *The Endangered Black Family: Coping with the Unisexualization and Coming Extinction of the Black Race* (San Francisco: Black Think Tank, 1984), p. 65.

17. Hare and Hare, *The Endangered Black Family*, p. 65.

18. Toni Morrison, *The Bluest Eye* (New York: Holt, Rinehart & Winston, 1970), p. 132.

19. Toni Morrison, *Tar Baby* (New York: Random House, 1981), p. 216.

20. Toni Morrison, *Beloved* (New York: Random House, 1988), p. 10.

21. Ibid.

22. Ibid.

23. Esteban Montejo, *The Autobiography of a Runaway Slave*, trans. Jocasta Innes, ed. Miguel Barnet (New York: Random House, 1968), p. 21.

24. Ibid., p. 41.

25. Ibid.

26. Ibid.

27. Ibid.

28. Ibid.

29. Ibid.

30. Ibid.

31. On the social practices surrounding the sexuality of slaves, see: John Blassingame, *The Slave Community: Plantation Life in the Antebellum South* (New York: Oxford University Press, 1979), pp. 154–191; Eugene Genovese, *Roll, Jordan, Roll: The World the Slaves Made* (New York: Random House, 1974), pp. 458–475; Mary Helen Washington, *Invented Lives: Narratives of Black Women: 1860–1960* (New York: Doubleday, 1987), pp. 4–8; Deborah Gray White, *Ar'n't I a Woman? Female Slaves in the Plantation South* (New York: Norton, 1985), pp. 142–160.

32. Jonathan Ned Katz, *Gay American History: Lesbians and Gay Men in the U.S.A.* (New York: Avon Books, 1976), p. 35; Jonathan Ned Katz, *Gay/Lesbian Almanac: A New Documentary* (New York: Harper & Row, 1983), p. 61.

33. Katz, *Gay American History*, pp. 35–36.

34. Ibid., p. 61.

35. A. Leon Higginbotham, Jr., *In the Matter of Color: Race and the American Legal Process: The Colonial Period* (New York: Oxford University Press, 1978), pp. 281–282; Katz, *Gay/Lesbian Almanac*, p. 61.

36. Martin Bauml Duberman, "Writhing Bedfellows," in *About Time: Exploring the Gay Past* (New York: Gay Presses of New York, 1986), pp. 13–14.

37. Tom Horner, *Jonathan Loved David: Homosexuality in Biblical Times* (Philadelphia: Westminster Press, 1978), pp. 91–99.

38. For example, toward the end of *The Normal Heart*, one of the indignities that befall a deceased person with AIDS is to be cremated by a black undertaker "for a thousand dollars,

no questions asked" (p. 106). The implication here is that the deceased was unable to have a decent or respectable burial, which would, of course, be by a white undertaker. This is significant because it is part of a tradition in Western aesthetics that associates blacks and Africans with indignity. This also reflects an instance of racism by the author.

39. An interesting case occurred in a serious article in the gay male pornography magazine *Stallion*. The author, Charles Jurrist, criticized the gay literary establishment for its exclusion of or, when included, stereotypical depiction of black men. However, the article perpetuated a stereotype by featuring a series of pictures of a spectacularly endowed Black man.

40. W. E. B. Du Bois, review of *Quicksand* by Nella Larson and *Home to Harlem* by Claude McKay, *Crisis* 35 (June 1928): 202; quoted in Lovie Gibson, "Du Bois' Propaganda Literature: An Outgrowth of His Sociological Studies," doctoral dissertation, State University of New York at Buffalo, 1977, p. 21.

41. Washington, *Invented Lives*, pp. xxiii–xxiv.

42. Michael G. Cooke, *Afro-American Literature in the Twentieth Century: The Achievement of Intimacy* (New Haven: Yale University Press, 1984), p. 95.

43. Samuel R. Delany, *The Motion of Light in Water* (New York: Morrow, 1988), p. 129.

44. Ibid., p. 175.

45. Ibid., p. 176.

46. William H. Grier and Price M. Cobbs, *Black Rage* (New York: Basic Books, 1968), pp. 91–100.

47. Larry Duplechan, *Eight Days a Week* (Boston: Alyson Publications, 1985), p. 28.

48. Essex Hemphill, *Conditions* (Washington, D.C.: Be Bop Books, 1986).

49. Albert Raboteau, *Slave Religion: The "Invisible Institution" in the Antebellum South* (New York: Oxford University Press, 1978), p. 290.

50. Jarena Lee, *Religious Experience and Journal of Mrs. Jarena Lee, Giving an Account of Her Call to Preach the Gospel* (Philadelphia, 1849); found in Ann Allen Shockley, *Afro-American Women Writers, 1746–1933* (New York: New American Library, 1988).

51. Leonard Patterson, "At Ebenezer Baptist Church," in *Black Men/White Men*, ed. Michael Smith (San Francisco: Gay Sunshine Press, 1983), p. 164.

52. Ibid., pp. 164–165.

53. Ibid., p. 165.

54. Ibid., p. 166.

55. James S. Tinney, "Struggles of a Black Pentecostal," in *Black Men/White Men*, ed. Michael Smith (San Francisco: Gay Sunshine Press, 1983), p. 167.

56. Ibid., p. 170.

57. Ibid.

58. Ibid., pp. 170–171.

59. Smitherman, *Talkin and Testifyin*, p. 120.

60. Larry Duplechan, *Blackbird* (New York: St. Martin's, 1986), p. 152.

61. Ibid., p. 153.

62. Ibid., p. 151.

63. Ibid., p. 153.

64. Ibid., p. 150.

65. Ibid., p. 152.

66. Ibid., p. 155.

67. Craig G. Harris, "Cut Off from among Their People," in *In the Life*, ed. by Joseph Beam (Boston: Alyson Publications, 1986), p. 66.

68. Ibid., p. 67.

69. Frederick Douglass, *Narrative of the Life of Frederick Douglass: An American Slave* (1845; New York: New American Library, 1968), p. 48.

70. Ibid.

71. Ibid., pp. 52–53.

72. Haki Madhubuti, "Don't Cry Scream," quoted in Smitherman, *Talkin and Testifyin*, p. 142.

73. Vito Russo, *The Celluloid Closet: Homosexuality in the Movies* (New York: Harper & Row, 1981), p. 229.

74. Julius Marcus Johnson, "Influence of Assimilation on the Psychosocial Adjustment of Black Homosexual Men," doctoral dissertation, California School of Professional Psychology at Berkeley, 1981.

75. Delany, *Motion of Light*, p. 219.

76. Ibid., p. 221.

77. Ibid., p. 220.

78. Ibid., p. 223.

79. George Wolfe, *The Colored Museum*, in *American Theatre*, ed. James Leverett and M. Elizabeth Osborn, February 1987, p. 4.

80. Ibid.

81. Ralph Ellison, *Invisible Man* (New York: New American Library, 1952), p. 7.

82. Wolfe, *Colored Museum*, p. 4.

83. Ibid.

84. Ibid.

85. See Thulani Davis, "Sapphire Attire: A Review," *Village Voice*, Nov. 11, 1986, p. 91; Roger Fristoe, "George C. Wolfe," *Louisville Courier-Journal*, p. 11; Jack Kroll, "Zapping Black Stereotypes," *Newsweek*, Nov. 17, 1986, p. 85.

WORKS CITED

Asante, Molefi. *Afrocentricity: A Theory of Social Change*. Buffalo, N.Y.: Amulefi, 1980.

Beam, Joseph. *In the Life: A Black Gay Anthology*. Boston: Alyson Publications, 1986.

Blassingame, John W. *The Slave Community: Plantation Life in the Antebellum South*. Rev. ed. New York: Oxford University Press, 1979.

Clarke, Cheryl. "The Failure to Transform: Homophobia in the Black Community." In *Home Girls: A Black Feminist Perspective*, ed. Barbara Smith, pp. 197–208. New York: Kitchen Table Press, 1983.

Cleaver, Eldridge. *Soul on Ice*. New York: Random House, 1969.

Darden, Norma Jean and Carole. *Spoonbread and Strawberry Wine*. New York: Fawcett, 1978.

Delany, Samuel R. *The Motion of Light in Water: Sex and Science Fiction Writing in the East Village, 1957–1965*. New York: Morrow, 1988.

Douglass, Frederick. *Narrative of the Life of Frederick Douglass: An American Slave*. 1845. New York: New American Library, 1968.

Duberman, Martin Bauml. *About Time: Exploring the Gay Past*. New York: Gay Presses of New York, 1986.

Duplechan, Larry. *Blackbird*. New York: St. Martin's, 1986.

————. *Eight Days a Week.* Boston: Alyson Publications, 1985.

Ellison, Ralph. *Invisible Man.* New York: Signet, 1952.

Fanon, Frantz, *Black Skin, White Masks.* Trans. Constance Farrington. New York: Grove Press, 1963.

Garrett, Daniel. "Other Countries: Importance of Difference." In *Other Countries: Black Gay Voices,* ed. Cary Alan Johnson, Colin Robinson, and Terence Taylor, pp. 17–28. New York: Other Countries, 1988.

Gates, Henry Louis, Jr. *Figures in Black: Words, Signs, and the "Racial" Self.* New York: Oxford University Press, 1987.

————. *The Signifying Monkey: A Theory of Afro-American Literary Criticism.* New York: Oxford University Press, 1988.

Genovese, Eugene. *Roll, Jordan, Roll: The World the Slaves Made.* New York: Random House, 1974.

Gibson, Lovie. "Du Bois' Propaganda Literature: An Outgrowth of His Sociological Studies." Doctoral dissertation, State University of New York at Buffalo, 1977.

Gordon, Billi. *You've Had Worse Things in Your Mouth.* San Francisco: West Graphics, 1985.

Grier, William H., and Cobbs, Price M. *Black Rage.* New York: Basic Books, 1968.

Hare, Nathan, and Hare, Julia. *The Endangered Black Family: Coping with the Unisexualization and Coming Extinction of the Black Race.* San Francisco: The Black Think Tank, 1984.

Hemphill, Essex. *Conditions.* Washington, D.C.: Be Bop Books, 1986.

Higginbotham, A. Leon. *In the Matter of Color: Race and the American Legal Process: The Colonial Period.* New York: Oxford University Press, 1978.

Horner, Tom. *Jonathan Loved David: Homosexuality in Biblical Times.* Philadelphia: Westminster Press, 1978.

Johnson, Julius Maurice. "Influence of Assimilation on the Psychosocial Adjustment of Black Homosexual Men." Doctoral dissertation, California School of Professional Psychology at Berkeley, 1981.

Jurrist, Charles. "Black Image." *Stallion,* December 1987, pp. 34–45.

Katz, Jonathan Ned. *Gay American History.* New York: Avon Books, 1976.

————. *Gay/Lesbian Almanac: A New Documentary.* New York: Harper & Row, 1983.

Kramer, Larry. *The Normal Heart.* New York: New American Library, 1985.

Mitchell-Kernan, Claudia. "Signifying as a Form of Verbal Art." In *Mother Wit From the Laughing Barrel: Readings in the Interpretation of Afro-American Folklore,* ed. Alan Dundes. Englewood Cliffs, N.J.: Prentice-Hall, 1973.

Montejo, Esteban. *The Autobiography of a Runaway Slave.* Trans. Jocasta Innes. Ed. Miguel Barnet. New York: Random House, 1968.

Morrison, Toni. *The Bluest Eye.* New York: Holt, Rinehart & Winston, 1970.

————. *Tar Baby.* New York: Random House, 1981.

————. *Beloved.* New York: Random House, 1987.

Poussaint, Alvin. "What Makes Them Tick?" *Ebony,* October 1978, p. 79+.

Raboteau, Albert J. *Slave Religion: The "Invisible Institution" in the Antebellum South.* New York: Oxford University Press, 1978.

Russo, Vito. *The Celluloid Closet: Homosexuality in the Movies.* New York: Harper & Row, 1981.

Scroggs, Robin. *The New Testament and Homosexuality: Contextual Background for Contemporary Debate.* Philadelphia: Fortress Press, 1983.

Shockley, Ann Allen. *Afro-American Women Writers, 1746–1933: An Anthology and Critical Guide*. New York: New American Library, 1988.

———. "The Illegitimates of Afro-American Literature." *Lambda Rising Book Report* 1, no. 4: 1+.

(Smart-Grosvenor), Vertamae. *Vibration Cookin; or The Travel Notes of a Geechee Girl*. New York: Doubleday, 1970.

Smith, Michael J. *Black Men/White Men: A Gay Anthology*. San Francisco: Gay Sunshine Press, 1983.

Smitherman, Geneva. *Talkin and Testifyin: The Language of Black America*. Detroit: Wayne State University Press, 1986.

Washington, Mary Helen. *Invented Lives: Narratives of Black Women, 1860–1960*. New York: Doubleday, 1987.

White, Deborah Gray. *Ar'n't I a Woman? Female Slaves in the Plantation South*. New York: Norton, 1985.

Wolfe, George. *The Colored Museum*. In *American Theatre*. Supplement, February 1987, pp. 1–11.

36 Theoretical Returns

Houston A. Baker, Jr.

(1991)

A theory is an explanation. Successful theories offer the possibility of global description and a predictive adequacy. Their goal is an order of understanding different from common sense or mere appreciation. They begin where such modes of thought end or at least where these modes fail to address questions that require for answer more than enumeration, cataloguing, impressionistic summary, selective list, or nonce formulation.

Proposed responses to the question "What is Afro-American literature?" might include anthologies, literary histories, bibliographies, survey courses, or reading lists. These responses—as useful as they may be—are not theory. For theory is occupied preeminently with assumptions, presuppositions, and principles of production rather than with the orderly handling of material products represented by anthologies and survey courses. Theory's relentless tendency is to go beyond the tangible in search of metalevels of explanation. A concern for metalevels, rather than tangible products, is also a founding condition of Afro-American intellectual discourse.

Africans uprooted from ancestral soil, stripped of material culture, and victimized by brutal contact with various European nations were compelled not only to maintain their cultural heritage at a meta (as opposed to a material) level but also to apprehend the operative metaphysics of various alien cultures. Primary to their survival was the work of consciousness, of nonmaterial counterintelligence.

The primacy of nonmaterial transactions in the African's initial negotiations of slavery and the slave trade led to a privileging of the roles and figures of medicine men, griots, conjurers, priests, and priestesses.[1] This emphasis on spiritual leadership (and leadings of the spirit) was embodied in at least one form as the founding institution of African American group life—the church, which in its very name sometimes expresses the spiritual syncretism of its founding: "African Methodist Episcopal."

The generative conditions of diasporic African life that privilege spiritual negotiation and the work of consciousness also make autobiography the premier genre of Afro-American discourse. Bereft of material, geographical or political inscriptions of a state and a common mind, diasporic Africans were compelled to seek a personal, spiritual assurance of worth. Their quest was analogous to Puritan religious meditations, such as Jonathan Edwards's *Personal Narrative*,[2] in the mainland British colonies of North America. For, like their Puritan fellows in deracination and forced immigration, Africans were compelled to verify a self's being. They were forced to construct and inscribe unique personhood in what appeared to be a blank and uncertain environment. Afro-American intellectual history, therefore, is keenly theoretical because it pays compulsory attention both to metalevels of cultural negotiation and to autobiographical inscription. Our intellectual history privileges the unseen and the intangibly personal. The trajectory of this process is from what might be called the workings of a distinctively syncretic spirit to autobiographical inscriptions of spirit work. Two images suggest themselves as illustrations of this trajectory.

One is the frontispiece of Phillis Wheatley's *Poems on Various Subjects Religious and Moral* (1773).[3] Clad in servant's clothing, the young and distinctively African-featured poet Phillis holds pen in hand and looks meditatively ahead, concentrating on something that remains invisible for viewers of her portrait. But the pen in her hand has obviously been at work. There are lines written on the parchment that we see. Perhaps they are the following ones:

> The happier *Terence* all the choir inspir'd,
> His soul replenish'd, and his bosom fir'd;
> But say, ye *Muses*, why this partial grace,
> To one alone of *Afric's* sable race:
> From age to age transmitting thus his name
> With the first glory in the rolls of fame? (4)

We do know that Phillis inscribed these lines in her poem "To Maecenas." In doing so, she wrote her male precursor African's name (Terence) into the discourse of eighteenth-century heroics. Further, she comes to us in these lines as African successor to Terence's precursorial spirit. She calls the question on the muses as it were—with her pen. That question, finally, is one of metalevels and canonicity. What is it, Phillis queries, that privileges Terence's name and why is there a situation of "partial grace" and perpetual exclusion?

The second image, this time from Frederick Douglass, reads as follows:

The hearing of those wild notes always depressed my spirit, and filled me with ineffable sadness. I have frequently found myself in tears while hearing them. The mere recurrence to those songs, even now, afflicts me; and while I am writing these lines, an expression of feeling has already found its way down my cheek. To those songs I trace my first glimmering conception of the dehumanizing character of slavery. I can never get rid of that conception. Those songs still follow me, to deepen my hatred of slavery, and quicken my sympathies for my brethren in bonds.[4]

Here the precursors are legion, but it is their sound that marks an expressive lineage. A self-conscious narrator of African ancestry can be envisioned staring straight ahead in the manner of Wheatley, hearing again from a position analytically outside the circle of song an informing sound. The tear on "these lines" is the unifying affective bond between a spirited and singing text and the written autobiography of Frederick Douglass. Theory's intangible province is captured in the image of the narrator writing black, lyrical first principles that he has extrapolated from his meditations on song. "Slaves sing most when they are most unhappy." Unhappiness, the tear, a soul-killing institutionalization of the African body bring the narrator's present writing and the songs' past sounding together under the controlled pen of African autobiographical genius. We might say the spirit comes through; the vernacular resounds in brilliant coalescence with the formally literary. The metalevel prompting the African slave impulse (an expressive impulse) to song is made readable.

The conflation of past and present, ineffable and readable, marked by Douglass's passage prepares the way for an entirely self-conscious translation of "unhappiness" in a soul-killing institution that brings the narrator into portrayed, pen-in-hand harmony with the Wheatley of *Poems on Various Subjects:*

> I had no bed. I must have perished with cold, but that, the coldest nights, I used to steal a bag which was used for carrying corn to the mill. I would crawl into this bag, and there sleep on the cold, damp, clay floor, with my head in and feet out. My feet have been so cracked with frost, *that the pen with which I am writing might be laid in the gashes.* (My emphasis; 72)

Deprivation, theft, commodification, the burlap (wool?) pulled over the slave's eyes, a sleep of reason that produces wounds ("cracked . . . gashes")—all of these merge in the meditation of a present narrator who has pen in hand. The spiritual bankruptcy of American slavery is expressed as the wounded and commodified ("a bag which was used for carrying corn to the mill") body of the African. The spiritual significance of such a scene emerges only through the pen laid, as poultice and portrayal, in the wound. The spirited response suggested by the pen's work is anticipated, however, by the counter-capital rebellion involved in "stealing" the bag. Finally, though, it is a single fissure ("gashes") that gives rise to written signification of immense proportions as Douglass, like his precursor Wheatley, calls the question.

The images of Wheatley and Douglass are images of Afro-American theory in its autobiographical resonance. They could be multiplied tenfold through a survey of Afro-American literary and critical traditions. One thinks of W. E. B. Du Bois's autobiographical situation at the close of his "Forethought" to *The Souls of Black Folk.* One summons to mind the autobiographical positioning of Richard Wright in "The Literature of the Negro in the United States," or of James Baldwin's narrator in the "Autobiographical Notes" that serve as prelude to *Notes of a Native Son.* There are, as well, Ralph Ellison's autobiographical "Introduction" to *Shadow and Act* and Amiri Baraka's introductory, autobiographical essay "Cuba Libre" in *Home.* Such enumerations, however, are not theory. They are certainly metatheoretical, though, in a way that will, one hopes, clarify the project in Afro-American intellectual traditions at work here. For the examples serve to adumbrate a lineage of autobiographical, metalevel negotiations that constitute Afro-American discourse in its most cogent form.

At present in the United States, there seems to have occurred quite a remarkable reversal of and aversion to this lineage. Imagistically, this reversal displays itself in the person and voice of Afro-American critics, with pen in hand, suggesting that theory is *alien* to African American discourse. Such critics claim that black discourse is most aptly characterized not as complexly theoretical, but as univocally humanistic and unambiguously moral. Critics such as R. Baxter Miller and Joyce Joyce want, in fact, to suggest that Afro-American discourse *must* be taken as the output of a loving, moral creature known as Man, or more charitably and inclusively, Humankind.[5] Implicit in the claims of Miller and Joyce is the notion that Homo Africanus is somehow comprehensible by standards of scholarship and fields of rhetoric that are not implicated in the sphere of metalevels, or "theory." For Joyce, Miller, and their compeers, an adequate picture of Afro-American discourse can be achieved only via assumptions of a traditional humanism and methods of standard disciplines such as social history, philosophy, and group psychology. Such claims situate their proponents with debunkers of a project in literary and expressive cultural study that has been disruptively influential for at least the past two decades in American, French, and British universities. It also situates them, I believe, at some remove from discernible contours of African American literary and critical traditions as I have tentatively envisioned them.

What I want to suggest is that the African American's negotiation of metalevels, in combination with his or her propensity for autobiography as a form of African survival, has always enabled him or her to control a variety of levels of discourse in the United States. Such control has placed African Americans in a position that refutes, it seems to me, any claims for a simplistic humanity, humanism, or affective purity of discourse.

The most forceful, expressive cultural spokespersons of Afro-America have traditionally been those who have first mastered a master discourse—at its most rarefied metalevels as well as at its quotidian performative levels—and then, autobiographically, written themselves and their own metalevels palimpsestically on the scroll of such mastery. Their acts of mastery have sometimes moved hostilely against claims of a traditional humanism, and they have seldom been characterized by any sentiment that might unambiguously or simply be designated "love."

A case in point from black discourse is resonantly before us in this time of celebration of the Constitution of the United States. When the writer David Walker issued his *Appeal* in 1829, in the form of a revolutionary document containing a "preamble" and four "articles," and maintained throughout that document an autobiographical voice, he accomplished the type of founding black theoretical negotiation I have in mind. As a document that, in a sense, writes itself on the enslaved body of the African, the Constitution of the United States contains both a foregrounded story of freedom and a variety of backgrounded narratives of suppression and enslavement. David Walker, like all theoretically adept Afro-American spokespeople, had absolute knowledge of one set of suppressions, and he took as his task an appealing writing (or re-righting) of the African body in the very foreground of the Constitution. Walker, in Henry Louis Gates's sense of the word,[6] signifies with, on, in the very face of the meta and performative levels of a founding (constitutive) discourse of Euramerican culture. He knew, of course, that such discourse as the Constitution had to be survived and syncretically refigured if African freedom and community were to become a United States of America reality.

Now, whether Walker was more loving, humanistic, convivial, or inherently humane than, say, the average white Boston citizen of his day, is a stunningly irrelevant issue where Afro-American expressive cultural theory is concerned. What is important is that Walker was both autobiographically astute and strikingly brilliant with respect to the foregrounded stories of such white citizenry. (His very title, in its long form, refers to colored citizens—a truly African heretical invocation of 1789.) He was, in short, a successful Afro-American theorist who knew that simplistic assertions of a distinguishable African American cultural and discursive practice would yield nothing. He knew that he had to master the very forms of enslavement in order to write let us say, "African flesh" in empowering ways.

Walker's act, thus, constitutes an autobiographical revolution, an explosive super-literacy that writes, not in the terms of the other, but in lines that adumbrate the suppressed story of an-other. His *Appeal* emerges as a new covenant, a new constitution. It repudiates a hypocritical Constitutional humanism and urges a robust hatred of slavery. Theory understood in terms of David Walker's *Appeal* is, I believe, of the essence of Afro-American intellectual traditions.

What most discourages readers about "theory"—specifically, as it has manifested itself in the academy in recent years—is its aloofness, difficulty, and refusal to supply material examples and enumerations that make for general recognition. Theory, in such a manifestation, seems merely self-indulgent, an endless spinning of solipsistic webs, or a ceaseless construction of what Elizabeth Bruss calls "beautiful theories."[7] Not only do such efforts fail to yield material examples of general reading, they may seem, finally, to have no practical consequences whatsoever, refusing to translate complex expressive cultural texts into enumerative, catalogued, or syllabused forms.

There is much to be said in support of the suspicion and charges of theory's detractors. There exist, for example, forceful, comprehensive, and usable accounts of expressive texts that derive from such seemingly "theory free" accountings as psychological and sociohistorical explanatory narratives. Still, the disparagement of theory in the expanded form in which it actually exists today seems slightly bizarre when it comes from Afro-American scholars. For it is surely theoretical discourse—conceived as autobiographical cultural commentary—that is the discursive foundation of Afro-American intellectual life in the United States. The incendiary deconstruction, defamiliarization, and signifying within the master discourse represented by Walker's *Appeal* or Du Bois's *Souls* or Baraka's *Home* (full as that text is of Wittgensteinian analytic philosophy) constitute a foundational writing and informed ritualization that is indispensable in any fleshing out of an African story in America.

Finally, it is not theory, I think, that Afro-American detractors mean when they attack the Afro-American literary theoretical project, but rather the politics of theory as they have unfolded. Afro-Americans have been the very first radically to call the question on the traditional exclusiveness of the American academy, and they have called it in traditionally Afro-American theoretical ways. At Yale, Cornell, and San Francisco State, for example, such workers as Armstead Robinson, Roy Bryce Laporte, Michael Thelwell, James Turner, Sonia Sanchez, and Nathan Hare astutely, personally (writing, talking, and thinking out of their own lives) adduced a different idea of the real story of higher education in the United States. Their endeavors were under the aegis of Black Studies. We might say that where the founding of Black Studies was concerned, the personal was the theoretical. The results of Black Studies initiatives have included new courses, revised canons of study, and the creation of possibilities for myriad formerly suppressed or backgrounded discourses to take to the open air in their unique significations. Still, Black Studies represented only an initial move. No matter how culturally specific its motivations, they were, nonetheless, subject to institutional constraints of an academy that demanded an historically grounded blackness. Only by achieving an academic superliteracy has Black Studies become Black (theoretical) Power. I have already discussed the theoretical distinctions between the two enterprises and want here merely to emphasize what might be termed an initiatory autobiographical energy marking Black Studies' inaugural instances.

From black actional autobiography, as it were, the academy has moved, on one hand, to other "studies" such as Women's, Chicano, Gay, Asian American, Lesbian, etc. On the other hand, the actively revisionist and committedly political energies that produced Black Studies have been recuperated by disciplines such as "English" as occasions for esoteric, leisurely "readings" of the same books by the same white-male authors who have marked syllabuses for decades. The traditionally privileged (as with the New Historicism's cast of authors and critics) maintain their access and control through renomination. A "new" academic generation in its thirties, forties, and fifties, therefore, looks almost as white—if not as male—as its forebears.

Represented in the manner that I have chosen, theory does seem somewhat useless, and Afro-American scholars who are academic theorists must appear traitors to a nativist purity, humanism, and love.

Still, neither the remissness of white academicians—men or women—nor the entrepreneurial or careerist motives of black academicians, men or women, should compel us to desert the most active traditions of Afro-American theory in our own intellectual lives. We must continue to seek—in our own currently possible negotiation of academic metalevels—to extrapolate from "theory" what is actionally and autobiographically necessary and useful for us. Only by doing so will we be able to move the founding and always resonantly in-action analytical project of our own culture beyond, let us say, the facile renominations within an academic elite's commodified, careerist pleasure dome.

In short, the task seems to me one of negotiating the unseen, presuppositional domains of current popular white theorizing in much the same way that Walker,

Douglass, Wheatley, Du Bois, or Baraka negotiated their respective eras—pen in hand, listening to sounds of African precursors, mastering (both intellectually and rhetorically) the public symbolic orders of the day. Like the workers of our cultural past, we must be fully informed—indeed brilliant—strategists of metalevels, trusting out own autobiographical impulses in a world that implores or intimidates us to a stolid historical essentialism.

There are several objections that I can envision to my proposals. First, there will arise the familiar and always paradoxical—considering its normal source—query about "exclusion." Does an autobiographical condition of existence and authenticity exclude non-Afro-American (say, "white") commentators from Afro-American expressive cultural theory? The answer is a painful No. Painful because the incumbency for the non-Afro-American critic is to finger the grains of a brutal experience in which—if he or she is white—he or she is historically implicated. In response to a white student's objection that James Baldwin's work was too full of "hatred," the author replied: "Your objection shows exactly why we need a white history month. Only when there is such education will we achieve a new moral vocabulary." "Autobiographical," in my proposal, means a personal negotiation of metalevels—one that foregrounds nuances and resonances of *an-other's* story. The white autobiographer who honestly engages his or her own autobiographical implication in a brutal past is as likely as an Afro-American to provide such nuances. What has usually been meant, however, in raising the objection of "exclusion" is that a vaguely specified "WE" should be concerned more with the universal (whatever that means) than with the autobiographical. Which brings us to the second possible objection: The situation of theory in the realm of autobiography seems to privilege delimited personal "experience" as a category of observation and analysis rather than general systematic, objective, empirical considerations of variables. The objection brought by practitioners of the latter against the "personal" is normally launched in the names of both moral and scientific objectivism. Morality and science (read: "rational truth") demand transcendence of the personal. Here, I think, we might enter a brief meditation on the personal as a way of addressing the objection and as a prelude to considerations of a poetics of Afro-American women's writing.

There are few moralists who fail to discover in their own lives indisputable evidence of an unimpeachable morality. Similarly, there are few scientific theorists who do not find in their work evidence of a stunning fidelity to the "spirit" of their subject. Neither the moralist nor the scientific theorist, however, is likely to see his or her evaluations as self-congratulatory. Governed by standards of a general virtue or a universalist objectivity, neither wishes to acknowledge the determinacy of language, vested interests, privileged interpretive postures, or a will to power in their analyses.

At least since Samuel Taylor Coleridge's reservations in the *Biographia Literaria* about the merely idiosyncratic features of Wordsworth's verse—or, perhaps, it is at least since Socrates set the ideal vision of the State against the idiosyncratic and merely personal reveries of the poets—moralists, poets, and analysts have been cautioned against the personal. We listen for a moment to T. S. Eliot: "One error, in fact, of eccentricity in poetry is to seek for new human emotions to express; and in this search for novelty in the wrong place it discovers the perverse. . . . poetry is not a turning loose of emotion, but an escape from emotion; it is not the expression of personality, but an escape from personality."[8] Eliot not only brings the classical argument home with full force but also states precisely the criteria by which any autobiographically situated project would be disqualified as standard or classical poetry and, perhaps, aptly characterized as "perverse." But before rushing to his judgment, we might attempt a series of counterclaims: Theorists follow, always, a purely personal line. In their most self-aware moments they have no doubt about the specifiable personal determinants of each of their essays, reviews, lectures, and pedagogical utterances. Now if they choose never to be "personal," that simply means they have made an entirely "personal" choice. Who, after all, in our most self-directing moments stands over us, saying "Now, you'll probably want to perform a search-and-replace operation when you're finished with the present essay, changing all 'I's to 'one's"? There are, to be sure, institutional conventions, career and market constraints, that serve as implicit censors for us. But, finally, we make our own choices and are seldom deceived, I think, about the "personal" determinacy of our work. The search-and-replace operation that normally forestalls recognition (sometimes even self-recognition) of the personal is the substitution of human or universal for what actually operates any given theoretical enterprise: namely, my values. The substitution of human or universal is always in the service of powerful interests (one's own included) that seek to maintain the status quo in the name of *la condition humaine*. But as the theorist normally works—even under such rigorously political circumstances as those of, say, Mikhail Bakhtin—the condition closest to hand is a very personal and interested one.

Thus, for a theorist to acknowledge autobiography as a driving force is for him or her to do no more than tell the truth. When I "analyze," for you my reader, a poem or a novel, or set forth a large-scale topos (e.g., "the daughters' departure") for an entire expressive domain, I am merely offering you a determinate recall of my experiences under the conventions of criticism, or theory—a peculiar and covering style, as it were. Now this is not to plump down squarely for a return to journeys of sensitive souls among the masterpieces. Both "sensitive" and "masterpieces" were overdetermined in that form of impressionism.

No, what "recall" implies here is a narrative, which begins, as Barbara Herrnstein Smith argues in *On the Margins of Discourse*, with the founding condition "something happened."[9] My critical position or theoretical project is a personal posture marked by the narration of what happened, *to me*. The decisive emphasis (mine) on "to me" suggests, of course, the work of Walter Pater and others. In *The Renaissance*, Pater says that Matthew Arnold's injunction to see the object "as in itself it really is" demands qualified restatement. The aim for Pater was to see a particular, unique object as it is to me. I am not, finally, advocating more than an autobiographical allowance that transforms the critic or theorist into a critic—a very particularly constructed and accounted-for figure.

Where Afro-American women's expressivity is concerned, the particular construction and accountability of the critic must allow him or her to negotiate metalevels of space, place, and time in order to figure forth a new expressive world. Like the autobiographical meditations of Wheatley and Douglass, the critic's work must be consciously theoretical if it is to be adequately figurative, and vice versa. The most thorough and persuasive work is that which is marked by a fit converse between consciousness and the figurative. Surely such converse is what Spillers implies when she calls us imaginatively to negotiate a presocial moment of the African "flesh"—to take back or secure a pre-European return upon African expressive energies silenced by an enslaving trade in our bodies. It is also such converse that Gaston Bachelard has in mind when he defines a phenomenological project in poetics. The convergence of poetics and Afro-American women's expressivity not only promotes a refiguration but leads, as well, to the revision of all American stories in the person of the "theorist"—say, a teller of metalevels such as Janie Crawford Killicks Starks Woods, who poetically refigures everyday black women's life in her own conscious autobiographical accountings. Bachelard's project is a resource with which we might enhance our general theoretical store in a way that enables us successfully to follow the world-renewing example of Hurston's protagonist.

Conditioned by Bachelard's allegiance to a phenomenology of the imagination, the "Introduction" to *The Poetics of Space* reads as follows:

> The image offered us by reading the poem now becomes really our own. It takes root in us. It has been given us by another, but we begin to have the impression that we could have created it, that we should have created it. It becomes a new being in our language, expressing us by making us what it expresses; in other words, it is at once a becoming of expression, and a becoming of our being. Here expression creates being. (xix)[10]

This statement implies a virtually shimmering instant when objective reality and all indicative experience are bracketed, compelling a reader to inhabit and to be inhabited by *the being* of the poetic image. For Bachelard, poetic images are the origin of consciousness. As reverberating products of poetic reverie, they enhance language and renew both us and the world in which we live.

More importantly, poetic images such as *house* serve as analytical tools. They allow us not only to map a topography of intimate human space but also to follow moments of human consciousness to the very functions (signaled by the verb "to inhabit") of intimacy and protection that are coextensive and coterminous with an image such as *house*. The "objective," "remembered," or "retained" corner of a childhood house is less important for an understanding of corners than felicitous images of *corner* presented by poetic reverie.

Hence, when he uses the word "poetics," Bachelard does not intend a peculiar set of conventions, rules, and procedures for the composition or analysis of creative writing. "Poetics" signals images and the consciousness-work through which they constitute the origin and foundation of a human world. "Space," for example, is conceivable only in terms of poetic images (such as *house* and *corner*) that figure it forth from and intersubjectively to human consciousness.

Bachelard wages a polemic against psychology and psychoanalysis because these disciplines strive to explain the "cause" or meaning of poetic images. For Bachelard, nothing prepares or "causes" a poetic image; its appearance and presentation are entirely new. Further, no psychobiography of a poet can make more effective the shimmering import of even one of his or her felicitous images.

The felicitous poetic image is, for Bachelard, not an objective phenomenon, but a reverberant event of consciousness that one enters in the office of renewal, comprehension, and liberation:

> A great verse awakens images that had been effaced, at the same time that it confirms the unforeseeable nature of speech. And if we render speech unforeseeable, is that not an apprenticeship to freedom? What delight the poetic imagination takes in making game of censors! (xxiii)

Bachelard's poetics and an effective criticism of Afro-American women's writing converge at the site of the felicitous poetic image.

One of the most important essays on the efficacy of Afro-American women's expressivity in the United States is Alice Walker's "In Search of Our Mothers' Gardens,"[11] in which the author recalls:

> I notice that it is only when my mother is working in her flowers that she is radiant, almost to the point of being invisible—except as Creator: hand and eye. She is involved in work her soul must have. Ordering the universe in the image of her personal conception of Beauty. (241)

This description—in its shimmering irradiance of subject and object—captures the splendid intersubjectivity detailed by Bachelard. The word "invisible" suggests a pure reverie in which the intuitively imaged garden is created as spiritual and eternal form.

Neither flowers nor mother is as important, finally, as an implied aboriginal creation in the garden. In a word, Walker as both reader and poet discovers through the image garden how the world is made anew.

By phenomenologically recovering her mother's vernacular garden and presenting it as literate poetic image (in the manner of Wheatley's "Terence" or Douglass's "songs"), Walker opens the field of Afro-American women's consciousness in its founding radiance and claims for herself an enduring spiritual legacy. Beginning her essay with a discussion of Jean Toomer's *Cane*, a book in which Afro-American women are tragically mute in their repressed spirituality, and Virginia Woolf's "A Room of One's Own," which discusses the traditional repression of women's creativity, Walker discovers rejoicing, celebration, and hope in her mother's imaged garden. If Bachelard's and Walker's formulations are combined, the prospect emerges for a theoretical approach to Afro-American women's writing called a "poetics."

But even as we project such an approach, the questions arise: "Why phenomenology in a poststructuralist world? How can the deployment of phenomenology be reconciled with adherence to a postmodernist problematic of sign production?" (These questions do not arise with equal interest to all, and the nonphilosophically disposed reader should know that he or she can avoid my proposed answers in this and the next section without losing the thread of my general argument. For those interested in the philosophical and, specifically, the Derridean strands of the thread, the two sections are indispensable.) After all, phenomenology seeks to move transcendently beyond indicative signs that govern "ordinary" communication. As a rationalist enterprise or method, it seeks its source of explanation in consciousness. For phenomenology objective validity is a function of intuition, not an "effect" of sign production. It is the quiddity or "what is" of phenomena, that is to say, that concerns phenomenology. Husserl's attempt to make philosophy "scientific" constitutes an inaugural move of the project.[12]

By "scientific," Husserl intended a status that would be methodologically adequate for certifying the unique givenness to consciousness of objectively valid knowledge. "Objectively valid" means givenness as such—in a manner adequate to demonstrate that the object of an intuition could not have been given otherwise. The phases of the epoche (or bracketing of the contingent), reduction (clearing away of phenomenal residue), and ideation (a perspectival "turning" or induction) are well known as Husserl's distinctive elaborations of method. The importance of his work is that it constitutes a critique of prior practices of philosophy. It attempts to escape metaphysics and the positivism of natural sciences that were contemporaneous with his *Logical Investigations*. Like Frege, Wittgenstein, Whitehead, Russell, and others at the beginning of the twentieth century, Husserl was concerned to start all over again, to solicit Western metaphysics and the traditional rationalism subsumed under the heading of "philosophy." It is the spirit of critique that makes his project compelling.

Taking philosophy as the science of being, he sought to provide a method for investigating absolute knowledge of absolute being. Such a method could only begin with the consciousness of the rational subject and the phenomenal data presented to that consciousness. For the only true being of objectivity is being in consciousness (*Bewusst-sein*), and the phenomenological description that reveals this being is objectively valid only insofar as it is valid for all time and all possible subjects.

Philosophy, thus, becomes a methodical reflection on consciousness as revelatory of being. Husserl designates the process implied here as "knowledge theory" and suggests that such theory

> investigate[s] the problems of the relationship between consciousness and being, . . . [and] can have before its eyes only being as the correlate of consciousness, as something 'intended' after the manner of consciousness: as perceived, remembered, expected, represented pictorially, imagined, identified, distinguished, believed, opined, evaluated, etc. It is clear, then, that the investigation must be directed toward a scientific essential knowledge of consciousness, toward that which consciousness itself "is" according to its essence in all its distinguishable forms.[13]

Subsequent to Husserl, Heidegger defined the same "knowledge theory" or phenomenological method as a leading back or re-duction of the investigative vision from a naively apprehended being to being.[14] But phenomenology, according to Heidegger, must not be confined to the pure negativity of a re-duction or retreat from beings (*res extensa*) toward being. It must also include a leading forward toward being. "Being does not become accessible like a being. We do not simply find it in front of us. As is to be shown, it must always be brought to view in a free projection. This projecting of the antecedently given being upon its being and the structures of its being we call *phenomenological construction*" (21–22). And there is yet a third component of phenomenological method that, according to Heidegger, involves the disentanglement of traditional concepts of philosophy from their historical situatedness and overdetermination:

> [A]ll philosophical discussion, even the most radical attempt to begin all over again, is pervaded by traditional concepts and thus by traditional horizons and traditional angles of approach, which we cannot assume with unquestionable certainty to have arisen originally and genuinely from the domain of being and the constitution of being they claim to comprehend. It is for this reason that there necessarily belongs to the conceptual interpretation of being and its structure, that is, to the reductive construction of being, a *destruction*—a critical process in which the traditional concepts, which at first must necessarily be employed, are de-constructed down to the sources from which they were drawn. Only by means of this destruction can ontology fully assure itself in a phenomenological way of the genuine character of its concepts. (22–23)

What prevails in my selective account is an air of critique. Phenomenology's aims seem to be a new rigor, a disentanglement or deconstruction of received tradition, an escape from metaphysics, and an order of explanation that provides objectively valid knowledge. Essential to this project is a rejection of the causality of natural science based on laws governing *res extensa*. *Res cogitans* and a language to fit them are preeminent.

In order to achieve its ends, phenomenology attempts to situate itself transcendently beyond the limitations of ordinary language. It rejects indication and communication in favor of expression and presentation. And it is in this linguistic aspect of its work that it is overtaken by the influential deconstructionist critique of Jacques Derrida in *Speech and Phenomena: Introduction to the Problem of Signs in Husserl's Phenomenology*.[15]

Derrida's monograph is one of the most influential poststructuralist interrogations of phenomenology. But his project is less a refutation, I think, than an inversion. Its most decisive move is privileging nonbeing and absence as, at least, philosophically coimplicated in all investigations of being and presence. His topsy-turvydom sounds as follows:

> To think of presence as the universal form of transcendental life [as phenomenology does] is to open myself to the knowledge that in my absence, beyond my empirical existence, before my birth and after my death, *the present is* . . . I have a strange and unique certitude that this universal form of presence, since it concerns no determined

being, will not be affected by it. The relationship with *my death* (my disappearance in general) thus lurks in this determination of being as presence, ideality, the absolute possibility of repetition . . . The I *am*, being experienced only as an I *am present*, itself presupposes the relationship with presence in general, with being as presence. . . . Therefore, I *am* originally means I *am mortal*. (54)

The nonbeing of death is, thus, thematized by Derrida in terms of language as *différance*. In a word, Derrida reminds us that repetition alone maintains presence, and repetition's motivation is preeminently a system of signs whose very possibility is founded in absence. A sign is a sign only insofar as its signifier and signifieds are systematically independent of a present speaking subject. The birth of the sign is precisely the death of the subject.

Signs are founded in difference—distinctions marked by phonemes and the infinite deferral of meaning, which is always indeterminately suspended between past and future.

To the extent that signs provide our only access to "repetition" and "presence," they can never be bracketed as contingent and inessential. The metaphysical paradox of phenomenology's quest for "present" "objective validity" of consciousness arises from its attempts at such bracketing.

Derrida, thus, argues that phenomenology forwards its project through an (at best) naive or (at worst) metaphysical privileging of voice, which the project deems an antithesis to the contingency of signs. (The original French title of Derrida's monograph was *La Voix et le phénomène*.) But this turn to voice is a dissimulation, since the verbal or spoken is already fissured, *differed*, as it were, by the *ur*-conditions of signification. The *différance, trace, supplément* that define the sign are anterior to and determinative of any possibility of "meaningful" voice or speech.

Hence, Derrida concludes that phenomenology's impulse to write a scientific philosophy free of metaphysics is betrayed by the project's own metaphysical privileging of a primordial expressive voice. The "metaphysics of presence"—with its formal logical requirements and teleological desire for truth—is palpably inscribed in phenomenology.

The phenomenologist, then, responds with questions of his own: "Is there life after Derrida? Or only death? Must phenomenology be abandoned in favor of its inversion? On what revised or expanded terms might one continue?"

If ideality, consciousness, being, and quiddity continue to interest us as themes of a project that contains, at least, the possibility of an escape from metaphysics, then I would think phenomenology remains of interest. It is, after all, precisely within the tradition of phenomenology that Derrida differs and defers: i.e., has any significance and import for us through a diacritical critique. Further, if we hope to avoid the optimistic existentialism of (natural) scientific explanation and the skeptical, sometimes tedious hermeneutics of representation, then we are compelled to investigate being and consciousness in the uniqueness of their constitution and relationships.

The Derridean critique of phenomenology is, in effect, the difference within that project that alerts us to both its vulnerabilities and possibilities. The "voice," as it were, of Derrida is like the hearing of itself of phenomenology. "Hearing oneself speak is not the inwardness of an inside that is closed in upon itself; it is the irreducible openness in the inside; it is the eye and the world within speech."[16]

Derrida's phenomenological *mundus inversus* is the site of intersection between phenomenology and its *différance*. It is a phenomenology of phenomenology that is in accord with Heidegger's specifications of a third moment in the project's method. Derrida's critique is the deconstruction of phenomenology that is always implicit in the project's goal—already anticipated, even invited. I think it is the aporia signaling, not an occasion for abandonment, but an opportunity for beginning again. But commencing not in a spirit of voluntaristic denial.

Derrida's dark auguries of death, closure, and endings cannot be willed out of account. Nor can they be considered sanctions for passive abandonment of the themes of phenomenology. Being, knowledge, consciousness, quiddity do arise to mind when we struggle to articulate the "whatness" and its mode of being of a tradition such as Afro-American women's expressivity. And metaphysical, historical, psychological, and positivistic models seem less promising than the possibility of an account that endeavors to discover the conditions and objects of consciousness of this expressivity.

Such an account would, in my estimation, be both metaphysical and Derridean. It would be "metaphysical," however, in a Johnsonian sense of yoking seemingly radically dissimilar projects together; Derridean insofar as radical dissimilarity reveals itself as the grounds of being (as well as the certainty of mortality) of the quest for being itself. A too simple way of stating the matter is to say that a phenomenological poetics proceeds today as a project whose "irreducible openness" has made available a methodologically tensioned mode of analysis that may lead to, at least, a semblance of both knowledge and theory.

If we continue to forward a phenomenological project through Derrida, then, we shall have done no more than seize upon the implications of what, to me, is the most significant utterance in *Speech and Phenomena*:

> [T]o restore the original and nonderivative character of signs, in opposition to classical metaphysics, is, by an apparent paradox, at the same time to eliminate a concept of signs whose whole history and meaning belong to the adventure of the metaphysics of presence. This also holds for the concepts of representation, repetition, difference, etc., as well as for the system they form. For the present and for some time to come, the movement of that schema will only be capable of working over the language of metaphysics from within, from a certain sphere of problems inside that language. No doubt this work has always already begun. (51–52)

Derrida is precisely that beginning for phenomenology, and, in a sense, all we do when we forward the project is read and re-read Derrida as a propaedeutic to a method of talking (again) about the themes of phenomenology.

In expressive cultural analysis, phenomenology offers a site that foregrounds the sign without minimizing the possibilities of unique access to and processing of being by human consciousness. Phenomenology does not augur a mimetic (sociohistorical, reflective, or "influence") theory of expressive culture, nor does it give place to pseudoscientific–new-critical models and allegories of reading. Rather, it assumes spirit and consciousness as agent and agency—through signs—of human expressive cultural production. It does not eradicate the material in its analyses, but seeks to constitute the being of the material in terms of a preeminent spirit work. If the sign is the limit of a material ideality or mortal immortality, then "the material" is the limit case coimplicated with spirit work.

Just as neither representation (v. presentation), reflection, nor deconstructive "reading" can upstage the consciousness of phenomenology, so the material itself takes its place not ahead of but onstage beside consciousness—paradoxically half-perceived and half-created through the very materiality of the sign. Signifying on a striking figure of Husserl's, Derrida locates the scene of his own phenomenology of phenomenology in the Dresden gallery:

> The gallery is the labyrinth which includes in itself its own exits: we have never come upon it as upon a particular *case* of experience—that which Husserl believes he is describing. It remains, then, for *us to speak*, to make our voices *resonate* throughout the corridors in order to make up for [*suppléer*] the breakup of presence. The phoneme, the *akoumenon*, is the *phenomenon of the labyrinth*. This is the *case* with the *phone*. Rising toward the sun of presence, it is the way of Icarus. (104)

Derrida, of course, retains flight (sight toward the sun) in the face of the repeated (as myth) possibilities of failure. And so, of course, does the expressive cultural critic seeking the "essence" or "being" of Afro-American women's creativity. Although writing, difference, supplement, and the sign may be always already determining, still the agency of spirit and consciousness motivates our analytical quest beyond a passive curator's desk and toward an investigation and sounding of corridors and works that are productions of an inferable and inspired past.

The "stage" of the Dresden gallery, like the work of the expressive cultural critic, summons the question of communication—that signal heat likely to dissolve the wings of Igarus. For of what use is an investigation of being that cannot be communicated?

The foundering place of phenomenology has, traditionally, been easily located at the site of *intersubjectivity*. In a footnote devoted to temporalization, Derrida writes,

> [D]etermination of "absolute subjectivity" would also have to be crossed out as soon as we conceive the present on the basis of difference, and not the reverse. The concept of *subjectivity* belongs *a priori and in general* to the order of the *constituted*. This holds *a fortiori* for the analogical appresentation that constitutes intersubjectivity. Intersubjectivity is inseparable from temporalization taken as the openness of the present upon an outside of itself, upon *another* absolute present. This being outside itself proper to time is its *spacing:* it is a proto-stage [*archi-scène*]. . . . There is no constituting subjectivity. (84–85)

And yet, Derrida realizes—even as Icarus must—that a denial of the sun is possible only in a flight toward it. To assert the negation is to open the possibility (in consciousness, at least) of the affirmation of a constituting subjectivity. The paradox of that subjectivity's claims for itself is what is at issue at the site of intersubjectivity. Quentin Lauer describes the paradox as follows:

> In a phenomenological context the problem of communication is really a double one. Though it is true that any cognition recognized by the subject as "objectively valid" will be recognized as being necessarily such for any possible other subjects, communication can be significant only if there are actual other subjects. The first problem, then, is that of knowing other actual subjects, in a framework where nothing is known unless it is constituted subjectively as an object of cognition. Thus the other subject must be an object constituted as a subject (i.e., as constituting its own subjects, including subjects other than itself).[17]

One way of characterizing this stumbling block is to call it the problem of a staged, monadic intuitionism. Rather than taking refuge from the logical paradox thus presented in paralyzing skepticism or solipsistic idealism, we can simply take the stance "nevertheless it moves."

That is to say, while we will have to qualify all claims to the absolute, and certainly to absolute and objectively valid "truth," we may nevertheless note that our phenomenological investigations move us beyond the tedious cleverness of skeptical "readings" that take comfort in a commitment to absolutely "nothing."

What we, in spite of our siting in a solitary self-consciousness, must communicate is a spirited, if tentative, sounding of culture work.

The paradox of constituting "other subjects" seems less formidable, perhaps, for an Afro-Americanist tradition in which the very spirited order of consciousness in and for itself, as either extant or being, has always already had to be constituted against a dominant culture's persistent "othering" and "objectifying." The pragmatic character of methodological effect tends—even through paradox—to win the day in Afro-American culture over logical completeness. Phenomenology may not communicate all that we wish to know—precisely because, as Derrida has demonstrated, it is locked into a communicative relationship to the world. But it is capable of providing a pragmatic and forceful accounting of Afro-American culture work. It succeeds, paradoxically, by acceding to the claims of its own deconstruction as to a treaty, let us say, with *différance*.

Hence, Bachelard's phenomenology and poetics of space should be impossible as moving cultural analysis, yet they move as persuasively as any account that one can imagine. Further, specifications for the intersubjectivity of poetic images should be impossible, yet they accord (even in an age of sophisticated cultural semiotics) well with what we know, or feel, or intuit of the workings of the expressive spirit in Afro-American culture. Phenomenology, then, seems to succeed in spite of itself—in conjunction, one might say, with its very paradoxes. Certainly it makes available, through a qualified deployment of Bachelard, a poetics for sounding Afro-American women's expressivity.

The "poetics of Afro-American women's writing" signals, then, a theory that seeks to arrive at the guiding spirit, or consciousness, of Afro-American women's writing by examining selected imagistic fields. Space, as conceived by Bachelard, is an imagistic field. It is a function of images (e.g., house or corner). We come to know space through an examination of such images. Furthermore, human space has attached to it both "protective value" and "imagined values, which soon become dominant" (xxxi–xxxii). By examining imagistic fields that compose space, therefore, we also come to apprehend values and beliefs that govern our lives. Our cultural geographies are, thus, comprehensible through images.

The word "cultural" must be taken as an independent variable. For Bachelard's approach is only effective, I believe, when it is combined with examinations of culturally specific creative or imaginative fields such as Walker's "In Search of Our Mothers' Gardens." A general or universal field such as space is, finally, only a motivating area of examination—one hypothesized as constitutive for all cultures.

We assume, for example, that space, place, and time as universal fields are, indeed, rife with images that Afro-Americans have both inhabited and been inhabited by. At the same time, we assume that there is a field of "particular" or vernacular imagery unique to the Afro-American imagination.

The task of a poetics, then, is to operate a universal category or imagistic field through a culturally specific field in order to enhance both. The project is, one might say, akin to the application of a course in general linguistics to the specifics of, say, Black English Vernacular. Again, it might be likened to the examination of Afro-American expressive culture under the prospect of general theories of textual production and performance. The axiological results of such operations include accessing the general, framing images and values of a culture as well as foregrounding the quite specific values or instances that modify and expand a general field.

For example, one might attempt to show how a "poetics of Afro-American women's expressivity" applied to a text such as Toni Morrison's *Sula*[18]—a text determined by place from its opening phrase "In that place"—sharply modifies and expands the field of place and, at the same time, foregrounds distinctive values and aspects of an Afro-American expressive field. Place, in a poetics of *Sula*, differentiates into European and Afro-American. Within the Afro-American, it undergoes further gender discrimination into a "standard" male province and a woman's cosmetological territory.

Correlatively, "the Bottom," which serves as *Sula*'s vernacular setting, becomes a field where specifically Afro-American women's places—Eva Peace's and Helene Wright's houses, Edna Finch's Mellow House, and Irene's Palace of Cosmetology—offer an energetic figuration of patterns of purity and danger, order and inversiveness in Afro-American life. The shack, or place, of Ajax's mother—where seven sons are taught respect, love, and admiration for women as well as the spiritedness of the art of conjure—becomes a generative image in the field of place and a foregrounded place of potential for spatial rearrangements of Afro-American life.

If one measure for determining the success of a poetics of Afro-American women's writing is the type of expansiveness and foregrounding just discussed, then surely another measure—indeed, one implicit in any project conditioned by phenomenology—is a palpable or felt "shift" of critical horizons. A theorist may always feel that his or her work has been successful in producing such a shift, but the essentialness of the shift can be confirmed only by the response of another. An example of the type of intersubjectivity that I have in mind occurs at the conclusion of Zora Neale Hurston's *Their Eyes Were Watching God*,[19] when Pheoby, the friend to whom Hurston's protagonist, Janie, tells her autobiographical story, responds:

> Lawd, . . . Ah done growed ten feet higher from just listen' tuh you, Janie. Ah ain't satisfied wid mahself no mo'. Ah means tuh make Sam [my husband] take me fishin' wid him after this. Nobody better not criticize you in mah hearin'. (284)

A sense of growth and change, a sense of dissatisfaction with the previously given are combined in Pheoby's words with a resolution to pursue a different course of action. Here, it seems to me, is one clearly figured success of poetics.

For, in a sense, what Janie has done—in a fictive and precursorial foreshadowing of Walker—is transform the quotidian rites of a black woman's passage through the world into a series of figures or images that are so resonant that they catapult Pheoby into new consciousness. Janie's revealed images become occasions for Pheoby to both read and write the world in new and liberating ways.

The type of intersubjective response that I have in mind is analyzed in Afro-Americanist terms by Michael Awkward in his fine work *Inspiriting Influences*.[20] Awkward views the process as akin to call-and-response—a necessarily communal communicative mode motivated by Afro-American double consciousness. As a split subject of slavery's "othering," the Afro-American strives for a participatory expressive return to wholeness or, in Awkward's term, "(comm)unity" (49–50). My suggestion is that the mode is coextensive with a general philosophical project and that project's projection of what might be called image work.

The life of Hurston's protagonist has its origins in the derogation and sexual exploitation of her grandmother and mother. The life itself is essentially a meditative one. It is recuperated in its potential, however, by an imagistic, autobiographical telling that receives attentive response. From two unfulfilling marriages and a tragically brief and fleetingly happy third one, Hurston's protagonist creates a poetics of Afro-American woman's everyday life.

What might be called Janie's "poetics" are of inestimable transformative value. To make Sam take her fishing is for Pheoby to alter expected relationships, transforming the black woman from worker (mule) of the world to a participant in male, ludic rituals that provide leisure and a space for spiritual growth. (We have but to recall how powerfully instructive for culture the one-day fishing expedition is in Hurston's

Mules and Men.) For Pheoby to forestall "criticism" of Janie is for her to exemplify a potential for the renewal of Afro-American tolerance and communality that is always immanent in black women's expressivity.

The correlations between universal and particular, critic and audience, that constitute measures of success for a poetics of Afro-American women's expressivity also suggest a third measure. Successful analyses, in their concentration on the essential spirit or immanent potential of Afro-American women's expressivity, move the criticism and theory of black women's writing beyond merely interested readings. Heretofore, the potentially liberating effects of Afro-American women's expressivity—like the poetic potential of Janie's autobiographical recall—have been hampered by the self-interested approaches of critical camps so busy, in Janie's phrase, "wid talk" that they have failed to provide the kind of comprehensive hearing offered by Pheoby.

As early as the appearance in the 1970s of Gayl Jones's *Corregidora*[21] and Toni Morrison's *The Bluest Eye*,[22] some blackmale [*sic*] critics insisted that Afro-American women's writing was but an Amazonian show of divisiveness, despair, and violence.[23] Such critics were particularly distressed by what they considered the exuberant black-male-bashing of black women writers. This earlier critical impulse to a self-interested concentration on aversive images in black women's writings persists in recent criticisms of Alice Walker's hugely successful *The Color Purple*.[24]

In response to such male criticism have come equally interested feminist responses suggesting that Afro-American women's writings are more amenable to feminist than to other kinds of critical readings.[25] The sound of this criticism is suggested by the guiding claim of one of Barbara Smith's notable essays: "Black women's existence, experience, and culture and the brutally complex systems of oppression which shape these are in the 'real world' of white and/or male consciousness beneath consideration, invisible, unknown" (157). Here, a phenomenological "unintelligibility" or inaccessibility to other than committed feminist critics is assumed as a ground for privileging radical feminist readings of black women's writings.

Finally, there are interested readings by both theorizing ideologues and rhetoricians (our new Sophists). The interested reading here is, perhaps, the most colonizing form of all. It shows no allegiance or obligation to the field of Afro-American particulars. Practitioners are often critics who feel that it is unnecessary for them to read an entire text before delivering sweeping critical judgments. They also feel no obligation to inform themselves, through even minimal study, of Afro-American culture or expressive consciousness before holding forth on novels, poems, essays, and short stories that are, at least in part, functions of such culture and consciousness.

But surely nothing could be more intensely "interested" than pointing to the limitations and excesses of critical orientations different from my own, and a poetics of Afro-American women's expressivity, as I advocate it, is indeed an interested enterprise. First, it proceeds from a theorist who began work under the aegis of the Black Aesthetic and whose nationalist orientation remains strong. Second, it derives from a male critic who has a decided interest in theory. These interests, obviously, condition my sense that there is a *sui generis* cultural spirit at work in quite specific ways in Afro-American women's expressivity and that this spirit can be elucidated through theoretical analysis.

But having acknowledged the interestedness of my own orientation (a subject position about which I shall have more to say later), I want still to claim that the success of a poetics of Afro-American women's expressivity should be measured by the extent to which the project avoids limitations of an exclusive self-interestedness and offers broadly comprehensive analyses of the guiding spirituality to be discovered in the imagistic fields of black women's creativity. And by "interestedness" I intend a preeminently defensive and ideological cast of mind that refuses to question the relativity of its judgments or to figure itself as figuring in an "open" field of inquiry. "Interestedness" marks, therefore, a negative limitation of the "self" rather than the type of inversive, challenging, autobiographical expansiveness that operates the most powerful theoretical analyses.

The spirit work that is imagistically projected by Afro-American women's expressivity is, I think, like what is called by the religion of voodoo *The Work*. In women's narratives such as Morrison's *Sula*, Zora Neale Hurston's *Mules and Men*,[26] and Ntozake Shange's *Sassafrass, Cypress and Indigo*,[27] spirit work is frequently imaged by the space, place, and time of the Conjure Woman. One might say, in fact, that a poetics of Afro-American women's writing is, in many ways, a phenomenology of conjure. In any case, the field most decisively analyzed by such a poetics is decidedly not one where pathological or aversive images dominate. Rather, what are revealed are felicitous images of the workings of a spirit that is so wonderfully captured by "In Search of Our Mothers' Gardens." Describing the task of her generation of Afro-American writers, Alice Walker asserts:

> We must fearlessly pull out of ourselves and look at and identify with our lives the living creativity some of our great-grandmothers were not allowed to know. I stress *some* of them because it is well known that the majority of our great-grandmothers knew, even without "knowing" it, the reality of their spirituality, even if they didn't recognize it beyond what happened in the singing at church—and they never had any intention of giving it up. (237–38)

Walkers's is a felicitous, as opposed to an "aversive," image not because it is visual or complimentary. "Felicitous" signals "well chosen, apt, appropriate," and I would add, comprehensive. What such an image entails is less a visual survey than a comprehensive hearing as in the case of Pheoby and Janie. "Comprehensive" signals a necessary attention to discordant or problematic cultural notes. After all, Walker's own epoche and reduction leading to her mother's garden begins not with a joyful noise but with a brutalizing and enforced silence. "Felicitous," then, signals an objectively valid act of consciousness that is sanctioned by all possible subjects' acquiescence in the givenness of the image. "Aversive," by contrast, suggests, perhaps, an exploitatively melodramatic or sensationalistic image in the service of a profitable ideology of shock. I believe Afro-American women creators have traditionally sought felicitous and multisensory images. Mae Henderson has also suggested to me in conversation that such images are "multimetaleveled," since they encode not simply explicitly racial but also complex gender negotiations of space, place, and time. Henderson believes that the specific "character" of the imagistic experience is dependent upon both the image as given and consciousness as giver and receiver. "Knowing" an image as felicitous or aversive, therefore, is a matter of a field, as it were, of consciousness that has always to be reconstructed, learned anew, renewed in manifold (as opposed to binary) ways.

My emphasis on "image," as I hope the extensiveness of my foregoing discussion suggests, is not intended as an appropriation of black women's expressivity through a colonizing gaze. Rather, a theory of the felicitous image suggests a comprehensive, conscious audition of the soundings of black women's expressivity in its intended fullness. One might say mine is an attempted listening to such expressivity in its very well-chosenness.

Hurston's "conjure" is one of the most well-chosen images of space that I know, and it unfolds its field of signification with persuasive energy in *Mules and Men*. The order of presentation of the poetics I wish to propose begins with space because Hurston has figured this field—in a striking return to southern territories of mothers and grandmothers—with poetic grandeur. The order also begins with space because Bachelard's siting of this category provides an account whose general specifications are both enhancing for and enhanced by Hurston's soundings and significations.

NOTES

1. For a discussion of the expressive cultural, or ritual, responses of Africans to the trade, see Sterling Stuckey's *Slave Culture* (New York: Oxford, 1987). See also: Lawrence W. Levine, *Black Culture and Black Consciousness* (New York: Oxford, 1977).

2. For a discussion of Afro-American autobiography, see: Houston Baker's "Autobiographical Acts and the Voice of the Southern Slave," in *The Journey Back* (Chicago: University of Chicago Press, 1980). See also, William Andrew's *To Tell a Free Story* (Urbana: University of Illinois Press, 1986).

3. *The Poems of Phillis Wheatley*, ed. Julian Mason (Chapel Hill: University of North Carolina Press, 1986). All citations refer to this edition.

4. *Narrative of the Life of Frederick Douglass*, ed. Houston A. Baker, Jr. (New York: Penguin, 1982), 58. All citations refer to this edition.

5. See *New Literary History*, XVIII (1986–87): 326–344; 371–384, for Joyce Joyce; see also R. Baxter Miller, ed., *Afro-American Literature and Humanism* (Lexington: University of Kentucky Press, 1978).

6. "The Blackness of Blackness: A Critique of the Sign and the Signifying Monkey," in *Black Literature and Literary Theory*, Henry Louis Gates, Jr., ed. (New York: Methuen, 1984), 285–321.

7. *Beautiful Theories* (Baltimore: Johns Hopkins University Press, 1979).

8. "Tradition and the Individual Talent," in *Selected Essays* (New York: Harcourt, 1950), 10.

9. Chicago: University of Chicago Press, 1978.

10. *The Poetics of Space*, Maria Jolas, trans. (Boston: Beacon, 1969), xix. All citations are to this edition and are hereafter marked by page numbers in parentheses.

11. Alice Walker, "In Search of Our Mothers' Gardens," *Ms.* (May 1974), and in *In Search of Our Mothers' Gardens: Womanist Prose* (San Diego: Harcourt, Brace, Jovanovich, 1983).

12. Edmund Husserl, *Phenomenology and the Crisis of Philosophy*, Quentin Lauer, trans. (New York: Harper, 1965). Lauer's extensive introduction was very helpful for my project. Hereafter, all Husserl citations refer to this edition of his work, which contains two seminal essays: "Philosophy as Rigorous Science" and "Philosophy and the Crisis of European Man."

13. "Philosophy as Rigorous Science" (see note 12), 89.

14. Martin Heidegger, *The Basic Problems of Phenomenology* (Bloomington: Indiana University Press, 1982). All citations refer to this work and are hereafter marked by page numbers in parentheses.

15. David B. Allison, trans. (Evanston: Northwestern University Press, 1973). All citations refer to this edition and are hereafter marked by page numbers in parentheses.

16. Ibid., 86.

17. In Husserl, *Phenomenology and the Crisis of Philosophy* (see note 12), 40–41.

18. Toni Morrison, *Sula* (New York: Knopf, 1974).

19. Zora Neale Hurston, *Their Eyes Were Watching God* (Urbana: University of Illinois Press, 1978).

20. Michael Awkward, *Inspiriting Influences* (New York: Columbia University Press, 1989).

21. Gayl Jones, *Corregidora* (New York: Random House, 1975).

22. Toni Morrison, *The Bluest Eye* (New York: Washington Square Press, 1972).

23. The school of critics known as "The Black Aesthetics" was preeminent in such charges.

24. Alice Walker, *The Color Purple: A Novel* (New York: Harcourt, Brace, Jovanovich, 1982).

25. See Barbara Smith, "Toward a Black Feminist Criticism," in *All The Women Are White, All the Blacks Are Men, but Some of Us Are Brave: Black Women's Studies*, Gloria T. Hull, Patricia Bell Scott, and Barbara Smith, eds. (Old Westbury, N.Y.: Feminist Press, 1982), 157–75.

26. Zora Neale Hurston, *Mules and Men* (Bloomington: Indiana University Press, 1978).

27. Ntozake Shange, *Sassafras, Cypress, and Indigo* (New York: St. Martin's Press, 1982).

37 Phallus(ies) of Interpretation
Toward Engendering the Black Critical "I"

Ann duCille

(1993)

" 'Love, Oh, love, Oh careless love.' That's the story. It's in the songs. It's in the books. And everybody knows it . . . The only problem is that the story almost everybody knows is almost totally false."[1]

Writing in *Ebony* in August of 1981, black historian Lerone Bennett, Jr., accused contemporary black writers of creating "a new literature based on the premise that Black America is a vast emotionless wasteland of hustlin' men and maimed women." As Bennett heard and read them, lines and lyrics about ceaseless sex and heedless love, like those immortalized by Bessie Smith in "Careless Love" and by Robert Hayden in "Homage to the Empress of the Blues," his tribute to Bessie, have helped construct a false history of tortuous gender relations among African Americans.[2] Such lyrics, like a great deal of modern black literature, in Bennett's view, tell a story of a "Black love deficit" almost entirely false. "As a matter of hard historical fact," he wrote, "the true story of Black love—love colored by, love *blackened* by the Black experience—is the exact opposite of the traditional myth." The "true story," as Bennett told it, is that "Black men and women—despite slavery, despite segregation, despite everything—created a modern love song in life and art that is the loveliest thing dreamed or sung this side of the seas" (32).

Bennett's "true story"—what black feminist critic Deborah McDowell might call his black family romance[3]—is seductive. It affirms what many of us (us being here African American men and women) would like to believe about our past and the possibilities for our future *together*. But, as Bennett argued in his essay, the story of an all-enduring black love is a plot many modern-day African American writers have rejected in favor of what he is hardly alone in labelling literary gender bating and male bashing.

Bennett named no one in particular in his generic indictment of artists who have gotten the story wrong, but throughout the past two decades, scores of other black male scholars and critics have pointed accusing fingers at such black women writers as Alice Walker, Toni Morrison, Gayl Jones, Ntozake Shange, and, most recently, Terry McMillan. These writers are chief among the many black women artists charged not only with historical inaccuracy but with racial infidelity as well—with in effect putting their gender before their race, their (white) feminism before their black family—and inventing historical fictions that serve a feminist rather than a black nationalist agenda.

Indeed, for black women, membership (real or assumed)[4] in the sisterhood of feminists is in some circles an unpardonable sin punishable by excommunication, if not from the race, certainly from the ranks of those who have authored the sacred texts of the race's canon. As one pair of critics put it: black feminists have drawn "a simplistic sex line in society" that has put them "on the wrong side of some fundamental questions"[5]—questions which presumably have more to do with race than with gender. One can be black or a woman, but claiming both identities places one on shaky familial ground, outside the black family romance.

In the minds or, more important, in the critiques of influential black men of letters such as critic Addison Gayle and poet/novelist Ishmael Reed, contemporary black women authors have not only miswritten the romance, they have slandered black men in the process of inventing their own feminist fictions. As McDowell notes in her incisive reading of this dubious battle of the sexes, while "female readers see an implicit affirmation of black women," many male readers see "a programmatic assault on black men" (75–76). What is for female writers like Alice Walker a commitment "to exploring the oppressions, the insanities, the loyalties, and the triumphs of black women," is for male readers like Gayle and Reed "a hatchet job" directed viciously against black men or a libel campaign akin to "the kind of propaganda spread by the Ku Klux Klan and the American Nazi party."[6] What for black women is an effort to write themselves into history is for Gayle and Reed a malicious form of myth-making that holds black men, black love, and black history hostage to a portrait of the past too painful to be anything but a lie. Addison Gayle has spoken in a particularly telling way to this nagging question of historical truth: "If we look at [Alice Walker's] work in history," he said in an interview with Roseann P. Bell, "particularly if there is any great deal of accuracy in her portrayal of Black men, then we're in more trouble than I thought we were, *and I thought we were okay*" (214).

In calling up these critiques, charges, and counter charges, I do not want merely to resurrect ancient arguments that pit black men and women against each other or simply to retrace ground already ably covered by scholars such as Deborah McDowell and Calvin Hernton,[7] who has also analyzed this text-based battle of the sexes. Nor in placing in opposition black women writers and black male critics do I mean to imply that male readers have been singularly disdainful of the "feminist fictions" of contemporary black women writers or that only male readers have offered such criticism.[8] Rather, what I hope to do in this essay is to explore from a slightly different angle some of the problematic, gender-loaded assumptions and racial imperatives that underpin many male-authored critiques of black women's fiction: (1) that there is an essential black experience; (2) that there is an absolute historical truth; (3) that art absolutely must tell the truth; (4) that black men and women in American are "okay" in their erotic relations with one another. I want to examine the different conceptions of I and You—Self and Other—that are at stake in a race-conscious, gender-bound criticism in which "black is beautiful" is the only "truth"—the sole story (or maybe soul story)—we are allowed to tell.

Because art is invention, "truth" is generally held to be a false standard by which to evaluate a writer's work. This should be the case whether the issue is Alice Walker's representation of black men or Spike Lee's treatment of black women. Yet, as I argue in this essay, this is precisely the leap of faith that critics of African American literature continue to make. Texts are transparent documents that must tell the truth as I know it. Failure to tell my truth not only invalidates the text, it also discredits, de-authorizes, and on occasion deracializes the writer. Truth, however, like beauty, is in the eye and perhaps the experience of the beholder.

The beholder metaphor suggests a problematic of the gaze—of power and perspective—worth pursuing. It invites us to question the authority of the critical *I* to constitute the *Other* it beholds, even in the midst of reading the *Other's* celebration of its own subjectivity. As black men and women, our racial alterity makes us always-already other—always-already beheld—but what happens when blacks read each other, when the beheld becomes the beholder, when black men read black women reading black men? How does a black male reader constitute himself as the center of seeing in a female-authored text? Must the beheld always be constituted in terms of her difference from the beholder? Is it possible for the male *I* to read the female text it others without reinscribing hierarchies of one kind or another, without in effect de-authorizing and even deracializing the female beheld?

While I generally shy away from efforts to define distinctly male and female ways of knowing, in this essay I want to take the risk of gender essentialism and codify this great divide as a battle between colliding and colluding subjectivities, between male and female stories, between phallocentric and gynocentric "truths." The collisions of gender I address in this essay are all the more difficult to tease out, it seems to me, because of the collusions of race—the shared racial alterity—that historically have made it hard to be at once black and woman.

While I readily acknowledge that my own readings of history and literature are colored by my indivisible blackwomanness, this essay is not intended as a black feminist manifesto or as an attack on male critics, on masculinism, on phallocentrism, or on what Elaine Showalter calls "phallic criticism": masculinist criticism which focuses on the phallus as principal signifier and on man as principal referent. I come in effect to praise Caesar, not to bury him—to legitimize phallic criticism, not to condemn it. Phallocentrism and masculinism have become for the most part loaded terms—pejoratives—whose invocation often makes men jumpy in the same way accusations of racism tend to make white people defensive. My own use of the terms, however, is practical rather than pejorative or metaphoric. It is based on my belief that as scholars, as critics, as intellectuals, we need to be up front about the roles that sex and gender, as well as race and culture, play in shaping our interpretive strategies. As I argue throughout this essay, we need to engender the critical I "who

reads here"—to use Houston Baker's phrase—and call masculinist, as well as feminist, criticism by its rightful name.

As I also argue, an important step in this naming ceremony is surrendering the
myth that our shared racial alterity—our common American experience of slavery,
institutionalized racism, and discrimination—makes black men and women "brothers under the skin," who are at heart "okay" with each other. "The enemy is not
Black men," Addison Gayle has said. "The enemy is not Black men, not Black
women, it's this country" (Bell 214). While I can hardly quarrel with the point that
both black men and black women have been victims of American racism, the "we're
okay" rendition of African American history carries with it a decidedly masculine
bias that factors out the sexism which has indeed made some black men the enemy.

If we didn't know it or refused to see it before, we have only to look as far as
Anita Hill and Clarence Thomas to see that black men and women in America are
no more "okay" than the patriarchal system that has reared us. Our dis-ease is
embedded in what Michele Wallace describes as our almost deliberate ignorance
about the sexual politics, power relations, and social pathology that have both
defined and been defined by our experience in this country.[9] While there may be an
advantage for black men in whitewashing "black love" into the "loveliest thing
dreamed or sung this side of the seas," many contemporary black female writers
realize that for women the costs of sustaining such myths are continued harassment,
brutalization, insanity, suicide, or even death.

Long before the Thomas/Hill hearings declared to the world the degree to which
black men and women in America are not okay, black women had ceased to sing the
lovely little love song that Bennett and Gayle would have us all claim as *the* true
story of black America. In singing a different tune, writers such as Walker, Morrison,
and Jones have committed what phallic criticism necessarily reads as racial heresy.
They have broken with what I call the "discourse of deference"—a nationalistic,
masculinist ideology of uplift, which has historically demanded female deference in
the cause of empowering the race by elevating its men.

As McDowell and others have demonstrated, this is precisely the charge Mel
Watkins levels against Jones, Shange, and Walker in his infamous review in the *New
York Times*. "[T]hose black women writers who have chosen black men as the target
have set themselves outside of a tradition as old as black American literature itself,"
he asserts. "They have, in effect, put themselves at odds with what seems to be an
unspoken but almost universally accepted covenant among black writers."[10]

Watkins suggests, in other words, that in naming as oppressors black men as well
as white, black women novelists are acting outside black history, writing outside the
racial fold, the colored community. But Watkins's community is first and foremost
the world of men. Since he acknowledges in the same article that until recently the
most acclaimed black fiction writers were men, the ancient tradition to which he
refers is not, it seems to me, a "universally accepted covenant," but an understanding
among men—a kind of gentlemen's agreement, as it were, that suborns female silence
in the name of racial empowerment.

In a perhaps more theoretically sophisticated, though ultimately no less male-identified, reading, W. Lawrence Hogue attributes this break with history and tradition to the influence of what he calls "the feminist discourse" of the sixties on the work of black women writers like Alice Walker. Rooting his analysis in Foucault's concept of discursive formation, Hogue argues that Walker's first novel *The Third Life of Grange Copeland* (1970)—along with other feminist texts such as Jones's *Corregidora* (1975) and *Eva's Man* (1976) and Morrison's *The Bluest Eye* (1970) and *Sula* (1973)—necessarily invents its own African American historical myths in order to validate its feminist assumptions about women's reality and existence. While he praises the novel for its attempt to show how the powers and pressures of white patriarchy cause black men "bruised and beaten by the system" to batter and abuse their wives and children, he also argues that the novel manipulates certain historical "facts" to meet its feminist ideologeme.[11] For while *The Third Life* indeed indicts the system, it also holds black men culpable for their own allegiance to and reinscription of the patriarchal values that reduce black women to mules of the world. While the Copeland men blame the white man for their own behavior ("white folks just don't let nobody *feel* like doing right"), the text blames as well black men's complicity in replicating an overarching system of domination.

Hogue, I think, makes the right theoretical move in acknowledging feminist fiction as invention. Unfortunately, however, this theoretical move is not fully realized in practice, for he ultimately treats the discursive strategies and emplotments he attributes to Walker, Jones, Morrison, et al., as if they are unique to feminist fiction rather than properties of textual production more generally. Novels like *The Third Life*, he argues, are completely silent about the thousands of black men who refused to be dehumanized by a dehumanizing system—men who "maintained their humanity, their integrity, and their sanity by turning honestly and genuinely to the church and Christianity"—men who "openly and vehemently defied the system, even at the expense of their own lives" (104–05).

As examples of such heroic black men, Hogue offers Ernest Gaines's characters Ned Douglass and Jimmy Aaron from *The Autobiography of Miss Jane Pittman* (1971) and Marcus Payne from *Of Love and Dust* (1967). Like Aaron and Douglass, Marcus Payne, Hogue writes, "refuses to accept the constrictions of the system. He strikes out against it and meets his death" (105). It seems from these and other similar examples that Hogue actually wants black women novelists to write Ernest Gaines's stories rather than their own. Like Bennett and Gayle, he seems ultimately to believe in a set of true historical "facts" that male writers such as Ernest Gaines have presented with greater fidelity to the African American experience than black women novelists.

Moreover, in the discursive formation of his own argument, Hogue transforms important textual "facts" and omits significant, telling details. He does not mention, for example, that Marcus Payne strikes out against the system in somewhat the same fashion as Alice Walker's character Brownfield Copeland—with his penis—by sleeping with the white boss's white wife. Seemingly following the advice of Eldridge

Cleaver, Ernest Gaines has created in Marcus Payne a character who fucks the white man by fucking his wife, a character who in effect uses his own tool to dismantle the master's house and is destroyed in the process.

Though far less caustic than the condemnations of Watkins, Gayle, and Reed, Hogue's analysis has inscribed in it precisely the gender blind spots and biases I want to illuminate in this essay. His reading of *The Third Life* and other feminist texts is dependent on his reading of such male-authored and authorized novels as *The Autobiography of Miss Jane Pittman* and *Of Love and Dust*. Here as elsewhere, the work of contemporary black women writers is evaluated in terms of its difference from the work of men—from the true history, from the normative master narrative. Curiously enough, however, this would-be normative narrative is based on an understanding of the past so inherently masculine—so subliminally rooted in the phallus—that sleeping with the white overseer's wife is read completely unself-consciously as a revolutionary act. Put another way, in this decidedly male-centered reading of African American literature and history, penile erection is equated with political insurrection.

The difference between Hogue's sense of history and heroism and Walker's is a critical difference—a critical difference that may cut to the core of the controversy over male and female texts, maculinist and feminist readings. It may be that at the heart of this controversy lie not only different notions of truth, art, and history, but very different readings of the phallus and the penis. What Houston Baker reads as the cosmic force of the black phallus in *Invisible Man*, for example, Toni Morrison exposes as the black penis that rapes and impregnates a twelve-year-old girl in *The Bluest Eye*. What for Ellison is symbolic action, is for Morrison a father's rape of his daughter. What for Baker is an aristocratic procreativity turned inward is in Morrison's novel "a bolt of desire [that] ran down [Cholly Breelove's] genitals, giving it length." What Baker calls "outgoing phallic energy," Morrison names inbreeding lust, a lust bordered by politeness that makes a father want to fuck his daughter— tenderly. "But the tenderness would not hold," Morrison writes in parodic undertones, which at least one male critic has mistaken for sympathy.[12] "The tightness of her vagina was more than he could bear. His soul seemed to slip down to his guts and fly out into her, and the gigantic thrust he made into her then provoked the only sound she made—a hollow suck of air in the back of her throat."[13]

It is interesting to note—and perhaps telling for my argument—that Baker repeatedly uses the term phallus—as Lacanian signifier, as originator of meaning—when he is talking about the action of the penis, a word that never appears in his extended reading of the Trueblood Incident. As he himself has argued elsewhere: "The PHALLUS is, of course, to be distinguished from the penis. The PHALLUS is not a material object but a signifier of the Father, or, better, of the Father's LAW."[14] Morrison's portrait of incest complicates what it seems to me both Ellison and Baker have oversimplified. It reminds us that signifier and signified are not so easily separable. For while the phallus may not be a material object, its action, its "phallic energy," its "Father LAW" are not immaterial—certainly not to Matty Lou Trueblood, Pecola Breedlove, and other objects of its power.

Baker's reading, like Ellison's narrative, erases the penis that rapes and impregnates the daughter as it privileges the phallus that fathers and rules what Baker describes as "the entire clan or tribe, of Afro-America." Baker's interpretation is, in perhaps the most literal sense possible, phallic criticism. But again, my motive in labelling it such is not to denigrate it but to denature it, to localize it, to wrest it of the illusion of universality and objectivity and to acknowledge that it, like feminist criticism, is situational, vested with a variety of imperatives.

The effort to denature phallic criticism or masculinist criticism must make an important second move, however—one that resists polarizing the interpretive process along easily drawn gender lines. For I do not mean to imply that only men do such readings or that such readings are the only kind male critics do. I would be remiss if I did not point out, for example, that one of the sharpest critiques of the gender biases of both Ellison's novel and Baker's reading has come from black male scholar Michael Awkward. Calling *The Bluest Eye* a "purposefully feminist revision" of Ellison's masculinist reading of incest, Awkward writes: "Baker's essay mirrors the strategies by which Trueblood (and Trueblood's creator) validates male perceptions of incest while, at the same time, silencing the female voice or relegating it to the evaluative periphery."[15]

In prose, in poetry, in song, modern black women artists speak, write, and sing through such silences. Complementing and by all means challenging male perspectives with their own, they offer up different and often difficult tunes—somebody-done-somebody-wrong songs that not only indict as oppressors black men as well as white, but that also identify love of men as the root of women's oppression.

Zora Neale Hurston's character Nanny makes such an identification in *Their Eyes Were Watching God* (1937). "'Dat's de very prong all us black women gits hung on,'" she tells her granddaughter Janie. "'Dis love! Dat's just whut's got us uh pullin' and uh haulin' and sweatin' and doin' from can't see in de mornin' till can't see at night.'"[16] In placing these words in her character's mouth—in identifying "dis love" as a potentially devastating force in the lives of black women—Hurston gave voice to a concern that reverberates throughout modern African American women's fiction. From Jessie Fauset and Nella Larsen writing in the 1920s to Alice Walker and Toni Morrison writing in the 1990s, black women novelists have been consistently concerned with exploring on paper what Hortense Spillers calls "the politics of intimacy"[17] and with confronting the consequences, burdens, and mixed blessings of love, men, and marriage in the lives of African American women.

But Hurston is also signifying, I think. For the prong on which women are impaled is not just simply "dis love" but "dat penis"—the domain of dominating power. At least one of my male colleagues has accused me of over-reading in making this claim. "'Dis love,'" he insists, "is just love." I remain convinced, however, that this sexual double entendre, like so many others in *Their Eyes*, is Hurston's invention, not mine. Part of what catches women up, Hurston seems to me to say, is not just their penchant for confusing and conflating sex and love, love and marriage, dream and truth, but their tendency to measure manliness by the same yardstick as men, to believe like men in the power vested in the penis.

Janie's implicit understanding of penile power is made explicit when she calls Joe out, as it were—when she finally responds in kind (and then some) to his harassment. After years of verbal and physical abuse, Janie delivers an ultimately fatal blow to her big-voiced husband's power source by telling him publicly that all he is is a big voice. To Joe's taunt that she "ain't no young gal no mo'" she replies:

> Naw, Ah ain't no young gal no mo' but den Ah ain't no old woman neither. Ah reckon Ah looks mah age too. But Ah'm uh woman every inch of me, and Ah know it. Dat's uh whole lot more'n *you* kin say. You big-bellies around here and puts out a lot of brag, but 'tain't nothin' to it but your big voice . . . When you pull down yo' britches, you look lak de change uh life. (122–23)

So saying, Janie announces to his male subjects that the mighty Mayor Joe Starks is sexually inadequate, that he can't get it up, that he's not enough man for "every inch" of woman she still is. It is significant, of course, that Janie reckons her sexuality by the male measurement of inches and signifies to all present that Joe's shriveled penis doesn't stand up. Hers is a series of well-placed punches that land below the belt, that not only rob Joe of "his illusion of irresistible maleness," but that meta-phorically *feminize* him by linking his impotence to female menopause—"de change uh life." In the wake of Janie's words, Joe's "vanity bled like a flood." It is a bloodletting—a symbolic castration—that ultimately ends in the mayor's death.

Like Janie, Mem Copeland, Brownfield's brutalized wife in *The Third Life*, even-tually effects a shift in the balance of power within her marriage by attacking her husband below the belt with a shotgun strategically aimed at his genitals. Thrusting the "cool hard gun barrel down between his thighs," Mem for a moment acts outside the submissive role she has accepted for nine years. " 'To think,' " she tells Brownfield at gunpoint, " 'I put myself to the trouble of wanting to git married to you . . . And just think how many times I done got my head beat by you just so you could feel a little bit like a man.' "[18] Wielding the shotgun (described as smooth and black and big) like a penis and threatening to shoot her husband's balls off if he doesn't abide by her rules, Mem negotiates a better life for herself and her family. She moves them out of their rat-infested country shack into a city house, "a 'mansion' of four sheet-rocked rooms" (102). The jobs she finds for herself and for Brownfield bring a sense of progress and new-found, if short-lived, prosperity to the Copeland household.

"If he had done any of it himself," the text tells us, "if he had insisted on the move, he might not have resisted the comfort" Mem's ingenuity brings the family (103). But instead Brownfield's bruised manhood flares tragically, and he plots to destroy his wife by using her own female body against her, twice impregnating her in a deliber-ate, calculated attempt to undermine her already fragile health. Mem's shotgun was a great equalizer, but ultimately Brownfield's penis proves the more powerful weapon. " '[Y]ou thought I fucked you 'cause I wanted it,' " he says to Mem in bitter triumph. " 'Your trouble is you just never learned how not to git pregnant' " (107). Some radical feminist readers might argue that in surrendering to heterosexual desire—in sleeping with her husband—Mem, in effect, collaborates with her own assassin. For, not content with nearly impregnating her to death, Brownfield eventually shoots and kills Mem with a shotgun. Patriarchy in this text is indeed black as well as white, and its penile oppression is lethal.

Toni Morrison gives a similarly oppressive, though less physically violent, face to patriarchy in *Song of Solomon*. And, like Hurston and Walker, she locates the source of man's abusive power between his legs. " 'You have never picked up anything heavier than your own feet or solved a problem harder than fourth-grade arithmetic,' " her character Lena says to her brother Milkman. " 'Where do you get the *right* to decide our lives? I'll tell you where,' " she continues. " 'From that hog's gut that hangs down between your legs.' "[19] As a parting shot at her brother and the value system and gender codes that have made his male life of greater value than her female one, Lena says: " 'You are a sad, pitiful, stupid, selfish, hateful man. I hope your little hog's gut stands you in good stead, and that you take good care of it, because you don't have anything else.' " Her message to Milkman resembles Janie's message to Joe. While this verbal assault on male genitalia does not kill or castrate, it does send Milkman Dead on a search that eventually brings him into a different quality of manhood.

Like Hurston and Walker, Morrison places the penis under scrutiny, at once acknowledging and problematizing its power. If dominative male power, as these writers suggest, is indeed located below the belt, disempowering men means not simply placing the penis under scrutiny, but under erasure. This is precisely the action the title character takes in Gayl Jones's highly controversial second novel *Eva's Man*.

After a month as "the willing prisoner of Davis Carter's love"[20]—to use one critic's characterization—Eva Medina Canada first poisons the man who has held her "captive" and then mutilates his dead body by severing his penis with her teeth:

> I opened his trousers and played with his penis. My mouth, my teeth, my tongue went inside his trousers. I raised blood . . . I got back on the bed and squeezed his dick in my teeth. I bit down hard . . .
>
> I got the silk handkerchief he used to wipe me after we made love, and wrapped his penis in it. I laid it back inside his trousers, zipped him up.[21]

Davis becomes for Eva and *Everyman*, and as such he is made to atone for the sins of a myriad of men (and an eight-year-old boy with a dirty popsicle stick) who have sexually abused her throughout her life. Here, too, however, it is not simply men who are under attack but the penis.

Coming on the heels of *Corregidora* the year before, the publication of *Eva's Man* in 1976 set off a hue and cry of foul among many black male critics, for whom Davis Carter's mutilated member is evidently more than just phallus, more than simply signifier. While the specter of a bloody, gnawed, dismembered member is surely horrifying for all audiences, it is, I suspect, particularly so for male readers whose connection to the severed organ is more than metaphorical. Yet there is more at issue in the negative critical reception of *Eva's Man* than mere castration anxiety, just as there is more at stake in the controversy over the feminist text than just negative portrayals of black men. Black men do not necessarily fare so well in such sacred, male-authored texts as *Native Son, Go Tell It on the Mountain,* and *Invisible Man.* Yet these novels continue to be championed by some of the same critics who have condemned *Eva's Man.* Moreover, the castration of the protagonist in *Invisible Man* is acknowledged and accepted as symbolic in a way that Davis Turner's castration is not, even though for all its graphic language it, too, I would argue, is metaphoric. What is actually at stake, it seems to me, are all the larger questions: Who holds the power? Who owns the black body? Who can tell the black story? Who can write the true black history? Who gets to say "I'm okay"? Who gets to sing the true blues? All of these larger questions are played out *masterfully* in Jones's first novel *Corregidora.*

Corregidora is literally and figuratively a blues novel; or, more specifically, in its treatment of erotic coupling and the marital relation, *Corregidora* is what I call "dearly beloved blues"—my name for a particular variety of prose, poetry, and song that focuses (often as a lament) on the problems of married life.[22] On the literal level, the text tells the story of blues singer Ursula "Ursa" Corregidora, the last in a long line of black women haunted and emotionally burdened by history—by a legacy of rape, incest, and patriarchal psychosexual abuse, passed down through four generations like a sacred family heirloom. The novel recounts the passions and pains of Ursa's brief marriage in 1947 to Mutt Thomas—their breakup after just four months of trying to work through and around Mutt's inability to accept Ursa's need to sing the blues—and the couple's eventual reunion twenty-two years later. In a figurative sense, the blues are the extended metaphor around which Jones works the magic of her text—the medium she uses to enable Ursa to tell her story.

Ursa is the great granddaughter of an unspeakably evil Portuguese slavemaster named Corregidora who prostituted and impregnated the women he owned, including his own daughter, Ursa's grandmother. Despite the unspeakable nature of Corregidora's crimes and the destruction of all record of those crimes, precisely the task with which Ursa, like her mother, grandmother, and great grandmother before her, has been entrusted is to speak Corregidora's evil: to "make generations" that bear witness to his cruelty and his abuses.

After a drunken Mutt causes Ursa to fall down a flight of stairs, she loses the child she is carrying and is forced to have a hysterectomy, leaving her physically unable to make generations. Her inability to live up to the charge of her mother and grandmothers is only part of her problem, however—only part of the difficulty Ursa has in loving Mutt or Tadpole (the cafe owner she marries briefly) or Cat or Jeffy (women friends who represent the perhaps intriguing but frightening possibility of lesbian love). Corregidora's larger problem lies in the contradiction and dishonesty inherent in Great Gram's charge to her to "make generations." Making generations, as Janice Harris has pointed out, means making love; but making love for the purpose of making human evidence turns what should be an act of love into an act of historical vengeance. As Harris says of this crippling contradiction: "The goal of lovemaking subverts the act; the end denies the means."[23]

What Ursula must ultimately face is not only the crippling contradiction inherent in Great Gram's charge, but the emotional ambivalence that underpins it: a tangle of mixed emotions and conflicting subjectivities that were no doubt present in a great many sexual liaisons between master and slave, owner and property. The question Ursa must confront in her own life is the question only her father Martin has had the courage to ask of her grandmothers: "How much was hate for Corregidora and how much was love?"

When at the end of the novel, a forty-seven-year-old Ursula is reunited with Mutt Thomas after a separation of twenty-two years, she asks herself the same question. " 'You never would suck it,' " Mutt says to Ursa, as she takes his penis in her mouth. " 'You never would suck it when I wanted you to. Oh, baby . . . I didn't think you would do this for me' " (184). At a moment in which she holds Mutt delicately suspended between pleasure and pain, Ursa understands what it was her great grandmother did to the man who owned her that made him hate her one minute and unable to get her out of his mind the next. "It had to be sexual . . . it had to be something sexual that Great Gram did to Corregidora." In this moment of understanding—in "a split second of hate and love"—Ursa realizes as well that she could kill Mutt: " 'I could kill you,' " she says (though it is unclear whether this is thought or spoken, for in the next line we are told " 'He came and I swallowed.' "). Love and hate for him, like Great Gram's love and hate for Corregidora, are so intimately intertwined that even or, perhaps, especially at the moment of giving intense sexual pleasure, she could kill him.

Unlike the psychosexually tormented heroine of *Eva's Man*, Ursa does not kill Mutt; she does not bite off his penis, as Eva does, or break the skin, as she imagines her great grandmother did. Instead, she swallows Mutt's semen in a sexual act that will not make generations, an act which can be read metaphorically as swallowing the past—not forgetting it, as Mutt would wish, but taking it inside as an act of reconciliation rather than carrying it outside as a weapon of revenge. The act of fellatio, then, particularly the swallowing, suggests a loosening of the bonds of history that have kept Ursa yoked to Corregidora; it signals Ursa's acceptance of the past, as Jones herself has said, as "an aspect of her own character, identity and present history."[24]

Melvin Dixon[25] suggests, however, that the climax of the novel is, in fact, an act of vengeance. "Ursa avenges herself on Mutt," he argues, "by performing fellatio on him—an act that places her in control of herself and Mutt." The mouth of the blues singer becomes, in Dixon's words, "an instrument of direct sexual power."[26] This is a possible and certainly popular reading, one a number of critics have endorsed, one the text surely invites. In such a reading, performing fellatio is said to empower the female because of her potential to disempower—to dismember—her male partner with a bite. I wonder if this empowerment isn't illusory, however, if the penis isn't, in this instance, indeed dematerialized as phallus. Just how long would a live specimen lie passive—recline (or sit) powerless—while his penis was being bitten off?

Jones elides this question in *Corregidora* by making the assault a fantasy, a theory, and in *Eva's Man* by having Eva poison Davis before she dismembers him. Critics, for the most part, have elided the question altogether. One exception is Richard Barksdale, who is so intent on making his case for female mandibular empowerment (Mother JAW as a counterpoint to Father LAW) that he goes so far as to rewrite

454 / Ann duCille

Jones's novel so that "during an act of fellatio [Eva] mutilates her lover *and leaves him to bleed to death*" (402, my emphasis).

In any case, if *Corregidora*'s poetic closure can be read as an act of revenge and empowerment, perhaps it can also be read as suggesting female submission and surrender. Ursa's mouth doesn't become a powerful instrument through the act of fellatio; it has always been a powerful instrument. In singing the blues—singing her mama's songs and her own—she has used her mouth as her mother and grandmothers used their wombs. She has, in effect, made generations in song; her survival has depended on her voice; she has sung "because it was something [she] had to do" (3). With her "hard voice," powerful, potent, penetrating like a penis, a voice so hard it "hurts you and makes you still want to listen," Ursa has both participated in and perpetuated an oral tradition. Her final act of oral *sexual* reconciliation may also be an act of self-silencing—an act in which Ursa's hard voice is not simply softened but quite literally silenced by Mutt's penis. I wonder: will Ursa still sing the blues in the morning and, if so, whose blues will they be?

I wonder also about the ideology of empowerment at work here. It troubles me that so many of our critical discussions about *Corregidora* define reconciliation and what Dixon calls "successful coupling" in terms of empowerment—who has power over whom sexually. Moreover, the role which so many critics (especially male critics) see as empowering the female—the privilege of "performing fellatio on" the man who for most of the novel has been more patriarch than partner—seems to me to confirm Ursa in precisely the role Mutt has wanted for her all along: as "his woman," as the instrument of his pleasure. The novel's climax can be read as a reconciliation certainly, but it also can be read as male sexual gratification: Ursa finally does *for him* what she would not do before. Mutt acknowledges as much himself: " 'You never would suck it when I wanted you to,' " he says to Ursa, as she goes to work between his legs. " 'I didn't think *you would do this for me*' " (my emphasis). Mutt cums, Ursa succombs.

The question of power and pleasure becomes even more complex if we consider it in terms of both *Corregidora* and *Eva's Man*. Eva achieves the climax with Elvira Moody, her woman cellmate, that Ursa does not with Mutt. Yet, the latter is read as the successful coupling. Mutt's pleasure is expressed: " 'Oh, baby.' " "He came and I swallowed." Ursa's is assumed (or perhaps consumed). Yet, it is this encounter that Melvin Dixon describes as the more active lovemaking—the better side of "the unrelenting violence, emotional silence, and passive disharmony in *Eva's Man*" (117).

" 'Tell me when it feels sweet,' " Elvira says to Eva in the final moments of *Eva's Man*. " 'Tell me when it feels sweet, honey.' " "I leaned back, squeezing her face between my legs," Eva says, "and told her, '*Now*' " (177, my emphasis). Eva, as Dixon reads her, allows herself to be seduced by Elvira Moody, "passively receiv[ing] her in the act of cunnilingus," unlike Ursa who, through the act of fellatio, "brings Mutt within the orbit of her physical control." I would argue, however, that the language of the encounter is hardly passive. Eva squeezes Elvira's face between her legs and *speaks* her own pleasure—" '*Now*' "—in a way she has not done before. Dixon's otherwise sensitive and provocative reading ultimately privileges the male principle, implying that it is better for a woman to give pleasure to a man than to take it with another woman. Throughout the novel, Eva has been "trapped in the prison of her own emotions," but will she remain there, trapped in her own silence, "forever singing solo," as Dixon suggests? " 'Now' " . . . I'm not so sure.

The novel ends in an ambiguity whose possibilities are both beautiful and ugly. Elvira Moody may be just another in a long line of men and women who abuse Eva, who take advantage of her. Or, as Ann Allen Shockley suggests, she may do no more in the novel than provide "a background litany of on-going seduction,"[27]—a seduction to which Eva finally submits simply because there is no man around, because she can't keep knocking Elvira out of bed. But when read in light of the fellatio with which *Corregidora* closes, the cunnilingus that brings Eva (and Eva's Man) to climax may suggest something else entirely. It may suggest a way off the prong "dat all us black women gits hung on"; not *necessarily* lesbian sexuality, but definitely paying less attention to male gratification and more to our own, to our own pleasure and our own pain. In other words: making ourselves the subjects of our own stories, our own lives.

Perhaps this is what has been difficult for many black male readers to accept: seeing themselves depicted as something other than the heroes of their women's lives, seeing the black penis portrayed as something other than the royally paternal black phallus. They have misread the refusal of a certain kind of male behavior as a rejection of black men. Such a misreading seems to me to underpin Addison Gayle's critique not of Gayl Jones's work, but of her. Protesting that black women novelists only write about black men as "white folks' Toms" or "brutes a la *Corregidora*," Gayle suggests that "if Gayl Jones believes that Black men are what she says they are, she ought to get a white man" (Bell 214–15). So saying, Gayle shifts the venue of literary criticism from the written fictions of the text to the assumed facts of the author's life, while at the same time questioning the writer's allegiance to the race she betrayed with her pen.

In appraisals like Gayle's, the beholder exceeds his authority as reader. He extrapolates a universal real—"all black men"—from the particular fiction—"a black man" or "some black men." At the same time, he denigrates the woman writer by assigning to her the attitudes, problems, proclivities, and conflicts of her characters, thus denying her the courtesy of a creative imagination.

In general, black women writers have weathered well the storms of criticism that their fictions have stirred up. But Gayl Jones, by her own admission, has been made "extremely 'double conscious' " by criticisms which, as she says (likely referring to Gayle, in particular), "suggest that the fictional invention must imply something about the personal relationships or the way I think 'black men are.' "[28] While she has not been completely silenced by such interpretive phallus(ies), the kind of vitriolic, overly personalized censure her first two novels received in certain circles has altered the course of her writing, particularly its attention to sexuality. "I had to force myself to go ahead with such scenes in *The Stone Dragon*," she says, "because they belonged there, but they're not as graphic and they don't use the same kind of vocabulary (that was true of the characters) of *Eva's Man* and *Corregidora*." Though she, like Walker, remains committed to exploring relationships between men and women, in most of her later work Jones either changes the race or gender of her antagonists or avoids sexual scenes altogether.

That Gayl Jones (or any other writer) would feel called upon to change the race, gender, or actions of her characters because some readers are unable, as she says, to "see beyond those details of erotic consciousness to other meanings" seems to me a travesty of both the creative and the critical process. It is a move which makes literary criticism an act of violence that ironically reinscribes the same oppressive, patriarchal attitudes the literature refracts.

CONCLUSION

Ishmael Reed, articulating the sentiments of many black male readers, has asked black women writers why they always feel the need to castrate the black man?[29] Perhaps the answer or, at least, one answer may be because, like the mountain, sexism is there. The novel and other literary forms have given black women a forum for exploring the oppression, insanities, sorrows, joys, and triumphs of women's lives and for transforming those experiences into art.

Clifford Geertz has suggested that all art forms render ordinary, everyday experience comprehensible.[30] Using Geertz's theory to explain the persistence of rape fantasies in white women's romantic fiction, Janice Radway has argued that "the romance's preoccupation with male brutality is an attempt to understand the meaning of an event that has become almost unavoidable in the real world."[31] Writing rape into the romance, then, Radway suggests, is a way for women to work through and deal with the misogynistic attitudes that are so deeply embedded in our society. A similar claim can be made for both the preoccupation with the politics of sexuality and the attention to male violence and penile oppression in the novels of writers such as Morrison, Walker, and Jones. Their fictions are not about doing a hatchet job on black men as mates, but about claiming women as the authors of their own lives rather than as objects of desire in a truth-as-I-know-it/I'm-okay-we're-okay history of blacks in America that is actually the "truths" of men.

Like a number of black male critics, Darryl Pinckney resists the effort to supplement male "truths" with female perceptions. He protests that in *The Color Purple*, "the black men are seen at a distance . . . entirely from the point of view of women."[32] From whose perspective should male characters in a woman-authored text be seen? From whose point of view is Ernest Gaines's Miss Jane Pittman seen or Bessie in *Native Son* or Matty Lou Trueblood in *Invisible Man*? Is a literature or a criticism utterly without (gender) perspective—without male or female perceptions—possible? In the realm of African American literary studies, both the texts and the interpretations of black men often have been treated as if they were indeed without such perspective—without male perceptions. They have been treated simply as *the truth*, like Bennett's true story of Black love.

Readings are never neutral. All criticisms are local, situational. My own critical interpretations, as I have acknowledged, are always-already colored by my race and my gender, by my blackness and my feminism. I readily (some might say too readily) label what I do "black feminist criticism." Masculinist criticism needs to be similarly willing to acknowledge and label itself and its biases. But what the field needs is not only more truth in advertising, as it were, but more introspection—more internal critique. For all of us—masculinists, feminists, womanists—the challenge of our critical practice is to see both inside and outside our own assumptions. Texts have a way of becoming what we say they are. But what's at stake is not just the fidelity we owe to the books we read, but the way we do our jobs, our own intellectual integrity. Many black male scholars have accused contemporary black women writers of wielding words like a sword, even as they have done so themselves. It remains to be seen whether the woman writer's sword is mightier than the pen is.

NOTES

1. Lerone Bennett, Jr., "The Roots of Black Love," *Ebony* (August 1981): 31.

2. Bennett exempts such writers as Paul Laurence Dunbar and such musicians as John Coltrane and the Commodores (all male) whom he sees as contributing to "the vitality of the Black love tradition" with poems like "When Malindy Sings" and songs like "Soul Eyes" and "Once, Twice, Three Times a Lady," all of which position black women not as active agents in history but as objects of male desire. "Careless Love," to which Bennett alludes in his essay, is an old folk song which Bessie Smith made famous. Poet Robert Hayden incorporates lyrics from "Careless Love" into his poetic tribute to Smith, "Homage to the Empress of the Blues," writing "Faithless Love/Twotiming Love Oh Love Oh Careless Aggravating Love." Bennett may be referring to Hayden's poem as well as to the song itself. Interestingly enough, Zora Neale Hurston also incorporates lyrics from this "old, old ballad" in her last novel, *Seraph on the Suwanee* (1948).

3. See McDowell's essay "Family Matters," in *Changing Our Own Words: Essays on Criticism, Theory, and Writing by Black Women*, ed. Cheryl Wall (New Brunswick, NJ: Rutgers University Press, 1989). Drawing on reviews and articles published primarily in the white literary media and popular press, McDowell brilliantly analyzes the often vitriolic responses that the fictions of writers like Walker, Morrison, and Jones have inspired from black male critics such as Mel Watkins and Darryl Pinckney. Part of the problem, McDowell points out, is that African American history has been written (by men) as a black family romance in which black men battle not their women but the oppressive forces of white racism. In representing black male abuse within the family, black women writers are writing outside the family, against the family romance.

4. A number of black women writers labelled "feminists" by some of their black male critics—Gayl Jones, for example—have not so identified themselves.

5. Don Alexander and Christine Wright, "Race, Sex and Class: The Clash over *The Color Purple,*" *Women and Revolution* 34 (Spring 1988): 20.

6. "Interview with Alice Walker," in *Interviews with Black Writers*, ed. John O'Brien (New York: Liveright, 1973): 192; Roseann P. Bell, "Judgment; Addison Gayle," in *Sturdy Black Bridges; Visions of Black Women in Literature* (Garden City, NY: Anchor Books, 1979): 214;

Ishmael Reed, *New Amsterdam News* (January-February, 1987). Quoted by Don Alexander and Christine Wright in "Race, Sex and Class: The Clash over *The Color Purple,*" *Women and Revolution* 34 (Spring 1988): 20.

7. See Calvin C. Hernton, *The Sexual Mountain and Black Women Writers: Adventures in Sex, Literature and Real Life* (New York: Doubleday, 1987).

8. As it has gained in popularity both in and outside the academy, black women's literature has acquired many champions among black male scholars. Some of the work of some of these male critics presents a problem of a kind slightly different from the one I address in this essay. Rather than denigrating feminism and its fictions, this criticism announces itself as feminist discourse, even as it remains primarily male-identified. It is also worth noting that several black feminist critics — Barbara Smith, Ann Allen Shockley, and Jewelle Gomez, for example — have been severely critical of what they read as either the silence about or the negative representation of lesbians in the fiction of such writers as Gayl Jones and Gloria Naylor.

9. See Michele Wallace, *Black Macho and the Myth of the Superwoman* (New York: Warner Books, 1978).

10. Mel Watkins, "Sexism, Racism and Black Women Writers," *New York Times Book Review* (15 June 1986): 36.

11. W. Lawrence Hogue, "History, the Feminist Discourse, and *The Third Life of Grange Copeland,*" chapter 5 in his book *Discourse and the Other* (Durham: Duke University Press, 1986): 86–106.

12. See Watkins, p. 35. While Watkins criticizes other black women writers for their negative portraits of black male brutality, he praises Morrison for her "subtle, intelligent prose," which he suggests directs our sympathies away from the actual horror of the rape to the swirl of emotions that motivate Cholly's actions.

13. Toni Morrison, *The Bluest Eye* (New York: Washington Square Press, 1970): 128–29. See also Houston A. Baker, Jr., *Blues, Ideology, and Afro-American Literature: A Vernacular Theory* (Chicago: University of Chicago Press, 1984): 177–88.

14. Houston A. Baker, Jr., *Workings of the Spirit: The Poetics of Afro-American Women's Writing* (Chicago: University of Chicago Press, 1991).

15. Michael Awkward, *Inspiring Influences: Tradition, Revision, and Afro-American Women's Novels* (New York: Columbia University Press, 1989): 82–83.

16. Zora Neale Hurston, *Their Eyes Were Watching God*, 1937, reprint with a foreword by Sherley Anne Williams (Urbana: University of Illinois Press, 1978): 41.

17. See Hortense Spillers, "The Politics of Intimacy: A Discussion," in *Sturdy Black Bridges*, 87–106.

18. Alice Walker, *The Third Life of Grange Copeland* (New York: Harcourt Brace Jovanovich, 1970): 94.

19. Toni Morrison, *Song of Solomon* (New York: New American Library, 1977): 217.

20. Richard K. Barksdale, "Castration Symbolism in Recent Black American Fiction," *CLA Journal* 29 (June 1986): 403.

21. Gayl Jones, *Eva's Man* (New York: Random House, 1976): 128–29.

22. My coinage of the term "dearly beloved blues" was inspired by Alice Walker's short story "Roselily," in which she interweaves the title character's thoughts as she is married to a Black Muslim with the words of the minister conducting the ceremony. From the simple but significant details that occupy Roselily's thoughts as the minister speaks — "ropes," "chains," "handcuffs," and "the stiff severity of [the groom's] plain black suit" — we know that this will not be a happy marriage. Also alluding to Walker, Gayl Jones calls male/female relationships

of the kind she deals with in *Corregidora* "blues relationships," coming out of a "tradition of 'love and trouble.'" See Alice Walker, "Roselily," in *In Love and Trouble: Stories of Black Women* (New York: Harcourt Brace Jovanovich, 1973): 3; "Gayl Jones: An Interview," *Chant of Saints: A Gathering of Afro-American Literature, Art, and Scholarship*, Michael S. Harper and Robert Stepto, eds. (Urbana: University of Illinois Press, 1979): 360.

23. Janice Harris, "Gayl Jones' *Corregidora*," *Frontiers* 3 (1981): 2.

24. Charles H. Rowell, "Interview with Gayl Jones," *Callaloo* 5 (October 1982): 45.

25. I cannot invoke Melvin Dixon without noting with sadness and regret his untimely passing in October of 1992. Melvin, Gayl Jones, and I were all graduate students together at Brown University in the early seventies. How remarkable it seems to me as I write this that our paths should cross textually in this way twenty years later.

26. Melvin Dixon, *Ride Out the Wilderness: Geography and Identity in Afro-American Literature* (Chicago: University of Illinois Press, 1987): 112.

27. Ann Allen Shockley, "The Black Lesbian in American Literature," in *Home Girls: A Black Feminist Anthology*, ed. Barbara Smith (New York: Women of Color Press, 1983): 89.

28. Rowell, 46–47.

29. See Reed's novel *Reckless Eyeballing*, among other sources.

30. Clifford Geertz, "Notes on the Balinese Cockfight," chapter in *The Interpretation of Culture* (New York: Basic Books, 1973): 443. Geertz writes: "Like any art form . . . the cockfight renders ordinary, everyday experience comprehensible by presenting it in terms of acts and objects which have had their practical consequences removed and been reduced . . . to the level of sheer appearances, where their meaning can be more powerfully articulated and more easily perceived."

31. Janice A. Radway, *Reading the Romance: Women, Patriarchy, and Popular Literature* (Chapel Hill: University of North Carolina Press, 1984): 71.

32. Darryl Pinckney, "Black Victims, Black Villains," *New York Review of Books* (19 January 1987): 18.

Nationalism and Social Division in Black Arts Poetry of the 1960s

Phillip Brian Harper

(1993)

BLACK RHETORIC AND THE NATIONALIST CALL

Who is being spoken to, and how, is a key in the material to which I now turn, as is the sort of dynamic of expulsion that characterized Magic Johnson's 1992 experiences in the NBA. At the same time, however, both of these issues signify differently in Johnson's situation—where they refer primarily to masculine identification—than they do in the context I am now considering, in which masculinity gives way to— and simultaneously grounds—black identity. I have already alluded to this process in my brief consideration of Haki Madhubuti's "Don't Cry, Scream" (1969); and it is perfectly emblematized in Nikki Giovanni's contemporaneous exhortation, "Learn to kill niggers / Learn to be Black men" ("True Import," p. 319), in which the accession to manhood that Giovanni demands coincides with the achievement of "Blackness" that she extols, both these developments deriving from the execution of cathartic violence against those who are yet "niggers" (according to a strict reading of the first line's syntax), by those very "niggers," who will thus emerge as "black men" (if we imagine a comma before "niggers" that renders it in the vocative case). Insofar as black identity thus depends upon identification specifically as man, however, then blackness will partake of the very uncertainty, tentativeness, and burden of proof that we have already seen to characterize conventional masculinity—a fact that is suggested by the nature of the distinction between "niggers" and "black men" that Giovanni invokes in the first place.

This chapter undertakes to explicate the way that distinction operates at a key moment in African-American cultural history—a moment for which the perfect epigraph might well be the one used by an influential literary figure to introduce a defining document in African-American poetics. Dudley Randall's anthology, *The Black Poets*, published in 1971, is significant not so much for the texts it provides of

460

folk verse and literary poetry from the mid-eighteenth through the early twentieth centuries as for its canonization of poetry from the contemporaneous Black Arts movement. The concluding (and by far the longest) section of Randall's anthology is titled "The Nineteen Sixties," and it is prefaced by the short poem "SOS" by Imamu Amiri Baraka (LeRoi Jones), which is printed not in the main text but on the title page for the section:

> Calling black people
> Calling all black people, man woman child
> Wherever you are, calling you, urgent, come in
> Black People, come in, wherever you are, urgent, calling
> you, calling all black people
> calling all black people, come in, black people, come
> on in. (P. 181)

Given the epigraphic function that Randall confers on it, we can reasonably conclude that Baraka's "SOS" is somehow emblematic of the poetic project of many young black writers of the late 1960s, and it is not particularly difficult to identify exactly in what this emblematic quality might consist. We know, after all, that radical black intellectual activism of the late 1960s was characterized by a drive for nationalistic unity among people of African descent. As Larry Neal put it in his defining essay of 1968, "The Black Arts Movement":

> Black Art is the aesthetic and spiritual sister of the Black Power concept. . . . The Black Arts and the Black Power concept both relate broadly to the Afro-American's desire for self-determination and nationhood. Both concepts are nationalistic. One is concerned with the relationship between art and politics; the other with the art of politics. (P. 272)

Addison Gayle also embraced the nationalist impulse in his conception of the movement, outlined in his 1971 introduction to *The Black Aesthetic*. According to Gayle, "The Black Aesthetic . . . is a corrective—a means of helping black people out of the polluted mainstream of Americanism" (p. xxiii). And in 1973, Stephen Henderson elaborated the development of this impulse through the late 1960s: "The poetry of the sixties is informed and unified by the new consciousness of Blackness . . . [, which has] shifted from Civil Rights to Black Power to Black Nationalism to Revolutionary Pan-Africanism . . ." (p. 183). Thus did three of the Black Aesthetic's most prominent theorists conceive the importance of nationalist unity to the Black Arts movement.[1] It probably goes without saying that such a nationalist impulse, having once been manifested, can develop in any number of different directions. For the sake of the present analysis, however, we can suspend consideration of this important point while we confirm the existence of that impulse, in however rudimentary a form, in Baraka's poem.

In the introduction to their authoritative anthology, *Black Nationalism in America* (1970), John Bracey, Jr., August Meier, and Elliott Rudwick identify as the basis of black nationalist thought "[t]he concept of racial solidarity," which, they assert, "is

462 / *Phillip Brian Harper*

essential to all forms of black nationalism" (p. xxvi). It is precisely this fundamental impulse to racial solidarity that is manifested in Baraka's "SOS." Considered with respect to nationalism, the political import of the poem inheres not in the stridency and exigency of its appeal, but rather in its breadth, in the fact that Baraka's call apparently embraces all members of the African diaspora, as it is directed explicitly and repeatedly to "all black people," thereby invoking a political Pan-Africanism posited as characteristic of the Black Arts project. Moreover, the enjambment of the last two lines and their modification of the injunction definitively transform the SOS from a mere distress signal into a general summons for assembly. What is striking about Baraka's poem, however, is not that it "calls" black people in this nationalistic way but that this is all it does; the objective for which it assembles the black populace is not specified in the piece itself, a fact I take to indicate fundamental difficulties in the nationalist agenda of the Black Arts poets, as will soon become clear.

In the meantime, I think it is useful to consider Baraka's "SOS" as a synecdoche for all of his poetic output of the 1960s, which constituted a challenge to other African-American poets to take up the nationalist ethic he espoused. As the source of this influential call, Baraka can certainly be seen as the founder of the Black Aesthetic of the 1960s, and "SOS" as representative of the standard to which his fellow poets rallied. "SOS" is part of Baraka's collection *Black Art*, comprising poems written in 1965 and 1966, and published, along with two other collections, in the volume *Black Magic Poetry, 1961–1967* (1969). Its message was subsequently engaged by other black writers from different generations and disparate backgrounds. For instance, in her 1972 autobiography, *Report from Part One*, Gwendolyn Brooks, who built her reputation on her expertly crafted lyrics of the 1940s and 1950s, made Baraka's enterprise her own as she described her new poetic mission in the early 1970s:

> My aim, in my next future, is to write poems that will somehow successfully "call" (see Imamu Baraka's "SOS") all black people: black people in taverns, black people in alleys, black people in gutters, schools, offices, factories, prisons, the consulate; I wish to reach black people in pulpits, black people in mines, on farms, on thrones(.)
> (P. 183)

Sonia Sanchez, on the other hand, in her 1969 poem, "blk/rhetoric," invoked Baraka's language to question what might happen after the calling had been done:

> who's gonna make all
> that beautiful blk/rhetoric
> mean something.
>   like
> i mean
>   who's gonna take
> the words
>   blk/beautiful
> and make more of it
> than blk/capitalism.

```
                    u dig?
             i mean
                   like who's gonna
     take all the young/long/haired/
     natural/brothers and sisters
     and let them
                   grow till
                        all that is
     imp't is them
                   selves
                        moving in straight/
     revolutionary/lines/toward the enemy
     (and we know who that is)
                        like.   man.
     who's gonna give our young
     blk people new heros
     (instead of catch/phrases)
     (instead of cad/ill/acs)
     (instead of pimps)
     (instead of white/whores)
     (instead of drugs)
     (instead of new/dances)
     (instead of chit/ter/lings)
     (instead of a 354 bottle of
                        ripple)
     (instead of quick/fucks
        in the hall/way of
                   white/america's
                        mind)
     like. this. is an S.O.S.
     me. calling. . . .
                   calling. . . .
                        some/one.
             pleasereplysoon.
```

Sanchez's call—prefaced as it is by her urgent question, and attended by the entreaty to her listeners in the final line—is more pleading than Baraka's, which is unabashedly imperative. I would suggest that the uncertainty that characterizes Sanchez's poem is the inevitable affective result of writing beyond the ending of Baraka's "SOS," which it seems to me is what "blk/rhetoric" does. By calling into question what will ensue among the black collectivity after it has heeded the general call—succumbed to the rhetoric, as it were—Sanchez points to the problematic nature of the black nationalist project that characterizes Black Arts poetry.

What remains certain, in Sanchez's rendering—so certain that it need not be stated explicitly—is the identity of the "enemy" against whom the assembled black troops must struggle. While Sanchez's elliptical reference might appear as somewhat ambiguous at this point, especially after the emergence in the early and mid-1970s of a strong black feminist movement that arrayed itself against racism and sexism, it seems clear enough that in the context of the 1969 Black Arts movement the enemy was most certainly the white "establishment." But this is the *only* thing that is "known" in Sanchez's poem, and while the identification of a generalized white foe is a central strategy in the Black Arts movement's effort to galvanize the black populace, here it provides a hedge against the overall uncertainty that characterizes the rest of the poem—a definitive core on which the crucial questions about the efficacy of nationalist rhetoric can center and thus themselves still be recognizable as nationalist discourse.

With its counterbalancing of fundamental inquiries about the future of the black nationalist enterprise by recourse to the trope of the white enemy, Sanchez's "blk/ rhetoric" verges on the problematic that I take to be constitutive of the Black Arts project. Insofar as that project is nationalistic in character, then its primary objective and continual challenge will be not to identify the external entity against which the black masses are distinguished—this is easy enough to do—but rather to negotiate division within the black population itself. I specifically invoke negotiation here and not, for instance, resolution because I want to claim that the response of Black Arts nationalism to social division within the black populace is not to strive to overcome it, but rather repeatedly to articulate it in the name of black consciousness.[2]

ANTIWHITE SENTIMENT AND THE BLACK AUDIENCE

It has been widely held that the fundamental characteristic of Black Arts poetry is its virulent antiwhite rhetoric. For instance, as Houston Baker (1988, p. 161) has noted, the influential black critic J. Saunders Redding disparaged the Black Aesthetic as representative of a discourse of "hate," a "naive racism in reverse." And it is true that Baraka himself became known for a generalized antiwhite sentiment, often manifested in highly particularized ethnic and religious slurs, especially anti-Semitic ones. His "Black Art" (1966, 1979) provides an exemplary litany, calling for

> [p]oems that wrestle cops into alleys
> and take their weapons leaving them dead
> with tongues pulled out and sent to Ireland. Knockoff
> poems for dope selling wops or slick halfwhite
> politicians Airplane poems . . .
> . . . Setting fire and death to
> whites ass. Look at the Liberal
> Spokesman for the jews clutch his throat
> & puke himself into eternity . . .

> . . . Another bad poem cracking
> steel knuckles in a jewlady's mouth[.] (P. 224)

"Black People!" calls for the "smashing [of] jellywhite faces. We must make our own / World, man, our own world, and we can not do this unless the white man / is dead. Let's get together and killhim [*sic*]" (pp. 226–27). Similarly, Nikki Giovanni, in the poem to which I have already referred (and to which I shall turn again soon), inquires urgently of the "nigger" she addresses, "Can you kill . . . / . . . Can you poison . . . / . . . Can you piss on a blond head / Can you cut it off . . . / . . . Can you kill a white man" ("True Import," p. 318).

While the affective power of such antiwhite sentiment in much of the poetry certainly cannot be denied, it seems to me that the drama of interracial strife that this rhetoric represents also serves to further another objective of Black Arts poetry—the establishment of intraracial distinctions that themselves serve to solidify the meaning of the Black Aesthetic. We can clarify this point through reference to a few poems that, while their authors may have since taken disparate poetic paths, function as archetypal Black Arts works: Baraka's "Poem for Half White College Students"; Giovanni's "The True Import of Present Dialogue: Black vs. Negro"; "Move Un-Noticed to Be Noticed: A Nationhood Poem," by Haki Madhubuti (Don L. Lee); Sanchez's "chant for young/brothas & sistuhs"; and "Okay 'Negroes,'" by June Jordan. These five poems . . . have been widely anthologized as exemplary of the Black Arts project, yet I would argue that they are exemplary not because they are representative of the poetics deployed in most Black Arts productions, but rather because they expose the logic of the Black Arts ethic that governs work from the movement generally, though its operation is carefully suppressed in most of that material.

These pieces certainly present disparaging references to white society—Jordan's "male white mammy," Sanchez's rendering of the heroin high, Baraka's invocation of film celebrities as representative of the shallowness of Euro-American culture—all of which fit neatly into characterizations of Black Arts poetry as essentially antiwhite. But while these works might engage conceptions of white America as a negative force, the rhetoric of the pieces is not addressed—not directly, at any rate—to the white society that is the ostensible target of their wrath. Rather, all the poems employ the second-person pronoun *you* in ways that are clearly meant to conjure a specifically black addressee, and thus to give the impression that the poetic works themselves are meant for consumption by a specifically black audience. In other words, the rhetoric of Black Arts poetry, in conjunction with the sociopolitical context in which it is produced, works a twist on John Stuart Mill's (1833, 1979, p. 1055) proclamation that "poetry is overheard," as it seems to effect a split in the audience for the work. Because of the way the poetry uses direct address and thus invites us to conflate addressee and audience, it appears that the material is meant to be heard by blacks, and overheard by whites, who would respond fearfully to the threat of mayhem it embodies. I think that this is appearance only, however, and it will be a secondary effect of my argument to demonstrate that, while Black Arts poetry very likely does depend for its power on the division of its audience along racial lines, it achieves its maximum impact in a context in which it is understood as being heard directly by whites, and overheard by blacks.

Clarification of this last point is forthcoming. In the meantime, it is necessary to acknowledge the substantial polemical effect that is achieved through the presentation of Black Arts poetry as meant for black ears only, for it is this presentation that commentators have seized on in characterizing the Black Arts movement as representing a completely Afrocentric impulse. As Gayle, for instance, put it in his introduction to *The Black Aesthetic* (1971, pp. xxi–xxii), the black artist of the 1960s "has given up the futile practice of speaking to whites, and has begun to speak to his brothers . . . to point out to black people the true extent of the control exercised upon them by the American society." Gayle's claim is, in itself, not earth-shaking; it typifies contemporary conceptions of the Black Arts movement's significance in African-American cultural history. What is notable is that Gayle's statement, in positing the Black Arts strategy as historically unique, established itself as a historical repetition, insofar as, nearly fifty years before, a black theorist of the Harlem Renaissance made a very similar claim about the nature of that movement. In his 1925 article on the contemporary flowering of African-American art, "Negro Youth Speaks," Alain Locke insisted that "[o]ur poets have now stopped speaking for the Negro—they speak as Negroes. Where formerly they spoke to others and tried to interpret, they now speak to their own and try to express" (p. 18). The full irony of this repetition lies in the fact that it was precisely on the basis of the perceived failure of the Harlem Renaissance to engage African-American interests that Black Arts theoreticians found fault with the earlier movement. Larry Neal (1968, p. 290) specifically charged that the Harlem Renaissance "failed" in that "[i]t did not address itself to the mythology and the life-styles of the Black community." Clearly, there is an anxiety of influence operative here, manifested in the powerful need among the Black Aestheticians to disassociate themselves from the Harlem Renaissance; and this disassociation would evidently be achieved through the later movement's presumedly uniquely effective manner of addressing itself to the interests of black people. By examining this strategy, we can see more clearly both how social division within the black community is fundamentally constitutive of Black Arts nationalism and, relatedly, why it is so difficult for the Black Arts movement to postulate concrete action beyond "black rhetoric," to project beyond the "call" manifested in Baraka's "SOS."

BLACKER THAN THOU

What is most striking about the way the poems under consideration—which I have suggested distill the logic of the Black Arts project—address themselves to the black community is their insistent use of the second-person pronoun. This aspect of the poetry is notable not only because it indicates both the Black Arts poets' keen awareness of issues of audience and their desire to appear to engage their audience directly (both of which I have already alluded to), but because the *you* references also—and paradoxically, given the Black Aesthetic's nation-building agenda—represent the implication of intraracial division within the Black Aesthetic's poetic strategy. It is clear, of course, that the use of the second-person pronoun of whatever number implies less inclusiveness than would, say, the use of the first-person plural, *we*. What remains to be explored is exactly on what this apparent exclusivity—this implicit social division—is founded, both grammatically and historically, in order for us to grasp more fully the significance of Black Arts poetics.

Theoretical work in the grammar of the linguistic "shifter"—of which pronouns are one type—has illuminated the peculiar character of the second-person singular pronoun, *you*, and its difference from *he, she*, or any other "third-person" entity. The pertinent findings of this work can be put fairly simply: Because it conjures an addressee to whom an iteration is directed, the invocation of *you* also necessarily implies a producing source of that iteration—namely, an *I*—against which you itself is defined; as linguist Emile Benveniste (1971, p. 201) has put it, *you* constitutes specifically and emphatically "the non-I person." And, because you thus exists in a contrastive relationship with *I*, any assertion made about you implies a converse characterization of *I*. Indeed, a statement about *you* can actually more effectively limn the traits of an iterating *I* than can a bona fide first-person proclamation since, to adduce one of the lessons of post-structuralist theory, the latter always implicates a disjuncture between the *I* who issues it and the *I* that is represented in it: in the Lacanian-influenced formulation of Antony Easthope (1983, p. 44), "the 'I' as represented in discourse . . . is always sliding away from the 'I' doing the speaking," rendering impossible any stably accurate first-person characterization.

Numerous commentators have discussed the ramifications of such post-structuralist–informed analysis for socially marginalized groups, whose political agendas have often been considered as based on a primary need to forge stable identities in the first place, and not on the deconstruction of such identity.[3] Certainly, the Black Arts movement can easily be understood as an attempt to establish a positive African-American subjectivity—based on nationalist ideals—in the face of major sociopolitical impediments to its construction. But post-structuralism's calling into question the unitary stability of the subjective *I* does not, I think, prohibit the Black Aesthetic's construction of a powerful black nationalist subject; it merely stipulates that such construction is possible only from a position externally and obliquely situated with respect to the discursive *I*. In that case, however—and in light of the analysis just presented—it is impossible for the Black Arts work examined here to posit an effective black nationalist collectivity. This is because the strategy necessarily deployed by Black Arts poetry to establish a strong black nationalist subject—and through which it derives its meaning and power—is founded on the oppositional logic that governs the pronominal language characteristic of the work. That opposition is thematized in the poetry, not in terms of the "us versus them" dichotomy that we might expect, however, with *us* representing blacks and *them* whites; rather, it is played out along the inherent opposition between *I* and *you*, both of these terms deriving their referents from within the collectivity of black subjects.

Thus the project of Black Arts poetry can be understood as the establishment of black nationalist subjectivity—the forcible fixing of the identity of the "speaking" *I*—by delineating it against the "non-*I* person," the *you* whose identity is clearly predicated in the poems we are considering. So the *you* in Baraka's "Poem for Half White College Students" is the African American who identifies with the Euro-American celebrity, against which the speaking *I* of the poem is implicitly contrasted. In Giovanni's and Lee's poems, *you* represents the Negro subject whose sense of self-worth and racial pride has yet to be proven. In Sanchez's "chant," *you* is the black junkie who finds solace in the "white" high of heroin, which is clearly associated with Euro-American corruption. And in June Jordan's "Okay 'Negroes,' " *you* is the African American who has not yet developed an understanding of the raciopolitical forces that impinge upon black subjectivity. Clearly, I oversimplify to the extent that the referent of any given *you* might well vary even within a single poem. But my point is that because, in spite of these shifts, the second person is much more readily identified than the speaking *I* for any utterance, any *you* that these Black Arts poets invoke can function as a negative foil against which the implicit *I* who speaks the poem can be distinguished as a politically aware, racially conscious black nationalist subject. It is this intraracial division on which the Black Arts project is founded, and not any sense of inclusiveness with respect to the African-American community that we might discern in Baraka's "SOS," which fact greatly problematizes the possibility of effective communal action after the issuance of Baraka's call.[4]

Indeed, once we have clarified the *I–you* division that underlies the Black Arts concept of African-American community, we can better understand the intraracial division that is implicit in movement references to the "black" subject itself. If it appears to us that Baraka's "SOS" embraces all members of the black diaspora, this is only because we are forgetting something that Lee's poem, on the other hand, usefully reminds us—that the designation *black*, from the middle 1960s through the early 1970s, represented an emergent identification among nationalist activists and intellectuals, and not a generic nomenclature by which any person of African descent might be referenced. Consequently, if Baraka is calling "all black people," he is already calling only those African Americans whose political consciousness is sufficiently developed for them to subscribe to the designation *black* in the first place. All others—designated by *you* in the poems that utilize the pronominal rhetoric—will be considered as *negroes*, as in the titles of Giovanni's and Jordan's poems—a term that is pointedly transmuted into *niggers* in Giovanni's text.

ANXIOUS IDENTITIES AND DIVISIONAL LOGIC

Having detailed these poems' method for authorizing their own black nationalist rhetoric, we must now consider how to account for it, since the intraracial division that it comprises evidently runs counter to the solidarity we have taken to found black nationalism. Undoubtedly, a number of specific, local contingencies contributed to the development of the Black Arts movement's agenda and practice. At the same time, it is possible, within the analytical context set up here, to identify a key concern that informed the enactment of its signal strategies. We have already noted that whatever political solidarity characterized the Black Arts movement did not necessarily bind it to its historical precursor, the Harlem Renaissance, whose cultural politics Black Aestheticians repudiated even as they recapitulated its rhetoric. That repudiation, as instanced in the writings by Larry Neal that we have examined, was based specifically on the sense that Harlem Renaissance artistic practice was fundamentally estranged from the concerns of the black community—that "[i]t failed," in Neal's (1968, p. 290) words, "to link itself concretely to the struggles of that community." By apparent contrast, rootedness in the day-to-day exigencies of black life was regularly invoked as a prime characteristic of Black Arts practice, with Baraka ("The Black Aesthetic," p. 5), for instance, coining alternative etymologies and manipulating typography to assert the essential groundedness of the Black Aesthetic: "What does aesthetic mean? A theory in the ether. Shdn't it mean for us Feelings about reality! . . . About REality." Thus commitment to black empowerment was conceived specifically in terms of engagement with the "hard facts" of African-American existence (to invoke a term with which Baraka was later to title a collection of his poems; see *Selected Poetry*, 1979, pp. 235–73), as opposed to the rather more "ethereal" concerns that putatively occupied the writers of the Harlem Renaissance.

And yet, four years prior to the 1969 publication of his "Black Aesthetic" essay, Baraka had already characterized as problematically disengaged from "reality" not the "Literary Negroes" he excoriated in that later piece (p. 6), but the entire class of white men, who, he charged, "devote their energies to the nonphysical, the nonrealistic," thereby becoming "estranged from" the physical and the real—evidently conceived here as one and the same (1965, 1966, p. 216). Anticipating the "Primeval Mitosis" analysis of Eldridge Cleaver's *Soul on Ice*, Baraka posited this estrangement not only as the critical and debilitating "alienation" frequently invoked by Euro-American intellectuals themselves (1965, 1966, p. 218), but specifically in terms of a failed masculinity the recognized horror of which powered the shock effect of his opening lines: "Most American white men are trained to be fags. For this reason it is no wonder their faces are weak and blank, left without the hurt that reality makes. . . . That red flush, those silk blue faggot eyes" (1965, 1966, p. 216). Given this categorical invalidation of Euro-American manhood by virtue of a perceived disengagement from the pressing demands of the physical world that supposedly constitute "real life," the comparable disengagement that Black Aestheticians discerned in the Harlem Renaissance (for instance) would indicate not only an inadequately developed black consciousness (particularly insofar as that disengagement would apparently constitute the adoption of a recognizably white social disposition), but a similarly inadequate masculinity that is coextensive with it. (This analysis is especially plausible with respect to the Harlem Renaissance itself, in light of the widely recognized—though generally only coyly acknowledged—homosexual orientation of many of its key male figures, including Countee Cullen, Wallace Thurman, and Alain Locke himself. See Rampersad, 1986, pp. 66–71, 165.) This logic allowed for

Black Arts judgments of insufficient racial identification to be figured specifically in terms of a failed manhood for which homosexuality, as always, was the primary signifier. Baraka's scathing "CIVIL RIGHTS POEM" is a quintessential case in point:

> Roywilkins is an eternal faggot
> His spirit is a faggot
> his projection
> and image, this is
> to say, that if i ever see roywilkins
> on the sidewalks
> imonna
> stick half my sandal
> up his
> ass

Indeed, so well understood was the identification between inadequacies of manhood and black consciousness in the Black Arts context that this poem needed never render explicit the grounds for its judgment of NAACP leader Roy Wilkins, for the perceived racial-political moderation of both him and his organization clearly bespoke his unforgivable "faggotry."

The Black Aestheticians' development of such a potent gender-political rhetoric through which to condemn perceived failures of black consciousness is significant for my analysis here for at least two reasons: First, it can clearly be seen as establishing a circular dynamic whereby Black Arts writers' own need not to be deemed racially effeminate fueled the ever-spiraling intensity of their repudiative formulations, including the divisional *I–you* constructions that we have examined;[5] second, it indicates the Black Aestheticians' preexistent anxiety regarding their own possible estrangement from the very demands of everyday black life that they repeatedly invoked as founding their practice. If the routine figuration of such estrangement as a voluntary and shameful effeminization was a powerful signal practice in Black Arts poetics, this may well be because the estrangement itself was experienced as the unavoidable effect of inexorable social processes—specifically, the attenuation of the Black Aestheticians' organic connection to the life of the folk (to invoke the Gramscian concept) by virtue of their increasing engagement with the traditional (Euro-American) categories of intellectual endeavor, through which they largely and inevitably developed their public profiles in the first place. The degree to which such *ressentiment* characterized Black Arts writers' relation to their undertakings in literature, say, or in the academy is suggested (for instance) by A. B. Spellman's arguably disingenuous condemnation of the emergent black-studies movement of the late 1960s and early 1970s as unacceptably "bourgie" (cited in Emanuel, 1971, p. 220). And the danger that the Black Aestheticians, in particular, might be accused of an intellectualized disengagement from concrete reality was evidenced as early as 1966, with Stokely Carmichael's highly charged proclamation: "We have to say, 'Don't play jive and start writing poems after Malcolm is shot.' We have to move from the point where the man left off and stop writing poems" (p. 472). Such suspicion regarding black intellectualism accounts for the will to linguistic performativity that characterizes Black Arts rhetoric—the anxious insistence that Black Arts verse constitutes substantive intervention in "real-world" affairs. Indeed, Baraka ("The Black Aesthetic," p. 6) tried mightily to disassociate the Black Arts movement from the ineffectuality connoted by "poetry": "Poetry is jingling lace without *purpose* . . . We are 'poets' because someone has used that word to describe us. What we are our children will have to define. We are creators and destroyers-firemakers, Bomb throwers and takers of heads"; and the poetry itself often seeks to instate the distinction, as when Nikki Giovanni considers her inability to produce a "tree poem" or a "sky poem" in "For Saundra" (1969, 1971, p. 322):

> so i thought again
> and it occurred to me
> maybe i shouldn't write
> at all
> but clean my gun
> and check my kerosene supply
>
> perhaps these are not poetic
> times
> at all

Giovanni herself provides a good indication, not only of the extent of the Black Arts poets concern about their relation to the black "community," but of the degree to which that concern was figured in terms of an anxiety regarding masculine potency. For while it is a truism that discussion of intraracial gender politics was generally suppressed in the Black Power context, indicating women's contested position within the movement,[6] Giovanni's work (as contrasted with that of Sanchez and Jordan, for instance) so insistently invokes a phallic standard of political engagement (the demand for avenging "Black men" in "True Import"; the reference to Richard Nixon as "no-Dick" in "For Saundra") as to suggest that no other term was available—not even to her who, in 1968, explicitly referenced herself as a "black female poet" ("My Poem," 1971, p. 319).

On the other hand, just beneath what appears as the all-too-uniformly status-anxious surface of the Black Arts poetic lurks a more profound wariness regarding the significance of the movement's own invocations—a wariness rendered explicit by Sonia Sanchez's worry that black-power rhetoric will lead only to "blk/capitalism." It seems to me that it is the threatening unpredictability of exactly what will issue from the essentially contradictory nationalist urge that accounts for Baraka's decision not to project beyond the call manifested in "SOS," with the result that the poem is driven by its first-order nationalist impulse rather than dissipated in the ambivalence with which that impulse would inevitably be followed up.

Ambivalence can have no place, after all, in the prosecution of such a revolutionary political program as the Black Aesthetic was supposed to represent. Indeed, the need to quell potential ambivalence might well explain the violent rhetoric that so much of the work employs, the extreme nature of which seems meant as much to desensitize black audiences to the contradictions of nationalist logic as to effect fantasmatically the white enemy's demise. At the same time, it is the fantasy of linguistic performativity apparently informing these invocations of violence that suggests that Black Arts poetry, as I have already proposed, is intended to be heard by whites and overheard by blacks. For according to this fantasy, not only would to be heard be to annihilate one's oppressors, but to be overheard would be to indicate to one's peers just how righteous, how nationalistic, how potently Black one is, in contradistinction to those very peers, who are figured as the direct addressee of the Black Arts works. And insofar as that Blackness is conceived in anxiously masculine terms, then the pronominal construct through which it is registered suggests, "I am a man, but you . . . ?"

All of which is to say that Black Arts rhetoric, whose ostensible objective is to promote racial solidarity, actually engenders a division among blacks that is paradoxically necessary to the nationalist project—a division that, furthermore, is predicated on a profoundly problematic masculinist ethic. While Black Arts politics—the most recent fully theorized version of African-American nationalism—is now a quarter-century old, its continuing import can be discerned in a range of rather more current phenomena, from the interest in accounts of the Black Power era by such authors as Elaine Brown, David Hilliard, and Hugh Pearson, to Afro-centric educational movements and certain aspects of hip-hop culture. It is as crucial as ever, then, to offer a cogent critique of black masculinism and the nationalist impulse. The point, of course, as is already clear, is not to sacrifice the one for the other—a practical impossibility in any event—but, by fully analyzing the workings of both, to expose and abolish the limits they present in promising liberation for "all black people," but not, evidently, for "you."

NOTES

1. For an overview of the development of black nationalism in the Black Arts movement, see Baker, *The Journey Back*, especially Chapter 4.

2. We might consider this project as one instantiation of the fundamental conservatism that Jennifer Jordan (1986) has suggested characterizes black cultural nationalism, whose negotiation in the Black Arts movements she reviews in her article on "Politics and Poetry."

3. For example, see Joyce A. Joyce's (1987) objection to the use of post-structuralist theory in African-Americanist literary criticism.

4. This is not to deny the power of such black collectivization as was generated, for example, in the context of public readings by Black Arts poets during the late 1960s and early 1970s (see Baker, 1980, pp. 128–29); rather, it is to point up the principle of intraracial division on which such collectivization—always necessarily partial—inevitably depends, which principle is evidenced in the published texts that must by definition outlast the live event itself.

5. It is also possible—to point in a direction that diverges substantially from my primary concerns in this volume—that the intraracial division effected in Black Arts poetry is a function of the African-American people's status as a sort of mutated colonial entity. During

the late 1960s, analyses of the colonialized nature of black communities in the United States were forthcoming from both social scientists and black activists. Indeed, in his introduction to *Black Nationalism in America*, John H. Bracey, Jr., posits just such a conception of black America, citing as his justification a number of contemporary studies in sociology and political science (1970, p. lvi; among the authors Bracey cites, Robert Blauner in particular clearly outlines the issues at stake in conceptualizing African-American communities as colonial entities). Given this, it is interesting to note that Abdul R. JanMohamed has identified as one of the cultural manifestations of colonialism a mapping of the social entity along a "manichean" duality that defines a morally "good" constituency—the colonizers, more often than not—against one that is seen as inherently "evil"—the colonized. (See both *Manichean Aesthetics* [1983] and "The Economy of Manichean Allegory" [1985].) While I do not believe that the situation of African Americans can be unproblematically posited as a colonial one, its historical sine qua non—the slave trade—can certainly be considered as a manifestation of the colonizing impulse. Consequently, it seems possible that, just as the economics of slavery developed in a particular manner after the initial appropriation of the "resources" from the African continent, there occurred concomitant mutations in the cultural realm in which we can still trace the remnants of an essential colonial logic. Thus, the I–you dichotomy that characterizes Black Arts poetry might represent the internalization within the African-American community of the manichean ethic that JanMohamed identifies with the colonial situation proper. Further work in this area, while clearly beyond the scope of my analysis here, might well prove critically useful.

6. Consider, for example, Emily Stoper's wry and telling 1989 reflection that the "[r]adical feminists" who emerged in the wake of the black power movement that she chronicled in her 1968 dissertation on the Student Nonviolent Coordinating Committee "never rested their hopes on political change; perhaps they knew better, since many of them were veterans of the New Left and even of SNCC itself" (p. xii). On the gender politics of the Black Power movement, see Wallace (1979, 1990).

WORKS CITED

Baker, Houston A., Jr. *Afro-American Poetics: Revisions of Harlem and the Black Aesthetic.* Madison: University of Wisconsin Press, 1988.

———. *The Journey Back: Issues in Black Literature and Criticism.* Chicago: University of Chicago Press, 1980.

Baraka, Imamu Amiri [LeRoi Jones]. "American Sexual Reference: Black Male." 1965. *Home: Social Essays.* New York: William Morrow, 1966, pp. 216–33.

———. "Black Art." 1966. *Selected Poetry*, pp. 106–7. Also in Randall, 1971, pp. 223–24.

———. *Black Magic: Poetry, 1961–1976.* Indianapolis and New York: Bobbs-Merrill, 1969.

———. "Poem for Half White College Students." 1965. In Randall, 1971, p. 225.

———. *Selected Poetry of Amiri Baraka/LeRoi Jones.* New York: William Morrow, 1979.

———. "SOS." 1966. In Randall, 1971, p. 181.

Benveniste, Emile. "Relationships of Person in the Verb." *Problems in General Linguistics.* Trans. Mary Elizabeth Meek. Miami Linguistics Series 8. Coral Gables, FL: University of Miami Press, 1971, pp. 195–204.

Bracey, John H., Jr., August Meier, and Elliott Rudwick, eds. *Black Nationalism in America.* Indianapolis and New York: Bobbs-Merrill, 1970.

Brooks, Gwendolyn. *Report from Part One*. Detroit: Broadside Press, 1972.

Carmichael, Stokely. Address of 28 July 1966. In Bracey, Meier, and Rudwick, 1970, pp. 470–76.

Easthope, Antony. *Poetry as Discourse*. London and New York: Methuen, 1983.

Emanuel, James A. "Blackness Can: A Quest for Aesthetics." In Gayle, 1971, pp. 192–223.

Gayle, Addison, Jr., ed. *The Black Aesthetic*. Garden City, NY: Doubleday, 1971.

Giovanni, Nikki. "For Saundra." 1969. In Randall, 1971, pp. 321–22.

———. "My Poem." 1969. In Randall, 1971, pp. 319–20.

———. "The True Import of Present Dialogue: Black vs. Negro." 1968. In Randall, 1971, pp. 318–19.

Henderson, Stephen. *Understanding the New Black Poetry: Black Speech and Black Music as Poetic References*. New York: William Morrow, 1973.

JanMohamed, Abdul R. *Manichean Aesthetics: The Politics of Literature in Colonial Africa*. Amherst: University of Massachusetts Press, 1983.

———. "The Economy of Manichean Allegory: The Function of Racial Difference in Colonialist Literature." *"Race," Writing, and Difference*. Ed. Gates. Spec. issue of *Critical Inquiry* 12.1 (Autumn 1985): 59–87.

Jordan, Jennifer. "Cultural Nationalism in the 1960s: Politics and Poetry." *Race, Politics, and Culture: Critical Essays on the Radicalism of the 1960s*. Ed. Adolph Reed, Jr. Contributions in Afro-American and African Studies 95. New York: Greenwood Press, 1986, pp. 29–60.

Jordan, June. "Okay 'Negroes.' " 1966. In Randall, 1971, p. 243.

Joyce, Joyce A. "The Black Canon: Reconstructing Black American Literary Criticism." *NLH* 18.2 (Winter 1987): 335–44.

Locke, Alain. "Negro Youth Speaks." 1925. In Gayle, 1971, pp. 17–23.

Madhubuti, Haki R. [Don L. Lee]. "Don't Cry, Scream." *Don't Cry, Scream*. Detroit: Broadside Press, 1969, pp. 27–31.

———. "Move Un-Noticed to Be Noticed: A Nationhood Poem." In Henderson, 1973, pp. 340–43.

Mill, John Stuart. "What Is Poetry?" 1833. *The Norton Anthology of English Literature*, 4th ed. Gen. ed. M. H. Abrams. Vol. 2. New York: Norton, 1979, 1051–59. 2 vols.

Rampersad, Arnold. *I, Too, Sing America*. New York: Oxford University Press, 1986. Vol. 1 of *The Life of Langston Hughes*. 2 vols. 1986–1988.

Randall, Dudley, ed. *The Black Poets*. New York: Bantam, 1971.

Sanchez, Sonia. "a chant for young / brothers & sistuhs." In Randall, 1971, pp. 240–42.

Stoper, Emily. *The Student Nonviolent Coordinating Committee: The Growth of Radicalism in a Civil Rights Organization*. Martin Luther King, Jr. and the Civil Rights Movement 17. Brooklyn: Carlson, 1989.

Wallace, Michele. *Black Macho and the Myth of the Superwoman*. 1979. The Haymarket Series. London and New York: Verso, 1990.

39 | The Problems with Silence and Exclusiveness in the African American Literary Community

Joyce A. Joyce

(1993/4)

Motivated solely by my staunch dedication to the historical tradition of African-American literature and criticism, I wrote the original essay, "The Black Canon: Reconstructing Black American Literature and Criticism." After accepting the essay for publication, Ralph Cohen, the editor of *New Literary History*, wanted to know if I would mind if he asked Henry Louis Gates, Jr., Houston Baker, Jr., and Michael Cooke, the three men I had mentioned in my essay, to write a response. Although Cooke chose not to respond, Gates' and Baker's documents are now well-known documents of African American literary history. After mailing the response to me, Ralph Cohen telephoned to confirm their arrival and to get a sense of how I was feeling. Because my own response was not due until June and because it was March and I was still reading, re-reading, and absorbing aspects of contemporary theory, I had not yet opened his package because I did not want to be distracted from my work. In May, when I finally did read them, I then clearly understood Ralph Cohen's concern that they would surely prove a distraction.

What is important about Cohen's call is the fact that he cared enough to want to know how I felt about Baker's and Gates' sexist, classicist, misogynist attacks. Also important is the fact that Cohen, too, was quite surprised about the nature of Baker's and Gates' essays. Contrary to the belief of numerous Black and white scholars who have suggested that Cohen "set me up," the responses were not what he expected. If anything, Baker and Gates set themselves up. Their essays clearly expose their hatred of at least one Black woman (and maybe all of us) and their better-than-thou attitude; they were shocked that a Black woman, or anyone else, would dare challenge their ideas.

I would like to take advantage of the opportunity presented by this special issue of *Black Books Bulletin: Words Work* to clarify some old ideas and present new ones that have surfaced since the publication of my original essay, since the publication of

Gates' and Baker's essays and since my responses to them (all in the Winter 1987 issue of *New Literary History*). Rather than suspecting Cohen, Gates and Baker conspired against me, the African-American literary community, including those white scholars who work with us, owe Cohen a debt of thanks for starting a tremendously needed dialogue that lies at the very core of African-American literary history and intellectual survival.

Since the publication of "The Black Canon" and my response to Baker and Gates, I have written another essay which was published both in the Summer 1991 issue of *New Literary History* and in *(En)Gendering Knowledge: Feminists in Academe* (edited by Joan E. Hartman and Ellen Messer-Davidow, 1991). In this last essay, I attempted to address the issues of sexism and misogyny that I did not emphasize in "'Who the Cap Fit': Unconsciousness and Unconscionableness in the Criticism of Houston A. Baker, Jr. and Henry Louis Gates, Jr." Instead I focused more on literary issues than on these Black male critics' responses to me as a woman. The lack of a public Black (or white) female response to the Winter 1987 issue of *New Literary History* charged my desire to document the ideas found in "Black Woman Scholar, Critic, and Teacher: The Inextricable Relationship between Race, Sex, and Class" (*New Literary History*, Summer 1987, and *(En)Gendering Knowledge: Feminists in Academe*). What is most interesting is that not a single Black woman scholar has published a defense or a challenge to the issue I presented in these essays that address not only the ideas espoused by Gates and Baker (especially Gates), but also their clear sexism and the power they wield over everyone in the African-American literary community.

To date, the only scholars who have responded in print in any sustained fashion to the dialogue between Baker, Gates and myself have been three Black males—Houston Baker's protégé, Michael Awkward, who defended Baker's position; Kwame Anthony Appiah, Gates' protégé, who defended him; Theodore Mason, who straddles the fence so effectively that he failed to take the dialogue forward or backwards—and one white male scholar, Harold Fromm, who cites the irresponsible nature of Gates' and Baker's essays. While Appiah's essay was published in *Black American Literature Forum* in 1989, Awkward's, Mason's and Fromm's essays all appeared in 1988. Thus, except for my essay, "Black Woman, Scholar, and Teacher," which was published in 1991, there has been no attention given to this debate except for a casual mentioning of its existence and of its heated nature by a handful of Black and white scholars.

The silence of African American scholars exist for several reasons: (1) more Black books are being published today than ever before in American history, (2) there are more Blacks teaching in predominately white institutions than ever before (though the number is small compared to the hegemony); there are more Black critics of African-American literature than ever before; and, thus, we have more Black faculty in predominately white institutions making more than $50,000 a year than ever before. These Black critics of African-American literature, with Gates as their mentor, are making more money than Black scholars have ever made in the history of this country. This desire for financial stability and institutional acceptance manifests itself in the language of the critical analyses on most African-American literature. Following Gates' lead, most scholars of African-American literature have adopted the language and ideology of contemporary theory that devalues or dismisses the importance of race, estranging the literature from the very people and issues that lie at its heart. My purpose here is not to dwell on the inappropriateness of this language and much of its ideology (I have addressed this issue at length in other places and will continue to do so). My goal is to address issues that are usually deemed inappropriate in literary analyses, yet they are at the core of those analyses.

African-American critics' lack of any public response to Henry Louis Gates' and Houston Baker's power over their critical praxis and the volume of their honorariums is also accompanied by their practices of inclusion and exclusion. In April 1987, Houston Baker sponsored a three-day conference at the University of Pennsylvania where he, in his own words,

> brought together twenty-one Afro-Americanists to present and consider a series of theoretical and critical papers devoted to major genres and areas of Afro-American literature and criticism. The conference was called "The Study of Afro-American Literature: An Agenda for the 1990s," and its purpose was to allow Afro-American literary scholars to discuss the past and future of the field in a forum designed to encourage sustained critical dialogue.

The word in the African American community was that both the participants and the audience could attend the conference by invitation only. Therefore, this "sustained critical dialogue" could only be carried on by scholars sanctioned by Houston Baker as the "leading scholars of Afro-American literature." This act of exclusion should have sent a very clear and negative message to the African-American literary community. It should have made all of us question the elitist nature of his action, the audacity of his desire for control, and the consequences of that power for all scholars of African-American literature—those who attended the conference, those who did not, whites as well as Blacks. The most important issue, though, is Baker's diversion from the inclusive tradition of African-American history and literature. It is a tradition that engages dialogue, and it excludes no one. Even the proponents of the Black Aesthetic did not practice such exclusiveness. And their goals were certainly not elitist.

Just as scholars spoke only privately of the problems they had with Baker's elitism, they continue to speak only privately of Gates's increased power over their careers. Before the publication of my essay "The Black Canon," numerous Black scholars, male and female, frequently spoke to me about their problems with Baker and Gates. Since the publication of "The Black Canon," I have been increasingly excluded from not only private discussions of Baker and Gates, but also from participating on panels at scholarly conferences. Some feminist scholars even shared the fact that some of their ideas had been co-opted by male scholars and that they had reason to suspect that their scholarly ideas might be used by them. And what happened to Eleanor Traylor's concept for a Center for African-American Literature and Culture is now no secret in the African-American literary community. Yet, I find that some of my feminist sisters have formed a clique that on some level includes Baker and Gates and excludes anyone whose ideas challenge their narrow concepts of Black feminism and question the nature of the relationship between their critical praxes and contemporary theory.

In his essay "Race, Gender, and the Politics of Reading," where he addresses the dialogue between Gates, Baker and me, Michel Awkward refuses to accept that literature, as Richard Wright demonstrates in "The Literature of the Negro in the United States," emerges out of an environment. Using Phyllis Wheatley, Alexander Dumas, George Moses Horton, Waring Cuney, W. E. B. Du Bois and others, Wright demonstrates that the Black writer's relationship to his/her environment or the extent to which a writer feels apart from or connected to environment determines the writer's sensibility, perspective even creative vision. It is this historical relationship between the Black writer and his work that critics like Gates, Baker and Awkward attempt to undermine. Yet their criticism aside, their politics alone demonstrate the truth of Wright's ingenious insight. Michael Awkward's essay is not an act of deconstructive play or arbitrariness, nor is its placement in the *Black American Literature Forum* arbitrary. For Awkward received his dissertation from the University of Pennsylvania, with Houston Baker as his dissertation director. Baker also happens to be one of the two associate editors of *BALF*. Furthermore, Gates was the book review editor of the issue that carried Awkward's essay. Indeed literature, in this case, springs out of a particular environment, or to use words antithetical to poststructuralist readings, Awkward's essay is in fact determined by environment. Moreover, a relationship exists between the politics of the literature and the determined personal lives of some of its editors and/or contributors.

It is quite provocative and evocative that the cover for the Spring 1988 issue of *Black American Literature Forum*, the so-called leading African-American literary journal, depicts Sudanese artist Mohammad Khalil, his white wife and their two very light-skinned children (the girl's head is on her mother, the son's rests on his father). While on the other hand it is appropriate to assure it is fitting the editors feature a picture of the issue's leading interviewee on the cover, we must question why they chose to use a picture which highlights Khalil is a Black man married to a white woman. Whether the editors were manifesting what they believed to be a progressive consciousness or simply a lack of careful thought, the picture stimulates much cause for alarm. If the editors refuse to address the historical and much debated issue of the sexual relationship between Blacks and whites, this particular use of a picture that suggests an intimate relationship between a Black man and a white woman is gratuitous. Its use springs out of an environment in which a number of the leading intellectual male figures are married to white women.

I want it to be clear here that I am not, under any circumstances, saying that Blacks should not marry whites. While I do question whether firm love can exist between Blacks and whites nurtured in a racist society, I do not intend to dictate whom another person should or should not marry. My point is that Black people in the position to affect the lives of many Blacks and who thus speak or write about important Black issues from positions of authority must consider how their personal lives affect the way their ideas will be received.

Any Black person married to a white person compromises his/her ability to act and speak against the white establishment. For the Black person married to a white person is not trusted or taken seriously by either the Black or the white community. Most importantly, it is very difficult, perhaps impossible, to fight the enemy once having become intimate with him or her. Both James Baldwin and Malcolm X, to varying degrees, have made this same point. Therefore, an interrelationship exists between environment (or biography) and critical praxis of those Black scholars who espouse post-structuralist theory that dismisses the role of race in African-American literary criticism.

It follows that if race does not affect critical praxis, racism does not play a role in determining who we are as Black and white people. Just as I chose to marry a Black man, I also chose to follow the critical influences of a host of Black writers, male and female, who address the role of race in Black literature and life. Ten years ago when I was titillated by a very well-known white scholar, two well-known Black women writers fulfilled the roles Black women play in a Toni Morrison novel by explaining to me that my personal life must be aligned with my politics in order to serve my community effectively. Of course, it should be clear that much contemporary African-American literary criticism reflects authors who are not concerned with serving a community. They are rather about the business of making money off the community without giving anything back in return.

While Howard University is the only predominately Black university in the United States that is a major research institution, it still has lost most of the renowned Black scholars once on its English faculty. Since Black schools cannot afford to recruit the most productive Black scholars, most well-established Black scholars do not concern themselves with the plight of these institutions. For these schools cannot afford to participate in the game of hiring the country's leading Black intellectuals. Henry Louis Gates, Jr. is the leading player in the game of hiring himself out to white institutions at a higher than market price. Not only has he moved from Yale to Cornell to Duke to Harvard, but he has also been able to take his protégé, Anthony Appiah, all along the way. Interestingly enough, Anthony Appiah and Manthia Diawara, who worked with Baker at the University of Pennsylvania, are two of the editors of *Callaloo*, the journal that carries Theodore Mason's essay mentioned above. Again, literature and institutional stability spring out of environment.

Why, in the 1980s and 1990s, does white America need a Black intellectual like Henry Louis Gates, Jr.? Gates' white appointed leadership served the racist Reagan and Bush administrations well. His critical praxis, social and political commentary that continue to appear in Black and white media substantiated the idea that race was no longer a problem in this country. Although his function is similar to Booker T. Washington's, the influence that Gates has on American race relations is far more destructive than Washington's. First of all, Gates does not have a figure to challenge him with the same force with which Du Bois challenged Washington. Secondly, and perhaps more importantly, Gates clearly does not maintain Black humility publicly or Black strength privately as historians have suggested Washington did. Gates has no private voice. He presents us with no ambiguities or ambivalences. His is the Black voice that commands a privately owned jet to fly him to Germany to speak at the premiere of Spike Lee's movie *Malcolm X*. We do not have to be told that the Black American intellectual community has a host of film critics far more knowledgeable of film than Gates. We also do not have to be told that Gates and Booker T. Washington do not frighten or threaten white people the way W. E. B. Du Bois did. While Washington bowed to the white ideology of Black intellectual inferiority, Gates, through his critical praxis, does not just downplay the role of race in literary criticism, he totally dismisses it. Therefore, his failure to engage in racial issues is soothing, non-threatening to whites. He forms a kind of camaraderie with them and unquestioningly sanctions their inclusion into the African-American literary dialogue. It is ironic that Gates represents the failure of Du Bois' talented tenth idea. Du Bois and others like him, such as Frances Ellen Watkins Harper, hoped that the talented tenth, those Blacks who were capable of pursuing the highest levels of education and could compete with whites on the highest intellectual levels, would work to improve the quality of the lives of their not-so-fortunate brothers and sisters.

A recent *Donahue* show demonstrated the need for more Black intellectuals (and white ones like Morris Dees and Andrew Hacker) to focus their attention on unearthing the now deeply buried root of racism. Derrick Bell and Morris Dees discussed their views on racism as espoused in their respective books with Donahue and the audience. The audience, as Donahue himself pointed out, was at least ninety percent white. Most of the whites who spoke in the audience were under thirty years of age, and nearly all believed that racism was not as much of a problem as Bell and Dees were proposing. They offered the fact that they welcomed social relationships with Blacks as "proof" of Dees' and Bell's exaggerations. Having experienced on a mass scale this same kind of willful ignorance (rather than innocence) while I was teaching in Nebraska, I immediately thought of my students and colleagues there and their fear of confronting the racism that lies within them. Bell responded to their comments by pointing out that it is this attitude of whites that is responsible for his belief that racism is permanent in America. What struck me so solidly was the fact that we Black scholars are now writing in a critical time in which Black intellectuals are bypassing the opportunity to change America in the way a Black social force changed America in the 1960s. The problem is no longer limited to white society; many Black intellectuals have accepted the same attitude toward Blackness and racism as the white mainstream.

Ironically, the young whites' belief that racism is not a problem directly undercuts Gates' theoretical notion that race is not important in discussing African-American literature. For just as Black literature grows out of an environment in which Blacks in this country have always experienced oppression, these young whites have lived free from oppression and, thus, from the reality of what it means to be white in America. The degree to which they deny their complicity in racist thinking and actions parallels not only the depths of their commodification of Gates but also the lack of progress in changing the statistics of Black infant mortality rates, Black males in prisons, single female headed households, Black-on-Black crimes, Black deaths from AIDS, cancer and heart attacks, Black miseducation, Black homelessness and Black unemployment.

Grassroots Black workers in the streets of the African-American community need their Black intellectuals. They need for us to stop titillating ourselves with white intellectual games and to understand that it is our responsibility to put each other in check, to pull each other's coat, to be honest with each other. We must understand what happens to a Black psyche when it has been educated in predominately white schools and when it is accustomed to being the only or one of a few Black scholars in a white environment. We must understand simply that we are not so very different from Pavlov's dogs. The reward of exclusiveness estranges us from our origins and our community. We must work toward a time when other Black scholars can write an essay like this one and not be scorned by their contemporaries who are the subjects, implied subjects or who feels because of their guilt that they are the subject. If we are going to change the quality of our lives, we must be active in challenging and keeping in check all those Black voices that compromise our dignity and self-respect. We cannot afford to leave these voices undisputed. We must engage in hard, painful self-criticism and not worry about washing our dirty laundry in front of whites. Such an attitude is merely a smoke screen that stifles growth.

NOTE

For a look at the essays mentioned above, see the following: Kwame Anthony Appiah, "The Conservation of 'Race.' " *Black American Literature* Forum 23, no. 1 (Spring 1989): 37–60; Michael Awkward, "Race, Gender, and the Politics of Reading." *Black American Literature Forum* 22, no. 1 (Spring 1988): 5–27; Houston A. Baker, Jr., "In Dubious Battle." *New Literary History* 18, no. 2 (Winter 1987): 363–369; Henry Louis Gates, "What's Love Got to Do with It." *New Literary History* 18. no. 2 (Winter 1987); 354–362; Harold Fromm, "Real Life, Literary Criticism, and the Perils of Bourgeoisification." *New Literary History* 20, no. 1 (Autumn 1988): 49–64; Joyce A. Joyce, "The Black Canon; Reconstructing African American Literary Criticism" and " 'Who the Cap Fit': Unconsciousness and Unconscionableness in the Criticism of Houston A. Baker, Jr. and Henry Louis Gates, Jr." *New Literary History*, 18, no. 2 (Winter 1987): 335–344 and 371–383 respectively; Joyce A. Joyce, "Black Woman Scholar, Critic, and Teacher: The Inextricable Relationship between Race, Sex, and Class." *New Literary History* 22, no. 3 (Summer 1991): 543–565; and Theodore Mason, "Between the Populist and the Scientist Ideology and Power in Recent Afro-American Literary Criticism or, 'The Dozens' as Scholarship." *Callaloo* 11, no. 3 (Summer 1988): 606–615.

40 Black (W)holes and the Geometry of Black Female Sexuality

Evelynn Hammonds

(1994)

> The female body in the West is not a unitary sign. Rather, like a coin, it has an obverse and a reverse: on the one side, it is white; on the other, not-white or, prototypically, black. The two bodies cannot be separated, nor can one body be understood in isolation from the other in the West's metaphoric construction of "woman." White is what woman is; not-white (and the stereotypes not-white gathers in) is what she had better not be. Even in an allegedly postmodern era, the not-white woman as well as the not-white man are symbolically and even theoretically excluded from sexual difference. Their function continues to be to cast the difference of white men and white women into sharper relief.
>
> —O'Grady (14)

When asked to write for the second special issue of *differences* on queer theory I must admit I was at first hesitant even to entertain the idea. Though much of what is now called queer theory I find engaging and intellectually stimulating, I still found the idea of writing about it disturbing. When I am asked if I am queer I usually answer yes even though the ways in which I am queer have never been articulated in the body of work that is now called queer theory. Where should I begin, I asked myself? Do I have to start by adding another adjective to my already long list of self-chosen identities? I used to be a black lesbian, feminist, writer, scientist, historian of science, and activist. Now would I be a black, queer, feminist, writer, scientist, historian of science, and activist? Given the rapidity with which new appellations are created I wondered if my new list would still be up to date by the time the article came out. More importantly, does this change or any change I might make to my list convey to anyone the ways in which I am queer?

Even a cursory reading of the first issue of *differences* on queer theory or a close reading of *The Lesbian and Gay Studies Reader* (Abelove, Barale, and Halperin)—

by now biblical in status—would lead me to answer no. So what would be the point of my writing for a second issue on queer theory? Well, I could perform that by now familiar act taken by black feminists and offer a critique of every white feminist for her failure to articulate a conception of a racialized sexuality. I could argue that while it has been acknowledged that race is not simply additive to or derivative of sexual difference, few white feminists have attempted to move beyond simply stating this point to describe the powerful effect that race has on the construction and representation of gender and sexuality. I could go further and note that even when race is mentioned it is a limited notion devoid of complexities. Sometimes it is reduced to biology and other times referred to as a social construction. Rarely is it used as a "global sign," a "metalanguage," as the "ultimate trope of difference, arbitrarily contrived to produce and maintain relations of power and subordination" (Higginbotham 255).

If I were to make this argument, I wonder under what subheading such an article would appear in *The Lesbian and Gay Studies Reader?* Assuming, of course, that they would want to include it in the second edition. How about "Politics and Sex"? Well, it would certainly be political but what would anybody learn about sex from it? As I look at my choices I see that I would want my article to appear in the section, "Subjectivity, Discipline, Resistance." But where would I situate myself in the group of essays that discuss "lesbian experience," "lesbian identity," "gender insubordination," and "Butch-Femme Aesthetic"? Perhaps they wouldn't want a reprint after all and I'd be off the hook. Maybe I've just hit one of those "constructed silences" that Teresa de Lauretis wrote about as one of the problems in lesbian and gay studies ("Queer" viii).

When *The Lesbian and Gay Studies Reader* was published, I followed my usual practice and searched for the articles on black women's sexuality. This reading practice has become such a commonplace in my life I have forgotten how and when I began it. I never open a book about lesbians or gays with the expectation that I will find some essay that will address the concerns of my life. Given that on the average most collections don't include writers of color, just the appearance of essays by African-Americans, Latinos, and Native Americans in this volume was welcome. The work of Barbara Smith, Stuart Hall, Phillip Brian Harper, Gloria Hall, Deborah McDowell, and, of course, Audre Lorde has deeply influenced my intellectual and political work for many years as has the work of many of the other writers in this volume.

Yet, despite the presence of these writers, this text displays the consistently exclusionary practices of lesbian and gay studies in general. In my reading, the canonical terms and categories of the field: "lesbian," "gay," "butch," "femme," "sexuality," and "subjectivity" are stripped of context in the works of those theorizing about these very categories, identities, and subject positions. Each of these terms is defined with white as the normative state of existence. This is an obvious criticism which many have expressed since the appearance of this volume. More interesting is the question of whether the essays engaging with the canonical terms have been in any way informed by the work of the writers of color that do appear in the volume. The essays by Hull and McDowell both address the point I am trying to make. Hull describes the life of Angelina Weld Grimké, a poet of the Harlem Renaissance whose poetry expressed desire for women. This desire is circumscribed, underwritten, and unspoken in her poetry. McDowell's critical reading of Nella Larsen's *Passing* also points to the submersion of sexuality and same-sex desire among black women. In addition, Harper's essay on the death of Max Robinson, one of the most visible African-Americans of his generation, foregrounds the silence in black communities on the issue of sexuality and AIDS. "Silence" is emphasized as well in the essay by Ana Maria Alonso and Maria Teresa Koreck on the AIDS crisis in "Hispanic" communities. But the issue of silence about so-called deviant sexuality in public discourse and its submersion in private spaces for people of color is never addressed in theorizing about the canonical categories of lesbian and gay studies in the reader. More important, public discourse on the sexuality of particular racial and ethnic groups is shaped by processes that pathologize those groups, which in turn produce the submersion of sexuality and the attendant silence(s). Lesbian and gay theory fails to acknowledge that these very processes are connected to the construction of the sexualities of whites, historically and contemporaneously.

QUEER WORDS AND QUEER PRACTICES

I am not by nature an optimist, although I do believe that change is possible and necessary. Does a shift from lesbian to queer relieve my sense of anxiety over whether the exclusionary practices of lesbian and gay studies can be resolved? If queer theory is, as de Lauretis notes in her introduction to the first special issue of differences, the place where "we [would] be willing to examine, make explicit, compare, or confront the respective histories, assumptions, and conceptual frameworks that have characterized the self-representations of North American lesbians and gay men, of color and white," and if it is "from there, [that] we could then go on to recast or reinvent the terms of our sexualities, to construct another discursive horizon, another way of thinking the sexual," then maybe I had found a place to explore the ways in which queer, black, and female subjectivities are produced (iv–v). Of course, I first had to gather more evidence about this shift before I jumped into the fray.

In her genealogy of queer theory, de Lauretis argues that the term was arrived at in the effort to avoid all the distinctions in the discursive protocols that emerged from the standard usage of the terms *lesbian* and *gay*. The kind of distinctions she notes include the need to add qualifiers of race or national affiliation to the labels, "lesbian" and "gay." De Lauretis goes on to address my central concern. She writes:

> The fact of the matter is, most of us, lesbians and gay men, do not know much about one another's sexual history, experiences, fantasies, desire, or modes of theorizing. And we do not know enough about ourselves, as well, when it comes to differences between and within lesbians, and between and within gay men, in relation to race and its attendant differences of class or ethnic culture, generational, geographical, and

socio-political location. *We do not know enough to theorize those differences.* (viii; emphasis added)

She continues:

> Thus an equally troubling question in the burgeoning field of "gay and lesbian studies" concerns the discursive constructions and constructed silences around the relations of race to identity and subjectivity in the practices of homosexualities and the representations of same sex desire. (viii)

In my reading of her essay, de Lauretis then goes on to attribute the problem of the lack of knowledge of the experiences of gays and lesbians of color to gays and lesbians of color. While noting the problems of their restricted access to publishing venues or academic positions, she concludes that "perhaps, to a gay writer and critic of color, defining himself gay is not of the utmost importance; he may have other more pressing priorities in his work and life" (ix). This is a woefully inadequate characterization of the problem of the visibility of gays and lesbians of color. Certainly institutional racism, homophobia, and the general structural inequalities in American society have a great deal more to do with this invisibility than personal choices. I have reported de Lauretis's words at length because her work is symptomatic of the disjuncture I see between the stated goals of the volume she edited and what it actually enacts.

Despite the presence of writers of writer of color, the authors of the essays in the *differences* volume avoid interrogating their own practices with respect to the issue of difference. That is to say to differences of race, ethnicity, and representation in analyzing subjectivity, desire, and the use of the psychoanalytic in gay and lesbian theory. Only Ekua Omosupe explicitly addresses the issue of black female subjectivity, and her essay foregrounds the very issue that queer theory ostensibly is committed to addressing. Omosupe still sees the need to announce her skepticism at the use of the term *lesbian* without the qualifier "black" and addresses the lack of attention to race in gay and lesbian studies in her analysis of Adrienne Rich's work (108). For her, the term "lesbian" without the racial qualifier is simply to be read as "white" lesbian. Despite her criticism, however, she too avoids confronting difference within the category of black lesbian, speaking of "the" black lesbian without attention to or acknowledgment of a multiplicity of identities or subject positions for black women. She notes that the title of Audre Lorde's collected essays is *Sister Outsider*, which she argues is "an apt metaphor for the Black lesbian's position in relation to the white dominant political cultures and to her own Black community as well" (106). But metaphors reveal as much as they conceal and Omosupe cannot tell us what kind of outsider Lorde is, that is to say what sexual practices, discourses, and subject positions within her black community she was rebelling against. As with the Hull and McDowell essays, Omosupe's article acknowledges silence, erasure, and invisibility as crucial issues in the dominant discourses about black female sexuality, while the essay and the volume as a whole continue to enact this silence.

Thus, queer theory as reflected in this volume has so far failed to theorize the very questions de Lauretis announces that the term "queer" will address. I disagree with her assertion that we do not know enough about one another's differences to theorize differences between and within gays and lesbians in relation to race. This kind of theorizing of difference, after all, isn't simply a matter of empirical examples. And we do know enough to delineate what queer theorists should want to know. For me it is a question of knowing specifically about the production of black female queer sexualities: if the sexualities of black women have been shaped by silence, erasure, and invisibility in dominant discourses, then are black lesbian sexualities doubly silenced? What methodologies are available to read and understand this perceived void and gauge its direct and indirect effects on that which is visible? Conversely, how does the structure of what is visible, namely white female sexualities, shape those not-absent-though-not-present black female sexualities which, as O'Grady argues, cannot be separated or understood in isolation from one another? And, finally, how do these racialized sexualities shaped by silence, erasure, and invisibility coexist with other sexualities, the closeted sexualities of white queers, for example? It seems to me that there are two projects here that need to be worked out. White feminists must refigure (white) female sexualities so that they are not theoretically dependent upon an absent yet-ever-present pathologized black female sexuality. I am not arguing that this figuration of (white) female sexuality must try to encompass completely the experiences of black women, but that it must include a conception of the power relations between white and black women as expressed in the representations of sexuality (Higginbotham 252).[1] This model of power, as Judith Butler has argued, must avoid setting up "racism and homophobia and misogyny as parallel or analogical relations," while recognizing that "what has to be thought through, is the ways in which these vectors of power require and deploy each other for the purpose of their own articulation" (18). Black feminist theorists must reclaim sexuality through the creation of a counternarrative that can reconstitute a present black female subjectivity and that includes an analysis of power relations between white and black women and among different groups of black women. In both cases I am arguing for the development of a complex, relational but not necessarily analogous, conception of racialized sexualities (JanMohamed 94). In order to describe more fully what I see as the project for black feminist theorists, I want to turn now to a review of some of the current discussions of black women's sexuality.

THE PROBLEMATIC OF SILENCE

> To name ourselves rather than be named we must first see ourselves. For some of us this will not be easy. So long unmirrored, we may have forgotten how we look. Nevertheless, we can't theorize in a void; we must have evidence.
>
> —O'GRADY (14)

Black feminist theorists have almost universally described black women's sexuality, when viewed from the vantage of the dominant discourses, as an absence. In one of the earliest and most compelling discussions of black women's sexuality, the literary critic Hortense Spillers wrote: "black women are the beached whales of the sexual universe, unvoiced, misseen, not doing, awaiting their verb" ("Interstices" 74). For writer Toni Morrison, black women's sexuality is one of the "unspeakable things unspoken," of the African-American experience. Black women's sexuality is often described in metaphors of speechlessness, space, or vision, as a "void" or empty space that is simultaneously ever visible (exposed) and invisible and where black women's bodies are always already colonized. In addition, this always already colonized black female body has so much sexual potential that it has none at all ("Interstices" 85). Historically, black women have reacted to this repressive force of the hegemonic discourses on race and sex with silence, secrecy, and a partially self-chosen invisibility.

Black feminist theorists, historians, literary critics, sociologists, lawyers, and cultural critics have drawn upon a specific historical narrative which purportedly describes the factors that have produced and maintained perceptions of black women's sexuality (including their own). Three themes emerge in this history: first, the construction of the black female as the embodiment of sex and the attendant invisibility of black women as the unvoiced, unseen everything that is not white; second, the resistance of black women both to negative stereotypes of their sexuality and to the material effects of those stereotypes on their lives; and finally, the evolution of a "culture of dissemblance" and a "politics of silence" by black women on the issue of their sexuality. The historical narrative begins with the production of the image of a pathologized black female "other" in the eighteenth century by European colonial elites and the new biological scientists. By the nineteenth century, with the increasing exploitation and abuse of black women during and after slavery, U.S. black women reformers began to develop strategies to counter negative stereotypes of their sexuality and their use as a justification for the rape, lynching, and other abuses of black women by whites. Although some of the strategies used by black women reformers might have initially been characterized as resistance to dominant and increasingly hegemonic constructions of their sexuality, by the early twentieth century black women reformers promoted a public silence about sexuality which, it could be argued, continues to the present.[2] This "politics of silence," as described by historian Evelyn Brooks Higginbotham, emerged as a political strategy by black women reformers who hoped by their silence and by the promotion of proper Victorian morality to demonstrate the lie of the image of the sexually immoral black woman (262). Historian Darlene Clark Hine argues that the "culture of dissemblance" that this politics engendered was seen as a way for black women to "protect the sanctity of inner aspects of their lives" (915). She defines this culture as "the behavior and attitudes of Black women that created the appearance of openness and disclosure but actually shielded the truth of their inner lives and selves from their oppressors" (915). "Only with secrecy," Hine argues, "thus achieving a self-imposed invisibility, could ordinary Black women accrue the psychic space and harness the resources needed to hold their own" (915). And by the projection of the image of a "super-moral" black woman, they hoped to garner greater respect, justice, and opportunity for all black Americans (915). Of course, as Higginbotham notes, there were problems with this strategy. First, it did not achieve its goal of ending the negative stereotyping of black women. And second, some middle-class black women engaged in policing the behavior of poor and working-class women and any who deviated from a Victorian norm in the name of protecting the "race."[3] My interpretation of the conservatizing and policing aspect of the "politics of silence" is that black women reformers were responding to the ways in which any black women could find herself "exposed" and characterized in racist sexual terms no matter what the truth of her individual life, and that they saw this so-called deviant individual behavior as a threat to the race as a whole. Finally, one of the most enduring and problematic aspects of the "politics of silence" is that in choosing silence black women also lost the ability to articulate any conception of their sexuality.

Without more detailed historical studies we will not know the extent of this "culture of dissemblance," and many questions will remain to be answered.[4] Was it expressed differently in rural and in urban areas; in the north, west, or south? How was it maintained? Where and how was it resisted? How was it shaped by class? And, furthermore, how did it change over time? How did something that was initially adopted as a political strategy in a specific historical period become so ingrained in black life as to be recognizable as a culture? Or did it? What emerges from the very incomplete history we have is a situation in which black women's sexuality is ideologically located in a nexus between race and gender, where the black female subject is not seen and has no voice. Methodologically, black feminists have found it difficult even to fully characterize this juncture, this point of erasure where African-American women are located. As legal scholar Kimberlé Crenshaw puts it, "Existing within the overlapping margins of race and gender discourse and the empty spaces between, it is a location whose very nature resists telling" (403). And this silence about sexuality is enacted individually and collectively by black women and by black feminist theorists writing about black women.

It should not surprise us that black women are silent about sexuality. The imposed production of silence and the removal of any alternative to the production of silence reflect the deployment of power against racialized subjects, "wherein those who could speak did not want to and those who did want to speak were prevented from doing so" (JanMohamed 105). It is this deployment of power at the level of the social and the individual which has to be historicized. It seems clear that we need a methodology that allows us to contest rather than reproduce the ideological system that has up to now defined the terrain of black women's sexuality. Spillers made this point over a decade ago when she wrote: "Because black American women do not participate, as a category of social and cultural agents, in the legacies of symbolic power, they maintain no allegiances to a strategic formation of texts, or ways of talking about sexual experience, that even remotely resemble the paradigm of symbolic domination, except that such a paradigm has been their concrete disaster" ("Interstices" 80). To date, through the work of black feminist literary critics, we know more about the elision of sexuality by black women than we do about the possible varieties of expression of sexual desire.[5] Thus what we have is a very narrow view of black women's sexuality. Certainly it is true, as Crenshaw notes, that "in feminist contexts, sexuality represents a central site of the oppression of women; rape and the rape trial are its dominant narrative trope. In antiracist discourse, sexuality is also a central site upon which the repression of blacks has been premised; the lynching narrative is embodied as its trope" (405). Sexuality is also, as Carol Vance defines it, "simultaneously a domain of restriction, repression, and danger as well as a domain of exploration, pleasure, and agency" (1). The restrictive, repressive, and dangerous aspects of black female sexuality have been emphasized by black feminist writers while pleasure, exploration, and agency have gone under-analyzed.

I want to suggest that black feminist theorists have not taken up this project in part because of their own status in the academy. Reclaiming the body as well as subjectivity is a process that black feminist theorists in the academy must go through themselves while they are doing the work of producing theory. Black feminist theorists are themselves engaged in a process of fighting to reclaim the body—the maimed immoral black female body—which can be and still is used by others to discredit them as producers of knowledge and as speaking subjects. Legal scholar Patricia Williams illuminates my point: "no matter what degree of professional I am, people will greet and dismiss my black femaleness as unreliable, untrustworthy, hostile, angry, powerless, irrational, and probably destitute" (95). When reading student evaluations, she finds comments about her teaching and her body: "I marvel, in a moment of genuine bitterness, that anonymous student evaluations speculating on dimensions of my anatomy are nevertheless counted into the statistical measurement of my teaching proficiency" (95). The hypervisibility of black women academics and the contemporary fascination with what bell hooks calls the "commodification of Otherness" (61) means that black women today find themselves precariously perched in the academy. Ann duCille notes:

> Mass culture, as hooks argues, produces, promotes, and perpetuates the commodifcation of Otherness through the exploitation of the black female body. In the 1990s, however, the principal sites of exploitation are not simply the cabaret, the speakeasy, the music video, the glamour magazine; they are also the academy, the publishing industry, the intellectual community. (592)

In tandem with the notion of silence, black women writers have repeatedly drawn on the notion of the "invisible" to describe aspects of black women's lives in general and sexuality in particular. Lorde writes that "within this country where racial difference creates a constant, if unspoken distortion of vision, Black women have on the one hand always been highly visible, and on the other hand, have been rendered invisible through the depersonalization of racism" (91). The hypervisibility of black women academics means that visibility too can be used to control the intellectual issues that black women can and cannot speak about. Already threatened with being sexualized and rendered inauthentic as knowledge producers in the academy by students and colleagues alike, this avoidance of theorizing about sexuality can be read as one contemporary manifestation of their structured silence. I want to stress here that the silence about sexuality on the part of black women academics is no more a "choice" than was the silence practiced by early twentieth-century black women. This production of silence instead of speech is an effect of the institutions such as the academy which are engaged in the commodification of Otherness. While hypervisibility can be used to silence black women academics it can also serve them. Lorde has argued that the "visibility which makes us most vulnerable," that of being black, "is that which is the source of our greatest strength." Patricia Hill Collins's interpretation of Lorde's comment is that "paradoxically, being treated as an invisible Other gives black women a peculiar angle of vision, the outsider-within stance that has served so many African-American women intellectuals as a source of tremendous strength" (*Sister Outsider*, 94).

Yet, while invisibility may be somewhat useful for academicians, the practice of a politics of silence belies the power of such a stance for social change. Most important, the outsider-within stance does not allow space for addressing the question of other outsiders, namely black lesbians. Black feminist theorizing about black female sexuality, with a few exceptions—Cheryl Clarke, Jewelle Gomez, Barbara Smith, and Audre Lorde—has been relentlessly focused on heterosexuality. The historical narrative that dominates discussion of black female sexuality does not address even the possibility of a black lesbian sexuality, or of a lesbian or queer subject. Spillers confirms this point when she notes that "the sexual realities of black American women across the spectrum of sexual preference and widened sexual styles tend to be a missing dialectical feature of the entire discussion" ("Interstices" 91).

At this juncture, then, I cannot cast blame for a lack of attention to black lesbian sexuality solely on white feminist theorists. De Lauretis argues that female homosexualities may be conceptualized as social and cultural forms in their own right, which are undercoded or discursively dependent upon more established forms. They (and male homosexualities) therefore act as "an agency of social process whose mode of functioning is both interactive and yet resistant, both participatory and yet distinct, claiming at once equality and difference, and demanding political and historical representation while insisting on its material and historical specificity" ("Queer" iii). If this is true, then theorizing about black lesbian sexuality is crucially dependent upon the existence of a conception of black women's sexuality in general. I am not arguing that black lesbian sexualities are derivative of black female heterosexualities, but only that we cannot understand the latter without understanding it in relation to the former. In particular, since discussions of black female sexuality often turn to the issue of the devastating effects of rape, incest, and sexual abuse, I want to argue that black queer female sexualities should be seen as one of the sites where black female desire is expressed.

Discussions of black lesbian sexuality have most often focused on differences from or equivalencies with white lesbian sexualities, with "black" added to delimit the fact that black lesbians share a history with other black women. However, this addition tends to obfuscate rather than illuminate the subject position of black lesbians. One obvious example of distortion is that black lesbians do not experience homophobia in the same way as do white lesbians. Here, as with other oppressions, the homophobia experienced by black women is always shaped by racism. What has to be explored and historicized is the specificity of black lesbian experience. I want to understand in what way black lesbians are "outsiders" within black communities. This, I think, would force us to examine the construction of the "closet" by black lesbians. Although this is the topic for another essay, I want to argue here that if we accept the existence of the "politics of silence" as an historical legacy shared by all black women, then certain expressions of black female sexuality will be rendered as dangerous, for individuals and for the collectivity. From this it follows then that the culture of dissemblance makes it acceptable for some heterosexual black women to cast black lesbians as proverbial traitors to the race.[6] And this in turn explains why black lesbians who would announce or act out desire for women—whose deviant sexuality exists within an already pre-existing deviant sexuality—have been wary of embracing the status of "traitor" and the attendant loss of community such an embrace engenders.[7] Of course, while some black lesbians have hidden the truth of their lives, there have been many forms of resistance to the conception of lesbian as traitor within black communities. Audre Lorde is one obvious example. Lorde's claiming of her black and lesbian difference "forced both her white and Black lesbian friends to contend with her historical agency in the face of [this] larger racial/sexual history that would reinvent her as dead" (Karla Scott, qtd. in de Lauretis, *Practice* 36). I would also argue that Lorde's writing, with its focus on the erotic, on passion and desire, suggests that black lesbian sexualities can be read as one expression of the reclamation of the despised black female body. Therefore, the works of Lorde and other black lesbian writers, because they foreground the very aspects of black female sexuality which are submerged—that is, female desire and agency—are critical to our theorizing of black female sexualities. Since silence about sexuality is being produced by black women and black feminist theorists, that silence itself suggests that black women do have some degree of agency. A focus on black lesbian sexualities, I suggest, implies that another discourse—other than silence—can be produced.

I also suggest that the project of theorizing black female sexualities must confront psychoanalysis. Given that the Freudian paradigm is the dominant discourse which defines how sexuality is understood in this post-modern time, black feminist theorists have to answer the question posed by Michele Wallace: "is the Freudian drama transformed by race in a way that would render it altered but usable?" (*Invisibility* 231). While some black feminists have called the psychoanalytic approach racist, others such as Spillers, Mae Henderson, and Valerie Smith have shown its usefulness in analyzing the texts of black women writers. As I am not a student of psychoanalytic theory, my suggested response to Wallace's question can only be tentative at best. Though I do not accept all aspects of the Freudian paradigm, I do see the need for exploring its strengths and limitations in developing a theory of black female sexualities.

It can readily be acknowledged that the collective history of black women has in some ways put them in a different relationship to the canonical categories of the Freudian paradigm, that is, to the father, the maternal body, to the female-sexed body (Spillers, "Mama's"). On the level of the symbolic, however, black women have created whole worlds of sexual signs and signifiers, some of which align with those of whites and some of which do not. Nonetheless, they are worlds which always have to contend with the power that the white world has to invade, pathologize, and disrupt those worlds. In many ways the Freudian paradigm implicitly depends on the presence of the black female other. One of its more problematic aspects is that in doing so it relegates black women's sexuality to the irreducibly abnormal category in which there are no distinctions between homosexual and heterosexual women. By virtue of this lack of distinction, there is a need for black women, both lesbian and heterosexual, to, as de Lauretis describes it, "reconstitute a female-sexed body as a body for the subject and for her desire" (*Practice* 200). This is a need that is perhaps expressed differently by black women than by white women, whose sexualities have not been subjected to the same forces of repression and domination. And this seems to me to be a critical place where the work of articulating black female sexualities must begin. Disavowing the designation of black female sexualities as inherently abnormal, while acknowledging the material and symbolic effects of the appellation, we could begin the project of understanding how differently located black women engage in reclaiming the body and expressing desire.

What I want to propose requires me to don one of my other hats, that of a student of physics. As I struggled with the ideas I cover in this essay, over and over again I found myself wrestling with the juxtaposed images of "white" (read normal) and "black" (read not white and abnormal) sexuality. In her essay, "Variations on Negation," Michele Wallace invokes the idea of the black hole as a trope that can be used to describe the invisibility of black creativity in general and black female creativity specifically (*Invisibility* 218). As a former physics student, I was immediately drawn to this image. Yet it also troubled me.[8] As Wallace rightfully notes, the observer outside of the hole sees it as a void, an empty place in space. However, it is not empty; it is a dense and full place in space. There seemed to me to be two problems: one, the astrophysics of black holes, i.e. how do you deduce the presence of a black hole? And second, what is it like inside of a black hole? I don't want to stretch this analogy too far so here are my responses. To the first question, I suggest that we can detect the presence of a black hole by its effects on the region of space where it is located. One way that physicists do this is by observing binary star systems. A binary star system is one that contains two bodies which orbit around each other under mutual gravitational attraction. Typically, in these systems one finds a visible apparently "normal" star in close orbit with another body such as a black hole, which is not seen optically. The existence of the black hole is inferred from the fact that the visible star is in orbit and its shape is distorted in some way or it is detected by the energy emanating from the region in space around the visible star that could not be produced by the visible star alone.[9] Therefore, the identification of a black hole requires the use of sensitive detectors of energy and distortion. In the case of black female sexualities, this implies that we need to develop reading strategies that allow us to make visible the distorting and productive effects these sexualities produce in relation to more visible sexualities. To the second question—what is it like inside of a black hole?—the answer is that we must think in terms of a different geometry. Rather than assuming that black female sexualities are structured along an axis of normal and perverse paralleling that of white women, we might find that for black women a different geometry operates. For example, acknowledging this difference I could read the relationship between Shug and Celie in Alice Walker's *The Color Purple* as one which depicts desire between women and men simultaneously, in dynamic relationship rather than in opposition. This mapping of the geometry of black female sexualities will perhaps require black feminist theorists to engage the Freudian paradigm more rigorously, or it may cause us to disrupt it.

CAN I GET HOME FROM HERE?

> I see my lesbian poetics as a way of entering into a dialogue—from the margins— with Black feminist critics, theorists and writers. My work has been to imagine an historical Black woman-to-woman eroticism and living—overt, discrete, coded, or latent as it might be. To imagine Black women's sexuality as a polymorphous erotic that does not exclude desire for men but also does not privilege it. To imagine, without apology, voluptuous Black women's sexualities.   —CLARKE (224)

So where has my search taken me? And why does the journey matter? I want to give a partial answer to the question I posed at the beginning of this essay. At this juncture queer theory has allowed me to break open the category of gay and lesbian and begin to question how sexualities and sexual subjects are produced by dominant discourses and then to interrogate the reactions and resistances to those discourses. However, interrogating sites of resistance and reaction did not take me beyond what is generally done in gay and lesbian studies. The turn to queer should allow me to explore, in Clarke's words, the "overt, discrete, coded, or latent" and "polymorphous" eroticism of differently located black women. It is still not clear to me, however, that other queer theorists will resist the urge to engage in a re-ranking, erasure, or appropriation of sexual subjects who are at the margins of dominant discourses.

Why does my search for black women's sexuality matter? Wallace once wrote that she feared being called elitist when she acted as though cultural criticism was as crucial to the condition of black women as health, the law, politics, economics, and the family. "But," she continued, "I am convinced that the major battle for the 'other' of the 'other' [Black women] will be to find voice, transforming the construction of dominant discourse in the process" (*Invisibility* 236). It is my belief that what is desperately needed is more rigorous cultural criticism detailing how power is deployed through issues like sexuality and the alternative forms that even an oppressed subject's power can take. Since 1987, a major part of my intellectual work as an historian of U.S. science and medicine has addressed the AIDS crisis in African-American communities. The AIDS epidemic is being used, as Simon Watney has said, to "inflect, condense and rearticulate the ideological meanings of race, sexuality, gender, childhood, privacy, morality and nationalism" (ix). The position of black women in this epidemic was dire from the beginning and worsens with each passing day. Silence, erasure, and the use of images of immoral sexuality abound in narratives about the experiences of black women with AIDS. Their voices are not heard in discussions of AIDS, while intimate details of their lives are exposed to justify their victimization. In the "war of representation" that is being waged through this epidemic, black women are victims that are once again the "other" of the "other," the deviants of the deviants, regardless of their sexual identities or practices. While white gay male activists are using the ideological space framed by this epidemic to contest the notion that homosexuality is "abnormal" and to preserve the right to live out their homosexual desires, black women are rendered silent. The gains made by queer activists will do nothing for black women if the stigma continues to be attached to their sexuality. The work of black feminist critics is to find ways to contest the historical construction of black female sexualities by illuminating how the dominant view was established and maintained and how it can be disrupted. This work might very well save some black women's lives. I want this epidemic to be used to foment the sexual revolution that black Americans never had (Giddings 462). I want it to be used to make visible black women's self-defined sexualities.

Visibility in and of itself, however, is not my only goal. Several writers, including bell hooks, have argued that one answer to the silence now being produced on the issue of black female sexuality is for black women to see themselves, to mirror themselves (61). The appeal to the visual and the visible is deployed as an answer to the legacy of silence and repression. As theorists, we have to ask what we assume such reflections would show. Would the mirror black women hold up to themselves and to each other provide access to the alternative sexual universe within the metaphorical black hole? Mirroring as a way of negating a legacy of silence needs to be explored in much greater depth than it has been to date by black feminist theorists. An appeal to the visual is not uncomplicated or innocent. As theorists we have to ask how vision is structured, and, following that, we have to explore how difference is established, how it operates, how and in what ways it constitutes subjects who *see* and *speak* in the world (Haraway, "Promises" 313). This we must apply to the ways in which black women are seen and not seen by the dominant society and to how they see themselves in a different landscape. But in overturning the "politics of silence" the goal cannot be merely to be seen: visibility in and of itself does not erase a history of silence nor does it challenge the structure of power and domination, symbolic and material, that determines what can and cannot be seen. The goal should be to develop a "politics of articulation." This politics would build on the interrogation of what makes it possible for black women to speak and act.

Finally, my search for black women's sexuality through queer theory has taught me that I need not simply add the label queer to my list as another naturalized identity. As I have argued, there is no need to re-produce black women's sexualities as a silent void. Nor are black queer female sexualities simply identities. Rather, they represent discursive and material terrains where there exists the possibility for the active production of speech, desire, and agency.

NOTES

1. Here I am referring to the work of Stuart Hall and especially Hazel Carby:

We need to recognize that we live in a society in which dominance and subordination are structured through processes of racialization that continuously interact with other forces of socialization. . . . But processes of racialization, when they are mentioned at all in multicultural debates are discussed as if they were the sole concern of those particular groups perceived to be racialized subjects. Because the politics of difference work with concepts of individual identity, rather than structures of inequality and exploitation, processes of racialization are marginalized and given symbolic meaning only when subjects are black. (Carby, "Multicultural" 193)

2. See Higginbotham; Hine; Giddings; Carby (*Reconstructing*); and Brown ("What").
3. See Carby, "Policing." Elsa Barkley Brown argues that the desexualization of black women was not just a middle-class phenomenon imposed on working-class women. Though many working-class women resisted Victorian notions of womanhood and developed their own notions of sexuality and respectability, some also, from their own experiences, embraced a desexualized image ("Negotiating" 144).
4. The historical narrative discussed here is very incomplete. To date there are no detailed historical studies of black women's sexuality.
5. See analyses of novels by Nella Larsen and Jessie Fauset in Carby (*Reconstructing*); McDowell; and others.
6. I participated in a group discussion of two novels written by black women, Jill Nelson's *Volunteer Slavery* and Audre Lorde's *Zami*, where one black woman remarked that while she thought Lorde's book was better written than Nelson's, she was disturbed that Lorde spoke so much about sex and "aired all of her dirty linen in public." She held to this even after it was pointed out to her that Nelson's book also included descriptions of her sexual encounters.
7. I am reminded of my mother's response when I "came out" to her. She asked me why, given that I was already black and that I had a nontraditional profession for a woman, I would want to take on one more thing that would make my life difficult. My mother's point, which is echoed by many black women, is that in announcing my homosexuality I was choosing to alienate myself from the black community.
8. I was disturbed by the fact that the use of the image of a black hole could also evoke a negative image of black female sexuality reduced to the lowest possible denominator, i.e. just a "hole."
9. The existence of the second body in a binary system is inferred from the periodic Doppler shift of the spectral lines of the visible star, which shows that it is in orbit, and by the production of X-ray radiation. My points are taken from the discussion of the astrophysics of black holes in Wald, chapters 8 and 9.

WORKS CITED

Abelove, Henry, Michèle Barale, and David Halperin, eds. *The Lesbian and Gay Studies Reader*. New York: Routledge, 1993.

Alonso, Ana Maria, and Maria Teresa Koreck. "Silences, 'Hispanics,' AIDS, and Sexual Practices." Abelove, Barale, and Halperin 110–126.

Brown, Elsa Barkley. "Negotiating and Transforming the Public Sphere: African American Political Life in the Transition From Slavery to Freedom." *Public Culture* 7.1 (1994): 117–46.

———. " 'What Has Happened Here'; The Politics of Difference in Women's History and Feminist Politics." *Feminist Studies* 18.2 (1992): 295–312.

Busia, Abena, and Stanlie James. *Theorizing Black Feminisms: The Visionary Pragmatism of Black Women*. New York: Routledge, 1993.

Butler, Judith. *Bodies That Matter: On the Discursive Limits of "Sex."* New York: Routledge, 1993.

Carby, Hazel. "The Multicultural Wars." Wallace and Dent 187–99.

———. "Policing the Black Woman's Body in the Urban Context." *Critical Inquiry* 18 (1992): 738–55.

———. *Reconstructing Womanhood: The Emergence of the Afro-American Woman Novelist*. New York: Oxford, 1987.

Clarke, Cheryl. "Living the Texts Out: Lesbians and the Uses of Black Women's Traditions." Busia and James 214–27.

Collins, Patricia Hill. *Black Feminist Thought, Knowledge, Consciousness, and the Politics of Empowerment*. Cambridge: Unwin Hyman, 1990.

Crenshaw, Kimberlé. "Whose Story Is It Anyway?: Feminist and Antiracist Appropriations of Anita Hill." Morrison 402–40.

de Lauretis, Teresa. *The Practice of Love: Lesbian Sexuality and Perverse Desire*. Bloomington: Indiana UP, 1994.

———. "Queer Theory: Lesbian and Gay Sexualities: An Introduction." *differences: A Journal of Feminist Cultural Studies* 3.2 (1991): iii–xviii.

duCille, Ann. "The Occult of True Black Womanhood: Critical Demeanor and Black Feminist Studies." *Signs* 19.3 (1994): 591–629.

Giddings, Paula. "The Last Taboo." Morrison 441–65.

Gomez, Jewelle. "A Cultural Legacy Denied and Discovered: Black Lesbians in Fiction by Women." B. Smith, *Home Girls*, 110–123.

Haraway, Donna. "The Promises of Monsters: A Regenerative Politics for Inappropriate/d Others." *Cultural Studies*. Ed. Laurence Grossberg, Cary Nelson, and Paula Treichler. New York: Routledge, 1992. 295–337.

———. "Situated Knowledges: The Science Question in Feminism and the Privilege of Partial Perspective." *Simians, Cyborgs, and Women: The Reinvention of Nature*. New York: Routledge, 1991.

Henderson, Mae Gwendolyn. "Speaking in Tongues: Dialogics, Dialectics, and the Black Woman Writer's Literary Tradition." Wall 16–37.

Higginbotham, Evelyn Brooks. "African-American Women's History and the Metalanguage of Race." *Signs* 17.2 (1992): 251–74.

Hine, Darlene Clark. "Rape and the Inner Lives of Black Women in the Middle West: Preliminary Thoughts on the Culture of Dissemblance." *Signs* 14.4 (1989): 915–20.

hooks, bell. "Selling Hot Pussy: Representations of Black Female Sexuality in the Cultural Marketplace." *Black Looks: Race and Representation*. Boston: South End, 1992. 61–76.

Hull, Gloria T. " 'Lines She Did Not Dare': Angela Weld Grimké, Harlem Renaissance Poet." Abelove, Barale, and Halperin 453–66.

JanMohamed, Abdul. "Sexuality on/of the Racial Border: Foucault, Wright, and the Articulation of 'Racialized Sexuality.'" *Discourses of Sexuality: From Artistotle to AIDS*. Ed. Domna Stanton. Ann Arbor: U of Michigan P, 1992. 94–116.

Lorde, Audre. *Sister Outsider, Essays and Speeches*. Trumansburg, NY: Crossing, 1984.

———. *Zami: A New Spelling of My Name*. Trumansburg, NY: Crossing, 1982.

McDowell, Deborah E. " 'It's Not Safe. Not Safe at All': Sexuality in Nella Larsen's *Passing*." Abelove, Barale, and Halperin 616–625.

Morrison, Toni, ed. *Race-ing Justice, En-gendering Power: Essays on Anita Hill, Clarence Thomas and the Construction of Social Reality*. New York: Pantheon, 1992.

Nelson, Jill. *Volunteer Slavery: My Authentic Negro Experience*. Chicago: Noble, 1993.

O'Grady, Lorraine. "Olympia's Maid: Reclaiming Black Female Subjectivity." *Afterimage* (1992): 14–23.

Omosupe, Ekus. "Black/Lesbian/Bulldagger." *differences: A Journal of Feminist Cultural Studies* 3.2 (1991): 101–11.

Smith, Barbara. "Toward a Black Feminist Criticism." *Conditions* 2 (1977): 25–44.

———, ed. *Home Girls: A Black Feminist Anthology*. New York: Kitchen Table, 1983.

Smith, Valerie. "Black Feminist Theory and the Representation of the 'Other.'" Wall 38–57.

Spillers, Hortense. "Interstices: A Small Drama of Words." Vance, *Pleasure* 73–100.

———. "Mama's Baby, Papa's Maybe: An American Grammar Book." *Diacritics* Summer 17.2 (1987): 65–81.

Vance, Carole, ed. *Pleasure and Danger: Exploring Female Sexuality*. London: Pandora, 1989.

———. "Pleasure and Danger; Toward a Politics of Sexuality." Vance, *Pleasure* 1–24.

Wald, Robert. *Space, Time, and Gravity: The Theory of the Big Bang and Black Holes*. 2nd edition. Chicago: U of Chicago P, 1992.

Wall, Cheryl, ed. *Changing Our Own Words: Essays on Criticism, Theory, and Writing by Black Women*. New Brunswick: Rutgers UP, 1989.

Wallace, Michele. *Invisibility Blues: From Pop to Theory*. New York: Verso, 1990.

Wallace, Michele, and Gina Dent, eds. *Black Popular Culture*. Seattle: Bay, 1992.

Walker, Alice. *The Color Purple*. New York: Harcourt, 1982.

Watney, Simon. *Policing Desire: Pornography, AIDS, and the Media*. Minneapolis: U of Minnesota P, 1989.

Williams, Patricia J. *The Alchemy of Race and Rights: Diary of a Law Professor*. Cambridge: Harvard UP, 1991.

41

Some Glances at the Black Fag

Race, Same-Sex Desire, and Cultural Belonging

Marlon B. Ross

(1994)

> This was how the people accepted it in the community. Nobody could be shocked at people being faggots. Nobody thought there was anything so crazy about it.
>
> —Claude Brown (1965, 205)

> Mass media images of contemporary Harlem reveal only a part of the actual texture of the lives of the people who inhabit that vast, richly varied, infinitely complex, and endlessly fascinating area uptown Manhattan. Those who create such images almost always restrict themselves to documenting the pathological.
>
> —Albert Murray (71)

When an open and autonomous culture of gays and lesbians began to form in America's urban centers during the late 1960s, there already existed largely integrated within the African American community an established and visible tradition of homosexuality. The consolidation of an openly gay culture had a direct impact on the ways in which black gays and lesbians could position themselves within the African American community, in relation to the emergent gay community, and in relation to American society at large. Given the ways in which European-American society has projected its own anxieties about sexual pathology and conformity onto African American culture, it is not surprising that issues of sexual diversity would be intimately tied to matters of racial community within the United States. The legitimate theoretical link between racial liberation and sexual liberation immediately became confused by the American tendency to associate sexual license with African American culture. If racial integration was projected as a threat to social order based on the myth of the African American as a promiscuous, pathological other, then it was a short step to conflating the social transgressions of homosexuality with deep-seated anxieties surrounding black sexuality. As the fear of cross-racial sexuality was intensified by the integration-oriented civil rights movement during the 1950s and 1960s, the fight for racial integration set the stage for viewing gay liberation in a similar light: as a cross-over phenomenon that operated by disrupting a social order based on maintaining the nuclear family, proper gender roles, and solid racial boundaries. The open display of homosexuality in the cities seemed to be but another symptom (and proof) of the breakdown of social order brought on by white America's impending loss of cultural control over black America.

Furthermore, by the 1960s a strong link had been established between African American culture and greater tolerance of homosexuality due to a long historical relation between more open urban homosexuals and African American urban communities. In the 1960s homosexuality was still largely an unspoken phenomenon in American society, even though its visibility had increased in larger cities since World War II. For some of the same reasons that African Americans had migrated from the rural South to Northern urban centers, gay men and lesbians had begun a pattern of migration from rural areas to major urban centers.[1] Homosexual activity was less hidden to African American eyes because those gays who were more open about their sexuality were beginning to share the same geographic terrain with blacks in Northern urban centers. The relation between white homosexuals and the African American community is a complicated, vexed history that can be traced at least as far back as the 1920s, but the African American community's reluctance to ostracize black homosexuals in the puritan European-American mode may go back much further.[2] On the one hand, white homosexuals, like bohemians and hipsters, saw African American communities as hip places to test their avante-garde status. Whites invaded black urban communities to make themselves feel more cosmopolitan, to give themselves license to feel unemcumbered by the puritanism and commercialism of middle-class white society. A significant aspect of this cosmopolitan ambiance was projected as sexual license—merely extenuating into vicarious pleasure the fearful tendency of white Americans to fantasize Africans as possessing a more deviant, and thus freer and richer, sexual life. Given the racial conditions, it is not surprising that white exploitation characterized one aspect of the relation between white homosexuals and the black community—a fact that has made any coalition between the two communities much more problematic.[3] On the other hand, the African American community was also seen as a genuinely safer place to experience homosexual relations without the stigma and judgment of middle-class white society. It provided a model of tolerance not available elsewhere in American society.

In "A Spectacle in Color: The Lesbian and Gay Subculture of Jazz Age Harlem," Eric Garber summarizes the attitude of white lesbians and gays who trekked up to Harlem to enjoy the liberties it afforded:

With its sexually tolerant population and its quasi-legal nightlife, Harlem offered an oasis to white homosexuals. For some, a trip to Harlem was part of a larger rebellion against the Prohibition Era's conservative moral and political climate. For Van Vechten, and for many other white lesbians and gay men, Harlem offered even deeper rewards. Blair Niles based her [novel] *Strange Brother* on her friend and confidant Leland Pettit, a young, white, gay man from Milwaukee and the organist at Grace

Church. According to *Strange Brother*, Pettit frequented the homosexual underworld in Harlem because he found social acceptance, and because he identified with others who were also outcasts from [white] American life. This identification and feeling of kinship, undoubtedly shared by other white lesbians and gay men, may have been the beginnings of homosexual "minority consciousness." (329)[4]

Garber's insight that gay "minority consciousness" may have formed in the black community's homosexual networks has much to recommend it—though we might question the way in which Garber segregates black same-sex activity to an "underworld."[5] The whole of pre-civil rights black life, from a white perspective, could be, and frequently has been, viewed as an "underworld." This relation between black neighborhoods and white homosexuals was by no means limited to Harlem, but was common in many urban centers. As a result, when gay men began to consolidate their own open communities in the 1960s, these communities often bordered the neighborhoods of blacks (and other people of color), and in most cases were developed not coincidentally in the midst of areas undergoing urban "blight." (In addition to New York City, this was the case in San Francisco, Chicago, Los Angeles, Detroit, Cleveland, Philadelphia, Washington, D.C., Boston, St. Louis, Milwaukee, New Orleans, Miami, Atlanta, Seattle, and Houston, as well as many smaller cities.) This "border" relationship helped to establish a further dialogue between white homosexuals and the black community, a complicated dialogue that academe and the media have not noticed until recently, and now tend to notice only in the most superficial, sensationalistic ways. This dialogue is most frequently characterized as contentious, pitting each side against the other by the press in such a way that both sides are wrong and neither side can win. The media tends to characterize blacks as being more homophobic than nonblacks—an astonishing conclusion, considering the history of relatively greater tolerance within the African American community. Gay men are characterized by the media as preying on the black community—taking attention away from the racial struggle and exploiting the successes of black civil rights in an attempt to parlay similar successes for themselves. Gay people are always portrayed in this context as all white and as male; the only blacks the media tends to interview are more socially conservative (male) ministers. As a result, the argument looks as though it is between the two figures that the media has portrayed as most frightening to mainstream America: the strong black (straight) male and the militant (white) gay male. The argument gets framed in such a way that the dominant stereotype of each figure is reinforced. The black (straight) male cannot protect his turf (the city) even against a faggot. The (white) homosexual is framed as an exploitative, narcissistic interloper, one who is more concerned about getting his sexual preference, that is his sexual license, validated than about the more serious problems of crime, unemployment, impoverishment, and genocide in the inner city. The media reacts as though the dialogue concerning the relation between homosexuality and race is a new phenomenon, one that came into existence only after mainstream white society was forced to begin to deal with questions of gay rights.

We should not be surprised by the media's distorted treatment of the relationship between white gays and the African American community. The media is simply doing what it always does well, picking up on a strain between two oppressed groups, and exploiting that strain to the disadvantage of each group and to the advantage of the status quo. In fact, there is a long, complicated history at stake, a history that tells us as much about the representation of black male sexuality as it does about the interplay of sex and race in American politics. The strain between white gays and the black community grows out of this history. When white gay men migrated to the cities, they came at an opportune moment. By concentrating their numbers in the cities, they were able to become an influential political block, both economically and at the ballot box, due to their relative affluence and to their growing visibility and political organization. In a sense, they began to replace the white "ethnics," who had begun to leave the urban centers for the suburbs, in competition with racial minorities for political control and influence in the cities. This political rivalry could only be intensified by the fact that gays have relied heavily on strategies, laws, and rhetoric originally fostered by black Americans in their fight for civil rights and group empowerment. The media's sensationalist and noisy attention to this rivalry, however, has silenced other aspects of this relationship, and has helped to suppress the rich, entangled history tying homosexual consciousness to the African American struggle for unity and empowerment. The broader and deeper nature of this relationship can be understood only through a double focus. First, we must clarify what the white homosexual, as a cultural concept and as a political entity, gains from a literal and figurative "border" relation to African American culture. Second, we must bring into view the cultural role of the black faggot, the male figure who is most frequently suppressed in the media's staging of an argument. The black homosexual does not obliterate the easy opposition between black and white, straight and gay, which fuels the American imagination and greases the oppressive engine of American politics, but this figure complicates those oppositions and helps us to flesh out a history in which homosexuality and race are not natural enemies.

Obviously, gays and lesbians looked to the civil rights movement as a model for their own awakening into social and political consciousness. More subtly, however, the more significant influence may have been the actual experience of how an outcast status could enable greater group solidarity and greater freedom within the group, a phenomenon that white gays experienced second-hand when visiting the homosexual networks of the black community. In homosexuals' attempt to establish a permanent, viable, open culture virtually from scratch against the grain of oppression and obscurity, the long history of African American culture had to prove a valuable resource for a homosexual consciousness in search of ways to consolidate and mobilize a fragmented, distorted, hidden proto-culture in which individuals necessarily start out as lonely queers bereft of a sympathetic community.

What did white homosexuals gain during the 1940s and 1950s by staying in and flocking to the urban centers at a point when these centers were being vacated by whites and were becoming unrespectable places to live from the viewpoint of an oppressing dominant culture?[6] Beyond the advantage of being left alone, white homosexuals gained, in effect, a nascent new identity as an oppressed group willing to acknowledge and work against its own oppression. Sharing the stigma of an inferior status with their neighbors of color, white homosexuals could attain the value of that stigma validated through their association with groups whose strength in adversity had been long proven, turning that stigma into a badge of cultural belonging. In his groundbreaking study *The Homosexual in America* (1951), Donald Webster Cory was the first to put forward a fully worked out theory of gay "subculture" based solely on the idea that gays and lesbians constitute an "unrecognized minority." Cory demonstrates how homosexuals already constituted a "minority" group, though not yet recognized as such, and more fundamentally a cultural group, though one whose culture was "submerged" or malformed due to the peculiar pressures of sexual oppression. At every turn of his elaborate and forceful argument, Cory relies on the comparison to African American "minority" culture to establish the legitimacy of a homosexual culture—the dominant strategy still relied on today by gay and lesbian activists of all political stripes.

Also at the heart of Cory's argument, however, is the idea that gays and lesbians constitute a fluid minority, whose particular virtue grows out of the fact that they exist inside of every other cultural group.

> The homosexual, cutting across all racial, religious, national, and caste lines, frequently reacts to rejection by a deep understanding of all others who have likewise been scorned because of belonging to an outcast group. "There, but for the grace of God . . ." it is said, and the homosexual, like those who are part of other dominated minorities, can "feel" as well as understand the meaning of that phrase. The person who has felt the sting of repudiation by the dominant culture can reflect that, after all, he might have been another religion or race or color, an untouchable in India, one of the mentally or physically handicapped. It is not for him to join with those who reject millions of their fellowmen of all types and groups, but to accept all men, an attitude forced upon him happily by the stigma of being cast out of the fold of society.
>
> It is no wonder, then, that a true and genuine democracy so frequently pervades the activities of the homosexual group . . . And today, the deeprooted prejudices that restrict marriages and friendships according to social strata—family, wealth, religion, color, and a myriad of other artifices—are conspicuously absent among the submerged groups that make up the homosexual society. (151–52)

Multi-culturalism is conceptualized here as an intrinsic and definitive determinant of gay culture, thus making the cross-over dynamic a founding principle of homosexuality. A culture that is ironically defined by its lack of cultural boundaries, rather than by its cultural singularity, becomes a guiding ideal within the gay and lesbian community. Cosmopolitanism defines this concept of open gay culture for whites in four interrelated ways.

First, as Cory points out, gays and lesbians represent every imaginable cultural group, and they bring this traditional cultural orientation with them when they enter into gay/lesbian culture. Second, their gay cultural affiliation is both secondary (always succeeding acculturation in some other racial, ethnic, religious group) and also invisible. Not only do nongays tend to project heterosexuality onto others; they also tend to defend against the invisible nature of the homosexual disposition by concocting elaborate myths about how homosexuals can be easily spotted. This means that a gay person can experience the stigma of oppression while appearing to be part of the dominant culture that oppresses. Whereas this experience of "passing" is also an option within other groups, it is an exception that requires the individual to abandon the formative culture. For the gay person, passing is the rule, not the exception, and the process and effect are just the opposite. Rather than abandoning the original cultural group in order to pass, the gay person passes by remaining totally assimilated by the original group. The gay person ceases to pass in a process of abandoning the original cultural group or in challenging its cultural priority and totality by coming out and identifying openly with gay/lesbian culture. For Cory this chameleon capacity forces the homosexual to cross boundaries and empathize with others in the most downcast groups ("an untouchable in India") without necessarily having to experience the external markers of that oppression. Whereas homosexuals from racially oppressed groups are used to the experience of being outcast from dominant society while being empowered within their own culture, for white homosexuals (especially men), this is a new experience.

Third, once homosexuals accept their variance (perceived as "deviance" in the 1950s and 1960s, as "difference" in the 1980s and 1990s), they not only are compelled to identify with downcast groups, but also are drawn into connections with individuals from these groups who also happen to be gay. The more openly gay the individual, the more she or he is pressed into relations with others who are also escaping the straightjacket of their original groups. Finally, the more openly gay the individual, the more she or he will become geographically marginalized in relation to the dominant culture, pressed into contact with those at the bottom of the American social scale in the urban centers. At each step and at every level in the gay person's developing awareness, the cosmopolitan impulse supposedly intensifies.[7]

Although we should not underestimate this utopian aspect of gay and lesbian settlement in the inner city, we should also remember that, as the most despised group in society, they had no choice but to settle among racial groups already outcast based on class and color. The diversity of homosexuality which makes gays and lesbians the most easily assimilable group also suggests an ideal—nowhere approached in practice—of "true and genuine democracy," once they begin to establish open geographic communities. Hoping that homosexuals will be able to stake a claim to a special contribution in the larger culture of America, Cory focuses on this innate cosmopolitan diversity and its attendant "democratic spirit" as axiomatic. "It is in this . . . that we find a reaction to being gay that is strength born of handicap. The sympathy for all mankind—including groups similarly despised in their own right—that is exhibited by so many homosexuals, can be a most rewarding factor, not only for the individual, but for society" (152).

This hope that gay culture will be instrumental in spreading cosmopolitan democracy is not as original as it first appears. For even in this cultural characteristic, gay/lesbian communities have been deeply influenced by the role of African American culture (as well as Jewish culture), especially since the 1920s, in creating the vanguard of modern cultural expression admired and imitated throughout the entire world.[8] By associating with African Americans from the 1920s to the 1940s and by actually settling open communities next to them in the 1950s and 1960s, homosexuals embarked on making visible the otherwise concealed mark of sexual deviation, and thus making valid, in the minds of white homosexuals, the *group* "identity" of homosexuality, which was normally considered a solitary, individual affliction. A white person venturing into a black neighborhood is already conspicuous, and any stigma and judgment brought down on him by African Americans would necessarily be different in effect, if not in kind. For a white person to be judged by blacks could not have the same ostracizing effect as being condemned by dominant white society. What white homosexuals gained from these largely economically impoverished African American neighborhoods was a cultural model for social tolerance, solidarity despite variance within the group, dignity in the face of oppression, and a drive for cultural expression that could determine the standard for cosmopolitanism.

The myth of greater sexual license within African American culture was easily confused with the reality of African American culture's great tolerance of black homosexuals. How could white homosexuals not observe with some envy the ways in which African American communities refused to ostracize even those native sons who were most "flamboyantly" homosexual? They could never have such freedom in their own mainstream white communities. How could the white homosexual understand that black society's embracing of their homosexual sons was not the same as black society's embracing of homosexuality itself?[9] What white homosexuals would have difficulty seeing is that the greater acceptance within the black community was not a result of greater sexual license per se, but instead was a result of a cultural value long held among African Americans that racial freedom could be gained only through racial solidarity, an understanding that the need for racial solidarity was much more important than the impulse to ostracize individuals whose sexuality seemed to vary from the norm. In effect, that "norm," like the rule of law itself, has been much more contested within African American culture, exactly because blacks have had to be wary of the endless attempts of mainstream society to whitewash black culture by imposing a standard of normalcy that is really just an excuse for oppressive behavior.

Unlike white homosexuals, who had the comparative luxury of being able to escape to urban centers and occasionally to go "slumming" in black neighborhoods within the city, black homosexuals had no such option before the 1960s, unless, as we shall see, they consented to becoming dependent, kept lovers of white gay men. If a black homosexual were to be ostracized from his community, where on earth could he go? This dramatic difference in social, economic, and historical conditions between the black and white homosexual necessarily has led to a different conception of sexual orientation and coming out. For the white homosexual, integrating same-sex desire into one's sense of self meant necessarily leaving one's community behind for a new community in a mixed urban environment. For the black homosexual, nothing could be further from the case. Integrating same-sex desire within the self meant finding a way to remain integrated within the home community while remaining true to one's desire. Even the black homosexual who might leave the rural South in search of homosexual community would possess a continuity not imaginable for the white homosexual. For even as black homosexuals might leave home behind, they would find it waiting for them in the black communities of the urban North. For the black homosexual, same-sex desire was a matter of finding a way to reaffirm continuity, rather than a matter of breaking with a dominant culture in order to gain a new identity through an awakened consciousness shared with others of a similarly oppressed status. After all, how could black gays break with dominant culture, since they had never been part of it?

This is why James Baldwin's refusal to identify as a homosexual is not necessarily the contradiction it is often seen as being. Though Baldwin felt compelled to expose the scandal of normalcy by bringing the reality of desire to the surface, he did not consider himself a homosexual. "Homosexual," he reminded us, is properly an adjective, not a noun. What Baldwin meant by this is that he viewed homosexuality as a practice or disposition of desire, not as an identity defining the existence of an individual's cultural belonging.

> A black gay person who is a sexual conundrum to society is already, long before the question of sexuality comes into it, menaced and marked because he's black or she's black. The sexual question comes after the question of color; it's simply one more aspect of the danger in which all black people live. I think white gay people feel cheated because they were supposed to be safe. The anomaly of their sexuality puts them in danger, unexpectedly. Their reaction seems to me in direct proportion to the sense of feeling cheated of the advantages which accrue to white people in a white society. There's an element, it has always seemed to me, of bewilderment and complaint. (In Goldstein 180)

Ironically, Baldwin's view of homosexuality is, in some ways, more similar to that of the black nationalists who blasted him than the white gay community, which has fully embraced the "gay" aspects of his work. Baldwin sees African American identity as both prior and more grounding. The same-sex disposition is, for him, not so much an identity as it is a variation within and among the bedrock of racial identity. Like Cory, he conceptualizes homosexuality as a fluid characteristic that traverses other identities that are assumed to be more stable, solid, and total. This idea that race is a more stable block of identity and that homosexuality is a more fluid, historically varied form of identity lives on in the 1990s and undergirds much of the academic and popular discourse on race and sexuality.[10] Often, this means that sexuality becomes a matter of "lifestyle," unfixable postmodern identification, and traveling alliances, whereas race becomes a matter of cultural tradition, fixed historical identification, and originary ties to specific geographical spheres (whiteness in Europe, blackness in Africa, etc.). Depending on the context, sexuality's unfixable nature is seen either as an advantage, especially when it is used as the exemplary characteristic that proves the cultural construction of identity, or as a disadvantage, especially when it is reduced to a mere lifestyle-choice in practical debates over civil rights legislation. For black homosexuals before the 1970s, to break with their racial culture as a way of embracing their variant desire made no sense. However, after the more militant movements of both black nationalism (which tended to scapegoat homosexuality) and gay liberation (which offered a rhetoric of racial inclusion) in the late 1960s and early 1970s, embracing European-American style autonomous gay identity began to make some sense for some black homosexuals. At first glance, it might appear to be the ultimate irony that Baldwin, the most famous openly gay black man and the one most responsible for initiating a popular discussion of homosexuality, did not believe in the existence of gay culture. But this irony is swept away once we remind ourselves of Baldwin's historical situation. However much homosexuality was damned to the inner "extremities" (the urban centers) of mainstream culture, the black who happened to be homosexual was already at home within those inner "extremities." As long as he remembered where he came from as a black man, homosexuality would normally not become a reason for his being banished from his own culture.

Within American society, there was every reason for a gay culture (or subculture) not to exist. Gays and lesbians did certainly have traditions, ways of thinking, even institutions (such as bars) before the 1960s (and perhaps even as early as the seventeenth century in Europe), but the important point is that these conditions existed in a strange limbo, a culture not yet born and yet always potentially operative.[11] This limbo was a comparatively safe place for them to visit temporarily in an escape from the hostilities of "real" culture, not a place to live, grow, work, prosper, and educate the next generation. Because gays and lesbians were thought to have no vital relation to procreation, they could have only a tangential relation to what was seen as legitimate culture, and, in the context of their own group, they were seen as isolated, lonely, misplaced individuals wrongly or rightly outcast from the permanence of real culture. At best, their social relations to each other could only diminish temporarily their loneliness by stressing the deeper reality of their essentially permanent isolation from culture. This mainstream American attitude toward the homosexual dominated through the 1960s. It is apparent in sociological and psychoanalytic studies on homosexuality, as well as in literary representations of homosexuality in novels like Gore Vidal's *City and the Pillar*, Chester Himes' *Cast the First Stone*, Baldwin's *Giovanni's Room*, James Barr's *Quatrefoil*, Fritz Peters' *Finistère*, Charles Wright's *The Messenger*, or the writings of Tennessee Williams, Truman Capote, and James Purdy. Even though all of these writers are sympathetic, they tend to disparage the social network available to homosexuals as a culture manqué, rather than a culture outright.

The best articulation of this dominant attitude comes not surprisingly from the most influential theoretical anthropologist of the '50s and '60s, Claude Lévi-Strauss. In his most popular book, *Tristes Tropiques* (1955), Lévi-Strauss searches for a way to describe the "weirdest" site of his travels into "primitive" South America, and he finds an appropriate geographic-anthropological analogy in Fire Island:

Both express the same kind of geographical and human absurdity, comic in the one instance and sinister in the other. Fire Island might have been invented by Swift. . . . The dunes on Fire Island are so shifting, and their hold on the sea so precarious, that further notices warn the public to keep off in case they should collapse into the water below. The place is like an inverted Venice, since it is the land which is fluid and the canals solid.

The "aquatic desert" of Porto Esperança is, like Fire Island's inverted relation between water and land, a freak of nature, a structure with "no reason for its existence" (169). The human factor in this absurd site is, of course, the homosexual population of Fire Island's major village, Cherry Grove, one of the earliest white American openly gay communities.

> To complete the picture, I must add that Cherry Grove is chiefly inhabited by male couples, attracted no doubt by the general pattern of inversion. Since nothing grows in the sand, apart from broad patches of poisonous ivy, provisions are collected once a day from the one and only shop, at the end of the landing-stage. In the tiny streets, on higher ground more stable than the dunes, the sterile couples can be seen returning to their chalets pushing prams (the only vehicles suitable for the narrow paths) containing little but the weekend bottles of milk that no baby will consume. (168–69)

Characterized by "farcical gaiety," Cherry Grove society is a parody of real culture solely because male couples cannot procreate. Lévi-Strauss' clever portrait of male couples pushing baby carriages laden with bottles of milk, instead of babies, assumes that any cultural group brought together without a procreative base will be sterile, both symbolically and literally. These fake couples are "attracted no doubt to the general pattern of inversion" on Fire Island. Underlying the farcical effect of this "sterile" community is a more sinister poisonousness. Just as the sterile couples must import their food because nothing but poison ivy grows on the island, so they must import their social relations from mainstream culture as they absurdly mock the heterosexual couple. For Lévi-Strauss this is all laughable only because it is so contained, so sterile, so unnatural, offering no real threat to real culture.

Lévi-Strauss' portrait of gay Fire Island relies on a confusion between the literal and the symbolic, a grounding fallacy in Western anthropological thinking.[12] Gay males are not literally sterile, and to call their relationships sterile can only make sense if the sole purpose for bonding is procreation, symbolic or literal. According to his logic, gay men must be literally attracted to literally sterile habitats, because homosexuals symbolize the inversion of culture's total purpose, the procreative drive. The symbolic correlation between social structure and geographic structure reveals, for the anthropologist, the literal relation between procreation and the reproduction of genuine cultural knowledge.

The Lévi-Strauss school of structural anthropology has been criticized for basing the reproduction of culture on abstract concepts and patterns that seem to diminish the role of instinct, practical physical needs, and the tactical give-and-take struggle that exists within any culture.[13] Actually, however, Lévi-Strauss' concept of culture places physical procreation as the cornerstone of legitimate culture in no less a way than his predecessors. His Cherry Grove example is not a whimsical aside, but a telling analogy. In his need to explain (and thus explain away) the existence of homosexuality among the Nambikwara, a native tribe of central Brazil, Lévi-Strauss again reveals the procreative logic at the heart of his anthropological system. Of course, this reveals nothing about the Nambikwara and everything about the peculiarly Western assumptions undergirding Lévi-Strauss' "science." According to Lévi-Strauss, the Nambikwara resort to homosexuality only as a clever way of solving the problem of a scarcity of female partners for young men, as a result of the practice which grants to the chief the privilege of polygamy:

> Such relationships are frequent between young men and take place far more publicly than *normal* relationships. The two partners do not withdraw into the bush like adults of opposite sexes. They settle down near the camp fire, while their neighbours look on with amusement. Such incidents are a source of jokes, which generally remain discreet; homosexual relationships are considered to be childish pastimes and little attention is paid to them. (354, italics added)

The anthropological question here *should be* what constitutes "normal relationships" for this tribal group; instead, it becomes *a priori* a matter of figuring out how behavior (male-male sexual relations) already defined by the anthropologist as abnormal can happen among such innocent primitives. If such relations are routine within Nambikwara society, then why is not such routineness itself a clue for the "normalcy" of such behavior? Among the Nambikwara, homosexuality is integrated within the culture in such a way that it is strange and threatening to Lévi-Strauss' observant Western eyes, but not so threatening as to alter his understanding of same-sex desire. In effect, he responds the same way to both the culturally integrated same-sex desire of the Nambikwara and the culturally segregated homosexuality of Cherry Grove. Given his assumptions, neither can be seen as deep structures within the cultural system; both are merely improvised rationales that, despite their instrinsic absurdity, give credence to the deepest structure of male-female bonding and procreation.

Lévi-Strauss' attitude was shared uniformly among social scientists throughout the 1950s and 1960s. As long as same-sex desire was seen as a form of inverted individual behavior dependent upon normal culture for its rationale, it could not be seen as a form of group behavior. In Western thinking, same-sex desire comes to make sense in itself only once it has been raised to the level of a cultural phenomenon, only once it is studied as a culture unto itself. Since Cory's study, white American gays and lesbians have understood that the only way to legitimate homosexual desire was first to segregate it culturally and demonstrate not only its "minority" status, but also its cultural value to the larger American society. This is difficult, if not impossible, to do by conceiving of homosexuality on an individual basis, for as individuals, gays and lesbians, according to the procreative logic of dominant society, will always be extraneous and detached loners. In the introduction to *Gay Culture in America*, Gilbert Herdt writes:

> It seems ideologically significant that a hundred years of research on homosexuality, marking its beginnings with Karl Ulrichs's twelve-volume study in the nineteenth century, have so very often been concerned with the causes rather than the outcomes of

"homosexuality." To ask, for instance, why people desire the same sex is very different from asking whether they are happy, or successful, or competent. Particularly in medical research and disease discourse, the issue has been fixated on individual development more than on the formation of a gay cultural community. Gradually, however, the focus of such studies—and the source of these studies as well—has shifted. Scholars of "homosexuality" are more and more gays or lesbians themselves, and they are concerned, not with the etiology of a "disease," but with the cultural history of lesbians and gays. (4–5)

The anthropological field essays in *Gay Culture in America* are themselves excellent examples of the shift Herdt refers to. It is not until after the actual formation of an open gay culture that this shift in scholarly procedure could take place, however.

While the focus on autonomous gay/lesbian culture works well for a post-Stonewall view of white homosexuality, it necessarily fails to account for the more integrated experience of same-sex desire within traditional African American culture, especially before the 1960s. The problem is that, once autonomous white gay and lesbian culture became the norm, as the object and subject of study, for understanding homosexuality, the same autonomous-culture approach was automatically applied to same-sex desire within African American communities. Attempts to apply the same autonomous-culture approach to black homosexuality, however, necessarily misrepresent the conditions of same-sex desire within the African American community. Predictably, the one essay on black gay men in *Gay Culture in America* returns to an individualist, causative approach, citing woefully inadequate statistics to try to understand why black gay men supposedly are less prone to come out, form relationships, and participate in the (white) lesbian/gay community. White homosexual culture becomes an unspoken norm which allows the anthropologist to understand (or misunderstand) same-gender relationships among African Americans. "Virtually all the data on sexual behavior of black men in the United States are confined to studies on their sexual behavior with females," John L. Peterson writes. "Similar studies of the same-sex behavior of black males have been largely neglected. This neglect results in insufficient knowledge of the social and psychological factors that influence same-sex behavior among black males" (147). These first sentences of the essay admit that there is not much statistical evidence about black gay men, so how can the statistical approach, used in Peterson's essay, provide anything more than speculative stereotypes, based on a flawed logic of etiology? If comparisons are to be made, it would be more appropriate to consider black homosexuality as a phenomenon more integrated into black life similar to the traditional culture of the Nambikwara, but in doing so, we must also steer clear of the kind of absurd Western assumptions besetting the observations of Lévi-Strauss.

Claude Brown's controversial 1965 documentary autobiography *Manchild in the Promised Land* is a much more compelling and helpful guide to understanding the relation between same-sex desire, black community, and masculinity. I am not suggesting that Brown, or any individual, can give us the key to knowing the "real" black fag. Cultural knowledge, as I have suggested in the Introduction, is always hedged in by the cognitive processes of synecdoche, metonymy, and projection.[14] Furthermore, my larger point has been and is that images of black manhood which come to dominate, though they may be based in reality, are always at the service of ideological purposes that can work both for and against the advancement of African American communities. I would not, however, go as far as Albert Murray, who argues that books like Claude Brown's and James Baldwin's merely repeat the pathology-oriented case studies favored by the social science "ghettologists." According to Murray, such authors are obsessed with proving that African American culture is sick in order to gain sympathy and money for fixing it (see 98–99). The ideological purpose of Murray's book is to suggest that blacks are American first, African second, like any other ethnic group, and that the real solution to economic and social problems within African American communities is to encourage advancement into the wrongly maligned black middle-class.[15] Murray wants to normalize the race by representing it as not really a race at all, but as a group of "omni-Americans" who contain within themselves everything that is in America, and whereby nothing that is in them is not also in all other Americans. In effect, this becomes another way of representing respectability. Traditionally, the black middle class has tried to hide or downplay those aspects of African American culture that might be seen as questionable to mainstream society. Ironically, during the civil rights era, these same cultural variations became exhibit A; they were now put forward by the black middle class as prime examples of why social reforms, like integration, needed broad political support. Whereas Murray sees through the flawed logic of exhibiting pathology as a basis for social change, Murray's shift to a focus on the continuity (good and bad aspects) between African American culture and mainstream American culture—assuring that the American norm is the African American norm—has its own liabilities, most notably a failure to question the legitimacy of norm-focused politics in any movement for social justice and self-empowerment.

Murray's criticism is instructive, however, in that it helps us to keep in mind that tendency in the social sciences, already pointed out in Lévi-Strauss, to pathologize every aspect of communities that are seen as deviating from mainstream European-American cultural practices. It is also true that at the height of the integrationist civil rights movement (mid-1950s to mid-1960s), African American authors developed a trend of exhibitionist writing. Geared toward making whites understand the predicament of black America, this trend encourages writers to exhibit in rich detail the social and sexual habits of life "on the street," in the "ghetto," or in the prison.[16] These ghettoized sites appeal to puritan-prurient white tastes exactly because they display black life as largely cut off from orderly mainstream America while also allowing white readers to experience vicariously what it might be like to lead a life that breaks the rules of an oppressive, hum-drum, work-driven, procreative social order. As Murray points out, Brown's book can be read within this trend, as can other such books that were popular during the time, including *Native Son* (perhaps the progenitor), Chester Himes, Ann Petry, Charles Wright, and, of course, James Baldwin.[17] But the more militant writers of the mid-1960s to early 1970s can also be read in this light, including Eldridge Cleaver, George Jackson, Malcolm X, and the early work of Imiri Baraka. Where Murray goes wrong is to discount totally the material discussed in these books due to the problematic nature of the trend in which they partake. Rather than suggesting that such books "distort" African American experience by stressing only the underside of it (as Murray contends), we would do better to consider how books like Brown's, even as they strive toward a necessarily flawed rhetorical strategy of nonjudgmental reportage, fall prey to the limitations inherent in the politics of cultural representativeness. The problem is that even though reportage might enable the writer to represent a slice of life as indexing a community spirit, such reportage gets transformed into an act of revelation. An African American, who necessarily lives his version of that experience, does not need it revealed as an experience. He does need, however, journalistic and artistic representations of that experience which can reveal its value and its shortcomings as a common, representable experience. Dependent largely upon a white media, a white publishing establishment, and a white critical response, the record of one man's experience of racial community inevitably gets contextualized as the black writer's astonishing revelation of salacious racial characteristics. Furthermore, it is difficult to disentangle the rhetorical strategy of reportage from the mainstream cultural value of scientific objectivity. It becomes easy for even African Americans to forget that what the writer reports is not some objectively validated, statistically justifiable social-science reality, or that such a thing can even exist, but instead what he reports is his own subjective experience of an objectifiable reality, one which can be reported on at all only when it is, in some sense, objectified. Brown's book especially seeks not only to explore what it is like on the street, but also what it means to view oneself on the street and what it means to represent the street as a sign of racial community.[18] Brown is clearly concerned with recording the conditions which enable a sense of community even under the most degrading and threatening circumstances, and thus with indexing a common experience of a people whose lives have been increasingly represented reductively by the media in terms of violence, despair, and moral rootlessness. The cultural index offers a slice of experience as a way of pointing toward and pointing out what the community at large may need to address as crucial; unfortunately, readers will tend to take this index as a wholistic representation of the race and will project the pressures bearing on the community at large as racial characteristics inhering in a racial whole. In effect, *Manchild* must be viewed in this context of the burden of cultural representation, as well as taken as an index that seeks to (re)present a frameable portrait, a readable account, of one aspect of African American experience.

Reflecting on his youth in Harlem during the 1940s and 1950s, Brown gives us a personal view from the inside of grassroots African American culture. His comments reflect, contrary to Murray's critique, no passing interest either in pathologizing or normalizing what he sees. His depiction helps us to see to what extent homosexuality has been a recognized, ordinary aspect of life within the African American community. This recognition of same-sex desire and sexual variance more generally hinges on a principled refusal to make sexual identity an overriding concern in an individual's make-up. Black cultural survival has depended much more on keeping "family" intact than on enforcing sexual norms that emphasize procreation within (white-identified) nuclear families. Rejecting or purging individuals who evidenced interest in same-sex desire would have also meant rejecting the talents and special gifts which such individuals might offer to the community at large. Even today, in a climate of sometimes heightened intolerance, homosexual individuals often take the role of providers for the young or as caretakers for the elderly in situations where parents or other adults cannot afford (in terms of time, money, and energy) to do so. In such situations, the attitude in the community tends to be to overlook the person's sexual disposition as irrelevant. Just as the individual's talents are seen as coming specially from God, so is the sexual disposition ("that God's doing"), which enables him to contribute in this special way. The community tendency to overlook homosexuality manifests itself in acknowledging the reality of the homosexual's existence but looking away, discounting its potential negative meaning in terms of religious and mainstream dogma, while valuing its positive significance in helping to fulfill needs in the community that might otherwise go unmet. This gesture of overlooking is virtually the opposite of the conventional European-American response in the decades before the 1970s. The convention there was to overlook as an act of totalized surveillance, whereby legally, politically, and socially the aim was to detect, ostracize, silence, and purge any sign of same-sex desire. In effect, African American culture has generally refused to treat homosexual individuals as an abstract phenomenon that threatens community survival and welfare, fully aware that the real threat to survival and welfare comes from economic deprivation, racist policies, and myriad other causes. Notably, recent attacks on homosexual individuals have come largely from an ideological camp, the Afrocentrists, who argue that homosexuality should be viewed as an abstract, segregatable phenomenon spawned and spread by a conspiracy of European-American origins. The most cogent, if not persuasive, statement of this case has been made by Nathan and Julia Hare in *The Endangered Black Family* (63–68). Significantly, the Hares advocate re-attaching the value of sexuality to procreation (125–136), as well as a return to strict gender-coded roles in terms of courtship, family, non-occupation related activities (137–150). However, even the Hares, illogically against the grain of their argument, reject the idea of ostracizing or purging homosexual individuals—recognizing, as they must, that this would go counter to what is best in African American history and counter to the objective of survival and unity (65).[19]

While Brown's refusal to exclude homosexuality from his documentary reflects a pragmatist and survivalist cultural attitude in which priorities are based on countering real threats and fulfilling basic needs, the contradictions in Brown's representation of black faggotry help us to see how the categories of sissy and swish and the tensions surrounding sexual respectability play themselves out, how such categories are constantly mediated by the common and varied experiences of African American people in everyday life.[20] The autobiography begins grippingly with Sonny, the author-observer-hero, being shot and then being awakened in the hospital:

> On my fourth day in the hospital, I was awakened by a male nurse at about 3 a.m.
> When he said hello in a very ladyish voice, I thought that he had come to the wrong

bed by mistake. After identifying himself, he told me that he had helped Dr. Freeman save my life. The next thing he said, which I didn't understand, had something to do with the hours he had put in working that day. He went on mumbling something about how tired he was and ended up asking me to rub his back. I had already told him that I was grateful to him for helping the doctor save my life. While I rubbed his back above the beltline, he kept pushing my hand down and saying, "Lower, like you are really grateful to me." I told him that I was sleepy from the needle a nurse had given me. He asked me to pat his behind. After I had done this, he left. (10–11)

As the narration moves through this episode, it does not skip a beat, but remains in the same routine, fast-paced, matter-of-fact reportage. The casual attitude toward such an encounter is unusual in the dominant culture, to say the least, and is rarely found even within white dominant culture today. Straight white men are expected to protest, to over-protest, any proximity to homosexuality, especially in a situation where the gay man has an advantage over the straight one, or is beholden to him. The treatment of the episode suggests, without having to say it, that this male nurse swish is part of the common fabric of African American life.

More importantly, it suggests that various forms of hyper-aversion, the response expected within mainstream culture even today, would have been rude in the context narrated here. The nurse asks Sonny to pat his behind; Sonny obliges. Sonny loses nothing in obliging, despite the fact that he has nothing to gain in obliging. The gesture of embracing the nurse's need to be touched is made significantly without protest, either by attempting, or over-attempting, to segregate the nurse either as an object of suspicion, scorn, or deviancy within the narrative sequence or as a discursive subject for focused attention outside of the narrative sequence. Brown does not use the introduction of this character as an opportunity to step outside of the narrative to discuss homosexuality, positively or negatively, as would be expected. In fact, the nurse is more a "character" in the sense of being a mildly amusing eccentric, whose impact is real but nonthreatening, than in the sense of a fictional construct placed within the narrative for the purposes of exploring the whys and hows of what makes such a "type" tick. The etiology of homosexuality is not an issue here. The episode is communicated literally as a real-life encounter, an impressionable one well remembered and casually retold.

On the one hand, the episode is matter-of-fact and inclusive—making the nurse as legitimate a part of Harlem life as any other person we encounter. On the other hand, we understand that the nurse is a swish, and our understanding is based on the stereotypical portrayal (the "ladyish" voice, the flaunting behavior, the self-parody). Furthermore, we understand that Sonny has no sexual interest in the nurse. This understanding is communicated playfully, not at the expense of the homosexual, who, after all, is the one who is playing around with Sonny's sexuality. As author, Brown only needs the slightest cue to indicate his sexual noninterest: "I rubbed his back above the beltline." As a character in the story, his noninterest is expressed in the same mild terms. In mainstream culture, a straight man's noninterest in homosexual desire is normally overemphasized by turning the homosexual into an object of verbal and/or physical violence. Moreover, this kind of violence is often acted out against men merely perceived to be gay, men who are not flaunting, who are not propositioning the straight, or showing any interest in the straight. Contrary to this mainstream attitude, Sonny communicates his noninterest in exactly the opposite way, through gentle touching, through verbally acknowledging the legitimacy of the swish's desire, and through playful setting of limits. The rejection of the swish's advances is carried out literally through inclusive verbal and physical gestures.

One of the stereotypes of the swish in African American folk culture is that he is always testing the boundaries and limits—not just sexually, but in all kinds of outrageous ways. He is always searching for sexual outlets without regard to rigid categories of sexual orientation. This is because he never knows when he might strike gold. Because homosexuality has tended to be more integrated into African American communities, there is naturally more interplay between "straight" men and gays, sexually and nonsexually.[21] Straight men can have sex with gay men and remain straight. Especially before the 1960s, there would be less psychological compulsion and less social pressure for the straight man to define his cultural orientation against homosexuality as an abstract unknown, since homosexual individuals were obviously integral contributors to the culture at large. Arbitrary violence against gay individuals was normally out of the question—unfortunately no longer the case in the volatilely mixed urban areas during the 1980s and 1990s. A swish could afford to be more casual and playful about what he desired from the object of his attention, who may be gay and interested, gay and not interested, straight and interested, straight and not interested, a circumspect sissy and interested, a circumspect sissy and not interested. Knowing that the swish's playful testing of limits is no reflection on the sexuality of the "straight" object of attention (which would be the normal presumption in white American culture), Sonny can reply just as playfully—without any hint of aversion or violence. The straight man can be just as playful about what he does not want as the swish can be about what he does.

Even more instructive than the episode itself is the response to it by Sonny's macho friends. Not only does Sonny casually tell us, his readers, about the swish; he just as casually tells his running buddies about the encounter in exactly the same tone:

> The next day when the fellows came to visit me, I told them about my early-morning visitor. Dunny said he would like to meet him. Tito joked about being able to get a dose of clap in the hospital. The guy with the tired back never showed up again, so the fellows never got a chance to meet him. Some of them were disappointed. (11)

Sonny's best pals, all of whom are straight, have their interest left tantalizingly piqued. Dunny's interest could be mere curiosity, or it could be more an interest in harmless sexual teasing to match the swish's own camp playfulness, or it could be genuine sexual interest. We have no way of knowing, just as the swish has no way of knowing without testing the waters and wading in to find what the actual circumstance brings up.

Tito's joke also indicates the flexibility of sexual encounters between swishes and straights in the black community. In the 1940s and 1950s, the folk wisdom was to be careful about going with gay men because many were supposedly infected with gonorrhea. (An obvious analogy could be made to AIDS in the 1980s, though there are significant differences due to both the deadly nature of the disease and the changed discourse on homosexuality in the black community by the 1980s.) This is a matter of the word on the street—from guys who know because they have been there. Tito's joke, however, suggests not only a caution to the wise, but also a humorous taunt that embraces, more than ridicules, the nurse. At the heart of the joke is the imaginable probability of sexual intercourse with the nurse: Is it not funny that you could go with this guy and get the clap right here in the hospital from the punk nurse who is supposed to be healing you? Despite their looking down on the swish as a kind of outrageous "character," Sonny and his friends clearly admire his boldness, and want to be entertained by the swish, who himself is entertained by entertaining them. This episode, and the ones that follow in the autobiography, contradict the common idea, expressed by Peterson, that the more flexible interplay between gay black men and straight black men is merely a matter of deprivation on the part of the straights. There is a much more fundamental cultural variation at stake here, one not easily explained away by applying European-American models of strict sexual labeling and white attitudes based on concepts of autonomous gay culture and segregated homosexual desire.

It is in juvenile prison that Sonny learns in depth about things he had taken for granted on the streets. "You learned something new from everybody you met" (144). Once again, homosexuality is just another case. Sonny comes to appreciate and understand something that he had taken for granted on the streets. It is with this coming into deeper awareness that we can begin to understand some of the African American cultural tensions that arise from overlaying the image of homosexuality over the actual experience of the black faggot.

> One of the most interesting things I learned was about faggots. Before I went to Warwick, I used to look down on faggots like they were something dirty. But while I was up there, I met some faggots who were pretty nice guys. We didn't play around or anything like that, but I didn't look down on them any more.
>
> These guys were young cats my age. It was the first time I'd been around guys who weren't afraid of being faggots. They were faggots because they wanted to be. Some cats were rape artists because they wanted to be, some cats were flunkies, some cats were thieves, and some cats were junkies. These guys were faggots because they wanted to be. And some of the faggots up there were pretty good with their hands. As a matter of fact, some of them were so good with their hands, they had the man they wanted just because he couldn't beat them.
>
> At Warwick, there was even a cottage just for faggots. If a cat came up there acting girlish, they'd put him right in there. They had a lot of guys in there—Puerto Ricans, white, colored, everything—young cats, sixteen and under, who had made up their minds that they liked guys, and that's all there was to it. (146–47)

There are obvious tensions between how Sonny has rather nonjudgmentally represented faggots before the prison meditations and the way he feels he has unfairly misjudged them in his own previous thinking. His behavior has been much less harsh toward gay men than his judgment is toward himself for merely thinking, not expressing, harsh things about them. In his mind, he thought dirty things about them, but in his behavior he has been more than tolerant. Once again, we have to remember that Sonny's behavior has been tolerant because he knows that homosexuals are not a real threat. Nonetheless, in his unexpressed, unformulated thinking about them, he thoughtlessly has imbibed the dominant image and prejudice espoused by some of the most "respectable" people in the community, inculcated by dominant culture, and enforced by the white legal establishment. To some extent, this is an expected tension between cultural doctrine (what respectable people think they ought to believe) and cultural practice (how respectful people negotiate firm beliefs into reasonable behavior). But at stake here is a much finer distinction between homosexual individuals who are an integral part of the community and the abstract concept of homosexuality as a segregated cultural identity, as a way of life significantly different from others' lives in the community.

There is tension between his portrayal of the gay nurse and his statement that "[i]t was the first time that I'd been around guys who were not afraid of being faggots." The nurse does not seem afraid; in fact, he seems outright self-confident. I would suggest that this is a tension between the African American projection of the swish's image and the actual, ordinary experience on the street. The projection is that the swish expects to be looked down on and is looked down on. The reality, not so much contradicting as overriding this image, is that the swish is admired for his daring testing of the waters, and that he knows how to play on that admiration. There is also a tension between the persistent viewing of the faggot as girlish and the awareness that some gay men can do macho things better than straight men. The prison officials immediately segregate the guys who act "girlish" in the "cottage just for faggots," despite the fact that you cannot tell the faggots from the straight men based on who is better at manly sports like boxing: "[S]ome of them were so good with their hands, they had the man they wanted just because he couldn't beat them" (147). Sexual variance was not a reason for segregating individuals in the black community. White society, on the other hand, has enforced its abstract concept of homosexuality as difference and deviation by enacting the same kind of policy against queer inmates that the American system enacted against African Americans in larger society. Segregation is the most efficient way to enforce categorical differences that otherwise might become insignificant as merely variable characteristics of a population. How ironic that the segregation of gay culture as an autonomous identity which occurred with the emergence of the gay rights movement should lead both to greater freedom and tolerance for homosexual expression in the larger society and to greater segregation and intolerance within African American community.

NOTES

This essay is excerpted from my study entitled *The Color of Manhood: Representations of Black Men in the Civil Rights Era*, which examines a complex of dialectically paired images of black masculinity—addict and entrepreneur, sissy and swish, agitator and athlete, integrationist and militant, prisoner and cop—and how they shape and are shaped by the racial and sexual politics of the civil rights era.

1. The cultural origins of the modern gay/lesbian community have been traced by a variety of scholars. See, for instance, John D'Emilio's *Sexual Politics, Sexual Communities*; Barry Adam's *The Rise of a Gay and Lesbian Movement*; Dennis Altman's *The Homosexualization of America, the Americanization of the Homosexual*; and Toby Marotta's *The Politics of Homosexuality*.

2. For a discussion of homosexuality in early African American culture, see Nero 233–35. Not surprisingly, reliable evidence concerning black male sexuality in early America is scant, but what evidence does exist makes absurd any presumption that there was no same-sex expression of desire.

3. For a concise, but incisive summary of the divisions between some leading African Americans and the gay/lesbian movement, see Henry Louis Gates, Jr.'s *New Yorker* essay "Blacklash." This observation is especially helpful:

> Much of the ongoing debate over gay rights has fixated, and foundered, on the vexed
> distinction between "status" and "behavior." The paradox here can be formulated as follows: Most people think of racial identity as a matter of (racial) status, but they respond to
> it as behavior. Most people think of sexual identity as a matter of (sexual) behavior, but
> they respond to it as status. (43)

The answer is not only to decode the false status-behavior dichotomy, but also, and more fundamentally, to demonstrate how "identity" historically comes to pit varying characteristics of and within cultural groups, of and within individuals, against one another.

4. Michael Bronski makes a similar point in *Culture Clash: The Making of Gay Sensibility* (72–76). Bronski points out also an important class difference within the black community: "Middle class blacks did not approve of the social or entertainment aspects of black culture that white cultural radicals were so enamoured of. This distaste continued through the 60s, when black nationalists demanded that Harlem's Apollo Theater cease its presentation of drag shows because 'it glorified the homosexual . . . and was a threat to black life and the black family'" (75–76). Bronski is right that the objection to overt homosexuality in the black community has a class basis, but the objection coming from black nationalists is more complicated. Black nationalism traditionally has sprung primarily from the grassroots, not from the more integration-oriented middle class, but, as we'll see in the next chapter, it does borrow its homophobia from middle-class concepts of family. For another account of a white gay trying to find community by turning to blacks, see Seymour Kleinberg's fascinating analysis of gay subcultures in Detroit and New York during the '60s and '70s in *Alienated Affections* (especially chapters 1 and 2).

5. I use the term "network" rather than "enclave" or "subculture" because network indicates both an active assembly constantly in motion, as well as a group not segregated from the larger community, but intimately tied to it while sustaining ties among themselves.

6. Another aspect of this question is dealt with later in the chapter in a section not included here. I argue that the white gay man turned the inner city into a "frontier" to be conquered with all of the connotations that accompany that concept in American culture and politics. By moving into the wilderness of the inner city, the white gay man proved his manhood to mainstream America, proved that he could survive the "extreme" conditions and make profitable and civilized settlements in a territory scarred by crime, violence, and declining profits.

The reward for this frontiersmanship was increasing political clout. Once the (white) gay man had conquered the inner city, he too could begin to move back into mainstream culture (into the suburbs), where his money and talents would be increasingly more accepted.

7. Much has been written on this utopian impulse in the early gay liberation movement, an impulse defined among white gay men as romantic and sexual license, the ability to bond with a variety of men from every racial, ethnic, and class background in an egalitarian setting. This cosmopolitan ideal was often seen as embodied in the gay bath-house, a site where all men were equally welcome and where all were equally desirable, desiring, and desired. Dennis Altman's *The Homosexualization of America* traces the history of, and offers an excellent critique of, this concept as it gets elided with the exploitative logic of consumer capitalism.

8. I do not mean to suggest here that African cultural expression was not influential before the 1920s; only that it was in this period that people of African descent became more self aware of their central role in world culture throughout history, thus forcing some whites (the bohemians and later the hipsters, beatniks, and hippies) to begin to recognize their own reliance on African forms of expression.

9. For instance, although Garber is careful to sketch the risks of being black and gay in Harlem during the 1920s, he still tends to conflate the black community's greater acceptance of black homosexuals with greater acceptance of homosexuality in general.

10. Biddy Martin has argued that much recent "queer theory" tends to rely on this dichotomy between race and sexuality, whereby race becomes the more totalized, determined experience of identity over against a playful, sophisticated, postmodern sexuality that is self-conscious of its own cultural construction.

11. Alan Bray has documented the presence of an urban homosexual subculture in England during the seventeenth century, as well as attempts made by governmental agencies to control and purge this subculture in his study *Homosexuality in Renaissance England*. See also Norton; and Trumbach. In many traditional African and Native American cultures, homosexuality was integrated into the "mainstream" of the cultures in various customs. Perhaps the most famous of these same-sex customs is the *berdache*, cross-dressing individuals who held an honorable status and were often taken as spouses by same-sex partners within many Native tribes. On the *berdache* tradition, see Williams; and Allen. A good compendium bringing together the extensive research on the variety of same-sex practices and homosexual expression in traditional cultures can be found in Greenberg 25–88.

12. By this I mean that anthropologists are necessarily very selective when it comes to explaining why a culture engages in its behaviors. What determines which behaviors need explanation and which behaviors are self-explanatory? The norm or standard of behavior already established in the anthropologist's own culture becomes the basis for selection and explanation.

13. See, for instance, Clifford Geertz's famous critique of Lévi-Strauss in The *Interpretation of Cultures* (345–59). Geertz writes:

> For what Lévi-Strauss has made for himself is an infernal culture machine. It annuls history, reduces sentiment to a shadow of the intellect, and replaces the particular minds of particular savages in particular jungles with the Savage Mind immanent in us all. It has made it possible for him to circumvent the impasse to which his Brazilian expedition led—physical closeness and intellectual distance—by what perhaps he always really wanted—intellectual closeness and physical distance. (355–56)

14. In the Introduction to my work in progress, *Color of Manhood*, I offer a concept of cultural knowledge based on the interdependent cognitive processes of synecdoche, meton-

ymy, and projection. I define synecdoche as the tendency to view specific characteristics perceived as common among a particular group as constituting a whole that can then be extrapolated back to every individual associated with the group. Cognitive metonymy is the tendency to exchange partial knowledge and ignorance about individuals perceived as belonging to a group for full knowledge about those individuals. Projection is the tendency to throw onto oppressed groups that which is most feared within an oppressing group as a form of scapegoating.

15. Murray is so uneasy with class analysis that he goes so far as to suggest that it is impossible to identify a black middle class, and yet his argument seems to rely on the need for a middle class (see his section the "Illusive Black Middle Class" in *The Omni-Americans* 86–96). For an analysis of the black middle class at the opposite end of the pole, see Cruse (especially 267–336); and Frazier. It is also ironic that Murray criticizes writers like Brown, Baldwin, and Cleaver for writing for white people when his own book is clearly written for white people in order to remold the image of African American culture into one of ethnic respectability.

16. Exhibitionist writing is closely related to the protest tradition in African American literature, a tradition which tends to represent the author as a spokesman for the race addressing a predominantly white audience. In *The Way of the New World*, Addison Gayle, Jr. develops a sophisticated cultural history of the African American novel based on the progression from protest to rebellion to revolution, as a progression from the desire for assimilation and American liberty to the reclamation of cultural identity and self-directed social revolution. From this perspective, exhibitionist writing like Baldwin's and Brown's becomes atavistic, going against the grain of African American literary history.

17. White interlopers in the black community also wrote books on the urban ghetto contributing to this trend. Murray uses Warren Miller's *The Cool World* (1959) as the prime example (see Albert Murray 127–83). Miller's portrayal of black men's sexual license, analyzed later in the chapter, participates in a tradition that goes at least as far back as Carl Van Vechten's 1926 novel about Harlem, *Nigger Heaven*.

18. Brown's 1973 book, *The Children of Ham*, is comprised of a series of interviews with young gang members, who talk about their lives on the street. As with *Manchild*, Brown aspires toward a documentary form, dissuading a judgmental response and encouraging vicarious sympathy, as a way of understanding the broader pressures bearing on the community at large. Mumps' description of prison homosexuality is noticeably different from the description given by Sonny, as Mumps relies much more on mainstream conventions of homophobia, rather than on attitudes toward sexual diversity indigenous to African American culture before the 1960s. This brief discussion of homosexuality in *Children of Ham* may index the attitudinal shift toward sexual variance resulting from a variety of changes within the African American community and within mainstream society concerning the status of gay men and lesbians (see 98–100).

19. In stressing the procreative value, and thus the father's place as inseminator or provider, Afrocentrists like the Hares are going against a long-honored, indigenous tradition within African American culture of stressing individual talent as contribution to community rather than strictly coded roles as the source of community stability. Traditionally, an individual gives according to the gifts and special talents given to him or her by God, not according to a social role predetermined by gender or sexuality and coded strictly according to one's place in a nuclear family. In this tradition, a homosexual or female provider is not a threat, but a necessity for mutual survival. According to the logic of some Afrocentrists, as in mainstream

white culture, the individual who provides outside of the prescribed gender role becomes a threat to patriarchal fathering and procreation.

20. In Chapter 2 of the *Color of Manhood*, I discuss in some detail the dialectically opposed images of the sissy and the swish, the two dominant representations of male homosexuality within African American culture. The sissy is an aspiring middle-class man who is very discreet about his same-sex desire. He courts and achieves respectability within the African American community, especially through the influential religious, educational, and social service institutions, either limiting or sacrificing his sexual expression for the sake of advancing the race. As a pillar of the community, he becomes a role model presentable to white America. The swisher, or swish, is as flamboyant and defiant as the sissy is circumspect and subservient. He is associated usually with life on the streets, and cultivates a cross-over dynamic with white homosexuals parallel to the sissy's cross-over influence as a representative spokesman for the race.

21. According to Peterson, "Black males have extensive homosexual experience, but it may not affect their homosexual identity" (149). This is one statistical notion that seems easily borne out in terms of the qualitative and representational literature on male homosexuality in the African American community. Nevertheless, Peterson goes on to apply inappropriate autonomous-culture models to this behavior, assuming—in a similar way that Lévi-Strauss does about the Nambikwara—that same-sex bonding behavior among men not self-identified as gay has to be explained away as acts of deprivation. "These heterosexual men may not label themselves homosexual because of the reasons they engage in homosexual behavior" (149). Peterson goes on to list economic motivations, high unemployment, and lack of access to female partners as the reasons for sex between self-identified gay black men and "heterosexual" black men. Peterson fails to see that the whole issue of labeling sexuality is different and plays a radically different role in African American culture from that in the dominant white culture. A similar pattern of behavior has been noted among Latino men. For a discussion of this issue in Chicano culture, see Almáquer and Carrier. Carrier writes, "One effect of homosexual role playing in Mexican society is that only the feminine male is labeled a 'homosexual.' By societal standards, the masculine self-image of Mexican males is not threatened by their homosexual behavior as long as they play the anal insertive role and also have a reputation for having sexual relations with women" (206). Carrier also points out that "[t]he major effect of this is that 'straight' Anglo males in general appear to be far more concerned about being approached by homosexual males than do 'straight' Mexican males. 'Queer bashing,' for example, is an Anglo phenomenon that occurs only rarely in Mexico" (207).

WORKS CITED

Adam, Barry D. *The Rise of a Gay and Lesbian Movement*. Boston: Twayne, 1987.

Allen, Paula Gunn. *The Sacred Hoop: Recovering the Feminine in Native American Traditions*. Boston: Beacon Press, 1986.

Almáquer, Tomás. "Chicano Men: A Cartography of Homosexual Identity and Behavior." *differences* 3.2 (1991): 75–100.

Altman, Dennis. *The Homosexualization of America, the Americanization of the Homosexual*. New York: St. Martin's, 1982.

Bray, Alan. *Homosexuality in Renaissance England*. London: Gay Men's Press, 1982.

Bronski, Michael. *Culture Clash: The Making of Gay Sensibility*. Boston: South End Press, 1984.

Brown, Claude. *Manchild in the Promised Land*. New York: Signet, 1965.

————. *The Children of Ham*. New York: Stein and Day, 1973.

Carrier, Joseph. "Miguel: Sexual Life History of a Gay Mexican American." *Gay Culture in America*, Ed. Gilbert Herdt. Boston: Beacon Press, 1992. 202–24.

Cory, Donald Webster. *The Homosexual in America: A Subjective Approach*. New York: Greenberg, 1951.

Cruse, Harold. *The Crisis of the Negro Intellectual*. New York: Quill, 1984.

D'Emilio, John. *Sexual Politics, Sexual Communities: The Making of a Homosexual Minority in the United States, 1940–1970*. Chicago: University of Chicago Press, 1983.

Frazier, E. Franklin. *Black Bourgeoisie: The Rise of a New Middle Class in the United States*. New York: Macmillan, 1957.

Garber, Eric. "A Spectacle in Color: The Lesbian and Gay Subculture of Jazz Age Harlem." *Hidden from History: Reclaiming the Gay and Lesbian Past*. Ed. Martin Bauml Duberman, Martha Vicinus and George Chauncey, Jr. New York: New American Library, 1989. 318–31.

Gates, Henry Louis, Jr. "Blacklash?" *The New Yorker*. 17 May 1993: 42–44.

Gayle, Addison, Jr. *The Way of the New World: The Black Novel in America*. Garden City, NY: Anchor/Doubleday, 1975.

Geertz, Clifford. *The Interpretation of Cultures*. New York: Basic Books, 1973.

Goldstein, Richard. "Go the Way Your Blood Beats: An Interview with James Baldwin." *James Baldwin: The Legacy*. Ed. Quincy Troupe. New York: Simon and Schuster, 1989. 173–85.

Greenberg, David F. *The Construction of Homosexuality*. Chicago: University of Chicago Press, 1988.

Hare, Nathan, and Julia Hare. *The Endangered Black Family: Coping with the Unisexualization and Coming Extinction of the Black Race*. San Francisco: Black Think Tank, 1984.

Herdt, Gilbert, ed. *Gay Culture in America: Essays from the Field*. Boston: Beacon Press, 1992.

Kleinberg, Seymour. *Alienated Affections: Being Gay in America*. New York: St. Martin's, 1977.

Lévi-Strauss, Claude. *Tristes Tropiques*. New York: Washington Square Press, 1955.

Marotta, Toby. *The Politics of Homosexuality*. Boston: Houghton Mifflin, 1981.

Martin, Biddy. "Sexualities without Genders and Other Queer Utopias." U of Michigan. 1 April 1993.

Murray, Albert. *The Omni-Americans: Black Experience and American Culture*. New York: Vintage, 1970.

Murray, Stephen O. "Components of Gay Community in San Francisco." *Gay Culture in America*. Ed. Gilbert Herdt. Boston: Beacon Press, 1992. 107–46.

Nero, Charles I. "Toward a Black Gay Aesthetic: Signifying in Contemporary Black Gay Literature." *Brother to Brother: New Writings by Black Gay Men*. Ed. Essex Hemphill. Conceived by Joseph Bean. Boston: Alyson, 1991. 229–52.

Norton, Rictor. *Mother Clap's Molly House: The Gay Subculture in England 1700–1830*. London: GMP, 1992.

Peterson, John L. "Black Men and Their Same-Sex Desires and Behaviors." *Gay Culture in America*. Ed. Gilbert Herdt. Boston: Beacon Press, 1992. 147–64.

Ross, Marlon B. *The Color of Manhood*. In progress.

Trumbach, Randolph. "The Birth of the Queen: Sodomy and the Emergence of Gender Equality in Modern Culture, 1660–1750." *Hidden from History: Reclaiming the Gay and Lesbian Past.* Ed. Martin Bauml Duberman, Martha Vicinus and George Chauncey, Jr. New York: New American Library, 1989. 129–40.

Williams, Walter L. *The Spirit and the Flesh: Sexual Diversity in American Indian Culture.* Boston: Beacon Press, 1986.

42 | The Crisis in Black American Literary Criticism and the Postmodern Cures of Houston A. Baker, Jr., and Henry Louis Gates, Jr.

Sandra Adell

(1994)

> Certainly one way to conceive of the Afro-American's attempt to resolve double-consciousness is as a struggle to be initiated into the larger American society. Such a struggle does not necessarily conclude in acceptance by that society. . . . In other words, Afro-American double-consciousness is not always resolved.
> —Michael Awkward, *Inspiring Influences*

This epigraph serves to remind us once again that Du Bois's "double consciousness," like the social myth that literary criticism can somehow speak for the absent and unrepresented other, is an abiding issue in Afro-American and black diaspora literature and literary criticism. And it is infused with the spirit of paradox. We can think of paradox as a rhetorical trope or as an inescapable logical principle of any system of thought. In either case, what we would find is that paradoxes are "profoundly self-critical." Rosalie Colie, who is perhaps the preeminent scholar of paradoxes, identifies three kinds of paradox: the rhetorical, the logical, and the epistemological. Each of these paradoxes carries out a critical function. They operate at the "limits of discourse" and redirect "thoughtful attention to the faulty or limited structures of thought" by commenting on their own method and technique. As Colie puts it, "paradoxes play back and forth across terminal and categorial boundaries—that is, they play with human understanding."[1]

In this chapter, I discuss how the current crisis in the critical reading of twentieth-century Afro-American writing has been deepened by certain philosophical and epistemological paradoxes arising from the incompleteness and inconsistencies of formal networks of principles such as the ones posited by Houston Baker in *Blues, Ideology, and Afro-American Literature: A Vernacular Theory*[2] and Henry Louis Gates, Jr., in *The Signifying Monkey*. But first, since I contend that this is a crisis in reading, I must also contend that I know how to read. Thus it becomes necessary to digress and briefly remark on the practice of the critical reading of literary texts.

Before the decline in the late 1930s of what Wlad Godzich calls the great age of literary history, reading was thought to be a simple horizontal process. The reader followed a line of writing or text in order to lay out its set and finite meanings and experience its truth. The critic, who occupied only two spaces in the academy—philology or literary history—was charged with securing the reader in the proper interpretation, and with establishing the texts and making them as reliable as possible so that they could be weaved into a "satisfactory narrative of national cultural achievement."[3] Later, literary criticism, under the influence of formalism and its interrogation of the meaning and truth of poetic analysis, began to turn its attention to reading as a problematic, as a complex relationship between the reader as decoder of signs and the text.

Among the questions this new criticism raised was, in the "transaction" that occurs between reader and text, who has control of the reading of the text? The reader, the critic, or the text itself?[4] Where are the meaning and the truth of the text lodged? Do they come out of the text, or are they brought to bear upon the text by the act of reading? In order to respond to these and other questions, criticism became divided into the "complementary opposition of primary text and secondary discourse." According to Godzich, what this opposition suggests is that the truth of the primary text, which "remains somehow burdened by its mode of representation," can be attained and "given a better representation" by the secondary work. "In other words, the primary vs. secondary opposition is predicated upon a prior opposition, which it locates in the primary text, between a truth or a meaning to be disclosed and the means of that disclosure."[5]

In many respects, Houston Baker's *Blues, Ideology, and Afro-American Literature* is symptomatic of this opposition. Baker wishes, among other things, to resolve the oppositions between the truth of what he calls "Afro-American expressive culture" and its modes of representation. To do so, he posits a spatial metaphor—the blues matrix—that does indeed "summon an image of the black blues singer at the railway junction lustily transforming experiences of a durative (unceasingly oppressive) landscape into the energies of rhythmic song" (7). This spatial metaphor also summons an image of the folk, the blues people who, in Baker's paradigm, "constitute the vernacular in the United States," cleaning the dirt and grime from their always already overworked bodies, exchanging their old work clothes for their very best clothes and heading for the function at the junction. Here, the field and foundry workers, the laborers and loggers, the garbage men and the yard men, the cooks and the cleaning women and the washerwomen and the just plain wild women temporarily suspend their worries and their fatigue. And with the "dance-beat elegance" intrinsic to a "dance-beat-oriented people," they sing and they shout and they shimmy and they swing and they boogie and they otherwise stomp their blues away.[6]

It is in this space that Baker hopes to find and develop a methodology that will allow him to disclose a "uniquely Afro-American discourse" from which the Afro-American "expressive work" emerges. Baker argues that "the blues . . . comprise a mediational site where familiar antinomies are resolved (or dissolved) in the office of adequate cultural understanding" (6). His text is structured around a "guiding pre-supposition . . . that Afro-American culture is a complex, reflexive enterprise which finds its proper figuration in blues considered as a matrix" (3). To restate the problematic, what Baker seeks through the blues matrix is a critique of American cultural values. He is also trying to find a new way of apprehending Afro-American expressive culture that would adhere to principles of understanding and history that somehow stand outside traditional American theoretical contexts.

Henry Louis Gates is likewise guided by a desire to identify and define a theory of criticism specific to the Afro-American tradition from *within* that tradition. In fact, he claims that his work in *The Signifying Monkey* tries to accomplish, through the Afro-American notion of "signifyin(g)," what he feels Baker accomplishes with the blues in *Blues, Ideology, and Afro-American Literature*, namely, the identification and isolation of an "authentic" Afro-American literary tradition grounded in the black vernacular. Paradoxically, however, as I will show, the methods employed by Baker and Gates make the very notion of such authenticity suspect, to say the least. For they both appropriate and marshal formidable epistemologies from structuralism, post-structuralism, and deconstruction in order to make certain truth claims on behalf of the tradition.

Let me state at the outset that I do not find these appropriations problematic with regard to the explanation and interpretation of Afro-American literature: our positions in the academy compel us to "master the master's tongue"; our positions as critics of Afro-American literature should compel us to rigorously interrogate the "complex relation between [Afro-American] literature and literary theory."[7] Neither am I concerned with passing judgments on Baker's and Gates's degree of commitment to the study of Afro-American literature or to the black community, although I believe that commitment is an issue about which those of us who are black and within the academy must do some serious thinking. What is at issue here is whether Baker and Gates, in the interest of the black vernacular, have not in fact subverted their own intentions. This leads me to raise the very questions posed by Gates in "Authority, (White) Power and the (Black) Critic." Specifically, "can we derive a valid, *integral* 'black' text of criticism or ideology from borrowed or appropriated forms? That is, can an authentic black text emerge in the forms of language inherited from the master's class, whether that be, for instance, the realistic novel or post-structuralist theory?"[8] In an attempt to respond to these questions, let us turn first to what I shall call the two master concepts—archaeology and ideology—of Houston Baker's *Blues, Ideology, and Afro-American Literature* and then to the coin of hermeneutics and rhetoric, which I feel governs Gates's rhetorical strategies in *The Signifying Monkey*.

In the first chapter of *Blues, Ideology, and Afro-American Literature*, Baker borrows his two master concepts, archaeology and ideology, in order to try to develop what he calls "Figurations for a New American Literary History." He uses these concepts in an effort to shift Afro-American literary study "from a 'traditional' to an economic perspective, from a humanistic to an ideologically-oriented frame of reference" (26). He relies on texts by Michel Foucault (the archaeology master-text) and Fredric Jameson and Hayden White (the ideology master-text) to effect this shift. Consequently, his discourse, indeed, his entire theoretical enterprise, is subtended by the spate of philosophical subtexts that prompt those of Foucault, Jameson, and White: the writings of Descartes, Nietzsche, Mallarmé, Heidegger, Hegel, Marx, Althusser, and Kenneth Burke, to name but a few. In any event, Baker's enterprise suggests a deep dissatisfaction—if not a crisis—with the way the fields of American and Afro-American literary history have been previously approached. But what, I ask, if anything, has been resolved in the crisis in the study of black writing by Baker's new technical elaboration of Eurocentric methods, concepts, paradigms, and so on? Does not his eclectic discursivity succeed only in more fully obscuring rather than revealing those modes of expression—the blues, for example, that are most firmly grounded in the black vernacular? I shall begin my interrogation by first taking up Baker's master concept, archaeology.

In his appropriation of *The Archaeology of Knowledge* Baker tends to reduce the text to a methodology, to a "method of analysis," in order to "discover certain primary linguistic functions" that he feels serve as governing statements for the discursive family of "American History." These statements, which include "religious man," "wilderness," "migratory errand," and the "New Jerusalem" are, according to Baker, the "primary conceptual structures" for the establishment of what he calls the "explicit boundaries" of "ethnic exclusion" in "traditional American literary history." He mentions Robert Spiller's *A Literary History of the United States* and an anthology, *American Literature*, edited by Cleanth Brooks, R. W. B. Lewis, and Robert Penn Warren in order to demonstrate his point that writing by people who do not fall within the category of the "Religious man," whom Baker describes as a "devout believer in God for whom matters of economics and wealth are minimal considerations" (19), constitutes a "category of the excluded" that exists "somewhere between secondary and non-literature" (21). In the first chapter, Baker aims to effect a movement from these "American historical statements" to a new structure. This new structure is governed by a statement, "commercial deportation," which he borrows from George Lamming's *Season of Adventure*. Baker feels that this "new governing statement" is capable of altering "the construction of traditional American historical discourse" since it signifies the involuntary transport, for profit, of human beings, "black gold" rather than courageous Pilgrims heading for "bleak and barren beginnings on New World shores yet to be civilized" (24). (While I do not intend to take it up here, it should be noted that Baker realizes that the statement also presents a fundamental problem for the archaeologist who undertakes to appropriate Foucault's archaeology of knowledge in English translation.) What Baker wishes to illustrate is that the "graphics" accompanying traditional American historical formations are derived from the category of statements that constitute the "New Jerusalem," whereas those accompanying the commercial deportation initiated by "an act of bizarre Western logic" are "strikingly different." Consequently, this new governing structure effects a shift in the larger historical view from a "New Jerusalem" to "Armageddon." Moreover, it "opens the way for a corollary shift in perspective on 'American literary history.' What comes starkly to the foreground are the conditions of a uniquely Afro-American historical and literary discourse" (24–25). In this way, the "archaeologist" Houston Baker feels that he had gone to a deeper level of discourse and has discovered certain formative principles—the economics and practice of slavery, for example—that subtend the explicit levels of American historical discourse. What is ironic, however, is that Baker can only discover European man engaged in commercial deportation through yet another "act of bizarre Western logic": through a massive importation of the theoretical and ideological constructs of European man.

This "act of bizarre Western logic" also clearly suggests that Baker sees Foucault's theoretical provocations as programmatic, although Foucault is not interested in constructing a method. While both Foucault and Baker are deeply concerned with knowledge of and the nature of historical change and with language as event or act, Foucault is perhaps more deeply concerned with the will to knowledge as such, that is, the "distinction between knowledge and the rules necessary to its acquisition; the difference between the will to knowledge and the will to truth; [and] the position of the subject and subjects in relation to this will."[9] Moreover, Foucault is acutely aware of the problems generated in the study of the theoretical problems themselves; for— and this is something that Baker seems not to have taken into consideration— problems are often generated by the very concepts one employs.

In the "History of Systems of Thought," Foucault writes that the series of individual analyses he initiated in a 1970–71 course was intended to gradually form a "morphology of the will to knowledge" from within the "history of systems of thought" (*Language* 199). His objective was to explore this theme "in relation to specific historical investigations and in its own right *in terms of its theoretical implications*" (*Language* 199, emphasis added). This latter objective necessitated the construction and definition of the tools that permit the analysis of the will to knowledge "according to the needs and possibilities that arise from a series of concrete studies" (*Language* 201). Furthermore, Foucault always starts his analysis from within a unified "field"—political economy for instance—and he goes to great lengths in order not to remain trapped within the codes of such a unity. But, more important, Foucault renounces systematic discourse and most certainly "structuralist ways." Following Nietzsche (who writes, "I mistrust all systematizers and I avoid them. The will to a system is a lack of integrity"),[10] Foucault in *The Archaeology of Knowledge* conceives of discourse as an "order" that, in his rejection of structuralism, he would like to subvert.

Baker does not ignore Foucault's disagreement with the "structuralist project." Yet, as he explains in a footnote, he brings Foucault together with Roland Barthes because he feels that in the conclusion to *The Archaeology of Knowledge* Foucault concedes "certain analytical successes" to structuralism (208n13). He also believes that Barthes, by focusing on the formation of historical discourse in his essay, "Historical Discourse," shares Foucault's concern with the "constraints of discourse" rather than with a "constraining subjectivity" (22). However, what Baker apparently overlooks in his reading of Barthes's essay, particularly in the third section, is the Nietzschean subtext shared by both the "semiotician" and the "archaeologist." Foucault makes explicit the extent to which his work is informed by that of Nietzsche in "Nietzsche, Genealogy, History." This has important implications for Baker's "archaeological" project because, in many respects, Foucault's concept of history mimes Nietzsche's genealogy. It therefore seeks to do away with the theme of anthropocentrism and the kinds of categories of cultural totalities that are essential to Baker's project. As Foucault explains in the introduction to *The Archaeology of Knowledge*, all of his work has been organized around an enterprise that seeks, as one of its objectives, to throw off the "anthropological constraints" he feels have prevented a close analysis of the methodological problems specific to the "field of history" in general. In return, he hopes to reveal how those constraints came about in the first place.[11] This enterprise therefore requires that history be mastered so that it can be turned to genealogical, or what Foucault refers to as "anti-Platonic purposes."

Foucault describes this historical sense as giving rise to three uses that oppose and correspond to the three Platonic modalities of history: the parodic, the dissociative, and the sacrificial. He writes that together "they imply a use of history that severs its connection to memory, its metaphysical and anthropological model, and constructs a counter-memory—a transformation of history into a totally different form of time" (160). Baker, on the other hand, is writing in the interest of "righting" American history and literary history, as we have seen (200). He also relies very heavily on anthropology. In fact, as he explains in chapter 2, he strongly favors the kind of "cultural-anthropological approach" to the study of Afro-American expressive culture taken by writers like Stephen Henderson and the Black Aestheticians (109). What he does not sufficiently discuss, however, are the limitations of his appropriated model for his own archaeological and anthropological enterprise.

Because Baker goes to great lengths to establish himself as a theorist—he even demotes Henry Louis Gates and Robert Stepto to the status of critics—certain sections of chapter 2 seem strangely out of place in his study (107). This can perhaps be attributed to the fact that the chapter is a revised version of an essay published in 1981 (64). What I find rather ironic about this chapter is that Baker takes issue with some of the same problems raised by Joyce A. Joyce in that very unfortunate exchange between Joyce, Gates, and Baker, which was published in the 1986–87 edition of *New Literary History*. Specifically, Baker criticizes the "reconstructionists" for being hampered by what he calls "literary-critical professionalism," a result of which is the "sometimes uncritical imposition upon Afro-American expressive culture of theories and theoretical terminologies borrowed from prominent white scholars" (89). He argues quite persuasively that the adoption by the "emergent" reconstructionists of the professional assumptions and jargon of white academic literary critics do little to further a "vernacular-oriented mode of analysis." It seems that Baker has not considered the possibility that his criticism of the would-be theorists Gates and Stepto could very well apply to himself. Baker has a penchant for uncritically stitching together concepts, methods, paradigms, and the like. Thus, what he says of the reconstructionists, that their early manifestations "reveal a vigorous, if quite often confused and confusing, engagement with establishment theoretical language," is tantamount to the pot calling the kettle black.

Baker's theorizing does, nevertheless, raise many important issues about Afro-American literature, criticism, and literary history that have not been previously addressed. Indeed, his readings in the third chapter of certain canonical Afro-American texts are nothing short of provocative. But his often wholesale appropriation has not served the interests of a "black vernacular" theory. Stated simply, Baker's theoretical intentions are badly undermined by his own eclectic moves. Consequently, what he observes about Robert B. Stepto's "critical rhetoric" is even more applicable to his own: it "plays him abysmally false" (93). It is not my intention, however, to rectify Baker's appropriations of Eurocentric philosophemes or his critical observations about other critics and theorists of Afro-American literature. I wish to comment, rather, on the imperatives—epistemological and ontological—that guide his theoretical shifts.

One of these imperatives has to do with Foucault's "alleged" decentering of the subject. Baker makes much of this, yet he is forced to inscribe these troublesome terms within quotation marks. For example, in an important footnote to the section called "Defining Blues," he writes,

> The description at this point is coextensive with the "decentering" of the subject mentioned at the outset of my introduction. What I wish to effect by noting a "subject" who is not *filled* is a displacement of the notion that knowledge, or "art," or "song," are manifestations of an ever more clearly defined individual consciousness of *Man*. In accord with Michel Foucault's explorations in his *Archaeology of Knowledge*, I want to claim that blues is like a discourse that comprises the "already said" of Afro-America. Blues' governing statements and sites are thus vastly more interesting in the process of cultural investigation than either a history of ideals or a history of individual, subjective consciousness vis-à-vis blues. (206n11)

It is worth noting here that Derrida, in "Structure, Sign, and Play,"[12] points to a problem that is relevant to Baker's discussion of the "decentering" of the subject, that is, the process by which a referred to "point of presence" or "fixed origin" neutralizes or reduces the structure itself. Derrida suggests that the "movement of any archaeology, like that of any eschatology," might be complicit in this reduction. That being the case, then,

> the whole history of the concept of structure . . . must be thought of as a series of substitutions of center for center, as a linked chain of determinations of the center. Successively, and in a regulated fashion, the center receives different forms or names. The history of metaphysics, like the history of the West, is the history of these metaphors and metonymies. Its matrix . . . is the determination of being as *presence* in all the senses of this word. (249)

We arrive, then, at Baker's spatial metaphor; we arrive, then, at the blues matrix, at the junction with its "substitutions of center for center," with the blues and the blues singer standing in for the "decentered subject," with the latter transforming and translating the former in a "lusty and ceaseless flux."

Through his spatial metaphors—intersection, juncture, and so forth—Baker points to the figure of the chiasm. One of the oldest rhetorical or grammatical devices, the chiasm shapes thought and allows it to both take discourse apart and bring together contradictory functions, to gather them within an identity—at the point of contact of *chi*, X, of movement. (I shall have more to say about the chiasm in my discussion of Gates.)

In *The Archaeology of Knowledge*, Foucault also employs spatial metaphors, but he does so in order to destroy the very notions of experience that Baker needs in order to place the blues and the blues singer at the juncture. For the blues singer is charged with interpreting the "experiencing of experience" and with mediating the "endless antinomies" generated by the juncture's "ever-changing scenes" (7). The metaphorics of space—even of an "original" textual space—dominates Baker's notion of understanding because he thinks it allows for "mediation," although he does not explain how antinomies can be mediated. In this space there is, at least for Baker's investigator, who "has to *be* there," a spectacle, a quiet spectacle with a beginning and an end. And so the disruptive play of the blues, I would like to suggest, is tamed in the interest of understanding and adequate explanation and interpretation.

Houston Baker appropriates his other master concept, ideology, from the ideological models of Fredric Jameson and Hayden White in an effort to avoid what he calls a "vulgar Marxism, or an idealistically polemical black nationalism." (Because certain limits must be drawn in any critical or theoretical undertaking, I will limit my discussion of the ideology master-text to Jameson.) Baker writes that his concern is with a "form of thought that grounds Afro-American discourse in concrete material situations" in such a way that one can gain the "subtextual dimensions" of that discourse which have yet to be effectively evaluated (25–26). However, in the process of trying to reach these "subtextual dimensions," Baker sidesteps a very complex problem: that of defining the status of the term ideology. To further complicate matters, in order to construct his own ideological model, Baker relies in part on Jameson's "The Symbolic Inference, or Kenneth Burke and Ideological Analysis," an essay that sparked a lively debate between Jameson and Burke precisely over what Burke calls Jameson's "over investment in the term 'ideology.' "[13]

Jameson is highly aware of the problematical nature of the ideological model, as Baker points out. In "The Symbolic Inference," Jameson calls ideology "the sign for a problem yet to be solved, a mental operation which remains to be executed" (Jameson 510). Its "usefulness" is as a "mediatory concept: that is, it is an imperative to re-invent a relationship between the linguistic or aesthetic or conceptual fact in question and its social ground" (Jameson 510). However, in describing his ideological analysis, which he claims to do phenomenologically, Jameson is careful not to argue for the priority of historical, social, or political reality over the literary artifacts themselves (Jameson 511). In fact, in another important essay, "Marxism and Historicism," Jameson deals with ideology as one aspect of the larger problem of what he calls a "properly Marxist *hermeneutic*": it is a problem in interpretation, which he "construes . . . as a rewriting operation."[14] What needs to be questioned is whether Jameson's alleged "over investment" in the term *ideology* and his privileging of the literary artifact over historical, social, or political reality is an attempt to avoid commitment and falling into a vulgar Marxism.

That question lies beyond the scope of this study, but I would like to point out that, contrary to critics like Joyce A. Joyce and Norman Harris,[15] who argue differently, Baker and Gates are as concerned with the historical, social, and political implications of Afro-American literature as they are with deepening its literary analyses. In fact, Baker interprets the literary texts included in his study within the conceptual framework of the capitalist "mode of production." His interpretations are therefore situated within the tropes of ideological and economic practice. The shortcoming, however, is that nowhere does he work out the specific modalities or relationships of this practice. He simply asserts what this shift from a traditional to an economic perspective is expected to signify, that is, a social system "that determined what, how, and for whom goods were produced to satisfy human wants. As a function of the European slave trade, the economy of the Old South was an exploitative mode of production embodied in the plantation system and spirited by a myth of aristocratic patriarchalism"(27).

This sort of critical endeavor requires a meticulous textual laying out of the combinatory of the specific mode of production being interrogated and all of its "practices," for as Balibar shows in *Reading Capital*, the concept of "mode of production" is extremely problematic.[16] This, Baker does not do. Instead he proceeds by simply asserting that the negotiation of the economics of slavery should lead to "black expressive wholeness," that is, to the appearance of blues energized expressive spaces in Afro-American expressive culture that have heretofore been neglected by critics untrained in the "vernacular" (114–15).

According to Baker, Paul Laurence Dunbar's *The Sport of that Gods* is a case in point. Baker claims that the novel "gestures" toward what he calls "a blues book most excellent." But in order to develop his interpretive strategy, he turns first, not to a "blues-ideology," or a "blues aesthetic," but to an essay by Victor Turner entitled "Myth and Symbol." Baker feels that an interpretive strategy grounded in the kind of discourse employed by Turner will somehow help to "clarify the nature of Dunbar's blues achievement." He tries to justify his strategy by asserting that since literary criticism constitutes a historical domain, in order to achieve status as an accepted and learned critic, "one must transmit readily comprehensible messages to a historical (i.e., human, and defined implicitly as possessing determinate needs, habits, customs, etc.) audience" in "ordinary language" (115–16). What this has to do with Dunbar's blues achievements in *The Sport of the Gods* is anyone's guess, for if it clarifies anything, it is only that Baker is unable to remain within his own archaeological and ideological models. This also serves to inform on Baker's position vis-à-vis "critical professionalism," for his concern with the critic's accepted and learned status certainly contradicts an earlier statement that "The necessity, in all paradigmatic blues analyses, is to leave the 'bitter . . . rotten,' and, one might add, 'overly professional or careerist' parts alone" (111).

Baker does make an important observation about the status of the Afro-American critic, however. Being betwixt and between, "He is bound to engage terms of a traditional historical criticism in order to demonstrate its limitations. At the same time, he is free to move decisively beyond the inadequacies of a past historical criticism and engage Afro-American expressive texts in their full symbolic potency"(117).

Needless to say, such pronouncements have much to recommend them, but only when the critic is also aware of how such an engagement actually positions him (or her, as the case may be). In other words, the critic must take into consideration the extent to which the discourse he employs helps to determine that position and, as in this case, may in fact remove him from the very tradition he is trying to establish. For, let us not forget, critique is a European concept. Therefore, any discourse falling under the aegis of critique is already heavily informed by certain preeminent (philosophical and quasi-philosophical) texts from which subsequent critical discourses, including my own, cannot easily extricate themselves. This means that all of us are unquestionably implicated in the tradition of critique. The problems raised by this theoretical topography are obviously immense, particularly for the black critic, for what remains to be asked is, Where does the critic in fact "stand"? Whence and what has the black critic received? Where do those who receive his writing "stand"? To properly treat these questions would require a painstaking account of the numerous mediations within this topography. Suffice it to say that as one who has "received" the writings of Baker and Gates, I am positioned in a way that compels me, in order to carry out this critique, to engage the very discourses being called into question. Stated differently, in order to adequately problematize the critical and theoretical projects undertaken by these critics, I must necessarily be traversed—criss-crossed— by their discourses. Theoretically, then, my "stand" makes me vulnerable to—or maybe it obliterates me from—the same kinds of criticisms I've made against them, for hasn't the pot once again called the kettle black? Perhaps. Or perhaps what is being demonstrated is how difficult it is for any critical or theoretical enterprise to support its claim against Eurocentrism. Perhaps what is being suggested is that for a literary tradition that has been established by dint of exclusion, Eurocentrism is the only ground.

I have indicated, albeit schematically, that Baker has in many and important ways misappropriated. The question remains, however, whether a more erudite appropriation of Foucault, Jameson, White, and all the other texts Baker grafts onto the blues matrix brings us any closer to specifying the black text. On this question I turn now to Henry Louis Gates, Jr.

Let us not forget that, like Baker, Gates is guided by a desire to identify and define a theory of criticism specific to the Afro-American literary tradition from within that very tradition. Before he can proceed, however, he must first clear the junction of the blues, the blues singer, and Houston Baker and place in their stead the figure of that sly simian himself. But, presumably in order to deepen the historical dimension of the Afro-American literary tradition, he must also invoke the Yoruba trickster figure, Esu-Elegbara, as the antecedent to the figure of the Signifying Monkey. As "points of conscious articulation of language traditions aware of themselves as traditions," these two figures presumably posit a "meta-discourse, a discourse about itself . . . in the black tradition, in the vernacular, far away from . . . those who do not speak the language of tradition" (xx–xxi).

The language of tradition, of the black vernacular, is to be disclosed through an examination, which Gates carries out in part 1 of *The Signifying Monkey*, of how these two "tricksters" reflect on the formal uses of language in their respective traditions and how they "stand for certain principles of verbal expression." Esu is described as "a figure for the nature and function of interpretation" and for what Gates calls "double-voiced utterance." The Signifying Monkey serves as a kind of master trope "in which are encoded several other peculiarly black rhetorical tropes." By exploring the "place each accords forms of language use in the production of meaning," Gates hopes, among other things, to show the historical relationship between the two figures and the extent to which they "articulate the black tradition's theory of its literature" (xxi). A ritual of renaming, substitution, and analogue is therefore obviously underway as tradition becomes both a site of struggle and an opposition to the regulative ideas of hermeneutics.

In Gates's historical account of the development of writing by blacks in "New World African-informed cultures," Hermes is replaced by Esu-Elegbara as "the guardian of the crossroads, master of style and of stylus, the phallic god of generation and fecundity, master of that elusive, mystical barrier that separates the divine world from the profane . . . the ultimate copula, connecting truth with understanding, the sacred with the profane, text with interpretation" (6). Hermeneutics, which Gates defines as "the study of methodological principles of interpretation of a text," is renamed Esu-tufunaalo, the Yoruba term for "one who unravels the knots of Esu" (8–9). What he leaves out of his definition of hermeneutics, however, is the role that understanding plays in interpretation. For all interpretation must operate in the "fore-structure" of understanding. It must proceed from an understanding of the world and what it means to be-in-the-world since "any interpretation which is to contribute understanding must already have understood what is to be interpreted."[17] It seems that what Gates seeks to uncover through the genealogy of Esu and the Signifying Monkey outlined in chapter 1 is the possibility for this "most primordial kind of knowing."[18] Esu-Elegbara is inscribed onto this genealogy as "the indigenous black metaphor for the literary critic" whereas the Signifying Monkey is "he who dwells at the margins of discourse, ever punning, ever troping, ever embodying the ambiguities of language, [he] is our trope for repetition and revision, indeed our trope of chiasmus, repeating and reversing simultaneously as he does in one deft discursive act" (52). Gates is obviously playing off of—signifyin(g) on—Baker's spatial metaphor (and Derrida's *Margins of Philosophy*). Esu is at the crossroads, the Signifying Monkey is "our trope of chiasmus."

And so, we are at once forced to confront Gates's Eurocentrism, for it seems that the more the black theorist writes in the interest of blackness, the greater his Euro-centrism reveals itself to be. As Lewis Nkosi remarks in *Home and Exile*, "It is interesting that the further back the African artist goes in exploring his tradition, the nearer he gets to the European avant-garde."[19] Similarly, as Gates goes back in an effort to resurrect the myth of Esu as "the primal figure in a truly black hermeneutic tradition" (42), he must employ the research technologies of postmodernism and post-structuralism, so much so that, terminologically, they effectively replace both Esu and his "Afro-American relative, the Signifying Monkey" (44). In the process, both are de-Africanized, as it were, and in Gates's version, they "speak" like trans-mogrifications of all the hermeneutical (Esu) and rhetorical (Signifying Monkey) paradigms post-structuralism has made ready-at-hand for him.

In some ways, Gates reminds one of his Yoruba-Nigerian friend, Wole Soyinka, particularly the Soyinka of *Myth, Literature and the African World*. Soyinka has made elaborate use of Nietzsche's notion of myth, and both Gates and Soyinka must have recourse to "mythic truth" in order to respond to the twin experiences of slavery and colonization and the cultural heritage left in their wake. In a sense, they both write in response to a critical, theoretical, and cultural hegemony, which they feel constrains African or Afro-American cultures. In a way, they also both seek to dislocate this hegemony by returning to—and supposedly arriving at—an "original" mythical locus that is inhabited by the gods, although Gates is aware that "origins are always occasions for speculation" (46). Both give priority to one god in the pantheon of Yoruba gods: Soyinka to Ogun, and Gates to Esu-Elegbara, who he places within the paradigms of origin and logos. "Esu's representations as the multi-plicity of meaning, as the logos, and as what I shall call the Ogboni Supplement encapsulate his role for the critic" (36). The figure of the god of hermeneutics, which Gates uses to underwrite his interpretations, is indeed, in the final analysis, written over by a grave rhetoricity. In this way what is "manufactured" or "fictioned," is a theory of criticism that brings starkly to the fore the extent to which the black literary tradition participates in the one created by "white men." For as Gates is careful to point out, "Our writers used that impressive tradition to define themselves, both with and against their concept of received order. We must do the same, with or against the Western critical canon. To name our tradition is to rename each of its antecedents, no matter how pale they might seem. To rename is to revise, and to revise is to Signify" (xxiii).

But how is renaming revising? What is the reality of these (re)names in the Afro-American context? Can this kind of nominalism in fact yield a "black signifyin(g) difference"? Keeping these questions in mind, let us turn to Gates once again: "Lest this theory of criticism, however, be thought of as only black, let me admit that the implicit premise of this study is that all texts Signify upon other texts, in motivated and unmotivated ways" (xxiv). Here, Gates undermines his own efforts to establish a principle of black cultural identity based on a "black signifyin(g) difference"; and unwittingly, perhaps, he points to the traditional conflict within the tradition between "Sameness" and "Otherness." For as I have tried to show in previous chapters, to identify itself, the Same needs the Other. The Master needs to define himself against the Slave and vice versa. In cases where there is no Other it has to be invented, for a tradition is an order that requires mechanisms of inclusion and exclusion in the interest of the Same. Gate's notion of "difference," accordingly, is, a notion of sameness. He therefore makes numerous gestures toward deconstruction only to end up in a kind of reconstruction.

For Gates, the Afro-American literary tradition is circumscribed by what he calls the "text of blackness," which he defines in terms of Ralph Ellison's notion of tradition: "a sharing of that 'concord of sensibilities' which the group *expresses*" (128). Gates is quick to point out, however, that this "shared sense of common experience" is not the primary factor in the sharing of the "text of blackness." He argues that the process of revision that tropes and topoi undergo when they are seized by writers as they read each other's texts is what grounds this "shared text of blackness" and the black writer in the tradition. For example, according to Gates, the Anglo-African tradition was inaugurated by John Marrant who used the text of Ukawsaw Gronniosaw as a model to be revised. Gates writes that his "idea of tradition, in part, turns upon this definition of texts read by an author and then Signified upon in some formal way, as an implicit commentary on grounding and on satisfactory modes of representation"(145).

These, then, are the grounds and the limits of the black literary tradition: to participate in the tradition one must read other authors in the tradition then signify on their works in some formal way, which would not be signifyin(g) at all. For as Gates so cogently argues in chapter 2 of *The Signifying Monkey*, an important aspect of signifyin(g) is its dreaded, yet playful "condition of ambiguity" (45). To signify is to engage in a spontaneous verbal game of one-up-manship that cannot be harnessed by writing. Consequently, to signify in "some formal way" is to deprive the game of that condition of ambiguity and the element of surprise intended to provoke a signifyin(g) response. Indeed, within Gates's critical paradigm, the disruptive play and subversiveness of the Signifying Monkey, like that of the blues in Baker, has been tamed, while the figures of the male and female slave and all they represent have been reduced to the figure of that lyin(g) monkey, and all in the interest of a "theory of the tradition." When this is considered in light of Gates's remarks in the introduction that the premise of his book is that "whatever is black about black American literature is to be found in this identifiable black Signifyin(g) difference," but that the implicit premise of the study is "that all texts Signify upon other texts, in motivated and unmotivated ways" (xxiv), one cannot help but wonder if Gates's "theory of the tradition" might more accurately be called the black tradition as Yale School rhetoricity!

As I stated earlier, Gates organizes and develops his theoretical enterprise around the practices of hermeneutics (Esu) and rhetoric (Signifying Monkey), with priority given to the latter as "the trope of literary revision itself" (44). Such a revision would therefore effectively mean that the tradition is beyond hermeneutics, for, let us not forget, all of the recent modalities of criticism that can be gathered under rhetoric eschew the hermeneutics of tradition. They see hermeneutics and rhetoric as antinomies. Thus, in spite of Gates, hermeneutics cannot be reduced to a methodology or somehow become a vehicle for myth-*emes*. It must, at least minimally, take up the problem of understanding's relationship to interpretation and try to grasp, in a given tradition, certain aspects of historical "consciousness." Textual aspects, therefore, participate in the cultural dimension known as heritage—or heritages—and are implicated in the Understanding. As I have previously suggested in my discussion of Baker's theoretical enterprise, ideological critique opposes this and finds alienation and distortion within the tradition. Similarly, a radical rhetoricity delights in pointing to discontinuity. Its operative mode is by definition deconstructive. This gives us an insight into why Gates is a reconstructionist in spite of his appropriation of the rhetorical mode of criticism.

This can all be more fully brought out by considering Gates's notion of chiasmus, which, as I showed earlier, is equated with the Signifying Monkey, "our trope of chiasmus" (52). I will have more to say on the figure of the simian after I have emphasized the centrality of the chiasmus in Gates's "theory of the tradition." Gates places his trope of chiasmus within a rhetorical field of "master tropes" which he claims have been identified by Vico, Burke, Nietzsche, de Man, and Bloom (52). He describes the chiasmus as the most commonly used rhetorical figure in black literature from the slave narratives onward. It "is figured in the black vernacular tradition by tropes of the crossroads, that liminal space where Esu resides" (128). Since it is the "master-trope" of literary revision, we should not be surprised to find that the chiasmus structures Gates's critical and theoretical project itself: "My movement, then, is from hermeneutics to rhetoric and semantics, only to return to hermeneutics again" (44). The question that must be asked is how can one return to hermeneutics [the tradition] after rhetoric?

At the heart of the problem is Gates's metaphor of movement in the junction. His revision is a sort of Hegelian synthesis that yields the tradition, for in contrast to rhetoric, the chiasmus in philosophy is, strictly speaking, a form of thought. Thus, what I am suggesting is that Gates's use of the chiasmus is fundamentally Hegelian.

Since Gates has quite explicitly structured his critical context in part around the works of such prominent figures as Paul de Man, Derrida, and Bloom—in chapter 2 he superimposes his "figures of signification" on Bloom's "map of misprision" in a "signifyin(g) riff" (87)—I feel justified in invoking Rodolphe Gasché, a consummate reader of Derrida and de Man, in my discussion of the chiasmus. Gasché, in his introduction to Andrzei Warminski's *Readings in Interpretation*, offers a most learned and interesting treatment of the chiasmus as "a form of thought in which differences are installed, preserved, and overcome in one grounding unity of totality. It is in this sense that the chiasm can be viewed as the primitive matrix of dialectics in its Hegelian form" (Warminski, xviii). In this sense, then, the chiasmus is hardly a trope of rhetoric.

In bringing hermenutics and rhetoric together, Gates does not take into consideration the problem of the tension and actual discontinuity between the two. Rhetorical theory, in what is perhaps its most powerful articulation, that of de Man, operates within the concept of discontinuity between grammar and rhetoric. Gasché points out that in *Allegories of Reading*, de Man makes it clear that, for him, the chiasm is more than a rhetorical structure based on reversal or substitution. For him it is the textual structure of all texts. As such it cannot serve as a figure of closure as does the concept of tradition (Warminski, xviii). In de Man there is no possibility for a hermeneutical dimension that would be capable of restoring the truth of the text and its tradition. This would be to neutralize the chiasm, since it preserves no textual hermeneutical truth. As the structure of texts as texts, the chiasm promotes and prolongs its own rhetorical delusions. That is what makes it a text. So in this context, the issue is not, as Gates suggests, one of a reversal. The chiasm as figure is beyond reversal and revision. Hence the possibility of movement from something to something and back again is nullified. Movement itself is forever deferred (Warminski xviii–xix).

In Derrida, all writing is chiasmic, at least according to Gasché. Time and space do not allow me to go into detail, but I should like to point out that the chiasm as a writing practice has the quality of undecidability, since it is "neither simply constitutive nor simply disruptive of totality; rather, it is the figure by which a totality constitutes itself in such a manner that the reference to the reserve or the medium of dissociation inseparably inscribed into the figure clearly marks the scope and limits of totality. No unity engendered chiasmically includes within itself the place of difference to which it must refer in order to constitute itself" (Warminski, xix). By definition, this conclusion would apply to the ensemble of *The Signifying Monkey*, which cannot itself be filled by that which it is trying to reverse.

It is not hard to see, therefore, that Gates is closer to the Master of dialectics, Hegel, than to the Masters of rhetorical disruption or the Masters of deferral and solicitation. But even if Gates were one of these Latter Day Masters, the following problems would remain: if rhetoric becomes literature or is literature's being, and if as such it is the phenomenon that, when analyzed specifically, would deconstruct the critical concept of the unity of tradition, then its a priori status would have to be demonstrated. To read rhetorically in the context presently under discussion means to effect such a deconstruction. Yet a principle of unity is essential to Gates's whole project, for without it the tradition would never start and Esu could not generate the Signifying Monkey. To some, this might be just as well, for there is a possibility that in the heritage of the Yoruba this particular simian would be unacceptable. According to one Yoruba scholar, Oyekan Owomoyela, Obotunde means "monkey has returned." He also informs us that "[w]ith the exception of Edun (Colonos monkey), which the twin-loving Yoruba associate with twins, monkeys in general are regarded with ridicule."[20] A more viable figure for Gates's project might have been the Signifying Slave or the Rebellious Slave, also of Yoruba origin, for, "Once, there was a solitary being [Ogun], the primogenitor of god and man, attended only by this slave, Atunda. We do not know where Atunda came from—myth is always careless about detail—perhaps the original one molded him from earth to assist him with domestic chores. However, the slave rebelled. For reasons best known to himself he rolled a huge boulder onto the god as he tended his garden on a hillside, sent him hurtling into the abyss in a thousand and one fragments."[21] But this would mean the deconstruction of the Signifying Monkey and the reconstruction of the Signifyin(g) Slave and a thousand and one godheads. Of such stuff are heritages and traditions made.

While *Blues, Ideology, and Afro-American Literature* and *The Signifying Monkey* fall short of their emancipatory goal of freeing Afro-American literature from the hegemony of Eurocentric discourses, both studies bring into sharp relief what can best be described as a nostalgia for tradition. For to summon a tradition, for example, by reconstructing it, is to search for an authority, that of the tradition itself. Such an enterprise, even as it pits two or more traditions against each other, or even as it attempts to fuse traditions, is inherently conservative. Something is always conserved; something always remains the Same. This is what makes the role of the black critic or anyone else concerned with advancing certain emancipatory ideas particularly burdensome.

Blues, Ideology, and Afro-American Literature and *The Signifying Monkey* most certainly seek, through their theories of the black vernacular, to relieve the critic of his or her burden. But to try to do so by employing the methodologies and critical practices of that "Other" tradition is very, very risky business. For, as Gates remarks in his analogy of Ralph Ellison's little man at Chehaw Station, "The 'little man' or *woman* is bound to surface when the literary critic begins to translate a signal concept from the black vernacular milieu into the discourse of critical theory" (65 emphasis added).

NOTES

A version of this essay first appeared in *Diacritics* (Winter 1990): 43–56. Reprinted with permission of the Journal.

1. Rosalie Colie, *Paradoxia Epidemica: The Renaissance Tradition of Paradox* (Princeton: Princeton University Press, 1966), 7.

2. Houston Baker, *Blues, Ideology, and Afro-American Literature* (All further references to this work are included in the text.)

3. Wlad Godzich, "Caution! Reader at Work!" in *Blindness and Insight*, ed. Paul de Man (Minneapolis: University of Minnesota Press, 1983), xvii.

4. This notion of reading as a *transaction* between a reader and a text was taken from Louise Rosenblatt's "On the Aesthetic as the Basic Model of the Reading Process," *Bucknell Review* 26, no. 1 (1981): 17–32.

5. Godzich, "Caution! Reader at Work!" xxiii.

6. Albert Murray, *Stomping the Blues* (New York: McGraw-Hill, 1976), 257.

7. Henry Louis Gates, Jr., "Authority, (White) Power and the (Black) Critic; It's All Greek to Me," *Cultural Critique* no.7 (Fall 1987): 36.

8. Ibid.

9. Michel Foucault, *Language, Counter-Memory, Practice*, trans. Donald Bouchard (Ithaca: Cornell University Press, 1977), 201.

10. Frederich Nietzsche, "Twilight of the Idols," in *The Portable Nietzsche*, ed. Walter Kaufmann (New York: Penguin Books, 1968), 470.

11. Foucault, *The Archaeology of Knowledge* (New York: Harper and Row, 1972), 15.

12. Jacques Derrida, "Structure, Sign, and Play in the Discourse of the Human Sciences," in *The Language of Criticism and the Sciences of Man*, ed. Richard Macksey and Eugenio Donato (Baltimore: Johns Hopkins Press, 1970), 247–72.

13. See Fredric Jameson, "The Symbolic Inference; or, Kenneth Burke and Ideological Analysis," *Critical Inquiry* 4 (1978): 507–22, and the Burke-Jameson critical responses in vol. 5, 401–22.

14. Jameson, "Marxism and Historicism," in *The Ideologies of Theory*, vol. 2 (Minneapolis: University of Minnesota Press, 1988), 148.

15. Norman Harris, "Who's Zoomin' Who: The New Black Formalism," *Journal of the Midwest Modern Language Association* 20, no. 1 (1987): 37–45. It should be noted that this essay does not mention Baker. It deals instead with Gates's and Robert Stepto's presumed lack of concern for the social and political in their critical practices.

16. Etienne Balibar, "On the Basic Concepts of Historical Materialism," in *Reading Capital* (London: The Gresham Press, 1977), 201–308. See especially pp. 230–33, 247.

17. Heidegger, *Being and Time*, 194.

18. Ibid., 194.

19. Lewis Nkosi, *Home and Exile* (London: Longmans, 1965), 113.

20. Oyekan Owomoyela, "The Phantom of Nigerian Theater," *African Studies Review* 22, no. 1 (Apr. 1979): 43.

21. Wole Soyinka, *Myth, Literature and the African World* (Cambridge: Cambridge University Press, 1976), 27.

43 A Black Man's Place in Black Feminist Criticism

Michael Awkward

(1995)

> The main theoretical task for male feminists, then, is to develop an analysis of their own position, and a strategy for how their awareness of their difficult and contradictory position in relation to feminism can be made explicit in discourse and practice.
>
> —Toril Mol, "Men against Patriarchy"

> She had been looking all along for a friend, and it took her a while to discover that a [male] lover was not a comrade and could never be—for a woman.
>
> —Toni Morrison, *Sula*

> Critics eternally become and embody the generative myths of their culture by half-perceiving and half-inventing their culture, their myths, and themselves.
>
> —Houston A. Baker, Jr., *Afro-American Poetics*

> Nor is any theorizing of feminism adequate without some positioning of the person who is doing the theorizing.
>
> —Cary Nelson, "Men, Feminism: The Materiality of Discourse"

Many essays by male and female scholars devoted to exploring the subject of male critics' place in feminism generally agree about the uses and usefulness of the autobiographical male "I." Such essays suggest that citing the male critical self reflects a response to (apparent) self-difference, an exploration of the disparities between the masculine's antagonistic position in feminist discourse on the one hand and, on the other, the desire of the individual male critic to represent his difference with and from the traditional androcentric perspectives of his gender and culture. Put another way, in male feminist acts, to identify the writing self as biologically male is to emphasize the desire not to be ideologically male; it is to explore the process of rejecting the phallocentric perspectives by which men traditionally have justified the subjugation of women.[1]

In what strikes me as a particularly suggestive theoretical formulation, Joseph Boone articulates his sense of the goals of such male feminist autobiographical acts:

> In exposing the latent multiplicity and difference in the word "me(n)," we can perhaps open up a space within the discourse of feminism where a male feminist voice *can* have something to say beyond impossibilities and apologies and unresolved ire. Indeed, if the male feminist can discover a position *from which* to speak that neither elides the importance of feminism to his work nor ignores the specificity of his gender, his voice may also find that it no longer exists as an abstraction . . . but that it in fact inhabits a body: its own sexual/textual body.[2]

Because of an awareness that androcentric perspectives are learned, are transmitted by means of specific sociocultural practices in such effective ways that they come to appear natural, male feminists such as Boone believe that, through an informed investigation of androcentric and feminist ideologies, individual men can work to resist the lure of the normatively masculine. That resistance for the aspiring male feminist requires, he says, exposing "the latent multiplicity and difference in the word 'men,' " in other words, disrupting both ideologies' unproblematized perceptions of monolithic and/or normative maleness (as villainous, antagonistic "other" for feminism, and, for androcentricism, powerful, domineering patriarch). At this early stage of male feminism's development, to speak self-consciously—autobiographically—is to explore, implicitly or explicitly, why and how the individual male experience (the "me" in men) has diverged from, has created possibilities for a rejection of, the androcentric norm.

And while there is not yet agreement as to what constitutes an identifiably male feminist act of criticism or about the usefulness of such acts for the general advancement of the feminist project, at least one possible explanation for a male critic's self-referential discourse is that it is a response to palpable mistrust—emanating from some female participants in feminism and perhaps from the writing male subject himself—about his motives. A skeptical strand of opinion with regard to male feminism is represented by Alice Jardine's "Men in Feminism: Odor di Uomo Or Campagnons de Route?" Having determined that the most useful measure of an adequately feminist text is its *"inscription of struggle—even of pain"*—an inscription of a struggle against patriarchy which Jardine finds absent from most male feminist acts, perhaps because "the historical fact that is the oppression of women [is] . . . one of their favorite blind spots"—she admits to some confusion as to the motivations for males' willing participation: "Why . . . would men want to be in feminism if it's about struggle? What do men want to be in—in pain?"[3]

In addition to seeking to cure its blindness where the history of female oppression is concerned, a male feminism must explore the motivations for its participation in what we might call, in keeping with Jardine's formulations, a discourse of (en)gendered pain. If one of the goals of male feminist self-referentiality is to demonstrate to females that individual males can indeed serve as allies in efforts to undermine androcentric power—and it seems that this is invariably the case—the necessary trust cannot be gained by insisting that motivation as such does not represent a crucial area that must be carefully negotiated. For example, I accept as accurate and, indeed, reflective of my own situation Andrew Ross's assertion that "there are those [men] for whom the *facticity* of feminism, for the most part, goes without saying . . . , who are young enough for feminism to have been a primary component of their intellectual formation."[4] However, in discussions whose apparent function is a foregrounding of both obstacles to and possibilities of a male feminism, men's relation(s) to the discourse can never go "without saying"; for the foreseeable future at least, this relation needs necessarily to be rigorously and judiciously theorized, and grounded explicitly in the experiential realm of the writing male subject.

But no matter how illuminating and exemplary one finds self-referential inscriptions of a male feminist critical self, if current views of the impossibility of a consistently truthful autobiographical act are correct, there are difficulties implicit in any such attempt to situate or inscribe that male self. Because, as recent theorizing on the subject of autobiography has demonstrated, acts of discursive self-rendering unavoidably involve the creation of an idealized version of a unified or unifiable self, we can be certain only of the fact that the autobiographical impulse yields but some of the truths of the male feminist critic's experiences.[5] As is also the case for female participants, a male can never possess or be able to tell the whole truth and nothing but the truth about his relationship to feminist discourse and praxis.

But while autobiographical criticism, like the genre of autobiography itself, is poised tenuously between the poles of closure and disclosure, between representation and re-presentation, between a lived life and an invented one, I believe that even in the recoverable half-truths of my life are some of the materials that have shaped my perceptions, my beliefs, the self or selves that I bring to the interpretive act. In these half-truths is the source of my desire both to inscribe a black male feminism and to inscribe myself as a self-consciously racialized version of what Jardine considers a potentially oxymoronic entity—"male feminist"—whose literal, if not ideological or performative "blackness" is indisputable, and whose adequacy vis-à-vis feminism others must determine. By examining discussions of the phenomenon of the male feminist—that is to say, by reading male and female explorations of men's places in feminist criticism—and exploring responses of others to my own professional and personal relationships to feminism, I will identify autobiographically and textually grounded sources for my belief that while gendered difference might be said to complicate the prospect of a non-phallocentric black male feminism, it does not render such a project impossible.

At the outset, I acknowledge that mine is a necessary participation with regard to black feminist criticism in the half-invention, half-perception which, in Houston Baker's compelling formulation, represents every scholar's relationship to cultural criticism.[6] Such an acknowledgment is not intended to indicate that my male relationship to feminism is that of an illegitimate child, as it were. Rather, it is meant to suggest, like Elizabeth Weed's insistence on "the impossibility" of both men's and women's "relationship to feminism," my belief that while feminism represents a complex, sometimes self-contradictory "utopian vision" which no one can fully possess, a biological male can "develop political, theoretical [and, more generally, interpretive] strategies" which, though at most perhaps half-true to all that feminist ideologies are, nevertheless can assist in a movement toward actualizing the goals of feminism.[7]

I have been forced to think in especially serious ways about my own relationship to feminist criticism since I completed the first drafts of *Inspiriting Influences*, my study of Afro-American women novelists.[8] I have questioned neither the explanatory power of feminism nor the essential importance of developing models adequate to the analysis of black female-authored texts, as my book—in harmony, I believe, with the black feminist project concerned with recovering and uncovering an Afro-American female literary tradition—attempts to provide on a limited scale. Instead, I have been confronted with suspicion about my gendered suitability for the task of explicating Afro-American women's texts, suspicion which has been manifested in the form of both specific responses to my project and general inquiries within literary studies into the phenomenon of the male feminist.

For example, a white female reader of the manuscript asserted—with undisguised surprise—that my work was "so feminist" and asked how I'd managed to offer such ideologically informed readings. Another scholar, a black feminist literary critic, recorded with no discernible hesitation her unease with my "male readings" of the texts of Zora Neale Hurston, Toni Morrison, Gloria Naylor, and Alice Walker. I wondered about the possibility of my being simultaneously "so feminist" and not so feminist (i.e., so "male"), about the meanings of these terms both for these scholars and for the larger interpretive communities in which they participate. Consequently, in what was perhaps initially an act of psychic self-protection, I began to formulate questions for which I still have found no consistently satisfactory answers. Were the differences in the readers' perceptions of the ideological adequacy of my study a function of their own views of feminist criticism, a product, in other words, of the differences not simply within me but within feminism itself? And if the differences within feminism are so significant, could I possibly satisfy everybody with "legitimate" interests in the texts of Hurston et al. by means of my own appropriated versions of black feminist discourse, my unavoidably half-true myth of what that discourse is, means, and does? Should my myth of feminism and its mobilization in critical texts be considered naturally less analytically compelling than that of a female scholar simply as a function of my biological maleness? And how could what I took to be a useful self-reflexivity avoid becoming a debilitating inquiry into a process that has come to seem for me, if not "natural," as Cary Nelson views his relationship to feminism, at least necessary?[9]

Compelled, and, to be frank, disturbed by such questions, I searched for answers in others' words, others' work. I purchased a copy of *Men in Feminism*, a collection which examines the possibility of men's participation as "comrades" (to use Toni Morrison's term) in feminist criticism and theory. Gratified by the appearance of such a volume, I became dismayed upon reading the editors' introductory remarks, which noted their difficulty in "locating intellectuals, who, having shown interest in the question, would offer, for instance, a gay or a black perspective on the problem."[10] While a self-consciously "gay . . . perspective" does find its way into the collection, the insights of nonwhite males and females are conspicuously absent.[11]

Even more troubling for me than the absence of black voices or, for that matter, of general inquiries into the effects of racial, cultural, and class differences on males' relationship to feminism, was the sense shared by many contributors of insurmountable obstacles to male feminism. In fact, the first essay, Stephen Heath's "Male Feminism," begins by insisting that "men's relation to feminism is an impossible one."[12] For me, Heath's formulations are insightful and provocative if not always persuasive, as when he claims: "This is, I believe, the most any man can do today: to learn and so to try to write and talk or act in response to feminism, and so to try not in any way to be anti-feminist, supportive of the old oppressive structures. Any more, any notion of writing a feminist book or being a feminist, is a myth, a male imaginary with the reality of appropriation and domination right behind."[13] Is male participation in feminism restricted to being either appropriative and domineering or not antifeminist? Must we necessarily agree with Heath and others who claim that men cannot be feminists? To put the matter differently, is gender really an adequate determinant of "class" position?

Despite the poststructuralist tenor of Heath's work generally and of many of his perspectives here, his is an easily problematized essentialist claim—that, in effect, biology determines destiny and, therefore, one's relationship to feminist ideology, that womanhood allows one to become feminist at the same time that manhood necessarily denies that status to men. And while Heath embraces its notions of history as a narrative of male "appropriation and domination" of gendered others, he appears resistant at this point in his discourse to evidence of a powerful feminist institutional present and presence. I believe that we must acknowledge that feminism represents, at least in areas of the American academy, an incomparably productive, influential, and resilient ideology and institution that men, no matter how cunning, duplicitous, or culturally powerful, will neither control nor overthrow in the foreseeable future, one whose perspectives have proved and might continue to prove convincing even to biological males. In surveying the potential implications of the participation of biological men in feminism, we must therefore be honest about feminism's current persuasiveness and indomitability, about its clarifying, transformative potential, and about the fact that the corruptive possibility of both the purposefully treacherous and the only half-convinced male is, for today at least, slight indeed. Surely it is neither naive, presumptuous, nor premature to suggest that feminism as ideology and reading strategy has assumed a position of exegetical and institutional strength capable of withstanding even the most energetically masculinist acts of subversion.

Below I want to focus specifically on the question of a black male feminism. Rather than seeing it as an impossibility or as a subtle new manifestation of and attempt at androcentric domination, I want to show that certain instances of Afrocentric feminism provide Afro-American men with an invaluable means of rewriting—of revis(ion)ing—our selves, our history and literary tradition, and our future.

Few would deny that black feminist literary criticism is an oppositional discourse constituted in large part as a response against black male participation in the subjugation of Afro-American women. From Barbara Smith's castigation of black male critics for their "virulently sexist . . . treatment" of black women writers and her insistence that they are "hampered by an inability to comprehend Black women's experience in sexual as well as racial terms" to Michele Wallace's characterization of the "black male Afro-Americanists who make pivotal use of Hurston's work" as "a gang," Afro-American men are generally perceived as non-allied others of black feminist discourse.[14] And, as is evident in Wallace's figuration of male Hurston scholars as intraracial street warriors, they are viewed at times as always already damned and unredeemable, even when they appear to take black women's writing seriously. We—I—must accept the fact that black male investigations informed by feminist principles, including this one, may never be good enough or ideologically correct enough for some black women who are feminists.

This sense of an unredeemable black male critic/reader is in stark contrast to perspectives offered in such texts as Sherley Anne Williams's "Some Implications of Womanist Theory." In her essay, she embraces Alice Walker's term "womanist"—which, according to Williams, connotes a commitment "to the survival and wholeness of an entire people, female and male, as well as a valorization of women's works in all their varieties and multitudes"—because she considers the black feminist project to be separatist in "its tendency to see not only a distinct black female culture but to see that culture as a separate cultural form" from "the facticity of Afro-American life."[15]

I believe that a black male feminism, whatever its connections to critical theory or its specific areas of concern, can profit immensely from what female feminists have to say about male participation. For example, Valerie Smith's suggestion in "Gender and Afro-Americanist Literary Theory and Criticism" that "Black male critics and theorists might explore the nature of the contradictions that arise when they undertake black feminist projects"[16] seems to me quite useful, as does Alice Jardine's advice to male feminists. Speaking for white female feminists, Jardine addresses white males who consider themselves to be feminists: "We do not want you to mimic us, to become the same as us; we don't want your pathos or your guilt; and we don't even want your admiration (even if it's nice to get it once in a while). What we want, I would even say what we need, is your work. We need you to get down to serious work. And like all serious work, that involves struggle and pain."[17] The womanist theoretical project that has been adopted by Williams, Smith, and others provides aspiring Afro-American male feminists with a useful model for the type of self-exploration that Smith and Jardine advocate. What Williams terms "womanist theory" is especially suggestive for Afro-American men because, while it calls for feminist discussions of black women's texts and for critiques of black androcentrism, womanism foregrounds a general black psychic health as a primary objective. Williams argues that "what is needed is a thoroughgoing examination of male images in the works of the black male writers"; her womanism, then, aims at "ending the separatist tendency in Afro-American criticism," at leading black feminism away from "the same hole The Brother has dug for himself—narcissism, isolation, inarticulation, obscurity," at the creation and or continuation of black "community and dialogue."[18]

If a black man is to become a useful contributor to black feminism, he must, as Boone argues, "discover a position from which to speak that neither elides the importance of feminism to his work nor ignores the specificity of his gender." However multiply split we perceive the subject to be, however deeply felt our sense of "maleness" and "femaleness" as a social construction, however heightened our sense of the historical consequences and current dangers of black androcenticism, a black male feminism cannot contribute to the continuation and expansion of the black feminist project by being so identified against or out of touch with itself as to fail to be both self-reflective and at least minimally self-interested. A black male feminist self-reflectivity of the type I have in mind necessarily would include examination of both the benefits and the dangers of situatedness in feminist discourse. The self-interestedness of a black male feminist would be manifested in part by his concern with exploring a man's place. Clearly if convincing mimicry of female-authored concerns and interpretive strategies—speaking like a female feminist—is not in and of itself an appropriate goal for aspiring male participants, then a male feminism necessarily must explore males' various situations in the contexts and texts of history and the present.

Perhaps the most difficult task for a black male feminist is striking a workable balance between male self-inquiry/interest and an adequately feminist critique of patriarchy. To this point, especially in response to the commercial and critical success of contemporary Afro-American women's literature, scores of black men have proved unsuccessful in this regard. As black feminist critics such as Valeril Smith and Deborah McDowell have argued, the contemporary moment of black feminist literature has been greeted by many Afro-American males with hostility self-interested misrepresentation, and a lack of honest intellectual introspection. In "Reading Family Matters," a useful discussion for black male feminism primarily as an exploration of what such a discourse ought not do and be, McDowell speaks of widely circulated androcentric male analyses of Afro-American feminist texts by writers such as Toni Morrison and Alice Walker:

> Critics leading the debate [about the representation of black men in black women's texts] have lumped all black women writers together and have focused on one tiny aspect of their immensely complex and diverse project—the image of black men—despite the fact that, if we can claim a center for these texts, it is located in the complexities of black female subjectivity and experience. In other words, though black women writers have made black women the subjects of their own family stories, these

male readers/critics are attempting to usurp that place for themselves and place it at the center of critical inquiry.[19]

Although I do not believe that "the image of black men" is as microscopic an element in Afro-American women's texts as McDowell claims, I agree with her about the reprehensible nature of unabashed androcentricism found in formulations she cites by such writers as Robert Staples, Mel Watkins, and Darryl Pinckney. Nevertheless, in relation to the potential development of a black male feminism, I am troubled by what appears to be a surprisingly explicit determination to protect turf. In their unwillingness to grant that exploration of how Afro-American males are delineated by contemporary black female novelists is a legitimate concern that might produce illuminating analyses, McDowell's formulations echo in unfortunate ways those of antifeminist male critics, white and black, who consider feminism to be an unredeemably myopic and unyielding interpretive strategy incapable of offering subtle readings of canonical, largely male-authored texts. Despite the circulation of reprehensibly masculinist responses to Afro-American women's literature, black feminist literary critics do not best serve the discourses that concern them by setting into motion homeostatic maneuvers intended to devalue all forms of inquiry except for those they hold to be most valuable (in this particular case, a female-authored scholarship that emphasizes Afro-American women's writings of black female subjectivity). If the Afro-American women's literary project is indeed "immensely complex and diverse," as McDowell claims, bringing to bear other angles of vision, including antipatriarchal male ones, can assist in analyzing aspects of that complexity.

While the views of Staples and others are clearly problematic, those problems do not arise specifically from their efforts to place males "at the center of critical inquiry" any more than feminism is implicitly flawed because it insists, in some of its manifestations, on a gynocritical foregrounding of representations of women. Rather, these problems appear to result from the fact that the particular readers who produce these perspectives do not seem sufficiently to be, in Toril Moi's titular phrase, "men against patriarchy."[20] Certainly, in an age when both gender studies and Afro-American women's literature have achieved a degree of legitimacy within the academy and outside of it, it is unreasonable for black women either to demand that black men not be concerned with the ways in which they are depicted by Afro-American women writers, or to see that concern as intrinsically troubling in feminist terms. If female feminist calls for a non-mimicking male feminism are indeed persuasive, then black men will have very little of substance to say about contemporary Afro-American women's literature, especially if we are also to consider as transgressive any attention to figurations of black manhood. It seems to me that the most black females in feminism can insist upon in this regard is that examinations which focus on male characters treat the complexity of contemporary Afro-American women novelists' delineations of black manhood with an antipatriarchal seriousness which the essays McDowell cites clearly lack.

From my perspective, what is potentially most valuable about the development of a black male feminism is not its capacity to reproduce black feminism as practiced by black females who focus primarily on "the complexities of black female subjectivity and experience."[21] Rather, its potential value lies in the possibility that, in being antipatriarchal and as self-inquiring about their relationship(s) to feminism as Afro-American women have been, black men can expand the range and utilization of feminist inquiry and explore other fruitful applications for feminist perspectives, including such topics as obstacles to a black male feminist project itself and new figurations of "family matters" and black male sexuality.

For the purpose of theorizing about a black male feminism, perhaps the most provocative, enlightening, and inviting moment in feminist or in "womanist" scholarship occurs in Hortense Spillers's "Mama's Baby, Papa's Maybe: An American Grammar Book." Indeed, Spillers's essay represents a fruitful starting point for new, potentially nonpatriarchal figurations of family and of black males' relationship to the female. Toward the end of this illuminating theoretical text, which concerns itself with slavery's debilitating effects on the Afro-American family's constitution, Spillers envisions black male identity formation as a process whose movement toward successful resolution seems to require a serious engagement of black feminist principles and perspectives. Spillers asserts that as a result of those specific familial patterns which functioned during American slavery and beyond and "removed the African-American male not so much from sight as from mimetic view as a partner in the prevailing social fiction of the Father's name, the Father's law," the African-American male "has been touched . . . by the *mother, handed* by her in ways that he cannot escape." Because of separation from traditional American paternal name and law, "the black American male embodies the only American community of males which has had the specific occasion to learn who the female is within itself. . . . It is the heritage of the mother that the African-American male must regain as an aspect of his own personhood—the power of 'yes' to the 'female' within."[22]

Rather than seeing the "female" strictly as other for the Afro-American male, Spillers's Afrocentric revisioning of psychoanalytic theory insists that we consider it an important aspect of the repressed in the black male self.[23] Employing Spillers's analyses as a starting point, we might regard Afro-American males' potential "inness" vis-à-vis feminism not, as Paul Smith insists in *Men in Feminism*, as a representation of male heterosexual desires to penetrate and violate female spaces[24] but rather as an acknowledgment of what Spillers considers the distinctive nature of the Afro-American male's connection to the "female." If Afro-American males are ever to have anything to say about or to black feminism beyond the types of reflex-action devaluations and diatribes about divisiveness that critics such as McDowell and Valerie Smith rightly decry, the investigative process of which womanist acts by Spillers and Williams speak is indispensable. Such a process, if pursued in an intellectually rigorous manner, offers a means by which black men can participate usefully in and contribute productively to the black feminist project.

Black womanism demands neither the erasure of the black gendered other's subjectivity, as have male movements to regain a putatively lost Afro-American manhood, nor the relegation of males to prone, domestic, or other limiting positions. What it does require, if it is indeed to become an ideology with widespread cultural impact, is a recognition on the part of both black females and males of the nature of the gendered inequities that have marked our past and present, and a resolute commitment to work for change. In that sense, black feminist criticism has not only created a space for an informed Afro-American male participation, but it heartily welcomes—in fact, insists upon—the joint participation of black males and females as comrades, to invoke, with a difference, this paper's epigraphic reference to *Sula*.

Reading "Mama's Baby, Papa's Maybe" was of special importance to me in part because it helped me to clarify and articulate my belief that my relationship to feminism need not mark me necessarily as a debilitatingly split subject. The source of that relationship can only be traced autobiographically, if at all. Having been raised by a mother who, like too many women of too many generations, was the victim of male physical and psychological brutality—a brutality which, according to my mother, resulted in large part from my father's frustrations about his inability to partake in what Spillers calls masculinity's "prevailing social fiction"—my earliest stories, my familial narratives, as it were, figured "maleness" in quite troubling terms. My mother told me horrific stories, one of which I was, in a sense, immediately involved in: my father—who left us before I was one year old and whom I never knew—kicked her in the stomach when my fetal presence swelled her body, because he believed she'd been unfaithful to him and that I was only "maybe" his baby.

As a youth, I pondered this and other such stories often and deeply, in part because of the pain I knew these incidents caused my mother, in part because, as someone without a consistent male familial role model, I actively sought a way to achieve a gendered self-definition. As one for whom maleness as manifested in the surrounding inner city culture seemed to be represented only by violence, familial abandonment, and the certainty of imprisonment, I found that I was able to define myself with regard to my gender primarily in oppositional ways. I had internalized the cautionary intent of my mother's narratives, which also served as her dearest wish for me: that I not grow up to be like my father, that I not adopt the definitions of "maleness" represented by his example and in the culture generally. Because the scars of male brutality were visibly etched—literally marked, as it were—on my mother's flesh and on her psyche, "maleness," as figured both in her stories and in my environment, seemed to me not to be a viable mimetic option. I grew up, then, not always sure of what or who I was with respect to prevailing social definitions of gender but generally quite painfully aware of what I could not become.

In order to begin to understand who my mother was, perhaps also who my father was, what "maleness" was and what extra-biological relationship I could hope to have to it, I needed answers that my mother was unable to provide. I found little of value in the black masculinist discourse of the time, which spoke endlessly of the dehumanization and castration of the Afro-American male by white men and black women—our central social narrative for too long—for this rhetoric seemed simplistic and unself-consciously concerned with justifying domestic violence and other forms of black male brutality.

Afro-American women's literature, to which I was introduced along with black feminism in 1977 as a sophomore at Brandeis University, helped me move toward a comprehension of the world, of aspects of my mother's life, and of what a man against patriarchy could be and do. These discourses provided me with answers, nowhere else available, to what had been largely unresolvable mysteries. I work within the paradigm of black feminist literary criticism because it explains elements of the world about which I care most deeply. I write and read what and as I do because I am incapable of escaping the meanings of my mother's narratives for my own life, because the pain and, in the fact of their enunciation to the next generation, the sense of hope for better days that characterizes these familial texts are illuminatingly explored in many narratives by black women. Afro-American women's literature has given me parts of myself that—incapable of a (biological) "fatherly reprieve"—I would not otherwise have had.

I have decided that it is ultimately irrelevant whether these autobiographical facts, which, of course, are not, and can never be, the whole story, are deemed by others sufficient to permit me to call myself "feminist." Like Toril Moi, I have come to believe that "the important thing for men is not to spend their time worrying about definitions and essences ('am I *really* a feminist?'), but to take up a recognizable anti-patriarchal position."[25] What is most important to me is that my work contribute, in however small a way, to the project whose goal is the dismantling of the phallocentric rule by which black females and, I am sure, countless other Afro-American sons have been injuriously "touched."

My indebtedness to Spillers's and other womanist perspectives is, then, great indeed, as is my sense of their potential as illuminating moments for a newborn—or not-yet-born—black male feminist discourse. But to utilize these perspectives requires that we be more inquiring than Spillers is in her formulations, not in envisioning liberating possibilities of an acknowledgment of the "female" within the black community and the male subject, but in noting potential dangers inherent in such an attempted adoption by historically brutalized Afro-American men whose relationship to a repressed "female" is not painstakingly (re)defined.

Clearly, more thinking is necessary not only about what the female within is but about what it can be said to represent for black males, as well as serious analysis of useful means and methods of interacting with a repressed female interiority and subject. Spillers's theorizing does not perform this task, in part because it has other, more compelling interests and emphases—among which is the righting/(re)writing of definitions of "woman" so that they will reflect Afro-American women's particular, historically conditioned "female social subject" status—but a black male feminism must be especially focused on exploring such issues if it is to mobilize Spillers's suggestive remarks as a means of developing a fuller understanding of the complex formulations of black manhood found in many texts and contexts, including Afro-American women's narratives.

I want to build briefly on Spillers's provocative theorizing about the Afro-American male's maturational process and situation on American shores. To this end, I will look at an illuminating moment in Toni Morrison's *Sula*, a text that is, to my mind, not only an unparalleled Afro-American woman's writing of the complexities of black female subjectivity and experience but also of black males' relationship to the female within as a consequence of their limited access to "the prevailing social fiction" of masculinity. In this novel, the difficulty of negotiating the spaces between black male lack and black female presence is plainly manifested in such figures as the undifferentiatable deweys; BoyBoy, whose name, in contrast to most of the authorial designations in *Sula*, speaks unambiguously for him; and Jude, whose difficulty in assuming the mantle of male provider leads him to view his union with Nel as that which "would make one Jude."[26]

The response of Plum, the most tragic of *Sula's* unsuccessful negotiators of the so-called white man's world, vividly represents for me some of the contemporary dangers of black male "in-ness" vis-à-vis the "female." Despite a childhood which included "float[ing] in a constant swaddle of love and affection" and his mother's intention to follow the Father's law by bequeathing "everything" to him (38), Plum appears incapable of embracing hegemonic notions of masculinity. Instead, he returns from World War I spiritually fractured but, unlike a similarly devastated Shadrack, lacking the imaginative wherewithal to begin to theorize or ritualize a new relationship to his world. He turns to drugs as a method of anesthetizing himself from the horrors of his devastation and, in his mother's view, seeks to compel her resumption of familiar/familial patterns of caretaking. In the following passage, Eva explains to Hannah her perception of Plum's desires, as well as the motivation for her participation in what amounts to an act of infanticide:

> When he came back from that war he wanted to git back in. After all that carryin' on, just gettin' him out and keepin' him alive, he wanted to crawl back in my womb and well . . . I ain't got the room no more even if he could do it. There wasn't space for him in my womb. And he was crawlin' back. Being helpless and thinking baby thoughts and dreaming baby dream and messing up his pants again and smiling all the time. I had room enough in my heart, but not in my womb, got no more. I birthed him once, couldn't do it again. He was growed, a big old thing. Godhavemercy, couldn't birth him twice. . . . A big man can't be a baby all wrapped up inside his mamma no more; he suffocate. I done everything I could to make him leave me and go on and live and be a man but he wouldn't and I had to keep him out so I just thought of a way he could die like a man not all scrunched up inside my womb, but like a man. (62)[27]

What is significant about this passage for an analysis of the possibilities of non-oppressive black male relationship to feminism—to female experience characterized by a refusal to be subjugated to androcentric desires—is its suggestiveness for our understanding of the obstacles to a revised male view of the repressed "female," obstacles which result in large part from black males' relative social powerlessness. If black feminism is persuasive in its analysis of the limitations of Afro-American masculinist ideology, emphasizing as it does achievement of black manhood at the expense of black female subjectivity, and if we can best describe an overwhelming number of Africa's American male descendants as males-in-crisis, the question a black male feminism must ask itself is, On what basis, according to what ideological perspective, can an Afro-American heterosexual male ground his notions of the female? Beyond its heterosexual dimension, can the "female" truly come to represent for a traditional black male-in-crisis more than a protective maternal womb from which he seeks to be "birthed" again? Can it serve as more than a site on which to find relief from or locate frustrations caused by an inability to achieve putatively normative American male socioeconomic status? If embracing normative masculinity requires an escape from the protection and life-sustaining aspects symbolized by maternal umbilical cords and apron strings and an achievement of an economic situation wherein the male provides domestic space and material sustenance for his dependents (including "his woman"), black manhood generally is, like Plum, in desperate trouble. And if, as has often been the case, a black female can be seen by an Afro-American male-in-crisis only if she has been emptied of subjectivity and selfhood, if she becomes visible for the male only when she is subsumed by male desire(s), then the types of refiguration and redefinition of black male subjectivity and engagement with the "female" central to Spillers's formulations are highly un-likely.

This question of seeing and not seeing, of the male gaze's erasure and recreation of the female, is crucial to *Sula's* general thematics. It seems to me that in all of her novels Morrison's figuration of black female subjectivity is largely incomprehensible without some serious attention both to her representation of black manhood and to her exploration of the relationships between socially constructed gendered (and ra-cial) positions. To return explicitly to the case of Eva: What Eva fears, what appears to be a self-interested motivation for her killing of her intended male heir, is that Plum's pitiful, infantile state has the potential to reduce *her* to a static female function of self-sacrificing mother, which, according to Bottom legend, had already provoked her decision to lose a leg in order to collect insurance money with which to provide for her children. Having personally lost so much already, Eva chooses, instead of sacrificing other essential parts of her self, to take the life of her self-described male heir. And if Plum dies "like a man" in Eva's estimation, his achievement of manhood has nothing to do with an assumption of traditional masculine traits, nothing to do with strength, courage, and a refusal to cry in the face of death. Instead, that achievement results from Eva's creation of conditions that have become essential components of her definition of manhood: death forces him to "leave" her and to "keep . . . out" of her womb. It would appear that manhood is defined here not as presence as typically represented in Western thought, but—by and for Eva at least— as liberating (domestic and uterine) absence.

One of the intentions of this chapter is to suggest that feminism represents a fruitful and potentially not oppressive means of reconceptualizing, of figuratively birthing twice, the black male subject. But, as a close reading of the aforementioned passage from *Sula* suggests, interactions between men and women motivated by male self-interest such as necessarily characterizes an aspect of male participation in feminism are fraught with possible dangers for the biological/ideological female body of an enactment of or a capitulation to hegemonic male power. Indeed, if it is the case that, as Spillers has argued in another context, "the woman who stays in man's company keeps alive the possibility of having, one day, an unwanted guest, or the guest, deciding 'to hump the hostess,' whose intentions turn homicidal," then male proximity to feminism generally creates the threat of a specifically masculinist violation.[28] If, as I noted earlier, the dangers of a hegemonic, heterosexual Euro-American male's "in-ness" vis-à-vis feminism include (sexualized) penetration and domination, then those associated with a heterosexual black male's interactions with the ideological female body are at least doubled, and potentially involve an envisioning of the black female body as self-sacrificingly maternal or self-sacrificingly sexual. Because of a general lack of access to the full force of hegemonic male power, Afro-American men could see in increasingly influential black female texts not only serious challenges to black male fictions of the self but also an appropriate location for masculine desires for control of the types of valuable resources that the discourses of black womanhood currently represent.

But a rigorous, conscientious black male feminism need not give in to traditional patriarchal desires for control and erasure of the female. To be of any sustained value to the feminist project, a discourse must provide illuminating and persuasive readings of gender as it is constituted for blacks in America and sophisticated, informed, contentious critiques of phallocentric practices in an effort to redefine our notions of black male and female textuality and subjectivity. And in its differences from black feminist texts that are produced by individual Afro-American women, a black male feminism must be both rigorous in engaging these texts and self-reflective enough to avoid, at all costs, the types of patronizing, marginalizing gestures that have traditionally characterized Afro-American male intellectuals' response to black womanhood. What a black male feminism must strive for, above all else, is to envision and enact the possibilities signaled by the differences feminism has exposed and created. In black feminist criticism, being an Afro-American male does not mean attempting to invade an/other political body like a lascivious soul snatcher or striving to erase its essence in order to replace it with one's own myth of what the discourse should be. Such a position for black men means, above all else, an acknowledgment and celebration of the incontrovertible fact that "the Father's law" is no longer the only law of the land.

NOTES

1. Joseph Boone's and Gerald MacLean's essays in *Gender and Theory* assume that the foregrounding of gendered subjectivity is essential to the production of a male feminism critical practice. Consequently, in an effort to articulate his perspectives on the possibilities of a male feminist discourse, Boone shares with us professional secrets—he writes of his disagreement with the male-authored essays in Alice Jardine and Paul Smith's *Men and Feminism*, and of being excluded, because of his gender, from a Harvard feminist group discussion of Elaine

Showalter's "Critical Cross-Dressing." And MacLean's essay discloses painfully personal information about his difficult relationship with his mother, his unsatisfying experience with psychoanalysis, and an incident of marital violence.

2. Joseph Boone, "Of Me(n) and Feminism: Who(se) is the Sex That Writes?" in *Gender and Theory*, 158–81. Here and below, I quote from p. 159. For my purposes, Boone's remarks are suggestive despite their use of language that might seem to mark them as a heterosexualization of men's participation in feminism ("open up a space," "discover a position"). I believe that Boone's passage implies less about any desire for domination on his part that it does about the pervasiveness in our language of terms which have acquired sexual connotations and, consequently, demonstrates the virtual unavoidability of using a discourse of penetration to describe interactions between males and females. But it also appears to reflect a sense of frustration motivated by Boone's knowledge that while feminism has had a tremendous impact on his thinking about the world he inhabits, many feminists do not see a place in their discourse for him or other like-minded males. In order to make such a place for himself, violation and transgression seem to Boone to be unavoidable.

3. Alice Jardine, "Men in Feminism: Odor di Uomo or Compagnons de Route?" in *Men in Feminism*, 58.

4. Andrew Ross, "No Question of Silence," in *Men in Feminism*, 86.

5. See Georges Poulet, "Criticism and the Experience of Interiority," in *Reader-Response Criticism From Formalism to Post-Structuralism*, ed. Jane P. Tompkins (Baltimore: Johns Hopkins University Press, 1980), 41–49.

6. Houston A. Baker, Jr., *Afro-American Poetics*, 8.

7. Elizabeth Weed, "A Man's Place," in Men in Feminism, 75.

8. Michael Awkward, *Inspiring Influences: Tradition, Revision, and Afro-American Women's Novels* (New York: Columbia University Press, 1989).

9. About his relationship to feminism, Nelson writes: "Feminism is part of my social and intellectual life, has been so for many years, and so, to the extent that writing is ever 'natural,' it is natural that I write about feminism" (153). Nelson's "Men, Feminism: The Materiality of Discourse" (*Men in Feminism*, 153–72) is, in my estimation, a model for self-referential male feminist inquiries that assume—or, at the very least, seek to demonstrate—a useful place for males in the discourse of feminism.

10. Jardine and Smith, *Men in Feminism*, vii–viii.

11. See Craig Owens, "Outlaws: Gay Men in Feminism," in *Men in Feminism*, 219–32. It is hard to believe that Jardine and Smith's difficulty reflected a lack of interest among Afro-Americans is exploring the relationship of men to black feminism. A number of texts give evidence of interest in "the problem": the 1979 *Black Scholar* special issue devoted to investigating black feminism as manifested primarily in Niozoke Shagne's *for colored girls* and Michele Wallace's *Black Macho and the Myth of the Superwoman*; Mel Watkins, "Sexism Racism, and Black Women Writers," *New York Times Book Review*, June 15, 1986; Darryl Pinckney, "Black Victims, Black Villains," *New York Review of Books* 34 (January 29 1987): 7–20; and essays by Valerie Smith and Deborah McDowell from which I draw below.

Jardine and Smith's difficulties might have stemmed from the facts that most of the men who had spoken publicly on the subject were open about their hostility to black feminism, and most of them did not speak the language of contemporary theory, a high academic idiom which demonstrates that the contributors to *Men in Feminism* are, despite significant differences among them, members of the same speech community.

12. Stephen Heath, "Male Feminism," *Men in Feminism*, 1.

13. Ibid., 9.

14. Barbara Smith, "Toward a Black Feminist Criticism," 173, 172; Michele Wallace, "Who Dat Say Dat When I Say Dat? Zora Neale Hurston Then and Now," *Village Voice Literary Supplement*, April 1988. p. 18.

15. Sherley Anne Williams, "Some Implications of Womanist Theory," *Callaloo 9* (1980): 304.

16. Valerie Smith, "Gender and Afro-Americans: Literary Theory and Criticism," in *Speaking of Gender*, 68.

17. Jardine, "Men in Feminism," *Men in Feminism*, 60.

18. Williams, "Some Implications," 307.

19. Deborah McDowell, "Reading Family Matters," in *Changing Our Own Words: Essays on Criticism, Theory, and the Writing by Black Women*, ed. Cheryl Wall (New Brunswick: Rutgers University Press, 1989), 84.

20. Toril Moi, "Men against Patriarchy," in *Gender and Theory*, 181–68.

21. McDowell's views notwithstanding, construction of black male and black female subjectivity are too obviously interrelated in black women's narratives for feminist criticism to profit in the long run from ignoring—or urging that others ignore—the important functions that delineations of black male subjectivity play in these narratives' thematics. Certainly the threat of antifeminist male critical bias is not cause to erase or minimize the significance of black male characters in these writers' work.

22. Spillers, "Mama's Baby, Papa's Maybe: An American Grammar Book," 80.

23. In this sense, Spillers's perspectives complement those of Shetley Anne Williams, for the latter demands, in effect, that we consider the extent to which black male repression of the "female" results from an attempt to follow the letter of the white Father's law.

24. Paul Smith, "Men in Feminism: Men and Feminist Theory," *Men in Feminism*, 33.

25. Moi, "Men against Patriarchy," 184.

26. Toni Morrison, *Sula* (New York: Plume, 1973), 71. Subsequent references to this novel appear in the text in parentheses.

27. At least one other reading of Eva's murder of her son is possible: as protection against the threat of incest. In a section of her explanation to Hannah—very little of which is contained in my textual citation of *Sula*—Eva discusses a dream she has had concerning Plum.

> I'd be laying here at night and he be downstairs in that room, but when I closed my eyes I'd see him . . . six feet tall smilin' and crawlin' up the stairs quietlike so I wouldn't hear and opening the door soft so I wouldn't hear and he'd be creepin' to the bed trying to spread my legs trying to get back up in my womb. He was a man, girl, a big old growed-up man. I didn't have that much room. I kept on dreaming it. Dreaming it and I knowed it was true. One night it wouldn't be no dream. It'd be true and I would have done it, would have let him if I'd've had the room but a big man can't be a baby all wrapped up inside his mamma no more; he suffocate. (72–73)

Morrison reverses to some extent the traditional dynamics of the most prevalent form of intergenerational incest. Instead of the male parent creeping to the bed and spreading the legs of his defenseless female child, in Eva's dream her man-child Plum is the active agent of violation. Eva's emphasis on Plum's immensity and her own uterus's size makes connections to incestuous creeping and spreading possible. It is not difficult to imagine, given Plum's constantly drugged state, that frustrations caused by an inability to re-insert his whole body into his mother's womb during what Eva views as an inevitable encounter might lead to a forced insertion of a part that "naturally" fits, his penis. At any rate, a reading of this scene that notes its use of language consistent with parent-child incest serves to ground what appear to be otherwise senseless fears on Eva's part concerning both the possible effects of Plum's desire for reentry into her uterine space and her own inability to deny her son access to that space ("I would have done it, would have let him").

28. Spillers, "Black, White, and in Color, or Learning How to Paint: Toward an Intramural Protocol of Reading."

44

Black Feminist Thinking

The "Practice" of "Theory"[1]

Deborah E. McDowell

(1995)

> The old patterns, no matter how cleverly rearranged to imitate progress, still condemn us to cosmetically altered repetitions of the same old exchanges.
>
> —Audre Lorde, "Age, Race, Class, and Sex"[2]

> To exist historically is to perceive the events one lives through as part of a story later to be told.
>
> —Arthur C. Danto, *Narration and Knowledge*[3]

That remembering is political and inextricably bound to culturally contested issues is now granted as freely as is the understanding that "why we remember and what we remember, the motive and the content, are inseparable."[4] . . . I want to consider the implications of memory and remembering in the construction of "historical knowledge" in general and of "critical theory" more specifically.

To speak of "historical knowledge" at all is to stage or enter a vigorous debate between those who see "history" and "knowledge" as ontological givens and those who don't. I identify with those who don't, with those who recognize that, despite its basis in the concrete certainties of "then" and "there," complete with recognizable names and familiar faces, history is a fantastical and slippery concept, a making, a construction.[5] I side with those who see history, to invoke the current *lingua franca*, as a "contested terrain" that often functions to repress and contain the conflicts and power asymmetries that mark the sociopolitical field.

That contemporary students of culture and its institutions have by and large willingly adjusted their assumptions and altered their practices to fit these axioms is a salutary development. But I share Renato Rosaldo's fear that in our zeal to establish historical contingency, to show that everything is constructed, human beings tend to "lose their specific gravity, their weight, and their density, and begin to float." We would do well to heed Rosaldo's warning against the dangers of declaring historical knowledge constructed and simply ending the discussion there, for we must show in nuanced historical perspective, however difficult that is, "how it was constructed, by whom, and with what consequences."[6]

Here, I want to take some liberties with time and construe the present moments as the future's past in order to determine what "historical knowledge" of "literary theory" we are constructing at this moment and with what consequences to what specific bodies. In other words, how are we telling the history or story of recent theoretical developments? Who are the principals in that story? What are the strategies of its emplotment? How does it reconstitute timeworn structures and strategies of dominance? Produce imagined divisions of scholarly labor that recode familiar hierarchical relations? I ask these questions because I share with many others a keen interest in how race and gender figure into our scholarly pursuits, drives, and desires. If we want an example of how "literary theory" gets historicized and of how social categories get woven into intellectual narrations, we need look no further than the representation of writings by African American women in contemporary academia. The period since 1977 provides a convenient point of access.

I agree with Hortense Spillers that "in a very real sense, black American women are invisible to various public discourses, and the state of invisibility for them has its precedent in an analogy on any patriarchal symbolic mode that we might wish to name."[7] And while some have tried to restore them to discursive sight, their efforts have been often compromised by the compulsions of historical legacy and the imperatives of contemporary social design. Such compulsions and imperatives are especially evident in debates of the past several years[8] about the supposed opposition between "theory" and "practice" (sometimes appearing as "theory" and "politics").[9] These debates illuminate how often the divisions and cleavages of scholarly labor exist in masked relation to the divisions and cleavages of social life.[10] More specifically, the theory/practice opposition is often racialized and gendered, especially in discussion of black feminist thinking, which, with precious few exceptions, gets constructed as "practice" or "politics," the negative obverse of "theory." While some black women have indeed helped to encourage this perception by viewing their writing as an enclosed and unified domain, fending off foreign intellectual invasions, they are neither the origins nor the primary agents of the theory/practice division that underwrites a familiar sociocultural contract.[11]

To raise questions about the social inflections of scholarly discourse is to confront the complex and steadily shifting contexts in which we position ourselves as intellectuals and in which we are positioned in turn. This situation leads, perhaps inescapably, to what Valerie Smith rightly terms the "split affinities" that render "inapplicable to the lives of black women any 'single-axis' theory about racism or sexism" and point to the difficulties of assuming any fixed critical position or pledging permanent allegiance to any one-dimensional idea of identity.[12]

What follows is not a singular narrative, but rather miscellaneous examples—call them "case studies"—about black feminist thinking that crop up in a variety of critical discussions. While I want to critique the treatment of "black feminist thinking" and "theory" as false unities, for purposes of easy reference I must refer to both in the singular, even as I am reminded that Hazel Carby's statements about black feminist criticism also apply to "theory," which must also be seen as a "locus of contradictions," a "sign that should be interrogated."[13] And although I select examples from a variety of critical denominations, I do so not to universalize or indict any whole, but rather to indicate the pervasiveness of the theory/practice division that has assumed a structural relevance and significance that can no longer be ignored.[14]

UNCOVERING THE TRUTH: COLORING "FEMINIST THEORY"

As we know, in the emplotment or narrativization of any history, much depends on familiar vocabularies of reference—on the circulation of names, proper names, and some names are more proper than others.[15] I want to talk briefly about the circulation of one name—Sojourner Truth—and the "knowledge" that name helps to construct about black feminist thinking within the general parameters of feminist discourse.[16]

In the opening chapter of her study *Am I That Name? Feminism and the Category of "Women" in History*, Denise Riley begins with a reference to Sojourner Truth and her famous and much-quoted question—"Ain't I a Woman?"—posed before the 1851 Women's Rights Convention in Akron, Ohio. Riley supposes that, in the current historical moment, Sojourner "might well—except for the catastrophic loss of grace in wording—issue another plea: 'Ain't I a Fluctuating Identity?'" The temptation here is simply to find the humor in Riley's rewriting and move on, except that to do so is to miss the sociocultural assumptions that attach to it, assumptions that escape the boundaries of Truth's time to project themselves boldly in our own.

Riley's move to appropriate Sojourner Truth introduces a subtle racial marker that distinguishes between Truth's original words and Riley's displacement. A familiar move in contemporary literary-critical discussion, Riley's "modernization" functions allegorically to make a common, if subtle, insinuation about black feminist thinking in general: It needs a new language. That language should serve a theory, preferably a poststructuralist theory, signaled in this context by the term fluctuating identity.[17]

To trace the move from Sojourner Truth's "Ain't I a Woman" to Riley's "Ain't I a Fluctuating Identity" is to plot, in effect, two crucial stages in a historical narrative of academic feminism's coming of age. Following this evolutionary logic, academic feminist discourse can be said to have "grown out of" an attachment to what Riley terms that "blatant[ly] disgrace[ful] and transparently suspicious" category—"Woman." That category happens to be personified by Sojourner's rhetorical and declarative question. Riley concedes that Sojourner represents one move in a necessary "double move" of feminist theory that recognizes that "both a concentration on and a refusal of the identity of 'woman' are essential to feminism."[18]

Constance Penley makes essentially the same point in *The Future of an Illusion*. Whereas in Riley's study Sojourner marks the point of departure, in Penley's she marks the point of closure. In the last two pages of the final chapter, she walks on to take a bow with Jacques Lacan. His "notorious bravura"—"the woman does not exist"—is counterposed to Sojourner Truth's "Ain't I a Woman?" Echoing Riley, Penley explains this counterposition as "two ideas or strategies . . . vitally important to feminism," though they might appear completely at odds. Penley classifies the one strategy—represented by Lacan, Althusser, and Derrida—as "epistemological" and "metaphysical"; the other—represented by Sojourner Truth—is "political." That Truth's declarative question—"Ain't I a Woman"—might be read as "political" and "epistemological" simultaneously seems not to have occurred to Penley, partly because she manipulates both these categories, consciously or not, to conform to an already polarized and preconceived understanding.[19]

Is it purely accidental that, in these two essays, Sojourner Truth comes to represent the politics but not the poetics that feminism needs? Is hers a purely neutral exemplarity? Agreeing with Gayatri Spivack that "it is at those borders of discourse where metaphor and example seem arbitrarily *chosen* that ideology breaks through,"[20] I would argue that Sojourner is far from an arbitrary example. Possible intentions notwithstanding, Sojourner Truth as a metonym for "black woman" is useful in this context both to a singular idea of academic feminism in general and, in particular, to ongoing controversies within that discourse over the often uneasy relations between theory and politics.

The belief that feminism and whiteness form a homogeneous unity has long persisted, along with the equally persistent directive to feminist theorists to "account" for the experiences of women of color in their discourses. The unexamined assumption that white feminist discourse bears a special responsibility to women of color helps to maintain the perception that feminism equates with whiteness and relates maternalistically to women of color.

Such assumptions are implied in the recently published *Feminist Theory in Practice and Process*. In "Naming the Politics of Theory," one section of the introduction, the editors challenge "feminist theory . . . to recognize the myriad forms of black women's race, gender, and class politics and to envision theories that encompass these lived realities and concrete practices."[21] Elizabeth Spelman's observation, from another context, is useful here: "It is not white middle-class women who are different from other women, but all other women who are different from them."[22]

That difference has become magnified and has assumed an even greater urgency since academic feminism, like all discursive communities on the contemporary scene, has accepted the constructive challenge to take its processes into self-conscious account; that is, since it has accepted the challenge to "theorize" about the work it does and the claims it makes. The strain to fulfill both requirements—to "theorize," on the one hand, and to recognize material "differences," on the other, has created a tension within academic feminist discourse (read *white*). That tension is often formulated as a contrast, if not a contest, between "theory" and "practice/politics," respectively.

I must rush to add that race (here, read *black*) and gender (here, read *female*) are not the only stigmatized markers on the practice/politics side of the border, for they trade places in a fluid system in which differences of nationality, sexuality, and class are interchangeable.[23] The now-quiescent French/American feminist theory debate—illustrated most controversially in Toril Moi's *Sexual/Textual Politics*—provides one example of what I mean. Moi clumps Anglo-American, black, and lesbian women on the practice/politics/criticism side of the border; French women, on the theory side. After blasting the claims of Anglo-American feminist criticism, Moi then turns to answer those who "might wonder why [she has] said nothing about black or lesbian (or black lesbian) feminist criticism in America . . . The answer is simple: this book purports to deal with the theoretical aspects of feminist criticism. So far, lesbian and/ or black feminist criticism have presented exactly the same *methodological* and *theoretical* problems as the rest of Anglo-American feminist criticism" (emphasis in text). Moi adds, "This is not to say that black and lesbian criticism have no . . . importance," but that importance is not to be "found at the level of *theory* . . . but the level of *politics*" (emphasis added).[24]

In the context of these critical developments, the use of "Sojourner Truth" projects myriad meanings needed to perform the work of distinction and differentiation in the culture of academe. To begin with, as a metonym for "black woman," the name can be read as a mark of racial difference and distinction within "feminist theory," which points up its internal conflicts and ambivalence over the relative merits and value of "political" discourse. That marks of racial difference can be hidden in itineraries represented as "purely" (and thus neutrally?) epistemological, is evident in the following summary by Jane Flax:

> Feminist theorists have tried to maintain two different epistemological positions. The first is that the mind, the self, and knowledge are socially constituted, and what we can know depends on our social practices and contexts. The second is that feminist theorists can uncover truths about the whole as it "really is." Those who support the second position reject many postmodern ideas and must depend upon certain assumptions about truth and the knowing subject.[25]

The assumptions about Sojourner Truth examined so far—both explicit and implied—cast her categorically in that second position, despite the fact that the short text of the "Ain't I a Woman?" speech is a compressed but powerful analysis and critique of the social practices within the context of slavery that depend on biases of class and race to construct an idea of universal or True Womanhood. She challenged that dominant knowledge, offering and authorizing her experiences under slavery as proof of its underlying illogicality.

The truth that Truth knows, then, is not reducible to a mere statement turned slogan that acts as theory's Other, or theory's shadow side. The politics contained within that epistemology, within that way of knowing Truth, must be interrogated and the foundations on which it rests laid bare. Those foundations are sharply exposed when we remember the moment in Truth's career perhaps most frequently remarked: the degrading demand to bare her breasts.

After delivering a speech in Silver Lake, Indiana, in 1851, one Dr. T. W. Strain alleged that she was a man. To prove that she wasn't, Truth bared her breasts.[26] The scene captures graphically Truth's fixity in the body and thus her distance from the "proper" white feminists enlisted to "verify" her sex. Her recuperation in these modern contexts forges a symbolic connection with that prior history, a conjunctive relationship to that past. It is precisely this earlier scene of verification that is being symbolically reenacted today. The demand in this present context is not to bare the breasts to verify black womanhood, but to bare the evidence that proves positively the qualifications of black feminist discourse as "theory."

But the selection of Sojourner Truth as metonym raises still other problems that connect to the relation between the symbolic and the social, the relation between the present and the past. The fact that Sojourner Truth was illiterate and that the words by which we know her were transcribed by stenographic reporters or admiring white friends has only begun to be interrogated with any complexity. Recent work by Nell Irvin Painter has begun to engage the nexus of paradoxes, ironies, and contradictions of these transcriptions and to inquire into why, until recently, Sojourner Truth, a "naive rather than an educated persona, seems to have better facilitated black women's entry into American memory" than any of her educated black female contemporaries. Painter's point is obviously not that only lettered or tutored black woman should have facilitated that memory, but that Sojourner Truth as figure keeps alive the "disparities of power and distinctions between European and Euro-Americans and natives, domestic and foreign."[27]

As a sign to a rematerializing critical discourse of its "sins of omission" around race, the utterance of "Sojourner Truth" or any other metonym for black women seems to perform for some an absolution of critical guilt; but the utterance is all. "Sojourner Truth"—or any other metonym for black women—is a name of which no more need be said. Truth's experiences beyond popularized clichés are not fully addressed.[28] She is useful simply as a name to drop in an era with at least nominal pretensions to interrogating race and the difference it makes in critical discussion.

But the repetition of Sojourner Truth's name makes no real difference. In dominant discourses it is a symbolic gesture masking the face of power and its operations in the present academic context. As a figure in remove, summoned from the seemingly safe and comfortable distance of a historical past, "Sojourner Truth" can thus act symbolically to absorb, defuse, and deflect a variety of conflicts and anxieties over race in present academic contexts. However, "Sojourner Truth" stirs up far more controversy than it settles, preventing any easy resolution of feminism's conflicts. Locked within that name is the timeless and unchanging knowledge (the very definition of "truth") of race and gender embedded in Western philosophy that now finds it way, like the return of the repressed, into the organization of knowledge in contemporary academe.

The repeated invocation of "Ain't I a Woman?"—detached from historical context—neither captures its immediacy for Truth's time nor reactivates it for our own. Put another way, the repeated invocation of "Sojourner Truth" functions not to document a moment in a developing discourse but to freeze that moment in time. Such a chronopolitics operates not so much as history but as an interruption of history, at least as black women might figure in it, a phenomenon recalling Hegel's description of Africa as outside the "real theatre of History" and of "no historical part of the World." "It has no movement or development to exhibit. . . . What we properly understand by Africa is the Unhistorical, Undeveloped Spirit, still involved in the conditions of mere nature, and which has to be presented . . . on the threshold of the World's history."[29]

The proposition that black feminist discourse is poised on the threshold of theory's history has predictable consequences. Not least, this view helps to reconstitute the structures and strategies of dominance, even in work that strives zealously in an opposite and oppositional direction.

GENDERING AFRICAN AMERICAN THEORY

We can observe such strategies of dominance in *Gender and Theory*, a recent anthology edited by Linda Kauffman. Kauffman tries studiously to prevent a reproduction of the simplistic divisions and antagonisms between black and white, male and female, "theory" and "politics." She explains in her introduction that while the title— *Gender and Theory*—posits a couple, the essays are arranged to permit men to respond to the essays by women and vice versa. That "structure is designed . . . to draw attention to such dichotomies in order to displace them by dissymmetry and dissonance."[30] Despite that goal, these very oppositions appear.

In fact, we could argue that if theory is often to practice/politics what Europe is to America, what white is to black, what straight is to gay, in Kauffman's anthology, theory is to practice what black male is to black female. This reductive accounting represents black women as categorically resistant to theory.

"Race" in Kauffman's anthology is constructed once again as synonymous with "blackness." Barbara Christian's "The Race for Theory" and Michael Awkward's response, "Appropriative Gestures: Theory and Afro-American Literary Criticism," are placed at the very end of the volume and thus apart from the preceding pairs of essays, none of which interrogates the racial inflections of "gender and theory." The racial opposition coordinates with oppositions of gender and genre, making theory male and practice female.

The question Kauffman poses in her introduction—"In what ways are Afro-American theory and Afro-American feminism complementary, and in what ways are they antagonistic?"—gets answered in the two concluding essays: "Afro-American theory" is gendered male and Afro-American feminism is gendered female, and they function effectively as structural antagonists. Such a seemingly innocent juxtaposition has already quickly decided its conclusion: Michael Awkward's response to Barbara Christian calls for a "theory" to her "practice."

One of the strengths of Awkward's response to Christian lies in its implicit recognition that poststructuralist theory cannot be homogenized, nor can it stand synecdochically for all theory. Although it is clear that he thinks Christian has missed the theoretical mark, he asserts that Barbara Smith's "Toward a Black Feminist Criticism" was "essentially a theoretical statement" "if not [a] poststructuralist discussion of critical practice and textual production." Smith's essay, he goes on to say, "theorizes despite its lack of a clearly informed awareness of deconstruction, reader-response theory, [and] semiotics."

Here, Awkward's vocabulary—"if not" and "lack of"—essentially negates whatever value he initially assigned Smith's essay, which is structured as the negative of the positive—an undifferentiated poststructuralism acting as the sole frame of reference. Making an uncritical link between black women as "writers" and black women as "critics" that holds the latter responsible for the survival of the former, Awkward offers a cautionary note: "If this field [black women's literature] is to continue to make inroads into the canon, if it is to gain the respect it doubtlessly deserves as an ideologically rich literary tradition, within an increasingly theoretical academy, it will require that its critics continue to move beyond description and master the discourse of contemporary theory."[31]

If, as Awkward suggests, "black women's literature still does not assume the prominent place in courses and criticism" that it merits, I would ask whether that marginality can be explained exclusively by a lack of theorizing on the part of black women or rather whether that marginalization is often structured into the very theories that Awkward wants black women to master. Again, my point should not be read as a simplistic rejection of "theory," even as it is narrowly associated, in Awkward's essay, with poststructuralist projects, but as a call for a more searching examination of the processes and procedures of marginalizing any historically subjugated knowledge.

Awkward's essay does more than close Kauffman's volume; it performs a kind of closure, or functions as a kind of "final word," that extends far beyond the boundaries of the collection *Gender and Theory*. He leaves intact the clichéd and unstudied distinctions between theory and practice represented by Paul de Man and Barbara Christian, respectively. It is paradoxical and ironic that an essay that privileges poststructuralist theory and extols de Man relies on an uncritical construction of theory as an autonomous entity with semantic stability and immanent properties that separate it from practice. It is all the more ironic that such a dichotomy should dominate in an essay that valorizes a body of theory identified most popularly with blurring such inherited and unmediated oppositions. But the dichotomies of Awkward's essay mark a difference and issue a set of limits—social limits—that extend beyond the academic realm. In identifying with Paul de Man, Awkward consolidates his own critical authority against Barbara Christian's, making theory a province shared between men.[32]

That theory is a province shared between men is nowhere more evident than in the wasteful *New Literary History* exchange between Joyce Joyce, Henry Louis Gates, and Houston Baker, which brought to the boiling point one of the most controversial shifts in the history of African American literary study: the "race" debate.[33] While this shift produced a schism among scholars in African American literary study, that schism has been oversimplified and exaggerated and construed, all too often, as a gender war over the uses and abuses of "theory" for African American literary study, a war with black men on the side of "theory" and black women against it.

Joyce Ann Joyce largely aided that perception with her much-discussed and critiqued essay "The Black Canon: Reconstructing Black American Literary Criticism." Recuperating the salient principles of the Black Aesthetic movement, Joyce argued for the responsibility of the black writer to his or her audience, for that writer's absolute and sovereign authority, for the use of the black literary text in fostering "Black pride and the dissolution of 'double consciousness,'" and the inappropriateness of "white" critical theories to analyses of black literature. In their responses to Joyce's essay, both Henry Louis Gates and Houston Baker were warranted in questioning these aspects of her argument, but they were less so in dismissing as naive and anachronistic her questions about "the historical interrelationship between literature, class, values, and the literary canon" (*New Literary History*, XVIII (1986): 326–334, 371–384. p. 336).[34] Gates and Baker choose to evade these questions in order to focus on Joyce's stubborn resistance to reading "race" as a pure signifier or arbitrary function of language. Joyce will not concede to her opponents in this debate that the complexities and irrationalities of social life in the United States are reducible to language games. And, even if they are, she comes just short of arguing, race still functions as a "transcendent signified" in the world.

Although he positions himself opposite Joyce in the *New Literary History* exchange, Houston Baker makes this same point eloquently in his essay "Caliban's Triple Play," a critical response to "Race, Writing and Difference," the special issue that Gates edited for *Critical Inquiry*.[35] Baker notes persuasively the power and resilience of "racial enunciative statements" that assert themselves painfully at the level of felt and lived experience. His compelling arguments in this essay indicate a clear reluctance to hypertextualize race, a stance that would seem to connect him with Joyce, but such a connection must be sacrificed in order to forge and secure a greater bond between Gates and Baker, one that transcends and papers over their critical differences. The rhetoric of erotics that tinges Gates's response to Joyce clearly indicates that much more is at issue and at stake than Joyce's alleged unexamined resistance to theory.

Gates's decision to use Tina Turner's pop hit "What's Love Got to Do with It," which Joyce rightly if reactively perceives as glorifying the objectification of women, clearly sexualizes this exchange:

> It is an act of love of the tradition—by which I mean *our* tradition—to bring to bear upon it honesty, insight and skepticism, as well as praise, enthusiasm, and dedication; all values fundamental to the blues and to signifying, those two canonical black discourses in which *Houston and I* locate the black critical difference. It is merely a mode of critical masturbation to praise a black text simply because it is . . . "black." (Gates, p. 347, emphasis added)

In identifying the "two canonical black discourses," associated in their critical articulations with himself and Baker, Gates prepares the way for Baker to further consolidate a growing chain of male theoretical authority distinct from the dragrope of "black women critics," who constitute a "new black conservatism." Although Baker argues that his critique is "directed against specific conservatisms, misjudgments, and errors," rather than "toward a group," it so happens that "black women" are linked to a widespread, if unspecified, group that shows "essential animosity toward recent modes of critical and theoretical discussion." It is black women who fail to seize the abundant opportunities for the kinds of "theoretical daring and critical inventiveness" that mark the age and set the agenda for a transformative politics.[36] In Baker's view, that daring and inventiveness are seen mainly in the work of Derrida, Althusser, Lacan, and Baudrillard.

Curiously, in Baker's reasoning, all positions and /or questions not readily assimilable to their projects are conservative and atheoretical. More curious is the fact that the agenda for a transformative politics must repress gender, for those questions asked by the "conservative" black women, whom Baker chastises and corrects, are questions about the relations between gender and artistic production, questions that a good many people might regard as interventions in clear service of a transformative politics. Further, those in that service might challenge Baker to consider the various ways feminists have found his agents of change—Derrida, Althusser, Lacan, and Baudrillard—both useful to and limited for feminist projects. Indeed, to borrow Baker's words, if not his meaning, "the towers of an old *mastery* are reconstituted" in any implied suggestion that feminist critique works against, rather than in harmony with, other varieties of transformative politics and discursive priorities.

NOTES TOWARD A COUNTER HISTORY

Where might we go from here? I would start with the forthright assertion that the challenge of any discourse identifying itself as black feminist is not necessarily or most immediately to vindicate itself as theory. Its challenge is to resist the theory/practice dichotomy, which is too broad, abbreviated, and compromised by hedging definitions to capture the range and diversity of contemporary critical projects, including the range and diversity of the contributions of black women to that discourse. A far more valuable and necessary project would proceed from the commonplace assumption that no consideration of any intellectual project is complete without an understanding of the process of that project's formation. And thus any responsible accounting of the work of black women in literary studies would have to provide a history of its emergence and consider that emergence first on its own terms.

Of course, part of the historical accounting of recent critical production is under way, but unfortunately it leaves questions of the relations between race and critical discourse largely unexplored. A counter history, a more urgent history, would bring "theory" and "practice" into a productive tension that would force a re-evaluation of each side. But that history could not be written without considering the determining, should I say the over-determining, influences of institutional life out of which all critical utterances emerge.

It follows, then, that we would have to submit to careful scrutiny the past two decades, which witnessed the uncanny convergence and confluence of significant historical moments, all contributing to the present shape and contours of literary studies. These are: the emergence of a second renaissance of black women writing to public acclaim; a demographic shift that brought the first generation of black intellectuals into the halls of predominantly white, male, and elitist institutions; the institutionalization and decline of African American studies and women's studies; and the rising command in the U.S. academy of poststructuralism, regarded as a synonym for theory.

Our historical narrative would have to dramatize the process by which deconstruction came to stand synecdochically for poststructuralist theory, its dominion extending from the pages of arcane journals of critical theory, to the pages of such privileged arbiters of culture as the *New York Times Magazine* and *The New York Review of Books*, to the less-illustrious pages of *Time* and *Newsweek*.[37] The analysis would have to explore how deconstruction became associated as much with an ideological position as a revitalizing and energetic intellectual project at roughly the same time that a few black women, following Barbara Smith's challenge, began to articulate a position identified as black feminist criticism. Smith focused on recuperating the writings of black women for critical examination and establishing reading strategies attentive to the intersections of gender, race, and class in their work.[38]

If we were to isolate the salient terms of black feminist criticism and poststructuralist theory for this historical narrative, they might run as follows:

(1) While black feminist criticism was asserting the significance of black women's experience, poststructuralism was dismantling the authority of experience.

(2) While black feminist criticism was calling for nonhostile interpretations of black women's writings, poststructuralism was calling interpretation into question.

(3) While black feminist criticism required that these interpretations be grounded in historical context, deconstruction denied history any authoritative value or truth claims and read context as just another text.

(4) While the black woman as author was central to black feminist writers efforts to construct a canon of new as well as unknown black women writers, poststructuralism had already rendered such efforts naive by asking, post-Foucault, "What *Is* an Author?" (1969) and trumpeting post-Barthes, "The Death of the Author" (1968).

(5) While black feminist critics and African Americanists more generally were involved in recuperating a canon of writers and outlining the features of a literary tradition, a critical vocabulary emerged to question the very idea of canons and traditions.

But the salient terms of these admittedly tendentious synopses would also have to reveal some useful correspondences. Both black feminist criticism and deconstruction perceived the regulation and exclusion of the marginal as essential to maintaining hegemonic structures. Both described the structural and hierarchical relations between the margins and the center. Our narrative might then pause to ponder how these two reading strategies came to be perceived as antithetical, how their specific *units* of critical interest came to be polarized and assigned an order of intellectual value that drew on a racist and sexist schema with heavy implications and investments in the sociopolitical arrangements of our time.

CHOOSING SIDES

It is important that this shorthand history not be read to mean that poststructuralist theories and their practitioners constitute a reaction formation against the emergent non-canonical literatures, and thus black feminist thinking would do well without them. No, my aim is not to demonize poststructuralist theories or to see them as having invented the present hierarchies that pervade critical inquiry. The hierarchical arrangements of knowledge within which black feminist thinking is marginalized extend far beyond and are well anterior to these theories. Such arrangements are part and parcel of what has already been written about black intellectuals, male and female alike, part and parcel of a general and historical devaluation of black intellectual activity in whatever form it takes.[39]

What viable position can then be taken in this context? We might begin to assert a provisional conclusion: When the writings of black women and other critics of color are excluded from the category of theory, it must be partly because theory has been reduced to a very particular practice. Since that reduction has been widely accepted, a great many ways of talking about literature have been excluded and a variety of discursive moves and strategies disqualified, in Terry Eagleton's words, as "invalid, illicit, non-critical."

The value of Eagleton's discussion of literary theory lies mainly in its understanding of how critical discourse is institutionalized. In that process, the power arrogated to some to police language, to decide that "certain statements must be excluded because they do not conform to what is acceptably sayable"[40] cannot be denied. The critical language of black women is represented, with few exceptions, as outside the bounds of the acceptably sayable and is heard primarily as an illicit and non-critical variety of critical discourse defined in opposition to theory. Its definition and identity continue to be constructed in contemporary critical discourses, all of which must be recognized, distinguished, and divided from each other in the academy's hierarchical system of classifying and organizing knowledge. To be sure, the discourses that exist at any given historical juncture compete with each other for dominance and meaning, compete with each other for status as knowledge, but we must be constantly on guard for what Biodun Jeyifo is right to term a misrecognition of theory, although this misrecognition has "achieved the status of that naturalization and transparency to which all ideologies aspire and which only the most hegemonic achieve."[41]

Given this misrecognition of theory and the privileged status it enjoys, even in moments of embattlement, it is readily understandable why some black feminists and other women of color in the academy would argue for the rightful recognition of their work as "theory." bell hooks offers only one example.[42] In evaluating the position of black women in theory, hooks goes directly to the necessary site of any such evaluation: the micropolitics of the corporate university. In analyzing the production of feminist theory, she perceives "only one type of theory is seen as valuable" in the academy—"that which is Eurocentric, linguistically convoluted, and rooted in Western white male sexist and racially biased philosophical frameworks" and rightly observes that, because this is the only "type of theory . . . seen as valuable," other varieties get overlooked.

Given hooks's astute understanding of the ways in which the parameters of "theory" have been constructed institutionally so as to eliminate the writings of black women, her observation that "little feminist theory is being written by black women and other women of color" (p. 38) runs oddly counter to her otherwise forceful critique. For her assessment is accurate only if "theory" is very narrowly conceived to fit the very definition she decries. Moreover, her lament for the paucity of theory by black women seems dependent on a false distinction between "theory" and "creative writing."[43]

In describing the pedagogical imperatives of the feminist classroom, hooks observes that in the economy of the average feminist syllabus, the "imaginative works [of black women] serve purposes that should be addressed by feminist theory," a tendency that does "disservice to black women writers and all women writers." However useful novels and confessional writings are in the larger projects of feminist theory, hooks adds "they cannot and do not take the place of theory" (p. 38).

hooks's fears that the tendency in classes on feminist theory to identify "writing by working-class . . . and women of color as 'experiential' while the writings of white women represent 'theory' " reinforces racism and elitism. Because of a long history that has constructed analytical thinking as the exclusive preserve of whites, hooks's concerns are fully understandable.[44] Although she is right to argue that "it does not serve the interests of feminist movement for feminist scholars to support this unnecessary and dangerous separation" between (theoretical) writing and writing that focuses on the experiential, her critique works only if she preserves that very distinction, ironically valorizing "theory" in the process.

While I would not presume to speak for or issue directives to "women of color," which would, in any case, assume a false and coherent totality, I openly share my growing skepticism about the tactical advantages of this position. I am far more interested, for the moment, in joining the growing number of critics—many of them "Third World"—who have begun to ask the difficult questions about the material conditions of institutional life and have begun to view theory, in its narrow usages (rather than in any intrinsic properties to be assigned to it), as an ideological category associated with the politically dominant. It is important that such a statement not be read as a resistance to "theory," but an insistence that we inquire into why that category is so reductively defined, and especially why its common definitions exclude so many marginalized groups within the academy. Such is Barbara Christian's point in "The Race for Theory," although in their rush to contain her inquiry, critics missed that aspect of her critique.

The question that Christian raises about the theory/practice distinction and the racial assumptions that it encodes is echoed in the writings of a growing number of students of minority and postcolonial discourses. For example, Rey Chow addressed the problem of "the asymmetrical structure between the 'West' as dominating subject and the 'non-West' or 'Third World' as the oppressed 'other'." She goes on to say, "contrary to the absolute difference that is often claimed *for* the 'Third World' . . . the work of a twentieth-century Chinese intellectual foretells much that is happening in the contemporary 'Western' theoretical scene."[45] Chow's observations go far beyond and far deeper than a plea for a liberal, pluralist position here, beyond a plea for "equal time." Neither she nor the growing number of Third World intellectuals who have begun to interrogate the uses to which "theory" is being increasingly put are so naive as to suggest that the power of its gravitational field in academic discourse can be so simply and reactively resisted. Most of us know that the debate over the uses and abuses of theory, formulated as such, followed by a growing demand to choose sides, is a sterile and boring debate that diverts us from the more difficult pursuit of understanding how theory has been constructed as an exclusively Western phenomenon.

The view that theory cannot exist outside that narrow orbit is especially apparent in what Edward Said refers to as a "maddening new critical shorthand" that "makes us no less susceptible to the dangers of received authority from canonical works and authors than we ever were. We make lackluster references to Nietzsche, Freud, Lacan as if the name alone carried enough value to override any objection or to settle any quarrel."[46] Said's list of names requires its constructed others to embody the most popular terms of critical opprobrium. I am concerned to note that often these are the names of black American women who become fetishized, to quote Valerie Smith, and "employed, if not sacrificed, to humanize their white [and male] superordinates, to teach them something about the content of their own subject positions."[47] And nowhere is this more apparent than in a recent exchange with Jane Gallop, Marianne Hirsch, and Nancy K. Miller in *Conflicts in Feminism*, edited by Marianne Hirsch and Evelyn Fox Keller.

REMEMORIES

This was not a story to pass on.   —*Beloved*

In that exchange, Gallop describes the process of her coming to write the history-in-process of feminist criticism through a reading of 1970s anthologies, a reading that would offer a more balanced version of the now largely disparaged seventies feminist criticism than recent years have seen. A part of the process of this project involved Gallop's own conversion to the idea of race. Asked by Hirsch how inclusive her history would be and whether she planned to include anthologies that foregrounded race, Gallop answered, and I quote in detail, perhaps in unseemly detail:

> I'm doing Pryse and Spillers's *Conjuring*. Race only posed itself as an urgent issue to me in the last couple of years. Obviously there has been a larger shift in the valent feminist discourses in which I participate. I didn't feel the necessity of discussing race

until I had moved myself out of a French poststructural orbit and began talking about American feminist literary criticism . . .

I was telling this guy in Syracuse that I thought in writing *Reading Lacan* I had worked through my transference both onto Lacan and onto things French in general. And he asked, "So who do you transfer onto now?" My first thought was to say, "no one." And then one of the things I thought of was a non-encounter with Deborah McDowell. I read work from my book last February at the University of Virginia. I had hoped Deborah McDowell would come to my talk: She was there, she was the one person in the audience that I was really hoping to please. Somebody in the audience asked me if I was writing about a black anthology. I answered no and tried to justify it, but my justification rang false in my ears. Some weeks later a friend of mine showed me a letter from McDowell which mentioned my talk and said that I was just doing the same old thing, citing that I was not talking about any books edited by black women. I obsessed over McDowell's comment until I decided to add a chapter on Pryse and Spillers's *Conjuring*. I had already vowed not to add any more chapters out of fear that I would never finish the book. As powerful as my fear of not finishing is, it was not as strong as my wish for McDowell's approval. *For McDowell, whom I do not know, read black feminist critic.* I realize that the set of feelings that I used to have about French men I now have about African American women. Those are the people I feel inadequate in relation to and try to please in my writing. It strikes me that this is not just idiosyncratic. This shift, for me, passed through a short stage when I felt like what I was saying was OK. The way McDowell has come to occupy the place of Lacan in my psyche does seem to correspond to the way that emphasis on race has replaced for me something like French vs. American feminism. (Emphasis added)[48]

It is important to note that Gallop sees her whole project as a "struggle over whose version of history is to be told to the next generation" (p. 362). She continues, "Mainly I am saying that feminist criticism has not been well enough understood. I am writing a history of something that is too known in the sense that it is familiar, but that we don't really perceive anymore because we have our set notions and categories for what is going on."

Gallop's reference to our "set notions and categories" is far more suggestive and incisive than perhaps even she intends. And the philosophy of history that her reference encodes encourages me to assert my own, by way of looking back in time and simultaneously returning to Sojourner Truth.

In 1863 Harriet Beecher Stowe published "Sojourner Truth: The Libyan Sibyl" in *Atlantic Monthly*. It begins:

Many years ago, the few readers of radical Abolitionist papers must often have seen the singular name of Sojourner Truth, announced as a frequent speaker at Anti-Slavery meetings, and as travelling on a sort of self-appointed agency through the country. *I had myself often remarked the name, but never met the individual.* On one occasion, when our house was filled with company, several eminent clergymen being our guests, notice was brought up to me that Sojourner Truth was below, and requested an interview. Knowing nothing of her but her singular name, I went down, prepared to make the interview short, as the pressure of many other engagements demanded. (Emphasis added)

Stowe's "I had myself often remarked the name, but never met the individual" has a striking ring or at least a structural similarity to Gallop's "For McDowell, whom I do not know, read black feminist critic." Having risked the dangers of a typological philosophy of history, let me suggest that in these two narratives, removed from each other by a century and a quarter, past and present become spectral adjacencies. While there are obvious risks in forging such a comparison, I do so out of understanding that intellectual inquiry is necessarily influenced and constrained by cultural traditions and social circumstances.

We might argue, then, that through the power of involuntary memory, the past is transferred to the present. While I obviously intend this play on words here, it is not idle play, for I want to capture that aspect of the transference that connotes a piece of repetition; the repetition is a transference of the forgotten past onto aspects of current situations. I want, moreover, to stress the rhetorical continuities between Stowe and Gallop in their own right as the legacy of a tradition of prefabricating blackness.

Both Stowe and Gallop commit what Ralph Ellison terms the "crime of reducing the humanity of others to that of a mere convenience, a counter in a banal game which involves no apparent risk to ourselves."[49] In "The Libyan Sibyl," Sojourner Truth is the counter to Stowe's conversion narrative, which assimilates Truth's complex life story to the civilizing rhetoric of Protestant evangelicism. In "Conflicts in Feminism," Deborah McDowell is the counter to an academic feminism now submitting to what Gallop calls the pressure of race.

But let me rush to insert here that my goal is neither to expose weaknesses in Jane Gallop's thinking nor to suggest that they are peculiar to her. In fact, in giving pause to her conversion narrative, I merely want to situate her within a general history. And Gallop would surely understand that, for as she prepares the reader for the delicate negotiations she must perform in the anthology study *Around 1981: Academic Feminist Literary Theory*, she takes care to note that

> We are [all] stuck inasmuch as we speak from within history. . . . [We] can only know from within history, with at best partial ideological awareness, and in specific relation to institutionalized discourses and *group interests*. (Emphasis added)[50]

As Gallop recounts the process of her own conversion or coming to race, she reveals again much more than she realizes. She confesses: "I can't discount being attacked in the name of Marxism or historicism or racial difference, things that I recognize as serious political, as opposed to what I think of as high theoretical" (Hirsch and Keller, p. 352). Racial difference figures in her confession as a proper name, my name.

The assignment so far of black women to the "serious political" as opposed to the "high theoretical" is an oversimplified taxonomic distinction based primarily on the convenience of the privileged few, and thus it is perhaps fitting that Gallop's truncated account of her intellectual development turns on references to class mobility:

> Around 1981, [I] experienced more anxiety about not being sophisticated enough whereas now my anxiety is about being bad, about having a white, middle-class outlook. . . . The anxiety about being a slob is an anxiety about not being high class enough, anxiety about being too low, whereas the other is anxiety about being too high. If you are looking up towards Derrida, Paris, sophistication, you feel like you're too low and you're anxious about not having something that comes from a higher class. . . . Now the situation is the opposite. (Hirsch and Keller, p. 353)

Race, in this context, equals lower class equals black feminist, a multiplication of equations that helps to construct an identity, a subjectivity for black feminist thinking among the general critical discourses of our time. Although black feminist criticism can be marked at one point on an as yet unfinished trajectory, it is consigned to the status of the permanent underclass. In that sense, the identity of black feminist criticism has so far been anything but fluctuating. It has been solidly fixed to a reference schemata and a racial stigmata in a history we've read before.

NOTES

1. This is a longer version of a talk presented at the Commonwealth Center for Literary and Cultural Change, University of Virginia, as part of a general symposium ("Is Knowledge Gendered?") and a specific panel on "Race and Gender in the Teaching of Historical Knowledge." I adapted the panel's focus in order to consider how "historical knowledge" gets constructed in the realm of literary studies. I thank Susan Fraiman and Rick Livingston for helpful comments and suggestions.

2. Audre Lorde, "Age, Race, and Class, and Sex," in *Sister Outsider: Essays and Speeches by Audre Lorde* (Trumansburg, N.Y.: Crossing, 1984), p. 123.

3. Arthur C. Danto, *Narration and Knowledge* (New York: Columbia University Press, 1985), p. 343.

4. See Richard King, "Memory and Phantasy," *Modern Language Notes 98* (December 1983): 1200. See also Pierra Nora, "Between History and Memory: Les Lieux de Memoire," *Representations* (Spring, 1989); Eric Hobsbawm and Terrence Ranger, eds., *The Invention of Tradition* (Cambridge: Cambridge University Press, 1983).

5. While certainly not peculiar to this tradition, this philosophy of history has long been prevalent in the writings of African Americans, especially in the historical, or documentary, fiction produced so insistently for the past twenty years. Random examples would include John A. Williams's two metahistorical novels, *The Man Who Cried I Am* and *Captain Blackman* (1972), in both of which history is a suspicious text constructed by paramilitary, conspiratorial agents. Other examples include Ishmael Reed's *Flight to Canada* (1976) and Sherley Anne Williams's *Dessa Rose*, derived from her short story "Meditations on History." For a discussion of history and documentation in African American fiction, see Barbara Foley, "The Afro-American Documentary Novel," in *Telling the Truth: The Theory and Practice of Documentary Fiction* (Ithaca, N.Y.: Cornell University Press, 1986). The now-familiar argument

that the generic conventions of narrative are evident in the construction of history has been articulated in works such as Hayden White's *Tropics of Discourse, The Content of the Form: Narrative Discourse and Historical Representation* (Baltimore: Johns Hopkins University Press, 1987), and *Metahistory* (Baltimore: Johns Hopkins University Press, 1973).

6. Renato Rosaldo, "Others of Invention: Ethnicity and Its Discontents," *Voice Literary Supplement*, February, 1990, p. 27.

7. Hortense Spillers, "Interstices: A Small Drama of Words," in Carole Vance, ed., *Pleasure and Danger: Exploring Female Sexuality*, p. 74.

8. In *Orientalism*, Edward Said also talks about the "powerful series of political and ultimately ideological realities [that] inform scholarship today. No one can escape dealing with, if not the East/West division, then the North/South one, the have/have not one, the imperialist/anti-imperialist one, the white/colored one" (New York: Vintage/Random House, 1979).

9. Definitions are in order here, but they are difficult to pin down. Although the term "theory" operates much like a mantra in contemporary criticism, it is difficult to find anything but vague definitions of the term. Randomly chosen attempts at definition would include Jonathan Culler's, which defines theory as a "nickname" used "to designate works that succeed in challenging and reorienting thinking in fields other than those to which they ostensibly belong because their analyses of language, or mind, or history, or culture offer novel and persuasive accounts of signification." See *Framing the Sign: Criticism and Its Institutions* (Norman: University of Oklahoma Press, 1988), p. 15. In *Criticism in the University*, Graff and Gibbon define theory as "simply a name for the questions which necessarily arise when principles and concepts once taken for granted become matters of controversy." Bruce Robbins uses theory to "refer to all those otherwise diverse conceptual innovations in the last twenty-five years or so which have combined to produce the single result of reshaping literary criticism." He goes on to say, "Theory is the body of external examiners, foreign and domestic, who have been called in and asked to put the status quo to the test, each applying her or his own criteria. In historical terms, theory has been an invitation to the critical examination and displacement of established practice." See "The Politics of Theory," *Social Text* 18 (1987): 5. What all these definitions lack, perhaps inevitably, is specificity and an awareness that "theory" is a term freighted with contemporary understandings and fraught with ambiguity. (Before 1960, the annual bibliography of the MLA contained no category of scholarly work designated by the term "theory.") Biodun Jeyifo draws an interesting and useful distinction between "theory," wrongly identified as a singular and uniform formation, and "theoreticism," the "specialized jargon through which 'theory' supposedly achieves its purchase on the power of generalization." See "Literary Theory and Theories of Decolonization," unpublished manuscript.

10. For further discussion of this idea, see Pierre Bourdieu, *Distinction: A Social Critique of the Judgment of Taste* (Cambridge: Harvard University Press, 1984). In "The Self-Evaluations of Critical Theory," Evan Watkins notes similarly that "how we tell ourselves the history of recent theoretical developments . . . takes place in [that] shady zone between the boundaries of intellectual work and social situation." *Boundary* 2 12–13 (1984): 359–78.

11. Such a perception derives in large part from the nasty battle waged on the pages of *New Literary History* 18 (1987). See Joyce Ann Joyce, "The Black Canon: Reconstructing Black American Literary Criticism"; Henry Louis Gates, Jr., " 'What's Love Got to Do with It?': Critical Theory, Integrity, and the Black Idiom"; Houston A. Baker, Jr., "In Dubious Battle"; and Joyce Ann Joyce, " 'Who the Cap Fit': Unconsciousness and Unconscionableness in the

Criticism of Houston A. Baker, Jr., and Henry Louis Gates, Jr." Barbara Christian's "The Race for Theory" added significantly to that perception.

12. Valerie Smith, "Split Affinities: The Case of Interracial Rape," in Marianne Hirsh and Evelyn Fox Keller, eds., *Conflicts in Feminism* (New York: Routledge, 1990).

13. Hazel Carby, *Reconstructing Womanhood*, p. 15.

14. One could raise at least two serious objections here. The first is that a focus on what has been written about black feminist thinking eclipses a more constructive, perhaps a more empowering, focus on what has been written by black feminists.

In her review of Patricia Hill Collins's *Black Feminist Thought*, for example, Farah Griffin commended Collins for moving black feminism "to a new level" by spending "little time castigating white feminists or black men for their failures in regard to black women." She praises Collins for focusing instead "on an exploration and analysis of thought produced by black women themselves. In so doing, she reinforces their status as subjects and agents of history." See *Women's Review of Books* 8 (February 1991): 14. While I would dispute Griffin's perception that the work of black feminists has been, to this point, determinedly other-directed, I regard her implied call for a necessary shift of focus and address within the work of black feminism as absolutely essential. But such a shift alone is insufficient, for it ignores the often unequally positioned sites of knowledge production and their influence on how and if the work of black feminists is read, on how and if it is read in a way that restructures, not simply annexes, knowledge in conditioned reflex acts.

One could raise a second objection: that my focus is too strictly and narrowly academicist, and curiously so if we consider that although its main address is now the UNIVERSITY, black feminist thinking does not stake its origins or find its shelter there, and even when academia is its central site, it strives to extend its borders. While the focus is narrow, its implications and imperatives for the organization and construction of "historical knowledge" are much broader.

15. For a discussion of the use of what Martin Jay terms "charismatic names" to legitimate critical arguments, see "Name Dropping or Dropping Names? Modes of Legitimation in the Humanities," in M. Kreiswirth and M. Cheetham, eds., *Theory between the Disciplines*.

16. For a discussion of Sojourner Truth as "standard exhibit in modern liberal historiography," see Phyllis Marynick Palmer, "White Women/Black Women: The Dualism of Female Identity and Experience in the United States," *Feminist Studies* 9 (Spring 1983): 151–69.

17. Rather than attempt to provide an extensive inventory here, let me call attention to certain benchmark statements from women of color about the injunction to theorize. In her controversial essay "The Race for Theory," Barbara Christian discusses the pressures she feels to "produce a black feminist literary theory as if [she] were a mechanical man," *Gender and Theory*, ed. Linda Kauffman (London and New York: Basil Blackwell, 1989), p. 227. Gloria Anzaldua notes that "what passes for theory these days is forbidden territory" for women of color, which makes it "*vital* that we occupy theorizing space," even as we understand that "what is considered theory in the dominant academic community is not necessarily what counts as theory for women of color," introduction, *Making Face, Making Soul/Haciendo Caras: Creative and Critical Perspectives by Women of Color* (San Francisco: Aunt Lute Foundation, 1990), p. xxv.

18. Denise Riley, *"Am I That Name?" Feminism and the Category of 'Women' in History* (Minneapolis: University of Minnesota, 1988), p. 1. By her admission, Riley's double move is a concession to pragmatism. She maintains that "it is compatible to suggest that 'women' don't exist—while maintaining a politics of 'as if they existed'—since the world behaves as if they unambiguously did" (p. 112).

19. Constance Penley, *The Future of an Illusion: Film, Feminism, and Psychoanalysis* (Minneapolis, 1989), p. 179.

20. Gayatri Spivack, "The Politics of Interpretation," in W. J. T. Mitchell, *The Politics of Interpretation* (Chicago: University of Chicago Press, 1982), p. 346.

21. Michelene Malson, Jean O'Barr, Sarah Westphal-Wihl, and Mary Wyer, eds., *Feminist Theory in Practice and Process* (Chicago: University of Chicago Press, 1989), p. 7.

22. Elizabeth Spelman, *Inessential Woman: Problems of Exclusion in Feminist Thought* (Boston: Beacon, 1988), p. 162.

23. In a very perceptive and persuasive chapter, Judith Roof argues that a "racial or lesbian commitment is defined as anachronistically political—'liberationist'—as activism instead of analysis." She asks, "Why for this moment are gender and class cerebral and race and sexual orientation experiential?" "All Analogies Are Faulty: The Fear of Intimacy in Feminist Criticism," in *A Lure of Knowledge: Lesbian Sexuality and Theory* (Columbia University Press, 1991).

24. Toril Moi, *Sexual/Textual Politics* (London and New York: Methuen, 1985), pp. 86, 87.

25. Jane Flax, *Thinking Fragments: Psychoanalysis, Feminism, and Postmodernism in the Contemporary West* (Berkeley: University of California Press, 1990), p. 140.

26. For a brilliant discussion of this scene and of the materiality in which black women were embedded more generally, see Haryette Mullen, " 'Indelicate Subjects': African American Women's Subjectivity," *Subversions* (Winter 1991): pp. 1–7. See also Valerie Smith, "Black Feminist Theory and the Representation of the Other,' " in Cheryl Wall, ed., *Changing Our Own Words: Essays on Criticism, Theory, and Writing by Black Women* (New Brunswick: Rutgers University Press, 1989), pp. 38–57. There Smith discusses tendencies prevalent in the discourses of Anglo-American feminists and male Afro-Americanists to invoke the experiences of black women, who become fetishized Others. She also links this association of black women as embodied others to classic Western philosophy as well as to nineteenth-century cultural ideas and ideals of womanhood. Such ideas of womanhood excluded slave women who were pinned in the body and therefore associated with "animal passions and slave labor" (p. 45).

27. Nell Irvin Painter, "Sojourner Truth in Life and Memory: Writing the Biography of an American Exotic," *Gender and History* 2 (Spring 1990):3–16. Painter traces the evolution of Sojourner Truth as historical legend and how the dominant representations of her, in both her time and ours, reflect various power asymmetries and hierarchies.

28. For example, it is seldom noted that during Reconstruction Truth assisted the resettlement of some blacks in the exodus to Kansas and worked on land reform.

29. Georg W. F. Hegel, "Geographical Basis of History," in *The Philosophy of History*, trans. J. Sibree (New York, 1991), p. 99.

30. Linda Kauffman, ed., *Gender and Theory* (New York, 1989), p. 2.

31. Michael Awkward, "Appropriative Gestures: Theory and Afro-American Literary Criticism," in Kauffman, *Gender and Theory*, p. 243.

32. Here I make an obvious allusion to Eve Sedgwick's influential study *Between Men: English Literature and Male Homosocial Desire* (New York: Columbia University Press, 1985), which examines the "bonds that link males to males," through and over the bodies of women.

33. Valerie Smith's observations about the trajectory of African American literary studies is well taken in this context. In "Gender and Afro-Americanist Literary Theory," in Elaine Showalter, ed., *Speaking of Gender* (New York: Routledge, 1989), she argues that the dynam-

ics of the male acquisition of power actually inform the critical positions of each generation. She refers specifically to Houston Baker's essay "Discovering America: Generational Shifts, Afro-American Literary Criticism, and the Study of Expressive Culture." She does well to note that in his epigraph to this essay, Baker "casts the connection of black expressive culture to literary criticism and theory in terms of the perennial battle between fathers and sons."

34. Such questions have received considerable attention in recent years. See, to name only a few examples, Jane Tompkins, *Sensational Designs: The Cultural Work of American Fiction, 1790–1860* (New York: Oxford University Press, 1985); Paul Lauter, *Canons and Contexts* (New York: Oxford University Press, 1991); John Guillory, "Canon," in Frank Lentricchia and Thomas McLaughlin, eds., *Critical Terms of Literary Study* (University of Chicago Press, 1990); and Richard Ohmann, "The Shaping of a Canon: U.S. Fiction, 1960–1975," in *Politics of Letters* (Middletown, Conn.: Wesleyan University Press, 1987).

35. The special issue and its responses are collected in Henry Louis Gates, Jr., ed., *"Race," Writing, and Difference* (Chicago: University of Chicago Press, 1986).

36. In *Essentially Speaking* (New York: Routledge, 1989), Diana Fuss makes essentially the same point. In " 'Race' Under Erasure? Poststructuralist Afro-American Literary Theory," while she praises Gates, who has "perhaps done the most to open the floodgates for Poststructuralist African American theory," and Baker, who "pioneers a fourth generational movement" (p. 81), Fuss, a white woman, asks, "What accounts . . . for the apparent resistance on the part of many minority women critics to what Barbara Christian has labeled 'the race for theory'?" (p. 95). A simple binarism between poststructuralism and essentialism structures Fuss's argument in this chapter, the former represented by Henry Louis Gates, Houston Baker, and Anthony Appiah (and, presumably, herself); the latter, by black women. In Fuss's analysis, "essentialism" is a kind of shorthand, catchall term for all that is not poststructuralist theory, a negation projected and branded onto black women. Moreover, essentialism acts very much like the proverbial poststructuralist "floating signifier," coming in a variety of brands. It slides up and down the scale of value and meaning, depending on its proximity to the moves and vocabularies of poststructuralism. Interestingly, Fuss acknowledges that a form of essentialism inheres in the work of Gates and Baker, but she redeems their variety of essentialism, primarily because she views it as redemptive, having "saved" African American literary study from what she terms the "bedrock of essentialism." Implying the now familiar theory/practice (politics) opposition, Fuss asks, "Is it possible that there might be an order of political necessity to these more essentialist arguments advanced by black women?"

37. Jonathan Arac, Wlad Godzich, and Wallace Martin described the spread of deconstruction in their preface to *The Yale Critics* (Minneapolis, 1987). In their estimation, "critics doing the new work most respected by a professionally authoritative screening group have drawn heavily from the Yale critics. In 35 essays that recently reached the editorial committee of PMLA, the American critics most cited were Miller . . . de Man, Bloom, Hartman and Derrida." Yet another and related sign of their powerful sway, Martin observed, was deconstruction's spread "from elite private institutions to public institutions," embracing "much more of the United States" and enrolling much "broader student bodies." While some have denied deconstruction's imperial status, arguing that it is only one of many discourses and, perhaps, one already displaced by competitors, a brief list of randomly chosen titles would suggest that even these "competing" discourses are often articulated through the language and tendencies of deconstruction. And though not simply mimicking deconstruction, many attempt to establish grounds of compatibility with it. In "Feminism and Deconstruction" (*Feminist Studies*, 14 [spring 1988]: 51–65), for example, Mary Poovey describes deconstruction as a discourse with

vast enabling possibilities for feminism. Michael Ryan's *Marxism and Deconstruction* (Baltimore: Johns Hopkins University Press, 1982) is an effort at what he calls a "critical articulation," which is not only a comparative reading of the two discourses, but also an "attempt to develop a new form of analysis which would be both marxism and deconstruction," an "alloy of the two" (pp. xv, xiii). In the introduction to his *Black Literature and Literary Theory* (New York: Methuen, 1984), Henry Louis Gates collects a group of essays that draw on various critical methodologies and reading strategies, but believes the signal challenge of black literary study is "to bring together, in a new fused form, the concepts of critical theory and the idiom of the Afro-American and African literary traditions." To undertake this complex process, he suggests that "Western critical theories [be used] to read black texts" (p. 10). Gates's inclusion of essays that do not effect such a fusion would seem to indicate no tendency on his part to prescribe; however, in the economy of the volume, the Yale School and its varieties of deconstruction predominate. Even though Gates's more recent essays call for black critics to "invent their own . . . black, text-specific theories," deriving from a "black formal cultural matrix," he also challenges them "not to shy away from white power—that is, literary theory," but to "translate it into the black idiom." The hegemony of "theory" (or white power) in this proposed hybridization is clear. The "New Historicism," one more recent contender for the throne of theory, derives, as Elizabeth Fox-Genovese is right to note, "in no small measure from its continuing affair with poststructuralist criticism—notably deconstruction with which it is much less at war than one might think."

38. Barbara Smith, "Toward a Black Feminist Criticism."

39. One of the most pointed historical antecedents to the cases I have been tracing in this chapter is Frederick Douglass's involvement with the abolitionist movement. As Douglass gained knowledge and confidence in the movement, he desired to break free of the confining role as "story-teller" handed him by the movement. He was admonished by John Collins, general agent of the Massachusetts Anti-Slavery Society, to "be yourself and tell your story. . . . Give us the facts, we will take care of the philosophy." Quoted in Waldo E. Martin, Jr. *The Mind of Frederick Douglass* (Chapel Hill: University of North Carolina Press, 1984), p. 22.

40. Terry Eagleton, *Literary Theory: An Introduction* (Minneapolis: University of Minnesota Press, 1983), p. 203.

41. Biodun Jeyifo, "Literary Theory and Theories of Decolonization," unpublished manuscript. Also see his "On Eurocentric Critical Theory: Some Paradigms from the Texts and Sub-Texts of Post-Colonial Writing," in Helen Tiffin and Stephen Slemon, eds., *After Europe: Critical Theory and Post-Colonial Writing* (Sydney: Dangaroo Press, 1989).

42. See her "Feminist Theory: A Radical Agenda" in *Talking Back: Thinking Feminist, Thinking Black* (Boston: South End Press, 1989), p. 36. See also Michele Wallace, who articulates a similar position in two essays from her collection *Invisibility Blues: From Pop to Theory* (London: Verso, 1990). In "Variations on Negation and the Heresy of Black Feminist Criticism," Wallace registers her concern that "black women writers and academics seem disproportionately under-represented in the sphere of knowledge production, in which literary criticism is included." While, in this essay, she concludes that "nobody in particular and everybody in general seems responsible for this situation" (pp. 215, 214), in "Negative Images: Toward a Black Feminist Cultural Criticism," she suggests that black women are largely responsible for this vacuum. She chastises them for producing "idealized and utopian black feminism, which remains almost entirely unarticulated and untheorized." Echoing Michael Awkward's point in "Appropriative Gestures: Theory and African American Literary Criti-

cism," Wallace asserts, "I am firmly convinced that if black feminism, or the feminism of women of color, is going to thrive on any level as a cultural analysis, it cannot continue to ignore the way that Freud, Marx, Saussure, Nietzsche, Levi-Strauss, Lacan, Derrida and Foucault have forever altered the credibility of obvious truth, 'common sense' or any unitary conception of reality" (p. 248). The importance of the work in this heterogeneous list is more asserted than argued, and recalls again Martin Jay's point about the "charismatic names," the ritualized forms of citation used to legitimate critical arguments simply through the act of reference. See "Name Dropping or Dropping Names? Modes of Legitimation in the Humanities."

43. The familiar and assumed distinction between "literature" and "criticism" has been widely problematized in contemporary critical discussion, as literary critics have rejected the "secondary" roles of servants to the master and "primary" texts and claimed for themselves a status equal to that of creative writers. As Barbara Hernsstein Smith puts it, "theory cannot be seen as distinct from and opposed to literary 'creation' but as a central and inevitable aspect of it," "Value/Evaluation," in Frank Lentricchia and Thomas McLaughlin, eds., *Critical Terms for Literary Study*, p. 181. In "The Race for Theory," Barbara Christian wants Smith's refusal of the distinction between "theory" and "creative writing" to work in reverse. That is, she wants to blur the distinction between the two in order to argue that if "theory" can be "creative writing," creative writing can be theory. But in arguing that "people of color have always theorized . . . in narrative forms, in the stories [they] create, in riddles and proverbs," she falls into the same logic that traps bell hooks. In other words, to reverse the theory/creative binarism in order to claim for the literatures of "people of color" status as "theory" is still to give primacy to "theory."

44. Cornel West makes a similar argument in "The Dilemma of the Black Intellectual," *Cultural Critique* 1 (1985): "Charges of intellectual inferiority can never be met upon the opponent's terrain." Rather, "the terrain itself must be viewed as . . . unworthy of setting the terms of contemporary discourse" (p. 117). West goes on to discuss the "place" of black intellectuals in Marxist thought, noting, "the Marxist privileging of black intellectuals often reeks of condescension that confines" the roles of black intellectuals to "spokespersons and organizers; only rarely are they allowed to function as creative thinkers who warrant serious critical attention" (p. 118).

45. Rey chow, " 'It's You, and Not Me': Domination and 'Othering' in Theorizing the 'Third World,' " in Elizabeth Weed, ed., *Coming to Terms: Feminism, Theory, Politics* (New York, 1989), p. 161.

46. Edward Said, *The World, the Text, and the Critic* (Cambridge: Harvard University Press, 1983), p. 143.

47. Valerie Smith, "Black Feminist Theory and the Representation of the 'Other,' " p. 46.

48. Jane Gallop, Marianne Hirsch, and Nancy K. Miller, "Criticizing Feminist Criticism," in Marianne Hirsch and Evelyn Fox Keller, eds., *Conflicts in Feminism* (New York: Routledge, 1990), pp. 364–65.

49. Ralph Ellison, "The World and the Jug," in *Shadow and Act* (New York: Vintage/Random House, 1972), p. 124.

50. Jane Gallop, *Around 1981: Academic Feminist Literary Theory* (New York: Routledge, 1992), p. 9.

45

"All the Things You Could Be by Now If Sigmund Freud's Wife Was Your Mother"

Psychoanalysis and Race

Hortense J. Spillers

(1996)

1

When I was young and free and used to wear silks[1] (and sat in the front pew, left of center, I might add), I used to think that my childhood minister occasionally made the oddest announcement. Whenever any one of our three church choirs was invited to perform at another congregation, our minister, suspecting that several of his members would stay home or do something else that afternoon, having already spent some hours at worship, skillfully anticipated them. Those who were not going with the choir were importuned to "send go." The injunction always tickled me, as I took considerable pleasure in conjuring up the image of a snaggle-toothed replica of my seven-year-old self going off in my place. But the minister meant "send money," so pass the collection plate. Decades later, I decided that the "send-go" of my childhood had an equivalent in the semiotic/philosophical discourse as the mark of substitution, the translated inflections of selves beyond the threshold of the fleshed, natural girl. It was not only a delightful but a useful idea to me that one herself need not always turn up. One and one did not always make two but might well yield some indeterminate sum, according to the context in which the arithmetic was carried out, indeed which arithmetic was performed. I have been suggesting that we need to work the double in this discussion.

Perhaps this is as factual as I know: In any investigatory procedure concerning African American culture, a given episteme fractures into negative and positive stresses that could be designated the crisis of inquiry that reveals where a kind of abandonment—we could also call it a gap—has occurred. Rather than running straight ahead toward a goal, the positivity (a given theoretical instrument) loops back and forward at once. For example, the notion of substitutive identity, not named as such in the literature of sociocultural critique, is analogous to the more familiar

580

concept of negation. On the one hand, negation is a time-honored concept of philosophical discourse and is already nuanced and absorbed, if not left behind, by linked discursive moves, from Hegel to Marx, from Kojève to Sartre and Lacan.[2] On the other hand, it is a useful concept to "introduce," alongside the psychoanalytic hermeneutic, to a particular historical order located in the postmodern time frame as a move toward self-empowerment, but in an era of discourse that needn't spell out the efficacy of either. (The same might be said for the concept of the subject.) We are confronted, then, by divergent temporal frames or beats that pose the problem of adequacy—how to reclaim an abandoned site of inquiry in the critical discourse when the very question that it articulates is carried along as a part of the methodological structure, as a feature of the paradigm that is itself under suspicion, while the question itself foregrounds a thematic that cannot be approached in any other way. If one needs a subject here, with its repertoire of shifts and transformations, and negation, with its successive generational closures and displacements, though both might be regarded as a disappeared quest-object at best, or a past tense for theory at worst, then we have come to the crisis that I have told, the instrument trapped in a looping movement or behind-time momentousness that need jump ahead. One tries in this fog of claims to keep her eyes on the prize. If by substitutive identities—the "send-go"—we mean the capacity to represent a self through masks of self-negation, then the dialectics of self-reflection and the strategies of a psychoanalytic hermeneutic come together at the site of a "new woman/man." That, I believe, is the aim of the cultural analysis.

A break toward the potentiality of becoming, or the formation of substitutive identities, consists in going beyond what is given; it is also the exceeding of necessity. While this gesture toward a theory of the transcendent is deeply implicated in the passage and itinerary of modern philosophy and the Cartesian subject, it is not so alien to the narratives and teachings of overcoming long associated not only with native traditions of philosophy in the lifeworld (via the teachings of the Christian church) but entirely consonant with the democratic principles on which the U.S. was founded (though immensely simplified in the discourses of liberal democracy). But the resonance that I would rely on here is less dependent on a narrative genealogy, whose plot line culminates in an epiphany of triumph, than on a different relation to the "Real," where I would situate the politics and the reality of "race." Even though it is fairly clear that "race" can be inflected (and should be) through the Lacanian dimensions, its face as an aspect of the "Real" brings to light its most persistent perversity. In Mikkel Borch-Jacobsen's reading of Lacan's "linguisteries," the "real" is said to be " 'pure and simple,' 'undifferentiated,' . . . 'without fissure,' " and " 'always in the same place' " (*L*, p. 192). As these Lacanian assertions seem to match precisely the mythical behavior of "race," or of any "myth today,"[3] they pointedly refer to the situation of the subject of enunciation—his or her own most "Real," or the status quo. In the classical narratives of psychoanalytic theory, the status quo, the standing pat, does not by error open onto death's corridor, inasmuch as it freezes and fixes subjectivity in a status permanently achieved. The outcome breezes by us in the very notion of status, with its play on *statue, sto, stant,* and so on. In this sense, overcoming is the cancellation of what is given. Borch-Jacobsen offers this explanation: "Thus language, the manifestation of the negativity of the subject who posits himself by negating (himself as) the Real, works the miracle of manifesting what is not; the tearing apart, the ek-sistence, and the perpetual self-overtaking that 'is' the subject who speaks himself in everything by negating everything" (*L*, p. 193). "Speaking" here is both process and paradigm to the extent that signifying enables the presence of an absence and registers the absence of a presence, but it is also a superior mark of the transformative, insofar as it makes something by cutting through the "pure and simple" of the "undifferentiated" in the gaps and spacings of signifiers. If potentiality, then, can be said to be the site of the human, rather than the nonhuman, fixedness; more precisely, if it is the "place" of the subjectivity, the condition of being/becoming subject, then its mission is to unfold—through "words, words, words" (*L*, p. 193), yes, but "words, words, words" as they lead us out to the re-presentational where the subject commences its journey in the looking glass of the symbolic.

Thus, to represent a self through masks of self-negation is to take on the work of discovering where one "is at"—the subject led back to his signifying dependence. Freud had thought a different idea—bringing unconsciousness under the domination of the preconscious—while Lacan, Freud's post-Saussurean poet, revised the idea as the "mapped" "network of signifiers" brought into existence at the place where the subject was, has always been: " 'Wo es war, soll Ich werden.' "[4] We could speak of this process as the subject making its mark through the transitivity of reobjectivations, the silent traces of desire on which the object of the subject hinges. This movement across an interior space demarcates the discipline of self-reflection, or the content of a self-interrogation that "race" always covers over as an already-answered. But for oneself another question is posed: What might I become, insofar as . . . ? To the extent that "I" "signs" itself "elsewhere," represents itself beyond the given, the onus of becoming boomerang[5]—Ralph Ellison's word—as it rebounds on the one putting the question. But what impedes the function of the question?

Once posed, the interrogative gesture, the interior intersubjectivity, would fill up the Fanonian *abîme*, "the great white error . . . the great black mirage."[6] But might we suggest that a different question could come about with the acquisition of a supplemental literacy, one that could be regarded as *alien* and for that very reason to be learned and pressed into service? Frantz Fanon assumed that his great positivities (conceptual narratives) were always and constantly equal to themselves, and he was exactly right. But he went further by saying that both of them were "not" in the sense that they were borne on the wings of an illusion and to the extent that they were both unsatisfactory as self-sufficient points of the stationary, and this seems right too. He did not, however; ask of himself and his formulation, So what? Such a question could not have been posed by him because his allegory had not only responded to the "so what?" but had preempted indeed any other impudent intervention. But if we move back in the direction of a "prior" moment, the seven-year-old in the front pew, for instance, we can then go forward with another set of competencies that originate, we might say, in the bone ignorance of curiosity, the child's gift for strange dreams of flying and bizarre, yet correct, notions about the adult bodies around her—how, for example, her father and brothers bent forward in a grimace when mischievously struck in a certain place above the knees by a little girl, propelling herself off a rollaway bed into their arms. The foreignness had already begun in the instant grasp of sexual and embodied division. But from that moment on, the imposition of homogeneity and sameness would also be understood as the great text of the "tradition" of "race." The Fanonian abyss requires this ur-text as the "answer" that fosters a two-way immobility. But before "race," something else has happened both within the context of "race" and alongside it.

Does tradition, then—depositories of discourse and ways of speaking, kinds of social practice and relations—enable some questions and not others? This seems so, but tradition, which hides its own crevices and interstices, is offered as the suture that takes on all the features of smoothness; in order to present itself as transparent, unruffled surface, it absorbs the rejects according to its most prominent configurations. But it seems that the move toward self-reflexivity demands a test of inherited portions of cultural content in order to discover not only what tradition conceals but, as a result, what one, under its auspices, is forced to blindside. What difference did it make that Fanon was a native speaker of French? That he had earned a significant place in French intellectual circles? His response seems appropriate—the sideways glance, the superbly ironical look. It was the effect of scission at the heart of the diasporic utterance. What he could not do, however, was read its outcome in reference to the "Negro of the Antilles," as well as to "Frantz Fanon." To have admitted that the diasporic African is cut on the bias to the West and not sharply at odds with it would have involved him in a contradiction that his polemic against the West could not abide. Nevertheless, the problematic that he carved out remains intact, and that is the extent to which the psychoanalytic hermeneutic has the least relevance to African diasporic lifeworlds.

Turning now to another protocol, we have the chance to pose the question again in an altered context, I want to look briefly at aspects of Marie-Cécile and Edmond Ortigues's *Oedipe africain* as an instance of psychoanalytic reference to a non-European community of subjects and as a systematic examination of symbolic currency (symbolization) as a response to the riddle that Fanon advances concerning the "Negro of the Antilles." Again, it is important to my mind to insist that even though diasporic African and continental African communities share "race," they pointedly differ in cultural ways and means; the contrary view, which flattens out black into the same thing despite time, weather, geography, and the entire range of complicating factors that go into the fashioning of persons, is difficult to put to rest, given, especially, what seems to be the unchanging face of racism. But unless we introduce cultural specificity to the picture, we run the risk of reenforcing the very myth that we would subvert. In that regard, the emphasis that *Oedipe africain* places on the processes of symbolization not only in the workings of psychoanalytic practice but in the making of human culture more broadly speaking offers a powerful antidote to reductive formulations. I have also examined aspects of Ibrâhîm Sow's *Les Structures anthropologiques de la folie en afrique noire* as a francophone reading from "inside" African culture. I try to bring the texts here into dialogue.

Oedipe africain is not available in English translation and was originally published in 1964 by French psychoanalysts who carried out clinical practice and observation in Dakar, Senegal from 1962–1966;[7] a redacted version, which text I use for this essay, came out in 1984. While the authors acknowledge that the analyst must attempt to understand the patient in the entire context of his or her lifeworld and that no point of comparison can be sustained between one culture and another along a particular line of stress without an examination of the whole, they do contend that the oedipal complex pertains to all human societies. Its nuances will differ, however, according to one's standing in the social order and the strategies of acculturation that are available to subjects within a given natal community. The authors suggest here that "a practitioner at work in a society foreign to his own definitely illustrates an essential characteristic of the analytic attitude; that is to say, no proposition can be understood without reference to a familial, social, and cultural context."[8]

If the knowledge that the analyst has about the total context is not exhaustive, "then what counts above all else is the analytical attitude that seeks to understand the place of the subject in what he says."[9] It seems to me that all dogmatic pronouncement, before and despite "what the subject says," is precisely the way in which traditional analyses, of various schools of thought, have failed, including all brands of nationalist thinking, as well as more informed opinions that have evolved a template of values to which "the black man" is supposed to conform, and including, moreover, "the black man" as a formulation itself. This whole vital soul, imagined to be snoring beneath the wisdom of the ages, conveniently poised for the exact liberatory moment, or "leader," is actually an unknown quantity in this very "soul" we thought we knew. Because the analyst, from the Ortigueses point of view, awaits a content, he has in effect no program to "sell." But the analyst here does not even do that much; he or she responds to a seeker.

Attempting to understand the subject in his or her discourse, the Ortigueses address the specificity of illness by way of a number of case studies (references to aggression, the persecution complex and its intricate functions, and so on). But in each instance the doctors, in touch with patients who have sought them out or have been referred to them by parents or school administrators, are not treating a single individual alone but an ensemble. Even the latter is not limited to the familial nucleus but may include ancestral and religious figures; in some cases, these might be the *rab*—an other-worldly figure—and the *marabout*, both of whom are active cultural figures in the Wolof, Lebu, and Serer communities of Senegal. The unseen seen, the "evidence" of things not seen, the *rab*, who may be either perverse of conduct "or possessively loving regarding a subject," is often felt to be responsible for certain facets of the subject's behavior. In this cultural setting, "illness is not a clinical entity at all" and certainly not foremost, but is "attributed by subjects to magical causality or the intervention of the divine."[10] The cultures in question are not only not of the West but are situated on the cultural map of Islam. The Western doctors, then, are attempting to work within the limitations posed by linguistic difference as well as differences of religious and ethnic reference.

If "the element of coherence" or consistency by which illness is represented is embodied in the *rab*, then this intervention would pose one more reason, among a variety of others, why "the doctors and their consultants might have been derailed in their interrogation."[11] In any case, however, this complicating factor in the relationship between a speaking subject and the grammar of his speaking brings to focus one of the key differences between tools of Western practice and the African context, as Sow will spell out: Who is the subject of treatment? In the African context, there are no lone subject of mental illness. A profoundly anthropological reading of subject disorder and its essentially communal and familiar character in traditional (and this distinction is crucial for Sow) African societies defines the project of *Les Structures anthropologiques de la folie en afrique noire*.

While the Ortigueses are aware that their project comes freighted with its own peculiar cultural baggage and bias, they nevertheless take their chances within the framework of certain psychoanalytic assumptions, as we have seen. Sow, on the other hand, locates the subject at last within a global scheme of reading that examines the basic tenets of West African culture. As informative as this method may be, it is in its own way as general and generalist as he claims that the classical descriptions of mental illnesses are to the African field. Too "superficial and artificial" to account for "psychological, social, human, and clinical realities" encountered in traditional African communities, the nosographical and nosological categories and tables, Sow argues, are themselves less objectionable to him than the inadequate supplement of their means with culture-specific strategies.[12] In *Les Structures anthropologiques*, he attempts to go beneath the manifestations of Western practice to penetrate its leading premises, to address and correct the problem, except that, in doing so, his chief actors are the macroelements of narrative and belief—the thematics of myth, of ancient tale and report. In that regard, he paints with a broader brush, as it were, and covers a canvas of wider scope, but ironically it seems that we lose the import of the psychoanalytic in the process precisely because, to Sow, it is unimpressively grounded in the messiness of the everyday world, in the utter evasion of the neat and rational category.

For example, madness in Sow's critique is similarly configured to the way it is sketched in *Oedipe africain*—as a mishap in an ensemble of sociocultural relations. Sow calls it a " 'sign' " that indicates straightaway that the subject is expressing conflict between himself and the constitutive authorities of his personality that are external to him (*SA*, p. 42; *AS*, p. 44). Sow consistently distinguishes between *personnalité* and *personne*.[13] It is the role of traditional therapy, then, alongside the interactive participation of family and community, to read and interpret the sign, to determine at what point in the constitutive network of the intimate structure of personality there has been breakdown or rupture in an otherwise highly articulated social function (see *SA*, p. 42; *AS*, p. 44). While it is fairly clear that Sow's "extérieures" look and behave suspiciously like the Lacanian "supports" through which the subject of enunciation is "spoken," Sow appears to so disjoin particular acts of enunciation from the culturally permissible that the neurosis itself erupts in "oneness." The double dose of narcissistic desire, therefore, follows from "individuality," when the neurotic *personne* behaves as if he were an end within himself:

In effect, what is signified for the neurotic is buried in his individuality and, in the final analysis, "doubles" or duplicates his narcissistic desire, which functions as if he were his own end in himself. For man confronting the sacred, however, what is signified is the Word, Law, Tradition—in short, man's Origin, in the sacrifice of the founding Ancestor; creator of the Law, guarantor of peace and coexistence among present-day human beings. [*AS*, p. 207][14]

But the real question for me in light of this formulation is, What is the relationship between Word and the word in which *personne*, neurotic and otherwise, is orchestrated? It appears that we pass here rather too quickly—dropping the ball is more like it—from a social dysfunction to a coerced repair in the formidable evocation of overwhelming devices, the great *di ex machina* that silence all before them—the Law, the Origin, the Tradition. "Man confronting the sacred" is a mighty idea, but who can stand before it? And isn't it quite possible that such standing would be unique? would represent an inimitable moment or an originary and irrecoverable act?

Nevertheless, Sow's insistence on a *constitutive network* restores the psychoanalytic hermeneutic to its social coherence, to its intersubjective function. As traditional therapy in his account seeks to transform mental illness into an articulated language, it would repair the broken link in which the individual is not alone located: "Reestablishing order in the subject reconstitutes the loose connection and reinserts the subject into the place from which he has been expelled, cut off from his source of nourishment by an 'aggressor' " (*AS*, p. 44).[15]

An "affliction" in the structure of communication implies an aversive meeting of *paroles*, and, to that extent, the anthropological elements of madness in African society do not deny, at the very least, conflict at the heart of human relations. Sow's "answer," however, by deferring or displacing the source of illness onto a global abstracted Outer, envisages an absolute otherness, whereas the struggle for meaning appears to "reduce" the absolute by dispersing its centrality. In other words, the subject, in a different order of things, must discover the degree to which he has engendered his own alienation. Consequently, the Western subject, it seems, sprouts guilt and big shoulders in taking on responsibility for an outcome, whereas his African counterpart, at least if Sow is right, does not acquire a discourse for the guilty conscience inasmuch as his ultimate ground of social and moral reference is situated "outside" himself.

In a sense, the universe projected in *Les Structures anthropologiques* is vestibular to both the historical and posthistorical insofar as it is finished and elegantly arranged according to an immemorial Law and Order that Sow elaborates at length. We can do no more than sketch some of its prominent features here. In West African cosmography, human and social order is based on an imbricated, yet hierarchical, grid of functions marked according to three levels of stress: (1) the sensible, given world of the microcosmos—the world that is immediate and given, the world of the social; (2) "the intermediary world of the genies, the spirits, and a repertoire of malevolent and beneficent forces of the *mesocosmos*"; and (3) "the *suprasensible* world of the Spirits elect, the Ancestors, the Godhead" (*SA*, p. 45; *AS*, p. 48). But there are ancestors and the Ancestor(s), as it seems apparent that the capitalized *Ancêtre* is the equivalent of the Godhead, if not exactly synonymous to it. Given this elaborate schematization, there is, in effect, "no one"—in a rather different sense from the *nothing* and *no one* of Western philosophical/psychoanalytic discourse—with its eye trained, finally, on an eclipsed God, or the One about whom silence is in order. In African discursive and social practice, as Sow narrates the scene, one is nothing more nor less than a link through which the three great valences of order reverberate. Therapy thus consists in bringing one back to harmonious relations with a cosmogonic principle whose intent can be teased out in various mythic narratives. There, "the prescriptions, rules, interdictions, and models of conduct" aim toward a definitive suggestion: that "cultural order and coherence repose on a delicate, subtle balance of the *differentiated* identity of each and all" (*SA*, p. 154; *AS*, p. 159), primarily the continuity of the generations in the passage of the biological age group, wave on wave of horizontal confraternities in progression toward the status of ancestry. In such a system, the strategies of rapprochement between God and human appear in language—"in speech, prayer, and dream, as the dialogue between distant interlocutors must pass through the privileged intercessory office of the Ancestors" (*AS*, p. 210 n. 9).[16]

From this perspective, mental illness is read as the interrupted circuitry between carefully delineated parts (see *SA*, pp. 10–11; *AS*, p. 6). But the texts of role and agency are not discoverable, inasmuch as they are already known from a transmitted structure of articulated cause and effect. Moreover, this symbolic economy, which rests in a transcendent signifier, generates a Story, unlike the discourse that breaks up into the atomized particles of evasive meaning, or a meaning delayed in the "effects" of the signifier: We would regard the latter as a symptom of modern social analysis that follows the trails of fragmented social objects—in short, a world defined by the loss of hierarchy, privileged moments, and ineluctably declarative—ambiguity expelled—utterances. We know this world as our own—the scene of scission and displacement.

But where would this buzz of the harmonious leave the culturally "illiterate," the one who misreads the traffic signals? In the opening chapter of *Les Structures anthropologiques*, Sow treats at length the occurrence and frequency of mental illness in West African communities. As he adopts nosographical categories of description familiar to Western psychiatric practice, he is convinced that the categories themselves are ill-equipped to treat key questions, such as "the problem of the stain, of the pure and impure, that dominates Swedish psychopathology, for instance" (*SA*, p. 31 n. 36; *AS*, p. 32 n. 10), or the phenomenon of "la bouffée psychotique": the most characteristic formal aspect of African psychiatry (*SA*, p. 31; *AS*, p. 31). If the "bouffée psychotique" is a characteristic form in African medicine, then persecution is the most frequently and meaningfully recurrent thematic of Continental practice (see *SA*, p. 34; *AS*, p. 35). He claims that it not only colors the entire field of practice but that it also occupies a privileged place in the anthropological system of representations across Black Africa. The ensemble of premises against which Sow leads up to his reading of the African conception of cosmos and its signifying role in the mental theatre might be summarized according to two binarily opposed tables of value. Traditional African institutions, in their preventive or prophylactic capacity, effectively maintain personal, interpersonal, and communal equilibrium. The psychological defenses are cultural and collective and may be compared with what we spoke of earlier as the Western implantation or interiorization of guilt.[17] In other words, the persecutor in African culture embodies the externalization of guilt, whereas in Western culture, the guilt function is assumed by the person. Sow evaluates the internalizing of guilt as (1) "the origin of the morbid structure" and (2) "the sociocultural context of sin and blame" (*SA*, p. 25 n. 20; *AS*, p. 24 n. 7). But is it possible that the binary disposition is less than dispositive, even in a traditional African setting? Is it possible that traditional structures, precisely because they are time honored, do not always respond to a particular demand?

Among the case studies presented in *Oedipe africain*, the Ortigueses' Samba C., a fourteen-year-old Wolof Muslim, might raise interesting problems for Sow's scheme. "According to the psychotherapeutic material presented to them," the authors believe that Samba did reach the internalization of conflict, which process Sow identifies as the origin of morbidity in Western disorders, and that a dream reported to them by the analysand not only signalled such internalization but announced it as the onset of a series of psychotic episodes. The dream, which led him to the Western doctors, is described this way: "The baobab tree [the renowned tree of African lore and legend] of Samba's initial vision, at the time of this dream . . . , cried out that the dead must be buried at his feet and not in the cemetery; the terrifying persona of Samba's hallucinations was transformed into a man who declared these words: 'It is the father of fathers.' "[18] Samba's confrontation with representative instances of the paternal image—in the baobab tree and the transformations that it induced—suggested to the doctors that Samba's troubles were related to the ancestors. In attempting to retrace the trajectory of the Ortigueses' conclusions, which follow below, we hope to see at least the divergence of interpretation between two styles of analytic practice and assumption. We can only guess how Sow might have read Samba's case.

> Samba C. first encountered trouble, when, passing under a baobab tree on returning to school one day, he heard a voice that called out to him by his family name three times. Samba does not answer, for responding would have been incorrect, but he does not continue on his way, and quite frightened, turns back toward home. He takes to his bed, trembling, vomiting during the night. For the rest of the following day and for some months afterward, Samba keeps his eyes closed, as if he feared a terrifying vision, "like children, something big, a devil." He suffered from migraine headaches in the course of things, refused to eat, and in any case only imbibed small amounts of food and drink. He remained inert, prostrate, arms bent in moaning. His groans would intensify for hours at a time, in extended and monotonous plaint. The words that escaped from him came torn, babbled, barely audible and were accompanied by an involuntary shaking of the head.

Samba's parents reported that the outbreak persisted for several months, and he was eventually led to neurological consultation and hospitalized. All the tests administered to him proved negative. During hospitalization, Samba's state was unchanged three weeks later; he left the hospital after insisting upon it, having attempted escapes daily. Shortly thereafter, he was hospitalized in the psychiatric unit. In the course of a year, he was hospitalized three times and during interim periods was treated as an outpatient, subjected, during each term of hospitalization, to a series of electroshocks at the same time as psychotherapy. A neuroleptic treatment was pursued as well.

In Samba's case, it is legitimate to speak of psychoanalytic psychotherapy in the most classic sense of the term. Samba's demand was clear: He came "to talk in order to get well." A rich transferential relation was quickly established, as his treatment lasted a year and included some fifty-one sessions with the doctors. Samba was regarded as intelligent and sought to verbalize everything that he lived.[19]

Summarizing, we can make the following observations: (1) After two months and nine sessions of treatment, Samba barely got beyond the hallucinations that haunted his nights. "The visual representations ranged from children, to snakes, to a very large black man, who frightened him." Samba reported auditory and visual hallucinations that included "snakes invading his body, drinking his blood, and the attacks made him feel that he would die soon."[20] The doctors were caught by the binary equation in Samba's description—"fear"/"bliss-happiness" ("peur"/"bonheur")—as they came to discover "that the voice of the baobab, which was the voice of the devil, was actually the projected persona of an older companion of Samba's, one Malik, who, in Samba's eyes, incorporated at once the manhood virtue of boldness, physical force, and endurance, as well as the temptations to fall that led to Samba's madness" (OA, p. 98). (2) "La folie" was understood by the doctors to have conformed to "désocialisation," into which Malik had led his younger companion over a few years— disobeying and deceiving parents, insolence toward authority, thievery, and the violation of a fundamental prohibition, "going out at night." The latter activity was strictly forbidden to children, especially treks into the bush or the countryside, those reputedly dangerous places thought to be inhabited by evil figures. This crossing the bar, we might say, manifested in various antisocial behaviors that challenged authority, was accompanied by gross misconduct toward Malik's and Samba's female peers. The doctors observed that "Malik's 'leadership' was exercised in a decidedly sadistic tonality" and that none of the authority figures, including parents and teachers, were ever able to bring him in line. "Above all, Malik embodied for Samba an element of undeniable fascination" (OA, p. 98). (3) Samba, then, "was frightened by his desire to look like Malik, *to be* Malik [*d'être un Malik*]. The temptation was projected as the 'devil' "—the "saytané." The attending *marabouts*, preceding consultation with the Western doctors, believed that the problem was the "devil," who wanted to harm Samba. But as it turned out, Samba's family, "his entourage," had themselves had similar experiences, "since childhood, with the evidentiary presence of djinns and devils" ("Pour le père et la mère de Samba, pour tout l'entourage, l'existence des djiné et saytané est une évidence quotidienne depuis l'enfance; chacun a une ou plusieurs expériences personnelles les concernant") (OA, p. 98).

4) "Samba finally arrived on the threshold of an interiorization" of guilt. The

"devil" was Malik, wanting him to do ill, yet "he realized that he admired the older boy and that the latter was a thug" ("celui-ci-était un voyou ignorant") (OA, p. 99). Over time, "his fantasies concerning the persona of the devil . . . terrifying and attractive at once, were doubled and divided among three or four persons, as this game of doubling, coupling, and dividing allowed Samba ever greater suppleness in projecting himself into variable positions regarding his desire and its related anxiety."[21]

Even though Samba's condition was ameliorated by treatment, the authors maintain that his state, for all that, proved irreversibly psychotic. To the question, What if the prognosis were inept, or unrelated to the strategies of cure available in Wolof society, the Ortigueses respond with what is, for all intents and purposes, a question of their own: "Did not Samba's culture impose on him, or propose to him in a privileged way the solution to his hallucinatory psychosis, vis-à-vis the theme of persecution?"[22] The doctors believed that Samba had "jumped"—my word—his circumstance by internalizing his dilemma, by seeking to resolve it at the level of personality. In a sense, cutting loose from certain communal beliefs, feeling himself driven to the wall, he had sought other means of address and "become a stranger to himself while doing so, acceding to the level of personal conscience that had situated him 'well ahead of the fathers."[23] In the culture in question, one did not reach for advancement beyond or away from the group, as they read the picture. At best, Samba's condition in the end "appeared fragile, as the 'devil' remained discretely present" (OA, p. 100).

What I have interpreted in the foregoing paragraphs as declarative assertions are advanced as inquiries in the text, and this is important to note, inasmuch as the doctors are themselves aware that their speculative instruments are adopted from a very different cultural framework. For instance, they question whether or not it is thinkable that Samba has arrived at the interiorization of the conflict that he clearly expressed and whose implications he could explain—"*Est-il pensable qu'il parvienne à intérioriser sa culpabilité?*" (OA, p. 99). Furthermore, they handle certain conclusions that they have tentatively reached in a subjunctive appeal: In effect, Samba's assumption of guilt would suppose that he had disconnected himself from certain communal values, and is such delinking not only possible but even desirable? The Ortigueses go on to say that everything during the course of initial treatment happened "as if" Samba, feeling no way out, had placed all his hope, had articulated all his demand in the opening dialogue of the first interviews and as if "he assumed the risk of an unknown outcome" ("il assumait le risque de l'issue inconnue") (OA, p. 100). His parents, "feeling anxious, powerless, and overwhelmed by Samba's auto-aggressive conduct," following the failure of traditional treatment, "sought to turn him over to 'the doctors' and also accepted the risks." During the course of the doctors' treatment, Samba's family consulted "un marabout 'plus fort' que les précédents," since the doctors were in accord with the decision. "This procedure, no more than prior consultations with the *marabout*, did not interrupt the psychoanalytic course," as the differing strategies were simultaneously pursued (OA, p. 100).

As readers going back and forth on this, grappling in another language, about a vastly different culture, not Western, French, English, or diasporic for that matter, trying to see through other eyes to the truth of the matter or even gain some clarity concerning it, we are confronted with mutually exclusive questions. Perhaps all the doctors and theorists are right, or more precisely, know how to be, within the particular parameters of insight and blindness that frame their discourse. But the affecting line "tout son espoir, toute sa demande" (OA, p. 100) sketches a face before us whose details are unreadable, except that we hear in its trace of the paraphrase the stunning bafflement of one at pains to know why he suffers, and it seems that we are captivated there—in the inscription of particular address. There is the society, doubtlessly so, but what about Samba? Another way to ask this question is the impossible, What does he say he wants? Unless I have misunderstood the matter, the "hermeneutic demand" of the psychoanalytic itinerary unfolds from each of the Sambas' articulated wannas-be, but in what world? Is it thinkable that a Samba was raising, in the depths of his being, a question that his culture could not answer; even though the latter had opened the place of the question by giving it its props, its materiality? Is the quest conditioned by the epistemic choices available to the want-to-be of the subject? And if the subject "overreaches" the given discursive conditions, does madness attend, no one quite knowing what he is saying, as indeed was reported to have happened at the onset of Samba's psychotic course? For the Ortigueses, Samba's dilemma raises the question of *recognition by the brothers*, which they contend is routed through "Oedipe africain." It is at heart an inquiry concerning *status* and the variable positions through which it is expressed.

In Samba's society, "the search for status recognition by the 'brothers' is a dominant mode of manhood affirmation" ("la recherche d'une reconnaissance de mon statut par les 'frères' est un mode dominant de l'affirmation virile" [OA, p. 135]). As we observed before, the brothers are the progressive, or processual, confraternity of age-mates precisely linked by the time of birth. "The wish to be a man expresses itself here in a form and content different from the ones that we know in European societies," say the Ortigueses. "In Europe, young Oedipus wishes to be a rival in tasks, actions, and realizations; it is a rivalry that is manifest by objective sanction," or we could say that the objectifiable nature of goals acts to mediate the rivalry— making a better boat, for instance, or hurling a discus farther than another. In brief, it seems that the socius of the objectifiable aim may be called competitive. In the Senegalese field, rivalry is accentuated by a

> stress on status, on prestige. It has to do with demonstrating or showing a certain image of the self to the "brothers," or of doing what they believe conforms with the image in the eyes of the brothers. . . .
>
> For the young Dakarois whom we saw, plans for the future . . . were hardly based on performance or personalized activity, as it was in small measure a question of inventing something, or exceeding some achievement, but was tied up with the theme of *giving oneself to be looked at*. A subject might have said, for instance, that he wanted to wear beautiful clothes, or have a good position, but the precise activity, the métier, the vocation that supported the good position or the beautiful clothes was not considered in and for itself. The wish, then, had less to do with a more interesting or

efficacious performance of some task, but more to do with achieving higher visibility for socially prominent reasons. . . . To improve one's status, one might say "I did this or that," or "such and such admires me," or "such and such said that I was intelligent" [or] . . . "great." . . . If a subject reported: "I have more success with the females than my buddies," he was appealing less to his relationship with the girls in question than reflecting on the admiration or the jealousy of his comrades.[24]

It is difficult to decide from what the authors report about such assertions whether or not bragging among the young is common across cultures. I actually think that it might well be, but one is nevertheless struck by the importance of the specular and the spectacular here, which is precisely where Du Bois placed the significance of the look regarding the "seventh son," albeit for radically different historical reasons.[25] Yet, I believe that this stunning thematic running through a milieu of West African society is well worth keeping in mind. Though far too quick a thought, as it were, to be considered for more than a passing moment, the concern about "how's it hanging"—which would mark an especially male anxiety—may actually "translate" into diasporic communities as the analogous stress on looks, prestige, success, and the entire repertoire of tensions that have to do with the outer trapping, that is, one's appearance. The Ortigueses suggest that with all their subjects, "references to fathers and uncles bore the character of spectacle, witness, and display offered to the look of others. The child felt empowered by the father, loved by the father, when he was well-dressed by him, when he imagined others looking at him well-dressed." Among Europeans, they contend, "a boy of a certain age might think: 'My father is stronger than a lion . . . my father has the biggest car . . . my father is rich and commanding,'" whereas among the young Dakarois, "the boy thinks: 'My father is going to buy me a beautiful shirt, a beautiful suit.'" The instances could be multiplied, they tell us, but they sum up the point: "The desire for better clothes, for more beautiful clothes, was the first desire expressed by the young men, the desire to show their father, and for those who suffered his indifference or estrangement, it was not rare to encounter an obsessive concern about appearance to the extent of seeking homosexual engagement in the search for ostentation."[26]

By "the look . . . the subject decides if he is mocked, held in contempt, thought to be disagreeable," and so on. "The frequency with which distressful sensations were triggered by the look of another, or perceived at the level of the skin or the superficial musculature" because of another's "regard," was considerable in their estimation. Relatedly, the Ortigueses evolved from the cases a veritable "grammar" of the look: "formidable," "contemptuous," "masked," "averted," "eyes turned sideways," "looks and laughs," "looks down (or lowers head)" ("formidable," "méprisant," "est masqué," "détourné," "les yeux de côté," "regard et il rit," "garde la tête baissée").[27] Prominently placed in the discourse of "the first interviews was the subject's concern about the troubling look; from instances of hysteria, having to do with a transient evil eye [*d'un mal aux yeux passager*] . . . to fantasies surging up in the here and now, we were always told: 'Je ne me donne pas le droit de voir.'" Because one's own look is disabled, or because one cannot seize the right to look, as I understand this, which frequently occurs in one's own bad dreams, perhaps we bear this rubric away from the scene: "The sight appears as a privileged place of castration" here (*OA*, p. 105).

By a detour off the customary path, the oedipal problematic travels in this instance through the peer group, snared in the coils of looking and being seen. The Ortigueses do not pause to elaborate on what is, to my mind, a point of saturation in their itinerary that could possibly bridge across Old and New World African cultures in a consideration of unconscious material, but I am not, for all that, claiming that there would be good reason on that basis to pose or even anticipate moments of a transhistorical (black) collective psyche. Nevertheless it seems to me that any sustained investigation along these lines might usefully isolate the gaze in its discrete cultural property as a route of organization for a comparative reading of intersubjective signals in divergent lifeworlds. But I should try to be clear about this. The inquiry that I am describing would occur under some other auspices than the psychoanalytic, even though it might be informed by its protocols. In any case, the look and its dynamics would bring to focus several topics that come together in the name of subjectivity, that is, the extent to which self-formation is authored elsewhere, in the split between the wanna-be and its objectivations in the place of another. The *eyes* in this case are nothing more nor less than the crucial relay of a "message" that either proffers or denies, though denial, as we know, is also a most powerful offer. The tales of the young Dakarois reenforce the unthinkable—it is all too often up to someone else—and for my money, we have little idea what this particular exchange of subtextual motive, "choreographed" in the rise and fall of the eyelid, actually "sounds" like in cultural theory concerning black communities. Relatedly, is there not this conundrum: If the young male consultants of the Ortigueses' "récits" are bound to the "look" of others—as feminist film theorists have suggested that the female "star" is[28]—then what revisionary notions might be introduced to the conceptualization of the gaze as heterosexual currency? At least to the extent that it induces more questions than it disposes of, the "récit" of the consultation expands the genre of narrative art.

The coil of the looks for the Ortigueses, however, is entirely related to the psychoanalytic aims of *Oedipe africain*, and that is to explore how the oedipal crisis—finding one's place in the social order—is resolved in a cultural context where the symbolic function of the father remains tied to the ancestors. We can only sketch out a few more details of this running narrative: (1) In the case where the father mediates between the dead ancestors and the living sons, the sons cannot think of themselves as the equal of the ancestor (and therefore not of the father either) and certainly not as his superior. What one must confront instead is the right to claim one's place within the group, as castration here is based on the collective register of obedience to the law of the dead, the law of the ancestors. To be excluded from the group or abandoned by it is the equivalent of castration (see *OA*, p. 75). When Samba, in the case that we have examined, was confronted by the baobab tree in his disturbing dream, he was essentially coming face to face, as it were, with a representative ancestral figure, as the baobab holds a privileged place in the culture as the site of the wisdom of the dead and of the living fathers. It is, therefore, collectively possessed. The appearance of the tree in the young man's dream apparently signalled his arrival on the threshold of manhood.

In contrasting the European Oedipus with its African equivalent, the Ortigueses suggest that the youth in the latter setting does not imagine killing the father but must be referred to the ancestors through him. Thus a second detail is added to the narrative: (2) Because the ancestors is "déjà mort" and "inattaquable," the sons constitute their own brothers in rivalry, the group that they must enter. This horizontal social arrangement yields two crucial representations—"the collective phallus and the unbeatable ancestor," which conduces to "the game of rivalry-solidarity between the brothers." In this setup, everything that the brothers do regarding one another acquires profound weight, inasmuch as one's successful achievement of status is predicated on it. "Rivalry, then, appears to be systematically displaced onto the 'brothers' who polarize the aggressive drives," as "aggression itself is primarily expressed under the form of persecutive reaction-formations." "The network of intersubjective relations would be strongly colored here by the fact that everyone is easily perceived as both vulnerable to persecution" and capable of serving its ends through the medium of a superior force or talisman. "Under all circumstances, it is appropriate to protect oneself against harmful intentions," against apparently aggressive moves in the other, which energy, the authors observe, is deflected away from self-affirmation through action toward self-defense. "Blame, then, is barely internalized or constituted as such," since the material cause of the harm "lies outside oneself," where the "badness" reigns: "Everything happens as if the individual cannot bear to be perceived as internally divided and driven by contradictory desires." *Les Structures anhropologiques* and *Oedipe africain* seem to strike a common chord on this point. We would also read Samba's predicament in this light.[29]

"To the extent that the aggressive drives are not projected onto another, the subject remains conscious of them, but represses them, tries to control them." "Aggressive fantasies and emotions might then take the route of the secretive, muted, destructive, unacknowledgeable material about which silence is deemed appropriate," because mouthing it might " 'discourage my parents,' " or " 'they would count against me,' " or expressing it would expose one's vulnerability, one's "locution," as it were. "Often, somatizations appeared as a means of inhibiting the instantaneous expression of fantasies and aggressive impulses." What might occur in the event of a repression is the dissimulation of mistrust and suspicion under the guise of an "imperturbable gentilesse" that is aimed at warding off a blow. But such a "separate peace" might not yield the expected "detente," but could well result in "immediate depression" or he "emergence of aggressive fantasies."

> Unless a subject sought solitude in order to protect himself against anxiety reactions that had become overwhelming, the young consultants described to us the high degree to which they felt compelled to be with their friends . . . , to be part of the group, of the crowd. Even if nothing of particular importance accrued from a sporting event, a

dance outing, an interminable round of talk . . . , the real thing was the presence of others—necessary and reassuring—in keeping the latent aggressive fantasies in the background.[30]

Could it be that male bonding or confraternity is based on keeping the latent aggressive fantasies at bay? In that sense, perhaps, the solidarity piece of the rivalrous relations would sheath, at all times, a decidedly violent possibility, all the more so for what it covers over. The "gang" in diasporic communities may well replicate this pattern of repression and closure.

We recall that the social formation of the brothers, banished in the Freudian myth for the crime of patricide and other impressive infamies, is the triggering mechanism of the incest taboo and the cut into human community. But Freud's exiled issue have the opportunity to "return" with the boon of guilt. As we think about the African Oedipus, according to the Ortigueses' sketch of it, several half-formed, obscure questions crowd in: Did African Oedipus show a break in the fabric of narrative, in the incontestable roll and continuity of generation after generation, reaching the shores of death and the "full fatherhood" ("père à part entière" [*OA*, p. 110]), by way of the Atlantic slave trade? The question springs to mind from a suggestive passage in Claude Meillassoux's *Maidens, Meal, and Money*, wherein Meillassoux, in elaborating the role of elders and juniors in the African "domestic community," cites other historical research on the matter: Populations that had been "brutally subjected to the effects of the European slave trade" often used the juniors not only as producers, "but ultimately commodities as well." Their severity toward them exaggerated by greed, the elders banished the juniors "for real or imagined crimes," as the young "were transformed into goods for the slave trade."[31] The slave trade, of course, bears none of the advantages of myth, but shows some of its earmarks, as the Atlantic trade might be thought of as one of the founding events of modern history and economy. But for our purposes here, the execrable trade, in radically altering the social system in Old and New World "domestic community," is as violent and disruptive as the never-did-happenstance of mythic and oneiric inevitability. In other words, this historical event, like a myth, marks so rigorous a transition in the order of things that it launches a new way of gauging time and human origin: It underwrites, in short, a new genealogy defined by a break with Tradition—with the Law of the Ancestors and the paternal intermediary.

From my perspective, then, African Oedipus is the term that mediates a new symbolic order. It allows us to see that "father" designates a function rather than, as Meillassoux points out, a "genitor": the father is "*he who nourishes* and protects you, and who claims your produce and labor in return."[32] In that regard, the African Oedipus removes the element of sentimentality from the myth and exposes it as a structure of relations instead. The riddle of origin that the Oedipus is supposed to constitute, first, as a crisis, then as a resolution of order and degree, was essentially cancelled by the Atlantic trade, as the "crisis," for all intents and purposes, has continued on the other side, the vantage from which I am writing. In the essay from which this writing is excerpted, I spoke about a subject in discourse, crossed by stigmata, as the psychoanalytic difference that has yet to be articulated. In the longer essay, I define the stigmatized subject as one whose access to discourse must be established as a human right and not assumed. I am referring specifically here to the history of slavery in the Americas and not only its traditions and practices of "chattel property," but, related to it, the strictures against literacy imposed on the bonded. Inasmuch as classical psychoanalytic practice works to transform symptomaticity into a narrative, I take it that discourse constitutes its primary value: The raced subject in an American context must, therefore, work his way through a layered imperative and impediment, which deeply implicates History in any autobiographical itinerary. I think that I am prepared to say that those markings on the social body of New World Africanity are the stripes of an oedipal crisis (for male and female children) that can only be cleared away now by a "confrontation" with the "scene" of its occurrence, but as if in myth. In other words, the discontinuity that the abandoned son demarcates here must be carried out as a kind of new article of faith in the non-Traditional, in the discovery of the Law of the living, not the dead, and in the circulation of a new social energy that confronts the future, not the past.

Carrying out that line of thinking, we might be able to see in an apposite psycho-analytic protocol for the subjects of "race," broken away from the point of origin, which rupture has left a hole that speech can only point to and circle around, an entirely new repertoire of inquiry into human relations. Perhaps I come out here where I least expected: Fanon, to that extent—my history must not imprison me, once I recognize it for what it is—might well have been right.

2

Among all the things you could be by now if Sigmund Freud's wife were your mother is someone who understands the dozens, the intricate verboseness of America's inner city. The big mouth brag, as much a sort of art form as a strategy of insult, the dozens takes the assaulted home to the backbone by "talking about" his mama and daddy. It is a choice weapon of defense and always changes the topic; bloodless, because it is all wounding words and outrageous combinations of imagery, and democratic, because anyone can play and be played, it outsmarts the Uzi—not that it is pleasant for all that—by re-siting (and "reciting"?) the stress. The game of living, after all, is played between the ears, up in the head. Instead of dispatching a body, one straightens its posture, instead of offering up a body, one sends his word. It is the realm of the ludic and the ludicrous that the late jazz bassist Charlie Mingus was playing around in when he concocted, as if on the spot, the title of the melody from which the title of this essay is borrowed. Responding to his own question—"What does it mean?"—that he poses to himself on the recording, he follows along the lines of his own cryptic signature, "Nothing. It means nothing." And what he proceeds to perform on the cut is certainly no thing we know. But that really is the point—to extend the realm of possibility for what might be known, and, not unlike the dozens, we will not easily decide if it is fun.

We traditionally understand the psychoanalytic in a pathological register, and there must be a very real question as to whether or not it remains psychoanalysis without its principal features—a "third ear," something like the "fourth wall," or the speech that unfolds in the pristinely silent arena of two star witnesses—a patient and he or she "who is supposed to know." The scene of assumptions is completed in the privileged relations of client and doctor in the atmosphere of the confessional. But my interest in this ethical self-knowing wants to unhook the psychoanalytic herme- neutic from its rigorous curative framework and try to recover it in a free-floating realm of self-didactic possibility that might decentralize and disperse the knowing one. We might need help here, for sure, but the uncertainty of where we'd be headed virtually makes no guarantee of that. Out here, the only music they are playing is Mingus's or much like it, and I should think that it would take a good long time to learn to hear it well.

NOTES

This essay is an excerpt from a longer work to be published under the same title in, first, *Boundary* 2 23 (Fall 1996) and, second, *Female Subjects in Black and White: Race, Psychoa- nalysis, Feminism*, ed. Elizabeth Abel, Barbara Christian, and Helene Moglen (forthcoming from University of California Press). Many thanks to Elizabeth Abel. Unless otherwise stated, all translations are my own.

1. This sentence alludes to a wonderful collection of short stories by the Barbadian Cana- dian writer Austin Clarke, *When He Was Free and Young and He Used to Wear Silks* (Toronto, 1971).

2. For a lucid reading of Lacan's indebtedness to Hegelian philosophy by way of Alexandre Kojève, see Mikkel Botch-Jacobsen, *Lacan: The Absolute Master*, trans. Douglas Brick (Stan- ford, Calif., 1991); hereafter abbreviated *L*.

3. Compare Roland Barthes, "Myth Today," *Mythologies*, trans. and ed. Annette Lavers (New York, 1972), pp. 109–59.

4. Sigmund Freud, quoted in Jacques Lacan, *The Four Fundamental Concepts of Psycho- Analysis*, trans. Alan Sheridan, ed. Jacques-Alain Miller (New York, 1978), p. 44.

5. For the boomerang effect and an inquiry into it, see Ralph Ellison, *Invisible Man* (1952; New York, 1992), in particular the "Prologue," pp. 3–14.

6. Frantz Fanon, *Toward the African Revolution—Political Essays*, trans. Hankon Cheva- lier (1964; New York, 1967), p. 27.

7. See Marie-Cécile and Edmond Ortigues, *Oedipe africain* (1966; Paris, 1984); hereafter abbreviated *O.1*.

8. "En décrivant dans ce chapitre la situation d'un psychanalyste travaillant dans une civilisation étrangère à la sienne, nous n'avons fait en définitive qu'illustrer un caractère essentiel de l'attitude analytique puisqu'aucun propos ne peutse comprendre sans référence au contexte familial, social, culturel" (*OA*, p. 57).

9. "Faudrait-il en conclure qu'une information sociologique poussée doit précéder le travail clinique? Nous répondrons que, si un minimum d'informations est nécessaire, ce qui importe avant tout c'est l'attitude analytique qui cherche à comprendre la place du sujet *dans ce qu'il dit*" (*OA*, p. 57; emphasis added).

10. "Et, en effet, ici, la maladie n'est pas une entité clinique. Pour les maladies mentales il n'y a de classification que par la causalité magique ou le destin voulu par Dieu.... On se réfère soit à une action contrariante des *rab*, soit à 'l'amour' possessif de *rab* liés à une famille, etc." (*OA*, p. 40.)

11. "L'élément de cohérence dans la représentation de la maladie c'est le *rab*.... C'est pourquoi nos consultants sont déroutés par nos interrogatoires" (*OA*, p. 40).

12. Ibrâhîm Sow, *Les Structures anthropologiques de la folie en afrique noire* (Paris, 1978). p. 48, hereafter abbreviated *SA*; trans. Joyce Diamanti, under the title *Anthropological Structures of Madness in Black Africa* (New York, 1980), p. 53, hereafter abbreviated *AS*; trans. mod. The translations used in this essay are mine.

At the time of the work's publication, the author was apparently a researcher and lecturer at the Laboratoire de Psychopathologie at the Sorbonne, Université René Descartes (Paris V) after having practiced psychiatric medicine in his native Senegal.

13. The French text reads: "En sa lecture la plus profonde, la folie est 'signe'; elle indique d'emblée que le sujet affecté exprime un conflit: conflit entre lui et les instances constitutives de sa personnalité qui lui sont extérieures, selon la conception traditionnelle" (*SA*, p. 42).

14.

En effet, on pourrait dire que le signifié du névrosé est enfoui dans son individualité et, au bout du compte, "double" son désir narcissique qui fonctionne comme s'il était, en lui-même, sa propre finalité: alors que le signifié de l'homme face au sacré, c'est le Verbe, la Loi, la Tradition, en un mot: l'Origine, dans le sacrifice de l'Ancêtre fondateur, créatur de la Loi, garant de la paix et de la coexistence entre les humains actuels. [*SA*, p. 162]

15. "Rétablir l'ordre dans le sujet affecté, victime, veut dire, en même temps, reconstituer le lien rompu, réinsérer le patient dans la place d'où il avait été exclu, coupé de ses instances constituantes par 'l'agresseur.' Ainsi, tout d'abord, il faudra transformer l'affection en structure de communication" (*SA*, p. 42).

16. "Parmi les moyens du rapprochement, il y a la parole, la prière et le rêve ... mais, comme toujours en Afrique, le dialogue entre Dieu et les hommes passe par l'intercesseur privilégié qu'est l'Ancêtre" (*SA*, p. 164 n. 27).

17. "Factors that are often cited are ... effective psychological—in effect, cultural—defenses, such as the externalization of conflict, with precise group identification of a persecutor" (*AS*, p. 38) ("On souligne souvent, en effet ... des défenses psychologiques—en fait, culturelles—efficaces telles que extériorité du conflit avec nomination collective précise d'un persécuteur" [*SA*, p. 36]).

18.

Le matériel de la psychothérapie montre qu'arrivé au seuil d'un affrontement assumé personnellement, Samba ... situe l'image paternelle et la castration dans le rapport aux ancêtres: le baobab de la vision initiale, lors d'un rêve (il figure dans le nombreux rêves), réclame que l'on enterre "le mort" à son pied et non au cimetière; le personnage terrifiant des hallucinations s'est mué en un homme au regard bon qui prononce ces seuls mots: "C'est le père des pères." [*OA*, p. 101]

19.

Les troubles de Samba ont commencé le jour où, passant sous un grand baobab en revenant de l'école, il entendit une viox qui l'appela trois fois par son nom de famille. Heureusement, il ne répondit pas car "quand on répond c'est mauvais, on devient fou, ou on est sale et seul dans la brousse" (comme un homme que Samba a vu jadis): il ne s'est pas retourné non plus. Il a eu très peur et est rentré chez lui en courant, s'est couché tremblant et a vomi dans la nuit. Depuis ce jour et des mois durant. Samba tient ses paupières closes comme s'il redoutait une vision terrifiante: "comme des enfants, quelque chose de gros, un diable." Il souffre de céphalées intenses, refuse de s'alimenter et en aucun cas ne porte lui-même à ses lèvres le peu de nourriture ou de boisson qu'il absorde. Il reste inerte, prostré, le dos voûté, en geignant. Ses gémissements peuvent, des heures durant, s'amplifier en de longues plaintes monotones. Les quelques mots que l'on parvient à lui arracher sont mur-murés, à peine audibles et accompagnés d'un mouvement de négation de la tête.

Ce tableau persistant plusieurs mois, au dire des parents, Samba est conduit à la consul-tation de neurologie et hospitalisé, tous les examens pratiqués sont négatifs. Son état étant inchangé trois semaines plus tard, Samba sort sur sa demande insistante, après de quoti-diennes tentatives de fugues. Il est hospitalisé peu après en psychiatrie. En un an il y sera hospitalisé à trois reprises et suivi entre-temps à titre externe. A chaque hospitalisation une série d'électro-chocs est pratiquée parallèlement à la psychothérapie. Un traitement par neuroleptiques est poursuivi également.

Dans le cas de Samba, il est légitime de parler de psychothérapie psychanalytique au sens le plus classique du terme. La demande de l'enfant est claire: il vient "parler pour être guéri." Une relation transférentielle riche s'établit rapidement. A ce jour le traitement dure depuis un an et a comporté 51 séances. Samba est intelligent et cherche à verbaliser tout ce qu'il vit. [*OA*, pp. 96–7]

20. "Des enfants ou un serpent ou un homme noir très, très grand, viennent lui faire peur, comme un diable . . . il une faisait peur: Il m'a montré le bonheur. . . . Des serpents sont dans son corps, sur corps, ils vont le mordre, ils boivent son sang, il va mourir dans l'instant" (*OA*, pp. 97–98).

21.

Dans ses fantasmes le personnage du diable, monolithique au départ, terrorisant et fasci-nant, s'est progressivement dédoublé puis scindé en un groupe de 3 ou 4 personnes, ce qui permettait à Samba un jeu de plus souple où il se projetait dans des positions variées à l'égard de son désir et de son anxiété. [*OA*, p. 99]

22. "Mais cela ne peut empêcher de se demander si la culture qui est celle de Samba ne lui impose pas ou ne lui propose pas de manière privilégiée la solution de la psychose hallucina-toire à thème de persécution" (*OA*, p. 100).

23.

Il est en effet bien difficile d'imaginer Samba guéri grâce à un traitement psychanalytique, après avoir intériorisé ses tensions, les avoir résolues "personnellement." Cela supposerait que, seul de son milieu, de sa famille, il se désolidarise des croyances communes, qu'il se singularise d'une manière telle qu'il deviendrait comme étranger chez lui, qu'il aurait ac-cédé à un niveau de conscience personnelle qui le situerait bien "en avant de ses pères" (il se trouve que l'on ne peut attendre aucune évolution du groupe familial). Est-ce possible? Est-ce souhaitable? [*OA*, p. 100]

24.

Ici l'accent est davantage mis sur l'affirmation d'un statut, d'un prestige. Il s'agit plutôt de montrer aux autres, aux "frères," une certaine image de soi-même, de faire qu'ils y croient pour pouvoir soi-même coïncider avec cette image . . .

Pour les jeones Dakarois que nous avous vus, les projects d'avenir, le "quand je serai grand," ne portent guère sur des performances ou des activités personnalisées: il est peu question d'inventer quoi que ce soit, ou de dépasser qui que ce soit, *sinon en se donnant a regarder.* On dira que l'ont veut porter de beaux vétements, que l'on veux avoir une bonne situation, mais l'activíté précise, disons le métier, que suppose la bonne situation ou l'acquisition des beaux vêtements, est peu considérée pour elle-même. Le voeu est moins celui d'une activité plus intéressante ou plus efficace que d'une place plus en vue, d'une raison sociale plus éminente. Le fantasme sous-jacent est d'imaginer ce que les autres pensent en vous regardant. Pour se valoriser on dira autant: "J'ai fait ceci ou cela," que: "Un tel m'admire . . . Un tel a dit que j'étais intelligent . . . Un tel a dit que j'étais un grand" (ce sont là paroles d'étudiants). Si l'on dit: "J'avais plus de succès féminins que mes camarades," ce sera moins pour évoquer ses relations avec les lilles que pour renvoyer à l'admiration ou à la jalousie des camarades. [*OA*, pp. 101–21]

25. W. E. B. Du Bois. *The Souls of Black Folk* (New York, 1989). pp. 2–3:

After the Egyptian and Indian, the Greek and Roman, the Teuton and Mongolian, the Negro is a sort of seventh son, born with a veil, and gifted with second-sight in this American world—a world which yields him no true self-consciousness, but only lets him see himself through the revelation of the other world. It is a peculiar sensation, this double-consciousness, this sense of always looking at one's self through the eyes of others.

26.

Chez tous nos sujets la reference au père ou à l'oncle a le caractère d'un spectacle, d'un témoignage offert au regard des autres. Avoir un père, *c'est étre habillé par lui* . . . L'enfant se sent en puissance de père, aimé du père, quand il est bien habillé, quand il imagine les autres le regardant bien habillé. Il n'est guère de cas où cette donnée ne soit présente. Chez nous, selon son âge, un garçon pensera: "Mon pére est plus fort qu'un lion . . . mon pére a la plus grosse voiture . . . mon pére est riche et commande . . ." Ici, l'enfant pense: "Mon pére va m'acheter une belle chemise, un beau costume . . ."

Le desir d'habits meilleurs, plus beaux, est le premier désir exprimé par les jeunes garçons, désir de montrer leur pére. Et chez ceux qui souffrent de son indifférence ou de son éloignement, il n'est pas rare de rencontrer un souci obsédant de leur apparence jusqu'à évoquer l'homosexualíté dans la recherche apportée aux colifichets. [*OA*, pp. 102–4]

27.

La fréquence avec laquelle le déclenchement de sensations douloureuses, perçues au niveau de la peau ou de la musculature superficielle, est attribué au regard des autres. Dans bien des cas, l'angoisse paraît être secondaire à la douleur perçue, à la crampe, comme si l'éprouvé corporel était directement modelé par le regard d'autrui. . . .

L'attention portée au regard dans les descriptions de comportement qui nous sont faites: il a un regard formidable; il a un regard méprisant; il est masqué; il a un regard détourné; il ne te regarde pas; il tient les yeux de côté; il regard et il rit, ce n'est pas l'enfant réglementaire; il garde la *tête baissée*. [*OA*, p. 104; my emphasis]

28. I am referring here to the very influential and suggestive writing by Laura Mulvey, "Visual Pleasure and Narrative Cinema," *Visual and Other Pleasures* (Bloomington, Ind., 1989), pp. 14–26.

29.

Dans le modèle européen du complexe d'Oedipe, le fils s'imagine tuant le père. Ici la pente typique serait plutôt: le fils se référant par l'intermédiaire du père à l'ancêtre déjà mort donc inattaquable et constituant ses "frères" en rivaux. C'est pourquoi les représentations que nous avons utilisées, phallus collectif, ancêtre inégalable, ne peuvent se comprendre qu'en fonction du terme où elles conduisent, le jeu de la rivalité-solidarité entre les frères. . . .

La rivalité nous parait tout d'abord être systématiquement déplacée sur les "frères" qui polarisent les pulsions agressives. . . . L'agressivité s'exprime principalement sous la forme de réactions persécutives. La culpabilité est peu intériorisée ou constituée comme telle. . . . L'ensemble des rapports interpersonnels est fortement coloré par le fait que chacun se perçoit facilement comme persécuté. On pourrait dire qu'une partie de l'énergie qui, dans un autre contexte, serait employée à s'affirmer en agissant, est ici consommée à se défendre. En toutes circonstances, il convient de se protéger des intentions menaçantes. . . .

La culpabilité est peu intériorisée ou constituée comme telle. Tout se passe comme si l'individu ne pouvait pas supporter de se percevoir divisé intérieurement, mobilisé par des désirs contradictoires. Le "mauvais" est toujours situé à l'extérieur de moi, il est du domaine de la fatalité, du sort, de la volonté de Dieu. [*OA*, pp. 79, 92, 93, 94]

30.

Dans la mesure où les pulsions agressives ne sont pas projetées, on peut constater qu'elles sont conscientes mais réprimées, contrôlées, non exprimées. Les fantasmes ou émois agressifs sont présents comme une longue souffrance, sourde et secrète, écrasante, inavouable qu'il convient de taire "pour ne pas décourager mes parents" . . . "parce qu'ils comptent sur moi" et aussi pour ne pas se montrer vulnérable. Bien souvent des somatisations apparaissent comme le moyen d'inhiber dans l'instant l'expression des fantasmes ou impulsions agressives. Le comportement de ces sujets est de méfiance dissimulée sous une imperturbable gentillesse visant à ne pas donner prise aux attaques . . . A moins qu'ils ne recherchent la solitude pour se protéger des contacts devenus trop anxiogènes, les jeunes gens décrivent tous comment ils sont poussés irrésistiblement à aller avec les amis, comment pour eux être "bien" (heureux, dynamique) c'est être partie d'un groupe, d'une foule. Peu importe souvent qu'il s'agisse d'une réunion sportive, dansante, de palabres interminables ("faire la nuit blanche") . . . La présence des autres est rassurante, nécessaire; elle désamorce ou repousse à l'arrière-plan les fantasmes agressifs latents. [*OA*, pp. 95–96]

31. Claude Meillassoux, *Maidens, Meal, and Money: Capitalism and the Domestic Community* (1975; Cambridge, 1981), p. 79.

32. Ibid., p. 47.

46

Tearing the Goat's Flesh

Homosexuality, Abjection, and the Production of a Late Twentieth-Century Black Masculinity

Robert F. Reid-Pharr

(1996)

> Thou shalt not seethe a kid in his mother's milk.
>
> —Exodus 23:19

> Chivo que rompe tambor con su pellejo paga.
>
> —Abakua proverb

Diana Fuss has argued in a recent discussion of contemporary gay and lesbian theory that the figure of what we might call the undead homosexual, the homosexual who continually reappears, even and especially in the face of the most grisly violence and degradation, is absolutely necessary to the production of positive heterosexual identity, at least heterosexual identity produced within bourgeois-dominated economies of desire that, as Eve Sedgwick demonstrates, deploy homophobia to check slippage between (male) homosociality and homosexuality.[1] The inside/out binarism, then, the distinction between normality and chaos, is maintained precisely through the mediation of the sexually liminal character, that is to say, the homosexual. Fuss writes:

> Those inhabiting, the inside . . . can only comprehend the outside through incorporation of a negative image. This process of negative interiorization involves turning homosexuality inside out, exposing not the homosexual's abjected insides but the homosexual as the abject, as the contaminated and expurgated insides of the heterosexual subject.[2]

Fuss's point is well taken. For she suggests not simply that the innate pathology of the homosexual must be revealed in order to produce the heterosexual community, but also that the homosexual works as the vehicle by which hetero-pathology itself might be negotiated; that is, the homosexual as "the contaminated and expurgated insides of the heterosexual subject."

In relating this insight to the production of African-American masculinity, I would

602

argue that the pathology that the homosexual must negotiate is precisely the specter of Black boundarylessness, the idea that there is no normal Blackness to which the Black subject, American, or otherwise, might refer. Following the work of René Girard, especially his 1986 study of the place of violence, real and imagined, in the production of communal identity, *The Scapegoat*,[3] I will suggest that homosexuality operates mimetically in the texts that I examine, standing itself as the sign of a prior violence, the violence of boundarylessness, or cultural eclipse—to borrow Girard's language—that has been continually visited upon the African-American community during its long sojourn in the new world. Indeed Orlando Patterson, Henry Louis Gates, and Paul Gilroy, among others, have argued that the Black has been conceptualized in modern (slave) culture as an inchoate, irrational non-subject, as the chaos that both defines and threatens the borders of logic, individuality, and basic subjectivity.[4] In that schema, all Blacks become interchangeable, creating among the population a sort of continual restlessness, a terror. Girard writes:

> The terror inspired in people by the eclipse of culture and the universal confusion of popular uprisings are signs of a community that is literally undifferentiated, deprived of all that distinguishes one person from another in time and space. As a consequence all are equally disordered in the same place and at the same time.[5]

Though Girard's discussion here proceedes from a consideration of societies suddenly thrown into confusion: plague-ridden medieval Europe, revolutionary France, his work suggests that all terror, all confusion, works to undifferentiate the subjects of the (newly) chaotic society such that the members of the society come to stand in for one another in their common experience of vertigo. The scapegoat, then, would be the figure who reproduces this undifferentiation, this chaos, this boundarylessness. The violence directed against the goat would mitigate against the prior violence, the erosion of borders that has beset the entire community.

I would add to this only that anti-homosexual violence operates in the production of Black masculinity on two levels. First, as I have argued already, the strike against the homosexual acts as a seemingly direct confrontation with the presumption of Black boundarylessness, or we might say the assumption of Black subhumanity and Black irrationality that has its roots deep in the history of slavery and the concomitant will to produce Africans as "Other." To strike the homosexual, the scapegoat, the sign of chaos and crisis, is to return the community to normality, to create boundaries around Blackness, rights that indeed white men are obliged to recognize.

Second, and perhaps more importantly, this violence allows for a reconnection to the very figure of boundarylessness that the assailant is presumably attempting to escape. As a consequence, Black subjects are able to transcend, if only for a moment, the very strictures of normality and rationality that have been defined in contradistinction to a necessarily amorphous Blackness. My point here is to argue for reconsideration of the process of abjection, a process referenced by Diana Fuss and developed most fruitfully by Julia Kristeva, in the *de*articulation of meaning and identity.[6] Rather, I would suggest that abjection is characterized by an excess of meaning. As a consequence, we might use the figure of the abject to access "slips" in the ideological structures of modernity, if not a complete reworking of the entire process. To put it bluntly, we must empty our consciousness of that which is contradictory and ambiguous and most especially that which disallows our differentiation. Still we seem not to be able to complete this process. We become uncomfortable with "realness" at precisely those moments when it appears to be most firmly established. Even as the profligate subject is destroyed, we retain "him" within the national consciousness, always on the brink of renewal, lest we find ourselves entrapped within a logic of subjectivity from which the Black is excluded already.

I

The formal and rhetorical strategies that link Eldridge Cleaver's *Soul on Ice*, James Baldwin's *Giovanni's Room*, and Piri Thomas's *Down These Mean Streets* are not immediately apparent. Cleaver and Thomas's texts are "autobiographical" and analytical while Baldwin's is fictional. Cleaver documents what has become one of the most recognizable, one might even say trite, markers of Black masculinity, incarceration, while both Thomas and Baldwin attempt to push against the confines of American Blackness altogether. Thomas charts the difficulty that a young, dark-skinned Puerto Rican encounters as he tries to make sense of an American racial economy that creates him as "Black" while Baldwin opts to step outside of the confines of American race literature altogether, producing a novel in which there are no Black characters, but, as I will argue below, in which race is one of the central signifiers.

At the same time, there is the pressing question of how we are to read Baldwin's "gay" novel in relation to the virulent homophobia of Eldridge Cleaver, a homophobia that reaches its apex at precisely those moments when it is directed specifically at Baldwin and his work, particularly *Another Country*. A similar question surrounds the work of Piri Thomas, whose antigay sentiment is just as apparent, if somewhat less virulent, than Cleaver's. One might argue, in fact, that Cleaver, Thomas and Baldwin belong to distinct literary camps such that any attempt to read the three together can proceed only by pointing out the variety of the diametric oppositions. Still, as Paul Gilroy has suggested in a discussion of John Singleton's *Boys in the Hood* and Marlon Riggs's *Tongues Untied*, even as the Black neo-masculinist heterosexual attempts to distance himself from homosexuality he draws attention to the "similarities and convergences in the way that love between men is the common factor."[7] It follows that the key to understanding the depth of Thomas and Cleaver's homophobia lies precisely in the fact that the universe that both represent in their literature is so consistently and insistently masculine and homosocial.

Much has been made of Cleaver's vicious and repeated attacks on women and gay men. In almost every treatment of this issue, however, Cleaver's misogyny and homophobia have been chalked up to his male privilege and antiquated notions of what constitutes properly Black gender and sexual relations. To date no one has examined seriously Cleaver's tragicomic struggle to construct a Black heterosexuality, to finally rid the Black consciousness of the dual specters of effeminacy and interracial homoeroticism. One might argue, in fact, that Cleaver's woman hating and fag bashing were, for all his bravado, failed attempts to assert himself and the Black community as "straight."

Soul on Ice is in large part an explication of the difficulties of Black subjectification within the highly homosocial, homosexual prison. Women, though present, operate only as the means by which social relations between men are communicated. Early in the text Cleaver confesses to having been a racially motivated rapist, perfecting his craft on the bodies of Black women before he "crossed the tracks" to seek out his "white prey."[8] Clearly the abuse of the Black female body acts as a means to an end, a type of cultural production in which Cleaver's manhood, his sense of self-worth, is established and articulated. I would be wrong, however, to suggest that Cleaver's ultimate goal is to possess and abuse white female bodies. Again women act only as conduits by which social relations, relations that take place exclusively between men, are represented. Cleaver may indeed be raping Black and white women, but it is white men whom he intends to hurt.

> Rape was an insurrectionary act. It delighted me that I was defying and trampling upon the white man's law, upon his system of values, and that I was defiling his women—and this point, I believe, was the most satisfying to me because I was very resentful over the historical fact of how the white man has used the black woman. I felt I was getting revenge.[9]

The peculiarity of Cleaver's twisted logic rests not so much in the fact that he saw sexual violence as an insurrectionary tool. On the contrary, the rape of women is used regularly to terrorize and subdue one's "enemies." The difficulty in Cleaver's logic rests in the fact that he raped both white *and* Black women. Was he, I must wonder, seeking revenge on the white man when he violated poor, Black female residents of his quintessentially Black ghettos?

This question is not simply rhetorical. Cleaver himself argues that there is a tendency within some segments of the Black community to understand the Black woman as having collaborated, particularly through the vehicle of sex, with the white master. Indeed Angela Davis attempts to contextualize this sentiment in her seminal essay, "Reflections on The Black Woman's Role in the Community of Slaves."[10] Raping the Black woman could be interpreted, then, as an attack on the white man's stooge. The Black woman becomes the means of telegraphing a message of rage and resistance to the white male oppressor, a figure Cleaver recodifies as the Omnipotent Administrator.

It becomes clear that the ultimate target of Cleaver's sexual attacks is always the white man. Both white and Black women act as pawns in an erotic conversation between Cleaver and his white male counterparts. This fact is emblematically represented in an exchange between Cleaver and a white prison guard who enters Cleaver's cell, rips a picture of a voluptuous white woman from the wall, tears it to bits, and then leaves the pieces floating in the toilet for Cleaver to find upon his return. The guard later tells Cleaver that he will allow him to keep pictures of Black women, but not whites.

The clue to how deeply homoerotic the exchange between Cleaver and the guard actually is lies in Cleaver's description of his initial reaction. He writes, "I was genuinely beside myself with anger: almost every cell, excepting those of the homosexuals, had a pin-up girl on the wall and the guards didn't bother them."[11] Cleaver's pin-up girl acts as not only a sign of interracial desire, but also a marker of his heterosexuality. This fact, which seems easy enough to understand, actually represents a deep contradiction within Cleaver's demonstration of the Black male heterosexual self. It points directly to the disjunction between the reality of the interracial homoerotic, homosexual environment, the prison, in which Cleaver actually lived and wrote and the fantasy of Black heterosexuality that he constructs in his narrative.

Indeed, Cleaver's one rather ethereal representation of heterosexual love seems artificial and contrived, coming as it does from the pen of an admitted serial rapist and committed homophobe. He spends some time in *Soul on Ice* describing the exchange of "love" letters between his lawyer, Beverly Axelrod, and himself. Strangely enough, there is little of Cleaver, the rapist, in these works. His love seemingly transcends the corporeal. By turns he describes Axelrod as a rebel and a revolutionary, a person of great intelligence, compassion, and humanity, a valiant defender of "civil rights demonstrators, sit-iners, and the Free Speech students." And just at the moment when he has produced her as bodiless, transcendent saint, he interjects,

> I suppose that I should be honest, and before going any further, admit that my lawyer is a woman . . . a very excellent, unusual, and beautiful woman. I know that she believes that I do not really love her and that I am confusing a combination of lust and gratitude for love. Lust and gratitude I feel abundantly, but I also love this woman.[12]

I am less concerned with pointing out the obvious homoerotic reference than with voicing how strikingly measured and cerebral his relationship with Beverly Axelrod actually was. Indeed lust and gratitude are distinct from "Love," which is presumably a type of transcendent, transsexual appreciation for the intrinsic worth of the individual.

Yet Cleaver's description of his non-corporeal, non-funky love for Beverly Axelrod can only redouble upon itself. It directly challenges the claim that Cleaver's work is a product of the stark reality he has experienced. Cleaver has, much like the white man, the Omnipotent Administrator he so despises, excised his own penis, his lust, his physical self from the conversation.

> The Omnipotent Administrator, having repudiated and abdicated his body, his masculine component which he has projected onto the men beneath him, cannot present his woman, the Ultrafeminine, with an image of masculinity capable of penetrating into the psychic depths where the treasure of her orgasm is buried.[13]

Still, even as Cleaver decries the bodilessness of the Omnipotent Administrator his love for Beverly Axelrod is no more physical than is the white man's for the ultrafeminine. Beverly Axelrod is unlike the victims of Cleaver's rapes in that she is all intellect and no body. The "sexual" passion between the two is even more rarefied than that of the Omnipotent Administrator and the Ultrafeminine because there is never even the promise of physical contact, raw sex, but only endless literary representations of their desire. Beverly Axelrod should be understood, then, as a fiction, or rather as the site of yet another fictional exchange. In this manner the idea of heterosexual normality becomes a sort of caricature of itself. The body gives way to the intellect, lust to love.

"Love" was for Cleaver always the terrain of conceptual struggle. Indeed "love" becomes in *Soul on Ice* the very site at which normality is constructed in contradistinction to the sense of boundary crisis that mitigates against the production of a stable Black masculinity. Perhaps the most telling moment, in this regard, is Cleaver's confrontation with his white intellectual mentor, Chris Lovdjieff, a prison teacher and a man whom Cleaver describes as "The Christ." Lovdjieff introduces Cleaver to what the great novelists and playwrights had said of love. He reads poetry on the subject and plays his students tapes of Ashley Montagu, then instructs them to write responsive essays. Cleaver writes that he cannot love whites, quoting Malcolm X as evidence:

> How can I love the man who raped my mother, killed my father, enslaved my ancestors, dropped atomic bombs on Japan, killed off the Indians and keeps me cooped up in the slums? I'd rather be tied up in a sack and tossed into the Harlem River first.[14]

Lovdjieff responds in a fit of tears to what he takes to be a personal attack. Cleaver remarks, "Jesus wept," then leaves. Soon thereafter the San Quentin officials begin to curtail Lovdjieff's access to the prisoners, finally barring him from entry altogether.

The ideological work that the reenactment of this oedipal ritual accomplishes is both to detach Cleaver and his narrative from the deeply homoerotic relationship he maintains with Lovdjieff and to clear the way for a purely Black masculinity. It is important to remember here that the country was in the midst of rather striking changes in the manner in which the official "reality" of both race and sexuality were articulated. In 1949, the United Nations Economic and Social Council (UNESCO) launched a study to identify means by which racism might be eradicated. The result of these efforts was a document, written by the same Ashley Montagu whose words Lovdjieff attempted to use as a bridge between his young protégé and himself.

Montagu, who began life as Israel Ehrenberg in London's east end, was trained as an anthropologist first at the University of London's University College and eventually at Columbia, where he received his graduate education under no less a light than Franz Boas.[15] By the time he wrote UNESCO's statement on race, he already had published widely in the field, developing a critical apparatus that not only called for a markedly relativistic understanding of "racial attributes," but that altogether called into question the efficacy of maintaining race as an analytical category.

For all practical social purposes, race is not so much a biological phenomenon as a social myth. . . . Biological differences between ethnic groups should be disregarded from the standpoint of social acceptance and social action. The unity of mankind is the main thing.[16]

I would suggest again that when Cleaver severs his ties with Lovdjieff he is helping to reestablish an ontological economy that would take racial difference as primary. The resolution of the crisis represented by their relationship leads to the renormalization of received racial thinking.

At the same time it is important to point out that the post–World War II period witnessed an incredible bifurcation in the means by which sexual desire was articulated and actualized. The typical narratives of the post-war sexual ethos would have it that Americans rushed into a sort of suffocating domesticity, erecting, in the process, an image of the nuclear family that would maintain a stranglehold on the nation's consciousness for at least two decades. There was also, however, a huge increase in the visibility of homosexual communities, particularly in the nation's cities, the same locations that were opening themselves more and more to Black immigrants.[17] Indeed the most prominent chroniclers of the Black urban males experience, including not only Cleaver, Baldwin and Thomas, but Claude Brown, Malcolm X, and Amiri Baraka, all reference the increased visibility of the urban homosexual. What I would argue, then, is that the homosexual, and in particular the racially marked homosexual, the Black homosexual, represented for the authors I am examining the very sign of deep crisis, a crisis of identity and community that threw into confusion, if only temporarily, the boundaries of (Black) normality.

II

Piri Thomas's narrative, *Down These Mean Streets*, proceeds in much the same manner as Cleaver's. Like his Anglo contemporary, Thomas gains his sense of manhood from within the confines of racist urban America. Moreover, like Cleaver, and indeed like a variety of late-twentieth-century Black male "autobiographers," most notably Malcolm X, his loss of freedom opens the path by which he gains his "freedom." Thomas uses the experience of prison to resurrect that part of himself that presumably has been squelched by the realities of racism and poverty, affecting in the process a counterscripting of the antebellum slave narratives. It is as if the literal loss of control over the self returns the narrators to the primal scene of Black subjectification, the moment when the Black, particularly the Black man, enmeshed within a system defined by the policing of Black bodies, turns for "escape" to the life of the mind, much as Douglass turns to literature and literacy in his struggle to construct himself as "free." The focus becomes, then, the immense effort necessary to maintain one's humanity or one's subjectivity, in the face of intense pressures to suppress or deny them. I would like to suggest, however, that unlike the antebellum slave narratives, in which the Black male slave risks being brutalized viciously or, worse yet, having his familial and conjugal prerogatives trampled upon by licentious white men, the twentieth-century Black male narrators are in danger of being homosexualized. I have discussed this phenomenon in the work of Cleaver already. I would add here that Thomas's understanding of himself is altogether mediated by his relationships with men. His adoration for his father gives way to his loyalty to the gang and then finally to his respect for the prison ethos. Throughout, the homosexual acts as the emblem of the border between the inside and the out. Thomas deploys the figure of the homosexual at precisely those moments when the complex ambiguity of his "standing" within his various communities is most apparent, that is to say, those moments when he cannot avoid a declaration of his status as either The Insider or The Out.

The great difficulty of maintaining the distinction between the homosexual and the homosocial is made explicit from almost the beginning of Thomas's narrative. The young man begins to develop as an adult, as a subject constructed by—but nevertheless greater than—the various identities he inhabits, at precisely that moment when he proves that he has heart, *corazon*, and is accepted into an all-male Puerto Rican gang. The test of his spirit, the challenge that he must accept if he is to be integrated fully into the gang's social life, is a fist fight, a strikingly physical struggle of wills between Thomas and the gang's leader, Waneko.

> He had *corazon*. He came on me. *Let him draw first blood*, I thought, *it's his block.* Smish, my nose began to bleed. His boys cheered, his heart cheered, his turf cheered. "Waste this chump," somebody shouted.
>
> *Okay, baby, now it's my turn.* He swung. I grabbed innocently, and forehead smashed into his nose. His eyes crossed. His fingernails went for my eye and landed in my mouth—crunch, I bit hard. I punched him in the mouth as he pulled away from me, and he slammed his foot into my chest.[18]

By standing his own in this fight, Thomas not only gains acceptance into the gang, but initiates a relationship with Waneko that lasts over many years. This fact is not, however, so terribly remarkable. The idea that violence often helps to strengthen the bonds between men is hardly new or surprising. Still, I would argue that the strikingly physical nature of the contest between Thomas and Waneko ought to alert us to the multiple levels on which this interchange resonates. Thomas allows Waneko to draw first blood out of deference to his position in the neighborhood and the gang. The abuse that the two young men mete out to one another in the course of their fight should not be understood, then, simply as a sign of masculine aggression. Thomas is not allowed into the gang solely because he is good with his fists. Instead the emphasis is on that elusive entity, heart, that place of deep feeling and masculine determination, to which the young Puerto Ricans gain access through ritualized violence. One might argue, then, that the fight between Thomas and Waneko is at once an act of aggression and an act of love.

I am supported in this claim by the fact that the gang members expend so much energy denying homoerotic feeling. This is even while all of them, including Thomas, seek out and willingly engage in (homo)sex. It is telling that only a few pages after the fight scene the young men decide to stretch themselves to the limits of their masculinity by visiting the apartment of a trio of stereotypically effeminate gay men. Indeed their interaction with the three homosexuals is itself designed to reflect their own hypermasculinity. They assure themselves, "Motherfuckers, who's a punk? Nobody, man," as they "jumped off the stoop and, grinning, shuffled towards the faggots' building" (p. 55).

The episode in the gay men's apartment is from the very outset overdetermined by the intense ambiguity that suffuses the extremely homosocial world of the gangs. The homosexuals, the *maricones*, stand in for the constant danger that the macho young men, with their relentless emphasis on masculinity and the male body, will stumble themselves, inadvertently, or not so inadvertently, across the line that separates the homosexual from the homosocial.

> I had heard that some of them fags had bigger joints than the guy that was screwing. *Oh shit, I ain't gonna screw no motherfuckin' fag. Agh—I'm not gonna get shit all over my peter, not for all the fuckin' coins in the world.* (P. 55)

The gay man refuses, in this passage, to conform to the boys' stereotypes. His joint, his penis, the marker of his worth within the logic of patriarchy, is larger than the guy doing the screwing, the real man who stands in for Thomas and his comrades. Even more striking is the fact that Thomas's fear, the fear that he will have sex with a homosexual (thereby, compromising his own masculinity), the fear against which he must assure himself constantly, turns upon the idea that he will get feces all over his penis. This aversion to feces points directly to the immense ambiguity, the boundary crisis, that the homosexual represents. Instead of Thomas's pulling blood from the gay body, much as he regularly pulls blood from the bodies of his fellow gang members and presumably also from the bodies of recently deflowered (female) virgins, he takes only feces from the homosexual, feces that acts as evidence of the nonproductive, perverse nature of the (homo)sexual act.

Let me make it perfectly clear that what I am interested in here is not the cataloging of homosexual content in the work of late twentieth-century Black male autobiographers, but instead a reading of homosexuality that pays attention to the way in which the homosexual stands in for the fear of crisis and chaos, or rather, the fear of slipping to the outside, that pervades the work of both nineteenth- and twentieth-century Black writers. As the young "heterosexual" Puerto Rican men enter the apartment of the young "homosexual" Puerto Rican men it becomes difficult, even in the face of the "straight" men's many protestations, to maintain a distinction between the two. Indeed it becomes nearly impossible to continue the inside/out binarism.

The rather lengthy group sex scene that Thomas describes takes on a strikingly surreal aspect. The air that they breathe is heavy with the smell of marijuana smoke, thereby pushing all the young men beyond their normal limits, creating the space of the gay men's apartment as a type of liminal terrain; we might even say a no-man's land. Moreover, the effect is not simply that the *normality* of their erotic lives is jettisoned, but also that the sexual act becomes transposed onto a variety of experiences and sites.

> I opened my eye a little. I saw a hand, and between its fingers was a stick of pot. I
> didn't look up at the face. I just plucked the stick from the fingers. I heard the
> feminine voice saying, 'You gonna like thees pot. Eet's good stuff.'
> I felt its size. It was a king-sized bomber. I put it to my lips and began to hiss my
> reserve away. It was going, going, going. I was gonna get a gone high. I inhaled. I held
> my nose, stopped up my mouth. I was gonna get a high . . . a gone high . . . a gone
> high . . . and then the stick was gone, burnt to a little bit of a roach. (P. 58)

Though this passage is taken from a scene that is heavily determined by the notion
of profligate sex and sexuality there is apparently no sexual activity at all. No penis,
vagina, breasts or buttocks are here to alert the reader that what we are experiencing
is a type of sexual intercourse. There is, moreover, neither blood nor feces to act as
evidence of the all-important penetration. I would argue, however, that the very fact
that this passage lacks the normal markers of sexual activity is precisely what produces it as a representation of profligacy. Here the erotic content is transferred from
the sexual organs to the lips, a key site of homoerotic, homosexual pleasure. As the
pot stick enters Thomas's lips, chipping away at his reserve until he is altogether
gone, or we might say, spent, sexuality is severed from its association with the genitals
and thus with heterosexual reproduction.

Moreover, Thomas accepts neither the passive nor active role. Though he receives
the stick of pot into his mouth, he does the penetration himself, plucking the stick
from between extended fingers, fingers attached to a never visible face. Still it is once
again the size of the homosexual's pot stick, or rather, his joint that intrigues the
youth. He is literally blown away by the innate power of this king-sized bomber,
reaching, in the process, a type of homoeroticized epiphany.

> Then it comes—the tight feeling, like a rubber band being squeezed around your
> forehead. You feel your Adam's apple doing an up-and-down act—gulp, gulp, gulp—
> and you feel great—great, dammit! So fine, so smooth. You like this feeling of being
> air-light, with your head tight. (P. 59)

Perhaps the most telling aspect of this rather remarkable scene in Thomas's narrative, is the fact that when he returns from what I will call his drug-induced orgasmic
moment, he immediately sets about tidying up the mess that he has just described. I
do not mean to suggest, however, that he denies the homosexual activity. On the
contrary, the descriptions of the various acts taking place between men are rather
straightforwardly rendered.

> I tried to make me get and move away from those squeezing fingers, but no good;
> . . . I pushed away at the fingers, but it grew independently. If I didn't like the scene,
> my pee-pee did. . . .
> I dug the lie before me. Antonia was blowin' Waneko and Indio at the same time.
> Alfredo was screwing La Vieja. The springs on the bed were squeaking like a million
> mice. . . . Indio's face was white and scared and expectant but his body was moving in
> time with Antonia's outrage. I tightened my own body. It was doing the same as
> Indio's. It was too late. I sucked my belly and felt the hot wetness of heat. I looked

down in time to see my pee-pee disappear into Concha's mouth. I felt the roughness of his tongue as it both scared and pleased me. *I like broads, I like muchachas. I like girls*, I chanted inside me. . . . Then I heard slurping sounds and it was all over . . . I smelled the odor of shit and heard Alfredo say, "Ya dirty *maricon*, ya shitted all over me."

"I'm sor-ree," said La Vieja, "I no could help eet."

"Ya stink'n faggot—". . . . I heard the last sounds of Alfredo's anger beating out against La Vieja—blap, blap, blap—and the faggot's wail. "Ayeeeeee, no heet me, no heet—" (P. 61)

We can see, in this passage, the reestablishment of the line separating the inside from the out at precisely the moment at which the spectacle of homosexual intercourse is realized most fully. Thomas maintains a distinction between himself and his sexual desire producing, for a moment, the former as the victim of the latter. It is his "pee-pee" that refuses to allow him to exit this scene. Moreover, the word pee-pee, with its connotations of childhood innocence, helps exonerate Thomas from any responsibility for the act in which he is engaged. Instead, by reasserting his genitalia as the privileged site of sexual pleasure, Thomas rescues himself from the never-never land of oral and anal eroticism. It is Concha, a name that can be translated as either shell or vagina, who steps to the nether side of the phallic economy, allowing his mouth to be "used" like the presumably (dis)empowered site of the vagina. Throughout, Thomas reminds himself that what he is experiencing is a lie. The satisfaction he feels is the product of a simple substitution, the mouth for the vagina, in which his pee-pee is fooled but he is not. He chants, "I like broads. I like *muchachas*, I like girls," as if to remind himself, in three different vernaculars, that the spectacle of his pee-pee within the homosexual's mouth is but a representation of, or perhaps, a signification upon the truth. And if this were not enough, the scene ends with the smell of the marijuana smoke giving way to the stench of shit, the proof that the boys have stumbled beyond the limits of normality, sullied themselves in the confusing, if always false, pleasures of the outside. As Alfredo beats *La Vieja*, the old woman, a man who despite his name is described as no more than thirty, the sexual and erotic economies seemingly have come back into order, the highly stylized—and stereotypical—rendering of *La Vieja's* screams: "Ayeeeeee, no heet me, no heet—" acting as irrefutable evidence of the incommensurability of *el macho* with *la maricon*.

It is striking that even as Thomas paints the homosexual as the quintessential outsider, he seems incapable of dispensing with him. Homosexuals and homosexuality intervene throughout the text to help Thomas give definition to his fledgling masculinity. It is during their attempt to rob a gay nightclub, or rather a site in which there are nothing but "faggots and soft asses," that leads to Thomas's arrest and incarceration. The would-be robbers: Thomas, his friend, Louie, and their two white accomplices, Danny and Billy, are thwarted in their efforts, precisely because they underestimate the ability of the homosexual to turn their expectations and desires back in on themselves. When Billy jumps to the stage and interrupts the drag show taking place, the audience refuses to respond in a fit of hysteria as he had expected.

Instead they laugh, taking him for one of the performers. It is as if the sight of a poor, undereducated white man attempting to assert his masculinity, his lack of lack, is itself a greater spectacle than the transvestite performance. It is only after he fires two shots over their heads, shattering the mirrors in the process, that they give him their full attention, or rather reflect back the image of himself that he wants to see. Of course the entire affair is bungled. Thomas is shot by an undercover police officer whose own incognito status within the gay bar implicates him as fully in the transvestite spectacle as any of the drag performers. Indeed the whole scene turns upon the recognition that things are not always what they seem. The "women" on stage are not really women. Thomas is not really a macho gangster, but instead just a Puerto Rican teenager who when struck by the bullet of an undercover police officer reverts to an infantile state: "I felt like a little baby, almost like I was waiting to get my diapers changed" (p. 237). "Mommie . . . I don't . . . Mommie, *no quiero morir*" (p. 238).

I have argued already that the prison acts as a primary site for the articulation of a late twentieth-century Black American masculinity. When the Black narrator enters prison he returns to the primal horde, as it were, a state in which the brothers are corralled together by the capricious violence and deprivation enacted by the father. Here the oedipal crisis has not been enacted, but only imagined. Thomas's focus remains on the unattainable female, his former girlfriend, Trina, even though the truth of his situation is that homosociality has given way altogether to homosexuality.

> [T]he real action was between men. If you weren't careful, if you didn't stand up for yourself and say, "Hands off, motherfucker," you became a piece of ass. And if you got by this hassle, there always was the temptation of wanting to cop some ass.
> (P. 262)

We have reached the point in Thomas's text when the danger—and the promise—of abjection become most apparent. In prison the rational norms no longer continue to operate. In spite of all his *corazon* and macho bravado, even Thomas is tempted to "cop some ass."

We should be careful not to slip into the trap of conceptualizing abjection as simply the opposite of normality. The abject is not the same as the object. The relationship of abject to subject is similar to that of the inside to the out, only in that the abject is not the subject and indeed that it may hold a contradictory or even confrontational relationship to it. As Julia Kristeva argues, abjection "lies outside, beyond the set, and does not seem to agree to the latter's rules of the game. And yet, from its place of banishment, the abject does not cease challenging its master."[19] The danger that Thomas confronts, then, when he gives voice to his own nascent homosexual desire is not simply that he will implicate himself further as an outsider. On the contrary, the episode in the apartment of the three effeminate gay men had proven already that he could maintain his macho image even in the midst of homosexual intercourse. The danger is that he will lose hold on the logic of the inside/out binarism, that he might forget that his desire for Trina is real, while his "desire" for men is only a substitution.

One time. That's all I have to do it. Just one time and it's gone time. I'll be screwing faggots as fast as I can get them. I'm not gonna get institutionalized. I don't want to lose my hatred of this damn place. Once you lose the hatred, then the can's got you. You can do all the time in the world and it doesn't bug you. You go outside and make it: you return to prison and you make it there, too. No sweat, no pain. No. Outside is real; inside is a lie. Outside is one kind of life, inside is another. And you make them the same if you lose your hate of prison.[20]

Thomas clearly sees the danger of blurring the distinction between the inside and the out. He is afraid to engage in (homo)sex not because it is displeasing, but because it will allow for the articulation—and actualization—of an alternate logic of pleasure. Prison becomes, in this schema, not simply the wretched underside of normal life, but an alternative site of meaning, truth, even love and life.

This is represented emblematically by two characters whom I will treat briefly here. The first, Claude, is a black man who is extremely attracted to Thomas and who offers his reluctant paramour a host of prison treasures if he will agree to be "his daddy-o." Thomas refuses. Claude then takes up with another prisoner, Big Jules, a man sentenced to a life sentence for cutting someone up into little pieces. The couple celebrate their union in a wedding complete with preacher, best man and attendants.

The second is Ruben, a muscular and exceptionally violent inmate, who is attracted to Thomas's "cousin," Tico. The naive youth accepts Ruben's many presents upon his arrival in prison until he receives a note from the older man, expressing his real intentions.

Dear Tico:
   Since the first moment I saw you, I knew you were for me. I fell in love with your young red lips and the hair to match it. I would like to keep on doing things for you and to take care of you and not let anybody mess with you. I promise not to let no one know about you being my old lady and you don't have to worry none, because I won't hurt you none at all. I know you might think it's gonna be bad, but it's not at all. I could meet you in the back part of the tier cell hall and nobody's going to know what's happening. I've been doing a lot for you and I never felt like this about no girl. If you let me cop you, I'll do it real easy to you. I'll use some hair oil and it will go in easy. You better not let me down 'cause I got it bad for you. I'd hate to mess you all up.

Love and Kisses
XXX
You know who
R.

P.S. Tear this up and flush it down the shit bowl.[21]

The most intriguing thing about Claude's desire for Thomas and especially Ruben's desire for Tico, particularly as it is represented within his note, is the fact that in both instances the emphasis is precisely *not* on sex, but instead on the production of a new type of (homosexual) romantic relationship. Claude wants not only an intercourse partner, but a husband, a daddy-o, one willing to express his commitment within a "public" ceremony. Moreover, one might argue that instead of pining away for some unattainable outside, some reality beyond his grasp, Claude empowers himself through the structures of the prison itself, subverting, in the process, the many constraints on his freedom. He refuses to understand Big Jules as solely a sadistic murderer, but instead reconfigures him as husband, lover, mate. Ruben, for his part, never even attempts to sever his tendency for violence from his love. He assures Tico that he will just as quickly "mess him up" as love him. Yet the highly romantic nature of his note is undeniable. Strikingly, his love for Tico does not begin at the penis or anus, but indeed at the lips and hair, the redness of which excite his passion. The beauty of the young man's red mouth and lips belies the necessity of the woman's (red) vagina. Ruben assures Tico, "I never felt like this for no girl" and then closes with a series of salutations that seem jarringly feminine and trite: Love and Kisses, XXX, You Know Who, R. He reminds Tico, in a postscript, to flush his note down the shit bowl, emphasizing once again the counterrationality of his desire.

III

I would like to turn, at this point, to the work of James Baldwin who achieves in his *Giovanni's Room* perhaps one of the most developed explications of the possibilities inherent within abjection yet written. The progress of Baldwin's early career might be narrated, in fact, as a series of successively more explicit and stark representations of the Black Abject, or as I will demonstrate below, the ghost of the homosexual. The whisper of adolescent longing for distant fathers and virile young men in *Go Tell It on the Mountain* gives way in *Another Country* to the tragically inverted "straight" man, Rufus, who, on the one hand, has passionate sex with his white girlfriend, a woman Cleaver refers to as a southern Jezebel, and, on the other, takes a white male southern lover, or again to quote Cleaver, "lets a white bisexual homosexual fuck him in the ass."

To be "fucked" by the white man is not simply to be overcome by white culture, white intellect, white notions of superiority. Nor can it be understood solely as the undeniable evidence of the desire to be white. Instead Cleaver's fear is that Baldwin opens up space for the reconstruction of the Black imaginary, such that the most sacrosanct of Black "truths" might be transgressed. The image of the white (male) southerner raping the (unwilling) Black woman resonates with a long history of African-American literature and lore in which the licentious white man acts as the absolute spoiler of Black desire. The image of the white (Southerner) "making love to" the Black *man*, however, throws all this into confusion.

On the one hand, we see a rescripting of Frederick Douglass's famous account of the whipping of his aunt Hester. The Black male subject is no longer able to remain, in the closet, as it were; instead he takes the woman's place on the joist, becoming himself the victim of the white man's scourge. On the other, it seems that the white man needs not force his "victim" at all. The reader cannot find comfort in the idea that the image of the white male "abuse" of the Black male body is but a deeper revelation of white barbarism. The Black subject willingly gives himself, becoming in the process the mirror image of the culpable female slave whom Angela Davis has described so ably. One might argue, in fact, that the spectacle of interracial homosexual desire puts such pressure on the ideological structures of the Black national literary tradition that it renders the continuation of the inside/out binarism nearly impossible.

These are the issues that shape the narrative of Baldwin's second novel, *Giovanni's Room*. This work, which is widely thought of as Baldwin's anomaly, the work with no Black characters, the work in which Baldwin stretches, some might say unsuccessfully, to demonstrate his grasp of the universal, has been neglected by both students of Black and gay literature, many of whom assume Baldwin had first to retreat from his Blackness in order to explore homosexuality and homophobia. I would argue, however, that the question of Blackness, precisely because of its very apparent absence, screams out at the turn of every page. As we have seen already, the nonexistence of the Black, particularly the Black homosexual, is a theme that Baldwin starts to develop as early as *Go Tell It on the Mountain*. My reading of *Giovanni's Room* will proceed, then, via an exploration of the absences in the text. I will suggest that Baldwin's explication of Giovanni's ghost-like non-presence, his non-subjectivity, parallels the absence of the Black from Western notions of rationality and humanity while at the same time pointing to the possibility of escape from this same Black-exclusive system of logic

Baldwin initiates his discussion of race in the very first paragraph, alerting the reader that even though there are no Blacks present, this is yet a race novel:

> I watch my reflection in the darkening gleam of the window pane. My reflection is tall, perhaps rather like an arrow, my blond hair gleams. My face is like a face you have seen many times. My ancestors conquered a continent, pushing across death-laden plains, until they came to an ocean which faced away from Europe into a darker past.[22]

There are a number of clues in this passage to alert the reader to the ideological work accomplished within Baldwin's text. His use of the autobiographical "I" both conflates his identity with that of his protagonist, David, and signals us that what he is interested in here is the subject of identity formation. David's consideration of his reflection, moreover, demonstrates Baldwin's fascination with the relationship of the Object to the Inverse, the One to the Other. David is indeed the real life (American) character who considers the fate of the already, or the almost already dead Giovanni. In the process, he faces away from Europe, away from whiteness, and from received notions of masculinity and sexuality to a nebulous darker past. Moreover, as Toni Morrison has recently suggested, the production of whiteness, American and otherwise, turns largely upon a complex process in which the Black is at once rendered invisible and omnipresent.[23]

Like Cleaver, then, Baldwin's task in *Giovanni's Room* is to examine the relation of the Black to the white, the body to the mind. Indeed it is the desire for the Other's

Body, in the person of Giovanni, that dictates the action of this text. Giovanni's nominally white, southern Italian body is bought and sold in the course of the novel. One might argue, in fact, that Giovanni becomes simply a creature of his body, a creature of sex and desire, by which other men are able to gauge their own humanity. That is to say, the paradox of the male homosexual is precisely that he usurps the woman's position as the site on which, or by which, fictional relationships between subjects are represented.

This explains why the central tragedy of the novel is the fact that Giovanni is never able to achieve his one true dream, the transcendence of the ideology of the corporeal: "Me, I want to escape . . . this dirty world, this dirty body. I never wish to make love again with anything more than the body."[24] It is not that Giovanni simply despises his flesh. On the contrary, he loves his flesh. It is the idea of his flesh, or rather, the fiction that his flesh represents that he so despises. He wishes to make love again, but only with his body, a body onto which others will no longer project notions of either filth and bestiality, or respectability and autonomy. Indeed Giovanni begins his process of pushing against the strictures of Western thought not in Paris, but in Italy, where he leaves behind his wife after their failed attempt to produce a child, the marker of both husband and wife's authenticity within the patriarchal economy. Giovanni struggles throughout not only to escape the position of the Other, but to produce a new identity, to move beyond the logic of self and other altogether. His work in Guillaume's bar, his relationship with David, and especially his squalid, overcrowded and never quite finished room are all testimony to his desire to achieve an alternative "realness," to enter the world of the living without becoming trapped there, to create a universe of his own making.

It is at this juncture that Baldwin's work so profoundly intersects with both Cleaver's and Thomas's. Like his heterosexually focused, heterosexist counterparts, Baldwin is concerned with both the body and the image of the body constructed by the white (European) mind. More importantly, all three men, even as they are divided by the yawning chasm of sexual desire and practice, give voice to the fear that the fiction of a pure heterosexuality no longer can be maintained, that the processes by which the "Black" male subject is imagined as autonomous, virile and invulnerable can no longer be rendered transparent. In each case, it is the homosexual who stands in for this concern, the homosexual who becomes the (scape)goat. It is almost as if the dissolution, in the gay body, of the strictures concerning "proper" Black male sexual desire and practice parallel the dissolution of a transparent Black American national consciousness. The homosexual is there when the "respectable" Black male protagonist gives way to the criminal Eldridge Cleaver. He stands by as Anglo-American-centered notions of race and "Blackness" are thrown into disarray by the Spanish-inflected "English" of the New York born Puerto Rican, Piri Thomas. Moreover, it is the search for the homosexual that drives the narrative of *Giovanni's Room*, a novel in which Baldwin, an author who has at times represented the apex of (Black) American liberal sentiment, abandons Black America, as it were, producing a text in which received racial thinking is inverted, if not subverted.

The character, Giovanni, might be read, in fact, as a rather odd and startling twist in Cleaver's notion of the Supermasculine Menial, the Black and immensely physical opposite of his Omnipotent Administrator. That is to say, the white bourgeoisie: the French Guillaume and the Belgian (American) Jacques, are competing constantly to claim both Giovanni's labor power and his sex, a process that necessarily restricts Giovanni to the realm of the corporeal and the dirty, and that creates him at once as both the brutalized Black male slave and the sexualized Black female slave. In this sense Giovanni has been dirtied, much as Puerto Rican boys are sullied with feces as they cross the line between the inside and the out, in their traffic with already marginal—and ambiguous—homosexuals. Indeed as Giovanni suggests, the central task of modern life is the struggle to rid oneself of the dirt:

> [W]hat distinguished the men was that they seemed incapable of age: they smelled of soap, which seemed indeed to be their preservative against the dangers and exigencies of any more intimate odor. (P. 118)

Strikingly, cleanliness acts as the very definition of manhood in this passage. The men are cleanly delineated from women, cleanly established as members of a community, cleanly recognized as insiders and subjects.

The struggle for cleanliness, the denial of the body that might protect one from the dangers of intimate odor, is precisely the struggle that David faces when he looks into his darker past. He attempts throughout to maintain a clean masculinity, to maintain his sense of respectability even as he, much like Thomas's gang, is pulled ever more deeply into the dirt muck. David's immersion into the Parisian demimonde has as much to do with his desire to understand himself as not dirty, as not vulnerable and indeed as *not* homosexual as with any real affinity for the people by whom he finds himself surrounded.

> Most of the people I knew in Paris were, as Parisians sometimes put it, of *le milieu* and while this milieu was certainly anxious enough to claim me, I was intent on proving, to them and to myself, that I was not of their company. I did this by being in their company a great deal and manifesting toward all of them a tolerance which placed me, I believed, above suspicion. (Pp. 32–33)

This precisely replicates the process of denial that I demonstrated in my discussion of *Soul on Ice* and *Down These Mean Streets*. Real identity, meaning heterosexual identity, is formed through concurrent acts of repression and projection. The homosexual non-subjects of *le milieu* not only reflect David's own subjectivity, creating him as a real man, they also stand in for the erasure of boundaries that render the entire real/not real logic unworkable.

David's abandonment of Giovanni for his female lover, Hella, a woman whom we only hear about in the second person until rather late in the novel, is both a demonstration of his heterosexuality and his authenticity. With Giovanni, David can only exist in the shadowy and confined spaces of back alley cafes, late night bars, and most especially Giovanni's cramped, suffocating and dishevelled room. It is this room, much like the gay men's apartment in Thomas's narrative, that acts as the marker of Giovanni's gallant, if quixotic, effort to construct a space for himself.

But it was not the room's disorder which was frightening; it was the fact that when one began searching for the key to this disorder, one realized that it was not to be found in any of the usual places. For this was not a matter of habit or circumstance or temperament; it was a matter of punishment or grief. (P. 115)

I think it important here that we not get stuck in a reading of this passage that would proceed solely from the assumption that the homosexual Giovanni has been punished for his efforts to break out of normality by being banished to the realm of "the never quite finished," "the always in process." That is not to say that I intend to disallow this reading altogether. Instead I would suggest also that the joy that David and Giovanni are able to achieve, however briefly, is itself a product of this same disorder. "In the beginning our life together held a joy and amazement which was newborn every day" (p. 99). The attraction for both David and Giovanni is that they are obliged to recreate themselves—and the room—daily. Each has refused already to settle down. Both have left their "homelands." Both throw off the strictures of male heterosexuality. Moreover, both leave behind the mores and values of *le milieu*. Perhaps, then, the greatest tragedy—and the promise—of this work is that while David and Giovanni are cast out of the "mainstream" neither is able—or willing— to inhabit the margin. They are not the other, but the vehicles of the abject.

It becomes impossible for either to claim status in the "real" world or even its underside. Giovanni cannot simply give in to the abuse and manipulation of Guillaume. Instead he kills him, creating himself as the marginal's marginal, the fugitive. Moreover, like both Cleaver and Thomas, he is eventually caught and incarcerated, remaining in prison until he undergoes the ultimate dissolution of the inside/out binarism, death. David had run away already from "America," which in this instance refers not simply to a geographical location, or a complex of political and social structures, but also to a patriarchal economy that produces maleness as the lack of lack, a fiction that David is never able to maintain. After the death of his mother, the family fiction is thrown into a profound crisis. His domineering aunt becomes the primary source of power and order in the household, re-embodying his father, in the process, such that the notion of masculine invulnerability is exploded. Indeed the tragedy that David brings with him from America is precisely that he both sees and knows his father. "Fathers ought to avoid utter nakedness before their sons. I did not want to know—not, anyway, from his mouth—that his flesh was as unregenerate as my own" (p. 26).

David can never go home again, as it were, to the wide open plains of America. And yet even as David attempts to create his (American) female lover, Hella, as a surrogate for his homeland, as he mounts one last desperate attempt to save himself, to create for himself an identity that can be seen and acknowledged within respectable (American) society, he is always haunted by the dual specters of Giovanni and his own homosexuality. David becomes himself a type of ghost, growing ever distant from Hella, retreating into a world of memory and denial to which she has no access.

And I look at my body, which is under sentence of death. It is lean, hard, and cold, the incarnation of a mystery. And I do not know what moves in this body, what this body is searching. It is trapped in my mirror as it is trapped in time and it hurries toward revelation. (P. 223)

Here again we see the reference to death, the site at which the distinctions between the inside and the out, the self and the other give way, allowing only the articulation of ghost-like subjectivities. Strikingly, David's ghost body becomes inexplicable. He can no longer fashion a narrative by which to describe it. It is distinct from the self which remains a victim to a type of body logic that he cannot yet understand.

It is at this point that we can see most clearly the process by which the figure of the homosexual is conflated with the figure of the ghost, a process that occurs throughout the production of African-American literature and that is intimately tied to the production of the abject. The specter of the non-productive, unauthentic, weak, effeminate, and anti-social homosexual had not, it seems, been exorcised with the virulently homophobic diatribes of Eldridge Cleaver, nor even with the deaths of Rufus and Giovanni. In the process of creating the authentic Black subject, a process that necessarily involves concurrent practices of negation and projection, one has always to resurrect the ghost of the Black devil, as it were. That is to say, we must point to that which is unauthentic, base and perverse in order to adequately define the borders of Black "realness." At the same time, in the process of travelling through the underworld, the muck, the feces that is represented by the Black homosexual, we are able to access, if only briefly, new modes of understanding and existence that seem to wait just beyond our grasp. As a consequence, the Black abject never dies. On the contrary, it is only more deeply woven into the fabric of the Black American (literary) imagination. As David says of Giovanni, "in fleeing from his body, I confirmed and perpetuated his body's power over me. Now, as though I had been branded his body was burned into my mind, into my dreams" (p. 191).

I opened this essay with two epigraphs: "Thou shalt not seethe a kid in his mother's milk," and *"Chivo que rompe tambor con su pellejo paga,"* or the goat who breaks the drum will pay with his hide. Both statements, taken from different, if not altogether dissimilar religious "texts," the Bible and the proverbs of the Cuban Abakua societies, reflect a profound concern with the question of perversity. To cook the goat in the same milk which it has been nourished is to subvert a number of "self-evident" truths, among them the distinctions between right and wrong, inside and out, such that it becomes impossible to maintain the coherency of the society's logical order. Moreover, the very existence of the prohibition bespeaks the reality of a desire that stands outside of received logics. Indeed it may be perverse to eat the kid prepared with its mother's milk, but this does not make it less enjoyable.

That the concern with boundary crisis, with the goat's tendency to break out of its prescribed roles within society should be repeated among Cuban Yoruba-based religious groups reflects not only the intersection of Christianity with New World religions, but also and importantly the fact that the articulation of the perverse and the grotesque is absolutely necessary to the production of a variety of national cultures. As Coco Fusco has suggested, even while the Abakua proverb points directly to the grave consequences of troublemaking,[25] it demonstrates the necessity of the untamed "outsider" to the continued creativity of the rest of the community. As James Baldwin's Giovanni is slaughtered and as Thomas' effeminate gay men are sexually tortured and beaten a type of music is produced, a music that points the way to new modes of existence, new ways of understanding, that allow the community to escape, however briefly, the systems of logic that have proven so enervating to the Black subject. The importance of the (scape)goat, then, is not so much that with its death peace returns to the village, or that crisis ends. The point is not simply to expurgate all that is ambiguous and contradictory. On the contrary, as the kid is consumed and the drum is beaten the community learns to gain pleasure from "the possibilities just beyond its grasp." It receives proof of its own authenticity and insider status while leaving open a space for change, perhaps even the possibility of new forms of joy. The boundaries are for a moment reestablished, but all are certain, even hopeful, that once again they will be erased.

NOTES

1. Eve Sedgwick, *Between Men: English Literature and Male Homosocial Desire* (New York: Columbia Univ. Press, 1985).

2. Diana Fuss, "Inside/Out," Diana Fuss, ed., *Inside/Out: Lesbian Theories, Gay Theories* (New York: Routledge, 1991), p. 3.

3. René Girard, *The Scapegoat* (Baltimore: Johns Hopkins Univ. Press, 1986).

4. See: Henry Louis Gates, *Figures in Black: Words, Signs and the "Racial" Self* (New York: Oxford Univ. Press, 1987); Paul Gilroy, *The Black Atlantic: Modernity and Double Consciousness* (Cambridge: Harvard Univ. Press, 1993); Orlando Patterson, *Slavery and Social Death* (Cambridge: Harvard Univ. Press. 1980).

5. Girard, pp. 15–16.

6. Julia Kristeva, *Powers of Horror: An Essay on Abjection* (New York: Columbia Univ. Press, 1982).

7. Paul Gilroy, "It's a Family Affair," Gina Dent, ed., *Black Popular Culture* (Seattle: Bay Press, 1992), p. 312.

8. Eldridge Cleaver, *Soul on Ice* (New York: Laurel, 1968), p. 26.

9. *Ibid.*, p. 26.

10. Angela Davis, "Reflections on the Black Woman's Role in the Community of Slaves," *Black Scholar* 3.4 (December 1971): 2–15.

11. Cleaver, p. 21.

12. *Ibid.*, pp. 32–33.

13. *Ibid.*, p. 175.

14. Quoted in Cleaver, p. 47.

15. See: Pat Shipman, *The Evolution of Racism: Human Differences and the Use and Abuse of Science* (New York: Simon and Schuster, 1994).

16. Quoted in Shipman, p. 163.

17. See: John D'Emilio and Estelle B. Freedman, *Intimate Matters: A History of Sexuality in America* (New York: Harper and Row, 1988); John D'Emilio, *Sexual Politics, Sexual Communities: The Making of the Homosexual Minority in the United States, 1940–1970* (Chicago: The Univ. of Chicago Press, 1983).

18. Piri Thomas, *Down These Mean Streets* (New York: Vintage, 1967), p. 50.

19. Kristeva, p. 2.

20. Thomas, p. 263.

21. *Ibid.*, p. 266.

22. James Baldwin, *Giovanni's Room* (New York: Laurel, 1956), p. 7.

23. Toni Morrison, *Playing in the Dark: Whiteness and the Literary Imagination* (Cambridge: Harvard Univ. Press, 1992). See also: Michael Banton, *Racial Theories* (New York: Cambridge Univ. Press, 1987); Alexander Saxton, *The Rise and Fall of the White Republic: Class Politics and Mass Culture in Nineteenth-Century America* (New York: Verso, 1990); David R. Reodiger, *The Wages of Whiteness* (New York: Verso, 1991); Eric Lott, *Love and Theft: Blackface Minstrels and the American Working Class* (New York: Oxford Univ. Press, 1993); Robert C. Toll, *Blacking Up: The Minstrel Show in Nineteenth-Century America* (New York: Oxford Univ. Press, 1974); Ruth Frankenberg, *White Women: Race Matters: The Social Construction of Whiteness* (Minneapolis: The Univ. of Minnesota Press, 1993); Shelly Fisher Fishkin, *Was Huck Black? Mark Twain and African American Voices* (New York: Oxford Univ. Press, 1993); George M. Fredrickson. *The Black Image in the White Mind: The Debate on Afro-American Character and Destiny, 1817–1914* (New York: Harper and Row, 1971).

24. Baldwin, p. 35.

25. Coco Fusco, "Pan-American Postnationalism: Another World Order," Gina Dent, ed., *Black Popular Culture* (Seattle: Bay Press, 1992), pp. 279–84.

47 African Signs and Spirit Writing

Harryette Mullen

(1996)

> The recording of an authentic black voice, a voice of deliverance
> from the deafening discursive silence which an "enlightened" Europe
> cited as proof of the absence of the African's humanity, was the
> millennial instrument of transformation through which the African
> would become the European, the slave become the ex-slave, the
> brute animal become the human being. So central was this idea to
> the birth of the black literary tradition that four of the first five
> eighteenth-century slave narratives drew upon the figure of the voice
> in the text as crucial "scenes of instruction" in the development of
> the slave on his road to freedom. James Gronniosaw in 1770, John
> Marrant in 1785, Ottobah Cuguano in 1787, Olaudah Equiano in
> 1789, and John Jea in 1815, all draw upon the figure of the voice in
> the text. . . . That the figure of the talking book recurs in these . . .
> black eighteenth-century texts says much about the degree of "inter-
> texuality" in early black letters, more than we heretofore thought.
> Equally important, however, this figure itself underscores the estab-
> lished correlation between silence and blackness we have been trac-
> ing, as well as the urgent need to make the text speak, the process
> by which the slave marked his distance from the master.
> —Davis and Gates, *The Slave's Narrative* xxvi–xxvii

Much of Henry Louis Gates's influential scholarship argues that black literary
traditions privilege orality. This critical position has become something of a commonplace, in part because it is based on accurate observation. From the "talking book"
featured in early slave narratives to "dialect poetry" and the "speakerly text," the
Afro-American tradition that Gates constructs and canonizes is that which seeks to
"speak" to readers with an "authentic black voice." Presumably, for the African-
American writer, there is no alternative to production of this "authentic black voice"
but silence, invisibility, or self-effacement. This speech-based and racially inflected
aesthetic that produces a "black poetic diction" requires that the writer acknowledge

and reproduce in the text a significant difference between the spoken and written language of African-Americans and that of other Americans. Without disputing, as George Schuyler did in his satiric novel, *Black No More*, that any such difference exists, I would like to argue that any theory of African-American literature that privileges a speech based poetics, or the trope of orality, to the exclusion of more writerly texts will cost us some impoverishment of the tradition. While Gates includes in his canon a consummately writerly text, such as Ralph Ellison's *Invisible Man*, because it also functions brilliantly as a speakerly text, and while Gates appreciates Zora Neale Hurston and celebrates Sterling A. Brown, he cannot champion Jean Toomer's *Cane* with the same degree of enthusiasm.[1] I would not worry so much about the criteria Gates has set for inclusion in his canon, if it did not seem to me that the requirement that a black text be "speakerly" will inevitably exclude certain African-American texts that draw more on the culture of books, writing, and print than they do on the culture of orality.

Another concern I have about Gates's argument is its seeming acceptance of an erroneous Eurocentric assumption that African cultures developed no indigenous writing or script systems. Although he is well aware of Job ben Solomon, a captive African sold into slavery in Maryland, and later ransomed and returned to Africa after it was discovered that he was literate in Arabic, Gates seems to overlook the possibility that non-Islamic slaves might also have been familiar with writing or indigenous script systems used for various religious purposes in their own cultural contexts. While the institutionalized illiteracy of African-American slaves born in the U.S. was enforced by laws forbidding anyone to teach them to read or write, the illiteracy of Africans cannot be accepted as given, although to speak of non-Islamic Africans as literate would require broader definitions of writing than Western scholars such as Walter J. Ong might find acceptable.

This essay is an attempt to explore connections between African signs and African-American spirit writing, traditions that may be traced more readily within a visual arts and art history context, where perhaps more continuity exists between African and African-American forms of visual expression, than within a canon of African-American literature or literary criticism, since the loss of African languages by African Americans constitutes a much more decisive rupture.

As a literary critic, another part of my project is to read the texts of ex-slave narratives and spiritual narratives as precursors of complementary traditions of African-American literacy, while at the same time keeping in mind that much of what is considered most authentically African in traditional African-American culture has been preserved and maintained through extraliterary forms, and has in fact often been the creation of illiterate or marginally literate African Americans whose aesthetic impact is all the more astonishing given their exclusion from the educational, cultural, and political institutions of the dominant bourgeois white culture of the United States. Looking at parallel traditions of African-American literacy inaugurated by ex-slave narratives and visionary texts mainly produced in the 19th century for possible answers, the larger question I am asking is this: How has the Western view of writing as a rational technology historically been received and transformed by

African Americans whose primary means of cultural transmission have been oral and visual rather than written, and for whom graphic systems have been associated not with instrumental human communication, but with techniques of spiritual power and spirit possession? In other words: How, historically, have African-Americans' attitudes toward literacy as well as their own efforts to acquire, use, and interiorize the technologies of literacy been shaped by what art historian Robert Farris Thompson calls "the flash of the spirit of a certain people armed with improvisatory drive and brilliance"?[2]

The ex-slave narratives offer one possible answer to this question.[3] Another possibility and an alternative tradition are suggested when Thompson notes that in African-American folk culture the printed text may provide ritual protection, as newspapers are used by "back-home architects" who "papered the walls of their cabins with newsprint to confuse jealous spirits with an excess of information," and writing may be employed to enclose and confine evil presences, as in the spirit-script of visionary artist J. B. Murray.[4] In what looks like illiterate scribbling or a handwriting exercise, Murray's noncommunicative spirit-writing or "textual glossolalia," Thompson finds an African-American manifestation of what may be a surviving element of Kongo prophetic practices in which a unique illegible script produced in a trance-like state functions as a graphic representation of spirit possession, "a visual equivalent to speaking in tongues" (Adele 14). In order to construct a cultural and material history of African America's embrace and transmutation of writing technologies, one might ask how writing and text functioned in a folk milieu that valued a script for its cryptographic incomprehensibility and uniqueness, rather than its legibility or reproducibility. How was the uniformity of print received by a folk culture in which perfect symmetry and straight, unbroken lines were avoided, an aesthetic preference for irregularity and variation that folklorist Gladys-Marie Fry attributes to "the folk belief of plantation slaves that evil spirits follow straight lines" (67)?[5]

Thompson imaginatively suggests that, just as in African and diasporic forms of oral expression, from the pygmy yodel to the field holler of the slave, from the blues wail to the gospel hum, from the bebopping scat of the jazz singer to the nonsense riffs erupting in the performance of the rap, dub, or reggae artist, it is apparent that the voice may be "unshackled" from meaningful words or from the pragmatic function of languages as a conveyor of cognitive information, so the written text, as spirit-script, may be unshackled from any phonetic representation of human speech or graphic representation of language. "Music brings down the spirit upon a prepared point in traditional Kongo culture," Thompson states. I might add that a reading of 19th-century African-American spiritual narratives suggests that, like music, the act of reading or writing, or the process of acquiring literacy itself may be a means for the visionary writer to attract a powerful presence to inhabit a spiritually focused imagination or a blank sheet of paper. Jarena Lee recalls the moment of her conversion, a flash of the spirit, inspired by hearing the Bible read aloud in church: "At the reading of the Psalms, a ray of renewed conviction darted into my soul" (Andrews 27). Zilpha Elaw, attending a camp meeting, experienced a "trance or ecstacy" that resulted in an unprecedented feeling of empowerment.

[M]y heart and soul were rendered completely spotless—as clean as a sheet of white paper, and I felt as if I had never sinned in all my life . . . when the prayer meeting afterwards commenced, the Lord opened my mouth in public prayer; and while I was thus engaged, it seemed as if I heard my God rustling in the tops of the mulberry-trees. Oh how precious was this day to my soul! (Andrews 67)

An African-American tradition of literacy as a secular technology and a tool for political empowerment, through appropriation of public symbols, and participation in mainstream cultural discourses, co-exists with a parallel tradition of visionary literacy as a spiritual practice in which divine inspiration, associated with Judeo-Christian biblical tradition, is syncretically merged with African traditions of spirit possession, as in the "spirit-writing" of Gertrude Morgan (1900–1980) and J. B. Murray (1910–1988), African-American visionary folk artists who were, respectively, literate and illiterate practitioners of what Robert Farris Thompson calls "arts of defense and affirmation" and "arts of black yearning" for transcendence and freedom.

The tradition of secular literacy may be traced in African-American tradition to the ex-slave narratives, with the 1845 narrative of Frederick Douglass as the paradigmatic text of the genre. The alternative tradition of visionary literacy may be traced to narratives and journals of spiritual awakening and religious conversion written by freeborn and emancipated Africans and African-Americans in the 18th and 19th centuries. Each of these traditions of literacy, the sacred and the secular, has a specific relation to African and diasporic orality as well as to the institutionalized illiteracy that resulted from the systematic exclusion of African Americans from equal educational opportunities. Both traditions have a common origin in the early narratives of African captives for whom emancipation had been associated with the conversion to the equally potent religions of Christianity and literacy.[6] By the 19th century, the bonds linking religious conversion and legal emancipation had been broken as masters complained that it made no sense economically to free slaves simply because they had become fellow Christians. It remained for 19th-century ex-slave narrators, notably Douglass, to preceive the legal codes forbidding literacy and social mobility to slaves as a secular analogue of the threat of spiritual alienation that had motivated Olaudah Equiano and others to learn to read in order to "talk to" the Bible.

The texts of ex-slave narratives signal a decisive movement of literate African Americans toward self-empowerment through the tools and technologies of literacy that are productive of bourgeois subjectivity, and away from the degradation imposed by slavery and compulsory illiteracy. The zealous pursuit of literacy embodied by ex-slave narrators, particularly Douglass, is an astute response to the disastrous assault on the collective cultural identities of African captives whose orally transmitted forms of knowledge brought from their various ethnic groups had been submerged, fragmented, or rendered irrelevant within a dominant bourgeois white culture that characterized whatever remained within slave culture of coherent African traditional aesthetic and spiritual systems as superstitious beliefs of primitive people.

Alongside the largely secular and overtly political ex-slave narratives, which of necessity are concerned with what happens to the slave's body, an alternate tradition of visionary literacy exists in the tradition of African-American spiritual autobiography, which concerned itself not with the legal status of the material body, but with the shackles placed on the soul and on the spiritual expressiveness of the freeborn or emancipated African American, whose religious conversion, sanctification, and worship were expected to conform to the stringent standards of the white Christian establishment. Until the founding of black churches and the calling of black preachers, and until the white clergy loosened its strictures against emotional displays of religious enthusiasm, African-American worship had been constrained in its expressive forms and rituals, which included communal dancing, the call and response by which the community and its leaders mutually affirmed one another, and the spontaneous vocalizations of the spirit-possessed. For African-American visionary writers and artists, the Bible as sacred text and sublime speech, as the written record of a divine voice inspiring its authors to write and its readers to speak holy words, mediates the historical and mythic dislocation from primarily oral cultures to one in which literacy has the power of a fetish.

Although equally zealous in their pursuit of freedom through literacy, spiritual autobiographers, unlike most ex-slave narrators, often forsake "bourgeois perception" of reality (Lowe) for "things unseen" or "signs in the heavens." Because of the stress they place on visionary experience, these texts have as much in common with the practice of literate and illiterate African-American visionary folk artists as with contemporaneous narratives written or dictated by emancipated or fugitive slaves in the 18th and 19th centuries. For visionary artists, as for these spiritual autobiographers, the art work or text is an extension of their call to preach. It functions as a spiritual signature or divine imprimatur, superseding human authority. The writer as well as the artist can become "an inspired device for the subconscious spirit," the African ancestor-spirit whose black yearning, unleashed as glossolalia, would be regarded in the dominant culture as mumbo jumbo. Through the visionary artist or writer who serves as a medium, it is possible for the surviving spirit of African cultural traditions "to manifest itself on the physical plane" through the artist's materials or the materiality of the writing process. The work of such individuals, while resonating with ancient traditions, "is conceived out of [a] deeply intuitive calling and spiritual need" (Nasisse).

In addition to stressing spiritual and personal over material and political forms of power, visionary writers were also much more likely to attribute their literacy to supernatural agency, rather than the realistically difficult and tedious work Douglass details in his attempt to "get hold of a book" and grasp the instrumentality of literacy (278). The secular ex-slave narrative tradition is exemplified by Douglass, who substituted abolitionist tracts for the Bible (Olaudah Equiano's "talking book")[7] as the text of desire motivating his acquisition of literacy, and who learned to write by copying the penmanship of his younger master, literally "writing in the spaces" of the master's copybook.

> I got hold of a book entitled "The Columbian Orator." Every opportunity I got, I used to read this book. . . . During this time, my copy-book was the board fence, brick

wall, and pavement; my pen and ink was a lump of chalk. With these, I learned mainly how to write. . . . By this time, my little Master Thomas had gone to school, and learned how to write, and had written over a number of copy-books. . . . When left thus [unsupervised in the master's house], I used to spend the time in writing in the spaces left in master Thomas's copy-book, copying what he had written. I continued to do this until I could write a hand very similar to that of Master Thomas. Thus, after a long, tedious effort for years, I finally succeeded in learning how to write. (Douglass 278–81)[8]

Both through his emphasis on the quotidian, his naming of the mundane material objects employed in his campaign of disciplinary self-instruction, as well as through his substitution of abolitionist writings where previous narratives had placed the Bible as the text of desire motivating the narrator to become literate, Douglass refigures and secularizes the trope of divine instruction employed in spiritual autobiographies of some free born or manumitted. African-Americans who claimed to have acquired literacy by supernatural means: through divine intervention after earnest prayer. The ethnographic and historical research that documents continuities between African and African-American aesthetic and spiritual practices now makes it possible to explore how, in the 18th and 19th centuries, Africans and African-Americans converting to Anglo-American/Protestant as well as Latin/Catholic Christianity, and interiorizing Western-style literacy, may themselves have transformed and refigured indigenous African concepts of protective religious writing, as Maude Southwell Wahlman suggests:

In Africa, among the Mande, Fon, Ejagham, and Kongo peoples, indigenous and imported writing is associated with knowledge, power, and intelligence, and thus is considered sacred and protective. African signs were sewn, dyed, painted or woven into cloth; and Central African artifacts were often read as aspects of a Kongo religious cosmogram. . . . In Nigeria, the Ejagham people are known for their 400-year-old writing system, called *Nsibidi* (Talbot, 1912). It was most likely invented by women since one sees it on their secret society buildings, fans, calabashes, skin-covered masks, textiles, and costumes made for secret societies. . . . In the New World various mixtures of West African (*Vai*) and Nigerian (*Nsibidi*) scripts and the Kongo cosmogram fused to create numerous new scripts. (29–30)

This phenomenon has been most extensively documented in the Latin/Catholic traditions in which religious syncretism thrives through the identification of Catholic saints with African deities, as well as through the church's hospitality to mysticism, and through incorporation of indigenous paganisms into elaborately layered and localized rites and rituals. Yet it can also be demonstrated that even the more austere traditions of Anglo-American/Protestant worship, particularly after the establishment of black churches, produced African-American syncretisms of African, European, and indigenous Native American spiritual practices. African-American preaching styles, call and response, spirituals, gospel singing, baptism and funeral rites, and ritual possession by "the Holy Ghost" are examples of such Protestant syncretisms.

Particularly in its insistence upon grassroots literacy training as an aspect of religious conversion and sanctification, so that the Holy Word might be transmitted directly to each individual through Bible reading, Protestantism fostered in African-American religious tropologies the figuring of acquisition and interiorization of literacy as a Christian form of spirit-possession compatible with African mystical traditions.

The tradition of spiritual writers includes John Jea, Jarena Lee, Zilpha Elaw, Julia Foote, and Rebecca Cox Jackson, whose spirituality links them to illiterate visionaries Harriet Tubman, Sojourner Truth, and Harriet Powers, to literate insurrectionists such as Nat Turner and Denmark Vesey, as well as to 20th-century visionary artists such as J. B. Murray and Gertrude Morgan. By comparing similarities in the imagery of visionary folk artists and the religious visions of 19th-century mystics, it is possible to see a continuum of syncretic survival of African spiritual traditions and aesthetic systems which could hide and thrive in the interstices of accepted Christian practices. According to Andy Nasisse, "The overwhelming evidence that certain images and religious ideas encoded in the work of Black American visions has verifiable trans-Atlantic connections to specific cultures in Africa . . . gives additional support to the notion that these images surface from a collective source. . . . Although many of these Africanisms could have been taught and otherwise handed down through genera-tions, there are numerous signs of the presence of tribal elements which seem to have spontaneously generated in an individual's art" (11).

Maude Southwell Wahlman locates visionary African-American art in a "creolized" tradition that blends cultural and aesthetic traditions of Africans, Native Americans, and Europeans. Because the artists, some of them illiterate, "could not always artic-ulate the African traditions that shaped their visions, dreams, and arts," they have seemed "idiosyncratic" to art critics and art historians schooled in European and Euro-American traditions (28–29). The creolized tradition of visionary folk artists, that has been "transmitted somewhat randomly through the generations, resulted in the retention of original African motifs although the symbolic meanings of the images were sometimes lost" (Adele 13).

This syncretic, or creolized, tradition is manifested in a most visually striking way in the work of African-American quilters. The narrative quilts of Harriet Powers offer a fascinating example of artifacts that incorporate African techniques and design elements, while also expressing the spiritual preoccupations of an artistically gifted individual, Powers, who could neither read nor write, was born into slavery in 1837 and died in 1911. According to folklorist Gladys-Marie Fry, "Harriet Powers's quilt forms a direct link to the tapestries traditionally made by the Fon people of Abomey, the ancient capital of Dahomey, West Africa" (85). Sterling Brown asserts that both Dahomean and Bakongo traditions are evident in Powers's Bible story quilts.

> Missionaries failed to halt African religion in Georgia because it took forms they did not understand or even recognize. Dahomean influence was even greater than one would have suspected by combining the insights of Bremer and Herskovits; it also appeared in a form and a place in which whites would least expect African religious

expression of any kind—in the quilts of slave women. Fashioned from throw-away cloth, slave quilts were used to clothe mysteries, to enfold those baptized with reinforcing symbols of their faith. Such quilts in Georgia bore a remarkable resemblance to Dahomean applique cloth. Harriet Powers's Bible quilt is a brilliant example both of that tradition and of Bakongo tradition, combining the two so naturally as to reflect the coming together of Dahomean and Bakongo people in American slavery. . . . Thus, her quilt is a symbol of the fusion of African ethnic traditions in slavery and later. . . . When asked about the meaning of her quilt, Harriet Powers responded at considerable length and in much detail, asserting that the quilt in every particular is Christian. (91–92)

The two extant Powers quilts memorialize historical, celestial, mythic, and biblical events, all drawn into the composition through the artist's imaginative system of visual representation. Powers's beautifully executed pictographic quilts also form an interesting link between folk material culture and the culture of literacy. Combining the distinctive applique techniques of Dahomey textile art with the distinctly American narrative quilt, Powers constructed visual narratives that could almost be described as storyboards. In the quilts themselves, textile approaches textuality; and dictated notes record Powers's recital of local, biblical, and apocryphal stories which had inspired the series of narrative frames, that "read" from left to right and top to bottom in her two extant quilts, now held in the collections of the Smithsonian Institution and Boston Museum of Fine Arts.

While I reject Nasisse's speculation that there may be some "genetic" reason for the recurrent images found in visionary folk art and their continuity with similar imagery found in African art and artifacts (other than the inherited tendency of human beings to make and preserve cultural symbols), certainly the persistence of such "Africanisms" in the work of Southern folk artists suggests that African cultural systems were not utterly destroyed by slavery, but rather survived in fragmentary, dispersed, and marginalized forms that continue to exist alongside dominant cultural traditions that also significantly influence African-American cultural production.

Sterling Stuckey, following Thompson's insight, argues that African-American culture was formed not only through the syncretism of African with European and indigenous native traditions, but also through the fusion of traditional practices that were familiar and comprehensible to individuals from different African ethnolinguistic groups. The slave community actually served to consolidate, reinforce, and preserve certain African customs that diverse cultural systems had shared in common, such as burial rituals that included decorating graves with sea shells, glass, or crockery.

Slaves found objects in North America similar to the shells and close enough to the earthenware of West Africa to decorate the grave in an African manner. . . . Africans from different points of the continent shared this vision, which could have *strengthened* an African trait under the conditions of North American slavery. . . . Being on good terms with the ancestral spirits was an overarching conceptual concern for Africans everywhere in slavery. . . . No one has yet demonstrated that skilled slaves sought to cut themselves off from their spiritual base in the slave community. If skilled slaves did not remove themselves from that base they remained connected to the African heritage on the profoundest possible level. (Stuckey 42–43)

What may seem to be the "spontaneous generation" of African symbols in the work of African-American folk artists may in fact indicate that the folk tradition has served as a repository of African spiritual practices since the arrival of the first captive Africans to this country. Such seemingly idiosyncratic imagery, that nevertheless alludes to dispersed and hidden fragments of coherent cultural systems, generally does not appear in the secular tradition initiated in the materially-based ex-slave narratives which tend to distance the narrator from "slave superstition" or "heathen" African spirituality, while providing a rationale for African-American displays of emotion. While Christianity strongly influences African-American spirituality, it is also evident that the visionary tradition allows within its spiritual matrix a space for a syncretic African-based spirituality or diasporic consciousness that a secular narrator such as Frederick Douglass specifically rejects as slave "superstition."

In his recollection of an incident in which an African-born slave offers and Douglass accepts a special root to serve as a protective charm against being whipped by the overseer, Douglass progressively dissociates himself from this superstitious belief in the power of the ritual object, while self-consciously using his text to suggest that his increasing grasp of literacy allowed Douglass eventually to transfer his youthful belief in the power associated in African cultures with ritual objects to the power associated in bourgeois Western culture with writing. First the written pass, which the slaves, significantly, swallow after a failed escape attempt, and finally the text of the narrative itself take on this aura of power that Douglass associates with his interiorization of literacy and its technologies.

Douglass's text registers cultural hybridity even as the narrator rejects the devalued alternative consciousness of the African captive in his determined pursuit of bourgeois subjectivity, the basic prerequisite of citizenship. His ambivalent portrayal of his own youthful belief in a spiritual technique later displaced in his regard by a belief in the greater efficacy of literacy might be read as Douglass's gloss on the failure of slave insurrections led by Denmark Vesey and Nat Turner.[9] Vesey, a free black, and Turner, a slave, sought to forge leadership at the interface of African orality/spirituality and an African-American visionary literacy founded on a prophetic reading of the Bible. Vesey's co-conspirator Gullah Jack, known among slaves as "the little man who can't be killed, shot, or taken," was, according to slave testimony, "born a conjuror and a physician, in his own country [Angola]," and possessed "a charm which rendered him invulnerable." Turner's insurrection relied upon his reading of "signs in the heavens" and "hieroglyphic characters" he had "found on the leaves in the woods" which corresponded with "the figures [he] had seen in the heavens," as well as his application of biblical prophecy to the historical circumstance of slavery in the United States. Eric Foner speculates that Turner "may have inherited some of his rebelliousness from his parents, for according to local tradition, his African-born mother had to be restrained from killing her infant son rather than see him a slave and his father escaped when Nat was a boy." In his dictated 1831 "confession," Turner notes that his family and the slave community had implicitly equated his predilection for prophetic vision with his precocious aptitude for literacy (*Nat Turner* 41–50). Although, like Douglass, he stressed his own extraordinary and individual brilliance, the leader of the most famous insurrection of slaves in the United States suggested that his uncanny knowledge of events that "had happened before I was born," quick intelligence, and easy acquisition of literacy were perceived by the African-American community as miraculous spiritual gifts, which signalled that "I surely would be a prophet."

> To a mind like mine, restless, inquisitive and observant of every thing that was passing, it is easy to suppose that religion was the subject to which it would be directed, and although this subject principally occupied my thoughts—there was nothing that I saw or heard to which my attention was not directed—The manner in which I learned to read and write, not only had great influence on my own mind, as I acquired it with the most perfect ease, so much so, that I have no recollection whatever of learning the alphabet—but to the astonishment of the family, one day, when a book was shewn to me to keep me from crying, I began spelling the names of different objects—this was a source of wonder to all in the neighborhood, particularly the blacks—and this learning was constantly improved at all opportunities. (*Nat Turner* 41–42)

While the black community that nurtured Nat Turner viewed literacy as compatible and continuous with African spiritual practice, Douglass's text stresses the divergence of the letter from the spirit as African spiritual traditions are uprooted by bourgeois literacy. Douglass's loss of faith in African power/knowledge is also echoed in Henry Bibb's *Narrative*, when as a young man Bibb tries but is disappointed by the inefficacy of charms procured from a slave conjuror. Given the stereotypical association of rational thought and behavior with masculinity as well as with humanity, there may have been an even greater sense of obligation on the part of men than on women to portray themselves in their narratives as rational rather than emotional or spiritual beings. Interestingly, at least two women who had been slaves, the illiterate Mary Prince and the literate Harriet Jacobs, included in their narratives tributes to the knowledge and skill of black women who practiced arts of traditional healing among the slaves.

Yet Robert Farris Thompson's insightful study of continuities between African and African-American art, drawing upon ethnographic research that regards cultural practices as coherent and comprehensible social "texts," suggests an alternate possibility of comprehensively "reading" African-American traditions of literacy. Rather than presuming that Western knowledge and literacy simply displaced African ignorance and illiteracy, as Douglass seems to imply, the visionary tradition, which encompasses both literate and illiterate spiritual practitioners, suggests alternatively that African-American literacy might be continuous rather than discontinuous with African ways of knowing, and with traditional systems of oral and visual communication that represent natural and supernatural forces as participants in an extralinguistic dialogue with human beings. Following the work of Melville Herskovits, as well as folklorist Zora Neale Hurston, Robert Farris Thompson has emphasized that ritual objects are invested with communicative power through the association of the names or qualities of objects with other objects, qualities, or actions.

> Kongo ritual experts have always worked with visionary objects. They call such objects *minkisi (nkisi,* in the singular). . . . The powers of such experts also resided in the ability to read and write the *nkisi* language of visual astonishment. Such signs (*bidimbu*) include chalked ideographs, plus myriad symbolic objects linked to mystic actions, through puns, on the name of the object and the sound of the verb. For example, a priest might place a grain (*luzibu*) in an *nkisi* so that it might spiritually open (*zibula*) up an affair. But Kongo writing also sometimes included mysterious ciphers, received by a person in a state of spiritual possession. This was "writing in the spirit," sometimes referred to as "visual glossolalia," this was writing as if copied from "a billboard in the sky." (1989, 101)

Nat Turner's prophetic interpretation of "signs in the heavens" suggests that the members of slave communities found in the text of the Bible a resonance with aspects of African spiritual techniques (41–50). Douglass's secular interpretation of the visionary object may have overlooked the spiritual power of the *nkisi* "visual language," suggested in the multivalent significance of the root, which might have been used by the conjuror in ritual practice to indicate the strength that comes of being rooted in a coherent culture and kinship structure.[10] In the twisted appearance of the gnarled root may be found an analogue, within nature, of the mystic scribbling that represents for J. B. Murray the possibility of mediumistic communication with the supernatural.

> "High John the Conqueror" or "Johnny the Conqueroo" is a gnarled root sold for love and gambling. "When you see a twisted root within a charm," Nigerian elder Fu-Kiau Bunseki told Robert Farris Thompson, "you know, like a tornado hidden in an egg, that this *nkisi* is very very strong." (*Flash of the Spirit* 131). [Contemporary African-American artist Alison] Saar has adapted this idea to a political image of Black power, a continuation of the concept of the extraordinary buried in the ordinary.[11]

The root's purported "magic" might lie simply in the power of language to aid in visualization as a healing technique, or as a psychological tool for self-affirmation. The effectiveness of visualization and affirmation as techniques of mental and physical health have only recently begun to be demonstrated through scientific experiment. Surely the African-American root doctor's "arts of defense and affirmation" also served as arts of survival for slaves barred from access to political power, and reliant upon religion for institutional structure, and upon their own visionary powers of imagination to "make a way out of no way" and thus conjure a better future for their descendants. Contemporary African Americans, armed with technical skill and tools of secular analysis, may equally rely upon the inspiration they derive from these African arts for "creative strategies of cohesion and survival" (Piper 19).

The transmission of two important African religious concepts—religious writing and healing charms—provides important examples of the influence of African cultural traditions on Afro-American visionary arts. Arts preserve cultural traditions even though the social context of traditions may change. In Africa the deeper significance of religious symbolism was revealed to those who had earned the title of elder. When religious ideas reappeared in the New World, they took different ways. They survived because they were essential tools of survival, and thus were encoded in a multiplicity of forms: visual arts, songs, dance, and black speech. Afro-American visionary arts can perhaps be classified into those more influenced by African script traditions or those more influenced by African charm traditions. (Wahlman 29)

If it can be demonstrated that aspects of African religious practice, such as spirit possession, survive in contemporary worship in many black churches, then it may not be too great a stretch to suppose that similar spiritual values, including even a "miniaturization" of spirit possession, might also survive in a compatible tradition of visionary writing. The ability to produce knowledge through "readings" of signs offered by the natural world, as well as the freedom African-American visionaries have found in submission to a spiritual force experienced as the interiorization of an external, self-validating power certainly have resonance with attributes Timothy Simone identifies with African cultural systems.

In traditional African cultures, the surfaces, depths, and beyonds were barely distinguishable from each other. Oscillating the demarcations with his own movements, man was simultaneously located in every dimension. Imprecision, fuzziness, and incomprehension were the very conditions which made it possible to develop a viable knowledge of social relations. Instead of these conditions being a problem to solve by resolute knowledge, they were viewed as the necessary limits to knowledge itself, determined by the value in which such knowledge was held, and the attitudes taken toward it.

There were choices among readings to be made. People looked for the best way to read things. That chosen as the best was not viewed as inherently the best to the exclusion of other readings. The best was one that added resiliency, validation, or sustenance to the *act* of reading. Africans did consider every surface as a surface to be read. Each reading was to add something else that could be said, neither to the detriment, exclusion, or undoing of any other reading. Not all surfaces were visible.

The position of being an individual with a capacity to articulate freely is expressed by the Songhai of Mali as: "I am a voice from elsewhere free to say exactly what they want". . . . Because he voices the thoughts of others, the speaker is not implicated, constrained, or held back in the speaking. His freedom to speak is not contingent upon what he has to say. He can make something happen—invent, undermine, posit, play—without it seeming that he is the one doing it. The speaker is not to be located in the situation he represents or creates with his speech and its concomitant assumptions and ideas. Some part of the speaker is always some place else. Therefore, no matter what happens as a result of the speaking, he is never fully captured, analyzed, apprehended, or pinned down by the listeners. Although this notion sounds like a

Western deconstructive position toward identity in general, the difference in the Songhai context is that this notion is consciously recognized as the precondition for speaking in general and descriptive of the psychological orientation assumed toward speaking. (153–54)

Of course, the Greek and Semitic cultures on which classical Western civilization is founded, and which had carried on a dialogue with Africa through Egypt, both viewed the inspired writer as the instrument of a divine spirit; and outside of scientific or critical discourses, this view of the artist still pertains, at least residually, in discussions of creativity. Also sometimes overlooked in discussions of African-American syncretism is the extent to which African cultures themselves typically have little interest in purity or orthodoxy, but have frequently sought to mesh tradition with exogenous influences.[12]

> Modern Kongo prophets, restructuring Christianity with the tenets of their classical religion, also use such mystic writing. The prophet submits to trance, and is the spirit, he taps unseen potencies, deriving from The Holy Spirit. . . . Vibrations of the spirit [may] blur the letters into undulating hints of powers streaming from the ancestors, from the woods or from the water. . . . This is not writing as the secular world understands such things. This is spiritual oscillography. These texts themselves embody *mayembo* (spiritual ecstasy) or *zakama* (spiritual happiness). In actual Kongo spirit-possession, ecstasy trembles the shoulder-blades of the ritual authority. Here, they ripple the body in a similar fashion, only miniaturized to the compass of a single writing hand.
>
> The spirit enters into the shaping of every single utterance. It leaves a unique impress . . . this is what ecstasy might read like in transcription. (Thompson, 1989, 101)

The Kongo concepts *mayembo* and *zakama* spiritual ecstasy and spiritual happiness, are paramount in the mystical experiences of those African-American preachers Jarena Lee, Zilpha Elaw, and Julia Foote, whose spiritual autobiographies are collected by William L. Andrews in *Sisters of the Spirit*. Each of these women had been disciplined and silenced during a childhood spent as an indentured servant in a white household, and each uses literacy to prepare herself for the visitation of the spirit that will "unbridle" the tongue and allow the reader of the Word to speak in God's name. Jarena Lee, in a spiritual autobiography published in 1836, asserts that her ecstatic experiences (which include visual, aural, and tactile impressions she believes are personal communications with God), derive from her continual preoccupation with spiritual matters.

> As to the nature of uncommon impressions, which the reader cannot but have noticed, and possibly sneered at in the course of these pages, they may be accounted for in this way: It is known that the blind have the sense of hearing in a manner much more acute than those who can see: also their sense of feeling is exceedingly fine, and is found to detect any roughness on the smoothest surface, where those who can see can find none. So it may be with such as [I] am, who has never had more than three months schooling; and wishing to know much of the way and law of God, have

therefore watched the more closely the operations of the spirit, and have in consequence been fed thereby. (Andrews 48)

For Julia Foote, the pursuit of literacy led to self-fulfillment through the fulfillment
of her spiritual aspirations:

> I was a poor reader and a poor writer; but the dear Holy Spirit helped me by quicken-
> ing my mental faculties. The more my besetting sin troubled me, the more anxious I
> became for an education. I believed that, if I were educated, God could make me
> understand what I needed; for, in spite of what others said, it would come to me, now
> and then, that I needed something more than what I had, but what that something
> was I could not tell. (Andrews 182)

Against the prevailing association of blackness with ignorance and sin, Zilpha Elaw,
much like Nat Turner, boldly asserts her intellectual authority and her intimacy with
spiritual power:

> At the commencement of my religious course, I was deplorably ignorant and dark; but
> the Lord himself was graciously pleased to become my teacher, instructing me by his
> Holy Spirit, in the knowledge of the Holy Scriptures. It was not by the aid of human
> instruments that I was first drawn to Christ; and it was by the Lord alone that I was
> upheld, confirmed, instructed, sanctified, and directed. (Andrews 60)

These writers are less interested than Douglass or other ex-slave narrators in providing credible documentary evidence of their literacy than in establishing a claim to
direct spiritual communication with the divine. Such claims authorized their spiritual
literacy, and ranged from attributing rapid learning to an eagerness to read the Bible,
to outright miracles of sudden comprehension, or instruction in the form of spiritual
guides sent in dreams or visions. Jarena Lee experienced her call to preach in a vision
"which was presented to [her] so plainly as if it had been a literal fact." This vision
had as its sequel a dream in which she responds to the call:

> In consequence of this, my mind became so exercised that during the night following, I
> took a text, and preached in my sleep. I thought there stood before me a great multi-
> tude, while I expounded to them the things of religion. So violent were my exertions,
> that I awoke from the sound of my own voice, which also awoke the family of the
> house where I resided. (Andrews 35)

Similar preoccupations with spiritual awakening pervade the journals of Rebecca
Cox Jackson, founder of an African-American Shaker community. Jean Humez argues persuasively that the Shaker religion attracted Jackson in part because of its
emphasis on sexual and racial equality. With the Shakers, who acknowledged her
"gifts of power" as a "spirit-instrument," Jackson found support and encouragement
of her desire to lead a self-sufficient black community. It is also worth noting that,
although the requirement of celibacy would have discouraged most African-
Americans from joining the Shakers, theirs was virtually the only Christian religion
that incorporated ecstatic dance into its worship. Most Protestant sects absolutely

prohibited dancing, and this forbidden pleasure was a temptation to more than one African-American convert.

Zilpha Elaw's parents made a vow to give up dancing and joined the Methodist church after a nearly fatal accident occurred on their way home from a frolic. Later, Elaw's older sister "would run away from home and go to dances—a place forbidden to us all," and Elaw herself, as a youthful Christian, "yielded to the persuasions of the old fiddler," but soon repented her supposed sin: "Had I persisted in dancing, I believe God would have smitten me dead on the spot. . . . What good is all this dissipation of the body and mind? Does dancing help to make you a better Christian?" (Andrews 178).

Among Rebecca Cox Jackson's gifts of power was the gift of literacy, which she explained as the result of divine instruction. Jackson wrote in her spiritual journal, kept from 1830–1864, that "the gift of literacy" came to her after praying to God when her literate brother, who was always too tired or too busy to teach her to read, failed to take accurate dictation of her spoken words when asked to write a letter. (The letter-writing sessions suggest to the reader of her journals the actual material site of her acquisition of literacy, as she alertly watches her brother write down her spoken words and then has him read them back to her.)

> After I received the blessing of God, I had a great desire to read the Bible. . . . And my brother so tired when he would come home that he had not power so to do, and it would grieve me. Then I would pray to God to give me power over my feelings that I might not think hard of my brother. Then I would be comforted. So I went to get my brother to write my letters and to read them. So he was awriting a letter in answer to one he had just read. I told him what to put in. Then I asked him to read. He did. I said, "Thee has put in more than I told thee." This he done several times. I then said, "I don't want thee to word my letter. I only want thee to write it." Then he said, "Sister, thee is the hardest one I ever wrote for!" These words, together with the manner that he had wrote my letter, pierced my soul like a sword. . . . And these words were spoken in my heart, "Be faithful, and the time shall come when you can write." . . . One day I was sitting finishing a dress in haste and in prayer. This word was spoken in my mind, "Who learned the first man on earth?" "Why God." "He is unchangeable, and if He learned the first man to read, He can learn you." I laid down my dress, picked up my Bible, ran upstairs, opened it, and kneeled down with it pressed to my breast, prayed earnestly to Almighty God if it was consisting to His holy will, to learn me to read His holy word. And when I looked on the word, I began to read. (107–8)

In her "dream of three books and a holy one," Jackson, who acquired literacy after age thirty-five, recalled:

> A white man took me by my right hand and led me on the north side of the room, where sat a square table. On it lay a book open. And he said to me, "Thou shall be instructed in the book, from Genesis to Revelations." And he took me on the west side, where stood a table. And it was like the first. And said, "Yea, thou shall be instructed from the beginning of creation to the end of time." And then he took me on

the east side of the room also, where stood a table and book like the two first, and said, "I will instruct thee—yea, thou shall be instructed from the beginning of all things to the end of all things. Yea, thou shall be well instructed, I will instruct." (146)

Jackson's image of the "holy one" who leads and instructs is sustained by the missionary efforts of white preachers as well as prevalent representations of the Christian deity and his angelic assistants. The association of literacy with white men (whose authority seems to be emphasized by the multiplication of books in Jackson's dream, and underlined by the symbolic significance of the square table and the right hand) is also common to early writings of African captives such as Equiano, who wrote in his 1792 narrative, "I had often seen my master and Dick employed in reading; and I had a great curiosity to talk to the books, as I thought they did; and so to learn how all things had a beginning" (43).

Yet Jackson differs from Equiano, and from Douglass, who, with the help of white boys and women, steals the thunder of white men. What distinguishes her representation of the acquisition of literacy is her belief that she learned to read not from any actual white person or persons in her community, nor even from her literate kindred, but from heavenly messengers (visualized as white and male) who appeared in dreams to instruct her. More often, Jackson's inspiration to acquire literacy is represented as encouraging "words spoken in [her] heart," and the extent to which both literacy and Christianity reinforced the authority of male speakers is suggested by the fact that even this inner voice of self-empowerment is described as words of "a tender father" (107–8). Thus the struggle for self-authorization is as dramatic for freeborn or emancipated visionary writers as it is for the ex-slave narrators. Yet it is striking to note that their reliance on visions, dreams, inner voices, and possession by The Holy Spirit, empowering them to speak and write, also may be seen as attempts of African-Americans, in the process of acquiring literacy, to fuse the inspiriting techniques of Christian prayer and biblical textuality with African traditions of oral and visual expressiveness. Protestantism in particular seems to have reinforced certain African cultural uses of "spirit-writing," while fostering an African-American visionary literacy that values and legitimates the protective power of writing over the use of ritual objects. Such objects or charms are now more closely associated in African-American culture with the persistence of African spiritual practices, while the links connecting African-American visionary literacy to African script-systems have, until recently, been obscured. The secular tradition of the blues paradoxically has circulated certain spiritual knowledge concerning the use of the *mojo*, while the Protestant religious tradition, with its emphasis on textuality, has been quite instrumental in promoting secular literacy among African Americans.

African-American literature of the 19th century registers the emergence of a specifically African-American culture marked by a productive tension between individuality and collectivity, and between the sacred and secular, aspects of everyday life that African cultures had worked to integrate seamlessly through communal rituals that forged collective identities and assured human beings of their significance in the universe. Certainly the ex-slave narrators' entry into the public discourse on slavery and freedom was politically and historically crucial, and their writings continue to resonate in the "call and response" that Robert Stepto designated as the characteristic mode of African-American literary influence. Yet it is also thanks to the complementary traditions of folk and visionary artists and writers who have preserved aspects of African and diasporic cultural consciousness in their syncretically visual and visionary works, that the secular and spiritual traditions of African-American literacy have begun once again to merge aesthetically, not in collective ritual, but in the work of contemporary visual and performance artists, such as Xenobia Bailey, Romare Bearden, John Biggers, Houston Conwill, Mel Edwards, David Hammons, Philip Jones, Ed Love, Robbie McCauley, Alison Saar, Betye Saar, Joyce Scott, Lorna Simpson, Renee Stout, Michael Cummings, Jawole Willa Jo Zollar, and others (whose works have been studied by art critics, curators, and art historians, including Mary Schmidt Campbell, Kellie Jones, Kinshasha Conwill, Judith McWillie, Lowery Sims, Alvia Wardlaw, and Judith Wilson) as well as in the work of contemporary African-American writers, such as Toni Cade Bambara, Octavia Butler, Randall Kenan, Ishmael Reed, Adrienne Kennedy, Nathaniel Mackey, Toni Morrison, Gloria Naylor, Ntozake Shange, and Alice Walker, in whose works and texts it is possible to read "the persistence of vision" (Mullen 10–13).

NOTES

1. See Henry Louis Gates's *Figures in Black*.
2. See Thompson's *Flash of the Spirit* and "The Song That Named the Land."
3. I have written more extensively about this tradition in *Gender and the Subjugated Body: Readings of Race, Subjectivity, and Difference in the Construction of Slave Narratives* (Ph.D. dissertation, University of California, Santa Cruz, 1990).
4. Similarly, the elaborately decorative, asymmetrically grid-like "devil houses" drawn in bichromatic red and blue colored pencil by illiterate prison artist Frank Jones were meant to confine and imprison the dangerous "spirits" that Jones had seen since childhood, as a result of having been "born with a veil over his left eye." Lynne Adele speculates, "Like the individuals Jones encountered in his physical world, the inhabitants of his spiritual world were often dangerous. The haints tormented and haunted Jones, but by capturing them on paper and enclosing them in the cell-like rooms of the houses, he could render them harmless" (42). Jones and Murray may share the African-American aesthetic of quilt-makers such as Pecolia Warner, whose work, according to Maude Southwell Wahlman, employs "multiple patterning, asymmetry, and unpredictable rhythms and tensions similar to those found in other Afro-American visual arts and in blues, jazz, Black English, and dance." Traditionally African-American tropes expressing tension between discontinuity/continuity, innovation/tradition, individuality/community, movement/stasis, passage/confinement and inclusion/exclusion are addressed not only in the literary canon, but also in the work of illiterate quilters and painters who improvise various, idiosyncratic, irregular rhythms upon the stable, containing structure of the grid. According to Wahlman, "Multiple patterning, and vestiges of script-like forms and designs, are especially evident in Afro-American [folk] paintings" (33).
5. See also Ruth Bass's "Mojo" and "The Little Man."

6. See Angelo Costanzo's *Surprising Narrative: Olaudah Equiano and the Beginnings of Black Autobiography*.

7. See Gates's *The Signifying Monkey* (127–69).

8. Douglass's acquisition of literacy alienates him from the culture of plantation slaves, whose attempt to create culture and community is increasingly viewed by the narrator as mere accommodation to their enslavement. Recent scholarship has expanded to include a broader spectrum of the slave community in addition to extraordinary individuals, such as Douglass, whose literacy and public stature allowed his immediate entry into the historical record. With a more extensive set of scholarly tools, it has become possible to appreciate the cultural contributions of slaves who left transcribed oral accounts and visual records of their existence. While Douglass's "copy-book" literacy implied a white male model, despite his oppositional stance, folklorist Gladys-Marie Fry shows that slave women making quilts for their own families rejected the patterns found in quilting copybooks they had followed when supervised by their mistresses. They used opportunities to make their own quilts as occasions for enjoying their own oral expressiveness, and preferred their own cultural aesthetic when it came to making quilts for their own use. My argument is that new insights into African-American literature emerge when texts are read in relation to a continuum of expressivity that includes forms which are oral, visual, tactile, kinesthetic, nonliterate, and extraliterate, as well as literate:

> [S]laves made two types of quilts: those for their personal use, made on their own time; and quilts for the big house, stitched under the supervision of the mistress. . . . The plantation mistress learned some traditional patterns from English copybooks. . . . Slave women, however, learned traditional quilting patterns not only from the mistress but also from each other. . . . Slave women also used original patterns for their personal quilts. . . . Slaves quilted during their 'own time'. . . . Often during more extended periods of free time, such as Sundays and holidays, authorized quilting parties were held in the quarters for slave women to pass the time making quilts while telling stories and passing along gossip about plantation events. . . . The glue that helped cement the fragile and uncertain existence of slave life was their oral lore. It was an ever-present force—sometimes the main event, as in the slave quilting party—and sometimes the background event while slaves sewed, mended, knitted, and such. But present it was. While the official learning of the master's literate world was denied the slave, it was the slave's oral lore that taught moral lessons, values, attitudes, strategies for survival, rites of passage, and humor! Folklore helped to preserve the slaves' sense of identity, of knowing who they were and how they perceived the world. Folk traditions also served as a buffer between the slaves and a hostile world, both on and off the plantation. For it was in the slave quarters that African traditions first met and intersected with Euro-American cultural forms. What emerged were transformations, adaptations, and reinterpretations. (39, 45–49, 63–64)

9. Perhaps for similar reasons as Douglass, Arna Bontemps also rejects the models of leadership and resistance offered by Vesey and Turner. Desiring to write a novel based on one of the most significant historically documented slave insurrections, Bontemps chose the rebellion led by Gabriel Prosser over the equally doomed plots of Vesey and Turner. While all three conspiracies failed, Prosser's style of leadership seemed preferable to the author. Bontemps wrote in his introduction to the novel, "Gabriel had not opened his mind too fully and hence had not been betrayed as had Vesey. He had by his own dignity and by the esteem in which he was held inspired and maintained loyalty. He had not depended on trance-like mumbo jumbo"

(xii, xiii). Yet Prosser's leadership was not devoid of a spiritual or religious component, since he was probably to some degree influenced by his brother Martin, a preacher and co-leader of the insurrection. See also Sterling Stuckey's *Slave Culture* and Herbert Aptheker's *American Negro Slave Revolts*.

10. Slave traders and masters deliberately mixed together Africans from diverse ethnolinguistic groups in order to prevent organized escape and rebellion. This uprooting and fragmentation of language and culture indeed destroyed the traditional bonds of kinship (and the kinship-based authority of the African patriarch) that had organized the collective identities of Africans. Although the common experience of the Middle Passage forged bonds among recent captives, many individuals did not begin to identify themselves racially with black people of other "nations" until slaves had forged a common African-American culture, while trying to hold together their slave families in their harsh, new environment. Their traditional group identification shattered, such displaced individuals (often adolescents who, like Equiano, were captured before they would have been ritually initiated into their clans) were sometimes easily manipulated by their masters, resulting in the disunity and betrayal of slaves who attempted to escape in groups or conspired to incite insurrection. Douglass's retrospective skepticism about the potency of the phallic root is in part the result of his strong suspicion that his first escape attempt had been betrayed by Sandy, the African-born conjuror. See also *American Negro Slavery*.

11. See Plate 13 (between pp. 88–90) in Lucy R. Lippard's *Mixed Blessings*.

12. Discussing contemporary race relations in the U.S., Timothy M. Simone points hopefully to this imaginative ability of black culture to embrace rather than repulsing otherness: "Although there is great variation among African societies . . . what is common among them is their ability to make the Other an integral aspect of their cultural and psychological lives. . . . When I ask my students to describe the basic difference between whites and blacks, the most-often-cited factor is the degree to which blacks are willing to extend themselves to the outside, to incorporate new ideas and influences with a minimum of a priori judgment. Minister Neal Massoud of the Nation of Islam: 'Our power has been our ability to extend ourselves to that which seems implausible, to that which makes little sense. . . . We have extended ourselves to both the unseen and the visible, to the fruits of our labor and the graves we have dug for them' " (57–58).

WORKS CITED

Adele, Lynne. *Black History/Black Vision: The Visionary Image in Texas*. The Gallery. Austin: University of Texas Press, 1989.

American Negro Slavery. Ed. Michael Mullin. New York: Harper and Row, 1976.

Andrews, William L. *Sisters of the Spirit: Three Black Women's Autobiographies of the Nineteenth Century*. Bloomington: Indiana University Press, 1986.

Aptheker, Herbert. *American Negro Slave Revolts*. New York: International Publishers, 1983; first published, New York: Columbia University Press, 1943.

Bass, Ruth. "Mojo" and "The Little Man." *Motherwit from the Laughing Barrel*. Ed. Alan Dundes. New York: Prentice Hall, 1973.

Bontemps, Arna. *Black Thunder*. Boston: Beacon Press, 1968; first published by Macmillan, 1936.

Costanzo, Angelo. *Surprising Narrative: Olaudah Equiano and the Beginnings of Black Autobiography*. New York: Greenwood Press, 1987.

Davis, Charles T., and Henry L. Gates, Jr. *The Slave's Narrative*. New York: Oxford University Press, 1985.

Douglass, Frederick. *Narrative*. *The Classic Slave Narratives*. Ed. Henry Louis Gates, Jr. New York: New American Library, 1987.

Equiano, Olaudah. *Travels*. *The Classic Slave Narratives*. Ed. Henry Louis Gates, Jr. New York: New American Library, 1987.

Fry, Gladys-Marie. *Stitched from the Soul: Slave Quilts from the Antebellum South*. New York: Dutton Studio Books/Museum of American Folk Art, 1990.

Gates, Henry Louis, Jr. *Figures in Black: Words, Signs, and the "Racial" Self*. New York: Oxford University Press, 1987.

———. *The Signifying Monkey*. New York: Oxford University Press, 1988.

Jackson, Rebecca Cox. *Gifts of Power: The Writings of Rebecca Jackson, Black Visionary, Shaker Eldress*. Ed. Jean McMahon Humez. Amherst: The University of Massachusetts Press, 1981.

Lippard, Lucy R. *Mixed Blessings: New Art in a Multicultural America*. New York: Pantheon Books, 1990.

Lowe, Donald. *History of Bourgeois Perception*. Chicago: University of Chicago Press, 1982.

Mullen, Kirsten. "The Persistence of Vision." *Rambling on My Mind: Black Folk Art in the Southwest*. Dallas: Museum of African-American Life and Culture, 1987.

Nasisse, Andy. "Aspects of Visionary Art." *Baking in the Sun: Visionary Images from the South*. University Art Museum. Lafayette: University of Southwestern Louisiana, 1987.

Nat Turner. Ed. Eric Foner. Englewood Cliffs, NJ: Prentice-Hall, 1971.

Piper, Adrian. "The Triple Negation of Colored Women Artists." *New Generation: Southern Black Aesthetic*. New York: Southeastern Center for Contemporary Art, 1990.

Simone, Timothy Maliqalim. *About Face: Race in Postmodern America*. Brooklyn: Autonomedia, 1989.

Stepto, Robert B. *From Behind the Veil: A Study of Afro-American Narrative*. Urbana: University of Illinois Press, 1979.

Stuckey, Sterling. *Slave Culture: Nationalist Theory and the Foundations of Black America*. New York: Oxford University Press, 1987.

Thompson, Robert Farris. "The Song That Named the Land: The Visionary Presence in African-American Art." *Black Art: Ancestral Legacy*. Dallas Museum of Art. New York: Harry N. Abrams, Inc., 1989. 97–141.

———. *Flash of the Spirit*. New York: Vintage Books/Random House, 1983.

Wahlman, Maude Southwell. "Africanisms in Afro-American Visionary Arts." *Baking in the Sun*. Ed. Herman Mhire. Lafayette: University Art Museum, University of Southwestern Louisiana, 1987.

48

Mapping the Interstices between Afro-American Cultural Discourse and Cultural Studies

A Prolegomenon

Wahneema Lubiano

(1996)

I

Afro-American cultural discourse in and of itself is a complicated terrain to negotiate. To comprehensively situate it alongside other politically engaged theoretical discourses requires a breadth and depth the finite constraints of this essay do not allow. Thus, my title: A Prolegomenon. What follows, then, is in the nature of an approach to a longer intervention that requires the work of others; as such an approach it raises the issues and goes over some of the ground of recently argued critiques of Afro-American Studies and literary discourse.

The problem of tackling the complexities of the relationship between something as amorphous as Afro-American[1] cultural studies (or cultural theory) is further exacerbated by how little is known about it. I begin, therefore, with a note about terms. For the purposes of my discussion here, when I refer to Afro-American cultural discourse, I include under that rubric Afro-American Studies and Afro-American literary discourse.

Afro-American Studies is a name for the institutionalization of a set of imperatives, approaches, political engagements, and privileged "interdisciplinariness" as paradigms and sites for counter-hegemonic cultural work. Historically, intellectuals involved in Afro-American Studies have seen their work as explicit and implicit interruptions (or attempts to interrupt) the traditional academic strangleholds on knowledge categories. The object of their interventions is to change the world by means of demystifying the relationship of "knowledge" producers to "knowledge," as well as to foreground the connection between "culture" and Afro-American "everyday life."

By *Afro-American literary discourse* I refer generally to the critical and theoretical discourse around the production and interpretation of texts by and about African

Americans. Afro-American literary discourse is not now nor has it ever been mono-lithic; however, what has been consistent within the explicit and implicit terms of that discourse (as well as within Afro-American Studies in its institutional manifes-tations within the academy itself) is a concern with relations of power and with social and economic history.

As an undergraduate and first-year graduate student at Howard University, I read C. L. R. James, Frantz Fanon, Aimé Césaire's *Discourse on Colonialism*, as well as the theories of language in which the Black Aesthetic critics engaged—notably Larry Neal, Stephen Henderson, and Addison Gayle—therefore, when I began to read post-structuralist theories (principally Derrida and Barthes) of language and cultural theory, my reaction was one of surprised recognition: how nice, I thought, they do this stuff, too. Deconstruction, for example, seemed to me to be an extension (within the dominant discourse) of the project of those already engaged in Afro-American or Black Studies—the project of theorizing about difference, absences, presences, and oppositionality. My response to the cultural studies discourse has been much the same.

Given my recognition of the salience of Afro-American cultural discourse to con-temporary debates, issues, and imperatives, I intend this essay not only to delineate the resonances in Afro-American Studies and cultural studies, but to foreground the problematic represented by particular uses of cultural studies vis-à-vis Afro-American Studies. That is to say, I want to intervene in framing and historicizing the discourse of contemporary Afro-American cultural discourse—especially given current discus-sions of cultural studies. I mean, by "cultural studies," to refer to cultural studies as an approach, as actual kinds of interdisciplinary work, and as politically engaged critique. Cultural studies focuses on the interstices between the structures of material life—economic and political—that determine the limits of human existence and means by which people imagine their relationship to their lives—the productions that result from that imagination.[2] According to Richard Johnson, "Cultural studies can be defined as an intellectual and political tradition, in its relations to academic disciplines, in terms of its theoretical paradigms, or by its characteristic objects of studies" (41–42). As I argue below, those characteristics describe African American Studies' imperatives and agenda. Stuart Hall's description of and work on cultural studies has in common with Afro-American Studies (as it has been theorized) both political purposefulness and "open-endedness"—neither paradigms that stake out the finality of a finished theoretical position. Because of the recent interest in cultural studies within universities and literature studies, its discourse is both important and problematic for Afro-American Studies, especially given certain critiques of Afro-American literary discourse that evoke cultural studies to the disadvantage of Afro-American literary discourse. The weight of such critiques is being added to the weight of more conventional critiques from pluralist Americanist critics. It is against this background that I want to make visible past invisible theorizing within Afro-American Studies and literary discourse—invisible to the dominant culture—and I want to extend further current theorizing within Afro-American Studies.

During the late 1960s, 1970s, and early 1980s, individuals and groups engaged in the work of Afro-American/Black Studies articulated the agenda of Afro-American Studies in terms of intellectual questions and political imperatives. The discussion went on primarily in marginalized places—historically Black colleges, associations (formal and informal) of professionals involved with Black Studies; within marginalized journals (*Journal of Negro Education, The Black Scholar, Western Journal of Black Studies, Black World, Journal of Afro-American Issues*, and numerous others)—and within the marginalized institutional spaces of Black colleges. Whether or not Afro-American Studies programs, approaches, or literature were taught in large, predominantly "White" research universities or Black colleges/universities, the various "institutions" of Afro-American Studies always occupied marginalized space. Even at Howard University, for example, the first Negro literature courses there, taught by Sterling Brown, were referred to by its administration as "nigger literature." Sterling Brown found it difficult to keep his job there, and Afro-American Studies came into being at Howard (as at other places) largely as the result of demands from politicized students. It has had a vexed existence ever since; the origins, ethos, and continued existence of Afro-American Studies, then, have been explicitly political.

The imperative of the work of Afro-American cultural discourse is and has been (whether explicitly stated or implicitly engaged) to engage itself in a two-part project: (1) what Frantz Fanon calls the necessary reclamation of a history and a culture as a revision of the "big lies" of the colonizer[3] and (2) what Abdul JanMohamed and David Lloyd have described as the resort to cultural modes of struggle necessary in the face of a global economy that marginalizes third world and minority people.[4] JanMohamed and Lloyd remind us that the physical survival of minority groups depends on the recognition of their cultures as viable (8). The history of Afro-American cultural production is and has been marked/driven by that awareness. And within its institutional manifestations it has been historically specific. Affirming Afro-American culture, then, is not to be confused with affirming the bourgeois status quo—the sum of the best produced by a ruling elite—but an insistence on the terms of another subjectivity, another marginalized subjectivity.

II

The late St. Clair Drake summed up the relationship of Black Studies to the dominant academy in language that should resonate with those engaged in cultural studies (he is quoted here from an early unpublished essay by Gerald McWhorter):

> The very use of the term Black Studies is by implication an indictment of American and Western European scholarship. It makes the bold assertion that what we have heretofore called "objective" intellectual activities were actually *white* studies in perspective and content; and that corrective bias, a shift in emphasis, is needed, even if

something called "truth" is set as a goal. . . . the present body of knowledge has an ideological element in it, and a counter-ideology is needed. Black Studies supply [*sic*] that counter-ideology.[5]

He later described the contestation, national and global, that inheres in Afro-American Studies as a dynamic that focuses on the tensions that inhere within a group as complicated as people of African descent across the world as well as between the group and the rest of the world.[6] The tension and global emphasis have been, according to Drake, "a historic concern of Afro-American intellectuals" because of the concerns of such intellectuals with the effect of worldwide conditions on their existence and the complexities of that existence (100). Along with a concern for the material existence of people of African descent in the United States and the world, Afro-American Studies, like cultural studies, has been cognizant of its contestatory relation to the dominant group within the realm of the academy. Johnnetta Cole asserts that scholars and activists of Black Studies charged that

> western scholarship suffered from a gender and class bias—a point that was tangential to the main charge of racism for some, but a point of equal centrality for others. . . . I am no less convinced than I was in the 1960s that Black Studies can be an essential corrective scholarship for certain biases in mainstream academics. (McWhorter and Bailey 23)

Cole's language delineates both the contestatory nature of the relation between Black Studies and the larger domain, but also that within the ranks itself—she is cognizant of the agenda as one still in flux, still fought over, in regard to gender and class.

Lucius Outlaw, in a review of a philosophy syllabi, speaks to the contestatory and political nature of Black Studies' engagement within and against the terrain of academic disciplines:

> The significance of this situation is understood when we take note of a basic feature and commitment of philosophical praxis: the articulation of a person's or peoples' understanding of themselves, or others, of the world and history, and of their place in them both, in the most fundamental sense. Western philosophy, along with religion and theology, continues to be the principal keep of the self-image in its most reflective, articulate form. More than that, in its dominant tendencies and driving orientations, it seeks to define and stand guard over what it means to be "a human being" as well. . . . At the same time, we must contribute to the construction of knowledge of and ideals for ourselves and the world's people that are more in keeping with the struggle to achieve a democratically just and liberated world. (McWhorter and Bailey 23)

Afro-American/Black Studies, then, has already engaged itself in the struggle that some cultural studies critics are at pains to suggest it undertake.

Of course, this sense of the contestatory nature of the domain of culture is not the only thing that Afro-American Studies and literary discourse has in common with cultural studies. Cultural studies takes as its subject of study the interstices between material life and cultural production. It focuses on subcultural style as a site for its examination. Such has also been the focus of African American intellectuals. Zora Neale Hurston's anthropological work resulted in representations and theorizing about everyday cultural practices of African Americans. She repeatedly emphasized the transformative value of vernacular cultural reworkings of the dominant culture's artifacts:

> So if we look at it squarely, the Negro is a very original being. While he lives and moves in the midst of a white civilization, everything that he touches is reinterpreted for his own use. He has modified the language, mode of food preparation, practice of medicine, and most certainly the religion of his new country, just as he adapted to suit himself the Sheik haircut made famous by Rudolph Valentino.
>
> Everyone is familiar with the Negro's modification of the whites' musical instruments, that his interpretation has been adapted by the white man himself and then reinterpreted.[7]

Consider that passage in relation to the following passage on subcultural style from the Center for Contemporary Cultural Studies:[8]

> They adopt and adapt material objects—goods and possessions and reorganize them into distinctive styles which express the collectivity of their being-as-a-group. These concerns, activities, relationships, materials become embodied in rituals of relationship and occasion and movement. Sometimes, the world is marked out, linguistically, by names or an *argot* which classifies the social world exterior to them in terms meaningful only within their group perspective, and maintains its boundaries. (Hall 471)

Hurston's project is only one site that offers fecund possibilities for cultural studies theorists to "discover" a pre-existing body of work with similar imperative with regard to readings of "everyday life" and "style" as subversion.

I've talked only very briefly about Hurston's work as fitting within cultural studies paradigms and imperatives, but I don't want to suggest that Afro-American Studies and Afro-American literary discourse be re-read solely in order to make its correspondences with other paradigms apparent. The emphasis within Afro-American Studies is to read Afro-American texts and cultural practices in ways that foreground their politicized historicity. Such reading is part of the larger project: to transform the world.

The attempt to control their histories and to be politically engaged on the part of African American intellectuals and other persons interested in Afro-American Studies stems from what Sylvia Wynter argues is an urge to constitute African American existence here and African existence on the continent as "institutional and therefore ontological fact" rather than allow those existences to remain simply "brute" or "empirical fact."[9]

Such strategic will to constitute a new institutional and ontological object of knowledge is present from the beginning of African American existence here, consistent across "history" within the discourse. What these nationalist projects argue— between antagonists within the field—is whether the agenda insists on a monolithic resistance, specific to the demands of momentary political imperatives—a Black countering essence—or whether each strategy engages another site of intra-group difference.

III

Against the exhortations of Americanist pluralists that African Americanists not engage in separatist agendas, Russell Adams reminds us that African Americanists do not have to promote intellectual separatism; the separatism is already present.[10] Still, Adams also argues in favor of the Afro-American Studies agenda "having as much influence on American epistemological thought as black musicians influenced the music of the Western world.[11] Whether imposed or claimed, separatism has to be abrogated, at carefully strategized sites, in order to contest the production of knowledge.

Those interested in reconstituting "Afro-Americanness" were both engaged in interventionist narrative and problematically enthralled, to various degrees, by the romance of particular methodologies. Precisely because of the necessary relation of their institutionalizing and cultural practice to the everyday material conditions and cultural practices for people held not to have any culture and therefore, like the "urban underclass" of the present, to be outside of the protections of civil liberties when the nation is caught in the grip of an emergency. This is only one, but a salient, example that is repeated in various violent and non-violent manifestations across the spectrum of African American lived life.

Following the pattern of continual reconstitution of Afro-Americanness established from as varied a group as one could imagine—both "off-campus" (Adams's ironic categorization of community Black Studies work from the early 18th century through the early 20th century)[12] and on-campus—ex-slaves, craftspersons, laborers, intellectuals, political activists, preachers, and the critics of the Harlem Renaissance rewrote African American history in order to rewrite African American identity and to transform the *material conditions of African American life.* They were interested in scientizing, in specialized professional discourses—something about which some later manifestations of Black Studies (as Drake, Cole, and Outlaw above note) would be suspicious, a suspicion embodied in critiques of "objectivity" and other paradigms of Western knowledge. The interest in what were perceived as Euro-American methods inhered in Alain Locke's counter-narratives of African art.[13] He saw African art as "rigid, controlled, disciplined, non-representational, and laconic" (254). All were characteristics that he opposed to Afro-American art (to that art's detriment), which he described as "emotional, sentimental, exuberant," due, he argued, to the peculiarly Euro-American tendencies of sentimentality (255). In other words, Locke counters stereotypes of Negroes and their production as emotional, overly exuberant, and sentimental by reference to "African" art, the characteristics of which were vastly different. He then attributes those normative markers (emotional, etc.) of "Negro" art to Euro-Americans—White folks. He constructs a new essence that draws on what he and others believed to be Western ideas (scientificity, professionalism, aesthetics) in order to unseat Western constructions of "Negroness." It was a cute move for that moment: his assertion that White people were the emotional, exuberant, sentimental ones, and that what we (African Americans) needed was to go, metaphorically at least, back to Africa. But lest we forget the contestatory nature of Afro-American cultural discourse, for every argument that deconstructed "Western" notions in order to posit African American positive counters, there was an argument within the group that insisted that we could not afford to do any such thing.

Arthur Schomberg shared Locke's (and Du Bois's, for that matter) insistence on the necessity, for the politically empowering possibilities, of "stating the truth." In his arguments, such drive for the truth took the form of an exhortation that African Americans needed professional, disciplinary history to be the hallmark of Afro-American Studies.[14] Schomberg's exhortation rests on at least 200 previous years of African American contestation of the specious truth claims of Euro-American professional histories of Africans and Africans in America as Gates's (and others) work has made clear. It is commonplace by now to recognize the parameters of dominant historiography that have variously inscribed in the public discourse the African (in and out of America) as the missing link between human kind and apes (at worst) or, (at best) the empty Black chalkboard upon which enlightened European and Euro-American civilization would make its mark.

Schomberg's response was also an exhortation to African American male scholars to do "real man" historiography, something especially salient among those angry with representations of the group as "feminized" by its history, its powerlessness—womanlike in its relation to male-like "Whiteness," a Whiteness constructed as civilized rationality. This notion, to which African American males responded so strongly, was in fact concretized in Robert Park's assertion that the Negro was the "lady of the races."[15]

IV

It isn't enough, however, to say that Afro-American Studies has always involved manifestations of what is now recognized as the cultural studies imperative. It is important to consider how things go on within the field, just what a properly historicized consideration of the terms of Afro-American literary discourse, an exercise of the kind of work Afro-American Studies has always encouraged, allows us to consider. Afro-American writers and writing fit into this discussion in a number of ways. Their position has been defined historically in terms of racial construction as a sub-group and an amalgamation of two groups: (1) people of African and/or African mixed with European descent, and (2) people whose lives are in the geopolitical sense North American. It is a position historically defined and complicated in terms of their relationship to "Americanness"—Americanness meaning autonomous; able to exercise the choice (always within the terms of a particular historical moment) of whether or not to work; free to choose (again, as always, qualified) work—the kind, the sites, the duration, free to have a family, to worship, to be educated, to make music, art, literature—in short, to make culture. Slaves did not enjoy any of those privileges, those freedoms—so geopolitical location—in North America—was meaningless as a marker of identity. Slaves could not be considered American under those terms. They lived lives of contradiction—bodies in but not of America. While the material condition of African Americans is no longer predicated on slavery, de jure physical autonomy has not completely undermined the ideology that perpetuates both economic and symbolic inequities or the power imbalance between African Americans and Euro-Americans as groups.

What interests me is a consideration of the differences within the group (African Americans) and between African Americans and Euro-Americans in the time since slavery. Vernacular analysis, as Gates, Baker, and others set it out, takes the differences within the group into account. It is important that the analysis do so, otherwise we would only talk to or argue against the dominant domain; we would exist only to oppose or resist the dominant discourse.

Certain Afro-American texts showcase the nexus of Afro-American material life and deconstructive politicized engagements with/against the terms of the dominant culture. Such texts allow us to theorize about the relationship to transformation of the African American quotidian—not in the romantic sense, but in the sense of considering the nexus of material costs and effective rebellions.

The Color Purple intervenes, in vernacular fashion, in the discourses of race and gender while unpacking the relationship of those constructions to the economic constraint imposed on an African American woman. One passage lays out the juxtapositions and foregrounds the attempted theft of a kind of emotional "surplus value" tied to forced maternalness. Sofia is forced to be a maid for the mayor's wife and nanny or mammy to the mayor's children. But Sofia has an emotional labor demanded of her also—a demand that she rejects in her exchange with Miss Eleanor Jane, one of her former charges, now a mother herself.[16] Eleanor Jane comes to visit Sofia with her small son, Reynolds Stanley Earl, and attempts to force Sofia to "admit" that she loves the child. Eleanor Jane, a child Sofia was forced to "mother," makes a demand for a re-energized and voluntary "mothering" from Sofia. It is a parodic "high noon" moment, only the OK Corral is the living room of Sofia's own family. Eleanor Jane's demand is that Sofia must "love" Reynolds Stanley as Sofia "loved" Eleanor Jane. This demand is especially outrageous given the beating, maiming, and imprisonment that Sofia has suffered at the hands of Eleanor Jane's father—the mayor—and the Sheriff.

The face-off ends with Sofia's refusal to say that she loves that child despite all of Eleanor Jane's attempts to make Sofia bear witness to the endearing quality of Reynolds Stanley and despite her reminders to Sofia of their own closeness:

> I just don't understand, say Miss Eleanor Jane. All the other colored women I know love children. The way you feel is something unnatural.
> I love children say Sofia. But all the colored women that say they love yours is lying. They don't love Reynolds Stanley any more than I do. But if you so badly raise as to ast 'em, what you expect them to say? Some colored people so scared of whitefolks they claim to love the cotton gin.

I got my own troubles, say Sofia, and when Reynolds Stanley grown up, he's gon be one of them.

But he won't, say Miss Eleanor Jane. I'm his mama and I won't let him be mean to colored.

You and whose army? say Sofia. The first word he likely to speak won't be nothing he learn from you.

You telling me I won't even be able to love my own son, say Miss Eleanor Jane.

No, say Sofia. That's not what I'm telling you. I'm telling you I won't be able to love your own son. You can love him just as much as you want to. But be ready to suffer the consequences. That's how the colored live. (272–73)

"How the colored live" ties together what cultural studies and vernacular theorists refer to as the styles of living as well as the material conditions under which "colored" live. This text makes the quotidian of African American life in that period—the cotton gin—the means by which Sofia engages both a critique of Eleanor Jane's manners, who is badly enough raised that she asks colored women whether they love white children, and a critique of the material conditions of their lives: they pick cotton and are further required to give up the surplus of their emotional production also. By first engaging in a style battle, the indirection of answering Eleanor Jane's questions without answering them, and then in a more directly analytical vein, Sofia represents a means to historicize love and ownership.

Given the fairly recent interest on the part of the dominant culture in Afro-American literature, however, complicating that attention is, or ought to be, of great importance to Afro-Americanists. My contribution in this brief essay is to try to interrupt the historical and contemporary dismissal of the discourse of African Americans around their own production.

Finally, the rest of the world is going to interest itself in the discourse of critics of Afro-American literature and of other cultural workers engaged in Afro-American Studies. Therefore, it behooves us (Afro-Americanists) to try to make sure the world does not simplify Afro-American cultural production, does not again rewrite Afro-American history or meta-commentary, does not leave us out of the discussion of ourselves. It is our imperative and that of scholars of minority discourses in general to complicate this "new" discovery of other "Americans." Otherwise our various groups' cultural productions will become simply new colonies for theoretical appropriation and exploitation.

NOTES

1. A note on names: Afro-American literature/Studies has been the customary nomenclature for a particular body of work, but I also follow the contemporary use "African American" to refer to individuals or the group as a way of historicizing the presence of folks of African descent who live here. Additionally, a historical study of Afro-American literature or Studies runs into the complication of the usage of the 1960s and 1970s (and sometimes earlier) when

Afro-American/Black Studies/literature programs were being constituted in the heat of the political moment and the common nomenclature was "Black." My variety of uses tries to pay attention to and sort out these complexities.

2. My understanding of cultural studies is drawn from Stuart Hall ("Subcultures, Cultures, and Class: A Theoretical Overview," *Resistance Through Ritual: Youth Subculture in Postwar Britain*, ed. Stuart Hall, J. Clarke, T. Jefferson, and B. Roberts [London: Hutchinson, 1976]) and Richard Johnson ("What Is Cultural Studies Anyway?" *Social Text* [1986–1987]: 38–80). Subsequent references appear parenthetically within the text.

3. Frantz Fanon, *The Wretched of the Earth* (1961; New York: Grove Press, 1968), 226.

4. Abdul JanMohamed and David Llyod, "Introduction: Minority Discourse—What Is to Be Done?" *Cultural Critique* (Fall 1987): 7–9. Subsequent references appear parenthetically within the text.

5. Gerald A. McWhorter and Ronald Bailey, "Black Studies Curriculum Development in the 1980s: Its Patterns and History," *Black Studies* 15.2 (1984): 22–23. Emphasis is mine. Subsequent references appear parenthetically within the text.

6. St. Clair Drake, "Black Studies and Global Perspectives: An Essay," *Journal of Negro Education* 53.3 (1984): 100. Subsequent references appear parenthetically within the text.

7. Zora Neale Hurston, "Characteristics of Negro Experience," *Voices from the Harlem Renaissance*, ed. Nathan Irvin Huggins (New York: Oxford University Press, 1976), 230.

8. Thanks to Eric Nelson for bringing this juxtaposition to my attention in my graduate seminar "The Harlem Renaissance and the Roots of African Literary Theory."

9. Sylvia Wynter, "On Disenchanting Discourse: 'Minority' Literary Criticism and Beyond," *Cultural Critique* (Fall 1987): 208.

10. Russell Adams, "Intellectual Questions and Imperatives in the Development of Afro-American Studies," *Journal of Negro Education* 53.3 (1984): 207. See also Henry Louis Gates, Jr., "On the Rhetoric of Racism in the Profession," *African Literature Association Bulletin* 15.1 (1989): 11–21.

11. Russell Adams, "Black Studies Perspectives," *Journal of Negro Education* 46.2 (1977): 225.

12. See Adams's "Black Studies Perspectives."

13. Alain Locke, "The Legacy of the Ancestral Arts," *The New Negro*, ed. Alain Locke (New York: Atheneum, 1977), 254–56. Subsequent references appear parenthetically within the text.

14. Arthur Schomberg, "The Negro Digs Up His Past," *The New Negro*, ed. Alain Locke (New York: Atheneum, 1977), 231–37.

15. Robert Park, *Race and Culture: Essays in the Sociology of Contemporary Man* (Glencoe, IL: Free Press, 1950), 280.

16. Alice Walker, *The Color Purple* (New York: Harcourt Brace Jovanovich, 1982), 270–73. Subsequent references appear parenthetically within the text.

49 Cultural Narratives Passed On

African American Mourning Stories

Karla F. C. Holloway

(1997)

Two Chicago stories frame this particular passed-on narrative. But that city is representative of other cities and their stories. New York and D.C., Atlanta and Birmingham and even L.A. stories reside as easily within this frame. Whether the stories are fictive or factual, the mourning stories of African American culture form a cultural narrative. These narratives are "passed on" in both senses of the expression—they are stories about death, and they are shared within the culture and from generation to generation. It is my argument as well that they constitute a cultural narrative because dimensions of African American ethnicity find a borderlined identity within their urban frames.

From the perspective of these stories, a nation's stories are excerpted, a community is demarcated, and in these ways, a culture's identity emerges as malignantly defined through shallow "blackface" impressions. The irony and sorrow of this narrow and negative glimpse at culture is that a community's culture can be isolated and identified through the narrative of its mourning stories, passed on.

This essay rehearses some of these twentieth-century narratives as they have appeared in our nation's history and as they have been represented in African American literature. Their coherence is troubling because it constructs the most damaging dimensions of stereotype. Despite the ways in which Ossie Davis's character Reverend Purlie Victorious described the "sweetness" of blackness as a "secret cup of gladness," black memories in African American culture are as painful as they are precious. Certainly, there are sweet black memories—Easter Sunday speeches in black churches, the swell of voices rising together in the Negro National Anthem, braiding a black girl's hair, and the practiced ritual recitation of James Weldon Johnson's "The Creation."

However, one could argue that some contemporary black memoirs that recall events like these have been insufficiently critical and that their over-romanticized

653

notions of racial memory have masked the complications of color and racial identity in the United States. The nostalgic return to a bathetic black past erases the ugly facts of a racist history where being black has been anything but beautiful. The fact is that cherished memories of black cultural histories reside in a troubled parallel with contemporary racist notions of "black cultural pathologies." So, although this essay's account of events in our culture and in our culture's literary history focuses on one dimension of this portraiture, I accept that the landscape of racial identities is complex and hybrid.

These are stories of loss. Their spectral coherence represents a sustained lament for a disappeared body, and it contextualizes a troubled and ambivalent narrative. Disembodiment is often the first indication of the spirit's persistence. (Consider the persistence of Sethe's daughter in Toni Morrison's *Beloved*.) Despite what seems to be a body's commitment to dying in fact, the fictive body contradicts this effort and perseveres in a literary construction.

My first Chicago story is from mid-century, the other limns this millennial moment. They share a text. In remembering the earliest story, a parent recalls bringing a child "to see what they do to us, and how his life and his youth were meaningless." It is early in September 1955 when this youngster looks into a coffin in the A.A. Raynor Funeral Home, and then later joins the crowds of other children and their parents at the Roberts Temple Church of God in Christ to see the maliciously mutilated face of Emmett Till. Myrlie Evers, widow of civil rights leader Medgar Evers, recalled that the event taught that "even a child is not safe from racism and bigotry and death" (Powledge 48).

Nearly half a century later, again in an early September, again at a Church of God in Christ, and also in Chicago, a *New York Times* journalist, Don Terry, quotes another parent's declaration: "I brought my grandson here to see what can happen . . . that's a baby in there and I'm scared to death for mine" (Terry A1). Once again, but this time in a ritual familiar to too many urban youth, children are brought to see a body that looks like them. In August 1994, the body of eleven-year-old Robert Sandifer, a.k.a. "Yummy," was discovered by Chicago police. He had been shot twice in the back of his head. His fellow gang members had committed the crime, determined to keep Robert away from police interrogation after his own random gunfire killed his neighbor, Shavon Dean. Like Emmett, Robert is funeralized in September. One newspaper account writes that his body, lying in the casket, looked as if it belonged to a seven-year-old playing dead in his big brother's tan suit. About four hundred people attended Yummy's funeral, far fewer than the estimated crowds of between one and six hundred thousand who filed past Emmett Till's open casket. Emmett's mother had demanded that the casket not be closed so that the world could see what had been done to him. She insisted that the ravages of racism etched into the poor dark body of the child she called "Bobo" would inscribe the cultural moment.

In *Celebrations of Death: The Anthropology of Mortuary Ritual*, Peter Metcalf and Richard Huffington note the critical role of a community's reflection on the constructedness, permeability, and violence of its borders as its members engage the ritual of death and dying. In African American literature, one finds representations of community reflection on death. Too often to be merely coincidental, the fictive stories incorporate real deaths; as writers reconstruct cultural death, fact and fiction edge into each other's territory—factual representation erupts into fiction in a violent transgression of narrative borders. The violence seems appropriate, given the text of death in the stories that accomplish this transgression. When fiction and fact collide in these mourning stories, the remembered event is often a violent narrative.

The stories constructed from reflection on these deaths are mourning stories. Their performance constructs a narrative that rehearses the permeability and violence of our culture's racialized boundary conditions. The narratives are imagined in fiction and are improvised in performative community rituals. (I am thinking here not only of the formal memorials like Maya Lin's sculpture for those Americans who died in the Vietnam War, but of those improvisational memorials like flowers, candles, and toys that are placed on a street corner or doorway—wherever the act of violence occurred and without attention to whether the space is formalized for such memorial. Such memorializing is now a familiar text in urban cultures.) They are persistent, despite what may seem to be a fiction writer's impulse toward improvisation, and herein lies the central problematic. Cultural deaths—African American mourning stories—perform perversely both a descriptive and a prescriptive ritual.

A black child's death enacts and enables a cultural narrative and encourages a ghostly presence. In consequence, we recognize these and even anticipate the texts that are engaged in mourning performances. Both the stories and the images haunt our fiction, our autobiographies and memoirs, our newsprint, our videotaping, and even our storytelling.

The magazine that enshrined our culture's stories for us was "the" *Jet*, as we labeled it in my community. *Jet* published a photograph of Emmett's disfigured corpse lying in his casket. In contrast to Bobo's mutilated body, Yummy's seemed almost pacific in its pose. Their route to the caskets, however, was similarly violent.

In African American families, recollections of Emmett Till's death are known across generations. The story is retold—like the "Where were you when . . . ?" narrative some in this nation still connect to John F. Kennedy's assassination. These mourning stories are ghostly touchstones—mooring places for cultural memorials.

When Emmett appears in Toni Morrison's *Song of Solomon*, there is barely a pause at the wonder of his factual presence in this fictive text. After all, the texture of our fictions is barely disturbed by the wrinkle of a fact. Freddie says to Milkman, "remember when Emmett Till was killed? Back in fifty-three . . . ?" (111). Freddie got the date wrong, but, after all, it is fiction. Many of our fictions incorporate this kind of spiritual persistence—Emmett Till's narrative emerges in more than one African American literary text, most recently in Bebe Moore Campbell's *Your Blues Ain't Like Mine* (1992).

Spiritual persistence also characterizes the way we die. It may be as simple as Sula's post-death pronouncement that "it didn't even hurt—wait'll I tell Nel" (Morrison, *Sula* 149). Or it may be the enduring image of four little girls' dying on a Birmingham Sunday, their tragedy seared into our memories and our stories, making certain that we do not leave their bodies behind. Sula's death is a poor comparison to theirs, but the loss similarly fixes itself within the most ambivalent narrative spaces of "passed on." In *Song of Solomon*, Guitar recalls the assassination of Cynthia Wesley, Addie Mae Collins, Carole Robertson, and Denise McNair:

> Every night now Guitar was seeing little scraps of Sunday dresses—white and purple, powder blue, pink and white, lace and voile, velvet. . . . Sunday dresses . . . [that] hung in the air quietly, like the whole notes in the last measure of an Easter hymn. . . .
>
> Four little colored girls had been blown out of a church. (Morrison, *Song of Solomon* 173)

Ernest Gaines also makes certain that we understand the heft of the spirit's obstinacy in his most recent novel, *A Lesson Before Dying*. Even though Jefferson (convicted and sentenced to die for his part in a robbery and murder) is the one who will die in this story, his dying and its manner become the means for the teacher Grant Wiggins to manage his living. Wiggins, the first-person narrator, visits Jefferson in prison:

> He had been crying. He raised his cuffed hands and wiped his eyes.
>
> "I need you," I told him. "I need you much more than you could ever need me. I need to know what to do with my life. . . . I need you to tell me, to show me . . .
>
> . . . *We need you to be and want you to be.* . . . Do you understand what I'm saying to you, Jefferson? Do you?"
>
> He looked at me in great pain. He may not have understood, but something was touched, something deep down in him—because he was still crying. (193; emphasis added)

What can this mean, "we need you to be and want you to be," other than a challenge to Jefferson to recall the cultural responsibility not to relinquish his being—his selfhood—despite his dying? His scheduled electrocution must be a fiction, because the community needed instead the fact of his body to make their "being" different—to manage their living. Jefferson's final lines in this novel are written in a journal that the teacher Wiggins encouraged him to keep. There Jefferson wrote: "good bye mr wigin, tell them i'm strong, tell them i'm a man good by mr wigin, i'm gon ax paul if he can bring you this" (234). How nearly these echoes disclaim the resemblance. Each of these deaths moved Chicago toward a familiar ritual, and toward a familiar language.

The parent who brings her child to another child's bier has a practiced recitation grown out of an experienced ritual. She performs the culture's mourning narrative for my community. "I came to bring my son," says one (Thomas). One man said he planned to bring his children back to the funeral home to let them know "you're not too young to die" (Fountain). "I wanted the world to see," said Emmett's mother (Powledge 48). "I brought my child because I wanted him to know," explained a parent who stood in line at Yummy's funeral (Terry). This series of interchangeable statements from Bobo's and Yummy's funerals uses as familiar a language as Wright's fictional account of the *Tribune* story that blames "a poor darky family of a shiftless and immoral variety."

Only a culture that could be even arguably identified with violence and abuse would find its aesthetic expression—its sustained black imaginary—ironically and perversely sustained through telling these stories of death and dying.

When that infamous Chicago narrative *Native Son* either races or plods to its inevitable conclusion, there is not enough wonder at Bigger's pronouncement, "What I killed for, I am." Poor Richard, whose own death left us with an ambiguous narrative of its circumstances, understood that the aesthetic resonance of black literature may well arise from its mourning stories.

Five years after Emmett's death, Richard Wright published *The Long Dream*. An early scene in this novel echoes Till's death. There, Fish's father Tyree, who is an undertaker, receives the mutilated body of Fish's best friend Chris, whose encounter with a white woman led to his lynching. His mother's lament echoes Emmett's mother's: "Mrs. Sims opened her eyes and saw her son's broken body and screamed and lunged forward, flinging herself upon the corpse. 'Chris baby, this ain't *you!*'" (75). Later, Tyree explains his funeral business to his son: "Fish, you know how I make my living?" Then without waiting for an answer he tells him: "I make money by gitting *black* dreams ready for the burial" (80).

Here lies the persistent trace of memory—its sketch, its reach, its limn of the boundaries between this world and the next, just its sliver of insistence that the bodies we would leave behind will challenge our own being unless we incorporate their stories into ours and, in so doing, claim their right to a memorial. I mean here the full sense of incorporate—to take into the body.

Our stories form the character of our cultural bodies. When it seems as if there is nothing left but a trace of language, or a disturbing photograph of the dead, or the threat of a dead daughter's return, or news cameras that glimpse the mere remains of our children, only mourning stories persist.

At the moment of her dying, Dorcas thinks, "I ought to be wide awake because something important is happening" (Morrison, *Jazz* 192). This is what matters the most. Something important is happening when the imaginary of our fictions is filled with the improvisational rituals of death in Chicago or L.A. or D.C. Something important is happening when the backlog of children's death make weekday (rather than weekend) funerals an ordinary event in Durham, North Carolina, or when the funeral homes in Buffalo, New York, turn away the funerals of children because "they come in here with guns and all" and "they act up." Something important is happening when some of the most memorable moments in our fictions and some of the most characteristic stories of our culture have been mourning stories.

Finally, critical to the social and aesthetic construction of mourning is the way in which the lesson learned before dying—that maleness and death often find identity in each other—is also a cultural narrative that particularizes a gendered imagery of African American ethnicity. In the final pages of *A Visitation of Spirits* Randall Kenan tells the story of a suicide:

Whether or not the malevolent spirit existed is irrelevant, in the end. For whether he caused it or not, the boy died. This is a fact. The bullet did break the skin . . . the blood did flow. . . . His heartbeat slowly decreased. Whether or not the demon was a ghost of his mind or a spirit of the netherworld, this did happen. And the man screamed, a helpless, affronted, high-pitched, terror-filled scream . . . a sobbing, moanful wail, unconsolable and primal. (253)

Kenan writes the text of a century of fictive and factual stories—Guitar's and Bigger's, Yummy's and Emmett's, the saga of the Atlanta child murders of the late 1970s and early '80s, and the tales of dead and dying youth in our contemporary urban landscapes. Then Kenan writes their pitiful epitaph:

Most importantly, the day did not halt in its tracks: clocks did not stop. The school buses rolled . . . dishes were washed . . . food was eaten. And that night the sun set with the full intention of rising on the morrow. (254).

In my African American literature classes, I explore the text of the 1994 exhibition on "The Black Male" held at the Whitney Gallery in New York City in the way many of us in our US literature classes discuss the 1913 Chicago Armory Show as the moment that modernism arrived on America's public scene. The "Black Male" exhibit, I believe, is a similar watershed moment in black culture and literature. It is aesthetically resonant and representative, and it is notable as well for its persistent performative text of mourning.

When we look back and wonder how we got over the hump of these millennial times, I think our mourning stories, carefully collected, will tell one way that the last century of the millennium was lived. Whether lynched like Emmett or lovingly relinquished, how we have died reflexively comments on how we have lived. This kind of memorial is not accomplished without cost to our faith and our certitude, but neither will our advancing through the coming years be manageable without a similar cost. The promise of culture, I am sure, is the certainty of our stories in its midst. Recalling the texts of our deaths and our dying alongside the stories of African American cultures rallies us against whatever it is that suggests we might "fly off and leave a body." Whatever it may signify for a culture's stories to reside in the ambivalent constructions of mourning, their text is nevertheless, as Morrison ambivalently reminds us in *Beloved*, "not a story to pass on."

WORKS CITED

Fountain, John. "Boy's Wake a Lesson for Roseland." *Chicago Tribune* 7 September 1994:1.
Gaines, Ernest. *A Lesson Before Dying*. New York: Knopf, 1993.
Kenan, Randall. *A Visitation of Spirits*. New York: Anchor/Doubleday, 1987.
Metcalf, Peter, and Richard Huffington. *Celebrations of Death: The Anthropology of Mortuary Ritual*. 2d ed. New York: Cambridge UP. 1991.
Morrison, Toni. *Beloved*. New York: Knopf, 1987.

———. *Jazz*. New York: Knopf, 1993.

———. *Song of Solomon*. New York: Knopf, 1978.

———. *Sula*. New York: Knopf, 1974.

Powledge, Fred. Free at Last: *The Civil Rights Movement and the People Who Made It.* Boston: Little Brown, 1991.

Terry, Don. "In an 11-Year-Old's Funeral, a Grim Lesson." *New York Times* 8 September 1994: A1, B11.

Thomas, Jerry. "Emmett's Legacy." *Chicago Tribune* 5 September 1995:5.

Wright, Richard. *Native Son*. 1940. New York: Vintage Library, 1994.

———. *The Long Dream*. 1958. New York: Harper and Row, 1987.

50 Introduction to *Race Men: The W. E. B. Du Bois Lectures*

Hazel V. Carby

(1998)

> [S]ince the dominant view holds prideful self-respect as the very essence of healthy African American identity, it also considers such identity to be fundamentally weakened wherever masculinity appears to be compromised. While this fact is rarely articulated, its influence is nonetheless real and pervasive. Its primary effect is that all debates over and claims to "authentic" African-American identity are largely animated by a profound anxiety about the status specifically of African-American masculinity.
>
> —Phillip Brian Harper

In these days of what is referred to as "global culture," the Nike corporation produces racialized images for the world by elevating the bodies of Michael Jordan and Tiger Woods to the status of international icons. Hollywood too now takes for granted that black bodies can be used to promote both products and style worldwide, and an increasing number of their "black" films are being produced and directed by black men. But despite the multimillion-dollar international trade in black male bodies, and encouragement to "just do it," there is no equivalent in international outrage, no marches or large-scale public protest, at the hundreds of thousands of black male bodies languishing out of sight of the media in the North American penal system.

Between the time that W. E. B. Du Bois published *The Souls of Black Folk*, and Danny Glover gained the status of international superstar in the *Lethal Weapon* series of films between 1987 and 1992, there has been a stark reversal in the nature of the visibility of the black male body, if not much of a change in the fortune of most black men. If the spectacle of the lynched black body haunts the modern age, then the slow disintegration of black bodies and souls in jail, urban ghettos, and beleaguered schools haunts our postmodern times.

This book traverses this history and asks questions about the nature of the cultural representation of various black masculinities at different historical moments and in different media: literature, photography, film, music and song. It does not seek to be a comprehensive history of the roles of black men in any one of these cultural forms but considers the cultural and political complexity of particular inscriptions, performances, and enactments of black masculinity on a variety of stages. Each stage is deliberately bounded and limited in its construction.

Ideologies of masculinity always exist in a dialectical relation to other ideologies— I have chosen to focus upon their articulation with discourses of race and nation in American culture. However, rather than analyze these discourses in representations of famous political figures, like Frederick Douglass, Malcolm X, or Martin Luther King, Jr., or through the work of established writers of fiction like Richard Wright, Ralph Ellison, and James Baldwin, I focus on a variety of artists and intellectuals.

For W. E. B. Du Bois, I have constructed the stage upon *The Souls of Black Folk*, because his book has become a canonical text in American culture and because its theory of double-consciousness has been so widely adopted to explain the nature of the African American soul. Though Du Bois led a long and varied intellectual and political life, I have limited his stage to this text because it is so frequently taken to be representative of black intellectual, psychological, and existential reality.

The stage for Paul Robeson, in the second chapter, is limited to the 1920s and 1930s in order to demonstrate the complexities of representations of race and gender within the modernist aesthetic. Robeson came to represent a form of black masculinity against which he eventually rebelled, seeking an alternative political and artistic aesthetic through activism and the Left Theatre Movement in England. (Robeson was perhaps the first internationally acclaimed black icon, and Michael Jordan, Tiger Woods, and Danny Glover would do well to reflect upon the politics of Robeson's response to this fame.) Whereas Du Bois argued for the importance of recognizing the centrality of black people and black culture to the formation of the United States, Robeson rejected the terms and conditions upon which his acclaim depended and, as a result, was declared a threat to national security.

The third chapter considers the stage of the spirituals and American folk song. Du Bois had argued for the historical significance of the sorrow songs, but interpretations of Robeson's performance of the spirituals repressed the history of exploitation and oppression out of which they grew. John and Alan Lomax's search for a representative of the American folk song led them to invent their own version of the dangerous, if gifted, black male, in the person of Huddie Ledbetter, known as Leadbelly, whose voice, though not his person, could be presented to the national archive.

In chapter four I argue that the cricket pitch is the stage upon which we should begin to understand the work of C. L. R. James. His cricket journalism recreates the world of body lines and color lines and represents the black male body as both autonomous and inspirational. James's descriptions of cricket as the site where lines of class, race, and gender are forged foreshadows his work on the Haitian revolutionary, Toussaint L'Ouverture.

The misogyny of Miles Davis and the world of jazz in the late 1950s and early 1960s provides the stage for a consideration of an alternative black masculinity performed in his music. Interwoven with this analysis of Davis's life and music is the work of Samuel Delany, a writer who consistently challenges his readers to expand their visions of masculinities and femininities through his revolutionary fiction and criticism.

Lastly, I propose that the film career of Danny Glover traces the development of an important Hollywood narrative of black masculinity. This narrative promises to resolve the racial contradictions and crises of the 1980s and 1990s through a revision of the traditional trope of the black male/white male partnership, a partnership which firmly excludes the democratic participation of women in modern public life.

There remains the question, what is a race man? Clearly, I think that it is a concept that encompasses all of the above, but is also much more than that. For a century, the figure of the race man has haunted black political and cultural thought, and this book seeks to conduct a feminist interrogation of this theme and of other definitions of black masculinity at work in American culture.

In 1945, in *Black Metropolis*, St. Clair Drake and Horace Cayton attempted to account for the emergence of the idea of a race man. "Race consciousness," they asserted, "is not the work of 'agitators,' or 'subversive influences'—it is forced upon Negroes by the very fact of their separate-subordinate status in American life." Since emancipation, Drake and Cayton argue, black people have had to prove, actively and consistently, that they were not the inferior beings that their status as second-class citizens declared them to be: hence an aggressive demonstration of their superiority in some field of achievement, either individually or collectively, was what established race pride: "the success of one Negro" was interpreted as "the success of all." The result of the pursuit of "race consciousness, race pride, and race solidarity" was the emergence of particular social types, among which was the Race Man.[1] Drake and Cayton add this cautionary note, however: "People try to draw a line between 'sincere Race Leaders' and those Race Men who are always clamoring everything for the race, just for the glory of being known."[2] The issue of acting as a race man for particular audiences is still relevant in a society where the mass media all too eagerly assign to a few carefully chosen voices the representation of the racialized many, and the chosen rarely reject their designation and transient moment of glory. What a race man signifies for the white segments of our society is not necessarily how a race man is defined for various black constituencies.[3]

While Drake and Cayton effectively situate the subtleties and complexities produced by and through processes of racialization in the United States, they, along with most contemporary black male intellectuals, take for granted the gendering at work in the other half of the concept "race man"—the part that is limited to man. What we have inherited from them and from others is a rarely questioned notion of masculinity as it is connected to ideas of race and nation.

In 1897, eighteen black men, under the leadership of Alexander Crummell, formally inaugurated the American Negro Academy. In his address to this august assembly, W. E. B. Du Bois declared: "For the development of Negro genius, of Negro literature and art, of Negro spirit, only Negroes bound and welded together, Negroes inspired by one vast ideal, can work out in its fullness the great message we have for humanity."[4] But only black men were to be "bound and welded together." Nothing was done to recruit black women into the Academy.[5]

Nevertheless, Crummell and the Negro Academies continue to stand as emblematic figures for the designation of black intellectual. The historian Wilson J. Moses has recently asserted that the life of Alexander Crummell "symbolizes the intricacy of the experience of black American intellectuals: their conflicting emotions with respect to the Western world, their discontent with 'civilization,' and their dependency on it, as they have labored to impose order on their existence both as racial beings and as individuals."[6] My position in this book is an outright rejection of the male-centered assumptions at work in such claims of representativeness.

In the late 1990s the work of black women intellectuals is still considered peripheral by the black male establishment. It is true that, superficially, the situation appears to have improved. The words "women and gender" are frequently added after the word "race" and the appropriate commas, and increasingly the word "sexuality" completes the litany. On occasion a particular black woman's name will be mentioned, like that of Toni Morrison. But the *intellectual work* of black women and gay men is not thought to be of enough significance to be engaged with, argued with, agreed or disagreed with. Thus terms like women, gender, and sexuality have a decorative function only. They color the background of the canvas to create the appropriate illusion of inclusion and diversity, but they do not affect the shape or texture of the subject. Indeed, we have recently been told by one of America's leading intellectuals that unless black intellectuals affect the demeanor and attire of the Victorian male in his dark three-piece suit, they will remain marginal and impotent.[7]

While contemporary black male intellectuals claim to challenge the hegemony of a racialized social formation, most fail to challenge the hegemony of their own assumptions about black masculinity and accept the consensus of a dominant society that "conceives African American society in terms of a perennial 'crisis' of black masculinity whose imagined solution is a proper affirmation of black male authority."[8] This apparent solution was at work in the Million Man March, but it is also at work in contemporary black intellectual life. On the contrary, rather than continue to dress ourselves in what Essex Hemphill calls "this threadbare masculinity," it is necessary to recognize the complex ways in which black masculinity has been, and still is, socially and culturally produced.

NOTES

1. St. Clair Drake and Horace Cayton, *Black Metropolis: A Study of Life in a Northern City* (New York: Harcourt Brace, 1945), pp. 390–392.

2. Drake and Cayton, *Black Metropolis*, p. 394.

3. It is interesting to note that in the white press the term "Race Man" appears in quotation marks, whereas in the black press it doesn't.

4. Alfred A. Moss, *The American Negro Academy: Voice of the Talented Tenth* (Baton Rouge: Louisiana State University Press, 1981), pp. 35, 49.

5. In 1898 Maritcha B. Lyons was asked to present a paper. It was read by F. D. Barrier, as Lyons could not attend. In 1908, at a panel discussion on education, a woman was asked her opinion. These are the only two occasions in which women were asked to participate. See Moss, *The American Negro Academy*, pp. 78, 134.

6. Wilson Jeremiah Moses (1989), *Alexander Crammell: A Study of Civilization and Discontent* (rpt. Amherst: University of Massachusetts Press, 1992), p. 10.

7. See Cornel West, *Race Matters* (Boston: Beacon Press, 1993), p. 40.

8. Phillip Brian Harper, *Are We Not Men? Masculine Anxiety and the Problem of African American Identity* (New York: Oxford University Press, 1996), p. x.

51

Malcolm's Conk and Danto's Colors; or, Four Logical Petitions Concerning Race, Beauty, and Aesthetics

Paul C. Taylor

(1999)

> It was at once the most fantastic and the most logical petition he had ever received. Here was an ugly little girl asking for beauty. . . . A little black girl who wanted to rise up out of the pit of her blackness and see the world with blue eyes. . . . For the first time he honestly wished he could work miracles.
>
> —Toni Morrison, *The Bluest Eye*

I have opened with this passage from Toni Morrison for a number of reasons. The passage reflects the long-standing preoccupation that African-American activists have had with standards of physical beauty, a preoccupation that I will soon call antiracist aestheticism. The passage also captures in singularly effective language the existential, social, and psychological conditions that motivate this preoccupation, and contributes the language of logical petitions that I will use to frame my discussion of aestheticism. Morrison's ugly little black girl, a character named Pecola, makes a request that would be ludicrous were it not for the nature of her circumstances. In this essay I want to consider how Pecola's circumstances motivate her petition and two others, after which I will offer my own petition concerning the practice of aesthetics.

First, a few words about the social and intellectual conditions that make Pecola's petition "logical." One of the cornerstones of the modern West has been the hierarchical valuation of human types along racial lines. (Unless I say otherwise, I will be concerned throughout with the modern West, particularly with England and its former possessions in the Americas.) The most prominent type of racialized ranking represents blackness as a condition to be despised, and most tokens of this type extend this attitude to cover the physical features that are central to the ascription of black identity. So a central assumption has been that black folks—with our kinky hair, flat noses, thick lips, dark skin, prognathism, and steatopygia—are ugly. (I call

665

to your attention the evaluative overtones of this standard descriptive language: imagine the difference if I had said broad noses, full lips, curly hair, and so on.)

To make matters worse, the most prominent type of racialist thought took shape under the same intellectual circumstances that in the eighteenth century produced efforts to define an aesthetic morality centered on the "beautiful soul" and in the nineteenth century led to the "science" of physiognomy. [1] The circumstances that I have in mind consist, as much as is pertinent for my purposes, of the widespread assumption that bodily beauty and deformity covary with moral beauty and deformity as well as with general cultural and intellectual capacity. This practice of conflating different categories of value—of running together the good, the beautiful, the intelligent, and the civilized—could only have made it easier for hierarchical racialism to become what I call thick racialism, which holds that the physical differences between races are signs of deeper, typically intellectual and moral, differences. Thus it became part of the content of the standard thick, hierarchical racialism—what I call classical racialism—that the physical ugliness of black people was a sign of a deeper ugliness and depravity.

The classical racialist order that presupposed the thoroughgoing odiousness of black people was composed of complex social formations that brought about the inequitable distribution of social goods along racial lines. (By "social goods" I mean material goods like property as well as other goods like freedom, self-esteem, and the right to own property.) This distributive project was both facilitated and constituted by ideological projects of justification that made the notion of black odiousness, inhumanity, and inferiority a part of commonsense sociology. These justifying projects made it possible for a humanist to be a slave holder without contradiction, for the dominance of capital and land to be concealed and maintained by the social and moral authority of racial hegemony, and, most important here, for imported Africans, stripped as much as could be of their own culture, to be socialized (though not, of course, universally and scamlessly) into the assumption of their own inferiority. Since the notion of black inferiority typically involves inferiority with respect to beauty, the modern black experience has been intimately bound up with a struggle against the cultural imperative to internalize the judgment of one's own thoroughgoing ugliness— hence the widespread sentiment among black people, in the nineteenth century especially, that black features are a problematic link to a "dark past" and to uncivilized ways.[2]

Given these conditions, it is logical for Pecola to think of blackness as a pit and to petition for escape from it. It is logical for her dream of escape to be expressed as the desire to transcend the physical features that are usually the most obvious signs of blackness. And it is logical for her to conceive of the whole process of personal improvement as a movement from ugliness to beauty.

But it is also logical for people interested in bettering the black condition to do as Morrison has done: to ask that we critically examine the conditions that make Pecola's petition reasonable. *The Bluest Eye* is just one example, though a particularly salutary one, of a strong and varied strain in the black antiracist tradition, a strain that I promised at the outset to call antiracist aestheticism. The participants in this subtradition—a group that includes writers like Gwendolyn Brooks and Zora Neale Hurston, academics like bell hooks and Cornel West, and filmmakers like Julie Dash and Spike Lee—have a double motivation.[3] They are motivated first by the realization that a white-dominated culture has racialized beauty, that it has defined beauty per se in terms of white beauty, in terms of the physical features that the people we consider white are more likely to have. They are motivated also by the worry that racialized standards of beauty reproduce the workings of racism by weaving racist assumptions into the daily practices and inner lives of the victims of racism—most saliently here, by encouraging them to accept and act on the supposition of their own ugliness. The problem of internalization that these activists are concerned with manifests itself in a variety of ways, some of which we will come to. But we can most efficiently discuss this worry in the context of what I will call the straight hair rule.

The straight hair rule is the presumption, long embraced in African-American communities (and, for not quite as long a time, in communities of African-descended peoples throughout the world), that straight hair is a necessary component of physical beauty. The necessity of this component is evident from the ordeals that people—including nonblack people unlucky enough to have curly hair[4]—will endure in its name. Consider Malcolm X's account of his first "conk," or chemically straightened hairstyle:

> The congolene just felt warm when Shorty started combing it in. But then my head caught fire. I gritted my teeth. . . . My eyes watered, my nose was running. I couldn't stand it any longer; I bolted to the washbasin. . . . My scalp still flamed, but not as badly. . . . My first view in the mirror blotted out the hurting. . . . The transformation, after the lifetime of kinks, is staggering. . . . On top of my head was this thick, smooth sheen of shining red hair . . . as straight as any white man's.[5]

The straight hair rule might be more precisely stated as the principle that long straight hair is a necessary component of female beauty. The aestheticist concern with beauty tends to be a concern with female beauty, as we might expect given the nature of the cultural forces in play: Since current social conditions make physical appearance central to the construction of womanhood and femininity and fairly peripheral to the construction of manhood and masculinity, talk about physical beauty more or less reduces to talk about womanhood, femininity, and women. Participants in the aestheticist tradition tend either to conduct the race-based critique alongside the gender critique, or, too often, to discuss the racial issues without any regard for the gender dynamics. I mention all of this because I will express myself below as if the problems of female beauty can stand in for the problems of racialized aesthetic standards in general. This is an attempt on my part to capture the overwhelming concern of the aestheticist tradition, not a denial of the need for gender critique.

The straight hair rule dominates African-American culture to such an extent that one commentator can meaningfully ask, "Have we reached the point where the only acceptable option for African American women is straight hair?"[6] This dominance should not be surprising, since the cultural imperative for black women to enact beauty engages most powerfully with the processes of racialization and internalization in connection with their hair. Until the fairly recent perfection of the technologies of colored contacts and cosmetic surgery, Pecola's dream of escape from the physical markers of blackness was most effectively focused on the hair, the part of the body that is most amenable to frequent, radical, and relatively inexpensive alteration in the direction of approximating "white" standards (since, at any rate, Madame C. J. Walker's work at the beginning of this century, about which more in a moment). Consequently, as Paulette Caldwell reports, "the writings of black women confirm the centrality of hair in the psychological abuse of black women. Virtually all novels and autobiographical works by black women writers contain some treatment of the issue of discrimination against black women because of . . . hair texture."[7]

In light of all this, the aestheticist tradition offers a logical petition of its own. The request takes different forms as it is stated by figures with different political affiliations, with different degrees of attachment to an essential black subject—the Form, as it were, of Blackness—and to one or another of the relevant psychological notions like pride or alienation. But the basic point remains the same. The aestheticist requests that we work to loosen the hold that hair-straightening has on the collective black consciousness, that we critically examine the conditions that make Pecola's request reasonable, and that we strive to cultivate the idea that we can be beautiful just as we are.

Stated broadly, the aestheticist account and critique should seem intuitively plausible. Given the present constitution of Western societies it seems right to say that the category of race tends to be central to the self-conception of the people we consider black, that physical features are central to the assignment and assumption of racial identities, and finally that, other things being equal, a person whose self-conception involves characteristics that she finds valuable is better off than someone whose identity is bound up with features she finds odious. But it is easy to narrow any broad statement of the aestheticist position in ways that make it more problematic. One might assume, for example, that the value of the aestheticist account is that it warrants inferences to the mental and moral states of individual agents, that it allows one to assume, in other words, that any person with straightened hair is, in the parlance of Spike Lee's "School Daze," a "wannabee"—someone who wants to be white. On such a view, straightening involves the moral failing of groundlessly devaluing huge portions of the human family, and it involves the psychological problems of alienation and self-hatred—of devaluing one's own portion of the human family, and hence devaluing oneself.

Some people are moved by the dangers of this crude version of aestheticism to offer a third logical petition: they urge that we take seriously the complexity of the processes by which individuals participate in patterns of social meaning. They point out that people can participate in meaning-laden practices like hair-straightening while, or as a way of, shifting the meanings; or that hair-straightening itself has taken on such racialized significance that participation in the practice can be a way of expressing black pride rather than a way of precluding it. So, for example, when Malcolm X attacks his earlier self for the "self-degradation" of "burning my flesh to have it look like a white man's hair,"[8] historian Robin Kelley suggests that this interpretation is too beholden to Malcolm's later politics to do justice to his earlier behavior. Kelley explains:

> [T]o claim that black working-class males who conked their hair were merely parrot-ing whites ignores the fact that specific stylizations created by black youth emphasized difference. . . . We cannot help but view the conk as part of a larger process by which black youth . . . reinscribed coded oppositional meanings onto styles derived from the dominant culture.[9]

Noliwe Rooks attempts a similar argument concerning Madame C. J. Walker, who amassed a fortune just after the turn of the twentieth century by popularizing the hot comb, the principal instrument for hair-straightening. Rooks explains that while "African Americans had long struggled with issues of inferiority, beauty, and the meaning of particular beauty practices. . . . [Walker] attempted to shift the signifi-cance of hair away from concerns of disavowing African ancestry."[10] Walker, it turns out, even rejected the claim that hair-straightening was principally what she was up to: she argued instead that she provided a way for black women to keep their hair healthy and, not coincidentally, to expand their economic and social opportunities in the process by becoming hairdressers.

This request that we take seriously the complexity of the relations between individ-uals and their cultures is an important addition, both as a corrective to the potential oversights of the aestheticist account and as a clarification of the aestheticist project. Rooks and Kelley help to affirm that the aestheticist argument at its best involves political criticism of culture, not moral criticism of individuals. They show that the aim should be to consider the extent to which an individual's actions presuppose, reproduce, maintain, and refashion broader and perhaps troubling patterns of behav-ior and structures of meaning, both consciously and unconsciously. They show, in short, that antiracist aestheticism is an indigenous mode of cultural criticism, pro-duced by efforts to come to grips with the uses and abuses of the concept of beauty in the experiences of black folks.

I want to insist for a moment on this last point, because it is the one that I have been aiming at all along. I have tried to discuss beauty here in a way that differs from what one usually finds in essays of philosophical aesthetics. Most often we consider beauty in its capacity as a property of artworks, either the property of general artistic merit or some more specific property that may not be necessary for the success of a work. But there is no reason for aestheticians to take up beauty only in the context of art—no reason, that is, apart from the widely held assumption that aesthetics just is the philosophy of art, an assumption that is deeply contingent as a matter of history and, though dominant, not universally accepted. I have discussed beauty in the context of cultural criticism because it seems to me that cultural criticism is one of the things that aesthetics can and should be. And that, of course, is the fourth of my eponymous petitions: that we explore the possibility that aesthe-ticians can examine something broader than and, in a sense, prior to the arts: the reciprocally constitutive relationships between cultures and individuals.

This is not, of course, a radical proposal. No less a figure than Arthur Danto has argued that aesthetics is "virtually as wide in scope as experience itself, whether it be experience of art or of insects." Aesthetics, he says, has to do with the "encoloration" of human cognition and perception by historical meaning and cultural value; to attend to something aesthetically is "to suspend practicality, to stand back and assume a detached view of the object, see its shapes and colors, enjoy and admire it for what it is, subtracting all considerations of utility." He goes on to suggest that the future of the discipline of aesthetics lies not simply in continued examination of the philosophical issues arising from the practices of fine art, but also in showing cognitive scientists how they have undermined their own prospects for success by "treating us in abstraction from our historical and cultural locations." Aesthetics becomes for him, then, in its role as something like the under-laborer to cognitive science, "a discipline which borders on philosophical psychology in one direction and the theory of knowledge in the other."[11]

I find Danto's proposal compelling except for the final step. Where he sees aesthetics bordering on the theory of knowledge and informing cognitive science, I see it bordering on political philosophy and informing social theory. I share his interest in the encoloration of cognition and perception by history and culture, but my concern has to do with how that process shapes our interactions with each other in the social realm. What more useful task could the discipline take up than that of excavating the hidden ways in which history and culture condition our choices, beliefs, desires, and preferences—such as the preference, say, for straight hair?

Recasting aesthetics as a kind of cultural criticism, as a discipline as ready to deal with the beauty of human bodies as with the beauty of art, would, I think, produce a number of benefits. First of all, cultural criticism relies heavily, and often obscurely, on the central aesthetic practice of interpretation. The much-ballyhooed (and sometimes overstated) clarity and rigor of philosophy could help to clear some of the ground here. Second, cultural criticism is, in the form of cultural studies, a thriving discipline in its own right. As such it represents a viable source of interdisciplinary cooperation, which makes it a useful intellectual and professional resource for a discipline that is often under attack both from the ax of downsizing administrations and from the arrogance of fellow philosophers. Finally, the move from aesthetics narrowly construed to an aesthetics "as broad in scope as experience itself" represents the opportunity to rebut once more the claim that philosophy is culturally detached and socially irrelevant.

I realize that I have said rather little about a number of crucial issues. I have simply gestured at what cultural criticism is; I have given no reason for the antiracist critic to stop at indexing judgments of beauty to racial body types instead of going on to question the whole framework of racialist (but, significantly, not necessarily classical racialist) thinking; and I have not been exactly clear about how the experience of being a black woman with hair that is not naturally straight, and can be made so only provisionally and with some expenditure of time and effort, differs from the experiences of similarly situated Jewish and Irish women. (As you might imagine, I mention these particular questions because I think I have answers to them, though I could not give them here.) My aim in this essay has not been to settle those issues but simply to point in a direction that seems to me to require, and likely to reward, further exploration. If I have done that adequately, then the rest can wait for another time.

NOTES

1. Robert E. Norto, *The Beautiful Soul: Aesthetic Morality in the Eighteenth Century* (Cornell University Press, 1995).

2. Noliwe Rooks, *Hair Raising* (Rutgers University Press, 1996), p. 35.

3. See especially Cornel West's essay, "A Geneaology of Modern Racism," in *Prophesy Deliverance* (Philadelphia: Westminster, 1982), pp. 47–65.

4. See Susan Bordo, *Unbearable Weight: Feminism, Western Culture, and the Body* (University of California Press, 1993), p. 255.

5. Alex Haley and Malcolm X, *The Autobiography of Malcolm X* (1965; New York: Ballantine Books, 1973), pp. 53–54.

6. Rooks, p. 132.

7. Paulette Caldwell, "A Hair Piece," *Duke Law Journal* 41, no. 2 (1991): 365–396, 391.

8. Haley, p. 54.

9. Robin D. G. Kelley, "The Riddle of the Zoot," in *Malcolm X*, ed. Joe Wood (New York: St. Martin's, 1992), pp. 155–182, 161–162.

10. Rooks, p. 52.

11. Arthur C. Danto, "A Future for Aesthetics," *The Journal of Aesthetics and Art Criticism* 51 (1993): 271–277, 274, 275; and *The Transfiguration of the Commonplace* (Harvard University Press, 1981), p. 22.

Suggested Readings since the 1970s for African American Literary/Cultural Theory

A Select Bibliography

LITERARY THEORY AND CRITICISM

GENERAL

Adell, Sandra. *Double-Consciousness/Double Bind: Theoretical Issues in Twentieth-Century Black Literature*. Urbana and Chicago: Illinois UP, 1994.

Awkward, Michael. *Negotiating Difference: Race, Gender, and the Politics of Positionality*. Chicago: Chicago UP, 1995.

Baker, Houston A. *Afro-American Poetics: Revisions of Harlem and the Black Aesthetic*. Madison: Wisconsin UP, 1988.

——. *Blues, Ideology, and Afro-American Literature: A Vernacular Theory*. Chicago: Chicago UP, 1984.

——. *The Journey Back: Issues in Black Literature and Criticism*. Chicago: Chicago UP, 1980.

——. *Long Black Song: Essays in Black American Literature and Culture*. Charlottesville: Virginia UP, 1972.

——. *Singers of Daybreak: Studies in Black American Literature*. Washington, D.C.: Howard UP, 1974.

Barksdale, Richard, and R. Baxter Miller. *Praisesong of Survival: Lectures and Essays, 1957–89*. Urbana: Illinois UP, 1992.

Blackshire-Belay, Carol Aisha, ed. *Language and Literature in the African American Imagination*. Westport, Conn.: Greenwood Press, 1972.

Britton, Celia M. *Edouard Glissant and Postcolonial Theory: Strategies of Language and Resistance*. Virginia UP, 1999.

Ervin, Hazel Arnett, ed. *American Literary Criticism: 1773 to 2000*. New York: Twayne, 1999.

Fisher, Dexter, and Robert B. Stepto, eds. *Afro-American Literature: The Reconstruction of Instruction*. New York: MLA, 1977.

673

Gates, Henry Louis, Jr., ed. *Black Literature and Literature Theory*. New York: Methuen, 1990.

———. *Figures in Black: Signs, and the "Racial" Self*. New York: Oxford UP, 1987.

———, ed. *"Race," Writing, and Difference*. Chicago: Chicago UP, 1985/86.

———. *The Signifying Monkey: A Theory of Afro-American Literary Criticism*. New York: Oxford UP, 1988.

Glissant, Edouard. *Poetics of Relation*. Trans. Betsy Wing. University of Michigan Press, 1997.

Hakutani, Yoshinobu, and Robert Butler, eds. *The City in African-American Literature*. Madison, N.J.: Fairleigh Dickinson UP, 1995.

Henderson, Stephen E. "The Form of Things Unknown." In his *Understanding the New Black Poetry, 1962–1977*. New York: William Morrow, 1973, pp. 1–69.

———. "The Heavy Blues of Sterling Brown: A Study of Craft and Tradition." *Black American Literature Forum* 14 (Spring 1980): 32–44.

———. "The Question of Form and Judgement in Contemporary Black American Poetry, 1962–1977." In *A Dark and Sudden Beauty: Two Essays on Black American Poetry by George Kent and Stephen Henderson*. Houston A. Baker, Jr., ed. Philadelphia: Afro-American Studies Program of the University of Pennsylvania, 1977.

Hord, Fred Lee. *Reconstructing Memory: Black Literary Criticism*. Chicago: Third World Press, 1991.

Joyce, Joyce Ann. *Warriors, Conjurers and Priests: Defining African-Centered Literary Criticism*. Chicago: Third World Press, 1994.

Lee, A. Robert. *Designs of Blackness: Mappings in the Literature and Culture of Afro-America*. London: Pluto Press, 1998.

McDowell, Deborah E., and Arnold Rampersad, eds. *Slavery and the Literary Imagination*. Baltimore: Johns Hopkins UP, 1990.

Miller, R. Baxter. *Black American Literature and Humanism*. Lexington: Kentucky UP, 1981.

Morrison, Toni. *Playing in the Dark: Whiteness and the Literary Imagination*. Cambridge, Mass.: Harvard UP, 1992.

Murray, Albert. *The Hero and the Blues*. New York: Vintage Books, 1996.

Nelson, Emmanuel S., ed. *Critical Essays: Gay and Lesbian Writers of Color*. New York: Haworth Press, 1993.

Nielsen, Aldon Lynn. *Writing between the Lines: Race and Intertextuality*. Athens: Georgia UP, 1994.

Saunders, James Robert. *Tightrope Walk: Identity, Survival and the Corporate World in African American Literature*. Jefferson, N.C.: McFarland & Co., 1997.

Smith, Felipe. *American Body Politics: Race, Gender, and Black Literary Renaissance*. Athens: Georgia UP, 1998.

Smith, Valerie, ed. *Representing Blackness*. New Brunswick, N.J.: Rutgers UP, 1996.

Sundquist, Eric J. *To Wake the Nations: Race in the Making of American Literature*. Cambridge, Mass.: Harvard UP, 1993.

Thiher, Allen. *The Power of Tautology: The Roots of Literary Theory*. Madison, N.J.: Fairleigh Dickinson UP, 1997.

Twagilimana, Aimable. *Race and Gender in the Making of an African American Literary Tradition*. New York: Garland, 1997.

Warren, Kenneth W. *Black and White Strangers: Race and American Literary Realism*. Chicago: Chicago UP, 1995.

Weixlmann, Joe, and Chester J. Fontenot, eds. *Black American Prose Theory: Studies in Black American Literature*, Vol. 1. Greenwood, Fla.: Penkeville, 1984.

————, eds. *Belief Versus Theory in Black American Literary Criticism: Studies in Black American Literature*, Vol. 2. Greenwood, Fla.: Penkeville, 1986.

———— and Houston A. Baker, Jr., eds. *Black Feminist Criticism and Critical Theory: Studies in Black American Literature*, Vol. 3. Greenwood, Fla.: Penkevill, 1988.

Williams, Sherley Ann. *Give Birth to Brightness: A Thematic Study in Neo-Black Literature.* New York: Dial Press, 1972.

Wonham, Henry B., ed. *Criticism and the Color Line: Desegregating American Literary Studies.* New Brunswick, N.J.: Rutgers UP, 1996.

GENRE STUDIES

Andrews, William L. *African American Autobiography: A Collection of Critical Essays.* Englewood Cliffs, N.J.: Prentice Hall, 1993.

Bell, Bernard W. *The Afro-American Novel and Its Tradition.* Amherst: Massachusetts UP, 1987.

Brown, Fahamisha P. *Performing the Word: African American Poetry as Vernacular Culture.* New Brunswick, N.J.: Rutgers UP, 1999.

Bryant, Jerry H. *Victims and Heroes: Racial Violence in the African American Novel.* Amherst: Massachusetts UP, 1997.

Cataliotti, Robert H. *The Music in African American Fiction.* New York: Garland, 1995.

Doyle, Laura. *Bordering on the Body: The Racial Matrix of Modern Fiction and Culture.* New York: Oxford UP, 1994.

Fox, Robert Elliot. *Conscientious Sorcerers: The Black Postmodernist Fiction of LeRoi Jones-Amiri Baraka, Ishmael Reed, and Samuel R. Delany.* Westport, Conn.: Greenwood Press, 1987.

————. *Masters of the Drum: Black Lit/oratures Across the Continuum.* Westport, Conn.: Greenwood Press, 1995.

Gayle, Addison. *The Way of the World: The Black Novel in America.* Garden City, N.Y.: Doubleday, 1975.

Gibson, Andrew. *Postmodernity, Ethics and the Novel: From Leavis to Levinas.* New York: Routledge, 1999.

————. *Toward a Postmodern Theory of the Novel.* Edinburgh: Edinburgh UP, 1997.

Gosselin, Adrienne Johnson. *Multicultural Detective Fiction: Murder from the "Other" Side.* New York: Garland, 1998.

Greene, J. Lee. *Blacks in Eden: The African American Novel's First Century.* Charlottesville: Virginia UP, 1996.

Griffin, Farah Jasmine. *"Who Set You Flowin'?": The African-American Migration Narrative.* New York: Oxford UP, 1995.

Hogue, W. Lawrence. *Discourse and the Other: The Production of the Afro-American Text.* Durham, N.C.: Duke UP, 1986.

Jablon, Madelyn. *Black Metafiction: Self-Consciousness in African American Literature.* Iowa City: Iowa UP, 1998.

Jones, Gayl. *Liberating Voices: Oral Tradition in African American Literature.* Cambridge, Mass.: Harvard UP, 1991.

Judy, Ronald A. *Disforming the American Canon: African-Arabic Slave Narratives and the Vernacular.* Minneapolis: Minnesota UP, 1993.

Kawash, Samira. *Dislocating the Color Line: Identity, Hybridity, and Singularity in African-American Narrative.* Palo Alto: Stanford UP, 1997.

Kester, Gunilla T. *Writing the Subject: Bildung and the African American Text*. New York: Peter Lang, 1997.

MacCann, Donnarae. *White Supremacy in Children's Literature: Characterizations of African Americans, 1830–1900*, Vol. 4. New York: Garland, 1998.

MacKey, Nathaniel. *Discrepant Engagement: Dissonance, Cross-Culturality, and Experimental Writing*. New York: Cambridge UP, 1993.

Montgomery, Maxine Lavon. *The Apocalypse in African-American Fiction*. Gainesville: Florida UP, 1998.

Mostern, Kenneth. *Autobiography and Black Identity Politics: Racialization in Twentieth-Century America*. New York: Cambridge UP, 1999.

Rodriguez, Barbara. *Autobiographical Inscriptions: Form, Personhood, and the American Woman Writer of Color*. New York: Oxford UP, 1999.

Rushdy, Ashraf. *Neoslave Narratives: Studies in the Social Logic of a Literary Form*. New York: Oxford UP, 1999.

Sanders, Mark A. *Afro-Modernist Aesthetics and the Poetry of Sterling A. Brown*. Athens: Georgia UP, 1999.

Sartwell, Crispin. *Act Like You Know: African-American Autobiography and White Identity*. Chicago UP, 1998.

Sekora, John, and Darwin T. Turner, eds. *The Art of Slave Narrative: Original Essays in Criticism and Theory*. Macomb: Western Illinois UP, 1982.

Smethurst, James Edward. *The New Red Negro: The Literary Left and African American Poetry, 1930–1946*. New York: Oxford UP, 1999.

Smith, Valerie. *Self-Discovery and Authority in Afro-American Narrative*. Cambridge, Mass.: Harvard UP, 1987.

Soitos, Stephen F. *The Blues Detective: A Study of African American Detective Fiction*. Amherst: Massachusetts UP, 1996.

Stepto, Robert. *From Behind the Veil: A Study of Afro-American Narrative*. Urbana: Illinois UP, 1979.

Tate, Claudia. *Psychoanalysis and Black Novels: Desire and the Protocols of Race*. New York: Oxford UP, 1998.

Watta, Oumarou. *Allegory for Real: A Theory of the Afro-American Novel: Essays*. Washington, D.C.: Pyramid Papyrus, 1992.

PERIOD STUDIES

Baker, Houston A. *Modernism and the Harlem Renaissance*. Chicago: Chicago UP, 1987.

Baker, Houston A., and Patricia Redmond, eds. *Afro-American Literary Study in the 1990s*. Chicago: Chicago UP, 1989.

Cooke, Michael G. *Afro-American Literature in the Twentieth Century: The Achievement of Intimacy*. New Haven: Yale UP, 1990.

De Jongh, James. *Vicious Modernism: Black Harlem and the Literary Imagination*. Cambridge: Cambridge UP, 1990.

Favor, J. Martin, *Authentic Blackness: The Folk in the New Negro Renaissance*. Durham, N.C.: Duke UP, 1999.

Flowers, Sandra Hollin. *African American Nationalist Literature of the 1960s: Pens of Fire*. New York: Garland, 1996.

Gayle, Addison, Jr., ed. *The Black Aesthetic*. Garden City, N.Y.: Doubleday, 1971.

Harper, Phillip Brian. *Framing the Margins: The Social Logic of Postmodern Culture.* New York: Oxford UP, 1994.

Hogue, W. Lawrence. *Race, Modernity, Postmodernity: A Look at the History and the Literatures of People of Color since the 1960s.* Albany: SUNY Press, 1996.

Jack, Belinda Elizabeth. *Negritude and Literary Criticism: The History and Theory of 'Negro-African' Literature in French.* Westport, Conn.: Greenwood Press, 1996.

Johnson, Abby A., and Ronald Johnson. *Propaganda and Aesthetics: The Literary Politics of Afro-American Magazines in the Twentieth Century.* Amherst: Massachusetts UP, 1991.

Johnson, Charles. *Being and Race: Black Writing since 1970.* Bloomington: Indiana UP, 1990.

Johnson, Eloise E. *Rediscovering the Harlem Renaissance: The Politics of Exclusion.* New York: Garland, 1997.

Leitch, Vincent B. *American Literary Criticism from the Thirties to the Eighties.* New York: Columbia UP, 1988.

Nielsen, Aldon Lynn. *Black Chant: Languages of African-American Postmodernism.* New York: Cambridge UP, 1996.

———. *Reading Race: White American Poets and the Racial Discourse in the Twentieth Century.* Athens: Georgia UP, 1990.

North, Michael. *The Dialect of Modernism: Race, Language, and Twentieth-Century Literature.* New York: Oxford UP, 1994.

Nunez, Elizabeth, and Brenda M. Greene, eds. *Defining Ourselves: Black Writers in the 90s.* New York: Peter Lang, 1999.

Roberts, John W. *From Trickster to Badman: The Black Folk Hero in Slavery and Freedom.* Pennsylvania State UP, 1990.

Singh, Amritjit. *The Novels of the Harlem Renaissance: Twelve Black Writers, 1923–1933.* University Park: Pennsylvania State UP, 1976.

Spillers, Hortense, ed. *Comparative American Identities: Race, Sex, and Nationality in the Modern Text.* New York: Routledge, 1991.

Thompson, Julius E. *Dudley Randall, Broadside Press, and the Black Arts Movement in Detroit, 1960–1995.* Jefferson, N.C.: McFarland, 1999.

Wall, Cheryl A. *Women of the Harlem Renaissance.* Bloomington: Indiana UP, 1995.

Wintz, Cary D. *Black Culture and the Harlem Renaissance.* Houston, Tex.: Rice UP, 1998.

———, ed. *The Emergence of the Harlem Renaissance.* New York: Garland, 1996.

———. *Politics and Aesthetics of "New Negro" Literature.* New York: Garland, 1996.

STUDY AND REFERENCE AIDS

Barry, Peter. *Beginning Theory: An Introduction to Literary and Cultural Theory.* Manchester: Manchester UP 1995.

Draper, James P, ed. *Black Literature Criticism: Excerpts from Criticism of the Most Significant Works of Black Authors over the Past 200 Years.* Detroit: Gale, 1991.

Earnshaw, Steven. *The Direction of Literary Theory: Generations of Meaning.* New York: St. Martin's, 1996.

Fowler, Carolyn, comp. *Black Arts and Black Aesthetics: A Bibliography.* Atlanta: First World, 1981.

Hawthorn, Jeremy. *A Concise Glossary of Contemporary Literary Theory.* New York: Oxford UP, 1998.

Hunter, Jeffrey W., and Timothy J. White, eds. *Contemporary Literary Criticism: Excerpts from Criticism of the Works of Today's Novelists, Poets, Playwrights, Short Story Writers, Scriptwriters, and Other Creative Writers*, Vol. 116. New York: Gale, 1999.

Makaryk, Irene R., general ed. *Encyclopedia of Contemporary Literary Theory: Approaches, Scholars, Terms*. Toronto: Toronto UP, 1993.

Marshall, Donald G., comp. *Contemporary Critical Theory: A Selective Bibliography*. New York: MLA, 1994.

Mishkin, Tracy, ed. *Literary Influence and African-American Writers: Collected Essays*. New York: Garland, 1995.

Mitchell, Angelyn, ed. *Within the Circle: An Anthology of African American Literary Criticism from the Harlem Renaissance to the Present*. Durham, N.C. Duke UP, 1994.

Murfin, Ross C., and Supryia M. Ray. *The Bedford Glossary of Critical and Literary Terms*. Boston: Bedford Books, 1997.

Payne Michael, Meenakshi Ponnuswami, and Jennifer Payne, eds. *A Dictionary of Cultural and Critical Theory*. New York: Blackwell, 1998.

Sollors, Werner, and Maria Diedrich, eds. *The Black Columbiad: Defining Moments in African American Literature and Culture*. Cambridge, Mass.: Harvard UP, 1994.

Steel, Melili. *Critical Confrontations: Literary Theories in Dialogue*. Columbia: South Carolina UP, 1997.

Tyson, Lois. *Critical Theory Today: A User-Friendly Guide*. New York: Garland, 1998.

Zima, Peter V. *The Philosophy of Modern Literary Theory*. New Brunswick, N.J. Athlone, 1999.

CULTURAL STUDIES AND THEORY

Abrahams, Roger D. *Singing the Master: The Emergence of African American Culture in the Plantation South*. New York: Pantheon Books, 1992.

Adjaye, Joseph K., and Adrianne R. Andrews, eds. *Language, Rhythm, and Sound: Black Popular Cultures into the Twenty-First Century*. Pittsburgh: Pittsburgh UP, 1997.

Appiah, Kwame Anthony, and Henry Louis Gates, Jr., eds. *Identities*. Chicago: Chicago UP, 1995.

Asante, Molefi K., and Mark T. Mattson. *The African-American Atlas: Black History and Culture—An Illustrated Reference*. New York: Macmillan, 1991; rpt. 1998.

Baker, Houston A. *Black Studies, Rap, and the Academy*. Chicago: Chicago UP, 1993.

BaNikongo, Nikongo, ed. *Leading Issues in African-American Studies*. Durham, N.C.: Carolina Academic Press, 1997.

Banner-Haley, Charles Pete T. *The Fruits of Integration: Black Middle-Class Ideology and Culture, 1960–1990*. Jackson: Mississippi UP 1994.

Barlow, William. *Voice Over: The Making of Black Radio*. Philadelphia: Temple UP, 1999.

Baugh, John. *Out of the Mouths of Slaves: African American Language and Educational Malpractice*. Austin: Texas UP, 1999.

Billington, Monroe Lee, and Roger D. Hardaway, eds. *African Americans on the Western Frontier*. Niwot: Colorado UP, 1998.

Blassingame, John W. *The Slave Community: Plantation Life in the Antebellum South*. New York: Oxford UP, 1972.

———. *Slave Testimony: Two Centuries of Letters, Speeches, Interviews, and Autobiographies*. Baton Rouge: Louisiana State UP, 1977.

Boyd, Todd. *Am I Black Enough for You?: Popular Culture from the' Hood and Beyond.* Bloomington: Indiana UP, 1997.

Budick, Emily Miller. *Blacks and Jews in Literary Conversation.* New York: Cambridge UP, 1998.

Cashmore, Ellis. *The Black Culture Industry.* London: Routledge, 1997.

Carby, Hazel. *Culture in Babylon: Black Britain and African America.* London: Verso, 1999.

Coleman. Robin R. Means. *African American Viewers and the Black Situation Comedy: Situating Racial Humor.* New York: Garland, 1998.

Conyers, James L., Jr., ed. *Africana Studies: A Disciplinary Quest for Both Theory and Method.* Jefferson, N.C.: McFarland & Company, 1997.

Cruz, Jon. *Culture on the Margins: The Black Spiritual and the Rise of American Cultural Interpretation.* Princeton: Princeton UP, 1999.

Dates, Jannette, and William Barlow, eds. *Split Image: African Americans in the Mass Media.* Washington, D.C.: Howard UP, 1990.

Davis, Angela, and Joy James. *Resisting State Violence: Radicalism, Gender, and Race in U.S. Culture.* Minneapolis: Minnesota UP, 1996.

Dent, Gina, ed. *Black Popular Culture: A Project by Michele Wallace.* Seattle: Bay Press, 1992.

Diedrich, Maria, Henry Louis Gates, Jr., and Carl Pederson, eds. *Black Imagination and the Middle Passage.* New York: Oxford UP, 1999.

Dorsey, Brian. *Who Stole the Soul?: Blaxploitation in the Harlem Renaissance.* Salzburg: Institut fur Anglistik und Amerikanistik, Universitat Salzburg, 1997.

Douglas, Debbie, Makeda Silvera, Douglas Stewart, and Courtnay McFarlane, eds. *Ma-KA Diasporic Juks: Contemporary Writing by Queers of African Descent.* Toronto: Sister Vision Press, 1997.

duCille, Ann. *Skin Trade.* Cambridge, Mass.: Harvard UP, 1996.

Dyson, Michael Eric. *Between God and Gangsta' Rap: Bearing Witness to Black Culture.* New York: Oxford UP, 1995.

———. *Reflecting Black: African American Cultural Criticism.* Minneapolis: Minnesota UP, 1993.

Early, Gerald. *One Nation under a Groove: Motown and American Culture.* Hopewell, N.J.: Ecco Press, 1995.

Foner, Philip Sheldon, ed. *The Black Panthers Speak.* Philadelphia: Lippincott, 1970.

Fout, John C., and Maura Shaw Tantillo, eds. *American Sexual Politics: Sex, Gender, and Race Since the Civil War.* Chicago: Chicago UP, 1993.

Gandhi, Leela. *Postcolonial Theory: A Critical Introduction.* New York: Columbia UP, 1998.

Gates, Henry Louis, Jr. *Loose Canons: Notes on the Culture War.* New York: Oxford UP, 1993.

———, Kwame Anthony Appiah, and Michael Colin Vazquez, eds. *Transition: Issue 69, Vol. 69.* Durham, N.C.: Duke UP, 1996.

Gates, Nathaniel, ed. *Cultural and Literary Critiques of the Concepts of "Race."* New York: Garland, 1997.

Gatewood, Willard B. *Aristocrats of Color: The Black Elite, 1880–1920.* Bloomington: Indiana UP, 1990.

George, Nelson. *Hip Hop America.* New York: Viking, 1998.

Gershon, Yekutiel. *Africans on African-Americans: The Creation and Uses of an African-American Myth.* New York: New York UP, 1997.

Gilroy, Paul. *The Black Atlantic: Modernity and Double Consciousness.* Cambridge, Mass.: Harvard UP, 1993.

———. *Small Acts: Thoughts on the Politics of Black Cultures.* New York: Serpent's Tail, 1994.

Graham, Lawrence Otis. *Our Kind of People: Inside America's Black Upper Class.* New York: Harper Collins, 1999.

Gray, Herman. *Watching Race: Television and the Struggle for the Sign of Blackness.* Minneapolis: Minnesota UP, 1997.

Gubar, Susan. *Racechanges: White Skin, Black Face in American Culture.* New York: Oxford UP, 1997.

Guillory, Monique, and Richard C. Green, eds. *Soul: Black Power, Politics, and Pleasure.* New York: New York UP, 1998.

Hall, Stuart, ed. *Representation: Cultural Representations and Signifying Practices.* London: Sage, in association with The Open University 1997.

———, and Paul Du Gay, eds. *Questions of Cultural Identity.* London: Sage, 1996.

Hall, Stuart, ed., with Paul Du Gay, Linda Janes, Hugh MacKay, Keith Negus, and Paul Du Gay. *Doing Cultural Studies: The Story of the Sony Walkman.* London: Sage, in association with The Open University, 1997.

Ham, Debra N. African-American Mosaic: *A Library of Congress Resource Guide for the Study of Black History and Culture.* Washington, D.C.: Library of Congress, 1993.

Harper, Phillip Brian. *Private Affairs: Critical Ventures in the Culture of Social Relatiions.* New York: New York UP, 1999.

Harris, Leonard, ed. *Critical Pragmatism of Alain Locke: A Reader on Value Theory, Aesthetics, Community, Culture, Race, and Education.* Lanham, Md.: Rowman & Littlefield, 1999.

———. *Philosophy Born of Struggle: Anthology of Afro-American Philosophy from 1917.* Dubuque, Iowa: Kendall/Hunt, 1983.

Harvey, David. *The Condition of Postmodernity: An Enquiry into the Origins of Cultural Change.* Oxford: Blackwell, 1989.

Hebdige, Dick. *Subculture: The Meaning of Style.* New York: Routledge, 1991.

Henderson, Mae Gwendolyn, ed. *Borders, Boundaries, and Frames: Essays in Cultural Criticism and Cultural Studies.* New York: Routledge, 1994.

Heuman, Gad J., ed. *Out of the House of Bondage: Runaways, Resistance and Marronage in Africa and the New World.* London: Frank Cass, 1986.

Holloway, John S. *Confronting the Veil: New Deal African American Intellectuals and the Evolution of a Radical Voice.* New York: Routledge, 1998.

Holloway, Karla F. C. *Codes of Conduct: Race, Ethics, and the Color of Our Character.* New Brunswick, N.J.: Rutgers UP, 1995.

James, Joy, and Lewis Gordon. *Transcending the Talented Tenth: Black Leaders and American Intellectuals.* New York: Routledge, 1996.

Jameson, Fredric. *The Cultural Turn: Selected Writings on the Postmodern, 1983–1998.* London: Verso, 1998.

Jordan, Winthrop D. *The White Man's Burden; Historical Origins of Racism in the United States.* New York: Oxford UP, 1974.

Kelley, Robin D. G. *Race Rebels: Culture, Politics, and the Black Working Class.* New York: Maxwell Macmillan International, 1994.

———. *Yo' Mama's Disfunktional!: Fighting the Culture Wars in Urban America.* Boston: Beacon, 1998.

Landrine, Hope, and Elizabeth A. Klonoff. *African American Acculturation: Deconstructing Race and Reviving Culture.* Thousand Oaks, Calif.: Sage, 1996.

Leitch, Vincent B. *Postmodernism: Local Effects, Global Flows*. Albany: SUNY Press, 1996.

Lott, Eric. *Love and Theft: Blackface Minstrelsy and the American Working Class*. New York: Oxford UP, 1995.

Lynch, Acklyn. *Nightmare Overhanging Darkly: Essays on African American Culture and Resistance*. Chicago: Third World Press, 1992.

Mama, Amina. *Beyond the Masks: Race, Gender and Subjectivity*. New York: Routledge, 1995.

Manring, M. M. *Slave in a Box: The Strange Career of Aunt Jemima*. Charlottesville: Virginia UP, 1998.

Maxwel, William J. *New Negro, Old Left: African-American Writing and Communism between the Wars*. New York: Columbia UP, 1999.

McClintock, Anne. *Imperial Leather: Race, Gender, and Sexuality in the Colonial Contest*. New York: Routledge, 1995.

McLaughlin, Thomas. *Street Smarts and Critical Theory: Listening to the Vernacular*. Madison: Wisconsin UP, 1996.

Meier, August, Elliott Rudwick, and Francis L. Broderick, eds. *Black Protest Thought in the Twentieth Century*. Indianapolis: Bobbs-Merrill, 1971.

Mellon, James. *Bullwhip Days: The Slaves Remember*. New York: Weidenfeld & Nicolson, 1988.

Mercer, Kobena. *Welcome to the Jungle: New Positions in Black Cultural Studies*. New York: Routledge, 1994.

Merelman, Richard M. *Representing Black Culture: Racial Conflict and Cultural Politics in the United States*. New York: Routledge, 1995.

Morley, David, and Kuan-Hsing Chen, eds. *Stuart Hall: Critical Dialogues in Cultural Studies*. London: Routledge, 1996.

Mufwene, Salikoko S., ed. *African-American English: Structure, History, and Use*. London: Routledge, 1998.

O'Meally, Robert G., and Genevieve E. Fabre, eds. *History and Memory in African American Culture*. New York: Oxford UP, 1994.

Padmini, Mongia. *Contemporary Postcolonial Theory: A Reader*. London: Edward Arnold, 1996.

Posnock, Ross. *Color and Culture: Black Writers and the Making of the Modern Intellectual*. Cambridge, Mass.: Harvard UP, 1998.

Potter, Russell A. *Spectacular Vernaculars: Hip-Hop and the Politics of Postmodernism*. Albany: SUNY Press, 1995.

Reagon, Bernice J., ed. *Black American Culture and Scholarship: Contemporary Issues*. Washington, D.C.: National Museum of American History, Smithsonian Institution, 1985.

Robinson, Cedric J. *Black Marxism: The Making of the Black Radical Tradition*. London: Zed; Totowa, N.J.: Biblio Distribution Center, 1983.

———. *Black Movements in America*. New York: Routledge, 1997.

Rooks, Noliwe M. *Hair Raising: Beauty, Culture, and African American Women*. New Brunswick, N.J.: Rutgers UP, 1996.

Ross, Andrew. *Real Love: In Pursuit of Cultural Justice*. New York: New York UP, 1998.

Rotenberg, Robert, and Gary McDonogh, eds. *The Cultural Meaning of Urban Space*. Westport, Conn.: Bergin and Garvey, 1993.

Sekayi, Dia N. R. *African American Intellectual-Activists: Legacies in the Struggle*. New York: Garland, 1997.

Shaw, Harry B. *Perspectives of Black Popular Culture*. Bowling Green, Ohio: Bowling Green Popular Press, 1990.

Silk, Catherine, and John Silk. *Racism and Anti-Racism in American Popular Culture: Portrayals of African-Americans in Fiction and Film*. Manchester: Manchester UP, 1990.

Smitherman, Geneva. *Talkin' and Testifyin': The Language of Black America*. Detroit: Wayne State UP, 1977.

Stewart, Jeffrey C., ed. *The Critical Temper of Alain Locke: A Selection of His Essays on Art and Culture*. New York: Garland, 1983.

Stuckey, Sterling. *The Ideological Origins of Black Nationalism*. Boston: Beacon Press, 1972.

————. *Slave Culture: Nationalist Theory and the Foundations of Black America*. New York: Oxford UP, 1987.

Tate, Greg. *Flyboy in the Buttermilk: Essays on Contemporary America*. New York: Simon & Schuster, 1992.

Thompson, Thompson. *Flash of the Spirit: African and Afro-American Art and Philosophy*. New York: Random House, 1984.

Turner, Patricia. A. *Ceramic Uncles and Celluloid Mammies: Black Images and Their Influence on Culture*. New York: Anchor Books, 1994.

Tyson, Timothy B. *Radio Free Dixie: Robert F. Williams and the Roots of Black Power*. Chapel Hill: North Carolina UP, 1999.

Valdivia, Angharad N. *Feminism, Multiculturalism, and the Media: Global Diversities*. Thousand Oaks, Calif.: Sage, 1995.

Van Deburg, William L. *Black Camelot: African-American Culture Heroes in Their Times, 1960–1980*. Chicago: Chicago UP, 1997.

————. *New Day in Babylon: The Black Power Movement and American Culture, 1965–1975*. Chicago: Chicago UP, 1992.

Vincent, Theodore G. *Voices of a Black Nation: Political Journalism in the Harlem Renaissance*. San Francisco: Ramparts Press, 1973.

Wallace, Michelle. *Invisibility Blues: From Pop to Theory*. London: Verso, 1990.

Watkins, Mel. *On the Real Side: Laughing, Lying, and Signifying: The Underground Tradition of African-American Humor that Transformed American Culture, from Slavery to Richard Pryor*. New York: Simon & Schuster, 1994.

Watts, Jerry Gafio. *Heroism and the Black Intellectual: Ralph Ellison, Politics, and Afro-American Intellectual Life*. Chapel Hill: North Carolina UP, 1994.

West, Cornel. *Beyond Eurocentrism and Multiculturalism*. Monroe, Me.: Common Courage Press, 1993.

White, Shane, and Graham White. *Stylin': African American Expressive Culture, from Its Beginnings to the Zoot Suit*. Ithaca, N.Y.: Cornell UP, 1998.

Wright, W. D. *Black Intellectuals, Black Cognition, and a Black Aesthetic*. Westport, Conn.: Greenwood Press, 1997.

Yancy, George, ed. *African-American Philosophers: 17 Conversations*. New York: Routledge, 1998.

Young, Mary E. *Mules and Dragons: Popular Culture Images in the Selected Writings of African-American and Chinese-American Women Writers*. Westport, Conn.: Greenwood Press, 1993.

Zook, Kristal Brent. *Color by Fox: The Fox Network and the Revolution in Black Television*. New York: Oxford UP, 1999.

FEMINIST THEORY AND CRITICISM

Abel, Elizabeth, Barbara Christian, and Helene Moglen, eds. *Female Subjects in Black and White: Race, Psychoanalysis, Feminism.* Berkeley: California UP, 1997.

Allan, Tuzyline Jita. *Womanist and Feminist Aesthetics: A Comparative Review.* Athens: Ohio UP, 1995.

Allen, Carol. *Black Women Intellectuals: Strategies of Nation, Family, and Neighborhood in the Works of Pauline Hopkins, Jessie Fauset, and Marita Bonner.* New York: Garland, 1998.

Awkward, Michael, and Carolyn G. Heilbrun, eds. *Inspiriting Influences: Tradition, Revision, and Afro-American Women's Novels.* New York: Columbia UP, 1991.

Baker, Houston A. *Workings of the Spirit: A Poetics of Afro-American Women's Writing.* Chicago: Chicago UP, 1991.

Baker-Fletcher, Karen. *A Singing Something: Womanist Reflections on Anna Julia Cooper.* New York: Crossroad, 1994.

Banks, Ingrid. *Hair Matters: Beauty, Power, and Black Women's Consciousness.* New York: New York UP, 2000.

Bassard, Katherine Clay. *Spiritual Interrogations: Culture, Gender, and Community in Early African American Women's Writing.* Princeton: Princeton UP, 1998.

Beaulieu, Elizabeth Ann. *Black Women Writers and the American Neo-Slave Narrative: Femininity Unfettered.* Westport, Conn.: Greenwood Press, 1999.

Bell, Roseann P., Bettye J. Parker, and Beverly Guy-Sheftall, eds. *Sturdy Black Bridges: Visions of Black Women in Literature.* Garden City, N.Y.: Anchor, 1975.

Bobo, Jacqueline. *Black Women as Cultural Readers.* New York: Columbia UP, 1995.

Braxton, Joanne M., and Andree Nicola McLaughlin, eds. *Wild Women in the Whirlwind: Afra-American Culture and the Contemporary Literary Renaissance.* New Brunswick, N.J.: Rutgers UP, 1990.

Brody, Jennifer Devere. *Impossible Purities: Blackness, Femininity, and Victorian Culture.* Durham, N.C.: Duke UP, 1998.

Butler-Evans, Elliot. *Race, Gender, and Desire: Narrative Strategies in the Fiction of Toni Cade Bambara, Toni Morrison, and Alice Walker.* Philadelphia: Temple UP, 1991.

Carby, Hazel V. *Reconstructing Womanhood: The Emergence of the Afro-American Woman Novelist.* New York: Oxford UP, 1990.

Carroll, Rebecca. *I Know What the Red Clay Looks Like: The Voice and Vision of Black Women Writers.* New York: Random House, 1994.

Christian, Barbara. *Black Feminist Criticism: Perspectives on Black Women Writers.* New York: Pergamon, 1985.

———. *Black Women Novelists: The Development of a Tradition, 1892–1976.* Westport, Conn.: Greenwood Press, 1980.

Clark, VeVe, A. Ruth-Ellen B. Joeres, and Madelon Sprengnether, eds. *Revising the Word and the World: Essays in Feminist Literary Criticism.* Chicago: Chicago UP, 1993.

Conboy, Katie, Nadia Medina, and Sarah Stanbury, eds. *Writing on the Body: Female Embodiment and Feminist Theory.* New York: Columbia UP, 1997.

Davies, Carole Boyce. *Black Women, Writing and Identity: Migrations of the Subject.* New York: Routledge, 1994.

Dubey, Madhu. *Black Women Novelists and the Nationalist Aesthetic.* Bloomington: Indiana UP, 1994.

duCille, Ann. *The Coupling Convention: Sex, Text, and Tradition in Black Women's Fiction.* New York: Oxford UP, 1993.

Gates, Henry Louis, Jr., ed. *Reading Black, Reading Feminist: A Critical Anthology.* New York: Meridian, 1990.

Giddings, Paula. *When and Where I Enter: The Impact of Black Women on Race and Sex in America.* New York: William Morrow, 1984.

Hall, Chekita T. *Gloria Naylor's Feminist Blues Aesthetic.* New York: Garland, 1998.

Hammonds, Evelynn, Barbara Laslett, Sally Gregory Kohlstedt, and Helen Longino, eds. *Gender and Scientific Authority.* Chicago: Chicago UP, 1996.

Hernton, Calvin. *The Sexual Mountain and Black Women Writers.* New York: Doubleday, 1987.

Hill-Collins, Patricia. *Black Feminist Thought: Knowledge, Consciousness, and the Politics of Empowerment.* Boston: Unwin Hyman, 1990.

————. *Fighting Words: Black Women and the Search for Justice.* Minneapolis: Minnesota UP, 1999.

————, and Margaret L. Andersen, eds. *Race, Class, and Gender: An Anthology.* Belmont, Calif.: Wadsworth, 1992.

Holloway, Karla F. C. *Moorings and Metaphors: Figures of Culture and Gender in Black Women's Literature.* New Brunswick, N.J.: Rutgers UP, 1992.

hooks, bell. *Ain't I a Woman: Black Women and Feminism.* Boston: South End Press, 1981.

————. *Feminist Theory from Margin to Center.* Boston: South End Press, 1984.

————. *Talking Back: Thinking Feminist, Thinking Black.* Boston: South End Press, 1989.

————. *Yearning: Race, Gender, and Cultural Politics.* Boston: South End Press, 1989.

Hull, Gloria T., Barbara Smith, and Patricia Bell Scott, eds. *All the Women Are White, All the Blacks Are Men, But Some of Us Are Brave: Black Women's Studies.* New York: Feminist Press at CUNY, 1981.

James, Joy. *Shadowboxing: Representation of Black Feminist Politics.* New York: St. Martins, 1999.

James, Stanlie M., and Abena P. A. Busia, eds. *Theorizing Feminisms: The Visionary Pragmatism of Black Women.* London: Routledge, 1993.

Johnson, Barbara. *The Feminist Difference: Literature, Psychoanalysis, Race, and Gender.* Cambridge, Mass.: Harvard UP, 1997.

Logan, Shirley Wilson. *"We Are Coming": The Persuasive Discourse of Nineteenth-Century Black Women.* Carbondale: Southern Illinois UP, 1999.

McDowell, Deborah E. *The Changing Same: Black Women's Literature, Criticism, and Theory.* Bloomington, Ind.: Indiana UP, 1995.

Meisenhelder, Susan Edwards. *Hitting a Straight Lick with a Crooked Stick: Race and Gender in the Work of Zora Neale Hurston.* Tuscaloosa: Alabama UP, 1999.

Mori, Aoi. *Toni Morrison and Womanist Discourse.* New York: Peter Lang, 1999.

Nordquist, Joan, comp. *Women of Color—Feminist Theory: A Bibliography.* Santa Cruz, Calif.: Reference and Research Services, 1995.

Parker, Patricia, and Margo Hendricks. *Women, "Race," and Writing in the Early Modern Period.* New York: Routledge, 1994.

Pearce, Lynne. *Feminism and the Politics of Reading.* London: Edward Arnold, 1997.

Plant, Deborah G. *Every Tub Must Sit on Its Own Bottom: The Philosophy and Politics of Zora Neale Hurston.* Urbana: Illinois UP, 1995.

Salvaggio, Ruth. *The Sounds of Feminist Theory.* Albany: SUNY Press, 1999.

Smith, Barbara, ed. *Home Girls: A Black Feminist Anthology*. New York: Kitchen Table—Women of Color Press, 1983.

———. *The Truth That Never Hurts: Writings on Race, Gender, and Freedom*. New Brunswick, NJ: Rutgers UP, 1998.

Smith, Dianne. *Womanlish Black Girls: Dancing Contradictions of Resistance*. New York: Peter Lang Publishing, 2000.

Smith, Valerie. *Not Just Race, Not Just Gender: Black Feminist Readings*. New York: Routledge, 1998.

Spillers, Hortense, and Marjorie Pryse, eds. *Conjuring: Black Women, Fiction, and Literary Tradition*. Bloomington: Indiana UP, 1985.

Stanley, Sandra Kumamoto; ed. *Other Sisterhoods: Literary Theory and U.S. Women of Color*. Urbana: Illinois UP, 1998.

Tate, Claudia. *Domestic Allegories of Political Desire: The Black Heroine's Text at the Turn of the Century*. New York: Oxford UP, 1992.

Wall, Cheryl A., ed. *Changing Our Own Words: Essays on Criticism, Theory, and Writing by Black Women*. New Brunswick, N.J.: Rutgers UP, 1989.

Wallace, Michelle. *Black Macho and the Myth of the Superwoman*. London: Calder, 1979.

White, Deborah Gray. *Too Heavy a Load: Black Women in Defense of Themselves, 1894–1994*. New York: W. W. Norton, 1998.

Willis, Susan. *Specifying: Black Women Writing the American Experience*. Madison: Wisconsin UP, 1990.

Wing, Adrien Katherine, ed. *Critical Race Feminism: A Reader*. New York: New York UP, 1996.

PERFORMANCE AND VISUAL ARTS

Anadolu-Okur, Nilgun. *Contemporary African American Theater: Afrocentricity in the Works of Larry Neal, Amiri Baraka, and Charles Fuller*. New York: Garland, 1997.

Anderson, Lisa M. *Mammies No More: The Changing Image of Black Women on Stage and Screen*. Lanham, Md.: Rowman & Littlefield, 1997.

Bailey, David A., and Catherine Ugwu. *Mirage: Enigmas of Race, Difference and Desire*. London: Institute of Contemporary Arts, Institute of International Visual Arts, 1995.

Bane, Michael. *White Boy Singin' the Blues: The Black Roots of White Rock*. New York: Penguin Books, 1982.

Baraka, Amiri. *The Music: Reflections on Jazz and Blues*. New York: William Morrow, 1987.

Cripps, Thomas. *Slow Fade to Black: The Negro in American Film, 1900–1942*. New York: Oxford UP, 1977.

Davis, Angela Y. *Blues Legacies and Black Feminism: Gertrude "Ma" Rainey, Bessie Smith, and Billie Holiday*. New York: Pantheon Books, 1998.

Diawara, Manthia. *Black American Cinema*. New York: Routledge, 1994.

Driskell, David C., ed. *African American Visual Aesthetics: A Postmodernist View*. Washington, D.C.: Smithsonian Institution, 1995.

Driskell, David C., David Levering Lewis, and Deborah Willis Ryan. *Harlem Renaissance: Art of Black America*. New York: Studio Museum in Harlem and Abrams, 1987.

Euba, Femi. *Archetypes, Imprecators, and Victims of Fate: Origins and Developments of Satire in Black Drama*. Westport, Conn.: Greenwood Press, 1989.

Friedman, Lester D. *Unspeakable Images: Ethnicity and the American Cinema*. Urbana: University of Illinois Press, 1991.

Gabbard, Erin, ed. *Jazz among the Discourses*. Durham, N.C.: Duke UP, 1995.

Gerard, Charley. *Jazz in Black and White: Race, Culture, and Identity in the Jazz Community*. Westport, Conn.: Praeger, 1998.

Guerreo, Ed. *Framing Blackness: The African American Image in Film (Culture and the Moving Image)*. Philadelphia: Temple UP. 1993.

Hazzard-Gordon, Katrina. *Jookin': The Rise of Social Dance Formations in African-American Culture*. Philadelphia: Temple UP, 1990.

Hill, Anthony D. *Pages from the Harlem Renaissance: A Chronicle of Performance*. New York: Peter Lang, 1996.

hooks, bell. *Reel to Real: Race, Sex, and Class at the Movies*. New York: Routledge, 1996.

James, Darius. *That's Blaxploitation!: Roots of the Baadasssss 'tude (Rated X by an All-Whyte Jury)*. New York: St. Martin's Griffin, 1995.

Kirschke, Amy Helene. *Aaron Douglas: Art, Race, and the Harlem Renaissance*. Jackson: Mississippi UP, 1995.

Krasner, David. *Resistance, Parody, and Double Consciousness in African American Theatre, 1895–1910*. New York: St. Martin's, 1997.

Lhamon, W. T., Jr. *Raising Cain: Blackface Performance from Jim Crow to Hip Hop*. Cambridge, Mass.: Harvard UP, 1997.

MacCabe, Colin, and Cornel West, eds. *White Screens, Black Images: Hollywood from the Dark Side/James Snead*. New York: Routledge, 1994.

Malone, Jacqui. *Steppin' on the Blues: The Visible Rhythms of African American Dance*. Urbana: Illinois UP, 1996.

Martin, Michael T., ed. *Cinemas of the Black Diaspora: Diversity, Dependence, and Oppositionality*. Detroit: Wayne State UP, 1995.

McKee, Margaret, and Fred Chisenhall. *Beale Black and Blue: Life and Music on Black America's Main Street*. Baton Rouge: Louisiana State UP, 1981.

Merlis, Bob, and Davin Seay. *Heart and Soul: A Celebration of Black Music Style in America 1930–1975*. New York: Stewart, Tabori & Chang, 1997.

Munoz, Jose Esteban. *Disidentifications: Queers of Color and the Performance of Politics*. Minneapolis: Minnesota UP, 1999.

Murray, Timothy. *Drama Trauma: Specters of Race and Sexuality in Performing Video and Art*. New York: Routledge, 1997.

Neal, Mark Anthony. *What the Music Said: Black Popular Music and Black Public Culture*. New York: Routledge, 1998.

Olaniyan, Tejumola. *Scars of Conquest/Masks of Resistance: The Invention of Cultural Identities in African-American, and Caribbean Drama*. New York: Oxford UP, 1995.

Panish, Jon. *The Color of Jazz: Race and Representation in Postwar American Culture*. Jackson: Mississippi UP, 1997.

Peretti, Burton. *The Creation of Jazz: Music, Race and Culture in Urban America*. Urbana: Illinois UP, 1992.

Perkins, William Eric, ed. *Droppin' Science: Critical Essays on Rap Music and Hip Hop Culture*. Philadelphia: Temple UP, 1995.

Pieterse, Jan Nederveen. *White on Black: Images of Africa and Blacks in Western Popular Culture*. New Haven: Yale UP, 1992.

Powell, Richard J. *Black Art and Culture in the 20th Century*. New York: Thames & Hudson, 1997.

————. *The Blues Aesthetic: Black Culture and Modernism.* Washington, D.C.: Washington Project for the Arts, 1989.

————, with David A. Bailey and Paul Gilroy. *Rhapsodies in Black: Art of the Harlem Renaissance.* Berkeley: California UP, 1997.

Reid, Mark A. *PostNegritude Visual and Literary Culture.* Albany: SUNY UP, 1997.

Rose, Tricia. *Black Noise: Rap Music and Black Culture in Contemporary America Music/Culture.* Hanover, NH: Wesleyan UP, 1994.

Rosenthal, David H. *Hard Bop: Jazz and Black Music 1955–1965.* New York: Oxford UP, 1992.

Sampson, Henry T. *That's Enough, Folks: Black Images in Animated Cartoons, 1900–1960.* Lanham, Md.: Scarecrow Press, 1998.

Schafer, William John, and Johannes Reidel. *The Art of Ragtime: Form and Meaning of an Original Black American Art.* Baton Rouge: Louisiana State UP, 1973.

Spencer, Jon Michael, ed. *Sacred Music of the Secular City: From Blues to Rap.* Durham, N.C.: Duke UP, 1992.

————. *The New Negroes and Their Music: The Success of the Harlem Renaissance.* Knoxville: Tennessee UP, 1997.

Stuckey, Sterling. *Going Through the Storm: The Influence of African American Art in History.* New York: Oxford UP, 1994.

Turner, Elizabeth Hutton, ed. *Jacob Lawrence: The Migration Series.* Washington, D.C.: Rappahannock Press in association with the Phillips Collection, 1993.

Tyler, Bruce Michael. *From Harlem to Hollywood: The Struggle for Racial and Cultural Democracy, 1920–1943.* New York: Garland, 1992.

Ward, Brian. *Just My Soul Responding: Rhythm and Blues, Black Consciousness, and Race Relations.* Berkeley: California UP, 1998.

Watkins, S. Craig. *Representing: Hip Hop Culture and the Production of Black Cinema.* Chicago: Chicago UP, 1998.

Werner, Craig Hansen. *Playing the Changes: From Afro-Modernism to the Jazz Impulse.* Urbana: Illinois UP, 1994.

Wheat, Ellen Harkins, ed. *Jacob Lawrence: The Frederick Douglass and Harriet Tubman Series of 1938–40.* Hampton, Va.: Hampton University Museum in association with Washington UP, Seattle, 1991.

Woll, Allen L. *Black Musical Theatre: From Coontown to Dreamgirls.* Baton Rouge: Louisiana State UP, 1989.

Yearwood, Gladstone L. *Black Film as a Signifying Practice: Cinema, Narration and the African American Aesthetic Tradition.* Lawrenceville, N.J.: Africa World Press, 1998.

RACE STUDIES

Adams, Michael Vannoy. *The Multicultural Imagination: "Race," Color, and the Unconscious.* London: Routledge, 1996.

Armour, Jody David. *Negrophobia and Reasonable Racism: The Hidden Costs of Being Black in America.* New York: New York UP, 1997.

Babbitt, Susan E., and Sue Campbell, eds. *Racism and Philosophy.* Ithacn, N.Y.: Cornell UP, 1999.

Baker, Lee D. *From Savage to Negro: Anthropology and the Construction of Race, 1896–1954.* Berkeley: California UP, 1998.

Banks, William M. *Black Intellectuals: Race and Responsibility in American Life*. New York: Norton, 1998.

Banton, Michael P. *The Idea of Race*. London: Tavistock, 1977.

Barrett, Lindon. *Blackness and Value: Seeing Double*. New York: Cambridge UP, 1998.

Bell, Bernard W., Emily Grosholz, and James B. Stewart, eds. *W. E. B. Du Bois on Race and Culture: Philosophy, Politics, and Poetics*. New York: Routledge, 1996.

Crenshaw, Kimberle, ed. *Critical Race Theory: The Key Writing That Formed the Movement*. New York: New Press, 1995.

Fossett, Judith Jackson, and Jeffrey A. Tucker, eds. *Race Consciousness: African-American Studies for the New Century*. New York: New York UP, 1997.

Frederickson, George M. *The Arrogance of Race: Historical Perspectives on Slavery, Racism, and Social Inequality*. Middletown, Conn.: Wesleyan UP, 1988.

————. *The Black Image in the White Mind: The Debate on Afro-American Character and Destiny, 1817–1914*. New York: Harper and Row, 1971.

Gates, Henry Louis, Jr., and Cornel West. *The Future of Race*. New York: Random House, 1997.

Gordon, Lewis, R. *Bad Faith and Antiblack Racism*. Atlantic Highlands, N.J.: Humanities Press, 1995.

————. *Her Majesty's Other Children: Sketches of Racism from a Neocolonial Age*. Lanham, Md.: Rowman & Littlefield, 1997.

————, ed. *Existence in Black: An Anthology of Black Existential Philosophy*. New York: Routledge, 1997.

————, and Renee T. White, eds. *Black Texts and Textuality: Constructing and Deconstructing Blackness*. New York: Rowman and Littlefield, 1999.

Gregory, Steven, and Roger Sanjek, eds. *Race*. New Brunswick, N.J.: Rutgers UP, 1994.

Haller, John S. *Outcasts from Evolution; Scientific Attitudes of Racial Inferiority, 1859–1900*. Urbana: Illinois UP, 1971.

Huemer, A. A. *Invention of "Race": The Columbian Turn in Modern Consciousness*. Lander, Wyo.: Agathon Books, 1998.

LaCapra, Dominick. *The Bounds of Race: Perspectives on Hegemony and Resistance*. Ithaca, N.Y.: Cornell UP, 1991.

Lorini, Alessandra. *Rituals of Race: American Public Culture and the Search for Racial Democracy*. Charlottesville: Virginia UP, 1999.

Lott, Tommy Lee. *The Invention of Race: Black Culture and the Politics of Representation*. Malden, Mass.: Blackwell, 1999.

Lubiano, Wahneema, ed. *The House that Race Built*. New York: Vintage Books, 1998.

Mills, Charles W. *Blackness Visible: Essays on Philosophy and Race*. Ithaca, N.Y.: Cornell UP, 1998.

Omi, Michael, and Howard Winant. *Racial Formation in the United States: From the 1960s to the 1990s*. New York: Routledge, 1994.

Outlaw, Lucius. *On Race and Philosophy*. New York: Routledge, 1996.

Scott-Childress, Reynolds J., and Rennie Childress, eds. *Race and the Production of Modern American Nationalism*. New York: Garland, 1998.

Voegelin, Eric. Ruth Hein, trans. *The History of the Race Idea: From Ray to Carus*. Baton Rouge: Louisiana State UP, 1998.

West, Cornel. *Keeping Faith: Philosophy and Race in America*. New York: Routledge, 1993.

————. *Race Matters*. Boston: Beacon Press, 1993.

Wiegman, Robyn. *American Anatomies: Theorizing Race and Gender*. Durham, N.C.: Duke UP, 1995.

Williams, Vernon J., Jr. *Rethinking Race: Franz Boas and His Contemporaries*. Lexington: Kentucky UP, 1996.

Williamson, Joel. *The Crucible of Race: Black-White Relations in the American South since Emancipation*. New York: Oxford UP, 1984.

Zack, Naomi, ed. *American Mixed Race: The Culture of Microdiversity*. Lanham, Md.: Rowman & Littlefield, 1995.

———. *Race and Mixed Race*. Philadelphia: Temple UP, 1993.

———. *Race/Sex: Their Sameness, Difference, and Interplay*. New York: Routledge, 1997.

———. *Thinking about Race*. Belmont, Calif.: Wadsworth, 1998.

MASCULINITY STUDIES

Bederman, Gail, and Catherine R. Stimpson. *Manliness and Civilization: A Cultural History of Gender and Race in the United States, 1880–1917*. Chicago: Chicago UP, 1996.

Belton, Don, ed. *Speak My Name: Black Men on Masculinity and the American Dream*. Boston: Beacon Press, 1995.

Black, Daniel P. *Dismantling Black Manhood: An Historical and Literary Analysis of the Legacy of Slavery*. New York: Garland, 1997.

Blount, Marcellus, and George P. Cunningham, eds. *Representing Black Men*. New York: Routledge, 1994.

Boyd, Herb, and Robert L. Allen, eds. *Brotherman: The Odyssey of Black Men in America*. New York: Ballantine Books, 1996.

Brod, Harry, ed. *The Making of Masculinities: The New Men's Studies*. New York: Viking, 1987.

Carbado, Devon, ed. *Black Men on Race, Gender, and Sexuality: A Critical Reader*. New York: New York UP, 1999.

Carby, Hazel V. *Race Men*. Cambridge, Mass.: Harvard UP, 1998.

Connor, Marlene K. *What Is Cool?: Black Manhood in America*. New York: Crown, 1995.

Gilmore, David. *Manhood in the Making: Cultural Concepts of Masculinity*. New Haven: Yale UP, 1990.

Golden, Thelma. *Black Male: Representations of Masculinity in Contemporary American Art*. New York: Whitney Museum of American Art, 1994.

Harper, Phillip Brian. *Are We Not Men?: Masculine Anxiety and the Problem of African Identity*. New York: Oxford UP, 1996.

———, Jose Esteban Munoz, and Trish Rosen, eds. *Queer Transexions of Race, Nation, and Gender*, Vol. 15. Durham, N.C.: Duke UP, 1997.

Leab, Daniel. J. *From Sambo to Super Spade*. Boston: Houghton Mifflin, 1976.

Majors, Richard G., and Jacob U. Gordon, eds. *The American Black Male: His Present Status and His Future*. Chicago: Nelson-Hall, 1994.

Majors, Richard G., and Janet Mancini. *Cool Pose: The Dilemmas of Black Manhood in America*. New York: Maxwell Macmillan International, 1992.

Pettiway, Leon E. *Honey, Honey, Miss Thang: Being Black, Gay and on the Streets*. Philadelphia: Temple UP, 1996.

Sale, Maggie Montesinos. *The Slumbering Volcano: American Slave Ship Revolts and the Production of Rebellious Masculinity*. Durham, N.C.: Duke UP, 1997.

Staples, Robert. *Black Masculinity: The Black Male's Role in American Society*. San Francisco: Black Scholar Press, 1982.

Stecopoulos, Harry, and Michael Uebel, eds. *Race and the Subject of Masculinities*. Durham, N.C.: Duke UP, 1997.

White, Joseph L., and James H. Cones III. *Black Man Emerging: Facing the Past and Seizing a Future in America*. New York: W. H. Freeman, 1999.

Contributors

SANDRA ADELL is Associate Professor in the Department of Afro-American Studies at the University of Wisconsin, Madison, where she specializes in literary criticism and theory. She is the author of *Double-Consciousness/Double Bind: Theoretical Issues in Twentieth-Century Black Literature.*

MICHAEL AWKWARD is Associate Professor of English and African American Studies at the University of Pennsylvania. He is the author of *Negotiating Difference: Race, Gender, and the Politics of Positionality and Inspiriting Influences: Tradition, Revision, and Afro-American Women's Novels.* He is also the editor of *New Essays on "Their Eyes Were Watching God."*

HOUSTON A. BAKER, JR., is the Susan Fox Beischer and George D. Beischer Arts and Sciences Professor of English at Duke University. A central force in the development of African American literary theory, he is the author of *Long Black Song: Essays in Black American Literature; Singers of daybreak: Studies in Black American Literature; Blues, Ideology, and Afro-American Literature: A Vernacular Theory; The Journey Back: Issues in Black Literature and Criticism;* and *Workings of the Spirit: The Politics of Afro-American Women's Writing.*

AMIRI BARAKA (LEROI JONES) is Professor Emeritus of Africana Studies at the State University of New York, Stony Brook. Playwright, poet, essayist, Baraka established himself during the 1960s and 1970s as the leading literary figure of the Black Cultural Revolution. His books on African American art and culture include *Blues People; Home: Social Essays; Raise, Race, Rays, Raze; Daggers and Javelins;* and *The Music: Reflections on Jazz and Blues.* He is also co-editor, with Larry Neal, of the seminal *Black Fire: An Anthology of Afro-American Writing.*

HAZEL V. CARBY is Professor of English and Director of the Department of African American Studies at Yale University. A feminist scholar and specialist in African American culture, she is the author of *Reconstructing Women: The Emergence of the Afro-American Women Novelist.* Other publications include *Race Men* and, most recently, *Culture in Babylon: Black Britain and African America.*

691

BARBARA CHRISTIAN is professor of English and African American Studies at the University of California, Berkeley. She is the author of *Black Women Novelists: The Development of a Tradition, 1892–1976* and *Black Feminist Criticism: Perspective on Black Women Writers*. She is also a co-editor, with Elizabeth Abel and Helen Moglen, of *Female Subjects in Black and White: Race, Psychoanalysis, Feminism*.

W. E. B. DU BOIS (1868–1963), sociologist, historian, novelist, poet, and race man, was the most formidable intellectual force in the early stages of twentieth-century African American history. His political and cultural commitment to black society resulted in the formation of the National Association for the Advancement of Colored People, and he served as editor of its Publication, *Crisis*, at one time the most popular and influential magazine for black America. The first African American to receive a Ph.D. from Harvard University, his dissertation, *The Suppression of the African Slave-Trade to the United States*, became the inaugurating volume for the Harvard Historical Studies project. Among his many other publications are *The Philadelphia Negro; The Souls of Black Folk; The Negro;* and *Darkwater: Voices within the Veil.*

ANN DUCILLE is Professor of African American and American Literature at the University of California, San Diego. She is the author of *The Coupling Convention: Sex, Text, and Tradition in Black Women's Fiction and Skin Trade.*

RALPH ELLISON (1914–1994) is best known for his novel *Invisible Man*. But he was also an important literary critic whose aesthetic adherence to the multicultural promise of democratic ideals provides some of our earliest articulation of politico-postmodern assumptions in African American culture. His literary critical writings are collected in the books *Shadow and Act* and *Going to the Territory*.

HENRY LOUIS GATES, JR., is W. E. B. Du Bois Professor of Humanities and Director of the Du Bois Institute for Afro-American Research at Harvard University. Considered a major force in African American literary thought, his books, *Figures in Black: Words, Signs, and the 'Racial' Self* and *The Signifying Monkey: A Theory of Afro-American Literary Criticism*, have made important theoretical contributions to the study of black literature and culture. His many publications as editor include *Black Literature and Literary Theory; "Race," Writing, and Difference* and *Reading Black, Reading Feminist: A Critical Anthology*.

ADDISON GAYLE, JR. (1932–1991), was Distinguished Professor of English at Baruch College. He is the author of *The Black Situation* and the editor of *Black Expression: Essays by and about Black Americans in the Creative Arts* and *Bondage Freedom and Beyond*. His landmark anthology, *The Black Aesthetic*, remains the most important assemblage of theoretical claims from the Black Arts Movement.

CAROLYN F. GERALD is a graduate of the University of California, Berkeley, where she also earned a master's degree. Her essays appeared widely in journals of black culture during the Black Arts Movement.

EVELYNN HAMMONDS is Assistant Professor of the History of Science at the Massachusetts Institute of Technology. She is a co-editor (with Barbara Laslett, Sally Gregory Kohlstedt, and Helen Longino) of *Gender and Scientific Authority*.

PHILLIP BRIAN HARPER is Professor of American Studies and English at New York University. His publications include *Framing the Margins: The Social Logic of Postmodern Culture* and *Are We Not Men? Masculine Anxiety and the Problem of African-American Identity.*

MAE GWENDOLYN HENDERSON is Professor of English at the University of North Carolina, Chapel Hill. She is the editor of *Borders, Boundaries, and Frames: Essays in Cultural Criticism and Cultural Studies* and co-editor (with John W. Blassingame and Jessica A. M. Dunn) of *Antislavery Newspapers and Periodicals: An Annotated Index of Letters, 1817–1871.* Her forthcoming book is entitled *Speaking in Tongues: Reading Black Women Writing.*

STEPHEN E. HENDERSON (1924–1996) was Professor of African American Studies at Howard University and Director of its Institute for the Humanities. Considered a seminal theoretical voice on black literature during the 1960s and 1970s, he is the author of *The Militant Black Writer in Africa and the United States* (with Mercer Cook) and the editor of *Understanding the New Black Poetry*, in which he introduced his theory of "saturation" in the introductory essay "The Form of Things Unknown."

KARLA F. C. HOLLOWAY is William R. Kenan, Jr., Professor of English and Dean of the Humanities and Social Sciences at Duke University. Her publications include *The Character of the Word: The Texts of Zora Neal Hurston; New Dimensions of Spirituality: A Biracial and Bicultural Reading of the Novels of Toni Morrison* (with Stephanie A. Demetrakopoulos); *Moorings and Metaphors: Figures of Culture and Gender in Black Women's Literature*; and *The Codes of Conduct: Race, Ethics, and the Color of Our Character.*

LANGSTON HUGHES (1902–1967) was one of the primary figures of the Harlem Renaissance. A prolific writer regarded mostly for his poetry, he adhered to an aesthetics that valued art as a means by which to celebrate the unique qualities of African American popular culture. This is especially apparent in works such as *Weary Blues* and *Fine Clothes to the Jew.*

ZORA NEALE HURSTON (1891–1960) studied African American culture at Howard University under the guidance of Carter G. Woodson and at Columbia University under the guidance of Franz Boas. These academic interests figure strongly into her creative writings, which reveal passionate attention to folk society and dialect. Her novels *Jonah's Gourd Vine* and *Their Eyes Were Watching God* exemplify best this integration of cultural anthropology and literary invention.

JOYCE A. JOYCE is Chairperson of the Department of African American Studies and Professor of English at Temple University. A highly respected critic, she is a co-editor (with Arthur P. Davis) of *The New Cavalcade: African American Writing from 1760 to the Present* and the editor of *Dawnsong!: The Epic Voice of Askia Toure.* She is author of *Richard Wright's Art of Tragedy* and *Warriors, Conjurers and Priests: Defining African-Centered Literary Criticism.* Her most recent book is *Ijala: Sonia Sanchez and the African Poetic Tradition.*

ALAIN LOCKE (1886–1954) was a professor of philosophy at Howard University. His celebration and nurturing of African American artistic culture played no small role in the discursive actualization of the Harlem Renaissance. His editing of the *New Negro*, in 1925, resulted in the most important documentation of thinkers and artists representing the progressive ethos popular among the American intelligentsia. With this book, Locke provided black America with its first manifesto of cultural reformation and goals, thereby helping to plant the seeds from which would grow the Black Cultural Revolution of the 1960s and 1970s. He was also a pioneer in racial and culture studies whose book *When We Meet*, a *Study in Race and Cultural Contacts* documents his philosophy of cultural pluralism.

WAHNEEMA LUBIANO is Associate Professor in the Department of Literature and the African American Studies Program at Duke University. She is the editor of *The House That Race Built: Black Americans, U.S. Terrain.* Her forthcoming books include *Messing with the Machine: Politics, Form, and African-American Fiction* and *Like Being Mugged by a Metaphor: "Deep Cover" and Other "Black" Fictions.*

DEBORAH E. MCDOWELL is Associate Professor of English at the University of Virginia. A widely published essayist, she is the general editor of the *Beacon Press Black Women Writers Series* and a co-editor (with Arnold Rampersad) of *Slavery and the Literary Imagination.* She is the author of *The Changing Same: Black Women's Literature, Criticism, and Theory* and, most recently, *Leaving Pipe Shop: Memories of Kin.*

HARRYETTE MULLEN is Associate Professor of English at the Center for African American Studies, University of California, Los Angels. She is an accomplished poet and short fiction writer whose forthcoming book is entitled *Freeing the Soul: Literacy and Liberty in Slave Narratives.*

LARRY NEAL (1937–1981) was a poet, playwright, and essayist whose explication of cultural nationalism during the sixties established him as a leading spokesperson for the Black Arts Movement. Selected essays on aesthetics and culture have been posthumously published in *Visions of a Liberated Future: Black Arts Movement Writings.* He is a co-editor, with Amiri Baraka, of *Black Fire: An Anthology of Afro-American Writing.* Among his collections of poetry are *Black Boogaloo: Notes on Black Liberation* and *Hoodoo Hollerin' Bebop Ghosts.*

CHARLES I. NERO is Associate Professor of African American Studies at Bates College, where he specializes in African American rhetoric and public address. Other areas of interest include the representation of blacks in film and slavery in the Americas.

ROBERT F. REID-PHARR is Assistant Professor of English and Director of the Comparative American Cultures Program at Johns Hopkins University. He is author of *Conjugal Union: The Body, The House and The Black American.*

MARLON B. ROSS is Associate Professor of English at the University of Michigan, Ann Arbor. A specialist in cultural criticism and gender theory, his publications include *The Contours of Masculine Desire: Romanticism and the Rise of Women's Poetry.*

GEORGE S. SCHUYLER (1895–1977) was a unique intellectual force in African American culture. Journalist, social critic, and novelist, he is the author of the first satirical novel produced by an African American, namely, *Black No More; Being an Account of the Strange and Wonderful Workings of Science in the Land of the Free* and also of the historical novel *Slaves Today.* His autobiography is titled *Black and Conservative.*

BARBARA SMITH is an innovative force in American culture whose 1977 essay, "Toward a Black Feminist Criticism," documents the canonical beginning of black feminist theory. She is one of the founding members of the Kitchen Table: Women of Color Press, the first publishing house of its kind in America. With Patricia Bell Scott and Gloria Hull, she is a co-editor of *All the Women Are White, All the Blacks Are Men, But Some of Us Are Brave*, the first anthology to focus on black feminist concerns. Along with Lorrain Bethel, she served as a guest editor of *Conditions Five: The Black Women's Issue*, producing the first publication to offer black lesbians a vehicle for concerted publication of their writings.

VALERIE SMITH is Associate Professor of English at the University of California, Los Angeles. A leading African American feminist theorist, she has published an impressive body of works on black expressive culture, including *Self-Discovery and Authority in Afro-American Narrative*. She is the editor of *New Essays on Song of Solomon* and *Representing Blackness: Issues in Film and Video*. Her most recent book is *Not Just Race, Not Just Gender: Black Feminist Readings*.

HORTENSE J. SPILLERS is Professor of English at Cornell University. Her essays have appeared in *Boundary 2, Critical Enquiry, Diacritics,* and *The African American Review*. She is the author of *Chosen Place, Timeless People: Some Figurations on the New World;* the editor of *Comparative American Identities: Race and Nationality in the Modern Text;* and a co-editor, with Majorie Pryse, of *Conjuring: Black Women, Fiction, and Literary Tradition*. Her forthcoming book on women and slavery is titled *In the Flesh: A Situation for Feminist Inquiry*.

PAUL C. TAYLOR is Assistant Professor of Philosophy at the University of Washington, where he specializes in American Pragmatism, aesthetics, and race theory.

SHERLEY ANNE WILLIAMS (1944–1999) was an accomplished critic, novelist, and poet. Her book *Give Birth to Brightness: A Thematic Study in Neo-Black Literature* exemplifies the revisionary black nationalist scholarship produced during the Black Cultural Revolution, while her novel *Dessa Rose* remains a critically acclaimed contribution to the canon of black feminist fiction. Her collections of poetry include *The Peacock Poems* and *Some One Sweet Angel Chile*.

RICHARD WRIGHT (1908–1960) is best known for his novel *Native Son*, which in the aesthetic spirit of Marxian and Freudian naturalism drew America's attention to the influence of the environment on the production of the antisocial psyche. The novel enhanced recognition of the writer as an important force whose works could provide valuable insight by which to improve understanding of the disfranchised and address distribution of economic and legal justice in American society.

Permissions

Every effort has been made to trace or contact copyright holders. The publishers will be pleased to make any corrections or additions in future editions or reprints.

W. E. B. Du Bois. "Criteria of Negro Art." *The Crisis* 32 (October 1926): 290–97. NYU Press wishes to thank *The Crisis* Publishing Co., Inc., the publisher of the magazine of the National Association for the Advancement of Colored People, for authorizing the use of this work.

George S. Schuyler. "The Negro-Art Hokum." *The Nation* (June 16, 1926): 662–663. Reprinted with permission.

Langston Hughes. "The Negro Artist and the Racial Mountain." *The Nation* (June 23, 1926): 692–694. Reprinted with permission.

Zora Neale Hurston. "Characteristics of Negro Expression," from *Negro: An Anthology*, coll. and ed. Nancy Cunard. © 1970 by Frederick Ungar Publishing. Reprinted by permission of The Continuum Publishing Company.

Richard Wright. "Blueprint for Negro Writing," from *New Challenge* 11 (1937): 53–65. © 1937 by Richard Wright. Reprinted by permission of Joan Hawkins & Associates, Inc.

Zora Neale Hurston. "What White Publishers Won't Print." *Negro Digest* V (April 1947): 85–89. In public domain.

Alain Locke. "Self-Criticism: The Third Dimension in Culture." *Phylon* 11, no.4 (1950): 391–94. Reprinted by permission.

LeRoi Jones (Amiri Baraka). "Expressive Language," from *Home: Social Essays* by LeRoi Jones (Amiri Baraka), pp. 166–72. Originally published in Kulchur magazine. © 1963, 1966 by LeRoi Jones. By permission of William Morrow and Company, Inc.

Ralph Ellison. "Brave Words for a Startling Occasion," from *Shadow and Act* by Ralph Ellison, 102–106. Copyright 1953. © 1964 by Ralph Ellison. Reprinted by permission of Random House, Inc.

Larry Neal. "And Shine Swam On: An Afterword," from *Black Fire: An Anthology of Afro-American Writing*, eds. Leroi Jones and Larry Neal, pp. 638–56. Reprinted by permission of Sterling Lord Literistic, Inc. © 1968 by Amiri Baraka.

Carolyn F. Gerald. "The Black Writer and His Role." *Negro Digest* (1969): 42–53; rpt. in *The Black Aesthetic*, ed. Addison Gayle. Garden City, New York: Doubleday, 1972, 349–56. Reprinted by permission of Johnson Publishing Company, Inc.

Larry Neal. "Some Reflections on The Black Aesthetic," from *The Black Aesthetic*, ed. Addison Gayle. Garden City, New York: Doubleday, 1972, 12–16. Reprinted by permission of Ms. Evelyn Neal.

Addison Gayle, Jr. "Cultural Strangulation: Black Literature and the White Aesthetic," from *The Black Aesthetic*, ed. Addison Gayle. Garden City, New York: Doubleday, 1972, 38–45. Reprinted by permission of Marie Brown Associates.

Stephen E. Henderson. "Inside the Funk Shop: A Word on Black Words." *Black Books Bulletin* 1 (Summer/Fall 1973): 9–12. Reprinted by permission of Mrs. Jeanne H. Henderson.

Stephen E. Henderson. "Saturation: Progress Report on a Theory of Black Poetry." *Black World* 24 (1975): 4–17. Reprinted by permission of Johnson Publishing Company, Inc.

Houston A. Baker, Jr. "On the Criticism of Black American Literature: One View of the Black Aesthetic," from *Reading Black: Essays in the Criticism of African, Caribbean, and Black American Literature*, ed. Houston Baker. Ithaca, New York: Cornell University Press, African Studies and Research Center Monograph Series, No. 4, 1976, 48–58. Reprinted by permission of Houston A. Baker, Jr.

Barbara Smith. "Toward a Black Feminist Criticism," from *Conditions: Two* 1, 1977, 25–44; rpt., *The New Feminist Criticism*, ed. Elaine Showalter. New York: Pantheon Books, 1985, 168–85. Reprinted by permission of the Charlotte Sheedy Literary Agency, Inc.

Henry Louis Gates, Jr. "Preface to Blackness: Text and Pretext," from *Afro-American Literature: The Reconstruction of Instruction*, eds. Dexter Fisher and Robert Stepto. New York: MLA, 1979, 44–69. Reprinted by permission of Modern Language Association.

Deborah E. McDowell. "New Directions for Black Feminist Criticism." *Black American Literature Forum* 14 (1980): 153–59.

Houston A. Baker, Jr. "Generational Shifts and the Recent Criticism of Afro-American Literature." *Black American Literature Forum* 15 (1981): 3–21. Reprinted by permission of Houston A. Baker, Jr. and *African American Review*.

Sherley Anne Williams. "Some Implications of Womanist Theory." Presented at the African Literature Association Conference, April 17, 1986. In *Reading Black, Reading Feminist: A Critical Anthology*, ed. Henry Louis Gates, Jr. New York: Meridian, 1990, 68–75. Reprinted by permission of Sherley Anne Williams.

Houston A. Baker, Jr. "Belief, Theory, and Blues: Notes for a Post-Structuralist Criticism of Afro-American Literature," from *Belief vs. Theory in Black American Literary Criticism*, eds. Joe Weixlmann and Chester J. Fontenot. Greenwood, Fla.: Penkeville, 1986, 5–30. Reprinted by permission of Houston A. Baker, Jr.

Hazel V. Carby. "Woman's Era: Rethinking Black Feminist Theory," from her *Reconstructing Womanhood: The Emergence of the Afro-American Woman Novelist*, pp. 3–19. © 1987 by Oxford University Press Inc. Used by permission of Oxford University Press, Inc.

Hortense Spillers. "Mama's Baby, Papa's Maybe: An American Grammar Book." *Diacritics* 17 (1987): 65–81. © 1987 The Johns Hopkins University Press.

Barbara Christian. "The Race for Theory." *Cultural Critique* 6: (Spring 1987): pp. 51–63. Used by permission of the University of Minnesota Press.

Joyce A. Joyce. "The Black Canon: Reconstructing Black American Literary Criticism." *New Literary History* 18 (Winter 1987): 335–44. © 1987 The University of Virginia. Reprinted by permission of The Johns Hopkins University Press.

Henry Louis Gates, Jr. " 'What's Love Got to Do with It?': Critical Theory, Integrity, and the

Black Idiom." *New Literary History* 18 (Winter 1987): 345–62. © 1987 The University of Virginia. Reprinted by permission of The Johns Hopkins University Press.

Houston A. Baker, Jr. "In Dubious Battle." *New Literary History* 18 (Winter 1987): 363–69. © 1987 The University of Virginia. Reprinted by permission of the Johns Hopkins University Press.

Joyce A. Joyce. " 'Who the Cap Fit': Unconsciousness and Unconscionableness in the Criticism of Houston A. Baker, Jr., and Henry Louis Gates, Jr." *New Literary History* 18 (Winter, 1987): 371–83. © 1987 The University of Virginia. Reprinted by permission of the Johns Hopkins University Press.

Michael Awkward. "Appropriative Gestures: Theory and Afro-American Literary Criticism," from *Gender and Theory: Dialogues on Feminist Criticism*, ed. Linda Kauffman. Oxford: Basil Blackwell, 1988, 238–46. Reprinted by permission of Blackwell Publishers Ltd.

Henry Louis Gates, Jr. Introduction from *The Signifying Monkey: A Theory of Afro-American Literary Criticism.* © 1988 by Henry Louis Gates, Jr. Used by permission of Oxford University Press, Inc.

Mae Gwendolyn Henderson. "Speaking in Tongues: Dialogics, Dialectics, and the Black Woman Writer's Literary Tradition," from *Changing Our Own Words: Essays on Criticism, Theory and Writing by Black Women*, ed. Cheryl Wall. New Brunswick, N.J.: Rutgers University Press, 1989, 16–37. Used by permission of Mae Gwendolyn Henderson.

Valerie Smith. "Black Feminist Theory and the Representation of the 'Other,' " from *Changing Our Own Words: Essays on Criticism, Theory and Writing by Black Women* by Cheryl Wall (pp. 38–57). © 1989 by Rutgers, the State University. Reprinted by permission of Rutgers University Press.

Karla F. C. Holloway. "Revision and (Re)membrance: A Theory of Literary Structures in Literature by African-American Women Writers." *Black American Literature Forum* 23 (Winter 1990): 617–31. Used by permission of Karla F. C. Holloway and the *African American Review.*

Charles I. Nero. "Toward a Black Gay Aesthetic: Signifying in Contemporary Black Gay Literature." From *Brother to Brother: New Writings by Black Gay Men*, ed. Essex Hemphill. Boston: Alyson, 1991, 229–52. Used by permission of Charles I. Nero.

Houston A. Baker, Jr. "Theoretical Returns." In his *Workings of the Spirit: The Poetics of Afro-American Women's Writing.* Chicago: University of Chicago Press, 1991, 38–68. Used by permission of University of Chicago Press and Houston A. Baker, Jr.

Ann duCille. "Phallus(ies) of Interpretation: Toward Engendering the Black Critical 'I.' " *Callaloo* 16:3 (Summer 1993): 559–73. © 1993 Charles H. Rowell. Reprinted by permission of the Johns Hopkins University Press.

Phillip Brian Harper. "Nationalism and Social Division in Black Arts Poetry of the 1960s," from *Are We Not Men: Masculine Anxiety and the Problem of African-American Identity.* *Critical Inquiry* 19 (2): 39–53. © 1996 by Phillip Brian Harper. Used by permission of Oxford University Press, Inc.

Joyce A. Joyce. "The Problems with Silence and Exclusiveness in the African American Literary Community." *Black Books Bulletin: WordsWork* 16 (Winter 1993/94): 48–52. Used by permission of Joyce Joyce.

Evelynn Hammonds. "Black (W)holes and the Geometry of Black Female Sexuality." *Differences: A Journal of Feminist Cultural Studies* 6 (1994): 126–45. Used by permission of Indiana University Press.

Marlon B. Ross. "Some Glances at the Black Fag: Race, Same-Sex Desire, and Cultural

Index

abjection, 602, 603–4, 613

abolitionists, 116–18, 147, 275, 578 n. 39

Abrahams, Roger, 109

Adams, Russell, 648

Adele, Lynne, 639 n. 4

Adell, Sandra, 8, 523–39

Adorno, Theodor, 302

aesthetics, racialization of, 665–71

African American. *See also under* black

African American literary theory: Baker on the criticism of black American literature, 113–31; Baker on generational shifts in, 179–217; and cultural studies, 11; female theorists, 12; Gates on blackness in black literature, 147–64; Henderson on saturation, 102–12; integrationism, 179, 180–82; in the 1970s, 87–164; in the 1980s, 165–384; in the 1990s, 385–651; professionalism in, 179, 195, 196, 528, 531–32; reformative spirit of, 1–2; resistance to theory in, 298, 300–304, 327–28, 331. *See also* black aesthetic; black feminist theory; black gay movement; cultural nationalism; poststructuralism; reconstructionists; structuralism

African Americans: as appropriative for Hurston, 336, 647; Black English, 101, 158, 208, 210, 282, 339; "black" versus "ne-gro," 468; conceptualized as irrational nonsubjects, 603; cultural inventiveness of, 6, 37–38; deconstructive use of language of, 6–7; Henderson on black words, 97–101; homosexuality as more open among, 498–500, 504, 512, 514, 517 n. 4, 518 n. 11; homosexuality as viewed negatively by, 401–4, 500–501; Hughes on class differences in, 27–29; Hurston on characteristics of Negro expression, 31–44; literacy for, 147–48; middle class emerging in 1970s, 195–96, 215 n. 30; Moynihan on family structure of, 257–59; the New Negro, 2–3, 58, 153; the Other made part of their lives by, 641 n. 12; racial standards of beauty, 665–71; reformative spirit of, 1–2; Schuyler on Americanness of, 25–26; at World's Columbian Exposition, 243; Wright on "black chauvinism," 48. *See also* black church; black literature; black music; black studies; folklore; signifying; slavery

African Methodist Episcopal Church, 199, 408, 421

African Methodist Episcopal Church Review, 149

African Methodist Episcopal Zion Church, 408

African sculpture, 34, 75

701